RANDOM HOUSE
WEBSTER'S

STUDENT
notebook
SPANISH
DICTIONARY

English Abbreviations/Abreviaturas inglesas

a.	adjective		*interrog.*	interrogative
abbr.	abbreviation		*Leg.*	legal
adv.	adverb		*m.*	masculine
Aero.	aeronautics		*Mech.*	mechanics
Agr.	agriculture		*Mex.*	Mexico
Anat.	anatomy		*Mil.*	military
art.	article		*Mus.*	music
Auto.	automotive		*n.*	noun
Biol.	biology		*Naut.*	nautical
Bot.	botany		*Phot.*	photography
Carib.	Caribbean		*pl.*	plural
Chem.	chemistry		*Pol.*	politics
Colloq.	colloquial		*prep.*	preposition
Com.	commerce		*pron.*	pronoun
conj.	conjunction		*Punct.*	punctuation
dem.	demonstrative		*rel.*	relative
Econ.	economics		*Relig.*	religion
Elec.	electrical		*S.A.*	Spanish America
esp.	especially		*Theat.*	theater
f.	feminine		*v.*	verb
Fig.	figurative			
Fin.	finance			
Geog.	geography			
Govt.	government			
Gram.	grammar			
interj.	interjection			

Note: If a main entry term is repeated in a boldface subentry in exactly the same form, it is abbreviated. Example: **comedor** *n.m.* dining room. **coche c.,** dining car.

Spanish Stress

In a number of words, spoken stress is marked by an accent (´): *nación, país, médico, día.*

Words which are not so marked are, generally speaking, stressed on the next-to-the-last syllable if they end in a vowel, *n,* or *s;* and on the last syllable if they end in a consonant other than *n* or *s.*

Note: An accent is placed over some words to distinguish them from others having the same spelling and pronunciation but differing in meaning.

Spanish Alphabetization

In Spanish, *ch* and *ll* are no longer considered to be separate letters of the alphabet. They are now alphabetized as they would be in English. However, words with *ñ* are alphabetized after *n.*

PRONUNCIATION KEY FOR SPANISH

IPA Symbols	Key Words	Approximate Equivalents
a	alba, banco, cera	father, depart
e	esto, del, parte, mesa	bet; like rain when e ends syllable and is not followed by r, rr, or t
i	ir, fino, adiós, muy	like beet, but shorter
o	oler, flor, grano	like vote, but shorter
u	un, luna, cuento, vergüenza, guarda	fool, group
b	bajo, ambiguo, vaca	by, abet
β	hablar, escribir, lavar	like vehicle, but with lips almost touching
d	dar, desde, andamio, dueña	deal, adept
ð	pedir, edredón, verdad	that, gather
f	fecha, afectar, golf	fan, after
g	gato, grave, gusto, largo, guerra	garden, ugly
h	gemelo, giro, junta, bajo	horse
k	cacao, claro, cura, cuenta, que, quinto	kind, actor
l	lado, lente, habla, papel	lot, altar
ʎ	(in Spain) llama, calle, olla	like million, but with tongue behind teeth
m	mal, amor	more, commit
n	nada, nuevo, mano, bien	not, enter
ɲ	ñapa, año	canyon, companion
ŋ	angosto, aunque	ring, anchor
p	peso, guapo	pill, applaud
r	real, faro, deber	like rice, but with single flap of tongue on roof of mouth
rr	perro, sierra	like rice, but with trill, or vibration of tongue, against upper teeth
s	sala, espejo, mas; (in Latin America) cena, hacer, vez	say, clasp
θ	(in Spain) cena, hacer, cierto, cine, zarzuela, lazo, vez	thin, myth
t	tocar, estado, cenit	table, attract
y	ya, ayer; (in Latin America) llama, calle	you, voyage
tʃ	chica, mucho	chill, batch

Diphthongs

ai, ay	baile, hay	high, rye
au	audacia, laudable	out, round
ei, ey	veinte, seis, rey	ray
ie	miel, tambien	fiesta
oi, oy	estoico, hoy	coin, loyal
ua	cuanto	quantity
ue	buena, suerte	sway, quaint

Guía de Pronunciación del Inglés

Símbolos del AFI	Ejemplos
/æ/	*ingl.* hat; como la **a** de *esp.* p**a**ro, pero más cerrada
/ei/	*ingl.* st**a**y; *esp.* r**ei**na
/ɛə/ [followed by /r/]	*ingl.* h**ai**r; *esp.* v**e**r
/ɑ/	*ingl.* f**a**ther; similar a las **a**s de *esp.* c**a**sa, pero más larga
/ɛ/	*ingl.* b**e**t; *esp.* **e**ntre
/i/	*ingl.* b**ee**; como la **i** de *esp.* v**i**da, pero más larga
/ɪə/ [followed by /r/]	*ingl.* h**ea**r; como la **i** de *esp.* ven**i**r, pero menos cerrada
/ɪ/	*ingl.* s**i**t; como la **i** de *esp.* Ch**i**le, pero menos cerrada
/ai/	*ingl.* tr**y**; *esp.* h**ay**
/ɒ/	*ingl.* h**o**t; *esp.* p**o**ner
/o/	*ingl.* b**oa**t; similar a la **o** de *esp.* s**a**co, pero más cerrada
/ɔ/	*ingl.* s**aw**; similar a la **o** de *esp.* c**o**rte, pero más cerrada
/ɔi/	*ingl.* t**oy**; *esp.* h**oy**
/ʊ/	*ingl.* b**oo**k; como la **u** de *esp.* ins**u**lto, pero menos cerrada
/u/	*ingl.* t**oo**; como la **u** de *esp.* l**u**na, pero más larga
/au/	*ingl.* c**ow**; *esp.* p**au**sa
/ʌ/	*ingl.* **u**p; entre la **o** de *esp.* b**o**rde y la **a** de *esp.* b**a**rro
/ɜ/ [followed by /r/]	*ingl.* b**u**rn; *fr.* fl**eu**r
/ə/	*ingl.* **a**lone; *fr.* d**e**main
/ɔ/	*ingl.* f**i**re (fi**ə**r); *fr.* bastill**e**
/b/	*ingl.* **b**oy; como la **b** de *esp.* **b**oca, pero más aspirada
/tʃ/	*ingl.* **ch**ild; *esp.* mu**ch**o
/d/	*ingl.* **d**ad; *esp.* **d**ar
/f/	*ingl.* **f**or; *esp.* **f**echa
/g/	*ingl.* **g**ive; *esp.* **g**ato
/h/	*ingl.* **h**appy; como la **j** de *esp.* **j**abón, pero más aspirada y menos aspera
/dʒ/	*ingl.* **j**ust; *it.* **g**iorno
/k/	*ingl.* **k**i**ck**; similar a la **k** de *esp.* **k**ilogramo, pero más aspirada
/l/	*ingl.* **l**ove; *esp.* **l**ibro
/m/	*ingl.* **m**other; *esp.* li**m**bo
/n/	*ingl.* **n**ow; *esp.* **n**oche
/ŋ/	*ingl.* si**ng**; *esp.* bla**n**co
/p/	*ingl.* **p**ot; como las **p**s de *esp.* **p**a**p**a, pero más aspirada
/r/	*ingl.* **r**ead; como la **r** de *esp.* pa**r**a, pero con la lengua elevada hacia el paladar, sin tocarlo
/s/	*ingl.* **s**ee; *esp.* ha**s**ta
/ʃ/	*ingl.* **sh**op; *fr.* **ch**ercher
/t/	*ingl.* **t**en; similar a la **t** de *esp.* **t**omar, pero más aspirada
/θ/	*ingl.* **th**ing; *esp.* (en España) **c**erdo, **z**apato
/ð/	*ingl.* fa**th**er; *esp.* co**d**o
/v/	*ingl.* **v**ictory; como la **b** de *esp.* ha**b**a, pero es labiodental en vez de bilabial
/w/	*ingl.* **w**itch; como la **u** de *esp.* p**u**esto, pero con labios más cerrados
/y/	*ingl.* **y**es; *esp.* **y**acer
/z/	*ingl.* **z**ipper; *fr.* **z**éro
/ʒ/	*ingl.* plea**s**ure; *fr.* **j**eune

Las consonantes /ḷ/, /ṃ/, y /ṇ/ son similar a las **l**, **m**, y **n** del español, pero alargada y resonante

Spanish–English

español–inglés

A

a /a/ *prep.* to; at.

abacería /aβaθe'ria; aβase'ria/ *n. f.* grocery store.

abacero /aβa'θero; aβa'sero/ *n. m.* grocer.

ábaco /'aβako/ *n. m.* abacus.

abad /a'βað/ *n. m.* abbot.

abadía /aβa'ðia/ *n. f.* abbey.

abajar /aβa'har/ *v.* lower; go down.

abajo /a'βaho/ *adv.* down; downstairs.

abandonar /aβando'nar/ *v.* abandon.

abandono /aβan'dono/ *n. m.* abandonment.

abanico /aβa'niko/ *n. m.* fan. **—abanicar,** *v.*

abaratar /aβara'tar/ *v.* cheapen.

abarcar /aβar'kar/ *v.* comprise; clasp.

abastecer /aβaste'θer; aβaste'ser/ *v.* supply, provide.

abatido /aβa'tiðo/ *a.* dejected, despondent.

abatir /aβa'tir/ *v.* knock down; dismantle; depress, dishearten.

abdicación /aβðika'θion; aβðika'sion/ *n. f.* abdication.

abdicar /aβði'kar/ *v.* abdicate.

abdomen /aβ'ðomen/ *n. m.* abdomen.

abdominal /aβðomi'nal/ *a.* **1.** abdominal. **—n. 2.** *m.* sit-up.

abecé /aβe'θe; aβe'se/ *n. m.* ABCs, rudiments.

abecedario /aβeθe'ðario; aβese'ðario/ *n. m.* alphabet; reading book.

abeja /a'βeha/ *n. f.* bee.

abejarrón /aβeha'rron/ *n. m.* bumblebee.

aberración /aβerra'θion; aβerra'sion/ *n. f.* aberration.

abertura /aβer'tura/ *n. f.* opening, aperture, slit.

abeto /a'βeto/ *n. m.* fir.

abierto /a'βierto/ *a.* open; overt.

abismal /aβis'mal/ *a.* abysmal.

abismo /a'βismo/ *n. m.* abyss, chasm.

ablandar /aβlan'dar/ *v.* soften.

abnegación /aβnega'θion; aβnega'sion/ *n. f.* abnegation.

abochornar /aβotʃor'nar/ *v.* overheat; embarrass.

abogado /aβo'gaðo/ **-da** *n.* lawyer, attorney.

abolengo /aβo'leŋgo/ *n. m.* ancestry.

abolición /aβoli'θion; aβoli'sion/ *n. f.* abolition.

abolladura /aβoʎa'ðura; aβoya'ðura/ *n. f.* dent. **—abollar,** *v.*

abominable /aβomi'naβle/ *a.* abominable.

abominar /aβomi'nar/ *v.* abhor.

abonado /aβo'naðo/ **-da** *n. m. & f.* subscriber.

abonar /aβo'nar/ *v.* pay; fertilize.

abonarse /aβo'narse/ *v.* subscribe.

abono /a'βono/ *n. m.* fertilizer; subscription; season ticket.

aborigen /aβor'ihen/ *a. & n.* aboriginal.

aborrecer /aβorre'θer; aβorre'ser/ *v.* hate, loathe, abhor.

abortar /aβor'tar/ *v.* abort, miscarry.

aborto /a'βorto/ *n. m.* abortion.

abovedar /aβoβe'ðar/ *v.* vault.

abrasar /aβra'sar/ *v.* burn.

abrazar /aβra'θar; aβra'sar/ *v.* embrace; clasp.

abrazo /a'βraθo; a'βraso/ *n. m.* embrace.

abrelatas /aβre'latas/ *n. m.* can opener.

abreviar /aβre'βiar/ *v.* abbreviate, abridge, shorten.

abreviatura /aβreβia'tura/ *n. f.* abbreviation.

abrigar /aβri'gar/ *v.* harbor, shelter.

abrigarse /aβri'garse/ *v.* bundle up.

abrigo /a'βrigo/ *n. m.* overcoat; shelter; (*pl.*) wraps.

abril /a'βril/ *n. m.* April.

abrir /a'βrir/ *v.* open; *Med.* lance.

abrochar /aβro'tʃar/ *v.* clasp.

abrogación /aβroga'θion; aβroga'sion/ *n. f.* abrogation, repeal.

abrogar /aβro'gar/ *v.* abrogate.

abrojo /a'βroho/ *n. m.* thorn.

abrumar /aβru'mar/ *v.* overwhelm, crush, swamp.

absceso /aβs'sθeso; aβ'sseso/ *n. m.* abscess.

absolución /aβsolu'θion; aβsolu'sion/ *n. f.* absolution; acquittal.

absoluto /aβso'luto/ *a.* absolute; downright.

absolver /aβsol'βer/ *v.* absolve, pardon.

absorbente /aβsor'βente/ *a.* absorbent.

absorber /aβsor'βer/ *v.* absorb.

absorción /aβsor'θion; aβsor'sion/ *n. f.* absorption.

abstemio /aβs'temio/ *a.* abstemious.

abstenerse /aβste'nerse/ *v.* abstain; refrain.

abstinencia /aβsti'nenθia; aβsti'nensia/ *n. f.* abstinence.

abstracción /aβstrak'θion; aβstrak'sion/ *n. f.* abstraction.

abstracto /aβ'strakto/ *a.* abstract.

abstraer /aβstra'er/ *v.* abstract.

absurdo /aβ'surðo/ *a.* **1.** absurd. **—n. 2.** *m.* absurdity.

abuchear /aβutʃe'ar/ *v.* boo.

abuela /a'βuela/ *n. f.* grandmother.

abuelo /a'βuelo/ *n. m.* grandfather; (*pl.*) grandparents.

abultado /aβul'taðo/ *a.* bulky.

abultamiento /aβulta'miento/ *n. m.* bulge. **—abultar,** *v.*

abundancia /aβun'danθia; aβun'dansia/ *n. f.* abundance, plenty.

abundante /aβun'dante/ *a.* abundant, plentiful.

abundar /aβun'dar/ *v.* abound.

aburrido /aβu'rriðo/ *a.* boring, tedious.

aburrimiento /aβurri'miento/ *n. m.* boredom.

aburrir /aβu'rrir/ *v.* bore.

abusar /aβu'sar/ *v.* abuse, misuse.

abusivo /aβu'siβo/ *a.* abusive.

abuso /a'βuso/ *n. m.* abuse.

abyecto /aβ'yekto/ *a.* abject, low.

a.C., *abbr.* (**antes de Cristo**) BC.

acá /a'ka/ *adv.* here.

acabar /aka'βar/ *v.* finish. **a. de...,** to have just....

acacia /a'kaθia; a'kasia/ *n. f.* acacia.

academia /aka'ðemia/ *n. f.* academy.

académico /aka'ðemiko/ *a.* academic.

acaecer /akae'θer; akae'ser/ *v.* happen.

acanalar /akana'lar/ *v.* groove.

acaparar /akapa'rar/ *v.* hoard; monopolize.

acariciar /akari'θiar; akari'siar/ *v.* caress, stroke.

acarrear /akarre'ar/ *v.* cart, transport; occasion, entail.

acaso /a'kaso/ *n. m.* chance. **por si a.,** just in case.

acceder /akθe'ðer; akse'ðer/ *v.* accede.

accesible /akθe'siβle; akse'siβle/ *a.* accessible.

acceso /ak'θeso; ak'seso/ *n. m.* access, approach.

accesorio /akθe'sorio; akse'sorio/ *a.* accessory.

accidentado /akθiðen'taðo; aksiðen'taðo/ *a.* hilly.

accidental /akθiðen'tal; aksiðen'tal/ *a.* accidental.

accidente /akθi'ðente; aksi'ðente/ *n. m.* accident, wreck.

acción /ak'θion; ak'sion/ *n. f.* action, act; *Com.* share of stock.

accionista /akθio'nista; aksio'nista/ *n. m. & f.* shareholder.

acechar /aθe'tʃar; ase'tʃar/ *v.* ambush, spy on.

acedia /a'θeðia; a'seðia/ *n. f.* heartburn.

aceite /a'θeite; a'seite/ *n. m.* oil.

aceite de hígado de bacalao /a'θeite de i'gaðo de baka'lao; a'seite/ cod-liver oil.

aceitoso /aθei'toso; asei'toso/ *a.* oily.

aceituna /aθei'tuna; asei'tuna/ *n. f.* olive.

aceleración /aθelera'θion; aselera'sion/ *n. f.* acceleration.

acelerar /aθele'rar; asele'rar/ *v.* accelerate, speed up.

acento /a'θento; a'sento/ *n. m.* accent.

acentuar /aθen'tuar; asen'tuar/ *v.* accent, accentuate, stress.

acepillar /aθepi'ʎar; asepi'yar/ *v.* brush; plane (wood).

aceptable /aθep'taβle; asep'taβle/ *a.* acceptable.

aceptación /aθepta'θion; asepta'sion/ *n. f.* acceptance.

aceptar /aθep'tar; asep'tar/ *v.* accept.

acequía /a'θekia; a'sekia/ *n. f.* ditch.

acera /a'θera; a'sera/ *n. f.* sidewalk.

acerca de /a'θerka de; a'serka de/ *prep.* about, concerning.

acercar /aθer'kar; aser'kar/ *v.* bring near.

acercarse /aθer'karse; aser'karse/ *v.* approach, come near, go near.

acero /a'θero; a'sero/ *n. m.* steel.

acero inoxidable /a'θero inoksi'ðaβle; a'sero inoksi'ðaβle/ stainless steel.

acertar /aθer'tar; aser'tar/ *v.* guess right. **a. en,** hit (a mark).

acertijo /aθer'tiho; aser'tiho/ *n. m.* puzzle, riddle.

achicar /atʃi'kar/ *v.* diminish, dwarf; humble.

acidez /aθi'ðeθ; asi'ðes/ *n. f.* acidity.

ácido /'aθiðo; 'asiðo/ *a.* **1.** sour. **—n. 2.** *m.* acid.

aclamación /aklama'θion; aklama'sion/ *n. f.* acclamation.

aclamar /akla'mar/ *v.* acclaim.

aclarar /akla'rar/ *v.* brighten; clarify, clear up.

acoger /ako'her/ *v.* welcome, receive.

acogida /ako'hiða/ *n. f.* welcome, reception.

acometer /akome'ter/ *v.* attack.

acomodador /akomoða'ðor/ *n. m.* usher.

acomodar /akomo'ðar/ *v.* accommodate, fix up.

acompañamiento /akompaɲa'miento/ *n. m.* accompaniment; following.

acompañar /akompa'ɲar/ *v.* accompany.

acondicionar /akondiθio'nar; akondisio'nar/ *v.* condition.

aconsejable /akonse'haβle/ *a.* advisable.

aconsejar /akonse'har/ *v.* advise.

acontecer /akonte'θer; akonte'ser/ *v.* happen.

acontecimiento /akonteθi'miento; akontesi'miento/ *n. m.* event, happening.

acorazado /akora'θaðo; akora'saðo/ *n.* **1.** *m.* battleship. **—a. 2.** armorplated, ironclad.

acordarse /akor'ðarse/ *v.* remember, recollect.

acordeón /akorðe'on/ *n. m.* accordion.

acordonar /akorðo'nar/ *v.* cordon off.

acortar /akor'tar/ *v.* shorten.

acosar /ako'sar/ *v.* beset, harry.

acostar /ako'star/ *v.* lay down; put to bed.

acostarse /akos'tarse/ *v.* lie down; go to bed.

acostumbrado /akostum'braðo/ *a.* accustomed; customary.

acostumbrar /akostum'brar/ *v.* accustom.

acrecentar /akreθen'tar; akresen'tar/ *v.* increase.

acreditar /akreði'tar/ *v.* accredit.

acreedor /akree'ðor/ **-ra** *n.* creditor.

acróbata /a'kroβata/ *n. m. & f.* acrobat.

acrobático /akro'βatiko/ *a.* acrobatic.

actitud /akti'tuð/ *n. f.* attitude.

actividad /aktiβi'ðað/ *n. f.* activity.

activista /akti'βista/ *a. & n.* activist.

activo /ak'tiβo/ *a.* active.

acto /'akto/ *n. m.* act.

actor /ak'tor/ *n. m.* actor.

actriz /ak'triθ; ak'tris/ *n. f.* actress.

actual /ak'tual/ *a.* present; present day.

actualidades /aktuali'ðaðes/ *n. f.pl.* current events.

actualmente /aktual'mente/ *adv.* at present; nowadays.

actuar /ak'tuar/ *v.* act.

acuarela /akua'rela/ *n. f.* watercolor.

acuario /a'kuario/ *n. m.* aquarium.

acuático /a'kuatiko/ *a.* aquatic.

acuchillar /akutʃi'ʎar; akutʃi'yar/ *v.* slash, knife.

acudir /aku'ðir/ *v.* rally; hasten; be present.

acuerdo /a'kuerðo/ *n. m.* accord, agreement; settlement. **de a.,** in agreement, agreed.

acumulación /akumula'θion; akumula'sion/ *n. f.* accumulation.

acumular /akumu'lar/ *v.* accumulate.

acuñar /aku'ɲar/ *v.* coin, mint.

acupuntura /akupun'tura/ *n. f.* acupuncture.

acusación /akusa'θion; akusa'sion/ *n. f.* accusation, charge.

acusado /aku'saðo/ **-da** *a. & n.* accused; defendant.

acusador /akusa'ðor/ **-ra** *n.* accuser.

acusar /aku'sar/ *v.* accuse; acknowledge.

acústica /a'kustika/ *n. f.* acoustics.

adaptación /aðapta'θion; aðapta'sion/ *n. f.* adaptation.

adaptador /aðapta'ðor/ *n. m.* adapter.

adaptar /aðap'tar/ *v.* adapt.

adecuado /aðe'kuaðo/ *a.* adequate.

adelantado /aðelan'taðo/ *a.* advanced; fast (clock).

adelantamiento /aðelanta'miento/ *n. m.* advancement, promotion.

adelantar /aðelan'tar/ *v.* advance.

adelante /aðe'lante/ *adv.* ahead, forward, onward, on.

adelanto /aðe'lanto/ *n. m.* advancement, progress, improvement.

adelgazar /aðelga'θar; aðelga'sar/ *v.* make thin.

ademán /aðe'man/ *n. m.* attitude; gesture.

además /aðe'mas/ *adv.* in addition, besides, also.

adentro /a'ðentro/ *adv.* in, inside.

adepto /a'ðepto/ *a.* adept.

aderezar /aðere'θar; aðere'sar/ *v.* prepare; trim.

adherirse /aðe'rirse/ *v.* adhere, stick.

adhesivo /aðe'siβo/ *a.* adhesive.

adicción /aðik'θion; aðik'sion/ *n. f.* adiction.

adición /aði'θion; aði'sion/ *n. f.* addition.

adicional /aðiθio'nal; aðisio'nal/ *a.* additional, extra.

adicto /a'ðikto/ **-ta** *a. & n.* addicted; addict.

adinerado /aðine'raðo/ **-a** *a.* wealthy.

adiós /a'ðios/ *n. m. & interj.* good-bye, farewell.

adivinar /aðiβi'nar/ *v.* guess.

adjetivo /aðhe'tiβo/ *n. m.* adjective.

adjunto /að'hunto/ *a.* enclosed.

administración /aðministra'θion; aðministra'sion/ *n. f.* administration.

administrador /aðministra'ðor/ **-ra** *n.* administrator.

administrar /aðminis'trar/ *v.* administer; manage.

administrativo /aðministra'tiβo/ *a.* administrative.

admirable /aðmi'raβle/ *a.* admirable.

admiración. /aðmira'θion; aðmira'prim;sion/ *n. f.* admiration; wonder.

admirar /aðmi'rar/ v. admire.

admisión /aðmi'sion/ n. f. admission.

admitir /aðmi'tir/ v. admit, acknowledge.

ADN, abbr. **(ácido deoxirribonucleico)** DNA (deoxyribonucleic acid).

adobar /aðo'βar/ v. marinate.

adolescencia /aðoles'θenθia; aðoles'sensia/ n. f. adolescence, youth.

adolescente /aðoles'θente; aðoles'sente/ a. & n. adolescent.

adónde /a'ðonde/ adv. where.

adondequiera /a,ðonde'kiera/ conj. wherever.

adopción /aðop'θion; aðop'sion/ n. f. adoption.

adoptar /aðop'tar/ v. adopt.

adoración /aðora'θion; aðora'sion/ n. f. worship, love, adoration. —**adorar,** v.

adormecer /aðorme'θer; aðorme'ser/ v. drowse.

adornar /aðor'nar/ v. adorn; decorate.

adorno /a'ðorno/ n. m. adornment, trimming.

adquirir /aðki'rir/ v. acquire, obtain.

adquisición /aðkisi'θion; aðkisi'sion/ n. f. acquisition, attainment.

aduana /a'ðuana/ n. f. custom house, customs.

adujada /aðu'haða/ n. f. Naut. coil of rope.

adulación /aðula'θion; aðula'sion/ n. f. flattery.

adular /aðu'lar/ v. flatter.

adulterar /aðulte'rar/ v. adulterate.

adulterio /aðul'terio/ n. m. adultery.

adulto /a'ðulto/ **-ta** a. & n. adult.

adusto /a'ðusto/ a. gloomy; austere.

adverbio /að'βerβio/ n. m. adverb.

adversario /aðβer'sario/ n. m. adversary.

adversidad /aðβersi'ðað/ n. f. adversity.

adverso /að'βerso/ a. adverse.

advertencia /aðβer'tenθia; aðβer'tensia/ n. f. warning.

advertir /aðβer'tir/ v. warn; notice.

adyacente /aðya'θente; aðya'sente/ a. adjacent.

aéreo /'aereo/ a. aerial; air.

aerodeslizador /aeroðesliθa'ðor; aeroðeslisa'ðor/ n. m. hovercraft.

aeromoza /aero'moθa; aero'mosa/ n. f. stewardess, flight attendant.

aeroplano /aero'plano/ n. m. light plane.

aeropuerto /aero'puerto/ n. m. airport.

aerosol /aero'sol/ n. m. aerosol, spray.

afable /a'faβle/ a. affable, pleasant.

afanarse /afa'narse/ v. toil.

afear /afe'ar/ v. deface, mar, deform.

afectación /afekta'θion; afekta'sion/ n. f. affectation.

afectar /afek'tar/ v. affect.

afecto /a'fekto/ n. m. affection, attachment.

afeitada /afei'taða/ n. f. shave. —**afeitarse,** v.

afeminado /afemi'naðo/ a. effeminate.

afición /afi'θion; afi'sion/ n. f. fondness, liking; hobby.

aficionado /afiθio'naðo; afisio'naðo/ a. fond.

aficionado -da n. fan, devotee; amateur.

aficionarse a /afiθio'narse a; afisio'narse a/ v. become fond of.

afilado /afi'laðo/ a. sharp.

afilar /afi'lar/ v. sharpen.

afiliación /afilia'θion; afilia'sion/ n. f. affiliation.

afiliado /afi'liaðo/ **-da** n. affiliate. —**afiliar,** v.

afinar /afi'nar/ v. polish; tune up.

afinidad /afini'ðað/ n. f. relationship, affinity.

afirmación /afirma'θion; afirma'sion/ n. f. affirmation, statement.

afirmar /afir'mar/ v. affirm, assert.

afirmativa /afirma'tiβa/ n. f. affirmative. —**afirmativo,** a.

aflicción /aflik'θion; aflik'sion/ n. f. affliction; sorrow, grief.

afligido /afli'hiðo/ a. sorrowful, grieved.

afligir /afli'hir/ v. grieve, distress.

aflojar /aflo'har/ v. loosen.

afluencia /a'fluenθia; a'fluensia/ n. f. influx.

afortunado /afortu'naðo/ a. fortunate, successful, lucky.

afrenta /a'frenta/ n. f. insult, outrage, affront. —**afrentar,** v.

afrentoso /afren'toso/ a. shameful.

africano /afri'kano/ **-na** a. & n. African.

afuera /a'fuera/ adv. out, outside.

afueras /a'fueras/ n. f.pl. suburbs.

agacharse /aga'tʃarse/ v. squat, crouch; cower.

agarrar /aga'rrar/ v. seize, grasp, clutch.

agarro /a'garro/ n. m. clutch, grasp.

agencia /a'henθia; a'hensia/ n. f. agency.

agencia de colocaciones /a'henθia de koloka'θiones; a'hensia de koloka'siones/ employment agency.

agencia de viajes /a'henθia de 'biahes; a'hensia de 'biahes/ travel agency.

agente /a'hente/ n. m. & f. agent, representative.

agente de aduana /a'hente de a'ðuana/ mf. customs officer.

agente inmobiliario /a'hente imoβi'liario/ **-ria** n. real-estate agent.

ágil /'ahil/ a. agile, spry.

agitación /ahita'θion; ahita'sion/ n. f. agitation, ferment.

agitado /ahi'taðo/ a. agitated; excited.

agitador /ahita'ðor/ n. m. agitator.

agitar /ahi'tar/ v. shake, agitate, excite.

agobiar /ago'βiar/ v. oppress, burden.

agosto /a'gosto/ n. m. August.

agotamiento /aɣota'miento/ n. m. exhaustion.

agotar /ago'tar/ v. exhaust, use up, sap.

agradable /agra'ðaβle/ a. agreeable, pleasant.

agradar /agra'ðar/ v. please.

agradecer /agraðe'θer; agraðe'ser/ v. thank; appreciate, be grateful for.

agradecido /agraðe'θiðo; agraðe'siðo/ a. grateful, thankful.

agradecimiento /agraðeθi'miento; agraðesi'miento/ n. m. gratitude, thanks.

agravar /agra'βar/ v. aggravate, make worse.

agravio /a'graβio/ n. m. wrong. —**agraviar,** v.

agregado /agre'gaðo/ a. & n. aggregate; Pol. attaché.

agregar /agre'gar/ v. add; gather.

agresión /agre'sion/ n. f. aggression; Leg. battery.

agresivo /agre'siβo/ a. aggressive.

agresor /agre'sor/ **-ra** n. aggressor.

agrícola /a'grikola/ a. agricultural.

agricultor /agrikul'tor/ n. m. farmer.

agricultura /agrikul'tura/ n. f. agriculture, farming.

agrio /'agrio/ a. sour.

agrupar /agru'par/ v. group.

agua /'agua/ n. f. water. —**aguar,** v.

aguacate /agua'kate/ n. m. avocado, alligator pear.

aguafuerte /,agua'fuerte/ n. f. etching.

agua mineral /'agua mine'ral/ mineral water.

aguantar /aguan'tar/ v. endure, stand, put up with.

aguardar /aguar'ðar/ v. await; expect.

aguardiente /aguar'ðiente/ n. m. brandy.

aguas abajo /'aguas a'βaho/ adv. downriver, downstream.

aguas arriba /'aguas a'rriβa/ adv. upriver, upstream.

agudo /a'guðo/ a. sharp, keen, shrill, acute.

agüero /a'guero/ n. m. omen.

águila /'agila/ n. f. eagle.

aguja /a'guha/ n. f. needle.

agujero /agu'hero/ n. m. hole.

aguzar /agu'θar; agu'sar/ v. sharpen.

ahí /a'i/ adv. there.

ahogar /ao'gar/ v. drown; choke; suffocate.

ahondar /aon'dar/ v. deepen.

ahora /a'ora/ adv. now.

ahorcar /aor'kar/ v. hang (execute).

ahorrar /ao'rrar/ v. save, save up; spare.

ahorros /a'orros/ n. m.pl. savings.

ahumar /au'mar/ v. smoke.

airado /ai'raðo/ a. angry, indignant.

aire /'aire/ n. m. air. —**airear,** v.

aire acondicionado /'aire akondi'θio'naðo; 'aire akondisio'naðo/ air conditioning.

aislamiento /aisla'miento/ n. m. isolation.

aislar /ais'lar/ v. isolate.

ajedrez /ahe'ðreθ; ahe'ðres/ n. m. chess.

ajeno /a'heno/ a. alien; someone else's.

ajetreo /ahe'treo/ n. m. hustle and bustle.

ají /a'hi/ n. m. chili.

ajo /'aho/ n. m. garlic.

ajustado /ahus'taðo/ a. adjusted; trim; exact.

ajustar /ahus'tar/ v. adjust.

ajuste /a'huste/ n. m. adjustment, settlement.

al /al/ contr. of a + el.

ala /'ala/ n. f. wing; brim (of hat).

alabanza /ala'βanθa; ala'βansa/ n. f. praise. —**alabar,** v.

alabear /alaβe'ar/ v. warp.

ala delta /'ala 'delta/ hang glider.

alambique /alam'bike/ n. m. still.

alambre /a'lambre/ n. m. wire. **a. de púas,** barbed wire.

alarde /a'larðe/ n. m. boasting, ostentation.

alargar /alar'gar/ v. lengthen; stretch out.

alarma /a'larma/ n. f. alarm. —**alarmar,** v.

alba /'alβa/ n. f. daybreak, dawn.

albanega /alβa'nega/ n. f. hair net.

albañil /alβa'ɲil/ n. m. bricklayer; mason.

albaricoque /alβari'koke/ n. m. apricot.

alberca /al'βerka/ n. f. swimming pool.

albergue /al'βerge/ n. m. shelter. —**albergar,** v.

alborotar /alβoro'tar/ v. disturb, make noise, brawl, riot.

alboroto /alβo'roto/ n. m. brawl, disturbance, din, tumult.

álbum /'alβum/ n. m. album.

álbum de recortes /'alβum de re'kortes/ scrapbook.

alcachofa /alka'tʃofa/ n. f. artichoke.

alcalde /al'kalde/ n. m. mayor.

alcance /al'kanθe; al'kanse/ n. m. reach; range, scope.

alcanfor /alkan'for/ n. m. camphor.

alcanzar /alkan'θar; alkan'sar/ v. reach, overtake, catch.

alcayata /alka'yata/ n. f. spike.

alce /'alθe; 'alse/ n. m. elk.

alcoba /al'koβa/ n. f. bedroom; alcove.

alcoba de huéspedes /al'koβa de 'uespeðes/ guest room.

alcoba de respeto /al'koβa de rres'peto/ guest room.

alcohol /al'kool/ n. m. alcohol.

alcohólico /alko'oliko/ **-ca** a. & n. alcoholic.

aldaba /al'daβa/ n. f. latch.

aldea /al'dea/ n. f. village.

alegación /alega'θion; alega'sion/ n. f. allegation.

alegar /ale'gar/ v. allege.

alegrar /ale'grar/ v. make happy, brighten.

alegrarse /ale'grarse/ v. be glad.

alegre /a'legre/ a. glad, cheerful, merry.

alegría /ale'gria/ n. f. gaiety, cheer.

alejarse /ale'harse/ v. move away, off.

alemán /ale'man/ **-ana** a. & n. German.

Alemania /ale'mania/ n. f. Germany.

alentar /alen'tar/ v. cheer up, encourage.

alergia /aler'hia/ n. f. allergy.

alerta /a'lerta/ adv. on the alert.

aleve /a'leβe/ **alevoso** a. treacherous.

alfabeto /alfa'βeto/ n. m. alphabet.

alfalfa /al'falfa/ n. f. alfalfa.

alfarería /alfare'ria/ n. f. pottery.

alférez /al'fereθ; al'feres/ n. m. (naval) ensign.

alfil /al'fil/ n. m. (chess) bishop.

alfiler /alfi'ler/ n. m. pin.

alfombra /al'fombra/ n. f. carpet, rug.

alforja /al'forha/ n. f. knapsack; saddlebag.

alga /'alga/ n. f. seaweed.

alga marina /'alga ma'rina/ seaweed.

algarabía /algara'βia/ n. f. jargon; din.

álgebra /'alheβra/ n. f. algebra.

algo /'algo/ pron. & adv. something, somewhat; anything.

algodón /algo'ðon/ n. m. cotton.

algodón hidrófilo /algo'ðon i'ðrofilo/ absorbent cotton.

alguien /'algien/ pron. somebody, someone; anybody, anyone.

algún /al'gun/ **-no -na** a. & pron. some; any.

alhaja /al'aha/ n. f. jewel.

aliado /a'liaðo/ **-da** a. & n. allied; ally. —**aliar,** v.

alianza /a'lianθa; a'liansa/ n. f. alliance.

alicates /ali'kates/ n. m.pl. pliers.

aliento /a'liento/ n. m. breath. **dar a.,** encourage.

aligerar /alihe'rar/ v. lighten.

alimentar /alimen'tar/ v. feed, nourish.

alimento /ali'mento/ n. m. nourishment, food.

alinear /aline'ar/ v. line up; Pol. align.

aliñar /ali'ɲar/ v. dress (a salad).

aliño /a'liɲo/ n. m. salad dressing.

alisar /ali'sar/ v. smooth.

alistamiento /alista'miento/ n. m. enlistment.

alistar /alis'tar/ v. make ready, prime.

alistarse /alis'tarse/ v. get ready; Mil. enlist.

aliviar /ali'βiar/ v. alleviate, relieve, ease.

alivio /a'liβio/ n. m. relief.

allá /a'ʎa; a'ya/ adv. there. **más a.,** beyond, farther on.

allanar /aʎa'nar; aya'nar/ v. flatten, smooth, plane.

allí /a'ʎi; a'yi/ adv. there. **por a.,** that way.

alma /'alma/ n. f. soul.

almacén /alma'θen; alma'sen/ n. m. department store; storehouse, warehouse.

almacenaje /almaθe'nahe; almase'nahe/ n. m. storage.

almacenar /almaθe'nar; almase'nar/ v. store.

almanaque /alma'nake/ n. m. almanac.

almeja /al'meha/ n. f. clam.

almendra /al'mendra/ n. f. almond.

almíbar /al'miβar/ n. m. syrup.

almidón /almi'ðon/ n. m. starch. —**almidonar,** v.

almirante /almi'rante/ n. m. admiral.

almohada /almo'aða/ n. f. pillow.

almuerzo /al'muerθo; al'muerso/ *n. m.* lunch. —**almorzar,** *v.*

alojamiento /aloha'miento/ *n. m.* lodging, accommodations.

alojar /alo'har/ *v.* lodge, house.

alojarse /alo'harse/ *v.* stay, room.

alquiler /alki'ler/ *n. m.* rent. —**alquilar,** *v.*

alrededor /alreðe'ðor/ *adv.* around.

alrededores /alreðe'ðores/ *n. m.pl.* environs.

altanero /alta'nero/ *a.* haughty.

altar /al'tar/ *n. m.* altar.

altavoz /ˌalta'βoθ/ /ˌalta'βos/ *n. m.* loudspeaker.

alteración /altera'θion; altera'sion/ *f.* alteration.

alterar /alte'rar/ *v.* alter.

alternativa /alterna'tiβa/ *n. f.* alternative. —**alternativo,** *a.*

alterno /al'terno/ *a.* alternate. —**alternar,** *v.*

alteza /al'teθa; al'tesa/ *n. f.* highness.

altivo /al'tiβo/ *a.* proud, haughty; lofty.

alto /'alto/ *a.* **1.** high, tall; loud. —*n.* **2.** *m.* height, story (house).

altura /al'tura/ *n. f.* height, altitude.

alud /a'luð/ *n. m.* avalanche.

aludir /alu'ðir/ *v.* allude.

alumbrado /alum'braðo/ *n. m.* lighting.

alumbrar /alum'brar/ *v.* light.

aluminio /alu'minio/ *n. m.* aluminum.

alumno /a'lumno/ **-na** *n.* student, pupil.

alusión /alu'sion/ *n. f.* allusion.

alza /'alθa; 'alsa/ *n. f.* rise; boost.

alzar /al'θar; al'sar/ *v.* raise, lift.

ama /'ama/ *n. f.* housewife, mistress (of house). **a. de llaves,** housekeeper.

amable /a'maβle/ *a.* kind; pleasant; sweet.

amalgamar /amalga'mar/ *v.* amalgamate.

amamantar /amaman'tar/ *v.* suckle, nurse.

amanecer /amane'θer; amane'ser/ *n.* **1.** *m.* dawn, daybreak. —*v.* **2.** dawn; awaken.

amante /a'mante/ *n. m. & f.* lover.

amapola /ama'pola/ *n. f.* poppy.

amar /a'mar/ *v.* love.

amargo /a'margo/ *a.* bitter.

amargón /amar'gon/ *n. m.* dandelion.

amargura /amar'gura/ *n. f.* bitterness.

amarillo /ama'riʎo; ama'riyo/ *a.* yellow.

amarradero /amarra'ðero/ *n. m.* mooring.

amarrar /ama'rrar/ *v.* hitch, moor, tie up.

amartillar /amarti'ʎar; amarti'yar/ *v.* hammer; cock (a gun).

amasar /ama'sar/ *v.* knead, mold.

ámbar /'ambar/ *n. m.* amber.

ambarino /amba'rino/ *a.* amber.

ambición /ambi'θion; ambi'sion/ *n. f.* ambition.

ambicionar /ambiθio'nar; ambisio'nar/ *v.* aspire to.

ambicioso /ambi'θioso; ambi'sioso/ *a.* ambitious.

ambientalista /ambienta'lista/ *n. m. & f.* environmentalist.

ambiente /am'biente/ *n. m.* environment, atmosphere.

ambigüedad /ambigue'ðað/ *n. f.* ambiguity.

ambiguo /am'biguo/ *a.* ambiguous.

ambos /'ambos/ *a. & pron.* both.

ambulancia /ambu'lanθia; ambu'lansia/ *n. f.* ambulance.

amenaza /ame'naθa; ame'nasa/ *n. f.* threat, menace.

amenazar /amena'θar; amena'sar/ *v.* threaten, menace.

ameno /a'meno/ *a.* pleasant.

americana /ameri'kana/ *n. f.* suit coat.

americano /ameri'kano/ **-na** *a. & n.* American.

ametralladora /ametraʎa'ðora; ametraya'ðora/ *n. f.* machine gun.

amigable /ami'gaβle/ *a.* amicable, friendly.

amígdala /a'migðala/ *n. f.* tonsil.

amigo /a'migo/ **-ga** *n.* friend.

aminorar /amino'rar/ *v.* lessen, reduce.

amistad /amis'tað/ *n. f.* friendship.

amistoso /amis'toso/ *a.* friendly.

amniocéntesis /amnioθen'tesis; amniosen'tesis/ *n. m.* amniocentesis.

amo /'amo/ *n. m.* master.

amonestaciones /amonesta'θiones; amonesta'siones/ *n. f.pl.* banns.

amonestar /amones'tar/ *v.* admonish.

amoníaco /amo'niako/ *n. m.* ammonia.

amontonar /amonto'nar/ *v.* amass, pile up.

amor /a'mor/ *n. m.* love. **a. propio,** self-esteem.

amorío /amo'rio/ *n. m.* romance, love affair.

amoroso /amo'roso/ *a.* amorous, loving.

amortecer /amorte'θer; amorte'ser/ *v.* deaden.

amparar /ampa'rar/ *v.* aid, befriend; protect, shield.

amparo /am'paro/ *n. m.* protection.

ampliar /amp'liar/ *v.* enlarge; elaborate.

amplificar /amplifi'kar/ *v.* amplify.

amplio /'amplio/ *a.* ample, roomy.

ampolla /am'poʎa; am'poya/ *n. f.* bubble; bulb; blister.

amputar /ampu'tar/ *v.* amputate.

amueblar /amue'βlar/ *v.* furnish.

analfabeto /analfa'βeto/ **-ta** *a. & n.* illiterate.

analgésico /anal'hesiko/ *n. m.* pain killer.

análisis /a'nalisis/ *n. m.* analysis.

analizar /anali'θar; anali'sar/ *v.* analyze.

analogía /analo'hia/ *n. f.* analogy.

análogo /a'nalogo/ *a.* similar, analogous.

anarquía /anar'kia/ *n. f.* anarchy.

anatomía /anato'mia/ *n. f.* anatomy.

ancho /'antʃo/ *a.* wide, broad.

anchoa /an'tʃoa/ *n. f.* anchovy.

anchura /an'tʃura/ *n. f.* width, breadth.

anciano /an'θiano; an'siano/ **-na** *a. & n.* old, aged (person).

ancla /'ankla/ *n. f.* anchor. —**anclar,** *v.*

anclaje /an'klahe/ *n. m.* anchorage.

andamio /an'damio/ *n. m.* scaffold.

andar /an'dar/ *v.* walk; move, go.

andén /an'den/ *n. m.* (railroad) platform.

andrajoso /andra'hoso/ *a.* ragged, uneven.

anécdota /a'nekðota/ *n. f.* anecdote.

anegar /ane'gar/ *v.* flood, drown.

anestesia /anes'tesia/ *n. f.* anesthetic.

anexar /anek'sar/ *v.* annex.

anexión /anek'sion/ *n. f.* annexation.

anfitrión /anfitri'on/ **-na** *n.* host.

ángel /'anhel/ *n. m.* angel.

angosto /aŋ'gosto/ *a.* narrow.

anguila /aŋ'gila/ *n. f.* eel.

angular /aŋgu'lar/ *a.* angular.

ángulo /'aŋgulo/ *n. m.* angle.

angustia /aŋ'gustia/ *n. f.* anguish, agony.

angustiar /aŋgus'tiar/ *v.* distress.

anhelar /ane'lar/ *v.* long for.

anidar /ani'ðar/ *v.* nest, nestle.

anillo /a'niʎo; a'niyo/ *n. m.* ring; circle.

animación /anima'θion; anima'sion/ *n. f.* animation; bustle.

animado /ani'maðo/ *a.* animated, lively; animate.

animal /ani'mal/ *a. & n.* animal.

ánimo /'animo/ *n. m.* state of mind, spirits; courage.

aniquilar /aniki'lar/ *v.* annihilate, destroy.

aniversario /aniβer'sario/ *n. m.* anniversary.

anoche /a'notʃe/ *adv.* last night.

anochecer /anotʃe'θer; anotʃe'ser/ *n.* **1.** *m.* twilight, nightfall. —*v.* **2.** get dark.

anónimo /a'nonimo/ *a.* anonymous.

anorexia /ano'reksia/ *n. f.* anorexia.

anormal /anor'mal/ *a.* abnormal.

anotación /anota'θion; anota'sion/ *f.* annotation.

anotar /ano'tar/ *v.* annotate.

ansia /'ansia/ **ansiedad** *n. f.* anxiety.

ansioso /an'sioso/ *a.* anxious.

antagonismo /antago'nismo/ *n. m.* antagonism.

antagonista /antago'nista/ *n. m. & f.* antagonist, opponent.

anteayer /antea'yer/ *adv.* day before yesterday.

antebrazo /ante'βraθo; ante'βraso/ *n. m.* forearm.

antecedente /anteθe'ðente; antese'ðente/ *a. & m.* antecedent.

anteceder /anteθe'ðer; antese'ðer/ *v.* precede.

antecesor /anteθe'sor; antese'sor/ *n. m.* ancestor.

antemano /ante'mano/ *de a.*, in advance.

antena /an'tena/ *n. f.* antenna.

antena parabólica /an'tena para'βolika/ satellite dish.

anteojos /ante'ohos/ *n. m.pl.* eyeglasses.

antepasado /antepa'saðo/ *n. m.* ancestor.

antepenúltimo /antepe'nultimo/ *a.* antepenultimate.

anterior /ante'rior/ *a.* previous, former.

antes /'antes/ *adv.* before; formerly.

antibala /anti'bala/ *a.* bulletproof.

anticipación /antiθipa'θion; antisipa'sion/ *n. f.* anticipation.

anticipar /antiθi'par; antisi'par/ *v.* anticipate; advance.

anticonceptivo /antikonθep'tiβo; antikonsep'tiβo/ *a. & n.* contraceptive.

anticongelante /antikoŋge'lante/ *n. m.* antifreeze.

anticuado /anti'kuaðo/ *a.* antiquated, obsolete.

antídoto /an'tiðoto/ *n. m.* antidote.

antigüedad /antigue'ðað/ *n. f.* antiquity; antique.

antiguo /an'tiguo/ *a.* former; old; antique.

antihistamínico /antiista'miniko/ *n. m.* antihistamine.

antílope /an'tilope/ *n. m.* antelope.

antinuclear /antinukle'ar/ *a.* antinuclear.

antipatía /antipa'tia/ *n. f.* antipathy.

antipático /anti'patiko/ *a.* disagreeable, nasty.

antiséptico /anti'septiko/ *a. & m.* antiseptic.

antojarse /anto'harse/ *v.* **se me antoja...** etc., I desire..., take a fancy to..., etc.

antojo /an'toho/ *n. m.* whim, fancy.

antorcha /an'tortʃa/ *n. f.* torch.

antracita /antra'θita; antra'sita/ *n. f.* anthracite.

anual /a'nual/ *a.* annual, yearly.

anudar /anu'ðar/ *v.* knot; tie.

anular /anu'lar/ *v.* annul, void.

anunciar /anun'θiar; anun'siar/ *v.* announce; proclaim, advertise.

anuncio /a'nunθio; a'nunsio/ *n. m.* announcement; advertisement.

añadir /aɲa'ðir/ *v.* add.

añil /a'ɲil/ *n. m.* bluing; indigo.

año /'aɲo/ *n. m.* year.

apacible /apa'θiβle; apa'siβle/ *a.* peaceful, peaceable.

apaciguamiento /aˌpaθigua'miento;

apacíguamiento /aˌpasigua'miento/ *n. m.* appeasement.

apaciguar /apaθi'guar; apasi'guar/ *v.* appease; placate.

apagado /apa'gaðo/ *a.* dull.

apagar /apa'gar/ *v.* extinguish, quench, put out.

apagón /apa'gn/ *n. m.* blackout.

aparador /apara'ðor/ *n. m.* buffet, cupboard.

aparato /apa'rato/ *n. m.* apparatus; machine; appliance, set.

aparcamiento /aparka'miento/ *n. m.* parking lot; parking space.

aparecer /apare'θer; apare'ser/ *v.* appear, show up.

aparejo /apa'reho/ *n. m.* rig. —**aparejar,** *v.*

aparentar /aparen'tar/ *v.* pretend; profess.

aparente /apa'rente/ *a.* apparent.

apariencia /apa'rienθia; apa'riensia/ **aparición** *n. f.* appearance.

apartado /apar'taðo/ *a.* **1.** aloof; separate. —*n.* **2.** *m.* post-office box.

apartamento /aparta'mento/ *n. m.* apartment. **a. en propiedad,** condominium.

apartar /apar'tar/ *v.* separate; remove.

aparte /a'parte/ *adv.* apart; aside.

apartheid /apar'teið/ *n. m.* apartheid.

apasionado /apasio'naðo/ *a.* passionate.

apatía /apa'tia/ *n. f.* apathy.

apearse /ape'arse/ *v.* get off, alight.

apedrear /apeðre'ar/ *v.* stone.

apelación /apela'θion; apela'sion/ *n. f.* appeal. —**apelar,** *v.*

apellido /ape'ʎiðo; ape'yiðo/ *n. m.* family name.

apellido materno /ape'ʎiðo ma'terno; ape'yiðo ma'terno/ mother's family name.

apellido paterno /ape'ʎiðo pa'terno; ape'yiðo pa'terno/ father's family name.

apenas /a'penas/ *adv.* scarcely, hardly.

apéndice /a'pendiθe; a'pendise/ *n. m.* appendix.

apercibir /aperθi'βir; apersi'βir/ *v.* prepare, warn.

aperitivo /aperi'tiβo/ *n. m.* appetizer.

aperos /a'peros/ *n. m.pl.* implements.

apestar /apes'tar/ *v.* infect; stink.

apetecer /apete'θer; apete'ser/ *v.* desire, have appetite for.

apetito /ape'tito/ *n. m.* appetite.

ápice /'apiθe; 'apise/ *n. m.* apex.

apilar /api'lar/ *v.* stack.

apio /'apio/ *n. m.* celery.

aplacar /apla'kar/ *v.* appease; placate.

aplastar /aplas'tar/ *v.* crush, flatten.

aplaudir /aplau'ðir/ *v.* applaud, cheer.

aplauso /a'plauso/ *n. m.* applause.

aplazar /apla'θar; apla'sar/ *v.* postpone, put off.

aplicable /apli'kaβle/ *a.* applicable.

aplicado /apli'kaðo/ *a.* industrious, diligent.

aplicar /apli'kar/ *v.* apply.

aplomo /a'plomo/ *n. m.* aplomb, poise.

apoderado /apoðe'raðo/ **-da** *n.* attorney.

apoderarse de /apoðe'rarse de/ *v.* get hold of, seize.

apodo /a'poðo/ *n. m.* nickname. —**apodar,** *v.*

apologético /apolo'hetiko/ *a.* apologetic.

apoplejía /apople'hia/ *n. f.* apoplexy.

aposento /apo'sento/ *n. m.* room, flat.

apostar /apos'tar/ *v.* bet, wager.

apóstol /a'postol/ *n. m.* apostle.

apoyar /apo'yar/ *v.* support, prop; lean.

apoyo /a'poyo/ *n. m.* support; prop; aid; approval.

apreciable /apreθia'βle; apresia'βle/ *a.* appreciable.

apreciar /apre'θiar; apre'siar/ v. appreciate, prize.

aprecio /a'preθio; a'presio/ n. m. appreciation, regard.

apremio /a'premio/ n. m. pressure, compulsion.

aprender /apren'der/ v. learn.

aprendiz /apren'diθ; apren'dis/ n. m. apprentice.

aprendizaje /aprendi'θahe; aprendi'sahe/ n. m. apprenticeship.

aprensión /apren'sion/ n. f. apprehension.

aprensivo /apren'siβo/ a. apprehensive.

apresurado /apresu'raðo/ a. hasty, fast.

apresurar /apresu'rar/ v. hurry, speed up.

apretado /apre'taðo/ a. tight.

apretar /apre'tar/ v. squeeze, press; tighten.

apretón /apre'ton/ n. m. squeeze.

aprieto /a'prieto/ n. m. plight, predicament.

aprobación /aproβa'θion; aproβa'sion/ n. f. approbation, approval.

aprobar /apro'βar/ v. approve.

apropiación /apropia'θion; apropia'sion/ n. f. appropriation.

apropiado /apro'piaðo/ a. appropriate. —**apropiar**, v.

aprovechar /aproβe't∫ar/ v. profit by.

aprovecharse /aproβe't∫arse/ v. take advantage.

aproximado /aproksi'maðo/ a. approximate.

aproximarse a /aproksi'marse a/ v. approach.

aptitud /apti'tuð/ n. f. aptitude.

apto /'apto/ a. apt.

apuesta /a'puesta/ n. f. bet, wager, stake.

apuntar /apun'tar/ v. point, aim; prompt; write down.

apunte /a'punte/ n. m. annotation, note; promptings, cue.

apuñalar /apuɲa'lar/ v. stab.

apurar /apu'rar/ v. hurry; worry.

apuro /a'puro/ n. m. predicament, scrape, trouble.

aquel /a'kel/ **aquella** dem. a. that.

aquél /a'kel/ **aquélla** dem. pron. that (one); the former.

aquello /a'keʎo; a'keyo/ dem. pron. that.

aquí /a'ki/ adv. here. **por a.**, this way.

aquietar /akie'tar/ v. allay; lull, pacify.

ara /'ara/ n. f. altar.

árabe /'araβe/ a. & n. Arab, Arabic.

arado /a'raðo/ n. m. plow. —**arar**, v.

arándano /a'randano/ n. m. cranberry.

araña /a'raɲa/ n. f. spider. **a. de luces**, chandelier.

arbitración /arβitra'θion; arβitra'sion/ n. f. arbitration.

arbitrador /arβitra'ðor/ **-ra** n. arbitrator.

arbitraje /arβi'trahe/ n. m. arbitration.

arbitrar /arβi'trar/ v. arbitrate.

arbitrario /arβi'trario/ a. arbitrary.

árbitro /'arβitro/ n. m. arbiter, umpire, referee.

árbol /'arβol/ n. m. tree; mast.

árbol genealógico /'arβol henea'lohiko/ family tree.

arbusto /ar'βusto/ n. m. bush, shrub.

arca /'arka/ n. f. chest; ark.

arcada /ar'kaða/ n. f. arcade.

arcaico /ar'kaiko/ a. archaic.

arce /'arθe; 'arse/ n. m. maple.

archipiélago /art∫i'pielago/ n. m. archipelago.

archivador /art∫iβa'ðor/ n. m. file cabinet.

archivo /ar't∫iβo/ n. m. archive; file. —**archivar**, v.

arcilla /ar'θiʎa; ar'siya/ n. f. clay.

arco /'arko/ n. m. arc; arch; (archer's) bow. **a. iris**, rainbow.

arder /ar'ðer/ v. burn.

ardid /ar'ðið/ n. m. stratagem, cunning.

ardiente /ar'ðiente/ a. ardent, burning, fiery.

ardilla /ar'ðiʎa; ar'ðiya/ n. f. squirrel.

ardor /ar'ðor/ n. m. ardor, fervor.

ardor de estómago /ar'ðor de es'tomago/ heartburn.

arduo /'arðuo/ a. arduous.

área /'area/ n. f. area.

arena /a'rena/ n. f. sand; arena.

arenoso /are'noso/ a. sandy.

arenque /a'renke/ n. m. herring.

arete /a'rete/ n. m. earring.

argentino /arhen'tino/ **-na** a. & n. Argentine.

argüir /ar'guir/ v. dispute, argue.

árido /'ariðo/ a. arid.

aristocracia /aristo'kraθia; aristo'krasia/ n. f. aristocracy.

aristócrata /aris'tokrata/ n. f. aristocrat.

aristocrático /aristo'kratiko/ a. aristocratic.

aritmética /arit'metika/ n. f. arithmetic.

arma /'arma/ n. f. weapon, arm.

armadura /arma'ðura/ n. f. armor; reinforcement; framework.

armamento /arma'mento/ n. m. armament.

armar /ar'mar/ v. arm.

armario /ar'mario/ n. m. cabinet, bureau, wardrobe.

armazón /arma'θon; arma'son/ n. m. framework, frame.

armería /arme'ria/ n. f. armory.

armisticio /armis'tiθio; armis'tisio/ n. m. armistice.

armonía /armo'nia/ n. f. harmony.

armonioso /armo'nioso/ a. harmonious.

armonizar /armoni'θar; armoni'sar/ v. harmonize.

arnés /ar'nes/ n. m. harness.

aroma /a'roma/ n. f. aroma, fragrance.

aromático /aro'matiko/ a. aromatic.

arpa /'arpa/ n. f. harp.

arquear /arke'ar/ v. arch.

arquitecto /arki'tekto/ n. m. architect.

arquitectura /arkitek'tura/ n. f. architecture.

arquitectural /arkitektu'ral/ a. architectural.

arrabal /arra'βal/ n. m. suburb.

arraigar /arrai'gar/ v. take root, settle.

arrancar /arran'kar/ v. pull out, tear out; start up.

arranque /a'rranke/ n. m. dash, sudden start; fit of anger.

arrastrar /arras'trar/ v. drag.

arrebatar /arreβa'tar/ v. snatch, grab.

arrebato /arre'βato/ n. m. sudden attack, fit of anger.

arrecife /arre'θife; arre'sife/ n. m. reef.

arreglar /arre'glar/ v. arrange; repair, fix; adjust, settle.

arreglárselas /arre'glarselas/ v. manage, shift for oneself.

arreglo /a'rreglo/ n. m. arrangement, settlement.

arremangarse /arremaɲ'garse/ v. roll up one's sleeves; roll up one's pants.

arremeter /arreme'ter/ v. attack.

arrendar /arren'dar/ v. rent.

arrepentimiento /arrepenti'miento/ n. m. repentance.

arrepentirse /arrepen'tirse/ v. repent.

arrestar /arres'tar/ v. arrest.

arriba /a'rriβa/ adv. up; upstairs.

arriendo /a'rriendo/ n. m. lease.

arriero /a'rriero/ n. m. muleteer.

arriesgar /arries'gar/ v. risk.

arrimarse /arri'marse/ v. lean.

arrodillarse /arroði'ʎarse; arroði'yarse/ v. kneel.

arrogancia /arro'ganθia; arro'gansia/ n. f. arrogance.

arrogante /arro'gante/ a. arrogant.

arrojar /arro'har/ v. throw, hurl; shed.

arrollar /arro'ʎar; arro'yar/ v. roll, coil.

arroyo /a'rroyo/ n. m. brook; gully; gutter.

arroz /a'rroθ; a'rros/ n. m. rice.

arruga /a'rruga/ n. f. ridge; wrinkle.

arrugar /arru'gar/ v. wrinkle, crumple.

arruinar /arrui'nar/ v. ruin, destroy, wreck.

arsenal /arse'nal/ n. m. arsenal; armory.

arsénico /ar'seniko/ n. m. arsenic.

arte /'arte/ n. m. (f. in pl.) art, craft; wiliness.

arteria /ar'teria/ n. f. artery.

artesa /ar'tesa/ n. f. trough.

artesano /arte'sano/ **-na** n. artisan, craftsman.

ártico /'artiko/ a. arctic.

articulación /artikula'θion; artikula'sion/ n. f. articulation; joint.

articular /artiku'lar/ v. articulate.

artículo /ar'tikulo/ n. m. article.

artífice /ar'tifiθe; ar'tifise/ n. m. & f. artisan.

artificial /artifi'θial; artifi'sial/ a. artificial.

artificio /arti'fiθio; arti'fisio/ n. m. artifice, device.

artificioso /artifi'θioso; artifi'sioso/ a. affected.

artillería /artiʎe'ria; artiye'ria/ n. f. artillery.

artista /ar'tista/ n. m. & f. artist.

artístico /ar'tistiko/ a. artistic.

artritis /ar'tritis/ n. f. arthritis.

arzobispo /arθo'βispo; arso'βispo/ n. m. archbishop.

as /as/ n. m. ace.

asado /a'saðo/ a. & n. roast.

asaltador /asalta'ðor/ **-ra** n. assailant.

asaltante /asal'tante/ n. m. & f. mugger.

asaltar /asal'tar/ v. assail, attack.

asalto /a'salto/ n. m. assault. —**asaltar**, v.

asamblea /asam'βlea/ n. f. assembly.

asar /a'sar/ v. roast; broil, cook (meat).

asaz /a'saθ; a'sas/ adv. enough; quite.

ascender /asθen'der; assen'der/ v. ascend, go up; amount.

ascenso /as'θenso; as'senso/ n. m. ascent.

ascensor /asθen'sor; assen'sor/ n. m. elevator.

ascensorista /asθenso'rista; assenso'rista/ n. m. & f. (elevator) operator.

asco /'asko/ n. m. nausea; disgusting thing. **qué a.**, how disgusting.

aseado /ase'aðo/ a. tidy. —**asear**, v.

asediar /ase'ðiar/ v. besiege.

asedio /a'seðio/ n. m. siege.

asegurar /asegu'rar/ v. assure; secure.

asegurarse /asegu'rarse/ v. make sure.

asemejarse a /aseme'harse a/ v. resemble.

asentar /asen'tar/ v. settle; seat.

asentimiento /asenti'miento/ n. m. assent. —**asentir**, v.

aseo /a'seo/ n. m. neatness, tidiness.

aseos /a'seos/ n. m.pl. restroom.

asequible /ase'kiβle/ a. attainable; affordable.

aserción /aser'θion; aser'sion/ n. f. assertion.

aserrar /ase'rrar/ v. saw.

asesinar /asesi'nar/ v. assassinate; murder, slay.

asesinato /asesi'nato/ n. m. assassination, murder.

asesino /ase'sino/ **-na** n. murderer, assassin.

aseveración /aseβera'θion; aseβera'sion/ n. f. assertion.

aseverar /aseβe'rar/ v. assert.

asfalto /as'falto/ n. m. asphalt.

así /a'si/ adv. so, thus, this way, that way. **a. como**, as well as. **a. que**, as soon as.

asiático /a'siatiko/ **-ca** a. & n. Asiatic.

asiduo /a'siðuo/ a. assiduous.

asiento /a'siento/ n. m. seat; chair; site.

asiento delantero /a'siento delan'tero/ front seat.

asiento trasero /a'siento tra'sero/ back seat.

asignar /asig'nar/ v. assign; allot.

asilo /a'silo/ n. m. asylum, sanctuary.

asimilar /asimi'lar/ v. assimilate.

asir /a'sir/ v. grasp.

asistencia /asis'tenθia; asistensia/ n. f. attendance, presence.

asistir /asis'tir/ v. be present, attend.

asno /'asno/ n. m. donkey.

asociación /asoθia'θion; asosia'sion/ n. f. association.

asociado /aso'θiaðo; aso'siaðo/ n. m. associate, partner.

asociar /aso'θiar; aso'siar/ v. associate.

asolar /aso'lar/ v. desolate; burn, parch.

asoleado /asole'aðo/ a. sunny.

asomar /aso'mar/ v. appear, loom up, show up.

asombrar /asom'βrar/ v. astonish, amaze.

asombro /a'sombro/ n. m. amazement, astonishment.

aspa /'aspa/ n. f. reel. —**aspar**, v.

aspecto /as'pekto/ n. m. aspect.

aspereza /aspe'reθa; aspe'resa/ n. f. harshness.

áspero /'aspero/ a. rough, harsh.

aspiración /aspira'θion; aspira'sion/ n. f. aspiration.

aspirador /aspira'ðor/ n. m. vacuum cleaner.

aspirar /aspi'rar/ v. aspire.

aspirina /aspi'rina/ n. f. aspirin.

asqueroso /aske'roso/ a. dirty, nasty, filthy.

asta /'asta/ n. f. shaft.

asterisco /aste'risko/ n. m. asterisk.

astilla /as'tiʎa; as'tiya/ n. f. splinter, chip. —**astillar**, v.

astillero /asti'ʎero; asti'yero/ n. m. dry dock.

astro /'astro/ n. m. star.

astronauta /astro'nauta/ n. m. & f. astronaut.

astronave /astro'naβe/ n. f. spaceship.

astronomía /astrono'mia/ n. f. astronomy.

astucia /as'tuθia; as'tusia/ n. f. cunning.

astuto /as'tuto/ a. astute, sly, shrewd.

asumir /asu'mir/ v. assume.

asunto /a'sunto/ n. m. matter, affair, business; subject.

asustar /asus'tar/ v. frighten, scare, startle.

atacar /ata'kar/ v. attack, charge.

atajo /a'taho/ n. m. shortcut.

ataque /a'take/ n. m. attack, charge; spell, stroke.

ataque cardíaco /a'take kar'ðiako/ heart attack.

atar /a'tar/ v. tie, bind, fasten.

atareado /atare'aðo/ a. busy.

atascar /atas'kar/ v. stall, stop, obstruct.

atasco /a'tasko/ n. m. traffic jam.

ataúd /ata'uð/ n. m. casket, coffin.

atavío /ata'βio/ n. m. dress; gear, equipment.

atemorizar /atemori'θar; atemori'sar/ v. frighten.

atención /aten'θion; aten'sion/ n. f. attention.

atender /aten'der/ v. heed; attend to, wait on.

atenerse a /ate'nerse a/ v. count on, depend on.

atentado /aten'taðo/ n. m. crime, offense.

atento /a'tento/ *a.* attentive, courteous.

ateo /a'teo/ *n. m.* atheist.

aterrizaje /aterri'θahe; aterri'sahe/ *n. m.* landing (of aircraft).

aterrizaje forzoso /aterri'θahe for-'θoso; aterri'sahe for'soso/ emergency landing, forced landing.

aterrizar /aterri'θar; aterri'sar/ *v.* land.

atesorar /ateso'rar/ *v.* hoard.

atestar /ates'tar/ *v.* witness.

atestiguar /atesti'guar/ *v.* attest, testify.

atinar /ati'nar/ *v.* hit upon.

atisbar /atis'βar/ *v.* scrutinize, pry.

Atlántico /at'lantiko/ *n. m.* Atlantic.

atlántico *a.* Atlantic.

atlas /'atlas/ *n. m.* atlas.

atleta /at'leta/ *n. m. & f.* athlete.

atlético /at'letiko/ *a.* athletic.

atletismo /atle'tismo/ *n. m.* athletics.

atmósfera /at'mosfera/ *n. f.* atmosphere.

atmosférico /atmos'feriko/ *a.* atmospheric.

atolladero /atoʎa'ðero; atoya'ðero/ *n. m.* dead end, impasse.

atómico /a'tomiko/ *a.* atomic.

átomo /'atomo/ *n. m.* atom.

atormentar /atormen'tar/ *v.* torment, plague.

atornillar /atorni'ʎar; atorni'yar/ *v.* screw.

atracción /atrak'θion; atrak'sion/ *n. f.* attraction.

atractivo /atrak'tiβo/ *a.* 1. attractive. —*n.* 2. *m.* attraction.

atraer /atra'er/ *v.* attract; lure.

atrapar /atra'par/ *v.* trap, catch.

atrás /a'tras/ *adv.* back; behind.

atrasado /atra'saðo/ *a.* belated; backward; slow (clock).

atrasar /atra'sar/ *v.* delay, retard; be slow.

atraso /a'traso/ *n. m.* delay; backwardness; (*pl.*) arrears.

atravesar /atraβe'sar/ *v.* cross.

atreverse /atre'βerse/ *v.* dare.

atrevido /atre'βiðo/ *a.* daring, bold.

atrevimiento /atreβi'miento/ *n. m.* boldness.

atribuir /atri'βuir/ *v.* attribute, ascribe.

atributo /atri'βuto/ *n. m.* attribute.

atrincherar /atrintʃe'rar/ *v.* entrench.

atrocidad /atroθi'ðað; atrosi'ðað/ *n. f.* atrocity, outrage.

atronar /atro'nar/ *v.* deafen.

atropellar /atrope'ʎar; atrope'yar/ *v.* trample; fell.

atroz /a'troθ; a'ntros/ *a.* atrocious.

atún /a'tun/ *n. m.* tuna.

aturdir /atur'ðir/ *v.* daze, stun, bewilder.

audacia /au'ðaθia; au'ðasia/ *n. f.* audacity.

audaz /au'ðaθ; au'ðas/ *a.* audacious, bold.

audible /au'ðiβle/ *a.* audible.

audífono /au'ðifono/ *n. m.* hearing aid.

audiovisual /auðioβi'sual/ *a.* audiovisual.

auditorio /auði'torio/ *n. m.* audience.

aula /'aula/ *n. f.* classroom, hall.

aullar /au'ʎar; au'yar/ *v.* howl, bay.

aullido /au'ʎiðo; au'yiðo/ *n. m.* howl.

aumentar /aumen'tar/ *v.* augment; increase, swell.

aun /a'un/ **aún** *adv.* still; even. **a. cuando,** even though, even if.

aunque /'aunke/ *conj.* although, though.

áureo /'aureo/ *a.* golden.

aureola /aure'ola/ *n. f.* halo.

auriculares /auriku'lares/ *n. m.pl.* headphones.

aurora /au'rora/ *n. f.* dawn.

ausencia /au'senθia; au'sensia/ *n. f.* absence.

ausentarse /ausen'tarse/ *v.* stay away.

ausente /au'sente/ *a.* absent.

auspicio /aus'piθio; aus'pisio/ *n. m.* auspice.

austeridad /austeri'ðað/ *n. f.* austerity.

austero /aus'tero/ *a.* austere.

austriaco /aus'triako/ **-ca** *a. & f.* Austrian.

auténtico /au'tentiko/ *a.* authentic.

auto /'auto/ **automóvil** *n. m.* auto, automobile.

autobús /auto'βus/ *n. m.* bus.

autocine /auto'θine; auto'sine/ **autocinema** *n. m.* drive-in (movie theater).

automático /auto'matiko/ *a.* automatic.

autonomía /autono'mia/ *n. f.* autonomy.

autopista /auto'pista/ *n. f.* expressway.

autor /au'tor/ *n. m.* author.

autoridad /autori'ðað/ *n. f.* authority.

autoritario /autori'tario/ *a.* authoritarian; authoritative.

autorizar /autori'θar; autori'sar/ *v.* authorize.

autostop /auto'stop/ *n. m.* hitchhiking. **hacer a.,** to hitchhike.

auxiliar /auksi'liar/ *a.* 1. auxiliary. —*v.* 2. assist, aid.

auxilio /auk'silio/ *n. m.* aid, assistance.

avaluar /aβa'luar/ *v.* evaluate, appraise.

avance /a'βanθe; a'βanse/ *n. m.* advance. —**avanzar,** *v.*

avaricia /aβa'riθia; aβa'risia/ *n. f.* avarice.

avariento /aβa'riento/ *a.* miserly, greedy.

avaro /a'βaro/ **-ra** *a. & m.* miser; miserly.

ave /'aβe/ *n. f.* bird.

avellana /aβe'ʎana; aβe'yana/ *n. f.* hazelnut.

Ave María /aβema'ria/ *n. m.* Hail Mary.

avena /a'βena/ *n. f.* oat.

avenida /aβe'niða/ *n. f.* avenue; flood.

avenirse /aβe'nirse/ *v.* compromise; agree.

aventajar /aβenta'har/ *v.* surpass, get ahead of.

aventar /aβen'tar/ *v.* fan; scatter.

aventura /aβen'tura/ *n. f.* adventure.

aventurar /aβentu'rar/ *v.* venture, risk, gamble.

aventurero /aβentu'rero/ **-ra** *a. & n.* adventurous; adventurer.

avergonzado /aβergon'θaðo; aβergon'saðo/ *a.* ashamed, abashed.

avergonzar /aβergon'θar; aβergon'sar/ *v.* shame, abash.

avería /aβe'ria/ *n. f.* damage. —**averiar,** *v.*

averiguar /aβeri'guar/ *v.* ascertain, find out.

aversión /aβer'sion/ *n. f.* aversion.

avestruz /aβes'truθ; aβes'trus/ *n. m.* ostrich.

aviación /aβia'θion; aβia'sion/ *n. f.* aviation.

aviador /aβia'ðor/ **-ra** *n.* aviator.

ávido /'aβiðo/ *a.* avid; eager.

avión /a'βion/ *n. m.* airplane.

avisar /aβi'sar/ *v.* notify, let know; warn, advise.

aviso /a'βiso/ *n. m.* notice, announcement; advertisement; warning.

avispa /a'βispa/ *n. f.* wasp.

avivar /aβi'βar/ *v.* enliven, revive.

axila /ak'sila/ *n. f.* armpit.

aya /'aya/ *n. f.* governess.

ayatolá /aya'tola/ *n. m.* ayatollah.

ayer /a'yer/ *adv.* yesterday.

ayuda /a'yuða/ *n. f.* help, aid. —**ayudar,** *v.*

ayudante /ayu'ðante/ *a.* assistant, helper; adjutant.

ayuno /a'yuno/ *n. m.* fast. —**ayunar,** *v.*

ayuntamiento /ayunta'miento/ *n. m.* city hall.

azada /a'θaða; a'saða/ *n. f.,* **azadón,** *m.* hoe.

azafata /aθa'fata; asa'fata/ *n. f.* stewardess, flight attendant.

azar /a'θar; a'sar/ *n. m.* hazard, chance. **al a.,** at random.

azotar /aθo'tar; aso'tar/ *v.* whip, flog; belabor.

azote /a'θote; a'sote/ *n. m.* scourge, lash.

azúcar /a'θukar; a'sukar/ *n. m.* sugar.

azucarero /aθuka'rero; asuka'rero/ *n. m.* sugar bowl.

azúcar moreno /a'θukar mo'reno; a'sukar mo'reno/ brown sugar.

azul /a'θul; a'sul/ *a.* blue.

azulado /aθu'laðo; asu'laðo/ *a.* blue, bluish.

azulejo /aθu'leho; asu'leho/ *n. m.* tile; bluebird.

azul marino /a'θul ma'rino; a'sul ma'rino/ navy blue.

B

baba /'baβa/ *n. f.* drivel. —**babear,** *v.*

babador /baβa'ðor, ba'βero/ *n. m.* bib.

babucha /ba'βutʃa/ *n. f.* slipper.

bacalao /baka'lao/ *n. m.* codfish.

bachiller /batʃi'ʎer; batʃi'yer/ **-ra** *n.* bachelor (degree).

bacía /ba'θia; ba'sia/ *n. f.* washbasin.

bacterias /bak'terias/ *n. f.pl.* bacteria.

bacteriología /bakteriolo'hia/ *n. f.* bacteriology.

bahía /ba'ia/ *n. f.* bay.

bailador /baila'ðor/ **-ra** *n.* dancer.

bailar /bai'lar/ *v.* dance.

bailarín /baila'rin/ **-ina** *n.* dancer.

baile /'baile/ *n. m.* dance.

baja /'baha/ *n. f.* fall (in price); *Mil.* casualty.

bajar /ba'har/ *v.* lower; descend.

bajeza /ba'heθa; ba'hesa/ *n. f.* baseness.

bajo /'baho/ *prep.* 1. under, below. —*a.* 2. low; short; base.

bala /'bala/ *n. f.* bullet; ball; bale.

balada /ba'laða/ *n. f.* ballad.

balancear /balanθe'ar; balanse'ar/ *v.* balance; roll, swing, sway.

balanza /ba'lanθa; ba'lansa/ *n. f.* balance; scales.

balbuceo /balβu'θeo; balβu'seo/ *n. m.* stammer; babble. —**balbucear,** *v.*

Balcanes /bal'kanes/ *n. m.pl.* Balkans.

balcón /bal'kon/ *n. m.* balcony.

balde /'balde/ *n. m.* bucket, pail. **de b.,** gratis. **en b.,** in vain.

balística /ba'listika/ *n. f.* ballistics.

ballena /ba'ʎena; ba'yena/ *n. f.* whale.

balneario /balne'ario/ *n. m.* bathing resort; spa.

balompié /balom'pie/ *n. m.* football.

balón /ba'lon/ *n. m.* football; *Auto.* balloon tire.

baloncesto /balon'θesto; balon'sesto/ *n. m.* basketball.

balota /ba'lota/ *n. f.* ballot, vote. —**balotar,** *v.*

balsa /'balsa/ *n. f.* raft.

bálsamo /'balsamo/ *n. m.* balm.

baluarte /ba'luarte/ *n. m.* bulwark.

bambolearse /bambole'arse/ *v.* sway.

bambú /bam'βu/ *n.* bamboo.

banal /ba'nal/ *a.* banal, trite.

banana /ba'nana/ *n. f.* banana.

banano /ba'nano/ *n. m.* banana tree.

bancarrota /banka'rrota/ *n. f.* bankruptcy.

banco /'banko/ *n. m.* bank; bench; school of fish.

banco cooperativo /'banko koopera'tiβo/ credit union.

banda /'banda/ *n. f.* band.

bandada /ban'daða/ *n. f.* covey; flock.

banda sonora /'banda so'nora/ *n. f.* soundtrack.

bandeja /ban'deha/ *n. f.* tray.

bandera /ban'dera/ *n. f.* flag; banner; ensign.

bandido /ban'diðo/ **-da** *n.* bandit.

bando /'bando/ *n. m.* faction.

bandolero /bando'lero/ **-ra** *n.* bandit, robber.

banquero /ban'kero/ **-ra** *n.* banker.

banqueta /ban'keta/ *n. f.* stool; (Mex.) sidewalk.

banquete /ban'kete/ *n. m.* feast, banquet.

banquillo /ban'kiʎo; ban'kiyo/ *n. m.* stool.

bañar /ba'nar/ *v.* bathe.

bañera /ba'nera/ *n. f.* bathtub.

baño /'bano/ *n. m.* bath; bathroom.

bar /bar/ *n. m.* bar, pub.

baraja /ba'raha/ *n. f.* pack of cards; game of cards.

baranda /ba'randa/ *n. f.* railing, banister.

barato /ba'rato/ *a.* cheap.

barba /'barβa/ *n. f.* beard; chin.

barbacoa /barβa'koa/ *n. f.* barbecue; stretcher.

barbaridad /barβari'ðað/ *n. f.* barbarity; *Colloq.* excess (in anything).

bárbaro /'barβaro/ *a.* barbarous; crude.

barbería /barβe'ria/ *n. f.* barbershop.

barbero /bar'βero/ *n. m.* barber.

barca /'barka/ *n. f.* (small) boat.

barcaza /bar'kaθa; bar'kasa/ *n. f.* barge.

barco /'barko/ *n. m.* ship, boat.

barniz /bar'niθ; bar'nis/ *n. m.* varnish. —**barnizar,** *v.*

barómetro /ba'rometro/ *n. m.* barometer.

barón /ba'ron/ *n. m.* baron.

barquilla /bar'kiʎa; bar'kiya/ *n. f. Naut.* log.

barra /'barra/ *n. f.* bar.

barraca /ba'rraka/ *n. f.* hut, shed.

barrear /barre'ar/ *v.* bar, barricade.

barreno /ba'rreno/ *n. m.* blast, blasting. —**barrenar,** *v.*

barrer /ba'rrer/ *v.* sweep.

barrera /ba'rrera/ *n. f.* barrier.

barricada /barri'kaða/ *n. f.* barricade.

barriga /ba'rriga/ *n. f.* belly.

barril /ba'rril/ *n. m.* barrel; cask.

barrio /'barrio/ *n. m.* district, ward, quarter.

barro /'barro/ *n. m.* clay, mud.

base /'base/ *n. f.* base; basis. —**basar,** *v.*

base de datos /'base de 'datos/ database.

bastante /bas'tante/ *a.* 1. enough, plenty of. —*adv.* 2. enough; rather, quite.

bastar /bas'tar/ *v.* suffice, be enough.

bastardo /bas'tarðo/ **-a** *a. & n.* bastard.

bastear /baste'ar/ *v.* baste.

bastidor /basti'ðor/ *n. m.* wing (in theater).

bastón /bas'ton/ *n. m.* (walking) cane.

bastos /'bastos/ *n. m.pl.* clubs (cards).

basura /ba'sura/ *n. f.* refuse, dirt; garbage; junk.

basurero /basu'rero/ **-ra** *n.* scavenger.

batalla /ba'taʎa; ba'taya/ *n. f.* battle. —**batallar,** *v.*

batallón /bata'ʎon; bata'yon/ *n. m.* battalion.

batata /ba'tata/ *n. f.* sweet potato.

bate /'bate/ *n. m.* bat. —**batear,** *v.*

batería /bate'ria/ *n. f.* battery.

batido /ba'tiðo/ *n. m.* (cooking) batter; milkshake.

batidora /bati'ðora/ *n. f.* mixer (for food).

batir /ba'tir/ v. beat; demolish; conquer.

baúl /ba'ul/ n. m. trunk.

bautismo /bau'tismo/ n. m. baptism.

bautista /bau'tista/ n. m. & f. Baptist.

bautizar /bauti'θar; bauti'sar/ v. christen, baptize.

bautizo /bau'tiθo; bau'tiso/ n. m. baptism.

baya /'baia/ n. f. berry.

bayoneta /bayo'neta/ n. f. bayonet.

beato /be'ato/ a. blessed.

bebé /be'βe/ n. m. baby.

beber /be'βer/ v. drink.

bebible /be'βiβle/ a. drinkable.

bebida /be'βiða/ n. f. drink, beverage.

beca /'beka/ n. f. grant, scholarship.

becado /be'kaðo/ **-da** n. scholar.

becerro /be'θerro; be'serro/ n. m. calf; calfskin.

beldad /bel'dað/ n. f. beauty.

belga /'belga/ a. & n. Belgian.

Bélgica /'belhika/ n. f. Belgium.

belicoso /beli'koso/ a. warlike.

beligerante /belihe'rante/ a. & n. belligerent.

bellaco /be'ʎako; be'yako/ a. **1.** sly, roguish. —n. **2.** m. rogue.

bellas artes /'beʎas 'artes; 'beyas 'artes/ n. f.pl. fine arts.

belleza /be'ʎeθa; be'yesa/ n. f. beauty.

bello /'beʎo; 'beyo/ a. beautiful.

bellota /be'ʎota; be'yota/ n. f. acorn.

bendecir /bende'θir; bende'sir/ v. bless.

bendición /bendi'θion; bendi'sion/ n. f. blessing, benediction.

bendito /ben'dito/ a. blessed.

beneficio /bene'fiθio; bene'fisio/ n. m. benefit. —**beneficiar**, v.

beneficioso /benefi'θioso; benefi'sioso/ a. beneficial.

benevolencia /beneβo'lenθia; beneβo'lensia/ n. f. benevolence.

benévolo /be'neβolo/ a. benevolent.

benigno /be'nigno/ a. benign.

beodo /be'oðo/ **-da** a. & n. drunk.

berenjena /beren'hena/ n. f. eggplant.

beso /'beso/ n. m. kiss. —**besar**, v.

bestia /'bestia/ n. f. beast, brute.

betabel /beta'βel/ n. m. beet.

Biblia /'biβlia/ n. f. Bible.

bíblico /'biβliko/ a. Biblical.

biblioteca /biβlio'teka/ n. f. library.

bicarbonato /bikarβo'nato/ n. m. bicarbonate.

bicicleta /biθi'kleta; bisi'kleta/ n. f. bicycle.

bien /bien/ adv. **1.** well. —n. **2.** good; (pl.) possessions.

bienes inmuebles /'bienes i'mueβles/ n. m.pl. real estate.

bienestar /bienes'tar/ n. m. well-being, welfare.

bienhechor /biene'tʃor/ **-ra** n. benefactor.

bienvenida /biembe'niða/ n. f. welcome.

bienvenido /biembe'niðo/ a. welcome.

biftec /bif'tek/ n. m. steak.

bifurcación /bifurka'θion; bifurka'sion/ n. f. fork. —**bifurcar**, v.

bigamia /bi'gamia/ n. f. bigamy.

bígamo /'bigamo/ **-a** n. bigamist.

bigotes /bi'gotes/ n. m.pl. mustache.

bikini /bi'kini/ n. m. bikini.

bilingüe /bi'lingue/ a. bilingual.

bilingüismo /bilin'guismo/ n. m. bilingualism.

bilis /'bilis/ n. f. bile.

billar /bi'ʎar; bi'yar/ n. m. billiards.

billete /bi'ʎete; bi'yete/ n. m. ticket; bank note, bill.

billete de banco /bi'ʎete de 'banko; bi'yete de 'banko/ bank note.

billón /bi'ʎon; bi'yon/ n. m. billion.

bingo /'biŋgo/ n. m. bingo.

biodegradable /bioðegra'ðaβle/ a. biodegradable.

biografía /biogra'fia/ n. f. biography.

biología /biolo'hia/ n. f. biology.

biombo /'biombo/ n. m. folding screen.

bisabuela /bisa'βuela/ n. f. great-grandmother.

bisabuelo /bisa'βuelo/ n. m. great-grandfather.

bisel /bi'sel/ n. m. bevel. —**biselar**, v.

bisonte /bi'sonte/ n. m. bison.

bisté /bis'te/ **bistec** n. m. steak.

bisutería /bisute'ria/ n. f. costume jewelry.

bizarro /bi'θarro; bi'sarro/ a. brave; generous; smart.

bizco /'biθko/ **-ca 1.** cross-eyed person. —a. **2.** cross-eyed, squinting.

bizcocho /biθ'kotʃo; bis'kotʃo/ n. m. biscuit, cake.

blanco /'blanko/ a. **1.** white; blank. —n. **2.** m. white; target.

blandir /blan'dir/ v. brandish, flourish.

blando /'blando/ a. soft.

blanquear /blanke'ar/ v. whiten; bleach.

blasfemar /blasfe'mar/ v. blaspheme, curse.

blasfemia /blas'femia/ n. f. blasphemy.

blindado /blin'daðo/ a. armored.

blindaje /blin'dahe/ n. m. armor.

bloque /'bloke/ n. m. block. —**bloquear**, v.

bloqueo /blo'keo/ n. m. blockade. —**bloquear**, v.

blusa /'blusa/ n. f. blouse.

bobada /bo'βaða/ n. f. stupid, silly thing.

bobo /'boβo/ **-ba** a. & n. fool; foolish.

boca /'boka/ n. f. mouth.

bocado /bo'kaðo/ n. m. bit; bite, mouthful.

bocanada /boka'naða/ n. f. puff (of smoke); mouthful (of liquor).

bocazas /bo'kaθas/ n. m. & f. Colloq. bigmouth.

bochorno /bo'tʃorno/ n. m. sultry weather; embarrassment.

bocina /bo'θina; bo'sina/ n. f. horn.

boda /'boða/ n. f. wedding.

bodega /bo'ðega/ n. f. wine cellar; Naut. hold; (Carib.) grocery store.

bofetada /bofe'taða/ n. f. **bofetón**, m. slap.

boga /'boga/ n. f. vogue; fad.

bogar /bo'gar/ v. row (a boat).

bohemio /bo'emio/ **-a** a. & n. Bohemian.

boicoteo /boiko'teo/ n. m. boycott. —**boicotear**, v.

boina /'boina/ n. f. beret.

bola /'bola/ n. f. ball.

bola de nieve /'bola de 'nieβe/ snowball.

bolas de billar /'bolas de bi'ʎar; 'bolas de bi'yar/ billiard balls.

bolera /bo'lera/ n. f. bowling alley.

boletín /bole'tin/ n. m. bulletin.

boletín informativo /bole'tin informa'tiβo/ news bulletin.

boleto /bo'leto/ n. m. ticket. **b. de embarque**, boarding pass.

boliche /bo'litʃe/ n. m. bowling alley.

bolígrafo /bo'ligrafo/ n. m. ballpoint pen.

boliviano /boli'βiano/ **-a** a. & n. Bolivian.

bollo /'boʎo; 'boyo/ n. m. bun, loaf.

bolos /'bolos/ n. m.pl. bowling.

bolsa /'bolsa/ n. f. purse; stock exchange.

bolsa de agua caliente /'bolsa de 'agua ka'liente/ hot-water bottle.

bolsillo /bol'siʎo; bol'siyo/ n. m. pocket.

bomba /'bomba/ n. f. pump; bomb; gas station.

bombardear /bombarðe'ar/ v. bomb, bombard, shell.

bombear /bombe'ar/ v. pump.

bombero /bom'βero/ n. m. fireman.

bombilla /bom'βiʎa; bom'βiya/ n. f. (light) bulb.

bonanza /bo'nanθa; bo'nansa/ n. f. prosperity; fair weather.

bondad /bon'dað/ n. f. kindness; goodness.

bondadoso /bonda'ðoso/ a. kind, kindly.

bongó /boŋ'go/ n. m. bongo drum.

bonito /bo'nito/ a. pretty.

bono /'bono/ n. m. bonus; Fin. bond.

boqueada /boke'aða/ n. f. gasp; gape. —**boquear**, v.

boquilla /bo'kiʎa; bo'kiya/ n. f. cigarette holder.

bordado /bor'ðaðo/ n. m., **bordadura**, f. embroidery.

bordar /bor'ðar/ v. embroider.

borde /'borðe/ n. m. border, rim, edge, brink, ledge.

borde de la carretera /'borðe de la karre'tera/ roadside.

borla /'borla/ n. f. tassel.

borracho /bo'rratʃo/ **-a** a. & n. drunk.

borrachón /borra'tʃon/ **-na** n. drunkard.

borrador /borra'ðor/ n. m. eraser.

borradura /borra'ðura/ n. f. erasure.

borrar /bo'rrar/ v. erase, rub out.

borrasca /bo'rraska/ n. f. squall, storm.

borrico /bo'rriko/ n. m. donkey.

bosque /'boske/ n. m. forest, wood.

bosquejo /bos'keho/ n. m. sketch, draft. —**bosquejar**, v.

bostezo /bos'teθo; bos'teso/ n. m. yawn. —**bostezar**, v.

bota /'bota/ n. f. boot.

botalón /bota'lon/ n. m. Naut. boom.

botánica /bo'tanika/ n. f. botany.

botar /bo'tar/ v. throw out, throw away.

bote /'bote/ n. m. boat; can, box.

bote salvavidas /'bote salβa'βiðas/ lifeboat.

botica /bo'tika/ n. f. pharmacy, drugstore.

boticario /boti'kario/ n. m. pharmacist, druggist.

botín /bo'tin/ n. m. booty, plunder, spoils.

botiquín /boti'kin/ n. m. medicine chest.

boto /'boto/ a. dull, stupid.

botón /bo'ton/ n. m. button.

botones /bo'tones/ n. m. bellboy (in a hotel).

bóveda /'boβeða/ n. f. vault.

boxeador /boksea'ðor/ n. m. boxer.

boxeo /bok'seo/ n. m. boxing. —**boxear**, v.

boya /'boya/ n. f. buoy.

boyante /bo'yante/ a. buoyant.

bozal /bo'θal; bo'sal/ n. m. muzzle.

bragas /'bragas/ n. f.pl. panties.

bramido /bra'miðo/ n. m. roar, bellow. —**bramar**, v.

brasa /'brasa/ n. f. embers, grill. —**brasear**, v.

brasileño /brasi'leɲo/ **-ña** a. & n. Brazilian.

bravata /bra'βata/ n. f. bravado.

bravear /braβe'ar/ v. bully.

braza /'braθa; 'brasa/ n. f. fathom.

brazada /bra'θaða; bra'saða/ n. f. (swimming) stroke.

brazalete /braθa'lete; brasa'lete/ n. m. bracelet.

brazo /'braθo; 'braso/ n. m. arm.

brea /'brea/ n. f. tar, pitch.

brecha /'bretʃa/ n. f. gap, breach.

brécol /'brekol/ n. m. broccoli.

bregar /bre'gar/ v. scramble.

breña /'breɲa/ n. f. rough country with brambly shrubs.

Bretaña /bre'taɲa/ n. f. Britain.

breve /'breβe/ a. brief, short. **en b.**, shortly, soon.

brevedad /breβe'ðað/ n. f. brevity.

bribón /bri'βon/ **-na** n. rogue, rascal.

brida /'briða/ n. f. bridle.

brigada /bri'gaða/ n. f. brigade.

brillante /bri'ʎante; bri'yante/ a. **1.** brilliant, shiny. —n. **2.** m. diamond.

brillo /'briʎo; 'briyo/ n. m. shine, glitter. —**brillar**, v.

brinco /'brinko/ n. m. jump; bounce, skip. —**brincar**, v.

brindis /'brindis/ n. m. toast. —**brindar**, v.

brío /'brio/ n. m. vigor.

brioso /'brioso/ a. vigorous, spirited.

brisa /'brisa/ n. f. breeze.

brisa marina /'brisa ma'rina/ sea breeze.

británico /bri'taniko/ a. British.

brocado /bro'kaðo/ **-da** a. & n. brocade.

brocha /'brotʃa/ n. f. brush.

broche /'brotʃe/ n. m. brooch, clasp, pin.

broma /'broma/ n. f. joke. —**bromear**, v.

bronca /'bronka/ n. f. Colloq. quarrel, row, fight.

bronce /'bronθe; 'bronse/ n. m. bronze; brass.

bronceador /bronθea'ðor; bronsea'ðor/ n. m. suntan lotion, suntan oil.

bronquitis /bron'kitis/ n. f. bronchitis.

brotar /bro'tar/ v. gush; sprout; bud.

brote /'brote/ n. m. bud, shoot.

bruja /'bruha/ n. f. witch.

brújula /'bruhula/ n. f. compass.

bruma /'bruma/ n. f. mist.

brumoso /bru'moso/ a. misty.

brusco /'brusko/ a. brusque; abrupt, curt.

brutal /bru'tal/ a. savage, brutal.

brutalidad /brutali'ðað/ n. f. brutality.

bruto /'bruto/ **-ta** a. **1.** brutish; ignorant. —n. **2.** blockhead.

bucear /buθe'ar; buse'ar/ v. dive.

bueno /'bueno/ a. good, fair; well (in health).

buey /buei/ n. m. ox, steer.

búfalo /'bufalo/ n. m. buffalo.

bufanda /bu'fanda/ n. f. scarf.

bufón /bu'fon/ **-ona** a. & n. fool, buffoon, clown.

búho /'buo/ n. m. owl.

buhonero /buo'nero/ n. m. peddler, vendor.

bujía /bu'hia/ n. f. spark plug.

bulevar /bule'βar/ n. m. boulevard.

bulimia /bu'limia/ n. f. bulimia.

bullicio /bu'ʎiθio; bu'yisio/ n. m. bustle, noise.

bullicioso /buʎi'θioso; buyi'sioso/ a. boisterous, noisy.

bulto /'bulto/ n. m. bundle; lump.

buñuelo /bu'ɲuelo/ n. m. bun.

buque /'buke/ n. m. ship.

buque de guerra /'buke de 'gerra/ warship.

buque de pasajeros /'buke de pasa'heros/ passenger ship.

burdo /'burðo/ a. coarse.

burgués /bur'ges/ **-esa** a. & n. bourgeois.

burla /'burla/ n. f. mockery; fun.

burlador /burla'ðor/ **-ra** n. trickster, jokester.

burlar /bur'lar/ v. mock, deride.

burlarse de /bur'larse de/ v. scoff at; make fun of.

burro /'burro/ n. m. donkey.

busca /'buska/ n. f. search, pursuit, quest.

buscar /bus'kar/ v. seek, look for; look up.

busto /'busto/ n. m. bust.

butaca /bu'taka/ n. f. armchair; Theat. orchestra seat.

buzo /'buθo; 'buso/ n. m. diver.

buzón /bu'θon; bu'son/ n. m. mailbox.

C

cabal /ka'βal/ a. exact; thorough.

cabalgar /kaβal'gar/ v. ride horseback.

caballeresco /kaβaʎeˈresko; kaβayeˈresko/ *a.* gentlemanly, chivalrous.

caballería /kaβaʎeˈria; kaβayeˈria/ *n. f.* cavalry; chivalry.

caballeriza /kaβaʎeˈriθa; kaβayeˈrisa/ *n. f.* stable.

caballero /kaβaˈʎero; kaβaˈyero/ *n. m.* gentleman; knight.

caballete /kaβaˈʎete; kaβaˈyete/ *n. m.* sawhorse; easel; ridge (of roof).

caballo /kaˈβaʎo; kaˈβayo/ *n. m.* horse.

cabaña /kaˈβaɲa/ *n. f.* cabin; booth.

cabaré /kaβaˈre/ *n. m.* nightclub.

cabaretero /kaβareˈtero/ **-a** *n. m. & f.* nightclub owner.

cabecear /kaβeθeˈar; kaβeseˈar/ *v.* pitch (as a ship).

cabecera /kaβeˈθera; kaβeˈsera/ *n. f.* head (of bed, table).

cabello /kaˈβeʎo; kaˈβeyo/ *n. m.* hair.

caber /kaˈβer/ *v.* fit into, be contained in. **no cabe duda,** there is no doubt.

cabeza /kaˈβeθa; kaˈβesa/ *n. f.* head; warhead.

cabildo /kaˈβildo/ *n. m.* city hall.

cabildo abierto /kaˈβildo aˈβierto/ town meeting.

cabizbajo /kaβiθˈβaho; kaβisˈβaho/ *a.* downcast.

cablegrama /kaβleˈgrama/ *n. m.* cablegram.

cabo /ˈkaβo/ *n. m.* end; *Geog.* cape; *Mil.* corporal. **llevar a c.,** carry out, accomplish.

cabra /ˈkaβra/ *n. f.* goat.

cacahuete /kakaˈuete/ *n. m.* peanut.

cacao /kaˈkao/ *n. m.* cocoa; chocolate.

cacerola /kaθeˈrola; kaseˈrola/ *n. f.* pan, casserole.

cachondeo /katʃonˈdeo/ *n. m.* fun, hilarity.

cachondo /kaˈtʃondo/ *a.* funny; *Colloq.* horny.

cachorro /kaˈtʃorro/ *n. m.* cub; puppy.

cada /ˈkaða/ *a.* each, every.

cadáver /kaˈðaβer/ *n. m.* corpse.

cadena /kaˈðena/ *n. f.* chain.

cadera /kaˈðera/ *n. f.* hip.

cadete /kaˈðete/ *n. m.* cadet.

caer /kaˈer/ *v.* fall.

café /kaˈfe/ *n. m.* coffee; café.

café exprés /kaˈfe eksˈpres/ espresso.

café soluble /kaˈfe soˈluβle/ instant coffee.

cafetal /kafeˈtal/ *n. m.* coffee plantation.

cafetera /kafeˈtera/ *n. f.* coffee pot.

caída /kaˈiða/ *n. f.* fall, drop; collapse.

caimán /kaiˈman/ *n. m.* alligator.

caja /ˈkaha/ *n. f.* box, case; checkout counter.

caja de ahorros /ˈkaha de aˈorros/ savings bank.

caja de cerillos /ˈkaha de θeˈriʎos; ˈkaha de seˈriyos/ matchbox.

caja de fósforos /ˈkaha de ˈfosfoˌros/ matchbox.

caja torácica /ˈkaha toˈraθika; ˈkaha toˈrasika/ rib cage.

cajero /kaˈhero/ **-ra** *n.* cashier.

cajón /kaˈhon/ *n. m.* drawer.

cal /kal/ *n. f.* lime.

calabaza /kalaˈβaθa; kalaˈβasa/ *n. f.* calabash, pumpkin.

calabozo /kalaˈβoθo; kalaˈβoso/ *n. m.* jail, cell.

calambre /kaˈlambre/ *n. m.* cramp.

calamidad /kalamiˈðað/ *n. f.* calamity, disaster.

calcetín /kalθeˈtin; kalseˈtin/ *n. m.* sock.

calcio /ˈkalθio; ˈkalsio/ *n. m.* calcium.

calcular /kalkuˈlar/ *v.* calculate, figure.

cálculo /ˈkalkulo/ *n. m.* calculation, estimate.

caldera /kalˈdera/ *n. f.* kettle, caldron; boiler.

caldo /ˈkaldo/ *n. m.* broth.

calefacción /kalefakˈθion; kalefakˈsion/ *n. f.* heat, heating.

calendario /kalenˈdario/ *n. m.* calendar.

calentar /kalenˈtar/ *v.* heat, warm.

calidad /kaliˈðað/ *n. f.* quality, grade.

caliente /kaˈliente/ *a.* hot, warm.

calificar /kalifiˈkar/ *v.* qualify.

callado /kaˈʎaðo; kaˈyaðo/ *a.* silent, quiet.

callarse /kaˈʎarse; kaˈyarse/ *v.* quiet down; keep still; stop talking.

calle /ˈkaʎe; ˈkaye/ *n. f.* street.

callejón /kaʎeˈhon; kayeˈhon/ *n. m.* alley.

calle sin salida /ˈkaʎe sin saˈliða; ˈkaye sin saˈliða/ dead end.

callo /ˈkaʎo; ˈkayo/ *n. m.* callus, corn.

calma /ˈkalma/ *n. f.* calm, quiet.

calmado /kalˈmaðo/ *a.* calm.

calmante /kalˈmante/ *a.* soothing, calming.

calmar /kalˈmar/ *v.* calm, quiet, lull, soothe.

calor /kaˈlor/ *n.* heat, warmth. **tener c.,** to be hot, warm; feel hot, warm. **hacer c.,** to be hot, warm (weather).

calorífero /kaloˈrifero/ *a.* **1.** heat-producing. —*n.* **2.** *m.* radiator.

calumnia /kaˈlumnia/ *n. f.* slander. —**calumniar,** *v.*

caluroso /kaluˈroso/ *a.* warm, hot.

calvario /kalˈβario/ *n. m.* Calvary.

calvo /ˈkalβo/ *a.* bald.

calzado /kalˈθaðo; kalˈsaðo/ *n. m.* footwear.

calzar /kalˈθar; kalˈsar/ *v.* wear (as shoes).

calzoncillos /kalθonˈθiʎos; kalsonˈsiyos/ *n. m.pl.* shorts.

calzones /kalˈθones; kalˈsones/ *n. m.pl.* trousers.

cama /ˈkama/ *n. f.* bed.

cámara /ˈkamara/ *n. f.* chamber; camera.

camarada /kamaˈraða/ *n. m. & f.* comrade.

camarera /kamaˈrera/ *n. f.* chambermaid; waitress.

camarero /kamaˈrero/ *n. m.* steward; waiter.

camarón /kamaˈron/ *n. m.* shrimp.

camarote /kamaˈrote/ *n. m.* stateroom, berth.

cambiar /kamˈβiar/ *v.* exchange, change, trade; cash.

cambio /ˈkambio/ *n. m.* change, exchange. **en c.,** on the other hand.

cambista /kamˈβista/ *n. m. & f.* money changer; banker, broker.

cambur /kamˈβur/ *n. m.* banana.

camello /kaˈmeʎo; kaˈmeyo/ *n. m.* camel.

camilla /kaˈmiʎa; kaˈmiya/ *n. f.* stretcher.

caminar /kamiˈnar/ *v.* walk.

caminata /kamiˈnata/ *n. f.* tramp, hike.

camino /kaˈmino/ *n. m.* road; way.

camión /kaˈmion/ *n. m.* truck.

camisa /kaˈmisa/ *n. f.* shirt.

camisería /kamiseˈria/ *n. f.* haberdashery.

camiseta /kamiˈseta/ *n. f.* undershirt; T-shirt.

campamento /kampaˈmento/ *n. m.* camp.

campana /kamˈpana/ *n. f.* bell.

campanario /kampaˈnario/ *n. m.* bell tower, steeple.

campaneo /kampaˈneo/ *n. m.* chime.

campaña /kamˈpaɲa/ *n. f.* campaign.

campeón /kampeˈon/ **-na** *n.* champion.

campeonato /kampeoˈnato/ *n. m.* championship.

campesino /kampeˈsino/ **-na** *n.* peasant.

campestre /kamˈpestre/ *a.* country, rural.

campo /ˈkampo/ *n. m.* field; (the) country.

campo de concentración /ˈkampo de konθentraˈθion; ˈkampo de konsentraˈsion/ concentration camp.

campo de golf /ˈkampo de ˈgolf/ golf course.

Canadá /kanaˈða/ *n. m.* Canada.

canadiense /kanaˈðiense/ *a. & n.* Canadian.

canal /kaˈnal/ *n. m.* canal; channel.

Canal de la Mancha /kaˈnal de la ˈmantʃa/ *n. m.* English Channel.

canalla /kaˈnaʎa; kaˈnaya/ *n. f.* rabble.

canario /kaˈnario/ *n. m.* canary.

canasta /kaˈnasta/ *n. f.* basket.

cáncer /ˈkanθer; ˈkanser/ *n. m.* cancer.

cancha de tenis /ˈkantʃa de ˈtenis/ *n. f.* tennis court.

canciller /kanθiˈʎer; kansiˈyer/ *n. m.* chancellor.

canción /kanˈθion; kanˈsion/ *n. f.* song.

candado /kanˈdaðo/ *n. m.* padlock.

candela /kanˈdela/ *n. f.* fire; light; candle.

candelero /kandeˈlero/ *n. m.* candlestick.

candidato /kandiˈðato/ **-ta** *n.* candidate; applicant.

candidatura /kandiðaˈtura/ *n. f.* candidacy.

canela /kaˈnela/ *n. f.* cinnamon.

cangrejo /kaŋˈgreho/ *n. m.* crab.

caníbal /kaˈniβal/ *n. m.* cannibal.

caniche /kaˈnitʃe/ *n. m.* poodle.

canje /ˈkanhe/ *n. m.* exchange, trade. —**canjear,** *v.*

cano /ˈkano/ *a.* gray.

canoa /kaˈnoa/ *n. f.* canoe.

cansado /kanˈsaðo/ *a.* tired, weary.

cansancio /kanˈsanθio; kanˈsansio/ *n. m.* fatigue.

cansar /kanˈsar/ *v.* tire, fatigue, wear out.

cantante /kanˈtante/ *n. m. & f.* singer.

cantar /kanˈtar/ *n.* **1.** *m.* song. —*v.* **2.** sing.

cántaro /ˈkantaro/ *n. m.* pitcher.

cantera /kanˈtera/ *n. f.* (stone) quarry.

cantidad /kantiˈðað/ *n. f.* quantity, amount.

cantina /kanˈtina/ *n. f.* bar, tavern; restaurant.

canto /ˈkanto/ *n. m.* chant, song, singing; edge.

caña /ˈkaɲa/ *n. f.* cane, reed; sugar cane; small glass of beer.

cañón /kaˈɲon/ *n. m.* canyon; cannon; gun barrel.

caoba /kaˈoβa/ *n. f.* mahogany.

caos /ˈkaos/ *n. m.* chaos.

caótico /kaˈotiko/ *a.* chaotic.

capa /ˈkapa/ *n. f.* cape, cloak; coat (of paint).

capacidad /kapaθiˈðað; kapasiˈðað/ *n. f.* capacity; capability.

capacitar /kapaθiˈtar; kapasiˈtar/ *v.* enable.

capataz /kapaˈtaθ; kapaˈtas/ *n. m.* foreman.

capaz /kaˈpaθ; kaˈpas/ *a.* capable, able.

capellán /kapeˈʎan; kapeˈyan/ *n. m.* chaplain.

caperuza /kapeˈruθa; kapeˈrusa/ *n. f.* hood.

capilla /kaˈpiʎa; kaˈpiya/ *n. f.* chapel.

capital /kapiˈtal/ *n.* **1.** *m.* capital. **2.** *f.* capital (city).

capitalista /kapitaˈlista/ *a. & n.* capitalist.

capitán /kapiˈtan/ *n. m.* captain.

capitular /kapituˈlar/ *v.* yield.

capítulo /kaˈpitulo/ *n. m.* chapter.

capota /kaˈpota/ *n. f.* hood.

capricho /kaˈpritʃo/ *n. m.* caprice; fancy, whim.

caprichoso /kapriˈtʃoso/ *a.* capricious.

cápsula /ˈkapsula/ *n. f.* capsule.

capturar /kaptuˈrar/ *v.* capture.

capucha /kaˈputʃa/ *n. f.* hood.

capullo /kaˈpuʎo; kaˈpuyo/ *n. m.* cocoon.

cara /ˈkara/ *n. f.* face.

caracol /karaˈkol/ *n. m.* snail.

carácter /kaˈrakter/ *n. m.* character.

característica /karakteˈristika/ *n. f.* characteristic.

característico /karakteˈristiko/ *a.* characteristic.

caramba /kaˈramba/ *n. f.* mild exclamation.

caramelo /karaˈmelo/ *n. m.* caramel; candy.

carátula /kaˈratula/ *n. f.* dial.

caravana /karaˈβana/ *n. f.* caravan.

carbón /karˈβon/ *n. m.* carbon; coal.

carbonizar /karβoniˈθar; karβoniˈsar/ *v.* char.

carburador /karβuraˈðor/ *n. m.* carburetor.

carcajada /karkaˈhaða/ *n. f.* burst of laughter.

cárcel /ˈkarθel; ˈkarsel/ *n. f.* prison, jail.

carcelero /karθeˈlero; karseˈlero/ *n. m.* jailer.

carcinogénico /karθinoˈheniko; karsinoˈheniko/ *a.* carcinogenic.

cardenal /karðeˈnal/ *n. m.* cardinal.

cardiólogo /karˈðiologo/ **-a** *m & f.* cardiologist.

carecer /kareˈθer; kareˈser/ *v.* lack.

carestía /karesˈtia/ *n. f.* scarcity; famine.

carga /ˈkarga/ *n. f.* cargo; load, burden; freight.

cargar /karˈgar/ *v.* carry; load; charge.

cargo /ˈkargo/ *n. m.* load; charge, office.

caricatura /karikaˈtura/ *n. f.* caricature; cartoon.

caricaturista /karikatuˈrista/ *n. m. & f.* caricaturist; cartoonist.

caricia /kaˈriθia; kaˈrisia/ *n. f.* caress.

caridad /kariˈðað/ *n. f.* charity.

cariño /kaˈriɲo/ *n. m.* affection, fondness.

cariñoso /kariˈɲoso/ *a.* affectionate, fond.

carisma /kaˈrisma/ *n. m.* charisma.

caritativo /karitaˈtiβo/ *a.* charitable.

carmesí /karmeˈsi/ *a. & m.* crimson.

carnaval /karnaˈβal/ *n. m.* carnival.

carne /ˈkarne/ *n. f.* meat, flesh; pulp.

carne acecinada /ˈkarne aθeθiˈnaða; ˈkarne asesiˈnaða/ *n. f.* corned beef.

carnero /karˈnero/ *n. m.* ram; mutton.

carnicería /karniθeˈria; karniseˈria/ *n. f.* meat market; massacre.

carnicero /karniˈθero; karniˈsero/ **-ra** *n.* butcher.

carnívoro /karˈniβoro/ *a.* carnivorous.

caro /ˈkaro/ *a.* dear, costly, expensive.

carpa /ˈkarpa/ *n. f.* tent.

carpeta /karˈpeta/ *n. f.* folder; briefcase.

carpintero /karpinˈtero/ *n. m.* carpenter.

carrera /kaˈrrera/ *n. f.* race; career.

carrera de caballos /kaˈrrera de kaˈβaʎos; kaˈrrera de kaˈβayos/ horse race.

carreta /kaˈrreta/ *n. f.* wagon, cart.

carrete /kaˈrrete/ *n. m.* reel, spool.

carretera /karreˈtera/ *n. f.* road, highway.

carril /kaˈrril/ *n. m.* rail.

carrillo /kaˈrriʎo; kaˈrriyo/ *n. m.* cart (for baggage or shopping).

carro /ˈkarro/ *n. m.* car, automobile; cart.

carroza /kaˈrroθa; kaˈrrosa/ *n. f.* chariot.

carruaje /kaˈrruahe/ *n. m.* carriage.

carta /ˈkarta/ *n. f.* letter; (*pl.*) cards.

cartel /karˈtel/ *n. m.* placard, poster; cartel.

cartelera /karteˈlera/ *n. f.* billboard.

cartera /karˈtera/ *n. f.* pocketbook, handbag, wallet; portfolio.

cartero /karˈtero/ **(-ra)** *n.* mail carrier.

cartón /kar'ton/ *n. m.* cardboard.

cartón piedra /kar'ton 'pieðra/ *n. m.* papier-mâché.

cartucho /kar'tutʃo/ *n. m.* cartridge; cassette.

casa /'kasa/ *n. f.* house, dwelling; home.

casaca /ka'saka/ *n. f.* dress coat.

casa de pisos /'kasa de 'pisos/ apartment house.

casado /ka'saðo/ *a.* married.

casamiento /kasa'miento/ *n. m.* marriage.

casar /ka'sar/ *v.* marry, marry off.

casarse /ka'sarse/ *v.* get married. **c. con**, marry.

cascabel /kaska'βel/ *n. m.* jingle bell.

cascada /kas'kaða/ *n. f.* waterfall, cascade.

cascajo /kas'kaho/ *n. m.* gravel.

cascanueces /kaska'nueθes; kaska'nueses/ *n. m.* nutcracker.

cascar /kas'kar/ *v.* crack, break, burst.

cáscara /'kaskara/ *n. f.* shell, rind, husk.

casco /'kasko/ *n. m.* helmet; hull.

casera /ka'sera/ *n. f.* landlady; housekeeper.

caserío /kase'rio/ *n. m.* settlement.

casero /ka'sero/ *a.* **1.** homemade. —*n.* **2.** *m.* landlord, superintendent.

caseta /ka'seta/ *n. f.* cottage, hut.

casi /'kasi/ *adv.* almost, nearly.

casilla /ka'siʎa; ka'siya/ *n. f.* booth; ticket office; pigeonhole.

casimir /kasi'mir/ *n. m.* cashmere.

casino /ka'sino/ *n. m.* club; clubhouse.

caso /'kaso/ *n. m.* case. **hacer c. a,** pay attention to.

casorio /ka'sorio/ *n. m.* informal wedding.

caspa /'kaspa/ *n. f.* dandruff.

casta /'kasta/ *n. f.* caste.

castaña /kas'taɲa/ *n. f.* chestnut.

castaño /kas'taɲo/ *a.* **1.** brown. —*n.* **2.** *m.* chestnut tree.

castañuela /kasta'ɲuela/ *n. f.* castanet.

castellano /kaste'ʎano; kaste'yano/ **-na** *a. & n.* Castilian.

castidad /kasti'ðað/ *n. f.* chastity.

castigar /kasti'gar/ *v.* punish, castigate.

castigo /kas'tigo/ *n. m.* punishment.

castillo /kas'tiʎo; kas'tiyo/ *n. m.* castle.

castizo /kas'tiθo; kas'tiso/ *a.* pure, genuine; noble.

casto /'kasto/ *a.* chaste.

castor /kas'tor/ *n. m.* beaver.

casual /ka'sual/ *adj.* accidental, coincidental.

casualidad /kasuali'ðað/ *n. f.* coincidence. **por c.,** by chance.

casuca /ka'suka/ *n. f.* hut, shanty, hovel.

cataclismo /kata'klismo/ *n. m.* cataclysm.

catacumba /kata'kumba/ *n. f.* catacomb.

catadura /kata'ðura/ *n. f.* act of tasting; appearance.

catalán /kata'lan/ **-na** *a. & n.* Catalonian.

catálogo /ka'talogo/ *n. m.* catalogue. —**catalogar,** *v.*

cataputta /kata'putta/ *n. f.* catapult.

catar /ka'tar/ *v.* taste; examine, try; bear in mind.

catarata /kata'rata/ *n. f.* cataract, waterfall.

catarro /ka'tarro/ *n. m.* head cold, catarrh.

catástrofe /ka'tastrofe/ *n. f.* catastrophe.

catecismo /kate'θismo; kate'sismo/ *n. m.* catechism.

cátedra /'kateðra/ *n. f.* professorship.

catedral /kate'ðral/ *n. f.* cathedral.

catedrático /kate'ðratiko/ **-ca** *n.* professor.

categoría /katego'ria/ *n. f.* category.

categórico /kate'goriko/ *a.* categorical.

catequismo /kate'kismo/ *n. m.* catechism.

catequizar /kateki'θar; kateki'sar/ *v.* catechize.

cátodo /'katoðo/ *n. m.* cathode.

catolicismo /katoli'θismo; katoli'sismo/ *n. m.* Catholicism.

católico /ka'toliko/ **-ca** *a. & n.* Catholic.

catorce /ka'torθe; ka'torse/ *a. & pron.* fourteen.

catre /'katre/ *n. m.* cot.

cauce /'kauθe; 'kause/ *n. m.* riverbed; ditch.

cauchal /kau'tʃal/ *n. m.* rubber plantation.

caucho /'kautʃo/ *n. m.* rubber.

caución /kau'θion; kau'sion/ *n. f.* precaution; security, guarantee.

caudal /kau'ðal/ *n. m.* means, fortune; (*pl.*) holdings.

caudaloso /kauða'loso/ *a.* prosperous, rich.

caudillaje /kauði'ʎahe; kauði'yahe/ *n. m.* leadership; tyranny.

caudillo /kau'ðiʎo; kau'ðiyo/ *n. m.* leader, chief.

causa /'kausa/ *n. f.* cause. —**causar,** *v.*

cautela /kau'tela/ *n. f.* caution.

cauteloso /kaute'loso/ *n. m.* cautious.

cautivar /kauti'βar/ *v.* captivate.

cautiverio /kauti'βerio/ *n. m.* captivity.

cautividad /kautiβi'ðað/ *n. f.* captivity.

cautivo /kau'tiβo/ **-va** *a. & n.* captive.

cauto /'kauto/ *a.* cautious.

cavar /ka'βar/ *v.* dig.

caverna /ka'βerna/ *n. f.* cavern, cave.

cavernoso /kaβer'noso/ *a.* cavernous.

cavidad /kaβi'ðað/ *n. f.* cavity, hollow.

cavilar /kaβi'lar/ *v.* criticize, cavil.

cayado /ka'yaðo/ *n. m.* shepherd's staff.

cayo /'kayo/ *n. m.* small rocky islet, key.

caza /'kaθa; 'kasa/ *n. f.* hunting, pursuit, game.

cazador /kaθa'ðor; kasa'ðor/ *n. m.* hunter.

cazar /ka'θar; ka'sar/ *v.* hunt.

cazatorpedero /kaθatorpe'ðero; kasatorpe'ðero/ *n. m.* torpedo-boat, destroyer.

cazo /'kaθo; 'kaso/ *n. m.* ladle, dipper; pot.

cazuela /ka'θuela; ka'suela/ *n. f.* crock.

cebada /θe'βaða; se'βaða/ *n. f.* barley.

cebiche /θe'bitʃe/ *n. m.* dish of marinated raw fish.

cebo /'θeβo; 'seβo/ *n. m.* bait. —**cebar,** *v.*

cebolla /θe'βoʎa; se'βoya/ *n. f.* onion.

cebolleta /θeβo'ʎeta; seβo'yeta/ *n. f.* spring onion.

ceceo /θe'θeo; se'seo/ *n. m.* lisp. —**cecear,** *v.*

cecina /θe'θina; se'sina/ *n. f.* dried beef.

cedazo /θe'ðaθo; se'ðaso/ *n. m.* sieve, sifter.

ceder /θe'ðer; se'ðer/ *v.* cede; transfer; yield.

cedro /'θeðro; 'seðro/ *n. m.* cedar.

cédula /'θeðula; 'seðula/ *n. f.* decree. **c. personal,** identification card.

cegar /θe'gar; se'gar/ *v.* blind.

ceguedad /θege'ðað, θe'gera; sege'ðað, se'gera/ **ceguera** *n. f.* blindness.

ceja /'θeha; 'seha/ *n. f.* eyebrow.

cejar /θe'har; se'har/ *v.* go backwards; yield, retreat.

celada /θe'laða; se'laða/ *n. f.* trap; ambush.

celaje /θe'lahe; se'lahe/ *n. m.* appearance of the sky.

celar /θe'lar; se'lar/ *v.* watch carefully, guard.

celda /'θelda; 'selda/ *n. f.* cell.

celebración /θeleβra'θion; seleβra'sion/ *n. f.* celebration.

celebrante /θele'βrante; sele'βrante/ *n. m.* officiating priest.

celebrar /θele'βrar; sele'βrar/ *v.* celebrate, observe.

célebre /'θeleβre; 'seleβre/ *a.* celebrated, noted, famous.

celebridad /θeleβri'ðað; seleβri'ðað/ *n. f.* fame; celebrity; pageant.

celeridad /θeleri'ðað; seleri'ðað/ *n. f.* speed, rapidity.

celeste /θe'leste; se'leste/ *a.* celestial.

celestial /θeles'tial; seles'tial/ *a.* heavenly.

celibato /θeli'βato; seli'βato/ *n. m.* celibacy.

célibe /'θeliβe; 'seliβe/ *a.* **1.** unmarried. —*n.* **2.** *m. & f.* unmarried person.

celista /θe'lista; se'lista/ *n. m. & f.* cellist.

cellisca /θe'ʎiska; se'yiska/ *n. f.* sleet. —**cellisquear,** *v.*

celo /'θelo; 'selo/ *n. m.* zeal; (*pl.*) jealousy.

celofán /θelo'fan; selo'fan/ *n. m.* cellophane.

celosía /θelo'sia; selo'sia/ *n. f.* Venetian blind.

celoso /θe'loso; se'loso/ *a.* jealous; zealous.

céltico /'θeltiko; 'seltiko/ *a.* Celtic.

célula /'θelula; 'selula/ *n. f. Biol.* cell.

celuloide /θelu'loiðe; selu'loiðe/ *n. m.* celluloid.

cementar /θemen'tar; semen'tar/ *v.* cement.

cementerio /θemen'terio; semen'terio/ *n. m.* cemetery.

cemento /θe'mento; se'mento/ *n. m.* cement.

cena /'θena; 'sena/ *n. f.* supper.

cenagal /θena'gal; sena'gal/ *n. m.* swamp, marsh.

cenagoso /θena'goso; sena'goso/ *a.* swampy, marshy, muddy.

cenar /θe'nar; se'nar/ *v.* dine, eat.

cencerro /θen'θerro; sen'serro/ *n. m.* cowbell.

cendal /θen'dal; sen'dal/ *n. m.* thin, light cloth; gauze.

cenicero /θeni'θero; seni'sero/ *n. m.* ashtray.

ceniciento /θeni'θiento; seni'siento/ *a.* ashen.

cenit /'θenit; 'senit/ *n. m.* zenith.

ceniza /θe'niθa; se'nisa/ *n. f.* ash, ashes.

censo /'θenso; 'senso/ *n. m.* census.

censor /θen'sor; sen'sor/ *n. m.* censor.

censura /θen'sura; sen'sura/ *n. f.* reproof, censure; censorship.

censurable /θensu'raβle; sensu'raβle/ *a.* objectionable.

censurar /θensu'rar; sensu'rar/ *v.* censure, criticize.

centavo /θen'taβo; sen'taβo/ *n. m.* cent.

centella /θen'teʎa; sen'teya/ *n. f.* thunderbolt, lightning.

centellear /θenteʎe'ar; senteye'ar/ *v.* twinkle, sparkle.

centelleo /θente'ʎeo; sente'yeo/ *n. m.* sparkle.

centenar /θente'nar; sente'nar/ *n. m.* (a) hundred.

centenario /θente'nario; sente'nario/ *n. m.* centennial, centenary.

centeno /θen'teno; sen'teno/ *n. m.* rye.

centígrado /θen'tigraðo; sen'tigraðo/ *a.* centigrade.

centímetro /θenti'metro; senti'metro/ *n. m.* centimeter.

céntimo /'θentimo; 'sentimo/ *n. m.* cent.

centinela /θenti'nela; senti'nela/ *n. m.* sentry, guard.

central /θen'tral; sen'tral/ *a.* central.

centralita /θentra'lita; sentra'lita/ *n. f.* switchboard.

centralizar /θentrali'θar; sentrali'sar/ *v.* centralize.

centrar /θen'trar; sen'trar/ *v.* center.

céntrico /'θentriko; 'sentriko/ *a.* central.

centro /'θentro; 'sentro/ *n. m.* center.

centroamericano /θentroameri'kano; sentroameri'kano/ **-na** *a. & n.* Central American.

centro de mesa /'θentro de 'mesa; 'sentro de 'mesa/ centerpiece.

ceñidor /θeɲi'ðor; seɲi'ðor/ *n. m.* belt, sash; girdle.

ceñir /θe'ɲir; se'ɲir/ *v.* gird.

ceño /'θeɲo; 'seɲo/ *n. m.* frown.

ceñudo /θe'ɲuðo; se'ɲuðo/ *a.* frowning, grim.

cepa /'θepa; 'sepa/ *n. f.* stump.

cepillo /θe'piʎo; se'piyo/ *n. m.* brush; plane. —**cepillar,** *v.*

cera /'θera; 'sera/ *n. f.* wax.

cerámica /θe'ramika; se'ramika/ *n. m.* ceramics.

cerámico /θe'ramiko; se'ramiko/ *a.* ceramic.

cerca /'θerka; 'serka/ *adv.* **1.** near. —*n.* **2.** *f.* fence, hedge.

cercado /θer'kaðo; ser'kaðo/ *n. m.* enclosure; garden.

cercamiento /θerka'miento; serka'miento/ *n. m.* enclosure.

cercanía /θerka'nia; serka'nia/ *n. f.* proximity.

cercano /θer'kano; ser'kano/ *a.* near, nearby.

cercar /θer'kar; ser'kar/ *v.* surround.

cercenar /θerθe'nar; serse'nar/ *v.* clip, lessen, reduce.

cerciorar /θerθio'rar; sersio'rar/ *v.* make sure; affirm.

cerco /'θerko; 'serko/ *n. m.* hoop; siege.

cerda /'θerða; 'serða/ *n. f.* bristle.

cerdo /'θerðo; 'serðo/ **-da** *n.* hog.

cerdoso /θer'ðoso; ser'ðoso/ *a.* bristly.

cereal /θere'al; sere'al/ *a. & m.* cereal.

cerebro /θe'reβro; se'reβro/ *n. m.* brain.

ceremonia /θere'monia; sere'monia/ *n. f.* ceremony.

ceremonial /θeremo'nial; seremo'nial/ *a. & m.* ceremonial, ritual.

ceremonioso /θeremo'nioso; seremo'nioso/ *a.* ceremonious.

cereza /θe'reθa; se'resa/ *n. f.* cherry.

cerilla /θe'riʎa; se'riya/ *n. f.,* **cerillo,** *m.* match.

cerner /θer'ner; ser'ner/ *v.* sift.

cero /'θero; 'sero/ *n. m.* zero.

cerrado /θe'rraðo; se'rraðo/ *a.* closed; cloudy; obscure; taciturn.

cerradura /θerra'ðura; serra'ðura/ *n. f.* lock.

cerrajero /θerra'hero; serra'hero/ *n. m.* locksmith.

cerrar /θe'rrar; se'rrar/ *v.* close, shut.

cerro /'θerro; 'serro/ *n. m.* hill.

cerrojo /θe'rroho; se'rroho/ *n. m.* latch, bolt.

certamen /θer'tamen; ser'tamen/ *n. m.* contest; competition.

certero /θer'tero; ser'tero/ *a.* accurate, exact; certain, sure.

certeza /θer'teθa; ser'tesa/ *n. f.* certainty.

certidumbre /θerti'ðumbre; serti'ðumβre/ *n. f.* certainty.

certificado /θertifi'kaðo; sertifi'kaðo/ *n. m.* certificate.

certificado de compra /θertifi'kaðo de 'kompra; sertifi'kaðo de 'kompra/ proof of purchase.

certificar /θertifi'kar; sertifi'kar/ *v.* certify; register (a letter).

cerúleo /θe'ruleo; se'ruleo/ *a.* cerulean, sky-blue.
cervecería /θerβeθe'ria; serβese'ria/ *n. f.* brewery; beer saloon.
cervecero /θerβe'θero; serβe'sero/ *n. m.* brewer.
cerveza /θer'βeθa; ser'βesa/ *n. f.* beer.
cesante /θe'sante; se'sante/ *a.* unemployed.
cesar /θe'sar; se'sar/ *v.* cease.
césped /'θespeð; 'sespeð/ *n. m.* sod, lawn.
cesta /'θesta; 'sesta/ *n. f.*, **cesto,** *m.* basket.
cetrino /θe'trino; se'trino/ *a.* yellow, lemon-colored.
cetro /'θetro; 'setro/ *n. m.* scepter.
chabacano /tʃaβa'kano/ *a.* vulgar.
chacal /tʃa'kal/ *n. m.* jackal.
chacó /'tʃako/ *n. m.* shako.
chacona /tʃa'kona/ *n. f.* chaconne.
chacota /tʃa'kota/ *n. f.* fun, mirth.
chacotear /tʃakote'ar/ *v.* joke.
chacra /'tʃakra/ *n. f.* small farm.
chafallar /tʃafa'ʎar; tʃafa'yar/ *v.* mend badly.
chagra /'tʃagra/ *n. m.* rustic; rural person.
chal /tʃal/ *n. m.* shawl.
chalán /tʃa'lan/ *n. m.* horse trader.
chaleco /tʃa'leko/ *n. m.* vest.
chaleco salvavidas /tʃa'leko salβa'βiðas/ life jacket.
chalet /tʃa'le; tʃa'let/ *n. m.* chalet.
challí /tʃa'ʎi; tʃa'yi/ *n. m.* challis.
chamada /tʃa'maða/ *n. f.* brushwood.
chamarillero /tʃamari'ʎero; tʃamari'yero/ *n. m.* gambler.
chamarra /tʃa'marra/ *n. f.* coarse linen jacket.
chambelán /tʃambe'lan/ *n. m.* chamberlain.
champaña /tʃam'paɲa/ *n. m.* champagne.
champú /tʃam'pu/ *n. m.* shampoo.
chamuscar /tʃamus'kar/ *v.* scorch.
chancaco /tʃan'kako/ *a.* brown.
chance /'tʃanθe/ *n. m. & f.* opportunity, break.
chancear /tʃanθe'ar; tʃanse'ar/ *v.* jest, joke.
chanciller /tʃanθi'ʎer; tʃansi'yer/ *n. m.* chancellor.
chancillería /tʃanθiʎe'ria; tʃansiye'ria/ *n. f.* chancery.
chancla /'tʃankla/ *n. f.* old shoe.
chancleta /tʃan'kleta/ *n. f.* slipper.
chanclos /'tʃanklos/ *n. m.pl.* galoshes.
chancro /'tʃankro/ *n. m.* chancre.
changador /tʃaŋga'ðor/ *n. m.* porter; handyman.
chantaje /tʃan'tahe/ *n. m.* blackmail.
chantajista /tʃanta'hista/ *n. m. & f.* blackmailer.
chantejear /tʃantehe'ar/ *v.* blackmail.
chanto /'tʃanto/ *n. m.* flagstone.
chantre /'tʃantre/ *n. m.* precentor.
chanza /'tʃanθa; 'tʃansa/ *n. f.* joke, jest. **—chancear,** *v.*
chanzoneta /tʃanθo'neta; tʃanso'neta/ *n. f.* chansonette.
chapa /'tʃapa/ *n. f.* (metal) sheet, plate; lock.
chapado en oro /tʃa'paðo en 'oro/ *a.* gold-plated.
chapado en plata /tʃa'paðo en 'plata/ *a.* silver-plated.
chaparrada /tʃapa'rraða/ *n. f.* downpour.
chaparral /tʃapa'rral/ *n. m.* chaparral.
chaparreras /tʃapa'rreras/ *n. f.pl.* chaps.
chaparrón /tʃapa'rron/ *n. m.* downpour.
chapear /tʃape'ar/ *v.* veneer.
chapeo /tʃa'peo/ *n. m.* hat.
chapero /tʃa'pero/ *n. m. Colloq.* male homosexual prostitute.
chapitel /tʃapi'tel/ *n. m.* spire, steeple; (architecture) capital.
chapodar /tʃapo'ðar/ *v.* lop.
chapón /tʃa'pon/ *n. m.* inkblot.
chapotear /tʃapote'ar/ *v.* paddle or splash in the water.
chapoteo /tʃapo'teo/ *n. m.* splash.
chapucear /tʃapuθe'ar; tʃapuse'ar/ *v.* fumble, bungle.
chapucero /tʃapu'θero; tʃapu'sero/ *a.* sloppy, bungling.
chapurrear /tʃapurre'ar/ *v.* speak (a language) brokenly.
chapuz /tʃa'puθ; tʃa'pus/ *n. m.* dive; ducking.
chapuzar /tʃapu'θar; tʃapu'sar/ *v.* dive; duck.
chaqueta /tʃa'keta/ *n. f.* jacket, coat.
chaqueta deportiva /tʃa'keta depor'tiβa/ sport jacket.
charada /tʃa'raða/ *n. f.* charade.
charamusca /tʃara'muska/ *n. f.* twisted candy stick.
charanga /tʃa'raŋga/ *n. f.* military band.
charanguero /tʃaraŋ'guero/ *n. m.* peddler.
charca /'tʃarka/ *n. f.* pool, pond.
charco /'tʃarko/ *n. m.* pool, puddle.
charla /'tʃarla/ *n. f.* chat; chatter, prattle. **—charlar,** *v.*
charladuría /tʃarlaðu'ria/ *n. f.* chatter.
charlatán /tʃarla'tan/ **-ana** *n.* charlatan.
charlatanismo /tʃarlata'nismo/ *n. m.* charlatanism.
charol /tʃa'rol/ *n. m.* varnish.
charolar /tʃaro'lar/ *v.* varnish; polish.
charquear /tʃarke'ar/ *v.* jerk (beef).
charquí /tʃar'ki/ *n. m.* jerked beef.
charrán /tʃa'rran/ *a.* roguish.
chascarillo /tʃaska'riʎo; tʃaska'riyo/ *n. m.* risqué story.
chasco /'tʃasko/ *n. m.* disappointment, blow; practical joke.
chasis /'tʃasis/ *n. m.* chassis.
chasquear /tʃaske'ar/ *v.* fool, trick; disappoint; crack (a whip).
chasquido /tʃas'kiðo/ *n. m.* crack (sound).
chata /'tʃata/ *n. f.* bedpan.
chatear /tʃate'ar/ *v.* chat (on the Internet).
chato /'tʃato/ *a.* flat-nosed, pugnosed.
chauvinismo /tʃauβi'nismo/ *n. m.* chauvinism.
chauvinista /tʃauβi'nista/ *n. & a.* chauvinist.
chelín /tʃe'lin/ *n. m.* shilling.
cheque /'tʃeke/ *n. m.* (bank) check.
chica /'tʃika/ *n. f.* girl.
chicana /tʃi'kana/ *n. f.* chicanery.
chicha /'tʃitʃa/ *n. f.* an alcoholic drink.
chícharo /'tʃitʃaro/ *n. f.* pea.
chicharra /tʃi'tʃarra/ *n. f.* cicada; talkative person.
chicharrón /tʃitʃa'rron/ *n. m.* crisp fried scrap of meat.
chichear /tʃitʃe'ar/ *v.* hiss in disapproval.
chichón /tʃi'tʃon/ *n. m.* bump, bruise, lump.
chicle /'tʃikle/ *n. m.* chewing gum.
chico /'tʃiko/ *a.* **1.** little. **—***n.* **2.** *m.* boy.
chicote /tʃi'kote/ *n. m.* cigar; cigar butt.
chicotear /tʃikote'ar/ *v.* whip, flog.
chifladura /tʃifla'ðura/ *n. f.* mania; whim; jest.
chiflar /tʃi'flar/ *v.* whistle; become insane.
chiflido /tʃi'fliðo/ *n. m.* shrill whistle.
chile /'tʃile/ *n. m.* chili.
chileno /tʃi'leno/ **-na** *a. & n.* Chilean.
chillido /tʃi'ʎiðo; tʃi'yiðo/ *n. m.* shriek, scream, screech. **—chillar,** *v.*
chillón /tʃi'ʎon; tʃi'yon/ *a.* shrill.
chimenea /tʃime'nea/ *n. f.* chimney, smokestack; fireplace.
china /'tʃina/ *n. f.* pebble; maid; Chinese woman.
chinarro /tʃi'narro/ *n. m.* large pebble, stone.
chinche /'tʃintʃe/ *n. f.* bedbug; thumbtack.
chincheta /tʃin'tʃeta/ *n. f.* thumbtack.
chinchilla /tʃin'tʃiʎa; tʃin'tʃiya/ *n. f.* chinchilla.
chinchorro /tʃin'tʃorro/ *n. m.* fishing net.
chinela /tʃi'nela/ *n. f.* slipper.
chinero /tʃi'nero/ *n. m.* china closet.
chino /'tʃino/ **-na** *a. & n.* Chinese.
chipirón /tʃipi'ron/ *n. m.* baby squid.
chiquero /tʃi'kero/ *n. m.* pen for pigs, goats, etc.
chiquito /tʃi'kito/ **-ta** *a.* **1.** small, tiny. **—***n.* **2.** *m. & f.* small child.
chiribitil /tʃiriβi'til/ *n. m.* small room, den.
chirimía /tʃiri'mia/ *n. f.* flageolet.
chiripa /tʃi'ripa/ *n. f.* stroke of good luck.
chirla /'tʃirla/ *n. f.* mussel.
chirle /'tʃirle/ *a.* insipid.
chirona /tʃi'rona/ *n. f.* prison, jail.
chirrido /tʃi'rriðo/ *n. m.* squeak, chirp. **—chirriar,** *v.*
chis /tʃis/ *interj.* hush!
chisgarabís /tʃisgara'βis/ *n.* meddler; unimportant person.
chisguete /tʃis'gete/ *n. m.* squirt, splash.
chisme /'tʃisme/ *n. m.* gossip. **—chismear,** *v.*
chismero /tʃis'mero/ **-ra** *n.* gossiper.
chismoso /tʃis'moso/ *adj.* gossiping.
chispa /'tʃispa/ *n. f.* spark.
chispeante /tʃispe'ante/ *a.* sparkling.
chispear /tʃispe'ar/ *v.* sparkle.
chisporrotear /tʃisporrote'ar/ *v.* emit sparks.
chistar /tʃis'tar/ *v.* speak.
chiste /'tʃiste/ *n. m.* joke, gag; witty saying.
chistera /tʃis'tera/ *n. f.* fish basket; top hat.
chistoso /tʃis'toso/ *a.* funny, comic, amusing.
chito /'tʃito/ *interj.* hush!
chiva /'tʃiβa/ *n. f.* female goat.
chivato /tʃi'βato/ *n. m.* kid, young goat.
chivo /'tʃiβo/ *n. m.* male goat.
chocante /tʃo'kante/ *a.* striking; shocking; unpleasant.
chocar /tʃo'kar/ *v.* collide, clash, crash; shock.
chocarrear /tʃokarre'ar/ *v.* joke, jest.
chochear /tʃotʃe'ar/ *v.* be in one's dotage.
chochera /tʃo'tʃera/ *n. f.* dotage, senility.
choclo /'tʃoklo/ *n. m.* clog; overshoe; ear of corn.
chocolate /tʃoko'late/ *n. m.* chocolate.
chocolate con leche /tʃoko'late kon 'letʃe/ milk chocolate.
chocolatería /tʃokolate'ria/ *n. f.* chocolate shop.
chofer /'tʃofer/ **chófer** *n. m.* chauffeur, driver.
chofeta /tʃo'feta/ *n. f.* chafing dish.
cholo /'tʃolo/ *n. m.* half-breed.
chopo /'tʃopo/ *n. m.* black poplar.
choque /'tʃoke/ *n. m.* collision, clash, crash; shock.
chorizo /tʃo'riθo; tʃo'riso/ *n. m.* sausage.
chorrear /tʃorre'ar/ *v.* spout; drip.
chorro /'tʃorro/ *n. m.* spout; spurt, jet. **llover a chorros,** to pour (rain).
choto /'tʃoto/ *n. m.* calf, kid.
choza /'tʃoθa; 'tʃosa/ *n. f.* hut, cabin.
chozno /'tʃoθno; 'tʃosno/ **-na** *n.* great-great-great-grandchild.
chubasco /tʃu'βasko/ *n. m.* shower, squall.
chubascoso /tʃuβas'koso/ *a.* squally.
chuchería /tʃutʃe'ria/ *n. f.* trinket, knickknack.
chucho /'tʃutʃo/ *n. m. Colloq.* mutt.
chulería /tʃule'ria/ *n. f.* pleasant manner.
chuleta /tʃu'leta/ *n. f.* chop, cutlet.
chulo /'tʃulo/ *n. m.* rascal, rogue; joker.
chupa /'tʃupa/ *n. f.* jacket.
chupada /tʃu'paða/ *n. f.* suck, sip.
chupado /tʃu'paðo/ *a.* very thin.
chupaflor /tʃupa'flor/ *n. m.* hummingbird.
chupar /tʃu'par/ *v.* suck.
churrasco /tʃu'rrasko/ *n. m.* roasted meat.
churros /'tʃuros/ *n. m.pl.* long, slender fritters.
chuscada /tʃus'kaða/ *n. f.* joke, jest.
chusco /'tʃusko/ *a.* funny, humorous.
chusma /'tʃusma/ *n. f.* mob, rabble.
chuzo /'tʃuθo; 'tʃuso/ *n. m.* pike.
CI, *abbr.* **(coeficiente intelectual)** IQ (intelligence quotient).
ciberespacio /θiβeres'paθio/ *n. m.* cyberspace.
cibernauta /θiβer'nauta/ *n. m. & f.* cybernaut.
cicatero /θika'tero; sika'tero/ *a.* stingy.
cicatriz /θika'triθ; sika'tris/ *n. f.* scar.
cicatrizar /θikatri'θar; sikatri'sar/ *v.* heal.
ciclamato /θi'klamato; si'klamato/ *n. m.* cyclamate.
ciclista /θi'klista; si'klista/ *m & f.* cyclist.
ciclo /'θiklo; 'siklo/ *n. m.* cycle.
ciclón /θi'klon; si'klon/ *n. m.* cyclone.
ciego /'θiego; 'siego/ **-ga** *a.* **1.** blind. **—***n.* **2.** blind person.
cielo /'θielo; 'sielo/ *n. m.* heaven; sky, heavens; ceiling.
ciempiés /θiem'pies; siem'pies/ *n. m.* centipede.
cien /θien; sien/ **ciento** *a. & pron.* hundred. **por c.,** per cent.
ciénaga /'θienaga; 'sienaga/ *n. f.* swamp, marsh.
ciencia /'θienθia; 'siensia/ *n. f.* science.
cieno /'θieno; 'sieno/ *n. m.* mud.
científico /θien'tifiko; sien'tifiko/ **-ca** *a.* **1.** scientific. **—***n.* **2.** scientist.
cierre /'θierre; 'sierre/ *n. m.* fastener, snap, clasp.
cierto /'θierto; 'sierto/ *a.* certain, sure, true.
ciervo /'θierβo; 'sierβo/ *n. m.* deer.
cierzo /'θierθo; 'sierso/ *n. m.* northerly wind.
cifra /'θifra; 'sifra/ *n. f.* cipher, number. **—cifrar,** *v.*
cigarra /θi'garra; si'garra/ *n. f.* locust.
cigarrera /θiga'rrera; siga'rrera/ **cigarrillera** *f.* cigarette case.
cigarrillo /θiga'rriʎo; siga'rriyo/ *n. m.* cigarette.
cigarro /θi'garro; si'garro/ *n. m.* cigar; cigarette.
cigüeña /θi'gueɲa; si'gueɲa/ *n. f.* stork.
cilíndrico /θi'lindriko; si'lindriko/ *a.* cylindrical.
cilindro /θi'lindro; si'lindro/ *n. m.* cylinder.
cima /'θima; 'sima/ *n. f.* summit, peak.
cimarrón /θima'rron; sima'rron/ *a.* **1.** wild, untamed. **—***n.* **2.** *m.* runaway slave.
címbalo /'θimbalo; 'simbalo/ *n. m.* cymbal.
cimbrar /θim'βrar, θimbre'ar; sim'βrar, simbre'ar/ *v.* shake, brandish.
cimientos /θi'mientos; si'mientos/ *n. m.pl.* foundation.
cinc /θink; sink/ *n. m.* zinc.
cincel /θin'θel; sin'sel/ *n. m.* chisel. **—cincelar,** *v.*
cincha /'θintʃa; 'sintʃa/ *n. f.* (harness) cinch. **—cinchar,** *v.*
cinco /'θinko; 'sinko/ *a. & pron.* five.
cincuenta /θin'kuenta; sin'kuenta/ *a. & pron.* fifty.

cine /'θine; 'sine/ *n. m.* movies; movie theater.
cíngulo /'θiŋgulo; 'siŋgulo/ *n. m.* cingulum.
cínico /'θiniko; 'siniko/ **-ca** *a.* & *n.* cynical; cynic.
cinismo /θi'nismo; si'nismo/ *n. m.* cynicism.
cinta /'θinta; 'sinta/ *n. f.* ribbon, tape; (movie) film.
cintilar /θinti'lar; sinti'lar/ *v.* glitter, sparkle.
cinto /'θinto; 'sinto/ *n. m.* belt; girdle.
cintura /θin'tura; sin'tura/ *n. f.* waist.
cinturón /θintu'ron; sintu'ron/ *n. m.* belt.
cinturón de seguridad /θintu'ron de seguri'ðað; sintu'ron de seguri'ðað/ safety belt.
ciprés /θi'pres; si'pres/ *n. m.* cypress.
circo /'θirko; 'sirko/ *n. m.* circus.
circuito /θir'kuito; sir'kuito/ *n. m.* circuit.
circulación /θirkula'θion; sirkula'sion/ *n. f.* circulation.
circular /θirku'lar; sirku'lar/ *a.* & *m.* **1.** circular. —*v.* **2.** circulate.
círculo /'θirkulo; 'sirkulo/ *n. m.* circle, club.
circundante /θirkun'dante; sirkun'dante/ *a.* surrounding.
circundar /θirkun'dar; sirkun'dar/ *v.* encircle, surround.
circunferencia /θirkunfe'renθia; sirkunfe'rensia/ *n. f.* circumference.
circunlocución /θirkunloku'θion; sirkunloku'sion/ *n.* circumlocution.
circunscribir /θirkunskri'βir; sirkunskri'βir/ *v.* circumscribe.
circunspección /θirkunspek'θion; sirkunspek'sion/ *n.* decorum, propriety.
circunspecto /θirkuns'pekto; sirkuns'pekto/ *a.* circumspect.
circunstancia /θirkuns'tanθia; sirkuns'tansia/ *n. f.* circumstance.
circunstante /θirkuns'tante; sirkuns'tante/ *n. m.* bystander.
circunvecino /θirkumbe'θino; sirkumbe'sino/ *a.* neighboring, adjacent.
cirio /'θirio; 'sirio/ *n. m.* candle.
cirrosis /θi'rrosis; si'rrosis/ *n. f.* cirrhosis.
ciruela /θi'ruela; si'ruela/ *n. f.* plum; prune.
cirugía /θiru'hia; siru'hia/ *n. f.* surgery.
cirujano /θiru'hano; siru'hano/ *n. m.* surgeon.
cisne /'θisne; 'sisne/ *n. m.* swan.
cisterna /θis'terna; sis'terna/ *n. f.* cistern.
cita /'θita; 'sita/ *n. f.* citation; appointment, date.
citación /θita'θion; sita'sion/ *n. f.* citation; (legal) summons.
citar /θi'tar; si'tar/ *v.* cite, quote; summon; make an appointment with.
cítrico /'θitriko; 'sitriko/ *a.* citric.
ciudad /θiu'ðað; siu'ðað/ *n. f.* city.
ciudadanía /θiuðaða'nia; siuðaða'nia/ *n. f.* citizenship.
ciudadano /θiuða'ðano; siuða'ðano/ **-na** *n.* citizen.
ciudadela /θiuða'ðela; siuða'ðela/ *n. f.* fortress, citadel.
cívico /'θiβiko; 'siβiko/ *a.* civic.
civil /θi'βil; si'βil/ *a.* & *n.* civil; civilian.
civilidad /θiβili'ðað; siβili'ðað/ *n. f.* politeness, civility.
civilización /θiβiliθa'θion; siβilisa'sion/ *n. f.* civilization.
civilizador /θiβiliθa'ðor; siβilisa'ðor/ *a.* civilizing.
civilizar /θiβili'θar; siβili'sar/ *v.* civilize.
cizallas /θi'θaʎas; si'sayas/ *n. f.pl.* shears. —**cizallar,** *v.*
cizaña /θi'θaɲa; si'saɲa/ *n. f.* weed; vice.
clamar /kla'mar/ *v.* clamor.
clamor /kla'mor/ *n. m.* clamor.
clamoreo /klamo'reo/ *n. m.* persistent clamor.
clamoroso /klamo'roso/ *a.* clamorous.
clandestino /klandes'tino/ *a.* secret, clandestine.
clara /'klara/ *n. f.* white (of egg).
claraboya /klara'βoya/ *n. m.* skylight; bull's-eye.
clara de huevo /'klara de 'ueβo/ egg white.
clarear /klare'ar/ *v.* clarify; become light, dawn.
clarete /kla'rete/ *n. m.* claret.
claridad /klari'ðað/ *n. f.* clarity.
clarificar /klarifi'kar/ *v.* clarify.
clarín /kla'rin/ *n. m.* bugle, trumpet.
clarinete /klari'nete/ *n. m.* clarinet.
clarividencia /klariβi'ðenθia; klariβi'ðensia/ *n. f.* clairvoyance.
clarividente /klariβi'ðente/ *a.* clairvoyant.
claro /'klaro/ *a.* clear; bright; light (in color); of course.
clase /'klase/ *n. f.* class; classroom; kind, sort.
clase nocturna /'klase nok'turna/ evening class.
clásico /'klasiko/ *a.* classic, classical.
clasificar /klasifi'kar/ *v.* classify, rank.
claustro /'klaustro/ *n. m.* cloister.
claustrofobia /klaustro'foβia/ *n. f.* claustrophobia.
cláusula /'klausula/ *n. f.* clause.
clausura /klau'sura/ *n. f.* cloister; inner sanctum; closing.
clavado /kla'βaðo/ *a.* **1.** nailed. —*n.* **2.** *m.* & *f.* dive.
clavar /kla'βar/ *v.* nail, peg, pin.
clave /'klaβe/ *n. f.* code; *Mus.* key.
clavel /kla'βel/ *n. m.* carnation.
clavetear /klaβete'ar/ *v.* nail.
clavícula /kla'βikula/ *n. f.* collarbone.
clavija /kla'βiha/ *n. f.* pin, peg.
clavo /'klaβo/ *n. m.* nail, spike; clove.
clemencia /kle'menθia; kle'mensia/ *n. f.* clemency.
clemente /kle'mente/ *a.* merciful.
clementina /klemen'tina/ *n. f.* tangerine.
clerecía /klere'θia; klere'sia/ *n. f.* clergy.
clerical /kleri'kal/ *a.* clerical.
clérigo /'klerigo/ *n. m.* clergyman.
clero /'klero/ *n. m.* clergy.
cliente /'kliente/ *n. m.* & *f.* customer, client.
clientela /klien'tela/ *n. f.* clientele, practice.
clima /'klima/ *n. m.* climate.
clímax /'klimaks/ *n. m.* climax.
clínica /'klinika/ *n. f.* clinic.
clínica de reposo /'klinika de rre'poso/ convalescent home.
clínico /'kliniko/ *a.* clinical.
clíper /'kliper/ *n. m.* clipper ship.
cloaca /klo'aka/ *n. f.* sewer.
cloquear /kloke'ar/ *v.* cluck, cackle.
cloqueo /klo'keo/ *n. m.* cluck.
cloro /'kloro/ *n. m.* chlorine.
club /kluβ/ *n. m.* club, association.
club juvenil /kluβ huβe'nil/ youth club.
clueca /'klueka/ *n. f.* brooding hen.
coacción /koak'θion; koak'sion/ *n.* compulsion.
coagular /koagu'lar/ *v.* coagulate, clot.
coágulo /ko'agulo/ *n. m.* clot.
coalición /koali'θion; koali'sion/ *n. f.* coalition.
coartada /koar'taða/ *n. f.* alibi.
coartar /koar'tar/ *v.* limit.
cobarde /ko'βarðe/ *a.* & *n.* cowardly; coward.
cobardía /koβar'ðia/ *n. f.* cowardice.
cobayo /ko'βayo/ *n. m.* guinea pig.
cobertizo /koβer'tiθo; koβer'tiso/ *n. m.* shed.
cobertor /koβer'tor/ *n. m.,* **cobija,** *f.* blanket.
cobertura /koβer'tura/ *n. f.* cover, wrapping.
cobijar /koβi'har/ *v.* cover; protect.
cobrador /koβra'ðor/ *n. m.* collector.
cobranza /ko'βranθa; ko'βransa/ *n. f.* collection or recovery of money.
cobrar /ko'βrar/ *v.* collect; charge; cash.
cobre /'koβre/ *n. m.* copper.
cobrizo /ko'βriθo; ko'βriso/ *a.* coppery.
cobro /'koβro/ *n. m.* collection or recovery of money.
coca /'koka/ *n. f.* coca leaves.
cocaína /koka'ina/ *n. f.* cocaine.
cocal /ko'kal/ *n. m.* coconut plantation.
cocear /koθe'ar; kose'ar/ *v.* kick; resist.
cocer /ko'θer; ko'ser/ *v.* cook, boil, bake.
coche /'kotʃe/ *n. m.* coach; car, automobile.
cochecito de niño /kotʃe'θito de 'niɲo; kotʃe'sito/ baby carriage.
coche de choque /'kotʃe de 'tʃoke/ dodgem.
cochera /ko'tʃera/ *n. f.* garage.
cochero /ko'tʃero/ *n. m.* coachman; cab driver.
cochinada /kotʃi'naða/ *n. f.* filth; herd of swine.
cochino /ko'tʃino/ *n. m.* pig, swine.
cocido /ko'θiðo; ko'siðo/ *n. m.* stew.
cociente /ko'θiente; ko'siente/ *n. m.* quotient.
cocimiento /koθi'miento; kosi'miento/ *n. m.* cooking.
cocina /ko'θina; ko'sina/ *n. f.* kitchen.
cocinar /koθi'nar; kosi'nar/ *v.* cook.
cocinero /koθi'nero; kosi'nero/ **-ra** *n.* cook.
coco /'koko/ *n. m.* coconut; coconut tree.
cocodrilo /koko'ðrilo/ *n. m.* crocodile.
cóctel /kok'tel/ *n. m.* cocktail.
codazo /ko'ðaθo; ko'ðaso/ *n. m.* nudge with the elbow.
codicia /ko'ðiθia; ko'ðisia/ *n. f.* avarice, greed; lust.
codiciar /koðiθi'ar; koðisi'ar/ *v.* covet.
codicioso /koðiθi'oso; koðisi'oso/ *a.* covetous; greedy.
código /'koðigo/ *n. m.* (law) code.
codo /'koðo/ *n. m.* elbow.
codorniz /koðor'niθ; koðor'nis/ *n. f.* quail.
coeficiente /koefi'θiente; koefi'siente/ *n. m.* quotient.
coeficiente intelectual /koefi'θiente intelek'tual; koefi'siente intelek'tual/ intelligence quotient.
coetáneo /koe'taneo/ *a.* contemporary.
coexistir /koeksis'tir/ *v.* coexist.
cofrade /ko'fraðe/ *n. m.* fellow member of a club, etc.
cofre /'kofre/ *n. m.* coffer; chest; trunk.
coger /ko'her/ *v.* (*except in S.A.*) catch; pick; take.
cogote /ko'gote/ *n. m.* nape.
cohecho /ko'etʃo/ *n. m.* bribe. —**cohechar,** *v.*
coheredero /koere'ðero/ **-ra** *n.* coheir.
coherente /koe'rente/ *a.* coherent.
cohesión /koe'sion/ *n. f.* cohesion.
cohete /ko'ete/ *n. m.* firecracker; rocket.
cohibición /koiβi'θion; koiβi'sion/ *n.* restraint; repression.
cohibir /koi'βir/ *v.* restrain; repress.
coincidencia /koinθi'ðenθia; koinsi'ðensia/ *n. f.* coincidence.
coincidir /koinθi'ðir; koinsi'ðir/ *v.* coincide.
cojear /kohe'ar/ *v.* limp.
cojera /ko'hera/ *n. m.* limp.
cojín /ko'hin/ *n. m.* cushion.
cojinete /kohi'nete/ *n. m.* small cushion, pad.
cojo /'koho/ **-a** *a.* **1.** lame. —*n.* **2.** lame person.
col /kol/ *n. f.* cabbage.
cola /'kola/ *n. f.* tail; glue; line, queue. **hacer c.,** stand in line.
colaboración /kolaβora'θion; kolaβora'sion/ *n. f.* collaboration.
colaborar /kolaβo'rar/ *v.* collaborate.
cola de caballo /'kola de ka'βaʎo; 'kola de ka'βayo/ ponytail.
coladera /kola'ðera/ *n. f.* strainer.
colador /kola'ðor/ *n. m.* colander, strainer.
colapso /ko'lapso/ *n. m.* collapse, prostration.
colar /ko'lar/ *v.* strain; drain.
colateral /kolate'ral/ *a.* collateral.
colcha /'koltʃa/ *n. f.* bedspread, quilt.
colchón /kol'tʃon/ *n. m.* mattress.
colear /kole'ar/ *v.* wag the tail.
colección /kolek'θion; kolek'sion/ *n. f.* collection, set.
coleccionar /kolekθio'nar; koleksio'nar/ *v.* collect.
colecta /ko'lekta/ *n. f.* collection; collect (a prayer).
colectivo /kolek'tiβo/ *a.* collective.
colector /kolek'tor/ *n. m.* collector.
colega /ko'lega/ *n. m.* & *f.* colleague.
colegial /kole'hial/ *n. m.* college student.
colegiatura /kolehia'tura/ *n. f.* scholarship; tuition.
colegio /ko'lehio/ *n. m.* (private) school, college.
colegir /kole'hir/ *v.* infer, deduce.
cólera /'kolera/ *n.* **1.** *f.* rage, wrath. **2.** *m.* cholera.
colérico /ko'leriko/ *adj.* angry, irritated.
colesterol /koleste'rol/ *n. m.* cholesterol.
coleta /ko'leta/ *n. f.* pigtail; postscript.
coleto /ko'leto/ *n. m.* leather jacket.
colgado /kol'gaðo/ **-da** *n.* **1.** crazy person. —*a.* **2.** hanging, pending.
colgador /kolga'ðor/ *n. m.* rack, hanger.
colgaduras /kolga'ðuras/ *n. f.pl.* drapery.
colgante /kol'gante/ *a.* hanging.
colgar /kol'gar/ *v.* hang up, suspend.
colibrí /koli'βri/ *n. m.* hummingbird.
coliflor /koli'flor/ *n. f.* cauliflower.
coligarse /koli'garse/ *v.* band together, unite.
colilla /ko'liʎa; ko'liya/ *n. f.* butt of a cigar or cigarette.
colina /ko'lina/ *n. f.* hill, hillock.
colinabo /koli'naβo/ *n. m.* turnip.
colindante /kolin'dante/ *a.* neighboring, adjacent.
colindar /kolin'dar/ *v.* neighbor, abut.
coliseo /koli'seo/ *n. m.* theater; coliseum.
colisión /koli'sion/ *n. f.* collision.
collado /ko'ʎaðo; ko'yaðo/ *n. m.* hillock.
collar /ko'ʎar; ko'yar/ *n. m.* necklace; collar.
colmar /kol'mar/ *v.* heap up, fill liberally.
colmena /kol'mena/ *n. f.* hive.
colmillo /kol'miʎo; kol'miyo/ *n. m.* eyetooth; tusk; fang.
colmo /'kolmo/ *n. m.* height, peak, extreme.
colocación /koloka'θion; koloka'sion/ *n. f.* place, position; employment, job; arrangement.
colocar /kolo'kar/ *v.* place, locate, put, set.
colombiano /kolom'biano/ **-na** *a.* & *n.* Colombian.
colon /'kolon/ *n. m.* colon (of intestines).
colonia /ko'lonia/ *n. f.* colony; eau de Cologne.
Colonia *n. f.* Cologne.
colonial /kolo'nial/ *a.* colonial.
colonización /koloniθa'θion; kolonisa'sion/ *n. f.* colonization.

colonizador /koloniθa'ðor; koloni-sa'ðor/ **-ra** n. colonizer.

colonizar /koloni'θar; koloni'sar/ v. colonize.

colono /ko'lono/ n. m. colonist; tenant farmer.

coloquio /ko'lokio/ n. m. conversation, talk.

color /ko'lor/ n. m. color. —**colorar,** v.

coloración /kolora'θion; kolora'sion/ n. f. coloring.

colorado /kolo'raðo/ a. red, ruddy.

colorar /kolo'rar/ v. color, paint; dye.

colorete /kolo'rete/ n. m. rouge.

colorformo /kolor'formo/ n. m. chloroform.

colorido /kolo'riðo/ n. m. color, coloring. —**colorir,** v.

colosal /kolo'sal/ a. colossal.

columbrar /kolum'brar/ v. discern.

columna /ko'lumna/ n. f. column, pillar, shaft.

columpiar /kolum'piar/ v. swing.

columpio /ko'lumpio/ n. m. swing.

coma /'koma/ n. f. coma; comma.

comadre /ko'maðre/ n. f. midwife; gossip; close friend.

comadreja /koma'ðreha/ n. f. weasel.

comadrona /koma'ðrona/ n. f. midwife.

comandancia /koman'danθia; koman'dansia/ n. m. command; command post.

comandante /koman'dante/ n. m. commandant; commander; major.

comandar /koman'dar/ v. command.

comandita /koman'dita/ n. f. silent partnership.

comanditario /komandi'tario/ **-ra** n. silent partner.

comando /ko'mando/ n. m. command.

comarca /ko'marka/ n. f. region; border, boundary.

comba /'komba/ n. f. bulge.

combar /kom'bar/ v. bend; bulge.

combate /kom'bate/ n. m. combat. —**combatir,** v.

combatiente /komba'tiente/ a. & m. combatant.

combinación /kombina'θion; kombina'sion/ n. f. combination; slip (garment).

combinar /kombi'nar/ v. combine.

combustible /kombus'tiβle/ a. **1.** combustible. —n. **2.** m. fuel.

combustión /kombus'tion/ n. f. combustion.

comedero /kome'ðero/ n. m. trough.

comedia /ko'meðia/ n. f. comedy; play.

comediante /kome'ðiante/ n. m. actor; comedian.

comedido /kome'ðiðo/ a. polite, courteous; obliging.

comedirse /kome'ðirse/ v. to be polite or obliging.

comedor /kome'ðor/ n. m. dining room. **coche c.,** dining car.

comendador /komenda'ðor/ n. m. commander.

comensal /komen'sal/ n. m. table companion.

comentador /komenta'ðor/ **-ra** n. commentator.

comentario /komen'tario/ n. m. commentary.

comento /ko'mento/ n. m. comment. —**comentar,** v.

comenzar /komen'θar; komen'sar/ v. begin, start, commence.

comer /ko'mer/ v. eat, dine.

comercial /komer'θial; komer'sial/ a. commercial.

comercializar /komerθiali'θar; komersiali'sar/ v. market.

comerciante /komer'θiante; komer'siante/ **-ta** n. merchant, trader, businessperson.

comerciar /komer'θiar; komer'siar/ v. trade, deal, do business.

comercio /ko'merθio; ko'mersio/ n. m. commerce, trade, business; store.

comestible /komes'tiβle/ a. **1.** edible. —n. **2.** m. (pl.) groceries, provisions.

cometa /ko'meta/ n. **1.** m. comet. **2.** f. kite.

cometer /kome'ter/ v. commit.

cometido /kome'tiðo/ n. m. commission; duty; task.

comezón /kome'θon; kome'son/ n. f. itch.

comicios /ko'miθios; ko'misios/ n. m.pl. primary elections.

cómico /'komiko/ **-ca** a. & n. comic, comical; comedian.

comida /ko'miða/ n. f. food; dinner; meal.

comidilla /komi'ðiʎa; komi'ðiya/ n. f. light meal; gossip.

comienzo /ko'mienθo; ko'mienso/ n. m. beginning.

comilitona /komili'tona/ n. f. spread, feast.

comillas /ko'miʎas; ko'miyas/ n. f.pl. quotation marks.

com²lón /komi'lon/ **-na** n. glutton; heavy eater.

comisario /komi'sario/ n. m. commissary.

comisión /komi'sion/ n. f. commission. —**comisionar,** v.

comisionado /komisio'naðo/ **-da** n. agent, commissioner.

comisionar /komisio'nar/ v. commission.

comiso /ko'miso/ n. m. (law) confiscation of illegal goods.

comistrajo /komis'traho/ n. m. mess, hodgepodge.

comité /komi'te/ n. m. committee.

comitiva /komi'tiβa/ n. f. retinue.

como /'komo/ conj. & adv. like, as.

cómo adv. how.

cómoda /'komoða/ n. f. bureau, chest (of drawers).

cómodamente /komoða'mente/ adv. conveniently.

comodidad /komoði'ðað/ n. f. convenience, comfort; commodity.

comodín /komo'ðin/ n. m. joker (playing card).

cómodo /'komoðo/ a. comfortable; convenient.

comodoro /komo'ðoro/ n. m. commodore.

compacto /kom'pakto/ a. compact.

compadecer /kompaðe'θer; kompaðe'ser/ v. be sorry for, pity.

compadraje /kompa'ðrahe/ n. m. clique.

compadre /kom'paðre/ n. m. close friend.

compaginar /kompahi'nar/ v. put in order; arrange.

compañerismo /kompaɲe'rismo/ n. m. companionship.

compañero /kompa'ɲero/ **-ra** n. companion, partner.

compañía /kompa'ɲia/ n. f. company.

comparable /kompa'raβle/ a. comparable.

comparación /kompara'θion; kompara'sion/ n. f. comparison.

comparar /kompa'rar/ v. compare.

comparativamente /komparatiβa'mente/ adv. comparatively.

comparativo /kompara'tiβo/ a. comparative.

comparecer /kompare'θer; kompare'ser/ v. appear.

comparendo /kompa'rendo/ n. m. summons.

comparsa /kom'parsa/ n. f. carnival masquerade; retinue.

compartimiento /komparti'miento/ n. m. compartment.

compartir /kompar'tir/ v. share.

compás /kom'pas/ n. m. compass; beat, rhythm.

compasar /kompa'sar/ v. measure exactly.

compasión /kompa'sion/ n. f. compassion.

compasivo /kompa'siβo/ a. compassionate.

compatibilidad /kompatiβili'ðað/ n. f. compatibility.

compatible /kompa'tiβle/ a. compatible.

compatriota /kompa'triota/ n. m. & f. compatriot.

compeler /kompe'ler/ v. compel.

compendiar /kompen'diar/ v. summarize; abridge.

compendiariamente /kompendiaria'mente/ adv. briefly.

compendio /kom'pendio/ n. m. summary; abridgment.

compendiosamente /kompendiosa'mente/ adv. briefly.

compensación /kompensa'θion; kompensa'sion/ n. f. compensation.

compensar /kompen'sar/ v. compensate.

competencia /kompe'tenθia; kompe'tensia/ n. f. competence; competition.

competente /kompe'tente/ a. competent.

competentemente /kompetente'mente/ adv. competently.

competición /kompeti'θion; kompeti'sion/ n. f. competition.

competidor /kompeti'ðor/ **-ra** a. & n. competitive; competitor.

competir /kompe'tir/ v. compete.

compilación /kompila'θion; kompila'sion/ n. f. compilation.

compilar /kompi'lar/ v. compile.

compinche /kom'pintʃe/ n. m. pal.

complacencia /kompla'θenθia; kompla'sensia/ n. f. complacency.

complacer /kompla'θer; kompla'ser/ v. please, oblige, humor.

complaciente /kompla'θiente; kompla'siente/ a. pleasing, obliging.

complejidad /komplehi'ðað/ n. f. complexity.

complejo /kom'pleho/ **-ja** a. & n. complex.

complemento /komple'mento/ n. m. complement; Gram. object.

completamente /kompleta'mente/ adv. completely.

completamiento /kompleta'miento/ n. m. completion, finish.

completar /komple'tar/ v. complete.

completo /kom'pleto/ a. complete, full, perfect.

complexión /komplek'sion/ n. f. nature, temperament.

complicación /komplika'θion; komplika'sion/ n. f. complication.

complicado /kompli'kaðo/ a. complicated.

complicar /kompli'kar/ v. complicate.

cómplice /'kompliθe; 'komplise/ n. m. & f. accomplice, accessory.

complicidad /kompliθi'ðað; komplisi'ðað/ n. f. complicity.

complot /kom'plot/ n. m. conspiracy, plot.

componedor /kompone'ðor/ **-ra** n. typesetter.

componenda /kompo'nenda/ n. f. compromise; settlement.

componente /kompo'nente/ a. & m. component.

componer /kompo'ner/ v. compose; fix, repair.

componible /kompo'niβle/ a. reparable.

comportable /kompor'taβle/ a. endurable.

comportamiento /komporta'miento/ n. m. behavior.

comportarse /kompor'tarse/ v. behave.

comporte /kom'porte/ n. m. behavior.

composición /komposi'θion; komposi'sion/ n. f. composition.

compositivo /komposi'tiβo/ a. synthetic; composite.

compositor /komposi'tor/ **-ra** n. composer.

compost /kom'post/ n. m. compost.

compostura /kompos'tura/ n. f. composure; repair; neatness.

compota /kom'pota/ n. f. (fruit) sauce.

compra /'kompra/ n. f. purchase. **ir de compras,** to go shopping.

comprador /kompra'ðor/ **-ra** n. buyer, purchaser.

comprar /kom'prar/ v. buy, purchase.

comprender /kompren'der/ v. comprehend, understand; include, comprise.

comprensibilidad /komprensiβili'ðað/ n. f. comprehensibility.

comprensible /kompren'siβle/ a. understandable.

comprensión /kompren'sion/ n. f. comprehension, understanding.

comprensivo /kompren'siβo/ n. m. comprehensive.

compresa /kom'presa/ n. f. medical compress.

compresión /kompre'sion/ n. f. compression.

comprimir /kompri'mir/ v. compress; restrain, control.

comprobación /komproβa'θion; komproβa'sion/ n. f. proof.

comprobante /kompro'βante/ a. **1.** proving. —n. **2.** m. proof.

comprobar /kompro'βar/ v. prove; verify, check.

comprometer /komprome'ter/ v. compromise.

comprometerse /komprome'terse/ v. become engaged.

compromiso /kompro'miso/ n. m. compromise; engagement.

compuerta /kom'puerta/ n. f. floodgate.

compuesto /kom'puesto/ n. m. composition; compound.

compulsión /kompul'sion/ n. f. compulsion.

compulsivo /kompul'siβo/ a. compulsive.

compunción /kompun'θion; kompun'sion/ n. f. compunction.

compungirse /kompuŋ'girse/ v. regret, feel remorse.

computación /komputa'θion; komputa'sion/ n. f. computation.

computador /komputa'ðor/ n. m. computer.

computadora de sobremesa /komputa'ðora de soβre'mesa/ n. f. desktop computer.

computadora doméstica /komputa'ðora do'mestika/ n. f. home computer.

computar /kompu'tar/ v. compute.

cómputo /'komputo/ n. m. computation.

comulgar /komul'gar/ v. take communion.

comulgatorio /komulga'torio/ n. m. communion altar.

común /ko'mun/ a. common, usual.

comunal /komu'nal/ a. communal.

comunero /komu'nero/ n. m. commoner.

comunicable /komuni'kaβle/ a. communicable.

comunicación /komunika'θion; komunika'sion/ n. f. communication.

comunicante /komuni'kante/ n. m. & f. communicant.

comunicar /komuni'kar/ v. communicate; convey.

comunicativo /komunika'tiβo/ a. communicative.

comunidad /komuni'ðað/ n. f. community.

comunión /komu'nion/ n. f. communion.

comunismo /komu'nismo/ n. m. communism.

comunista /komu'nista/ a. & n. communistic; communist.

comúnmente /komu'mente/ adv. commonly; usually; often.

con /kon/ prep. with.

concavidad /konkaβi'ðað/ n. f. concavity.

cóncavo /'konkaβo/ a. **1.** concave. —n. **2.** m. concavity.

concebible /konθe'βiβle; konse'βiβle/ *a.* conceivable.

concebir /konθe'βir; konse'βir/ *v.* conceive.

conceder /konθe'ðer; konse'ðer/ *v.* concede.

concejal /konθe'hal; konse'hal/ *n. m.* councilman.

concejo /kon'θeho; kon'seho/ *n. m.* city council.

concento /kon'θento; kon'sento/ *n. m.* harmony (of singing voices).

concentración /konθentra'θion; konsentra'sion/ *n. f.* concentration.

concentrar /konθen'trar; konsen'trar/ *v.* concentrate.

concepción /konθep'θion; konsep'sion/ *n. f.* conception.

conceptible /konθep'tiβle; konsep'tiβle/ *a.* conceivable.

concepto /kon'θepto; kon'septo/ *n. m.* concept; opinion.

concerniente /konθer'niente; konser'niente/ *a.* concerning.

concernir /konθer'nir; konser'nir/ *v.* concern.

concertar /konθer'tar; konser'tar/ *v.* arrange.

concertina /konθer'tina; konser'tina/ *n. f.* concertina.

concesión /konθe'sion; konse'sion/ *n. f.* concession.

concha /'kontʃa/ *n. f.* S.A. shell.

conciencia /kon'θienθia; kon'siensia/ *n. f.* conscience; consciousness; conscientiousness.

concienzudo /konθien'θuðo; konsien'suðo/ *a.* conscientious.

concierto /kon'θierto; kon'sierto/ *n. m.* concert.

conciliación /konθilia'θion; konsilia'sion/ *n. f.* conciliation.

conciliador /konθilia'ðor; konsilia'ðor/ **-ra** *n.* conciliator.

conciliar /konθi'liar; konsi'liar/ *v.* conciliate.

concilio /kon'θilio; kon'silio/ *n. m.* council.

concisión /konθi'sion; konsi'sion/ *n. f.* conciseness.

conciso /kon'θiso; kon'siso/ *a.* concise.

concitar /konθi'tar; konsi'tar/ *v.* instigate, stir up.

conciudadano /konθiuða'ðano; konsiuða'ðano/ **-na** *n.* fellow citizen.

concluir /kon'kluir/ *v.* conclude.

conclusión /konklu'sion/ *n. f.* conclusion.

conclusivo /konklu'siβo/ *a.* conclusive.

concluso /kon'kluso/ *a.* concluded; closed.

concluyentemente /konkluyente'mente/ *adv.* conclusively.

concomitante /konkomi'tante/ *a.* concomitant, attendant.

concordador /konkorða'ðor/ **-ra** *n.* moderator; conciliator.

concordancia /konkor'ðanθia; konkor'ðansia/ *n. f.* agreement, concord.

concordar /konkor'ðar/ *v.* agree; put or be in accord.

concordia /kon'korðia/ *n. f.* concord, agreement.

concretamente /konkreta'mente/ *adv.* concretely.

concretar /konkre'tar/ *v.* summarize; make concrete.

concretarse /konkre'tarse/ *v.* limit oneself to.

concreto /kon'kreto/ *a. & m.* concrete.

concubina /konku'βina/ *n. f.* concubine, mistress.

concupiscente /konkupis'θente; konkupis'sente/ *a.* lustful.

concurrencia /konku'rrenθia; konku'rrensia/ *n. f.* assembly; attendance; competition.

concurrente /konku'rrente/ *a.* concurrent.

concurrido /konku'rriðo/ *a.* heavily attended or patronized.

concurrir /konku'rrir/ *v.* concur; attend.

concurso /kon'kurso/ *n. m.* contest, competition; meeting.

conde /'konde/ *n. m.* (title) count.

condecente /konde'θente; konde'sente/ *a.* appropriate, proper.

condecoración /kondekora'θion; kondekora'sion/ *n. f.* decoration; medal; badge.

condecorar /kondeko'rar/ *v.* decorate with a medal.

condena /kon'dena/ *n. f.* prison sentence.

condenación /kondena'θion; kondena'sion/ *n. f.* condemnation.

condenar /konde'nar/ *v.* condemn; damn; sentence.

condensación /kondensa'θion; kondensa'sion/ *n. f.* condensation.

condensar /konden'sar/ *v.* condense.

condesa /kon'desa/ *n. f.* countess.

condescendencia /kondesθen'denθia; kondessen'densia/ *n. f.* condescension.

condescender /kondesθen'der; kondessen'der/ *v.* condescend, deign.

condescendiente /kondesθen'diente; kondessen'diente/ *a.* condescending.

condición /kondi'θion; kondi'sion/ *n. f.* condition.

condicional /kondiθio'nal; kondisio'nal/ *a.* conditional.

condicionalmente /kondiθional'mente; kondisional'mente/ *adv.* conditionally.

condimentar /kondimen'tar/ *v.* season, flavor.

condimento /kondi'mento/ *n. m.* condiment, seasoning, dressing.

condiscípulo /kondis'θipulo; kondis'sipulo/ **-la** *n.* schoolmate.

condolencia /kondo'lenθia; kondo'lensia/ *n. f.* condolence, sympathy.

condolerse de /kondo'lerse de/ *v.* sympathize with.

condominio /kondo'minio/ *n. m.* condominium.

condómino /kon'domino/ *n. m.* co-owner.

condonar /kondo'nar/ *v.* condone.

cóndor /'kondor/ *n. m.* condor (bird).

conducción /konduk'θion; konduk'sion/ *n. f.* conveyance.

conducente /kondu'θente; kondu'sente/ *a.* conducive.

conducir /kondu'θir; kondu'sir/ *v.* conduct, escort, lead; drive.

conducta /kon'dukta/ *n. f.* conduct, behavior.

conducto /kon'dukto/ *n. m.* pipe, conduit; sewer.

conductor /konduk'tor/ **-ra** *n.* driver; conductor.

conectar /konek'tar/ *v.* connect.

conejera /kone'hera/ *n. f.* rabbit warren; place of ill repute.

conejillo de Indias /kone'hiʎo de 'indias; kone'hiyo de 'indias/ guinea pig.

conejo /ko'neho/ **-ja** *n.* rabbit.

conexión /konek'sion/ *n. f.* connection; coupling.

conexivo /konek'siβo/ *a.* connective.

conexo /ko'nekso/ *a.* connected, united.

confalón /konfa'lon/ *n. m.* ensign, standard.

confección /konfek'θion; konfek'sion/ *n. f.* workmanship; ready-made article; concoction.

confeccionar /konfekθio'nar; konfeksio'nar/ *v.* concoct.

confederación /konfeðera'θion; konfeðera'sion/ *n. f.* confederation.

confederado /konfeðe'raðo/ **-da** *a. & n.* confederate.

confederar /konfeðe'rar/ *v.* confederate, unite, ally.

conferencia /konfe'renθia; konfe'rensia/ *n. f.* lecture; conference. **c. interurbana**, long-distance call.

conferenciante /konferen'θiante;

konferen'siante/ *n. m. & f.* lecturer, speaker.

conferenciar /konferen'θiar; konferen'siar/ *v.* confer.

conferencista /konferen'θista; konferen'sista/ *n. m. & f.* lecturer, speaker.

conferir /konfe'rir/ *v.* confer.

confesar /konfe'sar/ *v.* confess.

confesión /konfe'sion/ *n. f.* confession.

confesionario /konfesio'nario, konfeso'nario/ *n. m.* confessional.

confesor /konfe'sor/ **-ra** *n.* confessor.

confeti /kon'feti/ *n. m.pl.* confetti.

confiable /kon'fiaβle/ *a.* dependable.

confiado /kon'fiaðo/ *a.* confident; trusting.

confianza /kon'fianθa; kon'fiansa/ *n. f.* confidence, trust, faith.

confiar /kon'fiar/ *v.* entrust; trust, rely.

confidencia /konfi'ðenθia; konfi'ðensia/ *n. f.* confidence, secret.

confidencial /konfiðen'θial; konfiðen'sial/ *a.* confidential.

confidente /konfi'ðente/ *n. m. & f.* confidant.

confidentemente /konfiðente'mente/ *adv.* confidently.

confín /kon'fin/ *n. m.* confine.

confinamiento /konfina'miento/ *n. m.* confinement.

confinar /konfi'nar/ *v.* confine, imprison; border on.

confirmación /konfirma'θion; konfirma'sion/ *n. f.* confirmation.

confirmar /konfir'mar/ *v.* confirm.

confiscación /konfiska'θion; konfiska'sion/ *n. f.* confiscation.

confiscar /konfis'kar/ *v.* confiscate.

confitar /konfi'tar/ *v.* sweeten; make into candy or jam.

confite /kon'fite/ *n. m.* candy.

confitería /konfite'ria/ *n. f.* confectionery; candy store.

confitura /konfi'tura/ *n. f.* confection.

conflagración /konflagra'θion; konflagra'sion/ *n. f.* conflagration.

conflicto /kon'flikto/ *n. m.* conflict.

confluencia /kon'fluenθia; kon'fluensia/ *n. f.* confluence, junction.

confluir /kon'fluir/ *v.* flow into each other.

conformación /konforma'θion; konforma'sion/ *n. f.* conformation.

conformar /konfor'mar/ *v.* conform.

conforme /kon'forme/ *a.* 1. acceptable, right, as agreed; in accordance, in agreement. —*conj.* 2. according, as.

conformidad /konformi'ðað/ *n. f.* conformity; agreement.

conformismo /konfor'mismo/ *n. m.* conformism.

conformista /konfor'mista/ *n. m. & f.* conformist.

confortar /konfor'tar/ *v.* comfort.

confraternidad /konfraterni'ðað/ *n. f.* brotherhood, fraternity.

confricar /konfri'kar/ *v.* rub vigorously.

confrontación /konfronta'θion; konfronta'sion/ *n. f.* confrontation.

confrontar /konfron'tar/ *v.* confront.

confucianismo /konfuθia'nismo; konfusia'nismo/ *n. m.* Confucianism.

confundir /konfun'dir/ *v.* confuse; puzzle, mix up.

confusamente /konfusa'mente/ *adv.* confusedly.

confusión /konfu'sion/ *n. f.* confusion, mix-up; clutter.

confuso /kon'fuso/ *a.* confused; confusing.

confutación /konfuta'θion; konfuta'sion/ *n. f.* disproof.

confutar /konfu'tar/ *v.* refute, disprove.

congelable /konxe'laβle/ *a.* congealable.

congelación /konxela'θion; kon-

hela'sion/ *n. f.* congealment; deep freeze.

congelado /konxe'laðo/ *a.* frozen, congealed.

congelar /konxe'lar/ *v.* congeal, freeze.

congenial /konxe'nial/ *a.* congenial; analogous.

congeniar /konxe'niar/ *v.* be congenial.

congestión /konxes'tion/ *n. f.* congestion.

conglomeración /konglomera'θion; konglomera'sion/ *n. f.* conglomeration.

congoja /kon'goha/ *n. f.* grief, anguish.

congraciamiento /kongraθia'miento; kongrasia'miento/ *n. m.* flattery; ingratiation.

congraciar /kongra'θiar; kongra'siar/ *v.* flatter; ingratiate oneself.

congratulación /kongratula'θion; kongratula'sion/ *n. f.* congratulation.

congratular /kongratu'lar/ *v.* congratulate.

congregación /kongrega'θion; kongrega'sion/ *n. f.* congregation.

congregar /kongre'gar/ *v.* congregate.

congresista /kongre'sista/ *n. m. & f.* congressional representative.

congreso /kon'greso/ *n. m.* congress; conference.

conjetura /konxe'tura/ *n. f.* conjecture. —**conjeturar,** *v.*

conjetural /konxetu'ral/ *a.* conjectural.

conjugación /konxuga'θion; konxuga'sion/ *n. f.* conjugation.

conjugar /konxu'gar/ *v.* conjugate.

conjunción /konxun'θion; konxun'sion/ *n. f.* union; conjunction.

conjuntamente /konxunta'mente/ *adv.* together, jointly.

conjunto. /kon'xunto/ *a.* **1.** joint, unified. —*n.* **2.** *m.* whole.

conjuración /konxura'θion; konxura'sion/ *n. f.* conspiracy, plot.

conjurado /konxu'raðo/ **-da** *n.* conspirator, plotter.

conjurar /konxu'rar/ *v.* conjure.

conjuro /kon'xuro/ *n. m.* exorcism; spell; plea.

conllevador /konʎeβa'ðor; konyeβa'ðor/ *n. m.* helper, aide.

conmemoración /konmemora'θion; konmemora'sion/ *n. f.* commemoration; remembrance.

conmemorar /konmemo'rar/ *v.* commemorate.

conmemorativo /konmemora'tiβo/ *a.* commemorative, memorial.

conmensal /konmen'sal/ *n. m.* messmate.

conmigo /kon'migo/ *adv.* with me.

conmilitón /konmili'ton/ *n. m.* fellow soldier.

conminación /konmina'θion; konmina'sion/ *n. f.* threat, warning.

conminar /konmi'nar/ *v.* threaten.

conminatorio /konmina'torio/ *a.* threatening, warning.

conmiseración /konmisera'θion; konmisera'sion/ *n. f.* sympathy.

conmoción /konmo'θion; konmo'sion/ *n. f.* commotion, stir.

conmovedor /konmoβe'ðor/ *a.* moving, touching.

conmover /konmo'βer/ *v.* move, affect; touch.

conmutación /konmuta'θion; konmuta'sion/ *n. f.* commutation.

conmutador /konmuta'ðor/ *n. m.* electric switch.

conmutar /konmu'tar/ *v.* exchange.

connatural /konnatu'ral/ *a.* innate, inherent.

connotación /konnota'θion; konnota'sion/ *n. f.* connotation.

connotar /konno'tar/ *v.* connote.

connubial /konnu'βial/ *a.* connubial.

connubio /ko'nnuβio/ *n. m.* matrimony.

cono /'kono/ *n. m.* cone.

conocedor /konoθe'ðor; konose'ðor/ **-ra** *n.* expert, connoisseur.

conocer /kono'θer; kono'ser/ *v.* know, be acquainted with; meet, make the acquaintance of.

conocible /kono'θiβle; kono'siβle/ *a.* knowable.

conocido /kono'θiðo; kono'siðo/ **-da** *a.* 1. familiar, well-known. —*n.* 2. acquaintance, person known.

conocimiento /konoθi'miento; konosi'miento/ *n. m.* knowledge, acquaintance; consciousness.

conque /'konke/ *conj.* so then; and so.

conquista /kon'kista/ *n. f.* conquest.

conquistador /konkista'ðor/ **-ra** *n.* conqueror.

conquistar /konkis'tar/ *v.* conquer.

consabido /konsa'βiðo/ *a.* aforesaid.

consagración /konsagra'θion; konsagra'sion/ *n. f.* consecration.

consagrado /konsa'graðo/ *a.* consecrated.

consagrar /konsa'grar/ *v.* consecrate, dedicate, devote.

consanguinidad /konsaŋguini'ðað/ *n. f.* consanguinity.

consciente /kons'θiente; kons'siente/ *a.* conscious, aware.

conscientemente /konsθiente-'mente; konssiente'mente/ *adv.* consciously.

conscripción /konskrip'θion; konskrip'sion/ *n. f.* conscription for military service.

consecución /konseku'θion; konseku'sion/ *n. f.* attainment.

consecuencia /konse'kuenθia; konse'kuensia/ *n. f.* consequence.

consecuente /konse'kuente/ *a.* consequent; consistent.

consecuentemente /konsekuente-'mente/ *adv.* consequently.

consecutivamente /konsekutiβa-'mente/ *adv.* consecutively.

consecutivo /konseku'tiβo/ *a.* consecutive.

conseguir /konse'gir/ *v.* obtain, get, secure; succeed in, manage to.

conseja /kon'seha/ *n. f.* fable.

consejero /konse'hero/ **-ra** *n.* adviser, counselor.

consejo /kon'seho/ *n. m.* council; counsel; (piece of) advice. **c. de redacción,** editorial board.

consenso /kon'senso/ *n. m.* consensus.

consentido /konsen'tiðo/ *a.* spoiled, bratty.

consentimiento /konsenti'miento/ *n. m.* consent.

consentir /konsen'tir/ *v.* allow, permit.

conserje /kon'serhe/ *n. m.* superintendent, keeper.

conserva /kon'serβa/ *n. f.* conserve, preserve.

conservación /konserβa'θion; konserβa'sion/ *n. f.* conservation.

conservador /konserβa'ðor/ **-ra** *a. & n.* conservative.

conservar /konser'βar/ *v.* conserve.

conservativo /konserβa'tiβo/ *a.* conservative, preservative.

conservatorio /konserβa'torio/ *n. m.* conservatory.

considerable /konsiðe'raβle/ *a.* considerable, substantial.

considerablemente /konsiðeraβle'mente/ *adv.* considerably.

consideración /konsiðera'θion; konsiðera'sion/ *n. f.* consideration.

consideradamente /konsiðera-ða'mente/ *adv.* considerably.

considerado /konsiðe'raðo/ *a.* considerate; considered.

considerando /konsiðe'rando/ *conj.* whereas.

considerar /konsiðe'rar/ *v.* consider.

consigna /kon'signa/ *n. f.* watchword.

consignación /konsigna'θion; konsigna'sion/ *n. f.* consignment.

consignar /konsig'nar/ *v.* consign.

consignatorio /konsigna'torio/ **-ria** *n.* consignee; trustee.

consigo /kon'sigo/ *adv.* with herself, with himself, with oneself, with themselves, with yourself, with yourselves.

consiguiente /konsi'giente/ *a.* 1. consequent. —*n.* 2. *m.* consequence.

consiguientemente /konsigiente-'mente/ *adv.* consequently.

consistencia /konsis'tenθia; konsis'tensia/ *n. f.* consistency.

consistente /konsis'tente/ *a.* consistent.

consistir /konsis'tir/ *v.* consist.

consistorio /konsis'torio/ *n. m.* consistory.

consocio /kon'soθio; kon'sosio/ *n. m.* associate; partner; comrade.

consola /kon'sola/ *n. f.* console.

consolación /konsola'θion; konsola'sion/ *n. f.* consolation.

consolar /konso'lar/ *v.* console.

consolativo /konsola'tiβo/ *a.* consolatory.

consolidación /konsoliða'θion; konsoliða'sion/ *n.* consolidation.

consolidado /konsoli'ðaðo/ *a.* consolidated.

consolidar /konsoli'ðar/ *v.* consolidate.

consonancia /konso'nanθianb; konso'nansia/ *n. f.* agreement, accord, harmony.

consonante /konso'nante/ *a. & f.* consonant.

consonar /konso'nar/ *v.* rhyme.

consorte /kon'sorte/ *n. m. & f.* consort, mate.

conspicuo /kons'pikuo/ *a.* conspicuous.

conspiración /konspira'θion; konspira'sion/ *n. f.* conspiracy, plot.

conspirador /konspira'ðor/ **-ra** *n.* conspirator.

conspirar /konspi'rar/ *v.* conspire, plot.

constancia /kons'tanθia; kons'tansia/ *n. f.* perseverance; record.

constante /kons'tante/ *a.* constant.

constantemente /konstante'mente/ *adv.* constantly.

constar /kons'tar/ *v.* consist; be clear, be on record.

constelación /konstela'θion; konstela'sion/ *n. f.* constellation.

consternación /konsterna'θion; konsterna'sion/ *n. f.* consternation.

consternar /konster'nar/ *v.* dismay.

constipación /konstipa'θion; konstipa'sion/ *n. f.* head cold.

constipado /konsti'paðo/ *a.* 1. having a head cold. —*n.* 2. *m.* head cold.

constitución /konstitu'θion; konstitu'sion/ *n. f.* constitution.

constitucional /konstituθio'nal; konstitusio'nal/ *a.* constitutional.

constitucionalidad /konstituθion-ali'ðað; konstitusionali'ðað/ *n. f.* constitutionality.

constituir /konsti'tuir/ *v.* constitute.

constitutivo /konstitu'tiβo/ *n. m.* constituent.

constituyente /konstitu'yente; konstitu'tiβo/ *a.* constituent.

constreñidamente /konstreɲiða-'mente/ *adv.* compulsively; with constraint.

constreñimiento /konstreɲi'miento/ *n. m.* compulsion; constraint.

constreñir /konstre'ɲir/ *v.* constrain.

constricción /konstrik'θion; konstrik'sion/ *n. f.* constriction.

construcción /konstruk'θion; konstruk'sion/ *n. f.* construction.

constructivo /konstruk'tiβo/ *a.* constructive.

constructor /konstruk'tor/ **-ra** *n.* builder.

construir /kons'truir/ *v.* construct, build.

consuelo /kon'suelo/ *n. m.* consolation.

cónsul /'konsul/ *n. m.* consul.

consulado /konsu'laðo/ *n. m.* consulate.

consular /konsu'lar/ *a.* consular.

consulta /kon'sulta/ *n. f.* consultation.

consultación /konsulta'θion; konsulta'sion/ *n. f.* consultation.

consultante /konsul'tante/ *n. m. & f.* consultant.

consultar /konsul'tar/ *v.* consult.

consultivo /konsul'tiβo/ *a.* consultative.

consultor /konsul'tor/ **-ra** *n.* adviser.

consumación /konsuma'θion; konsuma'sion/ *n. f.* consummation; end.

consumado /konsu'maðo/ *a.* consummate, downright.

consumar /konsu'mar/ *v.* consummate.

consumidor /konsumi'ðor/ **-ra** *n.* consumer.

consumir /konsu'mir/ *v.* consume.

consumo /kon'sumo/ *n. m.* consumption.

consunción /konsun'θion; konsun'sion/ *n. m.* consumption, tuberculosis.

contabilidad /kontaβili'ðað/ *n. f.* accounting, bookkeeping.

contabilista /kontaβi'lista/ **contable** *n. m. & f.* accountant.

contacto /kon'takto/ *n. m.* contact.

contado /kon'taðo/ *a.* **al c.,** (for) cash.

contador /konta'ðor/ **-ra** *n.* accountant, bookkeeper; meter.

contagiar /konta'hiar/ *v.* infect.

contagio /kon'tahio/ *n. m.* contagion.

contagioso /konta'hioso/ *a.* contagious.

contaminación /kontamina'θion; kontamina'sion/ *n. f.* contamination, pollution. **c. del aire, c. atmosférica,** air pollution.

contaminar /kontami'nar/ *v.* contaminate, pollute.

contar /kon'tar/ *v.* count; relate, recount, tell. **c. con,** count on.

contemperar /kontempe'rar/ *v.* moderate.

contemplación /kontempla'θion; kontempla'sion/ *n. f.* contemplation.

contemplador /kontempla'ðor/ **-ra** *n.* thinker.

contemplar /kontem'plar/ *v.* contemplate.

contemplativamente /kontempla-tiβa'mente/ *adv.* thoughtfully.

contemplativo /kontempla'tiβo/ *a.* contemplative.

contemporáneo /kontempo'raneo/ **-nea** *a. & n.* contemporary.

contención /konten'θion; konten'sion/ *n. f.* contention.

contencioso /konten'θioso; konten'sioso/ *a.* quarrelsome; argumentative.

contender /konten'der/ *v.* cope, contend; conflict.

contendiente /konten'diente/ *n. m. & f.* contender.

contenedor /kontene'ðor/ *n. m.* container.

contener /konte'ner/ *v.* contain; curb, control.

contenido /konte'niðo/ *n. m.* contents.

contenta /kon'tenta/ *n. f.* endorsement.

contentamiento /kontenta'miento/ *n. m.* contentment.

contentar /konten'tar/ *v.* content, satisfy.

contentible /konten'tiβle/ *a.* contemptible.

contento /kon'tento/ *a.* 1. contented, happy. —*n.* 2. *m.* contentment, satisfaction, pleasure.

contérmino /kon'termino/ *a.* adjacent, abutting.

contestable /kontes'taβle/ *a.* disputable.

contestación /kontesta'θion; kontesta'sion/ *n. f.* answer. —**contestar,** *v.*

contestador automático /kontesta'ðor auto'matiko/ *n. m.* answering machine.

contextura /konteks'tura/ *n. f.* texture.

contienda /kon'tienda/ *n. f.* combat; match; strife.

contigo /kon'tigo/ *adv.* with you.

contiguamente /kontigua'mente/ *adv.* contiguously.

contiguo /kon'tiguo/ *a.* adjoining, next.

continencia /konti'nenθia; konti'nensia/ *n. f.* continence, moderation.

continental /konti'nental/ *a.* continental.

continente /konti'nente/ *n. m.* continent; mainland.

continentemente /kontinente-'mente/ *adv.* in moderation.

contingencia /kontin'henθia; kontin'hensia/ *n. f.* contingency.

contingente /kontin'hente/ *a.* contingent; incidental.

continuación /kontinua'θion; kontinua'sion/ *n. f.* continuation. **a c.,** thereupon, hereupon.

continuamente /kontinua'mente/ *adv.* continuously.

continuar /konti'nuar/ *v.* continue, keep on.

continuidad /kontinui'ðað/ *n. f.* continuity.

continuo /kon'tinuo/ *a.* continual; continuous.

contorcerse /kontor'θerse; kontor'serse/ *v.* writhe, twist.

contorción /kontor'θion; kontor'sion/ *n. f.* contortion.

contorno /kon'torno/ *n. m.* contour; profile, outline; neighborhood.

contra /'kontra/ *prep.* against.

contraalmirante /kontraalmi'rante/ *n. m.* rear admiral.

contraataque /kontraa'take/ *n. m.* counterattack.

contrabajo /kontra'βaho/ *n. m.* double bass.

contrabalancear /kontraβalanθe'ar; kontraβalanse'ar/ *v.* counterbalance.

contrabandear /kontraβande'ar/ *v.* smuggle.

contrabandista /kontraβan'dista/ *n. m. & f.* smuggler.

contrabando /kontra'βando/ *n. m.* contraband, smuggling.

contracción /kontrak'θion; kontrak'sion/ *n. f.* contraction.

contracepción /kontraθep'θion; kontrasep'sion/ *n. f.* contraception, birth control.

contractual /kontrak'tual/ *a.* contractual.

contradecir /kontraðe'θir; kontraðe'sir/ *v.* contradict.

contradicción /kontraðik'θion; kontraðik'sion/ *n. f.* contradiction.

contradictorio /kontraðik'torio/ *adj.* contradictory.

contraer /kontra'er/ *v.* contract; shrink.

contrahacedor /kontraaθe'ðor; kontraase'ðor/ **-ra** *n.* imitator.

contrahacer /kontraa'θer; kontraa'ser/ *v.* forge.

contralor /kontra'lor/ *n. m.* comptroller.

contramandar /kontraman'dar/ *v.* countermand.

contraorden /kontra'orðen/ *n. f.* countermand.

contraparte /kontra'parte/ *n. f.* counterpart.

contrapesar /kontrape'sar/ *v.* counterbalance; offset.

contrapeso /kontra'peso/ *n. m.* counterweight.

contraproducente /kontraproðu'θente; kontraproðu'sente/ *a.* counterproductive.

contrapunto /kontra'punto/ *n. m.* counterpoint.

contrariamente /kontraria'mente/ *adv.* contrarily.

contrariar /kontra'riar/ *v.* contradict; vex; antagonize; counteract.

contrariedad /kontrarie'ðað/ *n. f.* contrariness; opposition; contradiction; disappointment; trouble.

contrario /kon'trario/ *a. & m.* contrary, opposite.

contrarrestar /kontrarres'tar/ *v.* resist; counteract.

contrasol /kontra'sol/ *n. m.* sunshade.

contraste /kon'traste/ *n. m.* contrast. —**contrastar,** *v.*

contratar /kontra'tar/ *v.* engage, contract.

contratiempo /kontra'tiempo/ *n. m.* accident; misfortune.

contratista /kontra'tista/ *n. m. & f.* contractor.

contrato /kon'trato/ *n. m.* contract.

contribución /kontriβu'θion; kontriβu'sion/ *n. f.* contribution; tax.

contribuir /kontri'βuir/ *v.* contribute.

contribuyente /kontriβu'yente/ *n. m. & f.* contributor; taxpayer.

contrición /kontri'θion; kontri'sion/ *n. f.* contrition.

contristar /kontris'tar/ *v.* afflict.

contrito /kon'trito/ *a.* contrite, remorseful.

control /kon'trol/ *n. m.* control. —**controlar,** *v.*

controlador aéreo /kontrola'ðor a'ereo/ *n. m.* air traffic controller.

controversia /kontro'βersia/ *n. f.* controversy.

controversista /kontroβer'sista/ *n. m. & f.* controversialist.

controvertir /kontroβer'tir/ *v.* dispute.

contumacia /kontu'maθia; kontu'masia/ *n. f.* stubbornness.

contumaz /kontu'maθ; kontu'mas/ *adj.* stubborn.

contumelia /kontu'melia/ *n. f.* contumely; abuse.

conturbar /kontur'βar/ *v.* trouble, disturb.

contusión /kontu'sion/ *n. f.* contusion; bruise.

convalecencia /kombale'θenθia; kombale'sensia/ *n. f.* convalescence.

convalecer /kombale'θer; kombale'ser/ *v.* convalesce.

convaleciente /kombale'θiente; kombale'siente/ *a.* convalescent.

convecino /kombe'θino; kombe'sino/ **-na** *a.* **1.** near, close. —*n.* **2.** neighbor.

convencedor /kombenθe'ðor; kombense'ðor/ *adj.* convincing.

convencer /komben'θer; komben'ser/ *v.* convince.

convencimiento /kombenθi'miento; kombensi'miento/ *n. m.* conviction, firm belief.

convención /komben'θion; komben'sion/ *n. f.* convention.

convencional /kombenθio'nal; kombensio'nal/ *a.* conventional.

conveniencia /kombe'nienθia; kombe'niensia/ *n. f.* suitability; advantage, interest.

conveniente /kombe'niente/ *a.* suitable; advantageous, opportune.

convenio /kom'benio/ *n. m.* pact, treaty; agreement.

convenir /kombe'nir/ *v.* assent, agree, concur; be suitable, fitting, convenient.

convento /kom'bento/ *n. m.* convent.

convergencia /komber'henθia; komber'hensia/ *n. f.* convergence.

convergir /komber'hir/ *v.* converge.

conversación /kombersa'θion; kombersa'sion/ *n. f.* conversation.

conversar /komber'sar/ *v.* converse.

conversión /komber'sion/ *n. f.* conversion.

convertible /komber'tiβle/ *a.* convertible.

convertir /komber'tir/ *v.* convert.

convexidad /kombeksi'ðað/ *n. f.* convexity.

convexo /kom'bekso/ *a.* convex.

convicción /kombik'θion; kombik'sion/ *n. f.* conviction.

convicto /kom'bikto/ *a.* found guilty.

convidado /kombi'ðaðo/ **-da** *n.* guest.

convidar /kombi'ðar/ *v.* invite.

convincente /kombin'θente; kombin'sente/ *a.* convincing.

convite /kom'bite/ *n. m.* invitation, treat.

convocación /komboka'θion; komboka'sion/ *n. f.* convocation.

convocar /kombo'kar/ *v.* convoke, assemble.

convoy /kom'boi/ *n. m.* convoy, escort.

convoyar /kombo'yar/ *v.* convey; escort.

convulsión /kombul'sion/ *n. f.* convulsion.

convulsivo /kombul'siβo/ *a.* convulsive.

conyugal /konyu'gal/ *a.* conjugal.

cónyuge /'konyuhe/ *n. m. & f.* spouse, mate.

coñac /ko'nak/ *n. m.* cognac, brandy.

cooperación /koopera'θion; koopera'sion/ *n. f.* cooperation.

cooperador /koopera'ðor/ *a.* cooperative.

cooperar /koope'rar/ *v.* cooperate.

cooperativa /koopera'tiβa/ *n. f.* (food, etc.) cooperative, co-op.

cooperativo /koopera'tiβo/ *a.* cooperative.

coordinación /koorðina'θion; koorðina'sion/ *n. f.* coordination.

coordinar /koorði'nar/ *v.* coordinate.

copa /'kopa/ *n. f.* goblet.

copartícipe /kopar'tiθipe; kopar'tisipe/ *m & f.* partner.

copete /ko'pete/ *n. m.* tuft; toupee.

copia /'kopia/ *n. f.* copy. —**copiar,** *v.*

copiadora /kopia'ðora/ *n. f.* copier.

copioso /ko'pioso/ *a.* copious.

copista /ko'pista/ *n. f.* copyist.

copla /'kopla/ *n. f.* popular song.

coplero /kop'lero/ *n. m.* poetaster.

cópula /'kopula/ *n. f.* connection.

coqueta /ko'keta/ *n. f.* flirt. —**coquetear,** *v.*

coraje /ko'rahe/ *n. m.* courage, bravery; anger.

coral /ko'ral/ *a.* **1.** choral. —*n.* **2.** *m.* coral.

coralino /kora'lino/ *a.* coral.

Corán /ko'ran/ *n. m.* Koran.

corazón /kora'θon; kora'son/ *n. m.* heart.

corazonada /koraθo'naða; koraso'naða/ *n. f.* foreboding.

corbata /kor'βata/ *n. f.* necktie.

corbeta /kor'βeta/ *n. f.* corvette.

corcho /'kortʃo/ *n. m.* cork.

corcova /kor'koβa/ *n. f.* hump, hunchback.

corcovado /korko'βaðo/ **-da** *a. & n.* hunchback.

cordaje /kor'ðahe/ *n. m.* rigging.

cordel /kor'ðel/ *n. m.* string, cord.

cordero /kor'ðero/ *n. m.* lamb.

cordial /kor'ðial/ *a.* cordial; hearty.

cordialidad /korðiali'ðað/ *n. f.* cordiality.

cordillera /korði'ʎera; korði'yera/ *n. f.* mountain range.

cordón /kor'ðon/ *n. m.* cord; (shoe) lace.

cordura /kor'ðura/ *n. f.* sanity.

Corea /ko'rea/ *n. f.* Korea.

coreano /kore'ano/ **-a** *a. & n.* Korean.

coreografía /koreogra'fia/ *n. f.* choreography.

corista /ko'rista/ *n. f.* chorus girl.

corneja /kor'neha/ *n. f.* crow.

córneo /'korneo/ *a.* horny.

corneta /kor'neta/ *n. f.* bugle, horn, cornet.

corniforme /korni'forme/ *a.* horn-shaped.

cornisa /kor'nisa/ *n. f.* cornice.

cornucopia /kornu'kopia/ *n. f.* cornucopia.

coro /'koro/ *n. m.* chorus; choir.

corola /ko'rola/ *n. f.* corolla.

corolario /koro'lario/ *n. m.* corollary.

corona /ko'rona/ *n. f.* crown; halo; wreath.

coronación /korona'θion; korona'sion/ *n. f.* coronation.

coronamiento /korona'miento/ *n. m.* completion of a task.

coronar /koro'nar/ *v.* crown.

coronel /koro'nel/ *n. m.* colonel.

coronilla /koro'niʎa; koro'niya/ *n. f.* crown, top of the head.

corporación /korpora'θion; korpora'sion/ *n. f.* corporation.

corporal /korpo'ral/ *adj.* corporeal, bodily.

corpóreo /kor'poreo/ *a.* corporeal.

corpulencia /korpu'lenθia; korpu'lensia/ *n. f.* corpulence.

corpulento /korpu'lento/ *a.* corpulent, stout.

corpuscular /korpusku'lar/ *a.* corpuscular.

corpúsculo /kor'puskulo/ *n. m.* corpuscle.

corral /ko'rral/ *n. m.* corral, pen, yard.

correa /ko'rrea/ *n. f.* belt, strap.

correa transportadora /korrea transporta'ðora/ conveyor belt.

corrección /korrek'θion; korrek'sion/ *n. f.* correction.

correcto /ko'rrekto/ *a.* correct, proper, right.

corrector /korrek'tor/ **-ra** *n.* corrector, proofreader.

corredera /korre'ðera/ *n. f.* race course.

corredizo /korre'ðiθo; korre'ðiso/ *a.* easily untied.

corredor /korre'ðor/ *n. m.* corridor; runner.

corregible /korre'hiβle/ *a.* corrigible.

corregidor /korrehi'ðor/ *n. m.* corrector; magistrate, mayor.

corregir /korre'hir/ *v.* correct.

correlación /korrela'θion; korrela'sion/ *n. f.* correlation.

correlacionar /korrelaθio'nar; korrelasio'nar/ *v.* correlate.

correlativo /korrela'tiβo/ *a.* correlative.

correo /ko'rreo/ *n. m.* mail.

correoso /korre'oso/ *a.* leathery.

correr /ko'rrer/ *v.* run.

correría /korre'ria/ *n. f.* raid; escapade.

correspondencia /korrespon'denθia; korrespon'densia/ *n. f.* correspondence.

corresponder /korrespon'der/ *v.* correspond.

correspondiente /korrespon'diente/ *a. & m.* corresponding; correspondent.

corresponsal /korrespon'sal/ *n. m.* correspondent.

corretaje /korre'tahe/ *n. m.* brokerage.

correvedile /korreβe'ðile/ *n. m.* tale bearer; gossip.

corrida /ko'rriða/ *n. f.* race. **c. (de toros),** bullfight.

corrido /ko'rriðo/ *a.* abashed; expert.

corriente /ko'rriente/ *a.* **1.** current, standard. —*n.* **2.** *f.* current, stream. **3.** *m.* **al c.,** informed, up to date. **contra la c.,** against the current; upriver, upstream.

corroboración /korroβora'θion; korroβora'sion/ *n. f.* corroboration.

corroborar /korroβo'rar/ *v.* corroborate.

corroer /korro'er/ *v.* corrode.

corromper /korrom'per/ *v.* corrupt.

corrompido /korrom'piðo/ *a.* corrupt.

corrupción /korrup'θion; korrup'sion/ *n. f.* corruption.

corruptela /korrup'tela/ *n. f.* corruption; vice.

corruptibilidad /korruptiβili'ðað/ *n. f.* corruptibility.

corruptor /korrup'tor/ **-ra** *n.* corrupter.

corsario /kor'sario/ *n. m.* corsair.

corsé /kor'se/ *n. m.* corset.

corso /'korso/ *n. m.* piracy.

cortacésped /korta'θespeð; korta'sespeð/ *n. m.* lawnmower.

cortadillo /korta'ðiʎo; korta'ðiyo/ *n. m.* small glass.

cortado /kor'taðo/ *a.* cut.

cortadura /korta'ðura/ *n. f.* cut.

cortante /kor'tante/ *a.* cutting, sharp, keen.

cortapisa /korta'pisa/ *n. f.* obstacle.

cortaplumas /korta'plumas/ *n. m.* penknife.

cortar /kor'tar/ *v.* cut, cut off, cut out.

corte /'korte/ *n. f.* court, cut.

cortedad /korte'ðað/ *n. f.* smallness; shyness.

cortejar /korte'har/ *v.* pay court to, woo.

cortejo /kor'teho/ *n. m.* court; courtship; sweetheart.

cortés /kor'tes/ *a.* civil, courteous, polite.

cortesana /korte'sana/ *n. f.* courtesan.

cortesano. 1. /korte'sano/ *a.* **1.** courtly, courteous. —*n.* **2.** *m.* courtier.

cortesía /korte'sia/ *n. f.* courtesy.

corteza /kor'teθa; kor'tesa/ *n. f.* bark; rind; crust.

cortijo /kor'tiho/ *n. m.* farmhouse.

cortina /kor'tina/ *n. f.* curtain.

corto /'korto/ *a.* short.

corva /'korβa/ *n. f.* back of the knee.

cosa /'kosa/ *n. f.* thing. **c. de,** a matter of, roughly.

cosecha /ko'setʃa/ *n. f.* crop, harvest. —**cosechar,** *v.*

coser /ko'ser/ *v.* sew, stitch.

cosmético /kos'metiko/ *a. & m.* cosmetic.

cósmico /'kosmiko/ *a.* cosmic.

cosmonauta /kosmo'nauta/ *n. m. & f.* cosmonaut.

cosmopolita /kosmopo'lita/ *a. & n.* cosmopolitan.

cosmos /'kosmos/ *n. m.* cosmos.

coso /'koso/ *n. m.* arena for bull fights.

cosquilla /kos'kiʎa; kos'kiya/ *n. f.* tickle. —**cosquillar,** *v.*

cosquilloso /koski'ʎoso; koski'yoso/ *a.* ticklish.

costa /'kosta/ *n. f.* coast; cost, expense.

costado /kos'taðo/ *n. m.* side.

costal /kos'tal/ *n. m.* sack, bag.

costanero /kosta'nero/ *a.* coastal.

costar /kos'tar/ *v.* cost.

costarricense /kostarri'θense; kostarri'sense/ *a. & n.* Costa Rican.

coste /'koste/ *n. m.* cost, price.

costear /koste'ar/ *v.* defray, sponsor; sail along the coast of.

costilla /kos'tiʎa; kos'tiya/ *n. f.* rib; chop.

costo /'kosto/ *n. m.* cost, price.

costoso /kos'toso/ *a.* costly.

costra /'kostra/ *n. f.* crust.

costumbre /kos'tumbre/ *n. f.* custom, practice, habit.

costura /kos'tura/ *n. f.* sewing; seam.

costurera /kostu'rera/ *n. f.* seamstress, dressmaker.

costurero /kostu'rero/ *n. m.* sewing basket.

cota de malla /'kota de 'maʎa; 'kota de 'maya/ coat of mail.

cotejar /kote'har/ *v.* compare.

cotidiano /koti'ðiano/ *a.* daily; every-day.

cotillón /koti'ʎon; koti'yon/ *n. m.* cotillion.

cotización /kotiθa'θion; kotisa'sion/ *n. f.* quotation.

cotizar /koti'θar; koti'sar/ *v.* quote (a price).

coto /'koto/ *n. m.* enclosure; boundary.

cotón /ko'ton/ *n. m.* printed cotton cloth.

cotufa /ko'tufa/ *n. f.* Jerusalem artichoke.

coturno /ko'turno/ *n. m.* buskin.

covacha /ko'βatʃa/ *n. f.* small cave.

coxal /kok'sal/ *a.* of the hip.

coy /koi/ *n. m.* hammock.

coyote /ko'yote/ *n. m.* coyote.

coyuntura /koyun'tura/ *n. f.* joint; juncture.

coz /koθ; kos/ *n. f.* kick.

crac /krak/ *n. m.* failure.

cráneo /'kraneo/ *n. m.* skull.

craniano /kra'niano/ *a.* cranial.

crapuloso /krapu'loso/ *a.* drunken.

crasiento /kra'siento/ *a.* greasy, oily.

craso /'kraso/ *a.* fat; gross.

cráter /'krater/ *n. m.* crater.

craza /'kraθa; 'krasa/ *n. f.* crucible.

creación /krea'θion; krea'sion/ *n. f.* creation.

creador /krea'ðor/ **-ra** *a. & n.* creative; creator.

crear /kre'ar/ *v.* create.

creativo /krea'tiβo/ *a.* creative.

crébol /'kreβol/ *n. m.* holly tree.

crecer /kre'θer; kre'ser/ *v.* grow, grow up; increase.

creces /'kreθes; 'kreses/ *n. f.pl.* increase, addition.

crecidamente /kreθiða'mente; kresiða'mente/ *adv.* abundantly.

crecido /kre'θiðo; kre'siðo/ *a.* increased, enlarged; swollen.

creciente /kre'θiente; kre'siente/ *a.* **1.** growing. —*n.* **2.** *m.* crescent.

crecimiento /kreθi'miento; kresi'miento/ *n. m.* growth.

credenciales /kreðen'θiales; kreðen'siales/ *f.pl.* credentials.

credibilidad /kreðiβili'ðað/ *n. f.* credibility.

crédito /'kreðito/ *n. m.* credit.

credo /'kreðo/ *n. m.* creed, belief.

crédulamente /kreðula'mente/ *adv.* credulously, gullibly.

credulidad /kreðuli'ðað/ *n. f.* credulity.

crédulo /'kreðulo/ *a.* credulous.

creedero /kree'ðero/ *a.* credible.

creedor /kree'ðor/ *a.* credulous, believing.

creencia /kre'enθia; kre'ensia/ *n. f.* belief.

creer /kre'er/ *v.* believe; think.

creíble /kre'iβle/ *a.* credible, believable.

crema /'krema/ *n. f.* cream.

cremación /krema'θion; krema'sion/ *n. f.* cremation.

crema dentífrica /'krema den'tifrika/ toothpaste.

cremallera /krema'ʎera; krema'yera/ *n. f.* zipper.

crémor tártaro /'kremor 'tartaro/ *n. m.* cream of tartar.

cremoso /kre'moso/ *a.* creamy.

creosota /kreo'sota/ *n. f.* creosote.

crepitar /krepi'tar/ *v.* crackle.

crepuscular /krepusku'lar/ *a.* of or like the dawn or dusk; crepuscular.

crepúsculo /kre'puskulo/ *n. m.* dusk, twilight.

crescendo /kres'θendo; kres'sendo/ *n. m.* crescendo.

crespo /'krespo/ *a.* curly.

crespón /kres'pon/ *n. m.* crepe.

cresta /'kresta/ *n. f.* crest; heraldic crest.

crestado /kres'taðo/ *a.* crested.

creta /'kreta/ *n. f.* chalk.

cretáceo /kre'taθeo; kre'taseo/ *a.* chalky.

cretinismo /kreti'nismo/ *n. m.* cretinism.

cretino /kre'tino/ **-na** *n. & a.* cretin.

cretona /kre'tona/ *n. f.* cretonne.

creyente /kre'yente/ *a.* **1.** believing. —*n.* **2.** believer.

creyón /kre'yon/ *n. m.* crayon.

cría /'kria/ *n. f.* (stock) breeding; young (of an animal), litter.

criada /kri'aða/ *n. f.* maid.

criadero /kria'ðero/ *n. m. Agr.* nursery.

criado /kri'aðo/ **-da** *n.* servant.

criador /kria'ðor/ *a.* fruitful, prolific.

crianza /kri'anθa; kri'ansa/ *n. f.* breeding; upbringing.

criar /kri'ar/ *v.* raise, rear; breed.

criatura /kria'tura/ *n. f.* creature; infant.

criba /'kriβa/ *n. f.* sieve.

cribado /kri'βaðo/ *a.* sifted.

cribar /kri'βar/ *v.* sift.

crimen /'krimen/ *n. m.* crime.

criminal /krimi'nal/ *a. & n.* criminal.

criminalidad /kriminali'ðað/ *n. f.* criminality.

criminalmente /kriminal'mente/ *adv.* criminally.

criminología /kriminolo'hia/ *n. f.* criminology.

criminoso /krimi'noso/ *a.* criminal.

crines /'krines/ *n. f.pl.* mane of a horse.

crinolina /krino'lina/ *n. f.* crinoline.

criocirugía /krioθiru'hia; kriosiru'hia/ *n. f.* cryosurgery.

criollo /'krioʎo; 'krioyo/ **-lla** *a. & n.* native; Creole.

cripta /'kripta/ *n. f.* crypt.

criptografía /kriptogra'fia/ *n. f.* cryptography.

crisantemo /krisan'temo/ *n. m.* chrysanthemum.

crisis /'krisis/ *n. f.* crisis.

crisis nerviosa /'krisis ner'βiosa/ nervous breakdown.

crisma /'krisma/ *n. m.* chrism.

crisol /kri'sol/ *n. m.* crucible.

crispamiento /krispa'miento/ *n. m.* twitch, contraction.

crispar /kris'par/ *v.* contract (the muscles); twitch.

cristal /kris'tal/ *n. m.* glass; crystal; lens.

cristalería /kristale'ria/ *n. f.* glassware.

cristalino /krista'lino/ *a.* crystalline.

cristalización /kristaliθa'θion; kristalisa'sion/ *n. f.* crystallization.

cristalizar /kristali'θar; kristali'sar/ *v.* crystallize.

cristianar /kristia'nar/ *v.* baptize.

cristiandad /kristian'dað/ *n. f.* Christendom.

cristianismo /kristia'nismo/ *n. m.* Christianity.

cristiano /kris'tiano/ **-na** *a. & n.* Christian.

Cristo /'kristo/ *n. m.* Christ.

criterio /kri'terio/ *n. m.* criterion; judgment.

crítica /'kritika/ *n. f.* criticism; critique.

criticable /kriti'kaβle/ *a.* blameworthy.

criticador /kritika'ðor/ *a.* critical.

criticar /kriti'kar/ *v.* criticize.

crítico /'kritiko/ **-ca** *a. & n.* critical; critic.

croar /kro'ar/ *v.* croak.

crocante /kro'kante/ *n. m.* almond brittle.

crocitar /kroθi'tar; krosi'tar/ *v.* crow.

cromático /kro'matiko/ *a.* chromatic.

cromo /'kromo/ *n. m.* chromium.

cromosoma /kromo'soma/ *n. m.* chromosome.

cromotipia /kromo'tipia/ *n. f.* color printing.

crónica /'kronika/ *n. f.* chronicle.

crónico /'kroniko/ *a.* chronic.

cronicón /kroni'kon/ *n. m.* concise chronicle.

cronista /kro'nista/ *n. m. & f.* chronicler.

cronología /kronolo'hia/ *n. f.* chronology.

cronológicamente /kronolohika'mente/ *adv.* chronologically.

cronológico /krono'lohiko/ *a.* chronologic.

cronometrar /kronome'trar/ *v.* time.

cronómetro /kro'nometro/ *n. m.* stopwatch; chronometer.

croqueta /kro'keta/ *n. f.* croquette.

croquis /'krokis/ *n. m.* sketch; rough outline.

crótalo /'krotalo/ *n. m.* rattlesnake; castanet.

cruce /'kruθe; 'kruse/ *n. m.* crossing, crossroads, junction.

crucero /kru'θero; kru'sero/ *n. m.* cruiser.

crucífero /kru'θifero; kru'sifero/ *a.* cross-shaped.

crucificado /kruθifi'kaðo; krusifi'kaðo/ *a.* crucified.

crucificar /kruθifi'kar; krusifi'kar/ *v.* crucify.

crucifijo /kruθi'fiho; krusi'fiho/ *n. m.* crucifix.

crucifixión /kruθifik'sion; krusifik'sion/ *n. f.* crucifixion.

crucigrama /kruθi'grama; krusi'grama/ *n. m.* crossword puzzle.

crudamente /kruða'mente/ *adv.* crudely.

crudeza /kru'ðeθa; kru'ðesa/ *n. f.* crudeness.

crudo /'kruðo/ *a.* crude, raw.

cruel /kruel/ *a.* cruel.

crueldad /kruel'dað/ *n. f.* cruelty.

cruelmente /kruel'mente/ *adv.* cruelly.

cruentamente /kruenta'mente/ *adv.* bloodily.

cruento /'kruento/ *a.* bloody.

crujía /kru'hia/ *n. f.* corridor.

crujido /kru'hiðo/ *n. m.* creak.

crujir /kru'hir/ *v.* crackle; creak; rustle.

cruórico /'kruoriko/ *a.* bloody.

crup /krup/ *n. m.* croup.

crupié /kru'pie/ *n. m. & f.* croupier.

crustáceo /krus'taθeo; krus'taseo/ *n. & a.* crustacean.

cruz /kruθ; krus/ *n. f.* cross.

cruzada /kru'θaða; kru'saða/ *n. f.* crusade.

cruzado /kru'θaðo; kru'saðo/ **-da** *n.* crusader.

cruzamiento /kruθa'miento; krusa'miento/ *n. m.* crossing.

cruzar /kru'θar; kru'sar/ *v.* cross.

cruzarse con /kru'θarse kon; kru'sarse kon/ *v.* to (meet and) pass.

cuaderno /kua'ðerno/ *n. m.* notebook.

cuadra /'kuaðra/ *n. f.* block; (hospital) ward.

cuadradamente /kuaðraða'mente/ *adv.* exactly, precisely; completely, in full.

cuadradillo /kuaðra'ðiʎo; kuaðra'ðiyo/ *n. m.* lump of sugar.

cuadrado /kua'ðraðo/ **-da** *a. & n.* square.

cuadrafónico /kuaðra'foniko/ *a.* quadraphonic.

Cuadragésima /kuaðra'hesima/ *n. f.* Lent.

cuadragesimal /kuaðrahesi'mal/ *a.* Lenten.

cuadrángulo /kua'ðraŋgulo/ *n. m.* quadrangle.

cuadrante /kua'ðrante/ *n. m.* quadrant; dial.

cuadrar /kua'ðrar/ *v.* square; suit.

cuadricular /kuaðriku'lar/ *a.* in squares.

cuadrilátero /kuaðri'latero/ *a.* quadrilateral.

cuadrilla /kua'ðriʎa; kua'ðriya/ *n. f.* band, troop, gang.

cuadro /'kuaðro/ *n. m.* picture; painting; frame. **a cuadros,** checked, plaid.

cuadro de servicio /'kuaðro de ser'βiðio; 'kuaðro de ser'βisio/ timetable.

cuadrupedal /kuaðrupe'ðal/ *a.* quadruped.

cuádruplo /'kuaðruplo/ *a.* fourfold.

cuajada /kua'haða/ *n. f.* curd.

cuajamiento /kuaha'miento/ *n. m.* coagulation.

cuajar /kua'har/ *v.* coagulate; overdecorate.

cuajo /'kuaho/ *n. m.* rennet; coagulation.

cual /kual/ *rel. pron.* which.

cuál *a. & pron.* what, which.

cualidad /kuali'ðað/ *n. f.* quality.

cualitativo /kualita'tiβo/ *a.* qualitative.

cualquiera /kual'kiera/ *a. & pron.* whatever, any; anyone.

cuando /'kuando/ *conj.* when.

cuando *adv.* when. **de cuando en cuando,** from time to time.

cuantía /kuan'tia/ *n. f.* quantity; amount.

cuantiar /kuan'tiar/ *v.* estimate.

cuantiosamente /kuantiosa'mente/ *adv.* abundantly.

cuantioso /kuan'tioso/ *a.* abundant.

cuantitativo /kuantita'tiβo/ *a.* quantitative.

cuanto /'kuanto/ *a., adv. & pron.* as much as, as many as; all that which. **en c.,** as soon as. **en c. a,** as for. **c. antes,** as soon as possible. **c. más... tanto más,** the more... the more. **unos cuantos,** a few.

cuánto *a. & adv.* how much, how many.

cuaquerismo /kuake'rismo/ *n. m.* Quakerism.

cuáquero /'kuakero/ **-ra** *n. & a.* Quaker.

cuarenta /kua'renta/ *a. & pron.* forty.

cuarentena /kuaren'tena/ *n. f.* quarantine.

cuaresma /kua'resma/ *n. f.* Lent.

cuaresmal /kuares'mal/ *a.* Lenten.

cuarta /'kuarta/ *n. f.* quarter; quadrant; quart.

cuartear /kuarte'ar/ *v.* divide into quarters.

cuartel /kuar'tel/ *n. m. Mil.* quarters; barracks; *Naut.* hatch. **c. general,** headquarters. **sin c.,** giving no quarter.

cuartelada /kuarte'laða/ *n. f.* military uprising.

cuarterón /kuarte'ron/ *n. & a.* quadroon.

cuarteto /kuar'teto/ *n. m.* quartet.

cuartillo /kuar'tiʎo; kuar'tiyo/ *n. m.* pint.

cuarto /'kuarto/ *a.* **1.** fourth. —*n.* **2.** *m.* quarter; room.

cuarto de baño /'kuarto de 'baɲo/ bathroom.

cuarto de dormir /'kuarto de dor'mir/ bedroom.

cuarto para invitados /'kuarto para imbi'taðos/ guest room.

cuarzo /'kuarθo; 'kuarso/ *n. m.* quartz.

cuasi /'kuasi/ *adv.* almost, nearly.

cuate /'kuate/ *a. & n.* twin.

cuatrero /kua'trero/ *n. m.* cattle rustler.

cuatrillón /kuatri'ʎon; kuatri'yon/ *n. m.* quadrillion.

cuatro /'kuatro/ *a. & pron.* four.

cuatrocientos /kuatro'θientos; kuatro'sientos/ *a. & pron.* four hundred.

cuba /'kuβa/ *n. f.* cask, tub, vat.

cubano /ku'βano/ **-na** *a. & n.* Cuban.

cubero /ku'βero/ *n. m.* cooper.

cubeta /ku'βeta/ *n. f.* small barrel, keg.

cúbico /'kuβiko/ *a.* cubic.

cubículo /ku'βikulo/ *n. m.* cubicle.

cubierta /ku'βierta/ *n. f.* cover; envelope; wrapping; tread (of a tire); deck.

cubiertamente /kuβierta'mente/ *adv.* secretly, stealthily.

cubierto /ku'βierto/ *n. m.* place (at table).

cubil /ku'βil/ *n. m.* lair.

cubismo /ku'βismo/ *n. m.* cubism.

cubito de hielo /ku'βito de 'ielo/ *n. m.* ice cube.

cubo /'kuβo/ *n. m.* cube; bucket.

cubo de la basura /'kuβo de la ba'sura/ trash can.

cubrecama /kuβre'kama/ *n. f.* bedspread.

cubrir /ku'βrir/ *v.* cover.

cubrirse /ku'βrirse/ *v.* put on one's hat.

cucaracha /kuka'ratʃa/ *n. f.* cockroach.

cuchara /ku'tʃara/ *n. f.* spoon, tablespoon.

cucharada /kutʃa'raða/ *n. f.* spoonful.

cucharita /kutʃa'rita/ **cucharilla** *n. f.* teaspoon.

cucharón /kutʃa'ron/ *n. m.* dipper, ladle.

cuchicheo /kutʃi'tʃeo/ *n. m.* whisper. —**cuchichear**, *v.*

cuchilla /ku'tʃiʎa; ku'tʃiya/ *n. f.* cleaver.

cuchillada /kutʃi'ʎaða; kutʃi'yaða/ *n. f.* slash.

cuchillería /kutʃiʎe'ria; kutʃiye'ria/ *n. f.* cutlery.

cuchillo /ku'tʃiʎo; ku'tʃiyo/ *n. m.* knife.

cucho /'kutʃo/ *n. m.* fertilizer.

cuchufleta /kutʃu'fleta/ *n. f.* jest.

cuclillo /ku'kliʎo; ku'kliyo/ *n. m.* cuckoo.

cuco /'kuko/ *a.* sly.

cuculla /ku'kuʎa; ku'kuya/ *n. f.* hood, cowl.

cuelga /'kuelga/ *n. f.* cluster, bunch.

cuelgacapas /kuelga'kapas/ *n. m.* coat rack.

cuello /'kueʎo; 'kueyo/ *n. m.* neck; collar.

cuenca /'kuenka/ *n. f.* socket; (river) basin; wooden bowl.

cuenco /'kuenko/ *n. m.* earthen bowl.

cuenta /'kuenta/ *n. f.* account; bill. **darse c.,** to realize. **tener en c.,** to keep in mind.

cuenta bancaria /'kuenta ban'karia/ bank account.

cuenta de ahorros /'kuenta de a'orros/ savings account.

cuentagotas /kuenta'gotas/ *n. m.* dropper (for medicine).

cuentista /kuen'tista/ *n. m. & f.* storyteller; informer.

cuento /'kuento/ *n. m.* story, tale.

cuerda /'kuerða/ *n. f.* cord; chord; rope; string; spring (of clock). **dar c. a,** to wind (clock).

cuerdamente /kuerða'mente/ *adv.* sanely; prudently.

cuerdo /'kuerðo/ *a.* sane; prudent.

cuerno /'kuerno/ *n. m.* horn.

cuero /'kuero/ *n. m.* leather; hide.

cuerpo /'kuerpo/ *n. m.* body; corps.

cuervo /'kuerβo/ *n. m.* crow, raven.

cuesco /'kuesko/ *n. m.* pit, stone (of fruit).

cuesta /'kuesta/ *n. f.* hill, slope. **llevar a cuestas,** to carry on one's back.

cuestación /kuesta'θion; kuesta'sion/ *n. f.* solicitation for charity.

cuestión /kues'tion/ *n. f.* question; affair; argument.

cuestionable /kuestio'naβle/ *a.* questionable.

cuestionar /kuestio'nar/ *v.* question; discuss; argue.

cuestionario /kuestio'nario/ *n. m.* questionnaire.

cuete /'kuete/ *n. m.* firecracker.

[cue]va /'kueβa/ *n. f.* cave; cellar.

[cu]guar /'guar/ *n. m.* cougar.

[c]gu'haða/ *n. f.* lark.

---

cuidado /kui'ðaðo/ *n. m.* care, caution, worry. **tener c.,** to be careful.

cuidadosamente /kuiðaðosa'mente/ *adv.* carefully.

cuidadoso /kuiða'ðoso/ *a.* careful, painstaking.

cuidante /kui'ðante/ *n.* caretaker, custodian.

cuidar /kui'ðar/ *v.* take care of.

cuita /'kuita/ *n. f.* trouble, care; grief.

cuitado /kui'taðo/ *a.* unfortunate; shy, timid.

cuitamiento /kuita'miento/ *n. m.* timidity.

culata /ku'lata/ *n. f.* haunch, buttock; butt of a gun.

culatada /kula'taða/ *n. f.* recoil.

culatazo /kula'taðo; kula'taso/ *n. m.* blow with the butt of a gun; recoil.

culebra /ku'leβra/ *n. f.* snake.

culero /ku'lero/ *a.* lazy, indolent.

culinario /kuli'nario/ *a.* culinary.

culminación /kulmina'θion; kulmina'sion/ *n. f.* culmination.

culminar /kulmi'nar/ *v.* culminate.

culpa /'kulpa/ *n. f.* fault, guilt, blame. **tener la c.,** to be at fault. **echar la culpa a,** to blame.

culpabilidad /kulpaβili'ðað/ *n. f.* guilt, fault, blame.

culpable /kul'paβle/ *a.* at fault, guilty, to blame, culpable.

culpar /kul'par/ *v.* blame, accuse.

cultamente /kulta'mente/ *adv.* politely, elegantly.

cultivable /kulti'βaβle/ *a.* arable.

cultivación /kultiβa'θion; kultiβa'sion/ *n. f.* cultivation.

cultivador /kultiβa'ðor/ **-ra** *n.* cultivator.

cultivar /kulti'βar/ *v.* cultivate.

cultivo /kul'tiβo/ *n. m.* cultivation; (growing) crop.

culto /'kulto/ *a.* **1.** cultured, cultivated. —*n.* **2.** *m.* cult; worship.

cultura /kul'tura/ *n. f.* culture; refinement.

cultural /kultu'ral/ *a.* cultural.

culturar /kultu'rar/ *v.* cultivate.

culturismo /kultu'rismo/ *n. m.* body building.

culturista /kultu'rista/ *n. m. & f.* body builder.

cumbre /'kumbre/ *n. m.* summit, peak.

cumpleaños /kumple'aɲos/ *n. m.pl.* birthday.

cumplidamente /kumpliða'mente/ *adv.* courteously, correctly.

cumplido /kum'pliðo/ *a.* polite, polished.

cumplimentar /kumplimen'tar/ *v.* compliment.

cumplimiento /kumpli'miento/ *n. m.* fulfillment; compliment.

cumplir /kum'plir/ *v.* comply; carry out, fulfill; reach (years of age).

cumulativo /kumula'tiβo/ *a.* cumulative.

cúmulo /'kumulo/ *n. m.* heap, pile.

cuna /'kuna/ *n. f.* cradle.

cundir /kun'dir/ *v.* spread; expand; propagate.

cuneiforme /kunei'forme/ *a.* cuneiform, wedge-shaped.

cuneo /ku'neo/ *n. m.* rocking.

cuña /'kuɲa/ *n. f.* wedge.

cuñada /ku'ɲaða/ *n. f.* sister-in-law.

cuñado /ku'ɲaðo/ *n. m.* brother-in-law.

cuñete /ku'ɲete/ *n. m.* keg.

cuota /'kuota/ *n. f.* quota; dues.

cuotidiano /kuoti'ðiano/ *a.* daily.

cupé /ku'pe/ *n. m.* coupé.

Cupido /ku'piðo/ *n. m.* Cupid.

cupo /'kupo/ *n. m.* share; assigned quota.

cupón /ku'pon/ *n. m.* coupon.

cúpula /'kupula/ *n. f.* dome.

cura /'kura/ *n. m.* priest; *f.* treatment, (medical) care. **c. de urgencia,** first aid.

curable /ku'raβle/ *a.* curable.

---

curación /kura'θion; kura'sion/ *n. f.* healing; cure; (surgical) dressing.

curado /ku'raðo/ *a.* cured, healed.

curador /kura'ðor/ **-ra** *n.* healer.

curandero /kuran'dero/ **-ra** *n.* healer, medicine man.

curar /ku'rar/ *v.* cure, heal, treat.

curativo /kura'tiβo/ *a.* curative, healing.

curia /'kuria/ *n. f.* ecclesiastical court.

curiosear /kuriose'ar/ *v.* snoop, pry, meddle.

curiosidad /kuriosi'ðað/ *n. f.* curiosity.

curioso /ku'rioso/ *a.* curious.

curro /'kurro/ *a.* showy, loud, flashy.

cursante /kur'sante/ *n.* student.

cursar /kur'sar/ *v.* frequent; attend.

cursi /'kursi/ *a.* vulgar, shoddy, in bad taste.

curso /'kurso/ *n. m.* course.

curso por correspondencia /'kurso por korrespon'denθia; 'kurso por korrespon'densia/ *n. m.* correspondence course.

cursor /kur'sor/ *n. m.* cursor.

curtidor /kurti'ðor/ *n. m.* tanner.

curtir /kur'tir/ *v.* tan.

curva /'kurβa/ *n. f.* curve; bend.

curvatura /kurβa'tura, kurβi'ðað/ *n. f.* curvature.

cúspide /'kuspiðe/ *n. f.* top, peak.

custodia /kus'toðia/ *n. f.* custody.

custodiar /kusto'ðiar/ *v.* guard, watch.

custodio /kus'toðio/ *n. m.* custodian.

cutáneo /ku'taneo/ *a.* cutaneous.

cutícula /ku'tikula/ *n. f.* cuticle.

cutis /'kutis/ *n. m.* or *f.* skin, complexion.

cutre /'kutre/ *a.* shoddy.

cuyo /'kuyo/ *a.* whose.

D

dable /'daβle/ *a.* possible.

dactilógrafo /dakti'lografo/ **-fa** *n.* typist.

dádiva /'daðiβa/ *n. f.* gift.

dadivosamente /daðiβosa'mente/ *adv.* generously.

dadivoso /daði'βoso/ *a.* generous, bountiful.

dado /'daðo/ *n. m.* die.

dador /da'ðor/ **-ra** *n.* giver.

dados /'daðos/ *n. m.pl.* dice.

daga /'daga/ *n. f.* dagger.

dalia /'dalia/ *n. f.* dahlia.

dallador /da'ʎaðor; daya'ðor/ *n. m.* lawn mower.

dallar /da'ʎar; da'yar/ *v.* mow.

daltonismo /dalto'nismo/ *n. m.* color blindness.

dama /'dama/ *n. f.* lady.

damasco /da'masko/ *n. m.* apricot; damask.

damisela /dami'sela/ *n. f.* young lady, girl.

danés /da'nes/ **-esa** *a. & n.* Danish, Dane.

danza /'danθa; 'dansa/ *n. f.* (the) dance. —**danzar**, *v.*

danzante /dan'θante; dan'sante/ **-ta** *n.* dancer.

dañable /da'ɲaβle/ *a.* condemnable.

dañar /da'ɲar/ *v.* hurt, harm; damage.

dañino /da'ɲino/ *a.* harmful.

daño /'daɲo/ *n. m.* damage; harm.

dañoso /da'ɲoso/ *a.* harmful.

dar /dar/ *v.* give; strike (clock). **d. a,** face, open on. **d. con,** find, locate. **¡Dalo por hecho!** Consider it done!

dardo /'darðo/ *n. m.* dart.

dársena /'darsena/ *n. f.* dock.

datar /da'tar/ *v.* date.

dátil /'datil/ *n. m.* date (fruit).

dativo /da'tiβo/ *n. m. & a.* dative.

datos /'datos/ *n. m.pl.* data.

de /de/ *prep.* of; from; than.

debajo /de'βaho/ *adv.* underneath. **d. de,** under.

---

debate /de'βate/ *n. m.* debate.

debatir /de'βatir/ *v.* debate, argue.

debe /'deβe/ *n. m.* debit.

debelación /deβela'θion; deβela'sion/ *n. f.* conquest.

debelar /deβe'lar/ *v.* conquer.

deber /de'βer/ *v.* **1.** owe; must; be to, be supposed to. —*n.* **2.** *m.* obligation.

deberes /de'βeres/ *n. m.pl.* homework.

debido /de'βiðo/ *a.* due.

débil /'deβil/ *a.* weak, faint.

debilidad /deβili'ðað/ *n. f.* weakness.

debilitación /deβilita'θion; deβilita'sion/ *n. f.* weakness.

debilitar /deβili'tar/ *v.* weaken.

débito /'deβito/ *n. m.* debit.

debutar /deβu'tar/ *v.* make a debut.

década /'dekaða/ *n. f.* decade.

decadencia /deka'ðenθia; dekaðensia/ *n. f.* decadence, decline, decay.

decadente /deka'ðente/ *a.* decadent, declining, decaying.

decaer /deka'er/ *v.* decay, decline.

decalitro /deka'litro/ *n. m.* decaliter.

decálogo /de'kalogo/ *n. m.* decalogue.

decámetro /de'kametro/ *n. m.* decameter.

decano /de'kano/ *n. m.* dean.

decantado /dekan'taðo/ *a.* much discussed; overexalted.

decapitación /dekapita'θion; dekapitasion/ *n. f.* beheading.

decapitar /dekapi'tar/ *v.* behead.

decencia /de'θenθia; de'sensia/ *n. f.* decency.

decenio /de'θenio; de'senio/ *n. m.* decade.

decente /de'θente; de'sente/ *a.* decent.

decentemente /deθente'mente; desente'mente/ *adv.* decently.

decepción /deθep'θion; desep'sion/ *n. f.* disappointment, letdown; delusion.

decepcionar /deθepθio'nar; desepsio'nar/ *v.* disappoint, disillusion.

dechado /de'tʃaðo/ *n. m.* model; sample; pattern; example.

decibelio /deθi'βelio; desi'βelio/ *n. m.* decibel.

decididamente /deθiðiða'mente; desiðiða'mente/ *adv.* decidedly.

decidir /deθi'ðir; desi'ðir/ *v.* decide.

decigramo /deθi'gramo; desi'gramo/ *n. m.* decigram.

decilitro /deθi'litro; desi'litro/ *n. m.* deciliter.

décima /'deθima; 'desima/ *n. f.* tenline stanza.

decimal /deθi'mal; desi'mal/ *a.* decimal.

décimo /'deθimo; 'desimo/ *a.* tenth.

decir /de'θir; de'sir/ *v.* tell, say. **es d.,** that is (to say).

decisión /deθi'sion; desi'sion/ *n. f.* decision.

decisivamente /deθisiβa'mente; desisiβa'mente/ *adv.* decisively.

decisivo /deθi'siβo; desi'siβo/ *a.* decisive.

declamación /deklama'θion; deklama'sion/ *n. f.* declamation, speech.

declamar /dekla'mar/ *v.* declaim.

declaración /deklara'θion; deklara'sion/ *n. f.* declaration; statement; plea.

declaración de la renta /deklara'θion de la 'rrenta; deklara'sion de la 'rrenta/ tax return.

declarar /dekla'rar/ *v.* declare, state.

declarativo /deklara'tiβo, dekla'torio/ *a.* declarative.

declinación /deklina'θion; deklina'sion/ *n. f.* descent; decay; decline; declension.

declinar /dekli'nar/ *v.* decline.

declive /de'kliβe,/ *n. m.* declivity, slope.

decocción /dekok'θion; dekok'sion/ *n. f.* decoction.

decomiso /deko'miso/ *n. m.* seizure, confiscation.

decoración /dekora'θion; dekora'sion/ *n. f.* decoration, trimming.

decorado /deko'raðo/ *n. m. Theat.* scenery, set.

decorar /deko'rar/ *v.* decorate, trim.

decorativo /dekora'tiβo/ *a.* decorative, ornamental.

decoro /de'koro/ *n. m.* decorum; decency.

decoroso /deko'roso/ *a.* decorous.

decrecer /dekre'θer; dekre'ser/ *v.* decrease.

decrépito /de'krepito/ *a.* decrepit.

decreto /de'kreto/ *n. m.* decree. —**decretar,** *v.*

dedal /de'ðal/ *n. m.* thimble.

dédalo /'deðalo/ *n. m.* labyrinth.

dedicación /deðika'θion; deðika'sion/ *n. f.* dedication.

dedicar /deði'kar/ *v.* devote; dedicate.

dedicatoria /deðika'toria/ *n. f.* dedication, inscription.

dedo /'deðo/ *n. m.* finger, toe.

dedo anular /'deðo anu'lar/ ring finger.

dedo corazón /'deðo kora'θon; 'deðo kora'son/ middle finger.

dedo índice /'deðo 'indiθe; 'deðo 'indise/ index finger.

dedo meñique /'deðo me'ɲike/ little finger, pinky.

dedo pulgar /'deðo pul'gar/ thumb.

deducción /deðuk'θion; deðuk'sion/ *n. f.* deduction.

deducir /deðu'θir; deðu'sir/ *v.* deduce; subtract.

defectivo /defek'tiβo/ *a.* defective.

defecto /de'fekto/ *n. m.* defect, flaw.

defectuoso /defek'tuoso/ *a.* defective, faulty.

defender /defen'der/ *v.* defend.

defensa /de'fensa/ *n. f.* defense.

defensivo /defen'siβo/ *a.* defensive.

defensor /defen'sor/ **-ra** *n.* defender.

deferencia /defe'renθia; deferensia/ *n. f.* deference.

deferir /defe'rir/ *v.* defer.

deficiente /defi'θiente; defi'siente/ *a.* deficient.

déficit /'defiθit; 'defisit/ *n. m.* deficit.

definición /defini'θion; defini'sion/ *n. f.* definition.

definido /defi'niðo/ *a.* definite.

definir /defi'nir/ *v.* define; establish.

definitivamente /definitiβa'mente/ *adv.* definitely.

definitivo /defini'tiβo/ *a.* definitive.

deformación /deforma'θion; deforma'sion/ *n. f.* deformation.

deformar /defor'mar/ *v.* deform.

deforme /de'forme/ *a.* deformed; ugly.

deformidad /deformi'ðað/ *n. f.* deformity.

defraudar /defrau'ðar/ *v.* defraud.

defunción /defun'θion; defun'sion/ *n. f.* death.

degeneración /dehenera'θion; dehenera'sion/ *n. f.* degeneration.

degenerado /dehene'raðo/ *a.* degenerate. —**degenerar,** *v.*

deglutir /deglu'tir/ *v.* swallow.

degollar /dego'ʎar; dego'yar/ *v.* behead.

degradación /degraða'θion; degraða'sion/ *n. f.* degradation.

degradar /degra'ðar/ *v.* degrade, debase.

deidad /dei'ðað/ *n. f.* deity.

deificación /deifika'θion; deifika'sion/ *n. f.* deification.

deificar /deifi'kar/ *v.* deify.

deífico /de'ifiko/ *a.* divine, deific.

deísmo /de'ismo/ *n. m.* deism.

dejadez /deha'ðeθ; deha'ðes/ *n. f.* neglect, untidiness; laziness.

dejado /de'haðo/ *a.* untidy; lazy.

dejar /de'har/ *v.* let, allow; leave. **d. de,** stop, leave off. **no d. de,** not fail to.

dejo /'deho/ *n. m.* abandonment; negligence; aftertaste; accent.

del /del/ *contr. of* **de** + **el**.

delantal /delan'tal/ *n. m.* apron; pinafore. **delantal de niña,** pinafore.

delante /de'lante/ *adv.* ahead, forward; in front.

delantero /delan'tero/ *a.* forward, front, first.

delator /dela'tor/ *n. m.* informer; accuser.

delegación /delega'θion; delega'sion/ *n. f.* delegation.

delegado /dele'gaðo/ **-da** *n.* delegate. —**delegar,** *v.*

deleite /de'leite/ *n. m.* delight. —**deleitar,** *v.*

deleitoso /delei'toso/ *a.* delightful.

deletrear /deletre'ar/ *v.* spell; decipher.

delfín /del'fin/ *n. m.* dolphin; dauphin.

delgadez /delga'ðeθ; delgaðes/ *n. f.* thinness, slenderness.

delgado /del'gaðo/ *a.* thin, slender, slim, slight.

deliberación /deliβera'θion; deliβera'sion/ *n. f.* deliberation.

deliberadamente /deliβeraða'mente/ *adv.* deliberately.

deliberar /deliβe'rar/ *v.* deliberate.

deliberativo /deliβera'tiβo/ *a.* deliberative.

delicadamente /delikaða'mente/ *adv.* delicately.

delicadeza /delika'ðeθa; delika'ðesa/ *n. f.* delicacy.

delicado /deli'kaðo/ *a.* delicate, dainty.

delicia /deli'θia; deli'sia/ *n. f.* delight; deliciousness.

delicioso /deli'θioso; deli'sioso/ *a.* delicious.

delincuencia /delin'kuenθia; delin'kuensia/ *n. f.* delinquency.

delincuencia de menores /delin'kuenθia de me'nores; delin'kuensia de me'nores/ **delincuencia juvenil** juvenile delinquency.

delincuente /delin'kuente/ *a. & n.* delinquent; culprit, offender.

delineación /delinea'θion; delinea'sion/ *n. f.* delineation, sketch.

delinear /deline'ar/ *v.* delineate, sketch.

delirante /deli'rante/ *a.* delirious.

delirar /deli'rar/ *v.* rave, be delirious.

delirio /de'lirio/ *n. m.* delirium; rapture, bliss.

delito /de'lito/ *n. m.* crime, offense.

delta /'delta/ *n. m.* delta (of river); hang glider.

demacrado /dema'kraðo/ *a.* emaciated.

demagogia /dema'gohia/ *n. f.* demagogy.

demagogo /dema'gogo/ *n. m.* demagogue.

demanda /de'manda/ *n. f.* demand, claim.

demandador /demanda'ðor/ **-ra** *n.* plaintiff.

demandar /deman'dar/ *v.* sue; demand.

demarcación /demarka'θion; demarka'sion/ *n. f.* demarcation.

demarcar /demar'kar/ *v.* demarcate, limit.

demás /de'mas/ *a. & n.* other; (the) rest (of). **por d.,** too much.

demasía /dema'sia/ *n. f.* excess; audacity; iniquity.

demasiado /dema'siaðo/ *a. & adv.* too; too much; too many.

demencia /de'menθia; de'mensia/ *n. f.* dementia; insanity.

demente /de'mente/ *a.* demented.

democracia /demo'kraθia; demo'krasia/ *n. f.* democracy.

demócrata /de'mokrata/ *n. m. & f.* democrat.

democrático /demo'kratiko/ *a.* democratic.

demoler /demo'ler/ *v.* demolish, tear down.

demolición /demoli'θion; demoli'sion/ *n. f.* demolition.

demonio /de'monio/ *n. m.* demon, devil.

demontre /de'montre/ *n. m.* devil.

demora /de'mora/ *n. f.* delay, —**demorar,** *v.*

demostración /demostra'θion; demostra'sion/ *n. f.* demonstration.

demostrador /demostra'ðor/ **-ra** *n.* demonstrator.

demostrar /demos'trar/ *v.* demonstrate, show.

demostrativo /demostra'tiβo/ *a.* demonstrative.

demudar /demu'ðar/ *v.* change; disguise, conceal.

denegación /denega'θion; denega'sion/ *n. f.* denial; refusal.

denegar /dene'gar/ *v.* deny; refuse.

dengue /'dengue/ *n. m.* prudishness; dengue.

denigración /denigra'θion; denigra'sion/ *n. f.* defamation, disgrace.

denigrar /deni'grar/ *v.* defame, disgrace.

denodado /deno'ðaðo/ *a.* brave, dauntless.

denominación /denomina'θion; denomina'sion/ *n. f.* denomination.

denominar /denomi'nar/ *v.* name, call.

denotación /denota'θion; denota'sion/ *n. f.* denotation.

denotar /deno'tar/ *v.* denote, betoken, express.

densidad /densi'ðað/ *n. f.* density.

denso /'denso/ *a.* dense.

dentado /den'taðo/ *a.* toothed; serrated; cogged.

dentadura /denta'ðura/ *n. f.* set of teeth.

dentadura postiza /denta'ðura pos'tiθa; denta'ðura pos'tisa/ false teeth, dentures.

dental /den'tal/ *a.* dental.

dentífrico /den'tifriko/ *n. m.* dentifrice, toothpaste.

dentista /den'tista/ *n. m. & f.* dentist.

dentistería /dentiste'ria/ *n. f.* dentistry.

dentro /'dentro/ *adv.* within, inside. **d. de poco,** in a short while.

dentudo /den'tuðo/ *a.* toothy (person).

denuedo /de'nueðo/ *n. m.* bravery, courage.

denuesto /de'nuesto/ *n. m.* insult, offense.

denuncia /de'nunθia; de'nunsia/ *n. f.* denunciation; declaration; complaint.

denunciación /denunθia'θion; denunsia'sion/ *n. f.* denunciation.

denunciar /denun'θiar; denun'siar/ *v.* denounce.

deparar /depa'rar/ *v.* offer; grant.

departamento /departa'mento/ *n. m.* department, section.

departir /depar'tir/ *v.* talk, chat.

dependencia /depen'denθia; depen'densia/ *n. f.* dependence; branch office.

depender /depen'der/ *v.* depend.

dependiente /depen'diente/ *a. & m.* dependent; clerk.

depilar /depi'lar/ *v.* depilate, pluck.

depilatorio /depila'torio/ *a. & n.* depilatory.

depistar *v.* mislead, put off the track.

deplorable /deplo'raβle/ *a.* deplorable, wretched.

deplorablemente /deploraβle'mente/ *adv.* deplorably.

deplorar /deplo'rar/ *v.* deplore.

deponer /depo'ner/ *v.* depose.

deportación /deporta'θion; deporta'sion/ *n. f.* deportation; exile.

deportar /depor'tar/ *v.* deport.

deporte /de'porte/ *n. m.* sport. —**deportivo,** *a.*

deposición /deposi'θion; deposi'sion/ *n. f.* assertion, deposition; removal; movement.

depositante /deposi'tante/ *n. m. & f.* depositor.

depósito /de'posito/ *n. m.* deposit. —**depositar,** *v.*

depravación /depraβa'θion; depraβa'sion/ *n. f.* depravation; depravity.

depravado /depra'βaðo/ *a.* depraved, wicked.

depravar /depra'βar/ *v.* deprave, corrupt, pervert.

depreciación /depreθia'θion; depresia'sion/ *n. f.* depreciation.

depreciar /depre'θiar; depre'siar/ *v.* depreciate.

depredación /depreða'θion; depreða'sion/ *n. f.* depredation.

depredar /depre'ðar/ *v.* pillage, depredate.

depresión /depre'sion/ *n. f.* depression.

depresivo /depre'siβo/ *a.* depressive.

deprimir /depri'mir/ *v.* depress.

depurar /depu'rar/ *v.* purify.

derecha /de'retʃa/ *n. f.* right (hand, side).

derechera /dere'tʃera/ *n. f.* shortcut.

derecho /de'retʃo/ *a.* **1.** right; straight. —*n.* **2.** *m.* right; (the) law. **derechos,** *Com.* duty.

derechos civiles /de'retʃos θi'βiles; de'retʃos si'βiles/ *n. m.pl.* civil rights.

derechos de aduana /de'retʃos de a'ðuana/ *n. m.pl.* customs duty.

derechura /dere'tʃura/ *n. f.* straightness.

derelicto /dere'likto/ *a.* abandoned, derelict.

deriva /de'riβa/ *n. f. Naut.* drift.

derivación /deriβa'θion; deriβa'sion/ *n. f.* derivation.

derivar /deri'βar/ *v.* derive.

dermatólogo /derma'tologo/ **-a** *n.* dermatologist, skin doctor.

derogar /dero'gar/ *v.* derogate; repeal, abrogate.

derramamiento /derrama'miento/ *n. m.* overflow.

derramar /derra'mar/ *v.* spill, pour, scatter.

derrame /de'rrame/ *n. m.* overflow; discharge.

derretir /derre'tir/ *v.* melt, dissolve.

derribar /derri'βar/ *v.* demolish, knock down; bowl over, floor, fell.

derrocamiento /derroka'miento/ *n. m.* overthrow.

derrocar /derro'kar/ *v.* overthrow; oust; demolish.

derrochar /derro'tʃar/ *v.* waste.

derroche /de'rrotʃe/ *n. m.* waste.

derrota /de'rrota/ *n. f.* rout, defeat. —**derrotar,** *v.*

derrotismo /derro'tismo/ *n. m.* defeatism.

derrumbamiento /derrumba'miento/ **derrumbe** *m.* collapse; landslide.

derrumbarse /derrum'βarse/ *v.* collapse, tumble.

derviche /der'βitʃe/ *n. m.* dervish.

desabotonar /desaβoto'nar/ *v.* unbutton.

desabrido /desa'βriðo/ *a.* insipid, tasteless.

desabrigar /desaβri'gar/ *v.* uncover.

desabrochar /desaβro'tʃar/ *v.* unbutton, unclasp.

desacato /desa'kato/ *n. m.* disrespect, lack of respect.

desacierto /desa'θierto; desa'sierto/ *n. m.* error.

desacobardar /desakoβar'ðar/ *v.* remove fear; embolden.

desacomodadamente /desakomoðaða'mente/ *adv.* inconveniently.

desacomodado /desakomo'ðaðo/ *a.* unemployed.

desacomodar /desakomo'ðar/ *v.* molest; inconvenience; dismiss.

desacomodo /desako'moðo/ *n. m.* loss of employment.

desaconsejar /desakonse'har/ v. dissuade (someone); advise against (something).

desacordadamente /desakorða-ða'mente/ adv. unadvisedly.

desacordar /desakor'ðar/ v. differ, disagree; be forgetful.

desacorde /desa'korðe/ a. discordant.

desacostumbradamente /desakostumbraða'mente/ adv. unusually.

desacostumbrado /desakostum-'braðo/ a. unusual, unaccustomed.

desacostumbrar /desakostum'brar/ v. give up a habit or custom.

desacreditar /desakreði'tar/ v. discredit.

desacuerdo /desa'kuerðo/ n. m. disagreement.

desadeudar /desaðeu'ðar/ v. pay one's debts.

desadormecer /desaðorme'θer; desaðorme'ser/ v. waken, rouse.

desadornar /desaðor'nar/ v. divest of ornament.

desadvertidamente /desaðβertiða'mente/ adv. inadvertently.

desadvertido /desaðβer'tiðo/ a. imprudent.

desadvertimiento /desaðβerti-'miento/ n. m. imprudence, rashness.

desadvertir /desaðβer'tir/ v. act imprudently.

desafección /desafek'θion; desafek-'sion/ n. f. disaffection.

desafecto /desa'fekto/ a. disaffected.

desafiar /desa'fiar/ v. defy; challenge.

desafinar /desafi'nar/ v. be out of tune.

desafío /desa'fio/ n. m. defiance; challenge.

desaforar /desafo'rar/ v. infringe one's rights; be outrageous.

desafortunado /desafortu'naðo/ a. unfortunate.

desafuero /desa'fuero/ n. m. violation of the law; outrage.

desagraciado /desagra'θiaðo; desagra'siaðo/ a. graceless.

desagradable /desagra'ðaβle/ a. disagreeable, unpleasant.

desagradablemente /desagra-ðaβle'mente/ adv. disagreeably.

desagradecido /desagraðe'θiðo; desagraðe'siðo/ a. ungrateful.

desagradecimiento /desagraðe-θi'miento; desagraðesimiento/ n. m. ingratitude.

desagrado /desa'graðo/ n. m. displeasure.

desagraviar /desagra'βiar/ v. make amends.

desagregar /desagre'gar/ v. separate, disintegrate.

desagriar /desa'griar/ v. mollify, appease.

desaguadero /desagua'ðero/ n. m. drain, outlet; cesspool; sink.

desaguador /desagua'ðor/ n. m. water pipe.

desaguar /desa'guar/ v. drain.

desaguisado /desagi'saðo/ n. m. offense; injury.

desahogadamente /desaogaða-'mente/ adv. impudently; brazenly.

desahogado /desao'gaðo/ a. impudent, brazen; cheeky.

desahogar /desao'gar/ v. relieve.

desahogo /desa'ogo/ n. m. relief; nerve, cheek.

desahuciar /desau'θiar; desau'siar/ v. give up hope for; despair of.

desairado /desai'raðo/ a. graceless.

desaire /des'aire/ n. m. slight; scorn. —desairar, v.

desajustar /desahus'tar/ v. mismatch, misfit; make unfit.

desalar /desa'lar/ v. hurry, hasten.

desalentar /desalen'tar/ v. make out of breath; discourage.

desaliento /desa'liento/ n. m. dislment.

desalinar /desali'nar/ v. disarrange;

desaliño /desa'liɲo/ n. m. slovenliness, untidiness.

desalivar /desali'βar/ v. remove saliva from.

desalmadamente /desalmaða-'mente/ adv. mercilessly.

desalmado /desal'maðo/ a. merciless.

desalojamiento /desaloha'miento/ n. m. displacement; dislodging.

desalojar /desalo'har/ v. dislodge.

desalquilado /desalki'laðo/ a. vacant, unrented.

desamar /desa'mar/ v. cease loving.

desamasado /desama'saðo/ a. dissolved, disunited, undone.

desamistarse /desamis'tarse/ v. quarrel, disagree.

desamor /desa'mor/ n. m. disaffection, dislike; hatred.

desamorado /desamo'raðo/ a. cruel; harsh; rude.

desamparador /desampara'ðor/ n. m. deserter.

desamparar /desampa'rar/ v. desert, abandon.

desamparo /desam'paro/ n. m. desertion, abandonment.

desamueblado /desamue'βlaðo/ a. unfurnished.

desamueblar /desamue'βlar/ v. remove furniture from.

desandrajado /desandra'haðo/ a. shabby, ragged.

desanimadamente /desanimaða-'mente/ adv. in a discouraged manner; spiritlessly.

desanimar /desani'mar/ v. dishearten, discourage.

desánimo /des'animo/ n. m. discouragement.

desanudar /desanu'ðar/ v. untie; loosen; disentangle.

desapacible /desapa'θiβle; desapa'siβle/ a. rough, harsh; unpleasant.

desaparecer /desapare'θer; desapare'ser/ v. disappear.

desaparición /desapari'θion; desapari'sion/ n. f. disappearance.

desapasionadamente /desapa-sionaða'mente/ adv. dispassionately.

desapasionado /desapasio'naðo/ a. dispassionate.

desapego /desa'pego/ n. m. impartiality.

desapercibido /desaperθi'βiðo; desapersi'βiðo/ a. unnoticed; unprepared.

desapiadado /desapia'ðaðo/ a. merciless, cruel.

desaplicación /desaplika'θion; desaplika'sion/ n. f. indolence, laziness; negligence.

desaplicado /desapli'kaðo/ a. indolent, lazy; negligent.

desaposesionar /desaposesio'nar/ v. dispossess.

desapreciar /desapre'θiar; desapre'siar/ v. depreciate.

desapretador /desapreta'ðor/ n. m. screwdriver.

desapretar /desapre'tar/ v. loosen; relieve, ease.

desaprisionar /desaprisio'nar/ v. set free, release.

desaprobación /desaproβa'θion; desaproβa'sion/ n. f. disapproval.

desaprobar /desapro'βar/ v. disapprove.

desaprovechado /desaproβe't∫aðo/ a. useless, profitless; backward.

desaprovechar /desaproβe't∫ar/ v. waste; be backward.

desarbolar /desarβo'lar/ v. unmast.

desarmado /desar'maðo/ a. disarmed, defenseless.

desarmar /desar'mar/ v. disarm.

desarme /de'sarme/ n. m. disarmament.

desarraigado /desarrai'gaðo/ a. rootless.

desarraigar /desarrai'gar/ v. uproot; eradicate; expel.

desarreglar /desarre'glar/ v. disarrange, mess up.

desarrollar /desarro'ʎar; desarro'yar/ v. develop.

desarrollo /desa'rroʎo; des'arroyo/ n. m. development.

desarropar /desarro'par/ v. undress; uncover.

desarrugar /desarru'gar/ v. remove wrinkles from.

desaseado /desase'aðo/ a. dirty; disorderly.

desasear /desase'ar/ v. make dirty or disorderly.

desaseo /desa'seo/ n. m. dirtiness; disorder.

desasir /desa'sir/ v. loosen; disengage.

desasociable /desaso'θiaβle; desaso'siaβle/ a. unsociable.

desasosegar /desasose'gar/ v. disturb.

desasosiego /desaso'siego/ n. m. uneasiness.

desastrado /desas'traðo/ a. ragged, wretched.

desastre /de'sastre/ n. m. disaster.

desastroso /desas'troso/ a. disastrous.

desatar /desa'tar/ v. untie, undo.

desatención /desaten'θion; desaten'sion/ n. f. inattention; disrespect; rudeness.

desatender /desaten'der/ v. ignore; disregard.

desatentado /desaten'taðo/ a. inconsiderate; imprudent.

desatinado /desati'naðo/ a. foolish; insane, wild.

desatino /desa'tino/ n. m. blunder. —desatinar, v.

desatornillar /desatorni'ʎar; desatorni'yar/ v. unscrew.

desautorizado /desautori'θaðo; desautori'saðo/ a. unauthorized.

desautorizar /desautori'θar; desautori'sar/ v. deprive of authority.

desavenencia /desaβe'nenθia; desaβe'nensia/ n. f. disagreement, discord.

desaventajado /desaβenta'haðo/ a. disadvantageous.

desayuno /desa'yuno/ n. m. breakfast. —desayunar, v.

desazón /desa'θon; desa'son/ n. f. insipidity; uneasiness.

desazonado /desaθo'naðo; desaso'naðo/ a. insipid; uneasy.

desbandada /desβan'daða/ n. f. disbanding.

desbandarse /desβan'darse/ v. disband.

desbarajuste /desβara'huste/ n. m. disorder, confusion.

desbaratar /desβara'tar/ v. destroy.

desbastar /desβas'tar/ v. plane, smoothen.

desbocado /desβo'kaðo/ a. foulspoken, indecent.

desbocarse /desβo'karse/ v. use obscene language.

desbordamiento /desβorða'miento/ n. m. overflow; flood.

desbordar /desβor'ðar/ v. overflow.

desbrozar /desβro'θar; desβro'sar/ v. clear away rubbish.

descabal /deska'βal/ a. incomplete.

descabalar /deskaβa'lar/ v. render incomplete; impair.

descabellado /deskaβe'ʎaðo; deskaβe'yaðo/ a. absurd, preposterous.

descabezar /deskaβe'θar; deskaβe'sar/ v. behead.

descaecimiento /deskaeθi'miento; deskaesi'miento/ n. m. weakness; dejection.

descafeinado /deskafei'naðo/ a. decaffeinated.

descalabrar /deskala'βrar/ v. injure, wound (esp. the head).

descalabro /deska'laβro/ n. m. accident, misfortune.

descalzarse /deskal'θarse; deskal'sarse/ v. take off one's shoes.

descalzo /des'kalθo; des'kalso/ a. shoeless; barefoot.

descaminado /deskami'naðo/ a. wrong, misguided.

descaminar /deskami'nar/ v. mislead; lead into error.

descamisado /deskami'saðo/ a. shirtless; shabby.

descansillo /deskan'siʎo; deskan'siyo/ n. m. landing (of stairs).

descanso /des'kanso/ n. m. rest. —descansar, v.

descarado /deska'raðo/ a. saucy, fresh.

descarga /des'karga/ n. f. discharge.

descargar /deskar'gar/ v. discharge, unload, dump.

descargo /des'kargo/ n. m. unloading; acquittal.

descarnar /deskar'nar/ v. skin.

descaro /des'karo/ n. m. gall, effrontery.

descarriar /deska'rriar/ v. lead or go astray.

descarrilamiento /deskarrila-'miento/ n. m. derailment.

descarrilar /deskarri'lar/ v. derail.

descartar /deskar'tar/ v. discard.

descascarar /deskaska'rar/ v. peel; boast, brag.

descendencia /desθen'denθia; dessen'densia/ n. f. descent, origin; progeny.

descender /desθen'der; dessen'der/ v. descend.

descendiente /desθen'diente; dessen'diente/ n. m. & f. descendant.

descendimiento /desθendi'miento; dessendi'miento/ n. m. descent.

descenso /des'θenso; des'senso/ n. m. descent.

descentralización /desθentra-liθa'θion; dessentralisa'sion/ n. f. decentralization.

descifrar /desθi'frar; dessi'frar/ v. decipher, puzzle out.

descoco /des'koko/ n. m. boldness, brazenness.

descolgar /deskol'gar/ v. take down.

descollar /desko'ʎar; desko'yar/ v. stand out; excel.

descolorar /deskolo'rar/ v. discolor.

descolorido /deskolo'riðo/ a. pale, faded.

descomedido /deskome'ðiðo/ a. disproportionate; rude.

descomedirse /deskome'ðirse/ v. be rude.

descomponer /deskompo'ner/ v. decompose; break down, get out of order.

descomposición /deskomposi'θion; deskomposi'sion/ n. f. discomposure; disorder, confusion.

descompuesto /deskom'puesto/ a. impudent, rude.

descomulgar /deskomul'gar/ v. excommunicate.

descomunal /deskomu'nal/ a. extraordinary, huge.

desconcertar /deskonθer'tar; deskonser'tar/ v. disconcert, baffle.

desconcierto /deskon'θierto; deskon'sierto/ n. m. confusion, disarray.

desconectar /deskonek'tar/ v. disconnect.

desconfiado /deskon'fiaðo/ a. distrustful.

desconfianza /deskon'fianθa; deskon'fiansa/ n. f. distrust.

desconfiar /deskon'fiar/ v. distrust, mistrust; suspect.

descongelar /deskonhe'lar/ v. defrost.

descongestionante /deskonhestio-'nante/ n. m. decongestant.

desconocer /deskono'θer; deskono-'ser/ v. ignore, fail to recognize.

desconocido /deskono'θiðo; deskono'siðo/ **-da** n. stranger.

desconocimiento /deskonoθi'mien-to; deskonosi'miento/ n. m. ingratitude; ignorance.

desconsejado /deskonse'haðo/ a. imprudent, ill advised, rash.

desconsolado /deskonso'laðo/ *a.* disconsolate, wretched.

desconsuelo /deskon'suelo/ *n. m.* grief.

descontar /deskon'tar/ *v.* discount, subtract.

descontentar /deskonten'tar/ *v.* dissatisfy.

descontento /deskon'tento/ *n. m.* discontent.

descontinuar /deskonti'nuar/ *v.* discontinue.

desconvenir /deskombe'nir/ *v.* disagree.

descorazonar /deskoraθo'nar; deskoraso'nar/ *v.* dishearten.

descorchar /deskor't ʃar/ *v.* uncork.

descortés /deskor'tes/ *a.* discourteous, impolite, rude.

descortesía /deskorte'sia/ *n. f.* discourtesy, rudeness.

descortezar /deskorte'θar; deskor;te'sar/ *v.* peel.

descoyuntar /deskoyun'tar/ *v.* dislocate.

descrédito /des'kreðito/ *n. m.* discredit.

describir /deskri'βir/ *v.* describe.

descripción /deskrip'θion; deskrip'sion/ *n. f.* description.

descriptivo /deskrip'tiβo/ *a.* descriptive.

descuartizar /deskuarti'θar; deskuarti'sar/ *v.* dismember, disjoint.

descubridor /deskuβri'ðor/ **-ra** *n.* discoverer.

descubrimiento /deskuβri'miento/ *n. m.* discovery.

descubrir /desku'βrir/ *v.* discover; uncover; disclose.

descubrirse /desku'βrirse/ *v.* take off one's hat.

descuento /des'kuento/ *n. m.* discount.

descuidado /deskui'ðaðo/ *a.* reckless, careless; slack.

descuido /des'kuiðo/ *n. m.* neglect. —descuidar, *v.*

desde /'desðe/ *prep.* since; from. **d. luego,** of course.

desdén /des'ðen/ *n. m.* disdain. —desdeñar, *v.*

desdeñoso /desðe'ɲoso/ *a.* contemptuous, disdainful, scornful.

desdicha /des'ðit ʃa/ *n. f.* misfortune.

deseable /dese'aβle/ *a.* desirable.

desear /dese'ar/ *v.* desire, wish.

desecar /dese'kar/ *v.* dry, desiccate.

desechable /dese't ʃaβle/ *a.* disposable.

desechar /dese't ʃar/ *v.* scrap, reject.

desecho /de'set ʃo/ *n. m.* remainder, residue; (*pl.*) waste.

desembalar /desemba'lar/ *v.* unpack.

desembarazado /desembara'θaðo; desembara'saðo/ *a.* free; unrestrained.

desembarazar /desembara'θar; desembara'sar/ *v.* free; extricate; unburden.

desembarcar /desembar'kar/ *v.* disembark, go ashore.

desembocar /desembo'kar/ *v.* flow into.

desembolsar /desembol'sar/ *v.* disburse; expend.

desembolso /desem'bolso/ *n. m.* disbursement.

desemejante /deseme'hante/ *a.* unlike, dissimilar.

desempacar /desempa'kar/ *v.* unpack.

desempeñar /desempe'ɲar/ *v.* carry out; redeem.

desempeño /desem'peɲo/ *n. m.* fulfillment.

desencajar /desenka'har/ *v.* disjoint; disturb.

desencantar /desenkan'tar/ *v.* disillusion.

desencanto /desen'kanto/ *n. m.* disillusion.

desencarcelar /desenkarθe'lar; desenkarse'lar/ *v.* set free; release.

desenchufar /desent ʃu'far/ *v.* unplug.

desenfadado /desenfa'ðaðo/ *a.* free; unembarrassed; spacious.

desenfado /desen'faðo/ *n. m.* freedom; ease; calmness.

desenfocado /desenfo'kaðo/ *a.* out of focus.

desengaño /deseŋ'gaɲo/ *m.* disillusion. —desengañar *v.*

desenlace /desen'laθe; desen'lase/ *n. m.* outcome, conclusion.

desenredar /desenre'ðar/ *v.* disentangle.

desensartar /desensar'tar/ *v.* unthread (pearls).

desentenderse /desenten'derse/ *v.* overlook; avoid noticing.

desenterrar /desente'rrar/ *v.* disinter, exhume.

desenvainar /desembai'nar/ *v.* unsheath.

desenvoltura /desembol'tura/ *n. f.* confidence; impudence, boldness.

desenvolver /desembol'βer/ *v.* evolve, unfold.

deseo /de'seo/ *n. m.* wish, desire, urge.

deseoso /dese'oso/ *a.* desirous.

deserción /deser'θion; deser'sion/ *n. f.* desertion.

desertar /deser'tar/ *v.* desert.

desertor /deser'tor/ **-ra** *n.* deserter.

desesperación /desespera'θion; desespera'sion/ *n. f.* despair, desperation.

desesperado /desespe'raðo/ *a.* desperate; hopeless.

desesperar /desespe'rar/ *v.* despair.

desfachatez /desfat ʃa'teθ; desfat ʃa'tes/ *n. f.* cheek (gall).

desfalcar /desfal'kar/ *v.* embezzle.

desfase horario /des'fase o'rario/ *n. m.* jet lag.

desfavorable /desfaβo'raβle/ *a.* unfavorable.

desfigurar /desfigu'rar/ *v.* disfigure, mar.

desfiladero /desfila'ðero/ *n. m.* defile.

desfile /des'file/ *n. m.* parade. —desfilar, *v.*

desfile de modas /des'file de 'moðas/ fashion show.

desgaire /des'gaire/ *n. m.* slovenliness.

desgana /des'gana/ *n. f.* lack of appetite; unwillingness; repugnance.

desgarrar /desga'rrar/ *v.* tear, lacerate.

desgastar /desgas'tar/ *v.* wear away; waste; erode.

desgaste /des'gaste/ *n. m.* wear; erosion.

desgracia /des'graθia; des'grasia/ *n. f.* misfortune.

desgraciado /desgra'θiaðo; desgra'siaðo/ *a.* unfortunate.

desgranar /desgra'nar/ *v.* shell.

desgreñar /desgre'ɲar/ *v.* dishevel.

deshacer /desa'θer; desa'ser/ *v.* undo, take apart, destroy.

deshacerse de /desa'θerse de; desa'serse de/ *v.* get rid of, dispose of.

deshecho /des'et ʃo/ *a.* undone; wasted.

deshelar /dese'lar/ *v.* thaw; melt.

desheredamiento /desereða'miento/ *n. m.* disinheriting.

desheredar /desere'ðar/ *v.* disinherit.

deshielo /des'ielo/ *n. m.* thaw, melting.

deshinchar /desin't ʃar/ *v.* reduce a swelling.

deshojarse /deso'harse/ *v.* shed (leaves).

deshonestidad /desonesti'ðað/ *n. f.* dishonesty.

deshonesto /deso'nesto/ *a.* dishonest.

deshonra /de'sonra/ *n. f.* dishonor.

deshonrar /deson'rar/ *v.* disgrace; dishonor.

deshonroso /deson'roso/ *a.* dishonorable.

desierto /de'sierto/ *n. m.* desert, wilderness.

designar /desig'nar/ *v.* appoint, name.

designio /de'signio/ *n. m.* purpose, intent.

desigual /desi'gual/ *a.* uneven, unequal.

desigualdad /desigual'dað/ *n. f.* inequality.

desilusión /desilu'sion/ *n. f.* disappointment.

desinfección /desinfek'θion; desinfek'sion/ *n. f.* disinfection.

desinfectar /desinfek'tar/ *v.* disinfect.

desintegrar /desinte'grar/ *v.* disintegrate, zap.

desinterés /desinte'res/ *n. m.* indifference.

desinteresado /desintere'saðo/ *a.* disinterested, unselfish.

desistir /desis'tir/ *v.* desist, stop.

desleal /desle'al/ *a.* disloyal.

deslealtad /desleal'tað/ *n. f.* disloyalty.

desleir /desle'ir/ *v.* dilute, dissolve.

desligar /desli'gar/ *v.* untie, loosen; free, release.

deslindar /deslin'dar/ *v.* make the boundaries of.

deslinde /des'linde/ *n. m.* demarcation.

desliz /des'liθ; des'lis/ *n. m.* slip; false step; weakness.

deslizarse /desli'θarse; desli'sarse/ *v.* slide; slip; glide; coast.

deslumbramiento /deslumbra'miento/ *n. m.* dazzling glare; confusion.

deslumbrar /deslumb'rar/ *v.* dazzle; glare.

deslustre /des'lustre/ *n. m.* tarnish. —deslustrar, *v.*

desmán /des'man/ *n. m.* mishap; misbehavior; excess.

desmantelar /desmante'lar/ *v.* dismantle.

desmañado /desma'ɲaðo/ *a.* awkward, clumsy.

desmaquillarse /desmaki'ʎarse; desmaki'yarse/ *v.* remove one's makeup.

desmayar /desma'yar/ *v.* depress, dishearten.

desmayo /des'mayo/ *n. m.* faint. —desmayarse, *v.*

desmejorar /desmeho'rar/ *v.* make worse; decline.

desmembrar /desmem'brar/ *v.* dismember.

desmemoria /desme'moria/ *n. f.* forgetfulness.

desmemoriado /desmemo'riaðo/ *a.* forgetful.

desmentir /desmen'tir/ *v.* contradict, disprove.

desmenuzable /desmenu'θaβle; desmenu'saβle/ *a.* crisp, crumbly.

desmenuzar /desmenu'θar; desmenu'sar/ *v.* crumble, break into bits.

desmesurado /desmesu'raðo/ *a.* excessive.

desmobilizar /desmoβili'θar; desmoβili'sar/ *v.* demobilize.

desmonetización /desmonetiθa'θion; desmonetisa'sion/ *n. f.* demonetization.

desmonetizar /desmoneti'θar; desmoneti'sar/ *v.* demonetize.

desmontado /desmon'taðo/ *a.* dismounted.

desmontar /desmon'tar/ *v.* dismantle.

desmontarse /desmon'tarse/ *v.* dismount.

desmoralización /desmoraliθa'θion; desmoralisa'sion/ *n. f.* demoralization.

desmoralizar /desmorali'θar; desmorali'sar/ *v.* demoralize.

desmoronar /desmoro'nar/ *v.* crumble, decay.

desmovilizar /desmoβili'θar; desmoβili'sar/ *v.* demobilize.

desnatar /desna'tar/ *v.* skim.

desnaturalización /desnaturaliθa'θion; desnaturalisa'sion/ *n. f.* denaturalization.

desnaturalizar /desnaturali'θar; desnaturali'sar/ *v.* denaturalize.

desnegamiento /desnega'miento/ *n. m.* denial, contradiction.

desnervar /desner'βar/ *v.* enervate.

desnivel /desni'βel/ *n. m.* unevenness or difference in elevation.

desnudamente /desnuða'mente/ *adv.* nakedly.

desnudar /desnu'ðar/ *v.* undress.

desnudez /desnu'ðeθ; desnu'ðes/ *n. f.* bareness, nudity.

desnudo /des'nuðo/ *a.* bare, naked.

desnutrición /desnutri'θion; desnutri'sion/ *n. f.* malnutrition.

desobedecer /desoβeðe'θer; desoβeðe'ser/ *v.* disobey.

desobediencia /desoβeðien'θia; desoβeðien'sia/ *n. f.* disobedience.

desobediente /desoβe'ðiente/ *a.* disobedient.

desobedientemente /desoβeðiente'mente/ *adv.* disobediently.

desobligar /desoβli'gar/ *v.* release from obligation; offend.

desocupado /desoku'paðo/ *a.* idle, not busy; vacant.

desocupar /desoku'par/ *v.* vacate.

desolación /desola'θion; desola'sion/ *n. f.* desolation; ruin.

desolado /deso'laðo/ *a.* desolate. —desolar, *v.*

desollar /deso'ʎar; deso'yar/ *v.* skin.

desorden /de'sorðen/ *n. m.* disorder.

desordenar /desorðe'nar/ *v.* disarrange.

desorganización /desorganiθa'θion; desorganisa'sion/ *n. f.* disorganization.

desorganizar /desorgani'θar; desorgani'sar/ *v.* disorganize.

despabilado /despaβi'laðo/ *a.* vigilant, watchful; lively.

despachar /despa't ʃar/ *v.* dispatch, ship, send.

despacho /despa't ʃo/ *n. m.* shipment; dispatch, promptness; office.

despacio /des'paθio; des'pasio/ *adv.* slowly.

desparpajo /despar'paho/ *n. m.* glibness; fluency of speech.

desparramar /desparra'mar/ *v.* scatter.

despavorido /despaβo'riðo/ *a.* terrified.

despecho /des'pet ʃo/ *n. m.* spite.

despedazar /despeða'θar; despeða'sar/ *v.* tear up.

despedida /despe'ðiða/ *n. f.* farewell; leave-taking; discharge.

despedir /despe'ðir/ *v.* dismiss, discharge; see off.

despedirse de /despe'ðirse de/ *v.* say good-bye to, take leave of.

despegar /despe'gar/ *v.* unglue; separate; *Aero.* take off.

despego /des'pego/ *n. m.* indifference; disinterest.

despejar /despe'har/ *v.* clear, clear up.

despejo /des'peho/ *n. m.* sprightliness; clarity; without obstruction.

despensa /des'pensa/ *n. f.* pantry.

despensero /despen'sero/ *n. m.* butler.

despeñar /despe'ɲar/ *v.* throw down.

desperdicio /desper'ðiθio; desper'ðisio/ *n. m.* waste. —desperdiciar, *v.*

despertador /desperta'ðor/ *n. m.* alarm clock.

despertar /desper'tar/ *v.* wake, wake up.

despesar /despe'sar/ *n. m.* dislike.

despicar /despi'kar/ *v.* satisfy.

despidida /despi'ðiða/ *n. f.* gutter.

despierto /des'pierto/ *a.* awake; alert, wide-awake.

despilfarrado /despilfa'rraðo/ *a.* wasteful, extravagant.
despilfarrar /despilfa'rrar/ *v.* waste, squander.
despilfarro /despil'farro/ *n. m.* waste, extravagance.
despique /des'pike/ *n. m.* revenge.
despistar /despis'tar/ *v.* mislead, put off the track.
desplazamiento /desplaθa'miento; desplasa'miento/ *n. m.* displacement.
desplegar /desple'gar/ *v.* display; unfold.
desplome /des'plome/ *n. m.* collapse. **—desplomarse,** *v.*
desplumar /desplu'mar/ *v.* defeather, pluck.
despoblar /despo'βlar/ *v.* depopulate.
despojar /despo'har/ *v.* strip; despoil, plunder.
despojo /des'poho/ *n. m.* plunder, spoils; (*pl.*) remains, debris.
desposado /despo'saðo/ *a.* newly married.
desposar /despo'sar/ *v.* marry.
desposeer /despose'er/ *v.* dispossess.
déspota /'despota/ *n. m. & f.* despot.
despótico /des'potiko/ *a.* despotic.
despotismo /despo'tismo/ *n. m.* despotism, tyranny.
despreciable /despre'θiaβle; despre'siaβle/ *a.* contemptible.
despreciar /despre'θiar; despre'siar/ *v.* spurn, despise, scorn.
desprecio /des'preθio; des'presio/ *n. m.* scorn, contempt.
desprender /despren'der/ *v.* detach, unfasten.
desprenderse /despren'derse/ *v.* loosen, come apart. **d. de,** part with.
desprendido /despren'diðo/ *a.* disinterested.
despreocupado /despreoku'paðo/ *a.* unconcerned; unprejudiced.
desprevenido /despreβe'niðo/ *a.* unprepared, unready.
desproporción /despropor'θion; despropor'sion/ *n. f.* disproportion.
despropósito /despro'posito/ *n. m.* nonsense.
desprovisto /despro'βisto/ *a.* devoid.
después /des'pues/ *adv.* afterwards, later; then, next. **d. de, d. que,** after.
despuntar /despun'tar/ *v.* blunt; remove the point of.
desquiciar /deski'θiar; deski'siar/ *v.* unhinge; disturb, unsettle.
desquitar /deski'tar/ *v.* get revenge, retaliate.
desquite /des'kite/ *n. m.* revenge, retaliation.
desrazonable /desraθo'naβle; desraso'naβle/ *a.* unresonable.
destacamento /destaka'mento/ *n. m. Mil.* detachment.
destacarse /desta'karse/ *v.* stand out, be prominent.
destajero /desta'hero/ **-a** *n.* **destajista,** *m. & f.* pieceworker.
destapar /desta'par/ *v.* uncover.
destello /des'teʎo; deste'yo/ *n. m.* sparkle, gleam.
destemplar /destem'plar/ *v. Mus.* untune; disturb, upset.
desteñir /deste'ɲir/ *v.* fade, discolor.
desterrado /deste'rraðo/ **-da** *n.* exile.
desterrar /deste'rrar/ *v.* banish, exile.
destetar /deste'tar/ *v.* wean.
destierro /des'tierro/ *n. m.* banishment, exile.
destilación /destila'θion; destila'sion/ *n. f.* distillation.
destilar /desti'lar/ *v.* distill.
destilería /destile'ria/ *n. f.* distillery.
destilería de petróleo /destile'ria de pe'troleo/ oil refinery.
destinación /destina'θion; destina'sion/ *n. f.* destination.
destinar /desti'nar/ *v.* destine, intend.
destinatario /destina'tario/ **-ria** *n.* addressee (mail); payee (money).
destino /des'tino/ *n. m.* destiny, fate; destination.
destitución /destitu'θion; destitu'sion/ *n. f.* dismissal; abandonment.
destituido /desti'tuiðo/ *a.* destitute.
destorcer /destor'θer; destor'ser/ *v.* undo, straighten out.
destornillado /destorni'ʎaðo; destorni'yaðo/ *a.* reckless, careless.
destornillador /destorni'ʎaðor; destorni'yaðor/ *n. m.* screwdriver.
destraillar /destrai'ʎar; destrai'yar/ *v.* unleash; set loose.
destral /des'tral/ *n. m.* hatchet.
destreza /des'treθa; des'tresa/ *n. f.* cleverness; dexterity, skill.
destripar /destri'par/ *v.* eviscerate, disembowel.
destrísimo /des'trisimo/ *a.* extremely dexterous.
destronamiento /destrona'miento/ *n. m.* dethronement.
destronar /destro'nar/ *v.* dethrone.
destrozador /destroθa'ðor; destrosa'ðor/ *n. m.* destroyer, wrecker.
destrozar /destro'θar; destro'sar/ *v.* destroy, wreck.
destrozo /des'troθo; des'troso/ *n. m.* destruction, ruin.
destrucción /destruk'θion; destruk'sion/ *n. f.* destruction.
destructibilidad /destruktiβili'ðað/ *n. f.* destructibility.
destructible /destruk'tiβle/ *a.* destructible.
destructivamente /destruktiβa'mente/ *adv.* destructively.
destructivo /destruk'tiβo/ *a.* destructive.
destruir /destruir/ *v.* destroy; wipe out.
desuello /desue'ʎo; desue'yo/ *n. m.* impudence.
desunión /desu'nion/ *n. f.* disunion; discord; separation.
desunir /desu'nir/ *v.* disconnect, sever.
desusadamente /desusaða'mente/ *adv.* unusually.
desusado /desu'saðo/ *a.* archaic; obsolete.
desuso /de'suso/ *n. m.* disuse.
desvalido /des'βaliðo/ *a.* helpless; destitute.
desvalijador /desβaliha'ðor/ *n. m.* highwayman.
desván /des'βan/ *n. m.* attic.
desvanecerse /desβane'θerse; desβane'serse/ *v.* vanish; faint.
desvariado /desβa'riaðo/ *a.* delirious; disorderly.
desvarío /desβa'rio/ *n. m.* raving. **—desvariar,** *v.*
desvedado /desβe'ðaðo/ *a.* free; unrestrained.
desveladamente /desβelaða'mente/ *adv.* watchfully, alertly.
desvelado /desβe'laðo/ *a.* watchful; alert.
desvelar /desβe'lar/ *v.* be watchful; keep awake.
desvelo /des'βelo/ *n. m.* vigilance; uneasiness; insomnia.
desventaja /desβen'taha/ *n. f.* disadvantage.
desventar /desβen'tar/ *v.* let air out of.
desventura /desβen'tura/ *n. f.* misfortune.
desventurado /desβentu'raðo/ *a.* unhappy; unlucky.
desvergonzado /desβergon'θaðo; desβergonsaðo/ *a.* shameless, brazen.
desvergüenza /desβer'guenθa; desβer'guensa/ *n. f.* shamelessness.
desvestir /desβes'tir/ *v.* undress.
desviación /desβia'θion; desβia'sion/ *n. f.* deviation.
desviado /des'βiaðo/ *a.* deviant; remote.
desviar /des'βiar/ *v.* divert; deviate, detour.
desvío /des'βio/ *n. m.* detour; side track; indifference.
desvirtuar /desβir'tuar/ *v.* decrease the value of.
deszumar /desθu'mar; dessu'mar/ *v.* remove the juice from.
detalle /de'taʎe; de'taye/ *n. m.* detail. **—detallar,** *v.*
detective /de'tektiβe/ *n. m. & f.* detective.
detención /deten'θion; deten'sion/ *n. f.* detention, arrest.
detenedor /detene'ðor/ **-ra** *n.* stopper; catch.
detener /dete'ner/ *v.* detain, stop; arrest.
detenidamente /deteniða'mente/ *adv.* carefully, slowly.
detenido /dete'niðo/ *adv.* stingy; thorough.
detergente /deter'hente/ *a.* detergent.
deterioración /deteriora'θion; deteriora'sion/ *n. f.* deterioration.
deteriorar /deterio'rar/ *v.* deteriorate.
determinable /determi'naβle/ *a.* determinable.
determinación /determina'θion; determina'sion/ *n. f.* determination.
determinar /determi'nar/ *v.* determine, settle, decide.
determinismo /determi'nismo/ *n. m.* determinism.
determinista /determi'nista/ *n. & a.* determinist.
detestable /detes'taβle/ *a.* detestable, hateful.
detestablemente /detestaβle'mente/ *adv.* detestably, hatefully, abhorrently.
detestación /detesta'θion; detesta'sion/ *n. f.* detestation, hatefulness.
detestar /detes'tar/ *v.* detest.
detonación /detona'θion; detona'sion/ *n. f.* detonation.
detonar /deto'nar/ *v.* detonate, explode.
detracción /detrak'θion; detrak'sion/ *n. f.* detraction, defamation.
detractar /detrak'tar/ *v.* detract, defame, vilify.
detraer /detra'er/ *v.* detract.
detrás /de'tras/ *adv.* behind; in back.
detrimento /detri'mento/ *n. m.* detriment, damage.
deuda /'deuða/ *n. f.* debt.
deudo /'deuðo/ **-da** *n.* relative, kin.
deudor /deu'ðor/ **-ra** *n.* debtor.
Deuteronomio /deutero'nomio/ *n. m.* Deuteronomy.
devalar /deβa'lar/ *v.* drift off course.
devanar /deβa'nar/ *v.* to wind, as on a spool.
devanear /deβane'ar/ *v.* talk deliriously, rave.
devaneo /deβa'neo/ *n. m.* frivolity; idle pursuit; delirium.
devastación /deβasta'θion; deβasta'sion/ *n. f.* devastation, ruin, havoc.
devastador /deβasta'ðor/ *a.* devastating.
devastar /deβas'tar/ *v.* devastate.
devenir /deβe'nir/ *v.* happen, occur; become.
devoción /deβo'θion; deβo'sion/ *n. f.* devotion.
devocionario /deβoθio'nario; deβosio'nario/ *n. m.* prayer book.
devocionero /deβoθio'nero; deβosio'nero/ *a.* devotional.
devolver /deβol'βer/ *v.* return, give back.
devorar /deβo'rar/ *v.* devour.
devotamente /deβota'mente/ *adv.* devotedly, devoutly, piously.
devoto /de'βoto/ *a.* devout; devoted.
deyección /deiek'θion; deiek'sion/ *n. f.* depression, dejection.
día /dia/ *n. m.* day. **buenos días,** good morning.
diabetes /dia'βetes/ *n. f.* diabetes.
diabético /dia'βetiko/ *a.* diabetic.
diablear /diaβle'ar/ *v.* play pranks.
diablo /'diaβlo/ *n. m.* devil.
diablura /dia'βlura/ *n. f.* mischief.
diabólicamente /diaβolika'mente/ *adv.* diabolically.
diabólico /dia'βoliko/ *a.* diabolic, devilish.
diaconato /diako'nato/ *n. m.* deaconship.
diaconía /diako'nia/ *n. f.* deaconry.
diácono /'diakono/ *n. m.* deacon.
diacrítico /dia'kritiko/ *a.* diacritic.
diadema /dia'ðema/ *n. f.* diadem; crown.
diáfano /'diafano/ *a.* transparent.
diafragma /dia'fragma/ *n. m.* diaphragm.
diagnosticar /diagnosti'kar/ *v.* diagnose.
diagonal /diago'nal/ *n. f.* diagonal.
diagonalmente /diagonal'mente/ *adv.* diagonally.
diagrama /dia'grama/ *n. m.* diagram.
dialectal /dialek'tal/ *a.* dialectal.
dialéctico /dia'lektiko/ *a.* dialectic.
dialecto /dia'lekto/ *n. m.* dialect.
diálogo /'dialogo/ *n. m.* dialogue.
diamante /dia'mante/ *n. m.* diamond.
diamantista /diaman'tista/ *n. m. & f.* diamond cutter; jeweler.
diametral /diame'tral/ *a.* diametric.
diametralmente /diametral'mente/ *adv.* diametrically.
diámetro /'diametro/ *n. m.* diameter.
diana /'diana/ *n. f.* reveille; dartboard.
diapasón /diapa'son/ *n. m.* standard pitch; tuning fork.
diaplejía /diaple'hia/ *n. f.* paralysis.
diariamente /diaria'mente/ *adv.* daily.
diario /'diario/ *a. & m.* daily; daily paper; diary; journal.
diarrea /dia'rrea/ *n. f.* diarrhea.
diatriba /dia'triβa/ *n. f.* diatribe, harangue.
dibujo /di'βuho/ *n. m.* drawing, sketch. **—dibujar,** *v.*
dicción /dik'θion; dik'sion/ *n. f.* diction.
diccionario /dikθio'nario; diksio'nario/ *n. m.* dictionary.
diccionarista /dikθiona'rista; diksiona'rista/ *n. m. & f.* lexicographer.
dicha /'ditʃa/ *n. f.* happiness.
dicho /'ditʃo/ *n. m.* saying.
dichoso /di'tʃoso/ *a.* happy; fortunate.
diciembre /di'θiembre; di'siembre/ *n. m.* December.
dicotomía /dikoto'mia/ *n. f.* dichotomy.
dictado /dik'taðo/ *n. m.* dictation.
dictador /dikta'ðor/ **-ra** *n.* dictator.
dictadura /dikta'ðura/ *n. f.* dictatorship.
dictamen /dik'tamen/ *n. m.* dictate.
dictar /dik'tar/ *v.* dictate; direct.
dictatorial /diktato'rial/ **dictatorio** *a.* dictatorial.
didáctico /di'ðaktiko/ *a.* didactic.
diecinueve /dieθi'nueβe; diesi'nueβe/ *a. & pron.* nineteen.
dieciocho /die'θiotʃo; die'siotʃo/ *a. & pron.* eighteen.
dieciseis /dieθi'seis; diesi'seis/ *a. & pron.* sixteen.
diecisiete /dieθi'siete; diesi'siete/ *a. & pron.* seventeen.
diente /diente/ *n. m.* tooth.
diestramente /diestra'mente/ *adv.* skillfully, ably; ingeniously.
diestro /'diestro/ *a.* dexterous, skillful; clever.
dieta /'dieta/ *n. f.* diet; allowance.
dietética /die'tetika/ *n. f.* dietetics.
dietético /die'tetiko/ *a.* **1.** dietetic; dietary. **—***n.* **2. -ca.** dietician.
diez /dieθ; dies/ *a. & pron.* ten.
diezmal /dieθ'mal; dies'mal/ *a.* decimal.
diezmar /dieθ'mar; dies'mar/ *v.* decimate.
difamación /difama'θion; difama'sion/ *n. f.* defamation, smear.
difamar /difa'mar/ *v.* defame, smear, libel.

difamatorio /difama'torio/ *a.* defamatory.

diferencia /dife'renθia; dife'rensia/ *n. f.* difference.

diferencial /diferen'θial; diferen'sial/ *a. & f.* differential.

diferenciar /diferen'θiar; diferen'siar/ *v.* differentiate, distinguish.

diferente /dife'rente/ *a.* different.

diferentemente /diferente'mente/ *adv.* differently.

diferir /dife'rir/ *v.* differ; defer, put off.

difícil /di'fiθil; di'fisil/ *a.* difficult, hard.

difícilmente /difiθil'mente; difisil'mente/ *adv.* with difficulty or hardship.

dificultad /difikul'taδ/ *n. f.* difficulty.

dificultar /difikul'tar/ *v.* make difficult.

dificultoso /difikul'toso/ *a.* difficult, hard.

dificultoso /difikul'toso/ *a.* difficult, hard.

difidencia /difi'δenθia; difi'δensia/ *n. f.* diffidence.

difidente /difi'δente/ *a.* diffident.

difteria /dif'teria/ *n. f.* diphtheria.

difundir /difun'dir/ *v.* diffuse, spread.

difunto /di'funto/ *a.* **1.** deceased, dead, late. —*n.* **2. -ta,** deceased person.

difusamente /difusa'mente/ *adv.* diffusely.

difusión /difu'sion/ *n. f.* diffusion, spread.

digerible /dihe'riβle/ *a.* digestible.

digerir /dihe'rir/ *v.* digest.

digestible /dihes'tiβle/ *a.* digestible.

digestión /dihes'tion/ *n. f.* digestion.

digestivo /dihes'tiβo/ *a.* digestive.

digesto /di'hesto/ *n. m.* digest or code of laws.

digitado /dihi'taδo/ *a.* digitate.

digital /dihi'tal/ *a.* **1.** digital. —*n.* **2. f.** foxglove, digitalis.

dignación /digna'θion; digna'sion/ *f.* condescension; deigning.

dignamente /digna'mente/ *adv.* with dignity.

dignarse /dig'narse/ *v.* condescend, deign.

dignatario /digna'tario/ **-ra** *n.* dignitary.

dignidad /digni'δaδ/ *n. f.* dignity.

dignificar /dignifi'kar/ *v.* dignify.

digno /'digno/ *a.* worthy; dignified.

digresión /digre'sion/ *n. f.* digression.

digresivo /digre'siβo/ *a.* digressive.

dij, dije /'dih; 'dihe/ *n. m.* trinket, piece of jewelry.

dilación /dila'θion; dila'sion/ *n. f.* delay.

dilapidación /dilapiδa'θion; dilapi'δasion/ *n. f.* dilapidation.

dilapidado /dilapi'δaδo/ *a.* dilapidated.

dilatación /dilata'θion; dilata'sion/ *n. f.* dilatation, enlargement.

dilatar /dila'tar/ *v.* dilate; delay; expand.

dilatoria /dila'toria/ *n. f.* delay.

dilatorio /dila'torio/ *a.* dilatory.

dilecto /di'lekto/ *a.* loved.

dilema /di'lema/ *n. m.* dilemma.

diligencia /dili'henθia; dili'hensia/ *n. f.* diligence, industriousness.

diligente /dili'hente/ *a.* diligent, industrious.

diligentemente /dilihente'mente/ *adv.* diligently.

dilogía /dilo'hia/ *n. f.* ambiguous meaning.

dilución /dilu'θion; dilu'sion/ *n. f.* dilution.

diluir /di'luir/ *v.* dilute.

diluvial /dilu'βial/ *a.* diluvial.

diluvio /di'luβio/ *n. m.* flood, deluge.

dimensión /dimen'sion/ *n. f.* dimension; measurement.

diminución /diminu'θion; diminu'sion/ *n. f.* diminution.

diminuto /dimi'nuto/ **diminutivo** *a.* diminutive, little.

dimisión /dimi'sion/ *n. f.* resignation.

dimitir /dimi'tir/ *v.* resign.

Dinamarca /dina'marka/ *n. f.* Denmark.

dinamarqués /dinamar'kes/ **-esa** *a. & n.* Danish, Dane.

dinámico /di'namiko/ *a.* dynamic.

dinamita /dina'mita/ *n. f.* dynamite.

dinamitero /dinami'tero/ **-ra** *n.* dynamiter.

dínamo /'dinamo/ *n. m.* dynamo.

dinasta /di'nasta/ *n. m.* dynast, king, monarch.

dinastía /dinas'tia/ *n. f.* dynasty.

dinástico /di'nastiko/ *a.* dynastic.

dinero /di'nero/ *n. m.* money, currency.

dinosauro /dino'sauro/ *n. m.* dinosaur.

diócesis /'dioθesis; 'diosesis/ *n. f.* diocese.

Dios /dios/ *n. m.* God.

dios -sa *n.* god, goddess.

diploma /di'ploma/ *n. m.* diploma.

diplomacia /diplo'maθia; diplo'masia/ *n. f.* diplomacy.

diplomado /diplo'maδo/ **-da** *n.* graduate.

diplomarse /diplo'marse/ *v.* graduate (from a school).

diplomática /diplo'matika/ *n. f.* diplomacy.

diplomático /diplo'matiko/ **-ca** *a. & n.* diplomat; diplomatic.

dipsomanía /dipsoma'nia/ *n. f.* dipsomania.

diptongo /dip'tongo/ *n. m.* diphthong.

diputación /diputa'θion; diputa'sion/ *n. f.* deputation, delegation.

diputado /dipu'taδo/ **-da** *n.* deputy; delegate.

diputar /dipu'tar/ *v.* depute, delegate; empower.

dique /'dike/ *n. m.* dike; dam.

dirección /direk'θion; direk'sion/ *n. f.* direction; address; guidance; *Com.* management.

directamente /direkta'mente/ *adv.* directly.

directo /di'rekto/ *a.* direct.

director /direk'tor/ **-ra** *n.* director; manager.

directorio /direk'torio/ *n. m.* directory.

dirigente /diri'hente/ *a.* directing, controlling, managing.

dirigible /diri'hiβle/ *n. m.* dirigible.

dirigir /diri'hir/ *v.* direct; lead; manage.

dirigirse a /diri'hirse a/ *v.* address; approach, turn to; head for.

dirruir /di'rruir/ *v.* destroy, devastate.

disanto /di'santo/ *n. m.* holy day.

discantar /diskan'tar/ *v.* sing (esp. in counterpoint); discuss.

disceptación /disθepta'θion; dissepta'sion/ *n. f.* argument, quarrel.

disceptar /disθep'tar; dissep'tar/ *v.* argue, quarrel.

discernimiento /disθerni'miento; disserni'miento/ *n. m.* discernment.

discernir /disθer'nir; disser'nir/ *v.* discern.

disciplina /disθi'plina; dissi'plina/ *n. f.* discipline.

disciplinable /disθipli'naβle; dissipli'naβle/ *a.* disciplinable.

disciplinar /disθipli'nar; dissipli'nar/ *v.* discipline, train, teach.

discípulo /dis'θipulo; dis'sipulo/ **-la** *n.* disciple, follower; pupil.

disco /'disko/ *n. m.* disk; (phonograph) record.

disco compacto /'disko kom'pakto/ compact disk.

disco duro /'disko 'duro/ hard disk.

disco flexible /'disko flek'siβle/ floppy disk.

discontinuación /diskontinua'θion; diskontinua'sion/ *n. f.* discontinuation.

discontinuar /diskonti'nuar/ *v.* discontinue, break off, cease.

discordancia /diskor'δanθia; diskor'δansia/ *n. f.* discordance.

discordar /diskor'δar/ *v.* disagree, conflict.

discordia /dis'korδia/ *n. f.* discord.

discoteca /disko'teka/ *n. f.* disco, discotheque.

discreción /diskre'θion; diskre'sion/ *n. f.* discretion.

discrecional /diskreθio'nal; diskresio'nal/ *a.* optional.

discrecionalmente /diskreθional'mente; diskresional'mente/ *adv.* optionally.

discrepancia /diskre'panθia; diskre'pansia/ *n. f.* discrepancy.

discretamente /diskreta'mente/ *adv.* discreetly.

discreto /dis'kreto/ *a.* discreet.

discrimen /dis'krimen/ *n. m.* risk, hazard.

discriminación /diskrimina'θion; diskrimina'sion/ *n. f.* discrimination.

discriminar /diskrimi'nar/ *v.* discriminate.

disculpa /dis'kulpa/ *n. f.* excuse; apology.

disculpar /diskul'par/ *v.* excuse; exonerate.

disculparse /diskul'parse/ *v.* apologize.

discurrir /disku'rrir/ *v.* roam; flow; think; plan.

discursante /diskur'sante/ *n.* lecturer, speaker.

discursivo /diskur'siβo/ *a.* discursive.

discurso /dis'kurso/ *n. m.* speech, talk.

discusión /disku'sion/ *n. f.* discussion.

discutible /disku'tiβle/ *a.* debatable.

discutir /disku'tir/ *v.* discuss; debate; contest.

disecación /diseka'θion; diseka'sion/ *n. f.* dissection.

disecar /dise'kar/ *v.* dissect.

disección /disek'θion; disek'sion/ *n. f.* dissection.

diseminación /disemina'θion; disemina'sion/ *n. f.* dissemination.

diseminar /disemi'nar/ *v.* disseminate, spread.

disensión /disen'sion/ *n. f.* dissension; dissent.

disenso /di'senso/ *n. m.* dissent.

disentería /disente'ria/ *n. f.* dysentery.

disentir /disen'tir/ *v.* disagree, dissent.

diseñador /diseɲa'δor/ **-ra** *n.* designer.

diseño /di'seɲo/ *n. m.* design. —**diseñar,** *v.*

disertación /diserta'θion; diserta'sion/ *n. f.* dissertation.

disforme /dis'forme/ *a.* deformed, monstrous, ugly.

disformidad /disformi'δaδ/ *n. f.* deformity.

disfraz /dis'fraθ; dis'fras/ *n. m.* disguise. —**disfrazar,** *v.*

disfrutar /disfru'tar/ *v.* enjoy.

disfrute /dis'frute/ *n. m.* enjoyment.

disgustar /disgus'tar/ *v.* displease; disappoint.

disgusto /dis'gusto/ *n. m.* displeasure; disappointment.

disidencia /disi'δenθia; disi'δensia/ *n. f.* dissidence.

disidente /disi'δente/ *a. & n.* dissident.

disímil /di'simil/ *a.* unlike.

disimilitud /disimili'tuδ/ *n. f.* dissimilarity.

disimulación /disimula'θion; disimula'sion/ *n. f.* dissimulation.

disimulado /disimu'laδo/ *a.* dissembling, feigning; sly.

disimular /disimu'lar/ *v.* hide; dissemble.

disimulo /di'simulo/ *n. m.* pretense.

disipación /disipa'θion; disipa'sion/ *n. f.* dissipation.

disipado /disi'paδo/ *a.* dissipated; wasted; scattered.

disipar /disi'par/ *v.* waste; scatter.

dislexia /dis'leksia/ *n. f.* dyslexia.

disléxico /dis'leksiko/ *a.* dyslexic.

dislocación /disloka'θion; disloka'sion/ *n. f.* dislocation.

dislocar /dislo'kar/ *v.* dislocate; displace.

disminuir /dismi'nuir/ *v.* diminish, lessen, reduce.

disociación /disoθia'θion; disosia'sion/ *n. f.* dissociation.

disociar /diso'θiar; diso'siar/ *v.* dissociate.

disolubilidad /disoluβili'δaδ/ *n. f.* dissolubility.

disoluble /diso'luβle/ *a.* dissoluble.

disolución /disolu'θion; disolu'sion/ *n. f.* dissolution.

disolutamente /disoluta'mente/ *adv.* dissolutely.

disoluto /diso'luto/ *a.* dissolute.

disolver /disol'βer/ *v.* dissolve.

disonancia /diso'nanθia; diso'nansia/ *n. f.* dissonance; discord.

disonante /diso'nante/ *a.* dissonant; discordant.

disonar /diso'nar/ *v.* be discordant; clash in sound.

dísono /di'sono/ *a.* dissonant.

dispar /dis'par/ *a.* unlike.

disparadamente /disparaδa'mente/ *adv.* hastily, hurriedly.

disparar /dispa'rar/ *v.* shoot, fire (a weapon).

disparatado /dispara'taδo/ *a.* nonsensical.

disparatar /dispara'tar/ *v.* talk nonsense.

disparate /dispa'rate/ *n. m.* nonsense, tall tale.

disparejo /dispa'reho/ *a.* uneven, unequal.

disparidad /dispari'δaδ/ *n. f.* disparity.

disparo /dis'paro/ *n. m.* shot.

dispendio /dis'pendio/ *n. m.* extravagance.

dispendioso /dispen'dioso/ *a.* expensive; extravagant.

dispensa /dis'pensa/ **dispensación** *n. f.* dispensation.

dispensable /dispen'saβle/ *a.* dispensable; excusable.

dispensar /dispen'sar/ *v.* dispense, excuse; grant.

dispensario /dispen'sario/ *n. m.* dispensary.

dispepsia /dis'pepsia/ *n. f.* dyspepsia.

dispéptico /dis'peptiko/ *a.* dyspeptic.

dispersar /disper'sar/ *v.* scatter; dispel; disband.

dispersión /disper'sion/ *n. f.* dispersion, dispersal.

disperso /dis'perso/ *a.* dispersed.

displicente /displi'θente; displi'sente/ *a.* unpleasant.

disponer /dispo'ner/ *v.* dispose. **d. de,** have at one's disposal.

disponible /dispo'niβle/ *a.* available.

disposición /disposi'θion; disposi'sion/ *n. f.* disposition; disposal.

dispuesto /dis'puesto/ *a.* disposed, inclined; attractive.

disputa /dis'puta/ *n. f.* dispute, argument.

disputable /dispu'taβle/ *a.* disputable.

disputador /disputa'δor/ **-ra** *n.* disputant.

disputar /dispu'tar/ *v.* argue; dispute.

disquete /dis'kete/ *n. m.* diskette.

disquetera /diske'tera/ *n. f.* disk drive.

disquisición /diskisi'θion; diskisi'sion/ *n. f.* disquisition.

distancia /dis'tanθia; dis'tansia/ *n. f.* distance.

distante /dis'tante/ *a.* distant.

distantemente /distante'mente/ *adv.* distantly.

distar /dis'tar/ *v.* be distant, be far.

distender /disten'der/ *v.* distend, swell, enlarge.

distensión /disten'sion/ *n. f.* distension, swelling.

dístico /'distiko/ *n. m.* couplet.

distinción /distin'θion; distin'sion/ *n. f.* distinction, difference.

distingo /dis'tiŋgo/ *n. m.* restriction.

distinguible /distiŋ'guiβle/ *a.* distinguishable.

distinguido /distiŋ'guido/ *a.* distinguished, prominent.

distinguir /distiŋ'guir/ *v.* distinguish; make out, spot.

distintamente /distinta'mente/ *adv.* distinctly, clearly; differently.

distintivo /distin'tiβo/ *a.* distinctive.

distintivo del país /distin'tiβo del pa'is/ country code.

distinto /dis'tinto/ *a.* distinct; different.

distracción /distrak'θion; distrak'sion/ *n. f.* distraction, pastime; absent-mindedness.

distraer /distra'er/ *v.* distract.

distraídamente /distraida'mente/ *adv.* absent-mindedly, distractedly.

distraído /distra'ido/ *a.* absentminded; distracted.

distribución /distriβu'θion; distriβu'sion/ *n. f.* distribution.

distribuidor /distriβui'dor/ **-ra** *n.* distributor.

distribuir /distri'βuir/ *v.* distribute.

distributivo /distriβu'tiβo/ *a.* distributive.

distributor /distriβu'tor/ *n. m.* distributor.

distrito /dis'trito/ *n. m.* district.

disturbar /distur'βar/ *v.* disturb, trouble.

disturbio /dis'turβio/ *n. m.* disturbance, outbreak; turmoil.

disuadir /disua'dir/ *v.* dissuade.

disuasión /disua'sion/ *n. f.* dissuasion; deterrence.

disuasivo /disua'siβo/ *a.* dissuasive.

disyunción /disyun'θion; disyun'sion/ *n. f.* disjunction.

ditirambo /diti'rambo/ *n. m.* dithyramb.

diurno /'diurno/ *a.* diurnal.

diva /'diβa/ *n. f.* diva, prima donna.

divagación /diβaga'θion; diβaga'sion/ *n. f.* digression.

divagar /diβa'gar/ *v.* digress, ramble.

diván /di'βan/ *n. m.* couch.

divergencia /diβer'henθia; diβer'hensia/ *n. f.* divergence.

divergente /diβer'hente/ *a.* divergent, differing.

divergir /diβer'hir/ *v.* diverge.

diversamente /diβersa'mente/ *adv.* diversely.

diversidad /diβersi'dad/ *n. f.* diversity.

diversificar /diβersifi'kar/ *v.* diversify, vary.

diversión /diβer'sion/ *n. f.* diversion, pastime.

diverso /di'βerso/ *a.* diverse, different; (*pl.*) various, several.

divertido /diβer'tido/ *a.* humorous, amusing.

divertimiento /diβerti'miento/ *n. m.* diversion; amusement.

divertir /diβer'tir/ *v.* entertain, amuse.

divertirse /diβer'tirse/ *v.* enjoy oneself, have a good time.

dividendo /diβi'δendo/ *n. m.* dividend.

dividedero /diβiδi'δero/ *a.* to be divided.

dividido /diβi'δiδo/ *a.* divided.

dividir /diβi'δir/ *v.* divide; separate.

divieso /di'βieso/ *n. m.* Med. boil.

divinamente /diβina'mente/ *adv.* divinely.

divinidad /diβini'δaδ/ *n. f.* divinity.

divinizar /diβini'θar; diβini'sar/ *v.* deify.

divino /di'βino/ *a.* divine; heavenly.

divisa /di'βisa/ *n. f.* badge, emblem.

divisar /diβi'sar/ *v.* sight, make out.

divisibilidad /diβisiβili'δaδ/ *n. f.* divisibility.

divisible /diβi'siβle/ *a.* divisible.

división /diβi'sion/ *n. f.* division.

divisivo /diβi'siβo/ *a.* divisive.

divo /'diβo/ *n. m.* movie star.

divorcio /di'βorθio; di'βorsio/ *n. m.* divorce. —**divorciar**, *v.*

divulgable /diβul'gaβle/ *a.* divulgable.

divulgación /diβulga'θion; diβulga'sion/ *n. f.* divulgation.

divulgar /diβul'gar/ *v.* divulge, reveal.

dobladamente /doβlaδa'mente/ *adv.* doubly.

dobladillo /doβla'δiλo; doβla'δiyo/ *n. m.* hem of a skirt or dress.

dobladura /doβla'δura/ *n. f.* fold; bend.

doblar /do'βlar/ *v.* fold; bend.

doble /'doβle/ *a.* double.

doblegable /doβle'gaβle/ *a.* flexible, foldable.

doblegar /doβle'gar/ *v.* fold, bend; yield.

doblez /do'βleθ; doβles/ *n. m.* fold; duplicity.

doblón /do'βlon/ *n. m.* doubloon.

doce /'doθe; 'dose/ *a. & pron.* twelve.

docena /do'θena; do'sena/ *n. f.* dozen.

docente /do'θente; do'sente/ *a.* educational.

dócil /'doθil; 'dosil/ *a.* docile.

docilidad /doθili'δaδ; dosili'δaδ/ *n. f.* docility, tractableness.

dócilmente /doθil'mente; dosil'mente/ *adv.* docilely, meekly.

doctamente /dokta'mente/ *adv.* learnedly, profoundly.

docto /'dokto/ *a.* learned, expert.

doctor /dok'tor/ **-ra** *n.* doctor.

doctorado /dokto'raδo/ *n. m.* doctorate.

doctoral /dokto'ral/ *a.* doctoral.

doctrina /dok'trina/ *n. f.* doctrine.

doctrinador /doktrina'δor/ **-ra** *n.* teacher.

doctrinal /doktri'nal/ *n. m.* doctrinal.

doctrinar /doktri'nar/ *v.* teach.

documentación /dokumenta'θion; dokumenta'sion/ *n. f.* documentation.

documental /dokumen'tal/ *a.* documentary.

documento /doku'mento/ *n. m.* document.

dogal /do'gal/ *n. m.* noose.

dogma /'dogma/ *n. m.* dogma.

dogmáticamente /dog'matika-mente/ *adv.* dogmatically.

dogmático /dog'matiko/ *n. m.* dogmatic.

dogmatismo /dogma'tismo/ *n. m.* dogmatism.

dogmatista /dogma'tista/ *n. m. & f.* dogmatist.

dogo /'dogo/ *n. m.* bulldog.

dolar /do'lar/ *v.* cut, chop, hew.

dólar *n. m.* dollar.

dolencia /do'lenθia; do'lensia/ *n. f.* pain; disease.

doler /do'ler/ *v.* ache, hurt, be sore.

doliente /do'liente/ *a.* ill; aching.

dolor /do'lor/ *n. m.* pain; grief, sorrow, woe.

dolor de cabeza /do'lor de ka'βeθa; do'lor de ka'βesa/ headache.

dolor de espalda /do'lor de es'palda/ backache.

dolor de estómago /do'lor de es'tomago/ stomachache.

dolorido /dolo'riδo/ *a.* painful, sorrowful.

dolorosamente /dolorosa'mente/ *adv.* painfully, sorrowfully.

doloroso /dolo'roso/ *a.* painful, sorrowful.

dolosamente /dolosa'mente/ *adv.* deceitfully.

doloso /do'loso/ *a.* deceitful.

domable /do'maβle/ *a.* that can be tamed or managed.

domar /do'mar/ *v.* tame; subdue.

dombo /'dombo/ *n. m.* dome.

domesticable /domesti'kaβle/ *a.* that can be domesticated.

domesticación /domestika'θion; domestika'sion/ *n. f.* domestication.

domésticamente /domestika'mente/ *adv.* domestically.

domesticar /domesti'kar/ *v.* tame, domesticate.

domesticidad /domestiθi'δaδ; domestisi'δaδ/ *n. f.* domesticity.

doméstico /do'mestiko/ *a.* domestic.

domicilio /domi'θilio; domi'silio/ *n. m.* dwelling, home, residence, domicile.

dominación /domina'θion; domina'sion/ *n. f.* domination.

dominador /domina'δor/ *a.* dominating.

dominante /domi'nante/ *a.* dominant.

dominar /domi'nar/ *v.* rule, dominate; master.

dómine /'domine/ *n. m.* teacher.

domingo /do'mingo/ *n. m.* Sunday.

dominio /do'minio/ *n. m.* domain; rule; power.

dominó /domi'no/ *n. m.* domino.

Don /don/ *title used before a man's first name.*

don /don/ *n. m.* gift.

donación /dona'θion; dona'sion/ *n. f.* donation.

donador /dona'δor/ **-ra** *n.* giver, donor.

donaire /do'naire/ *n. m.* grace.

donairosamente /donairosa'mente/ *adv.* gracefully.

donairoso /donai'roso/ *a.* graceful.

donante /do'nante/ *n.* giver, donor.

donar /do'nar/ *v.* donate.

donativo /dona'tiβo/ *n. m.* donation, contribution; gift.

doncella /don'θeʎa; don'seya/ *n. f.* lass; maid.

donde /'donde/ **dónde** *conj. & adv.* where.

dondequiera /donde'kiera/ *adv.* wherever, anywhere.

donosamente /donosa'mente/ *adv.* gracefully; wittily.

donoso /do'noso/ *a.* graceful; witty.

donosura /dono'sura/ *n. f.* gracefulness; wittiness.

Doña /'doɲa/ *title used before a lady's first name.*

dopar /do'par/ *v.* drug, dope.

dorado /do'raδo/ *a.* gilded.

dorador /dora'δor/ **-ra** *n.* gilder.

dorar /do'rar/ *v.* gild.

dórico /'doriko/ *a.* Doric.

dormidero /dormi'δero/ *a.* sleep-inducing; soporific.

dormido /dor'miδo/ *a.* asleep.

dormir /dor'mir/ *v.* sleep.

dormirse /dor'mirse/ *v.* fall asleep, go to sleep.

dormitar /dormi'tar/ *v.* doze.

dormitorio /dormi'torio/ *n. m.* dormitory; bedroom.

dorsal /dor'sal/ *a.* dorsal.

dorso /'dorso/ *n. m.* spine.

dos /dos/ *a. & pron.* two. **los d.,** both.

dosañal /dosa'ɲal/ *a.* biennial.

doscientos /dos'θientos; dos'sientos/ *a. & pron.* two hundred.

dosel /do'sel/ *n. m.* canopy; platform, dais.

dosificación /dosifika'θion; dosifika'sion/ *n. f.* dosage.

dosis /'dosis/ *n. f.* dose.

dotación /dota'θion; dota'sion/ *n. f.* endowment; Naut. crew.

dotador /dota'δor/ **-ra** *n.* donor.

dotar /do'tar/ *v.* endow; give a dowry to.

dote /'dote/ *n. f.* dowry; (*pl.*) talents.

dragaminas /draga'minas/ *n. m.* mine sweeper.

dragar /dra'gar/ *v.* dredge; sweep.

dragón /dra'gon/ *n. m.* dragon; dragoon.

dragonear /dragone'ar/ *v.* pretend to be.

drama /'drama/ *n. m.* drama; play.

dramática /dra'matika/ *n. f.* drama, dramatic art.

dramáticamente /dramatika'mente/ *adv.* dramatically.

dramático /dra'matiko/ *a.* dramatic.

dramatizar /dramati'θar; dramati'sar/ *v.* dramatize.

dramaturgo /drama'turgo/ **-ga** *n.* playwright, dramatist.

drástico /'drastiko/ *a.* drastic.

drenaje /dre'nahe/ *n. m.* drainage.

dríada /'driaδa/ *n. f.* dryad.

dril /dril/ *n. m.* denim.

driza /'driθa; 'drisa/ *n. f.* halyard.

droga /'droga/ *n. f.* drug.

drogadicto /droga'δikto/ **-ta** *n.* drug addict.

droguería /droge'ria/ *n. f.* drugstore.

droguero /dro'gero/ *n. m.* druggist.

dromedario /drome'δario/ *n. m.* dromedary.

druida /'druiδa/ *n. m. & f.* Druid.

dualidad /duali'δaδ/ *n. f.* duality.

dubitable /duβi'taβle/ *a.* doubtful.

dubitación /duβita'θion; duβita'sion/ *n. f.* doubt.

ducado /du'kaδo/ *n. m.* duchy.

ducal /du'kal/ *a.* ducal.

ducha /'dutʃa/ *n. f.* shower (bath).

ducharse /du'tʃarse/ *v.* take a shower.

dúctil /'duktil/ *a.* ductile.

ductilidad /duktili'δaδ/ *n. f.* ductility.

duda /'duδa/ *n. f.* doubt.

dudable /du'δaβle/ *a.* doubtful.

dudar /du'δar/ *v.* doubt; hesitate; question.

dudosamente /duδosa'mente/ *adv.* doubtfully.

dudoso /du'δoso/ *a.* dubious; doubtful.

duela /'duela/ *n. f.* stave.

duelista /due'lista/ *n. m. & f.* duelist.

duelo /'duelo/ *n. m.* duel; grief; mourning.

duende /'duende/ *n. m.* elf, hobgoblin.

dueño /'dueɲo/ **-ña** *n.* owner; landlord -lady; master, mistress.

dulce /'dulθe; dulse/ *a.* **1.** sweet. **agua d.,** fresh water. —*n.* **2.** *m.* piece of candy; (*pl.*) candy.

dulcedumbre /dulθe'δumbre; dulse'δumbre/ *n. f.* sweetness.

dulcemente /dulθe'mente; dulse'mente/ *adv.* sweetly.

dulcería /dulθe'ria; dulse'ria/ *n. f.* confectionery; candy shop.

dulcificar /dulθifi'kar; dulsifi'kar/ *v.* sweeten.

dulzura /dul'θura; dul'sura/ *n. f.* sweetness; mildness.

duna /'duna/ *n. f.* dune.

dúo /'duo/ *n. m.* duo, duet.

duodenal /duoδe'nal/ *a.* duodenal.

duplicación /duplika'θion; duplika'sion/ *n. f.* duplication; doubling.

duplicadamente /duplikaδa'mente/ *adv.* doubly.

duplicado /dupli'kaδo/ *a. & m.* duplicate.

duplicar /dupli'kar/ *v.* double, duplicate, repeat.

duplicidad /dupliθi'δaδ; duplisi'δaδ/ *n. f.* duplicity.

duplo /'duplo/ *a.* double.

duque /'duke/ *n. m.* duke.

duquesa /du'kesa/ *n. f.* duchess.

durabilidad /duraβili'δaδ/ *n. f.* durability.

durable /du'raβle/ *a.* durable.

duración /dura'θion; dura'sion/ *n. f.* duration.

duradero /dura'ðero/ *a.* lasting, durable.

duramente /dura'mente/ *adv.* harshly, roughly.

durante /du'rante/ *prep.* during.

durar /du'rar/ *v.* last.

durazno /du'raθno; du'rasno/ *n. m.* peach; peach tree.

dureza /du'reθa; du'resa/ *n. f.* hardness.

durmiente /dur'miente/ *a.* sleeping.

duro /'duro/ *a.* hard; stiff; stern; stale.

dux /duks/ *n. m.* doge.

E

e /e/ *conj.* and.

ebanista /eβa'nista/ *n. m. & f.* cabinetmaker.

ebanizar /eβani'θar; eβani'sar/ *v.* give an ebony finish to.

ébano /'eβano/ *n. m.* ebony.

ebonita /eβo'nita/ *n. f.* ebonite.

ebrio /'eβrio/ *a.* drunken, inebriated.

ebullición /eβuʎi'θion; eβuyi'sion/ *n. f.* boiling.

echada /e't∫aða/ *n. f.* throw.

echadillo /et∫a'ðiʎo; et∫a'ðiyo/ *n. m.* foundling; orphan.

echar /e't∫ar/ *v.* throw, toss; pour. **e. a,** start to. **e. a perder,** spoil, ruin. **e. de menos,** miss.

echarse /e't∫arse/ *v.* lie down.

eclecticismo /eklekti'θismo; eklekti-'sismo/ *n. m.* eclecticism.

ecléctico /e'klektiko/ *n. & a.* eclectic.

eclesiástico /ekle'siastiko/ *a. & m.* ecclesiastic.

eclipse /e'klipse/ *n. m.* eclipse. —eclipsar, *v.*

écloga /'ekloga/ *n. f.* eclogue.

eco /'eko/ *n. m.* echo.

ecología /ekolo'hia/ *n. f.* ecology.

ecológico /eko'lohiko/ *n. f.* ecological.

ecologista /ekolo'hista/ *n. m. & f.* ecologist.

economía /ekono'mia/ *n. f.* economy; thrift; economics. **e. política,** political economy.

económicamente /ekonomika'mente/ *adv.* economically.

económico /eko'nomiko/ *a.* economic; economical, thrifty; inexpensive.

economista /ekono'mista/ *n. m. & f.* economist.

economizar /ekonomi'θar; ekonomi-'sar/ *v.* save, economize.

ecuación /ekua'θion; ekua'sion/ *n. f.* equation.

ecuador /ekua'ðor/ *n. m.* equator.

ecuanimidad /ekuanimi'ðað/ *n. f.* equanimity.

ecuatorial /ekuato'rial/ *a.* equatorial.

ecuatoriano /ekuato'riano/ **-na** *a. & n.* Ecuadorian.

ecuestre /e'kuestre/ *a.* equestrian.

ecuménico. /eku'meniko/ *a.* ecumenical.

edad /e'ðað/ *n. f.* age.

edecán /eðe'kan/ *n. m.* aide-de-camp.

Edén /e'ðen/ *n. m.* Eden.

edición /eði'θion; eði'sion/ *n. f.* edition; issue.

edicto /e'ðikto/ *n. m.* edict, decree.

edificación /eðifika'θion; eðifika-'sion/ *n. f.* construction; edification.

edificador /eðifika'ðor/ *n.* constructor; builder.

edificar /eðifi'kar/ *v.* build.

edificio /eði'fiθio; eði'fisio/ *n. m.* edifice, building.

editar /eði'tar/ *v.* publish, issue; edit.

editor /eði'tor/ *n. m.* publisher; editor.

editorial /eðito'rial/ *n. m.* editorial; publishing house.

edredón /eðre'ðon/ *n. m.* quilt.

educación /eðuka'θion; eðuka'sion/ *n. f.* upbringing; breeding; education.

educado /eðu'kaðo/ *a.* well-mannered; educated.

educador /eðuka'ðor/ **-ra** *n.* educator.

educar /eðu'kar/ *v.* educate; bring up; train.

educativo /eðuka'tiβo/ *a.* educational.

educción /eðuk'θion; eðuk'sion/ *n. f.* deduction.

educir /eðu'θir; eðu'sir/ *v.* educe.

efectivamente /efektiβa'mente/ *adv.* actually, really.

efectivo /efek'tiβo/ *a.* effective; actual, real. **en e.,** *Com.* in cash.

efecto /e'fekto/ *n. m.* effect.

efecto invernáculo /e'fekto imber'nakulo/ greenhouse effect.

efectuar /efek'tuar/ *v.* effect; cash.

eferente /efe'rente/ *a.* efferent.

efervescencia /eferβes'θenθia; eferβes'sensia/ *n. f.* effervescence; zeal.

eficacia /efi'kaθia; efi'kasia/ *n. f.* efficacy.

eficaz /efi'kaθ; efi'kas/ *a.* efficient, effective.

eficazmente /efikaθ'mente; efikas-'mente/ *adv.* efficaciously.

eficiencia /efi'θienθia; efi'siensia/ *n. f.* efficiency.

eficiente /efi'θiente; efi'siente/ *a.* efficient.

efigie /e'fihie/ *n. f.* effigy.

efímera /efi'mera/ *n. f.* mayfly.

efímero /e'fimero/ *a.* ephemeral, passing.

efluvio /e'fluβio/ *n. m.* effluvium.

efundir /efun'dir/ *v.* effuse; pour out.

efusión /efu'sion/ *n. f.* effusion.

egipcio /e'hipθio; e'hipsio/ **-cia** *a. n.* Egyptian.

Egipto /e'hipto/ *n. m.* Egypt.

egoísmo /ego'ismo/ *n. m.* egoism, egotism, selfishness.

egoísta /ego'ista/ *a. & n.* selfish, egoistic; egoist.

egotismo /ego'tismo/ *n. m.* egotism.

egotista /ego'tista/ *n. m. & f.* egotist.

egreso /e'greso/ *n. m.* expense, outlay.

eje /'ehe/ *n. m.* axis; axle.

ejecución /eheku'θion; eheku'sion/ *n. f.* execution; performance; enforcement.

ejecutar /eheku'tar/ *v.* execute; enforce; carry out.

ejecutivo /eheku''tiβo/ **-va** *a. & n.* executive.

ejecutor /eheku'tor/ **-ra** *n.* executor.

ejemplar /ehem'plar/ *a.* **1.** exemplary. —*n.* **2.** *m.* copy.

ejemplificación /ehemplifika'θion; ehemplifika'sion/ *n. f.* exemplification.

ejemplificar /ehemplifi'kar/ *v.* illustrate.

ejemplo /e'hemplo/ *n. m.* example.

ejercer /eher'θer; eher'ser/ *v.* exert; practice.

ejercicio /eher'θiθio; eher'sisio/ *n. m.* exercise, drill. —ejercitar, *v.*

ejercitación /eherθita'θion; ehersita-'sion/ *n. f.* exercise, training, drill.

ejercitar /eherθi'tar; ehersi'tar/ *v.* exercise, train, drill.

ejército /e'herθito; e'hersito/ *n. m.* army.

ejotes /e'hotes/ *n. m.pl.* string beans.

el /el/ *art. & pron.* the; the one.

él *pron.* he, him; it.

elaboración /elaβora'θion; elaβora-'sion/ *n. f.* elaboration; working up.

elaborado /elaβo'raðo/ *a.* elaborate.

elaborador /elaβora'ðor/ *n. m.* manufacturer, maker.

elaborar /elaβo'rar/ *v.* elaborate; manufacture; brew.

elación /ela'θion; ela'sion/ *n. f.* elation; magnanimity; turgid style.

elasticidad /elastiθi'ðað; elastisi'ðað/ *n. f.* elasticity.

elástico /e'lastiko/ *n. m.* elastic.

elección /elek'θion; elek'sion/ *n. f.* election; option, choice.

electivo /elek'tiβo/ *a.* elective.

electo /e'lekto/ *a.* elected, chosen, appointed.

electorado /elekto'raðo/ *n. m.* electorate.

electoral /elekto'ral/ *a.* electoral.

electricidad /elektriθi'ðað; elektrisi'ðað/ *n. f.* electricity.

electricista /elektri'θista; elektri'sista/ *n. m. & f.* electrician.

eléctrico /e'lektriko/ *a.* electric.

electrización /elektriθa'θion; elektrisa'sion/ *n. f.* electrification.

electrocardiograma /e,lektrokarðio'grama/ *n. m.* electrocardiogram.

electrocución /elektroku'θion; elektroku'sion/ *n. f.* electrocution.

electrocutar /elektroku'tar/ *v.* electrocute.

electrodo /elek'troðo/ *n. m.* electrode.

electrodoméstico /e,lektroðo'mestiko/ *n. m.* electrical appliance, home appliance.

electroimán /elektroi'man/ *n. m.* electromagnet.

electrólisis /elek'trolisis/ *n. f.* electrolysis.

electrólito /elek'trolito/ *n. m.* electrolyte.

electrón /elek'tron/ *n. m.* electron.

electrónico /elek'troniko/ *a.* electronic.

elefante /ele'fante/ *n. m.* elephant.

elegancia /ele'ganθia; ele'gansia/ *n. f.* elegance.

elegante /ele'gante/ *a.* elegant, smart, stylish, fine.

elegantemente /elegante'mente/ *adv.* elegantly.

elegía /ele'hia/ *n. f.* elegy.

elegibilidad /elehiβili'ðað/ *n. f.* eligibility.

elegible /ele'hiβle/ *a.* eligible.

elegir /ele'hir/ *v.* select, choose; elect.

elemental /elemen'tal/ *a.* elementary.

elementalmente /elemental'mente/ *adv.* elementally; fundamentally.

elemento /ele'mento/ *n. m.* element.

elepé /ele'pe/ *n. m.* long-playing (record), LP.

elevación /eleβa'θion; eleβa'sion/ *n. f.* elevation; height.

elevador /eleβa'ðor/ *n. m.* elevator.

elevamiento /eleβa'miento/ *n. m.* elevation.

elevar /ele'βar/ *v.* elevate; erect, raise.

elidir /eli'ðir/ *v.* elide.

eliminación /elimina'θion; elimina'sion/ *n. f.* elimination.

eliminar /elimi'nar/ *v.* eliminate.

elipse /e'lipse/ *n. f.* ellipse.

elipsis /e'lipsis/ *n. f.* ellipsis.

elíptico /e'liptiko/ *a.* elliptical.

ella /'eʎa; 'eya/ *pron.* she, her; it.

ello /'eʎo; 'eyo/ *pron.* it.

ellos /'eʎos; 'eyos/ **-as** *pron. pl.* they, them.

elocuencia /elo'kuenθia; elo'kuensia/ *n. f.* eloquence.

elocuente /elo'kuente/ *a.* eloquent.

elocuentemente /elokuente'mente/ *adv.* eloquently.

elogio /e'lohio/ *n. m.* praise, compliment. —elogiar, *v.*

elucidación /eluθiða'θion; elusiða-'sion/ *n. f.* elucidation.

elucidar /eluθi'ðar; elusi'ðar/ *v.* elucidate.

eludir /elu'ðir/ *v.* elude.

emanar /ema'nar/ *v.* emanate, stem.

emancipación /emanθipa'θion; emansipa'sion/ *n. f.* emancipation; freeing.

emancipador /emanθipa'ðor; emansipa'ðor/ **-ra** *n.* emancipator.

emancipar /emanθi'par; emansi'par/ *v.* emancipate; free.

embajada /emba'haða/ *n. f.* embassy; legation; *Colloq.* errand.

embajador /embaha'ðor/ **-ra** *n.* ambassador.

embalar /emba'lar/ *v.* pack, bale.

embaldosado /embaldo'saðo/ *n. m.* tile floor.

embalsamador /embalsama'ðor/ *n. m.* embalmer.

embalsamar /embalsa'mar/ *v.* embalm.

embarazada /embara'θaða; embara'saða/ *a.* pregnant.

embarazadamente /embaraθaða-'mente; embarasaða'mente/ *adv.* embarrassedly.

embarazar /embara'θar; embara'sar/ *v.* make pregnant; embarrass.

embarazo /emba'raθo; emba'raso/ *n. m.* embarrassment; pregnancy.

embarbascado /embarβas'kaðo/ *a.* difficult; complicated.

embarcación /embarka'θion; embarka'sion/ *n. f.* boat, ship; embarkation.

embarcadero /embarka'ðero/ *n. m.* wharf, pier, dock.

embarcador /embarka'ðor/ *n. m.* shipper, loader, stevedore.

embarcar /embar'kar/ *v.* embark, board ship.

embarcarse /embar'karse/ *v.* embark; sail.

embargador /embarga'ðor/ *n. m.* one who impedes; one who orders an embargo.

embargante /embar'gante/ *a.* impeding, hindering.

embargar /embar'gar/ *v.* impede, restrain; *Leg.* seize, embargo.

embargo /em'bargo/ *n. m.* seizure, embargo. **sin e.,** however, nevertheless.

embarnizar /embarni'θar; embarni'sar/ *v.* varnish.

embarque /em'barke/ *n. m.* shipment.

embarrador /embarra'ðor/ **-ra** *n.* plasterer.

embarrancar /embarran'kar/ *v.* get stuck in mud; *Naut.* run aground.

embarrar /emba'rrar/ *v.* plaster; besmear with mud.

embasamiento /embasa'miento/ *n. m.* foundation of a building.

embastecer /embaste'θer; embaste-'ser/ *v.* get fat.

embaucador /embauka'ðor/ **-ra** *n.* impostor.

embaucar /embau'kar/ *v.* deceive, trick, hoax.

embaular /embau'lar/ *v.* pack in a trunk.

embausamiento /embausa'miento/ *n. m.* amazement.

embebecer /embeβe'θer; embeβe-'ser/ *v.* amaze, astonish; entertain.

embeber /embe'βer/ *v.* absorb; incorporate; saturate.

embelecador /embeleka'ðor/ **-ra** *n.* impostor.

embeleco /embe'leko/ *n. m.* fraud, perpetration.

embeleñar /embele'ɲar/ *v.* fascinate, charm.

embelesamiento /embelesa'miento/ *n. m.* rapture.

embelesar /embele'sar/ *v.* fascinate, charm.

embeleso /embe'leso/ *n. m.* rapture, bliss.

embellecer /embeʎe'θer; embeye-'ser/ *v.* beautify, embellish.

embestida /embes'tiða/ *n. f.* violent assault; attack.

emblandecer /emblande'θer; emblande'ser/ *v.* soften; moisten; move to pity.

emblema /em'blema/ *n. m.* emblem.

emblemático /emble'matiko/ *a.* emblematic.

embocadura /emboka'ðura/ *n. f.* narrow entrance; mouth of a river.

embocar /embo'kar/ *v.* eat hastily; gorge.

embolia /em'bolia/ *n. f.* embolism.

émbolo /'embolo/ *n. m.* piston.

embolsar /embol'sar/ *v.* pocket.

embonar /embo'nar/ *v.* improve, fix, repair.

emborrachador /emborratʃa'ðor/ a. intoxicating.

emborrachar /emborra'tʃar/ v. get drunk.

emboscada /embos'kaða/ n. f. ambush.

emboscar /embos'kar/ v. put or lie in ambush.

embotado /embo'taðo/ a. blunt, dull (edged). —**embotar,** v.

embotadura /embota'ðura/ n. f. bluntness; dullness.

embotellamiento /emboteʎa'mien̪to; emboteya'miento/ n. m. bottling (liquids); traffic jam.

embotellar /embote'ʎar; embote'yar/ v. put in bottles.

embozado /embo'θaðo; embo'saðo/ v. muzzled; muffled.

embozar /embo'θar; embo'sar/ v. muzzle; muffle.

embozo /em'boθo; em'boso/ n. m. muffler.

embrague /em'braɣe/ n. m. Auto. clutch.

embravecer /embraβe'θer; embraβe'ser/ v. be or make angry.

embriagado /embria'ɣaðo/ a. drunken, intoxicated.

embriagar /embria'ɣar/ v. intoxicate.

embriaguez /embria'ɣeθ; embria'ɣes/ n. f. drunkenness.

embrión /em'brion/ n. m. embryo.

embrionario /embrio'nario/ a. embryonic.

embrochado /embro'tʃaðo/ a. embroidered.

embrollo /em'broʎo; em'broyo/ n. m. muddle. —**embrollar,** v.

embromar /embro'mar/ v. tease; joke.

embuchado /embu'tʃaðo/ n. m. pork sausage.

embudo /em'buðo/ n. m. funnel.

embuste /em'buste/ n. m. lie, fib.

embustear /embuste'ar/ v. lie, fib.

embustero /embus'tero/ **-ra** n. liar.

embutir /embu'tir/ v. stuff, cram.

emergencia /emer'henθia; emer'hensia/ n. f. emergency.

emérito /e'merito/ a. emeritus.

emético /e'metiko/ n. m. & a. emetic.

emigración /emiɣra'θion; emiɣra'sion/ n. f. emigration.

emigrante /emi'ɣrante/ a. & n. emigrant.

emigrar /emi'ɣrar/ v. emigrate.

eminencia /emi'nenθia; emi'nensia/ n. f. eminence, height.

eminente /emi'nente/ a. eminent.

emisario /emi'sario/ **-ria** n. emissary, spy; outlet.

emisión /emi'sion/ n. f. issue; emission.

emisor /emi'sor/ n. m. radio transmitter.

emitir /emi'tir/ v. emit.

emoción /emo'θion; emo'sion/ n. f. feeling, emotion, thrill.

emocional /emo'θional; emo'sional/ a. emotional.

emocionante /emoθio'nante; emosio'nante/ a. exciting.

emocionar /emoθio'nar; emosio'nar/ v. touch, move, excite.

emolumento /emolu'mento/ n. m. emolument; perquisite.

empacar /empa'kar/ v. pack.

empacho /em'patʃo/ n. m. shyness, timidity; embarrassment.

empadronamiento /empaðrona'miento/ n. m. census; list of taxpayers.

empalizada /empali'θaða; empali'saða/ n. f. palisade, stockade.

empanada /empa'naða/ n. f. meat pie.

empañar /empa'ɲar/ v. blur; soil, sully.

empapar /empa'par/ v. soak.

empapelado /empape'laðo/ n. m. wallpaper.

empapelar /empape'lar/ v. wallpaper.

empaque /em'pake/ n. m. packing; appearance, mien.

empaquetar /empake'tar/ v. pack, package.

emparedado /empare'ðaðo/ n. m. sandwich.

emparejarse /empare'harse/ v. match, pair off; level, even off.

emparentado /emparen'taðo/ a. related by marriage.

emparrado /empa'rraðo/ n. m. arbor.

empastadura /empasta'ðura/ n. f. (dental) filling.

empastar /empas'tar/ v. fill (a tooth); paste.

empate /em'pate/ n. m. tie, draw. —**empatarse,** v.

empecer /empe'θer; empe'ser/ v. hurt, harm, injure; prevent.

empedernir /empeðer'nir/ v. harden.

empeine /em'peine/ n. m. groin; instep; hoof.

empellar /empe'ʎar; empe'yar/ v. shove, jostle.

empellón /empe'ʎon; empe'yon/ m. hard push, shove.

empeñar /empe'ɲar/ v. pledge; pawn.

empeñarse en /empe'ɲarse en/ v. persist in, be bent on.

empeño /em'peɲo/ n. m. persistence; pledge; pawning.

empeoramiento /empeora'miento/ n. m. deterioration.

empeorar /empeo'rar/ v. get worse.

emperador /empera'ðor/ n. m. emperor.

emperatriz /empera'triθ; empera'tris/ n. f. empress.

empernar /emper'nar/ v. bolt.

empero /em'pero/ conj. however; but.

emperramiento /emperra'miento/ n. m. stubbornness.

empezar /empe'θar; empe'sar/ v. begin, start.

empinado /empi'naðo/ a. steep.

empinar /empi'nar/ v. raise; exalt.

empíreo /em'pireo/ a. celestial, heavenly; divine.

empíricamente /empirika'mente/ adv. empirically.

empírico /em'piriko/ a. empirical.

empirismo /empi'rismo/ n. m. empiricism.

emplastarse /emplas'tarse/ v. get smeared.

emplasto /em'plasto/ n. m. salve.

emplazamiento /emplaθa'miento; emplasa'miento/ n. m. court summons.

emplazar /empla'θar; empla'sar/ v. summon to court.

empleado /emple'aðo/ **-da** n. employee.

emplear /em'plear/ v. employ; use.

empleo /em'pleo/ n. m. employment; job; use.

empobrecer /empoβre'θer; empoβre'ser/ v. impoverish.

empobrecimiento /empoβreθi'miento; empoβresi'miento/ n. m. impoverishment.

empollador /empoʎa'ðor; empoya'ðor/ n. m. incubator.

empollar /empo'ʎar; empo'yar/ v. hatch.

empolvado /empol'βaðo/ a. dusty.

empolvar /empol'βar/ v. powder.

emporcar /empor'kar/ v. soil, make dirty.

emporio /em'porio/ n. m. emporium.

emprendedor /emprende'ðor/ a. enterprising.

emprender /empren'der/ v. undertake.

empreñar /empre'ɲar/ v. make pregnant; beget.

empresa /em'presa/ n. f. enterprise, undertaking; company.

empresario /empre'sario/ **-ria** n. businessperson; impresario.

empréstito /em'prestito/ n. m. loan.

empujón /empu'hon/ n. m. push; shove. —**empujar,** v.

empuñar /empu'ɲar/ v. grasp, seize; wield.

emulación /emula'θion; emula'sion/ n. f. emulation; envy; rivalry.

emulador /emula'ðor/ n. m. emulator; rival.

émulo /'emulo/ a. rival. —**emular,** v.

emulsión /emul'sion/ n. f. emulsion.

emulsionar /emulsio'nar/ v. emulsify.

en /en/ prep. in, on, at.

enaguas /e'naguas/ n. f.pl. petticoat; skirt.

enajenable /enahe'naβle/ a. alienable.

enajenación /enahena'θion; enahena'sion/ n. f. alienation; derangement, insanity.

enajenar /enahe'nar/ v. alienate.

enamoradamente /enamoraða'mente/ adv. lovingly.

enamorado /enamo'raðo/ a. in love.

enamorador /enamora'ðor/ n. m. wooer; suitor; lover.

enamorarse /enamo'rarse/ v. fall in love.

enano /e'nano/ **-na** n. midget; dwarf.

enardecer /enarðe'θer; enarðe'ser/ v. inflame.

enastado /enas'taðo/ a. horned.

encabestrar /enkaβe'strar/ v. halter.

encabezado /enkaβe'θaðo; enkaβe'saðo/ n. m. headline.

encabezamiento /enkaβeθa'miento; enkaβesa'miento/ n. m. title; census; tax roll.

encabezar /enkaβe'θar; enkaβe'sar/ v. head.

encachar /enka'tʃar/ v. hide.

encadenamiento /enkaðena'miento/ n. m. connection, linkage.

encadenar /enkaðe'nar/ v. chain; link, connect.

encajar /enka'har/ v. fit in, insert.

encaje /en'kahe/ n. m. lace.

encalar /enka'lar/ v. whitewash.

encallarse /enka'ʎarse; enka'yarse/ v. be stranded.

encallecido /enkaʎe'θiðo; enkaye'siðo/ a. hardened; calloused.

encalvecer /enkalβe'θer; enkalβe'ser/ v. lose one's hair.

encaminar /enkami'nar/ v. guide; direct; be on the way to.

encandilar /enkandi'lar/ v. dazzle; daze.

encantación /enkanta'θion; enkanta'sion/ n. f. incantation.

encantado /enkan'taðo/ a. charmed, fascinated, enchanted.

encantador /enkanta'ðor/ a. charming, delightful.

encante /en'kante/ n. m. public auction.

encanto /en'kanto/ n. m. charm, delight. —**encantar,** v.

encapillado /enkapi'ʎaðo; enkapi'yaðo/ n. m. clothes one is wearing.

encapotar /enkapo'tar/ v. cover, cloak; muffle.

encaprichamiento /enkapritʃa'miento/ n. m. infatuation.

encaramarse /enkara'marse/ v. perch; climb.

encararse con /enka'rarse kon/ v. face.

encarcelación /enkarθela'θion; enkarsela'sion/ n. f. imprisonment.

encarcelar /enkarθe'lar; enkarse'lar/ v. jail, imprison.

encarecer /enkare'θer; enkare'ser/ v. recommend; extol.

encarecidamente /enkareθiða'mente; enkaresiða'mente/ adv. extremely; ardently.

encargado /enkar'ɣaðo/ **-da** n. agent; attorney; representative.

encargar /enkar'ɣar/ v. entrust; order.

encargarse /enkar'ɣarse/ v. take charge, be in charge.

encargo /en'karɣo/ n. m. errand; assignment; Com. order.

encarnación /enkarna'θion; enkarna'sion/ n. f. incarnation.

encarnado /enkar'naðo/ a. red.

encarnar /enkar'nar/ v. embody.

encarnecer /enkarne'θer; enkarne'ser/ v. grow fat or heavy.

encarnizado /enkarni'θaðo; enkarni'saðo/ a. bloody, fierce.

encarrilar /enkarri'lar/ v. set right; put on the track.

encartar /enkar'tar/ v. ban, outlaw; summon.

encastar /enkas'tar/ v. improve by crossbreeding.

encastillar /enkasti'ʎar; enkasti'yar/ v. be obstinate or unyielding.

encatarrado /enkata'rraðo/ a. suffering from a cold.

encausar /enkau'sar/ v. prosecute; take legal action against.

encauzar /enkau'θar; enkau'sar/ v. channel; direct.

encefalitis /enθefa'litis; ensefa'litis/ n. f. encephalitis.

encelamiento /enθela'miento; ensela'miento/ n. m. envy, jealousy.

encelar /enθe'lar; ense'lar/ v. make jealous.

encenagar /enθena'gar; ensena'gar/ v. wallow in mud.

encendedor /enθende'ðor; ensende'ðor/ n. m. lighter.

encender /enθen'der; ensen'der/ v. light; set fire to, kindle; turn on.

encendido /enθen'diðo; ensen'diðo/ n. m. ignition.

encerado /enθe'raðo; ense'raðo/ n. m. oilcloth; tarpaulin.

encerar /enθe'rar; ense'rar/ v. wax.

encerrar /enθe'rrar; ense'rrar/ v. enclose; confine, shut in.

enchapado /entʃa'paðo/ n. m. veneer.

enchufe /en'tʃufe/ n. m. Elec. plug, socket.

encía /en'θia; en'sia/ n. f. gum.

encíclico /en'θikliko; en'sikliko/ a. 1. encyclic. —n. 2. f. encyclical.

enciclopedia /enθiklo'peðia; ensiklo'peðia/ n. f. encyclopedia.

enciclopédico /enθiklo'peðiko; ensiklo'peðiko/ a. encyclopedic.

encierro /en'θierro; en'sierro/ n. m. confinement; enclosure.

encima /en'θima; en'sima/ adv. on top. **e. de,** on. **por e. de,** above.

encina /en'θina; en'sina/ n. f. oak.

encinta /en'θinta; en'sinta/ a. pregnant.

enclavar /enkla'βar/ v. nail.

enclenque /en'klenke/ a. frail, weak, sickly.

encogerse /enko'herse/ v. shrink. **e. de hombros,** shrug the shoulders.

encogido /enko'hiðo/ a. shy, bashful, timid.

encojar /enko'har/ v. make or become lame; cripple.

encolar /enko'lar/ v. glue, paste, stick.

encolerizar /enkoleri'θar; enkoleri'sar/ v. make or become angry.

encomendar /enkomen'dar/ v. commend; recommend.

encomiar /enko'miar/ v. praise, laud, extol.

encomienda /enko'mienda/ n. f. commission, charge; (postal) package.

encomio /en'komio/ n. m. encomium, eulogy.

enconar /enko'nar/ v. irritate, annoy, anger.

encono /en'kono/ n. m. rancor, resentment.

enconoso /enko'noso/ a. rancorous, resentful.

encontrado /enkon'traðo/ a. opposite.

encontrar /enkon'trar/ v. find; meet.

encorajar /enkora'har/ v. encourage; incite.

encornar /enkor'nar/ v. gore.

encorralar /enkorra'lar/ v. corral.

encorvadura /enkorβa'ðura/ n. f. bend, curvature.

encorvar /enkor'βar/ *v.* arch, bend.

encorvarse /enkor'βarse/ *v.* stoop.

encrucijada /enkruθi'haða; enkrusi-'haða/ *n. f.* crossroads.

encuadrar /enkuað'rar/ *v.* frame.

encubierta /enku'βierta/ *a.* **1.** secret, fraudulent. —*n.* **2.** *f.* fraud.

encubrir /enkuβ'rir/ *v.* hide, conceal.

encuentro /en'kuentro/ *n. m.* encounter; match, bout.

encurtido /enkur'tiðo/ *n. m.* pickle.

endeble /en'deβle/ *a.* rail, weak, sickly.

enderezar /endere'θar; endere'sar/ *v.* straighten; redress.

endeudarse /endeu'ðarse/ *v.* get into debt.

endiablado /endia'βlaðo/ *a.* devilish.

endibia /en'diβia/ *n. f.* endive.

endiosar /endio'sar/ *v.* deify.

endorso /en'dorso/ **endoso** *n. m.* endorsement.

endosador /endosa'ðor/ **-ra** *n.* endorser.

endosar /endo'sar/ *v.* endorse.

endosatario /endosa'tario/ **-ria** *n.* endorsee.

endulzar /endul'θar; endul'sar/ *v.* sweeten; soothe.

endurar /endu'rar/ *v.* harden.

endurecer /endure'θer; endure'ser/ *v.* harden.

enemigo /ene'migo/ **-ga** *n.* foe, enemy.

enemistad /enemis'tað/ *n. f.* enmity.

éneo /'eneo/ *a.* brass.

energía /ener'hia/ *n. f.* energy.

energía nuclear /ener'hia nukle'ar/ atomic energy, nuclear energy.

energía vital /ener'hia bi'tal/ élan vital, vitality.

enérgicamente /e'nerhikamente/ *adv.* energetically.

enérgico /e'nerhiko/ *a.* forceful; energetic.

enero /e'nero/ *n. m.* January.

enervación /enerβa'θion; enerβa-'sion/ *n. f.* enervation.

enfadado /enfa'ðaðo/ *a.* angry.

enfadar /enfa'ðar/ *v.* anger, vex.

enfado /en'faðo/ *n. m.* anger, vexation.

énfasis /'enfasis/ *n. m. or f.* emphasis, stress.

enfáticamente /en'fatikamente/ *adv.* emphatically.

enfático /en'fatiko/ *a.* emphatic.

enfermar /enfer'mar/ *v.* make ill; fall ill.

enfermedad /enferme'ðað/ *n. f.* illness, sickness, disease.

enfermera /enfer'mera/ *n. f.* nurse.

enfermería /enferme'ria/ *n. f.* sanatorium.

enfermo /en'fermo/ **-ma** *a. & n.* ill, sick; sickly; patient.

enfilar /enfi'lar/ *v.* line up; put in a row.

enflaquecer /enflake'θer; enflake-'ser/ *v.* make thin; grow thin.

enfoque /en'foke/ *n. m.* focus. —**enfocar,** *v.*

enfrascamiento /enfraska'miento/ *n. m.* entanglement.

enfrascar /enfras'kar/ *v.* bottle; entangle oneself.

enfrenar /enfre'nar/ *v.* bridle, curb; restrain.

enfrentamiento /enfrenta'miento/ *n. m.* clash, confrontation.

enfrente /en'frente/ *adv.* across, opposite; in front.

enfriadera /enfria'ðera/ *n. f.* icebox; cooler.

enfriar /enf'riar/ *v.* chill, cool.

enfurecer /enfure'θer; enfure'ser/ *v.* infuriate, enrage.

engalanar /eŋgala'nar/ *v.* adorn, trim.

enganchar /eŋgan't ʃar/ *v.* hook, hitch, attach.

engañar /eŋga'ɲar/ *v.* deceive, cheat.

engaño /eŋ'gaɲo/ *n. m.* deceit; delusion.

engañoso /eŋga'ɲoso/ *a.* deceitful.

engarce /eŋ'garθe; eŋgarse/ *n. m.* connection, link.

engastar /eŋgas'tar/ *v.* to put (gems) in a setting.

engaste /eŋ'gaste/ *n. m.* setting.

engatusar /eŋgatu'sar/ *v.* deceive, trick.

engendrar /enhen'drar/ *v.* engender, beget, produce.

engendro /en'hendro/ *n. m.* fetus, embryo.

englobar /eŋglo'βar/ *v.* include.

engolfar /eŋgol'far/ *v.* be deeply absorbed.

engolosinar /eŋgolosi'nar/ *v.* allure, charm, entice.

engomar /eŋgo'mar/ *v.* gum.

engordador /eŋgor'ðaðor/ *a.* fattening.

engordar /eŋgor'ðar/ *v.* fatten; grow fat.

engranaje /eŋgra'nahe/ *n. m. Mech.* gear.

engranar /eŋgra'nar/ *v.* gear; mesh together.

engrandecer /eŋgrande'θer; eŋgrande'ser/ *v.* increase, enlarge; exalt; exaggerate.

engrasación /eŋgrasa'θion; eŋgrasa'sion/ *n. f.* lubrication.

engrasar /eŋgra'sar/ *v.* grease, lubricate.

engreído /eŋgre'iðo/ *a.* conceited.

engreimiento /eŋgrei'miento/ *n. m.* conceit.

engullidor /eŋguʎi'ðor; eŋguyi'ðor/ **-ra** *n.* devourer.

engullir /eŋgu'ʎir; eŋgu'yir/ *v.* devour.

enhebrar /ene'βrar/ *v.* thread.

enhestadura /enesta'ðura/ *n. f.* raising.

enhestar /enes'tar/ *v.* raise, erect, set up.

enhiesto /en'iesto/ *a.* erect, upright.

enhorabuena /enora'βuena/ *n. f.* congratulations.

enigma /e'nigma/ *n. m.* enigma, puzzle.

enigmáticamente /enigmatika'mente/ *adv.* enigmatically.

enigmático /enig'matiko/ *a.* enigmatic.

enjabonar /enhaβo'nar/ *v.* soap, lather.

enjalbegar /enhalβe'gar/ *v.* whitewash.

enjambradera /enhambra'ðera/ *n. f.* queen bee.

enjambre /en'hambre/ *n. m.* swarm. —**enjambrar,** *v.*

enjaular /enhau'lar/ *v.* cage, coop up.

enjebe /en'heβe/ *n. m.* lye.

enjuagar /enhua'gar/ *v.* rinse.

enjuague bucal /en'huage bu'kal/ *n. m.* mouthwash.

enjugar /enhu'gar/ *v.* wipe, dry off.

enjutez /enhu'teθ; enhu'tes/ *n. f.* dryness.

enjuto /en'huto/ *a.* dried; lean, thin.

enlace /en'laθe; en'lase/ *n. m.* attachment; involvement; connection.

enladrillador /enlaðriʎa'ðor; enlaðriya'ðor/ **-ra** *n.* bricklayer.

enlardar /enlar'ðar/ *v.* baste.

enlatado /enla'taðo/ **-da** *a.* canned (food).

enlatar /enla'tar/ *v.* can (food).

enlazar /enla'θar; enla'sar/ *v.* lace; join, connect; wed.

enlodar /enlo'ðar/ *v.* cover with mud.

enloquecer /enloke'θer; enloke'ser/ *v.* go insane; drive crazy.

enloquecimiento /enlokeθi'miento; enlokesi'miento/ *n. m.* insanity.

enlustrecer /enlustre'θer; enlustre-'ser/ *v.* polish, brighten.

enmarañar /emara'ɲar/ *v.* entangle.

enmendación /emenda'θion; emenda'sion/ *n. f.* emendation.

enmendador /emenda'ðor/ **-ra** *n.* emender, reviser.

enmendar /emen'dar/ *v.* amend, correct.

enmienda /e'mienda/ *n. f.* amendment; correction.

enmohecer /emoe'θer; emoe'ser/ *v.* rust; mold.

enmohecido /emoe'θiðo; emoe'siðo/ *a.* rusty; moldy.

enmudecer /emuðe'θer; emuðe'ser/ *v.* silence; become silent.

ennegrecer /ennegre'θer; ennegre-'ser/ *v.* blacken.

ennoblecer /ennoβle'θer; ennoβle-'ser/ *v.* ennoble.

enodio /e'noðio/ *n. m.* young deer.

enojado /eno'haðo/ *a.* angry, cross.

enojarse /eno'harse/ *v.* get angry.

enojo /e'noho/ *n. m.* anger. —**enojar,** *v.*

enojosamente /enohosa'mente/ *adv.* angrily.

enorme /e'norme/ *a.* enormous, huge.

enormemente /enorme'mente/ *adv.* enormously; hugely.

enormidad /enormi'ðað/ *n. f.* enormity; hugeness.

enraizar /enrai'θar; enrai'sar/ *v.* take root, sprout.

enramada /enra'maða/ *n. f.* bower.

enredadera /enreða'ðera/ *n. f.* climbing plant.

enredado /enre'ðaðo/ *a.* entangled, snarled.

enredar /enre'ðar/ *v.* entangle, snarl; mess up.

enredo /en'reðo/ *n. m.* tangle, entanglement.

enriquecer /enrike'θer; enrike'ser/ *v.* enrich.

enrojecerse /enrohe'θerse; enrohe-'serse/ *v.* color; blush.

enrollar /enro'ʎar; enro'yar/ *v.* wind, coil, roll up.

enromar /enro'mar/ *v.* make dull, blunt.

enronquecimiento /enronkeθi-'miento; enronkesi'miento/ *n. m.* hoarseness.

enroscar /enros'kar/ *v.* twist, curl, wind.

ensacar /ensa'kar/ *v.* put in a bag.

ensalada /ensa'laða/ *n. f.* salad.

ensaladera /ensala'ðera/ *n. f.* salad bowl.

ensalmo /en'salmo/ *n. m.* charm, enchantment.

ensalzamiento /ensalθa'miento; ensalsa'miento/ *n. m.* praise.

ensalzar /ensal'θar; ensal'sar/ *v.* praise, laud, extol.

ensamblar /ensam'blar/ *v.* join; unite; connect.

ensanchamiento /ensant ʃa'miento/ *n. m.* widening, expansion, extension.

ensanchar /ensan't ʃar/ *v.* widen, expand, extend.

ensangrentado /ensaŋgren'taðo/ *a.* bloody; bloodshot.

ensañar /ensa'ɲar/ *v.* enrage, infuriate; rage.

ensayar /ensa'yar/ *v.* try out; rehearse.

ensayista /ensa'yista/ *n. m. & f.* essayist.

ensayo /ensa'yo/ *n. m.* attempt; trial; rehearsal.

ensenada /ense'naða/ *n. f.* cove.

enseña /en'seɲa/ *n. f.* ensign, standard.

enseñador /enseɲa'ðor/ **-ra** *n.* teacher.

enseñanza /ense'ɲanθa; ense'ɲansa/ *n. f.* education; teaching.

enseñar /ense'ɲar/ *v.* teach, train; show.

enseres /en'seres/ *n. m.pl.* household goods.

ensilaje /ensi'lahe/ *n. m.* ensilage.

ensillar /ensi'ʎar; ensi'yar/ *v.* saddle.

ensordecedor /ensorðeθe'ðor; ensorðese'ðor/ *a.* deafening.

ensordecer /ensorðe'θer; ensorðe-'ser/ *v.* deafen.

ensordecimiento /ensorðeθi'miento; ensorðesi'miento/ *n. m.* deafness.

ensuciar /ensu'θiar; ensu'siar/ *v.* dirty, muddy, soil.

ensueño /en'sueɲo/ *n. m.* illusion, dream.

entablar /enta'βlar/ *v.* board up; initiate, begin.

entallador /entaʎa'ðor; entaya'ðor/ *n. m.* sculptor, carver.

entapizar /entapi'θar; entapi'sar/ *v.* upholster.

ente /'ente/ *n. m.* being.

entenada /ente'naða/ *n. f.* stepdaughter.

entenado /ente'naðo/ *n. m.* stepson.

entender /enten'der/ *v.* understand.

entendimiento /entendi'miento/ *n. m.* understanding.

entenebrecer /enteneβre'θer; enteneβre'ser/ *v.* darken.

enterado /ente'raðo/ *a.* aware, informed.

enteramente /entera'mente/ *adv.* entirely, completely.

enterar /ente'rar/ *v.* inform.

enterarse /ente'rarse/ *v.* find out.

entereza /ente'reθa; ente'resa/ *n. f.* entirety; integrity; firmness.

entero /en'tero/ *a.* entire, whole, total.

enterramiento /enterra'miento/ *n. m.* burial, interment.

enterrar /ente'rrar/ *v.* bury.

entestado /entes'taðo/ *a.* stubborn, willful.

entibiar /enti'βiar/ *v.* to cool; moderate.

entidad /enti'ðað/ *n. f.* entity.

entierro /en'tierro/ *n. m.* interment, burial.

entonación /entona'θion; entona'sion/ *n. f.* intonation.

entonamiento /entona'miento/ *n. m.* intonation.

entonar /ento'nar/ *v.* chant; harmonize.

entonces /en'tonθes; entonses/ *adv.* then.

entono /en'tono/ *n. m.* intonation; arrogance; affectation.

entortadura /entorta'ðura/ *n. f.* crookedness.

entortar /entor'tar/ *v.* make crooked; bend.

entrada /en'traða/ *n. f.* entrance; admission, admittance.

entrambos /en'trambos/ *a. & pron.* both.

entrante /en'trante/ *a.* coming, next.

entrañable /entra'ɲaβle/ *a.* affectionate.

entrañas /en'traɲas/ *n. f.pl.* entrails, bowels; womb.

entrar /en'trar/ *v.* enter, go in, come in.

entre /'entre/ *prep.* among; between.

entreabierto /entrea'βierto/ *a.* ajar, half-open.

entreabrir /entrea'βrir/ *v.* set ajar.

entreacto /entre'akto/ *n. m.* intermission.

entrecejo /entre'θeho; entre'seho/ *n. m.* frown; space between the eyebrows.

entrecuesto /entre'kuesto/ *n. m.* spine, backbone.

entredicho /entre'ðit ʃo/ *n. m.* prohibition.

entrega /en'trega/ *n. f.* delivery.

entregar /entre'gar/ *v.* deliver, hand; hand over.

entrelazar /entrela'θar; entrela'sar/ *v.* intertwine, entwine.

entremedias /entre'meðias/ *adv.* meanwhile; halfway.

entremés /entre'mes/ *n. m.* side dish.

entremeterse /entreme'terse/ *v.* meddle, intrude.

entremetido /entreme'tiðo/ **-da** *n.* meddler.

entrenador /entrena'ðor/ -ra n. coach. —**entrenar**, v.
entrenarse /entre'narse/ v. train.
entrepalado /entrepa'laðo/ a. variegated; spotted.
entrerenglonar /entrerenglo'nar/ v. interline.
entresacar /entresa'kar/ v. select, choose; sift.
entresuelo /entre'suelo/ n. m. mezzanine.
entretanto /entre'tanto/ adv. meanwhile.
entretenedor /entretene'ðor/ -ra n. entertainer.
entretener /entrete'ner/ v. entertain, amuse; delay.
entretenimiento /entreteni'miento/ n. m. entertainment, amusement.
entrevista /entre'βista/ n. f. interview. —**entrevistar**, v.
entrevistador /entreβista'ðor/ -ra n. interviewer.
entristecedor /entristeθe'ðor/ entriste'ðor/ a. sad.
entristecer /entriste'θer/ entriste'ser/ v. sadden.
entronar /entro'nar/ v. enthrone.
entroncar /entron'kar/ v. be related or connected.
entronización /entroniθa'θion; entronisa'sion/ n. f. enthronement.
entronque /entron'ke/ n. m. relationship; connection.
entumecer /entume'θer/ entume'ser/ v. become or be numb; swell.
entusiasmado /entusias'maðo/ a. enthusiastic.
entusiasmo /entu'siasmo/ n. m. enthusiasm.
entusiasta /entu'siasta/ n. m. & f. enthusiast.
entusiástico /entu'siastiko/ a. enthusiastic.
enumeración /enumera'θion; enumera'sion/ n. f. enumeration.
enumerar /enume'rar/ v. enumerate.
enunciación /enunθia'θion; enunsia'sion/ n. f. enunciation; statement.
enunciar /enun'θiar; enun'siar/ v. enunciate.
envainar /embai'nar/ v. sheathe.
envalentonar /embalento'nar/ v. encourage, embolden.
envanecimiento /embaneθimiento; embanesi'miento/ n. m. conceit, vanity.
envasar /emba'sar/ v. put in a container; bottle.
envase /em'base/ n. m. container.
envejecer /embehe'θer; embehe'ser/ v. age, grow old.
envejecimiento /embeheθi'miento; embehesi'miento/ n. m. oldness, aging.
envenenar /embene'nar/ v. poison.
envés /em'bes/ n. m. wrong side; back.
envestir /embes'tir/ v. put in office; invest.
enviada /em'biaða/ n. f. shipment.
enviado /em'biaðo/ -da n. envoy.
enviar /em'biar/ v. send; ship.
envidia /em'biðia/ n. f. envy. —**envidiar**, v.
envidiable /embi'ðiaβle/ a. enviable.
envidioso /embi'ðioso/ a. envious.
envilecer /embile'θer; embile'ser/ v. vilify, debase, disgrace.
envío /em'bio/ n. m. shipment.
envión /em'bion/ n. m. shove.
envoltura /embol'tura/ n. f. wrapping.
envolver /embol'βer/ v. wrap, wrap up.
enyesar /enye'sar/ v. plaster.
enyugar /enyu'gar/ v. yoke.
eperlano /eper'lano/ n. m. smelt (fish).
épica /'epika/ n. f. epic.
épico /'epiko/ a. epic.
epicureísmo /epikure'ismo/ n. m. epicureanism.

epicúreo /epi'kureo/ n. & a. epicurean.
epidemia /epi'ðemia/ n. f. epidemic.
epidémico /epi'ðemiko/ a. epidemic.
epidermis /epi'ðermis/ n. f. epidermis.
epigrama /epi'grama/ n. m. epigram.
epigramático /epigra'matiko/ -ca a. epigrammatic.
epilepsia /epi'lepsia/ n. f. epilepsy.
epiléptico /epi'leptiko/ -ca n. & a. epileptic.
epílogo /e'pilogo/ n. m. epilogue.
episcopado /episko'paðo/ n. m. bishopric; episcopate.
episcopal /episko'pal/ a. episcopal.
episódico /epi'soðiko/ a. episodic.
episodio /epi'soðio/ n. m. episode.
epístola /e'pistola/ n. f. epistle, letter.
epitafio /epi'tafio/ n. m. epitaph.
epitomadamente /epitomaða'mente/ adv. concisely.
epitomar /epito'mar/ v. epitomize, summarize.
época /'epoka/ n. f. epoch, age.
epopeya /epo'peya/ n. f. epic.
epsomita /epso'mita/ n. f. Epsom salts.
equidad /eki'ðað/ n. f. equity.
equilibrado /ekili'βraðo/ a. stable.
equilibrio /eki'liβrio/ n. m. equilibrium, balance.
equinoccio /eki'nokθio; ekinoksio/ n. m. equinox.
equipaje /eki'pahe/ n. m. luggage, baggage. **e. de mano,** luggage.
equipar /eki'par/ v. equip.
equiparar /ekipa'rar/ v. compare.
equipo /e'kipo/ n. m. equipment; team.
equitación /ekita'θion; ekita'sion/ f. horsemanship; horseback riding, riding.
equitativo /ekita'tiβo/ a. fair, equitable.
equivalencia /ekiβa'lenθia; ekiβa'lensia/ n. f. equivalence.
equivalente /ekiβa'lente/ a. equivalent.
equivaler /ekiβa'ler/ v. equal, be equivalent.
equivocación /ekiβoka'θion; ekiβoka'sion/ n. f. mistake.
equivocado /ekiβo'kaðo/ a. wrong, mistaken.
equivocarse /ekiβo'karse/ v. make a mistake, be wrong.
equívoco /e'kiβoko/ a. equivocal, ambiguous.
era /'era/ n. f. era, age.
erario /e'rario/ n. m. exchequer.
erección /erek'θion; erek'sion/ n. f. erection; elevation.
eremita /ere'mita/ n. m. hermit.
erguir /er'gir/ v. erect; straighten up.
erigir /eri'hir/ v. erect, build.
erisipela /erisi'pela/ n. f. erysipelas.
erizado /eri'θaðo; eri'saðo/ a. bristly.
erizarse /eri'θarse; eri'sarse/ v. bristle.
erizo /e'riθo; e'riso/ n. m. hedgehog; sea urchin.
ermita /er'mita/ n. f. hermitage.
ermitaño /ermi'taɲo/ n. m. hermit.
erogación /eroga'θion; eroga'sion/ n. f. expenditure. —**erogar**, v.
erosión /ero'sion/ n. f. erosion.
erótico /e'rotiko/ a. erotic.
erradicación /erraðika'θion; erraðika'sion/ n. f. eradication.
erradicar /erraði'kar/ v. eradicate.
errado /e'rraðo/ a. mistaken, erroneous.
errante /e'rrante/ a. wandering, roving.
errar /e'rrar/ v. be mistaken.
errata /e'rrata/ n. f. erratum.
errático /e'rratiko/ a. erratic.
erróneamente /erronea'mente/ adv. erroneously.
erróneo /e'rroneo/ a. erroneous.
error /e'rror/ n. m. error, mistake.

eructo /e'rukto/ n. m. belch. —**eructar**, v.
erudición /eruði'θion; eruði'sion/ n. f. scholarship, learning.
eruditamente /eruðita'mente/ adv. learnedly.
erudito /eru'ðito/ -ta n. **1.** scholar. —a. **2.** scholarly.
erupción /erup'θion; erup'sion/ n. f. eruption; rash.
eruptivo /erup'tiβo/ a. eruptive.
esbozo /es'βoθo; es'βoso/ n. m. outline, sketch. —**esbozar**, v.
escabechar /eskaβe'tʃar/ v. pickle; preserve.
escabeche /eska'βetʃe/ n. m. brine.
escabel /eska'βel/ n. m. small stool or bench.
escabroso /eska'βroso/ a. rough, irregular; craggy; rude.
escabullirse /eskaβu'ʎirse; eskaβu'yirse/ v. steal away, sneak away.
escala /es'kala/ n. f. scale; ladder. **hacer e.,** to make a stop.
escalada /eska'laða/ n. f. escalation.
escalador /eskala'ðor/ -ra n. climber.
escalar /eska'lar/ v. climb; scale.
escaldar /eskal'dar/ v. scald.
escalera /eska'lera/ n. f. stairs, staircase; ladder.
escalfado /eskal'faðo/ a. poached.
escalofriado /eskalo'friaðo/ a. chilled.
escalofrío /eskalo'frio/ n. m. chill.
escalón /eska'lon/ n. m. step.
escalonar /eskalo'nar/ v. space out, stagger.
escaloña /eska'loɲa/ n. f. scallion.
escalpar /eskal'par/ v. scalp.
escalpelo /eskal'pelo/ n. m. scalpel.
escama /es'kama/ n. f. (fish) scale. —**escamar**, v.
escamondar /eskamon'dar/ v. trim, cut; prune.
escampada /eskam'paða/ n. f. break in the rain, clear spell.
escandalizar /eskandali'θar; eskandali'sar/ v. shock, scandalize.
escandalizativo /eskandaliθa'tiβo; eskandalisa'tiβo/ a. scandalous.
escándalo /es'kandalo/ n. m. scandal.
escandaloso /eskanda'loso/ a. scandalous; disgraceful.
escandinavo /eskandi'naβo/ -va n. & a. Scandinavian.
escandir /eskan'dir/ v. scan.
escanear /eskane'ar/ v. scan (on a computer).
escáner /es'kaner/ v. scanner (of a computer).
escanilla /eska'niʎa; eska'niya/ n. f. cradle.
escañuelo /eska'ɲuelo/ n. m. small footstool.
escapada /eska'paða/ n. f. escapade.
escapar /eska'par/ v. escape.
escaparate /eskapa'rate/ n. m. shop window, store window.
escape /es'kape/ n. m. escape; Auto. exhaust.
escápula /es'kapula/ n. f. scapula.
escarabajo /eskara'βaho/ n. m. black beetle; scarab.
escaramucear /eskaramuθe'ar; eskaramuse'ar/ v. skirmish; dispute.
escarbadientes /eskarβa'ðientes/ n. m. toothpick.
escarbar /eskar'βar/ v. scratch; poke.
escarcha /es'kartʃa/ n. f. frost.
escardar /eskar'ðar/ v. weed.
escarlata /eskar'lata/ n. f. scarlet.
escarlatina /eskarla'tina/ n. f. scarlet fever.
escarmentar /eskarmen'tar/ v. correct severely.
escarnecedor /eskarneθe'ðor; eskarneseðor/ -ra n. scoffer; mocker.
escarnecer /eskarne'θer; eskarne'ser/ v. mock, make fun of.
escarola /eska'rola/ n. f. endive.
escarpa /es'karpa/ n. f. escarpment.

escarpado /eskar'paðo/ a. **1.** steep. —n. **2.** m. bluff.
escasamente /eskasa'mente/ adv. scarcely; sparingly; barely.
escasear /eskase'ar/ v. be scarce.
escasez /eska'seθ; eska'ses/ n. f. shortage, scarcity.
escaso /es'kaso/ a. scant; scarce.
escatimar /eskati'mar/ v. be stingy; skimp; save.
escatimoso /eskati'moso/ a. malicious; sly, cunning.
escena /es'θena; es'sena/ n. f. scene; stage.
escenario /esθe'nario; esse'nario/ n. m. stage (of theater); scenario.
escénico /es'θeniko; es'seniko/ a. scenic.
escépticamente /esθeptika'mente; esseptika'mente/ adv. skeptically.
escepticismo /esθepti'θismo; essepti'sismo/ n. m. skepticism.
escéptico /es'θeptiko; es'septiko/ -ca a. & n. skeptic; skeptical.
esclarecer /esklare'θer; esklare'ser/ v. clear up.
esclavitud /esklaβi'tuð/ n. f. slavery; bondage.
esclavizar /esklaβi'θar; esklaβi'sar/ v. enslave.
esclavo /es'klaβo/ -va n. slave.
escoba /es'koβa/ n. f. broom.
escocés /esko'θes; esko'ses/ -esa a. & n. Scotch, Scottish; Scot.
Escocia /es'koθia; eskosia/ n. f. Scotland.
escofinar /eskofi'nar/ v. rasp.
escoger /esko'her/ v. choose, select.
escogido /esko'hiðo/ a. chosen, selected.
escogimiento /eskohi'miento/ n. m. choice.
escolar /esko'lar/ a. **1.** scholastic, (of) school. —n. **2.** m.& f. student.
escolasticismo /eskolasti'θismo; eskolasti'sismo/ n. m. scholasticism.
escollo /es'koʎo; es'koyo/ n. m. reef.
escolta /es'kolta/ n. f. escort. —**escoltar**, v.
escombro /es'kombro/ n. m. mackerel.
escombros /es'kombros/ n. m.pl. debris, rubbish.
esconce /es'konθe; es'konse/ n. m. corner.
escondedero /eskonde'ðero/ n. m. hiding place.
esconder /eskon'der/ v. hide, conceal.
escondidamente /eskondiða'mente/ adv. secretly.
escondimiento /eskondi'miento/ n. m. concealment.
escondrijo /eskon'driho/ n. m. hiding place.
escopeta /esko'peta/ n. f. shotgun.
escopetazo /eskope'taθo; eskope'taso/ n. m. gunshot.
escoplo /es'koplo/ n. m. chisel.
escorbuto /eskor'βuto/ n. m. scurvy.
escorpena /eskor'pena/ n. f. grouper.
escorpión /eskor'pion/ n. m. scorpion.
escorzón /eskor'θon; eskor'son/ n. m. toad.
escotado /esko'taðo/ a. low-cut, with a low neckline.
escote /es'kote/ n. m. low neckline.
escribiente /eskri'βiente/ n. m. & f. clerk.
escribir /eskri'βir/ v. write.
escritor /eskri'tor/ -ra n. writer, author.
escritorio /eskri'torio/ n. m. desk.
escritura /eskri'tura/ n. f. writing, handwriting.
escrófula /es'krofula/ n. f. scrofula.
escroto /es'kroto/ n. m. scrotum.
escrúpulo /es'krupulo/ n. m. scruple.
escrupuloso /eskrupu'loso/ a. scrupulous.
escrutinio /eskru'tinio/ n. m. scrutiny; examination.

escuadra /es'kuaðra/ *n. f.* squad; fleet.

escuadrón /eskuað'ron/ *n. m.* squadron.

escualidez /eskuali'ðeθ; eskuali'ðes/ *n. f.* squalor; poverty; emaciation.

escuálido /es'kualiðo/ *a.* squalid.

escualo /es'kualo/ *n. m.* shark.

escuchar /esku't∫ar/ *v.* listen; listen to.

escudero /esku'ðero/ *n. m.* squire.

escudo /es'kuðo/ *n. m.* shield; protection; coin of certain countries.

escuela /es'kuela/ *n. f.* school.

escuela nocturna /es'kuela nok'turna/ night school.

escuela por correspondencia /es'kuela por korrespon'denθia; es'kuela por korrespon'densia/ correspondence school.

escuerzo /es'kuerθo; es'kuerso/ *n. m.* toad.

esculpir /eskul'pir/ *v.* carve, sculpture.

escultor /eskul'tor/ **-ra** *n.* sculptor.

escultura /eskul'tura/ *n. f.* sculpture.

escupidera /eskupi'ðera/ *n. f.* cuspidor.

escupir /esku'pir/ *v.* spit.

escurridero /eskurri'ðero/ *n. m.* drain board.

escurridor /eskurri'ðor/ *n. m.* colander, strainer.

escurrir /esku'rrir/ *v.* drain off; wring out.

escurrirse /esku'rrirse/ *v.* slip; sneak away.

ese /'ese/ **esa** *dem. a.* that.

ése, ésa *dem. pron.* that (one).

esencia /e'senθia; e'sensia/ *n. f.* essence; perfume.

esencial /esen'θial; esen'sial/ *a.* essential.

esencialmente /esenθial'mente; esensial'mente/ *adv.* essentially.

esfera /es'fera/ *n. f.* sphere.

esfinge /es'finhe/ *n. f.* sphinx.

esforzar /esfor'θar; esfor'sar/ *v.* strengthen.

esforzarse /esfor'θarse; esfor'sarse/ *v.* strive, exert oneself.

esfuerzo /es'fuerθo; es'fuerso/ *n. m.* effort, attempt; vigor.

esgrima /es'grima/ *n. f.* fencing.

esguince /es'ginθe; es'ginse/ *n. m.* sprain.

eslabón /esla'βon/ *n. m.* link (of a chain).

eslabonar /eslaβo'nar/ *v.* link, join, connect.

eslavo /es'laβo/ **-va** *a. & n.* Slavic; Slav.

esmalte /es'malte/ *n. m.* enamel, polish. —**esmaltar,** *v.*

esmerado /esme'raðo/ *a.* careful, thorough.

esmeralda /esme'ralda/ *n. f.* emerald.

esmerarse /esme'rarse/ *v.* take pains, do one's best.

esmeril /es'meril/ *n. m.* emery.

eso /'eso/ *dem. pron.* that.

esófago /e'sofago/ *n. m.* esophagus.

esotérico /eso'teriko/ *a.* esoteric.

espacial /espa'θial; espa'sial/ *a.* spatial.

espacio /es'paθio; es'pasio/ *n. m.* space. —**espaciar,** *v.*

espaciosidad /espaθiosi'ðað; espasiosi'ðað/ *n. f.* spaciousness.

espacioso /espa'θioso; espa'sioso/ *a.* spacious.

espada /es'paða/ *n. f.* sword; spade (in cards).

espadarte /espa'ðarte/ *n. m.* swordfish.

espaguetis /espa'getis/ *n. m.pl.* spaghetti.

espalda /es'palda/ *n. f.* back.

espaldera /espal'dera/ *n. f.* espalier.

espantar /espan'tar/ *v.* frighten, scare; scare away.

espanto /es'panto/ *n. m.* fright.

espantoso /espan'toso/ *a.* frightening, frightful.

España /es'paɲa/ *n. f.* Spain.

español /espa'ɲol/ **-ola** *a. & n.* Spanish; Spaniard.

esparcir /espar'θir; espar'sir/ *v.* scatter, disperse.

espárrago /es'parrago/ *n. m.* asparagus.

espartano /espar'tano/ **-na** *n. & a.* Spartan.

espasmo /es'pasmo/ *n. m.* spasm.

espasmódico /espas'moðiko/ *a.* spasmodic.

espata /es'pata/ *n. f.* spathe.

espato /es'pato/ *n. m.* spar (mineral).

espátula /es'patula/ *n. f.* spatula.

especia /es'peθia; es'pesia/ *n. f.* spice. —**especiar,** *v.*

especial /espe'θial; espe'sial/ *a.* special, especial.

especialidad /espeθiali'ðað; espesiali'ðað/ *n. f.* specialty.

especialista /espeθia'lista; espesia'lista/ *n. m. & f.* specialist.

especialización /espeθialiθa'θion; espesialisa'sion/ *n. f.* specialization.

especialmente /espeθial'mente; espesial'mente/ *adv.* especially.

especie /es'peθie; es'pesie/ *n. f.* species; sort.

especiería /espeθie'ria; espesie'ria/ *n. f.* grocery store; spice store.

especiero /espe'θiero; espe'siero/ **-ra** *n.* spice dealer; spice box.

especificar /espeθifi'kar; espesifi'kar/ *v.* specify.

específico /espe'θifiko; espe'sifiko/ *a.* specific.

espécimen /es'peθimen; es'pesimen/ *n. m.* specimen.

especioso /espe'θioso; espe'sioso/ *a.* neat; polished; specious.

espectacular /espektaku'lar/ *a.* spectacular.

espectáculo /espek'takulo/ *n. m.* spectacle, show.

espectador /espekta'ðor/ **-ra** *n.* spectator.

espectro /es'pektro/ *n. m.* specter, ghost.

especulación /espekula'θion; espekula'sion/ *n. f.* speculation.

especulador /espekula'ðor/ **-ra** *n.* speculator.

especular /espeku'lar/ *v.* speculate.

especulativo /espekula'tiβo/ *a.* speculative.

espejo /es'peho/ *n. m.* mirror.

espelunca /espe'lunka/ *n. f.* dark cave, cavern.

espera /es'pera/ *n. f.* wait.

esperanza /espe'ranθa; espe'ransa/ *n. f.* hope, expectation.

esperar /espe'rar/ *v.* hope; expect; wait, wait for, watch for.

espesar /espe'sar/ *v.* thicken.

espeso /es'peso/ *a.* thick, dense, bushy.

espesor /espe'sor/ *n. m.* thickness, density.

espía /es'pia/ *n. m. & f.* spy. —**espiar,** *v.*

espigón /espi'gon/ *n. m.* bee sting.

espina /es'pina/ *n. f.* thorn.

espinaca /espi'naka/ *n. f.* spinach.

espina dorsal /es'pina dor'sal/ spine.

espinal /espi'nal/ *a.* spinal.

espinazo /espi'naθo; espi'naso/ *n. m.* backbone.

espineta /espi'neta/ *n. f.* spinet.

espino /es'pino/ *n. m.* briar.

espinoso /espi'noso/ *a.* spiny, thorny.

espión /es'pion/ *n. m.* spy.

espionaje /espio'nahe/ *n. m.* espionage.

espiral /espi'ral/ *a. & m.* spiral.

espirar /espi'rar/ *v.* expire; breathe, exhale.

espíritu /es'piritu/ *n. m.* spirit.

espiritual /espiri'tual/ *a.* spiritual.

espiritualidad /espirituali'ðað/ *n. f.* spirituality.

espiritualmente /espiritual'mente/ *adv.* spiritually.

espita /es'pita/ *n. f.* faucet, spigot.

espléndido /es'plendiðo/ *a.* splendid.

esplendor /esplen'dor/ *n. m.* splendor.

espolear /espole'ar/ *v.* incite, urge on.

espoleta /espo'leta/ *n. f.* wishbone.

esponja /es'ponha/ *n. f.* sponge.

esponjoso /espon'hoso/ *a.* spongy.

esponsales /espon'sales/ *n. m.pl.* engagement, betrothal.

esponsalicio /esponsa'liθio; esponsa'lisio/ *a.* nuptial.

espontáneamente /espontanea'mente/ *adv.* spontaneously.

espontaneidad /espontanei'ðað/ *n. f.* spontaneity.

espontáneo /espon'taneo/ *a.* spontaneous.

espora /es'pora/ *n. f.* spore.

esporádico /espo'raðiko/ *a.* sporadic.

esposa /es'posa/ *n. f.* wife.

esposar /espo'sar/ *v.* shackle; handcuff.

esposo /es'poso/ *n. m.* husband.

espuela /es'puela/ *n. f.* spur. —**espolear,** *v.*

espuma /es'puma/ *n. f.* foam. —**espumar,** *v.*

espumadera /espuma'ðera/ *n. f.* whisk; skimmer.

espumajear /espumahe'ar/ *v.* foam at the mouth.

espumajo /espu'maho/ *n. m.* foam.

espumar /espu'mar/ *v.* foam, froth; skim.

espumoso /espu'moso/ *a.* foamy; sparkling (wine).

espurio /es'purio/ *a.* spurious.

esputar /espu'tar/ *v.* spit, expectorate.

esputo /es'puto/ *n. m.* spit, saliva.

esquela /es'kela/ *n. f.* note.

esqueleto /eske'leto/ *n. m.* skeleton.

esquema /es'kema/ *n. m.* scheme; diagram.

esquero /es'kero/ *n. m.* leather sack, leather pouch.

esquiar /es'kiar/ *v.* ski.

esquiciar /eski'θiar; eski'siar/ *v.* outline, sketch.

esquicio /es'kiθio; es'kisio/ *n. m.* rough sketch, rough outline.

esquife /es'kife/ *n. m.* skiff.

esquilar /eski'lar/ *v.* fleece, shear.

esquilmo /es'kilmo/ *n. m.* harvest.

esquimal /eski'mal/ *n. & a.* Eskimo.

esquina /es'kina/ *n. f.* corner.

esquivar /eski'βar/ *v.* evade, shun.

estabilidad /estaβili'ðað/ *n. f.* stability.

estable /es'taβle/ *a.* stable.

establecedor /estaβleθe'ðor; estaβlese'ðor/ *n. m.* founder, originator.

establecer /estaβle'θer; estaβle'ser/ *v.* establish, set up.

establecimiento /estaβleθi'miento; estaβlesi'miento/ *n. m.* establishment.

establero /estaβ'lero/ *n. m.* groom.

establo /es'taβlo/ *n. m.* stable.

estaca /es'taka/ *n. f.* stake.

estación /esta'θion; esta'sion/ *n. f.* station; season.

estacionamiento /estaθiona'miento; estasiona'miento/ *n. m.* parking; parking lot; parking space.

estacionar /estaθio'nar; estasio'nar/ *v.* station; park (a vehicle).

estacionario /estaθio'nario; estasio'nario/ *a.* stationary.

estación de servicio /esta'θion de ser'βiθio; esta'sion de ser'βisio/ service station.

estación de trabajo /esta'θion de tra'βaho; esta'sion de tra'βaho/ work station.

estadista /esta'ðista/ *n. m. & f.* statesman.

estadística /esta'ðistika/ *n. f.* statistics.

estadístico /esta'ðistiko/ *a.* statistical.

estado /es'taðo/ *n. m.* state; condition; status.

Estados Unidos /es'taðos u'niðos/ *n. m.pl.* United States.

estafa /es'tafa/ *n. f.* swindle, fake. —**estafar,** *v.*

estafeta /esta'feta/ *n. f.* post office.

estagnación /estagna'θion; estagna'sion/ *n. f.* stagnation.

estallar /esta'ʎar; esta'yar/ *v.* explode; burst; break out.

estallido /esta'ʎiðo; esta'yiðo/ *n. m.* crash; crack; explosion.

estampa /es'tampa/ *n. f.* stamp. —**estampar,** *v.*

estampado /estam'paðo/ *n. m.* printed cotton cloth.

estampida /estam'piða/ *n. f.* stampede.

estampilla /estam'piʎa; estam'piya/ *n. f.* (postage) stamp.

estancado /estan'kaðo/ *a.* stagnant.

estancar /estan'kar/ *v.* stanch, stop, check.

estancia /es'tanθia; es'tansia/ *n. f.* stay; (S.A.) small farm.

estanciero /estan'θiero; estan'siero/ **-ra** *n.* small farmer.

estandarte /estan'darte/ *n. m.* banner.

estanque /es'tanke/ *n. m.* pool; pond.

estante /es'tante/ *n. m.* shelf.

estaño /es'taɲo/ *n. m.* tin. —**estañar,** *v.*

estar /es'tar/ *v.* be; stand; look.

estática /es'tatika/ *n. f.* static.

estático /es'tatiko/ *a.* static.

estatua /es'tatua/ *n. f.* statue.

estatura /esta'tura/ *n. f.* stature.

estatuto /esta'tuto/ *n. m.* statute, law.

este /'este/ *n. m.* east.

este, esta *dem. a.* this.

éste, ésta *dem. pron.* this (one); the latter.

estelar /este'lar/ *a.* stellar.

estenografía /estenogra'fia/ *n. f.* stenography.

estenógrafo /este'nografo/ **-fa** *n.* stenographer.

estera /es'tera/ *n. f.* mat, matting.

estereofónico /estereo'foniko/ *a.* stereophonic.

estéril /es'teril/ *a.* barren; sterile.

esterilidad /esterili'ðað/ *n. f.* sterility, fruitlessness.

esterilizar /esterili'θar; esterili'sar/ *v.* sterilize.

esternón /ester'non/ *n. m.* breastbone.

estética /es'tetika/ *n. f.* esthetics.

estético /es'tetiko/ *a.* esthetic.

estetoscopio /esteto'skopio/ *n. m.* stethoscope.

estibador /estiβa'ðor/ *n. m.* stevedore.

estiércol /es'tierkol/ *n. m.* dung, manure.

estigma /es'tigma/ *n. m.* stigma; disgrace.

estilarse /esti'larse/ *v.* be in fashion, be in vogue.

estilo /es'tilo/ *n. m.* style; sort.

estilográfica /estilo'grafika/ *n. f.* (fountain) pen.

estima /es'tima/ *n. f.* esteem.

estimable /esti'maβle/ *a.* estimable, worthy.

estimación /estima'θion; estima'sion/ *n. f.* estimation.

estimar /esti'mar/ *v.* esteem; value; estimate; gauge.

estimular /estimu'lar/ *v.* stimulate.

estímulo /es'timulo/ *n. m.* stimulus.

estío /es'tio/ *n. m.* summer.

estipulación /estipula'θion; estipula'sion/ *n. f.* stipulation.

estipular /estipu'lar/ *v.* stipulate.

estirar /esti'rar/ *v.* stretch.

estirpe /es'tirpe/ *n. m.* stock, lineage.

esto /'esto/ *dem. pron.* this.

estocada /esto'kaða/ *n. f.* stab, thrust.

estofado /esto'faðo/ *n. m.* stew. —**estofar**, *v.*

estoicismo /estoi'θismo; estoi'sismo/ *n. m.* stoicism.

estoico /es'toiko/ *n. & a.* stoic.

estómago /es'tomago/ *n. m.* stomach.

estorbar /estor'βar/ *v.* bother, hinder, interfere with.

estorbo /es'torβo/ *n. m.* hindrance.

estornudo /estor'nuðo/ *n. m.* sneeze. —**estornudar**, *v.*

estrabismo /estra'βismo/ *n. m.* strabismus.

estrago /es'trago/ *n. m.* devastation, havoc.

estrangulación /estraŋgula'θion; estraŋgula'sion/ *n. f.* strangulation.

estrangular /estraŋgu'lar/ *v.* strangle.

estraperlista /estraper'lista/ *n. m. & f.* black marketeer.

estraperlo /estra'perlo/ *n. m.* black market.

estratagema /estrata'hema/ *n. f.* stratagem.

estrategia /estra'tehia/ *n. f.* strategy.

estratégico /estra'tehiko/ *a.* strategic.

estrato /es'trato/ *n. m.* stratum.

estrechar /estre'tʃar/ *v.* tighten; narrow.

estrechez /estre'tʃeθ; estre'tʃes/ *n. f.* narrowness; tightness.

estrecho /es'tretʃo/ *a.* **1.** narrow, tight. —*n.* **2.** strait.

estregar /estre'gar/ *v.* scour, scrub.

estrella /es'treʎa; es'treya/ *n. f.* star.

estrellamar /estreʎa'mar; estreya'mar/ *n. f.* starfish.

estrellar /estre'ʎar; estre'yar/ *v.* shatter, smash.

estremecimiento /estremeθi'miento; estremesi'miento/ *n. m.* shudder. —**estremecerse**, *v.*

estrenar /estre'nar/ *v.* wear for the first time; open (a play).

estreno /es'treno/ *n. m.* debut, first performance.

estrenuo /es'trenuo/ *a.* strenuous.

estreñido /estre'ɲiðo/ **-da** *a.* constipated.

estreñimiento /estreɲi'miento/ *n. m.* constipation.

estreñir /estre'ɲir/ *v.* constipate.

estrépito /es'trepito/ *n. m.* din.

estreptococo /estrepto'koko/ *n. m.* streptococcus.

estría /es'tria/ *n. f.* groove.

estribillo /estri'βiʎo; estri'βiyo/ *n. m.* refrain.

estribo /es'triβo/ *n. m.* stirrup.

estribor /estri'βor/ *n. m.* starboard.

estrictamente /estrikta'mente/ *adv.* strictly.

estrictez /estrik'teθ; estrik'tes/ *n. f.* strictness.

estricto /es'trikto/ *a.* strict.

estrofa /es'trofa/ *n. f.* stanza.

estropajo /estro'paho/ *n. m.* mop.

estropear /estrope'ar/ *v.* cripple, damage, spoil.

estructura /estruk'tura/ *n. f.* structure.

estructural /estruktu'ral/ *a.* structural.

estruendo /es'truendo/ *n. m.* din, clatter.

estuario /es'tuario/ *n. m.* estuary.

estuco /es'tuko/ *n. m.* stucco.

estudiante /estu'ðiante/ **-ta** *n.* student.

estudiar /estu'ðiar/ *v.* study.

estudio /es'tuðio/ *n. m.* study; studio.

estudioso /estu'ðioso/ *a.* studious.

estufa /es'tufa/ *n. f.* stove.

estufa de aire /es'tufa de 'aire/ fan heater.

estulto /es'tulto/ *a.* foolish.

estupendo /estu'pendo/ *a.* wonderful, grand, fine.

estupidez /estupi'ðeθ; estupi'ðes/ *n. f.* stupidity.

estúpido /es'tupiðo/ *a.* stupid.

estupor /estu'por/ *n. m.* stupor.

estuque /es'tuke/ *n. m.* stucco.

esturión /estu'rion/ *n. m.* sturgeon.

etapa /e'tapa/ *n. f.* stage.

éter /'eter/ *n. m.* ether.

etéreo /e'tereo/ *a.* ethereal.

eternal /eter'nal/ *a.* eternal.

eternidad /eterni'ðað/ *n. f.* eternity.

eterno /e'terno/ *a.* eternal.

ética /'etika/ *n. f.* ethics.

ético /'etiko/ *a.* ethical.

etimología /etimolo'hia/ *n. f.* etymology.

etiqueta /eti'keta/ *n. f.* etiquette; tag, label.

étnico /'etniko/ *a.* ethnic.

etrusco /e'trusko/ **-ca** *n. & a.* Etruscan.

eucaristía /eukaris'tia/ *n. f.* Eucharist.

eufemismo /eufe'mismo/ *n. m.* euphemism.

eufonía /eufo'nia/ *n. f.* euphony.

Europa /eu'ropa/ *n. f.* Europe.

europeo /euro'peo/ **-pea** *a. & n.* European.

eutanasia /euta'nasia/ *n. f.* euthanasia.

evacuación /eβakua'θion; eβakua'sion/ *n. f.* evacuation.

evacuar /eβa'kuar/ *v.* evacuate.

evadir /eβa'ðir/ *v.* evade.

evangélico /eβan'heliko/ *a.* evangelical.

evangelio /eβan'helio/ *n. m.* gospel.

evangelista /eβanhe'lista/ *n. m.* evangelist.

evaporación /eβapora'θion; eβapora'sion/ *n. f.* evaporation.

evaporarse /eβapo'rarse/ *v.* evaporate.

evasión /eβa'sion, eβa'siβa/ *n. f.* evasion.

evasivamente /eβasiβa'mente/ *adv.* evasively.

evasivo /eβa'siβo/ *a.* evasive.

evento /e'βento/ *n. m.* event, occurrence.

eventual /eβen'tual/ *a.* eventual.

eventualidad /eβentuali'ðað/ *n. f.* eventuality.

evicción /eβik'θion; eβik'sion/ *n. f.* eviction.

evidencia /eβi'ðenθia; eβiðensia/ *n. f.* evidence.

evidenciar /eβiðen'θiar; eβiðen'siar/ *v.* prove, show.

evidente /eβi'ðente/ *a.* evident.

evitación /eβita'θion; eβita'sion/ *n. f.* avoidance.

evitar /eβi'tar/ *v.* avoid, shun.

evocación /eβoka'θion; eβoka'sion/ *n. f.* evocation.

evocar /eβo'kar/ *v.* evoke.

evolución /eβolu'θion; eβolu'sion/ *n. f.* evolution.

exacerbar /eksaθer'βar; eksaser'βar/ *v.* irritate deeply; exacerbate.

exactamente /eksakta'mente/ *adv.* exactly.

exactitud /eksakti'tuð/ *n. f.* precision, accuracy.

exacto /ek'sakto/ *a.* exact, accurate.

exageración /eksahera'θion; eksahera'sion/ *n. f.* exaggeration.

exagerar /eksahe'rar/ *v.* exaggerate.

exaltación /eksalta'θion; eksalta'sion/ *n. f.* exaltation.

exaltamiento /eksalta'miento/ *n. m.* exaltation.

exaltar /eksal'tar/ *v.* exalt.

examen /ek'samen/ *n. m.* test, examination.

examen de ingreso /ek'samen de iŋ'greso/ entrance examination.

examinar /eksami'nar/ *v.* test, examine.

exánime /eksa'nime/ *a.* spiritless, weak.

exasperación /eksaspera'θion; eksaspera'sion/ *n. f.* exasperation.

exasperar /eksaspe'rar/ *v.* exasperate.

excavación /ekskaβa'θion; ekskaβa'sion/ *n. f.* excavation.

excavar /ekska'βar/ *v.* excavate.

exceder /eksθe'ðer; eksse'ðer/ *v.* exceed, surpass; outrun.

excelencia /eksθe'lenθia; eksse'lensia/ *n. f.* excellence.

excelente /eksθe'lente; eksse'lente/ *a.* excellent.

excéntrico /eks'θentriko; eks'sentriko/ *a.* eccentric.

excepción /eksθep'θion; ekssep'sion/ *n. f.* exception.

excepcional /eksθepθio'nal; ekssepsio'nal/ *a.* exceptional.

excepto /eks'θepto; eks'septo/ *prep.* except, except for.

exceptuar /eksθep'tuar; ekssep'tuar/ *v.* except.

excesivamente /eksθesiβa'mente; ekssesiβa'mente/ *adv.* excessively.

excesivo /eksθe'siβo; eksse'siβo/ *a.* excessive.

exceso /eks'θeso; eks'seso/ *n. m.* excess.

excitabilidad /eksθitaβili'ðað; ekssitaβili'ðað/ *n. f.* excitability.

excitación /eksθita'θion; ekssita'sion/ *n. f.* excitement.

excitar /eksθi'tar; ekssi'tar/ *v.* excite.

exclamación /eksklama'θion; ekssklama'sion/ *n. f.* exclamation.

exclamar /ekskla'mar/ *v.* exclaim.

excluir /eksk'luir/ *v.* exclude, bar, shut out.

exclusión /eksklu'sion/ *n. f.* exclusion.

exclusivamente /eksklusiβa'mente/ *adv.* exclusively.

exclusivo /eksklu'siβo/ *a.* exclusive.

excomulgar /ekskomul'gar/ *v.* excommunicate.

excomunión /ekskomu'nion/ *n. f.* excommunication.

excreción /ekskre'θion; ekskre'sion/ *n. f.* excretion.

excremento /ekskre'mento/ *n. m.* excrement.

excretar /ekskre'tar/ *v.* excrete.

exculpar /ekskul'par/ *v.* exonerate.

excursión /ekskur'sion/ *n. f.* excursion.

excursionista /ekskursio'nista/ *n. m. & f.* excursionist; tourist.

excusa /eks'kusa/ *n. f.* excuse. —**excusar**, *v.*

excusado /eksku'saðo/ *n. m.* toilet.

excusarse /eksku'sarse/ *v.* apologize.

exención /eksen'θion; eksen'sion/ *n. f.* exemption.

exento /ek'sento/ *a.* exempt. —**exentar**, *v.*

exhalación /eksala'θion; eksala'sion/ *n. f.* exhalation.

exhalar /eksa'lar/ *v.* exhale, breathe out.

exhausto /ek'sausto/ *a.* exhausted.

exhibición /eksiβi'θion; eksiβi'sion/ *n. f.* exhibit, exhibition.

exhibir /eksi'βir/ *v.* exhibit, display.

exhortación /eksorta'θion; eksorta'sion/ *n. f.* exhortation.

exhortar /eksor'tar/ *v.* exhort, admonish.

exhumación /eksuma'θion; eksuma'sion/ *n. f.* exhumation.

exhumar /eksu'mar/ *v.* exhume.

exigencia /eksi'henθia; eksi'hensia/ *n. f.* requirement, demand.

exigente /eksi'hente/ *a.* exacting, demanding.

exigir /eksi'hir/ *v.* require, exact, demand.

eximir /eksi'mir/ *v.* exempt.

existencia /eksis'tenθia; eksis'tensia/ *n. f.* existence; *Econ.* supply.

existente /eksis'tente/ *a.* existent.

existir /eksis'tir/ *v.* exist.

éxito /'eksito/ *n. m.* success.

éxodo /'eksoðo/ *n. m.* exodus.

exoneración /eksonera'θion; eksonera'sion/ *n. f.* exoneration.

exonerar /eksone'rar/ *v.* exonerate, acquit.

exorar /ekso'rar/ *v.* beg, implore.

exorbitancia /eksorβi'tanθia; eksorβi'tansia/ *n. f.* exorbitance.

exorbitante /eksorβi'tante/ *a.* exorbitant.

exorcismo /eksor'θismo; eksor'sismo/ *n. m.* exorcism.

exornar /eksor'nar/ *v.* adorn, decorate.

exótico /ek'sotiko/ *a.* exotic.

expansibilidad /ekspansiβili'ðað/ *n. f.* expansibility.

expansión /ekspan'sion/ *n. f.* expansion.

expansivo /ekspan'siβo/ *a.* expansive; effusive.

expatriación /ekspatria'θion; ekspatria'sion/ *n. f.* expatriation.

expatriar /ekspa'triar/ *v.* expatriate.

expectación /ekspekta'θion; ekspekta'sion/ *n. f.* expectation.

expectorar /ekspekto'rar/ *v.* expectorate.

expedición /ekspeði'θion; ekspeði'sion/ *n. f.* expedition.

expediente /ekspe'ðiente/ *n. m.* expedient; means.

expedir /ekspe'ðir/ *v.* send off, ship; expedite.

expeditivo /ekspeði'tiβo/ *a.* speedy, prompt.

expedito /ekspe'ðito/ *a.* speedy, prompt.

expeler /ekspe'ler/ *v.* expel, eject.

expendedor /ekspende'ðor/ **-ra** dealer.

expender /ekspen'der/ *v.* expend.

expensas /ek'spensas/ *n. f.pl.* expenses, costs.

experiencia /ekspe'rienθia; ekspe'riensia/ *n. f.* experience.

experimentado /eksperimen'taðo/ *a.* experienced.

experimental /eksperimen'tal/ *a.* experimental.

experimentar /eksperimen'tar/ *v.* experience.

experimento /eksperi'mento/ *n. m.* experiment.

expertamente /eksperta'mente/ *adv.* expertly.

experto /ek'sperto/ **-ta** *a. & n.* expert.

expiación /ekspia'θion; ekspia'sion/ *n. f.* atonement.

expiar /eks'piar/ *v.* atone for.

expiración /ekspira'θion; ekspira'sion/ *n. f.* expiration.

expirar /ekspi'rar/ *v.* expire.

explanación /eksplana'θion; eksplana'sion/ *n. f.* explanation.

explanar /ekspla'nar/ *v.* make level.

expletivo /eksple'tiβo/ *n. & a.* expletive.

explicable /ekspli'kaβle/ *a.* explicable.

explicación /eksplika'θion; eksplika'sion/ *n. f.* explanation.

explicar /ekspli'kar/ *v.* explain.

explicativo /eksplika'tiβo/ *a.* explanatory.

explícitamente /ekspliθita'mente; eksplisita'mente/ *adv.* explicitly.

explícito /eks'pliθito; eks'plisito/ *adj.* explicit.

exploración /eksplora'θion; eksplora'sion/ *n. f.* exploration.

explorador /eksplora'ðor/ **-ra** *n.* explorer; scout.

explorar /eksplo'rar/ *v.* explore; scout.

exploratorio /eksplora'torio/ *a.* exploratory.

explosión /eksplo'sion/ *n. f.* explosion; outburst.

explosivo /eksplo'siβo/ *a. & m.* explosive.

explotación /eksplota'θion; eksplota'sion/ *n. f.* exploitation.

explotar /eksplo'tar/ *v.* exploit.

exponer /ekspo'ner/ *v.* expose; set forth.

exportación /eksporta'θion; eksporta'sion/ *n. f.* exportation; export.

exportador /eksporta'ðor/ **-ra** *n.* exporter.

exportar /ekspor'tar/ *v.* export.

exposición /eksposi'θion; eksposi'sion/ *n. f.* exhibit; exposition; exposure.

expósito /eks'posito/ **-ta** *n.* foundling; orphan.

expresado /ekspre'saðo/ *a.* aforesaid.

expresamente /ekspresa'mente/ *adv.* clearly, explicitly.

expresar /ekspre'sar/ *v.* express.

expresión /ekspre'sion/ *n. f.* expression.

expresivo /ekspre'siβo/ *a.* expressive; affectionate.

expreso /eks'preso/ *a. & m.* express.

exprimidera de naranjas /eksprimi'ðera de na'ranhas/ *n. f.* orange squeezer.

exprimir /ekspri'mir/ *v.* squeeze.

expropiación /ekspropia'θion; ekspropia'sion/ *n. f.* expropriation.

expropiar /ekspro'piar/ *v.* expropriate.

expulsar /ekspul'sar/ *v.* expel, eject; evict.

expulsión /ekspul'sion/ *n. f.* expulsion.

expurgación /ekspurga'θion; ekspurga'sion/ *n. f.* expurgation.

expurgar /ekspur'gar/ *v.* expurgate.

exquisitamente /ekskisita'mente/ *adv.* exquisitely.

exquisito /eks'kisito/ *a.* exquisite.

éxtasis /'ekstasis/ *n. m.* ecstasy.

extemporáneo /ekstempo'raneo/ *a.* extemporaneous, impromptu.

extender /eksten'der/ *v.* extend; spread; widen; stretch.

extensamente /ekstensa'mente/ *adv.* extensively.

extensión /eksten'sion/ *n. f.* extension, spread, expanse.

extenso /eks'tenso/ *a.* extensive, widespread.

extenuación /ekstenua'θion; ekstenua'sion/ *n. f.* weakening; emaciation.

extenuar /ekstenu'ar/ *v.* extenuate.

exterior /ekste'rior/ *a. & m.* exterior; foreign.

exterminar /ekstermi'nar/ *v.* exterminate.

exterminio /ekster'minio/ *n. m.* extermination, ruin.

extinción /ekstin'θion; ekstin'sion/ *n. f.* extinction.

extinguir /ekstiŋ'guir/ *v.* extinguish.

extinto /eks'tinto/ *a.* extinct.

extintor /ekstin'tor/ *n. m.* fire extinguisher.

extirpar /ekstir'par/ *v.* eradicate.

extorsión /ekstor'sion/ *n. f.* extortion.

extra /'ekstra/ *n.* extra.

extracción /ekstrak'θion; ekstrak'sion/ *n. f.* extraction.

extractar /ekstrak'tar/ *v.* summarize.

extracto /eks'trakto/ *n. m.* extract; summary.

extradición /ekstraði'θion; ekstraði'sion/ *n. f.* extradition.

extraer /ekstra'er/ *v.* extract.

extranjero /ekstran'hero/ **-ra** **1.** foreign. —*n.* **2.** foreigner; stranger.

extrañar /ekstra'ɲar/ *v.* surprise; miss.

extraño /eks'traɲo/ *a.* strange, queer.

extraordinariamente /,ekstraorði-naria'mente/ *adv.* extraordinarily.

extraordinario /ekstraorði'nario/ *a.* extraordinary.

extravagancia /ekstraβa'ganθia; ekstraβa'gansia/ *n. f.* extravagance.

extravagante /ekstraβa'gante/ *a.* extravagant.

extraviado /ekstra'βiaðo/ *a.* lost, misplaced.

extraviarse /ekstra'βiarse/ *v.* stray, get lost.

extravío /ekstra'βio/ *n. m.* misplacement; aberration, deviation.

extremadamente /ekstremaða-'mente/ *adv.* extremely.

extremado /ekstre'maðo/ *a.* extreme.

extremaunción /ekstremaun'θion; ekstremaun'sion/ *n. f.* extreme unction.

extremidad /ekstremi'ðað/ *n. f.* extremity.

extremista /ekstre'mista/ *n. & a.* extremist.

extremo /eks'tremo/ *a. & m.* extreme, end.

extrínseco /ekstrin'seko/ *a.* extrinsic.

exuberancia /eksuβe'ranθia; eksuβe'ransia/ *n. f.* exuberance.

exuberante /eksuβe'rante/ *a.* exuberant.

exudación /eksuða'θion; eksuða'sion/ *n. f.* exudation.

exudar /eksu'ðar/ *v.* exude, ooze.

exultación /eksulta'θion; eksulta'sion/ *n. f.* exultation.

eyaculación /eyakula'θion; eyakula'sion/ *n. f.* ejaculation.

eyacular /eyaku'lar/ *v.* ejaculate.

eyección /eyek'θion; eyek'sion/ *n. f.* ejection.

eyectar /eyek'tar/ *v.* eject.

F

fábrica /'faβrika/ *n. f.* factory.

fabricación /faβrika'θion; faβrika-'sion/ *n. f.* manufacture, manufacturing.

fabricante /faβri'kante/ *n. m. & f.* manufacturer, maker.

fabricar /faβri'kar/ *v.* manufacture, make.

fabril /fa'βril/ *a.* manufacturing, industrial.

fábula /'faβula/ *n. f.* fable, myth.

fabuloso /faβu'loso/ *a.* fabulous.

facción /fak'θion; fak'sion/ *n. f.* faction, party; (*pl.*) features.

faccioso /fak'θioso; fak'sioso/ *a.* factious.

fachada /fa'tʃaða/ *n. f.* façade, front.

fácil /'faθil; 'fasil/ *a.* easy.

facilidad /faθili'ðað; fasili'ðað/ *n. f.* facility, ease.

facilitar /faθili'tar; fasili'tar/ *v.* facilitate, make easy.

fácilmente /,faθil'mente; ,fasil'mente/ *adv.* easily.

facsímile /fak'simile/ *n. m.* facsimile.

factible /fak'tiβle/ *a.* feasible.

factor /fak'tor/ *n. m.* factor.

factótum /fak'totum/ *n. m.* factotum; jack of all trades.

factura /fak'tura/ *n. f.* invoice, bill.

facturar /faktu'rar/ *v.* bill; check (baggage).

facultad /fakulta'ð/ *n. f.* faculty; ability.

facultativo /fakulta'tiβo/ *a.* optional.

faena /fa'ena/ *n. f.* task; work.

faisán /fai'san/ *n. m.* pheasant.

faja /'faha/ *n. f.* band; sash; zone.

falacia /fa'laθia; fa'lasia/ *n. f.* fallacy; deceitfulness.

falda /'falda/ *n. f.* skirt; lap.

falibilidad /faliβili'ðað/ *n. f.* fallibility.

falla /'faʎa; faya/ *n. f.* failure; fault.

fallar /fa'ʎar; fa'yar/ *v.* fail.

fallecer /faʎe'θer; faye'ser/ *v.* pass away, die.

fallo /'faʎo; 'fayo/ *n. m.* verdict; shortcoming.

falsear /false'ar/ *v.* falsify, counterfeit, forge.

falsedad /false'ðað/ *n. f.* falsehood; lie; falseness.

falsificación /falsifika'θion; falsifika'sion/ *n. f.* falsification; forgery.

falsificar /falsifi'kar/ *v.* falsify, counterfeit, forge.

falso /'falso/ *a.* false; wrong.

falta /'falta/ *n. f.* error, mistake; fault; lack. **hacer f.,** to be lacking, to be necessary. **sin f.,** without fail.

faltar /fal'tar/ *v.* be lacking, be missing; be absent.

faltriquera /faltri'kera/ *n. f.* pocket.

fama /'fama/ *n. f.* fame; reputation; glory.

familia /fa'milia/ *n. f.* family; household.

familiar /fami'liar/ *a.* familiar; domestic; (of) family.

familiaridad /familiari'ðað/ *n. f.* familiarity, intimacy.

familiarizar /familiari'θar; familiari'sar/ *v.* familiarize, acquaint.

famoso /fa'moso/ *a.* famous.

fanal /fa'nal/ *n. m.* lighthouse; lantern, lamp.

fanático /fa'natiko/ **-ca** *a. & n.* fanatic.

fanatismo /fana'tismo/ *n. m.* fanaticism.

fanfarria /fan'farria/ *n. f.* bluster. —**fanfarrear,** *v.*

fango /'faŋgo/ *n. m.* mud.

fantasía /fanta'sia/ *n. f.* fantasy; fancy, whim.

fantasma /fan'tasma/ *n. m.* phantom; ghost.

fantástico /fan'tastiko/ *a.* fantastic.

faquín /fa'kin/ *n. m.* porter.

faquir /fa'kir/ *n. m.* fakir.

farallón /fara'ʎon; fara'yon/ *n. m.* cliff.

Faraón /fara'on/ *n. m.* Pharaoh.

fardel /far'ðel/ *n. m.* bag; package.

fardo /far'ðo/ *n. m.* bundle.

farináceo /fari'naθeo; fari'naseo/ *a.* farinaceous.

faringe /fa'rinhe/ *n. f.* pharynx.

fariseo /fari'seo/ *n. m.* pharisee, hypocrite.

farmacéutico /farma'θeutiko; farma'seutiko/ **-ca** *a.* **1.** pharmaceutical. —*n.* **2.** pharmacist.

farmacia /far'maθia; far'masia/ *n. f.* pharmacy.

faro /'faro/ *n. m.* beacon; lighthouse; headlight.

farol /fa'rol/ *n. m.* lantern; (street) light, street lamp.

farra /'farra/ *n. f.* spree.

fárrago /'farrago/ *n. m.* medley; hodgepodge.

farsa /'farsa/ *n. f.* farce.

fascinación /fasθina'θion; fassina'sion/ *n. f.* fascination.

fascinar /fasθi'nar; fassi'nar/ *v.* fascinate, bewitch.

fase /'fase/ *n. f.* phase.

fastidiar /fasti'ðiar/ *v.* disgust; irk, annoy.

fastidio /fasti'ðio/ *n. m.* disgust; annoyance.

fastidioso /fasti'ðioso/ *a.* annoying; tedious.

fasto /'fasto/ *a.* happy, fortunate.

fatal /fa'tal/ *a.* fatal.

fatalidad /fatali'ðað/ *n. f.* fate; calamity, bad luck.

fatalismo /fata'lismo/ *n. m.* fatalism.

fatalista /fata'lista/ *n. & a.* fatalist.

fatiga /fa'tiga/ *n. f.* fatigue. —**fatigar,** *v.*

fauna /'fauna/ *n. f.* fauna.

fauno /'fauno/ *n. m.* faun.

favor /fa'βor/ *n. m.* favor; behalf. **por f.,** please.

¡Favor! Puh-lease!

favorable /faβo'raβle/ *a.* favorable.

favorablemente /faβoraβle'mente/ *adv.* favorably.

favorecer /faβore'θer; faβore'ser/ *v.* favor; flatter.

favoritismo /faβori'tismo/ *n. m.* favoritism.

favorito /faβo'rito/ **-ta** *a. & n.* favorite.

fax /faks/ *n. m.* fax.

faz /faθ; fas/ *n. f.* face.

fe /fe/ *n. f.* faith.

fealdad /feal'dað/ *n. f.* ugliness, homeliness.

febrero /fe'βrero/ *n. m.* February.

febril /fe'βril/ *a.* feverish.

fecha /'fetʃa/ *n. f.* date. —**fechar,** *v.*

fecha de caducidad /'fetʃa de kaðuθi'ðað; 'fetʃa de kaðusi'ðað/ expiration date.

fécula /'fekula/ *n. f.* starch.

fecundar /fekun'dar/ *v.* fertilize.

fecundidad /fekundi'ðað/ *n. f.* fecundity, fertility.

fecundo /fe'kundo/ *a.* fecund, fertile.

federación /feðera'θion; feðera'sion/ *n. f.* federation.

federal /feðe'ral/ *a.* federal.

felicidad /feliθi'ðað; felisi'ðað/ *n. f.* happiness; bliss.

felicitación /feliθita'θion; felisita'sion/ *n. f.* congratulation.

felicitar /feliθi'tar; felisi'tar/ *v.* congratulate.

feligrés /feli'gres/ **-esa** *n.* parishioner.

feliz /fe'liθ; fe'lis/ *a.* happy; fortunate.

felón /fe'lon/ *n. m.* felon.

felonía /felo'nia/ *n. f.* felony.

felpa /'felpa/ *n. f.* plush.

felpudo /fel'puðo/ *n. m.* doormat.

femenino /feme'nino/ *a.* feminine.

feminismo /femi'nismo/ *n. m.* feminism.

feminista /femi'nista/ *n. m. & f.* feminist.

fenecer /fene'θer; fene'ser/ *v.* conclude; die.

fénix /'feniks/ *n. m.* phoenix; model.

fenomenal /fenome'nal/ *a.* phenomenal.

fenómeno /fe'nomeno/ *n. m.* phenomenon.

feo /'feo/ *a.* ugly, homely.

feracidad /feraθi'ðað; ferasi'ðað/ *n. f.* feracity, fertility.

feraz /fe'raθ; 'feras/ *a.* fertile, fruitful; copious.

feria /'feria/ *n. f.* fair; market.

feriado /fe'riaðo/ *a.* **día f.,** holiday.

fermentación /fermenta'θion; fermenta'sion/ *n. f.* fermentation.

fermento /fer'mento/ *n. m.* ferment. —**fermentar,** *v.*

ferocidad /feroθi'ðað; ferosi'ðað/ *n. f.* ferocity, fierceness.

feroz /fe'roθ; fe'ros/ *a.* ferocious, fierce.

férreo /'ferreo/ *a.* of iron.

ferrería /ferre'ria/ *n. f.* ironworks.

ferretería /ferrete'ria/ *n. f.* hardware; hardware store.

ferrocarril /ferroka'rril/ *n. m.* railroad.

fértil /'fertil/ *a.* fertile.

fertilidad /fertili'ðað/ *n. f.* fertility.

fertilizar /fertili'θar; fertili'sar/ *v.* fertilize.

férvido /'ferβiðo/ *a.* fervid, ardent.

ferviente /fer'βiente/ *a.* fervent.

fervor /fer'βor/ *n. m.* fervor, zeal.

fervoroso /ferβo'roso/ *a.* zealous, eager.

festejar /feste'har/ *v.* entertain, fete.

festejo /feste'ho/ *n. m.* feast.

festín /fes'tin/ *n. m.* feast.

festividad /festiβi'ðað/ *n. f.* festivity.

festivo /fes'tiβo/ *a.* festive.

fétido /'fetiðo/ *adj.* fetid.

feudal /feu'ðal/ *a.* feudal.

feudo /'feuðo/ *n. m.* fief; manor.

fiado /'fiaðo, al/ *adj.* on trust, on credit.

fiambrera /fiam'brera/ *n. f.* lunch box.

fianza /'fianθa; 'fiansa/ *n. f.* bail.

fiar /fi'ar/ *v.* trust, sell on credit; give credit.

fiarse de /'fiarse de/ *v.* trust (in), rely on.

fiasco /'fiasko/ n. m. fiasco.
fibra /'fiβra/ n. f. fiber; vigor.
fibroso /fi'βroso/ a. fibrous.
ficción /fik'θion; fik'sion/ n. f. fiction.
ficha /'fitʃa/ n. f. slip, index card; chip.
fichero /fi'tʃero/ n. m. computer file, filing cabinet, card catalog.
ficticio /fik'tiθio; fik'tisio/ a. fictitious.
fidedigno /fiðe'ðigno/ a. trustworthy.
fideicomisario /fiðeikomi'sario/ **-ria** n. trustee.
fideicomiso /fiðeiko'miso/ n. m. trust.
fidelidad /fiðeli'ðað/ n. f. fidelity.
fideo /fi'ðeo/ n. m. noodle.
fiebre /'fieβre/ n. f. fever.
fiebre del heno /'fieβre del 'eno/ hayfever.
fiel /fiel/ a. faithful.
fieltro /'fieltro/ n. m. felt.
fiera /'fiera/ n. f. wild animal.
fiereza /fie'reθa; fie'resa/ n. f. fierceness, wildness.
fiero /'fiero/ a. fierce; wild.
fiesta /'fiesta/ n. f. festival, feast; party.
figura /fi'gura/ n. f. figure. —**figurar,** v.
figurarse /figu'rarse/ v. imagine.
figurón /figu'ron/ n. m. dummy.
fijar /fi'har/ v. fix; set, establish; post.
fijarse en /fi'harse en/ v. notice.
fijeza /fi'heθa; fi'hesa/ n. f. firmness.
fijo /'fiho/ a. fixed, stationary, permanent, set.
fila /'fila/ n. f. row, rank, file, line.
filantropía /filantro'pia/ n. f. philanthropy.
filatelia /fila'telia/ n. f. philately, stamp collecting.
filete /fi'lete/ n. m. fillet; steak.
film /film/ n. m. film. —**filmar,** v.
filo /'filo/ n. m. (cutting) edge.
filón /fi'lon/ n. m. vein (of ore).
filosofía /filoso'fia/ n. f. philosophy.
filosófico /filo'sofiko/ a. philosophical.
filósofo /fi'losofo/ **-fa** n. philosopher.
filtro /'filtro/ n. m. filter. —**filtrar,** v.
fin /fin/ n. m. end, purpose, goal. **a f. de que,** in order that. **en f.,** in short. **por f.,** finally, at last.
final /fi'nal/ a. **1.** final. —n. **2.** m. end.
finalidad /finali'ðað/ n. f. finality.
finalmente /final'mente/ adv. at last.
financiero /finan'θiero; finan'siero/ **-ra** a. **1.** financial. —n. **2.** financier.
finca /'finka/ n. f. real estate; estate; farm.
finés /fi'nes/ **-esa** a. & n. Finnish; Finn.
fineza /fi'neθa; fi'nesa/ n. f. courtesy, politeness; fineness.
fingimiento /finhi'miento/ n. m. pretense.
fingir /fin'hir/ v. feign, pretend.
fino /'fino/ a. fine; polite, courteous.
firma /'firma/ n. f. signature; Com. firm.
firmamento /firma'mento/ n. m. firmament, heavens.
firmar /fir'mar/ v. sign.
firme /'firme/ a. firm, fast, steady, sound.
firmemente /firme'mente/ adv. firmly.
firmeza /fir'meθa; fir'mesa/ n. f. firmness.
fisco /'fisko/ n. m. exchequer, treasury.
física /'fisika/ n. f. physics.
físico /'fisiko/ **-ca** a. & n. physical; physicist.
fisiología /fisiolo'hia/ n. f. physiology.
fláccido /'flakθiðo; 'flaksiðo/ a. flaccid, soft.
flaco /'flako/ a. thin, gaunt.
flagelación /flahela'θion; flahela'sion/ n. f. flagellation.
flagelar /flahe'lar/ v. flagellate, whip.
flagrancia /fla'granθia; fla'gransia/ n. f. flagrancy.
flagrante /fla'grante/ a. flagrant.
flama /'flama/ n. f. flame; ardor, zeal.
flamante /fla'mante/ a. flaming.
flamenco /fla'menko/ n. m. flamingo.
flan /flan/ n. m. custard.
flanco /'flanko/ n. m. side; Mil. flank.
flanquear /flanke'ar/ v. flank.
flaqueza /fla'keθa; fla'kesa/ n. f. thinness; weakness.
flauta /'flauta/ n. f. flute.
flautín /flau'tin/ n. m. piccolo.
flautista /flau'tista/ n. m. & f. flutist, piper.
flecha /'fletʃa/ n. f. arrow.
flechazo /fle'tʃaθo; fle'tʃaso/ n. m. love at first sight.
flechero /fle'tʃero/ **-ra** n. archer.
fleco /'fleko/ n. m. fringe; flounce.
flema /'flema/ n. f. phlegm.
flemático /fle'matiko/ a. phlegmatic.
flequillo /fle'kiʎo; fle'kiyo/ n. m. fringe; bangs (of hair).
flete /'flete/ n. m. freight. —**fletar,** v.
flexibilidad /fleksiβili'ðað/ n. f. flexibility.
flexible /fle'ksiβle/ a. flexible, pliable.
flirtear /flirte'ar/ v. flirt.
flojo /'floho/ a. limp; loose, flabby, slack.
flor /flor/ n. f. flower; compliment.
flora /'flora/ n. f. flora.
floral /flo'ral/ a. floral.
florecer /flore'θer; flore'ser/ v. flower, bloom; flourish.
floreo /flo'reo/ n. m. flourish.
florero /flo'rero/ n. m. flower pot; vase.
floresta /flo'resta/ n. f. forest.
florido /flo'riðo/ a. flowery; flowering.
florista /flo'rista/ n. m. & f. florist.
flota /'flota/ n. f. fleet.
flotante /flo'tante/ a. floating.
flotar /flo'tar/ v. float.
flotilla /flo'tiʎa; flo'tiya/ n. f. flotilla, fleet.
fluctuación /fluktua'θion; fluktua'sion/ n. f. fluctuation.
fluctuar /fluktu'ar/ v. fluctuate.
fluente /'fluente/ a. fluent; flowing.
fluidez /flui'ðeθ; flui'ðes/ n. f. fluency.
flúido /'fluiðo/ a. & m. fluid, liquid.
fluir /flu'ir/ v. flow.
flujo /'fluho/ n. m. flow, flux.
fluor /'fluor/ n. m. fluorine.
fluorescencia /fluores'θenθia; fluores'sensia/ n. f. fluorescence.
fluorescente /fluores'θente; fluores'sente/ a. fluorescent.
fobia /'foβia/ n. f. phobia.
foca /'foka/ n. f. seal.
foco /'foko/ n. m. focus, center; floodlight.
fogata /fo'gata/ n. f. bonfire.
fogón /fo'gon/ n. m. hearth, fireplace.
fogosidad /fogosi'ðað/ n. f. vehemence, ardor.
fogoso /fo'goso/ a. vehement, ardent.
folclore /fol'klore/ n. m. folklore.
follaje /fo'ʎahe; fo'yahe/ n. m. foliage.
folleto /fo'ʎeto; fo'yeto/ n. m. pamphlet, booklet.
follón /fo'ʎon; fo'yon/ n. m. mess, chaos.
fomentar /fomen'tar/ v. develop, promote, further, foster.
fomento /fo'mento/ n. m. fomentation.
fonda /'fonda/ n. f. eating house, inn.
fondo /'fondo/ n. m. bottom; back (part); background; (pl.) funds; finances. **a f.,** thoroughly.
fonética /fo'netika/ n. f. phonetics.
fonético /fo'netiko/ a. phonetic.
fonógrafo /fo'nografo/ n. m. phonograph.
fontanero /fonta'nero/ **-era** n. plumber.
forastero /foras'tero/ **-ra** a. **1.** foreign, exotic. —n. **2.** stranger.
forjar /for'har/ v. forge.
forma /'forma/ n. f. form, shape. —**formar,** v.
formación /forma'θion; forma'sion/ n. f. formation.
formal /for'mal/ a. formal.
formaldehido /formalde'iðo/ n. m. formaldehyde.
formalidad /formali'ðað/ n. f. formality.
formalizar /formali'θar; formali'sar/ v. finalize; formulate.
formidable /formi'ðaβle/ a. formidable.
formidablemente /formiðaβle'mente/ adv. formidably.
formón /for'mon/ n. m. chisel.
fórmula /'formula/ n. f. formula.
formular /formu'lar/ v. formulate, draw up.
formulario /formu'lario/ n. m. form.
foro /'foro/ n. m. forum.
forrado /fo'rraðo/ a. stuffed; Colloq. filthy rich.
forraje /fo'rrahe/ n. m. forage, fodder.
forrar /fo'rrar/ v. line.
forro /'forro/ n. m. lining; condom.
fortalecer /fortale'θer; fortale'ser/ v. fortify.
fortaleza /forta'leθa; forta'lesa/ n. f. fort, fortress; fortitude.
fortificación /fortifika'θion; fortifika'sion/ n. f. fortification.
fortitud /forti'tuð/ n. f. fortitude.
fortuitamente /fortuita'mente/ adv. fortuitously.
fortuito /for'tuito/ a. fortuitous.
fortuna /for'tuna/ n. f. fortune; luck.
forúnculo /fo'runkulo/ n. m. boil.
forzar /for'θar; for'sar/ v. force, compel, coerce.
forzosamente /forθosa'mente; forsosa'mente/ adv. compulsorily; forcibly.
forzoso /for'θoso; for'soso/ a. compulsory; necessary. **paro f.,** unemployment.
forzudo /for'θuðo; for'suðo/ a. powerful, vigorous.
fosa /'fosa/ n. f. grave; pit.
fósforo /'fosforo/ n. m. match; phosphorus.
fósil /'fosil/ n. m. fossil.
foso /'foso/ n. m. ditch, trench; moat.
fotocopia /foto'kopia/ n. f. photocopy.
fotocopiadora /fotokopia'ðora/ n. f. photocopier.
fotografía /fotogra'fia/ n. f. photograph; photography. —**fotografiar,** v.
frac /frak/ n. m. dress coat.
fracasar /fraka'sar/ v. fail.
fracaso /fra'kaso/ n. m. failure.
fracción /frak'θion; frak'sion/ n. f. fraction.
fractura /frak'tura/ n. f. fracture, break.
fragancia /fra'ganθia; fra'gansia/ n. f. fragrance; perfume; aroma.
fragante /fra'gante/ a. fragrant.
frágil /'frahil/ a. fragile, breakable.
fragilidad /frahili'ðað/ n. f. fragility.
fragmentario /fragmen'tario/ a. fragmentary.
fragmento /frag'mento/ n. m. fragment, bit.
fragor /fra'gor/ n. m. noise, clamor.
fragoso /fra'goso/ a. noisy.
fragua /'fragua/ n. f. forge. —**fraguar,** v.
fraile /'fraile/ n. m. monk.
frambuesa /fram'buesa/ n. f. raspberry.
francamente /franka'mente/ adv. frankly, candidly.
francés /fran'θes; fran'ses/ **-esa** a. & n. French; Frenchman, Frenchwoman.
Francia /'franθia; 'fransia/ n. f. France.
franco /'franko/ a. frank.
franela /fra'nela/ n. f. flannel.
frangible /fraŋ'giβle/ a. breakable.
franqueo /fran'keo/ n. m. postage.
franqueza /fran'keθa; fran'kesa/ n. f. frankness.
franquicia /fran'kiθia; fran'kisia/ n. f. franchise.
frasco /'frasko/ n. m. flask, bottle.
frase /'frase/ n. f. phrase; sentence.
fraseología /fraseolo'hia/ n. f. phraseology; style.
fraternal /frater'nal/ a. fraternal, brotherly.
fraternidad /fraterni'ðað/ n. f. fraternity, brotherhood.
fraude /'frauðe/ n. m. fraud.
fraudulento /frauðu'lento/ a. fraudulent.
frazada /fra'θaða; fra'saða/ n. f. blanket.
frecuencia /fre'kuenθia; fre'kuensia/ n. f. frequency.
frecuente /fre'kuente/ a. frequent.
frecuentemente /frekuente'mente/ adv. frequently, often.
fregadero /frega'ðero/ n. m. sink.
fregadura /frega'ðura/ n. f. scouring, scrubbing.
fregar /fre'gar/ v. scour, scrub, mop.
fregona /fre'gona/ n. f. mop.
freír /fre'ir/ v. fry.
fréjol /'frehol/ n. m. kidney bean.
frenazo /fre'naθo; fre'naso/ n. m. sudden braking, slamming on the brakes.
frenesí /frene'si/ n. m. frenzy.
frenéticamente /fre'netikamente/ adv. frantically.
frenético /fre'netiko/ a. frantic, frenzied.
freno /'freno/ n. m. brake. —**frenar,** v.
freno de auxilio /'freno de auk'silio/ emergency brake.
freno de mano /'freno de 'mano/ hand brake.
frente /'frente/ n. **1.** f. forehead. **2.** m. front. **en f., al f.,** opposite, across. **f. a,** in front of.
fresa /'fresa/ n. f. strawberry.
fresca /'freska/ n. f. fresh, cool air.
fresco /'fresko/ a. fresh; cool; crisp.
frescura /fres'kura/ n. f. coolness, freshness.
fresno /'fresno/ n. m. ash tree.
fresquería /freske'ria/ n. f. soda fountain.
friabilidad /friaβili'ðað/ n. f. brittleness.
friable /'friaβle/ a. brittle.
frialdad /frial'dað/ n. f. coldness.
fríamente /fria'mente/ adv. coldly; coolly.
fricandó /'frikando/ n. m. fricandeau.
fricar /fri'kar/ v. rub together.
fricción /frik'θion; frik'sion/ n. f. friction.
friccionar /frikθio'nar; friksio'nar/ v. rub.
friega /'friega/ n. f. friction; massage.
frigidez /frihi'ðeθ; frihi'ðes/ n. f. frigidity.
frígido /'frihiðo/ a. frigid.
frijol /fri'hol/ n. m. bean.
frío /'frio/ a. & n. cold. **tener f.,** to be cold, feel cold. **hacer f.,** to be cold (weather).
friolento /frio'lento/ **friolero** a. chilly; sensitive to cold.
friolera /frio'lera/ n. f. trifle, trinket.
friso /'friso/ n. m. frieze.
fritillas /fri'tiʎas; fri'tiyas/ n. f.pl. fritters.
frito /'frito/ a. fried.
fritura /fri'tura/ n. f. fritter.
frívolamente /'friβolamente/ adv. frivolously.
frivolidad /friβoli'ðað/ n. f. frivolity.
frívolo /'friβolo/ a. frivolous.
frondoso /fron'doso/ a. leafy.
frontera /fron'tera/ n. f. frontier; border.
frotar /fro'tar/ v. rub.

fructífero /fruk'tifero/ *a.* fruitful.
fructificar /fruktifi'kar/ *v.* bear fruit.
fructuosamente /fruktuosa'mente/ *adv.* fruitfully.
fructuoso /fruk'tuoso/ *a.* fruitful.
frugal /fru'gal/ *a.* frugal; thrifty.
frugalidad /frugali'ðað/ *n. f.* frugality; thrift.
frugalmente /frugal'mente/ *adv.* frugally, thriftily.
fruncir /frun'θir; frun'sir/ *v.* gather, contract. **f. el entrecejo,** frown.
fruslería /frusle'ria/ *n. f.* trinket.
frustrar /frus'trar/ *v.* frustrate, thwart.
fruta /'fruta/ *n. f.* fruit.
frutería /frute'ria/ *n. f.* fruit store.
fruto /'fruto/ *n. m.* fruit; product; profit.
fucsia /'fuksia/ *n. f.* fuchsia.
fuego /'fuego/ *n. m.* fire.
fuelle /'fueʎe; 'fueye/ *n. m.* bellows.
fuente /'fuente/ *n. f.* fountain; source; platter.
fuera /'fuera/ *adv.* without, outside.
fuero /'fuero/ *n. m.* statute.
fuerte /'fuerte/ *a.* **1.** strong; loud. —*n.* **2.** *m.* fort.
fuertemente /fuerte'mente/ *adv.* strongly; loudly.
fuerza /'fuerθa; 'fuersa/ *n. f.* force, strength.
fuga /'fuga/ *n. f.* flight, escape.
fugarse /fu'garse/ *v.* flee, escape.
fugaz /fu'gaθ; fu'gas/ *a.* fugitive, passing.
fugitivo /fuhi'tiβo/ **-va** *a.* & *n.* fugitive.
fulano /fu'lano/ **-na** *n.* Mr., Mrs. so-and-so.
fulcro /'fulkro/ *n. m.* fulcrum.
fulgor /ful'gor/ *n. m.* gleam, glow. —**fulgurar,** *v.*
fulminante /fulmi'nante/ *a.* explosive.
fumador /fuma'ðor/ **-ra** *n.* smoker.
fumar /fu'mar/ *v.* smoke.
fumigación /fumiga'θion; fumiga'sion/ *n. f.* fumigation.
fumigador /fumiga'ðor/ **-ra** *n.* fumigator.
fumigar /fumi'gar/ *v.* fumigate.
fumoso /fu'moso/ *a.* smoky.
función /fun'θion; fun'sion/ *n. f.* function; performance, show.
funcionar /funθio'nar; funsio'nar/ *v.* function; work, run.
funcionario /funθio'nario; funsio'nario/ **-ria** *n.* official, functionary.
funda /'funda/ *n. f.* case, sheath, slipcover.
fundación /funda'θion; funda'sion/ *n. f.* foundation.
fundador /funda'ðor/ **-ra** *n.* founder.
fundamental /funda'mental/ *a.* fundamental, basic.
fundamentalmente /fundamental'mente/ *adv.* fundamentally.
fundamento /funda'mento/ *n. m.* base, basis, foundation.
fundar /fun'dar/ *v.* found, establish.
fundición /fundi'θion; fundi'sion/ *n. f.* foundry; melting; meltdown.
fundir /fun'dir/ *v.* fuse; smelt.
fúnebre /'funeβre/ *a.* dismal.
funeral /fune'ral/ *n. m.* funeral.
funeraria /fune'raria/ *n. f.* funeral home, funeral parlor.
funestamente /funesta'mente/ *adv.* sadly.
fungo /'fuŋgo/ *n. m.* fungus.
furente /fu'rente/ *a.* furious, enraged.
furgoneta /furgo'neta/ *n. f.* van.
furia /'furia/ *n. f.* fury.
furiosamente /furiosa'mente/ *adv.* furiously.
furioso /fu'rioso/ *a.* furious.
furor /fu'ror/ *n. m.* furor; fury.
furtivamente /furtiβa'mente/ *adv.* furtively.
furtivo /fur'tiβo/ *a.* furtive, sly.
furúnculo /fu'runkulo/ *n. m.* boil.
fusibilidad /fusiβili'ðað/ *n. f.* fusibility.
fusible /fu'siβle/ *n. m.* fuse.
fusil /fu'sil/ *n. m.* rifle, gun.
fusilar /fusi'lar/ *v.* shoot, execute.
fusión /fu'sion/ *n. f.* fusion; merger.
fusionar /fusio'nar/ *v.* unite, fuse, merge.
fútbol /'futβol/ *n. m.* football, soccer.
fútil /'futil/ *a.* trivial.
futilidad /futili'ðað/ *n. f.* triviality.
futuro /fu'turo/ *a.* & *m.* future.
futurología /futurolo'hia/ *n. f.* futurology.

G

gabán /ga'βan/ *n. m.* overcoat.
gabardina /gaβar'ðina/ *n. f.* raincoat.
gabinete /gaβi'nete/ *n. m.* closet; cabinet; study.
gacela /ga'θela; ga'sela/ *n. f.* gazelle.
gaceta /ga'θeta; ga'seta/ *n. f.* gazette, newspaper.
gacetilla /gaθe'tiʎa; gase'tiya/ *n. f.* personal news section of a newspaper.
gaélico /ga'eliko/ *a.* Gaelic.
gafas /'gafas/ *n. f.pl.* eyeglasses.
gaguear /gage'ar/ *v.* stutter, stammer.
gaita /'gaita/ *n. f.* bagpipes.
gaje /'gahe/ *n. m.* salary; fee.
gala /'gala/ *n. f.* gala, ceremony; (*pl.*) regalia. **tener a g.,** be proud of.
galán /ga'lan/ *n. m.* gallant.
galano /ga'lano/ *a.* stylishly dressed; elegant.
galante /ga'lante/ *a.* gallant.
galantería /galante'ria/ *n. f.* gallantry, compliment.
galápago /ga'lapago/ *n. m.* freshwater turtle.
galardón /galar'ðon/ *n. m.* prize; reward.
gáleo /'galeo/ *n. m.* swordfish.
galera /ga'lera/ *n. f.* wagon; shed; galley.
galería /gale'ria/ *n. f.* gallery, *Theat.* balcony.
galés /'gales/ **-esa** *a.* & *n.* Welsh; Welshman, Welshwoman.
galgo /'galgo/ *n. m.* greyhound.
galillo /ga'liʎo; ga'liyo/ *n. m.* uvula.
galimatías /galima'tias/ *n. m.* gibberish.
gallardete /gaʎar'ðete; gayar'ðete/ *n. m.* pennant.
galleta /ga'ʎeta; ga'yeta/ *n. f.* cracker.
gallina /ga'ʎina; ga'yina/ *n. f.* hen.
gallinero /gaʎi'nero; gayi'nero/ *n. m.* chicken coop.
gallo /ga'ʎo; ga'yo/ *n. m.* rooster.
galocha /ga'lotʃa/ *n. f.* galosh.
galón /ga'lon/ *n. m.* gallon; *Mil.* stripe.
galope /ga'lope/ *n. m.* gallop. —**galopar,** *v.*
galopín /galo'pin/ *n. m.* ragamuffin, urchin (child).
gamba /'gamba/ *n. f.* prawn.
gamberro /gam'βerro/ **-ra** *n.* hooligan.
gambito /gam'bito/ *n. m.* gambit.
gamuza /ga'muθa; ga'musa/ *n. f.* chamois.
gana /'gana/ *n. f.* desire, wish, mind (to). **de buena g.,** willingly. **tener ganas de,** to feel like.
ganado /ga'naðo/ *n. m.* cattle.
ganador /gana'ðor/ **-ra** *n.* winner.
ganancia /ga'nanθia; ga'nansia/ *n. f.* gain, profit; (*pl.*) earnings.
ganapán /gana'pan/ *n. m.* drudge.
ganar /ga'nar/ *v.* earn; win; beat.
ganchillo /gan'tʃiʎo; gan'tʃiyo/ *n. m.* crochet work.
gancho /'gantʃo/ *n. m.* hook, hanger, clip, hairpin.
gandul /gan'dul/ **-la** *n.* idler, tramp, hobo.
ganga /'gaŋga/ *n. f.* bargain.
gangrena /gaŋ'grena/ *n. f.* gangrene.
gansarón /gansa'ron/ *n. m.* gosling.
ganso /'ganso/ *n. m.* goose.
garabato /gara'βato/ *n. m.* hook; scrawl, scribble.
garaje /ga'rahe/ *n. m.* garage.
garantía /garan'tia/ *n. f.* guarantee; collateral, security.
garantizar /garanti'θar; garanti'sar/ *v.* guarantee, secure, pledge.
garbanzo /gar'βanθo; gar'βanso/ *n. m.* chickpea.
garbo /'garβo/ *n. m.* grace.
garboso /gar'βoso/ *a.* graceful, sprightly.
gardenia /gar'ðenia/ *n. f.* gardenia.
garfa /'garfa/ *n. f.* claw, talon.
garganta /gar'ganta/ *n. f.* throat.
gárgara /'gargara/ *n. f.* gargle. —**gargarizar,** *v.*
garita /ga'rita/ *n. f.* sentry box.
garito /ga'rito/ *n. m.* gambling house.
garlopa /gar'lopa/ *n. f.* carpenter's plane.
garra /'garra/ *n. f.* claw.
garrafa /ga'rrafa/ *n. f.* decanter, carafe.
garrideza /garri'ðeθa; garri'ðesa/ *n. f.* elegance, handsomeness.
garrido /ga'rriðo/ *a.* elegant, handsome.
garrote /ga'rrote/ *n. m.* club, cudgel.
garrotillo /garro'tiʎo; garro'tiyo/ *n. m.* croup.
garrudo /ga'rruðo/ *a.* powerful, brawny.
garza /'garθa; 'garsa/ *n. f.* heron.
gas /gas/ *n. m.* gas.
gasa /'gasa/ *n. f.* gauze.
gaseosa /gase'osa/ *n. f.* carbonated water.
gaseoso /gase'oso/ *a.* gaseous.
gasolina /gaso'lina/ *n. f.* gasoline.
gasolinera /gasoli'nera/ *n. f.* gas station.
gastar /gas'tar/ *v.* spend; use up, wear out; waste.
gastritis /gas'tritis/ *n. f.* gastritis.
gastrómano /gas'tromano/ *n. m.* glutton.
gastrónomo /gas'tronomo/ **-ma** *n.* gourmet, epicure, gastronome.
gatear /gate'ar/ *v.* creep.
gatillo /ga'tiʎo; ga'tiyo/ *n. m.* trigger.
gato /'gato/ **-ta** *n.* cat.
gaucho /'gautʃo/ *n. m.* Argentine cowboy.
gaveta /ga'βeta/ *n. f.* drawer.
gavilla /ga'βiʎa; ga'βiya/ *n. f.* sheaf.
gaviota /ga'βiota/ *n. f.* seagull.
gayo /ga'yo/ *a.* merry, gay.
gayola /ga'yola/ *n. m.* cage; *Colloq.* prison.
gazapera /gaθa'pera; gasa'pera/ *n. f.* rabbit warren.
gazapo /ga'θapo; ga'sapo/ *n. m.* rabbit.
gazmoñada /gaθmo'ɲaða; gasmo'ɲaða/ *n. f.* prudishness.
gazmoño /gaθ'moɲo; gas'moɲo/ *n. m.* prude.
gaznate /gaθ'nate; gas'nate/ *n. m.* windpipe.
gazpacho /gaθ'patʃo; gas'patʃo/ *n. m.* cold tomato soup; gazpacho.
gelatina /hela'tina/ *n. f.* gelatine.
gemelo /he'melo/ **-la** *n.* twin.
gemelos /he'melos/ *n. m.pl.* cuff links; opera glasses; **-as,** twins.
gemido /he'miðo/ *n. m.* moan, groan, wail. —**gemir,** *v.*
genciana /hen'θiana; hen'siana/ *n. f.* gentian.
genealogía /henealo'hia/ *n. f.* genealogy, pedigree.
generación /henera'θion; henera'sion/ *n. f.* generation.
generador /henera'ðor/ *n. m.* generator.
general /hene'ral/ *a.* & *m.* general.
generalidad /henerali'ðað/ *n. f.* generality.
generalización /heneraliθa'θion; heneralisa'sion/ *n. f.* generalization.
generalizar /henerali'θar; henerali'sar/ *v.* generalize.
generalmente /heneral'mente/ *adv.* generally.
género /'henero/ *n.* **1.** *m.* gender; kind. **2.** (*pl.*) goods, material.
generosidad /henerosi'ðað/ *n. f.* generosity.
generoso /hene'roso/ *a.* generous.
génesis /'henesis/ *n. m.* genesis.
genético /he'netiko/ *a.* genetic.
genial /he'nial/ *a.* genial; brilliant.
genio /'henio/ *n. m.* genius; temper; disposition.
genitivo /heni'tiβo/ *n. m.* genitive.
genocidio /heno'θiðio; heno'siðio/ *n. m.* genocide.
gente /'hente/ *n. f.* people, folk.
gentil /hen'til/ *a.* gracious; graceful.
gentileza /henti'leθa; henti'lesa/ *n. f.* grace, graciousness.
gentío /hen'tio/ *n. m.* mob, crowd.
genuino /he'nuino/ *a.* genuine.
geografía /heogra'fia/ *n. f.* geography.
geográfico /heo'grafiko/ *a.* geographical.
geométrico /heo'metriko/ *a.* geometric.
geranio /he'ranio/ *n. m.* geranium.
gerencia /he'renθia; he'rensia/ *n. f.* management.
gerente /he'rente/ *n. m.* & *f.* manager, director.
germen /'hermen/ *n. m.* germ.
germinar /hermi'nar/ *v.* germinate.
gerundio /he'rundio/ *n. m.* gerund.
gesticulación /hestikula'θion; hestikula'sion/ *n. f.* gesticulation.
gesticular /hestiku'lar/ *v.* gesticulate, gesture.
gestión /hes'tion/ *n. f.* conduct; effort; action.
gesto /'hesto/ *n. m.* gesture, facial expression.
gigante /hi'gante/ *a.* & *n.* gigantic, giant.
gigantesco /higan'tesko/ *a.* gigantic, huge.
gilipollas /gili'poʎas; gili'poyas/ *n. m.* & *f. Colloq.* fool, idiot.
gimnasio /him'nasio/ *n. m.* gymnasium.
gimnástica /him'nastika/ *n. f.* gymnastics.
gimotear /himote'ar/ *v.* whine.
ginebra /hi'neβra/ *n. f.* gin.
ginecólogo /hine'kologo/ **-ga** *n.* gynecologist.
gira /'hira/ *n. f.* tour, trip.
girado /hi'raðo/ **-da** *n. Com.* drawee.
girador /hira'ðor/ **-ra** *n. Com.* drawer.
girar /hi'rar/ *v.* revolve, turn, spin, whirl.
giratorio /hira'torio/ *a.* rotary, revolving.
giro /'hiro/ *n. m.* whirl, turn, spin; *Com.* draft. **g. postal,** money order.
gitano /hi'tano/ **-na** *a.* & *n.* Gypsy.
glacial /gla'θial; gla'sial/ *a.* glacial, icy.
glaciar /gla'θiar; gla'siar/ *n. m.* glacier.
gladiador /glaðia'ðor/ *n. m.* gladiator.
glándula /'glandula/ *n. f.* gland.
glándula endocrina /'glandula endo'krina/ endocrine gland.
glándula pituitaria /'glandula pitui'taria/ pituitary gland.
glándula prostática /'glandula pros'tatika/ prostate gland.
glasé /gla'se/ *n. m.* glacé.
glicerina /gliθe'rina; glise'rina/ *n. f.* glycerine.
globo /'gloβo/ *n. m.* globe; balloon.
gloria /'gloria/ *n. f.* glory.
glorieta /glo'rieta/ *n. f.* bower.
glorificación /glorifika'θion; glorifika'sion/ *n. f.* glorification.
glorificar /glorifi'kar/ *v.* glorify.
glorioso /glo'rioso/ *a.* glorious.

glosa /'glosa/ n. f. gloss. —**glosar,** v.

glosario /glo'sario/ n. m. glossary.

glotón /glo'ton/ **-ona** a. & n. gluttonous; glutton.

glucosa /glu'kosa/ n. f. glucose.

gluten /'gluten/ n. m. gluten; glue.

gobernación /goβerna'θion; goβerna'sion/ n. f. government.

gobernador /goβerna'ðor/ **-ra** n. governor.

gobernalle /goβer'naʎe; goβer'naye/ n. m. rudder, tiller, helm.

gobernante /goβer'nante/ n. m. & f. ruler.

gobernar /goβer'nar/ v. govern.

gobierno /go'βierno/ n. m. government.

goce /'goθe; 'gose/ n. m. enjoyment.

gola /'gola/ n. f. throat.

golf /golf/ n. m. golf.

golfista /gol'fista/ n. m. & f. golfer.

golfo /'golfo/ n. m. gulf.

gollete /go'ʎete; go'yete/ n. m. upper portion of one's throat.

golondrina /golon'drina/ n. f. swallow.

golosina /golo'sina/ n. f. delicacy.

goloso /go'loso/ a. sweet-toothed.

golpe /'golpe/ n. m. blow, stroke. **de g.,** suddenly.

golpear /golpe'ar/ v. strike, beat, pound.

goma /'goma/ n. f. rubber; gum; glue; eraser.

góndola /'gondola/ n. f. gondola.

gordo /'gorðo/ a. fat.

gordura /gor'ðura/ n. f. fatness.

gorila /go'rila/ n. m. gorilla.

gorja /'gorha/ n. f. gorge.

gorjeo /gor'heo/ n. m. warble, chirp. —**gorjear,** v.

gorrión /go'rrion/ n. m. sparrow.

gorro /'gorro/ n. m. cap.

gota /'gota/ n. f. drop (of liquid).

gotear /gote'ar/ v. drip, leak.

goteo /go'teo/ n. m. leak.

gotera /go'tera/ n. f. leak; gutter.

gótico /'gotiko/ a. Gothic.

gozar /go'θar; go'sar/ v. enjoy.

gozne /'goθne; 'gosne/ n. m. hinge.

gozo /'goθo; 'goso/ n. m. enjoyment, delight, joy.

gozoso /go'θoso; go'soso/ a. joyful, joyous.

grabado /gra'βaðo/ n. **1.** m. engraving, cut, print. —a. **2.** recorded.

grabador /graβa'ðor/ n. m. engraver.

grabadora /graβa'ðora/ n. f. tape recorder.

grabar /gra'βar/ v. engrave; record.

gracia /'graθia; 'grasia/ n. f. grace; wit, charm. **hacer g.,** to amuse, strike as funny. **tener g.,** to be funny, to be witty.

gracias /'graθias; 'grasias/ n. f.pl. thanks, thank you.

gracioso /gra'θioso; gra'sioso/ a. witty, funny.

grada /'graða/ n. f. step.

gradación /graða'θion; graða'sion/ n. f. gradation.

grado /'graðo/ n. m. grade; rank; degree.

graduado /gra'ðuaðo/ **-da** n. graduate.

gradual /gra'ðual/ a. gradual.

graduar /gra'ðuar/ v. grade; graduate.

gráfico /'grafiko/ a. graphic, vivid.

grafito /gra'fito/ n. m. graphite.

grajo /'graho/ n. m. jackdaw.

gramática /gra'matika/ n. f. grammar.

gramo /'gramo/ n. m. gram.

gran /gran/ **grande** a. big, large; great.

granada /gra'naða/ n. f. grenade; pomegranate.

granar /gra'nar/ v. seed.

grandes almacenes /'grandes alma'θenes; 'grandes alma'senes/ n. m.pl. department store.

grandeza /gran'deθa; gran'desa/ n. f. greatness.

grandiosidad /grandiosi'ðað/ n. f. grandeur.

grandioso /gran'dioso/ a. grand, magnificent.

grandor /gran'dor/ n. m. size.

granero /gra'nero/ n. m. barn; granary.

granito /gra'nito/ n. m. granite.

granizada /grani'θaða; grani'saða/ n. f. hailstorm.

granizo /gra'niθo; gra'niso/ n. m. hail. —**granizar,** v.

granja /'granha/ n. f. grange; farm; farmhouse.

granjear /granhe'ar/ v. earn, gain; get.

granjero /gran'hero/ **-era** n. farmer.

grano /'grano/ n. m. grain; kernel.

granuja /gra'nuha/ n. m. waif, urchin.

grapa /'grapa/ n. f. clamp, clip.

grapadora /grapa'ðora/ n. f. stapler.

grasa /'grasa/ n. f. grease, fat.

grasiento /gra'siento/ a. greasy.

gratificación /gratifika'θion; gratifika'sion/ n. f. gratification; reward; tip.

gratificar /gratifi'kar/ v. gratify; reward; tip.

gratis /'gratis/ adv. gratis, free.

gratitud /grati'tuð/ n. f. gratitude.

grato /'grato/ a. grateful; pleasant.

gratuito /gra'tuito/ a. gratuitous; free.

gravamen /gra'βamen/ n. m. tax; burden; obligation.

grave /'graβe/ a. grave, serious, severe.

gravedad /graβe'ðað/ n. f. gravity, seriousness.

gravitación /graβita'θion; graβita'sion/ n. f. gravitation.

gravitar /graβi'tar/ v. gravitate.

gravoso /gra'βoso/ a. burdensome.

graznido /graθ'niðo; gras'niðo/ n. m. croak. —**graznar,** v.

Grecia /'greθia; 'gresia/ n. f. Greece.

greco /'greko/ **-ca** a. & n. Greek.

greda /'greða/ n. f. clay.

gresca /'greska/ n. f. revelry; quarrel.

griego /'griego/ **-ga** a. & n. Greek.

grieta /'grieta/ n. f. opening; crevice; crack.

grifo /'grifo/ n. m. faucet.

grillo /'griʎo; 'griyo/ n. m. cricket.

grima /'grima/ n. f. fright.

gringo /'gringo/ **-ga** n. foreigner (usually North American).

gripa /'gripa/ **gripe** n. f. grippe.

gris /gris/ a. gray.

grito /'grito/ n. m. shout, scream, cry. —**gritar,** v.

grosella /gro'seʎa; gro'seya/ n. f. currant.

grosería /grose'ria/ n. f. grossness; coarseness.

grosero /gro'sero/ a. coarse, vulgar, discourteous.

grotesco /gro'tesko/ a. grotesque.

grúa /'grua/ n. f. crane; tow truck.

gruesa /'gruesa/ n. f. gross.

grueso /'grueso/ a. **1.** bulky; stout; coarse, thick. —n. **2.** m. bulk.

grulla /'gruʎa; 'gruya/ n. f. crane.

gruñido /gru'niðo/ n. m. growl, snarl, mutter. —**gruñir,** v.

grupo /'grupo/ n. m. group, party.

gruta /'gruta/ n. f. cavern.

guacamol /guaka'mol/ **guacamole** n. m. avocado sauce; guacamole.

guadaña /gua'ðaɲa/ n. f. scythe. —**guadañar,** v.

guagua /'guagua/ n. f. (S.A.) baby; (Carib.) bus.

gualdo /'gualdo/ n. m. yellow, golden.

guano /'guano/ n. m. guano (fertilizer).

guante /'guante/ n. m. glove.

guantera /guan'tera/ n. f. glove compartment.

guapo /'guapo/ a. handsome.

guarda /'guarða/ n. m. or f. guard.

guardabarros /guarða'βarros/ n. m. fender.

guardacostas /guarða'kostas/ n. m. revenue ship.

guardaespaldas /,guarðaes'paldas/ n. m. & f. bodyguard.

guardameta /guarða'meta/ n. m. & f. goalkeeper.

guardar /guar'ðar/ v. keep, store, put away; guard.

guardarropa /guarða'rropa/ n. f. coat room.

guardarse de /guar'ðarse de/ v. beware of, avoid.

guardia /'guarðia/ n. **1.** f. guard; watch. —n. **2.** m. policeman.

guardián /guar'ðian/ **-na** n. guardian, keeper, watchman.

guardilla /guar'ðiʎa; guar'ðiya/ n. f. attic.

guarida /gua'riða/ n. f. den.

guarismo /gua'rismo/ n. m. number, figure.

guarnecer /guarne'θer; guarne'ser/ v. adorn.

guarnición /guarni'θion; guarni'sion/ n. f. garrison; trimming.

guasa /'guasa/ n. f. joke, jest.

guayaba /gua'yaβa/ n. f. guava.

gubernativo /guβerna'tiβo/ a. governmental.

guerra /'gerra/ n. f. war.

guerrero /ge'rrero/ **-ra** n. warrior.

guía /'gia/ n. **1.** m. & f. guide. **2.** f. guidebook, directory.

guiar /giar/ v. guide; steer, drive.

guija /'giha/ n. f. pebble.

guillotina /giʎo'tina; giyo'tina/ n. f. guillotine.

guindar /gin'dar/ v. hang.

guinga /'ginga/ n. f. gingham.

guiñada /gi'naða/ n. f., **guiño,** m. wink. —**guiñar,** v.

guión /gi'on/ n. m. dash, hyphen; script.

guirnalda /gir'nalda/ n. f. garland, wreath.

guisa /'gisa/ n. f. guise, manner.

guisado /gi'saðo/ n. m. stew.

guisante /gi'sante/ n. m. pea.

guisar /gi'sar/ v. cook.

guiso /'giso/ n. m. stew.

guita /'gita/ n. f. twine.

guitarra /gi'tarra/ n. f. guitar.

guitarrista /gita'rrista/ n. m. & f. guitarist.

gula /'gula/ n. f. gluttony.

gurú /gu'ru/ n. m. guru.

gusano /gu'sano/ n. m. worm, caterpillar.

gustar /gus'tar/ v. please; taste.

gustillo /gus'tiʎo; gus'tiyo/ n. m. aftertaste, slight pleasure.

gusto /'gusto/ n. m. pleasure; taste; liking.

gustoso /gus'toso/ a. pleasant; tasteful.

gutural /gutu'ral/ a. guttural.

H

haba /'aβa/ n. f. bean.

habanera /aβa'nera/ n. f. Cuban dance melody.

haber /a'βer/ v. have. **h. de,** be to, be supposed to.

haberes /a'βeres/ n. m.pl. property; worldly goods.

habichuela /aβi'tʃuela/ n. f. bean.

hábil /'aβil/ a. skillful; capable; clever.

habilidad /aβili'ðað/ n. f. ability; skill; talent.

habilidoso /aβili'ðoso/ a. able, skillful, talented.

habilitado /aβili'taðo/ **-da** n. paymaster.

habilitar /aβili'tar/ v. qualify; supply, equip.

hábilmente /'aβilmente/ adv. ably.

habitación /aβita'θion; aβita'sion/ n. f. dwelling; room. **h. individual,** single room.

habitante /aβi'tante/ n. m. & f. inhabitant.

habitar /aβi'tar/ v. inhabit; dwell.

hábito /'aβito/ n. m. habit; custom.

habitual /aβi'tual/ a. habitual.

habituar /aβi'tuar/ v. accustom, habituate.

habla /'aβla/ n. f. speech.

hablador /aβla'ðor/ a. talkative.

hablar /a'βlar/ v. talk, speak.

haca /'aka/ n. f. pony.

hacedor /aθe'ðor; ase'ðor/ n. m. maker.

hacendado /aθen'daðo; asen'daðo/ **-da** n. hacienda owner; farmer.

hacendoso /aθen'doso; asen'doso/ a. industrious.

hacer /a'θer; a'ser/ v. do; make. **hace dos años,** etc., two years ago, etc.

hacerse /a'θerse; a'serse/ v. become, get to be.

hacha /'atʃa/ n. f. ax, hatchet.

hacia /'aθia; 'asia/ prep. toward.

hacienda /a'θienda; a'sienda/ n. f. property; estate; ranch; farm; Govt. treasury.

hada /'aða/ n. f. fairy.

hado /'aðo/ n. m. fate.

halagar /ala'gar/ v. flatter.

halar /a'lar/ v. haul, pull.

halcón /al'kon/ n. m. hawk, falcon.

haleche /a'letʃe/ n. m. anchovy.

hallado /a'ʎaðo; a'yaðo/ a. found. **bien h.,** welcome. **mal h.,** uneasy.

hallar /a'ʎar; a'yar/ v. find, locate.

hallarse /a'ʎarse; a'yarse/ v. be located; happen to be.

hallazgo /a'ʎaðgo; a'yasgo/ n. m. find, thing found.

hamaca /a'maka/ n. f. hammock.

hambre /'ambre/ n. f. hunger. **tener h., estar con h.,** to be hungry.

hambrear /ambre'ar/ v. hunger; starve.

hambriento /am'briento/ a. starving, hungry.

hamburguesa /ambur'gesa/ n. f. beefburger, hamburger.

haragán /ara'gan/ **-na** n. idler, lazy person.

haraganear /aragane'ar/ v. loiter.

harapo /a'rapo/ n. m. rag, tatter.

haraposo /ara'poso/ a. ragged, shabby.

harén /a'ren/ n. m. harem.

harina /a'rina/ n. f. flour, meal.

harnero /ar'nero/ n. m. sieve.

hartar /ar'tar/ v. satiate.

harto /'arto/ a. stuffed; fed up.

hartura /ar'tura/ n. f. superabundance, glut.

hasta /'asta/ prep. **1.** until, till; as far as, up to. **h. luego,** good-bye, so long. —adv. **2.** even.

hastío /as'tio/ n. m. distaste, loathing.

hato /'ato/ n. m. herd.

hay /ai/ v. there is, there are. **h. que,** it is necessary to. **no h. de qué,** you're welcome, don't mention it.

haya /'aya/ n. f. beech tree.

haz /aθ; as/ n. f. bundle, sheaf; face.

hazaña /a'θaɲa; a'saɲa/ n. f. deed; exploit, feat.

hebdomadario /eβðoma'ðario/ a. weekly.

hebilla /e'βiʎa; e'βiya/ n. f. buckle.

hebra /'eβra/ n. f. thread, string.

hebreo /e'βreo/ **-rea** a. & n. Hebrew.

hechicero /etʃi'θero; etʃi'sero/ **-ra** n. wizard, witch.

hechizar /etʃi'θar; etʃi'sar/ v. bewitch.

hechizo /e'tʃiθo; e'tʃiso/ n. m. spell.

hecho /'etʃo/ n. m. fact; act; deed.

hechura /e'tʃura/ n. f. workmanship, make.

hediondez /eðion'deθ; eðion'des/ n. f. stench.

hégira /'ehira/ n. f. hegira.

helada /e'laða/ n. f. frost.

heladería /elaðe'ria/ n. f. ice-cream parlor.

helado /e'laðo/ n. m. ice cream.

helar /e'lar/ *v.* freeze.

helecho /e'letʃo/ *n. m.* fern.

hélice /'eliθe; 'elise/ *n. f.* propeller; helix.

helicóptero /eli'koptero/ *n. m.* helicopter.

helio /'elio/ *n. m.* helium.

hembra /'embra/ *n. f.* female.

hemisferio /emis'ferio/ *n. m.* hemisphere.

hemoglobina /emoglo'βina/ *n. f.* hemoglobin.

hemorragia /emo'rrahia/ *n. f.* hemorrhage.

hemorragia nasal /emo'rrahia na'sal/ nosebleed.

henchir /en'tʃir/ *v.* stuff.

hendedura /ende'ðura/ *n. f.* crevice, crack.

hendido /en'diðo/ *a.* cloven, cleft (lip).

heno /'eno/ *n. m.* hay.

hepática /e'patika/ *n. f.* liverwort.

hepatitis /epa'titis/ *n. f.* hepatitis.

heraldo /e'raldo/ *n. m.* herald.

herbáceo /er'βaθeo; er'βaseo/ *a.* herbaceous.

herbívoro /er'βiβoro/ *a.* herbivorous.

heredar /ere'ðar/ *v.* inherit.

heredero /ere'ðero/ **-ra** *n.* heir; successor.

hereditario /ereði'tario/ *a.* hereditary.

hereje /e'rehe/ *n. m. & f.* heretic.

herejía /ere'hia/ *n. f.* heresy.

herencia /e'renθia; e'rensia/ *n. f.* inheritance; heritage.

herético /e'retiko/ *a.* heretical.

herida /e'riða/ *n. f.* wound, injury.

herir /e'rir/ *v.* wound, injure.

hermafrodita /ermafro'ðita/ *a. & n.* hermaphrodite.

hermana /er'mana/ *n. f.* sister.

hermano /er'mano/ *n. m.* brother.

hermético /er'metiko/ *a.* airtight.

hermoso /er'moso/ *a.* beautiful, handsome.

hermosura /ermo'sura/ *n. f.* beauty.

hernia /'ernia/ *n. f.* hernia, rupture.

héroe /'eroe/ *n. m.* hero.

heroico /e'roiko/ *a.* heroic.

heroína /ero'ina/ *n. f.* heroine.

heroísmo /ero'ismo/ *n. m.* heroism.

herradura /erra'ðura/ *n. f.* horseshoe.

herramienta /erra'mienta/ *n. f.* tool; implement.

herrería /erre'ria/ *n. f.* blacksmith's shop.

herrero /e'rrero/ *n. m.* blacksmith.

herrumbre /e'rrumbre/ *n. f.* rust.

hertzio /'ertθio; 'ertsio/ *n. m.* hertz.

hervir /er'βir/ *v.* boil.

hesitación /esita'θion; esita'sion/ *n. f.* hesitation.

heterogéneo /etero'heneo/ *a.* heterogeneous.

heterosexual /eterosek'sual/ *a.* heterosexual.

hexagonal /eksago'nal/ *a.* hexagonal.

hexágono /e'ksagono/ *n. m.* hexagon.

hez /eθ; es/ *n. f.* dregs, sediment.

híbrido /'iβriðo/ **-da** *n. & a.* hybrid.

hidalgo /i'ðalgo/ **-ga** *a. & n.* noble.

hidalguía /iðal'gia/ *n. f.* nobility; generosity.

hidráulico /i'ðrauliko/ *a.* hydraulic.

hidroavión /iðroa'βion/ *n. m.* seaplane, hydroplane.

hidrofobia /iðro'foβia/ *n. f.* rabies.

hidrógeno /i'ðroheno/ *n. m.* hydrogen.

hidropesía /iðrope'sia/ *n. f.* dropsy.

hiedra /'ieðra/ *n. f.* ivy.

hiel /iel/ *n. f.* gall.

hielo /'ielo/ *n. m.* ice.

hiena /'iena/ *n. f.* hyena.

hierba /'ierβa/ *n. f.* grass; herb; marijuana.

hierbabuena /ierβa'βuena/ *n. f.* mint.

hierro /'ierro/ *n. m.* iron.

hígado /'igaðo/ *n. m.* liver.

higiene /i'hiene/ *n. f.* hygiene.

higiénico /i'hieniko/ *a.* sanitary, hygienic.

higo /'igo/ *n. m.* fig.

higuera /i'gera/ *n. f.* fig tree.

hija /'iha/ *n. f.* daughter.

hija adoptiva /'iha aðop'tiβa/ adopted daughter.

hijastro /i'hastro/ **-tra** *n.* stepchild.

hijo /'iho/ *n. m.* son.

hijo adoptivo /'iho aðop'tiβo/ *n. m.* adopted child, adopted son.

hila /'ila/ *n. f.* line.

hilandero /ilan'dero/ **-ra** *n.* spinner.

hilar /i'lar/ *v.* spin.

hilera /i'lera/ *n. f.* row, line, tier.

hilo /'ilo/ *n. m.* thread; string; wire; linen.

himno /'imno/ *n. m.* hymn.

hincar /in'kar/ *v.* drive, thrust; sink into.

hincarse /in'karse/ *v.* kneel.

hinchar /in'tʃar/ *v.* swell.

hindú /in'du/ *n. & a.* Hindu.

hinojo /i'noho/ *n. m.* knee.

hiperenlace /iperen'laθe, iperen'lase/ *n. m.* hyperlink.

hipermercado /ipermer'kaðo/ *n. m.* hypermarket.

hipertexto /iper'teksto/ *n. m.* hypertext.

hipnótico /ip'notiko/ *a.* hypnotic.

hipnotismo /ipno'tismo/ *n. m.* hypnotism.

hipnotista /ipno'tista/ *n. m. & f.* hypnotist.

hipnotizar /ipnoti'θar; ipnoti'sar/ *v.* hypnotize.

hipo /'ipo/ *n. m.* hiccough.

hipocresía /ipokre'sia/ *n. f.* hypocrisy.

hipócrita /i'pokrita/ *a. & n.* hypocritical; hypocrite.

hipódromo /i'poðromo/ *n. m.* race track.

hipoteca /ipo'teka/ *n. f.* mortgage. —**hipotecar,** *v.*

hipótesis /i'potesis/ *n. f.* hypothesis.

hirsuto /ir'suto/ *a.* hairy, hirsute.

hispano /is'pano/ *a.* Hispanic, Spanish American.

Hispanoamérica /ispanoa'merika/ *f.* Spanish America.

hispanoamericano /ispanoameri'kano/ **-na** *a. & n.* Spanish American.

histerectomía /isterekto'mia/ *n. f.* hysterectomy.

histeria /is'teria/ *n. f.* hysteria.

histérico /is'teriko/ *a.* hysterical.

historia /is'toria/ *n. f.* history; story.

historiador /istoria'ðor/ **-ra** *n.* historian.

histórico /is'toriko/ *a.* historic, historical.

histrión /is'trion/ *n. m.* actor.

hocico /o'θiko; o'siko/ *n. m.* snout, muzzle.

hogar /o'gar/ *n. m.* hearth; home.

hoguera /o'gera/ *n. f.* bonfire, blaze.

hoja /'oha/ *n. f.* leaf; sheet (of paper); pane; blade.

hoja de cálculo /'oha de 'kalkulo/ spreadsheet.

hoja de inscripción /'oha de inskrip'θion; 'oha de inskrip'sion/ entry blank.

hoja de pedidos /'oha de pe'ðiðos/ order blank.

hoja informativa /'oha informa'tiβa/ newsletter.

hojalata /oha'lata/ *n. f.* tin.

hojalatero /ohala'tero/ **-ra** *n.* tinsmith.

hojear /ohe'ar/ *v.* scan, skim through.

hola /'ola/ *interj.* hello.

Holanda /o'landa/ *n. f.* Holland, Netherlands.

holandés /olan'des/ **-esa** *a. & n.* Dutch; Hollander.

holganza /ol'ganθa; ol'gansa/ *n. f.* leisure; diversion.

holgazán /olga'θan; olga'san/ **-ana** *a.*

1. idle, lazy. —*n.* **2.** *m.* idler, loiterer, tramp.

holgazanear /olgaθane'ar; olgasane'ar/ *v.* idle, loiter.

hollín /o'ʎin; o'yin/ *n. m.* soot.

holografía /ologra'fia/ *n. f.* holography.

holograma /olo'grama/ *n. m.* hologram.

hombre /'ombre/ *n. m.* man.

hombría /om'βria/ *n. f.* manliness.

hombro /'ombro/ *n. m.* shoulder.

hombruno /om'bruno/ *a.* mannish, masculine (woman).

homenaje /ome'nahe/ *n. m.* homage.

homeópata /ome'opata/ *n. m.* homeopath.

homicidio /omi'θiðio; omi'siðio/ *n. m.* homicide.

homilía /omi'lia/ *n. f.* homily.

homosexual /omose'ksual/ *a.* homosexual, gay.

honda /'onda/ *n. f.* sling.

hondo /'ondo/ *a.* deep.

hondonada /ondo'naða/ *n. f.* ravine.

hondura /on'dura/ *n. f.* depth.

honestidad /onesti'ðað/ *n. f.* modesty, unpretentiousness.

honesto /o'nesto/ *a.* honest; pure; just.

hongo /'oŋgo/ *n. m.* fungus; mushroom.

honor /o'nor/ *n. m.* honor.

honorable /ono'raβle/ *a.* honorable.

honorario /ono'rario/ *a.* **1.** honorary. —*n.* **2.** *m.* honorarium, fee.

honorífico /ono'rifiko/ *a.* honorary.

honra /'onra/ *n. f.* honor. —**honrar,** *v.*

honradez /onra'ðeθ; onra'ðes/ *n. f.* honesty.

honrado /on'raðo/ *a.* honest, honorable.

hora /'ora/ *n. f.* hour; time (of day).

horadar /ora'ðar/ *v.* perforate.

hora punta /'ora 'punta/ rush hour.

horario /o'rario/ *n. m.* timetable, schedule.

horca /'orka/ *n. f.* gallows; pitchfork.

horda /'orða/ *n. f.* horde.

horizontal /oriθon'tal; orison'tal/ *a.* horizontal.

horizonte /ori'θonte; ori'sonte/ *n. m.* horizon.

hormiga /or'miga/ *n. f.* ant.

hormiguear /ormige'ar/ *v.* itch.

hormiguero /ormi'gero/ *n. m.* ant hill.

hornero /or'nero/ **-ra** *n.* baker.

hornillo /or'niʎo; or'nijo/ *n. m.* stove.

horno /'orno/ *n. m.* oven; kiln.

horóscopo /o'roskopo/ *n. m.* horoscope.

horrendo /o'rrendo/ *a.* dreadful, horrendous.

horrible /o'rriβle/ *a.* horrible, hideous, awful.

hórrido /'orriðo/ *a.* horrid.

horror /o'rror/ *n. m.* horror.

horrorizar /orrori'θar; orrori'sar/ *v.* horrify.

horroroso /orro'roso/ *a.* horrible, frightful.

hortelano /orte'lano/ *n. m.* horticulturist.

hospedaje /ospe'ðahe/ *n. m.* lodging.

hospedar /ospe'ðar/ *v.* give or take lodgings.

hospital /ospi'tal/ *n. m.* hospital.

hospitalario /ospita'lario/ *a.* hospitable.

hospitalidad /ospitali'ðað/ *n. f.* hospitality.

hospitalmente /ospital'mente/ *adv.* hospitably.

hostia /'ostia/ *n. f.* host; *Colloq.* hit, blow.

hostil /os'til/ *a.* hostile.

hostilidad /ostili'ðað/ *n. f.* hostility.

hotel /o'tel/ *n. m.* hotel.

hoy /oi/ *adv.* today. **h. día, h. en día,** nowadays.

hoya /'oya/ *n. f.* dale, valley.

hoyo /'oyo/ *n. m.* pit, hole.

hoyuelo /o'yuelo/ *n. m.* dimple.

hoz /oθ; os/ *n. f.* sickle.

hucha /'utʃa/ *n. f.* chest, money box; savings.

hueco /'ueko/ *a.* **1.** hollow, empty. —*n.* **2.** *m.* hole, hollow.

huelga /'uelga/ *n. f.* strike.

huelgista /uel'hista/ *n. m. & f.* striker.

huella /'ueʎa; 'ueya/ *n. f.* track, trace; footprint.

huérfano /'uerfano/ **-na** *a. & n.* orphan.

huero /'uero/ *a.* empty.

huerta /'uerta/ *n. f.* (vegetable) garden.

huerto /'uerto/ *n. m.* orchard.

hueso /'ueso/ *n. m.* bone; fruit pit.

huésped /'uespeð/ *n. m. & f.* guest.

huesudo /ue'suðo/ *a.* bony.

huevo /'ueβo/ *n. m.* egg.

huída /'uiða/ *n. f.* flight, escape.

huir /uir/ *v.* flee.

hule /'ule/ *n. m.* oilcloth.

humanidad /umani'ðað/ *n. f.* humanity, mankind; humaneness.

humanista /uma'nista/ *n. m. & f.* humanist.

humanitario /umani'tario/ *a.* humane.

humano /u'mano/ *a.* human; humane.

humareda /uma'reða/ *n. f.* dense cloud of smoke.

humear /ume'ar/ *v.* emit smoke or steam.

humedad /ume'ðað/ *n. f.* humidity, moisture, dampness.

humedecer /umeðe'θer; umeðe'ser/ *v.* moisten, dampen.

húmedo /'umeðo/ *a.* humid, moist, damp.

humildad /umil'dað/ *n. f.* humility, meekness.

humilde /u'milde/ *a.* humble, meek.

humillación /umiʎa'θion; umiya'sion/ *n. f.* humiliation.

humillar /umi'ʎar; umi'yar/ *v.* humiliate.

humo /'umo/ *n. m.* smoke; (*pl.*) airs, affectation.

humor /u'mor/ *n. m.* humor, mood.

humorista /umo'rista/ *n. m. & f.* humorist.

hundimiento /undi'miento/ *n. m.* collapse.

hundir /un'dir/ *v.* sink; collapse.

húngaro /'uŋgaro/ **-ra** *a. & n.* Hungarian.

Hungría /uŋ'gria/ *n. f.* Hungary.

huracán /ura'kan/ *n. m.* hurricane.

huraño /u'raɲo/ *a.* shy, bashful.

hurgar /ur'gar/ *v.* stir.

hurón /u'ron/ *n. m.* ferret.

hurtadillas /urta'ðiʎas; urta'ðiyas/ *n. f.pl.* **a h.,** on the sly.

hurtador /urta'ðor/ **-ra** *n.* thief.

hurtar /ur'tar/ *v.* steal, rob of; hide.

hurtarse /ur'tarse/ *v.* hide; withdraw.

husmear /usme'ar/ *v.* scent, smell.

huso /'uso/ *n. m.* spindle; bobbin.

huso horario /'uso o'rario/ time zone.

I

ibérico /i'βeriko/ *a.* Iberian.

iberoamericano /iβeroameri'kano/ **-na** *a. & n.* Latin American.

ida /'iða/ *n. f.* departure; trip out. **i. y vuelta,** round trip.

idea /i'ðea/ *n. f.* idea.

ideal /i'ðeal/ *a. & m.* ideal.

idealismo /iðea'lismo/ *n. m.* idealism.

idealista /iðea'lista/ *n. m. & f.* idealist.

idear /iðe'ar/ *v.* plan, conceive.

idéntico /i'ðentiko/ *a.* identical.

identidad /iðenti'ðað/ *n. f.* identity; identification.

identificar /iðentifi'kar/ v. identify.
idilio /i'ðilio/ n. m. idyll.
idioma /i'ðioma/ n. m. language.
idiota /i'ðiota/ a. & n. idiotic; idiot.
idiotismo /iðio'tismo/ n. m. idiom; idiocy.
idolatrar /iðola'trar/ v. idolize, adore.
ídolo /'iðolo/ n. m. idol.
idóneo /i'ðoneo/ a. suitable, fit, apt.
iglesia /i'glesia/ n. f. church.
ignición /igni'θion; igni'sion/ n. f. ignition.
ignominia /igno'minia/ n. f. ignominy, shame.
ignominioso /ignomi'nioso/ a. ignominious, shameful.
ignorancia /igno'ranθia; igno'ransia/ n. f. ignorance.
ignorante /igno'rante/ a. ignorant.
ignorar /igno'rar/ v. be ignorant of, not know.
ignoto /ig'noto/ a. unknown.
igual /i'gual/ a. equal; the same; (pl.) alike. m. equal.
igualar /igua'lar/ v. equal; equalize; match.
igualdad /igual'dað/ n. f. equality; sameness.
ijada /i'haða/ n. f. flank (of an animal).
ilegal /ile'gal/ a. illegal.
ilegítimo /ile'hitimo/ a. illegitimate.
ileso /i'leso/ a. unharmed.
ilícito /i'liθito; i'lisito/ a. illicit, unlawful.
iluminación /ilumina'θion; ilumina'sion/ n. f. illumination.
iluminar /ilumi'nar/ v. illuminate.
ilusión /ilu'sion/ n. f. illusion.
ilusión de óptica /ilu'sion de 'optika/ optical illusion.
ilusorio /ilu'sorio/ a. illusive.
ilustración /ilustra'θion; ilustra'sion/ n. f. illustration; learning.
ilustrador /ilustra'ðor/ **-ra** n. illustrator.
ilustrar /ilus'trar/ v. illustrate.
ilustre /i'lustre/ a. illustrious, honorable, distinguished.
imagen /i'mahen/ n. f. image.
imaginación /imahina'θion; imahina'sion/ n. f. imagination.
imaginar /imahi'nar/ v. imagine.
imaginario /imahi'nario/ a. imaginary.
imaginativo /imahina'tiβo/ a. imaginative.
imán /i'man/ n. m. magnet; imam.
imbécil /im'beθil; im'besil/ a. & n. imbecile; stupid, foolish; fool.
imbuir /im'buir/ v. imbue, instil.
imitación /imita'θion; imita'sion/ n. f. imitation.
imitador /imita'ðor/ **-ra** n. imitator.
imitar /imi'tar/ v. imitate.
impaciencia /impa'θienθia; impa'siensia/ n. f. impatience.
impaciente /impa'θiente; impa'siente/ a. impatient.
impar /im'par/ a. unequal, uneven, odd.
imparcial /impar'θial; impar'sial/ a. impartial.
impasible /impa'siβle/ a. impassive, unmoved.
impávido /im'paβiðo/ adj. fearless, intrepid.
impedimento /impeði'mento/ n. m. impediment, obstacle.
impedir /impe'ðir/ v. impede, hinder, stop, obstruct.
impeler /impe'ler/ v. impel; incite.
impensado /impen'saðo/ a. unexpected.
imperar /impe'rar/ v. reign; prevail.
imperativo /impera'tiβo/ a. imperative.
imperceptible /imperθep'tiβle; impersep'tiβle/ a. imperceptible.
imperdible /imper'ðiβle/ n. m. safety pin.
imperecedero /impereθe'ðero; imperese'ðero/ a. imperishable.

imperfecto /imper'fekto/ a. imperfect, faulty.
imperial /impe'rial/ a. imperial.
imperialismo /imperia'lismo/ n. m. imperialism.
impericia /impe'riθia; impe'risia/ n. f. inexperience.
imperio /im'perio/ n. m. empire.
imperioso /impe'rioso/ a. imperious, domineering.
impermeable /imperme'aβle/ a. waterproof. m. raincoat.
impersonal /imperso'nal/ a. impersonal.
impertinencia /impertinen'θia; impertinen'sia/ n. f. impertinence.
ímpetu /'impetu/ n. m. impulse; impetus.
impetuoso /impe'tuoso/ a. impetuous.
impiedad /impie'ðað/ n. f. impiety.
impío /im'pio/ a. impious.
implacable /impla'kaβle/ a. implacable, unrelenting.
implicar /impli'kar/ v. implicate, involve.
implorar /implo'rar/ v. implore.
imponente /impo'nente/ a. impressive.
imponer /impo'ner/ v. impose.
impopular /impopu'lar/ a. unpopular.
importación /importa'θion; importa'sion/ n. f. importation, importing.
importador /importa'ðor/ **-ra** n. importer.
importancia /impor'tanθia; impor'tansia/ n. f. importance.
importante /impor'tante/ a. important.
importar /impor'tar/ v. be important, matter; import.
importe /im'porte/ n. m. value; amount.
importunar /importu'nar/ v. beg, importune.
imposibilidad /imposiβili'ðað/ n. f. impossibility.
imposibilitado /imposiβili'taðo/ a. helpless.
imposible /impo'siβle/ a. impossible.
imposición /imposi'θion; imposi'sion/ n. f. imposition.
impostor /impos'tor/ **-ra** n. imposter, faker.
impotencia /impo'tenθia; impo'tensia/ n. f. impotence.
impotente /impo'tente/ a. impotent.
imprecar /impre'kar/ v. curse.
impreciso /impre'θiso; impre'siso/ adj. inexact.
impregnar /impreg'nar/ v. impregnate.
imprenta /im'prenta/ n. f. press; printing house.
imprescindible /impresθin'diβle; impressin'diβle/ a. essential.
impresión /impre'sion/ n. f. impression.
impresionable /impresio'naβle/ a. impressionable.
impresionar /impresio'nar/ v. impress.
impresor /impre'sor/ n. m. printer.
imprevisión /impreβi'sion/ n. f. oversight; thoughtlessness.
imprevisto /impre'βisto/ a. unexpected, unforeseen.
imprimir /impri'mir/ v. print; imprint.
improbable /impro'βaβle/ a. improbable.
improbo /im'proβo/ a. dishonest.
improductivo /improðuk'tiβo/ a. unproductive.
improperio /impro'perio/ n. m. insult.
impropio /im'propio/ a. improper.
improvisación /improβisa'θion; improβisa'sion/ n. f. improvisation.
improvisar /improβi'sar/ v. improvise.
improviso /impro'βiso, impro'βisto/ a. unforeseen.

imprudencia /impru'ðenθia; impru'ðensia/ n. f. imprudence.
imprudente /impru'ðente/ a. imprudent, reckless.
impuesto /im'puesto/ n. m. tax.
impuesto sobre la renta /im'puesto soβre la 'rrenta/ income tax.
impulsar /impul'sar/ v. prompt, impel.
impulsivo /impul'siβo/ a. impulsive.
impulso /im'pulso/ n. m. impulse.
impureza /impu'reθa; impu'resa/ n. f. impurity.
impuro /im'puro/ a. impure.
imputación /imputa'θion; imputa'sion/ n. f. imputation.
imputar /impu'tar/ v. impute, attribute.
inaccesible /inakθe'siβle; inakse'siβle/ a. inaccessible.
inacción /inak'θion; inak'sion/ n. f. inaction; inactivity.
inaceptable /inaθep'taβle; inasep'taβle/ a. unacceptable.
inactivo /inak'tiβo/ a. inactive; sluggish.
inadecuado /inaðe'kuaðo/ a. inadequate.
inadvertencia /inaðβer'tenθia; inaðβer'tensia/ n. f. oversight.
inadvertido /inaðβer'tiðo/ a. inadvertent, careless; unnoticed.
inagotable /inago'taβle/ a. inexhaustible.
inalterado /inalte'raðo/ a. unchanged.
inanición /inani'θion; inani'sion/ n. f. starvation.
inanimado /inani'maðo/ adj. inanimate.
inapetencia /inape'tenθia; inape'tensia/ n. f. lack of appetite.
inaplicable /inapli'kaβle/ a. inapplicable; unfit.
inaudito /inau'ðito/ a. unheard of.
inauguración /inaugura'θion; inaugura'sion/ n. f. inauguration.
inaugurar /inaugu'rar/ v. inaugurate, open.
incandescente /inkandes'θente; inkandes'sente/ a. incandescent.
incansable /inkan'saβle/ a. tireless.
incapacidad /inkapaθi'ðað; inkapasi'ðað/ n. f. incapacity.
incapacitar /inkapaθi'tar; inkapasi'tar/ v. incapacitate.
incapaz /inka'paθ; inka'pas/ a. incapable.
incauto /in'kauto/ a. unwary.
incendiar /inθen'diar; insen'diar/ v. set on fire.
incendio /in'θendio; in'sendio/ n. m. fire; conflagration.
incertidumbre /inθerti'ðumbre; inserti'ðumbre/ n. f. uncertainty, suspense.
incesante /inθe'sante; inse'sante/ a. continual, incessant.
incidente /inθi'ðente; insi'ðente/ n. m. incident, event.
incienso /in'θienso; in'sienso/ n. m. incense.
incierto /in'θierto; in'sierto/ a. uncertain, doubtful.
incinerar /inθine'rar; insine'rar/ v. incinerate; cremate.
incisión /inθi'sion; insi'sion/ n. f. incision, cut.
incitamiento /inθita'miento; insita'miento/ n. m. incitement, motivation.
incitar /inθi'tar; insi'tar/ v. incite, instigate.
incivil /inθi'βil; insi'βil/ a. impolite, rude.
inclemencia /inkle'menθia; inkle'mensia/ n. f. inclemency.
inclemente /inkle'mente/ a. inclement, merciless.
inclinación /inklina'θion; inklina'sion/ n. f. inclination, bent; slope.
inclinar /inkli'nar/ v. incline, influence.

inclinarse /inkli'narse/ v. slope; lean, bend over; bow.
incluir /in'kluir/ v. include; enclose.
inclusivo /inklu'siβo/ a. inclusive.
incluso /in'kluso/ prep. including.
incógnito /in'kognito/ a. unknown.
incoherente /inkoe'rente/ a. incoherent.
incombustible /inkombus'tiβle/ a. fireproof.
incomible /inko'miβle/ a. inedible.
incomodar /inkomo'ðar/ v. disturb, bother, inconvenience.
incomodidad /inkomoði'ðað/ n. f. inconvenience.
incómodo /in'komoðo/ n. m. uncomfortable; cumbersome; inconvenient.
incomparable /inkompa'raβle/ a. incomparable.
incompatible /inkompa'tiβle/ a. incompatible.
incompetencia /inkompe'tenθia; inkompe'tensia/ n. f. incompetence.
incompetente /inkompe'tente/ a. incompetent.
incompleto /inkom'pleto/ a. incomplete.
incondicional /inkondiθio'nal; inkondisio'nal/ a. unconditional.
inconexo /inkone'kso/ a. incoherent; unconnected.
incongruente /inkoŋgru'ente/ a. incongruous.
inconsciencia /inkon'sθienθia; inkon'ssiensia/ n. f. unconsciousness.
inconsciente /inkon'sθiente; inkon'ssiente/ a. unconscious.
inconsecuencia /inkonse'kuenθia; inkonse'kuensia/ n. f. inconsistency.
inconsecuente /inkonse'kuente/ a. inconsistent.
inconsiderado /inkonsiðe'raðo/ a. inconsiderate.
inconstancia /inkons'tanθia; inkons'tansia/ n. f. changeableness.
inconstante /inkons'tante/ a. changeable.
inconveniencia /inkombe'nienθia; inkombe'niensia/ n. f. inconvenience; unsuitability.
inconveniente /inkombe'niente/ a. unsuitable. m. disadvantage; objection.
incorporar /inkorpo'rar/ v. incorporate, embody.
incorporarse /inkorpo'rarse/ v. sit up.
incorrecto /inko'rrekto/ a. incorrect, wrong.
incredulidad /inkreðuli'ðað/ n. f. incredulity.
incrédulo /in'kreðulo/ a. incredulous.
increíble /inkre'iβle/ a. incredible.
incremento /inkre'mento/ n. m. increase.
incubadora /inkuβa'ðora/ n. f. incubator.
incubar /inku'βar/ v. hatch.
inculto /in'kulto/ a. uncultivated.
incumplimento de contrato /inkumpli'mento de kon'trato/ n. m. breach of contract.
incurable /inku'raβle/ a. incurable.
incurrir /inku'rrir/ v. incur.
indagación /indaga'θion; indaga'sion/ n. f. investigation, inquiry.
indagador /indaga'ðor/ **-ra** n. investigator.
indagar /inda'gar/ v. investigate, inquire into.
indebido /inde'βiðo/ a. undue.
indecencia /inde'θenθia; inde'sensia/ n. f. indecency.
indecente /inde'θente; inde'sente/ a. indecent.
indeciso /inde'θiso; inde'siso/ a. undecided.
indefenso /inde'fenso/ a. defenseless.
indefinido /indefi'niðo/ a. indefinite; undefined.
indeleble /inde'leβle/ a. indelible.
indemnización de despido /indem-

niθa'θion de des'piðo; indemnisa'sion de des'piðo/ *n. f.* severance pay.
indemnizar /indemni'θar; indemni'sar/ *v.* indemnify.
independencia /indepen'denθia; independ'densia/ *n. f.* independence.
independiente /indepen'diente/ *a.* independent.
indesmallable /indesma'ʎaβle; indesma'yaβle/ *a.* runproof.
India /'india/ *n. f.* India.
indicación /indika'θion; indika'sion/ *n. f.* indication.
indicar /indi'kar/ *v.* indicate, point out.
indicativo /indika'tiβo/ *a.* & *m.* indicative.
índice /'indiθe; 'indise/ *n. m.* index; forefinger.
índice de materias /'indiθe de ma'terias; 'indise de ma'terias/ table of contents.
indicio /in'diθio; in'disio/ *n. m.* hint, clue.
indiferencia /indife'renθia; indife'rensia/ *n. f.* indifference.
indiferente /indife'rente/ *a.* indifferent.
indígena /in'dihena/ *a.* & *n.* native.
indigente /indi'hente/ *a.* indigent, poor.
indignación /indigna'θion; indigna'sion/ *n. f.* indignation.
indignado /indig'naðo/ *a.* indignant, incensed.
indignar /indig'nar/ *v.* incense.
indigno /in'digno/ *a.* unworthy.
indio /'indio/ **-dia** *a.* & *n.* Indian.
indirecto /indi'rekto/ *a.* indirect.
indiscreción /indiskre'θion; indiskre'sion/ *n. f.* indiscretion.
indiscreto /indis'kreto/ *a.* indiscreet.
indiscutible /indisku'tiβle/ *a.* unquestionable.
indispensable /indispen'saβle/ *a.* indispensable.
indisposición /indisposi'θion; indisposi'sion/ *n. f.* indisposition, ailment; reluctance.
indistinto /indis'tinto/ *a.* indistinct, unclear.
individual /indiβi'ðual/ *a.* individual.
individualidad /indiβiðuali'ðað/ *n. f.* individuality.
individuo /indi'βiðuo/ *a.* & *m.* individual.
indócil /in'doθil; in'dosil/ *a.* headstrong, unruly.
índole /'indole/ *n. f.* nature, character, disposition.
indolencia /indo'lenθia; indo'lensia/ *n. f.* indolence.
indolente /indo'lente/ *a.* indolent.
indómito /in'domito/ *a.* untamed, wild; unruly.
inducir /indu'θir; indu'sir/ *v.* induce, persuade.
indudable /indu'ðaβle/ *a.* certain, indubitable.
indulgencia /indul'henθia; indul'hensia/ *n. f.* indulgence.
indulgente /indul'hente/ *a.* indulgent.
indultar /indul'tar/ *v.* free; pardon.
industria /in'dustria/ *n. f.* industry.
industrial /indus'trial/ *a.* industrial.
industrioso /indus'trioso/ *a.* industrious.
inédito /i'neðito/ *a.* unpublished.
ineficaz /inefi'kaθ; inefi'kas/ *a.* inefficient.
inepto /i'nepto/ *a.* incompetent.
inequívoco /ine'kiβoko/ *a.* unmistakable.
inercia /i'nerθia; i'nersia/ *n. f.* inertia.
inerte /i'nerte/ *a.* inert.
inesperado /inespe'raðo/ *a.* unexpected.
inestable /ines'taβle/ *a.* unstable.
inevitable /ineβi'taβle/ *a.* inevitable.
inexacto /ine'ksakto/ *a.* inexact.
inexperto /ineks'perto/ *a.* unskilled.
inexplicable /inekspli'kaβle/ *a.* inexplicable, unexplainable.
infalible /infa'liβle/ *a.* infallible.
infame /in'fame/ *a.* infamous, bad.
infamia /in'famia/ *n. f.* infamy.
infancia /in'fanθia; in'fansia/ *n. f.* infancy; childhood.
infante /in'fante/ **-ta** *n.* infant.
infantería /infante'ria/ *n. f.* infantry.
infantil /infan'til/ *a.* infantile, childish.
infarto (de miocardio) /in'farto de mio'karðio/ *n. m.* heart attack.
infatigable /infati'gaβle/ *a.* untiring.
infausto /in'fausto/ *a.* unlucky.
infección /infek'θion; infek'sion/ *n. f.* infection.
infeccioso /infek'θioso; infek'sioso/ *a.* infectious.
infectar /infek'tar/ *v.* infect.
infeliz /infe'liθ; infe'lis/ *a.* unhappy, miserable.
inferior /infe'rior/ *a.* inferior; lower.
inferir /infe'rir/ *v.* infer; inflict.
infernal /infer'nal/ *a.* infernal.
infestar /infes'tar/ *v.* infest.
infiel /in'fiel/ *a.* unfaithful.
infierno /in'fierno/ *n. m.* hell.
infiltrar /infil'trar/ *v.* infiltrate.
infinidad /infini'ðað/ *n. f.* infinity.
infinito /infi'nito/ *a.* infinite.
inflación /infla'θion; infla'sion/ *n. f.* inflation.
inflamable /infla'maβle/ *a.* flammable.
inflamación /inflama'θion; inflama'sion/ *n. f.* inflammation.
inflamar /infla'mar/ *v.* inflame, set on fire.
inflar /in'flar/ *v.* inflate, pump up, puff up.
inflexible /infle'ksiβle/ *a.* inflexible, rigid.
inflexión /infle'ksion/ *n. f.* inflection.
infligir /infli'hir/ *v.* inflict.
influencia /influ'enθia; influ'ensia/ *n. f.* influence.
influenza /in'fluenθa; in'fluensa/ *n. f.* influenza, flu.
influir /in'fluir/ *v.* influence, sway.
influyente /influ'yente/ *a.* influential.
información /informa'θion; informa'sion/ *n. f.* information.
informal /infor'mal/ *a.* informal.
informar /infor'mar/ *v.* inform; report.
informática /infor'matika/ *n. f.* computer science; information technology.
informe /in'forme/ *n. m.* report; (*pl.*) information, data.
infortunio /infor'tunio/ *n. m.* misfortune.
infracción /infrak'θion; infrak'sion/ *n. f.* violation.
infracetructura /infraθetruk'tura; infrasetruk'tura/ *n. f.* infrastructure.
infrascrito /infras'krito/ **-ta** *n.* signer, undersigned.
infringir /infrin'hir/ *v.* infringe, violate.
infructuoso /infruk'tuoso/ *a.* fruitless.
infundir /infun'dir/ *v.* instil, inspire with.
ingeniería /inhenie'ria/ *n. f.* engineering.
ingeniero /inhe'niero/ **-ra** *n.* engineer.
ingenio /in'henio/ *n. m.* wit; talent.
ingeniosidad /inheniosi'ðað/ *n. f.* ingenuity.
ingenioso /inhe'nioso/ *a.* witty; ingenious.
ingenuidad /inhenui'ðað/ *n. f.* candor; naïveté.
ingenuo /in'henuo/ *a.* ingenuous, naïve, candid.
Inglaterra /iŋgla'terra/ *n. f.* England.
ingle /'iŋgle/ *n. f.* groin.
inglés /iŋ'gles/ **-esa** *a.* & *n.* English; Englishman; Englishwoman.
ingratitud /iŋgrati'tuð/ *n. f.* ingratitude.
ingrato /iŋ'grato/ *a.* ungrateful.
ingravidez /iŋgraβi'ðeθ; iŋgraβi'ðes/ *n. f.* weightlessness.
ingrávido /iŋ'graβiðo/ *a.* weightless.
ingrediente /iŋgre'ðiente/ *n. m.* ingredient.
ingresar en /iŋgre'sar en/ *v.* enter; join.
ingreso /iŋ'greso/ *n. m.* entrance; (*pl.*) earnings, income.
inhábil /in'aβil/ *a.* unskilled; incapable.
inhabilitar /inaβili'tar/ *v.* disqualify.
inherente /ine'rente/ *a.* inherent.
inhibir /ini'βir/ *v.* inhibit.
inhumano /inu'mano/ *a.* cruel, inhuman.
iniciador /iniθia'ðor; inisia'ðor/ **-ra** *n.* initiator.
inicial /ini'θial; ini'sial/ *a.* initial.
iniciar /ini'θiar; ini'siar/ *v.* initiate, begin.
iniciativa /iniθia'tiβa; inisia'tiβa/ *n. f.* initiative.
inicuo /ini'kuo/ *a.* wicked.
iniquidad /iniki'ðað/ *n. f.* iniquity; sin.
injuria /in'huria/ *n. f.* insult. —**injuriar,** *v.*
injusticia /inhus'tiθia; inhus'tisia/ *n. f.* injustice.
injusto /in'husto/ *a.* unjust, unfair.
inmaculado /imaku'laðo/ *a.* immaculate; pure.
inmediato /ime'ðiato/ *a.* immediate.
inmensidad /imensi'ðað/ *n. f.* immensity.
inmenso /i'menso/ *a.* immense.
inmersión /imer'sion/ *n. f.* immersion.
inmigración /imigra'θion; imigra'sion/ *n. f.* immigration.
inmigrante /imi'grante/ *a.* & *n.* immigrant.
inmigrar /imi'grar/ *v.* immigrate.
inminente /imi'nente/ *a.* imminent.
inmoderado /imoðe'raðo/ *a.* immoderate.
inmodesto /imo'ðesto/ *a.* immodest.
inmoral /imo'ral/ *a.* immoral.
inmoralidad /imorali'ðað/ *n. f.* immorality.
inmortal /imor'tal/ *a.* immortal.
inmortalidad /imortali'ðað/ *n. f.* immortality.
inmóvil /i'moβil/ *a.* immobile, motionless.
inmundicia /imun'diθia; imun'disia/ *n. f.* dirt, filth.
inmune /i'mune/ *a.* immune; exempt.
inmunidad /imuni'ðað/ *n. f.* immunity.
innato /in'nato/ *a.* innate, inborn.
innecesario /inneθe'sario; innese'sario/ *a.* unnecessary, needless.
innegable /inne'gaβle/ *a.* undeniable.
innoble /in'noβle/ *a.* ignoble.
innocuo /inno'kuo/ *a.* innocuous.
innovación /innoβa'θion; innoβa'sion/ *n. f.* innovation.
innumerable /innume'raβle/ *a.* innumerable, countless.
inocencia /ino'θenθia; ino'sensia/ *n. f.* innocence.
inocentada /inoθen'taða; inosen'taða/ *n. f.* practical joke.
inocente /ino'θente; ino'sente/ *a.* innocent.
inocular /inoku'lar/ *v.* inoculate.
inodoro /ino'ðoro/ *n. m.* toilet.
inofensivo /inofen'siβo/ *a.* inoffensive, harmless.
inolvidable /inolβi'ðaβle/ *a.* unforgettable.
inoportuno /inopor'tuno/ *a.* inopportune.
inoxidable /inoksi'ðaβle/ *a.* stainless.
inquietante /inkie'tante/ *a.* disturbing, worrisome, worrying, upsetting.
inquietar /inkie'tar/ *v.* disturb, worry, trouble.
inquieto /in'kieto/ *a.* anxious, uneasy, worried; restless.
inquietud /inkie'tuð/ *n. f.* concern, anxiety, worry; restlessness.
inquilino /inki'lino/ **-na** *n.* occupant, tenant.
inquirir /inki'rir/ *v.* inquire into, investigate.
inquisición /inkisi'θion; inkisi'sion/ *n. f.* inquisition, investigation.
insaciable /insa'θiaβle; insa'siaβle/ *a.* insatiable.
insalubre /insa'luβre/ *a.* unhealthy.
insano /in'sano/ *a.* insane.
inscribir /inskri'βir/ *v.* inscribe; record.
inscribirse /inskri'βirse/ *v.* register, enroll.
inscripción /inskrip'θion; inskrip'sion/ *n. f.* inscription; registration.
insecticida /insekti'θiða; insekti'siða/ *n. m.* insecticide.
insecto /in'sekto/ *n. m.* insect.
inseguro /inse'guro/ *a.* unsure, uncertain; insecure, unsafe.
insensato /insen'sato/ *a.* stupid, senseless.
insensible /insen'siβle/ *a.* unfeeling, heartless.
inseparable /insepa'raβle/ *a.* inseparable.
inserción /inser'θion; inser'sion/ *n. f.* insertion.
insertar /inser'tar/ *v.* insert.
inservible /inser'βiβle/ *a.* useless.
insidioso /insi'ðioso/ *a.* insidious, crafty.
insigne /in'signe/ *a.* famous, noted.
insignia /in'signia/ *n. f.* insignia, badge.
insignificante /insignifi'kante/ *a.* insignificant, negligible.
insincero /insin'θero; insin'sero/ *a.* insincere.
insinuación /insinua'θion; insin;ua'sion/ *n. f.* insinuation; hint.
insinuar /insi'nuar/ *v.* insinuate, suggest, hint.
insipidez /insipi'ðeθ; insipi'ðes/ *n. f.* insipidity.
insípido /in'sipiðo/ *a.* insipid.
insistencia /insis'tenθia; insis'tensia/ *n. f.* insistence.
insistente /insis'tente/ *a.* insistent.
insistir /insis'tir/ *v.* insist.
insolación /insola'θion; insola'sion/ *n. f.* sunstroke.
insolencia /inso'lenθia; inso'lensia/ *n. f.* insolence.
insolente /inso'lente/ *a.* insolent.
insólito /in'solito/ *a.* unusual.
insolvente /insol'βente/ *a.* insolvent.
insomnio /in'somnio/ *n. m.* insomnia.
insonorizado /insonori'θaðo; insonori'saðo/ *a.* soundproof.
insonorizar /insonori'θar; insonori'sar/ *v.* soundproof.
insoportable /insopor'taβle/ *a.* unbearable.
inspección /inspek'θion; inspek'sion/ *n. f.* inspection.
inspeccionar /inspekθio'nar; inspeksio'nar/ *v.* inspect, examine.
inspector /inspek'tor/ **-ra** *n.* inspector.
inspiración /inspira'θion; inspira'sion/ *n. f.* inspiration.
inspirar /inspi'rar/ *v.* inspire.
instalación /instala'θion; instala'sion/ *n. f.* installation, fixture.
instalar /insta'lar/ *v.* install, set up.
instantánea /instan'tanea/ *n. f.* snapshot.
instantáneo /instan'taneo/ *a.* instantaneous.
instante /ins'tante/ *a.* & *m.* instant. **al i.,** at once.
instar /ins'tar/ *v.* coax, urge.
instigar /insti'gar/ *v.* instigate, urge.
instintivo /instin'tiβo/ *a.* instinctive.
instinto /ins'tinto/ *n. m.* instinct. **por i.,** by instinct, instinctively.
institución /institu'θion; institu'sion/ *n. f.* institution.

instituto /insti'tuto/ *n. m.* institute. —**instituir,** *v.*

institutriz /institu'triθ; institu'tris/ *n. f.* governess.

instrucción /instruk'θion; instruk'sion/ *n. f.* instruction; education.

instructivo /instruk'tiβo/ *a.* instructive.

instructor /instruk'tor/ **-ra** *n.* instructor.

instruir /ins'truir/ *v.* instruct, teach.

instrumento /instru'mento/ *n. m.* instrument.

insuficiente /insufi'θiente; insufi'siente/ *a.* insufficient.

insufrible /insu'friβle/ *a.* intolerable.

insular /insu'lar/ *a.* island, insular.

insulto /in'sulto/ *n. m.* insult. —**insultar,** *v.*

insuperable /insupe'raβle/ *a.* insuperable.

insurgente /insur'hente/ *n. & a.* insurgent, rebel.

insurrección /insurrek'θion; insurrek'sion/ *n. f.* insurrection, revolt.

insurrecto /insu'rrekto/ **-ta** *a. & n.* insurgent.

intacto /in'takto/ *a.* intact.

integral /inte'gral/ *a.* integral.

integridad /integri'ðað/ *n. f.* integrity; entirety.

íntegro /'integro/ *a.* entire; upright.

intelecto /inte'lekto/ *n. m.* intellect.

intelectual /intelek'tual/ *a. & n.* intellectual.

inteligencia /inteli'henθia; inteli'hensia/ *n. f.* intelligence.

inteligente /inteli'hente/ *a.* intelligent.

inteligible /inteli'hiβle/ *a.* intelligible.

intemperie /intem'perie/ *n. f.* bad weather.

intención /inten'θion; inten'sion/ *n. f.* intention.

intendente /inten'dente/ *n. m.* manager.

intensidad /intensi'ðað/ *n. f.* intensity.

intensificar /intensifi'kar/ *v.* intensify.

intensivo /inten'siβo/ *a.* intensive.

intenso /in'tenso/ *a.* intense.

intentar /inten'tar/ *v.* attempt, try.

intento /in'tento/ *n. m.* intent; attempt.

intercambiable /interkam'biaβle/ *a.* interchangeable.

intercambiar /interkam'βiar/ *v.* exchange, interchange.

interceptar /interθep'tar; intersep'tar/ *v.* intercept.

intercesión /interθe'sion; interse'sion/ *n. f.* intercession.

interés /inte'res/ *n. m.* interest; concern; appeal.

interesante /intere'sante/ *a.* interesting.

interesar /intere'sar/ *v.* interest, appeal to.

interfaz /inter'faθ; inter'fas/ *n. f.* interface.

interferencia /interfe'renθia; interfe'rensia/ *n. f.* interference.

interino /inte'rino/ *a.* temporary.

interior /inte'rior/ *a.* **1.** interior, inner. —*n.* **2.** *m.* interior.

interjección /interhek'θion; interhek'sion/ *n. f.* interjection.

intermedio /inter'meðio/ *a.* **1.** intermediate. —*n.* **2.** *m.* intermediary; intermission.

interminable /intermi'naβle/ *a.* interminable, endless.

intermisión /intermi'sion/ *n. f.* intermission.

intermitente /intermi'tente/ *a.* intermittent.

internacional /internaθio'nal; internasio'nal/ *a.* international.

internarse en /inter'narse en/ *v.* enter into, go into.

Internet, el /inter'net/ *n. m.* the Internet.

interno /in'terno/ *a.* internal.

interpelar /interpe'lar/ *v.* ask questions; implore.

interponer /interpo'ner/ *v.* interpose.

interpretación /interpreta'θion; interpreta'sion/ *n. f.* interpretation.

interpretar /interpre'tar/ *v.* interpret; construe.

intérprete /in'terprete/ *n. m. & f.* interpreter; performer.

interrogación /interroga'θion; interroga'sion/ *n. f.* interrogation.

interrogar /interro'gar/ *v.* question, interrogate.

interrogativo /interroga'tiβo/ *a.* interrogative.

interrumpir /interrum'pir/ *v.* interrupt.

interrupción /interrup'θion; interrup'sion/ *n. f.* interruption.

intersección /intersek'θion; intersek'sion/ *n. f.* intersection.

intervalo /inter'βalo/ *n. m.* interval.

intervención /interβen'θion; interβen'sion/ *n. f.* intervention.

intervenir /interβe'nir/ *v.* intervene, interfere.

intestino /intes'tino/ *n. m.* intestine.

intimación /intima'θion; intima'sion/ *n. f.* intimation, hint.

intimar /inti'mar/ *v.* suggest, hint.

intimidad /intimi'ðað/ *n. f.* intimacy.

intimidar /intimi'ðar/ *v.* intimidate.

íntimo /'intimo/ **-ma** *a. & n.* intimate.

intolerable /intole'raβle/ *a.* intolerable.

intolerancia /intole'ranθia; intole'ransia/ *n. f.* intolerance, bigotry.

intolerante /intole'rante/ *a.* intolerant.

intoxicación alimenticia /intoksika'θion alimen'tiθia; intoksika'sion alimen'tisia/ *n. f.* food poisoning.

intranquilo /intran'kilo/ *a.* uneasy.

intravenoso /intraβe'noso/ *a.* intravenous.

intrepidez /intrepi'ðeθ; intrepi'ðes/ *n. f.* daring.

intrépido /in'trepiðo/ *a.* intrepid.

intriga /in'triga/ *n. f.* intrigue, plot, scheme. —**intrigar,** *v.*

intrincado /intrin'kaðo/ *a.* intricate, involved; impenetrable.

introducción /introðuk'θion; introðuk'sion/ *n. f.* introduction.

introducir /introðu'θir; introðu'sir/ *v.* introduce.

intruso /in'truso/ **-sa** *n.* intruder.

intuición /intui'θion; intui'sion/ *n. f.* intuition.

inundación /inunda'θion; inunda'sion/ *n. f.* flood. —**inundar,** *v.*

inútil /i'nutil/ *a.* useless.

invadir /imba'ðir/ *v.* invade.

inválido /im'baliðo/ **-da** *a. & n.* invalid.

invariable /imba'riaβle/ *a.* constant.

invasión /imba'sion/ *n. f.* invasion.

invasor /imba'sor/ **-ra** *n.* invader.

invencible /imben'θiβle; imben'siβle/ *a.* invincible.

invención /imben'θion; imben'sion/ *n. f.* invention.

inventar /imben'tar/ *v.* invent; devise.

inventario /imben'tario/ *n. m.* inventory.

inventivo /imben'tiβo/ *a.* inventive.

invento /im'bento/ *n. m.* invention.

inventor /imben'tor/ **-ra** *n.* inventor.

invernáculo /imber'nakulo/ *n. m.* greenhouse.

invernal /imber'nal/ *a.* wintry.

inverosímil /imbero'simil/ *a.* improbable, unlikely.

inversión /imber'sion/ *n. f.* inversion; *Com.* investment.

inverso /im'berso/ *a.* inverse, reverse.

inversor /imber'sor/ **-ra** *n.* investor.

invertir /imber'tir/ *v.* invert; reverse; *Com.* invest.

investigación /imbestiga'θion; imbestiga'sion/ *n. f.* investigation.

investigador /imbestiga'ðor/ **-ra** *n.* investigator; researcher.

investigar /imbesti'gar/ *v.* investigate.

invierno /im'bierno/ *n. m.* winter.

invisible /imbi'siβle/ *a.* invisible.

invitación /imbita'θion; imbita'sion/ *n. f.* invitation.

invitar /imbi'tar/ *v.* invite.

invocar /imbo'kar/ *v.* invoke.

involuntario /imbolun'tario/ *a.* involuntary.

inyección /inyek'θion; inyek'sion/ *n. f.* injection.

inyectar /inyek'tar/ *v.* inject.

ir /ir/ *v.* go. **irse,** go away, leave.

ira /'ira/ *n. f.* anger, ire.

iracundo /ira'kundo/ *a.* wrathful, irate.

iris /'iris/ *n. m.* iris. **arco i.,** rainbow.

Irlanda /ir'landa/ *n. f.* Ireland.

irlandés /irlan'des/ **-esa** *a. & n.* Irish; Irishman, Irishwoman.

ironía /iro'nia/ *n. f.* irony.

irónico /i'roniko/ *a.* ironical.

irracional /irraθio'nal; irrasio'nal/ *a.* irrational; insane.

irradiación /irraðia'θion; irraðia'sion/ *n. f.* irradiation.

irradiar /irra'ðiar/ *v.* radiate.

irrazonable /irraθo'naβle; irraso'naβle/ *a.* unreasonable.

irregular /irregu'lar/ *a.* irregular.

irreligioso /irreli'hioso/ *a.* irreligious.

irremediable /irreme'ðiaβle/ *a.* irremediable, hopeless.

irresistible /irresis'tiβle/ *a.* irresistible.

irresoluto /irreso'luto/ *a.* irresolute, wavering.

irrespetuoso /irrespe'tuoso/ *a.* disrespectful.

irreverencia /irreβe'renθia; irreβe'rensia/ *n. f.* irreverence.

irreverente /irreβe'rente/ *adj.* irreverent.

irrigación /irriga'θion; irriga'sion/ *n. f.* irrigation.

irrigar /irri'gar/ *v.* irrigate.

irritación /irrita'θion; irrita'sion/ *n. f.* irritation.

irritar /irri'tar/ *v.* irritate.

irrupción /irrup'θion; irrup'sion/ *n. f.* raid, attack.

isla /'isla/ *n. f.* island.

isleño /is'leɲo/ **-ña** *n.* islander.

israelita /israe'lita/ *n. & a.* Israelite.

Italia /i'talia/ *n. f.* Italy.

italiano /ita'liano/ **-na** *a. & n.* Italian.

itinerario /itine'rario/ *n. m.* itinerary; timetable.

IVA, *abbrev.* (**impuesto sobre el valor añadido**) VAT (value-added tax).

izar /i'θar; i'sar/ *v.* hoist.

izquierda /iθ'kierða; is'kierða/ *n. f.* left (hand, side).

izquierdista /iθ'kierðista; is'kierðista/ *n. & a.* leftist.

izquierdo /iθ'kierðo; is'kierðo/ *a.* left.

J

jabalí /haβa'li/ *n. m.* wild boar.

jabón /ha'βon/ *n. m.* soap. **j. en polvo,** soap powder.

jabonar /haβo'nar/ *v.* soap.

jaca /'haka/ *n. f.* nag.

jacinto /ha'θinto; ha'sinto/ *n. m.* hyacinth.

jactancia /hak'tanθia; hak'tansia/ *n. f.* boast. —**jactarse,** *v.*

jactancioso /haktan'θioso; haktan'sioso/ *a.* boastful.

jadear /haðe'ar/ *v.* pant, puff.

jaez /ha'eθ; ha'es/ *n. m.* harness; kind.

jalar /ha'lar/ *v.* haul, pull.

jalea /ha'lea/ *n. f.* jelly.

jaleo /ha'leo/ *n. m.* row, uproar; hassle.

jamás /ha'mas/ *adv.* never, ever.

jamón /ha'mon/ *n. m.* ham.

Japón /ha'pon/ *n. m.* Japan.

japonés /hapo'nes/ **-esa** *a. & n.* Japanese.

jaqueca /ha'keka/ *n. f.* headache.

jarabe /ha'raβe/ *n. m.* syrup.

jaranear /harane'ar/ *v.* jest; carouse.

jardín /har'ðin/ *n. m.* garden.

jardín de infancia /har'ðin de in'fanθia; har'ðin de in'fansia/ nursery school.

jardinero /harði'nero/ **-ra** *n.* gardener.

jarra /'harra/ *n. f.* jar; pitcher.

jarro /'harro/ *n. m.* jug, pitcher.

jaspe /'haspe/ *n. m.* jasper.

jaula /'haula/ *n. f.* cage; coop.

jauría /hau'ria/ *n. f.* pack of hounds.

jazmín /haθ'min; has'min/ *n. m.* jasmine.

jefatura /hefa'tura/ *n. f.* headquarters.

jefe /'hefe/ **-fa** *n.* chief, boss.

jefe de comedor /'hefe de kome'ðor/ headwaiter.

jefe de sala /'hefe de 'sala/ maître d'.

jefe de taller /'hefe de ta'ʎer; 'hefe de ta'yer/ foreman.

Jehová /heo'βa/ *n. m.* Jehovah.

jengibre /hen'hiβre/ *n. m.* ginger.

jerez /he'reθ; he'res/ *n. m.* sherry.

jerga /'herga/ *n. f.* slang.

jergón /her'gon/ *n. m.* straw mattress.

jerigonza /heri'gonθa; heri'gonsa/ *n. f.* jargon.

jeringa /he'riŋga/ *n. f.* syringe.

jeringar /heriŋ'gar/ *v.* inject; annoy.

jeroglífico /hero'glifiko/ *n. m.* hieroglyph.

jersey /her'sei/ *n. m.* pullover; **j. de cuello alto,** turtleneck sweater.

Jerusalén /herusa'len/ *n. m.* Jerusalem.

jesuita /he'suita/ *n. m.* Jesuit.

Jesús /he'sus/ *n. m.* Jesus.

jeta /'heta/ *n. f.* snout.

jícara /'hikara/ *n. f.* cup.

jinete /hi'nete/ **-ta** *n.* horseman.

jingoísmo /hiŋgo'ismo/ *n. m.* jingoism.

jingoísta /hiŋgo'ista/ *n. & a.* jingoist.

jira /'hira/ *n. f.* picnic; outing.

jirafa /hi'rafa/ *n. f.* giraffe.

jiu-jitsu /hiu'hitsu/ *n. m.* jujitsu.

jocundo /ho'kundo/ *a.* jovial.

jornada /hor'naða/ *n. f.* journey; day's work.

jornal /hor'nal/ *n. m.* day's wage.

jornalero /horna'lero/ *n. m.* day laborer, workman.

joroba /ho'roβa/ *n. f.* hump.

jorobado /horo'βaðo/ *a.* humpbacked.

joven /'hoβen/ *a.* **1.** young. —*n.* **2.** *m. & f.* young person.

jovial /ho'βial/ *a.* jovial, jolly.

jovialidad /hoβiali'ðað/ *n. f.* joviality.

joya /'hoia/ *n. f.* jewel, gem.

joyas de fantasía /'hoias de fanta'sia/ *n. f.pl.* costume jewelry.

joyelero /hoie'lero/ *n. m.* jewel box.

joyería /hoie'ria/ *n. f.* jewelry; jewelry store.

joyero /ho'iero/ *n. m.* jeweler; jewel case.

juanete /hua'nete/ *n. m.* bunion.

jubilación /huβila'θion; huβila'sion/ *n. f.* retirement; pension.

jubilar /huβi'lar/ *v.* retire, pension.

jubileo /huβi'leo/ *n. m.* jubilee, public festivity.

júbilo /'huβilo/ *n. m.* glee, rejoicing.

jubiloso /huβi'loso/ *a.* joyful, gay.

judaico /hu'ðaiko/ *a.* Jewish.

judaísmo /huða'ismo/ *n. m.* Judaism.

judía /hu'ðia/ *n. f.* bean, string bean.

judicial /huði'θial; huði'sial/ *a.* judicial.

judío /hu'ðio/ **-día** *a. & n.* Jewish; Jew.

juego /'huego/ *n. m.* game; play;

gambling; set. **j. de damas,** checkers. **j. limpio,** fair play.
Juegos Olímpicos /huegos o'limpikos/ *n. m.pl.* Olympic Games.
juerga /'huerga/ *n. f.* spree.
jueves /'hueβes/ *n. m.* Thursday.
juez /hueθ; hues/ *n. m.* judge.
jugador /huga'ðor/ **-ra** *n.* player.
jugar /hu'gar/ *v.* play; gamble.
juglar /hug'lar/ *n. m.* minstrel.
jugo /'hugo/ *n. m.* juice. **j. de naranja,** orange juice.
jugoso /hu'goso/ *a.* juicy.
juguete /hu'gete/ *n. m.* toy, plaything.
juguetear /hugete'ar/ *v.* trifle.
juguetón /huge'ton/ *a.* playful.
juicio /'huiθio; 'huisio/ *n. m.* sense, wisdom, judgment; sanity; trial.
juicioso /hui'θioso; hui'sioso/ *a.* wise, judicious.
julio /'hulio/ *n. m.* July.
jumento /hu'mento/ *n. m.* donkey.
junco /'hunko/ *n. m.* reed, rush.
jungla /'huŋgla/ *n. f.* jungle.
junio /'hunio/ *n. m.* June.
junípero /hu'nipero/ *n. m.* juniper.
junquillo /hun'kiʎo; hun'kiyo/ *n. m.* jonquil.
junta /'hunta/ *n. f.* board, council; joint, coupling.
juntamente /hunta'mente/ *adv.* jointly.
juntar /hun'tar/ *v.* join; connect; assemble.
junto /'hunto/ *a.* together. **j. a,** next to.
juntura /hun'tura/ *n. f.* joint, juncture.
jurado /hu'raðo/ *n. m.* jury.
juramento /hura'mento/ *n. m.* oath.
jurar /hu'rar/ *v.* swear.
jurisconsulto /huriskon'sulto/ *n. m.* jurist.
jurisdicción /hurisðik'θion; hurisðik'sion/ *n. f.* jurisdiction; territory.
jurisprudencia /hurispru'ðenθia; hurispru'ðensia/ *n. f.* jurisprudence.
justa /'husta/ *n. f.* joust. **—justar,** *v.*
justicia /hus'tiθia; hus'tisia/ *n. f.* justice, equity.
justiciero /husti'θiero; husti'siero/ *a.* just.
justificación /hustifika'θion; hustifika'sion/ *n. f.* justification.
justificadamente /hustifikaða'mente/ *adv.* justifiably.
justificar /hustifi'kar/ *v.* justify, warrant.
justo /'husto/ *a.* right; exact; just; righteous.
juvenil /huβe'nil/ *a.* youthful.
juventud /huβen'tuð/ *n. f.* youth.
juzgado /huθ'gaðo; hus'gaðo/ *n. m.* court.
juzgar /huθ'gar; hus'gar/ *v.* judge, estimate.

K

káiser /'kaiser/ *n. m.* kaiser.
karate /ka'rate/ *n. m.* karate.
kepis /'kepis/ *n. m.* military cap.
kerosena /kero'sena/ *n. f.* kerosene.
kilo /'kilo/ **kilogramo** *n. m.* kilogram.
kilohercio /kilo'erθio; kilo'ersio/ *n. m.* kilohertz.
kilolitro /kilo'litro/ *n. m.* kiloliter.
kilometraje /kilome'trahe/ *n. m.* mileage.
kilómetro /ki'lometro/ *n. m.* kilometer.
kiosco /'kiosko/ *n. m.* newsstand; pavilion.

L

la /la/ *art. & pron.* **1.** the; the one. **—***pron.* **2.** her, it, you; (*pl.*) them, you.
laberinto /laβe'rinto/ *n. m.* labyrinth, maze.
labia /'laβia/ *n. f.* eloquence, fluency.
labio /'laβio/ *n. m.* lip.
labor /la'βor/ *n. f.* labor, work.
laborar /laβo'rar/ *v.* work; till.
laboratorio /laβora'torio/ *n. m.* laboratory.
laborioso /laβo'rioso/ *a.* industrious.
labrador /laβra'ðor/ *n. m.* farmer.
labranza /la'βranθa; la'βransa/ *n. f.* farming; farmland.
labrar /la'βrar/ *v.* work, till.
labriego /la'βriego/ **-ga** *n.* peasant.
laca /'laka/ *n. f.* shellac.
lacio /'laθio; 'lasio/ *a.* withered; limp; straight.
lactar /lak'tar/ *v.* nurse, suckle.
lácteo /'lakteo/ *a.* milky.
ladear /laðe'ar/ *v.* tilt, tip; sway.
ladera /la'ðera/ *n. f.* slope.
ladino /la'ðino/ *a.* cunning, crafty.
lado /'laðo/ *n. m.* side. **al l. de,** beside. **de l.,** sideways.
ladra /'laðra/ *n. f.* barking. **—ladrar,** *v.*
ladrillo /la'ðriʎo; la'ðriyo/ *n. m.* brick.
ladrón /la'ðron/ **-ona** *n.* thief, robber.
lagarto /la'garto/ *n. m.* lizard; (Mex.) alligator.
lago /'lago/ *n. m.* lake.
lágrima /'lagrima/ *n. f.* tear.
lagrimear /lagrime'ar/ *v.* weep, cry.
laguna /la'guna/ *n. f.* lagoon; gap.
laico /'laiko/ *a.* lay.
laja /'laha/ *n. f.* stone slab.
lamentable /lamen'taβle/ *a.* lamentable.
lamentación /lamenta'θion; lamenta'sion/ *n. f.* lamentation.
lamentar /lamen'tar/ *v.* lament; wail; regret, be sorry.
lamento /la'mento/ *n. m.* lament, wail.
lamer /la'mer/ *v.* lick; lap.
lámina /'lamina/ *n. f.* print, illustration.
lámpara /'lampara/ *n. f.* lamp.
lampiño /lam'piɲo/ *a.* beardless.
lana /'lana/ *n. f.* wool.
lanar /la'nar/ *a.* woolen.
lance /'lanθe; 'lanse/ *n. m.* throw; episode; quarrel.
lancha /'lantʃa/ *n. f.* launch; small boat.
lanchón /lan'tʃon/ *n. m.* barge.
langosta /laŋ'gosta/ *n. f.* lobster; locust.
langostino /laŋgos'tino/ *n. m.* king prawn.
languidecer /laŋguiðe'θer; laŋguiðe'ser/ *v.* languish, pine.
languidez /laŋgui'ðeθ; laŋgui'ðes/ *n. f.* languidness.
lánguido /'laŋguiðo/ *a.* languid.
lanza /'lanθa; 'lansa/ *n. f.* lance, spear.
lanzada /lan'θaða; lan'saða/ *n. f.* thrust, throw.
lanzar /lan'θar; lan'sar/ *v.* hurl; launch.
lañar /la'ɲar/ *v.* cramp; clamp.
lapicero /lapi'θero; lapi'sero/ *n. m.* mechanical pencil.
lápida /'lapiða/ *n. f.* stone; tombstone.
lápiz /'lapiθ; 'lapis/ *n. m.* pencil; crayon.
lápiz de ojos /'lapiθ de 'ohos; 'lapis de 'ohos/ *n. m.* eyeliner.
lapso /'lapso/ *n. m.* lapse.
lardo /'larðo/ *n. m.* lard.
largar /lar'gar/ *v.* loosen; free.
largo /'largo/ *a.* **1.** long. **a lo l. de,** along. **—***n.* **2.** *m.* length.
largometraje /largome'trahe/ *n. m.* feature film.
largor /lar'gor/ *n. m.* length.
largueza /lar'geθa; lar'gesa/ *n. f.* generosity; length.
largura /lar'gura/ *n. f.* length.
laringe /la'rinhe/ *n. f.* larynx.
larva /'larβa/ *n. f.* larva.
lascivia /las'θiβia; las'siβia/ *n. f.* lasciviousness.
lascivo /las'θiβo; las'siβo/ *a.* lascivious.
láser /'laser/ *n. m.* laser.
laso /'laso/ *a.* weary.
lástima /'lastima/ *n. f.* pity. **ser l.,** to be a pity, to be too bad.
lastimar /lasti'mar/ *v.* hurt, injure.
lastimoso /lasti'moso/ *a.* pitiful.
lastre /'lastre/ *n. m.* ballast. **—lastrar,** *v.*
lata /'lata/ *n. f.* tin can; tin (plate); *Colloq.* annoyance, bore.
latente /la'tente/ *a.* latent.
lateral /late'ral/ *a.* lateral, side.
latigazo /lati'gaθo; lati'gaso/ *n. m.* lash, whipping.
látigo /'latigo/ *n. m.* whip.
latín /la'tin/ *n. m.* Latin (language).
latino /la'tino/ *a.* Latin.
latir /la'tir/ *v.* beat, pulsate.
latitud /lati'tuð/ *n. f.* latitude.
latón /la'ton/ *n. m.* brass.
laúd /la'uð/ *n. m.* lute.
laudable /lau'ðaβle/ *a.* laudable.
láudano /'lauðano/ *n. m.* laudanum.
laurel /lau'rel/ *n. m.* laurel.
lava /'laβa/ *n. f.* lava.
lavabo /la'βaβo/ **lavamanos** *n. m.* washroom, lavatory.
lavadora /laβa'ðora/ *n. f.* washing machine.
lavandera /laβan'dera/ *n. f.* washerwoman, laundress.
lavandería /laβande'ria/ *f.* laundry; laundromat.
lavaplatos /laβa'platos/ *n.* **1.** *m.* dishwasher (machine). **—***n.* **2.** *m. & f.* dishwasher (person).
lavar /la'βar/ *v.* wash.
lavatorio /laβa'torio/ *n. m.* lavatory.
laya /'laia/ *n. f.* spade. **—layar,** *v.*
lazar /la'θar; la'sar/ *v.* lasso.
lazareto /laθa'reto; lasa'reto/ *n. m.* isolation hospital; quarantine station.
lazo /'laθo; 'laso/ *n. m.* tie, knot; bow; loop.
le /le/ *pron.* him, her, you; (*pl.*) them, you.
leal /le'al/ *a.* loyal.
lealtad /leal'tað/ *n. f.* loyalty.
lebrel /le'βrel/ *n. m.* greyhound.
lección /lek'θion; lek'sion/ *n. f.* lesson.
leche /'letʃe/ *n. f.* milk.
lechería /letʃe'ria/ *n. f.* dairy.
lechero /le'tʃero/ *n. m.* milkman.
lecho /'letʃo/ *n. m.* bed; couch.
lechón /le'tʃon/ *n. m.* pig.
lechoso /le'tʃoso/ *a.* milky.
lechuga /le'tʃuga/ *n. f.* lettuce.
lechuza /le'tʃuθa; le'tʃusa/ *n. f.* owl.
lecito /le'θito; le'sito/ *n. m.* yolk.
lector /lek'tor/ **-ra** *n.* reader.
lectura /lek'tura/ *n. f.* reading.
leer /le'er/ *v.* read.
legación /lega'θion; lega'sion/ *n. f.* legation.
legado /le'gaðo/ *n. m.* bequest.
legal /le'gal/ *a.* legal, lawful.
legalizar /legali'θar; legali'sar/ *v.* legalize.
legar /le'gar/ *v.* bequeath, leave, will.
legible /le'hiβle/ *a.* legible.
legión /le'hion/ *n. f.* legion.
legislación /lehisla'θion; lehisla'sion/ *n. f.* legislation.
legislador /lehisla'ðor/ **-ra** *n.* legislator.
legislar /lehis'lar/ *v.* legislate.
legislativo /lehisla'tiβo/ *a.* legislative.
legislatura /lehisla'tura/ *n. f.* legislature.
legítimo /le'hitimo/ *a.* legitimate.
lego /'lego/ *n. m.* layman.
legua /'legua/ *n. f.* league (measure).
legumbre /le'gumbre/ *n. f.* vegetable.
lejano /le'hano/ *a.* distant, far-off.
lejía /le'hia/ *n. f.* lye.
lejos /'lehos/ *adv.* far. **a lo l.,** in the distance.
lelo /'lelo/ *a.* stupid, foolish.
lema /'lema/ *n. m.* theme; slogan.
lengua /'leŋgua/ *n. f.* tongue; language.
lenguado /leŋ'guaðo/ *n. m.* sole, flounder.
lenguaje /leŋ'guahe/ *n. m.* speech; language.
lenguaraz /leŋgua'raθ; leŋgua'ras/ *a.* talkative.
lente /'lente/ *n.* **1.** *m. or f.* lens. **2.** *m.pl.* eyeglasses.
lenteja /len'teha/ *n. f.* lentil.
lentilla /len'tiʎa; len'tiya/ *n. f.* contact lens.
lentitud /lenti'tuð/ *n. f.* slowness.
lento /'lento/ *a.* slow.
leña /'leɲa/ *n. f.* wood, firewood.
león /le'on/ *n. m.* lion.
leopardo /leo'parðo/ *n. m.* leopard.
lerdo /'lerðo/ *a.* dull-witted.
lesbiana /les'βiana/ *n. f.* lesbian.
lesión /le'sion/ *n. f.* wound; damage.
letanía /leta'nia/ *n. f.* litany.
letárgico /le'tarhiko/ *a.* lethargic.
letargo /le'targo/ *n. m.* lethargy.
letra /'letra/ *n. f.* letter (of alphabet); print; words (of a song).
letrado /le'traðo/ *a.* **1.** learned. **—***n.* **2.** *m.* lawyer.
letrero /le'trero/ *n. m.* sign, poster.
leva /'leβa/ *n. f.* *Mil.* draft.
levadura /leβa'ðura/ *n. f.* yeast, leavening, baking powder.
levantador /leβanta'ðor/ *n. m.* lifter; rebel, mutineer.
levantar /leβan'tar/ *v.* raise, lift.
levantarse /leβan'tarse/ *v.* rise, get up; stand up.
levar /le'βar/ *v.* weigh (anchor).
leve /'leβe/ *a.* slight, light.
levita /le'βita/ *n. f.* frock coat.
léxico /'leksiko/ *n. m.* lexicon, dictionary.
ley /lei/ *n. f.* law, statute.
leyenda /le'ienda/ *n. f.* legend.
lezna /'leθna; 'lesna/ *n. f.* awl.
libación /liβa'θion; liβa'sion/ *n. f.* libation.
libelo /li'βelo/ *n. m.* libel.
libélula /li'βelula/ *n. f.* dragonfly.
liberación /liβera'θion; liβera'sion/ *n. f.* liberation, release.
liberal /liβe'ral/ *a.* liberal.
libertad /liβer'tað/ *n. f.* freedom.
libertador /liβerta'ðor/ **-ra** *n.* liberator.
libertar /liβer'tar/ *v.* free, liberate.
libertinaje /liβerti'nahe/ *n. m.* licentiousness.
libertino /liβer'tino/ **-na** *n.* libertine.
libídine /li'βiðine/ *n. f.* licentiousness; lust.
libidinoso /liβiði'noso/ *a.* lustful.
libra /'liβra/ *n. f.* pound.
libranza /li'βranθa; li'βransa/ *n. f.* draft, bill of exchange.
librar /li'βrar/ *v.* free, rid.
libre /'liβre/ *a.* free, unoccupied.
librería /liβre'ria/ *n. f.* bookstore.
librero /li'βrero/ **-ra** *n.* bookseller.
libreta /li'βreta/ *n. f.* notebook; booklet.
libreto /li'βreto/ *n. m.* libretto.
libro /'liβro/ *n. m.* book.
libro de texto /'liβro de 'teksto/ textbook.
licencia /li'θenθia; li'sensia/ *n. f.* permission, license, leave; furlough. **l. de armas,** gun permit.
licenciado /liθen'θiaðo; lisen'siaðo/ **-da** *n.* graduate.
licencioso /liθen'θioso; lisen'sioso/ *a.* licentious.
lícito /'liθito; 'lisito/ *a.* lawful.
licor /li'kor/ *n. m.* liquor.
licuadora /likua'ðora/ *n. f.* blender (for food).
lid /lið/ *n. f.* fight. **—lidiar,** *v.*
líder /'liðer/ *n. m. & f.* leader.
liebre /'lieβre/ *n. f.* hare.
lienzo /'lienθo; 'lienso/ *n. m.* linen.

liga /'liga/ *n. f.* league, confederacy; garter.
ligadura /liga'ðura/ *n. f.* ligature.
ligar /li'gar/ *v.* tie, bind, join.
ligero /li'hero/ *a.* light; fast, nimble.
ligustro /li'gustro/ *n. m.* privet.
lija /'liha/ *n. f.* sandpaper.
lijar /li'har/ *v.* sandpaper.
lima /'lima/ *n. f.* file; lime.
limbo /'limbo/ *n. m.* limbo.
limitación /limita'θion; limita'sion/ *n. f.* limitation.
límite /'limite/ *n. m.* limit. **—limitar,** *v.*
limo /'limo/ *n. m.* slime.
limón /li'mon/ *n. m.* lemon.
limonada /limo'naða/ *n. f.* lemonade.
limonero /limo'nero/ *n. m.* lemon tree.
limosna /li'mosna/ *n. f.* alms.
limosnero /limos'nero/ **-ra** *n.* beggar.
limpiabotas /limpia'βotas/ *n. m.* bootblack.
limpiadientes /limpia'ðientes/ *n. m.* toothpick.
limpiar /lim'piar/ *v.* clean, wash, wipe.
límpido /'limpiðo/ *a.* limpid, clear.
limpieza /lim'pieθa; lim'piesa/ *n. f.* cleanliness.
limpio /'limpio/ *n. m.* clean.
limusina /limu'sina/ *n. f.* limousine.
linaje /li'nahe/ *n. m.* lineage, ancestry.
linaza /li'naθa; li'nasa/ *n. f.* linseed.
lince /'linθe; 'linse/ *a.* sharp-sighted, observing.
linchamiento /lintʃa'miento/ *n. m.* lynching.
linchar /lin'tʃar/ *v.* lynch.
lindar /lin'dar/ *v.* border, bound.
linde /'linde/ *n. m.* boundary; landmark.
lindero /lin'dero/ *n. m.* boundary.
lindo /'lindo/ *a.* pretty, lovely, nice.
línea /'linea/ *n. f.* line.
línea de puntos /'linea de 'puntos/ dotted line.
lineal /line'al/ *a.* lineal.
linfa /'linfa/ *n. f.* lymph.
lingüista /liŋ'guista/ *n. m. & f.* linguist.
lingüístico /liŋ'guistiko/ *a.* linguistic.
linimento /lini'mento/ *n. m.* liniment.
lino /'lino/ *n. m.* linen; flax.
linóleo /li'noleo/ *n. m.* linoleum.
linterna /lin'terna/ *n. f.* lantern; flashlight.
lío /'lio/ *n. m.* pack, bundle; mess, scrape; hassle.
liquidación /likiða'θion; likiða'sion/ *n. f.* liquidation.
liquidar /liki'ðar/ *v.* liquidate; settle up.
líquido /'likiðo/ *a. & m.* liquid.
lira /'lira/ *n. f.* lyre.
lírico /'liriko/ *a.* lyric.
lirio /'lirio/ *n. m.* lily.
lirismo /li'rismo/ *n. m.* lyricism.
lis /lis/ *n. f.* lily.
lisiar /li'siar/ *v.* cripple, lame.
liso /'liso/ *a.* smooth, even.
lisonja /li'sonha/ *n. f.* flattery.
lisonjear /lisonhe'ar/ *v.* flatter.
lisonjero /lison'hero/ **-ra** *n.* flatterer.
lista /'lista/ *n. f.* list; stripe; menu.
lista negra /'lista 'negra/ blacklist.
listar /lis'tar/ *v.* list; put on a list.
listo /'listo/ *a.* ready; smart, clever.
listón /lis'ton/ *n. m.* ribbon.
litera /li'tera/ *n. f.* litter, bunk, berth.
literal /lite'ral/ *a.* literal.
literario /lite'rario/ *a.* literary.
literato /lite'rato/ *n. m.* literary person, writer.
literatura /litera'tura/ *n. f.* literature.
litigación /litiga'θion; litiga'sion/ *n. f.* litigation.
litigio /li'tihio/ *n. m.* litigation; lawsuit.
litoral /lito'ral/ *n. m.* coast.
litro /'litro/ *n. m.* liter.
liturgia /li'turhia/ *n. f.* liturgy.
liviano /li'βiano/ *a.* light (in weight).

lívido /'liβiðo/ *a.* livid.
llaga /'ʎaga; 'yaga/ *n. f.* sore.
llama /'ʎama; 'yama/ *n. f.* flame; llama.
llamada /ʎa'maða; ya'maða/ *n. f.* call; knock. **—llamar,** *v.*
llamarse /ʎa'marse; ya'marse/ *v.* be called, be named. **se llama...** etc., his name is... etc.
llamativo /ʎama'tiβo; yama'tiβo/ *a.* gaudy, showy.
llamear /ʎame'ar; yame'ar/ *v.* blaze.
llaneza /ʎa'neθa; ya'nesa/ *n. f.* simplicity.
llano /'ʎano; 'yano/ *a.* **1.** flat, level; plain. **—n. 2.** *m.* plain.
llanta /'ʎanta; 'yanta/ *n. f.* tire.
llanto /'ʎanto; 'yanto/ *n. m.* crying, weeping.
llanura /ʎa'nura; ya'nura/ *n. f.* prairie, plain.
llave /'ʎaβe; 'yaβe/ *n. f.* key; wrench; faucet; *Elec.* switch. **ll. inglesa,** monkey wrench.
llegada /ʎe'gaða; ye'gaða/ *n. f.* arrival.
llegar /ʎe'gar; ye'gar/ *v.* arrive; reach. **ll. a ser,** become, come to be.
llenar /ʎe'nar; ye'nar/ *v.* fill.
lleno /'ʎeno; 'yeno/ *a.* full.
llenura /ʎe'nura; ye'nura/ *n. f.* abundance.
llevadero /ʎeβa'ðero; yeβa'ðero/ *a.* tolerable.
llevar /ʎe'βar; ye'βar/ *v.* take, carry, bear; wear (clothes); **ll. a cabo,** carry out.
llevarse /ʎe'βarse; ye'βarse/ *v.* take away, run away with. **ll. bien,** get along well.
llorar /ʎo'rar; yo'rar/ *v.* cry, weep.
lloroso /ʎo'roso; yo'roso/ *a.* sorrowful, tearful.
llover /ʎo'βer; yo'βer/ *v.* rain.
llovido /ʎo'βiðo; yo'βiðo/ *n. m.* stowaway.
llovizna /ʎo'βiθna; yo'βisna/ *n. f.* drizzle, sprinkle. **—lloviznar,** *v.*
lluvia /'ʎuβia; 'yuβia/ *n. f.* rain.
lluvia ácida /'ʎuβia 'aθiða; 'yuβia 'asiða/ acid rain.
lluvioso /ʎu'βioso; yu'βioso/ *a.* rainy.
lo /lo/ *pron.* the; him, it, you; (*pl.*) them, you.
loar /lo'ar/ *v.* praise, laud.
lobina /lo'βina/ *n. f.* striped bass.
lobo /'loβo/ *n. m.* wolf.
lóbrego /'loβrego/ *a.* murky; dismal.
local /lo'kal/ *a.* **1.** local. **—n. 2.** *m.* site.
localidad /lokali'ðað/ *n. f.* locality, location; seat (in theater).
localizar /lokali'θar; lokali'sar/ *v.* localize.
loción /lo'θion; lo'sion/ *n. f.* lotion.
loco /'loko/ **-ca** *a.* **1.** crazy, insane, mad. **—n. 2.** lunatic.
locomotora /lokomo'tora/ *n. f.* locomotive.
locuaz /lo'kuaθ; lo'kuas/ *a.* loquacious.
locución /loku'θion; loku'sion/ *n. f.* locution, expression.
locura /lo'kura/ *n. f.* folly, madness, insanity.
lodo /'loðo/ *n. m.* mud.
lodoso /lo'ðoso/ *a.* muddy.
lógica /'lohika/ *n. f.* logic.
lógico /'lohiko/ *a.* logical.
lograr /lo'grar/ *v.* achieve; succeed in.
logro /'logro/ *n. m.* accomplishment.
lombriz /lom'βriθ; lom'βris/ *n. f.* earthworm.
lomo /'lomo/ *n. m.* loin; back (of an animal).
lona /'lona/ *n. f.* canvas, tarpaulin.
longevidad /lonheβi'ðað/ *n. f.* longevity.
longitud /lonhi'tuð/ *n. f.* longitude; length.
lonja /'lonha/ *n. f.* shop; market.
lontananza /lonta'nanθa; lonta'nansa/ *n. f.* distance.

loro /'loro/ *n. m.* parrot.
losa /'losa/ *n. f.* slab.
lote /'lote/ *n. m.* lot, share.
lotería /lote'ria/ *n. f.* lottery.
loza /'loθa; 'losa/ *n. f.* china, crockery.
lozanía /loθa'nia; losa'nia/ *n. f.* freshness, vigor.
lozano /lo'θano; lo'sano/ *a.* fresh, spirited.
lubricación /luβrika'θion; luβrika'sion/ *n. f.* lubrication.
lubricar /luβri'kar/ *v.* lubricate.
lucero /lu'θero; lu'sero/ *n. m.* (bright) star.
lucha /'lutʃa/ *n. f.* fight, struggle; wrestling. **—luchar,** *v.*
luchador /lutʃa'ðor/ **-ra** *n.* fighter, wrestler.
lúcido /'luθiðo; lu'siðo/ *a.* lucid, clear.
luciente /lu'θiente; lu'siente/ *a.* shining, bright.
luciérnaga /lu'θiernaga; lu'siernaga/ *n. f.* firefly.
lucimiento /luθi'miento; lusi'miento/ *n. m.* success; splendor.
lucir /lu'θir; lu'sir/ *v.* shine, sparkle; show off.
lucrativo /lukra'tiβo/ *a.* lucrative, profitable.
luego /'luego/ *adv.* right away; afterwards, next. **l. que,** as soon as. **desde l.,** of course. **hasta l.,** goodbye, so long.
lugar /lu'gar/ *n. m.* place, spot; space, room.
lúgubre /'luguβre/ *a.* gloomy; dismal.
lujo /'luho/ *n. m.* luxury. **de l.,** deluxe.
lujoso /lu'hoso/ *a.* luxurious.
lumbre /'lumbre/ *n. f.* fire; light.
luminoso /lumi'noso/ *a.* luminous.
luna /'luna/ *n. f.* moon.
lunar /lu'nar/ *n. m.* beauty mark, mole; polka dot.
lunático /lu'natiko/ **-ca** *a. & n.* lunatic.
lunes /'lunes/ *n. m.* Monday.
luneta /lu'neta/ *n. f. Theat.* orchestra seat.
lupa /'lupa/ *n. f.* magnifying glass.
lustre /'lustre/ *n. m.* polish, shine. **—lustrar,** *v.*
lustroso /lus'troso/ *a.* shiny.
luto /'luto/ *n. m.* mourning.
luz /luθ; lus/ *n. f.* light. **dar a l.,** give birth to.

M

maca /'maka/ *n. f.* blemish, flaw.
macaco /ma'kako/ *a.* ugly, horrid.
macareno /maka'reno/ *a.* boasting.
macarrones /maka'rrones/ *n. m.pl.* macaroni.
macear /maθe'ar; mase'ar/ *v.* molest, push around.
macedonia de frutas /maθe'ðonia de 'frutas; mase'ðonia de 'frutas/ *n. f.* fruit salad.
maceta /ma'θeta; ma'seta/ *n. f.* vase; mallet.
machacar /matʃa'kar/ *v.* pound; crush.
machina /ma'tʃina/ *n. f.* derrick.
machista /ma'tʃista/ *a.* macho.
macho /'matʃo/ *n. m.* male.
machucho /ma'tʃutʃo/ *a.* mature, wise.
macizo /ma'θiθo; ma'siso/ *a.* **1.** solid. **—n. 2.** *m.* bulk; flower bed.
macular /maku'lar/ *v.* stain.
madera /ma'ðera/ *n. f.* lumber; wood.
madero /ma'ðero/ *n. m.* beam, timber.
madrastra /ma'ðrastra/ *n. f.* stepmother.
madre /'maðre/ *n. f.* mother. **m. política,** mother-in-law.
madreperla /maðre'perla/ *n. f.* mother-of-pearl.
madriguera /maðri'gera/ *n. f.* burrow; lair, den.
madrina /ma'ðrina/ *n. f.* godmother.

madroncillo /maðron'θiʎo; maðron'siyo/ *n. m.* strawberry.
madrugada /maðru'gaða/ *n. f.* daybreak.
madrugar /maðru'gar/ *v.* get up early.
madurar /maðu'rar/ *v.* ripen.
madurez /maðu'reθ; maðu'res/ *n. f.* maturity.
maduro /ma'ðuro/ *a.* ripe; mature.
maestría /maes'tria/ *n. f.* mastery; master's degree.
maestro /ma'estro/ *n. m.* master; teacher.
mafia /'mafia/ *n. f.* mafia.
maganto /ma'ganto/ *a.* lethargic, dull.
magia /'mahia/ *n. f.* magic.
mágico /'mahiko/ *a. & m.* magic; magician.
magistrado /mahis'traðo/ *n. m.* magistrate.
magnánimo /mag'nanimo/ *a.* magnanimous.
magnético /mag'netiko/ *a.* magnetic.
magnetismo /magne'tismo/ *n. m.* magnetism.
magnetófono /magne'tofono/ *n. m.* tape recorder.
magnificar /magnifi'kar/ *v.* magnify.
magnificencia /magnifi'θenθia; magnifi'sensia/ *n. f.* magnificence.
magnífico /mag'nifiko/ *a.* magnificent.
magnitud /magni'tuð/ *n. f.* magnitude.
magno /'magno/ *a.* great, grand.
magnolia /mag'nolia/ *n. f.* magnolia.
mago /'mago/ *n. m.* magician; wizard.
magosto /ma'gosto/ *n. m.* chestnut roast; picnic fire for roasting chestnuts.
magro /'magro/ *a.* meager; thin.
magullar /magu'ʎar; magu'yar/ *v.* bruise.
mahometano /maome'tano/ *n. & a.* Mohammedan.
mahometismo /maome'tismo/ *n. m.* Mohammedanism.
maíz /ma'iθ; ma'is/ *n. m.* corn.
majadero /maha'ðero/ **-ra** *a. & n.* foolish; fool.
majar /ma'har/ *v.* mash.
majestad /mahes'tað/ *n. f.* majesty.
majestuoso /mahes'tuoso/ *a.* majestic.
mal /mal/ *adv.* **1.** badly; wrong. **—n. 2.** *m.* evil, ill; illness.
mala /'mala/ *n. f.* mail.
malacate /mala'kate/ *n. m.* hoist.
malandanza /malan'danθa; malan'dansa/ *n. f.* misfortune.
malaventura /malaβen'tura/ *n. f.* misfortune.
malcomido /malko'miðo/ *a.* underfed; malnourished.
malcontento /malkon'tento/ *a.* dissatisfied.
maldad /mal'dað/ *n. f.* badness; wickedness.
maldecir /malde'θir; malde'sir/ *v.* curse, damn.
maldición /maldi'θion; maldi'sion/ *n. f.* curse.
maldito /mal'dito/ *a.* accursed, damned.
malecón /male'kon/ *n. m.* embankment.
maledicencia /maleði'θenθia; maleði'sensia/ *n. f.* slander.
maleficio /male'fiθio; male'fisio/ *n. m.* spell, charm.
malestar /males'tar/ *n. m.* indisposition.
maleta /ma'leta/ *n. f.* suitcase, valise.
malévolo /ma'leβolo/ *a.* malevolent.
maleza /ma'leθa; ma'lesa/ *n. f.* weeds; underbrush.
malgastar /malgas'tar/ *v.* squander.
malhechor /male'tʃor/ **-ra** *n.* malefactor, evildoer.
malhumorado /malumo'raðo/ *a.* morose, ill-humored.

malicia /ma'liθia; ma'lisia/ *n. f.* malice.

maliciar /mali'θiar; mali'siar/ *v.* suspect.

malicioso /mali'θioso; mali'sioso/ *a.* malicious.

maligno /ma'ligno/ *a.* malignant, evil.

malla /'maʎa; 'maya/ *n. f.* mesh, net.

mallas /'maʎas; 'mayas/ *n. f.pl.* leotard.

mallete /ma'ʎete; ma'yete/ *n. m.* mallet.

malo /'malo/ *a.* bad; evil, wicked; naughty; ill.

malograr /malo'grar/ *v.* miss, lose.

malparto /mal'parto/ *n. m.* abortion, miscarriage.

malquerencia /malke'renθia; malke-'rensia/ *n. f.* hatred.

malquerer /malke'rer/ *v.* dislike; bear ill will.

malsano /mal'sano/ *a.* unhealthy; unwholesome.

malsín /mal'sin/ *n. m.* malicious gossip.

malta /'malta/ *n. f.* malt.

maltratar /maltra'tar/ *v.* mistreat.

malvado /mal'βaðo/ **-da** *a.* **1.** wicked. —*n.* **2.** villain.

malversar /malβer'sar/ *v.* embezzle.

malvís /mal'βis/ *n. m.* redwing.

mamá /'mama/ *n. f.* mama, mother.

mamar /ma'mar/ *v.* suckle; suck.

mamífero /ma'mifero/ *n. m.* mammal.

mampara /mam'para/ *n. f.* screen.

mampostería /mamposte'ria/ *n. f.* masonry.

mamut /ma'mut/ *n. m.* mammoth.

manada /ma'naða/ *n. f.* flock, herd, drove.

manantial /manan'tial/ *n. m.* spring (of water).

manar /ma'nar/ *v.* gush, flow out.

mancebo /man'θeβo; man'seβo/ *n. m.* young man.

mancha /'mantʃa/ *n. f.* stain, smear, blemish, spot. —**manchar,** *v.*

mancilla /man'θiʎa; man'siya/ *n. f.* stain; blemish.

manco /'manko/ *a.* armless; one-armed.

mandadero /manda'ðero/ *n. m.* messenger.

mandado /man'daðo/ *n. m.* order, command.

mandamiento /manda'miento/ *n. m.* commandment; command.

mandar /man'dar/ *v.* send; order, command.

mandatario /manda'tario/ *n. m.* attorney; representative.

mandato /man'dato/ *n. m.* mandate, command.

mandíbula /man'diβula/ *n. f.* jaw; jawbone.

mando /'mando/ *n. m.* command, order; leadership.

mando a distancia /'mando a dis'tanθia; 'mando a dis'tansia/ remote control.

mandón /man'don/ *a.* domineering.

mandril /man'dril/ *n. m.* baboon.

manejar /mane'har/ *v.* handle, manage; drive (a car).

manejo /ma'neho/ *n. m.* management; horsemanship.

manera /ma'nera/ *n. f.* way, manner, means. **de m. que,** so, as a result.

manga /'maŋga/ *n. f.* sleeve.

mangana /maŋ'gana/ *n. f.* lariat, lasso.

manganeso /maŋga'neso/ *n. m.* manganese.

mango /'maŋgo/ *n. m.* handle; mango (fruit).

mangosta /maŋ'gosta/ *n. f.* mongoose.

manguera /maŋ'guera/ *n. f.* hose.

manguito /maŋ'guito/ *n. m.* muff.

maní /ma'ni/ *n. m.* peanut.

manía /ma'nia/ *n. f.* mania, madness; hobby.

maníaco /ma'niako/ **-ca, maniático -ca** *a. & n.* maniac.

manicomio /mani'komio/ *n. m.* insane asylum.

manicura /mani'kura/ *n. f.* manicure.

manifactura /manifak'tura/ *n. f.* manufacture.

manifestación /manifesta'θion; manifesta'sion/ *n. f.* manifestation.

manifestar /manifes'tar/ *v.* manifest, show.

manifiesto /mani'fiesto/ *a. & m.* manifest.

manija /ma'niha/ *n. f.* handle; crank.

maniobra /ma'nioβra/ *n. f.* maneuver. —**maniobrar,** *v.*

manipulación /manipula'θion; manipula'sion/ *n. f.* manipulation.

manipular /manipu'lar/ *v.* manipulate.

maniquí /mani'ki/ *n. m.* mannequin.

manivela /mani'βela/ *n. f. Mech.* crank.

manjar /man'har/ *n. m.* food, dish.

manlieve /man'lieβe/ *n. m.* swindle.

mano /'mano/ *n. f.* hand.

manojo /ma'noho/ *n. m.* handful; bunch.

manómetro /ma'nometro/ *n. m.* gauge.

manopla /ma'nopla/ *n. f.* gauntlet.

manosear /manose'ar/ *v.* handle, feel, touch.

manotada /mano'taða/ *n. f.* slap, smack. —**manotear,** *v.*

mansedumbre /manse'ðumbre/ *n. f.* meekness, tameness.

mansión /man'sion/ *n. f.* mansion; abode.

manso /'manso/ *a.* tame, gentle.

manta /'manta/ *n. f.* blanket.

manteca /man'teka/ *n. f.* fat, lard; butter.

mantecado /mante'kaðo/ *n. m.* ice cream.

mantecoso /mante'koso/ *a.* buttery.

mantel /man'tel/ *n. m.* tablecloth.

mantener /mante'ner/ *v.* maintain, keep; sustain; support.

mantenimiento /manteni'miento/ *n. m.* maintenance.

mantequera /mante'kera/ *n. f.* butter dish; churn.

mantequilla /mante'kiʎa; mante'ki-ya/ *n. f.* butter.

mantilla /man'tiʎa; man'tiya/ *n. f.* mantilla; baby clothes.

mantillo /man'tiʎo; man'tiyo/ *n. m.* humus; manure.

manto /'manto/ *n. m.* mantle, cloak.

manual /ma'nual/ *a. & m.* manual.

manubrio /ma'nuβrio/ *n. m.* handle; crank.

manufacturar /manufaktu'rar/ *v.* manufacture; make.

manuscrito /manus'krito/ *n. m.* manuscript.

manzana /man'θana; man'sana/ *n. f.* apple; block (of street).

manzanilla /manθa'niʎa; mansa'niya/ *n. f.* dry sherry.

manzano /man'θano; man'sano/ *n. m.* apple tree.

maña /'maɲa/ *n. f.* skill; cunning; trick.

mañana /ma'ɲana/ *adv.* **1.** tomorrow. —*n.* **2.** *f.* morning.

mañanear /maɲane'ar/ *v.* rise early in the morning.

mañero /ma'ɲero/ *a.* clever; skillful; lazy.

mapa /'mapa/ *n. m.* map, chart.

mapache /ma'patʃe/ *n. m.* raccoon.

mapurito /mapu'rito/ *n. m.* skunk.

máquina /'makina/ *n. f.* machine. **m. de coser,** sewing machine. **m. de lavar,** washing machine.

maquinación /makina'θion; makina-'sion/ *n. f.* machination; plot.

maquinador /makina'ðor/ **-ra** *n.* plotter, schemer.

maquinal /maki'nal/ *a.* mechanical.

maquinar /maki'nar/ *v.* scheme, plot.

maquinaria /maki'naria/ *n. f.* machinery.

maquinista /maki'nista/ *n. m.* machinist; engineer.

mar /mar/ *n. m. or f.* sea.

marabú /mara'βu/ *n. m.* marabou.

maraña /ma'raɲa/ *n. f.* tangle; maze; snarl; plot.

maravilla /mara'βiʎa; mara'βiya/ *n. f.* marvel, wonder. —**maravillarse,** *v.*

maravilloso /maraβi'ʎoso; maraβi-'yoso/ *a.* marvelous, wonderful.

marbete /mar'βete/ *n. m.* tag, label; check.

marca /'marka/ *n. f.* mark, sign; brand, make.

marcador /marka'ðor/ *n. m.* highlighter.

marcapáginas /marka'pahinas/ *n. m.* bookmark.

marcar /mar'kar/ *v.* mark; observe, note.

marcha /'martʃa/ *n. f.* march; progress. —**marchar,** *v.*

marchante /mar'tʃante/ *n. m.* merchant; customer.

marcharse /mar'tʃarse/ *v.* go away, depart.

marchitable /martʃi'taβle/ *a.* perishable.

marchitar /martʃi'tar/ *v.* fade, wilt, wither.

marchito /mar'tʃito/ *a.* faded, withered.

marcial /mar'θial; mar'sial/ *a.* martial.

marco /'marko/ *n. m.* frame.

marea /ma'rea/ *n. f.* tide.

mareado /mare'aðo/ *a.* seasick.

marearse /mare'arse/ *v.* get dizzy; be seasick.

mareo /ma'reo/ *n. m.* dizziness; seasickness.

marfil /mar'fil/ *n. m.* ivory.

margarita /marga'rita/ *n. f.* pearl; daisy.

margen /'marhen/ *n. m. or f.* margin, edge, rim.

marido /ma'riðo/ *n. m.* husband.

marijuana /mari'huana/ *n. f.* marijuana.

marimacha /mari'matʃa/ *n. f.* lesbian.

marimacho /mari'matʃo/ *n. m.* mannish woman.

marimba /ma'rimba/ *n. f.* marimba.

marina /ma'rina/ *n. f.* navy; seascape.

marinero /mari'nero/ *n. m.* sailor, seaman.

marino /ma'rino/ *a. & m.* marine, (of) sea; mariner, seaman.

marión /ma'rion/ *n. m.* sturgeon.

mariposa /mari'posa/ *n. f.* butterfly.

mariquita /mari'kita/ *n. f.* ladybird.

mariscal /maris'kal/ *n. m.* marshal.

marisco /ma'risko/ *n. m.* shellfish; mollusk.

marital /mari'tal/ *a.* marital.

marítimo /ma'ritimo/ *a.* maritime.

marmita /mar'mita/ *n. f.* pot, kettle.

mármol /'marmol/ *n. m.* marble.

marmóreo /mar'moreo/ *a.* marble.

maroma /ma'roma/ *n. f.* rope.

marqués /mar'kes/ *n. m.* marquis.

marquesa /mar'kesa/ *n. f.* marquise.

Marruecos /ma'rruekos/ *n. m.* Morocco.

Marte /'marte/ *n. m.* Mars.

martes /'martes/ *n. m.* Tuesday.

martillo /mar'tiʎo; mar'tiyo/ *n. m.* hammer. —**martillar,** *v.*

mártir /'martir/ *n. m. & f.* martyr.

martirio /mar'tirio/ *n. m.* martyrdom.

martirizar /martiri'θar; martiri'sar/ *v.* martyrize.

marzo /'marθo; 'marso/ *n. m.* March.

mas /mas/ *conj.* but.

más *a. & adv.* more, most; plus. **no m.,** only; no more.

masa /'masa/ *n. f.* mass; dough.

masaje /ma'sahe/ *n. m.* massage.

mascar /mas'kar/ *v.* chew.

máscara /'maskara/ *n. f.* mask.

mascarada /maska'raða/ *n. f.* masquerade.

mascota /mas'kota/ *n. f.* mascot; good-luck charm.

masculino /masku'lino/ *a.* masculine.

mascullar /masku'ʎar; masku'yar/ *v.* mumble.

masón /ma'son/ *n. m.* Freemason.

masticar /masti'kar/ *v.* chew.

mástil /'mastil/ *n. m.* mast; post.

mastín /mas'tin/ *n. m.* mastiff.

mastín danés /mas'tin da'nes/ Great Dane.

mastuerzo /mas'tuerθo; mas'tuerso/ *n. m.* fool, ninny.

mata /'mata/ *n. f.* plant; bush.

matadero /mata'ðero/ *n. m.* slaughterhouse.

matador /mata'ðor/ **-ra** *n.* matador.

matafuego /mata'fuego/ *n. m.* fire extinguisher.

matanza /ma'tanθa; ma'tansa/ *n. f.* killing, bloodshed, slaughter.

matar /ma'tar/ *v.* kill, slay; slaughter.

matasanos /mata'sanos/ *n. m.* quack.

mate /'mate/ *n. m.* checkmate; Paraguayan tea.

matemáticas /mate'matikas/ *n. f.pl.* mathematics.

matemático /mate'matiko/ *a.* mathematical.

materia /ma'teria/ *n. f.* material; subject (matter).

material /mate'rial/ *a. & m.* material.

materialismo /materia'lismo/ *n. m.* materialism.

materializar /materiali'θar; materiali'sar/ *v.* materialize.

maternal /mater'nal/ **materno** *a.* maternal.

maternidad /materni'ðað/ *n. f.* maternity; maternity hospital.

matiné /mati'ne/ *n. f.* matinee.

matiz /ma'tiθ; ma'tis/ *n. m.* hue, shade.

matizar /mati'θar; mati'sar/ *v.* blend; tint.

matón /ma'ton/ *n. m.* bully.

matorral /mato'rral/ *n. m.* thicket.

matoso /ma'toso/ *a.* weedy.

matraca /ma'traka/ *n. f.* rattle. —**matraquear,** *v.*

matrícula /ma'trikula/ *n. f.* registration; tuition.

matricularse /matriku'larse/ *v.* enroll, register.

matrimonio /matri'monio/ *n. m.* matrimony, marriage; married couple.

matriz /ma'triθ; ma'tris/ *n. f.* womb; *Mech.* die, mold.

matrona /ma'trona/ *n. f.* matron.

maullar /mau'ʎar; mau'yar/ *v.* mew.

máxima /'maksima/ *n. f.* maxim.

máxime /'maksime/ *a.* principally.

máximo /'maksimo/ *a. & m.* maximum.

maya /'maya/ *n. f.* daisy.

mayo /'mayo/ *n. m.* May.

mayonesa /mayo'nesa/ *n. f.* mayonnaise.

mayor /ma'yor/ *a.* larger, largest; greater, greatest; elder, eldest, senior. **m. de edad,** major, of age. **al por m.,** at wholesale. **m.** major.

mayoral /mayo'ral/ *n. m.* head shepherd; boss; foreman.

mayordomo /mayor'ðomo/ *n. m.* manager; butler, steward.

mayoría /mayo'ria/ *n. f.* majority, bulk.

mayorista /mayo'rista/ *n. m. & f.* wholesaler.

mayúscula /ma'yuskula/ *n. f.* capital letter, upper-case letter.

mazmorra /maθ'morra; mas'morra/ *n. f.* dungeon.

mazorca /ma'θorka; ma'sorka/ *n. f.* ear of corn.

me /me/ *pron.* me; myself.

mecánico /me'kaniko/ **-ca** *a. & n.* mechanical; mechanic.

mecanismo /meka'nismo/ *n. m.* mechanism.

mecanizar /mekani'θar; mekani'sar/ *v.* mechanize.

mecanografía /mekanogra'fia/ *n. f.* typewriting.

mecanógrafo /meka'nografo/ **-fa** *n.* typist.

mecedor /meθe'ðor; mese'ðor/ *n. m.* swing.

mecedora /meθe'ðora; mese'ðora/ *n. f.* rocking chair.

mecer /me'θer; me'ser/ *v.* rock; swing, sway.

mecha /'metʃa/ *n. f.* wick; fuse.

mechón /me'tʃon/ *n. m.* lock (of hair).

medalla /me'ðaʎa; me'ðaya/ *n. f.* medal.

médano /'meðano/ *n. m.* sand dune.

media /'meðia/ *n. f.* stocking.

mediación /meðia'θion; meðia'sion/ *n. f.* mediation.

mediador /meðia'ðor/ **-ra** *n.* mediator.

mediados /me'ðiaðos/ *n. m.pl.* **a m. de,** about the middle of (a period of time).

medianero /meðia'nero/ *n. m.* mediator.

medianía /meðia'nia/ *n. f.* mediocrity.

mediano /me'ðiano/ *a.* medium; moderate; mediocre.

medianoche /meðia'notʃe/ *n. f.* midnight.

mediante /me'ðiante/ *prep.* by means of.

mediar /me'ðiar/ *v.* mediate.

medicamento /meðika'mento/ *n. m.* medicine, drug.

medicastro /meði'kastro/ *n. m.* quack.

medicina /meði'θina; meði'sina/ *n. f.* medicine.

medicinar /meðiθi'nar; meðisi'nar/ *v.* treat (as a doctor).

médico /'meðiko/ *a.* **1.** medical. —*n.* **2.** *m. & f.* doctor, physician.

medida /me'ðiða/ *n. f.* measure, step.

medidor /meði'ðor/ *n. m.* meter.

medieval /meðie'βal/ *a.* medieval.

medio /'meðio/ *a.* **1.** half; mid, middle of. —*n.* **2.** *m.* middle; means.

mediocre /me'ðiokre/ *a.* mediocre.

mediocridad /meðiokri'ðað/ *n. f.* mediocrity.

mediodía /meðio'ðia/ *n. m.* midday, noon.

medir /me'ðir/ *v.* measure, gauge.

meditación /meðita'θion; meðita'sion/ *n. f.* meditation.

meditar /meði'tar/ *v.* meditate.

mediterráneo /meðite'rraneo/ *a.* Mediterranean.

medrar /me'ðrar/ *v.* thrive; grow.

medroso /me'ðroso/ *a.* fearful, cowardly.

megáfono /me'gafono/ *n. m.* megaphone.

megahercio /mega'erθio; mega'ersio/ *n. f.* megahertz.

mejicano /mehi'kano/ **-na** *a. & n.* Mexican.

mejilla /me'hiʎa; me'hiya/ *n. f.* cheek.

mejillón /mehi'ʎon; mehi'yon/ *n. m.* mussel.

mejor /me'hor/ *a. & adv.* better; best. **a lo m.,** perhaps.

mejora /me'hora/ *n. f.*, **mejoramiento**, *m.* improvement.

mejorar /meho'rar/ *v.* improve, better.

mejoría /meho'ria/ *n. f.* improvement; superiority.

melancolía /melanko'lia/ *n. f.* melancholy.

melancólico /melan'koliko/ *a.* melancholy.

melaza /me'laθa; me'lasa/ *n. f.* molasses.

melena /me'lena/ *n. f.* mane; long or loose hair.

melenudo /mele'nuðo/ **-da** *a.* longhaired.

melindroso /melin'droso/ *a.* fussy.

mella /'meʎa; 'meya/ *n. f.* notch; dent. —**mellar,** *v.*

mellizo /me'ʎiθo; me'yiso/ **-za** *n. & a.* twin.

melocotón /meloko'ton/ *n. m.* peach.

melodía /melo'ðia/ *n. f.* melody.

melodioso /melo'ðioso/ *a.* melodious.

melón /me'lon/ *n. m.* melon.

meloso /me'loso/ *a.* like honey.

membrana /mem'brana/ *n. f.* membrane.

membrete /mem'brete/ *n. m.* memorandum; letterhead.

membrillo /mem'briʎo; mem'briyo/ *n. m.* quince.

membrudo /mem'bruðo/ *a.* strong, muscular.

memorable /memo'raβle/ *a.* memorable.

memorándum /memo'randum/ *n. m.* memorandum; notebook.

memoria /me'moria/ *n. f.* memory; memoir; memorandum.

mención /men'θion; men'sion/ *n. f.* mention. —**mencionar,** *v.*

mendigar /mendi'gar/ *v.* beg (for alms).

mendigo /men'digo/ **-a** *n.* beggar.

mendrugo /men'drugo/ *n. m.* (hard) crust, chunk.

menear /mene'ar/ *v.* shake, wag; stir.

menester /menes'ter/ *n. m.* need, want; duty, task. **ser m.,** to be necessary.

menesteroso /meneste'roso/ *a.* needy.

mengua /'meŋgua/ *n. f.* decrease; lack; poverty.

menguar /meŋ'guar/ *v.* abate, decrease.

meningitis /meniŋ'gitis/ *n. f.* meningitis.

menopausia /meno'pausia/ *n. f.* menopause.

menor /me'nor/ *a.* smaller, smallest; lesser, least; younger, youngest, junior. **m. de edad,** minor, under age. **al por m.,** at retail.

menos /'menos/ *a. & adv.* less, least; minus. **a m. que,** unless. **echar de m.,** to miss.

menospreciar /menospre'θiar; menospre'siar/ *v.* cheapen; despise; slight.

mensaje /men'sahe/ *n. m.* message.

mensajero /mensa'hero/ **-ra** *n.* messenger.

menstruar /menstru'ar/ *v.* menstruate.

mensual /men'sual/ *a.* monthly.

mensualidad /mensuali'ðað/ *n. f.* monthly income or allowance; monthly payment.

menta /'menta/ *n. f.* mint, peppermint.

mentado /men'taðo/ *a.* famous.

mental /men'tal/ *a.* mental.

mentalidad /mentali'ðað/ *n. f.* mentality.

menta romana /'menta rro'mana/ spearmint.

mente /'mente/ *n. f.* mind.

mentecato /mente'kato/ *a.* foolish, stupid.

mentir /men'tir/ *v.* lie, tell a lie.

mentira /men'tira/ *n. f.* lie, falsehood. **parece m.,** it seems impossible.

mentiroso /menti'roso/ *a.* lying, untruthful.

mentol /'mentol/ *n. m.* menthol.

menú /me'nu/ *n. m.* menu.

menudeo /menu'ðeo/ *n. m.* retail.

menudo /me'nuðo/ *a.* small, minute. **a m.,** often.

meñique /me'ɲike/ *a.* tiny.

meple /'meple/ *n. m.* maple.

merca /'merka/ *n. f.* purchase.

mercader /merka'ðer/ *n. m.* merchant.

mercaderías /merkaðe'rias/ *n. f.pl.* merchandise, commodities.

mercado /mer'kaðo/ *n. m.* market.

Mercado Común /mer'kaðo ko'mun/ Common Market.

mercado negro /mer'kaðo 'negro/ black market.

mercancía /merkan'θia; merkan'sia/ *n. f.* merchandise; (*pl.*) wares.

mercante /mer'kante/ *a.* merchant.

mercantil /merkan'til/ *a.* mercantile.

merced /mer'θeð; mer'seð/ *n. f.* mercy, grace.

mercenario /merθe'nario; merse'nario/ **-ria** *a. & n.* mercenary.

mercurio /mer'kurio/ *n. m.* mercury.

merecedor /mereθe'ðor; merese'ðor/ *a.* worthy.

merecer /mere'θer; mere'ser/ *v.* merit, deserve.

merecimiento /mereθi'miento; meresi'miento/ *n. m.* merit.

merendar /meren'dar/ *v.* eat lunch; snack.

merendero /meren'dero/ *n. m.* lunchroom.

meridional /meriðio'nal/ *a.* southern.

merienda /me'rienda/ *n. f.* midday meal, lunch; afternoon snack.

mérito /'merito/ *n. m.* merit, worth.

meritorio /meri'torio/ *a.* meritorious.

merla /'merla/ *n. f.* blackbird.

merluza /mer'luθa; mer'lusa/ *n. f.* haddock.

mermelada /merme'laða/ *n. f.* marmalade.

mero /'mero/ *a.* mere.

merodeador /meroðea'ðor/ **-ra** *n.* prowler.

mes /'mes/ *n. m.* month.

mesa /'mesa/ *n. f.* table.

meseta /me'seta/ *n. f.* plateau.

mesón /me'son/ *n. m.* inn.

mesonero /meso'nero/ **-ra** *n.* innkeeper.

mestizo /mes'tiθo; mes'tiso/ **-za** *a. & n.* half-caste.

meta /'meta/ *n. f.* goal, objective.

metabolismo /metaβo'lismo/ *n. m.* metabolism.

metafísica /meta'fisika/ *n. f.* metaphysics.

metáfora /me'tafora/ *n. f.* metaphor.

metal /me'tal/ *n. m.* metal.

metálico /me'taliko/ *a.* metallic.

metalurgia /metalur'hia/ *n. f.* metallurgy.

meteoro /mete'oro/ *n. m.* meteor.

meteorología /meteorolo'hia/ *n. f.* meteorology.

meter /me'ter/ *v.* put (in).

meterse /me'terse/ *v.* interfere, meddle; go into.

metódico /me'toðiko/ *a.* methodic.

método /'metoðo/ *n. m.* method, approach.

metralla /me'traʎa; me'traya/ *n. f.* shrapnel.

métrico /'metriko/ *a.* metric.

metro /'metro/ *n. m.* meter (measure); subway.

metrópoli /me'tropoli/ *n. f.* metropolis.

mexicano /meksi'kano/ **-na** *a. & n.* Mexican.

mezcla /'meθkla; 'meskla/ *n. f.* mixture; blend.

mezclar /meθ'klar; mes'klar/ *v.* mix; blend.

mezcolanza /meθko'lanθa; mesko'lansa/ *n. f.* mixture; hodgepodge.

mezquino /meθ'kino; mes'kino/ *a.* stingy; petty.

mezquita /meθ'kita; mes'kita/ *n. f.* mosque.

mi /'mi/ *a.* my.

mí /'mi/ *pron.* me; myself.

microbio /mi'kroβio/ *n. m.* microbe, germ.

microbús /mikro'βus/ *n. m.* minibus.

microchip /mikro'tʃip/ *n. m.* microchip.

microficha /mikro'fitʃa/ *n. f.* microfiche.

micrófono /mi'krofono/ *n. m.* microphone.

microforma /mikro'forma/ *n. f.* microform.

microscópico /mikros'kopiko/ *a.* microscopic.

microscopio /mikros'kopio/ *n. m.* microscope.

microtaxi /mikro'taksi/ *n. m.* minicab.

miedo /'mieðo/ *n. m.* fear. **tener m.,** fear, be afraid.

miedoso /mie'ðoso/ *a.* fearful.

miel /miel/ *n. f.* honey.

miembro /mi'embro/ *n. m. & f.* member; limb.

mientras /'mientras/ *conj.* while. **m. tanto,** meanwhile. **m. más... más,** the more... the more.

miércoles /'mierkoles/ *n. m.* Wednesday.

miércoles de ceniza /'mierkoles de θe'niθa; 'mierkoles de se'nisa/ Ash Wednesday.

miga /'miga/ **migaja** *n. f.* scrap; crumb.

migración /migra'θion; migra'sion/ *n. f.* migration.

migratorio /migra'torio/ *a.* migratory.

mil /mil/ *a. & pron.* thousand.

milagro /mi'lagro/ *n. m.* miracle.

milagroso /mila'groso/ *a.* miraculous.

milicia /mi'liθia; mi'lisia/ *n. f.* militia.

militante /mili'tante/ *a.* militant.

militar /mili'tar/ *a.* **1.** military. —*n.* **2.** *m.* military man.

militarismo /milita'rismo/ *n. m.* militarism.

milla /'miʎa; 'miya/ *n. f.* mile.

millar /mi'ʎar; mi'yar/ *n. m.* (a) thousand.

millón /mi'ʎon; mi'yon/ *n. m.* million.

millonario /miʎo'nario; miyo'nario/ **-ria** *n.* millionaire.

mimar /mi'mar/ *v.* pamper, spoil (a child).

mimbre /'mimbre/ *n. m.* willow; wicker.

mímico /'mimiko/ *a.* mimic.

mimo /'mimo/ *n. m.* mime, mimic.

mina /'mina/ *n. f.* mine. —**minar,** *v.*

mineral /mine'ral/ *a. & m.* mineral.

minero /mi'nero/ **-ra** *n.* miner.

miniatura /minia'tura/ *n. f.* miniature.

miniaturizar /miniaturi'θar; miniaturi'sar/ *v.* miniaturize.

mínimo /'minimo/ *a. & m.* minimum.

ministerio /minis'terio/ *n. m.* ministry; cabinet.

ministro /mi'nistro/ **-a** *n. Govt.* minister, secretary.

minoría /mino'ria/ *n. f.* minority.

minoridad /minori'ðað/ *n. f.* minority (of age).

minucioso /minu'θioso; minu'sioso/ *a.* minute; thorough.

minué /mi'nue/ *n. m.* minuet.

minúscula /mi'nuskula/ *n. f.* lowercase letter, small letter.

minuta /mi'nuta/ *n. f.* draft.

mío /'mio/ *a.* mine.

miopía /mio'pia/ *n. f.* myopia.

mira /'mira/ *n. f.* gunsight.

mirada /mi'raða/ *n. f.* look; gaze, glance.

miramiento /mira'miento/ *n. m.* consideration; respect.

mirar /mi'rar/ *v.* look, look at; watch. **m. a,** face.

miríada /mi'riaða/ *n. f.* myriad.

mirlo /'mirlo/ *n. m.* blackbird.

mirón /mi'ron/ **-ona** *n.* bystander, observer.

mirra /'mirra/ *n. f.* myrrh.

mirto /'mirto/ *n. m.* myrtle.

misa /'misa/ *n. f.* mass, church service.

misceláneo /misθe'laneo; misse'laneo/ *a.* miscellaneous.

miserable /mise'raβle/ *a.* miserable, wretched.

miseria /mi'seria/ *n. f.* misery.

misericordia /miseri'korðia/ *n. f.* mercy.

misericordioso /miserikor'ðioso/ *a.* merciful.

misión /mi'sion/ *n. f.* assignment; mission.

misionario /misio'nario/ **-ria, misionero -ra** *n.* missionary.

mismo /'mismo/ *a. & pron.* **1.** same; -self, -selves. —*adv.* **2.** right, exactly.

misterio /mis'terio/ *n. m.* mystery.

misterioso /miste'rioso/ *a.* mysterious, weird.

místico /'mistiko/ **-ca** *a. & n.* mystical, mystic.

mitad /mi'tað/ *n. f.* half.

mítico /'mitiko/ *a.* mythical.

mitigar /miti'gar/ *v.* mitigate.

mitin /'mitin/ *n. m.* meeting; rally.

mito /'mito/ *n. m.* myth.

mitón /mi'ton/ *n. m.* mitten.

mitra /'mitra/ *n. f.* miter (bishop's).

mixto /'miksto/ *a.* mixed.

mixtura /miks'tura/ *n. f.* mixture.

mobiliario /moβi'liario/ *n. m.* household goods.

mocasín /moka'sin/ *n. m.* moccasin.

mocedad /moθe'ðað; mose'ðað/ *n. f.* youthfulness.

mochila /mo'tʃila/ *n. f.* knapsack, backpack.

mocho /'motʃo/ *a.* cropped, trimmed, shorn.

moción /mo'θion; mo'sion/ *n. f.* motion.

mocoso /mo'koso/ **-sa** *n.* brat.

moda /'moða/ *n. f.* mode, fashion, style.

modales /mo'ðales/ *n. m.pl.* manners.

modelo /mo'ðelo/ *n. m.* model, pattern.

módem /'moðem/ *n. m.* modem.

moderación /moðera'θion; moðerasion/ *n. f.* moderation.

moderado /moðe'raðo/ *a.* moderate. —**moderar,** *v.*

modernizar /moðerni'θar; moðerni'sar/ *v.* modernize.

moderno /mo'ðerno/ *a.* modern.

modestia /mo'ðestia/ *n. f.* modesty.

modesto /mo'ðesto/ *a.* modest.

módico /'moðiko/ *a.* reasonable, moderate.

modificación /moðifi'kaθion; moðifika'sion/ *n. f.* modification.

modificar /moðifi'kar/ *v.* modify.

modismo /mo'ðismo/ *n. m.* Gram. idiom.

modista /mo'ðista/ *n. f.* dressmaker; milliner.

modo /'moðo/ *n. m.* way, means.

modular /moðu'lar/ *v.* modulate.

mofarse /mo'farse/ *v.* scoff, sneer.

mofletudo /mofle'tuðo/ *a.* fat-cheeked.

mohín /mo'in/ *n. m.* grimace.

moho /'moo/ *n. m.* mold, mildew.

mohoso /mo'oso/ *a.* moldy.

mojar /mo'har/ *v.* wet.

mojón /mo'hon/ *n. m.* landmark; heap.

molde /'molde/ *n. m.* mold, form.

molécula /mo'lekula/ *n. f.* molecule.

moler /mo'ler/ *v.* grind, mill.

molestar /moles'tar/ *v.* molest, bother, disturb, annoy, trouble.

molestia /mo'lestia/ *n. f.* bother, annoyance, trouble; hassle.

molesto /mo'lesto/ *a.* bothersome; annoyed; uncomfortable.

molicie /mo'liθie; mo'lisie/ *n. f.* softness.

molinero /moli'nero/ *n. m.* miller.

molino /mo'lino/ *n. m.* mill. **m. de viento,** windmill.

mollera /mo'ʎera; mo'yera/ *n. f.* top of the head.

molusco /mo'lusko/ *n. m.* mollusk.

momentáneo /momen'taneo/ *a.* momentary.

momento /mo'mento/ *n. m.* moment.

mona /'mona/ *n. f.* female monkey.

monarca /mo'narka/ *n. m. & f.* monarch.

monarquía /monar'kia/ *n. f.* monarchy.

monarquista /monar'kista/ *n. & a.* monarchist.

monasterio /mona'sterio/ *n. m.* monastery.

mondadientes /monda'ðientes/ *n. m.* toothpick.

moneda /mo'neða/ *n. f.* coin; money.

monetario /mone'tario/ *a.* monetary.

monición /moni'θion; moni'sion/ *n. m.* warning.

monigote /moni'gote/ *n. m.* puppet.

monja /'monha/ *n. f.* nun.

monje /'monhe/ *n. m.* monk.

mono /'mono/ **-na** *a.* **1.** Colloq. cute. —*n.* **2.** *m. & f.* monkey.

monólogo /mo'nologo/ *n. m.* monologue.

monopatín /monopa'tin/ *n. m.* skateboard.

monopolio /mono'polio/ *n. m.* monopoly.

monopolizar /monopoli'θar; monopoli'sar/ *v.* monopolize.

monosílabo /mono'silaβo/ *n. m.* monosyllable.

monotonía /monoto'nia/ *n. f.* monotony.

monótono /mo'notono/ *a.* monotonous, dreary.

monstruo /'monstruo/ *n. m.* monster.

monstruosidad /monstruosi'ðað/ *n. f.* monstrosity.

monstruoso /mon'struoso/ *a.* monstrous.

monta /'monta/ *n. f.* amount; price.

montaña /mon'taɲa/ *n. f.* mountain.

montañoso /monta'ɲoso/ *a.* mountainous.

montar /mon'tar/ *v.* mount, climb; amount; Mech. assemble. **m. a caballo,** ride horseback.

montaraz /monta'raθ; monta'ras/ *a.* wild, barbaric.

monte /'monte/ *n. m.* mountain; forest.

montón /mon'ton/ *n. m.* heap, pile.

montuoso /mon'tuoso/ *a.* mountainous.

montura /mon'tura/ *n. f.* mount; saddle.

monumental /monumen'tal/ *a.* monumental.

monumento /monu'mento/ *n. m.* monument.

mora /'mora/ *n. f.* blackberry.

morada /mo'raða/ *n. f.* residence, dwelling.

morado /mo'raðo/ *a.* purple.

moral /mo'ral/ *a.* **1.** moral. —*n.* **2.** *f.* morale.

moraleja /mora'leha/ *n. f.* moral.

moralidad /morali'ðað/ *n. f.* morality, morals.

moralista /mora'lista/ *n. m. & f.* moralist.

morar /mo'rar/ *v.* dwell, live, reside.

mórbido /'morβiðo/ *a.* morbid.

mordaz /mor'ðaθ; mor'ðas/ *a.* caustic, sarcastic.

mordedura /morðe'ðura/ *n. f.* bite.

morder /mor'ðer/ *v.* bite.

moreno /mo'reno/ **-na** *a. & n.* brown; dark-skinned; dark-haired, brunette.

morfina /mor'fina/ *n. f.* morphine.

moribundo /mori'βundo/ *a.* dying.

morir /mo'rir/ *v.* die.

morisco /mo'risko/ **-ca, moro -ra** *a. & n.* Moorish; Moor.

morriña /mo'rriɲa/ *n. f.* sadness.

morro /'morro/ *n. m.* bluff; snout.

mortaja /mor'taha/ *n. f.* shroud.

mortal /mor'tal/ *a. & n.* mortal.

mortalidad /mortali'ðað/ *n. f.* mortality.

mortero /mor'tero/ *n. m.* mortar.

mortífero /mor'tifero/ *a.* fatal, deadly.

mortificar /mortifi'kar/ *v.* mortify.

mortuorio /mor'tuorio/ *a.* funereal.

mosaico /mo'saiko/ *a. & m.* mosaic.

mosca /'moska/ *n. f.* fly.

mosquito /mos'kito/ *n. m.* mosquito.

mostacho /mos'tatʃo/ *n. m.* mustache.

mostaza /mos'taθa; mos'tasa/ *n. f.* mustard.

mostrador /mostra'ðor/ *n. m.* counter; showcase.

mostrar /mos'trar/ *v.* show, display.

mote /'mote/ *n. m.* nickname; alias.

motel /mo'tel/ *n. m.* motel.

motín /mo'tin/ *n. m.* mutiny; riot.

motivo /mo'tiβo/ *n. m.* motive, reason.

motocicleta /motoθi'kleta; motosi'kleta/ *n. f.* motorcycle.

motociclista /motoθi'klista; motosi'klista/ *n. m. & f.* motorcyclist.

motor /mo'tor/ *n. m.* motor.

motorista /moto'rista/ *n. m. & f.* motorist.

movedizo /moβe'ðiθo; moβe'ðiso/ *a.* movable; shaky.

mover /mo'βer/ *v.* move; stir.

movible /mo'βiβle/ *a.* movable.

móvil /'moβil/ *a.* mobile.

movilización /moβiliθa'θion; moβilisa'sion/ *n. f.* mobilization.

movilizar /moβili'θar; moβili'sar/ *v.* mobilize.

movimiento /moβi'miento/ *n. m.* movement, motion.

mozo /'moθo; 'moso/ *n. m.* boy; servant, waiter, porter.

muaré /mua're/ *n. m.* moiré.

muchacha /mu'tʃatʃa/ *n. f.* girl, youngster; maid (servant).

muchachez /mutʃa'tʃeθ; mutʃa'tʃes/ *n. m.* boyhood, girlhood.

muchacho /mu'tʃatʃo/ *n. m.* boy; youngster.

muchedumbre /mutʃe'ðumbre/ *n. f.* crowd, mob.

mucho /'mutʃo/ *a.* **1.** much, many. —*adv.* **2.** much.

mucoso /mu'koso/ *a.* mucous.

muda /'muða/ *n. f.* change.

mudanza /mu'ðanθa; muðansa/ *n. f.* change; change of residence.

mudar /mu'ðar/ *v.* change, shift.

mudarse /mu'ðarse/ *v.* change residence, move.

mudo /'muðo/ **-da** *a. & n.* mute.

mueble /'mueβle/ *n. m.* piece of furniture; (pl.) furniture.

mueca /'mueka/ *n. f.* grimace.

muela /'muela/ *n. f.* (back) tooth.

muelle /'mueʎe; 'mueye/ *n. m.* pier, wharf; Mech. spring.

muerte /'muerte/ *n. f.* death.

muerto /'muerto/ **-ta** *a.* **1.** dead. —*n.* **2.** dead person.

muesca /'mueska/ *n. f.* notch; groove.

muestra /'muestra/ *n. f.* sample, specimen; sign.

mugido /mu'hiðo/ *n. m.* lowing; mooing.

mugir /mu'hir/ *v.* low, moo.

mugre /'mugre/ *n. f.* filth, dirt.

mugriento /mu'griento/ *a.* dirty.

mujer /mu'her/ *n. f.* woman; wife. **m. de la limpieza,** cleaning lady, charwoman.

mujeril /muhe'ril/ *a.* womanly, feminine.

mula /'mula/ *n. f.* mule.

mulato /mu'lato/ **-ta** *a. & n.* mulatto.

muleta /mu'leta/ *n. f.* crutch; prop.

mulo /'mulo/ **-la** *n.* mule.

multa /'multa/ *n. f.* fine, penalty.

multicolor /multiko'lor/ *a.* many-colored.

multinacional /multinaθio'nal; multinasio'nal/ *a.* multinational.

múltiple /'multiple/ *a.* multiple.

multiplicación /multiplika'θion; multiplika'sion/ *n. f.* multiplication.

multiplicar /multipli'kar/ *v.* multiply.

multiplicidad /multipliθi'ðað; multiplisi'ðað/ *n. f.* multiplicity.

multitud /multi'tuð/ *n. f.* multitude, crowd.

mundanal /munda'nal, mun'dano/ *a.* worldly.

mundano /mun'dano/ *a.* worldly, mundane.

mundial /mun'dial/ *a.* worldwide; (of the) world.

mundo /'mundo/ *n. m.* world.

munición /muni'θion; muni'sion/ *n. f.* ammunition.

municipal /muniθi'pal; munisi'pal/ *a.* municipal.

municipio /muni'θipio; muni'sipio/ *n. m.* city hall.

muñeca /mu'ɲeka/ *n. f.* doll; wrist.

muñeco /mu'ɲeko/ *n. m.* doll; puppet.

mural /mu'ral/ *a. & m.* mural.

muralla /mu'raʎa; mu'raya/ *n. f.* wall.

murciélago /mur'θielago; mur'sielago/ *n. m.* bat.

murga /'murga/ *n. f.* musical band.

murmullo /mur'muʎo; mur'muyo/ *n. m.* murmur; rustle.

murmurar /murmu'rar/ *v.* murmur; rustle; grumble.

musa /'musa/ *n. f.* muse.

muscular /musku'lar/ *a.* muscular.

músculo /'muskulo/ *n. m.* muscle.

muselina /muse'lina/ *n. f.* muslin.

museo /mu'seo/ *n. m.* museum.

música /'musika/ *n. f.* music.

musical /musi'kal/ *a.* musical.

músico /'musiko/ **-ca** *a. & n.* musical; musician.

muslo /'muslo/ *n. m.* thigh.

mustio /'mustio/ *a.* sad.

musulmano /musul'mano/ **-na** *a. & n.* Muslim.

muta /'muta/ *n. f.* pack of hounds.

mutabilidad /mutaβili'ðað/ *n. f.* mutability.

mutación /muta'θion; muta'sion/ *n. f.* mutation.

mutilación /mutila'θion; mutila'sion/ *n. f.* mutilation.

mutilar /muti'lar/ *v.* mutilate; mangle.

mutuo /'mutuo/ *a.* mutual.

muy /'mui/ *adv.* very.

N Ñ

nabo /'naβo/ *n. m.* turnip.

nácar /'nakar/ *n. m.* mother-of-pearl.

nacarado /naka'raðo, na'kareo/ *a.* pearly.

nacer /na'θer; na'ser/ *v.* be born.

naciente /na'θiente; na'siente/ *a.* rising; nascent.

nacimiento /naθi'miento; nasi'miento/ *n. m.* birth.

nación /na'θion; na'sion/ *n. f.* nation.

nacional /naθio'nal; nasio'nal/ *a.* national.

nacionalidad /naθionali'ðað; nasionali'ðað/ *n. f.* nationality.

nacionalismo /naθiona'lismo; nasiona'lismo/ *n. m.* nationalism.

nacionalista /naθiona'lista; nasiona'lista/ *n. & a.* nationalist.

nacionalización /naθionaliθa'θion; nasionalisa'sion/ *n. f.* nationalization.

nacionalizar /naθionali'θar; nasionali'sar/ *v.* nationalize.

Naciones Unidas /na'θiones u'niðas; na'siones u'niðas/ *n. f.pl.* United Nations.

nada /'naða/ *pron.* **1.** nothing; anything. **de n.,** you're welcome. —*adv.* **2.** at all.

nadador /naða'ðor/ **-ra** *n.* swimmer.

nadar /na'ðar/ *v.* swim.

nadie /'naðie/ *pron.* no one, nobody; anyone, anybody.

nafta /'nafta/ *n. f.* naphtha.

naipe /'naipe/ n. m. (playing) card.
naranja /na'ranha/ n. f. orange.
naranjada /naran'haða/ n. f. orangeade.
naranjo /na'ranho/ n. m. orange tree.
narciso /nar'θiso; nar'siso/ n. m. daffodil; narcissus.
narcótico /nar'kotiko/ a. & m. narcotic.
nardo /'narðo/ n. m. spikenard.
nariz /na'riθ; na'ris/ n. f. nose; (pl.) nostrils.
narración /narra'θion; narra'sion/ n. f. account.
narrador /narra'ðor/ **-ra** n. narrator.
narrar /na'rrar/ v. narrate.
narrativa /narra'tiβa/ n. f. narrative.
nata /'nata/ n. f. cream.
nata batida /'nata ba'tiða/ whipped cream.
natación /nata'θion; nata'sion/ n. f. swimming.
natal /na'tal/ a. native; natal.
natalicio /nata'liθio; nata'lisio/ n. m. birthday.
natalidad /natali'ðað/ n. f. birth rate.
natillas /na'tiʎas; na'tiyas/ n. f.pl. custard.
nativo /na'tiβo/ a. native; innate.
natural /natu'ral/ a. **1.** natural. —n. **2.** m. & f. native. **3.** m. nature, disposition.
naturaleza /natura'leθa; natura'lesa/ n. f. nature.
naturalidad /naturali'ðað/ n. f. naturalness; nationality.
naturalista /natura'lista/ a. & n. naturalist; naturalist.
naturalización /naturaliθa'θion; naturalisa'sion/ n. f. naturalization.
naturalizar /naturali'θar; naturali'sar/ v. naturalize.
naufragar /naufra'gar/ v. be shipwrecked; fail.
naufragio /nau'frahio/ n. m. shipwreck; disaster.
náufrago /'naufrago/ **-ga** a. & n. shipwrecked (person).
náusea /'nausea/ n. f. nausea.
nausear /nause'ar/ v. feel nauseous.
náutico /'nautiko/ a. nautical.
navaja /na'βaha/ n. f. razor; pen knife.
naval /na'βal/ a. naval.
navasca /na'βaska/ n. f. blizzard, snowstorm.
nave /'naβe/ n. f. ship.
nave espacial /'naβe espa'θial; 'naβe es'pasial/ spaceship.
navegable /naβe'gaβle/ a. navigable.
navegación /naβega'θion; naβega'sion/ n. f. navigation.
navegador /naβega'ðor/ **-ra** n. navigator.
navegante /naβe'gante/ n. m. & f. navigator.
navegar /naβe'gar/ v. sail; navigate.
Navidad /naβi'ðað/ n. f. Christmas.
navío /na'βio/ n. m. ship.
neblina /ne'βlina/ n. f. mist, fog.
nebuloso /neβu'loso/ a. misty; nebulous.
necedad /neθe'ðað; nese'ðað/ n. f. stupidity; nonsense.
necesario /neθe'sario; nese'sario/ a. necessary.
necesidad /neθesi'ðað; nesesi'ðað/ n. f. necessity, need, want.
necesitado /neθesi'taðo; nesesi'taðo/ a. needy, poor.
necesitar /neθesi'tar; nesesi'tar/ v. need.
necio /'neθio; 'nesio/ **-cia** a. **1.** stupid, silly. —n. **2.** fool.
néctar /'nektar/ n. m. nectar.
nectarina /nekta'rina/ n. f. nectarine.
nefando /ne'fando/ a. nefarious.
nefasto /ne'fasto/ a. unlucky, ill-fated.
negable /ne'gaβle/ a. deniable.
negación /nega'θion; nega'sion/ n. f. denial, negation.
negar /ne'gar/ v. deny.
negarse /ne'garse/ v. refuse, decline.
negativa /nega'tiβa/ n. f. negative, refusal.
negativamente /negatiβa'mente/ adv. negatively.
negativo /nega'tiβo/ a. negative.
negligencia /negli'henθia; negli'hensia/ n. f. negligence, neglect.
negligente /negli'hente/ a. negligent.
negociación /negoθia'θion; negosia'sion/ n. f. negotiation, deal.
negociador /negoθia'ðor; negosia'ðor/ **-ra** n. negotiator.
negociante /nego'θiante; nego'siante/ **-ta** n. businessperson.
negociar /nego'θiar; nego'siar/ v. negotiate, trade.
negocio /ne'goθio; ne'gosio/ n. m. trade; business.
negro /'negro/ **-gra** a. **1.** black. —n. **2.** m. Black.
nene /'nene/ **-na** n. baby.
neo /'neo/ **neón** n. m. neon.
nervio /'nerβio/ n. m. nerve.
nerviosamente /nerβiosa'mente/ adv. nervously.
nervioso /ner'βioso/ a. nervous.
nesciencia /nesθien'θia; nessien'sia/ n. f. ignorance.
nesciente /nes'θiente; nes'siente/ a. ignorant.
neto /'neto/ a. net.
neumático /neu'matiko/ a. **1.** pneumatic. —n. **2.** m. (pneumatic) tire.
neumático de recambio /neu'matiko de rre'kambio/ spare tire.
neumonía /neumo'nia/ n. f. pneumonia.
neurótico /neu'rotiko/ a. neurotic.
neutral /neu'tral/ a. neutral.
neutralidad /neutrali'ðað/ n. f. neutrality.
neutro /'neutro/ a. neuter; neutral.
neutrón /neu'tron/ n. m. neutron.
nevada /ne'βaða/ n. f. snowfall.
nevado /ne'βaðo/ a. snow-white; snow-capped.
nevar /ne'βar/ v. snow.
nevera /ne'βera/ n. f. icebox.
nevoso /ne'βoso/ a. snowy.
ni /ni/ conj. **1.** nor. **ni... ni,** neither... nor. —adv. **2.** not even.
nicho /'nitʃo/ n. m. recess; niche.
nido /'niðo/ n. m. nest.
niebla /'nieβla/ n. f. fog; mist.
nieto /'nieto/ **-ta** n. grandchild.
nieve /'nieβe/ n. f. snow.
nilón /ni'lon/ n. m. nylon.
nimio /'nimio/ adj. stingy.
ninfa /'ninfa/ n. f. nymph.
ningún /niŋ'gun/ **-no -na** a. & pron. no, none, neither (one); any, either (one).
niñera /ni'ɲera/ n. f. nursemaid, nanny.
niñez /ni'ɲeθ; ni'ɲes/ n. f. childhood.
niño /'niɲo/ **-ña 1.** a. **1.** young; childish; childlike. —n. **2.** child.
níquel /'nikel/ n. m. nickel.
niquelado /nike'laðo/ a. nickel-plated.
nítido /'nitiðo/ a. neat, clean, bright.
nitrato /ni'trato/ n. m. nitrate.
nitro /'nitro/ n. m. niter.
nitrógeno /ni'troheno/ n. m. nitrogen.
nivel /ni'βel/ n. m. level; grade. —**nivelar,** v.
no /no/ adv. **1.** not. **no más,** only. —interj. **2.** no.
noble /'noβle/ a. & m. noble; nobleman.
nobleza /no'βleθa; no'βlesa/ n. f. nobility; nobleness.
noche /'notʃe/ n. f. night; evening.
Nochebuena /notʃe'βuena/ n. f. Christmas Eve.
noción /no'θion; no'sion/ n. f. notion, idea.
nocivo /no'θiβo; no'siβo/ a. harmful.
noctiluca /nokti'luka/ n. f. glowworm.
nocturno /nok'turno/ a. nocturnal.
nodriza /no'ðriθa; no'ðrisa/ n. f. wet nurse.
no fumador /no fuma'ðor/ **-ra** n. m. & f. nonsmoker.
nogal /no'gal/ n. m. walnut.
nombradía /nom'βraðia/ n. f. fame.
nombramiento /nombra'miento/ n. m. appointment, nomination.
nombrar /nom'βrar/ v. name, appoint, nominate; mention.
nombre /'nombre/ n. m. name; noun.
nombre y apellidos /'nombre i ape'ʎiðos; 'nombre i ape'yiðos/ (person's) full name.
nómina /'nomina/ n. f. list; payroll.
nominación /nomina'θion; nomina'sion/ n. f. nomination.
nominal /nomi'nal/ a. nominal.
nominar /nomi'nar/ v. nominate.
non /non/ a. uneven, odd.
nonada /no'naða/ n. f. trifle.
nordeste /nor'ðeste/ n. m. northeast.
nórdico /'norðiko/ a. Nordic; northerly.
norma /'norma/ n. f. norm, standard.
normal /nor'mal/ a. normal, standard.
normalidad /normali'ðað/ n. f. normality.
normalizar /normali'θar; normali'sar/ v. normalize; standardize.
noroeste /noro'este/ n. m. northwest.
norte /'norte/ n. m. north.
norteamericano /norteameri'kano/ **-na** a. & n. North American.
Noruega /no'ruega/ n. f. Norway.
noruego /no'ruego/ **-ga** a. & n. Norwegian.
nos /nos/ pron. us; ourselves.
nosotros /no'sotros, no'sotras/ **-as** pron. we, us; ourselves.
nostalgia /nos'talhia/ n. f. nostalgia, homesickness.
nostálgico /nos'talhiko/ a. nostalgic.
nota /'nota/ n. f. note; grade, mark.
notable /no'taβle/ a. notable, remarkable.
notación /nota'θion; nota'sion/ n. f. notation; note.
notar /no'tar/ v. note, notice.
notario /no'tario/ **-ria** n. notary.
noticia /no'tiθia; no'tisia/ n. f. notice; piece of news; (pl.) news.
noticia de última hora /no'tiθia de 'ultima 'ora; no'tisia de 'ultima 'ora/ news flash.
notificación /notifika'θion; notifika'sion/ n. f. notification.
notificación de reclutamiento /notifika'θion de rrekluta'miento; notifika'sion de rrekluta'miento/ draft notice.
notificar /notifi'kar/ v. notify.
notorio /no'torio/ a. well-known.
novato /no'βato/ **-ta** n. novice.
novecientos /noβe'θientos; noβe'sientos/ a. & pron. nine hundred.
novedad /noβe'ðað/ n. f. novelty; piece of news.
novel /no'βel/ a. new; inexperienced.
novela /no'βela/ n. f. novel.
novelista /noβe'lista/ n. m. & f. novelist.
novena /no'βena/ n. f. novena.
noveno /no'βeno/ a. ninth.
noventa /no'βenta/ a. & pron. ninety.
novia /'noβia/ n. f. bride; sweetheart; fiancée.
noviazgo /no'βiaθgo; no'βiasgo/ n. m. engagement.
novicio /no'βiθio; no'βisio/ **-cia** n. novice, beginner.
noviembre /no'βiembre/ n. m. November.
novilla /no'βiʎa; no'βiya/ n. f. heifer.
novio /'noβio/ n. m. bridegroom; sweetheart; fiancé.
nube /'nuβe/ n. f. cloud.
núbil /'nuβil/ a. marriageable.
nublado /nu'βlaðo/ a. cloudy.
nuclear /nukle'ar/ a. nuclear.
núcleo /'nukleo/ n. m. nucleus.
nudo /'nuðo/ n. m. knot.
nuera /'nuera/ n. f. daughter-in-law.
nuestro /'nuestro/ a. our, ours.
nueva /'nueβa/ n. f. news.
nueve /'nueβe/ a. & pron. nine.
nuevo /'nueβo/ a. new. **de n.,** again, anew.
nuez /nueθ; nues/ n. f. nut; walnut.
nulidad /nuli'ðað/ n. f. nonentity; nullity.
nulo /'nulo/ a. null, void.
numeración /numera'θion; numera'sion/ n. f. numeration.
numerar /nume'rar/ v. number.
numérico /nu'meriko/ a. numerical.
número /'numero/ n. m. number; size (of shoe, etc.) **n. impar,** odd number. **n. par,** even number.
numeroso /nume'roso/ a. numerous.
numismática /numis'matika/ n. f. numismatics.
nunca /'nunka/ adv. never; ever.
nupcial /nup'θial; nup'sial/ a. nuptial.
nupcias /'nupθias; 'nupsias/ n. f.pl. nuptials, wedding.
nutrición /nutri'θion; nutri'sion/ n. f. nutrition.
nutrimento /nutri'mento/ n. m. nourishment.
nutrir /nu'trir/ v. nourish.
nutritivo /nutri'tiβo/ a. nutritious.
nylon /'nilon/ n. m. nylon.
ñame /'ɲame/ n. m. yam.
ñapa /'ɲapa/ n. f. something extra.
ñoñeria /ɲoɲe'ria/ n. f. dotage.
ñoño /'ɲoɲo/ a. feeble-minded, senile.

O

o /o/ conj. or. **o... o,** either... or.
oasis /o'asis/ n. m. oasis.
obedecer /oβeðe'θer; oβeðe'ser/ v. obey, mind.
obediencia /oβe'ðienθia; oβe'ðiensia/ n. f. obedience.
obediente /oβe'ðiente/ a. obedient.
obelisco /oβe'lisko/ n. m. obelisk.
obertura /oβer'tura/ n. f. overture.
obeso /o'βeso/ a. obese.
obispo /o'βispo/ n. m. bishop.
obituario /oβi'tuario/ n. m. obituary.
objeción /oβhe'θion; oβhe'sion/ n. f. objection.
objetivo /oβhe'tiβo/ a. & m. objective.
objeto /oβ'heto/ n. m. object. —**objetar,** v.
objetor de conciencia /oβhe'tor de kon'θienθia; oβhe'tor de kon'siensia/ n. m. conscientious objector.
oblicuo /o'βlikuo/ a. oblique.
obligación /oβliga'θion; oβliga'sion/ n. f. obligation, duty.
obligar /oβli'gar/ v. oblige, require, compel; obligate.
obligatorio /oβliga'torio/ a. obligatory, compulsory.
oblongo /o'βloŋgo/ a. oblong.
oboe /o'βoe/ n. m. oboe.
obra /'oβra/ n. f. work. —**obrar,** v.
obrero /o'βrero/ **-ra** n. worker, laborer.
obscenidad /oβsθeni'ðað; oβsseni'ðað/ n. f. obscenity.
obsceno /oβs'θeno; oβs'seno/ a. obscene.
obscurecer /oβskure'θer; oβskure'ser/ v. obscure; darken.
obscuridad /oβskuri'ðað/ n. f. obscurity; darkness.
obscuro /oβs'kuro/ a. obscure; dark.
obsequiar /oβse'kiar/ v. court; make presents to, fete.
obsequio /oβ'sekio/ n. m. obsequiousness; gift; attention.
observación /oβserβa'θion; oβserβa'sion/ n. f. observation.
observador /oβserβa'ðor/ **-ra** n. observer.
observancia /oβser'βanθia; oβser'βansia/ n. f. observance.
observar /oβser'βar/ v. observe, watch.

observatorio /oβserβa'torio/ *n. m.* observatory.
obsesión /oβse'sion/ *n. f.* obsession.
obstáculo /oβs'takulo/ *n. m.* obstacle.
obstante /oβs'tante/ *adv.* **no o.,** however, yet, nevertheless.
obstar /oβs'tar/ *v.* hinder, obstruct.
obstetricia /oβste'triθia; oβste'trisia/ *n. f.* obstetrics.
obstinación /oβstina'θion; oβstina'sion/ *n. f.* obstinacy.
obstinado /oβsti'naðo/ *a.* obstinate, stubborn.
obstinarse /oβsti'narse/ *v.* persist, insist.
obstrucción /oβstruk'θion; oβstruk'sion/ *n. f.* obstruction.
obstruir /oβs'truir/ *v.* obstruct, clog, block.
obtener /oβte'ner/ *v.* obtain, get, secure.
obtuso /oβ'tuso/ *a.* obtuse.
obvio /'oββio/ *a.* obvious.
ocasión /oka'sion/ *n. f.* occasion; opportunity, chance. **de o.,** secondhand.
ocasional /okasio'nal/ *a.* occasional.
ocasionalmente /okasional'mente/ *adv.* occasionally.
ocasionar /okasio'nar/ *v.* cause, occasion.
occidental /okθiðen'tal; oksiðen'tal/ *a.* western.
occidente /okθi'ðente; oksi'ðente/ *n. m.* west.
océano /o'θeano; o'seano/ *n. m.* ocean.
Océano Atlántico /o'θeano a'tlantiko; o'seano a'tlantiko/ Atlantic Ocean.
Océano Pacífico /o'θeano pa'θifiko; o'seano pa'sifiko/ Pacific Ocean.
ocelote /oθe'lote; ose'lote/ *n. m.* ocelot.
ochenta /o'tʃenta/ *a. & pron.* eighty.
ocho /'otʃo/ *a. & pron.* eight.
ochocientos /otʃo'θientos; otʃo'sientos/ *a. & pron.* eight hundred.
ocio /'oθio; 'osio/ *n. m.* idleness, leisure.
ociosidad /oθiosi'ðað; osiosi'ðað/ *n. f.* idleness, laziness.
ocioso /o'θioso; o'sioso/ *a.* idle, lazy.
ocre /'okre/ *n. m.* ochre.
octagonal /oktago'nal/ *a.* octagonal.
octava /ok'taβa/ *n. f.* octave.
octavo /ok'taβo/ *a.* eighth.
octubre /ok'tuβre/ *n. m.* October.
oculista /oku'lista/ *n. m. & f.* oculist.
ocultación /okulta'θion; okulta'sion/ *n. f.* concealment.
ocultar /okul'tar/ *v.* hide, conceal.
oculto /o'kulto/ *a.* hidden.
ocupación /okupa'θion; okupa'sion/ *n. f.* occupation.
ocupado /oku'paðo/ *a.* occupied; busy.
ocupante /oku'pante/ *n. m. & f.* occupant.
ocupar /oku'par/ *v.* occupy.
ocuparse de /oku'parse de/ *v.* take care of, take charge of.
ocurrencia /oku'rrenθia; oku'rrensia/ *n. f.* occurrence; witticism.
ocurrente /oku'rrente/ *a.* witty.
ocurrir /oku'rrir/ *v.* occur, happen.
oda /'oða/ *n. f.* ode.
odio /'oðio/ *n. m.* hate. **—odiar,** *v.*
odiosidad /oðiosi'ðað/ *n. f.* odiousness; hatred.
odioso /o'ðioso/ *a.* obnoxious, odious.
odisea /oði'sea/ *n. f.* odyssey.
OEA, *abbr.* (**Organización de los Estados Americanos**). OAS (**Organization of American States**).
oeste /o'este/ *n. m.* west.
ofender /ofen'der/ *v.* offend, wrong.
ofenderse /ofen'derse/ *v.* be offended, take offense.
ofensa /o'fensa/ *n. f.* offense.
ofensiva /ofen'siβa/ *n. f.* offensive.
ofensivo /ofen'siβo/ *a.* offensive.
ofensor /ofen'sor/ **-ra** *n.* offender.
oferta /o'ferta/ *n. f.* offer, proposal.
ofertorio /ofer'torio/ *n. m.* offertory.
oficial /ofi'θial; ofi'sial/ *a. & m.* official; officer.
oficialmente /ofiθial'mente; ofisial'mente/ *adv.* officially.
oficiar /ofi'θiar; ofi'siar/ *v.* officiate.
oficina /ofi'θina; ofi'sina/ *n. f.* office.
oficio /o'fiθio; o'fisio/ *n. m.* office; trade; church service.
oficioso /ofi'θioso; ofi'sioso/ *a.* officious.
ofrecer /ofre'θer; ofre'ser/ *v.* offer.
ofrecimiento /ofreθi'miento; ofresi'miento/ *n. m.* offer, offering. **o. de presentación,** introductory offer.
ofrenda /o'frenda/ *n. f.* offering.
oftalmía /oftal'mia/ *n. f.* ophthalmia.
ofuscamiento /ofuska'miento/ *n. m.* obfuscation; bewilderment.
ofuscar /ofus'kar/ *v.* obfuscate; bewilder.
ogro /'ogro/ *n. m.* ogre.
oído /o'iðo/ *n. m.* ear; hearing.
oír /o'ir/ *v.* hear; listen.
ojal /o'hal/ *n. m.* buttonhole.
ojalá /oha'la/ *interj. expressing wish or hope.* **o. que...** would that...
ojeada /ohe'aða/ *n. f.* glance; peep; look.
ojear /ohe'ar/ *v.* eye, look at, glance at, stare at.
ojeriza /ohe'riθa; ohe'risa/ *n. f.* spite; grudge.
ojiva /o'hiβa/ *n. f.* pointed arch, ogive.
ojo /'oho/ *n. m.* eye. **¡Ojo!** Look out!
ola /'ola/ *n. f.* wave.
olaje /o'lahe/ *n. m.* surge of waves.
oleada /ole'aða/ *n. f.* swell.
oleo /'oleo/ *n. m.* oil; holy oil; extreme unction.
oleoducto /oleo'ðukto/ *n. m.* pipeline.
oleomargarina /oleomarga'rina/ *n. f.* oleomargarine.
oleoso /ole'oso/ *a.* oily.
oler /o'ler/ *v.* smell.
olfatear /olfate'ar/ *v.* smell.
olfato /ol'fato/ *n. m.* scent, smell.
oliva /o'liβa/ *n. f.* olive.
olivar /oli'βar/ *n. m.* olive grove.
olivo /o'liβo/ *n. m.* olive tree.
olla /'oʎa; 'oya/ *n. f.* pot, kettle. **o. podrida,** stew.
olmo /'olmo/ *n. m.* elm.
olor /o'lor/ *n. m.* odor, smell, scent.
oloroso /olo'roso/ *a.* fragrant, scented.
olvidadizo /olβiða'ðiθo; olβiða'ðiso/ *a.* forgetful.
olvidar /olβi'ðar/ *v.* forget.
olvido /ol'βiðo/ *n. m.* omission; forgetfulness.
ombligo /om'βligo/ *n. m.* navel.
ominar /omi'nar/ *v.* foretell.
ominoso /omi'noso/ *a.* ominous.
omisión /omi'sion/ *n. f.* omission.
omitir /omi'tir/ *v.* omit, leave out.
ómnibus /'omniβus/ *n. m.* bus.
omnipotencia /omnipo'tenθia; omnipo'tensia/ *n. f.* omnipotence.
omnipotente /omnipo'tente/ *a.* almighty.
omnipresencia /omnipre'senθia; omnipre'sensia/ *n. f.* omnipresence.
omnisciencia /omnis'θienθia; omnis'siensia/ *n. f.* omniscience.
omnívoro /om'niβoro/ *a.* omnivorous.
omóplato /omo'plato/ *n. m.* shoulder blade.
once /'onθe; 'onse/ *a. & pron.* eleven.
onda /'onda/ *n. f.* wave, ripple.
ondear /onde'ar/ *v.* ripple.
ondulación /ondula'θion; ondula'sion/ *n. f.* wave, undulation.
ondular /ondu'lar/ *v.* undulate, ripple.
onza /'onθa; 'onsa/ *n. f.* ounce.
opaco /o'pako/ *a.* opaque.
ópalo /'opalo/ *n. m.* opal.
opción /op'θion; op'sion/ *n. f.* option.
ópera /'opera/ *n. f.* opera.
operación /opera'θion; opera'sion/ *n. f.* operation.
operar /ope'rar/ *v.* operate; operate on.
operario /ope'rario/ **-ria** *n.* operator; (skilled) worker.
operarse /ope'rarse/ *v.* have an operation.
operativo /opera'tiβo/ *a.* operative.
opereta /ope'reta/ *n. f.* operetta.
opiato /o'piato/ *n. m.* opiate.
opinar /opi'nar/ *v.* opine.
opinión /opi'nion/ *n. f.* opinion, view.
opio /'opio/ *n. m.* opium.
oponer /opo'ner/ *v.* oppose.
Oporto /o'porto/ *n. m.* port (wine).
oportunidad /oportuni'ðað/ *n. f.* opportunity.
oportunismo /oportu'nismo/ *n. m.* opportunism.
oportunista /oportu'nista/ *n. & a.* opportunist.
oportuno /opor'tuno/ *a.* opportune, expedient.
oposición /oposi'θion; oposi'sion/ *n. f.* opposition.
opresión /opre'sion/ *n. f.* oppression.
opresivo /opre'siβo/ *a.* oppressive.
oprimir /opri'mir/ *v.* oppress.
oprobio /o'proβio/ *n. m.* infamy.
optar /op'tar/ *v.* select, choose.
óptica /'optika/ *n. f.* optics.
óptico /'optiko/ *a.* optic.
optimismo /opti'mismo/ *n. m.* optimism.
optimista /opti'mista/ *a. & n.* optimistic; optimist.
óptimo /'optimo/ *a.* best.
opuesto /o'puesto/ *a.* opposite; opposed.
opugnar /opug'nar/ *v.* attack.
opulencia /opu'lenθia; opu'lensia/ *n. f.* opulence, wealth.
opulento /opu'lento/ *a.* opulent, wealthy.
oración /ora'θion; ora'sion/ *n. f.* sentence; prayer; oration.
oráculo /o'rakulo/ *n. m.* oracle.
orador /ora'ðor/ **-ra** *n.* orator, speaker.
oral /o'ral/ *a.* oral.
orangután /oraŋgu'tan/ *n. m.* orangutan.
orar /o'rar/ *v.* pray.
oratoria /ora'toria/ *n. f.* oratory.
oratorio /ora'torio/ *a.* oratorical.
orbe /'orβe/ *n. m.* orb; globe.
órbita /'orβita/ *n. f.* orbit.
orden /'orðen/ *n. m. or f.* order.
ordenador /orðena'ðor/ *n. m.* computer; regulator.
ordenador de sobremesa /orðena'ðor de soβre'mesa/ desktop computer.
ordenador doméstico /orðena'ðor do'mestiko/ home computer.
ordenanza /orðe'nanθa; orðe'nansa/ *n. f.* ordinance.
ordenar /orðe'nar/ *v.* order; put in order; ordain.
ordeñar /orðe'ɲar/ *v.* milk.
ordinal /orði'nal/ *a. & m.* ordinal.
ordinario /orði'nario/ *a.* ordinary; common, usual.
oreja /o'reha/ *n. f.* ear.
orejera /ore'hera/ *n. f.* earmuff.
orfanato /orfa'nato/ *n. m.* orphanage.
organdí /organ'di/ *n. m.* organdy.
orgánico /or'ganiko/ *a.* organic.
organigrama /organi'grama/ *n. m.* flow chart.
organismo /orga'nismo/ *n. m.* organism.
organista /orga'nista/ *n. m. & f.* organist.
organización /organiθa'θion; organisa'sion/ *n. f.* organization.
organizar /organi'θar; organi'sar/ *v.* organize.
órgano /'organo/ *n. m.* organ.
orgía /or'hia/ *n. f.* orgy, revel.
orgullo /or'guʎo; or'guyo/ *n. m.* pride.
orgulloso /orgu'ʎoso; orgu'yoso/ *a.* proud.
orientación /orienta'θion; orienta'sion/ *n. f.* orientation.
oriental /orien'tal/ *a.* Oriental; eastern.
orientar /orien'tar/ *v.* orient.
oriente /o'riente/ *n. m.* orient, east.
orificación /orifika'θion; orifika'sion/ *n. f.* gold filling (for tooth).
origen /o'rihen/ *n. m.* origin; parentage, descent.
original /orihi'nal/ *a.* original.
originalidad /orihinali'ðað/ *n. f.* originality.
originalmente /orihinal'mente/ *adv.* originally.
originar /orihi'nar/ *v.* originate.
orilla /o'riʎa; o'riya/ *n. f.* shore; bank; edge.
orín /o'rin/ *n. m.* rust.
orina /o'rina/ *n. f.* urine.
orinar /ori'nar/ *v.* urinate.
orines /o'rines/ *n. m.pl.* urine.
oriol /o'riol/ *n. m.* oriole.
orla /'orla/ *n. f.* border; edging.
ornado /or'naðo/ *a.* ornate.
ornamentación /ornamenta'θion; ornamenta'sion/ *n. f.* ornamentation.
ornamento /orna'mento/ *n. m.* ornament. **—ornamentar,** *v.*
ornar /or'nar/ *v.* ornament, adorn.
oro /'oro/ *n. m.* gold.
oropel /oro'pel/ *n. m.* tinsel.
orquesta /or'kesta/ *n. f.* orchestra.
ortiga /or'tiga/ *n. f.* nettle.
ortodoxo /orto'ðokso/ *a.* orthodox.
ortografía /ortogra'fia/ *n. f.* orthography, spelling.
ortóptero /or'toptero/ *a.* orthopterous.
oruga /o'ruga/ *n. f.* caterpillar.
orzuelo /or'θuelo; or'suelo/ *n. m.* sty.
os /os/ *pron.* you (*pl.*); yourselves.
osadía /osa'ðia/ *n. f.* daring.
osar /o'sar/ *v.* dare.
oscilación /osθila'θion; ossila'sion/ *n. f.* oscillation.
oscilar /osθi'lar; ossi'lar/ *v.* oscillate, rock.
ósculo /'oskulo/ *n. m.* kiss.
oscurecer /oskure'θer; oskure'ser/ **oscuridad, oscuro** = obscur-.
oso /'oso/ **osa** *n.* bear.
oso de felpa /'oso de 'felpa/ teddy bear.
ostentación /ostenta'θion; ostenta'sion/ *n. f.* ostentation, showiness.
ostentar /osten'tar/ *v.* show off.
ostentoso /osten'toso/ *a.* ostentatious, flashy.
ostra /'ostra/ *n. f.* oyster.
ostracismo /ostra'θismo; ostra'sismo/ *n. m.* ostracism.
otalgia /o'talhia/ *n. f.* earache.
otero /o'tero/ *n. m.* hill, knoll.
otoño /o'toɲo/ *n. m.* autumn, fall.
otorgar /otor'gar/ *v.* grant, award.
otro /'otro/ *a. & pron.* other, another. **o. vez,** again. **el uno al o.,** one another, each other.
ovación /oβa'θion; oβa'sion/ *n. f.* ovation.
oval /o'βal/ **ovalado** *a.* oval.
óvalo /'oβalo/ *n. m.* oval.
ovario /o'βario/ *n. m.* ovary.
oveja /o'βeha/ *n. f.* sheep.
ovejero /oβe'hero/ *n. m.* sheep dog.
ovillo /o'βiʎo; o'βiyo/ *n. m.* ball of yarn.
OVNI /'oβni/ *abbr.* (objeto volador no identificado) UFO (unidentified flying object).
oxidación /oksiða'θion; oksiða'sion/ *n. f.* oxidation.
oxidar /oksi'ðar/ *v.* oxidize; rust.
óxido /'oksiðo/ *n. m.* oxide.
oxígeno /ok'siheno/ *n. m.* oxygen.
oyente /o'iente/ *n. m. & f.* hearer; (*pl.*) audience.

ozono /o'θono; o'sono/ *n. m.* ozone.

P

pabellón /paβe'ʎon; paβe'yon/ *n. m.* pavilion. **p. de deportes,** sports center.

pabilo /pa'βilo/ *n. m.* wick.

paciencia /pa'θienθia; pa'siensia/ *n. f.* patience.

paciente /pa'θiente; pa'siente/ *a. & n.* patient.

pacificar /paθifi'kar; pasifi'kar/ *v.* pacify.

pacífico /pa'θifiko; pa'sifiko/ *a.* pacific.

pacifismo /paθi'fismo; pasi'fismo/ *n. m.* pacifism.

pacifista /paθi'fista; pasi'fista/ *n. & a.* pacifist.

pacto /'pakto/ *n. m.* pact, treaty.

padecer /paðe'θer; paðe'ser/ *v.* suffer. **p. del corazón,** have heart trouble.

padrastro /pa'ðrastro/ *n. m.* stepfather.

padre /'paðre/ *n. m.* father; priest; (*pl.*) parents.

padrenuestro /paðre'nuestro/ *n. m.* paternoster; Lord's Prayer.

padrino /pa'ðrino/ *n. m.* godfather; sponsor.

paella /pa'eʎa; pa'eya/ *n. f.* dish of rice with meat or chicken.

paga /'paga/ *n. f.* pay, wages. **p. extra bonus.**

pagadero /paga'ðero/ *a.* payable.

pagador /paga'ðor/ **-ra** *n.* payer.

paganismo /paga'nismo/ *n. m.* paganism.

pagano /pa'gano/ **-na** *a. & n.* heathen, pagan.

pagar /pa'gar/ *v.* pay, pay for. **p. en metálico,** pay cash.

página /'pahina/ *n. f.* page.

pago /'pago/ *n. m.* pay, payment.

país /pa'is/ *n. m.* country, nation.

paisaje /pai'sahe/ *n. m.* landscape, scenery, countryside.

paisano /pai'sano/ **-na** *n.* countryman; compatriot; civilian.

paja /'paha/ *n. f.* straw.

pajar /pa'har/ *n. m.* barn.

pajarita /paha'rita/ *n. f.* bow tie.

pájaro /'paharo/ *n. m.* bird.

paje /'pahe/ *n. m.* page (person).

pala /'pala/ *n. f.* shovel, spade.

palabra /pa'laβra/ *n. f.* word.

palabrero /pala'βrero/ *a.* talkative; wordy.

palabrista /pala'βrista/ *n. m. & f.* talkative person.

palacio /pa'laθio; pa'lasio/ *n. m.* palace.

paladar /pala'ðar/ *n. m.* palate.

paladear /palaðe'ar/ *v.* taste; relish.

palanca /pa'lanka/ *n. f.* lever. **p. de cambio,** gearshift.

palangana /palaŋ'gana/ *n. f.* washbasin.

palco /'palko/ *n. m.* theater box.

palenque /pa'lenke/ *n. m.* palisade.

paleta /pa'leta/ *n. f.* mat, pallet.

paletilla /pale'tiʎa; pale'tiya/ *n. f.* shoulder blade.

palidecer /paliðe'θer; paliðe'ser/ *v.* turn pale.

palidez /pali'ðeθ; pali'ðes/ *n. f.* paleness.

pálido /'paliðo/ *a.* pale.

paliza /pa'liθa; pa'lisa/ *n. f.* beating.

palizada /pali'θaða; pali'saða/ *n. m.* palisade.

palma /'palma/ **palmera** *n. f.* palm (tree).

palmada /pal'maða/ *n. f.* slap, clap.

palmear /palme'ar/ *v.* applaud.

palo /'palo/ *n. m.* pole, stick; suit (in cards); *Naut.* mast.

paloma /pa'loma/ *n. f.* dove, pigeon.

palpar /pal'par/ *v.* touch, feel.

palpitación /palpita'θion; palpita'sion/ *n. f.* palpitation.

palpitar /palpi'tar/ *v.* palpitate.

paludismo /palu'ðismo/ *n. m.* malaria.

pampa /'pampa/ *n. f.* (*S.A.*) prairie, plain.

pan /pan/ *n. m.* bread; loaf. **p. de centeno,** rye bread.

pana /'pana/ *n. f.* corduroy.

panacea /pana'θea; pana'sea/ *n. f.* panacea.

panadería /panaðe'ria/ *n. f.* bakery.

panadero /pana'ðero/ **-ra** *n.* baker.

panameño /pana'meɲo/ **-ña** *a. & n.* Panamanian, of Panama.

panamericano /panameri'kano/ *a.* Pan-American.

páncreas /'pankreas/ *n. m.* pancreas.

pandeo /pan'deo/ *n. m.* bulge.

pandilla /pan'diʎa; pan'diya/ *n. f.* band, gang.

panecillo /pane'θiʎo; pane'siyo/ *n. m.* roll, muffin.

panegírico /pane'hiriko/ *n. m.* panegyric.

pánico /'paniko/ *n. m.* panic.

panocha /pa'notʃa/ *n. f.* ear of corn.

panorama /pano'rama/ *n. m.* panorama.

panorámico /pano'ramiko/ *a.* panoramic.

pantalla /pan'taʎa; pan'taya/ *n. f.* (movie) screen; lamp shade.

pantalones /panta'lones/ *n. m.pl.* trousers, pants.

pantano /pan'tano/ *n. m.* bog, marsh, swamp.

pantanoso /panta'noso/ *a.* swampy, marshy.

pantera /pan'tera/ *n. f.* panther.

pantomima /panto'mima/ *n. f.* pantomime.

pantorrilla /panto'rriʎa; panto'rriya/ *n. f.* calf (of body).

panza /'panθa; 'pansa/ *n. f.* belly, paunch.

pañal /pa'ɲal/ *n. m.* diaper.

paño /'paɲo/ *n. m.* piece of cloth.

pañuelo /pa'ɲuelo/ *n. m.* handkerchief.

Papa /'papa/ *n. m.* Pope.

papa *n. f.* potato.

papá *n. m.* papa, father.

papado /pa'paðo/ *n. m.* papacy.

papagayo /papa'gaio/ *n. m.* parrot.

papal /pa'pal/ *a.* papal.

Papá Noel /pa'pa no'el/ *n. m.* Santa Claus.

papel /pa'pel/ *n. m.* paper; role, part.

papel crespón /pa'pel kres'pon/ crepe paper.

papel de aluminio /pa'pel de alu'minio/ aluminum foil.

papel de escribir /pa'pel de es'kriβir/ writing paper.

papel de estaño /pa'pel de es'taɲo/ tin foil.

papel de lija /pa'pel de 'liha/ sandpaper.

papelera /pape'lera/ *n. f.* file cabinet; wastepaper basket.

papelería /papele'ria/ *n. f.* stationery store.

papel moneda /pa'pel mo'neða/ paper money.

paperas /pa'peras/ *n. f.pl.* mumps.

paquete /pa'kete/ *n. m.* package.

par /par/ *a.* **1.** even, equal. —*n.* **2.** pair; equal, peer. **abierto de p. en p.,** wide open.

para /'para/ *prep.* for; in order to. **p. que,** in order that. **estar p.,** to be about to.

parabién /para'βien/ *n. m.* congratulation.

parabrisa /para'βrisa/ *n. m.* windshield.

paracaídas /paraka'iðas/ *n. m.* parachute.

parachoques /para'tʃokes/ *n. m.* *Auto.* bumper.

parada /pa'raða/ *n. f.* stop, halt; stopover; parade.

paradero /para'ðero/ *n. m.* whereabouts; stopping place.

paradigma /para'ðigma/ *n. m.* paradigm.

paradoja /para'ðoha/ *n. f.* paradox.

parafina /para'fina/ *n. f.* paraffin.

parafrasear /parafrase'ar/ *v.* paraphrase.

paraguas /pa'raguas/ *n. m.* umbrella.

paraguayano /paragua'yano/ **-na** *n. & a.* Paraguayan.

paraíso /para'iso/ *n. m.* paradise.

paralelo /para'lelo/ *a. & m.* parallel.

parálisis /pa'ralisis/ *n. f.* paralysis.

paralizar /parali'θar; parali'sar/ *v.* paralyze.

paramédico /para'meðiko/ *n. m.* paramedic.

parámetro /pa'rametro/ *n. m.* parameter.

parapeto /para'peto/ *n. m.* parapet.

parar /pa'rar/ *v.* stop, stem, ward off; stay.

pararse /pa'rarse/ *v.* stop; stand up.

parasítico /para'sitiko/ *a.* parasitic.

parásito /pa'rasito/ *n. m.* parasite.

parcela /par'θela; par'sela/ *n. f.* plot of ground.

parcial /par'θial; par'sial/ *a.* partial.

parcialidad /parθiali'ðað; parsiali'ðað/ *n. f.* partiality; bias.

parcialmente /parθial'mente; parsial'mente/ *adv.* partially.

pardo /'parðo/ *a.* brown.

parear /pare'ar/ *v.* pair; match; mate.

parecer /pare'θer; pare'ser/ *n.* **1.** *m.* opinion. —*v.* **2.** seem, appear, look.

parecerse /pare'θerse; pare'serse/ *v.* look alike. **p. a,** look like.

parecido /pare'θiðo; pare'siðo/ *a.* similar.

pared /pa'reð/ *n. f.* wall.

pareja /pa'reha/ *n. f.* pair, couple; (dancing) partner.

parentela /paren'tela/ *n. f.* kinfolk.

parentesco /paren'tesko/ *n. m.* parentage, lineage; kin.

paréntesis /pa'rentesis/ *n. m.* parenthesis.

paria /'paria/ *n. m.* outcast, pariah.

paricipante /pariθi'pante; parisi'pante/ *n. m. & f.* participant.

paridad /pari'ðað/ *n. f.* parity.

pariente /pa'riente/ *n. m. & f.* relative.

parir /pa'rir/ *v.* give birth.

parisiense /pari'siense/ *n. & a.* Parisian.

parlamentario /parlamen'tario/ *a.* parliamentary.

parlamento /parla'mento/ *n. m.* parliament.

paro /'paro/ *n. m.* stoppage; strike. **p. forzoso,** unemployment.

parodia /pa'roðia/ *n. f.* parody.

parodista /paro'ðista/ *n. m. & f.* parodist.

paroxismo /parok'sismo/ *n. m.* paroxysm.

párpado /'parpaðo/ *n. m.* eyelid.

parque /'parke/ *n. m.* park.

parquímetro /par'kimetro/ *n. m.* parking meter.

parra /'parra/ *n. f.* grapevine.

párrafo /'parrafo/ *n. m.* paragraph.

parranda /pa'rranda/ *n. f.* spree.

parrandear /parrande'ar/ *v.* carouse.

parrilla /pa'rriʎa; pa'rriya/ *n. f.* grill; grillroom.

párroco /'parroko/ *n. m.* parish priest.

parroquia /pa'rrokia/ *n. f.* parish.

parroquial /parro'kial/ *a.* parochial.

parsimonia /parsi'monia/ *n. f.* economy, thrift.

parsimonioso /parsimo'nioso/ *a.* economical, thrifty.

parte /'parte/ *n. f.* part. **de p. de,** on behalf of. **alguna p.,** somewhere. **por otra p.,** on the other hand. **dar p. a,** to notify.

partera /par'tera/ *n. f.* midwife.

partición /parti'θion; parti'sion/ *n. f.* distribution.

participación /partiθipa'θion; partisipa'sion/ *n. f.* participation.

participar /partiθi'par; partisi'par/ *v.* participate; announce.

participio /parti'θipio; parti'sipio/ *n. m.* participle.

partícula /par'tikula/ *n. f.* particle.

particular /partiku'lar/ *a.* **1.** particular; private. —*n.* **2.** *m.* particular; detail; individual.

particularmente /partikular'mente/ *adv.* particularly.

partida /par'tiða/ *n. f.* departure; *Mil.* party; (sport) game.

partida de defunción /par'tiða de defun'θion; par'tiða de defun'sion/ death certificate.

partida de matrimonio /par'tiða de matri'monio/ marriage certificate.

partida de nacimiento /par'tiða de naθi'miento; par'tiða de nasi'miento/ birth certificate.

partidario /parti'ðario/ **-ria** *n.* partisan.

partido /par'tiðo/ *n. m.* side, party, faction; game, match.

partir /par'tir/ *v.* leave, depart; part, cleave, split.

parto /'parto/ *n. m.* delivery, childbirth.

pasa /'pasa/ *n. f.* raisin.

pasado /pa'saðo/ *a.* **1.** past; last. —*n.* **2.** *m.* past.

pasaje /pa'sahe/ *n. m.* passage, fare.

pasajero /pasa'hero/ **-ra** *a.* **1.** passing, transient. —*n.* **2.** passenger.

pasamano /pasa'mano/ *n. m.* banister.

pasaporte /pasa'porte/ *n. m.* passport.

pasar /pa'sar/ *v.* pass; happen; spend (time). **p. por alto,** overlook. **p. lista,** call the roll. **p. sin,** do without.

pasatiempo /pasa'tiempo/ *n. m.* pastime; hobby.

pascua /'paskua/ *n. f.* religious holiday; (*pl.*) Christmas (season). **P. Florida,** Easter.

pase de modelos /'pase de mo'ðelos/ *n. m.* fashion show.

paseo /pa'seo/ *n. m.* walk, stroll; drive. —**pasear,** *v.*

pasillo /pa'siʎo; pa'siyo/ *n. m.* aisle; hallway.

pasión /pa'sion/ *n. f.* passion.

pasivo /pa'siβo/ *a.* passive.

pasmar /pas'mar/ *v.* astonish, astound, stun.

pasmo /'pasmo/ *n. m.* spasm; wonder.

paso /'paso/ *a.* **1.** dried (fruit). —*n.* **2.** *m.* pace, step; (mountain) pass.

paso cebra /'paso 'θeβra; 'paso 'seβra/ crosswalk.

paso de ganso /'paso de 'ganso/ goose step.

paso de peatones /'paso de pea'tones/ pedestrian crossing.

pasta /'pasta/ *n. f.* paste; batter; plastic.

pasta dentífrica /'pasta den'tifrika/ toothpaste.

pastar /pas'tar/ *v.* graze.

pastel /pas'tel/ *n. m.* pastry; pie.

pastelería /pastele'ria/ *n. f.* pastry; pastry shop.

pasteurización /pasteuriθa'θion; pasteurisa'sion/ *n. f.* pasteurization.

pasteurizar /pasteuri'θar; pasteuri'sar/ *v.* pasteurize.

pastilla /pas'tiʎa; pas'tiya/ *n. f.* tablet, lozenge, coughdrop.

pasto /'pasto/ *n. m.* pasture; grass.

pastor /pas'tor/ *n. m.* pastor; shepherd.

pastorear /pastore'ar/ *v.* pasture, tend (a flock).

pastrón /pas'tron/ *n. m.* pastrami.

pastura /pas'tura/ *n. f.* pasture.

pata /'pata/ *n. f.* foot (of animal).

patada /pa'taða/ *n. f.* kick.

patán /pa'tan/ *n. m.* boor.

patanada /pata'naða/ *n. f.* rudeness.

patata /pa'tata/ *n. f.* potato. **p. asada,** baked potato.

patear /pate'ar/ *v.* stamp, tramp, kick.

patente /pa'tente/ *a. & m.* patent. —**patentar,** *v.*

paternal /pater'nal/ **paterno** *a.* paternal.

paternidad /paterni'ðað/ *n. f.* paternity, fatherhood.

patético /pa'tetiko/ *a.* pathetic.

patíbulo /pa'tiβulo/ *n. m.* scaffold; gallows.

patín /pa'tin/ *n. m.* skate. —**patinar,** *v.*

patín de ruedas /pa'tin de 'rrueðas/ roller skate.

patio /'patio/ *n. m.* yard, court, patio.

pato /'pato/ *n. m.* duck.

patria /'patria/ *n. f.* native land.

patriarca /pa'triarka/ *n. m. & f.* patriarch.

patrimonio /patri'monio/ *n. m.* inheritance.

patriota /pa'triota/ *n. m. & f.* patriot.

patriótico /pa'triotiko/ *a.* patriotic.

patriotismo /patrio'tismo/ *n. m.* patriotism.

patrocinar /patroθi'nar; patrosi'nar/ *v.* patronize, sponsor.

patrón /pa'tron/ **-ona** *n.* patron; boss; (dress) pattern.

patrulla /pa'truʎa; pa'truya/ *n. f.* patrol. —**patrullar,** *v.*

paulatino /paula'tino/ *a.* gradual.

pausa /'pausa/ *n. f.* pause. —**pausar,** *v.*

pausa para el café /'pausa 'para el ka'fe/ coffee break.

pauta /'pauta/ *n. f.* guideline.

pavesa /pa'βesa/ *n. f.* spark, cinder.

pavimentar /paβimen'tar/ *v.* pave.

pavimento /paβi'mento/ *n. m.* pavement.

pavo /'paβo/ *n. m.* turkey. **p. real,** peacock.

pavor /pa'βor/ *n. m.* terror.

payaso /pa'iaso/ **-sa** *n.* clown.

paz /paθ; pas/ *n. f.* peace.

peatón /pea'ton/ **-na** *n.* pedestrian.

peca /'peka/ *n. f.* freckle.

pecado /pe'kaðo/ *n. m.* sin. —**pecar,** *v.*

pecador /peka'ðor/ **-ra** *a. & n.* sinful; sinner.

pecera /pe'θera; pe'sera/ *n. f.* aquarium, fishbowl.

pechera /pe'tʃera/ *n. f.* shirt front.

pecho /'petʃo/ *n. m.* chest; breast; bosom.

pechuga /pe'tʃuga/ *n. f.* breast (of fowl).

pecoso /pe'koso/ *a.* freckled, freckly.

peculiar /peku'liar/ *a.* peculiar.

peculiaridad /pekuliari'ðað/ *n. f.* peculiarity.

pedagogía /peðago'hia/ *n. f.* pedagogy.

pedagogo /peða'gogo/ **-ga** *n.* pedagogue, teacher.

pedal /pe'ðal/ *n. m.* pedal.

pedantesco /peðan'tesko/ *a.* pedantic.

pedazo /pe'ðaθo; pe'ðaso/ *n. m.* piece.

pedernal /peðer'nal/ *n. m.* flint.

pedestal /peðes'tal/ *n. m.* pedestal.

pediatra /pe'ðiatra/ *n. m. & f.* pediatrician.

pediatría /peðia'tria/ *n. f.* pediatrics.

pedicuro /peði'kuro/ *n. m.* chiropodist.

pedir /pe'ðir/ *v.* ask, ask for, request; apply for; order.

pedo /'peðo/ *n. m.* fart; intoxication.

pedregoso /peðre'goso/ *a.* rocky.

pegajoso /pega'hoso/ *a.* sticky.

pegamento /pega'mento/ *n. m.* glue.

pegar /pe'gar/ *v.* beat, strike; adhere, fasten, stick.

peinado /pei'naðo/ *n. m.* coiffure, hairdo.

peine /'peine/ *n. m.* comb. —**peinar,** *v.*

peineta /pei'neta/ *n. f.* (ornamental) comb.

pelagra /pe'lagra/ *n. f.* pellagra.

pelar /pe'lar/ *v.* skin, pare, peel.

pelea /pe'lea/ *n. f.* fight, row. —**pelearse,** *v.*

pelícano /pe'likano/ *n. m.* pelican.

película /pe'likula/ *n. f.* movie, motion picture, film. **p. de terror** horror film.

peligrar /peli'grar/ *v.* be in danger.

peligro /pe'ligro/ *n. m.* peril, danger.

peligroso /peli'groso/ *a.* perilous, dangerous.

pelirrojo /peli'rroho/ **-ja** *a. & n.* redhead.

pellejo /pe'ʎeho; pe'yeho/ *n. m.* skin; peel (of fruit).

pellizco /pe'ʎiθko; pe'yisko/ *n. m.* pinch. —**pellizcar,** *v.*

pelo /'pelo/ *n. m.* hair.

pelota /pe'lota/ *n. f.* ball.

peltre /'peltre/ *n. m.* pewter.

peluca /pe'luka/ *n. f.* wig.

peludo /pe'luðo/ *a.* hairy.

peluquería /peluke'ria/ *n. f.* hairdresser's shop, beauty parlor.

peluquero /pelu'kero/ **-ra** *n.* hairdresser.

pena /'pena/ *n. f.* pain, grief, trouble, woe; penalty. **valer la p.,** to be worthwhile.

penacho /pe'natʃo/ *n. m.* plume.

penalidad /penali'ðað/ *n. f.* trouble; penalty.

pender /pen'der/ *v.* hang, dangle; be pending.

pendiente /pen'diente/ *a.* **1.** hanging; pending. —*n.* **2.** *m.* incline, slope; earring, pendant.

pendón /pen'don/ *n. m.* pennant, flag.

penetración /penetra'θion; penetra'sion/ *n. f.* penetration.

penetrar /pene'trar/ *v.* penetrate, pierce.

penicilina /peniθi'lina; penisi'lina/ *n. f.* penicillin.

península /pe'ninsula/ *n. f.* peninsula.

penitencia /peni'tenθia; peni'tensia/ *n. f.* penitence, penance.

penitenciaría /penitenθia'ria; penitensia'ria/ *n. f.* penitentiary.

penoso /pe'noso/ *a.* painful, troublesome, grievous, distressing.

pensador /pensa'ðor/ **-ra** *n.* thinker.

pensamiento /pensa'miento/ *n. m.* thought.

pensar /pen'sar/ *v.* think; intend, plan.

pensativo /pensa'tiβo/ *a.* pensive, thoughtful.

pensión /pen'sion/ *n. f.* pension; boardinghouse.

pensionista /pensio'nista/ *n. m. & f.* boarder.

pentagonal /pentago'nal/ *a.* pentagonal.

penúltimo /pe'nultimo/ *a.* next-to-the-last, last but one, penultimate.

penuria /pe'nuria/ *n. f.* penury, poverty.

peña /'peɲa/ *n. f.* rock.

peñascoso /peɲas'koso/ *a.* rocky.

peñón /pe'ɲon/ *n. m.* rock, crag.

Peñón de Gibraltar /pe'ɲon de hiβral'tar/ Rock of Gibraltar.

peón /pe'on/ *n. m.* unskilled laborer; infantryman.

peonada /peo'naða/ *n. f.* group of laborers.

peonía /peo'nia/ *n. f.* peony.

peor /pe'or/ *a.* worse, worst.

pepino /pe'pino/ *n. m.* cucumber.

pepita /pe'pita/ *n. f.* seed (in fruit).

pequeñez /peke'ɲeθ; peke'ɲes/ *n. f.* smallness; trifle.

pequeño /pe'keɲo/ **-ña** *a.* **1.** small, little, short, slight. —*n.* **2.** child.

pera /'pera/ *n. f.* pear.

peral /pe'ral/ *n. m.* pear tree.

perca /'perka/ *n. f.* perch (fish).

percal /per'kal/ *n. m.* calico, percale.

percance /per'kanθe; per'kanse/ *n. m.* mishap, snag, hitch.

percepción /perθep'θion; persep'sion/ *n. f.* perception.

perceptivo /perθep'tiβo; persep'tiβo/ *a.* perceptive.

percha /'pertʃa/ *n. f.* perch; clothes hanger, rack.

percibir /perθi'βir; persi'βir/ *v.* perceive, sense; collect.

perder /per'ðer/ *v.* lose; miss; waste. **echar a p.,** spoil. **p. el conocimiento,** lose consciousness.

perdición /perði'θion; perði'sion/ *n. f.* perdition, downfall.

pérdida /'perðiða/ *n. f.* loss.

perdiz /per'ðiθ; per'ðis/ *n. f.* partridge.

perdón /per'ðon/ *n. m.* pardon, forgiveness.

perdonar /perðo'nar/ *v.* forgive, pardon; spare.

perdurable /perðu'raβle/ *a.* enduring, everlasting.

perdurar /perðu'rar/ *v.* endure, last.

perecedero /pereθe'ðero; perese'ðero/ *a.* perishable.

perecer /pere'θer; pere'ser/ *v.* perish.

peregrinación /peregrina'θion; peregrina'sion/ *n. f.* peregrination; pilgrimage.

peregrino /pere'grino/ **-na** *n.* pilgrim.

perejil /pere'hil/ *n. m.* parsley.

perenne /pe'renne/ *a.* perennial.

pereza /pe'reθa; pe'resa/ *n. f.* laziness.

perezoso /pere'θoso; pere'soso/ *a.* lazy, sluggish.

perfección /perfek'θion; perfek'sion/ *n. f.* perfection.

perfeccionar /perfekθio'nar; perfeksio'nar/ *v.* perfect.

perfeccionista /perfekθio'nista; perfeksio'nista/ *a. & n.* perfectionist.

perfectamente /perfekta'mente/ *adv.* perfectly.

perfecto /per'fekto/ *a.* perfect.

perfidia /per'fiðia/ *n. f.* falseness, perfidy.

pérfido /'perfiðo/ *a.* perfidious.

perfil /per'fil/ *n. m.* profile.

perforación /perfora'θion; perfora'sion/ *n. f.* perforation.

perforar /perfo'rar/ *v.* pierce, perforate.

perfume /per'fume/ *n. m.* perfume, scent. —**perfumar,** *v.*

pergamino /perga'mino/ *n. m.* parchment.

pericia /pe'riθia; pe'risia/ *n. f.* skill, expertness.

perico /pe'riko/ *n. m.* parakeet.

perímetro /pe'rimetro/ *n. m.* perimeter.

periódico /pe'rioðiko/ *a.* **1.** periodic. —*n.* **2.** *m.* newspaper.

periodista /perio'ðista/ *n. m. & f.* journalist.

período /pe'rioðo/ *n. m.* period.

periscopio /peris'kopio/ *n. m.* periscope.

perito /pe'rito/ **-ta** *a. & n.* experienced; expert, connoisseur.

perjudicar /perhuði'kar/ *v.* damage, hurt; impair.

perjudicial /perhuði'θial; perhuði'sial/ *a.* harmful, injurious.

perjuicio /per'huiθio; per'huisio/ *n. m.* injury, damage.

perjurar /perhu'rar/ *v.* commit perjury.

perjurio /per'hurio/ *n. m.* perjury.

perla /'perla/ *n. f.* pearl.

permanecer /permane'θer; permane'ser/ *v.* remain, stay.

permanencia /perma'nenθia; perma'nensia/ *n. f.* permanence; stay.

permanente /perma'nente/ *a.* permanent.

permiso /per'miso/ *n. m.* permission; permit; furlough.

permitir /permi'tir/ *v.* permit, enable, let, allow.

permuta /per'muta/ *n. f.* exchange, barter.

pernicioso /perni'θioso; perni'sioso/ *a.* pernicious.

perno /'perno/ *n. m.* bolt.

pero /'pero/ *conj.* but.

peróxido /pe'roksiðo/ *n. m.* peroxide.

perpendicular /perpendiku'lar/ *n. m. & a.* perpendicular.

perpetración /perpetra'θion; perpetra'sion/ *n. f.* perpetration.

perpetrar /perpe'trar/ *v.* perpetrate.

perpetuar /perpe'tuar/ *v.* perpetuate.

perpetuidad /perpetui'ðað/ *n. f.* perpetuity.

perpetuo /per'petuo/ *a.* perpetual.

perplejo /per'pleho/ *a.* perplexed, puzzled.

perrito caliente /pe'rrito ka'liente/ *n. m.* hot dog.

perro /'perro/ **-rra** *n.* dog.

persecución /perseku'θion; perseku'sion/ *n. f.* persecution.

perseguir /perse'gir/ *v.* pursue; persecute.

perseverancia /perseβe'ranθia; perseβe'ransia/ *n. f.* perseverance.

perseverar /perseβe'rar/ *v.* persevere.

persiana /per'siana/ *n. f.* ʒhutter, Venetian blind.

persistente /persis'tente/ *a.* persistent.

persistir /persis'tir/ *v.* persist.

persona /per'sona/ *n. f.* person.

personaje /perso'nahe/ *n. m.* personage; *Theat.* character.

personal /perso'nal/ *a.* **1.** personal. —*n.* **2.** *m.* personnel, staff.

personalidad /personali'ðað/ *n. f.* personality.

personalmente /personal'mente/ *adv.* personally.

perspectiva /perspek'tiβa/ *n. f.* perspective; prospect.

perspicaz /perspi'kaθ; perspi'kas/ *a.* perspicacious, acute.

persuadir /persua'ðir/ *v.* persuade.

persuasión /persua'sion/ *n. f.* persuasion.

persuasivo /persua'siβo/ *a.* persuasive.

pertenecer /pertene'θer; pertene'ser/ *v.* pertain; belong.

pertinencia /perti'nenθia; perti'nensia/ *n. f.* pertinence.

pertinente /perti'nente/ *a.* pertinent; relevant.

perturbar /pertur'βar/ *v.* perturb, disturb.

peruano /pe'ruano/ **-na** *a. & n.* Peruvian.

perversidad /perβersi'ðað/ *n. f.* perversity.

perverso /per'βerso/ *a.* perverse.

pesadez /pesa'ðeθ; pesa'ðes/ *n. f.* dullness.

pesadilla /pesa'ðiʎa; pesa'ðiya/ *n. f.* nightmare.

pesado /pe'saðo/ *a.* heavy; dull, dreary, boring.

pésame /'pesame/ *n. m.* condolence.

pesar /pe'sar/ *n. m.* sorrow; regret. **a p. de,** in spite of. *v.* weigh.

pesca /'peska/ *n. f.* fishing; catch (of fish).

pescadería /peskaðe'ria/ *n. f.* fish store.

pescado /pes'kaðo/ *n. m.* fish. —**pescar,** *v.*

pescador /peska'ðor/ *n. m.* fisherman.

pesebre /pe'seβre/ *n. m.* stall, manger; crib.

peseta /pe'seta/ *n. f.* peseta (monetary unit).

pesimismo /pesi'mismo/ *n. m.* pessimism.

pesimista /pesi'mista/ *a. & n.* pessimistic; pessimist.

pésimo /'pesimo/ *a.* awful, terrible, very bad.

peso /'peso/ *n. m.* weight; load; peso (monetary unit).

pesquera /pes'kera/ *n. f.* fishery.

pesquisa /pes'kisa/ *n. f.* investigation.

pestaña /pes'taɲa/ *n. f.* eyelash.

pestañeo /pesta'ɲeo/ *n. m.* wink, blink. **—pestañear,** *v.*

peste /'peste/ *n. f.* plague.

pesticida /pesti'θiða; pesti'siða/ *n. m.* pesticide.

pestilencia /pesti'lenθia; pesti'lensia/ *n. f.* pestilence.

pétalo /'petalo/ *n. m.* petal.

petardo /pe'tarðo/ *n. m.* firecracker.

petición /peti'θion; peti'sion/ *n. f.* petition.

petirrojo /peti'rroho/ *n. m.* robin.

petrel /pe'trel/ *n. m.* petrel.

pétreo /'petreo/ *a.* rocky.

petrificar /petrifi'kar/ *v.* petrify.

petróleo /pe'troleo/ *n. m.* petroleum.

petrolero /petro'lero/ *n. m.* oil tanker.

petunia /pe'tunia/ *n. f.* petunia.

pez /peθ; pes/ *n.* **1.** *m.* fish (in the water). **—***n.* **2.** *f.* pitch, tar.

pezuña /pe'θuɲa; pe'suɲa/ *n. f.* hoof.

piadoso /pia'ðoso/ *a.* pious; merciful.

pianista /pia'nista/ *n. m.* & *f.* pianist.

piano /'piano/ *n. m.* piano.

picadero /pika'ðero/ *n. m.* riding school.

picadura /pika'ðura/ *n. f.* sting, bite, prick.

picamaderos /pikama'ðeros/ *n. m.* woodpecker.

picante /pi'kante/ *a.* hot, spicy.

picaporte /pika'porte/ *n. m.* latch.

picar /pi'kar/ *v.* sting, bite, prick; itch; chop up, grind up.

pícaro /'pikaro/ **-ra** *a.* **1.** knavish, mischievous. **—***n.* **2.** rogue, rascal.

picarse /pi'karse/ *v.* be offended, piqued.

picazón /pika'θon; pika'son/ *n. f.* itch.

pícea /'piθea; 'pisea/ *n. f.* spruce.

pichón /pi'tʃon/ *n. m.* pigeon, squab.

pico /'piko/ *n. m.* peak; pick; beak; spout; small amount.

picotazo /piko'taθo; piko'taso/ *n. m.* peck. **—picotear,** *v.*

pictórico /pik'toriko/ *a.* pictorial.

pie /pie/ *n. m.* foot. **al p. de la letra,** literally; thoroughly.

piedad /pie'ðað/ *n. f.* piety; pity, mercy.

piedra /'pieðra/ *n. f.* stone.

piel /piel/ *n. f.* skin, hide; fur.

pienso /'pienso/ *n. m.* fodder.

pierna /'pierna/ *n. f.* leg.

pieza /'pieθa; 'piesa/ *n. f.* piece; room; *Theat.* play.

pijama /pi'hama/ *n. m. or m.pl.* pajamas.

pila /'pila/ *n. f.* pile, stack; battery; sink.

pilar /pi'lar/ *n. m.* pillar, column.

píldora /'pildora/ *n. f.* pill.

pillo /'piʎo; 'piyo/ **-a** *n.* thief; rascal.

piloto /pi'loto/ *n. m.* & *f.* pilot.

pimentón /pimen'ton/ *n. m.* paprika.

pimienta /pi'mienta/ *n. f.* pepper (spice).

pimiento /pi'miento/ *n. m.* pepper (vegetable).

pináculo /pi'nakulo/ *n. m.* pinnacle.

pincel /pin'θel; pin'sel/ *n. m.* (artist's) brush.

pinchadiscos /pintʃa'ðiskos/ *m.* & *f.* disk jockey.

pinchazo /pin'tʃaθo; pin'tʃaso/ *n. m.* puncture; prick. **—pinchar,** *v.*

pingajo /piŋ'gaho/ *n. m.* rag, tatter.

pino /'pino/ *n. m.* pine.

pinta /'pinta/ *n. f.* pint.

pintar /pin'tar/ *v.* paint; portray, depict.

pintor /pin'tor/ **-ra** *n.* painter.

pintoresco /pinto'resko/ *a.* picturesque.

pintura /pin'tura/ *n. f.* paint; painting.

pinzas /'pinθas; 'pinsas/ *n. f.pl.* pincers, tweezers; claws.

piña /'piɲa/ *n. f.* pineapple.

pío /'pio/ *a.* pious; merciful.

piojo /'pioho/ *n. m.* louse.

pionero /pio'nero/ **-ra** *n.* pioneer.

pipa /'pipa/ *n. f.* tobacco pipe.

pique /'pike/ *n. m.* resentment, pique. **echar a p.,** sink (ship).

pira /'pira/ *n. f.* pyre.

piragua /pi'ragua/ *n. f.* canoe.

piragüismo /pira'guismo/ *n. m.* canoeing.

piragüista /pira'guista/ *n. m.* & *f.* canoeist.

pirámide /pi'ramiðe/ *n. f.* pyramid.

pirata /pi'rata/ *n. m.* & *f.* pirate. **p. de aviones,** hijacker.

pisada /pi'saða/ *n. f.* tread, step. **—pisar,** *v.*

pisapapeles /pisapa'peles/ *n. m.* paperweight.

piscina /pis'θina; pis'sina/ *n. f.* fishpond; swimming pool.

piso /'piso/ *n. m.* floor.

pista /'pista/ *n. f.* trace, clue, track; racetrack.

pista de tenis /'pista de 'tenis/ tennis court.

pistola /pis'tola/ *n. f.* pistol.

pistón /pis'ton/ *n. m.* piston.

pitillo /pi'tiʎo; pi'tiyo/ *n. m.* cigarette.

pito /'pito/ *n. m.* whistle. **—pitar,** *v.*

pizarra /pi'θarra; pi'sarra/ *n. f.* slate; blackboard.

pizca /'piθka; 'piska/ *n. f.* bit, speck; pinch.

pizza /'piθθa; 'pissa/ *n. f.* pizza.

placentero /plaθen'tero; plasen'tero/ *a.* pleasant.

placer /pla'θer; pla'ser/ *n.* **1.** *m.* pleasure. **—***v.* **2.** please.

plácido /'plaθiðo; 'plasiðo/ *a.* placid.

plaga /'plaga/ *n. f.* plague, scourge.

plagio /'plahio/ *n. m.* plagiarism; (*S.A.*) kidnapping.

plan /plan/ *n. m.* plan. **—planear,** *v.*

plancha /'plantʃa/ *n. f.* plate; slab, flatiron.

planchar /plan'tʃar/ *v.* iron, press.

planeta /pla'neta/ *n. m.* planet.

planificación /planifika'θion; planifika'sion/ *n. f.* planning.

planificar /planifi'kar/ *v.* plan.

plano /'plano/ *a.* **1.** level, flat. **—***n.* **2.** *m.* plan; plane.

planta /'planta/ *n. f.* plant; sole (of foot).

planta baja /'planta 'baha/ *n. f.* ground floor.

plantación /planta'θion; planta'sion/ *n. f.* plantation.

plantar /plan'tar/ *v.* plant.

plantear /plante'ar/ *v.* pose, present.

plantel /plan'tel/ *n. m.* educational institution; *Agr.* nursery.

plasma /'plasma/ *n. m.* plasma.

plástico /'plastiko/ *a.* & *m.* plastic.

plata /'plata/ *n. f.* silver; *Colloq.* money.

plataforma /plata'forma/ *n. f.* platform.

plátano /'platano/ *n. m.* plantain; banana.

platel /pla'tel/ *n. m.* platter.

plática /'platika/ *n. f.* chat, talk. **—platicar,** *v.*

platillo /pla'tiʎo; pla'tiyo/ *n. m.* saucer.

platillo volante /pla'tiʎo bo'lante; pla'tiyo bo'lante/ flying saucer.

plato /'plato/ *n. m.* plate, dish.

playa /'plaia/ *n. f.* beach, shore.

plaza /'plaθa; 'plasa/ *n. f.* square. **p. de toros,** bullring.

plazo /'plaθo; 'plaso/ *n. m.* term, deadline; installment.

plebe /'pleβe/ *n. f.* common people; masses.

plebiscito /pleβis'θito; pleβis'sito/ *n. m.* plebiscite.

plegable /ple'gaβle/ *a.* foldable, folding.

plegadura /plega'ðura/ *n. f.* fold, pleat. **—plegar,** *v.*

pleito /'pleito/ *n. m.* lawsuit; dispute.

plenitud /pleni'tuð/ *n. f.* fullness; abundance.

pleno /'pleno/ *a.* full. **en pleno...** in the middle of...

pliego /'pliego/ *n. m.* sheet of paper.

pliegue /'pliege/ *n. m.* fold, pleat, crease.

plomería /plome'ria/ *n. f.* plumbing.

plomero /plo'mero/ *n. m.* plumber.

plomizo /plo'miθo; plo'miso/ *a.* leaden.

plomo /'plomo/ *n. m.* lead; fuse.

pluma /'pluma/ *n. f.* feather; (writing) pen.

pluma estiglográfica /'pluma estiglo'grafika/ fountain pen.

plumafuente /pluma'fuente/ *n. f.* fountain pen.

plumaje /plu'mahe/ *n. m.* plumage.

plumero /plu'mero/ *n. m.* feather duster; plume.

plumoso /plu'moso/ *a.* feathery.

plural /plu'ral/ *a.* & *m.* plural.

pluriempleo /pluriem'pleo/ *n. m.* moonlighting.

PNB, *abbr.* (producto nacional bruto), GNP (gross national product).

población /poβla'θion; poβla'sion/ *n. f.* population; town.

poblador /poβla'ðor/ **-ra** *n.* settler.

poblar /po'βlar/ *v.* populate; settle.

pobre /'poβre/ *a.* & *n.* poor; poor person.

pobreza /po'βreθa; po'βresa/ *n. f.* poverty, need.

pocilga /po'θilga; po'silga/ *n. f.* pigpen.

poción /po'θion; po'sion/ *n. f.* drink; potion.

poco /'poko/ *a.* & *adv.* **1.** little, not much, (*pl.*) few. **por p.,** almost, nearly. **—***n.* **2.** *m.* **un p. (de),** a little, a bit (of).

poder /po'ðer/ *n.* **1.** *m.* power. **—***v.* **2.** be able to, can; be possible, may, might. **no p. menos de,** not be able to help.

poder adquisitivo /po'ðer aðkisi'tiβo/ purchasing power.

poderío /poðe'rio/ *n. m.* power, might.

poderoso /poðe'roso/ *a.* powerful, mighty, potent.

podrido /po'ðriðo/ *a.* rotten.

poema /po'ema/ *n. m.* poem.

poesía /poe'sia/ *n. f.* poetry; poem.

poeta /po'eta/ *n. m.* & *f.* poet.

poético /po'etiko/ *a.* poetic.

polaco /po'lako/ **-ca** *a.* & *n.* Polish; Pole.

polar /po'lar/ *a.* polar.

polaridad /polari'ðað/ *n. f.* polarity.

polea /po'lea/ *n. f.* pulley.

polen /'polen/ *n. m.* pollen.

policía /poli'θia; poli'sia/ *n.* **1.** *f.* police. **—***n.* **2.** *m.* policeman.

polideportivo /poliðepor'tiβo/ *n. m.* sports center.

poliéster /poli'ester/ *n. m.* polyester.

poligamia /poli'gamia/ *n. f.* polygamy.

polígloto /poli'gloto/ **-ta** *n.* polyglot.

polígono industrial /po'ligono indus'trial/ *n. m.* industrial park.

polilla /po'liʎa; po'liya/ *n. f.* moth.

política /po'litika/ *n. f.* politics; policy.

político /po'litiko/ **-ca** *a.* & *n.* politic; political; politician.

póliza /'poliθa; 'polisa/ *n. f.* (insurance) policy; permit, ticket.

polizonte /poli'θonte; poli'sonte/ *n. m.* policeman.

pollada /po'ʎaða; po'yaða/ *n. f.* brood.

pollería /poʎe'ria; poye'ria/ *n. f.* poultry shop.

pollino /po'ʎino; po'yino/ *n. m.* donkey.

pollo /'poʎo; 'poyo/ *n. m.* chicken.

polo /'polo/ *n. m.* pole; polo; popsicle.

polonés /polo'nes/ *a.* Polish.

Polonia /po'lonia/ *n. f.* Poland.

polvera /pol'βera/ *n. f.* powder box; powder puff.

polvo /'polβo/ *n. m.* powder; dust.

pólvora /'polβora/ *n. f.* gunpowder.

pompa /'pompa/ *n. f.* pomp.

pomposo /pom'poso/ *a.* pompous.

pómulo /'pomulo/ *n. m.* cheekbone.

ponche /'pontʃe/ *n. m.* punch (beverage).

ponchera /pon'tʃera/ *n. f.* punch bowl.

ponderar /ponde'rar/ *v.* ponder.

ponderoso /ponde'roso/ *a.* ponderous.

poner /po'ner/ *v.* put, set, lay, place.

ponerse /po'nerse/ *v.* put on; become, get; set (sun). **p. a,** start to.

poniente /po'niente/ *n. m.* west.

pontífice /pon'tifiθe; pon'tifise/ *n. m.* pontiff.

popa /'popa/ *n. f.* stern.

popular /popu'lar/ *a.* popular.

popularidad /populari'ðað/ *n. f.* popularity.

populazo /popu'laθo; popu'laso/ *n. m.* populace; masses.

por /por/ *prep.* by, through, because of; via; for. **p. qué,** why?

porcelana /porθe'lana; porse'lana/ *n. f.* porcelain, chinaware.

porcentaje /porθen'tahe; porsen'tahe/ *n. m.* percentage.

porche /'portʃe/ *n. m.* porch; portico.

porción /por'θion; por'sion/ *n. f.* portion, lot.

porfiar /por'fiar/ *v.* persist; argue.

pormenor /porme'nor/ *n. m.* detail.

pornografía /pornogra'fia/ *n. f.* pornography.

poro /'poro/ *n. m.* pore.

poroso /po'roso/ *a.* porous.

porque /'porke/ *conj.* because.

porqué *n. m.* reason, motive.

porra /'porra/ *n. f.* stick, club.

porrazo /po'rraθo; po'rraso/ *n. m.* blow.

porro /'porro/ *n. m. Colloq.* joint (marijuana).

portaaviones /portaa'βiones/ *n. m.* aircraft carrier.

portador /porta'ðor/ **-ra** *n.* bearer.

portal /por'tal/ *n. m.* portal.

portar /por'tar/ *v.* carry.

portarse /por'tarse/ *v.* behave, act.

portátil /por'tatil/ *a.* portable.

portavoz /porta'βoθ; porta'βos/ *n.* **1.** *m.* megaphone. **2.** *m.* & *f.* spokesperson.

porte /'porte/ *n. m.* bearing; behavior; postage.

portero /por'tero/ *n. m.* porter; janitor.

pórtico /'portiko/ *n. m.* porch.

portorriqueño /portorri'keɲo/ **-ña** *n.* & *a.* Puerto Rican.

portugués /portu'ges/ **-esa** *a.* & *n.* Portuguese.

posada /po'saða/ *n. f.* lodge, inn.

posar /po'sar/ *v.* pose.

posdata /pos'ðata/ *n. f.* postscript.

poseer /pose'er/ *v.* possess, own.

posesión /pose'sion/ *n. f.* possession.

posibilidad /posiβili'ðað/ *n. f.* possibility.

posible /po'siβle/ *a.* possible.

posiblemente /posiβle'mente/ *adv.* possibly.

posición /posi'θion; posi'sion/ *n. f.* position, stand.

positivo /posi'tiβo/ *a.* positive.

posponer /pospo'ner/ *v.* postpone.

postal /pos'tal/ *a.* postal; postcard.

poste /'poste/ *n. m.* post, pillar.

posteridad /posteri'ðað/ *n. f.* posterity.

posterior /poste'rior/ a. posterior, rear.

postizo /pos'tiθo; pos'tiso/ a. false, artificial.

postrado /pos'traðo/ a. prostrate. —**postrar**, v.

postre /'postre/ n. m. dessert.

póstumo /'postumo/ a. posthumous.

postura /pos'tura/ n. f. posture, pose; bet.

potable /po'taβle/ a. drinkable.

potaje /po'tahe/ n. m. porridge; pot stew.

potasa /po'tasa/ n. f. potash.

potasio /po'tasio/ n. m. potassium.

pote /'pote/ n. m. pot, jar.

potencia /po'tenθia; po'tensia/ f. potency, power.

potencial /poten'θial; poten'sial/ a. & m. potential.

potentado /poten'taðo/ n. m. potentate.

potente /po'tente/ a. potent, powerful.

potestad /potes'taθ/ n. f. power.

potro /'potro/ n. m. colt.

pozo /'poθo; 'poso/ n. m. well.

práctica /'praktika/ n. f. practice. —**practicar**, v.

práctico /'praktiko/ a. practical.

pradera /pra'ðera/ n. f. prairie, meadow.

prado /'praðo/ n. m. meadow; lawn.

pragmatismo /pragma'tismo/ n. m. pragmatism.

preámbulo /pre'ambulo/ n. m. preamble.

precario /pre'kario/ a. precarious.

precaución /prekau'θion; prekau'sion/ n. f. precaution.

precaverse /preka'βerse/ v. beware.

precavido /preka'βiðo/ a. cautious, guarded, wary.

precedencia /preθe'ðenθia; prese'ðensia/ n. f. precedence, priority.

precedente /preθe'ðente; prese'ðente/ a. & m. preceding; precedent.

preceder /preθe'ðer; prese'ðer/ v. precede.

precepto /pre'θepto; pre'septo/ n. m. precept.

preciar /pre'θiar; pre'siar/ v. value, prize.

preciarse de /pre'θiarse de; pre'siarse de/ v. take pride in.

precio /'preθio; 'presio/ n. m. price. **p. del billete de avión** air fare. **p. del cubierto** cover charge.

precioso /pre'θioso; pre'sioso/ a. precious; beautiful, gorgeous.

precipicio /preθi'piðio; presi'pisio/ n. m. precipice, cliff.

precipitación /preθipita'θion; presipita'sion/ n. f. precipitation.

precipitar /preθipi'tar; presipi'tar/ v. precipitate, rush; throw headlong.

precipitoso /preθipi'toso; presipi'toso/ a. precipitous; rash.

precisar /preθi'sar; presi'sar/ v. fix, specify; be necessary.

precisión /preθi'sion; presi'sion/ n. f. precision; necessity.

preciso /pre'θiso; pre'siso/ a. precise; necessary.

precocidad /prekoθi'ðaθ; prekosi'ðaθ/ n. f. precocity.

precocinado /prekoθi'naðo; prekosi'naðo/ a. precooked, ready-cooked.

precoz /pre'koθ; pre'kos/ a. precocious.

precursor /prekur'sor/ -ra a. **1.** preceding. —n. **2.** precursor, forerunner.

predecesor /preðeθe'sor; preðese'sor/ -ra a. & n. predecessor.

predecir /preðe'θir; preðe'sir/ v. predict, foretell.

predicación /preðika'θion; preðika'sion/ n. f. sermon.

predicador /preðika'ðor/ -ra n. preacher.

predicar /preði'kar/ v. preach.

predicción /preðik'θion; preðik'sion/ n. f. prediction.

predilecto /preði'lekto/ a. favorite, preferred.

predisponer /preðispo'ner/ v. predispose.

predisposición /preðisposi'θion; preðisposi'sion/ n. f. predisposition; bias.

predominante /preðomi'nante/ a. prevailing, prevalent, predominant.

predominar /preðomi'nar/ v. prevail, predominate.

predominio /preðo'minio/ n. m. predominance, sway.

prefacio /pre'faθio; pre'fasio/ n. m. preface.

preferencia /prefe'renθia; prefe'rensia/ n. f. preference.

preferentemente /preferente'mente/ adv. preferably.

preferible /prefe'riβle/ a. preferable.

preferir /prefe'rir/ v. prefer.

prefijo /pre'fiho/ n. m. prefix; area code, dialing code. —**prefijar**, v.

pregón /pre'gon/ n. m. proclamation; street cry.

pregonar /prego'nar/ v. proclaim; cry out.

pregunta /pre'gunta/ n. f. question, inquiry. **hacer una p.,** to ask a question.

preguntar /pregun'tar/ v. ask, inquire.

preguntarse /pregun'tarse/ v. wonder.

prehistórico /preis'toriko/ a. prehistoric.

prejuicio /pre'huiθio; pre'huisio/ n. m. prejudice.

prelacía /prela'θia; prela'sia/ n. f. prelacy.

preliminar /prelimi'nar/ a. & m. preliminary.

preludio /pre'luðio/ n. m. prelude.

prematuro /prema'turo/ a. premature.

premeditación /premeðita'θion; premeðita'sion/ n. f. premeditation.

premeditar /premeði'tar/ v. premeditate.

premiar /pre'miar/ v. reward; award a prize to.

premio /'premio/ n. m. prize, award; reward. **p. de consuelo,** consolation prize.

premisa /pre'misa/ n. f. premise.

premura /pre'mura/ n. f. pressure; urgency.

prenda /'prenda/ n. f. jewel; (personal) quality. **p. de vestir,** garment.

prender /pren'der/ v. seize, arrest, catch; pin, clip. **p. fuego a,** set fire to.

prensa /'prensa/ n. f. printing press; (the) press.

prensar /pren'sar/ v. press, compress.

preñado /pre'naðo/ a. pregnant.

preocupación /preokupa'θion; preokupa'sion/ n. f. worry, preoccupation.

preocupar /preoku'par/ v. worry, preoccupy.

preparación /prepara'θion; prepara'sion/ n. f. preparation.

preparar /prepa'rar/ v. prepare.

preparativo /prepara'tiβo/ n. m. preparation.

preparatorio /prepara'torio/ n. m. preparatory.

preponderante /preponde'rante/ a. preponderant.

preposición /preposi'θion; preposi'sion/ n. f. preposition.

prerrogativa /prerroga'tiβa/ n. f. prerogative, privilege.

presa /'presa/ n. f. capture; (water) dam.

presagiar /presa'hiar/ v. presage, forebode.

presbiteriano /presβite'riano/ -na n. & a. Presbyterian.

presbítero /pres'βitero/ n. m. priest.

prescindir de /presθin'dir de; pressin'dir de/ v. dispense with; omit.

prescribir /preskri'βir/ v. prescribe.

prescripción /preskrip'θion; preskrip'sion/ n. f. prescription.

presencia /pre'senθia; pre'sensia/ n. f. presence.

presenciar /presen'θiar; presen'siar/ v. witness, be present at.

presentable /presen'taβle/ a. presentable.

presentación /presenta'θion; presenta'sion/ n. f. presentation; introduction.

presentar /presen'tar/ v. present; introduce.

presente /pre'sente/ a. & m. present.

presentimiento /presenti'miento/ n. m. premonition.

preservación /preserβa'θion; preserβa'sion/ n. f. preservation.

preservar /preser'βar/ v. preserve, keep.

preservativo /preserβa'tiβo/ a. & m. preservative; condom.

presidencia /presi'ðenθia; presi'ðensia/ n. f. presidency.

presidencial /presiðen'θial; presiðen'sial/ a. presidential.

presidente /presi'ðente/ -ta n. president.

presidiario /presi'ðiario/ -ria n. m. & f. prisoner.

presidio /pre'siðio/ n. m. prison; garrison.

presidir /presi'ðir/ v. preside.

presión /pre'sion/ n. f. pressure.

presión arterial /pre'sion arte'rial/ blood pressure.

preso /'preso/ -sa n. prisoner.

presta /'presta/ n. f. mint (plant).

prestador /presta'ðor/ -ra n. lender.

prestamista /presta'mista/ n. m. & f. money lender.

préstamo /'prestamo/ n. m. loan.

prestar /pres'tar/ v. lend.

presteza /pres'teθa; pres'tesa/ n. f. haste, promptness.

prestidigitación /prestiðihita'θion; prestiðihita'sion/ n. f. sleight of hand.

prestigio /pres'tihio/ n. m. prestige.

presto /'presto/ a. **1.** quick, prompt; ready. —adv. **2.** quickly; at once.

presumido /presu'miðo/ a. conceited, presumptuous.

presumir /presu'mir/ v. presume; boast; claim; be conceited.

presunción /presun'θion; presun'sion/ n. f. presumption; conceit.

presunto /pre'sunto/ a. presumed; prospective.

presuntuoso /presun'tuoso/ a. presumptuous.

presupuesto /presu'puesto/ n. m. premise; budget.

pretender /preten'der/ v. pretend; intend; aspire.

pretendiente /preten'diente/ n. m. suitor; pretender (to throne).

pretensión /preten'sion/ n. f. pretension; claim.

pretérito /pre'terito/ a. & m. preterit, past (tense).

pretexto /pre'teksto/ n. m. pretext.

prevalecer /preβale'θer; preβale'ser/ v. prevail.

prevención /preβen'θion; preβen'sion/ n. f. prevention.

prevenir /preβe'nir/ v. prevent; forewarn; prearrange.

preventivo /preβen'tiβo/ a. preventive.

prever /pre'βer/ v. foresee.

previamente /preβia'mente/ adv. previously.

previo /'preβio/ a. previous.

previsible /preβi'siβle/ a. predictable.

previsión /preβi'sion/ n. f. foresight. **p. social,** social security.

prieto /'prieto/ a. blackish, very dark.

primacía /prima'θia; prima'sia/ n. f. primacy.

primario /pri'mario/ a. primary.

primavera /prima'βera/ n. f. spring (season).

primero /pri'mero/ a. & adv. first.

primitivo /primi'tiβo/ a. primitive.

primo /'primo/ -ma n. cousin.

primor /pri'mor/ n. m. beauty; excellence; lovely thing.

primoroso /primo'roso/ a. exquisite, elegant; graceful.

princesa /prin'θesa; prin'sesa/ n. f. princess.

principal /prinθi'pal; prinsi'pal/ a. **1.** principal, main. —n. **2.** m. chief, head, principal.

principalmente /prinθipal'mente; prinsipal'mente/ adv. principally.

príncipe /'prinθipe; 'prinsipe/ n. m. prince.

Príncipe Azul /'prinθipe a'θul; 'prinsipe a'sul/ Prince Charming.

principiar /prinθi'piar; prinsi'piar/ v. begin, initiate.

principio /prin'θipio; prin'sipio/ n. m. beginning, start; principle.

pringado /prin'gaðo/ n. m. low-life, loser.

prioridad /priori'ðaθ/ n. f. priority.

prisa /'prisa/ n. f. hurry, haste. **darse p.,** hurry, hasten. **tener p.,** be in a hurry.

prisión /pri'sion/ n. f. prison; imprisonment.

prisionero /prisio'nero/ -ra n. captive, prisoner.

prisma /'prisma/ n. m. prism.

prismático /pris'matiko/ a. prismatic.

privación /priβa'θion; priβa'sion/ n. f. privation, want.

privado /pri'βaðo/ a. private, secret; deprived.

privar /pri'βar/ v. deprive.

privilegio /priβi'lehio/ n. m. privilege.

pro /pro/ n. m. or f. benefit, advantage. **en p. de,** in behalf of. **en p. y en contra,** pro and con.

proa /'proa/ n. f. prow, bow.

probabilidad /proβaβili'ðaθ/ n. f. probability.

probable /pro'βaβle/ a. probable, likely.

probablemente /proβaβle'mente/ adv. probably.

probador /proβa'ðor/ n. m. fitting room.

probar /pro'βar/ v. try, sample; taste; test; prove.

probarse /pro'βarse/ v. try on.

probidad /proβi'ðaθ/ n. f. honesty, integrity.

problema /pro'βlema/ n. m. problem.

probo /'proβo/ a. honest.

procaz /pro'kaθ; pro'kas/ a. impudent, saucy.

proceder /proθe'ðer; prose'ðer/ v. proceed.

procedimiento /proθeði'miento; proseði'miento/ n. m. procedure.

procesar /proθe'sar; prose'sar/ v. prosecute; sue; process.

procesión /proθe'sion; prose'sion/ n. f. procession.

proceso /pro'θeso; pro'seso/ n. m. process; (court) trial.

proclama /pro'klama/ **proclamación** n. f. proclamation.

proclamar /prokla'mar/ v. proclaim.

procreación /prokrea'θion; prokrea'sion/ n. f. procreation.

procrear /prokre'ar/ v. procreate.

procurar /proku'rar/ v. try; see to it; get, procure.

prodigalidad /prodigali'ðaθ/ n. f. prodigality.

prodigar /proði'gar/ v. lavish; squander, waste.

prodigio /pro'ðihio/ n. m. prodigy.

pródigo /'proðigo/ a. prodigal; profuse; lavish.

producción /proðuk'θion; proðuk'sion/ n. f. production.

producir /proðu'θir; proðu'sir/ v. produce.

productivo /proðuk'tiβo/ a. productive.

producto /pro'ðukto/ *n. m.* product.

producto nacional bruto /pro'ðukto naθio'nal 'bruto; pro'ðukto nasio'nal 'bruto/ gross national product.

proeza /pro'eθa; pro'esa/ *n. f.* prowess.

profanación /profana'θion; profana'sion/ *n. f.* profanation.

profanar /profa'nar/ *v.* defile, desecrate.

profanidad /profani'ðað/ *n. f.* profanity.

profano /pro'fano/ *a.* profane.

profecía /profe'θia; profe'sia/ *n. f.* prophecy.

proferir /profe'rir/ *v.* utter, express.

profesar /profe'sar/ *v.* profess.

profesión /profe'sion/ *n. f.* profession.

profesional /profesio'nal/ *a.* professional.

profesor /profe'sor/ **-ra** *n.* professor, teacher.

profeta /pro'feta/ *n. m.* prophet.

profético /pro'fetiko/ *a.* prophetic.

profetizar /profeti'θar; profeti'sar/ *v.* prophesy.

proficiente /profi'θiente; profi'siente/ *a.* proficient.

profundamente /profunda'mente/ *adv.* profoundly, deeply.

profundidad /profundi'ðað/ *n. f.* profundity, depth.

profundizar /profundi'θar; profundi'sar/ *v.* deepen.

profundo /pro'fundo/ *a.* profound, deep.

profuso /pro'fuso/ *a.* profuse.

progenie /pro'henie/ *n. f.* progeny, offspring.

programa /pro'grama/ *n. m.* program; schedule.

programador /programa'ðor/ **-ra** *n.* (computer) programmer.

progresar /progre'sar/ *v.* progress, advance.

progresión /progre'sion/ *n. f.* progression.

progresista /progre'sista/ **progresivo** *a.* progressive.

progreso /pro'greso/ *n. m.* progress.

prohibición /proiβi'θion; proiβi'sion/ *n. f.* prohibition.

prohibir /proi'βir/ *v.* prohibit, forbid.

prohibitivo /proiβi'tiβo, proiβi'torio/ *a.* prohibitive.

prole /'prole/ *n. f.* progeny.

proletariado /proleta'riaðo/ *n. m.* proletariat.

proliferación /prolifera'θion; prolifera'sion/ *n. f.* proliferation.

prolijo /pro'liho/ *a.* prolix, tedious; long-winded.

prólogo /'prologo/ *n. m.* prologue; preface.

prolongar /prolon'gar/ *v.* prolong.

promedio /pro'meðio/ *n. m.* average.

promesa /pro'mesa/ *n. f.* promise.

prometer /prome'ter/ *v.* promise.

prometido /prome'tiðo/ *a.* promised; engaged (to marry).

prominencia /promi'nenθia; promi'nensia/ *n. f.* prominence.

promiscuamente /promiskua'mente/ *adv.* promiscuously.

promiscuo /pro'miskuo/ *a.* promiscuous.

promisorio /promi'sorio/ *a.* promissory.

promoción /promo'θion; promo'sion/ *n. f.* promotion.

promocionar /promoθio'nar; promosio'nar/ *v.* advertise, promote.

promover /promo'βer/ *v.* promote, further.

promulgación /promulga'θion; promulga'sion/ *n. f.* promulgation.

promulgar /promul'gar/ *v.* promulgate.

pronombre /pro'nombre/ *n. m.* pronoun.

pronosticación /pronostika'θion;

pronostikasion /n. f.* prediction, forecast.

pronosticar /pronosti'kar/ *v.* predict, forecast.

pronóstico /pro'nostiko/ *n. m.* prediction.

prontamente /pronta'mente/ *adv.* promptly.

prontitud /pronti'tuð/ *n. f.* promptness.

pronto /'pronto/ *a.* **1.** prompt; ready. —*adv.* **2.** soon; quickly. **de p.,** abruptly.

pronunciación /pronunθia'θion; pronunsia'sion/ *n. f.* pronunciation.

pronunciar /pronun'θiar; pronun'siar/ *v.* pronounce.

propagación /propaga'θion; propaga'sion/ *n. f.* propagation.

propaganda /propa'ganda/ *n. f.* propaganda.

propagandista /propagan'dista/ *n. m. & f.* propagandist.

propagar /propa'gar/ *v.* propagate.

propicio /pro'piθio; pro'pisio/ *a.* propitious, auspicious, favorable.

propiedad /propie'ðað/ *n. f.* property.

propietario /propie'tario/ **-ria** *n.* proprietor; owner; landlord, landlady.

propina /pro'pina/ *n. f.* gratuity, tip.

propio /'propio/ *a.* proper, suitable; typical; (one's) own; -self.

proponer /propo'ner/ *v.* propose.

proporción /propor'θion; propor'sion/ *n. f.* proportion.

proporcionado /proporθio'naðo; proporsio'naðo/ *a.* proportionate.

proporcionar /proporθio'nar; proporsio'nar/ *v.* provide with, supply, afford.

proposición /proposi'θion; proposi'sion/ *n. f.* proposition, offer; proposal.

propósito /pro'posito/ *n. m.* purpose; plan; **a p.,** by the way, apropos; on purpose.

propuesta /pro'puesta/ *n. f.* proposal, motion.

prorrata /pro'rrata/ *n. f.* quota.

prórroga /'prorroga/ *n. f.* renewal, extension.

prorrogar /prorro'gar/ *v.* renew, extend.

prosa /'prosa/ *n. f.* prose.

prosaico /pro'saiko/ *a.* prosaic.

proscribir /proskri'βir/ *v.* prohibit, proscribe, ban.

prosecución /proseku'θion; proseku'sion/ *n. f.* prosecution.

proseguir /prose'gir/ *v.* pursue; proceed, go on.

prosélito /pro'selito/ **-ta** *n.* proselyte.

prospecto /pros'pekto/ *n. m.* prospectus.

prosperar /prospe'rar/ *v.* prosper, thrive, flourish.

prosperidad /prosperi'ðað/ *n. f.* prosperity.

próspero /'prospero/ *a.* prosperous, successful.

prosternado /proster'naðo/ *a.* prostrate.

prostitución /prostitu'θion; prostitu'sion/ *n. f.* prostitution.

prostituir /prosti'tuir/ *v.* prostitute; debase.

prostituta /prosti'tuta/ *n. f.* prostitute.

protagonista /protago'nista/ *n. m. & f.* protagonist, hero, heroine.

protección /protek'θion; protek'sion/ *n. f.* protection.

protector /protek'tor/ **-ra** *a. & n.* protective; protector.

proteger /prote'her/ *v.* protect, safeguard. **p. contra escritura,** write-protect (diskette).

protegido /prote'hiðo/ **-da** *n.* **1.** protégé. —*a.* **2.** protected. **p. contra escritura,** write-protected.

proteína /prote'ina/ *n. f.* protein.

protesta /pro'testa/ *n. f.* protest. —**protestar,** *v.*

protestante /protes'tante/ *a. & n.* Protestant.

protocolo /proto'kolo/ *n. m.* protocol.

protuberancia /protuβe'ranθia; protuβe'ransia/ *n. f.* protuberance, lump.

protuberante /protuβe'rante/ *a.* bulging.

provecho /pro'βetʃo/ *n. m.* profit, gain, benefit. **¡Buen provecho!** May you enjoy your meal!

provechoso /proβe'tʃoso/ *a.* beneficial, advantageous, profitable.

proveer /proβe'er/ *v.* provide, furnish.

provenir de /proβe'nir de/ *v.* originate in, be due to, come from.

proverbial /proβer'βial/ *a.* proverbial.

proverbio /pro'βerβio/ *n. m.* proverb.

providencia /proβi'ðenθia; proβi'ðensia/ *n. f.* providence.

providente /proβi'ðente/ *a.* provident.

provincia /pro'βinθia; pro'βinsia/ *n. f.* province.

provincial /proβin'θial; proβin'sial/ *a.* provincial.

provinciano /proβin'θiano; proβin'siano/ **-na** *a. & n.* provincial.

provisión /proβi'sion/ *n. f.* provision, supply, stock.

provisional /proβisio'nal/ *a.* provisional.

provocación /proβoka'θion; proβoka'sion/ *n. f.* provocation.

provocador /proβoka'ðor/ **-ra** *n.* provoker.

provocar /proβo'kar/ *v.* provoke, excite.

provocativo /proβoka'tiβo/ *a.* provocative.

proximidad /proksimi'ðað/ *n. f.* proximity, vicinity.

próximo /'proksimo/ *a.* next; near.

proyección /proiek'θion; proiek'sion/ *n. f.* projection.

proyectar /proiek'tar/ *v.* plan, project.

proyectil /proyek'til/ *n. m.* projectile, missile, shell.

proyecto /pro'iekto/ *n. m.* plan, project, scheme.

proyector /proiek'tor/ *n. m.* projector.

prudencia /pru'ðenθia; pru'ðensia/ *n. f.* prudence.

prudente /pru'ðente/ *a.* prudent.

prueba /'prueβa/ *n. f.* proof; trial; test.

psicoanálisis /psikoa'nalisis/ *n. m.* psychoanalysis.

psicoanalista /psikoana'lista/ *n. m. & f.* psychoanalyst.

psicodélico /psiko'ðeliko/ *a.* psychedelic.

psicología /psikolo'hia/ *n. f.* psychology.

psicológico /psiko'lohiko/ *a.* psychological.

psicólogo /psi'kologo/ **-ga** *n.* psychologist.

psiquiatra /psi'kiatra/ *n. m. & f.* psychiatrist.

psiquiatría /psikia'tria/ *n. f.* psychiatry.

publicación /puβlika'θion; puβlika'sion/ *n. f.* publication.

publicar /puβli'kar/ *v.* publish.

publicidad /puβliθi'ðað; puβlisi'ðað/ *n. f.* publicity.

publicista /puβli'θista; puβli'sista/ *n. m. & f.* publicity agent.

público /'puβliko/ *a. & m.* public.

puchero /pu'tʃero/ *n. m.* pot.

pudiente /pu'ðiente/ *a.* powerful; wealthy.

pudín /pu'ðin/ *n. m.* pudding.

pudor /pu'ðor/ *n. m.* modesty.

pudoroso /puðo'roso/ *a.* modest.

pudrirse /pu'ðrirse/ *v.* rot.

pueblo /'pueβlo/ *n. m.* town, village; (the) people.

puente /'puente/ *n. m.* bridge.

puente para peatones /'puente para pea'tones/ *n. m.* footbridge.

puerco /'puerko/ **-ca** *n.* pig.

puericultura /puerikul'tura/ *n. f.* pediatrics.

pueril /pue'ril/ *a.* childish.

puerilidad /puerili'ðað/ *n. f.* puerility.

puerta /'puerta/ *n. f.* door; gate.

puerta giratoria /'puerta hira'toria/ revolving door.

puerta principal /'puerta prinθi'pal; 'puerta prinsi'pal/ front door.

puerto /'puerto/ *n. m.* port, harbor.

puertorriqueño /puertorri'keɲo/ **-ña** *n.* Puerto Rican.

pues /pues/ *adv.* **1.** well... —*conj.* **2.** as, since, for.

puesto /'puesto/ *n. m.* appointment, post, job; place; stand. **p. que,** since.

pugilato /puhi'lato/ *n. m.* boxing.

pugna /'pugna/ *n. f.* conflict.

pugnacidad /pugnaθi'ðað; pugnasi'ðað/ *n. f.* pugnacity.

pugnar /pug'nar/ *v.* fight; oppose.

pulcritud /pulkri'tuð/ *n. f.* neatness; exquisitness.

pulga /'pulga/ *n. f.* flea.

pulgada /pul'gaða/ *n. f.* inch.

pulgar /pul'gar/ *n. m.* thumb.

pulir /pu'lir/ *v.* polish; beautify.

pulmón /pul'mon/ *n. m.* lung.

pulmonía /pulmo'nia/ *n. f.* pneumonia.

pulpa /'pulpa/ *n. f.* pulp.

púlpito /'pulpito/ *n. m.* pulpit.

pulque /'pulke/ *n. m.* pulque (fermented maguey juice).

pulsación /pulsa'θion; pulsa'sion/ *n. f.* pulsation, beat.

pulsar /pul'sar/ *v.* pulsate, beat.

pulsera /pul'sera/ *n. f.* wristband; bracelet.

pulso /'pulso/ *n. m.* pulse.

pulverizar /pulβeri'θar; pulβeri'sar/ *v.* pulverize.

puma /'puma/ *n. f.* puma.

pundonor /pundo'nor/ *n. m.* point of honor.

punta /'punta/ *n. f.* point, tip, end.

puntada /pun'taða/ *n. f.* stitch.

puntapié /punta'pie/ *n. m.* kick.

puntería /punte'ria/ *n. f.* (marksman's) aim.

puntiagudo /puntia'guðo/ *a.* sharp-pointed.

puntillas /pun'tiʎas; pun'tiyas/ *n. f.pl.* **de p., en p.,** on tiptoe.

punto /'punto/ *n. m.* point; period; spot, dot. **dos puntos,** *Punct.* colon. **a p. de,** about to. **al p.,** instantly.

punto de admiración /'punto de aðmira'θion; 'punto de aðmira'sion/ exclamation mark.

punto de congelación /'punto de koŋgela'θion; 'punto de koŋgela'sion/ freezing point.

punto de ebullición /'punto de eβuʎi'θion; 'punto de eβuyi'sion/ boiling point.

punto de vista /'punto de 'bista/ point of view, viewpoint.

puntuación /puntua'θion; puntua'sion/ *n. f.* punctuation.

puntual /pun'tual/ *a.* punctual, prompt.

puntuar /pun'tuar/ *v.* punctuate.

puñada /pu'ɲaða/ *n. f.* punch.

puñado /pu'ɲaðo/ *n. m.* handful.

puñal /pu'ɲal/ *n. m.* dagger.

puñalada /puɲa'laða/ *n. f.* stab.

puñetazo /puɲe'taθo; puɲe'taso/ *n. m.* punch, fist blow.

puño /'puɲo/ *n. m.* fist; cuff; handle.

pupila /pu'pila/ *n. f.* pupil (of eye).

pupitre /pu'pitre/ *n. m.* writing desk, school desk.

pureza /pu'reθa; pu'resa/ *n. f.* purity; chastity.

purgante /pur'gante/ *n. m.* laxative.

purgar /pur'gar/ *v.* purge, cleanse.

purgatorio /purga'torio/ *n. m.* purgatory.

puridad /puri'ðað/ *n. f.* secrecy.

purificación /purifika'θion; purifika-'sion/ *n. f.* purification.

purificar /purifi'kar/ *v.* purify.

purismo /pu'rismo/ *n. m.* purism.

purista /pu'rista/ *n. m. & f.* purist.

puritanismo /purita'nismo/ *n. m.* puritanism.

puro /'puro/ *a.* **1.** pure. —*n.* **2.** *m.* cigar.

púrpura /'purpura/ *n. f.* purple.

purpúreo /pur'pureo/ *a.* purple.

purulencia /puru'lenθia; puru'lensia/ *n. f.* purulence.

purulento /puru'lento/ *a.* purulent.

pus /pus/ *n. m.* pus.

pusilánime /pusi'lanime/ *a.* pusillanimous.

puta /'puta/ **-to** *n.* prostitute.

putrefacción /putrefak'θion; putrefak'sion/ *n. f.* putrefaction, rot.

putrefacto /putre'fakto/ *a.* putrid, rotten.

pútrido /'putriðo/ *a.* putrid.

puya /'puya/ *n. f.* goad.

Q

que /ke/ *rel. pron.* **1.** who, whom; that, which. —*conj.* **2.** than.

qué *a. & pron.* what. **por q., para q.,** why? *adv.* how.

quebrada /ke'βraða/ *n. f.* ravine, gully, gulch; stream.

quebradizo /keβra'ðiθo; keβra'ðiso/ *a.* fragile, brittle.

quebraley /keβra'lei/ *n. m. & f.* lawbreaker, outlaw.

quebrar /ke'βrar/ *v.* break.

queda /'keða/ *n. f.* curfew.

quedar /ke'ðar/ *v.* remain, be located; be left. **q. bien a,** be becoming to.

quedarse /ke'ðarse/ *v.* stay, remain. **q. con,** keep, hold on to; remain with.

quedo /'keðo/ *a.* quiet; gentle.

quehacer /kea'θer; kea'ser/ *n. m.* task; chore.

queja /'keha/ *n. f.* complaint.

quejarse /ke'harse/ *v.* complain, grumble.

quejido /ke'hiðo/ *n. m.* moan.

quejoso /ke'hoso/ *a.* complaining.

quema /'kema/ *n. f.* burning.

quemadura /kema'ðura/ *n. f.* burn.

quemar /ke'mar/ *v.* burn.

querella /ke're λa; ke'reya/ *n. f.* quarrel; complaint.

querencia /ke'renθia; ke'rensia/ *n. f.* affection, liking.

querer /ke'rer/ *v.* want, wish; will; love (a person). **q. decir,** mean. **sin q.,** without meaning to; unwillingly.

querido /ke'riðo/ *a.* dear, loved, beloved.

quesería /kese'ria/ *n. f.* dairy.

queso /'keso/ *n. m.* cheese.

queso crema /'keso 'krema/ cream cheese.

quetzal /ket'θal; ket'sal/ *n. m.* quetzal.

quiche /'kitʃe/ *n. f.* quiche.

quiebra /'kieβra/ *n. f.* break, fracture; damage; bankruptcy.

quien /kien/ *rel. pron.* who, whom.

quién *interrog. pron.* who, whom.

quienquiera /kien'kiera/ *pron.* whoever, whomever.

quietamente /kieta'mente/ *adv.* quietly.

quieto /'kieto/ *a.* quiet, still.

quietud /kie'tuð/ *n. f.* quiet, quietude.

quijada /ki'haða/ *n. f.* jaw.

quijotesco /kiho'tesko/ *a.* quixotic.

quilate /ki'late/ *n. m.* carat.

quilla /'kiλa; 'kiya/ *n. f.* keel.

quimera /ki'mera/ *n. f.* chimera; vision; quarrel.

química /'kimika/ *n. f.* chemistry.

químico /'kimiko/ **-ca** *a. & n.* chemical; chemist.

quimoterapia /kimote'rapia/ *n. f.* chemotherapy.

quincalla /kin'kaλa; kin'kaya/ *n. f.* (computer) hardware.

quincallería /kinkaλe'ria; kinkaye-'ria/ *n. f.* hardware store.

quince /'kinθe; 'kinse/ *a. & pron.* fifteen.

quinientos /ki'nientos/ *a. & pron.* five hundred.

quinina /ki'nina/ *n. f.* quinine.

quintana /kin'tana/ *n. f.* country home.

quinto /'kinto/ *a.* fifth.

quirúrgico /ki'rurhiko/ *a.* surgical.

quiste /'kiste/ *n. m.* cyst.

quitamanchas /kita'mantʃas/ *n. m.* stain remover.

quitanieves /kita'nieβes/ *n. m.* snowplow.

quitar /ki'tar/ *v.* take away, remove.

quitarse /ki'tarse/ *v.* take off; get rid of.

quitasol /kita'sol/ *n. m.* parasol, umbrella.

quitasueño /kita'sueɲo/ *n. m. Colloq.* nightmare; worry.

quizá /ki'θa; ki'sa/ **quizás** *adv.* perhaps, maybe.

quórum /'korum/ *n. m.* quorum.

R

rábano /'rraβano/ *n. m.* radish.

rabí /rra'βi/ *rabino n. m.* rabbi.

rabia /'rraβia/ *n. f.* rage; grudge; rabies.

rabiar /rra'βiar/ *v.* rage, be furious.

rabieta /rra'βieta/ *n. f.* tantrum.

rabioso /rra'βioso/ *a.* furious; rabid.

rabo /'rraβo/ *n. m.* tail.

racha /'rratʃa/ *n. f.* streak.

racimo /rra'θimo; rra'simo/ *n. m.* bunch, cluster.

ración /rra'θion; rra'sion/ *n. f.* ration. —**racionar,** *v.*

racionabilidad /rraθionaβili'ðað; rrasionaβili'ðað/ *n. f.* rationality.

racional /rraθio'nal; rrasio'nal/ *a.* rational.

racionalismo /rraθiona'lismo; rrasiona'lismo/ *n. m.* rationalism.

racionalmente /rraθional'mente; rrasional'mente/ *adv.* rationally.

radar /rra'ðar/ *n. m.* radar.

radiación /rraðia'θion; rraðia'sion/ *n. f.* radiation.

radiador /rraðia'ðor/ *n. m.* radiator.

radiante /rra'ðiante/ *a.* radiant.

radical /rraði'kal/ *a. & n.* radical.

radicalismo /rraðika'lismo/ *n. m.* radicalism.

radicoso /rraði'koso/ *a.* radical.

radio /'rraðio/ *n. m.* or *f.* radio.

radioactividad /rraðioaktiβi'ðað/ *n. f.* radioactivity.

radioactivo /rraðioak'tiβo/ *a.* radioactive.

radiocasete /rraðioka'sete/ *n. m.* radio cassette.

radiodifundir /rraðioðifun'dir/ *v.* broadcast.

radiodifusión /rraðioðifu'sion/ *n. f.* (radio) broadcasting.

radiografía /rraðiogra'fia/ *n. f.* X-ray.

radiografiar /rraðiogra'fiar/ *v.* X-ray.

ráfaga /'rrafaga/ *n. f.* gust (of wind).

raíz /rra'iθ; rra'is/ *n. f.* root.

raja /'rraha/ *n. f.* rip; split; crack. —**rajar,** *v.*

ralea /rra'lea/ *n. f.* stock, breed.

ralo /'rralo/ *a.* thin, scattered.

rama /'rrama/ *n. f.* branch, bough.

ramillete /rrami'λete; rrami'yete/ *n. m.* bouquet.

ramo /'rramo/ *n. m.* branch, bough; bouquet.

ramonear /rramone'ar/ *v.* browse.

rampa /'rrampa/ *n. f.* ramp.

rana /'rrana/ *n. f.* frog.

ranchero /rran'tʃero/ **-ra** *n.* small farmer.

rancho /'rrantʃo/ *n. m.* ranch.

rancidez /rranθi'ðeθ; rransi'ðes/ *n. f.* rancidity.

rancio /'rranθio; 'rransio/ *a.* rancid, rank, stale, sour.

rango /'rraŋgo/ *n. m.* rank.

ranúnculo /rra'nunkulo/ *n. m.* ranunculus; buttercup.

ranura /rra'nura/ *n. f.* slot.

ranura de expansión /rra'nura de ekspan'sion/ expansion slot.

rapacidad /rrapaθi'ðað; rrapasi'ðað/ *n. f.* rapacity.

rapaz /rra'paθ; rra'pas/ *a.* **1.** rapacious. —*n.* **2.** *m.* young boy.

rapé /'rrape/ *n. m.* snuff.

rápidamente /rrapiða'mente/ *adv.* rapidly.

rapidez /rrapi'ðeθ; rrapi'ðes/ *n. f.* rapidity, speed.

rápido /'rrapiðo/ *a.* **1.** rapid, fast, speedy. —*n.* **2.** *m.* express (train).

rapiña /rra'piɲa/ *n. f.* robbery, plundering.

rapsodia /rrap'soðia/ *n. f.* rhapsody.

rapto /'rrapto/ *n. m.* kidnapping.

raquero /rra'kero/ **-ra** *n.* beachcomber.

raqueta /rra'keta/ *n. f.* (tennis) racket.

rareza /rra'reθa; rra'resa/ *n. f.* rarity; freak.

raridad /rrari'ðað/ *n. f.* rarity.

raro /'rraro/ *a.* rare, strange, unusual, odd, queer.

rasar /rra'sar/ *v.* skim.

rascacielos /rraska'θielos; rraska'sielos/ *n. m.* skyscraper.

rascar /rras'kar/ *v.* scrape; scratch.

rasgadura /rrasga'ðura/ *n. f.* tear, rip. —**rasgar,** *v.*

rasgo /'rrasgo/ *n. m.* trait.

rasgón /rras'gon/ *n. m.* tear.

rasguño /rras'guɲo/ *n. m.* scratch. —**rasguñar,** *v.*

raso /'rraso/ *a.* **1.** plain. **soldado r.,** *Mil.* private. —*n.* **2.** *m.* satin.

raspar /rras'par/ *v.* scrape; erase.

rastra /'rrastra/ *n. f.* trail, track. —**rastrear,** *v.*

rastrillar /rrastri'λar; rrastri'yar/ *v.* rake.

rastro /'rrastro/ *n. m.* track, trail, trace; rake; flea market.

rata /'rrata/ *n. f.* rat.

ratificación /rratifika'θion; rratifika-'sion/ *n. f.* ratification.

ratificar /rratifi'kar/ *v.* ratify.

rato /'rrato/ *n. m.* while, spell, short time.

ratón /rra'ton/ *n. m.* mouse.

ratonera /rrato'nera/ *n. f.* mousetrap.

raya /'rraya/ *n. f.* dash, line, streak, stripe.

rayar /rra'yar/ *v.* rule, stripe; scratch; cross out.

rayo /'rrayo/ *n. m.* lightning bolt; ray; flash.

rayón /rra'yon/ *n. m.* rayon.

raza /'rraθa; 'rrasa/ *n. f.* race; breed, stock.

razón /rra'θon; rra'son/ *n. f.* reason; ratio. **a r. de,** at the rate of. **tener r.,** to be right.

razonable /rraθo'naβle; rraso'naβle/ *a.* reasonable, sensible.

razonamiento /rraθona'miento; rrasona'miento/ *n. m.* argument.

razonar /rraθo'nar; rraso'nar/ *v.* reason.

reacción /rreak'θion; rreak'sion/ *n. f.* reaction.

reaccionar /rreakθio'nar; rreaksio-'nar/ *v.* react.

reaccionario /rreakθio'nario; rreaksio'nario/ **-ria** *a. & n.* reactionary.

reacondicionar /rreakondiθio'nar; rreakondisio'nar/ *v.* recondition.

reactivo /rreak'tiβo/ *a. & m.* reactive; *Chem.* reagent.

reactor /rreak'tor/ *n. m.* reactor.

real /rre'al/ *a.* royal, regal; real, actual.

realdad /rreal'dað/ *n. f.* royal authority.

realeza /rrea'leθa; rrea'lesa/ *n. f.* royalty.

realidad /rreali'ðað/ *n. f.* reality.

realidad virtual /rreali'ðað βir'tual/ virtual reality.

realista /rrea'lista/ *a. & n.* realistic; realist.

realización /rrealiθa'θion; rrealisa-'sion/ *n. f.* achievement, accomplishment.

realizar /rreali'θar; rreali'sar/ *v.* accomplish; fulfill; effect; *Com.* realize.

realmente /rreal'mente/ *adv.* in reality, really.

realzar /rreal'θar; rreal'sar/ *v.* enhance.

reata /rre'ata/ *n. f.* rope; lasso, lariat.

rebaja /rre'βaha/ *n. f.* reduction.

rebajar /rreβa'har/ *v.* cheapen; reduce (in price); lower.

rebanada /rreβa'naða/ *n. f.* slice. —**rebanar,** *v.*

rebaño /rre'βaɲo/ *n. m.* flock, herd.

rebato /rre'βato/ *n. m.* alarm; sudden attack.

rebelarse /rreβe'larse/ *v.* rebel, revolt.

rebelde /rre'βelde/ *a. & n.* rebellious; rebel.

rebelión /rreβe'lion/ *n. f.* rebellion, revolt.

reborde /rre'βorðe/ *n. m.* border.

rebotar /rreβo'tar/ *v.* rebound.

rebozo /rre'βoθo; rre'βoso/ *n. m.* shawl.

rebuscar /rreβus'kar/ *v.* search thoroughly.

rebuznar /rreβuθ'nar; rreβus'nar/ *v.* bray.

recado /rre'kaðo/ *n. m.* message; errand.

recaída /rreka'iða/ *n. f.* relapse. —**recaer,** *v.*

recalcar /rrekal'kar/ *v.* stress, emphasize.

recalentar /rrekalen'tar/ *v.* reheat.

recámara /rre'kamara/ *n. f.* (Mex.) bedroom.

recapitulación /rrekapitula'θion; rrekapitula'sion/ *n. f.* recapitulation.

recapitular /rrekapitu'lar/ *v.* recapitulate.

recatado /rreka'taðo/ *n. m.* coy; prudent.

recaudador /rrekauða'ðor/ **-ra** *n.* tax collector.

recelar /rreθe'lar; rrese'lar/ *v.* fear, distrust.

receloso /rreθe'loso; rrese'loso/ *a.* distrustful.

recepción /rreθep'θion; rresep'sion/ *n. f.* reception.

recepcionista /rreθepθio'nista; rresepsio'nista/ *n. m. & f.* desk clerk.

receptáculo /rreθep'takulo; rresep'takulo/ *n. m.* receptacle.

receptividad /rreθeptiβi'ðað; rreseptiβi'ðað/ *n. f.* receptivity.

receptivo /rreθep'tiβo; rresep'tiβo/ *a.* receptive.

receptor /rreθep'tor; rresep'tor/ *n. m.* receiver.

receta /rre'θeta; rre'seta/ *n. f.* recipe; prescription.

recetar /rreθe'tar; rrese'tar/ *v.* prescribe.

rechazar /rretʃa'θar; rretʃa'sar/ *v.* reject, spurn, discard.

rechinar /rretʃi'nar/ *v.* chatter.

recibimiento /rreθiβi'miento; rresiβi'miento/ *n. m.* reception; welcome; anteroom.

recibir /rreθi'βir; rresi'βir/ *v.* receive.

recibo /rre'θiβo; rre'siβo/ *n. m.* receipt.

reciclaje /rreθi'klahe; rresi'klahe/ *n. m.* recycling.

reciclar /rreθi'klar; rresi'klar/ *v.* recycle.

recidiva /rreθi'ðiβa; rresi'ðiβa/ *n. f.* relapse.

recién /rre'θien; rre'sien/ *adv.* recently, newly, just.

reciente /rre'θiente; rre'siente/ *a.* recent.

recinto /rre'θinto; rre'sinto/ *n. m.* enclosure.

recipiente /rreθi'piente; rresi'piente/ *n. m.* recipient.

reciprocación /rreθiproka'θion; rresiproka'sion/ *n. f.* reciprocation.

recíprocamente /rreθiproka'mente; rresiproka'mente/ *adv.* reciprocally.

reciprocar /rreθipro'kar; rresipro'kar/ *v.* reciprocate.

reciprocidad /rreθiproθi'ðað; rresiprosi'ðað/ *n. f.* reciprocity.

recitación /rreθita'θion; rresita'sion/ *n. f.* recitation.

recitar /rreθi'tar; rresi'tar/ *v.* recite.

reclamación /rreklama'θion; rreklama'sion/ *n. f.* claim; complaint.

reclamar /rrekla'mar/ *v.* claim; complain.

reclamo /rre'klamo/ *n. m.* claim; advertisement, advertising; decoy.

reclinar /rrekli'nar/ *v.* recline, repose, lean.

recluta /rre'kluta/ *n. m. & f.* recruit.

reclutar /rreklu'tar/ *v.* recruit, draft.

recobrar /rreko'βrar/ *v.* recover, salvage, regain.

recobro /rre'koβro/ *n. m.* recovery.

recoger /rreko'her/ *v.* gather; collect; pick up. **r. el conocimiento,** regain consciousness.

recogerse /rreko'herse/ *v.* retire (for night).

recolectar /rrekolek'tar/ *v.* gather, assemble; harvest.

recomendación /rrekomenda'θion; rrekomenda'sion/ *n. f.* recommendation; commendation.

recomendar /rrekomen'dar/ *v.* recommend; commend.

recompensa /rrekom'pensa/ *n. f.* recompense; compensation.

recompensar /rrekompen'sar/ *v.* reward; compensate.

reconciliación /rrekonθilia'θion; rrekonsilia'sion/ *n. f.* reconciliation.

reconciliar /rrekonθi'liar; rrekonsi'liar/ *v.* reconcile.

reconocer /rrekono'θer; rrekono'ser/ *v.* recognize; acknowledge; inspect, examine; *Mil.* reconnoiter.

reconocimiento /rrekonoθi'miento; rrekonosi'miento/ *n. m.* recognition; appreciation, gratitude.

reconstituir /rrekonsti'tuir/ *v.* reconstitute.

reconstruir /rrekons'truir/ *v.* reconstruct, rebuild.

record /'rrekorð/ *n. m.* (sports) record.

recordar /rrekor'ðar/ *v.* recall, recollect; remind.

recorrer /rreko'rrer/ *v.* go over; read over; cover (distance).

recorte /rre'korte/ *n. m.* clipping, cutting.

recostarse /rrekos'tarse/ *v.* recline, lean back, rest.

recreación /rrekrea'θion; rrekrea'sion/ *n. f.* recreation.

recreo /rre'kreo/ *n. m.* recreation.

recriminación /rrekrimina'θion; rrekrimina'sion/ *n. f.* recrimination.

rectangular /rrektaŋgu'lar/ *a.* rectangular.

rectángulo /rrek'taŋgulo/ *n. m.* rectangle.

rectificación /rrektifika'θion; rrektifika'sion/ *n. f.* rectification.

rectificar /rrektifi'kar/ *v.* rectify.

recto /'rrekto/ *a.* straight; just, fair. **ángulo r.,** right angle.

recuento /rre'kuento/ *n. m.* recount.

recuerdo /rre'kuerðo/ *n. m.* memory; souvenir; remembrance; (*pl.*) regards.

reculada /rreku'laða/ *n. f.* recoil. **—recular,** *v.*

recuperación /rrekupera'θion; rrekupera'sion/ *n. f.* recuperation.

recuperar /rrekupe'rar/ *v.* recuperate.

recurrir /rreku'rrir/ *v.* revert; resort, have recourse.

recurso /rre'kurso/ *n. m.* resource; recourse.

red /rreð/ *n. f.* net; trap. **r. local** local area network.

redacción /rreðak'θion; rreðak'sion/ *n. f.* (editorial) staff; composition (of written material).

redactar /rreðak'tar/ *v.* draft, draw up; edit.

redactor /rreðak'tor/ **-ra** *n.* editor.

redada /rre'ðaða/ *n. f.* netful, catch, haul.

redargución /rreðargu'θion; rreðargu'sion/ *n. f.* retort. **—redargüir,** *v.*

redención /rreðen'θion; rreðen'sion/ *n. f.* redemption, salvation.

redentor /rreðen'tor/ *n. m.* redeemer.

redimir /rreði'mir/ *v.* redeem.

redoblante /rreðo'βlante/ *n. m.* snare drum; snare dummer.

redonda /rre'ðonda/ *n. f.* neighborhood, vicinity.

redondo /rre'ðondo/ *a.* round, circular.

reducción /rreðuk'θion; rreðuk'sion/ *n. f.* reduction.

reducir /rreðu'θir; rreðu'sir/ *v.* reduce.

reembolso /rreem'βolso/ *n. m.* refund. **—reembolsar,** *v.*

reemplazar /rreempla'θar; rreempla'sar/ *v.* replace, supersede.

reencarnación /rreenkarna'θion; rreenkarna'sion/ *n. f.* reincarnation.

reexaminar /rreeksami'nar/ *v.* reexamine.

reexpedir /rreekspe'ðir/ *v.* forward (mail).

referencia /rrefe'renθia; rrefe'rensia/ *n. f.* reference.

referéndum /rrefe'rendum/ *n. m.* referendum.

referir /rrefe'rir/ *v.* relate, report on.

referirse /rrefe'rirse/ *v.* refer.

refinamiento /rrefina'miento/ *n. m.* refinement.

refinar /rrefi'nar/ *v.* refine.

refinería /rrefine'ria/ *n. f.* refinery.

reflejar /rrefle'har/ *v.* reflect; think, ponder.

reflejo /rre'fleho/ *n. m.* reflection; glare.

reflexión /rreflek'sion/ *n. f.* reflection, thought.

reflexionar /rrefleksio'nar/ *v.* reflect, think.

reflujo /rre'fluho/ *n. m.* ebb; ebb tide.

reforma /rre'forma/ *n. f.* reform. **—reformar,** *v.*

reformación /rreforma'θion; rreforma'sion/ *n. f.* reformation.

reformador /rreforma'ðor/ **-ra** *n.* reformer.

reforma tributaria /rre'forma triβu'taria/ tax reform.

reforzar /rrefor'θar; refor'sar/ *v.* reinforce, strengthen; encourage.

refractario /rrefrak'tario/ *a.* refractory.

refrán /rre'fran/ *n. m.* proverb, saying.

refrenar /rrefre'nar/ *v.* curb, rein; restrain.

refrescar /rrefres'kar/ *v.* refresh, freshen, cool.

refresco /rre'fresko/ *n. m.* refreshment; cold drink.

refrigeración /rrefrihera'θion; rrefrihera'sion/ *n. f.* refrigeration.

refrigerador /rrefrihera'ðor/ *n. m.* refrigerator.

refrigerar /rrefrihe'rar/ *v.* refrigerate.

refuerzo /rre'fuerθo; rre'fuerso/ *n. m.* reinforcement.

refugiado /rrefu'hiaðo/ **-da** refugee.

refugiarse /rrefu'hiarse/ *v.* take refuge.

refugio /rre'fuhio/ *n. m.* refuge, asylum, shelter.

refulgencia /rreful'henθia; rreful'hensia/ *n. f.* refulgence.

refulgente /rreful'hente/ *a.* refulgent.

refulgir /rreful'hir/ *v.* shine.

refunfuñar /rrefunfu'ɲar/ *v.* mutter, grumble, growl.

refutación /rrefuta'θion; rrefuta'sion/ *n. f.* refutation; rebuttal.

refutar /rrefu'tar/ *v.* refute.

regadera /rrega'ðera/ *n. f.* watering can.

regadizo /rrega'ðiθo; rrega'ðiso/ *a.* irrigable.

regadura /rrega'ðura/ *n. f.* irrigation.

regalar /rrega'lar/ *v.* give (a gift), give away.

regaliz /rrega'liθ; rrega'lis/ *n. m.* licorice.

regalo /rre'galo/ *n. m.* gift, present, **con r.,** in luxury.

regañar /rrega'ɲar/ *v.* reprove; scold.

regaño /rre'gaɲo/ *n. m.* reprimand; scolding.

regar /rre'gar/ *v.* water, irrigate.

regatear /rregate'ar/ *v.* haggle.

regateo /rrega'teo/ *n. m.* bargaining, haggling.

regazo /rre'gaθo; rre'gaso/ *n. m.* lap.

regencia /rre'henθia; rre'hensia/ *n. f.* regency.

regeneración /rrehenera'θion; rrehenera'sion/ *n. f.* regeneration.

regenerar /rrehene'rar/ *v.* regenerate.

regente /rre'hente/ **-ta** *a. & n.* regent.

régimen /'rrehimen/ *n. m.* regime; diet.

regimentar /rrehimen'tar/ *v.* regiment.

regimiento /rrehi'miento/ *n. m.* regiment.

región /rre'hion/ *n. f.* region.

regional /rrehio'nal/ *a.* regional, sectional.

regir /rre'hir/ *v.* rule; be in effect.

registrar /rrehis'trar/ *v.* register; record; search.

registro /rre'histro/ *n. m.* register; record; search.

regla /'rregla/ *n. f.* rule, regulation. **en r.,** in order.

reglamento /rregla'mento/ *n. m.* code of regulations.

regocijarse /rregoθi'harse; rregosi'harse/ *v.* rejoice, exult.

regocijo /rrego'θiho; rrego'siho/ *n. f.* rejoicing; merriment, joy.

regordete /rregor'ðete/ *a.* chubby, plump.

regresar /rregre'sar/ *v.* go back, return.

regresión /rregre'sion/ *n. f.* regression.

regresivo /rregre'siβo/ *a.* regressive.

regreso /rre'greso/ *n. m.* return.

regulación /rregula'θion; rregula'sion/ *n. f.* regulation.

regular /rregu'lar/ *a.* **1.** regular; fair, middling. **—***v.* **2.** regulate.

regularidad /rregulari'ðað/ *n. f.* regularity.

regularmente /rregular'mente/ *adv.* regularly.

rehabilitación /rreaβilita'θion; rreaβilita'sion/ *n. f.* rehabilitation.

rehabilitar /rreaβili'tar/ *v.* rehabilitate.

rehén /rre'en/ *n. m.* hostage.

rehogar /rreo'gar/ *v.* brown.

rehusar /rreu'sar/ *v.* refuse; decline.

reina /'rreina/ *n. f.* queen.

reinado /rrei'naðo/ *n. m.* reign. **—reinar,** *v.*

reino /'rreino/ *n. m.* kingdom; realm; reign.

reír /rre'ir/ *v.* laugh.

reiteración /rreitera'θion; rreitera'sion/ *n. f.* reiteration.

reiterar /rreite'rar/ *v.* reiterate.

reja /'rreha/ *n. f.* grating, grillwork.

relación /rrela'θion; rrela'sion/ *n. f.* relation; account, report.

relacionar /rrelaθio'nar; rrelasio'nar/ *v.* relate, connect.

relajamiento /rrelaha'miento/ *n. m.* laxity, laxness.

relajar /rrela'har/ *v.* relax, slacken.

relámpago /rre'lampago/ *n. m.* lightning; flash (of lightning).

relatador /rrelata'ðor/ **-ra** *n.* teller.

relatar /rrela'tar/ *v.* relate, recount.

relativamente /rrelatiβa'mente/ *adv.* relatively.

relatividad /rrelatiβi'ðað/ *n. f.* relativity.

relativo /rrela'tiβo/ *a.* relative.

relato /rre'lato/ *n. m.* account, story.

relegación /rrelega'θion; rrelega'sion/ *n. f.* relegation.

relegar /rrele'gar/ *v.* relegate.

relevar /rrele'βar/ *v.* relieve.

relicario /rreli'kario/ *n. m.* reliquary; locket.

relieve /rre'lieβe/ *n. m.* (sculpture) relief.

religión /rreli'hion/ *n. f.* religion.

religiosidad /rrelihiosi'ðað/ *n. f.* religiosity.

religioso /rreli'hioso/ **-sa** *a.* **1.** religious. **—***n.* **2.** *m.* member of a religious order.

reliquia /rre'likia/ *n. f.* relic.

rellenar /rreʎe'nar/ *v.* refill; fill up, stuff.

relleno /rre'ʎeno; rre'yeno/ *n. m.* filling; stuffing.

reloj /rre'loh/ *n. m.* clock; watch.

reloj de pulsera /rre'loh de pul'sera/ wrist watch.

relojería /rrelohe'ria/ *n. f.* watchmaker's shop.

relojero /rrelo'hero/ **-ra** *n.* watchmaker.

relucir /rrelu'θir; rrelu'sir/ *v.* glow, shine; excel.

relumbrar /rrelum'βrar/ *v.* glitter, sparkle.

remache /rre'matʃe/ *n. m.* rivet. **—remachar,** *v.*

remar /rre'mar/ *v.* row (a boat).

rematado /rrema'taðo/ *a.* finished; sold.

remate /rre'mate/ *n. m.* end, finish; auction. **de r.,** utterly, wholly.

remedador /rremeða'ðor/ **-ra** *n.* imitator.

remedar /rreme'ðar/ *v.* imitate.

remedio /rre'meðio/ *n. m.* remedy. **—remediar,** *v.*

remendar /rremen'dar/ *v.* mend, patch.

remesa /rre'mesa/ *n. f.* shipment; remittance.

remiendo /rre'miendo/ *n. m.* patch.

remilgado /rremil'gaðo/ *a.* prudish; affected.

reminiscencia /rreminis'θenθia; rreminis'sensia/ *n. f.* reminiscence.

remitir /rremi'tir/ *v.* remit.

remo /'rremo/ *n. m.* oar.

remolacha /rremo'latʃa/ *n. f.* beet.

remolcador /rremolka'ðor/ *n. m.* tug (boat); tow truck.

remolino /rremo'lino/ *n. m.* whirl; whirlpool; whirlwind.

remolque /rre'molke/ *n. m.* tow. **—remolcar,** *v.*

remontar /rremon'tar/ *v.* ascend, go up.

remontarse /rremon'tarse/ *v.* get excited; soar. **r. a,** date from; go back to (in time).

remordimiento /rremorði'miento/ *n. m.* remorse.

remotamente /rremota'mente/ *adv.* remotely.

remoto /rre'moto/ *a.* remote.

remover /rremo'βer/ *v.* remove; stir; shake; loosen.

rempujar /rrempu'har/ *v.* jostle.

remuneración /rremunera'θion; rremunera'sion/ *n. f.* remuneration.

remunerar /rremune'rar/ v. remunerate.

renacido /rrena'θiðo; rrena'siðo/ a. reborn, born-again.

renacimiento /rrenaθi'miento; rrenasi'miento/ n. m. rebirth; renaissance.

rencor /rren'kor/ n. m. rancor, bitterness, animosity; grudge.

rencoroso /rrenko'roso/ a. rancorous, bitter.

rendición /rrendi'θion; rrendi'sion/ n. f. surrender.

rendido /rren'diðo/ a. weary, worn out.

rendir /rren'dir/ v. yield; surrender, give up; win over.

renegado /rrene'gaðo/ **-da** n. renegade.

renglón /rren'glon/ n. m. line; Com. item.

reno /'rreno/ n. m. reindeer.

renombre /rre'nombre/ n. m. renown.

renovación /rrenoβa'θion; rrenoβa'sion/ f. renovation, renewal.

renovar /rreno'βar/ v. renew; renovate.

renta /'rrenta/ n. f. income; rent.

rentar /rren'tar/ v. yield; rent.

renuencia /rre'nuenθia; rre'nuensia/ n. f. reluctance.

renuente /rre'nuente/ a. reluctant.

renuncia /rre'nunθia; rre'nunsia/ n. f. resignation; renunciation.

renunciar /rrenun'θiar; rrenun'siar/ v. resign; renounce, give up.

reñir /rre'ɲir/ v. scold, berate; quarrel, wrangle.

reo /'rreo/ a. & n. criminal; convict.

reorganizar /rreorgani'θar; rreorgani'sar/ v. reorganize.

reparación /rrepara'θion; rrepara'sion/ n. f. reparation, atonement; repair.

reparar /rrepa'rar/ v. repair; mend; stop, stay over. **r. en**, notice; consider.

reparo /rre'paro/ n. m. repair; remark; difficulty; objection.

repartición /rreparti'θion; rreparti'sion/ n. f., **repartimiento, reparto**, m. division, distribution.

repartir /rrepar'tir/ v. divide, apportion, distribute; Theat. cast.

repaso /rre'paso/ n. m. review. —**repasar**, v.

repatriación /rrepatria'θion; rrepatria'sion/ n. f. repatriation.

repatriar /rrepa'triar/ v. repatriate.

repeler /rrepe'ler/ v. repel.

repente /rre'pente/ n. m. **de r.**, suddenly; unexpectedly.

repentinamente /rrepentina'mente/ adv. suddenly.

repentino /rrepen'tino/ a. sudden.

repercusión /rreperku'sion/ n. f. repercussion.

repertorio /rreper'torio/ n. m. repertoire.

repetición /rrepeti'θion; rrepeti'sion/ n. f. repetition; action replay.

repetidamente /rrepetiða'mente/ adv. repeatedly.

repetir /rrepe'tir/ v. repeat.

repisa /rre'pisa/ n. f. shelf.

réplica /'rreplika/ n. f. reply; objection; replica.

replicar /rrepli'kar/ v. reply; answer back.

repollo /rre'poʎo; rre'poyo/ n. m. cabbage.

reponer /rrepo'ner/ v. replace; repair.

reponerse /rrepo'nerse/ v. recover, get well.

reporte /rre'porte/ n. m. report; news.

repórter /rre'porter/ **reportero -ra** n. reporter.

reposado /rrepo'saðo/ a. tranquil, peaceful, quiet.

reposo /rre'poso/ n. m. repose, rest. —**reposar**, v.

reposte /rre'poste/ n. f. pantry.

represalia /rrepre'salia/ n. f. reprisal.

representación /rrepresenta'θion; rrepresenta'sion/ n. f. representation; Theat. performance.

representante /rrepresen'tante/ n. m. & f. representative, agent.

representar /rrepresen'tar/ v. represent; depict; Theat. perform.

representativo /rrepresenta'tiβo/ a. representative.

represión /rrepre'sion/ n. f. repression.

represivo /rrepre'siβo/ a. repressive.

reprimenda /rrepri'menda/ n. f. reprimand.

reprimir /rrepri'mir/ v. repress, quell.

reproche /rre'protʃe/ n. m. reproach. —**reprochar**, v.

reproducción /rreproðuk'θion; rreproðuk'sion/ n. f. reproduction.

reproducir /rreproðu'θir; rreproðu'sir/ v. reproduce.

reptil /rrep'til/ n. m. reptile.

república /rre'puβlika/ n. f. republic.

republicano /rrepuβli'kano/ **-na** a. & n. republican.

repudiación /rrepuðia'θion; rrepuðia'sion/ n. f. repudiation.

repudiar /rrepu'ðiar/ v. repudiate; disown.

repuesto /rre'puesto/ n. m. spare part. **de r.**, spare.

repugnancia /rrepug'nanθia; rrepug'nansia/ n. f. repugnance.

repugnante /rrepug'nante/ a. disgusting, repugnant, repulsive, revolting.

repugnar /rrepug'nar/ v. disgust.

repulsa /rre'pulsa/ n. f. refusal; repulse.

repulsivo /rrepul'siβo/ a. repulsive.

reputación /rreputa'θion; rreputa'sion/ n. f. reputation.

reputar /rrepu'tar/ v. repute; appreciate.

requerir /rreke'rir/ v. require.

requesón /rreke'son/ n. m. cottage cheese.

requisición /rrekisi'θion; rrekisi'sion/ n. f. requisition.

requisito /rreki'sito/ n. m. requisite, requirement.

res /rres/ n. f. head of cattle.

resaca /rre'saka/ n. f. hangover.

resbalar /rresβa'lar/ v. slide; slip.

resbaloso /rresβa'loso/ a. slippery.

rescate /rres'kate/ n. m. rescue; ransom. —**rescatar**, v.

rescindir /rresθin'dir; rressin'dir/ v. rescind.

resentimiento /rresenti'miento/ n. m. resentment.

resentirse /rresen'tirse/ v. resent.

reserva /rre'serβa/ n. f. reserve. —**reservar**, v.

reservación /rreserβa'θion; rreserβa'sion/ n. f. reservation.

resfriado /rres'friaðo/ n. m. Med. cold.

resfriarse /rres'friarse/ v. catch cold.

resguardar /rresguar'ðar/ v. guard, protect.

residencia /rresi'ðenθia; rresi'ðensia/ n. f. residence; seat, headquarters.

residente /rresi'ðente/ a. & n. resident.

residir /rresi'ðir/ v. reside.

residuo /rre'siðuo/ n. m. remainder.

resignación /rresigna'θion; rresigna'sion/ n. f. resignation.

resignar /rresig'nar/ v. resign.

resina /rre'sina/ n. f. resin; rosin.

resistencia /rresis'tenθia; rresis'tensia/ n. f. resistance.

resistir /rresis'tir/ v. resist; endure.

resolución /rresolu'θion; rresolu'sion/ n. f. resolution.

resolutivamente /rresolutiβa'mente/ adv. resolutely.

resolver /rresol'βer/ v. resolve; solve.

resonante /rreso'nante/ a. resonant.

resonar /rreso'nar/ v. resound.

resorte /rre'sorte/ n. m. Mech. spring.

respaldar /rrespal'dar/ v. endorse; back.

respaldo /rres'paldo/ n. m. back (of a seat).

respectivo /rrespek'tiβo/ a. respective.

respecto /rres'pekto/ n. m. relation, proportion; **r. a**, concerning, regarding.

respetabilidad /rrespetaβili'ðað/ n. f. respectability.

respetable /rrespe'taβle/ a. respectable.

respeto /rres'peto/ n. m. respect. —**respetar**, v.

respetuosamente /rrespetuosa'mente/ adv. respectfully.

respetuoso /rrespe'tuoso/ a. respectful.

respiración /rrespira'θion; rrespira'sion/ n. f. respiration, breath.

respirar /rrespi'rar/ v. breathe.

resplandeciente /rresplande'θiente; rresplande'siente/ a. resplendent.

resplandor /rresplan'dor/ n. m. brightness, glitter.

responder /rrespon'der/ v. respond, answer.

responsabilidad /rresponsaβili'ðað/ n. f. responsibility.

responsable /rrespon'saβle/ a. responsible.

respuesta /rres'puesta/ n. f. answer, response, reply.

resquicio /rres'kiθio; rres'kisio/ n. m. crack, slit.

resta /'rresta/ n. f. subtraction; remainder.

restablecer /rrestaβle'θer; rrestaβle'ser/ v. restore; reestablish.

restablecerse /rrestaβle'θerse; rrestaβle'serse/ v. recover, get well.

restar /rres'tar/ v. remain; subtract.

restauración /rrestaura'θion; rrestaura'sion/ n. f. restoration.

restaurante /rrestau'rante/ n. m. restaurant.

restaurar /rrestau'rar/ v. restore.

restitución /rrestitu'θion; rrestitu'sion/ n. f. restitution.

restituir /rresti'tuir/ v. restore, give back.

resto /'rresto/ n. m. remainder, rest; (pl.) remains.

restorán /rresto'ran/ n. m. restaurant.

restregar /rrestre'gar/ v. rub hard; scrub.

restricción /rrestrik'θion; rrestrik'sion/ n. f. restriction.

restrictivo /rrestrik'tiβo/ a. restrictive.

restringir /rrestriŋ'gir/ v. restrict, curtail.

resucitar /rresuθi'tar; rresusi'tar/ v. revive, resuscitate.

resuelto /rre'suelto/ a. resolute.

resultado /rresul'taðo/ n. m. result.

resultar /rresul'tar/ v. result; turn out; ensue.

resumen /rre'sumen/ n. m. résumé, summary, **en r.,** in brief.

resumir /rresu'mir/ v. sum up.

resurgir /rresur'hir/ v. resurge, reappear.

resurrección /rresurrek'θion; rresurrek'sion/ n. f. resurrection.

retaguardia /rreta'guarðia/ n. f. rear guard.

retal /rre'tal/ n. m. remnant.

retardar /rretar'ðar/ v. retard, slow.

retardo /rre'tarðo/ n. m. delay.

retención /rreten'θion; rreten'sion/ n. f. retention.

retener /rrete'ner/ v. retain, keep; withhold.

reticencia /rreti'θenθia; rreti'sensia/ n. f. reticence.

reticente /rreti'θente; rreti'sente/ a. reticent.

retirada /rreti'raða/ n. f. retreat, retirement.

retirar /rreti'rar/ v. retire, retreat, withdraw.

retiro /rre'tiro/ n. m. retirement.

retorcer /rretor'θer; rretor'ser/ v. wring.

retórica /rre'torika/ n. f. rhetoric.

retórico /rre'toriko/ a. rhetorical.

retorno /rre'torno/ n. m. return.

retozo /rre'toθo; rre'toso/ n. m. frolic, romp. —**retozar**, v.

retozón /rreto'θon; rreto'son/ a. frisky.

retracción /rretrak'θion; rretrak'sion/ n. f. retraction.

retractar /rretrak'tar/ v. retract.

retrasar /rretra'sar/ v. delay, set back.

retrasarse /rretra'sarse/ v. be slow.

retraso /rre'traso/ n. m. delay, lag, slowness.

retratar /rretra'tar/ v. portray; photograph.

retrato /rre'trato/ n. m. portrait; picture, photograph.

retreta /rre'treta/ n. f. Mil. retreat.

retrete /rre'trete/ n. m. toilet.

retribución /rretriβu'θion; rretriβu'sion/ n. f. retribution.

retroactivo /rretroak'tiβo/ a. retroactive.

retroalimentación /rretroalimenta'θion; rretroalimenta'sion/ n. f. feedback.

retroceder /rretroθe'ðer; rretrose'ðer/ v. recede, go back, draw back, back up.

retumbar /rretum'βar/ v. resound, rumble.

reumático /rreu'matiko/ a. rheumatic.

reumatismo /rreuma'tismo/ n. m. rheumatism.

reunión /rreu'nion/ n. f. gathering, meeting, party; reunion.

reunir /rreu'nir/ v. gather, collect, bring together.

reunirse /rreu'nirse/ v. meet, assemble, get together.

reutilizar /rreutili'zar/ v. reuse.

revelación /rreβela'θion; rreβela'sion/ n. f. revelation.

revelar /rreβe'lar/ v. reveal; betray; Phot. develop.

reventa /rre'βenta/ n. f. resale.

reventar /rreβen'tar/ v. burst; split apart.

reventón /rreβen'ton/ n. m. blowout (of tire).

reverencia /rreβeren'θia; rreβeren'sia/ n. f. reverence.

reverendo /rreβe'rendo/ a. reverend.

reverente /rreβe'rente/ a. reverent.

revertir /rreβer'tir/ v. revert.

revés /rre'βes/ n. m. reverse; back, wrong side. **al r.,** just the opposite; inside out.

revisar /rreβi'sar/ v. revise; review.

revisión /rreβi'sion/ n. f. revision.

revista /rre'βista/ n. f. magazine, periodical; review.

revivir /rreβi'βir/ v. revive.

revocación /rreβoka'θion; rreβoka'sion/ n. f. revocation.

revocar /rreβo'kar/ v. revoke, reverse.

revolotear /rreβolote'ar/ v. hover.

revolución /rreβolu'θion; rreβolu'sion/ n. f. revolution.

revolucionario /rreβoluθio'nario; rreβolusio'nario/ **-ria** a. & n. revolutionary.

revolver /rreβol'βer/ v. revolve, stir, agitate.

revólver n. m. revolver, pistol.

revuelta /rre'βuelta/ n. f. revolt; turn.

rey /rrei/ n. m. king.

reyerta /rre'yerta/ n. f. quarrel, wrangle.

rezar /rre'θar; rre'sar/ v. pray.

rezongar /rreθoŋ'gar; rresoŋ'gar/ v. grumble; mutter.

ría /'rria/ n. f. estuary.

riachuelo /rria'tʃuelo/ n. m. creek.

riba /'rriβa/ n. f. embankment.

rico /'rriko/ a. rich, wealthy; delicious.

ridículamente /rri'ðikulamente/ *adv.* ridiculously.
ridiculizar /rriðikuli'θar; rriðikuli'sar/ *v.* ridicule.
ridículo /rri'ðikulo/ *a.* & *m.* ridiculous; ridicule.
riego /'rriego/ *n. m.* irrigation.
rienda /'rrienda/ *n. f.* rein.
riesgo /'rriesgo/ *n. m.* risk, gamble.
rifa /'rrifa/ *n. f.* raffle; lottery; scuffle.
rifle /'rrifle/ *n. m.* rifle.
rígidamente /'rrihiðamente/ *adv.* rigidly.
rigidez /rrihi'ðeθ; rrihi'ðes/ *n. f.* rigidity.
rígido /'rrihiðo/ *a.* rigid, stiff.
rigor /rri'gor/ *n. m.* rigor.
riguroso /rrigu'roso/ *a.* rigorous, strict.
rima /'rrima/ *n. f.* rhyme. **—rimar,** *v.*
rimel /rri'mel/ *n. f.* mascara.
rincón /rrin'kon/ *n. m.* corner, nook.
rinoceronte /rrinoθe'ronte; rrinose'ronte/ *n. m.* rhinoceros.
riña /'rriɲa/ *n. f.* quarrel, feud.
riñón /rri'ɲon/ *n. m.* kidney.
río /'rrio/ *n. m.* river. **r. abajo** downstream, downriver. **r. arriba,** upstream, upriver.
ripio /'rripio/ *n. m.* debris.
riqueza /rri'keθa; rri'kesa/ *n. f.* wealth.
risa /'rrisa/ *n. f.* laugh; laughter.
risco /'rrisko/ *n. m.* cliff.
risibilidad /rrisiβili'ðað/ *n. f.* risibility.
risotada /rriso'taða/ *n. f.* peal of laughter.
risueño /rri'sueɲo/ *a.* cheerful, smiling.
rítmico /'rritmiko/ *a.* rhythmical.
ritmo /'rritmo/ *n. m.* rhythm.
rito /'rrito/ *n. m.* rite.
ritual /rri'tual/ *a.* & *m.* ritual.
rivalidad /rriβali'ðað/ *n. f.* rivalry.
rivera /rri'βera/ *n. f.* brook.
rizado /rri'θaðo; rri'saðo/ *a.* curly.
rizo /'rriθo; 'rriso/ *n. m.* curl. **—rizar,** *v.*
robar /rro'βar/ *v.* rob, steal.
roble /'rroβle/ *n. m.* oak.
roblón /rro'βlon/ *n. m.* rivet. **—roblar,** *v.*
robo /'rroβo/ *n. m.* robbery, theft.
robustamente /rroβusta'mente/ *adv.* robustly.
robusto /rro'βusto/ *a.* robust.
roca /'rroka/ *n. f.* rock; cliff.
rociada /rro'θiaða; rro'siaða/ *n. f.* spray, sprinkle. **—rociar,** *v.*
rocío /'rroθio; 'rrosio/ *n. m.* dew.
rocoso /rro'koso/ *a.* rocky.
rodar /rro'ðar/ *v.* roll; roam.
rodear /rroðe'ar/ *v.* surround, encircle.
rodeo /rro'ðeo/ *n. m.* turn, winding; roundup.
rodilla /rro'ðiʎa; rro'ðiya/ *n. f.* knee.
rodillo /rro'ðiʎo; rro'ðiyo/ *n. m.* roller.
rodio /'rroðio/ *n. m.* rhodium.
rododendro /rroðo'ðendro/ *n. m.* rhododendron.
roedor /rroe'ðor/ *n. m.* rodent.
roer /rro'er/ *v.* gnaw.
rogación /rroga'θion; rroga'sion/ *n. f.* request, entreaty.
rogar /rro'gar/ *v.* beg, plead with, supplicate.
rojizo /rro'hiθo; rro'hiso/ *a.* reddish.
rojo /'rroho/ *a.* red.
rollizo /rro'ʎiθo; rro'yiso/ *a.* chubby.
rollo /'rroʎo; 'rroyo/ *n. m.* roll; coil.
romadizo /rroma'ðiθo; rroma'ðiso/ *n. m.* head cold.
romance /rro'manθe; rro'manse/ *n. m.* romance; ballad.
románico /rro'maniko/ *a.* Romance.
romano /rro'mano/ **-na** *a.* & *n.* Roman.
romántico /rro'mantiko/ *a.* romantic.
romería /rrome'ria/ *n. f.* pilgrimage; picnic.
romero /rro'mero/ **-ra** *n.* pilgrim.
rompecabezas /rrompeka'βeθas; rrompeka'βesas/ *n. m.* puzzle (pastime).
romper /rrom'per/ *v.* break, smash, shatter; sever; tear.
rompible /rrom'piβle/ *a.* breakable.
ron /rron/ *n. m.* rum.
roncar /rron'kar/ *v.* snore.
ronco /'rronko/ *a.* hoarse.
ronda /'rronda/ *n. f.* round.
rondar /rron'dar/ *v.* prowl.
ronquido /rron'kiðo/ *n. m.* snore.
ronronear /rronrone'ar/ *v.* purr.
ronzal /rron'θal; rron'sal/ *n. m.* halter.
roña /'rroɲa/ *n. f.* scab; filth.
ropa /'rropa/ *n. f.* clothes, clothing. **r. blanca,** linen. **r. interior,** underwear.
ropa de marca /'rropa de 'marka/ designer clothing.
ropero /rro'pero/ *n. m.* closet.
rosa /'rrosa/ *n. f.* rose. **r. náutica,** compass.
rosado /rro'saðo/ *a.* pink, rosy.
rosal /rro'sal/ *n. m.* rose bush.
rosario /rro'sario/ *n. m.* rosary.
rosbif /rros'βif/ *n. m.* roast beef.
rosca /'rroska/ *n. f.* thread (of screw).
róseo /'rroseo/ *a.* rosy.
rostro /'rrostro/ *n. m.* face, countenance.
rota /'rrota/ *n. f.* defeat; *Naut.* course.
rotación /rrota'θion; rrota'sion/ *n. f.* rotation.
rotatorio /rrota'torio/ *a.* rotary.
rótula /'rrotula/ *n. f.* kneecap.
rotulador /rrotula'ðor/ *n. m.* felt-tipped pen.
rótulo /'rrotulo/ *n. m.* label. **—rotular,** *v.*
rotundo /rro'tundo/ *a.* round; sonorous.
rotura /rro'tura/ *n. f.* break, fracture, rupture.
rozar /rro'θar; rro'sar/ *v.* rub against, chafe; graze.
rubí /rru'βi/ *n. m.* ruby.
rubio /'rruβio/ **-bia** *a.* & *n.* blond.
rubor /rru'βor/ *n. m.* blush; bashfulness.
rúbrica /'rruβrika/ *n. f.* caption; scroll.
rucho /'rrutʃo/ *n. m.* donkey.
rudeza /rru'ðeθa; rru'ðesa/ *n. f.* rudeness; roughness.
rudimentario /rruðimen'tario/ *a.* rudimentary.
rudimento /rruði'mento/ *n. m.* rudiment.
rudo /'rruðo/ *a.* rude, rough.
rueda /'rrueða/ *n. f.* wheel.
rueda de feria /'rrueða de 'feria/ Ferris wheel.
ruego /'rruego/ *n. m.* plea; entreaty.
rufián /rru'fian/ *n. m.* ruffian.
rufo /'rrufo/ *a.* sandy haired.
rugir /rru'hir/ *v.* bellow, roar.
rugoso /rru'goso/ *a.* wrinkled.
ruibarbo /rrui'βarβo/ *n. m.* rhubarb.
ruido /'rruiðo/ *n. m.* noise.
ruidoso /rrui'ðoso/ *a.* noisy.
ruina /'rruina/ *n. f.* ruin, wreck.
ruinar /rrui'nar/ *v.* ruin, destroy.
ruinoso /rrui'noso/ *a.* ruinous.
ruiseñor /rruise'ɲor/ *n. m.* nightingale.
ruleta /rru'leta/ *n. f.* roulette.
rumba /'rrumba/ *n. f.* rumba (dance or music).
rumbo /'rrumbo/ *n. m.* course, direction.
rumor /rru'mor/ *n. m.* rumor; murmur.
runrún /rrun'run/ *n. m.* rumor.
ruptura /rrup'tura/ *n. f.* rupture, break.
rural /rru'ral/ *a.* rural.
Rusia /'rrusia/ *n. f.* Russia.
ruso /'rruso/ **-sa** *a.* & *n.* Russian.
rústico /'rrustiko/ **-ca** *a.* & *n.* rustic. **en r.,** paperback *f.*
ruta /'rruta/ *n. f.* route.
rutina /rru'tina/ *n. f.* routine.
rutinario /rruti'nario/ *a.* routine.

S

sábado /'saβaðo/ *n. m.* Saturday.
sábalo /'saβalo/ *n. m.* shad.
sábana /sa'βana/ *n. f.* sheet.
sabañon /saβa'ɲon/ *n. m.* chilblain.
saber /sa'βer/ *n.* **1.** *m.* knowledge. **—***v.* **2.** know; learn, find out; know how to; taste. **a s.,** namely, to wit.
sabiduría /saβiðu'ria/ *n. f.* wisdom; learning.
sabio /'saβio/ **-a** *a.* **1.** wise; scholarly. **—***n.* **2.** sage; scholar.
sable /'saβle/ *n. m.* saber.
sabor /sa'βor/ *n. m.* flavor, taste, savor.
saborear /saβore'ar/ *v.* savor, relish.
sabotaje /saβo'tahe/ *n. m.* sabotage.
sabroso /sa'βroso/ *a.* savory, tasty.
sabueso /sa'βueso/ *n. m.* hound.
sacacorchos /saka'kortʃos/ *n. m.* corkscrew.
sacapuntas /saka'puntas/ *n. f.* pencil sharpener.
sacar /sa'kar/ *v.* draw out; take out; take.
sacerdocio /saθer'ðoθio; saser'ðosio/ *n. m.* priesthood.
sacerdote /saθer'ðote; saser'ðote/ *n. m.* priest.
saciar /sa'θiar; sa'siar/ *v.* satiate.
saco /'sako/ *n. m.* sack, bag, pouch; suit coat, jacket.
sacramento /sakra'mento/ *n. m.* sacrament.
sacrificio /sakri'fiθio; sakri'fisio/ *n. m.* sacrifice. **—sacrificar,** *v.*
sacrilegio /sakri'lehio/ *n. m.* sacrilege.
sacristán /sakris'tan/ *n. m.* sexton.
sacro /'sakro/ *a.* sacred, holy.
sacrosanto /sakro'santo/ *a.* sacrosanct.
sacudir /saku'ðir/ *v.* shake, jerk, jolt.
sádico /'saðiko/ *a.* sadistic.
sadismo /sa'ðismo/ *n. m.* sadism.
sagacidad /sagaθi'ðað; sagasi'ðað/ *n. f.* sagacity.
sagaz /sa'gaθ; sa'gas/ *a.* sagacious, sage.
sagrado /sa'graðo/ *a.* sacred, holy.
sal /sal/ *n. f.* salt; *Colloq.* wit.
sala /'sala/ *n. f.* room; living room, parlor; hall, auditorium.
salado /sa'laðo/ *a.* salted, salty; *Colloq.* witty.
salar /sa'lar/ *v.* salt; steep in brine.
salario /sa'lario/ *n. m.* salary, wages.
salchicha /sal'tʃitʃa/ *n. f.* sausage.
sal de la Higuera /sal de la i'gera/ Epsom salts.
saldo /'saldo/ *n. m.* remainder, balance; (bargain) sale.
saldo acreedor /'saldo akree'ðor/ credit balance.
saldo deudor /'saldo deu'ðor/ debit balance.
salero /sa'lero/ *n. m.* salt shaker.
salida /sa'liða/ *n. f.* exit, outlet; departure.
salida de urgencia /sa'liða de ur'henθia; sa'liða de ur'hensia/ emergency exit, fire exit.
salir /salir/ *v.* go out, come out; set out, leave, start; turn out, result.
salirse de /sa'lirse de/ *v.* get out of. **s. con la suya,** have one's own way.
salitre /sa'litre/ *n. m.* saltpeter.
saliva /sa'liβa/ *n. f.* saliva.
salmo /'salmo/ *n. m.* psalm.
salmón /sal'mon/ *n. m.* salmon.
salmonete /salmo'nete/ *n. m.* red mullet.
salmuera /sal'muera/ *n. f.* pickle; brine.
salobre /sa'loβre/ *a.* salty.
salón /sa'lon/ *n. m.* parlor, living room; hall. **s. de baile,** dance hall. **s. de belleza** beauty parlor.
salpicar /salpi'kar/ *v.* spatter, splash.
salpullido /salpu'ʎiðo; salpu'yiðo/ *n. m.* rash.
salsa /'salsa/ *n. f.* sauce; gravy.
saltamontes /salta'montes/ *n. m.* grasshopper.
salteador /saltea'ðor/ *n. m.* highwayman.
saltear /salte'ar/ *v.* hold up, rob; sauté.
salto /'salto/ *n. m.* jump, leap, spring. **—saltar,** *v.*
saltón /sal'ton/ *n. m.* grasshopper.
salubre /sa'luβre/ *a.* salubrious, healthful.
salubridad /saluβri'ðað/ *n. f.* health.
salud /sa'luð/ *n. f.* health.
saludable /salu'ðaβle/ *a.* healthful, wholesome.
saludar /salu'ðar/ *v.* greet; salute.
saludo /sa'luðo/ *n. m.* greeting; salutation; salute.
salutación /saluta'θion; saluta'sion/ *n. f.* salutation.
salva /'salβa/ *n. f.* salvo.
salvación /salβa'θion; salβa'sion/ *n. f.* salvation; deliverance.
salvador /salβa'ðor/ **-ra** *n.* savior; rescuer.
salvaguardia /salβa'guarðia/ *n. m.* safeguard.
salvaje /sal'βahe/ *a.* & *n.* savage, wild (person).
salvamento /salβa'mento/ *n. m.* salvation; rescue.
salvar /sal'βar/ *v.* save; salvage; rescue; jump over.
salvavidas /salβa'βiðas/ *n. m.* life preserver.
salvia /'salβia/ *n. f.* sage (plant).
salvo /'salβo/ *a.* **1.** safe. **—***prep.* **2.** except, save (for). **s. que,** unless.
San /san/ *title.* Saint.
sanar /sa'nar/ *v.* heal, cure.
sanatorio /sana'torio/ *n. m.* sanatorium.
sanción /san'θion; san'sion/ *n. f.* sanction. **—sancionar,** *v.*
sancochar /sanko'tʃar/ *v.* parboil.
sandalia /san'dalia/ *n. f.* sandal.
sandez /san'deθ; san'des/ *n. f.* stupidity.
sandía /san'dia/ *n. f.* watermelon.
saneamiento /sanea'miento/ *n. m.* sanitation.
sangrar /saŋ'grar/ *v.* bleed.
sangre /'saŋgre/ *n. f.* blood.
sangriento /saŋ'griento/ *a.* bloody.
sanguinario /saŋgi'nario/ *a.* bloodthirsty.
sanidad /sani'ðað/ *n. f.* health.
sanitario /sani'tario/ *a.* sanitary.
sano /'sano/ *a.* healthy, sound, sane; healthful, wholesome.
santidad /santi'ðað/ *n. f.* sanctity, holiness.
santificar /santifi'kar/ *v.* sanctify.
santo /'santo/ **-ta** *a.* **1.** holy, saintly. **—***n.* **2.** *m.* saint.
Santo -ta *title.* Saint.
santuario /san'tuario/ *n. m.* sanctuary, shrine.
saña /'saɲa/ *n. f.* rage, anger.
sapiente /sa'piente/ *a.* wise.
sapo /'sapo/ *n. m.* toad.
saquear /sake'ar/ *v.* sack; ransack; plunder.
sarampión /saram'pion/ *n. m.* measles.
sarape /sa'rape/ *n. m.* (Mex.) woven blanket; shawl.
sarcasmo /sar'kasmo/ *n. m.* sarcasm.
sarcástico /sar'kastiko/ *a.* sarcastic.
sardina /sar'ðina/ *n. f.* sardine.
sargento /sar'hento/ *n. m.* sergeant.
sarna /'sarna/ *n. f.* itch.
sartén /sar'ten/ *n. m.* frying pan.
sastre /'sastre/ *n. m.* tailor.
satánico /sa'taniko/ *a.* satanic.
satélite /sa'telite/ *n. m.* satellite.

sátira /'satira/ n. f. satire.

satírico /sa'tiriko/ a. & m. satirical; satirist.

satirizar /satiri'θar; satiri'sar/ v. satirize.

sátiro /'satiro/ n. m. satyr.

satisfacción /satisfak'θion; satisfak'sion/ n. f. satisfaction.

satisfacer /satisfa'θer; satisfa'ser/ v. satisfy.

satisfactorio /satisfak'torio/ a. satisfactory.

saturación /satura'θion; satura'sion/ n. f. saturation.

saturar /satu'rar/ v. saturate.

sauce /'sauθe; 'sause/ n. m. willow.

sauna /'sauna/ n. f. sauna.

savia /'saβia/ n. f. sap.

saxofón /sakso'fon/ **saxófono** n. m. saxophone.

saya /'saya/ n. f. skirt.

sazón /sa'θon; sa'son/ n. f. season; seasoning. **a la s.,** at that time.

sazonar /saθo'nar; saso'nar/ v. flavor, season.

se /se/ pron. -self, -selves.

seca /'seka/ n. f. drought.

secador /seka'ðor/ **secador de pelo** n. m. hair dryer.

secante /se'kante/ a. **papel s.,** blotting paper.

secar /se'kar/ v. dry.

sección /sek'θion; sek'sion/ n. f. section.

seco /'seko/ a. dry; curt.

secreción /sekre'θion; sekre'sion/ n. f. secretion.

secretar /sekre'tar/ v. secrete.

secretaría /sekreta'ria/ n. f. secretary's office; secretariat.

secretario /sekre'tario/ **-ra** n. secretary.

secreto /se'kreto/ a. & m. secret.

secta /'sekta/ n. f. denomination; sect.

secuela /se'kuela/ n. f. result; sequel.

secuestrar /sekues'trar/ v. abduct, kidnap; hijack.

secuestro /se'kuestro/ n. m. abduction, kidnapping.

secular /seku'lar/ a. secular.

secundario /sekun'dario/ a. secondary.

sed /seð/ n. f. thirst. **tener s., estar con s.,** to be thirsty.

seda /'seða/ n. f. silk.

sedar /se'ðar/ v. quiet, allay.

sedativo /seða'tiβo/ a. & m. sedative.

sede /'seðe/ n. f. seat, headquarters.

sedentario /seðen'tario/ a. sedentary.

sedición /seði'θion; seði'sion/ n. f. sedition.

sedicioso /seði'θioso; seði'sioso/ a. seditious.

sediento /se'ðiento/ a. thirsty.

sedimento /seði'mento/ n. m. sediment.

sedoso /se'ðoso/ a. silky.

seducir /seðu'θir; seðu'sir/ v. seduce.

seductivo /seðuk'tiβo/ a. seductive, alluring.

segar /se'gar/ v. reap, harvest; mow.

seglar /seg'lar/ n. m. & f. layman, laywoman.

segmento /seg'mento/ n. m. segment.

segregar /segre'gar/ v. segregate.

seguida /se'giða/ n. f. succession. **en s.,** right away, at once.

seguido /se'giðo/ a. consecutive.

seguir /se'gir/ v. follow; continue, keep on, go on.

según /se'gun/ prep. **1.** according to. —conj. **2.** as.

segundo /se'gundo/ a. & m. second. —**segundar,** v.

seguridad /seguri'ðað/ n. f. safety, security; assurance.

seguro /se'guro/ a. **1.** safe, secure; sure, certain. —n. **2.** m. insurance.

seis /seis/ a. & pron. six.

seiscientos /seis'θientos; seis'sientos/ a. & pron. six hundred.

selección /selek'θion; selek'sion/ n. f. selection, choice.

seleccionar /selekθio'nar; seleksio'nar/ v. select, choose.

selecto /se'lekto/ a. select, choice, elite.

sello /'seʎo; 'seyo/ n. m. seal; stamp. —**sellar,** v.

selva /'selβa/ n. f. forest; jungle.

selvoso /sel'βoso/ a. sylvan.

semáforo /se'maforo/ n. m. semaphore; traffic light.

semana /se'mana/ n. f. week.

semana inglesa /se'mana iŋ'glesa/ five-day work week.

semanal /sema'nal/ a. weekly.

semana laboral /se'mana laβo'ral/ work week.

semántica /se'mantika/ n. f. semantics.

semblante /sem'βlante/ n. m. look, expression.

sembrado /sem'βraðo/ n. m. sown field.

sembrar /sem'βrar/ v. sow, seed.

semejante /seme'hante/ a. **1.** like, similar; such (a). —n. **2.** m. fellow man.

semejanza /seme'hanθa; seme'hansa/ n. f. similarity, likeness.

semejar /seme'har/ v. resemble.

semilla /se'miʎa; se'miya/ n. f. seed.

seminario /semi'nario/ n. m. seminary.

sémola /'semola/ n. f. semolina.

senado /se'naðo/ n. m. senate.

senador /sena'ðor/ **-ra** n. senator.

sencillez /senθi'ʎeθ; sensi'yes/ n. f. simplicity; naturalness.

sencillo /sen'θiʎo; sen'siyo/ a. simple, natural; single.

senda /'senda/ n. f. **sendero,** m. path, footpath.

senectud /senek'tuð/ n. f. old age.

senil /se'nil/ a. senile.

seno /'seno/ n. m. breast, bosom.

sensación /sensa'θion; sensa'sion/ n. f. sensation.

sensacional /sensaθio'nal; sensasio'nal/ a. sensational.

sensato /sen'sato/ a. sensible, wise.

sensibilidad /sensiβili'ðað/ n. f. sensibility; sensitiveness.

sensible /sen'siβle/ a. sensitive; emotional.

sensitivo /sensi'tiβo/ a. sensitive.

sensual /sen'sual/ a. sensual.

sensualidad /sensuali'ðað/ n. f. sensuality.

sentar /sen'tar/ v. seat. **s. bien,** fit well, be becoming.

sentarse /sen'tarse/ v. sit, sit down.

sentencia /sen'tenθia; sen'tensia/ n. f. (court) sentence.

sentidamente /sentiða'mente/ adv. feelingly.

sentido /sen'tiðo/ n. m. meaning, sense; consciousness.

sentido común /sen'tiðo ko'mun/ common sense.

sentimental /sentimen'tal/ a. sentimental.

sentimiento /senti'miento/ n. m. sentiment, feeling.

sentir /sen'tir/ v. feel, sense; hear; regret, be sorry.

seña /'seɲa/ n. f. sign, indication; (pl.) address.

señal /se'ɲal/ n. f. sign, signal; mark.

señalar /seɲa'lar/ v. designate, point out; mark.

señal de marcar /se'ɲal de mar'kar/ dial tone.

señor /se'ɲor/ n. m. gentleman; lord; (title) Mr., Sir.

señora /se'ɲora/ n. f. lady; wife; (title) Mrs., Madam.

señora de la limpieza /se'ɲora de la lim'pieθa; se'ɲora de la lim'piesa/ cleaning woman.

señorita /seɲo'rita/ n. f. young lady; (title) Miss.

sépalo /'sepalo/ n. m. sepal.

separación /separa'θion; separa'sion/ n. f. separation, parting.

separadamente /separaða'mente/ adv. separately.

separado /sepa'raðo/ a. separate; separated. —**separar,** v.

septentrional /septentrio'nal/ a. northern.

septiembre /sep'tiembre/ n. m. September.

séptimo /'septimo/ a. seventh.

sepulcro /se'pulkro/ n. m. sepulcher.

sepultar /sepul'tar/ v. bury, entomb.

sepultura /sepul'tura/ n. f. grave.

sequedad /seke'ðað/ n. f. dryness.

sequía /se'kia/ n. f. drought.

ser /ser/ v. be.

serenata /sere'nata/ n. f. serenade.

serenidad /sereni'ðað/ n. f. serenity.

sereno /se'reno/ a. **1.** serene, calm. —n. **2.** m. dew; watchman.

ser humano /ser u'mano/ n. human being.

serie /'serie/ n. f. series, sequence.

seriedad /serie'ðað/ n. f. seriousness.

serio /'serio/ a. serious. **en s.,** seriously.

sermón /ser'mon/ n. m. sermon.

seroso /se'roso/ a. watery.

serpiente /ser'piente/ n. f. serpent, snake.

serpiente de cascabel /ser'piente de kaska'βel/ rattlesnake.

serrano /se'rrano/ **-na** n. mountaineer.

serrar /se'rrar/ v. saw.

serrín /se'rrin/ n. m. sawdust.

servicial /serβi'θial; serβi'sial/ a. helpful, of service.

servicio /ser'βiθio; ser'βisio/ n. m. service; toilet.

servidor /serβi'ðor/ **-ra** n. servant.

servidumbre /serβi'ðumbre/ n. f. bondage; staff of servants.

servil /ser'βil/ a. servile, menial.

servilleta /serβi'ʎeta; serβi'yeta/ n. f. napkin.

servir /ser'βir/ v. serve. **s. para,** be good for.

servirse /ser'βirse/ v. help oneself.

sesenta /se'senta/ a. & pron. sixty.

sesgo /'sesgo/ n. m. slant. —**sesgar,** v.

sesión /se'sion/ n. f. session; sitting.

seso /'seso/ n. m. brain.

seta /'seta/ n. f. mushroom.

setecientos /sete'θientos; sete'sientos/ a. & pron. seven hundred.

setenta /se'tenta/ a. & pron. seventy.

seto /'seto/ n. m. hedge.

severamente /seβera'mente/ adv. severely.

severidad /seβeri'ðað/ n. f. severity.

severo /se'βero/ a. severe, strict, stern.

sexismo /sek'sismo/ n. m. sexism.

sexista /sek'sista/ a. & n. sexist.

sexo /'sekso/ n. m. sex.

sexto /'seksto/ a. sixth.

sexual /sek'sual/ a. sexual.

si /si/ conj. if; whether.

sí /si/ pron. **1.** -self, -selves. —interj. **2.** yes.

sico-. See psicoanálisis, psicología, etc.

sicómoro /siko'moro/ n. m. sycamore.

SIDA /'siða/ n. m. AIDS.

sidra /'siðra/ n. f. cider.

siempre /'siempre/ adv. always. **para s.,** forever. **s. que,** whenever; provided that.

sierra /'sierra/ n. f. saw; mountain range.

siervo /'sierβo/ **-va** n. slave; serf.

siesta /'siesta/ n. f. (afternoon) nap.

siete /'siete/ a. & pron. seven.

sifón /si'fon/ n. m. siphon; siphon bottle.

siglo /'siglo/ n. m. century.

signatura /signa'tura/ n. f. Mus. signature.

significación /signifika'θion; signifika'sion/ n. f. significance.

significado /signifi'kaðo/ n. m. meaning.

significante /signifi'kante/ a. significant.

significar /signifi'kar/ v. signify, mean.

significativo /signifika'tiβo/ a. significant.

signo /'signo/ n. m. sign, symbol; mark.

siguiente /si'giente/ a. following, next.

sílaba /'silaβa/ n. f. syllable.

silbar /sil'βar/ v. whistle; hiss, boo.

silbato /sil'βato/ **silbido** n. m. whistle.

silencio /si'lenθio; si'lensio/ n. m. silence, stillness.

silenciosamente /silenθiosa'mente; silensiosa'mente/ a. silently.

silencioso /silen'θioso; silen'sioso/ a. silent, still.

silicato /sili'kato/ n. m. silicate.

silicio /si'liθio; si'lisio/ n. m. silicon.

silla /'siʎa; 'siya/ n. f. chair; saddle.

sillón /si'ʎon; si'yon/ n. m. armchair.

silueta /si'lueta/ n. f. silhouette.

silvestre /sil'βestre/ a. wild, uncultivated. **fauna s.,** wildlife.

sima /'sima/ n. f. chasm; cavern.

simbólico /sim'boliko/ a. symbolic.

símbolo /'simbolo/ n. m. symbol.

simetría /sime'tria/ n. f. symmetry.

simétrico /si'metriko/ a. symmetrical.

símil /'simil/ similar a. similar, alike.

similitud /simili'tuð/ n. f. similarity.

simpatía /simpa'tia/ n. f. congeniality; friendly feeling.

simpático /sim'patiko/ a. likeable, nice, congenial.

simple /'simple/ a. simple.

simpleza /sim'pleθa; sim'plesa/ n. f. silliness; trifle.

simplicidad /simpliθi'ðað; simplisi'ðað/ n. f. simplicity.

simplificación /simplifika'θion; simplifika'sion/ n. f. simplification.

simplificar /simplifi'kar/ v. simplify.

simular /simu'lar/ v. simulate.

simultáneo /simul'taneo/ a. simultaneous.

sin /sin/ prep. without. **s. sentido,** meaningless.

sinagoga /sina'goga/ n. f. synagogue.

sinceridad /sinθeri'ðað; sinseri'ðað/ n. f. sincerity.

sincero /sin'θero; sin'sero/ a. sincere.

sincronizar /sinkroni'θar; sinkroni'sar/ v. synchronize.

sindicato /sindi'kato/ n. m. syndicate; labor union.

síndrome /'sindrome/ n. m. syndrome.

sinfonía /sinfo'nia/ n. f. symphony.

sinfónico /sin'foniko/ a. symphonic.

singular /singu'lar/ a. & m. singular.

siniestro /si'niestro/ a. sinister, ominous.

sino /'sino/ conj. but.

sinónimo /si'nonimo/ n. m. synonym.

sinrazón /sinra'θon; sinra'son/ n. f. wrong, injustice.

sinsabor /sinsa'βor/ n. m. displeasure, distaste; trouble.

sintaxis /sin'taksis/ n. f. syntax.

síntesis /'sintesis/ n. f. synthesis.

sintético /sin'tetiko/ a. synthetic.

síntoma /'sintoma/ n. m. symptom.

siquiera /si'kiera/ adv. **ni s.,** not even.

sirena /si'rena/ n. f. siren.

sirviente /sir'βiente/ **-ta** n. servant.

sistema /sis'tema/ n. m. system.

sistemático /siste'matiko/ a. systematic.

sistematizar /sistemati'θar; sistemati'sar/ v. systematize.

sitiar /si'tiar/ v. besiege.

sitio /'sitio/ n. m. site, location, place, spot.

situación /situa'θion; situa'sion/ n. f. situation; location.

situar /si'tuar/ v. situate; locate.

smoking /'smoking/ n. m. tuxedo, dinner jacket.

so /so/ prep. under.

soba /'soβa/ n. f. massage. —**sobar,** v.

sobaco /so'βako/ n. m. armpit.

sobaquero /soβa'kero/ n. m. armhole.

soberano /soβe'rano/ -na a. & n. sovereign.

soberbia /so'βerβia/ n. f. arrogance.

soberbio /so'βerβio/ a. superb; arrogant.

soborno /so'βorno/ n. m. bribe. —**sobornar,** v.

sobra /'soβra/ n. f. excess, surplus. **de sobra,** to spare.

sobrado /so'βraðo/ n. m. attic.

sobrante /so'βrante/ a. & m. surplus.

sobras /'soβras/ n. f.pl. leftovers.

sobre /'soβre/ prep. 1. about; above, over. —n. 2. m. envelope.

sobrecama /soβre'kama/ n. f. bedspread.

sobrecargo /soβre'kargo/ n. m. supercargo.

sobredicho /soβre'ðitʃo/ a. aforesaid.

sobredosis /soβre'ðosis/ n. f. overdose.

sobrehumano /soβreu'mano/ a. superhuman.

sobrenatural /soβrenatu'ral/ a. supernatural, weird.

sobrepasar /soβrepa'sar/ v. surpass.

sobresalir /soβresa'lir/ v. excel.

sobretodo /soβre'toðo/ n. m. overcoat.

sobrevivir /soβreβi'βir/ v. survive, outlive.

sobriedad /soβrie'ðað/ n. f. sobriety; moderation.

sobrina /so'βrina/ n. f. niece.

sobrino /so'βrino/ n. m. nephew.

sobrio /'soβrio/ a. sober, temperate.

socarrén /soka'rren/ n. m. eaves.

sociable /so'θiaβle; so'siaβle/ a. sociable.

social /so'θial; so'sial/ a. social.

socialismo /soθia'lismo; sosia'lismo/ n. m. socialism.

socialista /soθia'lista; sosia'lista/ a. & n. socialist.

sociedad /soθie'ðað; sosie'ðað/ n. f. society; association.

sociedad de consumo /soθie'ðað de kon'sumo; sosie'ðað de kon'sumo/ consumer society.

socio /'soθio; 'sosio/ -cia n. associate, partner; member.

sociología /soθiolo'hia; sosiolo'hia/ n. f. sociology.

sociológico /soθio'lohiko; sosio'lohiko/ a. sociological.

sociólogo /so'θiologo; so'siologo/ -ga n. sociologist.

socorrista /soko'rrista/ n. m. & f. lifeguard.

socorro /so'korro/ n. m. help, aid. —**socorrer,** v.

soda /'soða/ n. f. soda.

sodio /'soðio/ n. m. sodium.

soez /so'eθ; so'es/ a. vulgar.

sofá /so'fa/ n. m. sofa, couch.

sofisma /so'fisma/ n. m. sophism.

sofista /so'fista/ n. m. sophist.

sofocación /sofoka'θion; sofoka'sion/ n. f. suffocation.

sofocar /sofo'kar/ v. smother, suffocate, stifle, choke.

sofrito /so'frito/ n. m. sauce of sautéed tomatoes, peppers, onions, and garlic.

software /'sofθwer/ n. m. software.

soga /'soga/ n. f. rope.

soja /'soha/ n. f. soya.

sol /sol/ n. m. sun.

solada /so'laða/ n. f. dregs.

solanera /sola'nera/ n. f. sunburn.

solapa /so'lapa/ n. f. lapel.

solar /so'lar/ a. 1. solar. —n. 2. m. building lot.

solaz /so'laθ; so'las/ n. m. solace, comfort. —**solazar,** v.

soldado /sol'daðo/ n. m. soldier.

soldar /sol'dar/ v. solder, weld.

soledad /sole'ðað/ n. f. solitude, privacy.

solemne /so'lemne/ a. solemn.

solemnemente /solemne'mente/ adv. solemnly.

solemnidad /solemni'ðað/ n. f. solemnity.

soler /so'ler/ v. be in the habit of.

solicitador /soliθita'ðor; solisita'ðor/ -ra n. applicant, petitioner.

solicitar /soliθi'tar; solisi'tar/ v. solicit; apply for.

solícito /so'liθito; so'lisito/ a. solicitous.

solicitud /soliθi'tuð; solisi'tuð/ n. f. solicitude; application.

sólidamente /soliða'mente/ adv. solidly.

solidaridad /soliðari'ðað/ n. f. solidarity.

solidez /soli'ðeθ; soli'ðes/ n. f. solidity.

solidificar /soliðifi'kar/ v. solidify.

sólido /'soliðo/ a. & m. solid.

soliloquio /soli'lokio/ n. m. soliloquy.

solitario /soli'tario/ a. solitary, lone.

sollozo /so'ʎoθo; so'yoso/ n. m. sob. —**sollozar,** v.

solo /'solo/ a. 1. only; single; alone; lonely. **a solas,** alone. —n. 2. m. Mus. solo.

sólo /'solo/ adv. only, just.

solomillo /solo'miʎo; solo'miyo/ n. m. sirloin.

soltar /sol'tar/ v. release; loosen.

soltero /sol'tero/ -ra a. & n. single, unmarried (person).

soltura /sol'tura/ n. f. poise, ease, facility.

solubilidad /soluβili'ðað/ n. f. solubility.

solución /solu'θion; solu'sion/ n. f. solution.

solucionar /soluθio'nar; solusio'nar/ v. solve, settle.

solvente /sol'βente/ a. solvent.

sombra /'sombra/ n. f. shade; shadow. —**sombrear,** v.

sombra de ojos /'sombra de 'ohos/ eye shadow.

sombrerera /sombre'rera/ n. f. hatbox.

sombrero /som'βrero/ n. m. hat.

sombrilla /som'βriʎa; som'βriya/ n. f. parasol.

sombrío /som'βrio/ a. somber, bleak, gloomy.

sombroso /som'βroso/ a. very shady.

someter /some'ter/ v. subject; submit.

somnífero /som'nifero/ n. m. sleeping pill.

somnolencia /somno'lenθia; somno'lensia/ n. f. drowsiness.

son /son/ n. m. sound. —**sonar,** v.

sonata /so'nata/ n. f. sonata.

sondar /son'dar/ v. sound, fathom.

sonido /so'niðo/ n. m. sound.

sonoridad /sonori'ðað/ n. f. sonority.

sonoro /so'noro/ a. sonorous.

sonrisa /son'risa/ n. f. smile. —**sonreír,** v.

sonrojo /son'roho/ n. m. flush, blush. —**sonrojarse,** v.

soñador /soɲa'ðor/ -ra a. & n. dreamy; dreamer.

soñar /so'ɲar/ v. dream.

soñoliento /soɲo'liento/ a. sleepy.

sopa /'sopa/ n. f. soup.

soplar /so'plar/ v. blow.

soplete /so'plete/ n. m. blowtorch.

soplo /'soplo/ n. m. breath; puff, gust.

soportar /sopor'tar/ v. abide, bear, stand.

soprano /so'prano/ n. m. & f. soprano.

sorbete /sor'βete/ n. m. sherbet.

sorbo /'sorβo/ n. m. sip. —**sorber,** v.

sordera /sor'ðera/ n. f. deafness.

sórdidamente /sorðiða'mente/ adv. sordidly.

sordidez /sorði'ðeθ; sorði'ðes/ n. f. sordidness.

sórdido /'sorðiðo/ a. sordid.

sordo /'sorðo/ a. deaf; muffled, dull.

sordomudo /sorðo'muðo/ -da a. & n. deaf-mute.

sorpresa /sor'presa/ n. f. surprise. —**sorprender,** v.

sorteo /sor'teo/ n. m. drawing lots; raffle.

sortija /sor'tiha/ n. f. ring.

sosa /'sosa/ n. f. Chem. soda.

soso /'soso/ a. dull, insipid, tasteless.

sospecha /sos'petʃa/ n. f. suspicion.

sospechar /sospe'tʃar/ v. suspect.

sospechoso /sospe'tʃoso/ a. suspicious.

sostén /sos'ten/ n. m. bra, brassiere; support.

sostener /soste'ner/ v. hold, support; maintain.

sostenimiento /sosteni'miento/ n. m. sustenance.

sota /'sota/ n. f. jack (in cards).

sótano /'sotano/ n. m. basement, cellar.

soto /'soto/ n. m. grove.

soviet /so'βiet/ n. m. soviet.

soya /'soya/ n. f. soybean.

su /su/ a. his, her, its, their, your.

suave /'suaβe/ a. smooth; gentle, soft, mild.

suavidad /suaβi'ðað/ n. f. smoothness; gentleness, softness, mildness.

suavizar /suaβi'θar; suaβi'sar/ v. soften.

subalterno /suβal'terno/ -na a. & n. subordinate.

subasta /su'βasta/ n. f. auction.

subcampeón /suβkampe'on/ -na n. runner-up.

subconsciencia /suβkons'θienθia; suβkons'siensia/ n. f. subconscious.

súbdito /'suβðito/ -ta n. subject.

subestimar /suβesti'mar/ v. underestimate.

subida /su'βiða/ n. f. ascent, rise.

subilla /su'βiʎa; su'βiya/ n. f. awl.

subir /su'βir/ v. rise, climb, ascend, mount. **s. a,** amount to.

súbito /'suβito/ a. sudden.

subjetivo /suβhe'tiβo/ a. subjective.

subjuntivo /suβhun'tiβo/ a. & m. subjunctive.

sublimación /suβlima'θion; suβlima'sion/ n. f. sublimation.

sublimar /suβli'mar/ v. elevate; sublimate.

sublime /su'βlime/ a. sublime.

submarinismo /suβmari'nismo/ n. m. scuba diving.

submarino /suβma'rino/ a. & m. submarine.

subordinación /suβorðina'θion; suβorðina'sion/ n. f. subordination.

subordinado /suβorði'naðo/ -da a. & n. subordinate. —**subordinar,** v.

subrayar /suβra'yar/ v. underline.

subscribirse /suβskri'βirse/ v. subscribe; sign one's name.

subscripción /suβskrip'θion; suβskrip'sion/ n. f. subscription.

subsecuente /suβse'kuente/ a. subsequent.

subsidiario /suβsi'ðiario/ a. subsidiary.

subsiguiente /suβsi'giente/ a. subsequent.

substancia /suβs'tanθia; suβs'tansia/ n. f. substance.

substancial /suβs'tanθial; suβs'tansial/ a. substantial.

substantivo /suβstan'tiβo/ n. m. substantive, noun.

substitución /suβstitu'θion; suβstitu'sion/ n. f. substitution.

substituir /suβsti'tuir/ v. replace; substitute.

substitutivo /suβstitu'tiβo/ a. substitute.

substituto /suβsti'tuto/ -ta n. substitute.

substraer /suβstra'er/ v. subtract.

subsuelo /suβ'suelo/ n. m. subsoil.

subterfugio /suβter'fuhio/ n. m. subterfuge.

subterráneo /suβte'rraneo/ a. 1. subterranean, underground. —n. 2. m. place underground; subway.

subtítulo /suβ'titulo/ n. m. subtitle.

suburbio /su'βurβio/ n. m. suburb.

subvención /suββen'θion; suββen'sion/ n. f. subsidy, grant.

subversión /suββer'sion/ n. f. subversion.

subversivo /suββer'siβo/ a. subversive.

subvertir /suββer'tir/ v. subvert.

subyugación /suβyuga'θion; suβyuga'sion/ n. f. subjugation.

subyugar /suβyu'gar/ v. subjugate, quell.

succión /suk'θion; suk'sion/ n. f. suction.

suceder /suθe'ðer; suse'ðer/ v. happen, occur, befall. **s. a,** succeed, follow.

sucesión /suθe'sion; suse'sion/ n. f. succession.

sucesivo /suθe'siβo; suse'siβo/ a. successive. **en lo s.,** in the future.

suceso /su'θeso; su'seso/ n. m. event.

sucesor /suθe'sor; suse'sor/ -ra n. successor.

suciedad /suθie'ðað; susie'ðað/ n. f. filth, dirt.

sucio /'suθio; 'susio/ a. filthy, dirty.

suculento /suku'lento/ a. succulent.

sucumbir /sukum'βir/ v. succumb.

sud /suð/ n. m. south.

sudadera /suða'ðera/ n. f. sweatshirt.

Sudáfrica /su'ðafrika/ n. f. South Africa.

sudafricano /suðafri'kano/ -na a. & n. South African.

sudamericano /suðameri'kano/ -na a. & n. South American.

sudar /su'ðar/ v. perspire, sweat.

sudeste /su'ðeste/ n. m. southeast.

sudoeste /suðo'este/ n. m. southwest.

sudor /su'ðor/ n. m. perspiration, sweat.

Suecia /'sueθia; 'suesia/ n. f. Sweden.

sueco /'sueko/ -ca a. & n. Swedish; Swede.

suegra /'suegra/ n. f. mother-in-law.

suegro /'suegro/ n. m. father-in-law.

suela /'suela/ n. f. sole.

sueldo /'sueldo/ n. m. salary, wages.

suelo /'suelo/ n. m. soil; floor; ground.

suelto /'suelto/ a. 1. loose; free; odd, separate. —n. 2. loose change.

sueño /'sueɲo/ n. m. sleep; sleepiness; dream. **tener s.,** to be sleepy.

suero /'suero/ n. m. serum.

suerte /'suerte/ n. f. luck; chance; lot.

suéter /'sueter/ n. m. sweater.

suficiente /sufi'θiente; sufi'siente/ a. sufficient.

sufragio /su'frahio/ n. m. suffrage.

sufrimiento /sufri'miento/ n. m. suffering, agony.

sufrir /su'frir/ v. suffer; undergo; endure.

sugerencia /suhe'renθia; suhe'rensia/ n. f. suggestion.

sugerir /suhe'rir/ v. suggest.

sugestión /suhes'tion/ n. f. suggestion.

sugestionar /suhestio'nar/ v. influence; hypnotize.

suicida /sui'θiða; sui'siða/ n. m. & f. suicide (person).

suicidarse /suiθi'ðarse; suisi'ðarse/ v. commit suicide.

suicidio /sui'θiðio; sui'siðio/ n. m. (act of) suicide.

Suiza /'suiθa; 'suisa/ n. f. Switzerland.

suizo /'suiθo; 'suiso/ -za a. & n. Swiss.

sujeción /suhe'θion; suhe'sion/ *n. f.* subjection.

sujetador /suheta'ðor/ *n. m.* bra, brassiere.

sujetapapeles /su'hetapa'peles/ *n. m.* paper clip.

sujetar /suhe'tar/ *v.* hold, fasten, clip.

sujeto /su'heto/ *a.* **1.** subject, liable. —*n.* **2.** *m. Gram.* subject.

sulfato /sul'fato/ *n. m.* sulfate.

sulfuro /sul'furo/ *n. m.* sulfide.

sultán /sul'tan/ *n. m.* sultan.

suma /'suma/ *n. f.* sum, amount. **en s.,** in short. **s. global,** lump sum.

sumar /su'mar/ *v.* add up.

sumaria /su'maria/ *n. f.* indictment.

sumario /su'mario/ *a. & m.* summary.

sumergir /sumer'hir/ *v.* submerge.

sumersión /sumer'sion/ *n. f.* submersion.

sumisión /sumi'sion/ *n. f.* submission.

sumiso /su'miso/ *a.* submissive.

sumo /'sumo/ *a.* great, high, utmost.

suntuoso /sun'tuoso/ *a.* sumptuous.

superar /supe'rar/ *v.* overcome, surpass.

superficial /superfi'θial; superfi'sial/ *a.* superficial, shallow.

superficie /super'fiθie; super'fisie/ *f.* surface.

supérfluo /su'perfluo/ *a.* superfluous.

superhombre /super'ombre/ *n. m.* superman.

superintendente /superinten'dente/ *n. m. & f.* superintendent.

superior /supe'rior/ *a.* **1.** superior; upper, higher. —*n.* **2.** *m.* superior.

superioridad /superiori'ðað/ *n. f.* superiority.

superlativo /superla'tiβo/ *n. m. & a.* superlative.

superstición /supersti'θion; supersti'sion/ *n. f.* superstition.

supersticioso /supersti'θioso; supersti'sioso/ *a.* superstitious.

supervisar /superβi'sar/ *v.* supervise.

supervivencia /superβi'βenθia; superβi'βensia/ *n. f.* survival.

suplantar /suplan'tar/ *v.* supplant.

suplementario /suplemen'tario/ *a.* supplementary.

suplemento /suple'mento/ *n. m.* supplement. —**suplementar,** *v.*

suplente /su'plente/ *a. & n.* substitute.

súplica /'suplika/ *n. f.* request, entreaty, plea.

suplicación /suplika'θion; suplika'sion/ *n. f.* supplication; request, entreaty.

suplicar /supli'kar/ *v.* request, entreat; implore.

suplicio /su'pliθio; su'plisio/ *n. m.* torture, ordeal.

suplir /su'plir/ *v.* supply.

suponer /supo'ner/ *v.* suppose, presume, assume.

suposición /suposi'θion; suposi'sion/ *n. f.* supposition, assumption.

supositorio /suposi'torio/ *n. m.* suppository.

supremacía /suprema'θia; suprema'sia/ *n. f.* supremacy.

supremo /su'premo/ *a.* supreme.

supresión /supre'sion/ *n. f.* suppression.

suprimir /supri'mir/ *v.* suppress; abolish.

supuesto /su'puesto/ *a.* supposed. **por s.,** of course.

sur /sur/ *n. m.* south.

surco /'surko/ *n. m.* furrow. —**surcar,** *v.*

surgir /sur'hir/ *v.* arise; appear suddenly.

surtido /sur'tiðo/ *n. m.* assortment; supply, stock.

surtir /sur'tir/ *v.* furnish, supply.

susceptibilidad /susθeptiβili'ðað; susseptiβili'ðað/ *n. f.* susceptibility.

susceptible /susθep'tiβle; sussep'tiβle/ *a.* susceptible.

suscitar /susθi'tar; sussi'tar/ *v.* stir up.

suscri- = subscri-

suspender /suspen'der/ *v.* withhold; suspend; fail (in a course).

suspensión /suspen'sion/ *n. f.* suspension.

suspenso /sus'penso/ *n. m.* failing grade. **en s.,** in suspense.

suspicacia /suspi'kaθia; suspi'kasia/ *n. f.* suspicion, distrust.

suspicaz /suspi'kaθ; suspi'kas/ *a.* suspicious.

suspicazmente /suspikaθ'mente; suspikas'mente/ *adv.* suspiciously.

suspiro /sus'piro/ *n. m.* sigh. —**suspirar,** *v.*

sustan- = substan-

sustentar /susten'tar/ *v.* sustain, support.

sustento /sus'tento/ *n. m.* sustenance, support, living.

susti- = substi-

susto /'susto/ *n. m.* fright, scare.

sustraer /sustra'er/ = substraer.

susurro /su'surro/ *n. m.* rustle; whisper. —**susurrar,** *v.*

sutil /'sutil/ *a.* subtle.

sutileza /suti'leθa, sutili'ðað; suti'lesa, sutili'ðað/ **sutilidad** *n. f.* subtlety.

sutura /su'tura/ *n. f.* suture.

suyo /'suyo/ *a.* his, hers, theirs, yours.

T

tabaco /ta'βako/ *n. m.* tobacco.

tábano /'taβano/ *n. m.* horsefly.

tabaquería /taβake'ria/ *n. f.* tobacco shop.

taberna /ta'βerna/ *n. f.* tavern, bar.

tabernáculo /taβer'nakulo/ *n. m.* tabernacle.

tabique /ta'βike/ *n. m.* dividing wall, partition.

tabla /'taβla/ *n. f.* board, plank; table, list. **t. de planchar,** ironing board.

tablado /ta'βlaðo/ *n. m.* stage, platform.

tablero /ta'βlero/ *n. m.* panel.

tableta /ta'βleta/ *n. f.* tablet.

tablilla /ta'βliʎa; ta'βliya/ *n. f.* bulletin board.

tabú /ta'βu/ *n. m.* taboo.

tabular /taβu'lar/ *a.* tabular.

tacaño /ta'kaɲo/ *a.* stingy.

tacha /'tatʃa/ *n. f.* fault, defect.

tachar /ta'tʃar/ *v.* find fault with; cross out.

tachuela /ta'tʃuela/ *n. f.* tack.

tácitamente /'taθitamente; 'tasitamente/ *adv.* tacitly.

tácito /'taθito; 'tasito/ *a.* tacit.

taciturno /taθi'turno; tasi'turno/ *a.* taciturn.

taco /'tako/ *n. m.* heel (of shoe); billiard cue.

tacón /ta'kon/ *n. m.* heel (of shoe).

táctico /'taktiko/ *a.* tactical.

tacto /'takto/ *n. m.* (sense of) touch; tact.

tafetán /tafe'tan/ *n. m.* taffeta.

taimado /tai'maðo/ *a.* sly.

tajada /ta'haða/ *n.* cut, slice. —**tajar,** *v.*

tajea /ta'hea/ *n. f.* channel.

tal /tal/ *a.* such. **con t. que.,** provided that. **t. vez,** perhaps.

taladrar /tala'ðrar/ *v.* drill.

taladro /ta'laðro/ *n. m. Mech.* drill.

talante /ta'lante/ *n. m.* humor, disposition.

talco /'talko/ *n. m.* talc.

talega /ta'lega/ *n. f.* bag, sack.

talento /ta'lento/ *n. m.* talent.

talla /'taʎa; 'taya/ *n. f.* engraving; stature; size (of suit).

tallador /taʎa'ðor; taya'ðor/ **-ra** *n.* engraver; dealer (at cards).

talle /'taʎe; 'taye/ *n. m.* figure; waist; fit.

taller /ta'ʎer; ta'yer/ *n. m.* workshop, factory.

tallo /'taʎo; 'tayo/ *n. m.* stem, stalk.

talón /ta'lon/ *n. m.* heel (of foot); (baggage) check, stub.

tamal /ta'mal/ *n. m.* tamale.

tamaño /ta'maɲo/ *n. m.* size.

tambalear /tambale'ar/ *v.* stagger, totter.

también /tam'bien/ *adv.* also, too.

tambor /tam'bor/ *n. m.* drum.

tamiz /ta'miθ; ta'mis/ *n. m.* sieve, sifter.

tampoco /tam'poko/ *adv.* neither, either.

tan /tan/ *adv.* so.

tanda /'tanda/ *n. f.* turn, relay.

tándem /'tandem/ *n. m.* tandem; pair.

tangencia /taŋ'genθia; taŋ'gensia/ *n. f.* tangency.

tangible /taŋ'giβle/ *a.* tangible.

tango /'taŋgo/ *n. m.* tango (dance or music).

tanque /'tanke/ *n. m.* tank.

tanteo /tan'teo/ *n. m.* estimate. —**tantear,** *v.*

tanto /'tanto/ *a. & pron.* **1.** so much, so many; as much, as many. **entre t.,** meanwhile. **por lo t.,** therefore. **un t.,** somewhat, a bit. —*n.* **2.** *m.* point (in games) **3.** *(pl.)* score. **estar al t.,** to be up to date.

tañer /ta'ɲer/ *v.* play (an instrument); ring (bells).

tapa /'tapa/ *n. f.* cap, cover; snack served in a bar. —**tapar,** *v.*

tapadero /tapa'ðero/ *n. m.* stopper, lid.

tápara /'tapara/ *n. f.* caper.

tapete /ta'pete/ *n. m.* small rug, mat, cover.

tapia /'tapia/ *n. f.* wall.

tapicería /tapiθe'ria; tapise'ria/ *n. f.* tapestry.

tapioca /ta'pioka/ *n. f.* tapioca.

tapiz /ta'piθ; ta'pis/ *n. m.* tapestry; carpet.

tapizado (de pared) /tapi'θaðo de pa'reð tapi'saðo de pa'reð/ *n. m.* (wall) covering.

tapón /ta'pon/ *n. m.* plug; cork.

taquigrafía /takigra'fia/ *n. f.* shorthand.

taquilla /ta'kiʎa; ta'kiya/ *n. f.* ticket office; box office; ticket window.

tara /'tara/ *n. f.* hang-up.

tarántula /ta'rantula/ *n. f.* tarantula.

tararear /tarare'ar/ *v.* hum.

tardanza /tar'ðanθa; tar'ðansa/ *n. f.* delay; lateness.

tardar /tar'ðar/ *v.* delay; be late; take (of time). **a más t.,** at the latest.

tarde /'tarðe/ *adv.* **1.** late. —*n.* **2.** *f.* afternoon.

tardío /tar'ðio/ *a.* late, belated.

tarea /ta'rea/ *n. f.* task, assignment.

tarifa /ta'rifa/ *n. f.* rate; tariff; price list.

tarjeta /tar'heta/ *n. f.* card.

tarjeta bancaria /tar'heta ban'karia/ bank card.

tarjeta de crédito /tar'heta de 'kreðito/ credit card.

tarjeta de embarque /tar'heta de em'βarke/ boarding pass.

tarta /'tarta/ *n. f.* tart.

tartamudear /tartamuðe'ar/ *v.* stammer, falter.

tasa /'tasa/ *n. f.* rate.

tasación /tasa'θion; tasa'sion/ *n. f.* valuation.

tasar /ta'sar/ *v.* assess, appraise.

tasca /'taska/ *n. f.* bar, pub.

tasugo /ta'sugo/ *n. m.* badger.

tatuar /tatu'ar/ *v.* tattoo.

tautología /tautolo'hia/ *n. f.* tautology.

taxi /'taksi/ **taxímetro** *n. m.* taxi.

taxista /tak'sista/ *n. m. & f.* taxi driver.

taxonomía /taksono'mia/ *n. f.* taxonomy.

taza /'taθa; 'tasa/ *n. f.* cup.

te /te/ *pron.* you; yourself.

té *n. m.* tea.

team /tim/ *n. m.* team.

teátrico /te'atriko/ *a.* theatrical.

teatro /te'atro/ *n. m.* theater.

tebeo /te'βeo/ *n. m.* comic book.

techo /'tetʃo/ *n. m.* roof. —**techar,** *v.*

tecla /'tekla/ *n. f.* key (of a piano, etc.).

teclado /te'klaðo/ *n. m.* keyboard.

teclado numérico /te'klaðo nu'meriko/ numeric keypad.

técnica /'teknika/ *n. f.* technique.

técnicamente /'teknikamente/ *adv.* technically.

técnico /'tekniko/ *a.* **1.** technical; —*m.* **2.** repairman, technician.

tecnología /teknolo'hia/ *n. f.* technology.

tedio /'teðio/ *n. m.* tedium, boredom.

tedioso /te'ðioso/ *a.* tedious.

teísmo /te'ismo/ *n. m.* theism.

teja /'teha/ *n. f.* tile.

tejado /te'haðo/ *n. m.* roof.

tejano /te'hano/ **-na** *a. & n.* Texan.

tejanos /te'hanos/ *n. m.pl.* jeans.

tejer /te'her/ *v.* weave; knit.

tejido /te'hiðo/ *n. m.* fabric; weaving.

tejón /te'hon/ *n. m.* badger.

tela /'tela/ *n. f.* cloth, fabric, web. **t. metálica,** screen; screening. **t. vaquera,** denim.

telar /te'lar/ *n. m.* loom.

telaraña /tela'raɲa/ *n. f.* cobweb, spiderweb.

telefonista /telefo'nista/ *n. m. & f.* (telephone) operator.

teléfono /te'lefono/ *n. m.* telephone. —**telefonear,** *v.*

teléfono gratuito /te'lefono gra'tuito/ toll-free number.

teléfono público /te'lefono 'puβliko/ pay phone, public telephone.

teléfono rojo /te'lefono 'rroho/ hotline.

telégrafo /te'legrafo/ *n. m.* telegraph. —**telegrafear,** *v.*

telegrama /tele'grama/ *n. m.* telegram.

telescopio /teles'kopio/ *n. m.* telescope.

televisión /teleβi'sion/ *n. f.* television.

telón /te'lon/ *n. m. Theat.* curtain.

telurio /te'lurio/ *n. m.* tellurium.

tema /'tema/ *n. m.* theme, subject.

temblar /tem'blar/ *v.* tremble, quake; shake, shiver.

temblor /tem'blor/ *n. m.* tremor; shiver.

temer /te'mer/ *v.* fear, be afraid of, dread.

temerario /teme'rario/ *a.* rash.

temeridad /temeri'ðað/ *n. f.* temerity.

temerosamente /temerosa'mente/ *adv.* timorously.

temeroso /teme'roso/ *a.* fearful.

temor /te'mor/ *n. m.* fear.

témpano /'tempano/ *n. m.* kettledrum; iceberg.

temperamento /tempera'mento/ *n. m.* temperament.

temperancia /tempe'ranθia; tempe'ransia/ *n. f.* temperance.

temperatura /tempera'tura/ *n. f.* temperature.

tempestad /tempes'tað/ *n. f.* tempest, storm.

tempestuoso /tempes'tuoso/ *a.* tempestuous, stormy.

templado /tem'plaðo/ *a.* temperate, mild, moderate.

templanza /tem'planθa; tem'plansa/ *n. f.* temperance; mildness.

templar /tem'plar/ *v.* temper; tune (an instrument).

templo /'templo/ *n. m.* temple.

temporada /tempo'raða/ *n. f.* season, time, spell.

temporal /tempo'ral/ **temporáneo** a. temporary.

temprano /tem'prano/ a. & adv. early.

tenacidad /tenaθi'ðað; tenasi'ðað/ n. f. tenacity.

tenaz /te'naθ; te'nas/ a. tenacious, stubborn.

tenazmente /tenaθ'mente; tenas'mente/ adv. tenaciously.

tendencia /ten'denθia; tendensia/ n. f. tendency, trend.

tender /ten'der/ v. stretch, stretch out.

tendero /ten'dero/ -ra n. shopkeeper, storekeeper.

tendón /ten'don/ n. m. tendon, sinew.

tenebrosidad /teneβrosi'ðað/ n. f. gloom.

tenebroso /tene'βroso/ a. dark, gloomy.

tenedor /tene'ðor/ n. **1.** m. & f. keeper; holder. **2.** m. fork.

tener /te'ner/ v. have; own; hold. **t. que,** have to, must.

teniente /te'niente/ n. m. lieutenant.

tenis /'tenis/ n. m. tennis; (pl.) sneakers.

tenor /te'nor/ n. m. tenor.

tensión /ten'sion/ n. f. tension, stress, strain.

tenso /'tenso/ a. tense.

tentación /tenta'θion; tenta'sion/ n. f. temptation.

tentáculo /ten'takulo/ n. m. tentacle.

tentador /tenta'ðor/ a. alluring, tempting.

tentar /ten'tar/ v. tempt, lure; grope, probe.

tentativa /tenta'tiβa/ n. f. attempt.

tentativo /tenta'tiβo/ a. tentative.

teñir /te'ɲir/ v. tint, dye.

teología /teolo'hia/ n. f. theology.

teológico /teo'lohiko/ a. theological.

teoría /teo'ria/ n. f. theory.

teórico /te'oriko/ a. theoretical.

terapéutico /tera'peutiko/ a. therapeutic.

tercero /ter'θero; ter'sero/ a. third.

tercio /'terθio; 'tersio/ n. m. third.

terciopelo /terθio'pelo; tersio'pelo/ n. m. velvet.

terco /'terko/ a. obstinate, stubborn.

termal /ter'mal/ a. thermal.

terminación /termina'θion; termina'sion/ n. f. termination; completion.

terminal aérea /termi'nal 'airea/ n. f. air terminal.

terminar /termi'nar/ v. terminate, finish.

término /'termino/ n. m. term; end.

terminología /terminolo'hia/ n. f. terminology.

termómetro /ter'mometro/ n. m. thermometer.

termos /'termos/ n. m. thermos.

termostato /ter'mostato/ n. m. thermostat.

ternero /ter'nero/ -ra n. calf.

ternura /ter'nura/ n. f. tenderness.

terquedad /terke'ðað/ n. f. stubbornness.

terraza /te'rraθa; te'rrasa/ n. f. terrace.

terremoto /terre'moto/ n. m. earthquake.

terreno /te'rreno/ a. **1.** earthly, terrestrial. —n. **2.** m. ground, terrain; lot, plot.

terrible /te'rriβle/ a. terrible, awful.

terrífico /te'rrifiko/ a. terrifying.

territorio /terri'torio/ n. m. territory.

terrón /te'rron/ n. m. clod, lump; mound.

terror /te'rror/ n. m. terror.

terso /'terso/ a. smooth, glossy; terse.

tertulia /ter'tulia/ n. f. social gathering, party.

tesis /'tesis/ n. f. thesis.

tesorería /tesore'ria/ n. f. treasury.

tesorero /teso'rero/ -ra n. treasurer.

tesoro /te'soro/ n. m. treasure.

testamento /testa'mento/ n. m. will, testament.

testarudo /testa'ruðo/ a. stubborn.

testificar /testifi'kar/ v. testify.

testigo /tes'tigo/ n. m. & f. witness.

testimonial /testimo'nial/ a. testimonial.

testimonio /testi'monio/ n. m. testimony.

teta /'teta/ n. f. teat.

tetera /te'tera/ n. f. teapot.

tétrico /'tetriko/ a. sad; gloomy.

texto /'teksto/ n. m. text.

textura /teks'tura/ n. f. texture.

tez /teθ; tes/ n. f. complexion.

ti /ti/ pron. you; yourself.

tía /'tia/ n. f. aunt.

tibio /'tiβio/ a. lukewarm.

tiburón /tiβu'ron/ n. m. shark.

tiemblo /'tiemblo/ n. m. aspen.

tiempo /'tiempo/ n. m. time; weather; Gram. tense.

tienda /'tienda/ n. f. shop, store, tent.

tientas /'tientas/ n. f.pl. **andar a t.,** to grope (in the dark).

tierno /'tierno/ a. tender.

tierra /'tierra/ n. f. land; ground; earth, dirt, soil.

tieso /'tieso/ a. taut, stiff, hard, strong.

tiesto /'tiesto/ n. m. flower pot.

tiesura /tie'sura/ n. f. stiffness; harshness.

tifo /'tifo/ n. m. typhus.

tifoideo /tifoi'ðeo/ n. m. typhoid fever.

tigre /'tigre/ n. m. tiger.

tijeras /ti'heras/ n. f.pl. scissors.

tila /'tila/ n. f. linden.

timbre /'timbre/ n. m. seal, stamp; tone; (electric) bell.

tímidamente /'timiðamente/ adv. timidly.

timidez /timi'ðeθ; timi'ðes/ n. f. timidity.

tímido /'timiðo/ a. timid, shy.

timón /ti'mon/ n. m. rudder, helm.

tímpano /'timpano/ n. m. kettledrum; eardrum.

tina /'tina/ n. f. tub, vat.

tinaja /ti'naha/ n. f. jar.

tinta /'tinta/ n. f. ink.

tinte /'tinte/ n. m. tint, shade.

tintero /tin'tero/ n. m. inkwell.

tinto /'tinto/ a. wine-colored; red (of wine).

tintorería /tintore'ria/ n. f. dry cleaning shop.

tintorero /tinto'rero/ -ra n. dyer; dry cleaner.

tintura /tin'tura/ n. f. tincture; dye.

tiñoso /ti'ɲoso/ a. scabby; stingy.

tío /'tio/ n. m. uncle.

tiovivo /tio'βiβo/ n. m. merry-go-round.

típico /'tipiko/ a. typical.

tipo /'tipo/ n. m. type, sort; (interest) rate; Colloq. guy, fellow.

tipo de cambio /'tipo de 'kambio/ exchange rate.

tipo de interés /'tipo de inte'res/ interest rate.

tira /'tira/ n. f. strip.

tirabuzón /tiraβu'θon; tiraβu'son/ n. m. corkscrew.

tirada /ti'raða/ n. f. edition.

tirado /ti'raðo/ -da a. dirt-cheap.

tiranía /tira'nia/ n. f. tyranny.

tiránico /ti'raniko/ n. m. tyrannical.

tirano /ti'rano/ -na n. tyrant.

tirante /ti'rante/ a. **1.** tight, taut; tense. —n. **2.** m.pl. suspenders.

tirar /ti'rar/ v. throw; draw; pull; fire (a weapon).

tiritar /tiri'tar/ v. shiver.

tiro /'tiro/ n. m. throw; shot.

tirón /ti'ron/ n. m. pull. **de un t.,** at a stretch, at one stroke.

tísico /'tisiko/ a. & a. consumptive.

tisis /'tisis/ n. f. consumption, tuberculosis.

titanio /ti'tanio/ n. m. titanium.

títere /'titere/ n. m. puppet.

titilación /titila'θion; titila'sion/ n. f. twinkle.

titubear /tituβe'ar/ v. stagger; totter; waver.

titulado /titu'laðo/ a. entitled; so-called.

titular /titu'lar/ a. **1.** titular. —v. **2.** entitle.

título /'titulo/ n. m. title, headline.

tiza /'tiθa; 'tisa/ n. f. chalk.

tiznar /tiθ'nar; tis'nar/ v. smudge; stain.

toalla /to'aʎa; to'aya/ n. f. towel. **t. sanitaria,** sanitary napkin.

toalleta /toa'ʎeta; toa'yeta/ n. f. small towel.

tobillo /to'βiʎo; to'βiyo/ n. m. ankle.

tobogán /toβo'gan/ n. m. toboggan.

tocadiscos /toka'ðiskos/ n. m. record player.

tocadiscos compacto /toka'ðiskos kom'pakto/ **tocadiscos digital** CD player.

tocado /to'kaðo/ n. m. hairdo.

tocador /toka'ðor/ n. m. boudoir; dressing table.

tocante /to'kante/ a. touching. **t. a,** concerning, relative to.

tocar /to'kar/ v. touch; play (an instrument). **t. a uno,** be one's turn; be up to one.

tocayo /to'kayo/ -ya n. namesake.

tocino /to'θino; to'sino/ n. m. bacon.

tocólogo /to'kologo/ -ga n. obstetrician.

todavía /toða'βia/ adv. yet, still.

todo /'toðo/ a. **1.** all, whole. **todos los,** every. —pron. **2.** all, everything. **con t.,** still, however. **del t.,** wholly, at all.

todopoderoso /toðopoðe'roso/ a. almighty.

toldo /'toldo/ n. m. awning.

tolerancia /tole'ranθia; tole'ransia/ n. f. tolerance.

tolerante /tole'rante/ a. tolerant.

tolerar /tole'rar/ v. tolerate.

toma /'toma/ n. f. taking, capture, seizure.

tomaína /to'maina/ n. f. ptomaine.

tomar /to'mar/ v. take; drink. **t. el sol,** sunbathe.

tomate /to'mate/ n. m. tomato.

tomillo /to'miʎo; to'miyo/ n. m. thyme.

tomo /'tomo/ n. m. volume.

tonada /to'naða/ n. f. tune.

tonel /to'nel/ n. m. barrel, cask.

tonelada /tone'laða/ n. f. ton.

tonelaje /tone'lahe/ n. m. tonnage.

tónico /'toniko/ a. & m. tonic.

tono /'tono/ n. m. tone, pitch, shade. **darse t.,** to put on airs.

tonsila /ton'sila/ n. f. tonsil.

tonsilitis /tonsi'litis/ n. f. tonsilitis.

tontería /tonte'ria/ n. f. nonsense, foolishness.

tontifútbol /tonti'futβol/ n. m. excessively defensive strategy (in soccer).

tonto /'tonto/ -ta a. & n. foolish, silly; fool.

topacio /to'paθio; to'pasio/ n. m. topaz.

topar /to'par/ v. run into. **t. con,** come upon.

tópico /'topiko/ a. **1.** topical. —n. **2.** m. cliché.

topo /'topo/ n. m. mole (animal).

toque /'toke/ n. m. touch.

tórax /'toraks/ n. m. thorax.

torbellino /torβe'ʎino; torβe'yino/ n. m. whirlwind.

torcer /tor'θer; tor'ser/ v. twist; wind; distort.

toreador /torea'ðor/ -a n. toreador.

torero /to'rero/ -ra n. bullfighter.

torio /'torio/ n. m. thorium.

tormenta /tor'menta/ n. f. storm.

tormento /tor'mento/ n. m. torment.

tornado /tor'naðo/ n. m. tornado.

tornar /tor'nar/ v. return; turn.

tornarse en /tor'narse en/ v. turn into, become.

torneo /tor'neo/ n. m. tournament.

tornillo /tor'niʎo; tor'niyo/ n. m. screw.

toro /'toro/ n. m. bull.

toronja /to'ronha/ n. f. grapefruit.

torpe /'torpe/ a. awkward, clumsy; sluggish.

torpedero /torpe'ðero/ n. m. torpedo boat.

torpedo /tor'peðo/ n. m. torpedo.

torre /'torre/ n. f. tower.

torre de mando /'torre de 'mando/ control tower.

torrente /to'rrente/ n. m. torrent.

tórrido /'torriðo/ a. torrid.

torta /'torta/ n. f. cake; loaf.

tortilla /tor'tiʎa; tor'tiya/ n. f. omelet; (Mex.) tortilla, pancake.

tórtola /'tortola/ n. f. dove.

tortuga /tor'tuga/ n. f. turtle.

tortuoso /tor'tuoso/ a. tortuous.

tortura /tor'tura/ n. f. torture. —**torturar,** v.

tos /tos/ n. m. cough. —**toser,** v.

tosco /'tosko/ a. coarse, rough, uncouth.

tosquedad /toske'ðað/ n. f. coarseness, roughness.

tostador /tosta'ðor/ n. m. toaster.

tostar /'tostar/ v. toast; tan.

total /to'tal/ a. & m. total.

totalidad /totali'ðað/ n. f. totality, entirety, whole.

totalitario /totali'tario/ a. totalitarian.

totalmente /total'mente/ adv. totally; entirely.

tótem /'totem/ n. m. totem.

tóxico /'toksiko/ a. toxic.

toxicómano /toksi'komano/ -na n. m. & f. drug addict.

trabajador /traβaha'ðor/ -ra a. **1.** hardworking. —n. **2.** worker.

trabajo /tra'βaho/ n. m. work; labor. —**trabajar,** v.

trabar /tra'βar/ v. fasten, shackle; grasp; strike up.

tracción /trak'θion; trak'sion/ n. f. traction.

tracto /'trakto/ n. m. tract.

tractor /trak'tor/ n. m. tractor.

tradición /traði'θion; traði'sion/ n. f. tradition.

tradicional /traðiθio'nal; traðisio'nal/ a. traditional.

traducción /traðuk'θion; traðuk'sion/ n. f. translation.

traducir /traðu'θir; traðu'sir/ v. translate.

traductor /traðuk'tor/ -ra n. translator.

traer /tra'er/ v. bring; carry; wear.

tráfico /'trafiko/ n. m. traffic. —**traficar,** v.

tragaperras /traga'perras/ n. f. slot machine, one-armed bandit.

tragar /tra'gar/ v. swallow.

tragedia /tra'heðia/ n. f. tragedy.

trágicamente /'trahikamente/ adv. tragically.

trágico /'trahiko/ -ca a. **1.** tragic. —n. **2.** tragedian.

trago /'trago/ n. m. swallow; drink.

traición /trai'θion; trai'sion/ n. f. treason, betrayal.

traicionar /traiθio'nar; traisio'nar/ v. betray.

traidor /trai'ðor/ -ra a. & n. traitorous; traitor.

traje /'trahe/ n. m. suit; dress; garb, apparel.

traje de baño /'trahe de 'baɲo/ bathing suit.

trama /'trama/ v. plot (of a story).

tramador /trama'ðor/ -ra n. weaver; plotter.

tramar /tra'mar/ v. weave; plot, scheme.

trámite /'tramite/ n. m. (business) deal, transaction.

tramo /'tramo/ *n. m.* span, stretch, section.

trampa /'trampa/ *n. f.* trap, snare.

trampista /tram'pista/ *n. m. & f.* cheater; swindler.

trance /'tranθe; 'transe/ *n. m.* critical moment or stage. **a todo t.,** at any cost.

tranco /'tranko/ *n. m.* stride.

tranquilidad /trankili'ðað/ *n. f.* tranquility, calm, quiet.

tranquilizante /trankili'θante; trankili'sante/ *n. m.* tranquilizer.

tranquilizar /trankili'θar; trankili'sar/ *v.* quiet, calm down.

tranquilo /tran'kilo/ *a.* tranquil, calm.

transacción /transak'θion; transak'sion/ *n. f.* transaction.

transbordador /transβorða'ðor/ *n. m.* ferry.

transbordador espacial /transβorða'ðor espa'θial; transβorða'ðor espa'sial/ space, shuttle.

transcribir /transkri'βir/ *v.* transcribe.

transcripción /transkrip'θion; transkrip'sion/ *n. f.* transcription.

transcurrir /transku'rrir/ *v.* elapse.

transeúnte /tran'seunte/ *a. & n.* transient; passerby.

transexual /transek'sual/ *a.* transsexual.

transferencia /transfe'renθia; transfe'rensia/ *n. f.* transference.

transferir /transfe'rir/ *v.* transfer.

transformación /transforma'θion; transforma'sion/ *n. f.* transformation.

transformar /transfor'mar/ *v.* transform.

transfusión /transfu'sion/ *n. f.* transfusion.

transgresión /transgre'sion/ *n. f.* transgression.

transgresor /transgre'sor/ **-ra** *n.* transgressor.

transición /transi'θion; transi'sion/ *n. f.* transition.

transigir /transi'hir/ *v.* compromise, settle; agree.

transistor /transis'tor/ *n. m.* transistor.

transitivo /transi'tiβo/ *a.* transitive.

tránsito /'transito/ *n. m.* transit, passage.

transitorio /transi'torio/ *a.* transitory.

transmisión /transmi'sion/ *n. f.* transmission; broadcast.

transmisora /transmi'sora/ *n. f.* broadcasting station.

transmitir /transmi'tir/ *v.* transmit; broadcast.

transparencia /transpa'renθia; transpa'rensia/ *n. f.* transparency.

transparente /transpa'rente/ *a.* **1.** transparent. —*n.* **2.** *m.* (window) shade.

transportación /transporta'θion; transporta'sion/ *n. f.* transportation.

transportar /transpor'tar/ *v.* transport, convey.

transporte /trans'porte/ *n. m.* transportation; transport.

tranvía /tram'bia/ *n. m.* streetcar, trolley.

trapacero /trapa'θero; trapa'sero/ **-ra** *n.* cheat; swindler.

trapo /'trapo/ *n. m.* rag.

tráquea /'trakea/ *n. f.* trachea.

tras /tras/ *prep.* after; behind.

trasegar /trase'gar/ *v.* upset, overturn.

trasero /tra'sero/ *a.* rear, back.

traslado /tras'laðo/ *n. m.* transfer. —**trasladar,** *v.*

traslapo /tras'lapo/ *n. m.* overlap. —**traslapar,** *v.*

trasnochar /trasno't ʃar/ *v.* stay up all night.

traspalar /traspa'lar/ *v.* shovel.

traspasar /traspa'sar/ *v.* go beyond; cross; violate; pierce.

trasquilar /traski'lar/ *v.* shear; clip.

trastornar /trastor'nar/ *v.* overturn, overthrow, upset.

trastorno /tras'torno/ *m.* overthrow; upheaval.

trastorno mental /tras'torno men'tal/ mental disorder.

trasvasar /trasβa'sar/ *v.* download; download.

tratado /tra'taðo/ *n. m.* treaty; treatise.

tratamiento /trata'miento/ *n. m.* treatment.

tratar /tra'tar/ *v.* treat, handle. **t. de,** deal with; try to; call (a name).

tratarse de /tra'tarse de/ *v.* be a question of.

trato /'trato/ *n. m.* treatment; manners; *Com.* deal.

través /tra'βes/ *adv.* **a t. de,** through, across. **de t.,** sideways.

travesía /traβe'sia/ *n. f.* crossing, voyage.

travesti /tra'βesti/ *n. m.* transvestite.

travestido /traβes'tiðo/ *a.* disguised.

travesura /traβe'sura/ *n. f.* prank; mischief.

travieso /tra'βieso/ *a.* naughty, mischievous.

trayectoria /trayek'toria/ *n. f.* trajectory.

trazar /tra'θar; tra'sar/ *v.* plan, devise; trace; draw.

trazo /'traθo; 'traso/ *n.* plan, outline; line, stroke.

trébol /'treβol/ *n. m.* clover.

trece /'treθe; 'trese/ *a. & pron.* thirteen.

trecho /'tretʃo/ *n. m.* space, distance, stretch.

tregua /'tregua/ *n. f.* truce; respite, lull.

treinta /'treinta/ *a. & pron.* thirty.

tremendo /tre'mendo/ *a.* tremendous.

tremer /tre'mer/ *v.* tremble.

tren /tren/ *n. m.* train.

trenza /'trenθa; 'trensa/ *n. f.* braid. —**trenzar,** *v.*

trepar /tre'par/ *v.* climb, mount.

trepidación /trepiða'θion; trepiða'sion/ *n. f.* trepidation.

tres /tres/ *a. & pron.* three.

trescientos /tres'θientos; tres'sientos/ *a. & pron.* three hundred.

triángulo /tri'angulo/ *n. m.* triangle.

triar /triar/ *v.* sort, separate.

tribu /'triβu/ *n. f.* tribe.

tribulación /triβula'θion; triβula'sion/ *n. f.* tribulation.

tribuna /tri'βuna/ *n. f.* rostrum, stand; (*pl.*) grandstand.

tribunal /triβu'nal/ *n. m.* court, tribunal.

tributario /triβu'tario/ *a. & m.* tributary.

tributo /tri'βuto/ *n. m.* tribute.

triciclo /tri'θiklo; tri'siklo/ *n. m.* tricycle.

trigo /'trigo/ *n. m.* wheat.

trigonometría /trigonome'tria/ *n. f.* trigonometry.

trigueño /tri'geɲo/ *a.* swarthy, dark.

trilogía /trilo'hia/ *n. f.* trilogy.

trimestral /trimes'tral/ *a.* quarterly.

trinchar /trin'tʃar/ *v.* carve (meat).

trinchera /trin'tʃera/ *n. f.* trench, ditch.

trineo /tri'neo/ *n. m.* sled; sleigh.

trinidad /trini'ðað/ *n. f.* trinity.

tripa /'tripa/ *n. f.* tripe, entrails.

triple /'triple/ *a.* triple. —**triplicar,** *v.*

trípode /'tripoðe/ *n. m.* tripod.

tripulación /tripula'θion; tripula'sion/ *n. f.* crew.

tripulante /tripu'lante/ *m & f.* crew member.

tripular /tripu'lar/ *v.* man.

triste /'triste/ *a.* sad, sorrowful; dreary.

tristemente /triste'mente/ *adv.* sadly.

tristeza /tris'teθa; tris'tesa/ *n. f.* sadness; gloom.

triunfal /triun'fal/ *a.* triumphal.

triunfante /triun'fante/ *a.* triumphant.

triunfo /'triunfo/ *n. m.* triumph; trump. —**triunfar,** *v.*

trivial /tri'βial/ *a.* trivial, commonplace.

trivialidad /triβiali'ðað/ *n. f.* triviality.

trocar /tro'kar/ *v.* exchange, switch; barter.

trofeo /tro'feo/ *n. m.* trophy.

trombón /trom'bon/ *n. m.* trombone.

trompa /'trompa/ **trompeta** *n. f.* trumpet, horn.

tronada /tro'naða/ *n. f.* thunderstorm.

tronar /tro'nar/ *v.* thunder.

tronco /'tronko/ *n. m.* trunk, stump.

trono /'trono/ *n. m.* throne.

tropa /'tropa/ *n. f.* troop.

tropel /tro'pel/ *n. m.* crowd, throng.

tropezar /trope'θar; trope'sar/ *v.* trip, stumble. **t. con,** come upon, run into.

trópico /'tropiko/ *a.* tropical; tropics.

tropiezo /tro'pieθo; tro'pieso/ *n. m.* stumble; obstacle; slip, error.

trote /'trote/ *n. m.* trot. —**trotar,** *v.*

trovador /troβa'ðor/ *n. m.* troubadour.

trozo /'troθo; 'troso/ *n. m.* piece, portion, fragment; selection, passage.

trucha /'trutʃa/ *n. f.* trout.

trueco /'trueko/ **trueque** *n. m.* exchange, barter.

trueno /'trueno/ *n. m.* thunder.

trufa /'trufa/ *n. f.* truffle.

tu /tu/ *a.* your.

tú *pron.* you.

tuberculosis /tuβerku'losis/ *n. f.* tuberculosis.

tubo /'tuβo/ *n. m.* tube, pipe.

tubo de ensayo /'tuβo de en'sayo/ test tube.

tubo de escape /'tuβo de es'kape/ exhaust pipe.

tuerca /'tuerka/ *n. f. Mech.* nut.

tulipán /tuli'pan/ *n. m.* tulip.

tumba /'tumba/ *n. f.* tomb, grave.

tumbar /tum'bar/ *v.* knock down.

tumbarse /tum'βarse/ *v.* lie down.

tumbo /'tumbo/ *n. m.* tumble; somersault.

tumbona /tum'βona/ *n. f.* deck chair.

tumor /tu'mor/ *n. m.* tumor; growth.

tumulto /tu'multo/ *n. m.* tumult, commotion.

tumultuoso /tumul'tuoso/ *a.* tumultuous, boisterous.

tunante /tu'nante/ *n. m.* rascal, rogue.

tunda /'tunda/ *n. f.* spanking, whipping.

túnel /'tunel/ *n. m.* tunnel.

túnel del Canal de la Mancha /'tunel del ka'nal de la 'mantʃa/ Channel Tunnel, Chunnel.

tungsteno /tuŋs'teno/ *n. m.* tungsten.

túnica /'tunika/ *n. f.* tunic, robe.

tupir /tu'pir/ *v.* pack tight, stuff; stop up.

turbación /turβa'θion; turβa'sion/ *n. f.* confusion, turmoil.

turbamulta /turβa'multa/ *n. f.* mob, disorderly crowd.

turbar /tur'βar/ *v.* disturb, upset; embarrass.

turbina /tur'βina/ *n. f.* turbine.

turbio /'turβio/ *a.* turbid; muddy.

turco /'turko/ **-ca** *a. & n.* Turkish; Turk.

turismo /tu'rismo/ *n. m.* touring, (foreign) travel, tourism.

turista /tu'rista/ *n. m. & f.* tourist.

turno /'turno/ *n. m.* turn; (work) shift.

turquesa /tur'kesa/ *n. f.* turquoise.

Turquía /tur'kia/ *n. f.* Turkey.

turrón /tu'rron/ *n. m.* nougat.

tusa /'tusa/ *n. f.* corncob; corn.

tutear /tute'ar/ *v.* use the pronoun **tú,** etc., in addressing a person.

tutela /tu'tela/ *n. f.* guardianship; aegis.

tutor /tu'tor/ **-ra** *n.* tutor; guardian.

tuyo /'tuyo/ *a.* your, yours.

U

u /u/ *conj.* or.

ubre /'uβre/ *n. f.* udder.

Ucrania /u'krania/ *n. f.* Ukraine.

ucranio /u'kranio/ **-ia** *a. & n.* Ukrainian.

ufano /u'fano/ *a.* proud, haughty.

úlcera /'ulθera; 'ulsera/ *n. f.* ulcer.

ulterior /ulte'rior/ *a.* ulterior.

último /'ultimo/ *a.* last, final; ultimate; latest. **por ú.,** finally. **ú. minuto,** last minute, eleventh hour.

ultraje /ul'trahe/ *n. m.* outrage. —**ultrajar,** *v.*

ultrasónico /ultra'soniko/ *a.* ultrasonic.

umbral /um'bral/ *n. m.* threshold.

umbroso /um'broso/ *a.* shady.

un /un/ **una** *art.* *a.* a, an; one; (*pl.*) some.

unánime /u'nanime/ *a.* unanimous.

unanimidad /unanimi'ðað/ *n. f.* unanimity.

unción /un'θion; un'sion/ *n. f.* unction.

ungüento /uŋ'guento/ *n. m.* ointment, salve.

único /'uniko/ *a.* only, sole; unique.

unicornio /uni'kornio/ *n. m.* unicorn.

unidad /uni'ðað/ *n. f.* unit; unity.

unidad de cuidados intensivos /uni'ðað de kui'ðaðos inten'siβos/ **unidad de vigilancia intensiva** intensive-care unit.

unidad de disco /uni'ðað de 'disko/ disk drive.

unificar /unifi'kar/ *v.* unify.

uniforme /uni'forme/ *a. & m.* uniform.

uniformidad /uniformi'ðað/ *n. f.* uniformity.

unión /u'nion/ *n. f.* union; joining.

unir /u'nir/ *v.* unite, join.

universal /uniβer'sal/ *a.* universal.

universalidad /uniβersali'ðað/ *n. f.* universality.

universidad /uniβersi'ðað/ *n. f.* university; college.

universo /uni'βerso/ *n. m.* universe.

uno /'uno/ **una** *pron.* one; (*pl.*) some.

untar /un'tar/ *v.* spread; grease; anoint.

uña /'uɲa/ *n. f.* fingernail.

urbanidad /urβani'ðað/ *n. f.* urbanity; good breeding.

urbanismo /urβa'nismo/ *n. m.* city planning.

urbano /ur'βano/ *a.* urban; urbane; well-bred.

urbe /'urβe/ *n. f.* large city.

urgencia /ur'henθia; ur'hensia/ *n. f.* urgency.

urgente /ur'hente/ *a.* urgent, pressing. **entrega u.,** special delivery.

urgir /ur'hir/ *v.* be urgent.

urna /'urna/ *n. f.* urn; ballot box; (*pl.*) polls.

urraca /u'rraka/ *n. f.* magpie.

usanza /u'sanθa; u'sansa/ *n. f.* usage, custom.

usar /u'sar/ *v.* use; wear.

uso /'uso/ *n. m.* use; usage; wear.

usted /us'teð/ *pron.* you.

usual /u'sual/ *a.* usual.

usualmente /usual'mente/ *adv.* usually.

usura /u'sura/ *n. f.* usury.

usurero /usu'rero/ **-ra** *n.* usurer.

usurpación /usurpa'θion; usurpa'sion/ *n. f.* usurpation.

usurpar /usur'par/ *v.* usurp.

utensilio /uten'silio/ *n. m.* utensil.

útero /'utero/ *n. m.* uterus.

útil /'util/ *a.* useful, handy.

utilidad /utili'ðað/ *n. f.* utility, usefulness.

utilizar /utili'θar; utili'sar/ *v.* use, utilize.

útilmente /util'mente/ *adv.* usefully.

utópico /u'topiko/ *a.* utopian.

uva /'uβa/ *n. f.* grape.

V

vaca /'baka/ *n. f.* cow; beef.

vacaciones /baka'θiones; baka'siones/ *n. f.pl.* vacation, holidays.

vacancia /ba'kanθia; ba'kansia/ *n. f.* vacancy.

vacante /ba'kante/ *a.* **1.** vacant. —*n.* **2.** *f.* vacancy.

vaciar /ba'θiar; ba'siar/ *v.* empty; pour out.

vacilación /baθila'θion; basila'sion/ *n. f.* vacillation, hesitation.

vacilante /baθi'lante; basi'lante/ *a.* vacillating.

vacilar /baθi'lar; basi'lar/ *v.* falter, hesitate; waver; stagger.

vacío /ba'θio; ba'sio/ *a.* **1.** empty. —*n.* **2.** *m.* void, empty space.

vacuna /ba'kuna/ *n. f.* vaccine.

vacunación /bakuna'θion; bakuna'sion/ *n. f.* vaccination.

vacunar /baku'nar/ *v.* vaccinate.

vacuo /'bakuo/ *a.* **1.** empty, vacant. —*n.* **2.** *m.* vacuum.

vadear /baðe'ar/ *v.* wade through, ford.

vado /'baðo/ *n. m.* ford.

vagabundo /baga'βundo/ **-da** *a. & n.* vagabond.

vagar /ba'gar/ *v.* wander, rove, roam; loiter.

vago /'bago/ **-ga** *a.* **1.** vague, hazy; wandering, vagrant. —*n.* **2.** vagrant, tramp.

vagón /ba'gon/ *n. m.* railroad car.

vahído /ba'iðo/ *n. m.* dizziness.

vaina /'baina/ *n. f.* sheath; pod.

vainilla /bai'niʎa; bai'niya/ *n. f.* vanilla.

vaivén /bai'βen/ *n. m.* vibration, sway.

vajilla /ba'hiʎa; ba'hiya/ *n. f.* (dinner) dishes.

valentía /balen'tia/ *n. f.* valor, courage.

valer /ba'ler/ *n.* **1.** *m.* worth. —*v.* **2.** be worth.

valerse de /ba'lerse de/ *v.* make use of, avail oneself of.

valía /ba'lia/ *n. f.* value.

validez /bali'ðeθ; bali'ðes/ *n. f.* validity.

válido /'baliðo/ *a.* valid.

valiente /ba'liente/ *a.* valiant, brave, courageous.

valija /ba'liha/ *n. f.* valise.

valioso /ba'lioso/ *a.* valuable.

valla /'baʎa; 'baya/ *n. f.* fence, barrier.

valle /'baʎe; 'baye/ *n. m.* valley.

valor /ba'lor/ *n. m.* value, worth; bravery, valor; (*pl., Com.*) securities.

valoración /balora'θion; balora'sion/ *n. f.* appraisal.

valorar /balo'rar/ *v.* value, appraise.

vals /bals/ *n. m.* waltz.

valsar /bal'sar/ *v.* waltz.

valuación /balua'θion; balua'sion/ *n. f.* valuation.

valuar /balu'ar/ *v.* value; rate.

válvula /'balβula/ *n. f.* valve.

válvula de seguridad /'balβula de seguri'ðað/ safety valve.

vandalismo /banda'lismo/ *n. m.* vandalism.

vándalo /'bandalo/ **-la** *n.* vandal.

vanidad /bani'ðað/ *n. f.* vanity.

vanidoso /bani'ðoso/ *a.* vain, conceited.

vano /'bano/ *a.* vain; inane.

vapor /ba'por/ *n. m.* vapor; steam; steamer, steamship.

vaquero /ba'kero/ **-ra** *n.* cowboy.

vara /'bara/ *n. f.* wand, stick, switch.

varadero /bara'ðero/ *n. m.* shipyard.

varar /ba'rar/ *v.* launch; be stranded; run aground.

variable /ba'riaβle/ *a.* variable.

variación /baria'θion; baria'sion/ *n. f.* variation.

variar /ba'riar/ *v.* vary.

varicela /bari'θela; bari'sela/ *n. f.* chicken pox.

variedad /barie'ðað/ *n. f.* variety.

varios /'barios/ *a. & pron. pl.* various; several.

variz /ba'riθ; ba'ris/ *n. f.* varicose vein.

varón /ba'ron/ *n. m.* man; male.

varonil /baro'nil/ *a.* manly, virile.

vasallo /ba'saʎo; ba'sayo/ *n. m.* vassal.

vasectomía /basekto'mia/ *n. f.* vasectomy.

vasija /ba'siha/ *n. f.* bowl, container (for liquids).

vaso /'baso/ *n. m.* water glass; vase. **v. de papel,** paper cup.

vástago /'bastago/ *n. m.* bud, shoot; twig; offspring.

vasto /'basto/ *a.* vast.

vecindad /beθin'dað; besin'dað/ *n. f.* **vecindario,** *m.* neighborhood, vicinity.

vecino /be'θino; be'sino/ **-na** *a. & n.* neighboring; neighbor.

vedar /be'ðar/ *v.* forbid; impede.

vega /'bega/ *n. f.* meadow.

vegetación /beheta'θion; beheta'sion/ *n. f.* vegetation.

vegetal /behe'tal/ *n. m.* vegetable.

vehemente /bee'mente/ *a.* vehement.

vehículo /be'ikulo/ *n. m.* vehicle; conveyance.

veinte /'beinte/ *a. & pron.* twenty.

vejez /be'heθ; be'hes/ *n. f.* old age.

vejiga /be'higa/ *n. f.* bladder.

vela /'bela/ *n. f.* vigil, watch; candle; sail.

velar /be'lar/ *v.* stay up, sit up; watch over.

vellón /be'ʎon; be'yon/ *n. m.* fleece.

velloso /be'ʎoso; be'yoso/ *a.* hairy; fuzzy.

velludo /be'ʎuðo; be'yuðo/ *a.* downy.

velo /'belo/ *n. m.* veil.

velocidad /beloθi'ðað; belosi'ðað/ *n. f.* velocity, speed; rate. **v. máxima,** speed limit.

velomotor /belomo'tor/ *n. m.* motorbike, moped.

veloz /be'loθ; be'los/ *a.* speedy, fast, swift.

vena /'bena/ *n. f.* vein.

venado /be'naðo/ *n. m.* deer.

vencedor /benθe'ðor; bense'ðor/ **-ra** *n.* victor.

vencer /ben'θer; ben'ser/ *v.* defeat, overcome, conquer; *Com.* become due, expire.

vencimiento /benθi'miento; bensi'miento/ *n. m.* defeat; expiration.

venda /'benda/ *n. f.* **vendaje,** *m.* bandage. —**vendar,** *v.*

vendedor /bende'ðor/ **-ra** *n.* seller, trader; sales clerk.

vender /ben'der/ *v.* sell.

vendimia /ben'dimia/ *n. f.* vintage; grape harvest.

Venecia /be'neθia; be'nesia/ *n. f.* Venice.

veneciano /bene'θiano; bene'siano/ **-na** *a. & n.* Venetian.

veneno /be'neno/ *n. m.* poison.

venenoso /bene'noso/ *a.* poisonous.

veneración /benera'θion; benera'sion/ *n. f.* veneration.

venerar /bene'rar/ *v.* venerate, revere.

venero /be'nero/ *n. m.* spring; origin.

véneto /'beneto/ *a.* Venetian.

venezolano /beneθo'lano; beneso'lano/ **-na** *a. & n.* Venezuelan.

vengador /beŋga'ðor/ **-ra** *n.* avenger.

venganza /beŋ'ganθa; beŋ'gansa/ *n. f.* vengeance, revenge.

vengar /beŋ'gar/ *v.* avenge.

venida /be'niða/ *n. f.* arrival, advent, coming.

venidero /beni'ðero/ *a.* future; coming.

venir /be'nir/ *v.* come.

venta /'benta/ *n. f.* sale; sales.

ventaja /ben'taha/ *n. f.* advantage; profit.

ventajoso /benta'hoso/ *a.* advantageous; profitable.

ventana /ben'tana/ *n. f.* window.

ventero /ben'tero/ **-ra** *n.* innkeeper.

ventilación /bentila'θion; bentila'sion/ *n. m.* ventilation.

ventilador /bentila'ðor/ *n. m.* ventilator, fan.

ventilar /benti'lar/ *v.* ventilate, air.

ventisquero /bentis'kero/ *n. m.* snowdrift; glacier.

ventoso /ben'toso/ *a.* windy.

ventura /ben'tura/ *n. f.* venture; happiness; luck.

ver /ber/ *v.* see. **tener que v. con,** have to do with.

vera /'bera/ *n. f.* edge.

veracidad /beraθi'ðað; berasi'ðað/ *n. f.* truthfulness, veracity.

verano /be'rano/ *n. m.* summer. —**veranear,** *v.*

veras /'beras/ *n. f.pl.* **de v.,** really, truly.

veraz /be'raθ; be'ras/ *a.* truthful.

verbigracia /berβi'graθia; berβi'grasia/ *adv.* for example.

verbo /'berβo/ *n. m.* verb.

verboso /ber'βoso/ *a.* verbose.

verdad /ber'ðað/ *n. f.* truth. **ser v.,** to be true.

verdadero /berða'ðero/ *a.* true, real.

verde /'berðe/ *a.* green; risqué, off-color.

verdor /ber'ðor/ *n. m.* greenness, verdure.

verdugo /ber'ðugo/ *n. m.* hangman.

verdura /ber'ðura/ *n. f.* verdure, vegetation; (*pl.*) vegetables.

vereda /be'reða/ *n. f.* path.

veredicto /bere'ðikto/ *n. m.* verdict.

vergonzoso /bergon'θoso; bergon'soso/ *a.* shameful, embarrassing; shy, bashful.

vergüenza /ber'guenθa; ber'guensa/ *n. f.* shame; disgrace; embarrassment.

verificar /berifi'kar/ *v.* verify, check.

verja /'berha/ *n. f.* grating, railing.

verosímil /bero'simil/ *a.* likely, plausible.

verraco /be'rrako/ *n. m.* boar.

verruga /be'rruga/ *n. f.* wart.

versátil /ber'satil/ *a.* versatile.

verse /'berse/ *v.* look, appear.

versión /ber'sion/ *n. f.* version.

verso /'berso/ *n. m.* verse, stanza; line (of poetry).

verter /ber'ter/ *v.* pour, spill; shed; empty.

vertical /berti'kal/ *a.* vertical.

vertiente /ber'tiente/ *n. f.* slope; watershed.

vertiginoso /bertihi'noso/ *a.* dizzy.

vértigo /'bertigo/ *n. m.* vertigo, dizziness.

vestíbulo /bes'tiβulo/ *n. m.* vestibule, lobby.

vestido /bes'tiðo/ *n. m.* dress; clothing.

vestigio /bes'tihio/ *n. m.* vestige, trace.

vestir /bes'tir/ *v.* dress, clothe.

veterano /bete'rano/ **-na** *a. & n.* veteran.

veterinario /beteri'nario/ **-ria** *a.* **1.** veterinary. —*n.* **2.** veterinarian.

veto /'beto/ *n. m.* veto.

vetusto /be'tusto/ *a.* ancient, very old.

vez /beθ; bes/ *n. f.* time; turn. **tal v.,** perhaps. **a la v.,** at the same time. **en v. de,** instead of. **una v.,** once. **otra v.,** again.

vía /'bia/ *n. f.* track; route, way.

viaducto /bia'ðukto/ *n. m.* viaduct.

viajante /bia'hante/ *a. & n.* traveling; traveler.

viajar /bia'har/ *v.* travel; journey; tour.

viaje /'biahe/ *n. m.* trip, journey, voyage; (*pl.*) travels.

viaje de estudios /'biahe de es'tuðios/ field trip.

viajero /bia'hero/ **-ra** *n.* traveler; passenger.

viaje todo incluido /'biahe 'toðo in'kluiðo/ package tour.

viandas /'biandas/ *n. f.pl.* victuals, food.

víbora /'biβora/ *n. f.* viper.

vibración /biβra'θion; biβra'sion/ *n. f.* vibration.

vibrar /bi'βrar/ *v.* vibrate.

vicepresidente /biθepresi'ðente; bisepresi'ðente/ **-ta** *n.* vice president.

vicio /'biθio; 'bisio/ *n. m.* vice.

vicioso /bi'θioso; bi'sioso/ *a.* vicious; licentious.

víctima /'biktima/ *n. f.* victim.

victoria /bik'toria/ *n. f.* victory.

victorioso /bikto'rioso/ *a.* victorious.

vid /bið/ *n. f.* grapevine.

vida /'biða/ *n. f.* life; living.

vídeo /'biðeo/ *n. m.* videotape.

videocámara /biðeo'kamara/ *n. f.* video camera.

videodisco /biðeo'ðisko/ *n. m.* videodisc.

videojuego /biðeo'huego/ *n. m.* video game.

vidrio /'biðrio/ *n. m.* glass.

viejo /'bieho/ **-ja** *a. & n.* old; old person.

viento /'biento/ *n. m.* wind. **hacer v.,** to be windy.

vientre /'bientre/ *n. m.* belly.

viernes /'biernes/ *n. m.* Friday.

viga /'biga/ *n. f.* beam, rafter.

vigente /bi'hente/ *a.* in effect (prices, etc.).

vigilante /bihi'lante/ *a. & m.* vigilant, watchful; watchman.

vigilante nocturno /bihi'lante nok'turno/ night watchman.

vigilar /bihi'lar/ *v.* guard, watch over.

vigilia /bi'hilia/ *n. f.* vigil, watchfulness; *Relig.* fast.

vigor /bi'gor/ *n. m.* vigor. **en v.,** in effect, in force.

vil /bil/ *a.* vile, low, contemptible.

vileza /bi'leθa; bi'lesa/ *n. f.* baseness; vileness.

villa /'biʎa; 'biya/ *n. f.* town; country house.

villancico /biʎan'θiko; biyan'siko/ *n. m.* Christmas carol.

villanía /biʎa'nia; biya'nia/ *n. f.* villainy.

villano /bi'ʎano; bi'yano/ *n. m.* boor.

vinagre /bi'nagre/ *n. m.* vinegar.

vinagrera /bina'grera/ *n. f.* cruet.

vínculo /'binkulo/ *n. m.* link. —**vincular,** *v.*

vindicar /bindi'kar/ *v.* vindicate.

vino /'bino/ *n. m.* wine.

viña /'biɲa/ *n. f.* vineyard.

violación /biola'θion; biola'sion/ *n. f.* violation; rape.

violador /biola'ðor/ **-ra** *n. m. & f.* rapist.

violar /bio'lar/ *v.* violate; rape.

violencia /bio'lenθia; bio'lensia/ *n. f.* violence.

violento /bio'lento/ *a.* violent; impulsive.

violeta /bio'leta/ *n. f.* violet.

violín /bio'lin/ *n. m.* violin.

violón /bio'lon/ *n. m.* bass viol.

virar /bi'rar/ *v.* veer, change course.

virgen /bir'hen/ *n. f.* virgin.

viril /bi'ril/ *a.* virile, manly.

virilidad /birili'ðað/ *n. f.* virility, manhood.

virtual /bir'tual/ *a.* virtual.

virtud /bir'tuð/ *n. f.* virtue; efficacy, power.

virtuoso /bir'tuoso/ *a.* virtuous.

viruela /bi'ruela/ *n. f.* smallpox.

viruelas locas /bi'ruelas 'lokas/ *n. f.pl.* chicken pox.

virus /'birus/ *n. m.* virus.

visa /'bisa/ *n. f.* visa.

visaje /bi'sahe/ *n. m.* grimace.

visera /bi'sera/ *n. f.* visor.

visible /bi'siβle/ *a.* visible.

visión /bi'sion/ *n. f.* vision.

visionario /bisio'nario/ **-ria** *a. & n.* visionary.

visita /bi'sita/ *n. f.* visit; *m. & f.* visitor, caller. **v. con guía, v. explicada, v. programada,** guided tour.

visitación /bisita'θion; bisita'sion/ *n. f.* visitation.

visitante /bisi'tante/ *a. & n.* visiting; visitor.

visitar /bisi'tar/ *v.* visit; inspect, examine.

vislumbrar /bislum'βrar/ *v.* glimpse.

vislumbre /bis'lumbre/ *n. f.* glimpse.

viso /'biso/ *n. m.* looks; outlook.

víspera /'bispera/ *n. f.* eve, day before.

vista /'bista/ *n. f.* view; scene; sight.

vista de pájaro /'bista de 'paharo/ bird's-eye view.

vistazo /bis'taθo; bis'taso/ *n. m.* glance, glimpse.

vistoso /bis'toso/ *a.* beautiful; showy.

visual /bi'sual/ *a.* visual.

vital /bi'tal/ *a.* vital.

vitalidad /bitali'ðað/ *n. f.* vitality.

vitamina /bita'mina/ *n. f.* vitamin.

vitando /bi'tando/ *a.* hateful.

vituperar /bitupe'rar/ *v.* vituperate; revile.

viuda /'biuða/ *n. f.* widow.

viudo /'biuðo/ *n. m.* widower.

vivaz /bi'βaθ; bi'βas/ *a.* vivacious, buoyant; clever.

víveres /'biβeres/ *n. m.pl.* provisions.

viveza /bi'βeθa; bi'βesa/ *n. f.* animation, liveliness.

vívido /bi'βiðo/ *a.* vivid, bright.

vivienda /bi'βienda/ *n. f.* (living) quarters, dwelling.

vivificar /biβifi'kar/ *v.* vivify, enliven.

vivir /bi'βir/ *v.* live.

vivo /'biβo/ *a.* live, alive, living; vivid; animated, brisk.

vocablo /bo'kaβlo/ *n. m.* word.

vocabulario /bokaβu'lario/ *n. m.* vocabulary.

vocación /boka'θion; boka'sion/ *n. f.* vocation, calling.

vocal /bo'kal/ *a.* **1.** vocal. —*n.* **2.** *f.* vowel.

vocear /boθe'ar; bose'ar/ *v.* vociferate.

vodca /'boðka/ *n. m.* vodka.

vodevil /boðe'βil/ *n. m.* vaudeville.

volante /bo'lante/ *a.* **1.** flying. —*n.* **2.** *m.* memorandum; (steering) wheel.

volar /bo'lar/ *v.* fly; explode.

volcán /bol'kan/ *n. m.* volcano.

volcar /bol'kar/ *v.* upset, capsize.

voltaje /bol'tahe/ *n. m.* voltage.

voltear /bolte'ar/ *v.* turn, whirl; overturn.

voltio /'boltio/ *n. m.* volt.

volumen /bo'lumen/ *n. m.* volume.

voluminoso /bolumi'noso/ *a.* voluminous.

voluntad /bolun'tað/ *n. f.* will. **buena v.** goodwill.

voluntario /bolun'tario/ **-ria** *a. & n.* voluntary; volunteer.

voluntarioso /bolunta'rioso/ *a.* willful.

volver /bol'βer/ *v.* turn; return, go back, come back. **v. a hacer** (etc.), do (etc.) again.

volverse /bol'βerse/ *v.* turn around; turn, become.

vómito /'bomito/ *n. m.* vomit. —**vomitar,** *v.*

voracidad /boraθi'ðað; borasi'ðað/ *n. f.* voracity; greed.

voraz /bo'raθ; bo'ras/ *a.* greedy, ravenous.

vórtice /'bortiθe; 'bortise/ *n. m.* whirlpool.

vosotros /bo'sotros, bo'sotras/ **-as** *pron.pl.* you; yourselves.

votación /bota'θion; bota'sion/ *n. f.* voting; vote.

voto /'boto/ *n. m.* vote; vow. —**votar,** *v.*

voz /boθ; bos/ *n. f.* voice; word. **a voces,** by shouting. **en v. alta,** aloud.

vuelco /'buelko/ *n. m.* upset.

vuelo /'buelo/ *n. m.* flight. **v. libre,** hang gliding.

vuelo chárter /'buelo 'tʃarter/ charter flight.

vuelo regular /'buelo rregu'lar/ scheduled flight.

vuelta /'buelta/ *n. f.* turn, bend; return. **a la v. de,** around. **dar una v.,** to take a walk.

vuestro /'buestro/ *a.* your, yours.

vulgar /bul'gar/ *a.* vulgar, common.

vulgaridad /bulgari'ðað/ *n. f.* vulgarity.

vulgo /'bulgo/ *n. m.* (the) masses, (the) common people.

vulnerable /bulne'raβle/ *a.* vulnerable.

Y Z

y /i/ *conj.* and.

ya /ya/ *adv.* already; now; at once. **y. no,** no longer, any more. **y. que,** since.

yacer /ya'θer; ya'ser/ *v.* lie.

yacimiento /yaθi'miento; yasi'miento/ *n. m.* deposit.

yanqui /'yanki/ *a. & n.* North American.

yate /'yate/ *n. m.* yacht.

yegua /'yegua/ *n. f.* mare.

yelmo /'yelmo/ *n. m.* helmet.

yema /'yema/ *n. f.* yolk (of an egg).

yerba /'yerβa/ *n. f.* grass; herb.

yerno /'yerno/ *n. m.* son-in-law.

yerro /'yerro/ *n. m.* error, mistake.

yeso /'yeso/ *n. m.* plaster.

yídish /'yiðis/ *n. m.* Yiddish.

yo /yo/ *pron.* I.

yodo /'yoðo/ *n. m.* iodine.

yoduro /jo'ðuro/ *n. m.* iodide.

yonqui /'yonki/ *m. & f. Colloq.* drug addict, junkie.

yugo /'yugo/ *n. m.* yoke.

yunque /'yunke/ *n. m.* anvil.

yunta /'yunta/ *n. f.* team (of animals).

zafarse /θa'farse; sa'farse/ *v.* run away, escape. **z. de,** get rid of.

zafio /'θafio; 'safio/ *a.* coarse, uncivil.

zafiro /θa'firo; sa'firo/ *n. m.* sapphire.

zaguán /θa'guan; sa'guan/ *n. m.* vestibule, hall.

zalamero /θala'mero; sala'mero/ **-ra** *n.* flatterer, wheedler.

zambullir /θambu'ʎir; sambu'yir/ *v.* plunge, dive.

zampar /θam'par; sam'par/ *v. Colloq.* gobble down, wolf down.

zanahoria /θana'oria; sana'oria/ *n. f.* carrot.

zanja /'θanha; 'sanha/ *n. f.* ditch, trench.

zapatería /θapate'ria; sapate'ria/ *n. f.* shoe store; shoemaker's shop.

zapatero /θapa'tero; sapa'tero/ *n. m.* shoemaker.

zapato /θa'pato; sa'pato/ *n. m.* shoe.

zar /θar/ *n. m.* czar.

zaraza /θa'raθa; sa'rasa/ *n. f.* calico; chintz.

zarza /'θarθa; 'sarsa/ *n. f.* bramble.

zarzuela /θar'θuela; sar'suela/ *n. f.* musical comedy.

zodíaco /θo'ðiako; so'ðiako/ *n. m.* zodiac.

zona /'θona; 'sona/ *n. f.* zone.

zoología /θoolo'hia; soolo'hia/ *n. f.* zoology.

zoológico /θoo'lohiko; soo'lohiko/ *a.* zoological.

zorro /'θorro; 'sorro/ **-rra** *n.* fox.

zozobra /θo'θoβra; so'soβra/ *n. f.* worry, anxiety; capsizing.

zozobrar /θoθo'βrar; soso'βrar/ *v.* capsize; worry.

zumba /'θumba; 'sumba/ *n. f.* spanking.

zumbido /θum'βiðo; sum'βiðo/ *n. m.* buzz, hum. —**zumbar,** *v.*

zumo /'θumo; 'sumo/ *n. m.* juice. **z. de naranja,** orange juice.

zurcir /θur'θir; sur'sir/ *v.* darn, mend.

zurdo /'θurðo; 'surðo/ *a.* left-handed.

zurrar /θu'rrar; su'rrar/ *v.* flog, drub.

English–Spanish

inglés–español

A

a /ə, *when stressed* ā/ *art.* un, una.
abacus /'æbəkəs/ *n.* ábaco *m.*
abandon /ə'bændən/ *n.* **1.** desenfreno, abandono *m.* —*v.* **2.** abandonar, desamparar.
abandoned /ə'bændənd/ *a.* abandonado.
abandonment /ə'bændənmənt/ *n.* abandono, desamparo *m.*
abase /ə'beis/ *v.* degradar, humillar.
abasement /ə'beismənt/ *n.* degradación, humillación *f.*
abash /ə'bæʃ/ *v.* avergonzar.
abate /ə'beit/ *v.* menguar, moderarse.
abatement /ə'beitmənt/ *n.* disminución *f.*
abbess /'æbɪs/ *n.* abadesa *f.*
abbey /'æbi/ *n.* abadía *f.*
abbot /'æbət/ *n.* abad *m.*
abbreviate /ə'brivi,eit/ *v.* abreviar.
abbreviation /ə,brivi'eiʃən/ *n.* abreviatura *f.*
abdicate /'æbdɪ,keit/ *v.* abdicar.
abdication /,æbdɪ'keiʃən/ *n.* abdicación *f.*
abdomen /'æbdəmən/ *n.* abdomen *m.*
abdominal /æb'dɒmənl/ *a.* abdominal.
abduct /æb'dʌkt/ *v.* secuestrar.
abduction /æb'dʌkʃən/ *n.* secuestra *f.*
abductor /æb'dʌktər/ *n.* secuestrador -ra.
aberrant /ə'bɛrənt, 'æbər-/ *a.* aberrante.
aberration /,æbə'reiʃən/ *n.* aberración *f.*
abet /ə'bɛt/ *v.* apoyar, favorecer.
abetment /ə'bɛtmənt/ *n.* apoyo *m.*
abettor /ə'bɛtər/ *n.* cómplice *m. & f.*
abeyance /ə'beiəns/ *n.* suspensión *f.*
abhor /æb'hɔr/ *v.* abominar, odiar.
abhorrence /æb'hɔrəns/ *n.* detestación *f.;* aborrecimiento *m.*
abhorrent /æb'hɔrənt/ *a.* detestable, aborrecible.
abide /ə'baid/ *v.* soportar. **to a. by,** cumplir con.
abiding /ə'baidɪŋ/ *a.* perdurable.
ability /ə'bɪliti/ *n.* habilidad *f.*
abject /'æbdʒɛkt/ *a.* abyecto; desanimado.
abjuration /,æbdʒə'reiʃən/ *n.* renuncia *f.*
abjure /æb'dʒʊr/ *v.* renunciar.
ablative /'æblətɪv/ *a. & n. Gram.* ablativo *m.*
ablaze /ə'bleiz/ *a.* en llamas.
able /'eibəl/ *a.* capaz; competente. **to be a.,** poder.
able-bodied /'eibəl 'bɒdid/ *a.* robusto.
ablution /ə'bluʃən/ *n.* ablución *f.*
ably /'eibli/ *adv.* hábilmente.
abnegate /'æbnɪ,geit/ *v.* repudiar; negar.
abnegation /,æbnɪ'geiʃən/ *n.* abnegación; repudiación *f.*
abnormal /æb'nɔrməl/ *a.* anormal.
abnormality /,æbnɔr'mæliti/ *n.* anormalidad, deformidad *f.*
abnormally /æb'nɔrməli/ *adv.* anormalmente.
aboard /ə'bɔrd/ *adv.* a bordo.
abode /ə'boud/ *n.* residencia *f.*
abolish /ə'bɒliʃ/ *v.* suprimir.
abolishment /ə'bɒliʃmənt/ *n.* abolición *f.*
abolition /,æbə'liʃən/ *n.* abolición *f.*
abominable /ə'bɒmənəbəl/ *a.* abominable.
abominate /ə'bɒmə,neit/ *v.* abominar, detestar.
abomination /ə,bɒmə'neiʃən/ *n.* abominación *f.*
aboriginal /,æbə'rɪdʒənl/ *a. & n.* aborigen *f.*
abortion /ə'bɔrʃən/ *n.* aborto *m.*
abortive /ə'bɔrtɪv/ *a.* abortivo.

abound /ə'baund/ *v.* abundar.
about /ə'baut/ *adv.* **1.** como. **about to,** para; a punto de. —*prep.* **2.** de, sobre, acerca de.
about-face /ə'baut,feis, ə'baut'feis/ *n. Mil.* media vuelta.
above /ə'bʌv/ *adv.* **1.** arriba. —*prep.* **2.** sobre; por encima de.
aboveboard /ə'bʌv,bɔrd/ *a. & adv.* sincero, franco.
abrasion /ə'breiʒən/ *n.* raspadura *f.; Med.* abrasión *f.*
abrasive /ə'breisɪv/ *a.* raspante. *n.* abrasivo *m.*
abreast /ə'brɛst/ *adv.* de frente.
abridge /ə'brɪdʒ/ *v.* abreviar.
abridgment /ə'brɪdʒmənt/ *n.* abreviación *f.;* compendio *m.*
abroad /ə'brɔd/ *adv.* en el extranjero, al extranjero.
abrogate /'æbrə,geit/ *v.* abrogar, revocar.
abrogation /,æbrə'geiʃən/ *n.* abrogación, revocación *f.*
abrupt /ə'brʌpt/ *a.* repentino; brusco.
abruptly /ə'brʌptli/ *adv.* bruscamente, precipitadamente.
abruptness /ə'brʌptnɪs/ *n.* precipitación; brusquedad *f.*
abscess /'æbsɛs/ *n.* absceso *m.*
abscond /æb'skɒnd/ *v.* fugarse.
absence /'æbsəns/ *n.* ausencia, falta *f.*
absent /'æbsənt/ *a.* ausente.
absentee /,æbsən'ti/ *a. & n.* ausente *m. & f.*
absent-minded /'æbsənt 'maindɪd/ *a.* distraído.
absinthe /'æbsɪnθ/ *n.* absenta *f.*
absolute /'æbsə,lut/ *a.* absoluto.
absolutely /,æbsə'lutli/ *adv.* absolutamente.
absoluteness /,æbsə'lutnɪs/ *n.* absolutismo *m.*
absolution /,æbsə'luʃən/ *n.* absolución *f.*
absolutism /'æbsəlu,tɪzəm/ *n.* absolutismo, despotismo *m.*
absolve /æb'zɒlv/ *v.* absolver.
absorb /æb'sɔrb/ *v.* absorber; preocupar.
absorbed /æb'sɔrbd/ *a.* absorbido; absorto.
absorbent /æb'sɔrbənt/ *a.* absorbente.
absorbent cotton algodón hidrófilo *m.*
absorbing /æb'sɔrbɪŋ/ *a.* interesante.
absorption /æb'sɔrpʃən/ *n.* absorción; preocupación *f.*
abstain /æb'stein/ *v.* abstenerse.
abstemious /æb'stimiəs/ *a.* abstemio, sobrio.
abstinence /'æbstənəns/ *n.* abstinencia *f.*
abstract /*a, v* æb'strækt, 'æbstrækt; *n* 'æbstrækt/ *a.* **1.** abstracto. —*n.* **2.** resumen. —*v.* **3.** abstraer.
abstracted /æb'stræktɪd/ *a.* distraído.
abstraction /æb'strækʃən/ *n.* abstracción *f.*
abstruse /æb'strus/ *a.* abstruso.
absurd /æb'sɜrd/ *a.* absurdo, ridículo.
absurdity /æb'sɜrditi/ *n.* absurdo *m.*
absurdly /æb'sɜrdli/ *adv.* absurdamente.
abundance /ə'bʌndəns/ *n.* abundancia *f.*
abundant /ə'bʌndənt/ *a.* abundante.
abundantly /ə'bʌndəntli/ *adv.* abundantemente.
abuse /*n* ə'byus; *v* ə'byuz/ *n.* **1.** abuso *m.* —*v.* **2.** abusar de; maltratar.
abusive /ə'byusɪv/ *a.* abusivo.
abusively /ə'byusɪvli/ *adv.* abusivamente, ofensivamente.
abutment /ə'bʌtmənt/ *n.* (building) estribo, contrafuerte *m.*
abut (on) /ə'bʌt/ *v.* terminar (en); lindar (con).
abyss /ə'bɪs/ *n.* abismo *m.*
Abyssinian /,æbə'sɪniən/ *a. & n.* abisinio -nia.
acacia /ə'keiʃə/ *n.* acacia *f.*

academic /,ækə'dɛmɪk/ *a.* académico.
academy /ə'kædəmi/ *n.* academia *f.*
acanthus /ə'kænθəs/ *n. Bot.* acanto *m.*
accede /æk'sid/ *v.* acceder; consentir.
accelerate /æk'sɛlə,reit/ *v.* acelerar.
acceleration /æk,sɛlə'reiʃən/ *n.* aceleración *f.*
accelerator /æk'sɛlə,reitər/ *n. Auto.* acelerador *m.*
accent /'æksɛnt/ *n.* **1.** acento *m.* —*v.* **2.** acentuar.
accentuate /æk'sɛntʃu,eit/ *v.* acentuar.
accept /æk'sɛpt/ *v.* aceptar.
acceptability /æk,sɛptə'bɪliti/ *n.* aceptabilidad *f.*
acceptable /æk'sɛptəbəl/ *a.* aceptable.
acceptably /æk'sɛptəbli/ *adv.* aceptablemente.
acceptance /æk'sɛptəns/ *n.* aceptación *f.*
access /'æksɛs/ *n.* acceso *m.,* entrada *f.*
accessible /æk'sɛsəbəl/ *a.* accesible.
accessory /æk'sɛsəri/ *a.* **1.** accesorio. —*n.* **2.** cómplice *m. & f.*
accident /'æksɪdənt/ *n.* accidente *m.* **by a.,** por casualidad.
accidental /,æksɪ'dɛntl/ *a.* accidental.
accidentally /,æksɪ'dɛntli/ *adv.* accidentalmente, casualmente.
acclaim /ə'kleim/ *v.* aclamar.
acclamation /,æklə'meiʃən/ *n.* aclamación *f.*
acclimate /'æklə,meit/ *v.* aclimatar.
acclivity /ə'klɪvɪti/ *n.* subida *f.*
accolade /'ækə,leid/ *n.* acolada *f.*
accommodate /ə'kɒmə,deit/ *v.* acomodar.
accommodating /ə'kɒmə,deitɪŋ/ *a.* bondadoso, complaciente.
accommodation /ə,kɒmə'deiʃən/ *n.* servicio *m.;* (pl.) alojamiento *m.*
accompaniment /ə'kʌmpənimənt/ *n.* acompañamiento *m.*
accompanist /ə'kʌmpənɪst/ *n.* acompañante *m. & f.*
accompany /ə'kʌmpəni/ *v.* acompañar.
accomplice /ə'kɒmplɪs/ *n.* cómplice *m. & f.*
accomplish /ə'kɒmplɪʃ/ *v.* llevar a cabo; realizar.
accomplished /ə'kɒmplɪʃt/ *a.* acabado, cumplido; culto.
accomplishment /ə'kɒmplɪʃmənt/ *n.* realización *f.;* logro *m.*
accord /ə'kɔrd/ *n.* **1.** acuerdo *m.* —*v.* **2.** otorgar.
accordance /ə'kɔrdns/ *n.:* **in a. with,** de acuerdo con.
accordingly /ə'kɔrdɪŋli/ *adv.* en conformidad.
according to /ə'kɔrdɪŋ/ *prep.* según.
accordion /ə'kɔrdiən/ *n.* acordeón *m.*
accost /ə'kɒst/ *v.* dirigirse a.
account /ə'kaunt/ *n.* **1.** relato *m.; Com.* cuenta *f.* **on a. of,** a causa de. **on no a.,** de ninguna manera. —*v.* **2. a. for,** explicar.
accountable /ə'kauntəbəl/ *a.* responsable.
accountant /ə'kauntnt/ *n.* contador -ra.
accounting /ə'kauntɪŋ/ *n.* contabilidad *f.*
accouter /ə'kutər/ *v.* equipar, ataviar.
accouterments /ə'kutərmənts/ *n.* equipo, atavío *m.*
accredit /ə'krɛdɪt/ *v.* acreditar.
accretion /ə'kriʃən/ *n.* aumento *m.*
accrual /ə'kruəl/ *n.* aumento, incremento *m.*
accrue /ə'kru/ *v.* provenir; acumularse.
accumulate /ə'kyumyə,leit/ *v.* acumular.
accumulation /ə,kyumyə'leiʃən/ *n.* acumulación *f.*
accumulative /ə'kyumyə,leitɪv/ *a.* acumulativo.

accumulator /ə'kyumyə,leitər/ *n.* acumulador *m.*
accuracy /'ækyərəsi/ *n.* exactitud, precisión *f.*
accurate /'ækyərɪt/ *a.* exacto.
accursed /ə'kɜrsɪd, ə'kɜrst/ *a.* maldito.
accusation /,ækyu'zeiʃən/ *n.* acusación *f.,* cargo *m.*
accusative /ə'kyuzətɪv/ *a. & n.* acusativo *m.*
accuse /ə'kyuz/ *v.* acusar.
accused /ə'kyuzd/ *a. & n.* acusado -da, procesado -da.
accuser /ə'kyuzər/ *n.* acusador -ra.
accustom /ə'kʌstəm/ *v.* acostumbrar.
accustomed /ə'kʌstəmd/ *a.* acostumbrado.
ace /eis/ *a.* **1.** sobresaliente. —*n.* **2.** as *m.*
acerbity /ə'sɜrbiti/ *n.* acerbidad, amargura *f.*
acetate /'æsɪ,teit/ *n. Chem.* acetato *m.*
acetic /ə'sitɪk/ *a.* acético.
acetylene /ə'sɛtl,in/ *a.* **1.** acetilénico. —*n.* **2.** *Chem.* acetileno *m.*
ache /eik/ *n.* **1.** dolor *m.* —*v.* **2.** doler.
achieve /ə'tʃiv/ *v.* lograr, llevar a cabo.
achievement /ə'tʃivmənt/ *n.* realización *f.;* hecho notable *m.*
acid /'æsɪd/ *a. & n.* ácido *m.*
acidify /ə'sɪdə,fai/ *v.* acidificar.
acidity /ə'sɪdɪti/ *n.* acidez *f.*
acidosis /,æsɪ'dousɪs/ *n. Med.* acidismo *m.*
acid rain lluvia ácida *f.*
acid test prueba decisiva.
acidulous /ə'sɪdʒələs/ *a.* agrio, acídulo.
acknowledge /æk'nɒlɪdʒ/ *v.* admitir; (receipt) acusar.
acme /'ækmi/ *n.* apogeo, colmo *m.*
acne /'ækni/ *n. Med.* acné *m. & f.*
acolyte /'ækə,lait/ *n.* acólito *m.*
acorn /'eikɔrn/ *n.* bellota *f.*
acoustics /ə'kustɪks/ *n.* acústica *f.*
acquaint /ə'kweint/ *v.* familiarizar. **to be acquainted with,** conocer.
acquaintance /ə'kweintns/ *n.* conocimiento *m.;* (person known) conocido -da. **to make the a. of,** conocer.
acquiesce /,ækwi'ɛs/ *v.* consentir.
acquiescence /,ækwi'ɛsəns/ *n.* consentimiento *m.*
acquire /ə'kwaiər/ *v.* adquirir.
acquirement /ə'kwaiərmənt/ *n.* adquisición *f.;* (pl.) conocimientos *m.pl.*
acquisition /,ækwə'zɪʃən/ *n.* adquisición *f.*
acquisitive /ə'kwɪzɪtɪv/ *a.* adquisitivo.
acquit /ə'kwɪt/ *v.* exonerar, absolver.
acquittal /ə'kwɪtl/ *n.* absolución *f.*
acre /'eikər/ *n.* acre *m.*
acreage /'eikərɪdʒ/ *n.* número de acres.
acrid /'ækrɪd/ *a.* acre, punzante.
acrimonious /,ækrə'mouniəs/ *a.* acrimonioso, mordaz.
acrimony /'ækrə,mouni/ *n.* acrimonia, aspereza *f.*
acrobat /'ækrə,bæt/ *n.* acróbata *m. & f.*
acrobatic /,ækrə'bætɪk/ *a.* acrobático.
across /ə'krɔs/ *adv.* **1.** a través, al otro lado. —*prep.* **2.** al otro lado de, a través de.
acrostic /ə'krɔstɪk/ *n.* acróstico *m.*
act /ækt/ *n.* **1.** acción *f.;* acto *m.* —*v.* **2.** actuar, portarse. **act as,** hacer de. **act on,** decidir sobre.
acting /'æktɪŋ/ *a.* **1.** interino. —*n.* **2.** acción *f.; Theat.* representación *f.*
actinism /'æktə,nɪzəm/ *n.* actinismo *m.*
actinium /æk'tɪniəm/ *n. Chem.* actinio *m.*
action /'ækʃən/ *n.* acción *f.* **take a.,** tomar medidas.
action replay /'ri,plei/ repetición *f.*
activate /'æktə,veit/ *v.* activar.

activation /ˌæktəˈveiʃən/ *n.* activación *f.*
activator /ˈæktəˌveitər/ *n. Chem.* activador *m.*
active /ˈæktɪv/ *a.* activo.
activity /ækˈtɪvɪti/ *n.* actividad *f.*
actor /ˈæktər/ *n.* actor *m.*
actress /ˈæktrɪs/ *n.* actriz *f.*
actual /ˈæktʃuəl/ *a.* real, efectivo.
actuality /ˌæktʃuˈælɪti/ *n.* realidad, actualidad *f.*
actually /ˈæktʃuəli/ *adv.* en realidad.
actuary /ˈæktʃuˌɛri/ *n.* actuario *m.*
actuate /ˈæktʃuˌeit/ *v.* impulsar, mover.
acumen /əˈkyumən/ *n.* cacumen *m.*, perspicacia *f.*
acupuncture /ˈækyʊˌpʌŋktʃər/ *n.* acupuntura *f.*
acute /əˈkyut/ *a.* agudo; perspicaz.
acutely /əˈkyutli/ *adv.* agudamente.
acuteness /əˈkyutnɪs/ *n.* agudeza *f.*
adage /ˈædɪdʒ/ *n.* refrán, proverbio *m.*
adamant /ˈædəmənt/ *a.* firme.
Adam's apple /ˈædəmz/ nuez de la garganta.
adapt /əˈdæpt/ *v.* adaptar.
adaptability /əˌdæptəˈbɪlɪti/ *n.* adaptabilidad *f.*
adaptable /əˈdæptəbəl/ *a.* adaptable.
adaptation /ˌædəpˈteiʃən/ *n.* adaptación *f.*
adapter /əˈdæptər/ *n. Elec.* adaptador *m.; Mech.* ajustador *m.*
adaptive /əˈdæptɪv/ *a.* adaptable, acomodable.
add /æd/ *v.* agregar, añadir. **a. up,** sumar.
adder /ˈædər/ *n.* víbora; serpiente *f.*
addict /ˈædɪkt/ *n.* adicto -ta; (fan) aficionado -da.
addition /əˈdɪʃən/ *n.* adición *f.* **in a. to,** además de.
additional /əˈdɪʃənl̩/ *a.* adicional.
addle /ˈædl̩/ *v.* confundir.
address /*n* əˈdrɛs, ˈædrɛs; *v* əˈdrɛs/ *n.* **1.** dirección *f.*; señas *f.pl.*; (speech) discurso. —*v.* **2.** dirigirse a.
addressee /ˌædrɛˈsi/ *n.* destinatario -ia.
adduce /əˈdus/ *v.* aducir.
adenoid /ˈædn̩ˌɔid/ *a.* adenoidea.
adept /əˈdɛpt/ *a.* adepto.
adeptly /əˈdɛptli/ *adv.* diestramente.
adeptness /əˈdɛptnɪs/ *n.* destreza *f.*
adequacy /ˈædɪkwəsi/ *n.* suficiencia *f.*
adequate /ˈædɪkwɪt/ *a.* adecuado.
adequately /ˈædɪkwɪtli/ *adv.* adecuadamente.
adhere /ædˈhɪər/ *v.* adherirse, pegarse.
adherence /ædˈhɪərəns/ *n.* adhesión *f.*; apego *m.*
adherent /ædˈhɪərənt/ *n.* adherente *m.*, partidario -ria.
adhesion /ædˈhiʒən/ *n.* adhesión *f.*
adhesive /ædˈhisɪv/ *a.* adhesivo. **a. tape,** esparadrapo *m.*
adhesiveness /ædˈhisɪvnɪs/ *n.* adhesividad *f.*
adieu /əˈdu/ *interj.* **1.** adiós. —*n.* **2.** despedida *f.*
adjacent /əˈdʒeisənt/ *a.* adyacente.
adjective /ˈædʒɪktɪv/ *n.* adjetivo *m.*
adjoin /əˈdʒɔin/ *v.* lindar (con).
adjoining /əˈdʒɔinɪŋ/ *a.* contiguo.
adjourn /əˈdʒɜrn/ *v.* suspender, levantar.
adjournment /əˈdʒɜrnmənt/ *n.* suspensión *f.*; *Leg.* espera *f.*
adjunct /ˈædʒʌŋkt/ *n.* adjunto *m.*; *Gram.* atributo *m.*
adjust /əˈdʒʌst/ *v.* ajustar, acomodar; arreglar.
adjuster /əˈdʒʌstər/ *n.* ajustador -ra.
adjustment /əˈdʒʌstmənt/ *n.* ajuste; arreglo *m.*
adjutant /ˈædʒətənt/ *n. Mil.* ayudante *m.*
administer /ædˈmɪnəstər/ *v.* administrar.
administration /ædˌmɪnəˈstreiʃən/ *n.* administración *f.*; gobierno *m.*
administrative /ædˈmɪnəˌstreitɪv/ *a.* administrativo.
administrator /ædˈmɪnəˌstreitər/ *n.* administrador -ra.
admirable /ˈædmərəbəl/ *a.* admirable.
admirably /ˈædmərəbli/ *adv.* admirablemente.
admiral /ˈædmərəl/ *n.* almirante *m.*
admiralty /ˈædmərəlti/ *n.* Ministerio de Marina.
admiration /ˌædməˈreiʃən/ *n.* admiración *f.*
admire /ædˈmaiᵊr/ *v.* admirar.
admirer /ædˈmaiᵊrər/ *n.* admirador -ra; enamorado -da.
admiringly /ædˈmaiᵊrɪŋli/ *adv.* admirativamente.
admissible /ædˈmɪsəbəl/ *a.* admisible, aceptable.
admission /ædˈmɪʃən/ *n.* admisión; entrada *f.*
admit /ædˈmɪt/ *v.* admitir.
admittance /ædˈmɪtn̩s/ *n.* entrada *f.*
admittedly /ædˈmɪtɪdli/ *adv.* reconocidamente.
admixture /ædˈmɪkstʃər/ *n.* mezcla *f.*
admonish /ædˈmɒnɪʃ/ *v.* amonestar.
admonition /ˌædməˈnɪʃən/ *n.* admonición *f.*
adolescence /ˌædl̩ˈɛsəns/ *n.* adolescencia *f.*
adolescent /ˌædl̩ˈɛsənt/ *n.* & *a.* adolescente.
adopt /əˈdɒpt/ *v.* adoptar.
adopted child /əˈdɒptɪd/ hija adoptiva *f.*, hijo adoptivo *m.*
adoption /əˈdɒpʃən/ *n.* adopción *f.*
adorable /əˈdɔrəbəl/ *a.* adorable.
adoration /ˌædəˈreiʃən/ *n.* adoración *f.*
adore /əˈdɔr/ *v.* adorar.
adorn /əˈdɔrn/ *v.* adornar.
adornment /əˈdɔrnmənt/ *n.* adorno *m.*
adrenalin /əˈdrɛnl̩ɪn/ *n.* adrenalina *f.*
adrift /əˈdrɪft/ *adv.* a la ventura.
adroit /əˈdrɔit/ *a.* diestro.
adulate /ˈædʒəˌleit/ *v.* adular.
adulation /ˌædʒəˈleiʃən/ *n.* adulación *f.*
adult /əˈdʌlt/ *a.* & *n.* adulto -a.
adulterant /əˈdʌltərənt/ *a.* & *n.* adulterante *m.*
adulterate /əˈdʌltəˌreit/ *v.* adulterar.
adulterer /əˈdʌltərər/ *n.* adúltero -ra.
adulteress /əˈdʌltərɪs/ *n.* adúltera *f.*
adultery /əˈdʌltəri/ *n.* adulterio *m.*
advance /ædˈvæns/ *n.* **1.** avance; adelanto *m.* **in a.,** de antemano, antes. —*v.* **2.** avanzar, adelantar.
advanced /ædˈvænst/ *a.* avanzado, adelantado.
advancement /ædˈvænsmənt/ *n.* adelantamiento *m.*; promoción *f.*
advantage /ædˈvæntɪdʒ/ *n.* ventaja *f.* **take a. of,** aprovecharse de.
advantageous /ˌædvənˈteidʒəs/ *a.* provechoso, ventajoso.
advantageously /ˌædvənˈteidʒəsli/ *adv.* ventajosamente.
advent /ˈædvɛnt/ *n.* venida, llegada *f.*
adventitious /ˌædvənˈtɪʃəs/ *a.* adventicio, espontáneo.
adventure /ædˈvɛntʃər/ *n.* aventura *f.*
adventurer /ædˈvɛntʃərər/ *n.* aventurero -ra.
adventurous /ædˈvɛntʃərəs/ *a.* aventurero, intrépido.
adventurously /ædˈvɛntʃərəsli/ *adv.* arriesgadamente.
adverb /ˈædvɜrb/ *n.* adverbio *m.*
adverbial /ædˈvɜrbiəl/ *a.* adverbial.
adversary /ˈædvərˌsɛri/ *n.* adversario -a.
adverse /ædˈvɜrs/ *a.* adverso.
adversely /ædˈvɜrsli/ *adv.* adversamente.
adversity /ædˈvɜrsɪti/ *n.* adversidad *f.*
advert /ædˈvɜrt/ *v.* hacer referencia a.
advertise /ˈædvərˌtaiz/ *v.* avisar, anunciar; (promote) promocionar.
advertisement /ˌædvərˈtaizmənt, ædˈvɜrtɪsmənt/ *n.* aviso, anuncio *m.*
advertiser /ˈædvərˌtaizər/ *n.* anunciante *m.* & *f.*, avisador -ra.
advertising /ˈædvərˌtaizɪŋ/ *n.* publicidad *f.*
advice /ædˈvais/ *n.* consejos *m.pl.*
advisability /ædˌvaizəˈbɪlɪti/ *n.* prudencia, propiedad *f.*
advisable /ædˈvaizəbəl/ *a.* aconsejable, prudente.
advisably /ædˈvaizəbli/ *adv.* prudentemente.
advise /ædˈvaiz/ *v.* aconsejar. **a. against,** desaconsejar.
advisedly /ædˈvaizɪdli/ *adv.* avisadamente, prudentemente.
advisement /ædˈvaizmənt/ *n.* consideración *f.*; **take under a.,** someter a estudio.
adviser /ædˈvaizər/ *n.* consejero -ra.
advocacy /ˈædvəkəsi/ *n.* abogacía; defensa *f.*
advocate /*n* ˈædvəkɪt; *v* -ˌkeit/ *n.* **1.** abogado -da. —*v.* **2.** apoyar.
aegis /ˈidʒɪs/ *n.* amparo *m.*
aerate /ˈɛəreit/ *v.* airear, ventilar.
aeration /ˌɛəˈreiʃən/ *n.* aeración, ventilación *f.*
aerial /ˈɛəriəl/ *a.* aéreo.
aerie /ˈɛəri/ *n.* nido de águila.
aeronautics /ˌɛərəˈnɔtɪks/ *n.* aeronáutica *f.*
aerosol bomb /ˈɛərəˌsɔl/ bomba insecticida.
afar /əˈfɑr/ *adv.* lejos. **from a.,** de lejos, desde lejos.
affability /ˌæfəˈbɪlɪti/ *n.* afabilidad, amabilidad *f.*
affable /ˈæfəbəl/ *a.* afable.
affably /ˈæfəbli/ *adv.* afablemente.
affair /əˈfɛər/ *n.* asunto *m.* **love a.,** aventura amorosa.
affect /əˈfɛkt/ *v.* afectar; (emotionally) conmover.
affectation /ˌæfɛkˈteiʃən/ *n.* afectación *f.*
affected /əˈfɛktɪd/ *a.* artificioso.
affecting /əˈfɛktɪŋ/ *a.* conmovedor.
affection /əˈfɛkʃən/ *n.* cariño *m.*
affectionate /əˈfɛkʃənɪt/ *a.* afectuoso, cariñoso.
affectionately /əˈfɛkʃənɪtli/ *adv.* afectuosamente, con cariño.
affiance /əˈfaiəns/ *v.* dar palabra de casamiento; **become affianced,** comprometerse.
affidavit /ˌæfɪˈdeivɪt/ *n. Leg.* declaración, deposición *f.*
affiliate /*n* əˈfɪliˌɪt; *v* əˈfɪliˌeit/ *n.* **1.** afiliado -da. —*v.* **2.** afiliar.
affiliation /əˌfɪliˈeiʃən/ *n.* afiliación *f.*
affinity /əˈfɪnɪti/ *n.* afinidad *f.*
affirm /əˈfɜrm/ *v.* afirmar.
affirmation /ˌæfərˈmeiʃən/ *n.* afirmación, aserción *f.*
affirmative /əˈfɜrmətɪv/ *n.* **1.** afirmativa *f.* —*a.* **2.** afirmativo.
affirmatively /əˈfɜrmətɪvli/ *adv.* afirmativamente, aseveradamente.
affix /*n* ˈæfɪks; *v* əˈfɪks/ *n.* **1.** *Gram.* afijo *m.* —*v.* **2.** fijar, pegar, poner.
afflict /əˈflɪkt/ *v.* afligir.
affliction /əˈflɪkʃən/ *n.* aflicción *f.*; mal *m.*
affluence /ˈæfluəns/ *n.* abundancia, opulencia *f.*
affluent /ˈæfluənt/ *a.* opulento, afluente.
afford /əˈfɔrd/ *v.* proporcionar. **be able to a.,** tener con que comprar.
affordable /əˈfɔrdəbəl/ *a.* asequible.
affront /əˈfrʌnt/ *n.* **1.** afrenta *f.* —*v.* **2.** afrentar, insultar.
afield /əˈfild/ *adv.* lejos de casa; lejos del camino; lejos del asunto.
afire /əˈfaiᵊr/ *adv.* ardiendo.
afloat /əˈflout/ *adv. Naut.* a flote.
aforementioned /əˈfɔrˌmɛnʃənd/ *a.* dicho, susodicho.
afraid /əˈfreid/ *a.* **to be a.,** tener miedo, temer.
African /ˈæfrɪkən/ *n.* & *a.* africano -na.
aft /æft/ *adv. Naut.* a popa, en popa.
after /ˈæftər/ *prep.* **1.** después de. —*conj.* **2.** después que.
aftermath /ˈæftərˌmæθ/ *n.* resultados *m.pl.*, consecuencias *f.pl.*
afternoon /ˌæftərˈnun/ *n.* tarde *f.* **good a.,** buenas tardes.
aftertaste /ˈæftərˌteist/ *n.* gustillo *m.*
afterthought /ˈæftərˌθɔt/ *n.* idea tardía.
afterward(s) /ˈæftərwərdz/ *adv.* después.
again /əˈgɛn/ *adv.* otra vez, de nuevo. **to do a.,** volver a hacer.
against /əˈgɛnst/ *prep.* contra; en contra de.
agape /əˈgeip/ *adv.* con la boca abierta.
agate /ˈægɪt/ *n.* ágata *f.*
age /eidʒ/ *n.* **1.** edad *f.* **of a.,** mayor de edad. **old a.,** vejez *f.* —*v.* **2.** envejecer.
aged /eidʒd; ˈeidʒɪd/ *a.* viejo, anciano, añejo.
ageism /ˈeidʒɪzəm/ *n.* discriminación contra las personas de edad.
ageless /ˈeidʒlɪs/ *a.* sempiterno.
agency /ˈeidʒənsi/ *n.* agencia *f.*
agenda /əˈdʒɛndə/ *n.* agenda *f.*, orden *m.*
agent /ˈeidʒənt/ *n.* agente; representante *m.* & *f.*
agglutinate /əˈglutn̩ˌeit/ *v.* aglutinar.
agglutination /əˌglutn̩ˈeiʃən/ *n.* aglutinación *f.*
aggrandize /əˈgrændaiz/ *v.* agrandar; elevar.
aggrandizement /əˈgrændɪzmənt/ *n.* engrandecimiento *m.*
aggravate /ˈægrəˌveit/ *v.* agravar; irritar.
aggravation /ˌægrəˈveiʃən/ *n.* agravamiento; empeoramiento *m.*
aggregate /ˈægrɪgɪt, -ˌgeit/ *a.* & *n.* agregado *m.*
aggregation /ˌægrɪˈgeiʃən/ *n.* agregación *f.*
aggression /əˈgrɛʃən/ *n.* agresión *f.*
aggressive /əˈgrɛsɪv/ *a.* agresivo.
aggressively /əˈgrɛsɪvli/ *adv.* agresivamente.
aggressiveness /əˈgrɛsɪvnɪs/ *n.* agresividad *f.*
aggressor /əˈgrɛsər/ *n.* agresor -ra.
aghast /əˈgæst/ *a.* horrorizado.
agile /ˈædʒəl/ *a.* ágil.
agility /æˈdʒɪlɪti/ *n.* agilidad, ligereza, prontitud *f.*
agitate /ˈædʒɪˌteit/ *v.* agitar.
agitation /ˌædʒɪˈteiʃən/ *n.* agitación *f.*
agitator /ˈædʒɪˌteitər/ *n.* agitador -ra.
agnostic /ægˈnɒstɪk/ *a.* & *n.* agnóstico -ca.
ago /əˈgou/ *adv.* hace. **two days a.,** hace dos días.
agonized /ˈægəˌnaizd/ *a.* angustioso.
agony /ˈægəni/ *n.* sufrimiento *m.*; angustia *f.*
agrarian /əˈgrɛəriən/ *a.* agrario.
agree /əˈgri/ *v.* estar de acuerdo; convenir. **a. with one,** sentar bien.
agreeable /əˈgriəbəl/ *a.* agradable.
agreeably /əˈgriəbli/ *adv.* agradablemente.
agreement /əˈgrimənt/ *n.* acuerdo *m.*
agriculture /ˈægrɪˌkʌltʃər/ *n.* agricultura *f.*
ahead /əˈhɛd/ *adv.* adelante.
aid /eid/ *n.* **1.** ayuda *f.* —*v.* **2.** ayudar.
aide /eid/ *n.* ayudante -ta.
AIDS /eidz/ *n.* SIDA *m.*
ailing /ˈeilɪŋ/ *adj.* enfermo.
ailment /ˈeilmənt/ *n.* enfermedad *f.*
aim /eim/ *n.* **1.** puntería *f.*; (purpose) propósito *m.* —*v.* **2.** apuntar.
aimless /ˈeimlɪs/ *a.* sin objeto.
air /ɛər/ *n.* **1.** aire *m.* **by a.** por avión. —*v.* **2.** ventilar, airear.

airbag /ˈɛərˌbæg/ *n.* (in automobiles) saco de aire *m.*
air-conditioned /ˈɛər kənˌdɪʃənd/ *a.* con aire acondicionado.
air-conditioning /ɛər kənˌdɪʃənɪŋ/ acondicionamiento del aire.
aircraft /ˈɛərˌkræft/ *n.* avión *m.*
aircraft carrier portaaviones *m.*
airfare /ˈɛərˌfɛər/ *n.* precio del billete de avión *m.*
airing /ˈɛərɪŋ/ *n.* ventilación *f.*
airline /ˈɛərˌlain/ *n.* línea aérea *f.*
airliner /ˈɛərˌlainər/ *n.* avión de pasajeros.
airmail /ˈɛərˌmeil/ *n.* correo aéreo.
airplane /ˈɛərˌplein/ *n.* avión, aeroplano *m.*
air pollution contaminación atmosférica, contaminación del aire.
airport /ˈɛərˌpɔrt/ *n.* aeropuerto *m.*
air pressure presión atmosférica.
air raid ataque aéreo.
airsick /ˈɛərˌsɪk/ *a.* mareado.
air terminal terminal aérea *f.*
airtight /ˈɛərˌtait/ *a.* hermético.
air traffic controller controlador aéreo *m.*
aisle /ail/ *n.* pasillo *m.*
ajar /əˈdʒɑr/ *a.* entreabierto.
akin /əˈkɪn/ *a.* emparentado, semejante.
alacrity /əˈlækrɪti/ *n.* alacridad, presteza *f.*
alarm /əˈlɑrm/ *n.* **1.** alarma *f.* —*v.* **2.** alarmar.
alarmist /əˈlɑrmɪst/ *n.* alarmista *m.* & *f.*
albino /ælˈbainou/ *n.* albino -na.
album /ˈælbəm/ *n.* álbum *m.*
alcohol /ˈælkəˌhɔl/ *n.* alcohol *m.*
alcoholic /ˌælkəˈhɔlɪk/ *a.* alcohólico.
alcove /ˈælkouv/ *n.* alcoba *f.*
ale /eil/ *n.* cerveza inglesa.
alert /əˈlɜrt/ *n.* **1.** alarma *f.* **on the a.,** alerta, sobre aviso. —*a.* **2.** listo, vivo. —*v.* **3.** poner sobre aviso.
alfalfa /ælˈfælfə/ *n.* alfalfa *f.*
algebra /ˈældʒəbrə/ *n.* álgebra *f.*
alias /ˈeiliəs/ *n.* alias *m.*
alibi /ˈæləˌbai/ *n.* excusa *f.*; *Leg.* coartada *f.*
alien /ˈeiliən/ *a.* **1.** ajeno, extranjero. —*n.* **2.** extranjero -ra.
alienate /ˈeiliəˌneit/ *v.* enajenar.
alight /əˈlait/ *v.* bajar, apearse.
align /əˈlain/ *v.* alinear.
alike /əˈlaik/ *a.* **1.** semejante, igual. —*adv.* **2.** del mismo modo, igualmente.
alimentary canal /ˌæləˈmɛntəri/ *n.* tubo digestivo *m.*
alive /əˈlaiv/ *a.* vivo; animado.
alkali /ˈælkəˌlai/ *n.* *Chem.* álcali, cali *m.*
alkaline /ˈælkəˌlain/ *a.* alcalino.
all /ɔl/ *a.* & *pron.* todo. **not at a.,** de ninguna manera, nada.
allay /əˈlei/ *v.* aquietar.
allegation /ˌælɪˈgeiʃən/ *n.* alegación *f.*
allege /əˈlɛdʒ/ *v.* alegar; pretender.
allegiance /əˈlidʒəns/ *n.* lealtad *f.*; (to country) homenaje *m.*
allegory /ˈæləˌgɔri/ *n.* alegoría *f.*
allergy /ˈælərdʒi/ *n.* alergia *f.*
alleviate /əˈliviˌeit/ *v.* aliviar.
alley /ˈæli/ *n.* callejón *m.* **bowling a.,** bolera *f.*, boliche *m.*
alliance /əˈlaiəns/ *n.* alianza *f.*
allied /ˈælaid/ *a.* aliado.
alligator /ˈælɪˌgeitər/ *n.* caimán *m.*; (Mex.) lagarto *m.* **a. pear,** aguacate *m.*
allocate /ˈæləˌkeit/ *v.* colocar, asignar.
allot /əˈlɒt/ *v.* asignar.
allotment /əˈlɒtmənt/ *n.* lote, porción *f.*
allow /əˈlau/ *v.* permitir, dejar.
allowance /əˈlauəns/ *n.* abono *m.*; dieta *f.* **make a. for,** tener en cuenta.
alloy /ˈælɔi/ *n.* mezcla *f.*; (metal) aleación *f.*
all right está bien.
allude /əˈlud/ *v.* aludir.
allure /əˈlʊr/ *n.* **1.** atracción *f.* —*v.* **2.** atraer, tentar.
alluring /əˈlʊrɪŋ/ *a.* tentador, seductivo.
allusion /əˈluʒən/ *n.* alusión *f.*
ally /*n* ˈælai, *v* əˈlai/ *n.* **1.** aliado -da. —*v.* **2.** aliar.
almanac /ˈɔlməˌnæk/ *n.* almanaque *m.*
almighty /ɔlˈmaiti/ *a.* todopoderoso.
almond /ˈɑmənd/ *n.* almendra *f.*
almost /ˈɔlmoust/ *adv.* casi.
alms /ɑmz/ *n.* limosna *f.*
aloft /əˈlɔft/ *adv.* arriba, en alto.
alone /əˈloun/ *adv.* solo, a solas. **to leave a.,** dejar en paz.
along /əˈlɔŋ/ *prep.* por; a lo largo de. **a. with,** junto con.
alongside /əˈlɔŋˈsaid/ *adv.* **1.** al lado. —*prep.* **2.** junto a.
aloof /əˈluf/ *a.* apartado.
aloud /əˈlaud/ *adv.* en voz alta.
alpaca /ælˈpækə/ *n.* alpaca *f.*
alphabet /ˈælfəˌbɛt/ *n.* alfabeto *m.*
alphabetical /ˌælfəˈbɛtɪkəl/ *a.* alfabético.
alphabetize /ˈælfəbɪˌtaiz/ *v.* alfabetizar.
already /ɔlˈrɛdi/ *adv.* ya.
also /ˈɔlsou/ *adv.* también.
altar /ˈɔltər/ *n.* altar *m.*
alter /ˈɔltər/ *v.* alterar.
alteration /ˌɔltəˈreiʃən/ *n.* alteración *f.*
alternate /*a, n* ˈɔltərnɪt; *v* -ˌneit/ *a.* **1.** alterno. —*n.* **2.** substituto -ta. —*v.* **3.** alternar.
alternative /ɔlˈtɜrnətɪv/ *a.* **1.** alternativo. —*n.* **2.** alternativa *f.*
although /ɔlˈðou/ *conj.* aunque.
altitude /ˈæltɪˌtud/ *n.* altura *f.*
alto /ˈæltou/ *n.* contralto *m.*
altogether /ˌɔltəˈgɛðər/ *adv.* en junto; enteramente.
altruism /ˈæltruˌɪzəm/ *n.* altruismo *m.*
alum /ˈæləm/ *n.* alumbre *m.*
aluminum /əˈlumənəm/ *n.* aluminio *m.*
aluminum foil papel de aluminio *m.*
always /ˈɔlweiz/ *adv.* siempre.
amalgam /əˈmælgəm/ *n.* amalgama *f.*
amalgamate /əˈmælgəˌmeit/ *v.* amalgamar.
amass /əˈmæs/ *v.* amontonar.
amateur /ˈæməˌtʃʊr/ *n.* aficionado -da.
amaze /əˈmeiz/ *v.* asombrar; sorprender.
amazement /əˈmeizmənt/ *n.* asombro *m.*
amazing /əˈmeizɪŋ/ *a.* asombroso, pasmoso.
ambassador /æmˈbæsədər/ *n.* embajador -ra.
amber /ˈæmbər/ *a.* **1.** ambarino. —*n.* **2.** ámbar *m.*
ambidextrous /ˌæmbɪˈdɛkstrəs/ *a.* ambidextro.
ambiguity /ˌæmbɪˈgyuɪti/ *n.* ambigüedad *f.*
ambiguous /æmˈbɪgyuəs/ *a.* ambiguo.
ambition /æmˈbɪʃən/ *n.* ambición *f.*
ambitious /æmˈbɪʃəs/ *a.* ambicioso.
ambulance /ˈæmbyələns/ *n.* ambulancia *f.*
ambush /ˈæmbʊʃ/ *n.* **1.** emboscada *f.* —*v.* **2.** acechar.
ameliorate /əˈmilyəˌreit/ *v.* mejorar.
amenable /əˈminəbəl/ *a.* tratable, dócil.
amend /əˈmɛnd/ *v.* enmendar.
amendment /əˈmɛndmənt/ *n.* enmienda *f.*
amenity /əˈmɛnɪti/ *n.* amenidad *f.*
American /əˈmɛrɪkən/ *a.* & *n.* americano -na, norteamericano -na.
amethyst /ˈæməθɪst/ *n.* amatista *f.*
amiable /ˈeimiəbəl/ *a.* amable.
amicable /ˈæmɪkəbəl/ *a.* amigable.
amid /əˈmɪd/ *prep.* entre, en medio de.
amidships /əˈmɪdˌʃɪps/ *adv.* *Naut.* en medio del navío.
amiss /əˈmɪs/ *adv.* mal. **to take a.,** llevar a mal.
amity /ˈæmɪti/ *n.* amistad, armonía *f.*
ammonia /əˈmounyə/ *n.* amoníaco *m.*
ammunition /ˌæmyəˈnɪʃən/ *n.* municiones *f.pl.*
amnesia /æmˈniʒə/ *n.* amnesia *f.*
amnesty /ˈæmnəsti/ *n.* amnistía *f.*, indulto *m.*
amniocentesis /ˌæmniousɛnˈtisɪs/ *n.* amniocéntesis *f.*
amoeba /əˈmibə/ *n.* amiba *f.*
among /əˈmʌŋ/ *prep.* entre.
amoral /eiˈmɔrəl/ *a.* amoral.
amorous /ˈæmərəs/ *a.* amoroso.
amorphous /əˈmɔrfəs/ *a.* amorfo.
amortize /ˈæmərˌtaiz/ *v.* *Com.* amortizar.
amount /əˈmaunt/ *n.* **1.** cantidad, suma *f.* —*v.* **2. a. to,** subir a.
ampere /ˈæmpɪər/ *n.* *Elec.* amperio *m.*
amphibian /æmˈfɪbiən/ *a.* & *n.* anfibio *m.*
amphitheater /ˈæmfəˌθiətər/ *n.* anfiteatro, circo *m.*
ample /ˈæmpəl/ *a.* amplio; suficiente.
amplify /ˈæmpləˌfai/ *v.* amplificar.
amputate /ˈæmpyʊˌteit/ *v.* amputar.
amuse /əˈmyuz/ *v.* entretener, divertir.
amusement /əˈmyuzmənt/ *n.* diversión *f.*
an /ən, *when stressed* an/ *art.* un, una.
anachronism /əˈnækrəˌnɪzəm/ *n.* anacronismo, *m.*
analogous /əˈnæləgəs/ *a.* análogo, parecido.
analogy /əˈnælədʒi/ *n.* analogía *f.*
analysis /əˈnæləsɪs/ *n.* análisis *m.*
analyst /ˈænl̩ɪst/ *n.* analista *m.* & *f.*
analytic /ˌænl̩ˈɪtɪk/ *a.* analítico.
analyze /ˈænl̩ˌaiz/ *v.* analizar.
anarchy /ˈænərki/ *n.* anarquía *f.*
anatomy /əˈnætəmi/ *n.* anatomía *f.*
ancestor /ˈænsɛstər/ *n.* antepasado *m.*
ancestral /ænˈsɛstrəl/ *a.* de los antepasados, hereditario.
ancestry /ˈænsɛstri/ *n.* linaje, abolengo *m.*
anchor /ˈæŋkər/ *n.* **1.** ancla *f.* **weigh a.,** levar el ancla. —*v.* **2.** anclar.
anchorage /ˈæŋkərɪdʒ/ *n.* *Naut.* ancladero, anclaje *m.*
anchovy /ˈæntʃouvi/ *n.* anchoa *f.*
ancient /ˈeinʃənt/ *a.* & *n.* antiguo -ua.
and /ænd, ənd/ *conj.* y, (before *i-*, *hi-*) e.
anecdote /ˈænɪkˌdout/ *n.* anécdota *f.*
anemia /əˈnimiə/ *n.* *Med.* anemia *f.*
anesthetic /ˌænəsˈθɛtɪk/ *n.* anestesia *f.*
anew /əˈnu/ *adv.* de nuevo.
angel /ˈeindʒəl/ *n.* ángel *m.*
anger /ˈæŋgər/ *n.* **1.** ira *f.*, enojo *m.* —*v.* **2.** enfadar, enojar.
angle /ˈæŋgəl/ *n.* ángulo *m.*
angry /ˈæŋgri/ *a.* enojado, enfadado.
anguish /ˈæŋgwɪʃ/ *n.* angustia *f.*
angular /ˈæŋgyələr/ *a.* angular.
aniline /ˈænl̩ɪn/ *n.* *Chem.* anilina *f.*
animal /ˈænəməl/ *a.* & *n.* animal *m.*
animate /*v* ˈænəˌmeit; *a* -mɪt/ *v.* **1.** animar. —*a.* **2.** animado.
animated /ˈænəˌmeitɪd/ *a.* vivo, animado.
animation /ˌænəˈmeiʃən/ *n.* animación, viveza *f.*
animosity /ˌænəˈmɒsɪti/ *n.* rencor *m.*
anise /ˈænɪs/ *n.* anís *m.*
ankle /ˈæŋkəl/ *n.* tobillo *m.*
annals /ˈænl̩z/ *n.pl.* anales *m.pl.*
annex /*n* ˈænɛks; *v* əˈnɛks, ˈænɛks/ *n.* **1.** anexo *m.*, adición *f.* —*v.* **2.** anexar.
annexation /ˌænɪkˈseiʃən/ *n.* anexión, adición *f.*
annihilate /əˈnaiəˌleit/ *v.* aniquilar, destruir.
anniversary /ˌænəˈvɜrsəri/ *n.* aniversario *m.*
annotate /ˈænəˌteit/ *v.* anotar.
annotation /ˌænəˈteiʃən/ *n.* anotación *f.*, apunte *m.*
announce /əˈnauns/ *v.* anunciar.
announcement /əˈnaunsmənt/ *n.* anuncio, aviso *m.*
announcer /əˈnaunsər/ *n.* anunciador -ra; (radio) locutor -ra.
annoy /əˈnɔi/ *v.* molestar.
annoyance /əˈnɔiəns/ *n.* molestia, incomodidad *f.*
annual /ˈænyuəl/ *a.* anual.
annuity /əˈnuɪti/ *n.* anualidad, pensión *f.*
annul /əˈnʌl/ *v.* anular, invalidar.
anode /ˈænoud/ *n.* *Elec.* ánodo *m.*
anoint /əˈnɔint/ *v.* untar; *Relig.* ungir.
anomalous /əˈnɒmələs/ *a.* anómalo, irregular.
anonymous /əˈnɒnəməs/ *a.* anónimo.
anorexia /ˌænəˈrɛksiə/ *n.* anorexia *f.*
another /əˈnʌðər/ *a.* & *pron.* otro.
answer /ˈænsər, ˈɑn-/ *n.* **1.** contestación, respuesta *f.* —*v.* **2.** contestar, responder. **a. for,** ser responsable de.
answerable /ˈænsərəbəl/ *a.* discutible, refutable.
answering machine /ˈænsərɪŋ/ contestador automático *m.*
ant /ænt/ *n.* hormiga *f.*
antacid /æntˈæsɪd/ *a.* & *n.* antiácido *m.*
antagonism /ænˈtægəˌnɪzəm/ *n.* antagonismo *m.*
antagonist /ænˈtægənɪst/ *n.* antagonista *m.* & *f.*
antagonistic /ænˌtægəˈnɪstɪk/ *a.* antagónico, hostil.
antagonize /ænˈtægəˌnaiz/ *v.* contrariar.
antarctic /æntˈɑrktɪk/ *a.* & *n.* antártico *m.*
antecedent /ˌæntəˈsidn̩t/ *a.* & *n.* antecedente *m.*
antedate /ˈæntɪˌdeit/ *v.* antedatar.
antelope /ˈæntl̩ˌoup/ *n.* antílope *m.*, gacela *f.*
antenna /ænˈtɛnə/ *n.* antena *f.*
antepenultimate /ˌæntipɪˈnʌltəmɪt/ *a.* antepenúltimo.
anterior /ænˈtɪəriər/ *a.* anterior.
anteroom /ˈæntiˌrum/ *n.* antecámara *f.*
anthem /ˈænθəm/ *n.* himno *m.*; (religious) antífona *f.*
anthology /ænˈθɒlədʒi/ *n.* antología *f.*
anthracite /ˈænθrəˌsait/ *n.* antracita *f.*
anthrax /ˈænθræks/ *n.* *Med.* ántrax *m.*
anthropology /ˌænθrəˈpɒlədʒi/ *n.* antropología *f.*
antiaircraft /ˌæntiˈɛərˌkræft, ˌæntai-/ *a.* antiaéreo.
antibody /ˈæntɪˌbɒdi/ *n.* anticuerpo *m.*
anticipate /ænˈtɪsəˌpeit/ *v.* esperar, anticipar.
anticipation /ænˌtɪsəˈpeiʃən/ *n.* anticipación *f.*
anticlerical /ˌæntiˈklɛrɪkəl, ˌæntai-/ *a.* anticlerical.
anticlimax /ˌæntiˈklaimæks, ˌæntai-/ *n.* anticlímax *m.*
antidote /ˈæntɪˌdout/ *n.* antídoto *m.*
antifreeze /ˈæntɪˌfriz/ *n.* anticongelante *m.*
antihistamine /ˌæntiˈhɪstəˌmin, -mɪn, ˌæntai-/ *n.* antihistamínico *m.*
antimony /ˈæntəˌmouni/ *n.* antimonio *m.*
antinuclear /ˌæntiˈnukliər, æntai-/ *a.* antinuclear.
antipathy /ænˈtɪpəθi/ *n.* antipatía *f.*
antiquated /ˈæntɪˌkweitɪd/ *a.* anticuado.
antique /ænˈtik/ *a.* **1.** antiguo. —*n.* **2.** antigüedad *f.*
antiquity /ænˈtɪkwɪti/ *n.* antigüedad *f.*
antiseptic /ˌæntəˈsɛptɪk/ *a.* & *n.* antiséptico *m.*
antisocial /ˌæntiˈsouʃəl, ˌæntai-/ *a.* antisocial.

antitoxin /ˌæntɪˈtɒksɪn/ *n. Med.* antitoxina *f.*
antler /ˈæntlər/ *n.* asta *f.*
anvil /ˈænvɪl/ *n.* yunque *m.*
anxiety /æŋˈzaiɪti/ *n.* ansia, ansiedad *f.*
anxious /ˈæŋkʃəs, ˈæŋʃəs/ *a.* inquieto, ansioso.
any /ˈɛni/ *a.* alguno; (at all) cualquiera; (after *not*) ninguno.
anybody /ˈɛniˌbɒdi/ *pron.* alguien; (at all) cualquiera; (after *not*) nadie.
anyhow /ˈɛniˌhau/ *adv.* de todos modos; en todo caso.
anyone /ˈɛniˌwʌn/ *pron.* = anybody.
anything /ˈɛniˌθɪŋ/ *pron.* algo; (at all) cualquier cosa; (after *not*) nada.
anyway /ˈɛniˌwei/ *adv.* = anyhow.
anywhere /ˈɛniˌwɛər/ *adv.* en alguna parte; (at all) dondequiera; (after *not*) en ninguna parte.
apart /əˈpɑrt/ *adv.* aparte. **to take a.,** deshacer.
apartheid /əˈpɑrtheit, -hait/ *n.* apartheid *m.*
apartment /əˈpɑrtmənt/ *n.* apartamento, piso *m.*
apartment house casa de pisos *f.*
apathetic /ˌæpəˈθɛtɪk/ *a.* apático.
apathy /ˈæpəθi/ *n.* apatía *f.*
ape /eip/ *n.* **1.** mono *-na.* —*v.* **2.** imitar.
aperture /ˈæpərtʃər/ *n.* abertura *f.*
apex /ˈeipɛks/ *n.* ápice *m.*
aphorism /ˈæfəˌrɪzəm/ *n.* aforismo *m.*
apiary /ˈeipiˌɛri/ *n.* colmenario, abejar *m.*
apiece /əˈpis/ *adv.* por persona; cada uno.
apologetic /əˌpɒləˈdʒɛtɪk/ *a.* apologético.
apologist /əˈpɒlədʒɪst/ *n.* apologista *m. & f.*
apologize /əˈpɒləˌdʒaiz/ *v.* excusarse, disculparse.
apology /əˈpɒlədʒi/ *n.* excusa; apología *f.*
apoplectic /ˌæpəˈplɛktɪk/ *a.* apopléctico.
apoplexy /ˈæpəˌplɛksi/ *n.* apoplejía *f.*
apostate /əˈpɒsteit/ *n.* apóstata *m. & f.*
apostle /əˈpɒsəl/ *n.* apóstol *m.*
apostolic /ˌæpəˈstɒlɪk/ *a.* apostólico.
appall /əˈpɔl/ *v.* horrorizar; consternar.
apparatus /ˌæpəˈrætəs/ *n.* aparato *m.*
apparel /əˈpærəl/ *n.* ropa *f.*
apparent /əˈpærənt/ *a.* aparente; claro.
apparition /ˌæpəˈrɪʃən/ *n.* aparición *f.*; fantasma *m.*
appeal /əˈpil/ *n.* **1.** súplica *f.*; interés *m.*; *Leg.* apelación *f.* —*v.* **2.** apelar, suplicar; interesar.
appear /əˈpɪər/ *v.* aparecer, asomar; (seem) parecer; *Leg.* comparecer.
appearance /əˈpɪərəns/ *n.* apariencia *f.*, aspecto *m.*; aparición *f.*
appease /əˈpiz/ *v.* aplacar, apaciguar.
appeasement /əˈpizmənt/ *n.* apaciguamiento *m.*
appeaser /əˈpizər/ *n.* apaciguador -ra, pacificador -ra.
appellant /əˈpɛlənt/ *n.* apelante, demandante *m. & f.*
appellate /əˈpɛlɪt/ *a. Leg.* de apelación.
appendage /əˈpɛndɪdʒ/ *n.* añadidura *f.*
appendectomy /ˌæpənˈdɛktəmi/ *n.* apendectomía *f.*
appendicitis /əˌpɛndəˈsaitɪs/ *n.* apendicitis *f.*
appendix /əˈpɛndɪks/ *n.* apéndice *m.*
appetite /ˈæpɪˌtait/ *n.* apetito *m.*
appetizer /ˈæpɪˌtaizər/ *n.* aperitivo *m.*
appetizing /ˈæpɪˌtaizɪŋ/ *a.* apetitoso.
applaud /əˈplɔd/ *v.* aplaudir.
applause /əˈplɔz/ *n.* aplauso *m.*
apple /ˈæpəl/ *n.* manzana *f.* **a. tree,** manzano *m.*
applesauce /ˈæpəlˌsɔs/ *n.* compota de manzana.
appliance /əˈplaiəns/ *n.* aparato *m.*
applicable /ˈæplɪkəbəl/ *a.* aplicable.
applicant /ˈæplɪkənt/ *n.* suplicante *m. & f.*; candidato -ta.
application /ˌæplɪˈkeiʃən/ *n.* solicitud *f.*, (computer) programa *m.*
applied /əˈplaid/ *a.* aplicado. **a. for,** pedido.
appliqué /ˌæplɪˈkei/ *n.* (sewing) aplicación *f.*
apply /əˈplai/ *v.* aplicar. **a. for,** solicitar, pedir.
appoint /əˈpɔint/ *v.* nombrar.
appointment /əˈpɔintmənt/ *n.* nombramiento *m.*; puesto *m.*
apportion /əˈpɔrʃən/ *v.* repartir.
apposition /ˌæpəˈzɪʃən/ *n. Gram.* aposición *f.*
appraisal /əˈpreizəl/ *n.* valoración *f.*
appraise /əˈpreiz/ *v.* evaluar; tasar; estimar.
appreciable /əˈpriʃiəbəl/ *a.* apreciable; notable.
appreciate /əˈpriʃiˌeit/ *v.* apreciar, estimar.
appreciation /əˌpriʃiˈeiʃən/ *n.* aprecio; reconocimiento *m.*
apprehend /ˌæprɪˈhɛnd/ *v.* prender, capturar.
apprehension /ˌæprɪˈhɛnʃən/ *n.* aprensión *f.*; detención *f.*
apprehensive /ˌæprɪˈhɛnsɪv/ *a.* aprensivo.
apprentice /əˈprɛntɪs/ *n.* aprendiz -iza.
apprenticeship /əˈprɛntɪsˌʃɪp/ *n.* aprendizaje *m.*
apprise /əˈpraiz/ *v.* informar.
approach /əˈproutʃ/ *n.* **1.** acceso; método *m.* —*v.* **2.** acercarse.
approachable /əˈproutʃəbəl/ *a.* accesible.
approbation /ˌæprəˈbeiʃən/ *n.* aprobación *f.*
appropriate /*a* əˈproupriɪt; *v* -ˌeit/ *a.* **1.** apropiado. —*v.* **2.** apropiar.
appropriation /əˌproupriˈeiʃən/ *n.* apropiación *f.*
approval /əˈpruvəl/ *n.* aprobación *f.*
approve /əˈpruv/ *v.* aprobar.
approximate /*a* əˈprɒksəmɪt; *v* -ˌmeit/ *a.* **1.** aproximado. —*v.* **2.** aproximar.
approximately /əˈprɒksəmɪtli/ *adv.* aproximadamente.
approximation /əˌprɒksəˈmeiʃən/ *n.* aproximación *f.*
appurtenance /əˈpɜrtn̩əns/ *n.* dependencia *f.*
apricot /ˈæprɪˌkɒt/ *n.* albaricoque, damasco *m.*
April /ˈeiprəl/ *n.* abril *m.*
apron /ˈeiprən/ *n.* delantal *m.*
apropos /ˌæprəˈpou/ *adv.* a propósito.
apt /æpt/ *a.* apto; capaz.
aptitude /ˈæptɪˌtud/ *n.* aptitud; facilidad *f.*
aquarium /əˈkwɛəriəm/ *n.* acuario *m.*, pecera *f.*
aquatic /əˈkwætɪk/ *a.* acuático.
aqueduct /ˈækwɪˌdʌkt/ *n.* acueducto *m.*
aqueous /ˈækwiəs/ *a.* ácueo, acuoso, aguoso.
aquiline /ˈækwəˌlain/ *a.* aquilino, aguileño.
Arab /ˈærəb/ *a. & n.* árabe *m. & f.*
arable /ˈærəbəl/ *a.* cultivable.
arbitrary /ˈɑrbɪˌtrɛri/ *a.* arbitrario.
arbitrate /ˈɑrbɪˌtreit/ *v.* arbitrar.
arbitration /ˌɑrbɪˈtreiʃən/ *n.* arbitraje *m.*, arbitración *f.*
arbitrator /ˈɑrbɪˌtreitər/ *n.* arbitrador -ra.
arbor /ˈɑrbər/ *n.* emparrado *m.*
arboreal /ɑrˈbɔriəl/ *a.* arbóreo.
arc /ɑrk/ *n.* arco *m.*
arch /ɑrtʃ/ *n.* **1.** arco *m.* —*v.* **2.** arquear, encorvar.
archaeology /ˌɑrkiˈɒlədʒi/ *n.* arqueología *f.*
archaic /ɑrˈkeiɪk/ *a.* arcaico.
archbishop /ˈɑrtʃˈbɪʃəp/ *n.* arzobispo *m.*
archdiocese /ˌɑrtʃˈdaiəˌsis, -sɪs/ *n.* archidiócesis *f.*
archduke /ˈɑrtʃˈduk/ *n.* archiduque *m.*
archer /ˈɑrtʃər/ *n.* arquero *m.*
archery /ˈɑrtʃəri/ *n.* ballestería *f.*
archipelago /ˌɑrkəˈpɛləˌgou/ *n.* archipiélago *m.*
architect /ˈɑrkɪˌtɛkt/ *n.* arquitecto -ta.
architectural /ˌɑrkɪˈtɛktʃərəl/ *a.* arquitectural.
architecture /ˈɑrkɪˌtɛktʃər/ *n.* arquitectura *f.*
archive /ˈɑrkaiv/ *n.* archivo *m.*
archway /ˈɑrtʃˌwei/ *n.* arcada *f.*
arctic /ˈɑrktɪk, ˈɑrtɪk/ *a.* ártico.
ardent /ˈɑrdn̩t/ *a.* ardiente.
ardor /ˈɑrdər/ *n.* ardor *m.*, pasión *f.*
arduous /ˈɑrdʒuəs/ *a.* arduo, difícil.
area /ˈɛəriə/ *n.* área; extensión *f.*
area code prefijo *m.*
arena /əˈrinə/ *n.* arena *f.*
Argentine /ˈɑrdʒəntɪn, -ˌtain/ *a. & n.* argentino -na.
argue /ˈɑrgyu/ *v.* disputar; sostener.
argument /ˈɑrgyəmənt/ *n.* disputa *f.*; razonamiento *m.*
argumentative /ˌɑrgyəˈmɛntətɪv/ *a.* argumentoso.
aria /ˈɑriə/ *n.* aria *f.*
arid /ˈærɪd/ *a.* árido, seco.
arise /əˈraiz/ *v.* surgir; alzarse.
aristocracy /ˌærəˈstɒkrəsi/ *n.* aristocracia *f.*
aristocrat /əˈrɪstəˌkræt/ *n.* aristócrata *m.*
aristocratic /əˌrɪstəˈkrætɪk/ *a.* aristocrático.
arithmetic /əˈrɪθmətɪk/ *n.* aritmética *f.*
ark /ɑrk/ *n.* arca *f.*
arm /ɑrm/ *n.* **1.** brazo *m.*; (weapon) arma *f.* —*v.* **2.** armar.
armament /ˈɑrməmənt/ *n.* armamento *m.*
armchair /ˈɑrmˌtʃɛər/ *n.* sillón *m.*, butaca *f.*
armed forces /ˈɑrmd ˈfɔrsɪz/ fuerzas militares.
armful /ˈɑrmˌfʊl/ *n.* brazada *f.*
armhole /ˈɑrmˌhoul/ *n.* (sew.) sobaquera *f.*
armistice /ˈɑrməstɪs/ *n.* armisticio *m.*
armor /ˈɑrmər/ *n.* armadura *f.*, blindaje *m.*
armored /ˈɑrmərd/ *a.* blindado.
armory /ˈɑrməri/ *n.* armería *f.*, arsenal *m.*
armpit /ˈɑrmˌpɪt/ *n.* axila *f.*, sobaco *m.*
army /ˈɑrmi/ *n.* ejército *m.*
arnica /ˈɑrnɪkə/ *n.* árnica *f.*
aroma /əˈroumə/ *n.* fragancia *f.*
aromatic /ˌærəˈmætɪk/ *a.* aromático.
around /əˈraund/ *prep.* alrededor de, a la vuelta de; cerca de. **a. here,** por aquí.
arouse /əˈrauz/ *v.* despertar; excitar.
arraign /əˈrein/ *v. Leg.* procesar criminalmente.
arrange /əˈreindʒ/ *v.* arreglar; concertar; *Mus.* adaptar.
arrangement /əˈreindʒmənt/ *n.* arreglo; orden *m.*
array /əˈrei/ *n.* **1.** orden; adorno *m.* —*v.* **2.** adornar.
arrears /əˈrɪərz/ *n.* atrasos *m.pl.*
arrest /əˈrɛst/ *n.* **1.** detención *f.* —*v.* **2.** detener, arrestar.
arrival /əˈraivəl/ *n.* llegada *f.*
arrive /əˈraiv/ *v.* llegar.
arrogance /ˈærəgəns/ *n.* arrogancia *f.*
arrogant /ˈærəgənt/ *a.* arrogante.
arrogate /ˈærəˌgeit/ *v.* arrogarse, usurpar.
arrow /ˈærou/ *n.* flecha *f.*
arrowhead /ˈærouˌhɛd/ *n.* punta de flecha *f.*
arsenal /ˈɑrsənl̩/ *n.* arsenal *m.*
arsenic /ˈɑrsənɪk/ *n.* arsénico *m.*
arson /ˈɑrsən/ *n.* incendio premeditado.
art /ɑrt/ arte *m.* (*f.* in *pl.*); (skill) maña *f.*
arterial /ɑrˈtɪəriəl/ *a.* arterial.
arteriosclerosis /ɑrˌtɪəriousklәˈrousɪs/ *n.* arteriosclerosis *f.*
artery /ˈɑrtəri/ *n.* arteria *f.*
artesian well /ɑrˈtiʒən/ pozo artesiano.
artful /ˈɑrtfəl/ *a.* astuto.
arthritis /ɑrˈθraitɪs/ *n.* artritis *f.*
artichoke /ˈɑrtɪˌtʃouk/ *n.* alcachofa *f.*
article /ˈɑrtɪkəl/ *n.* artículo *m.*
articulate /ɑrˈtɪkyəˌleit/ *v.* articular.
articulation /ɑrˌtɪkyəˈleiʃən/ *n.* articulación *f.*
artifice /ˈɑrtəfɪs/ *n.* artificio *m.*
artificial /ˌɑrtəˈfɪʃəl/ *a.* artificial.
artificially /ˌɑrtəˈfɪʃəli/ *adv.* artificialmente.
artillery /ɑrˈtɪləri/ *n.* artillería *f.*
artisan /ˈɑrtəzən/ *n.* artesano -na.
artist /ˈɑrtɪst/ *n.* artista *m. & f.*
artistic /ɑrˈtɪstɪk/ *a.* artístico.
artistry /ˈɑrtɪstri/ *n.* arte *m. & f.*
artless /ˈɑrtlɪs/ *a.* natural, cándido.
as /æz/ *adv. & conj.* como; **as... as** tan... como.
asbestos /æsˈbɛstəs/ *n.* asbesto *m.*
ascend /əˈsɛnd/ *v.* ascender.
ascendancy /əˈsɛndənsi/ *n.* ascendiente *m.*
ascendant /əˈsɛndənt/ *a.* ascendente.
ascent /əˈsɛnt/ *n.* subida *f.*, ascenso *m.*
ascertain /ˌæsərˈtein/ *v.* averiguar.
ascetic /əˈsɛtɪk/ *a.* **1.** ascético. —*n.* **2.** asceta *m. & f.*
ascribe /əˈskraib/ *v.* atribuir.
ash /æʃ/ *n.* ceniza *f.*
ashamed /əˈʃeimd/ *a.* avergonzado.
ashen /ˈæʃən/ *a.* pálido.
ashore /əˈʃɔr/ *adv.* a tierra. **go a.,** desembarcar.
ashtray /ˈæʃˌtrei/ *n.* cenicero *m.*
Ash Wednesday miércoles de ceniza *m.*
Asiatic /ˌeiʒiˈætɪk/ *a. & n.* asiático -ca.
aside /əˈsaid/ *adv.* al lado. **a. from.** aparte de.
ask /æsk/ *v.* preguntar; invitar; (request) pedir. **a. for,** pedir. **a. a question,** hacer una pregunta.
askance /əˈskæns/ *adv.* de soslayo; con recelo.
asleep /əˈslip/ *a.* dormido. **to fall a.,** dormirse.
asparagus /əˈspærəgəs/ *n.* espárrago *m.*
aspect /ˈæspɛkt/ *n.* aspecto *m.*, apariencia *f.*
asperity /əˈspɛrɪti/ *n.* aspereza *f.*
aspersion /əˈspɜrʒən/ *n.* calumnia *f.*
asphalt /ˈæsfɔlt/ *n.* asfalto *m.*
asphyxia /æsˈfɪksiə/ *n.* asfixia *f.*
asphyxiate /æsˈfɪksiˌeit/ *v.* asfixiar, sofocar.
aspirant /ˈæspərənt/ *a. & n.* aspirante *m. & f.*
aspirate /ˈæspəˌreit/ *v.* aspirar.
aspiration /ˌæspəˈreiʃən/ *n.* aspiración *f.*
aspirator /ˈæspəˌreitər/ *n.* aspirador *m.*
aspire /əˈspaiᵊr/ *v.* aspirar. **a. to,** ambicionar.
aspirin /ˈæspərɪn/ *n.* aspirina *f.*
ass /æs/ *n.* asno, burro *m.*
assail /əˈseil/ *v.* asaltar, acometer.
assailant /əˈseilənt/ *n.* asaltador -ra.
assassin /əˈsæsɪn/ *n.* asesino -na.
assassinate /əˈsæsəˌneit/ *v.* asesinar.
assassination /əˌsæsəˈneiʃən/ *n.* asesinato *m.*
assault /əˈsɔlt/ *n.* **1.** asalto *m.* —*v.* **2.** asaltar, atacar.
assay /ˈæsei/ *v.* examinar; ensayar.
assemblage /əˈsɛmblɪdʒ/ *n.* asamblea *f.*
assemble /əˈsɛmbəl/ *v.* juntar, convocar; (mechanism) montar.

assembly /ə'sɛmbli/ *n.* asamblea, concurrencia *f.*
assent /ə'sɛnt/ *n.* **1.** asentimiento *m.* —*v.* **2.** asentir, convenir.
assert /ə'sɜrt/ *v.* afirmar, aseverar. **a. oneself,** hacerse sentir.
assertion /ə'sɜrʃən/ *n.* aserción, aseveración *f.*
assertive /ə'sɜrtɪv/ *a.* asertivo.
assess /ə'sɛs/ *v.* tasar, evaluar.
assessor /ə'sɛsər/ *n.* asesor -ra.
asset /'æsɛt/ *n.* ventaja *f.* **assets,** *Com.* capital *m.*
asseverate /ə'sɛvə,reit/ *v.* aseverar, afirmar.
asseveration /ə,sɛvə'reiʃən/ *n.* aseveración *f.*
assiduous /ə'sɪdʒuəs/ *a.* asiduo.
assiduously /ə'sɪdʒuəsli/ *adv.* asiduamente.
assign /ə'sain/ *v.* asignar; destinar.
assignable /ə'sainəbəl/ *a.* asignable, transferible.
assignation /,æsɪg'neiʃən/ *n.* asignación *f.*
assignment /ə'sainmənt/ *n.* misión; tarea *f.*
assimilate /ə'sɪmə,leit/ *v.* asimilar.
assimilation /ə,sɪmə'leiʃən/ *n.* asimilación *f.*
assimilative /ə'sɪmələtɪv/ *a.* asimilativo.
assist /ə'sɪst/ *v.* ayudar, auxiliar.
assistance /ə'sɪstəns/ *n.* ayuda *f.*, auxilio *m.*
assistant /ə'sɪstənt/ *n.* ayudante -ta, asistente -ta.
associate /*n* ə'sousiɪt; *v* -si,eit/ *n.* **1.** socio -cia. —*v.* **2.** asociar.
association /ə,sousi'eiʃən/ *n.* asociación; sociedad *f.*
assonance /'æsənəns/ *n.* asonancia *f.*
assort /ə'sɔrt/ *v.* surtir con variedad.
assorted /ə'sɔrtɪd/ *a.* variado, surtido.
assortment /ə'sɔrtmənt/ *n.* surtido *m.*
assuage /ə'sweidʒ/ *v.* mitigar, aliviar.
assume /ə'sum/ *v.* suponer; asumir.
assuming /ə'sumɪŋ/ *a.* presuntuoso. **a. that,** dado que.
assumption /ə'sʌmpʃən/ *n.* suposición; *Relig.* asunción *f.*
assurance /ə'ʃʊrəns/ *n.* seguridad; confianza *f.*; garantía *f.*
assure /ə'ʃʊr/ *v.* asegurar; dar confianza.
assured /ə'ʃʊrd/ *a.* **1.** seguro. —*a.* & *n.* **2.** *Com.* asegurado -da.
assuredly /ə'ʃʊrɪdli/ *adv.* ciertamente.
aster /'æstər/ *n.* aster *f.*
asterisk /'æstərɪsk/ *n.* asterisco *m.*
astern /ə'stɜrn/ *adv. Naut.* a popa.
asteroid /'æstə,rɔid/ *n.* asteroide *m.*
asthma /'æzmə/ *n. Med.* asma *f.*
astigmatism /ə'stɪgmə,tɪzəm/ *n.* astigmatismo *m.*
astir /ə'stɜr/ *adv.* en movimiento.
astonish /ə'stɒnɪʃ/ *v.* asombrar, pasmar.
astonishment /ə'stɒnɪʃmənt/ *n.* asombro *m.*, sorpresa *f.*
astound /ə'staund/ *v.* pasmar, sorprender.
astral /'æstrəl/ *a.* astral, estelar.
astray /ə'strei/ *a.* desviado.
astride /ə'straid/ *adv.* a horcajadas.
astringent /ə'strɪndʒənt/ *a.* & *n.* astringente *m.*
astrology /ə'strɒlədʒi/ *n.* astrología *f.*
astronaut /'æstrə,nɔt/ *n.* astronauta *m.* & *f.*
astronomy /ə'strɒnəmi/ *n.* astronomía *f.*
astute /ə'stut/ *a.* astuto; agudo.
asunder /ə'sʌndər/ *adv.* en dos.
asylum /ə'sailəm/ *n.* asilo, refugio *m.*
asymmetry /ei'sɪmɪtri/ *n.* asimetría *f.*
at /æt/ *prep.* a, en; cerca de.
ataxia /ə'tæksiə/ *n. Med.* ataxia *f.*
atheist /'eiθiɪst/ *n.* ateo -tea.
athlete /'æθlit/ *n.* atleta *m.* & *f.*
athletic /æθ'lɛtɪk/ *a.* atlético.
athletics /æθ'lɛtɪks/ *n.* atletismo *m.*, deportes *m.pl.*
athwart /ə'θwɔrt/ *prep.* a través de.
Atlantic /æt'læntɪk/ *a.* **1.** atlántico. —*n.* **2.** Atlántico *m.*
Atlantic Ocean Océano Atlántico *m.*
atlas /'ætləs/ *n.* atlas *m.*
atmosphere /'ætməs,fɪər/ *n.* atmósfera *f.*; *Fig.* ambiente *m.*
atmospheric /,ætməs'fɛrɪk/ *a.* atmosférico.
atoll /'ætɔl/ *n.* atolón *m.*
atom /'ætəm/ *n.* átomo *m.*
atomic /ə'tɒmɪk/ *a.* atómico.
atomic bomb bomba atómica *f.*
atomic energy energía atómica, energía nuclear *f.*
atomic theory teoría atómica. *f.*
atomic weight peso atómico *m.*
atonal /ei'tounl/ *a. Mus.* atonal.
atone /ə'toun/ *v.* expiar, compensar.
atonement /ə'tounmənt/ *n.* expiación; reparación *f.*
atrocious /ə'trouʃəs/ *a.* atroz.
atrocity /ə'trɒsɪti/ *n.* atrocidad *f.*
atrophy /'ætrəfi/ *n.* **1.** *Med.* atrofia *f.* —*v.* **2.** atrofiar.
atropine /'ætrə,pin, -pɪn/ *n.* atropina *f.*
attach /ə'tætʃ/ *v.* juntar; prender; (hook) enganchar; *Fig.* atribuir.
attaché /ætæ'ʃei/ *n.* agregado -da.
attachment /ə'tætʃmənt/ enlace *m.*; accesorio *m.*; (emotional) afecto, cariño *m.*
attack /ə'tæk/ *n.* **1.** ataque *m.* —*v.* **2.** atacar.
attacker /ə'tækər/ *n.* asaltador -ra.
attain /ə'tein/ *v.* lograr, alcanzar.
attainable /ə'teinəbəl/ *a.* accesible, realizable.
attainment /ə'teinmənt/ *n.* logro; *(pl.)* dotes *f.pl.*
attempt /ə'tɛmpt/ *n.* **1.** ensayo; esfuerzo *m.*; tentativa *f.* —*v.* **2.** ensayar, intentar.
attend /ə'tɛnd/ *v.* atender; (a meeting) asistir a.
attendance /ə'tɛndəns/ *n.* asistencia; presencia *f.*
attendant /ə'tɛndənt/ *a.* **1.** concomitante. —*n.* **2.** servidor -ra.
attention /ə'tɛnʃən/ *n.* atención *f.*; obsequio *m.* **to pay a. to,** hacer caso a.
attentive /ə'tɛntɪv/ *a.* atento.
attentively /ə'tɛntɪvli/ *adv.* atentamente.
attenuate /ə'tɛnyu,eit/ *v.* atenuar, adelgazar.
attest /ə'tɛst/ *v.* confirmar, atestiguar.
attic /'ætɪk/ *n.* desván *m.*, guardilla *f.*
attire /ə'taiᵊr/ *n.* **1.** traje *m.* —*v.* **2.** vestir.
attitude /'ætɪ,tud/ *n.* actitud *f.*, ademán *m.*
attorney /ə'tɜrni/ *n.* abogado -da, apoderado -da.
attract /ə'trækt/ *v.* atraer. **a. attention,** llamar la atención.
attraction /ə'trækʃən/ *n.* atracción *f.*, atractivo *m.*
attractive /ə'træktɪv/ *a.* atractivo; simpático.
attributable /ə'trɪbyʊtəbəl/ *a.* atribuible, imputable.
attribute /*n* 'ætrə,byut; *v* ə'trɪbyut/ *n.* **1.** atributo *m.* —*v.* **2.** atribuir.
attrition /ə'trɪʃən/ *n.* roce, desgaste *m.*; atrición *f.*
attune /ə'tun/ *v.* armonizar.
auction /'ɔkʃən/ *n.* subasta *f.*, *S.A.* venduta *f.*
auctioneer /,ɔkʃə'nɪər/ *n.* subastador -ra, *S.A.* martillero -ra.
audacious /ɔ'deiʃəs/ *a.* audaz.
audacity /ɔ'dæsɪti/ *n.* audacia *f.*
audible /'ɔdəbəl/ *a.* audible.
audience /'ɔdiəns/ *n.* auditorio, público *m.*; entrevista *f.*
audiovisual /,ɔdiou'vɪʒuəl/ *a.* audiovisual.
audit /'ɔdɪt/ *n.* **1.** revisión de cuentas *f.* —*v.* **2.** revisar cuentas.
audition /ɔ'dɪʃən/ *n.* audición *f.*
auditor /'ɔdɪtər/ *n.* interventor -ora, revisor -ora.
auditorium /,ɔdɪ'tɔriəm/ *n.* sala *f.*; teatro *m.*
auditory /'ɔdɪ,tɔri/ *a.* & *n.* auditorio *m.*
augment /ɔg'mɛnt/ *v.* aumentar.
augur /'ɔgər/ *v.* augurar, pronosticar.
August /'ɔgəst/ *n.* agosto *m.*
aunt /ænt, ɑnt/ *n.* tía *f.*
auspice /'ɔspɪs/ *n.* auspicio *m.*
auspicious /ɔ'spɪʃəs/ *a.* favorable; propicio.
austere /ɔ'stɪər/ *a.* austero.
austerity /ɔ'stɛrɪti/ *n.* austeridad, severidad *f.*
Austrian /'ɔstriən/ *a.* & *n.* austríaco -ca.
authentic /ɔ'θɛntɪk/ *a.* auténtico.
authenticate /ɔ'θɛntɪ,keit/ *v.* autenticar.
authenticity /,ɔθɛn'tɪsɪti/ *n.* autenticidad *f.*
author /'ɔθər/ *n.* autor -ra, escritor -ra.
authoritarian /ə,θɔrɪ'tɛəriən/ *a.* & *n.* autoritario -ria.
authoritative /ə'θɔrɪ,teitɪv/ *a.* autoritativo; autorizado.
authoritatively /ə'θɔrɪ,teitɪvli/ *adv.* autoritativamente.
authority /ə'θɔrɪti/ *n.* autoridad *f.*
authorization /,ɔθərə'zeiʃən/ *n.* autorización *f.*
authorize /'ɔθə,raiz/ *v.* autorizar.
auto /'ɔtou/ *n.* auto, automóvil *m.*
autobiography /,ɔtəbai'ɒgrəfi/ *n.* autobiografía *f.*
autocracy /ɔ'tɒkrəsi/ *n.* autocracia *f.*
autocrat /'ɔtə,kræt/ *n.* autócrata *m.* & *f.*
autograph /'ɔtə,græf/ *n.* autógrafo *m.*
automatic /,ɔtə'mætɪk/ *a.* automático.
automatically /,ɔtə'mætɪkəli/ *adv.* automáticamente.
automobile /,ɔtəmə'bil/ *n.* automóvil, coche *m.*
automotive /,ɔtə'moutɪv/ *a.* automotriz.
autonomy /ɔ'tɒnəmi/ *n.* autonomía *f.*
autopsy /'ɔtɒpsi/ *n.* autopsia *f.*
autumn /'ɔtəm/ *n.* otoño *m.*
auxiliary /ɔg'zɪlyəri/ *a.* auxiliar.
avail /ə'veil/ *n.* **1. of no a.,** en vano. —*v.* **2. a. oneself of,** aprovecharse.
available /ə'veiləbəl/ *a.* disponible.
avalanche /'ævə,læntʃ/ *n.* alud *m.*
avarice /'ævərɪs/ *n.* avaricia, codicia *f.*
avariciously /,ævə'rɪʃəsli/ *adv.* avaramente.
avenge /ə'vɛndʒ/ *v.* vengar.
avenger /ə'vɛndʒər/ *n.* vengador -ra.
avenue /'ævə,nu/ *n.* avenida *f.*
average /'ævərɪdʒ/ *a.* **1.** medio; común. —*n.* **2.** promedio, término medio *m.* —*v.* **3.** calcular el promedio.
averse /ə'vɜrs/ *a.* **to be a. to,** tener antipatía a, opuesto a.
aversion /ə'vɜrʒən/ *n.* aversión *f.*
avert /ə'vɜrt/ *v.* desviar; impedir.
aviary /'eivi,ɛri/ *n.* pajarera, avería *f.*
aviation /,eivi'eiʃən/ *n.* aviación *f.*
aviator /'eivi,eitər/ *n.* aviador -ra.
aviatrix /,eivi'eitrɪks/ *n.* aviatriz *f.*
avid /'ævɪd/ *a.* ávido.
avocado /,ævə'kɑdou, ,ɑvə-/ *n.* aguacate *m.*
avocation /,ævə'keiʃən/ *n.* pasatiempo *f.*
avoid /ə'vɔid/ *v.* evitar.
avoidable /ə'vɔidəbəl/ *a.* evitable.
avoidance /ə'vɔidn̩s/ *n.* evitación *f.*; *Leg.* anulación *f.*
avow /ə'vau/ *v.* declarar; admitir.
avowal /ə'vauəl/ *n.* admisión *f.*
avowed /ə'vaud/ *a.* reconocido; admitido.
avowedly /ə'vauɪdli/ *adv.* reconocidamente; confesadamente.
await /ə'weit/ *v.* esperar, aguardar.
awake /ə'weik/ *a.* despierto.
awaken /ə'weikən/ *v.* despertar.
award /ə'wɔrd/ *n.* **1.** premio *m.* —*v.* **2.** otorgar.
aware /ə'wɛər/ *a.* enterado, consciente.
awash /ə'wɒʃ/ *a.* & *adv. Naut.* a flor de agua.
away /ə'wei/ *adv.* (see under verb: **go away, put away, take away,** etc.)
awe /ɔ/ *n.* pavor *m.*
awesome /'ɔsəm/ *a.* pavoroso; aterrador.
awful /'ɔfəl/ *a.* horrible, terrible, muy malo, pésimo.
awhile /ə'wail/ *adv.* por un rato.
awkward /'ɔkwərd/ *a.* torpe, desmañado; *Fig.* delicado, embarazoso.
awning /'ɔnɪŋ/ *n.* toldo *m.*
awry /ə'rai/ *a.* oblicuo, torcido.
ax /æks/ *n.* hacha *f.*
axiom /'æksiəm/ *n.* axioma *m.*
axis /'æksɪs/ *n.* eje *m.*
axle /'æksəl/ *n.* eje *m.*
ayatollah /,ɑyə'toulə/ *n.* ayatolá *m.*
azure /'æʒər/ *a.* azul.

B

babble /'bæbəl/ *n.* **1.** balbuceo, murmullo *m.* —*v.* **2.** balbucear.
babbler /'bæblər/ *n.* hablador -ra, charlador -ra.
baboon /bæ'bun/ *n.* mandril *m.*
baby /'beibi/ *n.* nene, bebé *m.*
baby carriage cochecito de niño *m.*
babyish /'beibiɪʃ/ *a.* infantil.
baby squid /skwɪd/ chipirón *m.*
bachelor /'bætʃələr/ *n.* soltero *m.*
bacillus /bə'sɪləs/ *n.* bacilo, microbio *m.*
back /bæk/ *adv.* **1.** atrás. **to be b.,** estar de vuelta. **b. of,** detrás de. —*n.* **2.** espalda *f.*; (of animal) lomo *m.*
backache /'bæk,eik/ *n.* dolor de espalda *m.*
backbone /'bæk,boun/ *n.* espinazo *m.*; *Fig.* firmeza *f.*
backer /'bækər/ *n.* sostenedor -ra.
background /'bæk,graund/ *n.* fondo *m.* antecedentes *m.pl.*
backing /'bækɪŋ/ *n.* apoyo *m.*, garantía *f.*
backlash /'bæk,læʃ/ *n.* repercusión negativa.
backlog /'bæk,lɔg/ *n.* atrasos *m.pl.*
backpack /'bæk,pæk/ *n.* mochila *f.*
back seat asiento trasero *m.*
backstage /'bæk'steidʒ/ *n.* entre bastidores *m.*
backup /'bæk,ʌp/ *n.* copia de seguridad *f.*
backward /'bækwərd/ *a.* **1.** atrasado. —*adv.* **2.** hacia atrás.
backwardness /'bækwərdnɪs/ *n.* atraso *m.*
backwater /'bæk,wɔtər/ *n.* parte de río estancada *f.*
backwoods /'bæk'wʊdz/ *n.* región del monte apartada *f.*
bacon /'beikən/ *n.* tocino *m.*
bacteria /bæk'tɪəriə/ *n.* bacterias *f.pl.*
bacteriologist /,bæktɪəri'ɒlədʒɪst/ *n.* bacteriólogo -a.
bacteriology /,bæktɪəri'ɒlədʒi/ *n.* bacteriología *f.*
bad /bæd/ *a.* malo.
badge /bædʒ/ *n.* insignia, divisa *f.*
badger /'bædʒər/ *n.* **1.** tejón *m.* —*v.* **2.** atormentar.
badly /'bædli/ *adv.* mal.
badness /'bædnɪs/ *n.* maldad *f.*
bad-tempered /'bæd'tɛmpərd/ *a.* de mal humor.
baffle /'bæfəl/ *v.* desconcertar.
bafflement /'bæfəlmənt/ *n.* contrariedad; confusión *f.*

bag /bæg/ *n.* **1.** saco *m.;* bolsa *f.* —*v.* **2.** ensacar, cazar.
baggage /ˈbægɪdʒ/ *n.* equipaje *m.* **b. check,** talón *m.*
baggage cart (airport) carrillo para llevar equipaje.
baggy /ˈbægi/ *a.* abotagado; bolsudo; hinchado.
bagpipe /ˈbæg,paip/ *n.* gaita *f.*
bail /beil/ *n.* **1.** fianza *f.* —*v.* **2.** desaguar.
bailiff /ˈbeilɪf/ *n.* alguacil *m.*
bait /beit/ *n.* **1.** cebo *m.* —*v.* **2.** cebar.
bake /beik/ *v.* cocer en horno.
baked potato /beikt/ patata asada *f.*
baker /ˈbeikər/ *n.* panadero -ra, hornero -ra.
bakery /ˈbeikəri, ˈbeikri/ *n.* panadería *f.*
baking /ˈbeikɪŋ/ *n.* hornada *f.* **b. powder,** levadura *f.*
balance /ˈbæləns/ *n.* balanza *f.;* equilibrio *m.; Com.* saldo *m.*
balcony /ˈbælkəni/ *n.* balcón *m.; Theat.* galería *f.*
bald /bɔld/ *a.* calvo.
baldness /ˈbɔldnɪs/ *n.* calvicie *f.*
bale /beil/ *n.* **1.** bala *f.* —*v.* **2.** embalar.
balk /bɔk/ *v.* frustrar; rebelarse.
Balkans /ˈbɔlkənz/ *n.pl.* Balcanes *m.pl.*
balky /ˈbɔki/ *a.* rebelón.
ball /bɔl/ *n.* bola, pelota *f.;* (dance) baile *m.*
ballad /ˈbæləd/ *n.* romance, *m.;* balada *f.*
ballast /ˈbæləst/ *n.* **1.** lastre *m.* —*v.* **2.** lastrar.
ball bearing cojinete de bolas *m.*
ballerina /,bæləˈrinə/ *n.* bailarina *f.*
ballet /bæˈlei/ *n.* danza *f.;* ballet *m.*
ballistics /bəˈlɪstɪks/ *n.* balística *f.*
balloon /bəˈlun/ *n.* globo *m.* **b. tire,** neumático de balón.
ballot /ˈbælət/ *n.* **1.** balota *f.,* voto *m.* —*v.* **2.** balotar, votar.
ballpoint pen /ˈbɔl,pɔint/ bolígrafo *m.*
ballroom /ˈbɔl,rum/ *n.* salón de baile *m.*
balm /bɑm/ *n.* bálsamo; ungüento *m.*
balmy /ˈbɑmi/ *a.* fragante; reparador; calmante.
balsa /ˈbɔlsə/ *n.* balsa *f.*
balsam /ˈbɔlsəm/ *n.* bálsamo *m.*
balustrade /ˈbælə,streid/ *n.* barandilla *f.*
bamboo /bæmˈbu/ *n.* bambú *m.,* caña *f.*
ban /bæn/ *n.* **1.** prohibición *f.* —*v.* **2.** prohibir; proscribir.
banal /bəˈnæl/ *a.* trivial; vulgar.
banana /bəˈnænə/ *n.* banana *f.,* cambur *m.* **b. tree,** banano, plátano *m.*
band /bænd/ *n.* **1.** banda *f.;* (of men) banda, cuadrilla, partida *f.* —*v.* **2.** asociarse.
bandage /ˈbændɪdʒ/ *n.* **1.** vendaje *m.* —*v.* **2.** vendar.
bandanna /bænˈdænə/ *n.* pañuelo (grande) *m.;* bandana *f.*
bandbox /ˈbænd,bɒks/ *n.* caja de cartón.
bandit /ˈbændɪt/ *n.* bandido -da.
bandmaster /ˈbænd,mæstər/ *n.* director de una banda musical *m.*
bandstand /ˈbænd,stænd/ *n.* kiosco de música.
bang /bæŋ/ *interj.* **1.** ¡pum! —*n.* **2.** ruido de un golpe. —*v.* **3.** golpear ruidosamente.
banish /ˈbænɪʃ/ *v.* desterrar.
banishment /ˈbænɪʃmənt/ *n.* destierro *m.*
banister /ˈbænəstər/ *n.* pasamanos *m.pl.*
bank /bæŋk/ *n.* **1.** banco *m.;* (of a river) margen *f.* —*v.* **2.** depositar.
bank account cuenta bancaria *f.*
bankbook /ˈbæŋk,bʊk/ *n.* libreta de depósitos *f.*
bank card tarjeta bancaria *f.*
banker /ˈbæŋkər/ *n.* banquero -ra.
banking /ˈbæŋkɪŋ/ *a.* bancaria. *n.* banca *f.*
bank note billete de banco *m.*
bankrupt /ˈbæŋkrʌpt/ *a.* insolvente.
bankruptcy /ˈbæŋkrʌptsi/ *n.* bancarrota *f.*
banner /ˈbænər/ *n.* bandera *f.;* estandarte *m.*
banquet /ˈbæŋkwɪt/ *n.* banquete *m.*
banter /ˈbæntər/ *n.* **1.** choteo *m.;* zumba; burla *f.* —*v.* **2.** chotear; zumbar; burlarse.
baptism /ˈbæptɪzəm/ *n.* bautismo, bautizo *m.*
baptismal /bæpˈtɪzməl/ *a.* bautismal.
Baptist /ˈbæptɪst/ *n.* bautista *m.* & *f.*
baptize /bæpˈtaiz, ˈbæptaiz/ *v.* bautizar.
bar /bɑr/ *n.* **1.** barra *f.;* obstáculo *m.;* (tavern) taberna *f.,* bar *m.* —*v.* **2.** barrear; prohibir, excluir.
barbarian /bɑrˈbɛəriən/ *a.* bárbaro. *n.* bárbaro -ra.
barbarism /ˈbɑrbə,rɪzəm/ *n.* barbarismo *m.,* barbarie *f.*
barbarous /ˈbɑrbərəs/ *a.* bárbaro, cruel.
barbecue /ˈbɑrbɪ,kyu/ *n.* animal asado entero; (Mex.) barbacoa *f.*
barber /ˈbɑrbər/ *n.* barbero *m.* **b. shop,** barbería *f.*
barbiturate /bɑrˈbɪtʃərɪt/ *n.* barbitúrico *m.*
bar code código de barras *m.*
bare /bɛər/ *a.* **1.** desnudo; descubierto. —*v.* **2.** desnudar; descubrir.
bareback /ˈbɛər,bæk/ *adv.* sin silla.
barefoot(ed) /ˈbɛər,fʊtɪd/ *a.* descalzo.
barely /ˈbɛərli/ *adv.* escasamente, apenas.
bareness /ˈbɛərnɪs/ *n.* desnudez *f.;* pobreza *f.*
bargain /ˈbɑrgən/ *n.* **1.** ganga *f.,* compra ventajosa *f.;* contrato *m.* —*v.* **2.** regatear; negociar.
barge /bɑrdʒ/ *n.* lanchón *m.,* barcaza *f.*
baritone /ˈbærɪ,toun/ *n.* barítono *m.*
barium /ˈbɛəriəm/ *n.* bario *m.*
bark /bɑrk/ *n.* **1.** corteza *f.;* (of dog) ladrido *f.* —*v.* **2.** ladrar.
barley /ˈbɑrli/ *n.* cebada *f.*
barn /bɑrn/ *n.* granero *m.*
barnacle /ˈbɑrnəkəl/ *n.* lapa *f.*
barnyard /ˈbɑrn,yɑrd/ *n.* corral *m.*
barometer /bəˈrɒmɪtər/ *n.* barómetro *m.*
barometric /,bærəˈmɛtrɪk/ *a.* barométrico.
baron /ˈbærən/ *n.* barón *m.*
baroness /ˈbærənɪs/ *n.* baronesa *f.*
baronial /bəˈrouniəl/ *a.* baronial.
baroque /bəˈrouk/ *a.* barroco.
barracks /ˈbærəks/ *n.* cuartel *m.*
barrage /bəˈrɑʒ/ *n.* cortina de fuego *f.*
barred /bɑrd/ *a.* excluído; prohibido.
barrel /ˈbærəl/ *n.* barril *m.;* (of gun) cañón *m.*
barren /ˈbærən/ *a.* estéril.
barrenness /ˈbærən,nɪs/ *n.* esterilidad *f.*
barricade /ˈbærɪ,keid/ *n.* barricada, barrera *f.*
barrier /ˈbæriər/ *n.* barrera *f.;* obstáculo *m.*
barroom /ˈbɑr,rum, -,rʊm/ *n.* cantina *f.*
bartender /ˈbɑr,tɛndər/ *n.* tabernero; cantinero *m.*
barter /ˈbɑrtər/ *n.* **1.** cambio, trueque *m.* —*v.* **2.** cambiar, trocar.
base /beis/ *a.* **1.** bajo, vil. —*n.* **2.** base *f.* —*v.* **3.** basar.
baseball /ˈbeis,bɔl/ *n.* béisbol *m.*
baseboard /ˈbeis,bɔrd/ *n.* tabla de resguardo.
basement /ˈbeismənt/ *n.* sótano *m.*
baseness /ˈbeisnɪs/ *n.* bajeza, vileza *f.*
bashful /ˈbæʃfəl/ *a.* vergonzoso, tímido.
bashfully /ˈbæʃfəli/ *adv.* tímidamente; vergonzosamente.
bashfulness /ˈbæʃfəlnɪs/ *n.* vergüenza; timidez *f.*
basic /ˈbeisɪk/ *a.* fundamental, básico.
basin /ˈbeisən/ *n.* bacía *f.;* (of river) cuenca *f.*
basis /ˈbeisɪs/ *n.* base *f.*
bask /bæsk/ *v.* tomar el sol.
basket /ˈbæskɪt/ *n.* cesta, canasta *f.*
bass /bæs; beis/ *n.* (fish) lobina *f.; Mus.* bajo profundo *m.* **b. viol.** violón *m.*
bassinet /,bæsəˈnɛt/ *n.* bacinete *m.*
bassoon /bæˈsun/ *n.* bajón *m.*
bastard /ˈbæstərd/ *a.* & *n.* bastardo -da; hijo -a natural.
baste /beist/ *v.* (sew) bastear; (cooking) pringar.
bat /bæt/ *n.* **1.** (animal) murciélago *m.;* (baseball) bate *m.* —*v.* **2.** batear.
batch /bætʃ/ *n.* cantidad de cosas.
bath /bæθ/ *n.* baño *m.*
bathe /beið/ *v.* bañar, bañarse.
bather /ˈbeiðər/ *n.* bañista *m.* & *f.*
bathing resort /ˈbeiðɪŋ/ balneario *m.*
bathing suit /ˈbeiðɪŋ/ traje de baño.
bathrobe /ˈbæθ,roub/ *n.* bata de baño *f.*
bathroom /ˈbæθ,rum, -,rʊm/ *n.* cuarto de baño.
bathtub /ˈbæθ,tʌb/ *n.* bañera *f.*
baton /bəˈtɒn/ *n.* bastón *m.; Mus.* batuta *f.*
battalion /bəˈtælyən/ *n.* batallón *m.*
batter /ˈbætər/ *n.* **1.** (cooking) batido *m.;* (baseball) voleador *m.* —*v.* **2.** batir; derribar.
battery /ˈbætəri/ *n.* batería; *Elec.* pila *f.*
batting /ˈbætɪŋ/ *n.* agramaje, moldeaje *m.*
battle /ˈbætl̩/ *n.* **1.** batalla *f.;* combate *m.* —*v.* **2.** batallar.
battlefield /ˈbætl̩,fild/ *n.* campo de batalla.
battleship /ˈbætl̩,ʃɪp/ *n.* acorazado *m.*
bauxite /ˈbɔksait, ˈbouzait/ *n.* bauxita *f.*
bawl /bɔl/ *v.* gritar; vocear.
bay /bei/ *n.* bahía *f. v.* aullar.
bayonet /ˈbeiənɛt/ *n.* bayoneta *f.*
bazaar /bəˈzɑr/ *n.* bazar *m.,* feria *f.*
BC *abbr.* (**before Christ**) a.C. (antes de Cristo).
be /bi/ *v.* ser; estar. (See **hacer; hay; tener** in Sp.-Eng. section.)
beach /bitʃ/ *n.* playa *f.*
beachcomber /ˈbitʃ,koumər/ *n.* raquero -ra *m.* & *f.*
beacon /ˈbikən/ *n.* faro *m.*
bead /bid/ *n.* cuenta *f.; pl. Relig.* rosario *m.*
beading /ˈbidɪŋ/ *n.* abalorio *m.*
beady /ˈbidi/ *a.* globuloso; burbujoso.
beak /bik/ *n.* pico *m.*
beaker /ˈbikər/ *n.* vaso con pico *m.*
beam /bim/ *n.* viga *f.;* (of wood) madero *m.;* (of light) rayo *m.*
beaming /ˈbimɪŋ/ *a.* radiante.
bean /bin/ *n.* haba, habichuela *f.,* frijol *m.*
bear /bɛər/ *n.* **1.** oso -sa. —*v.* **2.** llevar; (endure) aguantar.
bearable /ˈbɛərəbəl/ *a.* sufrible; soportable.
beard /bɪərd/ *n.* barba *f.*
bearded /ˈbɪərdɪd/ *a.* barbado; barbudo
beardless /ˈbɪərdlɪs/ *a.* lampiño; imberbe.
bearer /ˈbɛərər/ *n.* portador -ra.
bearing /ˈbɛərɪŋ/ *n.* porte, aguante *m.*
bearskin /ˈbɛər,skɪn/ *n.* piel de oso *f.*
beast /bist/ *n.* bestia *f.;* bruto -ta.
beat /bit/ *v.* golpear; batir; pulsar; (in games) ganar, vencer.
beaten /ˈbitn̩/ *a.* vencido; batido.
beatify /biˈætə,fai/ *v.* beatificar.
beating /ˈbitɪŋ/ *n.* paliza *f.*
beau /bou/ *n.* novio *m.*
beautiful /ˈbyutəfəl/ *a.* hermoso, bello.
beautifully /ˈbyutəfəli/ *adv.* bellamente.
beautify /ˈbyutə,fai/ *v.* embellecer.
beauty /ˈbyuti/ *n.* hermosura, belleza *f.* **b. parlor,** salón de belleza.
beaver /ˈbivər/ *n.* castor *m.*
becalm /bɪˈkɑm/ *v.* calmar; sosegar; encalmarse.
because /bɪˈkɔz/ *conj.* porque. **b. of,** a causa de.
beckon /ˈbɛkən/ *v.* hacer señas.
become /bɪˈkʌm/ *v.* hacerse; ponerse.
becoming /bɪˈkʌmɪŋ/ *a.* propio, correcto; **be b.,** quedar bien, sentar bien.
bed /bɛd/ *n.* cama *f.;* lecho *m.;* (of river) cauce *m.*
bedbug /ˈbɛd,bʌg/ *n.* chinche *m.*
bedclothes /ˈbɛd,klouz, -,klouðz/ *n.* ropa de cama *f.*
bedding /ˈbɛdɪŋ/ *n.* colchones *m.pl.*
bedfellow /ˈbɛd,fɛlou/ *n.* compañero -ra de cama.
bedizen /bɪˈdaizən, -ˈdɪzən/ *v.* adornar; aderezar.
bedridden /ˈbɛd,rɪdn̩/ *a.* postrado (en cama).
bedrock /ˈbɛd,rɒk/ *n.* (mining) lecho de roca *m.; Fig.* fundamento *m.*
bedroom /ˈbɛd,rum/ *n.* alcoba *f.;* (Mex.) recámara *f.*
bedside /ˈbɛd,said/ *n.* al lado de una cama *m.*
bedspread /ˈbɛd,sprɛd/ *n.* cubrecama, sobrecama *f.*
bedstead /ˈbɛd,stɛd/ *n.* armadura de cama *f.*
bedtime /ˈbɛd,taim/ *n.* hora de acostarse.
bee /bi/ *n.* abeja *f.*
beef /bif/ *n.* carne de vaca.
beefburger /ˈbif,bɜrgər/ *n.* hamburguesa *f.*
beefsteak /ˈbif,steik/ *n.* bistec, bisté *m.*
beehive /ˈbi,haiv/ *n.* colmena *f.*
beer /bɪər/ *n.* cerveza *f.*
beeswax /ˈbiz,wæks/ *n.* cera de abejas.
beet /bit/ *n.* remolacha *f.;* (Mex.) betabel *m.*
beetle /ˈbitl̩/ *n.* escarabajo *m.*
befall /bɪˈfɔl/ *v.* suceder, sobrevenir.
befitting /bɪˈfɪtɪŋ/ *a.* conveniente; propio; digno.
before /bɪˈfɔr/ *adv.* antes. *prep.* antes de; (in front of) delante de. *conj.* antes que.
beforehand /bɪˈfɔr,hænd/ *adv.* de antemano.
befriend /bɪˈfrɛnd/ *v.* amparar.
befuddle /bɪˈfʌdl̩/ *v.* confundir; aturdir.
beg /bɛg/ *v.* rogar, suplicar; (for alms) mendigar.
beget /bɪˈgɛt/ *v.* engendrar; producir.
beggar /ˈbɛgər/ *n.* mendigo -ga; *S.A.* limosnero -ra.
beggarly /ˈbɛgərli/ *a.* pobre, miserable.
begin /bɪˈgɪn/ *v.* empezar, comenzar, principiar.
beginner /bɪˈgɪnər/ *n.* principiante -ta.
beginning /bɪˈgɪnɪŋ/ *n.* principio, comienzo *m.*
begrudge /bɪˈgrʌdʒ/ *v.* envidiar.
behalf /bɪˈhæf/ *n.:* **in, on b. of,** a favor de, en pro de.
behave /bɪˈheiv/ *v.* portarse, comportarse.
behavior /bɪˈheivyər/ *n.* conducta *f.;* comportamiento *m.*
behead /bɪˈhɛd/ *v.* decapitar.
behind /bɪˈhaind/ *adv.* atrás, detrás. *prep.* detrás de.
behold /bɪˈhould/ *v.* contemplar.
beige /beiʒ/ *a.* beige.
being /ˈbiɪŋ/ *n.* existencia *f.;* (person) ser *m.*

bejewel /bɪ'dʒuəl/ v. adornar con joyas.

belated /bɪ'leitɪd/ a. atrasado, tardío.

belch /bɛltʃ/ n. **1.** eructo m. —v. **2.** vomitar; eructar.

belfry /'bɛlfri/ n. campanario m.

Belgian /'bɛldʒən/ a. & n. belga m. & f.

Belgium /'bɛldʒəm/ n. Bélgica f.

belie /bɪ'lai/ v. desmentir.

belief /bɪ'lif/ n. creencia f.; parecer m.

believable /bɪ'livəbəl/ a. creíble.

believe /bɪ'liv/ v. creer.

believer /bɪ'livər/ n. creyente m. & f.

belittle /bɪ'lɪtl/ v. dar poca importancia a.

bell /bɛl/ n. campana f.; (of house) campanilla f.; (electric) timbre m.

bellboy /'bɛl,bɔi/ n. mozo, botones m.

bellicose /'bɛlɪ,kous/ a. guerrero.

belligerence /bə'lɪdʒərəns/ n. beligerancia f.

belligerent /bə'lɪdʒərənt/ a. & n. beligerante m. & f.

belligerently /bə'lɪdʒərəntli/ adv. belicosamente.

bellow /'bɛlou/ v. bramar, rugir.

bellows /'bɛlouz/ n. fuelle m.

belly /'bɛli/ n. vientre m.; panza, barriga f.

belong /bɪ'lɔŋ/ v. pertenecer.

belongings /bɪ'lɔŋɪŋz/ n. propiedad f.

beloved /bɪ'lʌvɪd/ a. querido, amado.

below /bɪ'lou/ adv. **1.** debajo, abajo. —prep. **2.** debajo de.

belt /bɛlt/ n. cinturón m.

bench /bɛntʃ/ n. banco m.

bend /bɛnd/ n. vuelta; curva f. v. encorvar, doblar.

beneath /bɪ'niθ/ adv. **1.** debajo, abajo. —prep. **2.** debajo de.

benediction /,bɛnɪ'dɪkʃən/ n. bendición f.

benefactor /'bɛnə,fæktər/ n. bienhechor -ra.

benefactress /'bɛnə,fæktrɪs/ n. bienhechora f.

beneficial /,bɛnə'fɪʃəl/ a. provechoso, beneficioso.

beneficiary /,bɛnə'fɪʃi,ɛri/ n. beneficiario -ria, beneficiado -da.

benefit /'bɛnəfɪt/ n. **1.** provecho, beneficio m. —v. **2.** beneficiar.

benevolence /bə'nɛvələns/ n. benevolencia f.

benevolent /bə'nɛvələnt/ a. benévolo.

benevolently /bə'nɛvələntli/ adv. benignamente.

benign /bɪ'nain/ bɪ'nɪgnənt/ a. benigno.

benignity /bɪ'nɪgnɪti/ n. benignidad f.; bondad f.

bent /bɛnt/ a. **1.** encorvado. **b. on,** resuelto a. —n. **2.** inclinación f.

benzene /'bɛnzin, bɛn'zin/ n. benceno m.

bequeath /bɪ'kwið/ v. legar.

bequest /bɪ'kwɛst/ n. legado m.

berate /bɪ'reit/ v. reñir, regañar.

bereave /bɪ'riv/ v. despojar; desolar.

bereavement /bɪ'rivmənt/ n. privación f.; despojo m.; (mourning) luto m.

berry /'bɛri/ n. baya f.

berth /bɜrθ/ n. camarote m.; Naut. litera f.; (for vessel) amarradero m.

beseech /bɪ'sitʃ/ v. suplicar; implorar.

beseechingly /bɪ'sitʃɪŋli/ adv. suplicantemente.

beset /bɪ'sɛt/ v. acosar; rodear.

beside /bɪ'said/ prep. al lado de.

besides /bɪ'saidz/ adv. además, por otra parte.

besiege /bɪ'sidʒ/ v. sitiar; asediar.

besieged /bɪ'sidʒd/ a. sitiado.

besieger /bɪ'sidʒər/ n. sitiador -ra.

besmirch /bɪ'smɜrtʃ/ v. manchar; deshonrar.

best /bɛst/ a. & adv. mejor. **at b.,** a lo más.

bestial /'bɛstʃəl/ a. bestial; brutal.

bestir /bɪ'stɜr/ v. incitar; intrigar.

best man n. padrino de boda.

bestow /bɪ'stou/ v. conferir.

bestowal /bɪ'stouəl/ n. dádiva; presentación f.

bet /bɛt/ n. **1.** apuesta f. —v. **2.** apostar.

betoken /bɪ'toukən/ v. presagiar, anunciar.

betray /bɪ'trei/ v. traicionar; revelar.

betrayal /bɪ'treiəl/ n. traición f.

betroth /bɪ'trouð/ v. contraer esponsales; prometerse.

betrothal /bɪ'trouðəl/ n. esponsales m.pl.

better /'bɛtər/ a. & adv. **1.** mejor. —v. **2.** mejorar.

between /bɪ'twin/ prep. entre, en medio de.

bevel /'bɛvəl/ n. **1.** cartabón m. —v. **2.** cortar al sesgo.

beverage /'bɛvərɪdʒ/ n. bebida f.; (cold) refresco m.

bewail /bɪ'weil/ v. llorar; lamentar.

beware /bɪ'wɛər/ v. guardarse, precaverse.

bewilder /bɪ'wɪldər/ v. aturdir.

bewildered /bɪ'wɪldərd/ a. descarriado.

bewildering /bɪ'wɪldərɪŋ/ a. aturdente.

bewilderment /bɪ'wɪldərmənt/ n. aturdimiento m.; perplejidad f.

bewitch /bɪ'wɪtʃ/ v. hechizar; embrujar.

beyond /bi'ɒnd/ prep. más allá de.

biannual /bai'ænyuəl/ a. semianual; semestral.

bias /'baiəs/ n. **1.** parcialidad f.; prejuicio m. **on the b.,** al sesgo. —v. **2.** predisponer, influir.

bib /bɪb/ n. babador m.

Bible /'baibəl/ n. Biblia f.

Biblical /'bɪblɪkəl/ a. bíblico.

bibliography /,bɪbli'ɒgrəfi/ n. bibliografía f.

bicarbonate /bai'kɑrbənɪt/ n. bicarbonato m.

bicentennial /,baisɛn'tɛniəl/ a. & n. bicentenario m.

biceps /'baisɛps/ n. bíceps m.

bicker /'bɪkər/ v. altercar.

bicycle /'baisɪkəl/ n. bicicleta f.

bicyclist /'baisɪklɪst/ n. biciclista m. & f.

bid /bɪd/ n. **1.** proposición, oferta f. —v. **2.** mandar; ofrecer.

bidder /'bɪdər/ n. postor -ra.

bide /baid/ v. aguardar; esperar.

bier /bɪər/ n. ataúd m.

bifocal /bai'foukəl/ a. bifocal.

big /bɪg/ a. grande.

bigamist /'bɪgəmɪst/ n. bígamo -ma.

bigamy /'bɪgəmi/ n. bigamia f.

bigot /'bɪgət/ n. persona intolerante.

bigotry /'bɪgətri/ n. intolerancia f.

bikini /bɪ'kini/ n. bikini m.

bilateral /bai'lætərəl/ a. bilateral.

bile /bail/ n. bilis f.

bilingual /bai'lɪŋgwəl/ a. bilingüe.

bilingualism /bai'lɪŋgwə,lɪzəm/ n. bilingüismo m.

bilious /'bɪlyəs/ a. bilioso.

bill /bɪl/ **1.** n. cuenta, factura f.; (money) billete m.; (of bird) pico m. —v. **2.** facturar.

billboard /'bɪl,bɔrd/ n. cartelera f.

billet /'bɪlɪt/ n. **1.** billete m.; Mil. boleta f. —v. **2.** aposentar.

billfold /'bɪl,fould/ n. cartera f.

billiard balls /'bɪlyərd bɔlz/ bolas de billar.

billiards /'bɪlyərdz/ n. billar m.

billion /'bɪlyən/ n. billón m.

bill of health n. certificado de sanidad.

bill of lading /'leidɪŋ/ n. conocimiento de embarque.

bill of sale n. escritura de venta.

billow /'bɪlou/ n. ola; oleada f.

bimetallic /,baimə'tælɪk/ a. bimetálico.

bimonthly /bai'mʌnθli/ a. & adv. bimestral.

bin /bɪn/ n. hucha f.; depósito m.

bind /baind/ v. atar; obligar; (book) encuadernar.

bindery /'baindəri/ n. taller de encuadernación m.

binding /'baindɪŋ/ n. encuadernación f.

bingo /'bɪŋgou/ n. bingo m.

binocular /bə'nɒkyələr/ a. binocular. n.pl. gemelos m.pl.

biochemistry /,baiou'kɛməstri/ n. bioquímica f.

biodegradable /,baioudɪ'greidəbəl/ a. biodegradable.

biofeedback /,baiou'fid,bæk/ n. biofeedback.

biographer /bai'ɒgrəfər/ n. biógrafo -fa.

biographical /,baiə'græfɪkəl/ a. biográfico.

biography /bai'ɒgrəfi/ n. biografía f.

biological /,baiə'lɒdʒɪkəl/ a. biológico.

biologically /,baiə'lɒdʒɪkəli/ adv. biológicamente.

biology /bai'ɒlədʒi/ n. biología f.

bipartisan /bai'pɑrtəzən/ a. bipartito.

biped /'baipɛd/ n. bípedo m.

bird /bɜrd/ n. pájaro m.; ave f.

birdie /'bɜrdi/ n. (golf) uno bajo par m.

bird of prey n. ave de rapiña f.

bird's-eye view /'bɜrdz,ai/ n. vista de pájaro f.

birth /bɜrθ/ n. nacimiento m. **give b. to,** dar a luz.

birth certificate partida de nacimiento f.

birth control n. contracepción f.

birthday /'bɜrθ,dei/ n. cumpleaños m.

birthmark /'bɜrθ,mɑrk/ n. marca de nacimiento f.

birthplace /'bɜrθ,pleis/ n. natalicio m.

birth rate n. natalidad f.

birthright /'bɜrθ,rait/ n. primogenitura f.

biscuit /'bɪskɪt/ n. bizcocho m.

bisect /bai'sɛkt/ v. bisecar.

bishop /'bɪʃəp/ n. obispo m.; (chess) alfil m.

bishopric /'bɪʃəprɪk/ n. obispado m.

bismuth /'bɪzməθ/ n. bismuto m.

bison /'baisən/ n. bisonte m.

bit /bɪt/ n. pedacito m.; Mech. taladro m.; (for horse) bocado m.; (computer) bit m.

bitch /bɪtʃ/ n. perra f.

bite /bait/ n. **1.** bocado m.; picada f. —v. **2.** morder; picar.

biting /'baitɪŋ/ a. penetrante; mordaz.

bitter /'bɪtər/ a. amargo.

bitterly /'bɪtərli/ adv. amargamente; agriamente.

bitterness /'bɪtərnɪs/ n. amargura f.; rencor m.

bivouac /'bɪvu,æk/ n. **1.** vivaque m. —v. **2.** vivaquear.

biweekly /bai'wikli/ a. quincenal.

black /blæk/ a. negro.

Black /blæk/ n. (person) negro -gra; persona de color.

blackberry /'blæk,bɛri/ n. mora f.

blackbird /'blæk,bɜrd/ n. mirlo m.

blackboard /'blæk,bɔrd/ n. pizarra f.

blacken /'blækən/ v. ennegrecer.

black eye n. ojo amoratado.

blackguard /'blægɑrd/ n. tunante; pillo m.

blacklist /'blæk,lɪst/ n. lista negra f.

blackmail /'blæk,meil/ n. **1.** chantaje m. —v. **2.** amenazar con chantaje, chantajear.

black market mercado negro, estraperlo m.

black marketeer /,mɑrkɪ'tir/ estraperlista mf.

blackout /'blæk,aut/ n. oscurecimiento, apagamiento m.

blacksmith /'blæk,smɪθ/ n. herrero -ra.

bladder /'blædər/ n. vejiga f.

blade /bleid/ n. (sword) hoja f.; (oar) pala f.; (grass) brizna f.

blame /bleim/ v. culpar, echar la culpa a.

blameless /'bleimlɪs/ a. inculpable.

blanch /blæntʃ/ v. blanquear; escaldar.

bland /blænd/ a. blando.

blank /blæŋk/ a. & n. en blanco.

blanket /'blæŋkɪt/ n. manta f.; cobertor m.

blare /blɛər/ n. sonido de trompeta. v. sonar como trompeta.

blaspheme /blæs'fim/ v. blasfemar.

blasphemer /blæs'fimər/ n. blasfemo -ma, blasfemador -ra.

blasphemous /'blæsfəməs/ a. blasfemo, impío.

blasphemy /'blæsfəmi/ n. blasfemia f.

blast /blæst/ n. **1.** barreno m.; (wind) ráfaga f. —v. **2.** barrenar.

blatant /'bleitnt/ a. bramante; descarado.

blaze /bleiz/ n. **1.** llama, hoguera f. —v. **2.** encenderse en llama.

blazing /'bleizɪŋ/ a. flameante.

bleach /blitʃ/ n. **1.** lejía, blanqueador m. —v. **2.** blanquear.

bleachers /'blitʃərz/ n. asientos al aire libre.

bleak /blik/ a. frío y sombrío.

bleakness /'bliknɪs/ n. desolación f.

bleed /blid/ v. sangrar.

blemish /'blɛmɪʃ/ n. **1.** mancha f.; lunar m. —v. **2.** manchar.

blend /blɛnd/ n. **1.** mezcla f. —v. **2.** mezclar, combinar.

blended /'blɛndɪd/ a. mezclado.

blender /'blɛndər/ n. (for food) licuadora f.

bless /blɛs/ v. bendecir.

blessed /'blɛsɪd/ a. bendito.

blessing /'blɛsɪŋ/ a. bendición f.

blight /blait/ n. **1.** plaga f.; tizón m. —v. **2.** atizonar.

blind /blaind/ a. ciego.

blindfold /'blaind,fould/ v. vendar los ojos.

blinding /'blaindɪŋ/ a. deslumbrante; ofuscante.

blindly /'blaindli/ adv. ciegamente.

blindness /'blaindnɪs/ n. ceguedad, ceguera f.

blink /blɪŋk/ n. **1.** guiñada f. —v. **2.** guiñar.

bliss /blɪs/ n. felicidad f.

blissful /'blɪsfəl/ a. dichoso; bienaventurado.

blissfully /'blɪsfəli/ adv. felizmente.

blister /'blɪstər/ n. ampolla f.

blithe /blaið/ a. alegre; jovial; gozoso.

blizzard /'blɪzərd/ n. nevasca f.

bloat /blout/ v. hinchar.

bloc /blɒk/ n. grupo (político); bloc.

block /blɒk/ n. **1.** bloque m.; (street) manzana, cuadra f. —v. **2.** bloquear.

blockade /blɒ'keid/ n. **1.** bloqueo m. —v. **2.** bloquear.

blond /blɒnd/ a. & n. rubio -ia.

blood /blʌd/ n. sangre f.; parentesco, linaje m.

bloodhound /'blʌd,haund/ n. sabueso m.

bloodless /'blʌdlɪs/ a. exangüe; desangrado.

blood poisoning /'pɔizənɪŋ/ envenenamiento de sangre.

blood pressure presión arterial.

bloodshed /'blʌd,ʃɛd/ n. matanza f.

bloodthirsty /'blʌd,θɜrsti/ a. cruel, sanguinario.

bloody /'blʌdi/ a. ensangrentado, sangriento.

bloom /blum/ n. **1.** flor f. —v. **2.** florecer.

blooming /'blumɪŋ/ a. lozano; fresco; floreciente.

blossom /'blɒsəm/ n. **1.** flor f. —v. **2.** florecer.

blot /blɒt/ *n.* **1.** mancha *f.* —*v.* **2.** manchar.

blotch /blɒtʃ/ *n.* **1.** mancha, roncha *f.* —*v.* **2.** manchar.

blotter /ˈblɒtər/ *n.* papel secante.

blouse /blaus/ *n.* blusa *f.*

blow /blou/ *n.* **1.** golpe *m.; Fig.* chasco *m.* —*v.* **2.** soplar.

blowout /ˈblouˌaut/ *n.* reventón de neumático *m.*

blubber /ˈblʌbər/ *n.* grasa de ballena.

bludgeon /ˈblʌdʒən/ *n.* porra *f. v.* apalear.

blue /blu/ *a.* azul; triste, melancólico.

bluebird /ˈbluˌbɜrd/ *n.* azulejo *m.*

blue jeans jeans; vaqueros *m.pl.*

blueprint /ˈbluˌprɪnt/ *n.* heliografía *f.*

bluff /blʌf/ *n.* risco *m. v.* alardear; baladronar.

bluing /ˈbluɪŋ/ *n.* añil *m.*

blunder /ˈblʌndər/ *n.* **1.** desatino *m.* —*v.* **2.** desatinar.

blunderer /ˈblʌndərər/ *n.* desatinado -da.

blunt /blʌnt/ *a.* embotado; descortés. *v.* embotar.

bluntly /ˈblʌntli/ *a.* bruscamente.

bluntness /ˈblʌntnɪs/ *n.* grosería *f.;* brusquedad.

blur /blɜr/ *n.* **1.** trazo confuso. —*v.* **2.** hacer indistinto.

blush /blʌʃ/ *n.* **1.** rubor, sonrojo *m.* —*v.* **2.** sonrojarse.

bluster /ˈblʌstər/ *n.* **1.** fanfarria *f.* —*v.* **2.** fanfarrear.

boar /bɔr/ *n.* verraco *m.* **wild b.,** jabalí.

board /bɔrd/ *n.* **1.** tabla; *Govt.* consejo *m.;* junta *f.* **b. and room,** cuarto y comida, casa y comida. —*v.* **2.** (ship) abordar.

boarder /ˈbɔrdər/ *n.* pensionista *m.* & *f.*

boardinghouse /ˈbɔrdɪŋ/ *n.* pensión *f.*, casa de huéspedes.

boarding pass /ˈbɔrdɪŋ/ boleto de embarque *m.*, tarjeta de embarque *f.*

boast /boust/ *n.* **1.** jactancia *f.* —*v.* **2.** jactarse.

boaster /ˈboustər/ *n.* fanfarrón -na.

boastful /ˈboustfəl/ *a.* jactancioso.

boastfulness /ˈboustfəlnɪs/ *n.* jactancia *f.*

boat /bout/ *n.* barco, buque, bote *m.*

boathouse /ˈboutˌhaus/ *n.* casilla de botes *f.*

boatswain /ˈbousən/ *n.* contramaestre *m.*

bob /bɒb/ *v.* menear.

bobbin /ˈbɒbɪn/ *n.* bobina *f.*

bobby pin /ˈbɒbi/ *n.* gancho *m.*, horquilla.

bodice /ˈbɒdɪs/ *n.* corpiño *m.*

bodily /ˈbɒdl̩i/ *a.* corporal.

body /ˈbɒdi/ *n.* cuerpo *m.*

body builder culturista *mf.*

body building culturismo *m.*

bodyguard /ˈbɒdiˌgɑrd/ *n.* guardaespaldas.

bog /bɒg/ *n.* pantano *m.*

bogey /ˈbougi/ *n.* (golf) uno sobre par *m.*

Bohemian /bouˈhimiən/ *a.* & *n.* bohemio -mia.

boil /bɔil/ *n.* **1.** hervor *m.; Med.* divieso *m.* —*v.* **2.** hervir.

boiler /ˈbɔilər/ *n.* marmita; caldera *f.*

boiling point /ˈbɔilɪŋ/ punto de ebullición *m.*

boisterous /ˈbɔistərəs/ *a.* tumultuoso.

boisterously /ˈbɔistərəsli/ *adv.* tumultuosamente.

bold /bould/ *a.* atrevido, audaz.

boldface /ˈbouldˌfeis/ *n.* (type) letra negra.

boldly /ˈbouldli/ *adv.* audazmente; descaradamente.

boldness /ˈbouldnɪs/ *n.* atrevimiento *m.;* osadía *f.*

Bolivian /bouˈlɪviən/ *a.* & *n.* boliviano -na.

bologna /bəˈlouni/ *n.* salchicha *f.*, mortadela.

bolster /ˈboulstər/ *n.* **1.** travesero, cojín *m.* —*v.* **2.** apoyar, sostener.

bolt /boult/ *n.* perno *m.;* (of door) cerrojo *m.;* (lightning) rayo *m. v.* acerrojar.

bomb /bɒm/ *n.* **1.** bomba *f.* —*v.* **2.** bombardear.

bombard /bɒmˈbɑrd/ *v.* bombardear.

bombardier /ˌbɒmbərˈdɪər/ *n.* bombardero -ra.

bombardment /bɒmˈbɑrdmənt/ *n.* bombardeo *m.*

bomber /ˈbɒmər/ *n.* avión de bombardeo.

bombproof /ˈbɒmˌpruf/ *a.* a prueba de granadas.

bombshell /ˈbɒmˌʃɛl/ *n.* bomba *f.*

bonbon /ˈbɒnˌbɒn/ *n.* dulce, bombón *m.*

bond /bɒnd/ *n.* lazo *m.; Com.* bono *m.*

bondage /ˈbɒndɪdʒ/ *n.* esclavitud, servidumbre *f.*

bonded /ˈbɒndɪd/ *a.* garantizado.

bone /boun/ *n.* hueso *m.*

boneless /ˈbounlɪs/ *a.* sin huesos.

bonfire /ˈbɒnˌfaiᵊr/ *n.* hoguera, fogata *f.*

bonnet /ˈbɒnɪt/ *n.* gorra *f.*

bonus /ˈbounəs/ *n.* sobrepaga *f.*

bony /ˈbouni/ *a.* huesudo.

boo /bu/ *v.* abuchear.

book /bʊk/ *n.* libro *m.*

bookbinder /ˈbʊkˌbaindər/ *n.* encuadernador -ora.

bookcase /ˈbʊkˌkeis/ *n.* armario para libros.

bookkeeper /ˈbʊkˌkipər/ *n.* tenedor -ra de libros.

bookkeeping /ˈbʊkˌkipɪŋ/ *n.* contabilidad *f.*

booklet /ˈbʊklɪt/ *n.* folleto *m.*, libreta *f.*

bookmark /ˈbʊkˌmɑrk/ *n.* marcapáginas *m.*

bookseller /ˈbʊkˌsɛlər/ *n.* librero -ra.

bookstore /ˈbʊkˌstɔr/ *n.* librería *f.*

boom /bum/ *n. Naut.* botalón *m.;* prosperidad repentina.

boon /bun/ *n.* dádiva *f.*

boor /bʊr/ *n.* patán, rústico *m.*

boorish /ˈbʊrɪʃ/ *a.* villano.

boost /bust/ *n.* **1.** alza; ayuda *f.* —*v.* **2.** levantar, alzar; fomentar.

booster /ˈbustər/ *n.* fomentador *m.*

boot /but/ *n.* bota *f.*

bootblack /ˈbutˌblæk/ *n.* limpiabotas *m.*

booth /buθ/ *n.* cabaña; casilla *f.*

booty /ˈbuti/ *n.* botín *m.*

border /ˈbɔrdər/ *n.* **1.** borde *m.;* frontera *f.* —*v.* **2. b. on,** lindar con.

borderline /ˈbɔrdərˌlain/ *a.* marginal. *n.* margen *m.*

bore /bɔr/ *n.* lata *f.;* persona pesada. *v.* aburrir, fastidiar; *Mech.* taladrar.

boredom /ˈbɔrdəm/ *n.* aburrimiento *m.*

boric acid /ˈbɔrɪk/ *n.* ácido bórico *m.*

boring /ˈbɔrɪŋ/ *a.* aburrido, pesado.

born /bɔrn/ *a.* nacido. **be born,** nacer.

born-again /ˈbɔrn əˈgɛn/ *a.* renacido.

borrow /ˈbɒrou/ *v.* pedir prestado.

bosom /ˈbʊzəm/ *v.* seno, pecho *m.*

boss /bɒs/ *n.* jefe, patrón *m.*

botany /ˈbɒtn̩i/ *n.* botánica *f.*

both /bouθ/ *pron.* & *a.* ambos, los dos.

bother /ˈbɒðər/ *n.* molestia *f. v.* molestar, incomodar.

bothersome /ˈbɒðərsəm/ *a.* molesto.

bottle /ˈbɒtl̩/ *n.* **1.** botella *f.* —*v.* **2.** embotellar.

bottling /ˈbɒtl̩ɪŋ/ *n.* embotellamiento *m.*

bottom /ˈbɒtəm/ *n.* fondo *m.*

boudoir /ˈbudwɑr/ *n.* tocador *m.*

bough /bau/ *n.* rama *f.*

boulder /ˈbouldər/ *n.* canto rodado.

boulevard /ˈbʊləˌvɑrd/ *n.* bulevar *m.*

bounce /bauns/ *n.* **1.** brinco *m.* —*v.* **2.** brincar; hacer saltar.

bound /baund/ *n.* **1.** salto *m.* —*v.* **2.** limitar.

boundary /ˈbaundəri/ *n.* límite, lindero *m.*

bouquet /bouˈkei, bu-/ *n.* ramillete de flores.

bourgeois /bʊrˈʒwɑ/ *a.* & *n.* burgués -esa.

bout /baut/ *n.* encuentro; combate *m.*

bow /n bau, bou; *v* bau/ *n.* **1.** saludo *m.;* (of ship) proa *f.;* (archery) arco *m.;* (ribbon) lazo *m.* —*v.* **2.** saludar, inclinar.

bowels /ˈbauəlz/ *n.* intestinos *m.pl.;* entrañas *f.pl.*

bowl /boul/ *n.* **1.** vasija *f.;* platón *m.* —*v.* **2.** jugar a los bolos. **b. over,** derribar.

bowlegged /ˈbouˌlɛgɪd/ *a.* perniabierto.

bowling /ˈboulɪŋ/ *n.* bolos *m.pl.*

bow tie /bou/ pajarita *f.*

box /bɒks/ *n.* **1.** caja *f.; Theat.* palco *m.* —*v.* **2.** (sports) boxear.

boxcar /ˈbɒksˌkɑr/ *n.* vagón *m.*

boxer /ˈbɒksər/ *n.* boxeador -ra, pugilista *m.* & *f.*

boxing /ˈbɒksɪŋ/ *n.* boxeo *m.*

box office *n.* taquilla *f.*

boy /bɔi/ *n.* muchacho, chico, niño *m.*

boycott /ˈbɔikɒt/ *n.* **1.** boicoteo *m.* —*v.* **2.** boicotear.

boyhood /ˈbɔihʊd/ *n.* muchachez *f.*

boyish /ˈbɔiɪʃ/ *a.* pueril.

boyishly /ˈbɔiɪʃli/ *adv.* puerilmente.

bra /brɑ/ *n.* sujetador, sostén *m.*

brace /breis/ *n.* **1.** grapón *m.; pl.* tirantes *m.pl.* —*v.* **2.** reforzar.

bracelet /ˈbreislɪt/ *n.* brazalete *m.*, pulsera *f.*

bracket /ˈbrækɪt/ *n.* ménsula *f.*

brag /bræg/ *v.* jactarse.

braggart /ˈbrægərt/ *a.* **1.** jactancioso. —*n.* **2.** jaque *m.*

braid /breid/ *n.* **1.** trenza *f.* —*v.* **2.** trenzar.

brain /brein/ *n.* cerebro, seso *m.*

brainy /ˈbreini/ *a.* sesudo, inteligente.

brake /breik/ *n.* **1.** freno *m.* —*v.* **2.** frenar.

bran /bræn/ *n.* salvado *m.*

branch /bræntʃ, brɑntʃ/ *n.* ramo *m.;* (of tree) rama *f.*

brand /brænd/ *n.* marca *f.*

brandish /ˈbrændɪʃ/ *v.* blandir.

brand-new /ˈbrænˈnu/ *a.* enteramente nuevo.

brandy /ˈbrændi/ *n.* aguardiente, coñac *m.*

brash /bræʃ/ *a.* impetuoso.

brass /bræs/ *n.* bronce, latón *m.*

brassiere /brəˈzɪər/ *n.* corpiño, sujetador, sostén *m.*

brat /bræt/ *n.* mocoso *m.*

bravado /brəˈvɑdou/ *n.* bravata *f.*

brave /breiv/ *a.* valiente.

bravery /ˈbreivəri/ *n.* valor *m.*

brawl /brɔl/ *n.* alboroto *m. v.* alborotar.

brawn /brɔn/ *n.* músculo *m.*

bray /brei/ *v.* rebuznar.

brazen /ˈbreizən/ *a.* desvergonzado.

Brazil /brəˈzɪl/ *n.* Brasil *m.*

Brazilian /brəˈzɪlyən/ *a.* & *n.* brasileño -ña.

breach /britʃ/ *n.* rotura; infracción *f.*

breach of contract incumplimiento de contrato *m.*

bread /brɛd/ *n.* pan *m.*

breadth /brɛdθ/ *n.* anchura *f.*

break /breik/ *n.* **1.** rotura; pausa *f.* —*v.* **2.** quebrar, romper.

breakable /ˈbreikəbəl/ *a.* rompible, frágil.

breakage /ˈbreikɪdʒ/ *n.* rotura *f.*, destrozo *m.*

breakfast /ˈbrɛkfəst/ *n.* **1.** desayuno, almuerzo *m.* —*v.* **2.** desayunar, almorzar.

breakneck /ˈbreikˌnɛk/ *a.* rápido, precipitado, atropellado.

breast /brɛst/ *n.* (of human) pecho, seno *m.;* (of fowl) pechuga *f.*

breastbone /ˈbrɛstˌboun/ *n.* esternón *m.*

breath /brɛθ/ *n.* aliento; soplo *m.*

breathe /brið/ *v.* respirar.

breathless /ˈbrɛθlɪs/ *a.* desalentado.

breathlessly /ˈbrɛθlɪsli/ *adv.* jadeantemente, intensamente.

bred /brɛd/ *a.* criado; educado.

breeches /ˈbrɪtʃɪz/ *n.pl.* calzones; pantalones, *m.pl.*

breed /brid/ *n.* **1.** raza *f.* —*v.* **2.** engendrar; criar.

breeder /ˈbridər/ *n.* criador -ra.

breeding /ˈbridɪŋ/ *n.* cría *f.*

breeze /briz/ *n.* brisa *f.*

breezy /ˈbrizi/ *a.:* **it is b.,** hace brisa.

brevity /ˈbrɛvɪti/ *n.* brevedad *f.*

brew /bru/ *v.* fraguar; elaborar.

brewer /ˈbruər/ *n.* cervecero -ra.

brewery /ˈbruəri/ *n.* cervecería *f.*

bribe /braib/ *n.* **1.** soborno, cohecho *m.* —*v.* **2.** sobornar, cohechar.

briber /ˈbraibər/ *n.* sobornador -ra.

bribery /ˈbraibəri/ *n.* soborno, cohecho *m.*

brick /brɪk/ *n.* ladrillo *m.*

bricklayer /ˈbrɪkˌleiər/ *n.* albañil *m.*

bridal /ˈbraidl̩/ *a.* nupcial.

bride /braid/ *n.* novia *f.*

bridegroom /ˈbraidˌgrum/ *n.* novio *m.*

bridesmaid /ˈbraidzˌmeid/ *n.* madrina de boda.

bridge /brɪdʒ/ *n.* puente *m.*

bridged /brɪdʒd/ *a.* conectado.

bridgehead /ˈbrɪdʒˌhɛd/ *n. Mil.* cabeza de puente.

bridle /ˈbraidl̩/ *n.* brida *f.*

brief /brif/ *a.* breve.

briefcase /ˈbrifˌkeis/ *n.* maletín *m.*

briefly /ˈbrifli/ *adv.* brevemente.

briefness /ˈbrifnɪs/ *n.* brevedad *f.*

brier /ˈbraiər/ *n.* zarza *f.*

brig /brɪg/ *n.* bergantín *m.*

brigade /brɪˈgeid/ *n.* brigada *f.*

bright /brait/ *a.* claro, brillante.

brighten /ˈbraitn̩/ *v.* abrillantar; alegrar.

brightness /ˈbraitnɪs/ *n.* resplandor *m.*

brilliance /ˈbrɪlyəns/ *n.* brillantez *f.*

brilliant /ˈbrɪlyənt/ *a.* brillante.

brim /brɪm/ *n.* borde *m.;* (of hat) ala *f.*

brine /brain/ *n.* escabeche, *m.* salmuera *f.*

bring /brɪŋ/ *v.* traer. **b. about,** efectuar, llevar a cabo.

brink /brɪŋk/ *n.* borde *m.*

briny /ˈbraini/ *a.* salado.

brisk /brɪsk/ *a.* vivo; enérgico.

briskly /ˈbrɪskli/ *adv.* vivamente.

briskness /ˈbrɪsknɪs/ *n.* viveza *f.*

bristle /ˈbrɪsəl/ *n.* cerda *f.*

bristly /ˈbrɪsli/ *a.* hirsuto.

Britain /ˈbrɪtn̩/ *n.* **Great B.,** Gran Bretaña *f.*

British /ˈbrɪtɪʃ/ *a.* británico.

British Empire imperio británico *m.*

British Isles /ailz/ islas británicas *f.*

Briton /ˈbrɪtn̩/ *n.* inglés *m.*

brittle /ˈbrɪtl̩/ *a.* quebradizo, frágil.

broad /brɔd/ *a.* ancho.

broadcast /ˈbrɔdˌkæst/ *n.* **1.** radiodifusión *f.* —*v.* **2.** radiodifundir.

broadcaster /ˈbrɔdˌkæstər/ *n.* locutor -ra.

broadcloth /ˈbrɔdˌklɔθ/ *n.* paño fino.

broaden /ˈbrɔdn̩/ *v.* ensanchar.

broadly /ˈbrɔdli/ *adv.* ampliamente.

broadminded /ˈbrɔdˈmaindɪd/ *a.* tolerante, liberal.

brocade /brouˈkeid/ *n.* brocado *m.*

brocaded /brouˈkeidɪd/ *a.* espolinado.

broccoli /ˈbrɒkəli/ *n.* brécol *m.*

broil /brɔil/ *v.* asar.

broiler /ˈbrɔilər/ *n.* parrilla *f.*

broken /ˈbroukən/ *a.* roto, quebrado.

broken-hearted /ˈbroukənˈhɑrtɪd/ *a.* angustiado.

broker /ˈbroukər/ n. corredor -ra, bolsista m. & f.

brokerage /ˈbroukərɪdʒ/ n. corretaje m.

bronchial /ˈbrɒŋkiəl/ a. bronquial.

bronchitis /brɒŋˈkaitɪs/ n. bronquitis f.

bronze /brɒnz/ n. bronce m.

brooch /broutʃ/ n. broche m.

brood /brud/ n. **1.** cría, progenie f. —v. **2.** empollar; cobijar.

brook /brʊk/ n. arroyo m., quebrada f.

broom /brum/ n. escoba f.

broomstick /ˈbrumˌstɪk/ n. palo de escoba.

broth /brɔθ/ n. caldo m.

brothel /ˈbrɒθəl/ n. burdel m.

brother /ˈbrʌðər/ n. hermano m.

brotherhood /ˈbrʌðərˌhʊd/ n. fraternidad f.

brother-in-law /ˈbrʌðər ɪn ˌlɔ/ n. cuñado m.

brotherly /ˈbrʌðərli/ a. fraternal.

brow /brau/ n. ceja; frente f.

brown /braun/ a. pardo, moreno; marrón. v. rehogar.

brown sugar azúcar moreno m.

browse /brauz/ v. curiosear; ramonear.

browser /ˈbrauzər/ n. (Internet) navegador m., visualizador m., visor m.

bruise /bruz/ n. **1.** contusión f. —v. **2.** magullar.

brunette /bruˈnɛt/ a. & n. moreno -na, trigueño -ña.

brush /brʌʃ/ n. **1.** cepillo m.; brocha f. —v. **2.** cepillar.

brushwood /ˈbrʌʃˌwʊd/ n. matorral m.

brusque /brʌsk/ a. brusco.

brusquely /ˈbrʌskli/ adv. bruscamente.

brutal /ˈbrutl̩/ a. brutal.

brutality /bruˈtælɪti/ n. brutalidad f.

brutalize /ˈbrutl̩ˌaiz/ v. embrutecer.

brute /brut/ n. bruto -ta, bestia f.

bubble /ˈbʌbəl/ n. ampolla f.

bucket /ˈbʌkɪt/ n. cubo m.

buckle /ˈbʌkəl/ n. hebilla f.

buckram /ˈbʌkrəm/ n. bucarán m.

bucksaw /ˈbʌkˈsɔ/ n. sierra de bastidor.

buckshot /ˈbʌkˌʃɒt/ n. posta f.

buckwheat /ˈbʌkˌwit/ n. trigo sarraceno.

bud /bʌd/ n. **1.** brote m. —v. **2.** brotar.

budding /ˈbʌdɪŋ/ a. en capullo.

budge /bʌdʒ/ v. moverse.

budget /ˈbʌdʒɪt/ n. presupuesto m.

buffalo /ˈbʌfəˌlou/ n. búfalo m.

buffer /ˈbʌfər/ n. parachoques m.

buffet /bəˈfei/ n. bufet m.; (furniture) aparador m.

buffoon /bəˈfun/ n. bufón m.

bug /bʌg/ n. insecto m.; (computer) error m.

bugle /ˈbyugəl/ n. clarín m.; corneta f.

build /bɪld/ v. construir.

builder /ˈbɪldər/ n. constructor -ra.

building /ˈbɪldɪŋ/ n. edificio m.

bulb /bʌlb/ n. bulbo m.; (of lamp) bombilla, ampolla f.

bulge /bʌldʒ/ n. abultamiento m. v. abultar.

bulging /ˈbʌldʒɪŋ/ a. protuberante.

bulimia /buˈlimiə/ n. bulimia f.

bulk /bʌlk/ n. masa f.; grueso m.; mayoría f.

bulkhead /ˈbʌlkˌhɛd/ n. frontón m.

bulky /ˈbʌlki/ a. grueso, abultado.

bull /bʊl/ n. toro m.

bulldog /ˈbʊlˌdɔg/ n. perro de presa.

bullet /ˈbʊlɪt/ n. bala f.

bulletin /ˈbʊlɪtɪn/ n. boletín m.

bulletproof /ˈbʊlɪtˌpruf/ a. a prueba de bala.

bullfight /ˈbʊlˌfait/ n. corrida de toros.

bullfighter /ˈbʊlˌfaitər/ n. torero -ra.

bullfinch /ˈbʊlˌfɪntʃ/ n. pinzón real m.

bully /ˈbʊli/ n. **1.** rufián m. —v. **2.** bravear.

bulwark /ˈbʊlwərk/ n. baluarte m.

bum /bʌm/ n. holgazán m.

bump /bʌmp/ n. **1.** golpe, choque m. —v. **2. b. into,** chocar contra.

bumper /ˈbʌmpər/ n. parachoques m.

bun /bʌn/ n. bollo m.

bunch /bʌntʃ/ n. racimo; montón m.

bundle /ˈbʌndl̩/ n. **1.** bulto m. —v. **2. b. up,** abrigar.

bungalow /ˈbʌŋgəˌlou/ n. casa de un solo piso.

bungle /ˈbʌŋgəl/ v. estropear.

bunion /ˈbʌnyən/ n. juanete m.

bunk /bʌŋk/ n. litera f.

bunny /ˈbʌni/ n. conejito -ta.

bunting /ˈbʌntɪŋ/ n. lanilla; banderas f.

buoy /ˈbui/ n. boya f.

buoyant /ˈbɔiənt/ a. boyante; vivaz.

burden /ˈbɜrdn̩/ n. **1.** carga f. —v. **2.** cargar.

burdensome /ˈbɜrdn̩səm/ a. gravoso.

bureau /ˈbyʊrou/ n. (furniture) cómoda f.; departamento m.

burglar /ˈbɜrglər/ n. ladrón -ona.

burglarize /ˈbɜrgləˌraiz/ v. robar.

burglary /ˈbɜrgləri/ n. robo m.

burial /ˈbɛriəl/ n. entierro m.

burlap /ˈbɜrlæp/ n. arpillera f.

burly /ˈbɜrli/ a. corpulento.

burn /bɜrn/ v. quemar; arder.

burner /ˈbɜrnər/ n. mechero m.

burning /ˈbɜrnɪŋ/ a. ardiente.

burnish /ˈbɜrnɪʃ/ v. pulir; acicalar.

burrow /ˈbɜrou/ v. minar; horadar.

burst /bɜrst/ v. reventar.

bury /ˈbɛri/ v. enterrar.

bus /bʌs/ n. autobús m.

bush /bʊʃ/ n. arbusto m.

bushy /ˈbʊʃi/ a. matoso; peludo.

business /ˈbɪznɪs/ n. negocios m.pl.; comercio m.

businesslike /ˈbɪznɪsˌlaik/ a. directo, práctico.

businessman /ˈbɪznɪsˌmæn/ n. hombre de negocios, comerciante m.

businesswoman /ˈbɪznɪsˌwʊmən/ n. mujer de negocios.

bust /bʌst/ n. busto; pecho m.

bustle /ˈbʌsəl/ n. bullicio m.; animación f.

busy /ˈbɪzi/ a. ocupado, atareado.

busybody /ˈbɪziˌbɒdi/ n. entremetido -da.

but /bʌt/ conj. pero; sino.

butcher /ˈbʊtʃər/ n. carnicero -ra.

butchery /ˈbʊtʃəri/ n. carnicería; matanza f.

butler /ˈbʌtlər/ n. mayordomo m.

butt /bʌt/ n. punta f.; cabo extremo m.

butter /ˈbʌtər/ n. manteca, mantequilla f.

buttercup /ˈbʌtərˌkʌp/ n. ranúnculo m.

butterfat /ˈbʌtərˌfæt/ n. mantequilla f.

butterfly /ˈbʌtərˌflai/ n. mariposa f.

buttermilk /ˈbʌtərˌmɪlk/ n. suero (de leche) m.

button /ˈbʌtn̩/ n. botón m.

buttonhole /ˈbʌtn̩ˌhoul/ n. ojal m.

buttress /ˈbʌtrɪs/ n. sostén; refuerzo m.

buxom /ˈbʌksəm/ a. regordete.

buy /bai/ v. comprar.

buyer /ˈbaiər/ n. comprador -ra.

buzz /bʌz/ n. **1.** zumbido m. —v. **2.** zumbar.

buzzard /ˈbʌzərd/ n. gallinazo m.

buzzer /ˈbʌzər/ n. zumbador m.; timbre m.

buzz saw n. sierra circular f.

by /bai/ prep. por; (near) cerca de, al lado de; (time) para.

by-and-by /ˌbaiənˈbai/ adv. pronto; luego.

bygone /ˈbaiˌgɔn/ a. pasado.

bylaw /ˈbaiˌlɔ/ n. estatuto, reglamento m.

bypass /ˈbaiˌpæs/ n. desvío m.

byproduct /ˈbaiˌprɒdəkt/ n. subproducto m.

bystander /ˈbaiˌstændər/ n. espectador -ra; mirón -na.

byte /bait/ n. en teoría de la información: ocho bits, byte m.

byway /ˈbaiˌwei/ n. camino desviado m.

C

cab /kæb/ n. taxi, coche de alquiler m.

cabaret /ˌkæbəˈrei/ n. cabaret m.

cabbage /ˈkæbɪdʒ/ n. repollo m.

cabin /ˈkæbɪn/ n. cabaña f.

cabinet /ˈkæbənɪt/ n. gabinete; ministerio m.

cabinetmaker /ˈkæbənɪtˌmeikər/ n. ebanista m.

cable /ˈkeibəl/ n. cable m.

cablegram /ˈkeibəlˌgræm/ n. cablegrama m.

cache /kæʃ/ n. escondite m.

cackle /ˈkækəl/ n. charla f.; cacareo m. v. cacarear.

cacophony /kəˈkɒfəni/ n. cacofonía f.

cactus /ˈkæktəs/ n. cacto m.

cad /kæd/ n. persona vil.

cadaver /kəˈdævər/ n. cadáver m.

cadaverous /kəˈdævərəs/ a. cadavérico.

caddie /ˈkædi/ n. (golf) ayudante m. & f.

cadence /ˈkeidns/ n. cadencia f.

cadet /kəˈdɛt/ n. cadete m.

cadmium /ˈkædmiəm/ n. cadmio m.

cadre /ˈkædri, ˈkɑdrei/ n. núcleo; Mil. cuadro m.

café /kæˈfei/ n. café m., cantina f.

cafeteria /ˌkæfɪˈtɪəriə/ n. cafetería f.

caffeine /kæˈfin/ n. cafeína f.

cage /keidʒ/ n. jaula f. v. enjaular.

caged /keidʒd/ a. enjaulado.

caisson /ˈkeisɒn, -sən/ n. arcón m.; Mil. furgón m.

cajole /kəˈdʒoul/ v. lisonjear; adular.

cake /keik/ n. torta f.; bizcocho m.

calamitous /kəˈlæmɪtəs/ a. calamitoso.

calamity /kəˈlæmɪti/ n. calamidad f.

calcify /ˈkælsəˌfai/ v. calcificar.

calcium /ˈkælsiəm/ n. calcio m.

calculable /ˈkælkyələbəl/ a. calculable.

calculate /ˈkælkyəˌleit/ v. calcular.

calculating /ˈkælkyəˌleitɪŋ/ a. interesado.

calculation /ˌkælkyəˈleiʃən/ n. calculación f.; cálculo m.

calculus /ˈkælkyələs/ n. cálculo m.

caldron /ˈkɔldrən/ n. caldera f.

calendar /ˈkæləndər/ n. calendario m.

calf /kæf/ n. ternero m. (animal); pantorrilla f. (of the body).

calfskin /ˈkæfˌskɪn/ n. piel de becerro.

caliber /ˈkælɪbər/ n. calibre m.

calico /ˈkælɪˌkou/ n. calicó m.

caliper /ˈkæləpər/ n. calibrador m.

calisthenics /ˌkæləsˈθɛnɪks/ n. calistenia, gimnasia f.

calk /kɔk/ v. calafatear; rellenar.

calker /ˈkɔkər/ n. calafate -ta.

call /kɔl/ n. **1.** llamada f. —v. **2.** llamar.

calligraphy /kəˈlɪgrəfi/ n. caligrafía f.

calling /ˈkɔlɪŋ/ n. vocación f.

calling card tarjeta (de visita) f.

callously /ˈkæləsli/ adv. insensiblemente.

callow /ˈkælou/ a. sin experiencia.

callus /ˈkæləs/ n. callo m.

calm /kɑm/ a. **1.** tranquilo, calmado. —n. **2.** calma f. —v. **3.** calmar.

calmly /ˈkɑmli/ adv. serenamente.

calmness /ˈkɑmnɪs/ n. calma f.

caloric /kəˈlɔrɪk/ a. calórico.

calorie /ˈkæləri/ n. caloría f.

calorimeter /ˌkæləˈrɪmɪtər/ n. calorímetro m.

calumniate /kəˈlʌmniˌeit/ v. calumniar.

calumny /ˈkæləmni/ n. calumnia f.

Calvary /ˈkælvəri/ n. Calvario m.

calve /kæv/ v. parir (la vaca).

calyx /ˈkeilɪks/ n. cáliz m.

camaraderie /ˌkɑməˈrɑdəri/ n. compañerismo m., compadrería f.

cambric /ˈkeimbrɪk/ n. batista f.

camcorder /ˈkæmˌkɔrdər/ n. videocámara f.

camel /ˈkæməl/ n. camello -lla.

camellia /kəˈmilyə/ n. camelia f.

camel's hair /ˈkæməlz/ pelo de came;llo.

cameo /ˈkæmiˌou/ n. camafeo m.

camera /ˈkæmərə/ n. cámara f.

camouflage /ˈkæməˌflɑʒ/ n. camuflaje m.

camouflaging /ˈkæməˌflɑʒɪŋ/ n. simulacro, disfraz m.

camp /kæmp/ n. **1.** campamento m. —v. **2.** acampar.

campaign /kæmˈpein/ n. campaña f.

camper /ˈkæmpər/ n. acampado m.

campfire /ˈkæmpˌfaiᵊr/ n. fogata de campamento.

camphor /ˈkæmfər/ n. alcanfor m.

camphor ball bola de alcanfor.

campus /ˈkæmpəs/ n. campo de colegio (o universidad), campus m.

can /kæn/ v. (be able) poder.

can /kæn/ n. **1.** lata f. —v. **2.** conservar en latas, enlatar.

Canada /ˈkænədə/ n. Canadá m.

Canadian /kəˈneidiən/ a. & n. canadiense.

canal /kəˈnæl/ n. canal m.

canalize /ˈkænl̩ˌaiz/ v. canalizar.

canard /kəˈnɑrd/ n. embuste m.

canary /kəˈnɛəri/ n. canario -ria.

cancel /ˈkænsəl/ v. cancelar.

cancellation /ˌkænsəˈleiʃən/ n. cancelación f.

cancer /ˈkænsər/ n. cáncer m.

candelabrum /ˌkændl̩ˈɑbrəm/ n. candelabro m.

candid /ˈkændɪd/ a. cándido, sincero.

candidacy /ˈkændɪdəsi/ n. candidatura f.

candidate /ˈkændɪˌdeit/ n. candidato -ta.

candidly /ˈkændɪdli/ adv. cándidamente.

candidness /ˈkændɪdnɪs/ n. candidez; sinceridad f.

candied /ˈkændid/ a. garapiñado.

candle /ˈkændl̩/ n. vela f.

candlestick /ˈkændl̩ˌstɪk/ n. candelero m.

candor /ˈkændər/ n. candor m.; sinceridad f.

candy /ˈkændi/ n. dulces m.pl.

cane /kein/ n. caña f.; (for walking) bastón m.

canine /ˈkeinain/ a. canino.

canister /ˈkænəstər/ n. frasco m.; lata f.

canker /ˈkæŋkər/ n. llaga; úlcera f.

cankerworm /ˈkæŋkərˌwɜrm/ n. oruga f.

canned /kænd/ a. envasado, enlatado.

canner /ˈkænər/ n. envasador m.

cannery /ˈkænəri/ n. fábrica de conservas alimenticias f.

cannibal /ˈkænəbəl/ n. caníbal m. & f.

cannon /ˈkænən/ n. cañón m.

cannonade /ˌkænəˈneid/ n. cañoneo m.

cannoneer /ˌkænəˈnɪər/ n. cañonero -ra.

canny /ˈkæni/ a. sagaz; prudente.

canoe /kəˈnu/ n. canoa, piragua f.

canoeing /kəˈnuɪŋ/ n. piragüismo m.

canoeist /kəˈnuɪst/ n. piragüista m. & f.

canon /ˈkænən/ n. canon m.; Relig. canónigo m.

canonical /kəˈnɒnɪkəl/ a. canónico.

canonize /ˈkænəˌnaiz/ v. canonizar.

can opener /ˈoupənər/ abrelatas m.

canopy /ˈkænəpi/ n. dosel m.

cant /kænt/ *n.* hipocresía *f.*
cantaloupe /ˈkæntḷˌoup/ *n.* melón *m.*
canteen /kænˈtin/ *n.* cantina *f.*
canter /ˈkæntər/ *n.* **1.** medio galope *m.* —*v.* **2.** galopar.
cantonment /kænˈtɒnmənt/ *n. Mil.* acuartelamiento *m.*
canvas /ˈkænvəs/ *n.* lona *f.*
canyon /ˈkænyən/ *n.* cañón, desfiladero *m.*
cap /kæp/ *n.* **1.** tapa *f.*; (headwear) gorro *m.* —*v.* **2.** tapar.
capability /ˌkeipəˈbɪlɪti/ *n.* capacidad *f.*
capable /ˈkeipəbəl/ *a.* capaz.
capably /ˈkeipəbli/ *adv.* hábilmente.
capacious /kəˈpeiʃəs/ *a.* espacioso.
capacity /kəˈpæsɪti/ *n.* capacidad *f.*
cape /keip/ *n.* capa *f.*, *Geog.* cabo *m.*
caper /ˈkeipər/ *n.* zapateta *f.*; *Bot.* alcaparra *f.*
capillary /ˈkæpəˌlɛri/ *a.* capilar.
capital /ˈkæpɪtḷ/ *n.* capital *m.*; *Govt.* capital *f.*
capitalism /ˈkæpɪtḷˌɪzəm/ *n.* capitalismo *m.*
capitalist /ˈkæpɪtḷɪst/ *n.* capitalista *m.* & *f.*
capitalistic /ˌkæpɪtḷˈɪstɪk/ *a.* capitalista.
capitalization /ˌkæpɪtḷəˈzeiʃən/ *n.* capitalización *f.*
capitalize /ˈkæpɪtḷˌaiz/ *v.* capitalizar.
capital letter *n.* mayúscula *f.*
capitulate /kəˈpɪtʃəˌleit/ *v.* capitular.
capon /ˈkeipɒn/ *n.* capón *m.*
caprice /kəˈpris/ *n.* capricho *m.*
capricious /kəˈprɪʃəs/ *a.* caprichoso.
capriciously /kəˈprɪʃəsli/ *adv.* caprichosamente.
capriciousness /kəˈprɪʃəsnɪs/ *n.* capricho *m.*
capsize /ˈkæpsaiz/ *v.* zozobrar, volcar.
capsule /ˈkæpsəl/ *n.* cápsula *f.*
captain /ˈkæptən/ *n.* capitán -tana.
caption /ˈkæpʃən/ *n.* título *m.*; (motion pictures) subtítulo *m.*
captious /ˈkæpʃəs/ *a.* capcioso.
captivate /ˈkæptəˌveit/ *v.* cautivar.
captivating /ˈkæptəˌveitɪŋ/ *a.* encantador.
captive /ˈkæptɪv/ *n.* cautivo -va, prisionero -ra.
captivity /kæpˈtɪvɪti/ *n.* cautividad *f.*
captor /ˈkæptər/ *n.* apresador -ra.
capture /ˈkæptʃər/ *n.* **1.** captura *f.* —*v.* **2.** capturar.
car /kɑr/ *n.* coche, carro *m.*; (of train) vagón, coche *m.* **baggage c.,** vagón de equipajes. **parlor c.,** coche salón.
carafe /kəˈræf/ *n.* garrafa *f.*
caramel /ˈkærəməl/ *n.* caramelo *m.*
carat /ˈkærət/ *n.* quilate *m.*
caravan /ˈkærəˌvæn/ *n.* caravana *f.*
caraway /ˈkærəˌwei/ *n.* alcaravea *f.*
carbide /ˈkɑrbaid/ *n.* carburo *m.*
carbine /ˈkɑrbin/ *n.* carabina *f.*
carbohydrate /ˌkɑrbouˈhaidreit/ *n.* hidrato de carbono.
carbon /ˈkɑrbən/ *n.* carbón *m.*
carbon dioxide /daiˈɒksaid/ anhídrido carbónico.
carbon monoxide /mɒnˈɒksaid/ monóxido de carbono.
carbon paper papel carbón *m.*
carbuncle /ˈkɑrbʌŋkəl/ *n.* carbúnculo *m.*
carburetor /ˈkɑrbəˌreitər/ *n.* carburador *m.*
carcinogenic /ˌkɑrsənəˈdʒɛnɪk/ *a.* carcinogénico.
card /kɑrd/ *n.* tarjeta *f.* **playing c.,** naipe *m.*
cardboard /ˈkɑrdˌbɔrd/ *n.* cartón *m.*
cardiac /ˈkɑrdiˌæk/ *a.* cardíaco.
cardigan /ˈkɑrdɪgən/ *n.* chaqueta de punto.
cardinal /ˈkɑrdṇl/ *a.* **1.** cardinal. —*n.* **2.** cardenal *m.*
cardiologist /ˌkɑrdiˈɒlədʒɪst/ *n.* cardiólogo, -ga *m.* & *f.*
care /kɛər/ *n.* **1.** cuidado. —*v.* **2. c. for,** cuidar.
careen /kəˈrin/ *v.* carenar; echarse de costado.
career /kəˈrɪər/ *n.* carrera *f.*
carefree /ˈkɛərˌfri/ *a.* descuidado.
careful /ˈkɛərfəl/ *a.* cuidadoso. **be. c.,** tener cuidado.
carefully /ˈkɛərfəli/ *adv.* cuidadosamente.
carefulness /ˈkɛərfəlnɪs/ *n.* esmero; cuidado *m.*; cautela *f.*
careless /ˈkɛərlɪs/ *a.* descuidado.
carelessly /ˈkɛərlɪsli/ *adv.* descuidadamente; negligentemente.
carelessness /ˈkɛərlɪsnɪs/ *n.* descuido *m.*
caress /kəˈrɛs/ *n.* **1.** caricia *f.* —*v.* **2.** acariciar.
caretaker /ˈkɛərˌteikər/ *n.* guardián -ana.
cargo /ˈkɑrgou/ *n.* carga *f.*
caricature /ˈkærɪkətʃər/ *n.* caricatura *f.*
caricaturist /ˈkærɪkəˌtʃʊrɪst/ *n.* caricaturista *m.* & *f.*
caries /ˈkɛəriz/ *n.* caries *f.*
carjacking /ˈkɑrˌdʒækɪŋ/ *n.* robo de coche *m.*
carload /ˈkɑrˌloud/ *a.* furgonada, vagonada.
carnal /ˈkɑrnḷ/ *a.* carnal.
carnation /kɑrˈneiʃən/ *n.* clavel *m.*
carnival /ˈkɑrnəvəl/ *n.* carnaval *m.*
carnivorous /kɑrˈnɪvərəs/ *a.* carnívoro.
carol /ˈkærəl/ *n.* villancico *m.*
carouse /kəˈrauz/ *v.* parrandear.
carpenter /ˈkɑrpəntər/ *n.* carpintero -ra.
carpet /ˈkɑrpɪt/ *n.* alfombra *f.*
carpeting /ˈkɑrpɪtɪŋ/ *n.* alfombrado *m.*
car pool /ˈkɑrˌpul/ uso habitual, por varias personas, de un automóvil perteneciente a una de ellas.
carriage /ˈkærɪdʒ/ *n.* carruaje; (bearing) porte *m.*
carrier /ˈkæriər/ *n.* portador -ra.
carrier pigeon paloma mensajera.
carrot /ˈkærət/ *n.* zanahoria *f.*
carrousel /ˌkærəˈsɛl/ *n.* volantín, carrusel *m.*
carry /ˈkæri/ *v.* llevar, cargar. **c. out,** cumplir, llevar a cabo.
cart /kɑrt/ *n.* carreta *f.*
cartage /ˈkɑrtɪdʒ/ *n.* acarreo, carretaje *m.*
cartel /kɑrˈtɛl/ *n.* cartel *m.*
cartilage /ˈkɑrtḷɪdʒ/ *n.* cartílago *m.*
carton /ˈkɑrtṇ/ *n.* caja de cartón.
cartoon /kɑrˈtun/ *n.* caricatura *f.*
cartoonist /kɑrˈtunɪst/ *n.* caricaturista *m.* & *f.*
cartridge /ˈkɑrtrɪdʒ/ *n.* cartucho *m.*
carve /kɑrv/ *v.* esculpir; (meat) trinchar.
carver /ˈkɑrvər/ *n.* tallador -ra; grabador -ra.
carving /ˈkɑrvɪŋ/ *n.* entalladura *f.*; arte de trinchar. **c. knife,** trinchante *m.*
cascade /kæsˈkeid/ *n.* cascada *f.*
case /keis/ *n.* caso *m.*; (box) caja *f.* **in any c.,** sea como sea.
cash /kæʃ/ *n.* **1.** dinero contante. —*v.* **2.** efectuar, cambiar.
cashier /kæˈʃɪər/ *n.* cajero -ra.
cashmere /ˈkæʒmɪər/ *n.* casimir *m.*
casino /kəˈsinou/ *n.* casino *m.*
cask /kæsk/ *n.* barril *m.*
casket /ˈkæskɪt/ *n.* ataúd *m.*
casserole /ˈkæsəˌroul/ *n.* cacerola *f.*
cassette /kəˈsɛt/ *n.* cassette *m.*, cartucho *m.*
cast /kæst/ *n.* **1.** *Theat.* reparto de papeles. —*v.* **2.** echar; *Theat.* repartir.
castanet /ˌkæstəˈnɛt/ *n.* castañuela *f.*
castaway /ˈkæstəˌwei/ *n.* náufrago -ga.
caste /kæst/ *n.* casta *f.*
caster /ˈkæstər/ *n.* tirador *m.*
castigate /ˈkæstɪˌgeit/ *v.* castigar.
Castilian /kæˈstɪlyən/ *a.* castellano.
cast iron *n.* hierro colado *m.*
castle /ˈkæsəl/ *n.* castillo *m.*
castoff /ˈkæstˌɔf/ *a.* descartado.
casual /ˈkæʒuəl/ *a.* casual.
casually /ˈkæʒuəli/ *adv.* casualmente.
casualness /ˈkæʒuəlnɪs/ *n.* casualidad *f.*
casualty /ˈkæʒuəlti/ *n.* víctima *f.*; *Mil.* baja *f.*
cat /kæt/ *n.* gato -ta.
cataclysm /ˈkætəˌklɪzəm/ *n.* cataclismo *m.*
catacomb /ˈkætəˌkoum/ *n.* catacumba *f.*
catalogue /ˈkætḷˌɔg/ *n.* catálogo *m.*
catapult /ˈkætəˌpʌlt/ *n.* catapulta *f.*
cataract /ˈkætəˌrækt/ *n.* catarata *f.*
catarrh /kəˈtɑr/ *n.* catarro *m.*
catastrophe /kəˈtæstrəfi/ *n.* catástrofe *f.*
catch /kætʃ/ *v.* alcanzar, atrapar, coger.
catchy /ˈkætʃi/ *a.* contagioso.
catechism /ˈkætɪˌkɪzəm/ *n.* catequismo *m.*
catechize /ˈkætɪˌkaiz/ *v.* catequizar.
categorical /ˌkætɪˈgɔrɪkəl/ *a.* categórico.
category /ˈkætɪˌgɔri/ *n.* categoría *f.*
cater /ˈkeitər/ *v.* abastecer; proveer. **c. to,** complacer.
caterpillar /ˈkætəˌpɪlər/ *n.* gusano *m.*
catgut /ˈkætˌgʌt/ *n.* cuerda (de tripa).
catharsis /kəˈθɑrsɪs/ *n.* catarsis, purga *f.*
cathartic /kəˈθɑrtɪk/ *a.* **1.** catártico; purgante. —*n.* **2.** purgante *m.*
cathedral /kəˈθidrəl/ *n.* catedral *f.*
cathode /ˈkæθoud/ *n.* cátodo *m.*
Catholic /ˈkæθəlɪk/ *a.* católico & *n.* católico -ca.
Catholicism /kəˈθɒləˌsɪzəm/ *n.* catolicismo *m.*
catnap /ˈkætˌnæp/ *n.* siesta corta.
catsup /ˈkætsəp, ˈkɛtʃəp/ *n.* salsa de tomate.
cattle /ˈkætḷ/ *n.* ganado *m.*
cattleman /ˈkætḷmən, -ˌmæn/ *n.* ganadero *m.*
cauliflower /ˈkɔləˌflauər/ *n.* coliflor *m.*
causation /kɔˈzeiʃən/ *n.* causalidad *f.*
cause /kɔz/ *n.* causa *f.*
causeway /ˈkɔzˌwei/ *n.* calzada elevada *f.*; terraplén *m.*
caustic /ˈkɔstɪk/ *a.* cáustico.
cauterize /ˈkɔtəˌraiz/ *v.* cauterizar.
cautery /ˈkɔtəri/ *n.* cauterio *m.*
caution /ˈkɔʃən/ *n.* cautela *f.*
cautious /ˈkɔʃəs/ *a.* cauteloso.
cavalcade /ˌkævəlˈkeid/ *n.* cabalgata *f.*
cavalier /ˌkævəˈlɪər/ *n.* caballero *m.*
cavalry /ˈkævəlri/ *n.* caballería *f.*
cave /keiv/ **cavern** *n.* caverna, gruta *f.*
cave-in /ˈkeiv ˌɪn/ *n.* hundimiento *m.*
caviar /ˈkæviˌɑr/ *n.* caviar *m.*
cavity /ˈkævɪti/ *n.* hueco *m.*
cayman /ˈkeimən/ *n.* caimán *m.*
CD player tocadiscos compacto, tocadiscos digital *m.*
cease /sis/ *v.* cesar.
ceaseless /ˈsislɪs/ *a.* incesante.
cedar /ˈsidər/ *n.* cedro *m.*
cede /sid/ *v.* ceder.
ceiling /ˈsilɪŋ/ *n.* techo; cielo *m.*
celebrant /ˈsɛləbrənt/ *n.* celebrante -ta.
celebrate /ˈsɛləˌbreit/ *v.* celebrar.
celebration /ˌsɛləˈbreiʃən/ *n.* celebración *f.*
celebrity /səˈlɛbrɪti/ *n.* celebridad.
celerity /səˈlɛrɪti/ *n.* celeridad; prontitud *f.*
celery /ˈsɛləri/ *n.* apio *m.*
celestial /səˈlɛstʃəl/ *a.* celeste.
celibacy /ˈsɛləbəsi/ *n.* celibato -ta.
celibate /ˈsɛləbɪt/ *a.* & *n.* célibe *m.* & *f.*
cell /sɛl/ *n.* celda *f.*; *Biol.* célula *f.*
cellar /ˈsɛlər/ *n.* sótano *m.*
cellist /ˈtʃɛlɪst/ *a.* celista *m.* & *f.*
cello /ˈtʃɛlou/ *n.* violonchelo *m.*
cellophane /ˈsɛləˌfein/ *n.* celofán *m.*
cellular /ˈsɛlyələr/ *a.* celular.
cellular phone /foun/ teléfono móvil *m.*
celluloid /ˈsɛlyəˌlɔid/ *n.* celuloide *m.*
cellulose /ˈsɛlyəˌlous/ *a.* **1.** celuloso. —*n.* **2.** celulosa *f.*
Celtic /ˈkɛltɪk, ˈsɛl-/ *a.* céltico.
cement /sɪˈmɛnt/ *n.* cemento *m.*
cemetery /ˈsɛmɪˌtɛri/ *n.* cementerio *m.*; campo santo *m.*
censor /ˈsɛnsər/ *n.* censor -ra.
censorious /sɛnˈsɔriəs/ *a.* severo; crítico.
censorship /ˈsɛnsərˌʃɪp/ *n.* censura *f.*
censure /ˈsɛnʃər/ *n.* **1.** censura *f.* —*v.* **2.** censurar.
census /ˈsɛnsəs/ *n.* censo *m.*
cent /sɛnt/ *n.* centavo, céntimo *m.*
centenary /sɛnˈtɛnəri/ *a.* & *n.* centenario *m.*
centennial /sɛnˈtɛniəl/ *a.* & *n.* centenario *m.*
center /ˈsɛntər/ *n.* centro *m.*
centerfold /ˈsɛntərˌfould/ *n.* página central desplegable en una revista.
centerpiece /ˈsɛntərˌpis/ *n.* centro de mesa.
centigrade /ˈsɛntɪˌgreid/ *a.* centígrado.
centigrade thermometer termómetro centígrado.
central /ˈsɛntrəl/ *a.* central.
Central American *a.* & *n.* centroamericano -na.
centralize /ˈsɛntrəˌlaiz/ *v.* centralizar.
century /ˈsɛntʃəri/ *n.* siglo *m.*
century plant maguey *m.*
ceramic /səˈræmɪk/ *a.* cerámico.
ceramics /səˈræmɪks/ *n.* cerámica *f.*
cereal /ˈsɪəriəl/ *n.* cereal *m.*
cerebral /səˈribrəl/ *a.* cerebral.
ceremonial /ˌsɛrəˈmouniəl/ *a.* ceremonial.
ceremonious /ˌsɛrəˈmouniəs/ *a.* ceremonioso.
ceremony /ˈsɛrəˌmouni/ *n.* ceremonia *f.*
certain /ˈsɜrtṇ/ *a.* cierto, seguro.
certainly /ˈsɜrtṇli/ *adv.* sin duda, seguramente.
certainty /ˈsɜrtṇti/ *n.* certeza *f.*
certificate /sərˈtɪfɪkɪt/ *n.* certificado *m.*
certification /ˌsɜrtəfɪˈkeiʃən, sərˌtɪfə-/ *n.* certificación *f.*
certified /ˈsɜrtəˌfaid/ *a.* certificado.
certify /ˈsɜrtəˌfai/ *v.* certificar.
certitude /ˈsɜrtɪˌtyud/ *n.* certeza *f.*
cessation /sɛˈseiʃən/ *n.* cesación, descontinuación *f.*
cession /ˈsɛʃən/ *n.* cesión *f.*
chafe /tʃeif/ *v.* irritar.
chafing dish /ˈtʃeifɪŋ/ *n.* escalfador *m.*
chagrin /ʃəˈgrɪn/ *n.* disgusto *m.*
chain /tʃein/ *n.* **1.** cadena *f.* —*v.* **2.** encadenar.
chair /tʃɛər/ *n.* silla *f.*
chairman /ˈtʃɛərmən/ *n.* presidente -ta.
chairperson /ˈtʃɛərˌpɜrsən/ *n.* presidente -ta; persona que preside.
chalk /tʃɔk/ *n.* tiza *f.*
challenge /ˈtʃælɪndʒ/ *n.* **1.** desafío *m.* —*v.* **2.** desafiar.
challenger /ˈtʃælɪndʒər/ *n.* desafiador -ra.
chamber /ˈtʃeimbər/ *n.* cámara *f.*
chamberlain /ˈtʃeimbərlɪn/ *n.* camarero *m.*
chambermaid /ˈtʃeimbərˌmeid/ *n.* camarera *f.*
chameleon /kəˈmiliən/ *n.* camaleón *m.*
chamois /ˈʃæmi/ *n.* gamuza *f.*
champagne /ʃæmˈpein/ *n.* champán *m.*, champaña *f.*
champion /ˈtʃæmpiən/ *n.* **1.** campeón -na —*v.* **2.** defender.
championship /ˈtʃæmpiənˌʃɪp/ *n.* campeonato *m.*

chance /tʃæns/ *n.* oportunidad, ocasión *f.* **by c.,** por casualidad, por acaso. **take a c.,** aventurarse.
chancel /'tʃænsəl/ *n.* antealtar *m.*
chancellery /'tʃænsələri/ *n.* cancillería *f.*
chancellor /'tʃænsələr/ *n.* canciller *m.*
chandelier /ˌʃændl̩'ɪər/ *n.* araña de luces.
change /tʃeindʒ/ *n.* **1.** cambio; (from a bill) moneda *f.* —*v.* **2.** cambiar.
changeability /ˌtʃeindʒə'bɪlɪti/ *n.* mutabilidad *f.*
changeable /'tʃeindʒəbəl/ *a.* variable, inconstante.
changer /'tʃeindʒər/ *n.* cambiador -ra.
channel /'tʃænl̩/ *n.* **1.** canal *m.* —*v.* **2.** encauzar.
Channel Tunnel túnel del Canal de la Mancha *m.*
chant /tʃænt/ *n.* **1.** canto llano *m.* —*v.* **2.** cantar.
chaos /'keiɒs/ *n.* caos *m.*
chaotic /kei'ɒtɪk/ *a.* caótico.
chap /tʃæp/ *n.* **1.** *Colloq.* tipo *m.* —*v.* **2.** rajar.
chapel /'tʃæpəl/ *n.* capilla *f.*
chaperon /'ʃæpəˌroun/ *n.* acompañante -ta de señorita.
chaplain /'tʃæplɪn/ *n.* capellán *m.*
chapter /'tʃæptər/ *n.* capítulo *m.*
char /tʃɑr/ *v.* carbonizar.
character /'kærɪktər/ *n.* carácter *m.*
characteristic /ˌkærɪktə'rɪstɪk/ *a.* **1.** característico. —*n.* **2.** característica *f.*
characterization /ˌkærɪktərə'zeiʃən/ *n.* caracterización *f.*
characterize /'kærɪktəˌraiz/ *v.* caracterizar.
charcoal /'tʃɑrˌkoul/ *n.* carbón leña.
charge /tʃɑrdʒ/ *n.* **1.** acusación *f.*; ataque *m.* —*v.* **2.** cargar; acusar; atacar.
chariot /'tʃæriət/ *n.* carroza *f.*
charisma /kə'rɪzmə/ *n.* carisma *m.*
charitable /'tʃærɪtəbəl/ *a.* caritativo.
charitableness /'tʃærɪtəbəlnɪs/ *n.* caridad *f.*
charitably /'tʃærɪtəbli/ *adv.* caritativamente.
charity /'tʃærɪti/ *n.* caridad *f.*; (alms) limosna *f.*
charlatan /'ʃɑrlətn̩/ *n.* charlatán -na.
charlatanism /'ʃɑrlətn̩ˌɪzəm/ *n.* charlatanería *f.*
charm /tʃɑrm/ *n.* **1.** encanto *m.*; (witchcraft) hechizo *m.* —*v.* **2.** encantar; hechizar.
charming /'tʃɑrmɪŋ/ *a.* encantador.
charred /tʃɑrd/ *a.* carbonizado.
chart /tʃɑrt/ *n.* tabla, esquema *f.*
charter /'tʃɑrtər/ *n.* **1.** carta *f.* —*v.* **2.** alquilar.
charter flight vuelo chárter *m.*
charwoman /'tʃɑrˌwʊmən/ *n.* mujer de la limpieza *f.*
chase /tʃeis/ *n.* **1.** caza *f.* —*v.* **2.** cazar; perseguir.
chaser /'tʃeisər/ *n.* perseguidor -ra.
chasm /'kæzəm/ *n.* abismo *m.*
chassis /'tʃæsi/ *n.* chasis *m.*
chaste /tʃeist/ *a.* casto.
chasten /'tʃeisən/ *v.* corregir, castigar.
chastise /tʃæs'taiz/ *v.* castigar.
chastisement /tʃæs'taizmənt/ *n.* castigo *m.*
chastity /'tʃæstɪti/ *n.* castidad, pureza *f.*
chat /tʃæt/ *n.* **1.** plática, charla *f.* —*v.* **2.** platicar, charlar.
chateau /ʃæ'tou/ *n.* castillo *m.*
chattels /'tʃætəlz/ *n.pl.* bienes *m.*
chatter /'tʃætər/ *v.* **1.** cotorrear; (teeth) rechinar. —*n.* **2.** cotorreo *m.*
chatterbox /'tʃætˌər bɒks/ *n.* charlador -ra.
chauffeur /'ʃoufər/ *n.* chofer *m.*
cheap /tʃip/ *a.* barato.
cheapen /'tʃipən/ *v.* rebajar, menospreciar.
cheaply /'tʃipli/ *adv.* barato.
cheapness /'tʃipnɪs/ *n.* baratura *f.*
cheat /tʃit/ *v.* engañar.
cheater /'tʃitər/ *n.* engañador -ra.
check /tʃɛk/ *n.* **1.** verificación *f.*; (bank) cheque *m.*; (restaurant) cuenta *f.*; (chess) jaque *m.* —*v.* **2.** verificar.
checkers /'tʃɛkərz/ *n.* juego de damas.
checkmate /'tʃɛkˌmeit/ *v.* dar mate.
checkout counter /'tʃɛkˌaut/ caja *f.*
cheek /tʃik/ *n.* mejilla *f.* (of face), desfachatez *f.* (gall).
cheekbone /'tʃikˌboun/ *n.* pómulo *m.*
cheeky /'tʃiki/ *a.* fresco, descarado, chulo.
cheer /tʃɪər/ *n.* **1.** alegría *f.*; aplauso *m.* —*v.* **2.** alegrar; aplaudir.
cheerful /'tʃɪərfəl/ *a.* alegre.
cheerfully /'tʃɪərfəli/ *adv.* alegremente.
cheerfulness /'tʃɪərfəlnɪs/ *n.* alegría *f.*
cheerless /'tʃɪərlɪs/ *a.* triste.
cheery /'tʃɪəri/ *a.* alegre.
cheese /tʃiz/ *n.* queso *m.* **cottage c.,** requesón *m.*
chef /ʃɛf/ *n.* cocinero en jefe.
chemical /'kɛmɪkəl/ *a.* **1.** químico. —*n.* **2.** reactivo *m.*
chemically /'kɛmɪkli/ *adv.* químicamente.
chemist /'kɛmɪst/ *n.* químico -ca.
chemistry /'kɛməstri/ *n.* química *f.*
chemotherapy /ˌkimou'θɛrəpi/ *n.* quimioterapia *f.*
chenille /ʃə'nil/ *n.* felpilla *f.*
cherish /'tʃɛrɪʃ/ *v.* apreciar.
cherry /'tʃɛri/ *n.* cereza *f.*
cherub /'tʃɛrəb/ *n.* querubín *m.*
chess /tʃɛs/ *n.* ajedrez *m.*
chest /tʃɛst/ *n.* arca *f.*; (physiology) pecho *m.*
chestnut /'tʃɛsˌnʌt/ *n.* castaña *f.*
chevron /'ʃɛvrən/ *n.* sardineta *f.*
chew /tʃu/ *v.* mascar, masticar.
chewer /'tʃuər/ *n.* mascador -ra.
chic /ʃik/ *a.* elegante, paquete.
chicanery /ʃɪ'keinəri/ *n.* trampería *f.*
chick /tʃɪk/ *n.* pollito -ta.
chicken /'tʃɪkən/ *n.* pollo *m.*, gallina *f.*
chicken-hearted /'tʃɪkən 'hɑrtɪd/ *a.* cobarde.
chicken pox /pɒks/ viruelas locas, varicela *f.*
chicle /'tʃɪkəl/ *n.* chicle *m.*
chicory /'tʃɪkəri/ *n.* achicoria *f.*
chide /tʃaid/ *v.* regañar, reprender.
chief /tʃif/ *a.* **1.** principal. —*n.* **2.** jefe -fa.
chiefly /'tʃifli/ *adv.* principalmente, mayormente.
chieftain /'tʃiftən/ *n.* caudillo *m.*; (Indian c.) cacique *m.*
chiffon /ʃɪ'fɒn/ *n.* chifón *m.*, gasa *f.*
chilblain /'tʃɪlblein/ *n.* sabañón *m.*
child /tʃaild/ *n.* niño -ña; hijo -ja.
childbirth /'tʃaildˌbɜrθ/ *n.* parto *m.*
childhood /'tʃaildhʊd/ *n.* niñez *f.*
childish /'tʃaildɪʃ/ *a.* pueril.
childishness /'tʃaildɪʃnɪs/ *n.* puerilidad *f.*
childless /'tʃaildlɪs/ *a.* sin hijos.
childlike /'tʃaildˌlaik/ *a.* infantil.
Chilean /'tʃɪliən/ *a.* & *n.* chileno -na.
chili /'tʃɪli/ *n.* chile, ají *m.*
chill /tʃɪl/ *n.* **1.** frío; escalofrío *m.* —*v.* **2.** enfriar.
chilliness /'tʃɪlinɪs/ *n.* frialdad *f.*
chilly /'tʃɪli/ *a.* frío; friolento.
chimes /tʃaimz/ *n.* juego de campanas.
chimney /'tʃɪmni/ *n.* chimenea *f.*
chimpanzee /ˌtʃɪmpæn'zi, tʃɪm'pænzi/ *n.* chimpancé *m.*
chin /tʃɪn/ *n.* barba *f.*
china /'tʃainə/ *n.* loza *f.*
chinchilla /tʃɪn'tʃɪlə/ *n.* chinchilla *f.*
Chinese /tʃai'niz/ *a.* & *n.* chino -na.
chink /tʃɪŋk/ *n.* grieta *f.*
chintz /tʃɪnts/ *n.* zaraza *f.*
chip /tʃɪp/ *n.* **1.** astilla *f.* —*v.* **2.** astillar.
chiropodist /kɪ'rɒpədɪst/ *n.* pedicuro -ra.
chiropractor /'kairəˌpræktər/ *n.* quiropráctico -ca.
chirp /tʃɜrp/ *n.* **1.** chirrido *m.* —*v.* **2.** chirriar, piar.
chisel /'tʃɪzəl/ *n.* **1.** cincel *m.* —*v.* **2.** cincelar, talar.
chivalrous /'ʃɪvəlrəs/ *a.* caballeroso.
chivalry /'ʃɪvəlri/ *n.* caballería *f.*
chive /tʃaiv/ *n.* cebollino *m.*
chloride /'klɔraid/ *n.* cloruro *m.*
chlorine /'klɔrin/ *n.* cloro *m.*
chloroform /'klɔrəˌfɔrm/ *n.* cloroformo *m.*
chlorophyll /'klɔrəfɪl/ *n.* clorofila *f.*
chock-full /'tʃɒk'fʊl/ *a.* repleto, colmado.
chocolate /'tʃɔkəlɪt/ *n.* chocolate *m.*
choice /tʃɔis/ *a.* **1.** selecto, escogido. —*n.* **2.** selección *f.*; escogimiento *m.*
choir /kwaiᵊr/ *n.* coro *m.*
choke /tʃouk/ *v.* sofocar, ahogar.
cholera /'kɒlərə/ *n.* cólera *f.*
choleric /'kɒlərɪk/ *a.* colérico, irascible.
cholesterol /kə'lɛstəˌroul/ *n.* colesterol *m.*
choose /tʃuz/ *v.* elegir, escoger.
chop /tʃɒp/ *n.* **1.** chuleta, costilla *f.* —*v.* **2.** tajar; cortar.
chopper /'tʃɒpər/ *n.* tajador -ra.
choppy /'tʃɒpi/ *a.* agitado.
choral /'kɔrəl/ *a.* coral.
chord /kɔrd/ *n.* cuerda *f.*; acorde *m.*
chore /tʃɔr/ *n.* tarea *f.*, quehacer *m.*
choreography /ˌkɔri'ɒgrəfi, ˌkour-/ *n.* coreografía *f.*
chorister /'kɔrəstər/ *n.* corista *m.*
chorus /'kɔrəs/ *n.* coro *m.*
christen /'krɪsən/ *v.* bautizar.
Christendom /'krɪsəndəm/ *n.* cristiandad *f.*
Christian /'krɪsʃən/ *a.* & *n.* cristiano -na.
Christianity /ˌkrɪsʃi'ænɪti/ *n.* cristianismo *m.*
Christmas /'krɪsməs/ *n.* Navidad, Pascua *f.* **Merry C.,** felices Pascuas. **C. Eve,** Nochebuena *f.*
chromatic /krou'mætɪk/ *a.* cromático.
chromium /'kroumiəm/ *n.* cromo *m.*
chromosome /'krouməˌsoum/ *n.* cromosoma *m.*
chronic /'krɒnɪk/ *a.* crónico.
chronicle /'krɒnɪkəl/ *n.* crónica *f.*
chronological /ˌkrɒnl̩'ɒdʒɪkəl/ *a.* cronológico.
chronology /krə'nɒlədʒi/ *n.* cronología *f.*
chrysalis /'krɪsəlɪs/ *n.* crisálida *f.*
chrysanthemum /krɪ'sænθəməm/ *n.* crisantemo *m.*
chubby /'tʃʌbi/ *a.* regordete, rollizo.
chuck /tʃʌk/ *v.* (cluck) cloquear; (throw) echar, tirar.
chuckle /'tʃʌkəl/ *v.* reír entre dientes.
chum /tʃʌm/ *n.* amigo -ga; compinche *m.*
chummy /'tʃʌmi/ *a.* íntimo.
chunk /tʃʌŋk/ *n.* trozo *m.*
chunky /'tʃʌŋki/ *a.* fornido, trabado.
Chunnel /'tʃʌnl̩/ *n.* túnel del Canal de la Mancha *m.*
church /tʃɜrtʃ/ *n.* iglesia *f.*
churchman /'tʃɜrtʃmən/ *n.* eclesiástico *m.*
churchyard /'tʃɜrtʃˌyɑrd/ *n.* cementerio *m.*
churn /tʃɜrn/ *n.* **1.** mantequera *f.* —*v.* **2.** agitar, revolver.
chute /ʃut/ *n.* conducto; canal *m.*
cicada /sɪ'keidə/ *n.* cigarra, chicharra *f.*
cider /'saidər/ *n.* sidra *f.*
cigar /sɪ'gɑr/ *n.* cigarro, puro *m.*
cigarette /ˌsɪgə'rɛt/ *n.* cigarrillo, cigarro, pitillo *m.* **c. case,** cigarrillera *f.* **c. lighter,** encendedor *m.*
cinchona /sɪŋ'kounə/ *n.* cinchona *f.*
cinder /'sɪndər/ *n.* ceniza *f.*
cinema /'sɪnəmə/ *n.* cine *m.*
cinnamon /'sɪnəmən/ *n.* canela *f.*
cipher /'saifər/ *n.* cifra *f.*
circle /'sɜrkəl/ *n.* círculo *m.*
circuit /'sɜrkɪt/ *n.* circuito *m.*
circuitous /sər'kyuɪtəs/ *a.* tortuoso.
circuitously /sər'kyuɪtəsli/ *adv.* tortuosamente.
circular /'sɜrkyələr/ *a.* circular, redondo.
circularize /'sɜrkyələˌraiz/ *v.* hacer circular.
circulate /'sɜrkyəˌleit/ *v.* circular.
circulation /ˌsɜrkyə'leiʃən/ *n.* circulación *f.*
circulator /'sɜrkyəˌleitər/ *n.* diseminador -ra.
circulatory /'sɜrkyələˌtɔri/ *a.* circulatorio.
circumcise /'sɜrkəmˌsaiz/ *v.* circuncidar.
circumcision /ˌsɜrkəm'sɪʒən/ *n.* circuncisión *f.*
circumference /sər'kʌmfərəns/ *n.* circunferencia *f.*
circumlocution /ˌsɜrkəmlou'kyuʃən/ *n.* circunlocución *f.*
circumscribe /'sɜrkəmˌskraib/ *v.* circunscribir; limitar.
circumspect /'sɜrkəmˌspɛkt/ *a.* discreto.
circumstance /'sɜrkəmˌstæns/ *n.* circunstancia *f.*
circumstantial /ˌsɜrkəm'stænʃəl/ *a.* circunstancial, indirecto.
circumstantially /ˌsɜrkəm'stænʃəli/ *adv.* minuciosamente.
circumvent /ˌsɜrkəm'vɛnt/ *v.* evadir, evitar.
circumvention /ˌsɜrkəm'vɛnʃən/ *n.* trampa *f.*
circus /'sɜrkəs/ *n.* circo *m.*
cirrhosis /sɪ'rousɪs/ *n.* cirrosis *f.*
cistern /'sɪstərn/ *n.* cisterna *f.*
citadel /'sɪtədl̩/ *n.* ciudadela *f.*
citation /sai'teiʃən/ *n.* citación *f.*
cite /sait/ *v.* citar.
citizen /'sɪtəzən/ *n.* ciudadano -na.
citizenship /'sɪtəzənˌʃɪp/ *n.* ciudadanía *f.*
citric /'sɪtrɪk/ *a.* cítrico.
city /'sɪti/ *n.* ciudad *f.*
city hall ayuntamiento, municipio *m.*
city planning urbanismo *m.*
civic /'sɪvɪk/ *a.* cívico.
civics /'sɪvɪks/ *n.* ciencia del gobierno civil.
civil /'sɪvəl/ *a.* civil; cortés.
civilian /sɪ'vɪlyən/ *a.* & *n.* civil *m.* & *f.*
civility /sɪ'vɪlɪti/ *n.* cortesía *f.*
civilization /ˌsɪvələ'zeiʃən/ *n.* civilización *f.*
civilize /'sɪvəˌlaiz/ *v.* civilizar.
civil rights /raits/ derechos civiles *m. pl.*
civil service *n.* servicio civil oficial *m.*
civil war *n.* guerra civil *f.*
clabber /'klæbər/ *n.* **1.** cuajo *m.* —*v.* **2.** cuajarse.
clad /klæd/ *a.* vestido.
claim /kleim/ *n.* **1.** demanda; pretensión *f.* —*v.* **2.** demandar, reclamar.
claimant /'kleimənt/ *n.* reclamante -ta.
clairvoyance /klɛər'vɔiəns/ *n.* clarividencia *f.*
clairvoyant /klɛər'vɔiənt/ *a.* clarividente.
clam /klæm/ *n.* almeja *f.*
clamber /'klæmbər/ *v.* trepar.
clamor /'klæmər/ *n.* **1.** clamor *m.* —*v.* **2.** clamar.
clamorous /'klæmərəs/ *a.* clamoroso.
clamp /klæmp/ *n.* **1.** prensa de sujeción *f.* —*v.* **2.** asegurar, sujetar.
clan /klæn/ *n.* tribu *f.*, clan *m.*
clandestine /klæn'dɛstɪn/ *a.* clandestino.
clandestinely /klæn'dɛstɪnli/ *adv.* clandestinamente.
clangor /'klæŋər, 'klæŋgər/ *n.* estruendo *m.*, estrépito *m.*

clannish /'klænɪʃ/ a. unido; exclusivista.

clap /klæp/ v. aplaudir.

clapboard /'klæbərd, 'klæp,bɔrd/ n. chilla f.

claque /klæk/ n. claque f.

claret /'klærɪt/ n. clarete m.

clarification /,klærəfə'keɪʃən/ n. clarificación f.

clarify /'klærə,faɪ/ v. clarificar.

clarinet /,klærə'nɛt/ n. clarinete m.

clarinetist /,klærə'nɛtɪst/ n. clarinetista m. & f.

clarity /'klærɪti/ n. claridad f.

clash /klæʃ/ n. 1. choque, enfrentamiento m. —v. 2. chocar.

clasp /klæsp/ n. 1. broche m. —v. 2. abrochar.

class /klæs/ n. clase f.

classic, /'klæsɪk/ classical a. clásico.

classicism /'klæsə,sɪzəm/ n. clasicismo m.

classifiable /'klæsə,faɪəbəl/ a. clasificable, calificable.

classification /,klæsəfɪ'keɪʃən/ n. clasificación f.

classify /'klæsə,faɪ/ v. clasificar.

classmate /'klæs,meɪt/ n. compañero -ra de clase.

classroom /'klæs,rum, -,rʊm/ n. sala de clase.

clatter /'klætər/ n. 1. alboroto m. —v. 2. alborotar.

clause /klɔz/ n. cláusula f.

claustrophobia /,klɔstrə'foʊbiə/ n. claustrofobia f.

claw /klɔ/ n. garra f.

clay /kleɪ/ n. arcilla f.; barro m.

clean /klin/ a. 1. limpio. —v. 2. limpiar.

cleaner /'klinər/ n. limpiador -ra.

cleaning lady, cleaning woman /'klinɪŋ/ señora de la limpieza, mujer de la limpieza f.

cleanliness /'klɛnlinɪs/ n. limpieza f.

cleanse /klɛnz/ v. limpiar, purificar.

cleanser /'klɛnzər/ n. limpiador m., purificador m.

clear /klɪər/ a. claro.

clearance /'klɪərəns/ n. espacio libre. **c. sale,** venta de liquidación.

clearing /'klɪərɪŋ/ n. despejo m.; desmonte m.

clearly /'klɪərli/ adv. claramente, evidentemente.

clearness /'klɪərnɪs/ n. claridad f.

cleavage /'klivɪdʒ/ n. resquebradura f.

cleaver /'klivər/ n. partidor m., hacha f.

clef /klɛf/ n. clave, llave f.

clemency /'klɛmənsi/ n. clemencia f.

clench /klɛntʃ/ v. agarrar.

clergy /'klɜrdʒi/ n. clero m.

clergyman /'klɜrdʒimən/ n. clérigo m.

clerical /'klɛrɪkəl/ a. clerical. **c. work,** trabajo de oficina.

clericalism /'klɛrɪkə,lɪzəm/ n. clericalismo m.

clerk /klɜrk/ n. dependiente, escribiente m.

clerkship /'klɜrkʃɪp/ n. escribanía f., secretaría f.

clever /'klɛvər/ a. diestro, hábil.

cleverly /'klɛvərli/ adv. diestramente, hábilmente.

cleverness /'klɛvərnɪs/ n. destreza f.

cliché /kli'ʃeɪ/ n. tópico m.

client /'klaɪənt/ n. cliente -ta.

clientele /,klaɪən'tɛl/ n. clientela f.

cliff /klɪf/ n. precipicio, risco m.

climate /'klaɪmɪt/ n. clima m.

climatic /klaɪ'mætɪk/ a. climático.

climax /'klaɪmæks/ n. colmo m., culminación f.

climb /klaɪm/ v. escalar; subir.

climber /'klaɪmər/ n. trepador -ra, escalador -ra; Bot. enredadera f.

climbing plant /'klaɪmɪŋ/ enredadera f.

clinch /klɪntʃ/ v. afirmar.

cling /klɪŋ/ v. pegarse.

clinic /'klɪnɪk/ n. clínica f.

clinical /'klɪnɪkəl/ a. clínico.

clinically /'klɪnɪkəli/ adv. clínicamente.

clip /klɪp/ n. 1. grapa f. **paper c.,** gancho m. —v. 2. prender; (shear) trasquilar.

clipper /'klɪpər/ n. recortador m.; Aero. clíper m.

clipping /'klɪpɪŋ/ n. recorte m.

clique /klik/ n. camarilla f., compadraje m.

cloak /kloʊk/ n. capa f., manto m.

clock /klɒk/ n. reloj m. **alarm c.,** despertador m.

clod /klɒd/ n. terrón m.; césped m.

clog /klɒg/ v. obstruir.

cloister /'klɔɪstər/ n. claustro m.

clone /kloʊn/ n. clon m. & f. v. clonar.

close /a, adv. kloʊs; v klouz/ a. 1. cercano. —adv. 2. cerca. **c. to,** cerca de. —v. 3. cerrar; tapar.

closely /'kloʊsli/ adv. (near) de cerca; (tight) estrechamente; (care) cuidadosamente.

closeness /'kloʊsnɪs/ n. contigüidad f., apretamiento m.; (airless) falta de ventilación f.

closet /'klɒzɪt/ n. gabinete m. **clothes c.,** ropero m.

clot /klɒt/ n. 1. coágulo f. —v. 2. coagularse.

cloth /klɒθ/ n. paño m.; tela f.

clothe /kloʊð/ v. vestir.

clothes /kloʊz/ n. ropa f.

clothing /'kloʊðɪŋ/ n. vestidos m., ropa f.

cloud /klaʊd/ n. nube f.

cloudburst /'klaʊd,bɜrst/ n. chaparrón m.

cloudiness /'klaʊdinɪs/ n. nebulosidad f.; obscuridad f.

cloudless /'klaʊdlɪs/ a. despejado, sin nubes.

cloudy /'klaʊdi/ a. nublado.

clove /kloʊv/ n. clavo m.

clover /'kloʊvər/ n. trébol m.

clown /klaʊn/ n. bufón -na, payaso -sa.

clownish /'klaʊnɪʃ/ a. grosero; bufonesco.

cloy /klɔɪ/ v. saciar, empalagar.

club /klʌb/ n. 1. porra f.; (social) círculo, club m.; (cards) basto m. —v. 2. golpear con una porra.

clubfoot /'klʌb,fʊt/ n. pateta m., pie zambo m.

clue /klu/ n. seña, pista f.

clump /klʌmp/ n. grupo m., masa f.

clumsiness /'klʌmzinɪs/ n. tosquedad f.; desmaña f.

clumsy /'klʌmzi/ a. torpe, desmañado.

cluster /'klʌstər/ n. 1. grupo m.; (fruit) racimo m. —v. 2. agrupar.

clutch /klʌtʃ/ n. 1. Auto. embrague m. —v. 2. agarrar.

clutter /'klʌtər/ n. 1. confusión f. —v. 2. poner en desorden.

coach /koʊtʃ/ n. 1. coche, vagón m.; coche ordinario; (sports) entrenador m. —v. 2. entrenar.

coachman /'koʊtʃmən/ n. cochero -ra.

coagulate /koʊ'ægyə,leɪt/ v. coagular.

coagulation /koʊ,ægyə'leɪʃən/ n. coagulación f.

coal /koʊl/ n. carbón m.

coalesce /,koʊə'lɛs/ v. unirse, soldarse.

coalition /,koʊə'lɪʃən/ n. coalición f.

coal oil n. petróleo m.

coal tar n. alquitrán m.

coarse /kɔrs/ a. grosero, burdo; (material) tosco, grueso.

coarsen /'kɔrsən/ v. vulgarizar.

coarseness /'kɔrsnɪs/ n. grosería; tosquedad f.

coast /koʊst/ n. 1. costa, litoral m. —v. 2. deslizarse.

coastal /'koʊstl/ a. costanero.

coast guard guardacostas m. & f.

coat /koʊt/ n. 1. saco m., chaqueta f.; (paint) capa f. —v. 2. cubrir.

coat of arms /ɑrmz/ n. escudo m.

coax /koʊks/ v. instar.

cobalt /'koʊbɔlt/ n. cobalto m.

cobbler /'kɒblər/ n. zapatero -ra.

cobblestone /'kɒbəl,stoʊn/ n. guijarro m.

cobra /'koʊbrə/ n. cobra f.

cobweb /'kɒb,wɛb/ n. telaraña f.

cocaine /koʊ'keɪn/ n. cocaína f.

cock /kɒk/ n. (rooster) gallo m.; (water, etc.) llave f.; (gun) martillo m.

cockfight /'kɒk,faɪt/ n. riña de gallos f.

cockpit /'kɒk,pɪt/ n. gallera f.; reñidero de gallos m.; Aero. cabina f.

cockroach /'kɒk,roʊtʃ/ n. cucaracha f.

cocktail /'kɒk,teɪl/ n. cóctel m.

cocky /'kɒki/ a. confiado, atrevido.

cocoa /'koʊkoʊ/ n. cacao m.

coconut /'koʊkə,nʌt/ n. coco m.

cocoon /kə'kun/ n. capullo m.

cod /kɒd/ n. bacalao m.

code /koʊd/ n. código m.; clave f.

codeine /'koʊdin/ n. codeína f.

codfish /'kɒd,fɪʃ/ n. bacalao m.

codify /'kɒdə,faɪ/ v. compilar.

cod-liver oil /'kɒd 'lɪvər/ aceite de hígado de bacalao m.

coeducation /,koʊɛdʒʊ'keɪʃən/ n. coeducación f.

coequal /koʊ'ikwəl/ a. mutuamente igual.

coerce /koʊ'ɜrs/ v. forzar.

coercion /koʊ'ɜrʃən/ n. coerción f.

coercive /koʊ'ɜrsɪv/ a. coercitivo.

coexist /,koʊɪg'zɪst/ v. coexistir.

coffee /'kɔfi/ n. café m. **c. plantation,** cafetal m. **c. shop,** café m.

coffee break pausa para el café f.

coffer /'kɔfər/ n. cofre m.

coffin /'kɔfɪn/ n. ataúd m.

cog /kɒg/ n. diente de rueda m.

cogent /'koʊdʒənt/ a. convincente.

cogitate /'kɒdʒɪ,teɪt/ v. pensar, reflexionar.

cognizance /'kɒgnəzəns/ n. conocimiento m., comprensión f.

cognizant /'kɒgnəzənt/ a. conocedor, informado.

cogwheel /'kɒg,wil/ n. rueda dentada f.

cohere /koʊ'hɪər/ v. pegarse.

coherent /koʊ'hɪərənt/ a. coherente.

cohesion /koʊ'hiʒən/ n. cohesión f.

cohesive /koʊ'hisɪv/ a. cohesivo.

cohort /'koʊhɔrt/ n. cohorte f.

coiffure /kwɑ'fyʊr/ n. peinado, tocado m.

coil /kɔɪl/ n. 1. rollo m.; Naut. adujada f. —v. 2. enrollar.

coin /kɔɪn/ n. moneda f.

coinage /'kɔɪnɪdʒ/ n. sistema monetario m.

coincide /,koʊɪn'saɪd/ v. coincidir.

coincidence /koʊ'ɪnsɪdəns/ n. coincidencia; casualidad f.

coincident /koʊ'ɪnsɪdənt/ a. coincidente.

coincidental /koʊ,ɪnsɪ'dɛntl/ a. coincidental.

coincidentally /koʊ,ɪnsɪ'dɛntli/ adv. coincidentalmente, al mismo tiempo.

colander /'kɒləndər/ n. colador m.

cold /koʊld/ a. & n. frío -a; Med. resfriado m. **to be c.,** tener frío; (weather) hacer frío.

coldly /'koʊldli/ adv. fríamente.

coldness /'koʊldnɪs/ n. frialdad f.

collaborate /kə'læbə,reɪt/ v. colaborar.

collaboration /kə,læbə'reɪʃən/ n. colaboración f.

collaborator /kə'læbə,reɪtər/ n. colaborador -ra.

collapse /kə'læps/ n. 1. desplome m.; Med. colapso m. —v. 2. desplomarse.

collar /'kɒlər/ n. cuello m.

collarbone /'kɒlər,boʊn/ n. clavícula f.

collate /koʊ'leɪt/ v. comparar.

collateral /kə'lætərəl/ a. 1. colateral. —n. 2. garantía f.

collation /kə'leɪʃən/ n. comparación f.; (food) colación f., merienda f.

colleague /'kɒlig/ n. colega m. & f.

collect /kə'lɛkt/ v. cobrar; recoger; coleccionar.

collection /kə'lɛkʃən/ n. colección f.

collective /kə'lɛktɪv/ a. colectivo.

collectively /kə'lɛktɪvli/ adv. colectivamente, en masa.

collector /kə'lɛktər/ n. colector -ra; coleccionista m. & f.

college /'kɒlɪdʒ/ n. colegio m.; universidad f.

collegiate /kə'lidʒɪt/ n. colegiado m.

collide /kə'laɪd/ v. chocar.

collision /kə'lɪʒən/ n. choque m.

colloquial /kə'loʊkwiəl/ a. familiar.

colloquially /kə'loʊkwiəli/ adv. familiarmente.

colloquy /'kɒləkwi/ n. conversación f., coloquio m.

collusion /kə'luʒən/ n. colusión f., connivencia f.

Cologne /kə'loʊn/ n. Colonia f.

Colombian /kə'lʌmbiən/ a. & n. colombiano -na.

colon /'koʊlən/ n. colon m.; Punct. dos puntos.

colonel /'kɜrnl/ n. coronel m.

colonial /kə'loʊniəl/ a. colonial.

colonist /'kɒlənɪst/ n. colono -na.

colonization /,kɒlənə'zeɪʃən/ n. colonización f.

colonize /'kɒlə,naɪz/ v. colonizar.

colony /'kɒləni/ n. colonia f.

color /'kʌlər/ n. 1. color; colorido m. —v. 2. colorar; colorir.

coloration /,kʌlə'reɪʃən/ n. colorido m.

colored /'kʌlərd/ a. de color.

colorful /'kʌlərfəl/ a. vívido.

colorless /'kʌlərlɪs/ a. descolorido, sin color.

colossal /kə'lɒsəl/ a. colosal.

colt /koʊlt/ n. potro m.

column /'kɒləm/ n. columna f.

coma /'koʊmə/ n. coma m.

comb /koʊm/ n. 1. peine m. —v. 2. peinar.

combat /n 'kɒmbæt; v kəm'bæt/ n. 1. combate m. —v. 2. combatir.

combatant /kəm'bætnt/ n. combatiente -ta.

combative /kəm'bætɪv/ a. combativo.

combination /,kɒmbə'neɪʃən/ n. combinación f.

combine /kəm'baɪn/ v. combinar.

combustible /kəm'bʌstəbəl/ a. & n. combustible m.

combustion /kəm'bʌstʃən/ n. combustión f.

come /kʌm/ v. venir. **c. back,** volver. **c. in,** entrar. **c. out,** salir. **c. up,** subir. **c. upon,** encontrarse con.

comedian /kə'midiən/ n. cómico -ca.

comedienne /kə,midi'ɛn/ n. cómica f., actriz f.

comedy /'kɒmɪdi/ n. comedia f.

comet /'kɒmɪt/ n. cometa m.

comfort /'kʌmfərt/ n. 1. confort m.; solaz m. —v. 2. confortar; solazar.

comfortable /'kʌmftəbəl/ a. cómodo.

comfortably /'kʌmftəbli/ adv. cómodamente.

comforter /'kʌmfərtər/ n. colcha f.

comfortingly /'kʌmfərtɪŋli/ adv. confortantemente.

comfortless /'kʌmfərtlɪs/ a. sin consuelo; sin comodidades.

comic /'kɒmɪk/ **comical** a. cómico.

comic book n. tebeo m.

coming /'kʌmɪŋ/ n. 1. venida f., llegada f. —a. 2. próximo, que viene, entrante.

comma /'kɒmə/ n. coma f.

command /kə'mænd/ n. 1. mando m. —v. 2. mandar.

commandeer /,kɒmən'dɪər/ v. reclutir forzosamente, expropiar.

commander /kə'mændər/ *n.* comandante -ta.

commander in chief *n.* generalísimo, jefe supremo.

commandment /kə'mændmənt/ *n.* mandato; mandamiento *m.*

commemorate /kə'mɛmə,reit/ *v.* conmemorar.

commemoration /kə,mɛmə'reiʃən/ *n.* conmemoración *f.*

commemorative /kə'mɛmə,reitiv/ *a.* conmemorativo.

commence /kə'mɛns/ *v.* comenzar, principiar.

commencement /kə'mɛnsmənt/ *n.* comienzo *m.*; graduación *f.*

commend /kə'mɛnd/ *v.* encomendar; elogiar.

commendable /kə'mɛndəbəl/ *a.* recomendable.

commendably /kə'mɛndəbli/ *adv.* loablemente.

commendation /,kɒmən'deiʃən/ *n.* recomendación *f.*; elogio *m.*

commensurate /kə'mɛnsərit/ *a.* proporcionado.

comment /'kɒmɛnt/ *n.* **1.** comentario *m.* —*v.* **2.** comentar.

commentary /'kɒmən,tɛri/ *n.* comentario *m.*

commentator /'kɒmən,teitər/ *n.* comentador -ra.

commerce /'kɒmərs/ *n.* comercio *m.*

commercial /kə'mɜrʃəl/ *a.* comercial.

commercialism /kə'mɜrʃə,lizəm/ *n.* comercialismo *m.*

commercialize /kə'mɜrʃə,laiz/ *v.* mercantilizar, explotar.

commercially /kə'mɜrʃəli/ *a. & adv.* comercialmente.

commiserate /kə'mizə,reit/ *v.* compadecerse.

commissary /'kɒmə,sɛri/ *n.* comisario *m.*

commission /kə'miʃən/ *n.* **1.** comisión *f.* —*v.* **2.** comisionar.

commissioner /kə'miʃənər/ *n.* comisario -ria.

commit /kə'mit/ *v.* cometer.

commitment /kə'mitmənt/ *n.* compromiso *m.*

committee /kə'miti/ *n.* comité *m.*

commodious /kə'moudiəs/ *a.* cómodo.

commodity /kə'mɒditi/ *n.* mercadería *f.*

common /'kɒmən/ *a.* común; ordinario.

commonly /'kɒmənli/ *adv.* comúnmente, vulgarmente.

Common Market Mercado Común *m.*

commonplace /'kɒmən,pleis/ *a.* trivial, banal.

common sense sentido común *m.*

commonwealth /'kɒmən,wɛlθ/ *n.* estado *m.*; nación *f.*

commotion /kə'mouʃən/ *n.* tumulto *m.*

communal /kə'myunḷ/ *a.* comunal, público.

commune /'kɒmyun/ *n.* **1.** distrito municipal *m.*; comuna *f.* —*v.* **2.** conversar.

communicable /kə'myunɪkəbəl/ *a.* comunicable; *Med.* transmisible.

communicate /kə'myunɪ,keit/ *v.* comunicar.

communication /kə,myunɪ'keiʃən/ *n.* comunicación *f.*

communicative /kə'myunɪ,keitiv/ *a.* comunicativo.

communion /kə'myunyən/ *n.* comunión *f.* **take c.**, comulgar.

communiqué /kə,myunɪ'kei/ *n.* comunicación *f.*

communism /'kɒmyə,nizəm/ *n.* comunismo *m.*

communist /'kɒmyənɪst/ *n.* comunista *m. & f.*

communistic /,kɒmyə'nɪstɪk/ *a.* comunístico.

community /kə'myunɪti/ *n.* comunidad *f.*

commutation /,kɒmyə'teiʃən/ *n.* conmutación *f.*

commuter /kə'myutər/ *n.* empleado que viaja diariamente desde su domicilio hasta la ciudad donde trabaja.

compact /*a* kəm'pækt; *n* 'kɒmpækt/ *a.* **1.** compacto. —*n.* **2.** pacto *m.*; (lady's) polvera *f.*

compact disk disco compacto *m.*

companion /kəm'pænyən/ *n.* compañero -ra.

companionable /kəm'pænyənəbəl/ *a.* sociable.

companionship /kəm'pænyən,ʃip/ *n.* compañerismo *m.*

company /'kʌmpəni/ *n.* compañía *f.*

comparable /'kɒmpərəbəl/ *a.* comparable.

comparative /kəm'pærətiv/ *a.* comparativo.

comparatively /kəm'pærətivli/ *a.* relativamente.

compare /kəm'pɛər/ *v.* comparar.

comparison /kəm'pærəsən/ *n.* comparación *f.*

compartment /kəm'pɑrtmənt/ *n.* compartimiento *m.*

compass /'kʌmpəs/ *n.* compás *m.*; *Naut.* brújula *f.*

compassion /kəm'pæʃən/ *n.* compasión *f.*

compassionate /kəm'pæʃənit/ *a.* compasivo.

compassionately /kəm'pæʃənitli/ *adv.* compasivamente.

compatible /kəm'pætəbəl/ *a.* compatible.

compatriot /kəm'peitriət/ *n.* compatriota *m. & f.*

compel /kəm'pɛl/ *v.* obligar.

compensate /'kɒmpən,seit/ *v.* compensar.

compensation /,kɒmpən'seiʃən/ *n.* compensación *f.*

compensatory /kəm'pɛnsə,tori/ *a.* compensatorio.

compete /kəm'pit/ *v.* competir.

competence /'kɒmpitəns/ *n.* competencia *f.*

competent /'kɒmpitənt/ *a.* competente, capaz.

competently /'kɒmpitəntli/ *adv.* competentemente.

competition /,kɒmpi'tiʃən/ *n.* concurrencia *f.*; concurso *m.*

competitive /kəm'pɛtitiv/ *a.* competidor.

competitor /kəm'pɛtitər/ *n.* competidor -ra.

compile /kəm'pail/ *v.* compilar.

complacency /kəm'pleisənsi/ *n.* complacencia *f.*

complacent /kəm'pleisənt/ *a.* complaciente.

complacently /kəm'pleisəntli/ *adv.* complacientemente.

complain /kəm'plein/ *v.* quejarse.

complaint /kəm'pleint/ *n.* queja *f.*

complement /'kɒmpləmənt/ *n.* complemento *m.*

complete /kəm'plit/ *a.* **1.** completo —*v.* **2.** completar.

completely /kəm'plitli/ *adv.* completamente, enteramente.

completeness /kəm'plitnis/ *n.* integridad *f.*

completion /kəm'pliʃən/ *n.* terminación *f.*

complex /kəm'plɛks/ *a.* complejo.

complexion /kəm'plɛkʃən/ *n.* tez *f.*

complexity /kəm'plɛksiti/ *n.* complejidad *f.*

compliance /kəm'plaiəns/ *n.* consentimiento *m.* **in c. with**, de acuerdo con.

compliant /kəm'plaiənt/ *a.* dócil; complaciente.

complicate /'kɒmpli,keit/ *v.* complicar.

complicated /'kɒmpli,keitid/ *a.* complicado.

complication /,kɒmpli'keiʃən/ *n.* complicación *f.*

complicity /kəm'plisiti/ *n.* complicidad *f.*

compliment /*n* 'kɒmpləmənt; *v* -,mɛnt/ *n.* **1.** elogio *m. Fig.* —*v.* **2.** felicitar; echar flores.

complimentary /,kɒmplə'mɛntəri/ *a.* galante, obsequioso, regaloso.

comply /kəm'plai/ *v.* cumplir.

component /kəm'pounənt/ *a. & n.* componente *m.*

comport /kəm'port/ *v.* portarse.

compose /kəm'pouz/ *v.* componer.

composed /kəm'pouzd/ *a.* tranquilo; (made up) compuesto.

composer /kəm'pouzər/ *n.* compositor -ra.

composite /kəm'pɒzit/ *a.* compuesto.

composition /,kɒmpə'ziʃən/ *n.* composición *f.*

composure /kəm'pouʒər/ *n.* serenidad *f.*; calma *f.*

compote /'kɒmpout/ *n.* compota *f.*

compound /'kɒmpaund/ *a. & n.* compuesto *m.*

comprehend /,kɒmpri'hɛnd/ *v.* comprender.

comprehensible /,kɒmpri'hɛnsəbəl/ *a.* comprensible.

comprehension /,kɒmpri'hɛnʃən/ *n.* comprensión *f.*

comprehensive /,kɒmpri'hɛnsiv/ *a.* comprensivo.

compress /*n* 'kɒmprɛs; *v* kəm'prɛs/ *n.* **1.** cabezal *m.* —*v.* **2.** comprimir.

compressed /kəm'prɛst/ *a.* comprimido.

compression /kəm'prɛʃən/ *n.* compresión *f.*

compressor /kəm'prɛsər/ *n.* compresor *m.*

comprise /kəm'praiz/ *v.* comprender; abarcar.

compromise /'kɒmprə,maiz/ *n.* **1.** compromiso *m.* —*v.* **2.** comprometer.

compromiser /'kɒmprə,maizər/ *n.* compromisario *m.*

compulsion /kəm'pʌlʃən/ *n.* compulsión *f.*

compulsive /kəm'pʌlsiv/ *a.* compulsivo.

compulsory /kəm'pʌlsəri/ *a.* obligatorio.

compunction /kəm'pʌŋkʃən/ *n.* compunción *f.*; escrúpulo *m.*

computation /,kɒmpyu'teiʃən/ *n.* computación *f.*

compute /kəm'pyut/ *v.* computar, calcular.

computer /kəm'pyutər/ *n.* computadora *f.*, ordenador *m.*

computerize /kəm'pyutə,raiz/ *v.* procesar en computadora, computerizar.

computer programmer /'prougræmər/ programador -ra de ordenadores.

computer science informática *f.*

comrade /'kɒmræd/ *n.* camarada *m. & f.*; compañero -ra.

comradeship /'kɒmræd,ʃip/ *n.* camaradería *f.*

concave /kɒn'keiv/ *a.* cóncavo.

conceal /kən'sil/ *v.* ocultar, esconder.

concealment /kən'silmənt/ *n.* ocultación *f.*

concede /kən'sid/ *v.* conceder.

conceit /kən'sit/ *n.* amor propio; engreimiento *m.*

conceited /kən'sitid/ *a.* engreído.

conceivable /kən'sivəbəl/ *a.* concebible.

conceive /kən'siv/ *v.* concebir.

concentrate /'kɒnsən,treit/ *v.* concentrar.

concentration /,kɒnsən'treiʃən/ *n.* concentración *f.*

concentration camp campo de concentración *m.*

concept /'kɒnsɛpt/ *n.* concepto *m.*

conception /kən'sɛpʃən/ *n.* concepción *f.*; concepto *m.*

concern /kən'sɜrn/ *n.* **1.** interés *m.*; inquietud *f.*; *Com.* negocio *m.* —*v.* **2.** concernir.

concerning /kən'sɜrnɪŋ/ *prep.* respecto a.

concert /'kɒnsɜrt/ *n.* concierto *m.*

concerted /kən'sɜrtid/ *a.* convenido.

concession /kən'sɛʃən/ *n.* concesión *f.*

conciliate /kən'sili,eit/ *v.* conciliar.

conciliation /kən,sili'eiʃən/ *n.* conciliación *f.*

conciliator /kən'sili,eitər/ *n.* conciliador -ra.

conciliatory /kən'siliə,tori/ *a.* conciliatorio.

concise /kən'sais/ *a.* conciso.

concisely /kən'saisli/ *adv.* concisamente.

conciseness /kən'saisnis/ *n.* concisión *f.*

conclave /'kɒnkleiv/ *n.* conclave *m.*

conclude /kən'klud/ *v.* concluir.

conclusion /kən'kluʒən/ *n.* conclusión *f.*

conclusive /kən'klusiv/ *a.* conclusivo, decisivo.

conclusively /kən'klusivli/ *adv.* concluyentemente.

concoct /kɒn'kɒkt/ *v.* confeccionar.

concomitant /kɒn'kɒmitənt/ *n. & a.* concomitante *m.*

concord /'kɒnkɔrd/ *n.* concordia *f.*

concordat /kɒn'kɔrdæt/ *n.* concordato *m.*

concourse /'kɒnkɔrs/ *n.* concurso *m.*; confluencia *f.*

concrete /'kɒnkrit/ *a.* concreto.

concretely /kɒn'kritli/ *adv.* concretamente.

concubine /'kɒŋkyə,bain/ *n.* concubina, amiga *f.*

concur /kən'kɜr/ *v.* concurrir.

concurrence /kən'kɜrəns/ *n.* concurrencia *f.*; casualidad *f.*

concurrent /kən'kɜrənt/ *a.* concurrente.

concussion /kən'kʌʃən/ *n.* concusión *f.*; (c. of the brain) conmoción cerebral *f.*

condemn /kən'dɛm/ *v.* condenar.

condemnable /kən'dɛmnəbəl/ *a.* culpable, condenable.

condemnation /,kɒndɛm'neiʃən/ *n.* condenación *f.*

condensation /,kɒndɛn'seiʃən/ *n.* condensación *f.*

condense /kən'dɛns/ *v.* condensar.

condenser /kən'dɛnsər/ *n.* condensador *m.*

condescend /,kɒndə'sɛnd/ *v.* condescender.

condescension /,kɒndə'sɛnʃən/ *n.* condescendencia *f.*

condiment /'kɒndəmənt/ *n.* condimento *m.*

condition /kən'diʃən/ *n.* **1.** condición *f.*; estado *m.* —*v.* **2.** acondicionar.

conditional /kən'diʃənḷ/ *a.* condicional.

conditionally /kən'diʃənḷi/ *adv.* condicionalmente.

condole /kən'doul/ *v.* condolerse.

condolence /kən'douləns/ *n.* pésame *m.*

condom /'kɒndəm/ *n.* forro, preservativo *m.*

condominium /,kɒndə'miniəm/ *n.* condominio *m.*

condone /kən'doun/ *v.* condonar.

conducive /kən'dusiv, -'dyu-/ *a.* conducente.

conduct /*n* 'kɒndʌkt; *v* kən'dʌkt/ *n.* **1.** conducta *f.* —*v.* **2.** conducir.

conductivity /,kɒndʌk'tiviti/ *n.* conductividad *f.*

conductor /kən'dʌktər/ *n.* conductor *m.*

conduit /'kɒnduit/ *n.* caño *m.*, canal *f.*; conducto *m.*

cone /koun/ *n.* cono *m.* **ice-cream c.**, barquillo de helado.

confection /kən'fɛkʃən/ *n.* confitura *f.*

confectioner /kən'fɛkʃənər/ *n.* confitero -ra.

confectionery /kən'fɛkʃə,nɛri/ n. dulcería f.

confederacy /kən'fɛdərəsi/ n. federación f.

confederate / kən'fɛdərɪt/ a. & n. confederado m.

confederation /kən,fɛdə'reiʃən/ n. confederación f.

confer /kən'fɜr/ v. conferenciar; conferir.

conference /'kɒnfərəns/ n. conferencia f.; congreso m.

confess /kən'fɛs/ v. confesar.

confession /kən'fɛʃən/ n. confesión f.

confessional /kən'fɛʃəl/ n. 1. confesionario m. —a. 2. confesional.

confessor /kən'fɛsər/ n. confesor m.

confetti /kən'fɛti/ n. confetti m.

confidant /'kɒnfɪ,dænt/ **confidante** n. confidente m. & f.

confide /kən'faid/ v. confiar.

confidence /'kɒnfɪdəns/ n. confianza f.

confident /'kɒnfɪdənt/ a. confiado; cierto.

confidential /,kɒnfɪ'dɛnʃəl/ a. confidencial.

confidentially /,kɒnfɪ'dɛnʃəli/ adv. confidencialmente, en secreto.

confidently /'kɒnfɪdəntli/ adv. confiadamente.

confine /kən'fain/ n. 1. confín m. —v. 2. confinar; encerrar.

confirm /kən'fɜrm/ v. confirmar.

confirmation /,kɒnfər'meiʃən/ n. confirmación f.

confiscate /'kɒnfə,skeit/ v. confiscar.

confiscation /,kɒnfə'skeiʃən/ n. confiscación f.

conflagration /,kɒnflə'greiʃən/ n. incendio m.

conflict /n 'kɒnflɪkt; v kən'flɪkt/ n. 1. conflicto m. —v. 2. oponerse; estar en conflicto.

conform /kən'fɔrm/ v. conformar.

conformation /,kɒnfɔr'meiʃən/ n. conformación f.

conformer /kən'fɔrmər/ n. conformista m. & f.

conformist /kən'fɔrmɪst/ n. conformista m. & f.

conformity /kən'fɔrmɪti/ n. conformidad f.

confound /kɒn'faund/ v. confundir.

confront /kən'frʌnt/ v. confrontar.

confrontation /,kɒnfrən'teiʃən/ n. enfrentamiento m.

confuse /kən'fyuz/ v. confundir.

confusion /kən'fyuʒən/ n. confusión f.

congeal /kən'dʒil/ v. congelar, helar.

congealment /kən'dʒilmənt/ n. congelación f.

congenial /kən'dʒinyəl/ a. congenial.

congenital /kən'dʒɛnɪtl̩/ a. congénito.

congenitally /kən'dʒɛnɪtli/ adv. congenitalmente.

congestion /kən'dʒɛstʃən/ n. congestión f.

conglomerate /v kən'glɒmə,reit; a, n kən'glɒmərɪt/ v. 1. conglomerar. —a. & n. 2. conglomerado.

conglomeration /kən,glɒmə'reiʃən/ n. conglomeración f.

congratulate /kən'grætʃə,leit/ v. felicitar.

congratulation /kən,grætʃə'leiʃən/ n. felicitación f.

congratulatory /kən'grætʃələ,tɔri/ a. congratulatorio.

congregate /'kɒŋgrɪ,geit/ v. congregar.

congregation /,kɒŋgrɪ'geiʃən/ n. congregación f.

congress /'kɒŋgrɪs/ n. congreso m.

conic /'kɒnɪk/ n. 1. cónica f. —a. 2. cónico.

conjecture /kən'dʒɛktʃər/ n. 1. conjetura f. —v. 2. conjeturar.

conjugal /'kɒndʒəgəl/ a. conyugal, matrimonial.

conjugate /'kɒndʒə,geit/ v. conjugar.

conjugation /,kɒndʒə'geiʃən/ n. conjugación f.

conjunction /kən'dʒʌŋkʃən/ n. conjunción f.

conjunctive /kən'dʒʌŋktɪv/ n. 1. Gram. conjunción f. —a. 2. conjuntivo.

conjunctivitis /kən,dʒʌŋktə'vaitɪs/ n. conjuntivitis f.

conjure /'kɒndʒər/ v. conjurar.

connect /kə'nɛkt/ v. juntar; relacionar.

connection /kə'nɛkʃən/ n. conexión f.

connivance /kə'naivəns/ n. consentimiento m.

connive /kə'naiv/ v. disimular.

connoisseur /,kɒnə'sɜr/ n. perito -ta.

connotation /,kɒnə'teiʃən/ n. connotación f.

connote /kə'nout/ v. connotar.

connubial /kə'nubiəl/ a. conyugal.

conquer /'kɒŋkər/ v. conquistar.

conquerable /'kɒŋkərəbəl/ a. conquistable, vencible.

conqueror /'kɒŋkərər/ n. conquistador -ra.

conquest /'kɒnkwɛst/ n. conquista f.

conscience /'kɒnʃəns/ n. conciencia f.

conscientious /,kɒnʃi'ɛnʃəs/ a. concienzudo.

conscientiously /,kɒnʃi'ɛnʃəsli/ adv. escrupulosamente.

conscientious objector /ɒb'dʒɛktər/ objetor de conciencia m.

conscious /'kɒnʃəs/ a. consciente.

consciously /'kɒnʃəsli/ adv. con conocimiento.

consciousness /'kɒnʃəsnɪs/ n. conciencia f.

conscript /n 'kɒnskrɪpt; v kən'skrɪpt/ n. 1. conscripto m., recluta m. —v. 2. reclutar, alistar.

conscription /kən'skrɪpʃən/ n. conscripción f., alistamiento m.

consecrate /'kɒnsɪ,kreit/ v. consagrar.

consecration /,kɒnsɪ'kreiʃən/ n. consagración f.

consecutive /kən'sɛkyɪtɪv/ a. consecutivo, seguido.

consecutively /kən'sɛkyɪtɪvli/ adv. consecutivamente, de seguida.

consensus /kən'sɛnsəs/ n. consenso m., acuerdo general m.

consent /kən'sɛnt/ n. 1. consentimiento m. —v. 2. consentir.

consequence /'kɒnsɪ,kwɛns/ n. consecuencia f.

consequent /'kɒnsɪ,kwɛnt/ a. consiguiente.

consequential /,kɒnsɪ'kwɛnʃəl/ a. importante.

consequently /'kɒnsɪ,kwɛntli/ adv. por lo tanto, por consiguiente.

conservation /,kɒnsər'veiʃən/ n. conservación f.

conservatism /kən'sɜrvə,tizəm/ n. conservatismo m.

conservative /kən'sɜrvətɪv/ a. conservador, conservativo.

conservatory /kən'sɜrvə,tɔri/ n. (plants) invernáculo m.; (school) conservatorio m.

conserve /kən'sɜrv/ v. conservar.

consider /kən'sɪdər/ v. considerar. C. it done! ¡Dalo por hecho!

considerable /kən'sɪdərəbəl/ a. considerable.

considerably /kən'sɪdərəbli/ adv. considerablemente.

considerate /kən'sɪdərɪt/ a. considerado.

considerately /kən'sɪdərɪtli/ adv. consideradamente.

consideration /kən,sɪdə'reiʃən/ n. consideración f.

considering /kən'sɪdərɪŋ/ prep. visto que, en vista de.

consign /kən'sain/ v. consignar.

consignment /kən'sainmənt/ n. consignación f., envío m.

consist /kən'sɪst/ v. consistir.

consistency /kən'sɪstənsi/ n. consistencia f.

consistent /kən'sɪstənt/ a. consistente.

consolation /,kɒnsə'leiʃən/ n. consolación f.

consolation prize premio de consuelo m.

console /'kɒnsoul/ v. consolar.

consolidate /kən'sɒlɪ,deit/ v. consolidar.

consommé /,kɒnsə'mei/ n. caldo m.

consonant /'kɒnsənənt/ n. consonante f.

consort /n 'kɒnsɔrt, v kən'sɔrt/ n. 1. cónyuge m. & f.; socio. —v. 2. asociarse.

conspicuous /kən'spɪkyuəs/ a. conspicuo.

conspicuously /kən'spɪkyuəsli/ adv. visiblemente, llamativamente.

conspicuousness /kən'spɪkyuəsnɪs/ n. visibilidad f.; evidencia f.; fama f.

conspiracy /kən'spɪrəsi/ n. conspiración f.; complot m.

conspirator /kən'spɪrətər/ n. conspirador -ra.

conspire /kən'spaiᵊr/ v. conspirar.

conspirer /kən'spaiᵊrər/ n. conspirante m. & f.

constancy /'kɒnstənsi/ n. constancia f., lealtad f.

constant /'kɒnstənt/ a. constante.

constantly /'kɒnstəntli/ adv. constantemente, de continuo.

constellation /,kɒnstə'leiʃən/ n. constelación f.

consternation /,kɒnstər'neiʃən/ n. consternación f.

constipate /'kɒnstə,peit/ v. estreñir.

constipated /'kɒnstə,peitɪd/ a. estreñido, m.

constipation /,kɒnstə'peiʃən/ n. estreñimiento, m.

constituency /kən'stɪtʃuənsi/ n. distrito electoral m.

constituent /kən'stɪtʃuənt/ a. 1. constituyente. —n. 2. elector m.

constitute /'kɒnstɪ,tut/ v. constituir.

constitution /,kɒnstɪ'tuʃən/ n. constitución f.

constitutional /,kɒnstɪ'tuʃənl/ a. constitucional.

constrain /kən'strein/ v. constreñir.

constraint /kən'streint/ n. constreñimiento m., compulsión f.

constrict /kən'strɪkt/ v. apretar, estrechar.

construct /kən'strʌkt/ v. construir.

construction /kən'strʌkʃən/ n. construcción f.

constructive /kən'strʌktɪv/ a. constructivo.

constructively /kən'strʌktɪvli/ adv. constructivamente; por deducción.

constructor /kən'strʌktər/ n. constructor m.

construe /kən'stru/ v. interpretar.

consul /'kɒnsəl/ n. cónsul m.

consular /'kɒnsələr/ a. consular.

consulate /'kɒnsəlɪt/ n. consulado m.

consult /kən'sʌlt/ v. consultar.

consultant /kən'sʌltənt/ n. consultor -ora.

consultation /,kɒnsəl'teiʃən/ n. consulta f.

consume /kən'sum/ v. consumir.

consumer /kən'sumər/ n. consumidor -ra.

consumer society sociedad de consumo f.

consummation /,kɒnsə'meiʃən/ n. consumación f.

consumption /kən'sʌmpʃən/ n. consumo m.; Med. tisis.

consumptive /kən'sʌmptɪv/ n. 1. tísico m. —a. 2. consuntivo.

contact /'kɒntækt/ n. 1. contacto m. —v. 2. ponerse en contacto con.

contact lens lentilla f.

contagion /kən'teidʒən/ n. contagio m.

contagious /kən'teidʒəs/ a. contagioso.

contain /kən'tein/ v. contener.

container /kən'teinər/ n. envase m.

contaminate /kən'tæmə,neit/ v. contaminar.

contemplate /'kɒntəm,pleit/ v. contemplar.

contemplation /,kɒntəm'pleiʃən/ n. contemplación f.

contemplative /kən'tɛmplətɪv/ a. contemplativo.

contemporary /kən'tɛmpə,rɛri/ n. & a. contemporáneo -nea.

contempt /kən'tɛmpt/ n. desprecio m.

contemptible /kən'tɛmptəbəl/ a. vil, despreciable.

contemptuous /kən'tɛmptʃuəs/ a. desdeñoso.

contemptuously /kən'tɛmptʃuəsli/ adv. desdeñosamente.

contend /kən'tɛnd/ v. contender; competir.

contender /kən'tɛndər/ n. competidor -ra.

content /a, v kən'tɛnt; n 'kɒntɛnt/ a. 1. contento. —n. 2. contenido m. —v. 3. contentar.

contented /kən'tɛntɪd/ a. contento.

contention /kən'tɛnʃən/ n. contención f.

contentment /kən'tɛntmənt/ n. contentamiento m.

contest /n 'kɒntɛst; v kən'tɛst/ n. 1. concurso m. —v. 2. disputar.

contestable /kən'tɛstəbəl/ a. contestable.

context /'kɒntɛkst/ n. contexto m.

contiguous /kən'tɪgyuəs/ a. contiguo.

continence /'kɒntn̩əns/ n. continencia f., castidad f.

continent /'kɒntn̩ənt/ n. continente m.

continental /,kɒntn̩'ɛntl̩/ a. continental.

contingency /kən'tɪndʒənsi/ n. eventualidad f., casualidad f.

contingent /kən'tɪndʒənt/ a. contingente.

continual /kən'tɪnyuəl/ a. continuo.

continuation /kən,tɪnyu'eiʃən/ n. continuación f.

continue /kən'tɪnyu/ v. continuar.

continuity /,kɒntn̩'uiti/ n. continuidad f.

continuous /kən'tɪnyuəs/ a. continuo.

continuously /kən'tɪnyuəsli/ adv. continuamente.

contour /'kɒntur/ n. contorno m.

contraband /'kɒntrə,bænd/ n. contrabando m.

contraception /,kɒntrə'sɛpʃən/ n. contracepción f.

contraceptive /,kɒntrə'sɛptɪv/ n. & a. anticeptivo m.

contract /n 'kɒntrækt; v kən'trækt/ n. 1. contrato m. —v. 2. contraer.

contraction /kən'trækʃən/ n. contracción f.

contractor /'kɒntræktər/ n. contratista m. & f.

contradict /,kɒntrə'dɪkt/ v. contradecir.

contradiction /,kɒntrə'dɪkʃən/ n. contradicción f.

contradictory /,kɒntrə'dɪktəri/ a. contradictorio.

contralto /kən'træltou/ n. contralto m.

contrary /'kɒntrɛri/ a. & n. contrario -ria.

contrast /n 'kɒntræst; v kən'træst/ n. 1. contraste m. —v. 2. contrastar.

contribute /kən'trɪbyut/ v. contribuir.

contribution /,kɒntrə'byuʃən/ n. contribución f.

contributor /kən'trɪbyətər/ n. contribuidor -ra.

contributory /kən'trɪbyə,tɔri/ a. contribuyente.

contrite /kən'trait/ a. contrito.

contrition /kən'trɪʃən/ n. contrición f.

contrivance /kən'traivəns/ n. aparato m.; estratagema f.

contrive /kən'traiv/ v. inventar, tramar; darse maña.

control /kən'troul/ n. **1.** control m. —v. **2.** controlar.

controllable /kən'trouləbəl/ a. controlable, dominable.

controller /kən'troulər/ n. interventor -ra; contralor -ra.

control tower torre de mando f.

controversial /ˌkɒntrə'vɜrʃəl/ a. contencioso.

controversy /'kɒntrə,vɜrsi/ n. controversia f.

contusion /kən'tuʒən/ n. contusión f.

convalesce /ˌkɒnvə'lɛs/ v. convalecer.

convalescence /ˌkɒnvə'lɛsəns/ n. convalecencia f.

convalescent /ˌkɒnvə'lɛsənt/ n. convaleciente m. & f.

convalescent home clínica de reposo f.

convene /kən'vin/ v. juntarse; convocar.

convenience /kən'vinyəns/ n. comodidad f.

convenient /kən'vinyənt/ a. cómodo; oportuno.

conveniently /kən'vinyəntli/ adv. cómodamente.

convent /'kɒnvɛnt/ n. convento m.

convention /kən'vɛnʃən/ n. convención f.

conventional /kən'vɛnʃənl/ a. convencional.

conventionally /kən'vɛnʃənli/ adv. convencionalmente.

converge /kən'vɜrdʒ/ v. convergir.

convergence /kən'vɜrdʒəns/ n. convergencia f.

convergent /kən'vɜrdʒənt/ a. convergente.

conversant /kən'vɜrsənt/ a. versado; entendido (de).

conversation /ˌkɒnvər'seiʃən/ n. conversación, plática f.

conversational /ˌkɒnvər'seiʃənl/ a. de conversación.

conversationalist /ˌkɒnvər'seiʃənlɪst/ n. conversador -ra.

converse /kən'vɜrs/ v. conversar.

conversely /kən'vɜrsli/ adv. a la inversa.

convert /n 'kɒnvɜrt; v kən'vɜrt/ n. **1.** convertido da-. —v. **2.** convertir.

converter /kən'vɜrtər/ n. convertidor m.

convertible /kən'vɜrtəbəl/ a. convertible.

convex /kɒn'vɛks/ a. convexo.

convey /kən'vei/ v. transportar; comunicar.

conveyance /kən'veiəns/ n. transporte; vehículo m.

conveyor /kən'veiər/ n. conductor m.; Mech. transportador m.

conveyor belt correa transportadora f.

convict /n 'kɒnvɪkt; v kən'vɪkt/ n. **1.** reo m. —v. **2.** declarar culpable.

conviction /kən'vɪkʃən/ n. convicción f.

convince /kən'vɪns/ v. convencer.

convincing /kən'vɪnsɪŋ/ a. convincente.

convivial /kən'vɪviəl/ a. convival.

convocation /ˌkɒnvə'keiʃən/ n. convocación; asamblea f.

convoke /kən'vouk/ v. convocar, citar.

convoy /'kɒnvɔi/ n. convoy m.; escolta f.

convulse /kən'vʌls/ v. convulsionar; agitar violentamente.

convulsion /kən'vʌlʃən/ n. convulsión f.

convulsive /kən'vʌlsɪv/ a. convulsivo.

---

cook /kuk/ n. **1.** cocinero -ra. —v. **2.** cocinar, cocer.

cookbook /'kuk,buk/ n. libro de cocina m.

cookie /'kuki/ n. galleta dulce f.

cool /kul/ a. **1.** fresco. —v. **2.** refrescar.

cooler /'kulər/ n. enfriadera f.

coolness /'kulnɪs/ n. frescura f.

coop /kup/ n. **1.** jaula f. **chicken c.,** gallinero m. —v. **2.** enjaular.

cooperate /kou'ɒpə,reit/ v. cooperar.

cooperation /kou,ɒpə'reiʃən/ n. cooperación f.

cooperative /kou'ɒpərətɪv/ a. cooperativo.

cooperatively /kou'ɒpərətɪvli/ adv. cooperativamente.

coordinate /kou'ɔrdn,eit/ v. coordinar.

coordination /kou,ɔrdn'eiʃən/ n. coordinación f.

coordinator /kou'ɔrdn,eitər/ n. coordinador -ra.

cope /koup/ v. contender. **c. with,** superar, hacer frente a.

copier /'kɒpiər/ n. copiadora f.

copious /'koupiəs/ a. copioso, abundante.

copiously /'koupiəsli/ adv. copiosamente.

copiousness /'koupiəsnɪs/ n. abundancia f.

copper /'kɒpər/ n. cobre m.

copy /'kɒpi/ n. **1.** copia f.; ejemplar m. —v. **2.** copiar.

copyist /'kɒpiɪst/ n. copista m. & f.

copyright /'kɒpi,rait/ n. derechos de propiedad literaria m.pl.

coquetry /'koukɪtri/ n. coquetería f.

coquette /kou'kɛt/ n. coqueta f.

coral /'kɒrəl/ n. coral m.

cord /kɔrd/ n. cuerda f.

cordial /'kɔrdʒəl/ a. cordial.

cordiality /kɔr'dʒælɪti/ n. cordialidad f.

cordially /'kɔrdʒəli/ adv. cordialmente.

cordon off /'kɔrdn/ v. acordonar.

cordovan /'kɔrdəvən/ n. cordobán m.

corduroy /'kɔrdə,rɔi/ n. pana f.

core /kɔr/ n. corazón; centro m.

cork /kɔrk/ n. corcho m.

corkscrew /'kɔrk,skru/ n. tirabuzón m.

corn /kɔrn/ n. maíz m.

cornea /'kɔrniə/ n. córnea f.

corned beef /kɔrnd/ carne acecinada f.

corner /'kɔrnər/ n. rincón m.; (of street) esquina f.

cornet /kɔr'nɛt/ n. corneta f.

cornetist /kɔr'nɛtɪst/ n. cornetín m.

cornice /'kɔrnɪs/ n. cornisa f.

cornstarch /'kɔrn,stɑrtʃ/ n. maicena f.

corollary /'kɒrə,lɛri/ n. corolario m.

coronary /'kɒrə,nɛri/ a. coronario.

coronation /ˌkɒrə'neiʃən/ n. coronación f.

corporal /'kɔrpərəl/ a. **1.** corpóreo. —n. **2.** cabo m.

corporate /'kɔrpərɪt/ a. corporativo.

corporation /ˌkɔrpə'reiʃən/ n. corporación f.

corps /kɔr/ n. cuerpo m.

corpse /kɔrps/ n. cadáver m.

corpulent /'kɔrpyələnt/ a. corpulento.

corpuscle /'kɔrpəsəl/ n. corpúsculo m.

corral /kə'ræl/ n. **1.** corral m. —v. **2.** acorralar.

correct /kə'rɛkt/ a. **1.** correcto. —v. **2.** corregir.

correction /kə'rɛkʃən/ n. corrección; enmienda f.

corrective /kə'rɛktɪv/ n. & a. correctivo.

correctly /kə'rɛktli/ adv. correctamente.

correctness /kə'rɛktnɪs/ n. exactitud f.

---

correlate /'kɔrə,leit/ v. correlacionar.

correlation /ˌkɔrə'leiʃən/ n. correlación f.

correspond /ˌkɔrə'spɒnd/ v. corresponder.

correspondence /ˌkɔrə'spɒndəns/ n. correspondencia f.

correspondence course curso por correspondencia m.

correspondence school escuela por correspondencia f.

correspondent /ˌkɔrə'spɒndənt/ a. & n. correspondiente m. & f.

corresponding /ˌkɔrə'spɒndɪŋ/ a. correspondiente.

corridor /'kɔrɪdər/ n. corredor, pasillo m.

corroborate /kə'rɒbə,reit/ v. corroborar.

corroboration /kə,rɒbə'reiʃən/ n. corroboración f.

corroborative /kə'rɒbə,reitɪv/ a. corroborante.

corrode /kə'roud/ v. corroer.

corrosion /kə'rouʒən/ n. corrosión f.

corrugate /'kɔrə,geit/ v. arrugar; ondular.

corrupt /kə'rʌpt/ a. **1.** corrompido. —v. **2.** corromper.

corruptible /kə'rʌptəbəl/ a. corruptible.

corruption /kə'rʌpʃən/ n. corrupción f.

corruptive /kə'rʌptɪv/ a. corruptivo.

corset /'kɔrsɪt/ n. corsé m., (girdle) faja f.

cortege /kɔr'tɛʒ/ n. comitiva f., séquito m.

corvette /kɔr'vɛt/ n. corbeta f.

cosmetic /kɒz'mɛtɪk/ a. & n. cosmético m.

cosmic /'kɒzmɪk/ a. cósmico.

cosmonaut /'kɒzmə,nɔt/ n. cosmonauta m. & f.

cosmopolitan /ˌkɒzmə'pɒlɪtn/ a. & n. cosmopolita m. & f.

cosmos /'kɒzməs/ n. cosmos m.

cost /kɔst/ n. **1.** coste m.; costa f. —v. **2.** costar.

Costa Rican /'kɒstə'rikən/ a. & n. costarricense m. & f.

costly /'kɒstli/ a. costoso, caro.

costume /'kɒstum/ n. traje; disfraz m.

costume jewelry bisutería f., joyas de fantasía f.pl.

cot /kɒt/ n. catre m.

coterie /'koutəri/ n. camarilla f.

cotillion /kə'tɪlyən/ n. cotillón m.

cottage /'kɒtɪdʒ/ n. casita f.

cottage cheese requesón m.

cotton /'kɒtn/ n. algodón m.

cottonseed /'kɒtn,sid/ n. semilla del algodón f.

couch /kautʃ/ n. sofá m.

cougar /'kugər/ n. puma m.

cough /kɔf/ n. **1.** tos f. —v. **2.** toser.

council /'kaunsəl/ n. consejo, concilio m.

counsel /'kaunsəl/ n. **1.** consejo; (law) abogado -da. —v. **2.** aconsejar. **to keep one's c.,** no decir nada.

counselor /'kaunsələr/ n. consejero -ra; (law) abogado -da.

count /kaunt/ n. **1.** cuenta f.; (title) conde m. —v. **2.** contar.

countenance /'kauntnəns/ n. **1.** aspecto m.; cara f. —v. **2.** aprobar.

counter /'kauntər/ adv. **1. c. to,** contra, en contra de. —n. **2.** mostrador m.

counteract /ˌkauntər'ækt/ v. contrarrestar.

counteraction /ˌkauntər'ækʃən/ n. neutralización f.

counterbalance /'kauntər,bæləns/ n. **1.** contrapeso m. —v. **2.** contrapesar.

counterfeit /'kauntər,fɪt/ a. **1.** falsificado. —v. **2.** falsear.

countermand /ˌkauntər'mænd/ v. contramandar.

counteroffensive /ˌkauntərə'fɛnsɪv/ n. contraofensiva f.

---

counterpart /'kauntər,pɑrt/ n. contraparte f.

counterproductive /ˌkauntərprə'dʌktɪv/ a. contraproducente.

countess /'kauntɪs/ n. condesa f.

countless /'kauntlɪs/ a. innumerable.

country /'kʌntri/ n. campo m.; Pol. país m.; (homeland) patria f.

country code distintivo del país m.

countryman /'kʌntrimən/ n. paisano m. **fellow c.,** compatriota m.

countryside /'kʌntri,said/ n. campo, paisaje m.

county /'kaunti/ n. condado m.

coupé /kup/ n. cupé m.

couple /'kʌpəl/ n. **1.** par m. —v. **2.** unir.

coupon /'kupɒn/ n. cupón, talón m.

courage /'kɜrɪdʒ/ n. valor m.

courageous /kə'reidʒəs/ a. valiente.

course /kɔrs/ n. curso m. **of c.,** por supuesto, desde luego.

court /kɔrt/ n. **1.** corte f.; cortejo m.; (of law) tribunal m. —v. **2.** cortejar.

courteous /'kɜrtiəs/ a. cortés.

courtesy /'kɜrtəsi/ n. cortesía f.

courthouse /'kɔrt,haus/ n. palacio de justicia m., tribunal m.

courtier /'kɔrtiər/ n. cortesano m.

courtly /'kɔrtli/ a. cortés, galante.

courtroom /'kɔrt,rum, -,rʊm/ n. sala de justicia f.

courtship /'kɔrtʃɪp/ n. cortejo m.

courtyard /'kɔrt,yɑrd/ n. patio m.

cousin /'kʌzən/ n. primo -ma.

covenant /'kʌvənənt/ n. contrato, convenio m.

cover /'kʌvər/ n. **1.** cubierta, tapa f. —v. **2.** cubrir, tapar.

cover charge precio del cubierto m.

covet /'kʌvɪt/ v. ambicionar, suspirar por.

covetous /'kʌvɪtəs/ a. codicioso.

cow /kau/ n. vaca f.

coward /'kauərd/ n. cobarde m. & f.

cowardice /'kauərdɪs/ n. cobardía f.

cowardly /'kauərdli/ a. cobarde.

cowboy /'kau,bɔi/ n. vaquero, gaucho m.

cower /'kauər/ v. agacharse (de miedo).

cowhide /'kau,haid/ n. cuero m.

coy /kɔi/ a. recatado, modesto.

coyote /kai'outi/ n. coyote m.

cozy /'kouzi/ a. cómodo y agradable.

crab /kræb/ n. cangrejo m.

crab apple n. manzana silvestre f.

crack /kræk/ n. **1.** hendedura f.; (noise) crujido m. —v. **2.** hender; crujir.

cracker /'krækər/ n. galleta f.

cradle /'kreidl/ n. cuna f.

craft /kræft/ n. arte m.

craftsman /'kræftsmən/ n. artesano -na.

craftsmanship /'kræftsmən,ʃɪp/ n. artesanía f.

crafty /'kræfti/ a. ladino.

crag /kræg/ n. despeñadero m.; peña f.

cram /kræm/ v. rellenar, hartar.

cramp /kræmp/ n. calambre m.

cranberry /'kræn,bɛri/ n. arándano m.

crane /krein/ n. (bird) grulla f.; Mech. grúa f.

cranium /'kreiniəm/ n. cráneo m.

crank /kræŋk/ n. Mech. manivela f.

cranky /'kræŋki/ a. chiflado, caprichoso.

crash /kræʃ/ n. **1.** choque; estallido m. —v. **2.** estallar.

crate /kreit/ n. canasto m.

crater /'kreitər/ n. cráter m.

crave /kreiv/ v. desear; anhelar.

craven /'kreivən/ a. cobarde.

craving /'kreivɪŋ/ n. sed m., anhelo m.

crawl /krɔl/ v. andar a gatas, arrastrarse.

crayon /'kreiɒn/ n. creyón; lápiz m.

crazy /'kreizi/ a. loco.

creak /krik/ v. crujir.

creaky /'kriki/ a. crujiente.

cream /krim/ n. crema f.

cream cheese queso crema m.

creamery /'kriməri/ n. lechería f.

creamy /'krimi/ a. cremoso.

crease /kris/ n. **1.** pliegue m. —v. **2.** plegar.

create /kri'eit/ v. crear.

creation /kri'eiʃən/ n. creación f.

creative /kri'eitiv/ a. creativo, creador.

creator /kri'eitər/ n. creador -ra.

creature /'kritʃər/ n. criatura f.

credence /'kridns/ n. creencia f.

credentials /krɪ'dɛnʃəlz/ n. credenciales f.pl.

credibility /,krɛdə'bɪlɪti/ n. credibilidad f.

credible /'krɛdəbəl/ a. creíble.

credit /'krɛdɪt/ n. **1.** crédito m. **on c.,** al fiado. —v. **2.** Com. abonar.

creditable /'krɛdɪtəbəl/ a. fidedigno.

credit balance saldo acreedor.

credit card n. tarjeta de crédito f.

creditor /'krɛdɪtər/ n. acreedor -ra.

credit union banco cooperativo m.

credo /'kridou/ n. credo m.

credulity /krə'dulɪti/ n. credulidad f.

credulous /'krɛdʒələs/ a. crédulo.

creed /krid/ n. credo m.

creek /krik/ n. riachuelo m.

creep /krip/ v. gatear.

cremate /'krimeit/ v. incinerar.

crematory /'krimə,tɔri/ n. crematorio m.

creosote /'kriə,sout/ n. creosota f.

crepe /kreip/ n. crespón m.

crepe paper papel crespón m.

crescent /'krɛsənt/ a. & n. creciente f.

crest /krɛst/ n. cresta; cima f.; (heraldry) timbre m.

cretonne /krɪ'tɒn/ n. cretona f.

crevice /'krɛvɪs/ n. grieta f.

crew /kru/ n. tripulación f.

crew member tripulante m. & f.

crib /krɪb/ n. pesebre m.; cuna.

cricket /'krɪkɪt/ n. grillo m.

crime /kraim/ n. crimen m.

criminal /'krɪmənl/ a. & n. criminal m. & f.

criminologist /,krɪmə'nɒlədʒɪst/ n. criminólogo -ga, criminalista m. & f.

criminology /,krɪmə'nɒlədʒi/ n. criminología f.

crimson /'krɪmzən, -sən/ a. & n. carmesí m.

cringe /krɪndʒ/ v. encogerse, temblar.

cripple /'krɪpəl/ n. **1.** lisiado -da. —v. **2.** estropear, lisiar.

crisis /'kraisis/ n. crisis f.

crisp /krɪsp/ a. crespo, fresco.

crispness /'krɪspnɪs/ n. encrespadura f.

crisscross /'krɪs,krɔs/ a. entrelazado.

criterion /krai'tɪəriən/ n. criterio m.

critic /'krɪtɪk/ n. crítico -ca.

critical /'krɪtɪkəl/ a. crítico.

criticism /'krɪtə,sɪzəm/ n. crítica; censura f.

criticize /'krɪtə,saiz/ v. criticar; censurar.

critique /krɪ'tik/ n. crítica f.

croak /krouk/ n. **1.** graznido m. —v. **2.** graznar.

crochet /krou'ʃei/ n. **1.** crochet m. —v. **2.** hacer crochet.

crochet work ganchillo m.

crock /krɒk/ n. cazuela f.; olla de barro.

crockery /'krɒkəri/ n. loza f.

crocodile /'krɒkə,dail/ n. cocodrilo m.

crony /'krouni/ n. compinche m.

crooked /'krʊkɪd/ a. encorvado; deshonesto.

croon /krun/ v. canturrear.

crop /krɒp/ n. cosecha f.

croquet /krou'kei/ n. juego de croquet m.

croquette /krou'kɛt/ n. croqueta f.

cross /krɔs/ a. **1.** enojado, mal humorado. —n. **2.** cruz f. —v. **3.** cruzar, atravesar.

crossbreed /'krɔs,brid/ n. **1.** mestizo m. —v. **2.** cruzar (animales o plantas).

cross-examine /'krɔs ɪg,zæmɪn/ v. interrogar.

cross-eyed /'krɔs ,aid/ a. bizco.

cross-fertilization /'krɔs ,fɜrtlə-'zeiʃən/ n. alogamia f.

crossing /'krɔsɪŋ/ **crossroads** n. cruce m.

cross section corte transversal m.

crosswalk /'krɔs,wɔk/ n. paso cebra m.

crossword puzzle /'krɔs ,wɜrd/ crucigrama m.

crotch /krɒtʃ/ n. bifurcación f.; Anat. bragadura f.

crouch /krautʃ/ v. agacharse.

croup /krup/ n. Med. crup m.

croupier /'krupiər/ n. crupié m. & f.

crow /krou/ n. cuervo m.

crowd /kraud/ n. **1.** muchedumbre f.; tropel m. —v. **2.** apretar.

crowded /'kraudɪd/ a. lleno de gente.

crown /kraun/ n. **1.** corona f. —v. **2.** coronar.

crown prince príncipe heredero m.

crucial /'kruʃəl/ a. crucial.

crucible /'krusəbəl/ n. crisol m.

crucifix /'krusəfɪks/ n. crucifijo m.

crucifixion /,krusə'fɪkʃən/ n. crucifixión f.

crucify /'krusə,fai/ v. crucificar.

crude /krud/ a. crudo; (oil) bruto.

crudeness /'krudnɪs/ a. crudeza f.

cruel /'kruəl/ a. cruel.

cruelty /'kruəlti/ n. crueldad f.

cruet /'kruit/ n. vinagrera f.

cruise /kruz/ n. **1.** viaje por mar. —v. **2.** navegar.

cruiser /'kruzər/ n. crucero m.

crumb /krʌm/ n. miga; migaja f.

crumble /'krʌmbəl/ v. desmigajar; desmoronar.

crumple /'krʌmpəl/ v. arrugar; encogerse.

crusade /kru'seid/ n. cruzada f.

crusader /kru'seidər/ n. cruzado m.

crush /krʌʃ/ v. aplastar.

crust /krʌst/ n. costra; corteza f.

crustacean /krʌ'steiʃən/ n. crustáceo m.

crutch /krʌtʃ/ n. muleta f.

cry /krai/ n. **1.** grito m. —v. **2.** gritar; (weep) llorar.

cryosurgery /,kraiou'sɜrdʒəri/ n. criocirugía f.

crypt /krɪpt/ n. gruta f., cripta f.

cryptic /'krɪptɪk/ a. secreto.

cryptography /krɪp'tɒgrəfi/ n. criptografía f.

crystal /'krɪstl/ n. cristal m.

crystalline /'krɪstlɪn/ a. cristalino, transparente.

crystallize /'krɪstl,aiz/ v. cristalizar.

cub /kʌb/ n. cachorro m.

Cuban /'kyubən/ n. & a. cubano -na.

cube /kyub/ n. cubo m.

cubic /'kyubɪk/ a. cúbico.

cubicle /'kyubɪkəl/ n. cubículo m.

cubic measure medida de capacidad f.

cubism /'kyubɪzəm/ n. cubismo m.

cuckoo /'kuku/ n. cuco m.

cucumber /'kyukʌmbər/ n. pepino m.

cuddle /'kʌdl/ v. abrazar.

cudgel /'kʌdʒəl/ n. palo m.

cue /kyu/ n. apunte m.; (billiards) taco m.

cuff /kʌf/ n. puño de camisa. **c. links,** gemelos.

cuisine /kwɪ'zin/ n. arte culinario m.

culinary /'kyulə,nɛri/ a. culinario.

culminate /'kʌlmə,neit/ v. culminar.

culmination /,kʌlmə'neiʃən/ n. culminación f.

culpable /'kʌlpəbəl/ a. culpable.

culprit /'kʌlprɪt/ n. criminal; delincuente m. f.

cult /kʌlt/ n. culto m.

cultivate /'kʌltə,veit/ v. cultivar.

cultivated /'kʌltə,veitɪd/ a. cultivado.

cultivation /,kʌltə'veiʃən/ n. cultivo m.; cultivación f.

cultivator /'kʌltə,veitər/ n. cultivador -ra.

cultural /'kʌltʃərəl/ a. cultural.

culture /'kʌltʃər/ n. cultura f.

cultured /'kʌltʃərd/ a. culto.

cumbersome /'kʌmbərsəm/ a. pesado, incómodo.

cumulative /'kyumyələtɪv/ a. acumulativo.

cunning /'kʌnɪŋ/ a. **1.** astuto. —n. **2.** astucia f.

cup /kʌp/ n. taza, jícara f.

cupboard /'kʌbərd/ n. armario, aparador m.

cupidity /kyu'pɪdɪti/ n. avaricia f.

curable /'kyurəbəl/ a. curable.

curator /kyu'reitər/ n. guardián -ana.

curb /kɜrb/ n. **1.** freno m. —v. **2.** refrenar.

curd /kɜrd/ n. cuajada f.

curdle /'kɜrdl/ v. cuajarse, coagularse.

cure /kyur/ n. **1.** remedio m. —v. **2.** curar, sanar.

curfew /'kɜrfyu/ n. toque de queda m.

curio /'kyuri,ou/ n. objeto curioso.

curiosity /,kyuri'ɒsɪti/ n. curiosidad f.

curious /'kyuriəs/ a. curioso.

curl /kɜrl/ n. **1.** rizo m. —v. **2.** rizar.

curly /'kɜrli/ a. rizado.

currant /'kɜrənt/ n. grosella f.

currency /'kɜrənsi/ n. circulación f.; dinero m.

current /'kɜrənt/ a. & n. corriente f.

current events /ɪ'vɛnts/ actualidades f.pl.

currently /'kɜrəntli/ adv. corrientemente.

curriculum /kə'rɪkyələm/ n. plan de estudio m.

curse /kɜrs/ n. **1.** maldición f. —v. **2.** maldecir.

cursor /'kɜrsər/ n. cursor m.

cursory /'kɜrsəri/ a. sumario.

curt /kɜrt/ a. brusco.

curtail /kər'teil/ v. reducir; restringir.

curtain /'kɜrtn/ n. cortina f.; Theat. telón m.

curtsy /'kɜrtsi/ n. **1.** reverencia f. —v. **2.** hacer una reverencia.

curvature /'kɜrvətʃər/ n. curvatura f.

curve /kɜrv/ n. **1.** curva f. —v. **2.** encorvar.

cushion /'kuʃən/ n. cojín m.; almohada f.

cuspidor /'kʌspɪ,dɔr/ n. escupidera f.

custard /'kʌstərd/ n. flan m.; natillas f.pl.

custodian /kʌ'stoudiən/ n. custodio m.

custody /'kʌstədi/ n. custodia f.

custom /'kʌstəm/ n. costumbre f.

customary /'kʌstə,mɛri/ a. acostumbrado, usual.

customer /'kʌstəmər/ n. cliente m. & f.

customhouse /'kʌstəm,haus/ **customs** n. aduana f.

customs duty /'kʌstəmz/ derechos de aduana m.pl.

customs officer /'kʌstəmz/ agente de aduana m. & f.

cut /kʌt/ n. **1.** corte m.; cortada f.; tajada f.; (printing) grabado m. —v. **2.** cortar; tajar.

cute /kyut/ a. mono, lindo.

cut glass cristal tallado m.

cuticle /'kyutɪkəl/ n. cutícula f.

cutlery /'kʌtləri/ n. cuchillería f.

cutlet /'kʌtlɪt/ n. chuleta f.

cutter /'kʌtər/ n. cortador -ra; Naut. cúter m.

cutthroat /'kʌt,θrout/ n. asesino -na.

cyberpunk /'saibər,pʌŋk/ n. ciberpunk m. & f.

cyberspace /'saibər,speis/ n. ciberespacio m.

cyclamate /'saiklə,meit, 'sɪklə-/ n. ciclamato m.

cycle /'saikəl/ n. ciclo m.

cyclist /'saiklɪst/ n. ciclista m. & f.

cyclone /'saikloun/ n. ciclón, huracán m.

cyclotron /'saiklə,trɒn, 'sɪklə-/ n. ciclotrón m.

cylinder /'sɪlɪndər/ n. cilindro m.

cylindrical /sɪ'lɪndrɪkəl/ a. cilíndrico.

cymbal /'sɪmbəl/ n. címbalo m.

cynic /'sɪnɪk/ n. cínico -ca.

cynical /'sɪnɪkəl/ a. cínico.

cynicism /'sɪnə,sɪzəm/ n. cinismo m.

cypress /'saiprəs/ n. ciprés m. **c. nut,** piñuela f.

cyst /sɪst/ n. quiste m.

D

dad /dæd/ n. papá m., papito m.

daffodil /'dæfədɪl/ n. narciso m.

dagger /'dægər/ n. puñal m.

dahlia /'dælyə/ n. dalia f.

daily /'deili/ a. diario, cotidiano.

daintiness /'deintɪnɪs/ n. delicadeza f.

dainty /'deinti/ a. delicado.

dairy /'dɛəri/ n. lechería, quesería f.

dais /'deiɪs/ n. tablado m.

daisy /'deizi/ n. margarita f.

dale /deil/ n. valle m.

dally /'dæli/ v. holgar; perder el tiempo.

dam /dæm/ n. presa f.; dique m.

damage /'dæmɪdʒ/ n. **1.** daño m. —v. **2.** dañar.

damask /'dæməsk/ n. damasco m.

damn /dæm/ v. condenar.

damnation /dæm'neiʃən/ n. condenación f.

damp /dæmp/ a. húmedo.

dampen /'dæmpən/ v. humedecer.

dampness /'dæmpnɪs/ n. humedad f.

damsel /'dæmzəl/ n. doncella f.

dance /dæns/ n. **1.** baile m.; danza f. —v. **2.** bailar.

dance hall salón de baile m.

dancer /'dænsər/ n. bailador -ra; (professional) bailarín -na.

dancing /'dænsɪŋ/ n. baile m.

dandelion /'dændl,aiən/ n. amargón m.

dandruff /'dændrəf/ n. caspa f.

dandy /'dændi/ n. petimetre m.

danger /'deindʒər/ n. peligro m.

dangerous /'deindʒərəs/ a. peligroso.

dangle /'dæŋgəl/ v. colgar.

Danish /'deinɪʃ/ a. & n. danés -sa; dinamarqués -sa.

dapper /'dæpər/ a. gallardo.

dare /dɛər/ v. atreverse, osar.

daredevil /'dɛər,dɛvəl/ n. atrevido m., -da f.

daring /'dɛərɪŋ/ a. **1.** atrevido. —n. **2.** osadía f.

dark /dark/ a. **1.** obscuro; moreno. —n. **2.** obscuridad f.

darken /'darkən/ v. obscurecer.

darkness /'darknɪs/ n. obscuridad f.

darkroom /'dark,rum, -,rʊm/ n. cámara obscura f.

darling /'darlɪŋ/ a. & n. querido -da, amado -da f.

darn /darn/ v. zurcir.

darning needle /'darnɪŋ/ aguja de zurcir m.

dart /dart/ n. dardo m.

dartboard /'dart,bɔrd/ n. diana f.

dash /dæʃ/ n. arranque m.; Punct. guión m.

data /'deitə/ n. datos m.

database /'deitə,beis/ n. base de datos m.

data processing /'prɒsɛsɪŋ/ proceso de datos m.

date /deit/ n. fecha f.; (engagement) cita f.; (fruit) dátil m.

daughter /'dɔtər/ n. hija f.

daughter-in-law /'dɔ,tər ɪn lɔ/ n. nuera f.

daunt /dɔnt, dɑnt/ v. intimidar.

dauntless /'dɔntlɪs/ a. intrépido.

davenport /'dævən,pɔrt/ n. sofá m.

dawn /dɔn/ n. **1.** alba, madrugada f. —v. **2.** amanecer.

day /dei/ n. día m. **good d.,** buenos días.

daybreak /'dei,breik/ n. alba, madrugada f.

daydream /'dei,drim/ n. fantasía f.

daylight /'dei,lait/ n. luz del día.

daze /deiz/ v. aturdir.

dazzle /'dæzəl/ v. deslumbrar.

deacon /'dikən/ n. diácono m.

dead /dɛd/ a. muerto.

deaden /'dɛdn/ v. amortecer.

dead end atolladero m. (impasse); callejón sin salida m. (street).

deadline /'dɛd,lain/ n. fecha límite f.

deadlock /'dɛd,lɒk/ n. paro m.

deadly /'dɛdli/ a. mortal.

deaf /dɛf/ a. sordo.

deafen /'dɛfən/ v. ensordecer.

deafening /'dɛfənɪŋ/ a. ensordecedor.

deaf-mute /'dɛf 'myut/ n. sordomudo -da.

deafness /'dɛfnɪs/ n. sordera f.

deal /dil/ n. **1.** trato m.; negociación f. **a great d., a good d.,** mucho. —v. **2.** tratar; negociar.

dealer /'dilər/ n. comerciante m., (at cards) tallador -ra.

dean /din/ n. decano -na.

dear /dɪər/ a. querido; caro.

dearth /dɜrθ/ n. escasez f.

death /dɛθ/ n. muerte f.

death certificate partida de defunción f.

deathless /'dɛθlɪs/ a. inmortal.

debacle /də'bakəl/ n. desastre m.

debase /dɪ'beis/ v. degradar.

debatable /dɪ'beitəbəl/ a. discutible.

debate /dɪ'beit/ n. **1.** debate m. —v. **2.** disputar, deliberar.

debauch /dɪ'bɔtʃ/ v. corromper.

debilitate /dɪ'bɪlɪ,teit/ v. debilitar.

debit /'dɛbɪt/ n. débito m.

debit balance saldo deudor m.

debonair /,dɛbə'nɛər/ a. cortés; alegre, vivo.

debris /dei'bri/ n. escombros m.pl.

debt /dɛt/ n. deuda f. **get into d.** endeudarse.

debtor /'dɛtər/ n. deudor -ra.

debug /di'bʌg/ v. depurar, limpiar.

debunk /dɪ'bʌŋk/ v. desacreditar; desenmascarar.

debut /dei'byu/ n. debut, estreno m.

debutante /'dɛbyu,tɑnt/ n. debutante f.

decade /'dɛkeid/ n. década f.

decadence /'dɛkədəns/ n. decadencia f.

decadent /'dɛkədənt/ a. decadente.

decaffeinated /di'kæfɪ,neitɪd/ a. descafeinado.

decalcomania /dɪ,kælkə'meiniə/ n. calcomanía f.

decanter /dɪ'kæntər/ n. garrafa f.

decapitate /dɪ'kæpɪ,teit/ v. descabezar.

decay /dɪ'kei/ n. **1.** descaecimiento m.; (dental) caries f. —v. **2.** decaer; (dental) cariarse.

deceased /dɪ'sist/ a. muerto, difunto.

deceit /dɪ'sit/ n. engaño m.

deceitful /dɪ'sitfəl/ a. engañoso.

deceive /dɪ'siv/ v. engañar.

December /dɪ'sɛmbər/ n. diciembre m.

decency /'disənsi/ n. decencia f.; decoro m.

decent /'disənt/ a. decente.

decentralize /di'sɛntrə,laiz/ v. descentralizar.

deception /dɪ'sɛpʃən/ n. decepción f.

deceptive /dɪ'sɛptɪv/ a. deceptivo.

decibel /'dɛsə,bɛl/ n. decibelio m.

decide /dɪ'said/ v. decidir.

decimal /'dɛsəməl/ a. decimal.

decipher /dɪ'saifər/ v. descifrar.

decision /dɪ'sɪʒən/ n. decisión f.

decisive /dɪ'saisɪv/ a. decisivo.

deck /dɛk/ n. cubierta f.

deck chair tumbona f.

declamation /,dɛklə'meiʃən/ n. declamación f.

declaration /,dɛklə'reiʃən/ n. declaración f.

declarative /dɪ'klærətɪv/ a. declarativo.

declare /dɪ'klɛər/ v. declarar.

declension /dɪ'klɛnʃən/ n. declinación f.

decline /dɪ'klain/ n. **1.** decadencia f. —v. **2.** decaer; negarse; Gram. declinar.

decompose /,dikəm'pouz/ v. descomponer.

decongestant /,dikən'dʒɛstənt/ n. descongestionante m.

decorate /'dɛkə,reit/ v. decorar, adornar.

decoration /,dɛkə'reiʃən/ n. decoración f.

decorative /'dɛkərətɪv/ a. decorativo.

decorator /'dɛkə,reitər/ n. decorador -ra.

decorous /'dɛkərəs/ a. correcto.

decorum /dɪ'kɔrəm/ n. decoro m.

decrease /dɪ'kris/ v. disminuir.

decree /dɪ'kri/ n. decreto m.

decrepit /dɪ'krɛpɪt/ a. decrépito.

decry /dɪ'krai/ v. desacreditar.

dedicate /'dɛdɪ,keit/ v. dedicar; consagrar.

dedication /,dɛdɪ'keiʃən/ n. dedicación; dedicatoria f.

deduce /dɪ'dus/ v. deducir.

deduction /dɪ'dʌkʃən/ n. rebaja; deducción f.

deductive /dɪ'dʌktɪv/ a. deductivo.

deed /did/ n. acción; hazaña f.

deem /dim/ v. estimar.

deep /dip/ a. hondo, profundo.

deepen /'dipən/ v. profundizar, ahondar.

deep freeze congelación f.

deeply /'dipli/ adv. profundamente.

deer /dɪər/ n. venado, ciervo m.

deface /dɪ'feis/ v. mutilar.

defamation /,dɛfə'meiʃən/ n. calumnia f.

defame /dɪ'feim/ v. difamar.

default /dɪ'fɔlt/ n. **1.** defecto m. —v. **2.** faltar.

defeat /dɪ'fit/ n. **1.** derrota f. —v. **2.** derrotar.

defeatism /dɪ'fitɪzəm/ n. derrotismo m.

defect /'difɛkt, dɪ'fɛkt/ n. defecto m.

defective /dɪ'fɛktɪv/ a. defectivo.

defend /dɪ'fɛnd/ v. defender.

defendant /dɪ'fɛndənt/ n. acusado -da.

defender /dɪ'fɛndər/ n. defensor -ra.

defense /dɪ'fɛns/ n. defensa f.

defensive /dɪ'fɛnsɪv/ a. defensivo.

defer /dɪ'fɜr/ v. aplazar; deferir.

deference /'dɛfərəns/ n. deferencia f.

defiance /dɪ'faiəns/ n. desafío m.

defiant /dɪ'faiənt/ a. desafiador.

deficiency /dɪ'fɪʃənsi/ n. defecto m.

deficient /dɪ'fɪʃənt/ a. deficiente.

deficit /'dɛfəsɪt/ n. déficit, descubierto m.

defile /dɪ'fail/ n. **1.** desfiladero m. —v. **2.** profanar.

define /dɪ'fain/ v. definir.

definite /'dɛfənɪt/ a. exacto; definitivo.

definitely /'dɛfənɪtli/ adv. definitivamente.

definition /,dɛfə'nɪʃən/ n. definición f.

definitive /dɪ'fɪnɪtɪv/ a. definitivo.

deflation /dɪ'fleiʃən/ n. desinflación f.

deflect /dɪ'flɛkt/ v. desviar.

deform /dɪ'fɔrm/ v. deformar.

deformity /dɪ'fɔrmɪti/ n. deformidad f.

defraud /dɪ'frɔd/ v. defraudar.

defray /dɪ'frei/ v. costear.

defrost /dɪ'frɔst/ v. descongelar.

deft /dɛft/ a. diestro.

defy /dɪ'fai/ v. desafiar.

degenerate /a dɪ'dʒɛnərɪt; v -,reit/ a. **1.** degenerado. —v. **2.** degenerar.

degeneration /dɪ,dʒɛnə'reiʃən/ n. degeneración f.

degradation /,dɛgrɪ'deiʃən/ n. degradación f.

degrade /dɪ'greid/ v. degradar.

degree /dɪ'gri/ n. grado m.

deign /dein/ v. condescender.

deity /'diiti/ n. deidad f.

dejected /dɪ'dʒɛktɪd/ a. abatido.

dejection /dɪ'dʒɛkʃən/ n. tristeza f.

delay /dɪ'lei/ n. **1.** retardo m., demora f. —v. **2.** tardar, demorar.

delegate /n 'dɛlɪgɪt; v -,geit/ n. **1.** delegado -da. —v. **2.** delegar.

delegation /,dɛlɪ'geiʃən/ n. delegación f.

delete /dɪ'lit/ v. suprimir, tachar.

deliberate /a dɪ'lɪbərɪt; v -ə,reit/ a. **1.** premeditado. —v. **2.** deliberar.

deliberately /dɪ'lɪbərɪtli/ adv. deliberadamente.

deliberation /dɪ,lɪbə'reiʃən/ n. deliberación f.

deliberative /dɪ'lɪbərətɪv/ a. deliberativo.

delicacy /'dɛlɪkəsi/ n. delicadeza f.

delicate /'dɛlɪkɪt/ a. delicado.

delicious /dɪ'lɪʃəs/ a. delicioso.

delight /dɪ'lait/ n. deleite m.

delightful /dɪ'laitfəl/ a. deleitoso.

delinquency /dɪ'lɪŋkwənsi/ a. delincuencia f.

delinquent /dɪ'lɪŋkwənt/ a. & n. delincuente. m. & f.

delirious /dɪ'lɪəriəs/ a. delirante.

deliver /dɪ'lɪvər/ v. entregar.

deliverance /dɪ'lɪvərəns/ n. liberación; salvación f.

delivery /dɪ'lɪvəri/ n. entrega f.; Med. parto m.

delude /dɪ'lud/ v. engañar.

deluge /'dɛlyudʒ/ n. inundación f.

delusion /dɪ'luʒən/ n. decepción f.; engaño m.

delve /dɛlv/ v. cavar, sondear.

demagogue /'dɛmə,gɒg/ n. demagogo -ga.

demand /dɪ'mænd/ n. **1.** demanda f. —v. **2.** demandar; exigir.

demarcation /,dimar'keiʃən/ n. demarcación f.

demeanor /dɪ'minər/ n. conducta f.

demented /dɪ'mɛntɪd/ a. demente, loco.

demilitarize /di'mɪlɪtə,raiz/ v. desmilitarizar.

demobilize /di'moubə,laiz/ v. desmovilizar.

democracy /dɪ'mɒkrəsi/ n. democracia f.

democrat /'dɛmə,kræt/ n. demócrata m. & f.

democratic /,dɛmə'krætɪk/ a. democrático.

demolish /dɪ'mɒlɪʃ/ v. demoler.

demon /'dimən/ n. demonio m.

demonstrate /'dɛmən,streit/ v. demostrar.

demonstration /,dɛmən'streiʃən/ n. demostración f.

demonstrative /də'mɒnstrətɪv/ a. demostrativo.

demoralize /dɪ'mɔrə,laiz, -'mɒr-/ v. desmoralizar.

demure /dɪ'myur/ a. modesto, serio.

den /dɛn/ n. madriguera, caverna f.

denature /di'neitʃər/ v. alterar.

denial /dɪ'naiəl/ n. negación f.

denim /'dɛnəm/ n. dril, tela vaquera.

Denmark /'dɛnmark/ n. Dinamarca f.

denomination /dɪ,nɒmə'neiʃən/ n. denominación; secta f.

denote /dɪ'nout/ v. denotar.

denounce /dɪ'nauns/ v. denunciar.

dense /dɛns/ a. denso, espeso; estúpido.

density /'dɛnsɪti/ n. densidad f.

dent /dɛnt/ n. **1.** abolladura f. —v. **2.** abollar.

dental /'dɛntl/ a. dental.

dentist /'dɛntɪst/ n. dentista m. & f.

dentistry /'dɛntəstri/ n. odontología f.

denture /'dɛntʃər/ n. dentadura f.

denunciation /dɪ,nʌnsi'eiʃən/ n. denunciación f.

deny /dɪ'nai/ v. negar, rehusar.

deodorant /di'oudərənt/ n. desodorante m.

depart /dɪ'part/ v. partir; irse, marcharse.

department /dɪ'partmənt/ n. departamento m.

departmental /dɪ,part'mɛntl/ a. departamental.

department store grandes almacenes m.pl.

departure /dɪ'partʃər/ n. salida; desviación f.

depend /dɪ'pɛnd/ v. depender.

dependability /dɪ,pɛndə'bɪlɪti/ n. confiabilidad f.

dependable /dɪ'pɛndəbəl/ a. confiable.

dependence /dɪ'pɛndəns/ n. dependencia f.

dependent /dɪ'pɛndənt/ a. & n. dependiente m. & f.

depict /dɪ'pɪkt/ v. pintar; representar.

deplete /dɪ'plit/ v. agotar.

deplorable /dɪ'plɔrəbəl/ a. deplorable.

deplore /dɪ'plɔr/ v. deplorar.

deport /dɪ'pɔrt/ v. deportar.

deportation /,dipɔr'teiʃən/ n. deportación f.

deportment /dɪ'pɔrtmənt/ n. conducta f.

depose /dɪ'pouz/ v. deponer.

deposit /dɪ'pɒzɪt/ n. **1.** depósito m. (of money); yacimiento (of ore, etc.) m. —v. **2.** depositar.

depositor /dɪ'pɒzɪtər/ n. depositante m. & f.

depot /'dipou/ n. depósito m.; (railway) estación f.

depravity /dɪ'prævɪti/ n. depravación f.

deprecate /'dɛprɪ,keit/ v. deprecar.

depreciate /dɪ'priʃi,eit/ v. depreciar.

depreciation /dɪ,priʃi'eiʃən/ n. depreciación f.

depredation /,dɛprə'deiʃən/ n. depredación f.

depress /dɪ'prɛs/ v. deprimir; desanimar.

depression /dɪ'prɛʃən/ n. depresión f.

deprive /dɪ'praiv/ v. privar.

depth /dɛpθ/ n. profundidad, hondura f.

depth charge carga de profundidad f.

deputy /'dɛpyəti/ n. diputado -da.

deride /dɪ'raid/ v. burlar.

derision /dɪ'rɪʒən/ n. burla f.

derivation /,dɛrə'veiʃən/ n. derivación f.

derivative /dɪ'rɪvətɪv/ a. derivativo.

derive /dɪ'raiv/ v. derivar.

dermatologist /,dɜrmə'tɒlədʒɪst/ n. dermatólogo -ga.

derogatory /dɪ'rɒgə,tɔri/ a. derogatorio.

derrick /'dɛrɪk/ n. grúa f.

descend /dɪ'sɛnd/ v. descender, bajar.

descendant /dɪ'sɛndənt/ n. descendiente m. & f.

descent /dɪ'sɛnt/ n. descenso m.; origen m.

describe /dɪ'skraib/ v. describir.

description /dɪ'skrɪpʃən/ n. descripción f.

descriptive /dɪ'skrɪptɪv/ a. descriptivo.

desecrate /'dɛsɪ,kreit/ v. profanar.

desert /n 'dɛzərt; v dɪ'zɜrt/ n. **1.** desierto m. —v. **2.** abandonar.

deserter /dɪ'zɜrtər/ n. desertor -ra.

desertion /dɪ'zɜrʃən/ n. deserción f.

deserve /dɪ'zɜrv/ v. merecer.

design /dɪ'zain/ *n.* **1.** diseño *m.* —*v.* **2.** diseñar.
designate /'dɛzɪg,neit/ *v.* señalar, apuntar; designar.
designation /,dɛzɪg'neiʃən/ *n.* designación *f.*
designer /dɪ'zainər/ *n.* diseñador -ra; (technical) proyectista *m.* & *f.*
designer clothes, designer clothing ropa de marca *f.*
desirability /dɪ,zaiᵊrə'bɪlɪti/ *n.* conveniencia *f.*
desirable /dɪ'zaiᵊrəbəl/ *a.* deseable.
desire /dɪ'zaiᵊr/ *n.* **1.** deseo *m.* —*v.* **2.** desear.
desirous /dɪ'zaiᵊrəs/ *a.* deseoso.
desist /dɪ'sɪst/ *v.* desistir.
desk /dɛsk/ *n.* escritorio *m.*
desk clerk recepcionista *m.* & *f.*
desktop computer /'dɛsk,tɒp/ computadora de sobremesa *f.*, ordenador de sobremesa *f.*
desolate /*a* 'dɛsəlɪt; *v* -,leit/ *a.* **1.** desolado. —*v.* **2.** desolar.
desolation /,dɛsə'leiʃən/ *n.* desolación, ruina *f.*
despair /dɪ'spɛər/ *n.* **1.** desesperación *f.* —*v.* **2.** desesperar.
despatch /dɪ'spætʃ/ **dispatch** *n.* **1.** despacho *m.*; prontitud *f.* —*v.* **2.** despachar.
desperado /,dɛspə'rɑdou/ *n.* bandido *m.*
desperate /'dɛspərɪt/ *a.* desesperado.
desperation /,dɛspə'reiʃən/ *n.* desesperación *f.*
despicable /'dɛspɪkəbəl/ *a.* vil.
despise /dɪ'spaiz/ *v.* despreciar.
despite /dɪ'spait/ *prep.* a pesar de.
despondent /dɪ'spɒndənt/ *a.* abatido; desanimado.
despot /'dɛspət/ *n.* déspota *m.* & *f.*
despotic /dɛs'pɒtɪk/ *a.* despótico.
dessert /dɪ'zɜrt/ *n.* postre *m.*
destination /,dɛstə'neiʃən/ *n.* destinación *f.*
destine /'dɛstɪn/ *v.* destinar.
destiny /'dɛstəni/ *n.* destino *m.*
destitute /'dɛstɪ,tut/ *a.* destituído, indigente.
destitution /,dɛstɪ'tuʃən/ *n.* destitución *f.*
destroy /dɪ'strɔi/ *v.* destrozar, destruir.
destroyer /dɪ'strɔiər/ *n.* destruidor -ra; (naval) destructor *m.*
destruction /dɪ'strʌkʃən/ *n.* destrucción *f.*
destructive /dɪ'strʌktɪv/ *a.* destructivo.
desultory /'dɛsəl,tɔri/ *a.* inconexo; casual.
detach /dɪ'tætʃ/ *v.* separar, desprender.
detachment /dɪ'tætʃmənt/ *n.* *Mil.* destacamento; desprendimiento *m.*
detail /dɪ'teil/ *n.* **1.** detalle *m.* —*v.* **2.** detallar.
detain /dɪ'tein/ *v.* detener.
detect /dɪ'tɛkt/ *v.* descubrir.
detection /dɪ'tɛkʃən/ *n.* detección *f.*
detective /dɪ'tɛktɪv/ *n.* detective *m.* & *f.*
deténte /dei'tɑnt/ *n.* distensión *f.*; *Pol.* deténte.
detention /dɪ'tɛnʃən/ *n.* detención; cautividad *f.*
deter /dɪ'tɜr/ *v.* disuadir.
detergent /dɪ'tɜrdʒənt/ *n.* & *a.* detergente *m.*
deteriorate /dɪ'tɪəriə,reit/ *v.* deteriorar.
deterioration /dɪ,tɪəriə'reiʃən/ *n.* deterioración *f.*
determination /dɪ,tɜrmə'neiʃən/ *n.* determinación *f.*
determine /dɪ'tɜrmɪn/ *v.* determinar.
deterrence /dɪ'tɜrəns/ *n.* disuasión *f.*
detest /dɪ'tɛst/ *v.* detestar.
detonate /'dɛtn,eit/ *v.* detonar.
detour /'ditʊr/ *n.* desvío *m.* *v.* desviar.
detract /dɪ'trækt/ *v.* disminuir.
detriment /'dɛtrəmənt/ *n.* detrimento *m.*, daño *m.*
detrimental /,dɛtrə'mɛntl/ *a.* dañoso.
devaluate /di'vælyu,eit/ *v.* depreciar.
devastate /'dɛvə,steit/ *v.* devastar.
develop /dɪ'vɛləp/ *v.* desarrollar; *Phot.* revelar.
developing nation /dɪ'vɛləpɪŋ/ nación en desarrollo.
development /dɪ'vɛləpmənt/ *n.* desarrollo *m.*
deviate /'divi,eit/ *v.* desviar.
deviation /,divi'eiʃən/ *n.* desviación *f.*
device /dɪ'vais/ *n.* aparato; artificio *m.*
devil /'dɛvəl/ *n.* diablo, demonio *m.*
devious /'diviəs/ *a.* desviado.
devise /dɪ'vaiz/ *v.* inventar.
devoid /dɪ'vɔid/ *a.* desprovisto.
devote /dɪ'vout/ *v.* dedicar, consagrar.
devoted /dɪ'voutɪd/ *a.* devoto.
devotee /,dɛvə'ti/ *n.* aficionado -da.
devotion /dɪ'vouʃən/ *n.* devoción *f.*
devour /dɪ'vaur/ *v.* devorar.
devout /dɪ'vaut/ *a.* devoto.
dew /du/ *n.* rocío, sereno *m.*
dexterity /dɛk'stɛrɪti/ *n.* destreza *f.*
dexterous /'dɛkstrəs/ *a.* diestro.
diabetes /,daiə'bitɪs/ *n.* diabetes *f.*
diabolic /,daiə'bɒlɪk/ *a.* diabólico.
diadem /'daiə,dɛm/ *n.* diadema *f.*
diagnose /'daiəg,nous/ *v.* diagnosticar.
diagnosis /,daiəg'nousɪs/ *n.* diagnóstico *m.*
diagonal /dai'ægənl/ *n.* diagonal *f.*
diagram /'daiə,græm/ *n.* diagrama *m.*
dial /'daiəl/ *n.* **1.** cuadrante *m.*, carátula *f.* —*v.* **2. dial up** marcar.
dialect /'daiə,lɛkt/ *n.* dialecto *m.*
dialing code /'daiəlɪŋ/ prefijo *m.*
dialogue /'daiə,lɔg/ *n.* diálogo *m.*
dial tone señal de marcar *f.*
diameter /dai'æmɪtər/ *n.* diámetro *m.*
diamond /'daimənd/ *n.* diamante, brillante *m.*
diaper /'daipər/ *n.* pañal *m.*
diarrhea /,daiə'riə/ *n.* diarrea *f.*
diary /'daiəri/ *n.* diario *m.*
diathermy /'daiə,θɜrmi/ *n.* diatermia *f.*
dice /dais/ *n.* dados *m.pl.*
dictate /'dɪkteit/ *n.* **1.** mandato *m.* —*v.* **2.** dictar.
dictation /dɪk'teiʃən/ *n.* dictado *m.*
dictator /'dɪkteitər/ *n.* dictador -ra.
dictatorship /dɪk'teitər,ʃɪp/ *n.* dictadura *f.*
diction /'dɪkʃən/ *n.* dicción *f.*
dictionary /'dɪkʃə,nɛri/ *n.* diccionario *m.*
die /dai/ *n.* **1.** matriz *f.*; (game) dado *m.* —*v.* **2.** morir.
diet /'daiɪt/ *n.* dieta *f.*
dietary /'daiɪ,tɛri/ *a.* dietético.
dietitian /,daiɪ'tɪʃən/ *n.* & *a.* dietético -ca.
differ /'dɪfər/ *v.* diferir.
difference /'dɪfərəns/ *n.* diferencia *f.* **to make no d.,** no importar.
different /'dɪfərənt/ *a.* diferente, distinto.
differential /,dɪfə'rɛnʃəl/ *n.* diferencial *f.*
differentiate /,dɪfə'rɛnʃi,eit/ *v.* diferenciar.
difficult /'dɪfɪ,kʌlt/ *a.* difícil.
difficulty /'dɪfɪ,kʌlti/ *n.* dificultad *f.*
diffident /'dɪfɪdənt/ *a.* tímido.
diffuse /dɪ'fyuz/ *v.* difundir.
diffusion /dɪ'fyuʒən/ *n.* difusión *f.*
dig /dɪg/ *v.* cavar.
digest /*n* 'daidʒɛst; *v* dɪ'dʒɛst, dai-/ *n.* **1.** extracto *m.* —*v.* **2.** digerir.
digestible /dɪ'dʒɛstəbəl, dai-/ *a.* digerible.
digestion /dɪ'dʒɛstʃən, dai-/ *n.* digestión *f.*
digestive /dɪ'dʒɛstɪv, dai-/ *a.* digestivo.
digital /'dɪdʒɪtl/ *a.* digital.
digitalis /,dɪdʒɪ'tælɪs/ *n.* digital *f.*
dignified /'dɪgnə,f aid/ *a.* digno.
dignify /'dɪgnə,f ai/ *v.* dignificar.
dignitary /'dɪgnɪ,tɛri/ *n.* dignatario -ria.
dignity /'dɪgnɪti/ *n.* dignidad *f.*
digress /dɪ'grɛs, dai-/ *v.* divagar.
digression /dɪ'grɛʃən, dai-/ *n.* digresión *f.*
dike /daik/ *n.* dique *m.*
dilapidated /dɪ'læpɪ,deitɪd/ *a.* dilapidado.
dilapidation /dɪ,læpə'deiʃən/ *n.* dilapidación *f.*
dilate /dai'leit/ *v.* dilatar.
dilatory /'dɪlə,tɔri/ *a.* dilatorio.
dilemma /dɪ'lɛmə/ *n.* dilema *m.*
dilettante /'dɪlɪ,tɑnt/ *n.* diletante *m.* & *f.*
diligence /'dɪlɪdʒəns/ *n.* diligencia *f.*
diligent /'dɪlɪdʒənt/ *a.* diligente, aplicado.
dilute /dɪ'lut, dai-/ *v.* diluir.
dim /dɪm/ *a.* **1.** oscuro. —*v.* **2.** oscurecer.
dimension /dɪ'mɛnʃən/ *n.* dimensión *f.*
diminish /dɪ'mɪnɪʃ/ *v.* disminuir.
diminution /,dɪmə'nuʃən/ *n.* disminución *f.*
diminutive /dɪ'mɪnyətɪv/ *a.* diminutivo.
dimness /'dɪmnɪs/ *n.* oscuridad *f.*
dimple /'dɪmpəl/ *n.* hoyuelo *m.*
din /dɪn/ *n.* alboroto, estrépito *m.*
dine /dain/ *v.* comer, cenar.
diner /'dainər/ *n.* coche comedor *m.*
dingy /'dɪndʒi/ *a.* deslucido, deslustrado.
dining room /'dainɪŋ/ comedor *m.*
dinner /'dɪnər/ *n.* comida, cena *f.*
dinosaur /'dainə,sɔr/ *n.* dinosauro *m.*
diocese /'daiəsɪs/ *n.* diócesis *f.*
dip /dɪp/ *v.* sumergir, hundir.
diphtheria /dɪf'θɪəriə/ *n.* difteria *f.*
diploma /dɪ'ploumə/ *n.* diploma *m.*
diplomacy /dɪ'plouməsi/ *n.* diplomacia *f.*
diplomat /'dɪplə,mæt/ *n.* diplomático -ca.
diplomatic /,dɪplə'mætɪk/ *a.* diplomático.
dipper /'dɪpər/ *n.* cucharón *m.*
dire /daiᵊr/ *a.* horrendo.
direct /dɪ'rɛkt, dai-/ *a.* **1.** directo. —*v.* **2.** dirigir.
direction /dɪ'rɛkʃən, 'dai-/ *n.* dirección *f.*
directive /dɪ'rɛktɪv, dai-/ *n.* directiva *f.*
directly /dɪ'rɛktli, dai-/ *adv.* directamente.
director /dɪ'rɛktər, dai-/ *n.* director -ra.
directory /dɪ'rɛktəri, dai-/ *n.* directorio *m.*, guía *f.*
dirigible /'dɪrɪdʒəbəl/ *n.* dirigible *m.*
dirt /dɜrt/ *n.* basura *f.*; (earth) tierra *f.*
dirt-cheap /'dɜrt 'tʃip/ *a.* tirado.
dirty /'dɜrti/ *a.* sucio.
dis /dɪs/ *v.* *Colloq.* ofender, faltar al respeto.
disability /,dɪsə'bɪlɪti/ *n.* inhabilidad *f.*
disable /dɪs'eibəl/ *v.* incapacitar.
disabuse /,dɪsə'byuz/ *v.* desengañar.
disadvantage /,dɪsəd'væntɪdʒ/ *n.* desventaja *f.*
disagree /,dɪsə'gri/ *v.* desconvenir; disentir.
disagreeable /,dɪsə'griəbəl/ *a.* desagradable.
disagreement /,dɪsə'grimənt/ *n.* desacuerdo *m.*
disappear /,dɪsə'pɪər/ *v.* desaparecer.
disappearance /,dɪsə'pɪərəns/ *n.* desaparición *f.*
disappoint /,dɪsə'pɔint/ *v.* disgustar, desilusionar.
disappointment /,dɪsə'pɔintmənt/ *n.* disgusto *m.*, desilusión *f.*
disapproval /,dɪsə'pruvəl/ *n.* desaprobación *f.*
disapprove /,dɪsə'pruv/ *v.* desaprobar.
disarm /dɪs'ɑrm/ *v.* desarmar.
disarmament /dɪs'ɑrməmənt/ *n.* desarme *m.*
disarrange /,dɪsə'reindʒ/ *v.* desordenar; desarreglar.
disaster /dɪ'zæstər/ *n.* desastre *m.*
disastrous /dɪ'zæstrəs/ *a.* desastroso.
disavow /,dɪsə'vau/ *v.* repudiar.
disavowal /,dɪsə'vauəl/ *n.* repudiación *f.*
disband /dɪs'bænd/ *v.* dispersarse.
disbelieve /,dɪsbɪ'liv/ *v.* descreer.
disburse /dɪs'bɜrs/ *v.* desembolsar, pagar.
discard /dɪ'skɑrd/ *v.* descartar.
discern /dɪ'sɜrn/ *v.* discernir.
discerning /dɪ'sɜrnɪŋ/ *a.* discernidor, perspicaz.
discernment /dɪ'sɜrnmənt/ *n.* discernimiento *m.*
discharge /dɪs'tʃɑrdʒ/ *v.* descargar; despedir.
disciple /dɪ'saipəl/ *n.* discípulo -la.
disciplinary /'dɪsəplə,nɛri/ *a.* disciplinario.
discipline /'dɪsəplɪn/ *n.* disciplina *f.*
disclaim /dɪs'kleim/ *v.* repudiar.
disclaimer /dɪs'kleimər/ *n.* negación *f.*
disclose /dɪ'sklouz/ *v.* revelar.
disclosure /dɪ'sklouʒər/ *n.* revelación *f.*
disco /'dɪskou/ *n.* discoteca *f.*
discolor /dɪs'kʌlər/ *v.* descolorar.
discomfort /dɪs'kʌmfərt/ *n.* incomodidad *f.*
disconcert /,dɪskən'sɜrt/ *v.* desconcertar.
disconnect /,dɪskə'nɛkt/ *v.* desunir; desconectar.
disconnected /,dɪskə'nɛktɪd/ *a.* desunido.
disconsolate /dɪs'kɒnsəlɪt/ *a.* desconsolado.
discontent /,dɪskən'tɛnt/ *n.* descontento *m.*
discontented /,dɪskən'tɛntɪd/ *a.* descontento.
discontinue /,dɪskən'tɪnyu/ *v.* descontinuar.
discord /'dɪskɔrd/ *n.* discordia *f.*
discordant /dɪs'kɔrdənt/ *a.* disonante.
discotheque /'dɪskə,tɛk/ *n.* discoteca *f.*
discount /'dɪskaunt/ *n.* descuento *m.*
discourage /dɪ'skɜrɪdʒ/ *v.* desalentar, desanimar.
discouragement /dɪ'skɜrɪdʒmənt/ *n.* desaliento, desánimo *m.*
discourse /'dɪskɔrs/ *n.* discurso *m.*
discourteous /dɪs'kɜrtiəs/ *a.* descortés.
discourtesy /dɪs'kɜrtəsi/ *n.* descortesía *f.*
discover /dɪ'skʌvər/ *v.* descubrir.
discoverer /dɪ'skʌvərər/ *n.* descubridor -ra.
discovery /dɪ'skʌvəri/ *n.* descubrimiento *m.*
discreet /dɪ'skrit/ *a.* discreto.
discrepancy /dɪ'skrɛpənsi/ *n.* discrepancia *f.*
discretion /dɪ'skrɛʃən/ *n.* discreción *f.*
discriminate /dɪ'skrɪm,əneit/ *v.* distinguir. **d. against** discriminar contra.
discrimination /dɪ,skrɪmə'neiʃən/ *n.* discernimiento *m.*; discriminación *f.*
discuss /dɪ'skʌs/ *v.* discutir.
discussion /dɪ'skʌʃən/ *n.* discusión *f.*
disdain /dɪs'dein/ *n.* **1.** desdén *m.* —*v.* **2.** desdeñar.
disdainful /dɪs'deinfəl/ *a.* desdeñoso.
disease /dɪ'ziz/ *n.* enfermedad *f.*, mal *m.*
disembark /,dɪsɛm'bɑrk/ *v.* desembarcar.

disentangle /ˌdɪsɛn'tæŋgəl/ v. desenredar.

disfigure /dɪs'fɪgyər/ v. desfigurar.

disgrace /dɪs'greis/ n. **1.** vergüenza; deshonra f. —v. **2.** deshonrar.

disgraceful /dɪs'greisfəl/ a. vergonzoso.

disguise /dɪs'gaiz/ n. **1.** disfraz m. —v. **2.** disfrazar.

disgust /dɪs'gʌst/ n. **1.** repugnancia —v. **2.** fastidiar; repugnar.

dish /dɪʃ/ n. plato m.

dishearten /dɪs'hɑrtn/ v. desanimar; descorazonar.

dishonest /dɪs'ɒnɪst/ a. deshonesto.

dishonesty /dɪs'ɒnəsti/ n. deshonestidad f.

dishonor /dɪs'ɒnər/ n. **1.** deshonra f. —v. **2.** deshonrar.

dishonorable /dɪs'ɒnərəbəl/ a. deshonroso.

dishwasher /dɪʃ,wɒʃər/ n. lavaplatos m.

disillusion /ˌdɪsɪ'luʒən/ n. **1.** desengaño m. —v. **2.** desengañar.

disinfect /ˌdɪsɪn'fɛkt/ v. desinfectar.

disinfectant /ˌdɪsɪn'fɛktənt/ n. desinfectante m.

disinherit /ˌdɪsɪn'hɛrɪt/ v. desheredar.

disintegrate /dɪs'ɪntə,greit/ v. desintegrar.

disinterested /dɪs'ɪntə,rɛstɪd, -trɪstɪd/ a. desinteresado.

disk /dɪsk/ n. disco m.

disk drive disquetera f.

diskette /dɪs'kɛt/ n. disquete m.

disk jockey pinchadiscos m. & f.

dislike /dɪs'laik/ n. **1.** antipatía f. —v. **2.** no gustar de.

dislocate /'dɪslou,keit/ v. dislocar.

dislodge /dɪs'lɒdʒ/ v. desalojar; desprender.

disloyal /dɪs'lɔiəl/ a. desleal; infiel.

disloyalty /dɪs'lɔialti/ n. deslealtad f.

dismal /'dɪzməl/ a. lúgubre.

dismantle /dɪs'mæntl/ v. desmantelar, desmontar.

dismay /dɪs'mei/ n. **1.** consternación f. —v. **2.** consternar.

dismiss /dɪs'mɪs/ v. despedir.

dismissal /dɪs'mɪsəl/ n. despedida f.

dismount /dɪs'maunt/ v. apearse, desmontarse.

disobedience /ˌdɪsə'bidiəns/ n. desobediencia f.

disobedient /ˌdɪsə'bidiənt/ a. desobediente.

disobey /ˌdɪsə'bei/ v. desobedecer.

disorder /dɪs'ɔrdər/ n. desorden m.

disorderly /dɪs'ɔrdərli/ a. desarreglado, desordenado.

disown /dɪs'oun/ v. repudiar.

dispassionate /dɪs'pæʃənɪt/ a. desapasionado; templado.

dispatch /dɪs'pætʃ/ n. **1.** despacho m. —v. **2.** despachar.

dispel /dɪs'pɛl/ v. dispersar.

dispensary /dɪs'pɛnsəri/ n. dispensario m.

dispensation /ˌdɪspən'seiʃən/ n. dispensación f.

dispense /dɪs'pɛns/ v. dispensar.

dispersal /dɪs'pərsəl/ n. dispersión f.

disperse /dɪs'pərs/ v. dispersar.

displace /dɪs'pleis/ v. dislocar.

display /dɪs'plei/ n. **1.** despliegue m., exhibición f. —v. **2.** desplegar, exhibir.

displease /dɪs'pliz/ v. disgustar; ofender.

displeasure /dɪs'plɛʒər/ n. disgusto, sinsabor m.

disposable /dɪs'pouzəbəl/ a. disponible; desechable.

disposal /dɪs'pouzəl/ n. disposición f.

dispose /dɪs'pouz/ v. disponer.

disposition /ˌdɪspə'zɪʃən/ n. disposición f.; índole f., genio m.

dispossess /ˌdɪspə'zɛs/ v. desposeer.

disproportionate /ˌdɪsprə'pɔrʃənɪt/ a. desproporcionado.

disprove /dɪs'pruv/ v. confutar.

dispute /dɪ'spyut/ n. **1.** disputa f. —v. **2.** disputar.

disqualify /dɪs'kwɒlə,fai/ v. inhabilitar.

disregard /ˌdɪsrɪ'gɑrd/ n. **1.** desatención f. —v. **2.** desatender.

disrepair /ˌdɪsrɪ'pɛər/ n. descompostura f.

disreputable /dɪs'rɛpyətəbəl/ a. desacreditado.

disrespect /ˌdɪsrɪ'spɛkt/ n. falta de respeto, f., desacato m.

disrespectful /ˌdɪsrɪ'spɛktfəl/ a. irrespetuoso.

disrobe /dɪs'roub/ v. desvestir.

disrupt /dɪs'rʌpt/ v. romper; desbaratar.

dissatisfaction /ˌdɪssætɪs'fækʃən/ n. descontento m.

dissatisfy /dɪs'sætɪs,fai/ v. descontentar.

dissect /dɪ'sɛkt/ v. disecar.

dissemble /dɪ'sɛmbəl/ v. disimular.

disseminate /dɪ'sɛmə,neit/ v. diseminar.

dissension /dɪ'sɛnʃən/ n. disensión f.

dissent /dɪ'sɛnt/ n. **1.** disensión f. —v. **2.** disentir.

dissertation /ˌdɪsər'teiʃən/ n. disertación f.

dissimilar /dɪ'sɪmələr/ a. desemejante.

dissipate /'dɪsə,peit/ v. disipar.

dissipation /ˌdɪsə'peiʃən/ n. disipación f.; libertinaje m.

dissolute /'dɪsə,lut/ a. disoluto.

dissolution /ˌdɪsə'luʃən/ n. disolución f.

dissolve /dɪ'zɒlv/ v. disolver; derretirse.

dissonant /'dɪsənənt/ a. disonante.

dissuade /dɪ'sweid/ v. disuadir.

distance /'dɪstəns/ n. distancia f. **at a d., in the d.,** a lo lejos.

distant /'dɪstənt/ a. distante, lejano.

distaste /dɪs'teist/ n. disgusto, sinsabor m.

distasteful /dɪs'teistfəl/ a. desagradable.

distill /dɪ'stɪl/ v. destilar.

distillation /ˌdɪstl'eiʃən/ n. destilación f.

distillery /dɪ'stɪləri/ n. destilería f.

distinct /dɪ'stɪŋkt/ a. distinto.

distinction /dɪ'stɪŋkʃən/ n. distinción f.

distinctive /dɪ'stɪŋktɪv/ a. distintivo; característico.

distinctly /dɪ'stɪŋktli/ adv. distintamente.

distinguish /dɪ'stɪŋgwɪʃ/ v. distinguir.

distinguished /dɪ'stɪŋgwɪʃt/ a. distinguido.

distort /dɪ'stɔrt/ v. falsear; torcer.

distract /dɪ'strækt/ v. distraer.

distraction /dɪ'strækʃən/ n. distracción f.

distraught /dɪ'strɔt/ a. aturrullado; demente.

distress /dɪ'strɛs/ n. **1.** dolor m. —v. **2.** afligir.

distressing /dɪ'strɛsɪŋ/ a. penoso.

distribute /dɪ'strɪbyut/ v. distribuir.

distribution /ˌdɪstrə'byuʃən/ n. distribución f.; reparto m.

distributor /dɪ'strɪbyətər/ n. distribuidor -ra.

district /'dɪstrɪkt/ n. distrito m.

distrust /dɪs'trʌst/ n. **1.** desconfianza f. —v. **2.** desconfiar.

distrustful /dɪs'trʌstfəl/ a. desconfiado; sospechoso.

disturb /dɪ'stɜrb/ v. incomodar; inquietar.

disturbance /dɪ'stɜrbəns/ n. disturbio m.

disturbing /dɪ'stɜrbɪŋ/ a. inquietante.

ditch /dɪtʃ/ n. zanja f.; foso m.

divan /dɪ'væn/ n. diván m.

dive /daiv/ n. **1.** clavado m.; Colloq. leonera f. —v. **2.** echar un clavado; bucear.

diver /'daivər/ n. buzo m.

diverge /dɪ'vɜrdʒ/ v. divergir.

divergence /dɪ'vɜrdʒəns/ n. divergencia f.

divergent /dɪ'vɜrdʒənt/ a. divergente.

diverse /dɪ'vɜrs/ a. diverso.

diversion /dɪ'vɜrʒən/ n. diversión f.; pasatiempo m.

diversity /dɪ'vɜrsɪti/ n. diversidad f.

divert /dɪ'vɜrt/ v. desviar; divertir.

divest /dɪ'vɛst/ v. desnudar, despojar.

divide /dɪ'vaid/ v. dividir.

dividend /'dɪvɪ,dɛnd/ n. dividendo m.

divine /dɪ'vain/ a. divino.

divinity /dɪ'vɪnɪti/ n. divinidad f.

division /dɪ'vɪʒən/ n. división f.

divorce /dɪ'vɔrs/ n. **1.** divorcio m. —v. **2.** divorciar.

divorcee /dɪvɔr'sei/ n. divorciado -da.

divulge /dɪ'vʌldʒ/ v. divulgar, revelar.

dizziness /'dɪzi:nɪs/ n. vértigo, mareo m.

dizzy /'dɪzi/ a. mareado.

DNA abbr. (deoxyribonucleic acid) ADN (ácido deoxirribonucleico) m.

do /du/ v. hacer.

docile /'dɒsəl/ a. dócil.

dock /dɒk/ n. **1.** muelle m. **dry d.,** astillero m. —v. **2.** entrar en muelle.

doctor /'dɒktər/ n. médico m.; doctor -ra.

doctorate /'dɒktərɪt/ n. doctorado m.

doctrine /'dɒktrɪn/ n. doctrina f.

document /'dɒkyəmənt/ n. documento m.

documentary /ˌdɒkyə'mɛntəri/ a. documental.

documentation /ˌdɒkyəmɛn'teiʃən/ n. documentación f.

dodge /dɒdʒ/ n. **1.** evasión f. —v. **2.** evadir.

dodgem /'dɒdʒɪm/ n. coche de choque m.

doe /dou/ n. gama f.

dog /dɔg/ n. perro -a.

dogma /'dɔgmə/ n. dogma m.

dogmatic /dɔg'mætɪk/ a. dogmático.

dogmatism /'dɔgmə,tɪzəm/ n. dogmatismo m.

doily /'dɔili/ n. servilletita f.

doleful /'doulfəl/ a. triste.

doll /dɒl/ n. muñeca -co.

dollar /'dɒlər/ n. dólar m.

dolorous /'doulərəs/ a. lastimoso.

dolphin /'dɒlfɪn/ n. delfín m.

domain /dou'mein/ n. dominio m.

dome /doum/ n. domo m.

domestic /də'mɛstɪk/ a. doméstico.

domesticate /də'mɛstɪ,keit/ v. domesticar.

domicile /'dɒmə,sail/ n. domicilio m.

dominance /'dɒmənəns/ n. dominación f.

dominant /'dɒmənənt/ a. dominante.

dominate /'dɒmə,neit/ v. dominar.

domination /ˌdɒmə'neiʃən/ n. dominación f.

domineer /ˌdɒmə'nɪər/ v. dominar.

domineering /ˌdɒmə'nɪərɪŋ/ a. tiránico, mandón.

dominion /də'mɪnyən/ n. dominio; territorio m.

domino /'dɒmə,nou/ n. dominó m.

donate /'douneit/ v. donar; contribuir.

donation /dou'neiʃən/ n. donación f.

donkey /'dɒŋki/ n. asno, burro m.

doom /dum/ n. **1.** perdición, ruina f. —v. **2.** perder, ruinar.

door /dɔr/ n. puerta f.

doorman /'dɔr,mæn, -mən/ n. portero m.

doormat /'dɔr,mæt/ n. felpudo m.

doorway /'dɔr,wei/ n. entrada f.

dope /doup/ n. Colloq. narcótico m.; idiota m.

dormant /'dɔrmənt/ a. durmiente; inactivo.

dormitory /'dɔrmɪ,tɔri/ n. dormitorio m.

dosage /'dousɪdʒ/ n. dosificación f.

dose /dous/ n. dosis f.

dot /dɒt/ n. punto m.

dotted line /'dɒtɪd/ línea de puntos f.

double /'dʌbəl/ a. **1.** doble. —v. **2.** duplicar.

double bass /beis/ contrabajo m.

double-breasted /'dʌbəl 'brɛstɪd/ a. cruzado.

double-cross /'dʌbəl 'krɔs/ v. traicionar.

doubly /'dʌbli/ adv. doblemente.

doubt /daut/ n. **1.** duda f. —v. **2.** dudar.

doubtful /'dautfəl/ a. dudoso, incierto.

doubtless /'dautlɪs/ a. **1.** indudable. —adv. **2.** sin duda.

dough /dou/ n. pasta, masa f.

doughnut /'dounət, -,nʌt/ n. buñuelo m.

dove /duv/ n. paloma f.

dowager /'dauədʒər/ n. viuda (con título) f.

down /daun/ adv. **1.** abajo. —prep. **2.** **d. the street,** etc. calle abajo, etc.

downcast /'daun,kæst/ a. cabizbajo.

downfall /'daun,fɔl/ n. ruina, perdición f.

downhearted /'daun'hɑrtɪd/ a. descorazonado.

download /'daun,loud/ v. bajar, descargar.

downpour /'daun,pɔr/ n. chaparrón m.

downright /'daun,rait/ a. absoluto, completo.

downriver /'daun'rɪvər/ adv. aguas abajo, río abajo.

downstairs /'daun'stɛərz/ adv. **1.** abajo. —n. **2.** primer piso.

downstream /'daun'strim/ adv. aguas abajo, río abajo.

downtown /'daun'taun/ adv. al centro, en el centro.

downward /'daunwərd/ a. **1.** descendente. —adv. **2.** hacia abajo.

dowry /'dauri/ n. dote f.

doze /douz/ v. dormitar.

dozen /'dʌzən/ n. docena f.

draft /dræft/ n. **1.** dibujo m.; Com. giro m.; Mil. conscripción f. —v. **2.** dibujar; Mil. reclutar.

draftee /dræf'ti/ n. conscripto m.

draft notice notificación de reclutamiento f.

drag /dræg/ v. arrastrar.

dragon /'drægən/ n. dragón m.

drain /drein/ n. **1.** desaguadero m. —v. **2.** desaguar.

drainage /'dreinɪdʒ/ n. drenaje m.

drain board escurridero m.

drama /'drɑmə/ n. drama m.

dramatic /drə'mætɪk/ a. dramático.

dramatics /drə'mætɪks/ n. dramática f.

dramatist /'dræmətɪst, 'drɑmə-/ n. dramaturgo -ga.

dramatize /'dræmə,taiz, 'drɑmə-/ v. dramatizar.

drape /dreip/ n. cortinas f.pl. v. vestir; adornar.

drapery /'dreipəri/ n. colgaduras f.pl.; ropaje m.

drastic /'dræstɪk/ a. drástico.

draw /drɔ/ v. dibujar; atraer. **d. up,** formular.

drawback /'drɔ,bæk/ n. desventaja f.

drawer /drɔr/ n. cajón m.

drawing /'drɔɪŋ/ n. dibujo m.; rifa f.

dread /drɛd/ n. **1.** terror m. —v. **2.** temer.

dreadful /'drɛdfəl/ a. terrible.

dreadfully /'drɛdfəli/ adv. horrendamente.

dream /drim/ n. **1.** sueño, ensueño m. —v. **2.** soñar.

dreamer /'drimər/ n. soñador -ra; visionario -ia.

dreamy /'drimi/ a. soñador, contemplativo.

dreary /'drɪəri/ a. monótono y pesado.

dredge /drɛdʒ/ n. **1.** rastra f. —v. **2.** rastrear.
dregs /drɛgz/ n. sedimento m.
drench /drɛntʃ/ v. mojar.
dress /drɛs/ n. **1.** vestido; traje m. —v. **2.** vestir.
dresser /'drɛsər/ n. (furniture) tocador.
dressing /'drɛsɪŋ/ n. Med. curación f.; (cookery) relleno m., salsa f.
dressing gown bata f.
dressing table tocador m.
dressmaker /'drɛs,meikər/ n. modista m. & f.
drift /drɪft/ n. **1.** tendencia f.; Naut. deriva f. —v. **2.** Naut. derivar; (snow) amontonarse.
drill /drɪl/ n. **1.** ejercicio m.; Mech. taladro m. —v. **2.** Mech. taladrar.
drink /drɪŋk/ n. **1.** bebida f. —v. **2.** beber, tomar.
drinkable /'drɪŋkəbəl/ a. potable, bebible.
drip /drɪp/ v. gotear.
drive /draiv/ n. **1.** paseo m. —v. **2.** impeler; Auto. guiar, conducir.
drive-in (movie theater) /'draiv ,ɪn/ n. autocine, autocinema m.
driver /'draivər/ n. conductor -ra; chofer m. **d.'s license**, permiso de conducir.
driveway /'draiv,wei/ n. entrada para coches.
drizzle /'drɪzəl/ n. **1.** llovizna f. —v. **2.** lloviznar.
dromedary /'drɒmɪ,dɛri/ n. dromedario m.
droop /drup/ v. inclinarse.
drop /drɒp/ n. **1.** gota f. —v. **2.** soltar; dejar caer.
dropout /'drɒp,aut/ n. joven que abandona sus estudios.
dropper /'drɒpər/ n. cuentagotas f.
dropsy /'drɒpsi/ n. hidropesía f.
drought /draut/ n. sequía f.
drove /drouv/ n. manada f.
drown /draun/ v. ahogar.
drowse /drauz/ v. adormecer.
drowsiness /'drauzinɪs/ n. somnolencia f.
drowsy /'drauzi/ a. soñoliento.
drudge /drʌdʒ/ n. ganapán m.
drudgery /'drʌdʒəri/ n. trabajo penoso.
drug /drʌg/ n. **1.** droga f. —v. **2.** narcotizar.
drug addict drogadicto -ta, toxicómano -na m. & f.
druggist /'drʌgɪst/ n. farmacéutico -ca, boticario -ria.
drugstore /'drʌg,stɔr/ n. farmacia, botica, droguería f.
drum /drʌm/ n. tambor m.
drummer /'drʌmər/ n. tambor m.
drumstick /'drʌm,stɪk/ n. palillo m.; Leg. pierna f.
drunk /drʌŋk/ a. & n. borracho, -a.
drunkard /'drʌŋkərd/ n. borrachón m.
drunken /'drʌŋkən/ a. borracho; ebrio.
drunkenness /'drʌŋkənnɪs/ n. embriaguez f.
dry /drai/ a. **1.** seco, árido. —v. **2.** secar.
dry cell n. pila seca f.
dry cleaner tintorero -ra.
dryness /'drainɪs/ n. sequedad f.
dual /'duəl/ a. doble.
dubious /'dubiəs/ a. dudoso.
duchess /'dʌtʃɪs/ n. duquesa f.
duck /dʌk/ n. **1.** pato m. —v. **2.** zambullir; (avoid) esquivar.
duct /dʌkt/ n. canal m.
due /du/ a. **1.** debido; Com. vencido. —n. **2.** dues cuota f.
duel /'duəl/ n. duelo f.
duelist /'duəlɪst/ n. duelista m.
duet /du'ɛt/ n. dúo m.
duke /duk/ n. duque m.
dull /dʌl/ a. apagado, desteñido; sin punta; Fig. pesado, soso.

dullness /'dʌlnɪs/ n. estupidez; pesadez f.; deslustre m.
duly /'duli/ adv. debidamente.
dumb /dʌm/ a. mudo; Colloq. estúpido.
dumbwaiter /'dʌm,weitər/ n. montaplatos m.
dumfound /dʌm'faund/ v. confundir.
dummy /'dʌmi/ n. maniquí m.
dump /dʌmp/ n. **1.** depósito m. —v. **2.** descargar.
dune /dun/ n. duna f.
dungeon /'dʌndʒən/ n. calabozo m.
dunk /dʌŋk/ v. mojar.
dupe /dup/ v. engañar.
duplicate /a, n 'duplikɪt; v -,keit/ a. & n. **1.** duplicado m. —v. **2.** duplicar.
duplication /,dupli'keiʃən/ n. duplicación f.
duplicity /du'plɪsiti/ n. duplicidad f.
durability /,durə'bɪliti/ n. durabilidad f.
durable /'durəbəl/ a. durable, duradero.
duration /du'reiʃən/ n. duración f.
duress /du'rɛs/ n. compulsión f.; encierro m.
during /'durɪŋ/ prep. durante.
dusk /dʌsk/ n. crepúsculo m.
dusky /'dʌski/ a. oscuro; moreno.
dust /dʌst/ n. **1.** polvo m. —v. **2.** polvorear; despolvorear.
dusty /'dʌsti/ a. empolvado.
Dutch /dʌtʃ/ a. holandés -sa.
dutiful /'dutəfəl/ a. respetuoso.
dutifully /'dutəfəli/ adv. respetuosamente, obedientemente.
duty /'duti/ n. deber m.; Com. derechos m.pl.
duty-free /'duti 'fri/ a. libre de derechos.
dwarf /dwɔrf/ n. **1.** enano -na. —v. **2.** achicar.
dwell /dwɛl/ v. habitar, residir. **d. on**, espaciarse en.
dwelling /'dwɛlɪŋ/ n. morada, casa f.
dwindle /'dwɪndl/ v. disminuirse.
dye /dai/ n. **1.** tintura f. —v. **2.** teñir.
dyer /'daiər/ n. tintorero -ra.
dynamic /dai'næmɪk/ a. dinámico.
dynamite /'dainə,mait/ n. dinamita f.
dynamo /'dainə,mou/ n. dínamo m.
dynasty /'dainəsti/ n. dinastía f.
dysentery /'dɪsən,tɛri/ n. disentería f.
dyslexia /dɪs'lɛksiə/ n. dislexia f.
dyslexic /dɪs'lɛksɪk/ a. disléxico.
dyspepsia /dɪs'pɛpʃə/ n. dispepsia f.

E

each /itʃ/ a. **1.** cada. —pron. **2.** cada uno -na. **e. other**, el uno al otro.
eager /'igər/ a. ansioso.
eagerly /'igərli/ adv. ansiosamente.
eagerness /'igərnɪs/ n. ansia f.
eagle /'igəl/ n. águila f.
ear /ɪər/ n. oído m.; (outer) oreja f.; (of corn) mazorca f.
earache /'ɪər,eik/ n. dolor de oído m.
earl /ɜrl/ n. conde m.
early /'ɜrli/ a. & adv. temprano.
earn /ɜrn/ v. ganar.
earnest /'ɜrnɪst/ a. serio.
earnestly /'ɜrnɪstli/ adv. seriamente.
earnings /'ɜrnɪŋz/ n. ganancias f.pl.; Com. ingresos m.pl.
earphone /'ɪər,foun/ n. auricular m.
earring /'ɪər,rɪŋ/ n. pendiente, arete m.
earth /ɜrθ/ n. tierra f.
earthquake /'ɜrθ,kweik/ n. terremoto m.
ease /iz/ n. **1.** reposo m.; facilidad f. —v. **2.** aliviar.
easel /'izəl/ n. caballete m.
easily /'izəli/ adv. fácilmente.
east /ist/ n. oriente, este m.
Easter /'istər/ n. Pascua Florida.
eastern /'istərn/ a. oriental.
eastward /'istwərd/ adv. hacia el este.

easy /'izi/ a. fácil.
eat /it/ v. comer.
eau de Cologne /'ou də kə'loun/ colonia f.
eaves /ivz/ n. socarrén m.
ebb /ɛb/ n. **1.** menguante f. —v. **2.** menguar.
ebony /'ɛbəni/ n. ébano m.
eccentric /ɪk'sɛntrɪk/ a. excéntrico.
eccentricity /,ɛksən'trɪsiti/ n. excentricidad f.
ecclesiastic /ɪ,klizi'æstɪk/ a. & n. eclesiástico.
echelon /'ɛʃə,lɒn/ n. escalón m.
echo /'ɛkou/ n. eco m.
eclipse /ɪ'klɪps/ n. **1.** eclipse m. —v. **2.** eclipsar.
ecological /,ɛkə'lɒdʒɪkəl/ a. ecológico.
ecology /ɪ'kɒlədʒi/ n. ecología f.
economic /,ɛkə'nɒmɪk, ,ikə-/ a. económico.
economical /,ɛkə'nɒmɪkəl, ,ikə-/ a. económico.
economics /,ɛkə'nɒmɪks, ,ikə-/ n. economía política.
economist /ɪ'kɒnəmɪst/ n. economista m. & f.
economize /ɪ'kɒnə,maiz/ v. economizar.
economy /ɪ'kɒnəmi/ n. economía f.
ecstasy /'ɛkstəsi/ n. éxtasis m.
Ecuadorian /,ɛkwə'dɔriən/ a. & n. ecuatoriano -na.
ecumenical /,ɛkyu'mɛnikəl/ a. ecuménico.
eczema /'ɛksəmə/ n. eczema f.
eddy /'ɛdi/ n. **1.** remolino m. —v. **2.** remolinar.
edge /ɛdʒ/ n. **1.** filo; borde m. —v. **2. e. one's way**, abrirse paso.
edible /'ɛdəbəl/ a. comestible.
edict /'idɪkt/ n. edicto m.
edifice /'ɛdəfɪs/ n. edificio m.
edify /'ɛdə,fai/ v. edificar.
edition /ɪ'dɪʃən/ n. edición f.
editor /'ɛdɪtər/ n. redactor -ra.
editorial /,ɛdɪ'tɔriəl/ n. editorial m. **e. board**, consejo de redacción m. **e. staff**, redacción f.
educate /'ɛdʒu,keit/ v. educar.
education /,ɛdʒu'keiʃən/ n. instrucción; enseñanza f.
educational /,ɛdʒu'keiʃənl/ a. educativo.
educator /'ɛdʒu,keitər/ n. educador -ra, pedagogo -ga.
eel /il/ n. anguila f.
efface /ɪ'feis/ v. tachar.
effect /ɪ'fɛkt/ n. **1.** efecto m. **in e.**, en vigor. —v. **2.** efectuar, realizar.
effective /ɪ'fɛktɪv/ a. eficaz; efectivo; en vigor.
effectively /ɪ'fɛktɪvli/ adv. eficazmente.
effectiveness /ɪ'fɛktɪvnɪs/ n. efectividad f.
effectual /ɪ'fɛktʃuəl/ a. eficaz.
effeminate /ɪ'fɛmənɪt/ a. afeminado.
efficacy /'ɛfɪkəsi/ n. eficacia f.
efficiency /ɪ'fɪʃənsi/ n. eficiencia f.
efficient /ɪ'fɪʃənt/ a. eficaz.
efficiently /ɪ'fɪʃəntli/ adv. eficazmente.
effigy /'ɛfɪdʒi/ n. efigie f.
effort /'ɛfərt/ n. esfuerzo m.
effrontery /ɪ'frʌntəri/ n. impudencia f.
effusive /ɪ'fyusɪv/ a. efusivo.
egg /ɛg/ n. huevo m. **fried e.**, huevo frito. **soft-boiled e.**, h. pasado por agua. **scrambled eggs**, huevos revueltos.
eggplant /'ɛg,plænt/ n. berenjena f.
egg white clara de huevo f.
egoism /'igou,ɪzəm/ **egotism** n. egoísmo m.
egoist /'igouɪst/ **egotist** n. egoísta m. & f.
egotism /'igə,tɪzəm/ n. egotismo m.
egotist /'igətɪst/ n. egotista m. & f.
Egypt /'idʒɪpt/ n. Egipto m.

Egyptian /ɪ'dʒɪpʃən/ a. & n. egipcio -ia.
eight /eit/ a. & pron. ocho.
eighteen /'ei'tin/ a. & pron. dieciocho.
eighth /eitθ, eiθ/ a. octavo.
eightieth /'eitiɪθ/ n. octogésimo m.
eighty /'eiti/ a. & pron. ochenta.
either /'iðər/ a. & pron. **1.** cualquiera de los dos. —adv. **2.** tampoco. —conj. **3. either... or,** o... o.
ejaculate /ɪ'dʒækyə,leit/ v. exclamar; eyacular.
ejaculation /ɪ,dʒækyə'leiʃən/ n. eyaculación f.
eject /ɪ'dʒɛkt/ v. expeler; eyectar.
ejection /ɪ'dʒɛkʃən/ n. expulsión f.; eyección f.
elaborate /a ɪ'læbərɪt; v -ə,reit/ a. **1.** elaborado. —v. **2.** elaborar; ampliar.
elapse /ɪ'læps/ v. transcurrir; pasar.
elastic /ɪ'læstɪk/ a. & n. elástico m.
elasticity /ɪlæ'stɪsiti/ n. elasticidad f.
elate /ɪ'leit/ v. exaltar.
elation /ɪ'leiʃən/ n. exaltación f.
elbow /'ɛlbou/ n. codo m.
elder /'ɛldər/ a. **1.** mayor. —n. **2.** anciano -na.
elderly /'ɛldərli/ a. de edad.
eldest /'ɛldɪst/ a. mayor.
elect /ɪ'lɛkt/ v. elegir.
election /ɪ'lɛkʃən/ n. elección f.
elective /ɪ'lɛktɪv/ a. electivo.
electorate /ɪ'lɛktərɪt/ n. electorado m.
electric /ɪ'lɛktrɪk/ **electrical** a. eléctrico.
electrician /ɪlɛk'trɪʃən/ n. electricista m. & f.
electricity /ɪlɛk'trɪsiti/ n. electricidad f.
electrocardiogram /ɪ,lɛktrou'kardiə,græm/ n. electrocardiograma m.
electrocute /ɪ'lɛktrə,kyut/ v. electrocutar.
electrode /ɪ'lɛktroud/ n. electrodo m.
electrolysis /ɪlɛk'trɒləsɪs/ n. electrólisis f.
electron /ɪ'lɛktrɒn/ n. electrón m.
electronic /ɪlɛk'trɒnɪk/ a. electrónico.
electronics /ɪlɪk'trɒnɪks/ n. electrónica f.
elegance /'ɛligəns/ n. elegancia f.
elegant /'ɛligənt/ a. elegante.
elegy /'ɛlɪdʒi/ n. elegía f.
element /'ɛləmənt/ n. elemento m.
elemental /,ɛlə'mɛntl/ a. elemental.
elementary /,ɛlə'mɛntəri/ a. elemental.
elephant /'ɛləfənt/ n. elefante -ta.
elevate /'ɛlə,veit/ v. elevar.
elevation /,ɛlə'veiʃən/ n. elevación f.
elevator /'ɛlə,veitər/ n. ascensor m.
eleven /ɪ'lɛvən/ a. & pron. once.
eleventh /ɪ'lɛvənθ/ a. undécimo.
eleventh hour último minuto m.
elf /ɛlf/ n. duende m.
elicit /ɪ'lɪsɪt/ v. sacar; despertar.
eligibility /,ɛlɪdʒə'bɪliti/ n. elegibilidad f.
eligible /'ɛlɪdʒəbəl/ a. elegible.
eliminate /ɪ'lɪmə,neit/ v. eliminar.
elimination /ɪ,lɪmə'neiʃən/ n. eliminación f.
elixir /ɪ'lɪksər/ n. elixir m.
elk /ɛlk/ n. alce m., anta m.
elm /ɛlm/ n. olmo m.
elocution /,ɛlə'kyuʃən/ n. elocución f.
elongate /ɪ'lɔŋgeit/ v. alargar.
elope /ɪ'loup/ v. fugarse.
eloquence /'ɛləkwəns/ n. elocuencia f.
eloquent /'ɛləkwənt/ a. elocuente.
eloquently /'ɛləkwəntli/ adv. elocuentemente.
else /ɛls/ adv. más. **someone e.,** otra persona. **something e.,** otra cosa. **or e.,** de otro modo.
elsewhere /'ɛls,wɛər/ adv. en otra parte.

elucidate /ɪ'lusɪ,deit/ v. elucidar.
elude /ɪ'lud/ v. eludir.
elusive /ɪ'lusɪv/ a. evasivo.
emaciated /ɪ'meiʃi,eitɪd/ a. demacrado, enflaquecido.
e-mail /'i,meil/ n. correo electrónico m.
emanate /'ɛmə,neit/ v. emanar.
emancipate /ɪ'mænsə,peit/ v. emancipar.
emancipation /ɪ,mænsə'peiʃən/ n. emancipación f.
emancipator /ɪ'mænsə,peitər/ n. libertador -ra.
embalm /ɛm'bɑm/ v. embalsamar.
embankment /ɛm'bæŋkmənt/ n. malecón, dique m.
embargo /ɛm'bɑrgou/ n. embargo m.
embark /ɛm'bɑrk/ v. embarcar.
embarrass /ɛm'bærəs/ v. avergonzar; turbar.
embarrassing /ɛm'bærəsɪŋ/ a. penoso, vergonzoso.
embarrassment /ɛm'bærəsmənt/ n. turbación; vergüenza f.
embassy /'ɛmbəsi/ n. embajada f.
embellish /ɛm'bɛlɪʃ/ v. hermosear, embellecer.
embellishment /ɛm'bɛlɪʃmənt/ n. embellecimiento m.
embezzle /ɛm'bɛzəl/ v. desfalcar, malversar.
emblem /'ɛmbləm/ n. emblema m.
embody /ɛm'bɒdi/ v. incorporar; personificar.
embrace /ɛm'breis/ n. 1. abrazo m. —v. 2. abrazar.
embroider /ɛm'brɔidər/ v. bordar.
embroidery /ɛm'brɔidəri, -dri/ n. bordado m.
embryo /'ɛmbri,ou/ n. embrión m.
embryonic /,ɛmbri'ɒnɪk/ a. embrionario.
emerald /'ɛmərəld/ n. esmeralda f.
emerge /ɪ'mɜrdʒ/ v. salir.
emergency /ɪ'mɜrdʒənsi/ n. emergencia f.
emergency brake freno de auxilio m.
emergency exit salida de urgencia f.
emergency landing aterrizaje forzoso m.
emergent /ɪ'mɜrdʒənt/ a. emergente.
emery /'ɛməri/ n. esmeril m.
emetic /ɪ'mɛtɪk/ n. emético m.
emigrant /'ɛmɪgrənt/ a. & n. emigrante m. & f.
emigrate /'ɛmɪ,greit/ v. emigrar.
emigration /,ɛmə'greiʃən/ n. emigración f.
eminence /'ɛmənəns/ n. altura; eminencia f.
eminent /'ɛmənənt/ a. eminente.
emissary /'ɛmə,sɛri/ n. emisario m.
emission /ɪ'mɪʃən/ n. emisión f.
emit /ɪ'mɪt/ v. emitir.
emolument /ɪ'mɒlyəmənt/ n. emolumento m.
emotion /ɪ'mouʃən/ n. emoción f.
emotional /ɪ'mouʃənl/ a. emocional; sentimental.
emperor /'ɛmpərər/ n. emperador m.
emphasis /'ɛmfəsɪs/ n. énfasis m. or f.
emphasize /'ɛmfə,saiz/ v. acentuar, recalcar.
emphatic /ɛm'fætɪk/ a. enfático.
empire /'ɛmpaiᵊr/ n. imperio m.
empirical /ɛm'pɪrɪkəl/ a. empírico.
employ /ɛm'plɔi/ v. emplear.
employee /ɛm'plɔii/ n. empleado -da.
employer /ɛm'plɔiər/ n. patrón -ona.
employment /ɛm'plɔimənt/ n. empleo m.
employment agency agencia de colocaciones f.
empower /ɛm'pauər/ v. autorizar.
emptiness /'ɛmptɪnɪs/ n. vaciedad; futilidad f.
empty /'ɛmpti/ a. 1. vacío. —v. 2. vaciar.
emulate /'ɛmyə,leit/ v. emular.
emulsion /ɪ'mʌlʃən/ n. emulsión f.

enable /ɛn'eibəl/ v. capacitar; permitir.
enact /ɛn'ækt/ v. promulgar, decretar.
enactment /ɛn'æktmənt/ n. ley f., estatuto m.
enamel /ɪ'næməl/ n. 1. esmalte m. —v. 2. esmaltar.
enamored /ɪ'næmərd/ a. enamorado.
enchant /ɛn'tʃænt/ v. encantar.
enchantment /ɛn'tʃæntmənt/ n. encanto m.
encircle /ɛn'sɜrkəl/ v. circundar.
enclose /ɛn'klouz/ v. encerrar. **enclosed,** (in letter) adjunto.
enclosure /ɛn'klouʒər/ n. recinto m.; (in letter) incluso m.
encompass /ɛn'kʌmpəs/ v. circundar.
encounter /ɛn'kauntər/ n. 1. encuentro m. —v. 2. encontrar.
encourage /ɛn'kɜrɪdʒ/ v. animar.
encouragement /ɛn'kɜrɪdʒmənt/ n. estímulo m.
encroach /ɛn'kroutʃ/ v. usurpar; meterse.
encryption /ɛn'krɪpʃən/ n. encriptación f., cifrado m.
encyclical /ɛn'sɪklɪkəl/ n. encíclica f.
encyclopedia /ɛn,saiklə'pidiə/ n. enciclopedia f.
end /ɛnd/ n. 1. fin, término, cabo; extremo; (aim) propósito m. —v. 2. acabar; terminar.
endanger /ɛn'deindʒər/ v. poner en peligro.
endear /ɛn'dɪər/ v. hacer querer.
endeavor /ɛn'dɛvər/ n. 1. esfuerzo m. —v. 2. esforzarse.
ending /'ɛndɪŋ/ n. conclusión f.
endless /'ɛndlɪs/ a. sin fin.
endocrine gland /'ɛndəkrɪn/ glándula endocrina f.
endorse /ɛn'dɔrs/ v. endosar; apoyar.
endorsement /ɛn'dɔrsmənt/ n. endoso m.
endow /ɛn'dau/ v. dotar, fundar.
endowment /ɛn'daumənt/ n. dotación f., fundación f.
endurance /ɛn'dʊrəns/ n. resistencia f.
endure /ɛn'dʊr/ v. soportar, resistir, aguantar.
enema /'ɛnəmə/ n. enema; lavativa f.
enemy /'ɛnəmi/ n. enemigo -ga.
energetic /,ɛnər'dʒɛtɪk/ a. enérgico.
energy /'ɛnərdʒi/ n. energía f.
enervate /'ɛnər,veit/ v. enervar.
enervation /,ɛnər'veiʃən/ n. enervación f.
enfold /ɛn'fould/ v. envolver.
enforce /ɛn'fɔrs/ v. ejecutar.
enforcement /ɛn'fɔrsmənt/ n. ejecución f.
engage /ɛn'geidʒ/ v. emplear; ocupar.
engaged /ɛn'geidʒd/ a. (to marry) prometido.
engagement /ɛn'geidʒmənt/ n. combate; compromiso; contrato m.; cita f.
engine /'ɛndʒən/ n. máquina f. (railroad) locomotora f.
engineer /,ɛndʒə'nɪər/ n. ingeniero -ra; maquinista m.
engineering /,ɛndʒə'nɪərɪŋ/ n. ingeniería f.
England /'ɪŋglənd/ n. Inglaterra f.
English /'ɪŋglɪʃ/ a. & n. inglés -esa.
English Channel Canal de la Mancha m.
Englishman /'ɪŋglɪʃmən/ n. inglés m.
Englishwoman /'ɪŋglɪʃ,wumən/ n. inglesa f.
engrave /ɛn'greiv/ v. grabar.
engraver /ɛn'greivər/ n. grabador m.
engraving /ɛn'greivɪŋ/ n. grabado m.
engross /ɛn'grous/ v. absorber.
enhance /ɛn'hæns/ v. aumentar en valor; realzar.
enigma /ə'nɪgmə/ n. enigma m.
enigmatic /,ɛnɪg'mætɪk/ a. enigmático.
enjoy /ɛn'dʒɔi/ v. gozar de; disfrutar de. **e. oneself,** divertirse.
enjoyable /ɛn'dʒɔiəbəl/ a. agradable.
enjoyment /ɛn'dʒɔimənt/ n. goce m.

enlarge /ɛn'lɑrdʒ/ v. agrandar; ampliar.
enlargement /ɛn'lɑrdʒmənt/ n. ensanchamiento m., ampliación f.
enlarger /ɛn'lɑrdʒər/ n. amplificador m.
enlighten /ɛn'laitn/ v. informar.
enlightenment /ɛn'laitnmənt/ n. esclarecimiento m.; cultura f.
enlist /ɛn'lɪst/ v. reclutar; alistarse.
enlistment /ɛn'lɪstmənt/ n. alistamiento m.
enliven /ɛn'laivən/ v. avivar.
enmesh /ɛn'mɛʃ/ v. entrampar.
enmity /'ɛnmɪti/ n. enemistad f.
enormity /ɪ'nɔrmɪti/ v. enormidad f.
enormous /ɪ'nɔrməs/ a. enorme.
enough /ɪ'nʌf/ a. & adv. bastante. **to be e.,** bastar.
enrage /ɛn'reidʒ/ v. enfurecer.
enrich /ɛn'rɪtʃ/ v. enriquecer.
enroll /ɛn'roul/ v. registrar; matricularse.
enrollment /ɛn'roulmənt/ n. matriculación f.
ensign /'ɛnsən/ n. bandera f.; (naval) subteniente m.
enslave /ɛn'sleiv/ v. esclavizar.
ensue /ɛn'su/ v. seguir, resultar.
entail /ɛn'teil/ v. acarrear, ocasionar.
entangle /ɛn'tæŋgəl/ v. enredar.
enter /'ɛntər/ v. entrar.
enterprise /'ɛntər,praiz/ n. empresa f.
enterprising /'ɛntər,praizɪŋ/ a. emprendedor.
entertain /,ɛntər'tein/ v. entretener; divertir.
entertainment /,ɛntər'teinmənt/ n. entretenimiento m.; diversión f.
enthrall /ɛn'θrɔl/ v. esclavizar; cautivar.
enthusiasm /ɛn'θuzi,æzəm/ n. entusiasmo m.
enthusiast /ɛn'θuzi,æst, -ɪst/ n. entusiasta m. & f.
enthusiastic /ɛn,θuzi'æstɪk/ a. entusiasmado.
entice /ɛn'tais/ v. inducir.
entire /ɛn'taiᵊr/ a. entero.
entirely /ɛn'taiᵊrli/ adv. enteramente.
entirety /ɛn'taiᵊrti/ n. totalidad f.
entitle /ɛn'taitl/ v. autorizar; (book) titular.
entity /'ɛntɪti/ n. entidad f.
entrails /'ɛntreilz/ n. entrañas f.pl.
entrance /'ɛntrəns/ n. entrada f.
entrance examination examen de ingreso m.
entrant /'ɛntrənt/ n. competidor -ra.
entreat /ɛn'trit/ v. rogar, suplicar.
entreaty /ɛn'triti/ n. ruego m., súplica f.
entrench /ɛn'trɛntʃ/ v. atrincherar.
entrust /ɛn'trʌst/ v. confiar.
entry /'ɛntri/ n. entrada f.; Com. partida f.
entry blank hoja de inscripción f.
enumerate /ɪ'numə,reit/ v. enumerar.
enumeration /ɪ,numə'reiʃən/ n. enumeración f.
enunciate /ɪ'nʌnsi,eit/ v. enunciar.
enunciation /ɪ,nʌnsi'eiʃən/ n. enunciación f.
envelop /ɛn'vɛləp/ v. envolver.
envelope /'ɛnvə,loup/ n. sobre m.; cubierta f.
enviable /'ɛnviəbəl/ a. envidiable.
envious /'ɛnviəs/ a. envidioso.
environment /ɛn'vairənmənt/ n. ambiente m.
environmentalist /ɛn,vairən'mɛntlɪst/ n. ambientalista, ecologista m. & f.
environmental protection /ɛn,vairən'mɛntəl/ protección del ambiente.
environs /ɛn'vairənz/ n. alrededores m.
envoy /'ɛnvɔi/ n. enviado m.
envy /'ɛnvi/ n. 1. envidia f. —v. 2. envidiar.
eon /'iən/ n. eón m.

ephemeral /ɪ'fɛmərəl/ a. efímero.
epic /'ɛpɪk/ a. 1. épico. —n. 2. epopeya f.
epicure /'ɛpɪ,kyur/ n. epicúreo m.
epidemic /,ɛpɪ'dɛmɪk/ a. 1. epidémico. —n. 2. epidemia f.
epidermis /,ɛpɪ'dɜrmɪs/ n. epidermis f.
epigram /'ɛpɪ,græm/ n. epigrama m.
epilepsy /'ɛpə,lɛpsi/ n. epilepsia f.
epilogue /'ɛpə,lɔg/ n. epílogo m.
episode /'ɛpə,soud/ n. episodio m.
epistle /ɪ'pɪsəl/ n. epístola f.
epitaph /'ɛpɪ,tæf/ n. epitafio m.
epithet /'ɛpə,θɛt/ n. epíteto m.
epitome /ɪ'pɪtəmi/ n. epítome m.
epoch /'ɛpək/ n. época, era f.
Epsom salts /'ɛpsəm/ n.pl. sal de la Higuera f.
equal /'ikwəl/ a. & n. 1. igual m. —v. 2. igualar; equivaler.
equality /ɪ'kwɒlɪti/ n. igualdad f.
equalize /'ikwə,laiz/ v. igualar.
equanimity /,ikwə'nɪmɪti/ n. ecuanimidad f.
equate /ɪ'kweit/ v. igualar.
equation /ɪ'kweiʒən/ n. ecuación f.
equator /ɪ'kweitər/ n. ecuador m.
equatorial /,ikwə'tɔriəl/ a. ecuatorial
equestrian /ɪ'kwɛstriən/ n. 1. jinete m. —a. 2. ecuestre.
equilibrium /,ikwə'lɪbriəm/ n. equilibrio m.
equinox /'ikwə,nɒks/ n. equinoccio m.
equip /ɪ'kwɪp/ v. equipar.
equipment /ɪ'kwɪpmənt/ n. equipo m.
equitable /'ɛkwɪtəbəl/ a. equitativo.
equity /'ɛkwɪti/ n. equidad, justicia f.
equivalent /ɪ'kwɪvələnt/ a. & n. equivalente m.
equivocal /ɪ'kwɪvəkəl/ a. equívoco, ambiguo.
era /'ɪərə, 'ɛrə/ n. era, época, edad f.
eradicate /ɪ'rædɪ,keit/ v. extirpar.
erase /ɪ'reis/ v. borrar.
eraser /ɪ'reisər/ n. borrador m.
erasure /ɪ'reiʃər/ n. borradura f.
erect /ɪ'rɛkt/ a. 1. derecho, erguido. —v. 2. erigir.
erection /ɪ'rɛkʃən/ **erectness** n. erección f.
ermine /'ɜrmɪn/ n. armiño m.
erode /ɪ'roud/ v. corroer.
erosion /ɪ'rouʒən/ n. erosión f.
erotic /ɪ'rɒtɪk/ a. erótico.
err /ɜr, ɛr/ v. equivocarse.
errand /'ɛrənd/ n. encargo, recado m.
errant /'ɛrənt/ a. errante.
erratic /ɪ'rætɪk/ a. errático.
erroneous /ə'rouniəs/ a. erróneo.
error /'ɛrər/ n. error m.
erudite /'ɛryu,dait/ a. erudito.
erudition /,ɛryu'dɪʃən/ n. erudición f.
eruption /ɪ'rʌpʃən/ n. erupción, irrupción f.
erysipelas /,ɛrə'sɪpələs/ n. erisipela f.
escalate /'ɛskə,leit/ v. escalar; intensificarse.
escalator /'ɛskə,leitər/ n. escalera mecánica f.
escapade /'ɛskə,peid/ n. escapada; correría f.
escape /ɪ'skeip/ n. 1. fuga, huída f. **fire e.,** escalera de salvamento. —v. 2. escapar; fugarse.
eschew /ɛs'tʃu/ v. evadir.
escort /n 'ɛskɔrt; v ɪ'skɔrt/ n. 1. escolta f. —v. 2. escoltar.
escrow /'ɛskrou/ n. plica f.
escutcheon /ɪ'skʌtʃən/ n. escudo de armas m.
esophagus /ɪ'sɒfəgəs/ n. esófago m.
esoteric /,ɛsə'tɛrɪk/ a. esotérico.
especially /ɪ'spɛʃəli/ adv. especialmente.
espionage /'ɛspiə,nɑʒ/ n. espionaje m.
espresso /ɛ'sprɛsou/ n. café exprés, m.
essay /'ɛsei/ n. ensayo m.

essayist /'εseɪɪst/ n. ensayista m. & f.

essence /'εsəns/ n. esencia f.; perfume m.

essential /ə'sεntʃəl/ a. esencial.

essentially /ə'sεntʃəli/ adv. esencialmente.

establish /ɪ'stæblɪʃ/ v. establecer.

establishment /ɪ'stæblɪʃmənt/ n. establecimiento m.

estate /ɪ'steɪt/ n. estado m.; hacienda f.; bienes m.pl.

esteem /ɪ'stim/ n. 1. estima f. —v. 2. estimar.

estimable /'εstəməbəl/ a. estimable.

estimate /n 'εstə,mɪt; v -,meɪt/ n. 1. cálculo; presupuesto m. —v. 2. estimar.

estimation /,εstə'meɪʃən/ n. estimación f.; cálculo m.

estrange /ɪ'streɪndʒ/ v. extrañar; enajenar.

estuary /'εstʃu,εri/ n. estuario m.

etch /εtʃ/ v. grabar al agua fuerte.

etching /'εtʃɪŋ/ n. aguafuerte.

eternal /ɪ'tɜrnl/ a. eterno.

eternity /ɪ'tɜrnɪti/ n. eternidad f.

ether /'iθər/ n. éter m.

ethereal /ɪ'θɪəriəl/ a. etéreo.

ethical /'εθɪkəl/ a. ético.

ethics /'εθɪks/ n. ética f.

ethnic /'εθnɪk/ a. étnico.

etiquette /'εtɪkɪt/ n. etiqueta f.

etymology /,εtə'mɒlədʒi/ n. etimología f.

eucalyptus /,yukə'lɪptəs/ n. eucalipto m.

eugenic /yu'dʒεnɪk/ a. eugenésico.

eugenics /yu'dʒεnɪks/ n. eugenesia f.

eulogize /'yulə,dʒaiz/ v. elogiar.

eulogy /'yulədʒi/ n. elogio m.

eunuch /'yunək/ n. eunuco m.

euphonious /yu'founiəs/ a. eufónico.

Europe /'yʊrəp/ n. Europa f.

European /,yʊrə'piən/ a. & n. europeo -pea.

euthanasia /,yuθə'neɪʒə, -ʒiə, -ziə/ n. eutanasia f.

evacuate /ɪ'vækyu,eɪt/ v. evacuar.

evade /ɪ'veɪd/ v. evadir.

evaluate /ɪ'vælyu,eɪt/ v. evaluar.

evaluation /ɪ,vælyu'eɪʃən/ n. valoración f.

evangelist /ɪ'vændʒəlɪst/ n. evangelista m. & f.

evaporate /ɪ'væpə,reɪt/ v. evaporarse.

evaporation /ɪ,væpə'reɪʃən/ n. evaporación f.

evasion /ɪ'veɪʒən/ n. evasión f.

evasive /ɪ'veɪsɪv/ a. evasivo.

eve /iv/ n. víspera f.

even /'ivən/ a. 1. llano; igual. —adv. 2. aun; hasta. **not e.**, ni siquiera.

evening /'ivnɪŋ/ n. noche, tarde f. **good e.!** ¡buenas tardes! ¡buenas noches!

evening class clase nocturna f.

evenness /'ivənɪs/ n. uniformidad f.

even number número par m.

event /ɪ'vεnt/ n. acontecimiento, suceso m.

eventful /ɪ'vεntfəl/ a. memorable.

eventual /ɪ'vεntʃuəl/ a. eventual.

ever /'εvər/ adv. alguna vez; (after not) nunca. **e. since**, desde que.

everlasting /,εvər'læstɪŋ/ a. eterno.

every /'εvri/ a. cada, todos los.

everybody /'εvri,bɒdi, -,bʌdi/ pron. todo el mundo; cada uno.

everyday /'εvri,deɪ/ a. ordinario, de cada día.

everyone /'εvri,wʌn/ pron. todo el mundo; cada uno; cada cual.

everything /'εvri,θɪŋ/ pron. todo m.

everywhere /'εvri,wεər/ adv. por todas partes, en todas partes.

evict /ɪ'vɪkt/ v. expulsar.

eviction /ɪ'vɪkʃən/ n. evicción f.

evidence /'εvɪdəns/ n. evidencia f.

evident /'εvɪdənt/ a. evidente.

evidently /'εvɪdəntli/ adv. evidentemente.

evil /'ivəl/ a. 1. malo; maligno. —n. 2. mal m.

evince /ɪ'vɪns/ v. revelar.

evoke /ɪ'vouk/ v. evocar.

evolution /,εvə'luʃən/ n. evolución f.

evolve /ɪ'vɒlv/ v. desenvolver; desarrollar.

ewe /yu/ v. oveja f.

exact /ɪg'zækt/ a. 1. exacto. —v. 2. exigir.

exacting /ɪg'zæktɪŋ/ a. exigente.

exactly /ɪg'zæktli/ adv. exactamente.

exaggerate /ɪg'zædʒə,reɪt/ v. exagerar.

exaggeration /ɪg,zædʒə'reɪʃən/ n. exageración f.

exalt /ɪg'zɔlt/ v. exaltar.

exaltation /,εgzɔl'teɪʃən/ n. exaltación f.

examination /ɪg,zæmə'neɪʃən/ n. examen m.; (legal) interrogatorio m.

examine /ɪg'zæmɪn/ v. examinar.

example /ɪg'zæmpəl/ n. ejemplo m.

exasperate /ɪg'zæspə,reɪt/ v. exasperar.

exasperation /ɪg,zæspə'reɪʃən/ n. exasperación f.

excavate /'εkskə,veɪt/ v. excavar, cavar.

exceed /ɪk'sid/ v. exceder.

exceedingly /ɪk'sidɪŋli/ adv. sumamente, extremadamente.

excel /ɪk'sεl/ v. sobresalir.

excellence /'εksələns/ n. excelencia f.

Excellency /'εksələnsi/ n. (title) Excelencia f.

excellent /'εksələnt/ a. excelente.

except /ɪk'sεpt/ prep. 1. salvo, excepto. —v. 2. exceptuar.

exception /ɪk'sεpʃən/ n. excepción f.

exceptional /ɪk'sεpʃənl/ a. excepcional.

excerpt /'εksərpt/ n. extracto m.

excess /ɪk'sεs, 'εksεs/ n. exceso m.

excessive /ɪk'sεsɪv/ a. excesivo.

exchange /ɪks'tʃeɪndʒ/ n. 1. cambio; canje m. **stock e.**, bolsa f. **telephone e.**, central telefónica. —v. 2. cambiar, canjear, intercambiar.

exchangeable /ɪks'tʃeɪndʒəbəl/ a. cambiable.

exchange rate tipo de cambio m.

excise /n 'εksaiz; v ɪk'saiz/ n. 1. sisa f. —v. 2. extirpar.

excite /ɪk'saɪt/ v. agitar; provocar; emocionar.

excitement /ɪk'saɪtmənt/ n. agitación, conmoción f.

exciting /ɪk'saɪtɪŋ/ a. emocionante.

exclaim /ɪk'skleɪm/ v. exclamar.

exclamation /,εksklə'meɪʃən/ n. exclamación f.

exclamation mark punto de admiración m.

exclude /ɪk'sklud/ v. excluir.

exclusion /ɪk'skluʒən/ n. exclusión f.

exclusive /ɪk'sklusɪv/ a. exclusivo.

excommunicate /,εkskə'myunɪ,keɪt/ v. excomulgar, descomulgar.

excommunication /,εkskə,myunɪ'keɪʃən/ n. excomunión f.

excrement /'εkskrəmənt/ n. excremento m.

excruciating /ɪk'skruʃi,eɪtɪŋ/ a. penosísimo.

exculpate /'εkskʌl,peɪt/ v. exculpar.

excursion /ɪk'skɜrʒən/ n. excursión, jira f.

excuse /n ɪk'skyus; v ɪk'skyuz/ n. 1. excusa f. —v. 2. excusar, perdonar, disculpar; dispensar.

execrable /'εksɪkrəbəl/ a. execrable.

execute /'εksɪ,kyut/ v. ejecutar.

execution /,εksɪ'kyuʃən/ n. ejecución f.

executioner /,εksɪ'kyuʃənər/ n. verdugo m.

executive /ɪg'zεkyətɪv/ a. & n. ejecutivo -va.

executor /ɪg'zεkyətər/ n. testamentario m.

exemplary /ɪg'zεmpləri/ a. ejemplar.

exemplify /ɪg'zεmplə,faɪ/ v. ejemplificar.

exempt /ɪg'zεmpt/ a. 1. exento. —v. 2. exentar.

exercise /'εksər,saiz/ n. 1. ejercicio m. —v. 2. ejercitar.

exert /ɪg'zɜrt/ v. esforzar.

exertion /ɪg'zɜrʃən/ n. esfuerzo m.

exhale /εks'heɪl/ v. exhalar.

exhaust /ɪg'zɔst/ n. 1. Auto. escape m. —v. 2. agotar.

exhaustion /ɪg'zɔstʃən/ n. agotamiento m.

exhaustive /ɪg'zɔstɪv/ a. exhaustivo.

exhaust pipe tubo de escape m.

exhibit /ɪg'zɪbɪt/ n. 1. exhibición, exposición f. —v. 2. exhibir.

exhibition /,εksə'bɪʃən/ n. exhibición f.

exhilarate /ɪg'zɪlə,reɪt/ v. alegrar; estimular.

exhort /ɪg'zɔrt/ v. exhortar.

exhortation /,εgzɔr'teɪʃən/ n. exhortación f.

exhume /ɪg'zum/ v. exhumar.

exigency /'εksɪdʒənsi/ n. exigencia f., urgencia f.

exile /'εgzaɪl/ n. 1. destierro m., (person) desterrado m. —v. 2. desterrar.

exist /ɪg'zɪst/ v. existir.

existence /ɪg'zɪstəns/ n. existencia f.

existent /ɪg'zɪstənt/ a. existente.

exit /'εgzɪt, 'εksɪt/ n. salida f.

exodus /'εksədəs/ n. éxodo m.

exonerate /ɪg'zɒnə,reɪt/ v. exonerar.

exorbitant /ɪg'zɔrbɪtənt/ a. exorbitante.

exorcise /'εksɔr,saiz/ v. exorcizar.

exotic /ɪg'zɒtɪk/ a. exótico.

expand /ɪk'spænd/ v. dilatar; ensanchar.

expanse /ɪk'spæns/ n. espacio m.; extensión f.

expansion /ɪk'spænʃən/ n. expansión f.

expansion slot ranura de expansión f.

expansive /ɪk'spænsɪv/ a. expansivo.

expatiate /ɪk'speɪʃi,eɪt/ v. espaciarse.

expatriate /n, a εks'peɪtriɪt; v εks'peɪtri,eɪt/ n. & a. 1. expatriado m. —v. 2. expatriar.

expect /ɪk'spεkt/ v. esperar; contar con.

expectancy /ɪk'spεktənsi/ n. esperanza f.

expectation /,εkspεk'teɪʃən/ n. esperanza f.

expectorate /ɪk'spεktə,reɪt/ v. expectorar.

expediency /ɪk'spidiənsi/ n. conveniencia f.

expedient /ɪk'spidiənt/ a. 1. oportuno. —n. 2. expediente m.

expedite /'εkspɪ,daɪt/ v. acelerar, despachar.

expedition /,εkspɪ'dɪʃən/ n. expedición f.

expel /ɪk'spεl/ v. expeler; expulsar.

expend /ɪk'spεnd/ v. desembolsar, expender.

expenditure /ɪk'spεndɪtʃər/ n. desembolso; gasto m.

expense /ɪk'spεns/ n. gasto m.; costa f.

expensive /ɪk'spεnsɪv/ a. caro, costoso.

expensively /ɪk'spεnsɪvli/ adv. costosamente.

experience /ɪk'spɪəriəns/ n. 1. experiencia f. —v. 2. experimentar.

experienced /ɪk'spɪəriənst/ a. experimentado, perito.

experiment /n ɪk'spεrəmənt; v -,mεnt/ n. 1. experimento m. —v. 2. experimentar.

experimental /ɪk,spεrə'mεntl/ a. experimental.

expert /'εkspɜrt/ a. & n. experto -ta.

expertise /,εkspər'tiz/ n. pericia f.

expiate /'εkspi,eɪt/ v. expiar.

expiration /,εkspə'reɪʃən/ n. expiración f.

expiration date fecha de caducidad f.

expire /ɪk'spaiər/ v. expirar; Com. vencerse.

explain /ɪk'spleɪn/ v. explicar.

explanation /,εksplə'neɪʃən/ n. explicación f.

explanatory /ɪk'splænə,tɔri/ a. explicativo.

expletive /'εksplɪtɪv/ n. 1. interjección f. —a. 2. expletivo.

explicit /ɪk'splɪsɪt/ a. explícito, claro.

explode /ɪk'sploud/ v. estallar, volar; refutar.

exploit /ɪk'splɔɪt/ n. 1. hazaña f. —v. 2. explotar.

exploitation /,εksplɔɪ'teɪʃən/ n. explotación f.

exploration /,εksplə'reɪʃən/ n. exploración f.

exploratory /ɪk'splɔrə,tɔri/ a. exploratorio.

explore /ɪk'splɔr/ v. explorar.

explorer /ɪk'splɔrər/ n. explorador -ra.

explosion /ɪk'splouʒən/ n. explosión f.

explosive /ɪk'splousɪv/ a. explosivo.

export /n 'εkspɔrt; v ɪk'spɔrt/ n. 1. exportación f. —v. 2. exportar.

exportation /,εkspɔr'teɪʃən/ n. exportación f.

expose /ɪk'spouz/ v. exponer; descubrir.

exposition /,εkspə'zɪʃən/ n. exposición f.

expository /ɪk'spɒzɪ,tɔri/ a. expositivo.

expostulate /ɪk'spɒstʃə,leɪt/ v. altercar.

exposure /ɪk'spouʒər/ n. exposición f.

expound /ɪk'spaund/ v. exponer, explicar.

express /ɪk'sprεs/ a. & n. 1. expreso m. **e. company**, compañía de porteo. —v. 2. expresar.

expression /ɪk'sprεʃən/ n. expresión f.

expressive /ɪk'sprεsɪv/ a. expresivo.

expressly /ɪk'sprεsli/ adv. expresamente.

expressman /ɪk'sprεsmən, -,mæn/ n. empresario de expresos m.

expressway /ɪk'sprεs,weɪ/ n. autopista f.

expropriate /εks'proupri,eɪt/ v. expropriar.

expulsion /ɪk'spʌlʃən/ n. expulsión f.

expunge /ɪk'spʌndʒ/ v. borrar, expurgar.

expurgate /'εkspər,geɪt/ v. expurgar.

exquisite /ɪk'skwɪzɪt/ a. exquisito.

extant /'εkstənt/ a. existente.

extemporaneous /ɪk,stεmpə'reiniəs/ a. improvisado.

extend /ɪk'stεnd/ v. extender.

extension /ɪk'stεnʃən/ n. extensión f.

extensive /ɪk'stεnsɪv/ a. extenso.

extensively /ɪk'stεnsɪvli/ adv. extensamente.

extent /ɪk'stεnt/ n. extensión f.; grado m. **to a certain e.**, hasta cierto punto.

extenuate /ɪk'stεnyu,eɪt/ v. extenuar.

exterior /ɪk'stɪəriər/ a. & n. exterior m.

exterminate /ɪk'stɜrmə,neɪt/ v. exterminar.

extermination /ɪk,stɜrmə'neɪʃən/ n. exterminio m.

external /ɪk'stɜrnl/ a. externo, exterior.

extinct /ɪk'stɪŋkt/ a. extinto.

extinction /ɪk'stɪŋkʃən/ n. extinción f.

extinguish /ɪk'stɪŋgwɪʃ/ v. extinguir, apagar.

extol /ɪk'stoul/ v. alabar.

extort /ɪk'stɔrt/ v. exigir dinero sin derecho.

extortion /ɪk'stɔrʃən/ n. extorsión f.

extra /'εkstrə/ a. 1. extraordinario;

adicional. —n. **2.** (newspaper) extra m.

extract /n 'ɛkstrækt; v ɪk'strækt/ n. **1.** extracto m. —v. **2.** extraer.

extraction /ɪk'strækʃən/ n. extracción f.

extraneous /ɪk'streiniəs/ a. extraño; ajeno.

extraordinary /ɪk'strɔrdn̩,ɛri/ a. extraordinario.

extravagance /ɪk'strævəgəns/ n. extravagancia f.

extravagant /ɪk'strævəgənt/ a. extravagante.

extreme /ɪk'strim/ a. & n. extremo m.

extremity /ɪk'strɛmɪti/ n. extremidad f.

extricate /'ɛkstrɪ,keit/ v. desenredar.

exuberant /ɪg'zubərənt/ a. exuberante.

exude /ɪg'zud/ v. exudar.

exult /ɪg'zʌlt/ v. regocijarse.

exultant /ɪg'zʌltn̩t/ a. triunfante.

eye /ai/ n. **1.** ojo m. —v. **2.** ojear.

eyeball /'ai,bɔl/ n. globo del ojo.

eyebrow /'ai,brau/ n. ceja f.

eyeglasses /'ai,glæsɪz/ n. lentes m.pl.

eyelash /'ai,læʃ/ n. pestaña f.

eyelid /'ai,lɪd/ n. párpado m.

eyeliner /'ai,lainər/ n. lápiz de ojos m.

eye shadow n. sombra de ojos f.

eyesight /'ai,sait/ n. vista f.

F

fable /'feibəl/ n. fábula; ficción f.

fabric /'fæbrɪk/ n. tejido m., tela f.

fabricate /'fæbrɪ,keit/ v. fabricar.

fabulous /'fæbyələs/ a. fabuloso.

façade /fə'sɑd/ n. fachada f.

face /feis/ n. **1.** cara f. **make faces,** hacer muecas. —v. **2.** encararse con. **f. the street,** dar a la calle.

facet /'fæsɪt/ n. faceta f.

facetious /fə'siʃəs/ a. chistoso.

facial /'feiʃəl/ n. **1.** masaje facial m. —a. **2.** facial.

facile /'fæsɪl/ a. fácil.

facilitate /fə'sɪlɪ,teit/ v. facilitar.

facility /fə'sɪlɪti/ n. facilidad f.

facsimile /fæk'sɪməli/ n. facsímile m.

fact /fækt/ n. hecho m. **in f.,** en realidad.

faction /'fækʃən/ n. facción f.

factor /'fæktər/ n. factor m.

factory /'fæktəri/ n. fábrica f.

factual /'fæktʃuəl/ a. verdadero.

faculty /'fækəlti/ n. facultad f.

fad /fæd/ n. boga; novedad f.

fade /feid/ v. desteñirse; (flowers) marchitarse.

fail /feil/ v. **1. without f.,** sin falla. —v. **2.** fallar; fracasar. **not to f. to,** no dejar de.

failure /'feilyər/ n. fracaso m.

faint /feint/ a. **1.** débil; vago; pálido. —n. **2.** desmayo m. —v. **3.** desmayarse.

faintly /'feintli/ adv. débilmente; indistintamente.

fair /fɛər/ a. **1.** razonable, justo; (hair) rubio; (weather) bueno. —n. **2.** feria f.

fairly /'fɛərli/ adv. imparcialmente; regularmente; claramente; bellamente.

fairness /'fɛərnɪs/ n. justicia f.

fair play juego limpio m.

fairway /'fɛər,wei/ n. (golf) calle f.

fairy /'fɛəri/ n. hada f., duende m.

faith /feiθ/ n. fe; confianza f.

faithful /'feiθfəl/ a. fiel.

fake /feik/ a. **1.** falso; postizo. —n. **2.** imitación; estafa f. —v. **3.** imitar; fingir.

faker /'feikər/ n. imitador m.; farsante m.

falcon /'fɔlkən/ n. halcón m.

fall /fɔl/ n. **1.** caída; catarata f.; (season) otoño m.; (in price) baja f. —v.

2. caer; bajar. **f. asleep,** dormirse; **f. in love,** enamorarse.

fallacious /fə'leiʃəs/ a. falaz.

fallacy /'fæləsi/ n. falacia f.

fallible /'fæləbəl/ a. falible.

fallout /'fɔl,aut/ n. lluvia radiactiva, polvillo radiactivo.

fallow /'fælou/ a. sin cultivar; barbecho.

false /fɔls/ a. falso; postizo.

falsehood /'fɔlshud/ n. falsedad; mentira f.

falseness /'fɔlsnɪs/ n. falsedad, perfidia f.

false teeth /tiθ/ dentadura postiza f.

falsetto /fɔl'sɛtou/ n. falsete m.

falsification /,fɔlsəfɪ'keiʃən/ n. falsificación f.

falsify /'fɔlsəfai/ v. falsificar.

falter /'fɔltər/ v. vacilar; (in speech) tartamudear.

fame /feim/ n. fama f.

familiar /fə'mɪlyər/ a. familiar; conocido. **be f. with,** estar familiarizado con.

familiarity /fə,mɪli'ærɪti/ n. familiaridad f.

familiarize /fə'mɪlyə,raiz/ v. familiarizar.

family /'fæməli/ n. familia; especie f.

family name apellido m.

family tree árbol genealógico m.

famine /'fæmɪn/ n. hambre; carestía f.

famished /'fæmɪʃt/ a. hambriento.

famous /'feiməs/ a. famoso, célebre.

fan /fæn/ n. abanico; ventilador m. (sports) aficionado -da.

fanatic /fə'nætɪk/ a. & n. fanático -ca.

fanatical /fə'nætɪkəl/ a. fanático.

fanaticism /fə'nætə,sɪzəm/ n. fanatismo m.

fanciful /'fænsɪfəl/ a. caprichoso; fantástico.

fancy /'fænsi/ a. **1.** fino, elegante. **f. foods,** novedades f.pl. —n. **2.** fantasía f.; capricho m. —v. **3.** imaginar.

fanfare /'fænfɛər/ n. fanfarria f.

fang /fæŋ/ n. colmillo m.

fan heater estufa de aire f.

fantastic /fæn'tæstɪk/ a. fantástico.

fantasy /'fæntəsi/ n. fantasía f.

FAQ /fæk/ n. (Frequently Asked Questions) preguntas más frecuentes f.pl.

far /fɑr/ a. **1.** lejano, distante. —adv. **2.** lejos. **how f.,** a qué distancia. **as f. as,** hasta. **so f., thus f.,** hasta aquí.

farce /fɑrs/ n. farsa f.

fare /fɛər/ n. pasaje m.

farewell /,fɛər'wɛl/ n. **1.** despedida f. **to say f.** despedirse. —interj. **2.** ¡adiós!

farfetched /'fɑr'fɛtʃt/ a. forzado, inverosímil.

farm /fɑrm/ n. **1.** granja; hacienda f. —v. **2.** cultivar, labrar la tierra.

farmer /'fɑrmər/ n. labrador, agricultor m.

farmhouse /'fɑrm,haus/ n. hacienda, alquería f.

farming /'fɑrmɪŋ/ n. agricultura f.; cultivo m.

fart /fɑrt/ n. Colloq. pedo m.

fascinate /'fæsə,neit/ v. fascinar, embelesar.

fascination /,fæsə'neiʃən/ n. fascinación f.

fascism /'fæʃ,ɪzəm/ n. fascismo m.

fashion /'fæʃən/ n. **1.** moda; costumbre; guisa f. **be in f.,** estilarse. —v. **2.** formar.

fashionable /'fæʃənəbəl/ a. de moda, en boga.

fashion show desfile de modas, pase de modelos m.

fast /fæst/ a. **1.** rápido, veloz; (watch) adelantado; (color) firme. —adv. **2.** ligero, de prisa. —n. **3.** ayuno m. —v. **4.** ayunar.

fasten /'fæsən/ v. afirmar; atar; fijar.

fastener /'fæsənər/ n. asegurador m.

fastidious /fæ'stɪdiəs/ a. melindroso.

fat /fæt/ a. **1.** gordo. —n. **2.** grasa, manteca f.

fatal /'feitl/ a. fatal.

fatality /fei'tælɪti/ n. fatalidad f.

fatally /'feitli/ adv. fatalmente.

fate /feit/ n. destino m.; suerte f.

fateful /'feitfəl/ a. fatal; ominoso.

father /'fɑðər/ n. padre m.

fatherhood /'fɑðər,hud/ n. paternidad f.

father-in-law /'fɑ,ðər ɪn lɔ/ n. suegro m.

fatherland /'fɑðər,lænd/ n. patria f.

fatherly /'fɑðərli/ a. **1.** paternal. —adv. **2.** paternalmente.

fathom /'fæðəm/ n. **1.** braza f. —v. **2.** sondar; Fig. penetrar en.

fatigue /fə'tig/ n. **1.** fatiga f., cansancio m. —v. **2.** fatigar, cansar.

fatten /'fætn/ v. engordar, cebar.

faucet /'fɔsɪt/ n. grifo m., llave f.

fault /fɔlt/ n. culpa f.; defecto m. **at f.,** culpable.

faultless /'fɔltlɪs/ a. sin tacha, perfecto.

faultlessly /'fɔltlɪsli/ adv. perfectamente.

faulty /'fɔlti/ a. defectuoso, imperfecto.

fauna /'fɔnə/ n. fauna f.

favor /'feivər/ n. **1.** favor m. —v. **2.** favorecer.

favorable /'feivərəbəl/ a. favorable.

favorite /'feivərɪt/ a. & n. favorito -ta.

favoritism /'feivərɪ,tɪzəm/ n. favoritismo m.

fawn /fɔn/ n. **1.** cervato m. —v. **2.** halagar, adular.

fax /fæks/ n. **1.** fax m. —v. **2.** mandar un fax.

faze /feiz/ v. desconcertar.

fear /fɪər/ n. **1.** miedo, temor m. —v. **2.** temer.

fearful /'fɪərfəl/ a. temeroso, medroso.

fearless /'fɪərlɪs/ a. intrépido; sin temor.

fearlessness /'fɪərlɪsnɪs/ n. intrepidez f.

feasible /'fizəbəl/ a. factible.

feast /fist/ n. banquete m.; fiesta f.

feat /fit/ n. hazaña f.; hecho m.

feather /'fɛðər/ n. pluma f.

feature /'fitʃər/ n. **1.** facción f.; rasgo m.; (movies) película principal f., largometraje m. —v. **2.** presentar como atracción especial.

February /'fɛbru,ɛri, 'fɛbyu-/ n. febrero m.

federal /'fɛdərəl/ a. federal.

federation /,fɛdə'reiʃən/ n. confederación, federación f.

fee /fi/ n. honorarios m.pl.

feeble /'fibəl/ a. débil.

feeble-minded /'fibəl 'maindɪd/ a. imbécil.

feebleness /'fibəlnɪs/ a. debilidad f.

feed /fid/ n. **1.** pasto m. —v. **2.** alimentar; dar de comer. **fed up with,** harto de.

feedback /'fid,bæk/ n. feedback m., retroalimentación f.

feel /fil/ n. **1.** sensación f. —v. **2.** sentir; palpar. **f. like,** tener ganas de.

feeling /'filɪŋ/ n. sensación; sentimiento m.

feign /fein/ v. fingir.

felicitate /fɪ'lɪsɪ,teit/ v. felicitar.

felicitous /fɪ'lɪsɪtəs/ a. feliz.

felicity /fɪ'lɪsɪti/ n. felicidad f., dicha f.

feline /'filain/ a. felino.

fellow /'fɛlou/ n. compañero; socio m.; Colloq. tipo m.

fellowship /'fɛlou,ʃɪp/ n. compañerismo m.; (for study) beca f.

felon /'fɛlən/ n. reo m. & f., felón -ona.

felony /'fɛləni/ n. felonía f.

felt /fɛlt/ n. fieltro m.

felt-tipped pen /'fɛlt ,tɪpt/ rotulador m.

female /'fimeil/ a. & n. hembra f.

feminine /'fɛmənɪn/ a. femenino.

feminist /'fɛmənɪst/ a. & n. feminista m. & f.

fence /fɛns/ n. **1.** cerca f. —v. **2.** cercar.

fender /'fɛndər/ n. guardabarros m.pl.

ferment /n 'fɜrmɛnt; v fər'mɛnt/ n. **1.** fermento m.; Fig. agitación f. —v. **2.** fermentar.

fermentation /,fɜrmɛn'teiʃən/ n. fermentación f.

fern /fɜrn/ n. helecho m.

ferocious /fə'rouʃəs/ a. feroz, fiero.

ferociously /fə'rouʃəsli/ adv. ferozmente.

ferocity /fə'rɒsɪti/ n. ferocidad, fiereza f.

Ferris wheel /'fɛrɪs/ rueda de feria f.

ferry /'fɛri/ n. transbordador m., barca de transporte.

fertile /'fɜrtl/ a. fecundo; (land) fértil.

fertility /fər'tɪlɪti/ n. fertilidad f.

fertilization /,fɜrtlə'zeiʃən/ n. fertilización f.

fertilize /'fɜrtl,aiz/ v. fertilizar, abonar.

fertilizer /'fɜrtl,aizər/ n. abono m.

fervency /'fɜrvənsi/ n. ardor m.

fervent /'fɜrvənt/ a. fervoroso.

fervently /'fɜrvəntli/ adv. fervorosamente.

fervid /'fɜrvɪd/ a. férvido.

fervor /'fɜrvər/ n. fervor m.

fester /'fɛstər/ v. ulcerarse.

festival /'fɛstəvəl/ n. fiesta f.

festive /'fɛstɪv/ a. festivo.

festivity /fɛ'stɪvɪti/ n. festividad f.

festoon /fɛ'stun/ n. **1.** festón m. —v. **2.** festonear.

fetch /fɛtʃ/ v. ir por; traer.

fete /feit/ n. **1.** fiesta f. —v. **2.** festejar.

fetid /'fɛtɪd/ a. fétido.

fetish /'fɛtɪʃ/ n. fetiche m.

fetter /'fɛtər/ n. **1.** grillete m. —v. **2.** engrillar.

fetus /'fitəs/ n. feto m.

feud /fyud/ n. riña f.

feudal /'fyudl/ a. feudal.

feudalism /'fyudl,ɪzəm/ n. feudalismo m.

fever /'fivər/ n. fiebre f.

feverish /'fivərɪʃ/ a. febril.

feverishly /'fivərɪʃli/ adv. febrilmente.

few /fyu/ a. pocos. **a. f.,** algunos, unos cuantos.

fiancé, fiancée /,fiɑn'sei/ n. novio -via.

fiasco /fi'æskou/ n. fiasco m.

fiat /'fiat/ n. fiat m., orden f.

fib /fɪb/ n. **1.** mentira f. —v. **2.** mentir.

fiber /'faibər/ n. fibra f.

fibrous /'faibrəs/ a. fibroso.

fickle /'fɪkəl/ a. caprichoso.

fickleness /'fɪkəlnɪs/ n. inconstancia f.

fiction /'fɪkʃən/ n. ficción f.; (literature) novelas f.pl.

fictitious /fɪk'tɪʃəs/ a. ficticio.

fidelity /fɪ'dɛlɪti/ n. fidelidad f.

fidget /'fɪdʒɪt/ v. inquietar.

field /fild/ n. campo m.

field trip viaje de estudios m.

fiend /find/ n. demonio m.

fiendish /'findɪʃ/ a. diabólico, malvado.

fierce /fɪərs/ a. fiero, feroz.

fiery /'faiəri/ a. ardiente.

fiesta /fi'ɛstə/ n. fiesta f.

fife /faif/ n. pífano m.

fifteen /'fɪf'tin/ a. & pron. quince.

fifteenth /'fɪf'tinθ/ n. & a. décimoquinto.

fifth /fɪfθ/ a. quinto.

fifty /'fɪfti/ a. & pron. cincuenta.

fig /fɪg/ n. higo m. **f. tree,** higuera f.

fight /fait/ n. **1.** lucha, pelea f. —v. **2.** luchar, pelear.

fighter /'faitər/ n. peleador -ra, luchador -ra.

figment /ˈfɪgmənt/ *n.* invención *f.*
figurative /ˈfɪgyərətɪv/ *a.* metafórico.
figuratively /ˈfɪgyərətɪvli/ *adv.* figuradamente.
figure /ˈfɪgyər/ *n.* **1.** figura; cifra *f.* —*v.* **2.** figurar; calcular.
filament /ˈfɪləmənt/ *n.* filamento *m.*
file /fail/ *n.* **1.** archivo *m.;* (instrument) lima *f.;* (row) fila *f.* —*v.* **2.** archivar; limar.
file cabinet archivador *m.*
filial /ˈfɪliəl/ *a.* filial.
filigree /ˈfɪləˌgri/ *n.* filigrana *f.*
fill /fɪl/ *v.* llenar.
fillet /ˈfɪlɪt/ *n.* filete *m.*
filling /ˈfɪlɪŋ/ *n.* relleno *m.;* (dental) empastadura *f.* **f. station,** gasolinera *f.*
film /fɪlm/ *n.* **1.** película *f.,* film *m.* —*v.* **2.** filmar.
filter /ˈfɪltər/ *n.* **1.** filtro *m.* —*v.* **2.** filtrar.
filth /fɪlθ/ *n.* suciedad, mugre *f.*
filthy /ˈfɪlθi/ *a.* sucio.
fin /fɪn/ *n.* aleta *f.*
final /ˈfainl/ *a.* **1.** final, último. —*n.* **2.** examen final. **finals** (sports) final *f.*
finalist /ˈfainlɪst/ *n.* finalista *m.* & *f.*
finally /ˈfainli/ *adv.* finalmente.
finances /ˈfainænsəz/ *n.* recursos, fondos *m.pl.*
financial /fɪˈnænʃəl/ *a.* financiero.
financier /ˌfɪnənˈsɪər, ˌfainən-/ *n.* financiero -ra.
find /faind/ *n.* **1.** hallazgo *m.* —*v.* **2.** hallar; encontrar. **f. out,** averiguar, enterarse, saber.
fine /fain/ *a.* **1.** fino; bueno. —*adv.* **2.** muy bien. —*n.* **3.** multa *f.* —*v.* **4.** multar.
fine arts /ɑrts/ bellas artes *f.pl.*
finery /ˈfainəri/ *n.* gala *f.,* adorno *m.*
finesse /fɪˈnɛs/ *n.* **1.** artificio *m.* —*v.* **2.** valerse de artificio.
finger /ˈfɪŋgər/ *n.* dedo *m.*
finger bowl *n.* enjuagatorio *m.*
fingernail /ˈfɪŋgərˌneil/ *n.* uña *f.*
fingerprint /ˈfɪŋgərˌprɪnt/ *n.* **1.** impresión digital *f.* —*v.* **2.** tomar las impresiones digitales.
finicky /ˈfɪnɪki/ *a.* melindroso.
finish /ˈfɪnɪʃ/ *n.* **1.** conclusión *f.* —*v.* **2.** acabar, terminar.
finished /ˈfɪnɪʃt/ *a.* acabado.
finite /ˈfainait/ *a.* finito.
fir /fɜr/ *n.* abeto *m.*
fire /fai^{ə}r/ *n.* **1.** fuego; incendio *m.* —*v.* **2.** disparar, tirar; *Colloq.* despedir.
fire alarm *n.* alarma de incendio *f.*
firearm /ˈfai^{ə}rˌɑrm/ *n.* arma de fuego.
firecracker /ˈfai^{ə}rˌkrækər/ *n.* triquitraque *m.,* buscapiés *m.,* petardo *m.*
fire engine bomba de incendios *f.*
fire escape escalera de incendios *f.*
fire exit salida de urgencia *f.*
fire extinguisher /ɪkˈstɪŋgwɪʃər/ matafuego *m.*
firefly /ˈfai^{ə}rˌflai/ *n.* luciérnaga *f.*
fireman /ˈfai^{ə}rmən/ *n.* bombero *m.;* (railway) fogonero *m.*
fireplace /ˈfai^{ə}rˌpleis/ *n.* hogar, fogón *m.*
fireproof /ˈfai^{ə}rˌpruf/ *a.* incombustible.
fireside /ˈfai^{ə}rˌsaid/ *n.* hogar, fogón *m.*
fireworks /ˈfai^{ə}rˌwɜrks/ *n.* fuegos artificiales.
firm /fɜrm/ *a.* **1.** firme. —*n.* **2.** firma, empresa *f.*
firmness /ˈfɜrmnɪs/ *n.* firmeza *f.*
first /fɜrst/ *a.* & *adv.* primero. **at f.,** al principio.
first aid primeros auxilios.
first-class /ˈfɜrst ˈklæs/ *a.* de primera clase.
fiscal /ˈfɪskəl/ *a.* fiscal.
fish /fɪʃ/ *n.* **1.** (food) pescado *m.;* (alive) pez *m.* —*v.* **2.** pescar.
fisherman /ˈfɪʃərmən/ *n.* pescador *m.*
fishhook /ˈfɪʃˌhʊk/ *n.* anzuelo *m.*
fishing /ˈfɪʃɪŋ/ *n.* pesca *f.* **go f.,** ir de pesca.
fishmonger /ˈfɪʃˌmʌŋgər/ *n.* pescadero *m.*
fish store pescadería *f.*
fission /ˈfɪʃən/ *n.* fisión *f.*
fissure /ˈfɪʃər/ *n.* grieta *f.,* quebradura *f.;* fisura.
fist /fɪst/ *n.* puño *m.*
fit /fɪt/ *a.* **1.** capaz; justo. —*n.* **2.** corte, talle *m.; Med.* convulsión *f.* —*v.* **3.** caber; quedar bien, sentar bien.
fitful /ˈfɪtfəl/ *a.* espasmódico; caprichoso.
fitness /ˈfɪtnɪs/ *n.* aptitud; conveniencia *f.*
fitting /ˈfɪtɪŋ/ *a.* **1.** conveniente. **be f.,** convenir. —*n.* **2.** ajuste *m.*
fitting room probador *m.*
five /faiv/ *a.* & *pron.* cinco.
five-day work week /ˈfaiv ˈdei/ semana inglesa *f.*
fix /fɪks/ *n.* **1.** apuro *m.* —*v.* **2.** fijar; arreglar; componer, reparar.
fixation /fɪkˈseiʃən/ *n.* fijación *f.;* fijeza *f.*
fixed /fɪkst/ *a.* fijo.
fixture /ˈfɪkstʃər/ *n.* instalación; guarnición *f.*
flabby /ˈflæbi/ *a.* flojo.
flaccid /ˈflæksɪd, ˈflæsɪd/ *a.* flojo; flácido.
flag /flæg/ *n.* bandera *f.*
flagellant /ˈflædʒələnt/ *n.* & *a.* flagelante *m.*
flagon /ˈflægən/ *n.* frasco *m.*
flagrant /ˈfleigrənt/ *a.* flagrante.
flagrantly /ˈfleigrəntli/ *adv.* notoriamente.
flair /flɛər/ *n.* aptitud especial *f.*
flake /fleik/ *n.* **1.** escama *f.;* copo de nieve. —*v.* **2.** romperse en láminas.
flamboyant /flæmˈbɔiənt/ *a.* flamante, llamativo.
flame /fleim/ *n.* **1.** llama *f.* —*v.* **2.** llamear.
flaming /ˈfleimɪŋ/ *a.* llameante, flamante.
flamingo /fləˈmɪŋgou/ *n.* flamenco *m.*
flammable /ˈflæməbəl/ *a.* inflamable.
flank /flæŋk/ *n.* **1.** ijada *f.; Mil.* flanco *m.* —*v.* **2.** flanquear.
flannel /ˈflænl/ *n.* franela *f.*
flap /flæp/ *n.* **1.** cartera *f.* —*v.* **2.** aletear; sacudirse.
flare /flɛər/ *n.* **1.** llamarada *f.* —*v.* **2.** brillar; *Fig.* enojarse.
flash /flæʃ/ *n.* **1.** resplandor *m.;* (lightning) rayo, relámpago *m.; Fig.* instante *m.* —*v.* **2.** brillar.
flashcube /ˈflæʃˌkyub/ *n.* cubo de flash *m.*
flashlight /ˈflæʃˌlait/ *n.* linterna (eléctrica).
flashy /ˈflæʃi/ *a.* ostentoso.
flask /flæsk/ *n.* frasco *m.*
flat /flæt/ *a.* **1.** llano; (tire) desinflado. —*n.* **2.** llanura *f.;* apartamento *m.*
flatness /ˈflætnɪs/ *n.* llanura *f.*
flatten /ˈflætn/ *v.* aplastar, allanar; abatir.
flatter /ˈflætər/ *v.* adular, lisonjear.
flatterer /ˈflætərər/ *n.* lisonjero -ra; zalamero -ra.
flattery /ˈflætəri/ *n.* adulación, lisonja *f.*
flaunt /flɔnt/ *v.* ostentar.
flavor /ˈfleivər/ *n.* **1.** sabor *m.* —*v.* **2.** sazonar.
flavoring /ˈfleivərɪŋ/ *n.* condimento *m.*
flaw /flɔ/ *n.* defecto *m.*
flax /flæks/ *n.* lino *m.*
flay /flei/ *v.* despellejar; excoriar.
flea /fli/ *n.* pulga *f.*
flea market rastro *m.*
fleck /flɛk/ *n.* **1.** mancha *f.* —*v.* **2.** varetear.
flee /fli/ *v.* huir.
fleece /flis/ *n.* **1.** vellón *m.* —*v.* **2.** esquilar.
fleet /flit/ *a.* **1.** veloz. —*n.* **2.** flota *f.*
fleeting /ˈflitɪŋ/ *a.* fugaz, pasajero.
flesh /flɛʃ/ *n.* carne *f.*
fleshy /ˈflɛʃi/ *a.* gordo; carnoso.
flex /flɛks/ *n.* **1.** doblez *m.* —*v.* **2.** doblar.
flexibility /ˌflɛksəˈbɪlɪti/ *n.* flexibilidad *f.*
flexible /ˈflɛksəbəl/ *a.* flexible.
flier /ˈflaiər/ *n.* aviador -ra.
flight /flait/ *n.* vuelo *m.;* fuga *f.*
flight attendant *n.* azafata *f.;* ayudante de vuelo *m.*
flimsy /ˈflɪmzi/ *a.* débil.
flinch /flɪntʃ/ *v.* acobardarse.
fling /flɪŋ/ *v.* lanzar.
flint /flɪnt/ *n.* pedernal *m.*
flip /flɪp/ *v.* lanzar.
flippant /ˈflɪpənt/ *a.* impertinente.
flippantly /ˈflɪpəntli/ *adv.* impertinentemente.
flirt /flɜrt/ *n.* **1.** coqueta *f.* —*v.* **2.** coquetear, flirtear.
flirtation /flɜrˈteiʃən/ *n.* coqueteo *m.*
float /flout/ *v.* flotar.
flock /flɒk/ *n.* **1.** rebaño *m.* —*v.* **2.** congregarse.
flog /flɒg/ *v.* azotar.
flood /flʌd/ *n.* **1.** inundación *f.* —*v.* **2.** inundar.
floor /flɔr/ *n.* **1.** suelo, piso *m.* —*v.* **2.** derribar.
floppy disk /ˈflɒpi/ floppy, *m.,* disquete, *m.*
floral /ˈflɔrəl/ *a.* floral.
florid /ˈflɔrɪd/ *a.* florido.
florist /ˈflɔrɪst/ *n.* florista *m.* & *f.*
flounce /flauns/ *n.* **1.** (sewing) volante *m.* —*v.* **2.** pernear.
flounder /ˈflaundər/ *n.* rodaballo *m.*
flour /flau^{ə}r/ *n.* harina *f.*
flourish /ˈflɜrɪʃ/ *n.* **1.** *Mus.* floreo *m.* —*v.* **2.** florecer; prosperar; blandir.
flow /flou/ *n.* **1.** flujo *m.* —*v.* **2.** fluir.
flow chart organigrama *m.*
flower /ˈflauər/ *n.* **1.** flor *f.* —*v.* **2.** florecer.
flowerpot /ˈflauərˌpɒt/ *n.* maceta *f.*
flowery /ˈflauəri/ *a.* florido.
fluctuate /ˈflʌktʃuˌeit/ *v.* fluctuar.
fluctuation /ˌflʌktʃuˈeiʃən/ *n.* fluctuación *f.*
flue /flu/ *n.* humero *m.*
fluency /ˈfluənsi/ *n.* fluidez *f.*
fluent /ˈfluənt/ *a.* fluido; competente.
fluffy /ˈflʌfi/ *a.* velloso.
fluid /ˈfluɪd/ *a.* & *n.* fluido *m.*
fluidity /fluˈɪdɪti/ *n.* fluidez *f.*
fluoroscope /ˈflʊrəˌskoup/ *n.* fluoroscopio *m.*
flurry /ˈflɜri/ *n.* agitación *f.*
flush /flʌʃ/ *a.* **1.** bien provisto. —*n.* **2.** sonrojo *m.* —*v.* **3.** limpiar con un chorro de agua; sonrojarse.
flute /flut/ *n.* flauta *f.*
flutter /ˈflʌtər/ *n.* **1.** agitación *f.* —*v.* **2.** agitarse.
flux /flʌks/ *n.* flujo *m.*
fly /flai/ *n.* **1.** mosca *f.* —*v.* **2.** volar.
flying saucer /ˈflaiɪŋ/ platillo volante *m.*
foam /foum/ *n.* **1.** espuma *f.* —*v.* **2.** espumar.
focal /ˈfoukəl/ *a.* focal.
focus /ˈfoukəs/ *n.* **1.** enfoque *m.* —*v.* **2.** enfocar.
fodder /ˈfɒdər/ *n.* forraje *m.,* pienso *m.*
foe /fou/ *n.* adversario -ria, enemigo -ga.
fog /fɒg/ *n.* niebla *f.*
foggy /ˈfɒgi/ *a.* brumoso.
foil /fɔil/ *v.* frustrar.
foist /fɔist/ *v.* imponer.
fold /fould/ *n.* **1.** pliegue *m.* —*v.* **2.** doblar, plegar.
foldable /ˈfouldəbəl/ *a.* plegable.
folder /ˈfouldər/ *n.* circular *m.;* (for filing) carpeta *f.*
folding /ˈfouldɪŋ/ *a.* plegable.
foliage /ˈfouliɪdʒ/ *n.* follaje *m.*
folio /ˈfouliˌou/ *n.* infolio; folio *m.*
folklore /ˈfoukˌlɔr/ *n.* folklore *m.*
folks /fouks/ *n.* gente; familia *f.*
follicle /ˈfɒlɪkəl/ *n.* folículo *m.*
follow /ˈfɒlou/ *v.* seguir.
follower /ˈfɒlouər/ *n.* partidario -ria.
folly /ˈfɒli/ *n.* locura *f.*
foment /fouˈmɛnt/ *v.* fomentar.
fond /fɒnd/ *a.* cariñoso, tierno. **be f. of,** ser aficionado a.
fondle /ˈfɒndl/ *v.* acariciar.
fondly /ˈfɒndli/ *adv.* tiernamente.
fondness /ˈfɒndnɪs/ *n.* afición *f.;* cariño *m.*
food /fud/ *n.* alimento *m.;* comida *f.*
foodie /ˈfudi/ *n. Colloq.* gastrónomo -ma, gourmet *m.* & *f.*
food poisoning /ˈpɔizənɪŋ/ intoxicación alimenticia *f.*
foodstuffs /ˈfudˌstʌfs/ *n.pl.* comestibles, víveres *m.pl.*
fool /ful/ **1.** tonto -ta; bobo -ba; bufón -ona. —*v.* **2.** engañar.
foolhardy /ˈfulˌhɑrdi/ *a.* temerario.
foolish /ˈfulɪʃ/ *a.* bobo, tonto, majadero.
foolproof /ˈfulˌpruf/ *a.* seguro.
foot /fʊt/ *n.* pie *m.*
footage /ˈfʊtɪdʒ/ *n.* longitud en pies.
football /ˈfʊtˌbɔl/ *n.* fútbol, balompié *m.*
footbridge /ˈfʊtˌbrɪdʒ/ *n.* puente para peatones *m.*
foothold /ˈfʊtˌhould/ *n.* posición establecida.
footing /ˈfʊtɪŋ/ *n.* base *f.,* fundamento *m.*
footlights /ˈfʊtˌlaits/ *n.pl.* luces del proscenio.
footnote /ˈfʊtˌnout/ *n.* nota al pie de una página.
footpath /ˈfʊtˌpæθ/ *n.* sendero *m.*
footprint /ˈfʊtˌprɪnt/ *n.* huella *f.*
footstep /ˈfʊtˌstɛp/ *n.* paso *m.*
footstool /ˈfʊtˌstul/ *n.* escañuelo *m.,* banqueta *f.*
fop /fɒp/ *n.* petimetre *m.*
for /fɔr; *unstressed* fər/ *prep.* **1.** para; por. **as f.,** en cuanto a. **what f.,** ¿para qué? —*conj.* **2.** porque, pues.
forage /ˈfɔrɪdʒ/ *n.* **1.** forraje *m.* —*v.* **2.** forrajear.
foray /ˈfɔrei/ *n.* correría *f.*
forbear /fɔrˈbɛər/ *v.* cesar; abstenerse.
forbearance /fɔrˈbɛərəns/ *n.* paciencia *f.*
forbid /fərˈbɪd/ *v.* prohibir.
forbidding /fərˈbɪdɪŋ/ *a.* repugnante.
force /fɔrs/ *n.* **1.** fuerza *f.* —*v.* **2.** forzar.
forced landing /fɔrst/ aterrizaje forzoso *m.*
forceful /ˈfɔrsfəl/ *a.* fuerte; enérgico.
forcible /ˈfɔrsəbəl/ *a.* a la fuerza; enérgico.
ford /fɔrd/ *n.* **1.** vado *m.* —*v.* **2.** vadear.
fore /fɔr/ *a.* **1.** delantero. —*n.* **2.** delantera *f.*
fore and aft de popa a proa.
forearm /fɔrˈɑrm/ *n.* antebrazo *m.*
forebears /ˈfɔrˌbɛərz/ *n.pl.* antepasados *m.pl.*
forebode /fɔrˈboud/ *v.* presagiar.
foreboding /fɔrˈboudɪŋ/ *n.* presentimiento *m.*
forecast /ˈfɔrˌkæst/ *n.* **1.** pronóstico *m.;* profecía *f.* —*v.* **2.** pronosticar.
forecastle /ˈfouksəl/ *n. Naut.* castillo de proa.
forefathers /ˈfɔrˌfɑðərz/ *n.* antepasados *m.pl.*
forefinger /ˈfɔrˌfɪŋgər/ *n.* índice *m.*
forego /fɔrˈgou/ *v.* renunciar.
foregone /fɔrˈgɔn/ *a.* predeterminado.
foreground /ˈfɔrˌgraund/ *n.* primer plano.
forehead /ˈfɔrɪd/ *n.* frente *f.*
foreign /ˈfɔrɪn/ *a.* extranjero.
foreign aid *n.* ayuda exterior *f.*
foreigner /ˈfɔrənər/ *n.* extranjero -ra; forastero -ra.

foreleg /ˈfɔrˌlɛg/ *n.* pierna delantera.
foreman /ˈfɔrmən/ *n.* capataz, jefe de taller *m.*
foremost /ˈfɔrˌmoust/ *a.* **1.** primero. —*adv.* **2.** en primer lugar.
forenoon /ˈfɔrˌnun/ *n.* mañana *f.*
forensic /fəˈrɛnsɪk/ *a.* forense.
forerunner /ˈfɔrˌrʌnər/ *n.* precursor -ra.
foresee /fɔrˈsi/ *v.* prever.
foreshadow /fɔrˈʃædou/ *v.* prefigurar, anunciar.
foresight /ˈfɔrˌsait/ *n.* previsión *f.*
forest /ˈfɔrɪst/ *n.* bosque *m.;* selva *f.*
forestall /fɔrˈstɔl/ *v.* anticipar; prevenir.
forester /ˈfɔrəstər/ *n.* silvicultor -ra; guardamontes *m.pl.* & *f.pl.*
forestry /ˈfɔrəstri/ *n.* silvicultura *f.*
foretell /fɔrˈtɛl/ *v.* predecir.
forever /fɔrˈɛvər/ *adv.* por siempre, para siempre.
forevermore /fɔrˌɛvərˈmɔr/ *adv.* siempre.
forewarn /fɔrˈwɔrn/ *v.* advertir, avisar.
foreword /ˈfɔrˌwɜrd/ *n.* prefacio *m.*
forfeit /ˈfɔrfɪt/ *n.* **1.** prenda; multa *f.* —*v.* **2.** perder.
forfeiture /ˈfɔrfɪtʃər/ *n.* decomiso *m.*, multa *f.;* pérdida.
forgather /fɔrˈgæðər/ *v.* reunirse.
forge /fɔrdʒ/ *n.* **1.** fragua *f.* —*v.* **2.** forjar; falsear.
forger /ˈfɔrdʒər/ *n.* forjador -ra; falsificador -ra.
forgery /ˈfɔrdʒəri/ *n.* falsificación *f.*
forget /fərˈgɛt/ *v.* olvidar.
forgetful /fərˈgɛtfəl/ *a.* olvidadizo.
forgive /fərˈgɪv/ *v.* perdonar.
forgiveness /fərˈgɪvnɪs/ *n.* perdón *m.*
fork /fɔrk/ *n.* **1.** tenedor *m.;* bifurcación *f.* —*v.* **2.** bifurcarse.
forlorn /fɔrˈlɔrn/ *a.* triste.
form /fɔrm/ *n.* **1.** forma *f.;* (document) formulario *m.* —*v.* **2.** formar.
formal /ˈfɔrməl/ *a.* formal; ceremonioso. **f. dance,** baile de etiqueta. **f. dress,** traje de etiqueta.
formality /fɔrˈmælɪti/ *n.* formalidad *f.*
formally /ˈfɔrməli/ *adv.* formalmente.
format /ˈfɔrmæt/ *n.* formato *m.*
formation /fɔrˈmeiʃən/ *n.* formación *f.*
formative /ˈfɔrmətɪv/ *a.* formativo.
formatting /ˈfɔrmætɪŋ/ *n.* formateo *m.*
former /ˈfɔrmər/ *a.* anterior; antiguo. **the f.,** aquél.
formerly /ˈfɔrmərli/ *adv.* antiguamente.
formidable /ˈfɔrmɪdəbəl/ *a.* formidable.
formless /ˈfɔrmlɪs/ *a.* sin forma.
formula /ˈfɔrmyələ/ *n.* fórmula *f.*
formulate /ˈfɔrmyəˌleit/ *v.* formular.
formulation /ˌfɔrmyˈleiʃən/ *n.* formulación *f.;* expresión *f.*
forsake /fɔrˈseik/ *v.* abandonar.
fort /fɔrt/ *n.* fortaleza *f.;* fuerte *m.*
forte /ˈfɔrtei/ *a.* & *adv.* *Mus.* forte; fuerte.
forth /fɔrθ/ *adv.* adelante. **back and f.,** de aquí allá. **and so f.,** etcétera.
forthcoming /ˈfɔrθˈkʌmɪŋ/ *a.* futuro, próximo.
forthright /ˈfɔrθˌrait/ *a.* franco.
forthwith /ˌfɔrθˈwɪθ/ *adv.* inmediatamente.
fortification /ˌfɔrtəfɪˈkeiʃən/ *n.* fortificación *f.*
fortify /ˈfɔrtəˌfai/ *v.* fortificar.
fortissimo /fɔrˈtɪsəˌmou/ *a.* & *adv.* *Mus.* fortísimo.
fortitude /ˈfɔrtɪˌtud/ *n.* fortaleza; fortitud *f.*
fortnight /ˈfɔrtˌnait/ *n.* quincena *f.*
fortress /ˈfɔrtrɪs/ *n.* fuerte *m.*, fortaleza *f.*
fortuitous /fɔrˈtuɪtəs/ *a.* fortuito.
fortunate /ˈfɔrtʃənɪt/ *a.* afortunado.
fortune /ˈfɔrtʃən/ *n.* fortuna; suerte *f.*
fortune-teller /ˈfɔrtʃən ˌtɛlər/ *n.* sortílego -ga, adivino -na.
forty /ˈfɔrti/ *a.* & *pron.* cuarenta.
forum /ˈfɔrəm/ *n.* foro *m.*
forward /ˈfɔrwərd/ *a.* **1.** delantero; atrevido. —*adv.* **2.** adelante. —*v.* **3.** trasmitir, reexpedir.
foster /ˈfɔstər/ *n.* **1. f. child,** hijo adoptivo. —*v.* **2.** fomentar; criar.
foul /faul/ *a.* sucio; impuro.
found /faund/ *v.* fundar.
foundation /faunˈdeiʃən/ *n.* fundación *f.;* (of building) cimientos *m.pl.*
founder /ˈfaundər/ *n.* **1.** fundador -ra. —*v.* **2.** irse a pique.
foundry /ˈfaundri/ *n.* fundición *f.*
fountain /ˈfauntn̩/ *n.* fuente *f.*
fountain pen pluma estilográfica, plumafuente *f.*
four /fɔr/ *a.* & *pron.* cuatro.
fourteen /ˈfɔrˈtin/ *a.* & *pron.* catorce.
fourth /fɔrθ/ *a.* & *n.* cuarto *m.*
fowl /faul/ *n.* ave *f.*
fox /fɒks/ *n.* zorro -rra.
fox-trot /ˈfɒksˌtrɒt/ *n.* foxtrot *m.*
foxy /ˈfɒksi/ *a.* astuto.
foyer /ˈfɔiər/ *n.* salón de entrada.
fracas /ˈfreikəs, ˈfrækəs/ *n.* riña *f.*
fraction /ˈfrækʃən/ *n.* fracción *f.*
fracture /ˈfræktʃər/ *n.* **1.** fractura, rotura *f.* —*v.* **2.** fracturar, romper.
fragile /ˈfrædʒəl/ *a.* frágil.
fragment /ˈfrægmənt/ *n.* fragmento, trozo *m.*
fragmentary /ˈfrægmənˌtɛri/ *a.* fragmentario.
fragrance /ˈfreigrəns/ *n.* fragancia *f.*
fragrant /ˈfreigrənt/ *a.* fragante.
frail /freil/ *a.* débil, frágil.
frailty /ˈfreilti/ *n.* debilidad, fragilidad *f.*
frame /freim/ *n.* **1.** marco; armazón; cuadro; cuerpo *m.* —*v.* **2.** fabricar; formar; encuadrar.
frame-up /ˈfreim ˌʌp/ *n.* *Colloq.* conspiración *f.*
framework /ˈfreimˌwɜrk/ *n.* armazón *m.*
France /fræns/ *n.* Francia *f.*
franchise /ˈfræntʃaiz/ *n.* franquicia *f.*
frank /fræŋk/ *a.* **1.** franco. —*n.* **2.** carta franca. —*v.* **3.** franquear.
frankfurter /ˈfræŋkfərtər/ *n.* salchicha *f.*
frankly /ˈfræŋkli/ *adv.* francamente.
frankness /ˈfræŋknɪs/ *n.* franqueza *f.*
frantic /ˈfræntɪk/ *a.* frenético.
fraternal /frəˈtɜrnl̩/ *a.* fraternal.
fraternity /frəˈtɜrnɪti/ *n.* fraternidad *f.*
fraternization /ˌfrætərnəˈzeiʃən/ *n.* fraternización *f.*
fraternize /ˈfrætərˌnaiz/ *v.* confraternizar.
fratricide /ˈfrætrɪˌsaid/ *n.* fratricida *m.* & *f.;* fratricidio *m.*
fraud /frɔd/ *n.* fraude *m.*
fraudulent /ˈfrɔdʒələnt/ *a.* fraudulento.
fraudulently /ˈfrɔdʒələntli/ *adv.* fraudulentamente.
fraught /frɔt/ *a.* cargado.
freak /frik/ *n.* rareza *f.;* monstruosidad.
freckle /ˈfrɛkəl/ *n.* peca *f.*
freckled /ˈfrɛkəld/ *a.* pecoso.
free /fri/ *a.* **1.** libre; gratis. —*v.* **2.** libertar, librar.
freedom /ˈfridəm/ *n.* libertad *f.*
freeze /friz/ *v.* helar, congelar.
freezer /ˈfrizər/ *n.* heladora *f.*
freezing point /ˈfrizɪŋ/ punto de congelación *m.*
freight /freit/ *n.* **1.** carga *f.;* flete *m.* —*v.* **2.** cargar; fletar.
freighter /ˈfreitər/ *n.* *Naut.* fletador *m.*
French /frɛntʃ/ *a.* & *n.* francés -esa.
Frenchman /ˈfrɛntʃmən/ *n.* francés *m.*
Frenchwoman /ˈfrɛntʃˌwumən/ *n.* francesa *f.*
frenzied /ˈfrɛnzid/ *a.* frenético.
frenzy /ˈfrɛnzi/ *n.* frenesí *m.*
frequency /ˈfrikwənsi/ *n.* frecuencia *f.*
frequency modulation /ˌmɒdʒəˈleiʃən/ modulación de frequencia.
frequent /ˈfrikwənt/ *a.* frecuente.
frequently /ˈfrikwəntli/ *adv.* frecuentemente.
fresco /ˈfrɛskou/ *n.* fresco.
fresh /frɛʃ/ *a.* fresco. **f. water,** agua dulce.
freshen /ˈfrɛʃən/ *v.* refrescar.
freshness /ˈfrɛʃnɪs/ *n.* frescura *f.*
fret /frɛt/ *v.* quejarse, irritarse; *Mus.* traste *m.*
fretful /ˈfrɛtfəl/ *a.* irritable.
fretfully /ˈfrɛtfəli/ *adv.* de mala gana.
fretfulness /ˈfrɛtfəlnɪs/ *n.* mal humor.
friar /ˈfraiər/ *n.* fraile *m.*
fricassee /ˌfrɪkəˈsi/ *n.* fricasé *m.*
friction /ˈfrɪkʃən/ *n.* fricción *f.*
Friday /ˈfraidei/ *n.* viernes *m.* **Good F.,** Viernes Santo *m.*
fried /fraid/ *a.* frito.
friend /frɛnd/ *n.* amigo -ga.
friendless /ˈfrɛndlɪs/ *a.* sin amigos.
friendliness /ˈfrɛndlinɪs/ *n.* amistad *f.*
friendly /ˈfrɛndli/ *a.* amistoso.
friendship /ˈfrɛndʃɪp/ *n.* amistad *f.*
fright /frait/ *n.* susto *m.*
frighten /ˈfraitn̩/ *v.* asustar, espantar.
frightful /ˈfraitfəl/ *a.* espantoso.
frigid /ˈfrɪdʒɪd/ *a.* frígido; frío.
frill /frɪl/ *n.* (sewing) lechuga *f.*
fringe /frɪndʒ/ *n.* fleco; borde *m.*
frisky /ˈfrɪski/ *a.* retozón.
fritter /ˈfrɪtər/ *n.* fritura *f.*
frivolity /frɪˈvɒlɪti/ *n.* frivolidad *f.*
frivolous /ˈfrɪvələs/ *a.* frívolo.
frivolousness /ˈfrɪvələsnɪs/ *n.* frivolidad *f.*
frock /frɒk/ *n.* vestido de mujer. **f. coat,** levita *f.*
frog /frɒg/ *n.* rana *f.*
frolic /ˈfrɒlɪk/ *n.* **1.** retozo *m.* —*v.* **2.** retozar.
from /frʌm, *unstressed* frəm/ *prep.* de; desde.
front /frʌnt/ *n.* frente; (of building) fachada *f.* **in f. of,** delante de.
frontal /ˈfrʌntl̩/ *a.* frontal.
front door puerta principal *f.*
frontier /frʌnˈtɪər/ *n.* frontera *f.*
front seat asiento delantero *m.*
frost /frɔst/ *n.* helada, escarcha *f.*
frosty /ˈfrɔsti/ *a.* helado.
froth /frɔθ/ *n.* espuma *f.*
frown /fraun/ *n.* **1.** ceño *m.* —*v.* **2.** fruncir el entrecejo.
frowzy /ˈfrauzi/ *a.* desaliñado.
frozen /ˈfrouzən/ *a.* helado; congelado.
fructify /ˈfrʌktəˌfai/ *v.* fructificar.
frugal /ˈfrugəl/ *a.* frugal.
frugality /fruˈgælɪti/ *n.* frugalidad *f.*
fruit /frut/ *n.* fruta *f.;* (benefits) frutos *m.pl.* **f. tree,** árbol frutal.
fruitful /ˈfrutfəl/ *a.* productivo.
fruition /fruˈɪʃən/ *n.* fruición *f.*
fruitless /ˈfrutlɪs/ *a.* inútil, en vano.
fruit salad macedonia de frutas *f.*
fruit store frutería *f.*
frustrate /ˈfrʌstreit/ *v.* frustrar.
frustration /frʌˈstreiʃən/ *n.* frustración *f.*
fry /frai/ *v.* freír.
fuel /ˈfyuəl/ *n.* combustible *m.*
fugitive /ˈfyudʒɪtɪv/ *a.* & *n.* fugitivo -va.
fugue /fyug/ *n.* fuga *f.*
fulcrum /ˈfulkrəm/ *n.* fulcro *m.*
fulfill /fulˈfɪl/ *v.* cumplir.
fulfillment /fulˈfɪlmənt/ *n.* cumplimiento *m.;* realización *f.*
full /ful/ *a.* lleno; completo; pleno.
full name nombre y apellidos.
fullness /ˈfulnɪs/ *n.* plenitud *f.*
fulminate /ˈfʌlməˌneit/ *v.* volar; fulminar.
fulmination /ˌfʌlməˈneiʃən/ *n.* fulminación; detonación *f.*
fumble /ˈfʌmbəl/ *v.* chapucear.
fume /fyum/ *n.* **1.** humo *m.* —*v.* **2.** humear.
fumigate /ˈfyumɪˌgeit/ *v.* fumigar.
fumigator /ˈfyumɪˌgeitər/ *n.* fumigador *m.*
fun /fʌn/ *n.* diversión *f.* **to make f. of,** burlarse de. **to have f.,** divertirse.
function /ˈfʌŋkʃən/ *n.* **1.** función *f.* —*v.* **2.** funcionar.
functional /ˈfʌŋkʃənl̩/ *a.* funcional.
fund /fʌnd/ *n.* fondo *m.*
fundamental /ˌfʌndəˈmɛntl̩/ *a.* fundamental.
funeral /ˈfyunərəl/ *n.* funeral *m.*
funeral home, funeral parlor funeraria *f.*
fungus /ˈfʌŋgəs/ *n.* hongo *m.*
funnel /ˈfʌnl̩/ *n.* embudo *m.;* (of ship) chimenea *f.*
funny /ˈfʌni/ *a.* divertido, gracioso. **to be f.,** tener gracia.
fur /fɜr/ *n.* piel *f.*
furious /ˈfyʊriəs/ *a.* furioso.
furlough /ˈfɜrlou/ *n.* permiso *m.*
furnace /ˈfɜrnɪs/ *n.* horno *m.*
furnish /ˈfɜrnɪʃ/ *v.* surtir, proveer; (a house) amueblar.
furniture /ˈfɜrnɪtʃər/ *n.* muebles *m.pl.*
furrow /ˈfɜrou/ *n.* **1.** surco *m.* —*v.* **2.** surcar.
further /ˈfɜrðər/ *a.* & *adv.* **1.** más. —*v.* **2.** adelantar, fomentar.
furthermore /ˈfɜrðərˌmɔr/ *adv.* además.
fury /ˈfyʊri/ *n.* furor *m.;* furia *f.*
fuse /fyuz/ *n.* **1.** fusible *m.* —*v.* **2.** fundir.
fuss /fʌs/ *n.* **1.** alboroto *m.* —*v.* **2.** preocuparse por pequeñeces.
fussy /ˈfʌsi/ *a.* melindroso.
futile /ˈfyutl̩/ *a.* fútil.
future /ˈfyutʃər/ *a.* **1.** futuro. —*n.* **2.** porvenir *m.*
futurology /ˌfyutʃəˈrɒlədʒi/ *n.* futurología *f.*
fuzzy logic /ˈfʌzi/ lógica matizada *f.*
FYI *abbr.* (For Your Information) para su información.

G

gag /gæg/ *n.* chiste *m.;* mordaza *f.*
gaiety /ˈgeiɪti/ *n.* alegría *f.*
gain /gein/ *n.* **1.** ganancia *f.* —*v.* **2.** ganar.
gait /geit/ *n.* paso *m.*
gale /geil/ *n.* ventarrón *m.*
gall /gɔl/ *n.* hiel *f.;* *Fig.* amargura *f.;* descaro *m.*
gallant /ˈgælənt, gəˈlænt, -ˈlɑnt/ *a.* **1.** galante. —*n.* **2.** galán *m.*
gallery /ˈgæləri/ *n.* galería *f.;* *Theat.* paraíso *m.*
gallon /ˈgælən/ *n.* galón *m.*
gallop /ˈgæləp/ *n.* **1.** galope *m.* —*v.* **2.** galopar.
gallows /ˈgælouz/ *n.* horca *f.*
gamble /ˈgæmbəl/ *n.* **1.** riesgo *m.* —*v.* **2.** jugar, aventurar.
game /geim/ *n.* juego *m.;* (match) partida *f.;* (hunting) caza *f.*
gang /gæŋ/ *n.* cuadrilla; pandilla *f.*
gangster /ˈgæŋstər/ *n.* rufián *m.*
gap /gæp/ *n.* raja *f.*
gape /geip/ *v.* boquear.
garage /gəˈrɑʒ/ *n.* garaje *m.*
garbage /ˈgɑrbɪdʒ/ *n.* basura *f.*
garden /ˈgɑrdn̩/ *n.* jardín *m.;* (vegetable) huerta *f.*
gardener /ˈgɑrdnər/ *n.* jardinero -ra.
gargle /ˈgɑrgəl/ *n.* **1.** gárgara *f.* —*v.* **2.** gargarizar.
garland /ˈgɑrlənd/ *n.* guirnalda *f.*
garlic /ˈgɑrlɪk/ *n.* ajo *m.*
garment /ˈgɑrmənt/ *n.* prenda de vestir.
garrison /ˈgærəsən/ *n.* guarnición *f.*

garter /ˈgɑrtər/ *n.* liga *f.*; atadera *f.pl.*
gas /gæs/ *n.* gas *m.*
gasohol /ˈgæsəˌhɔl, -ˌhɒl/ *n.* gasohol *m.*
gasoline /ˌgæsəˈlin/ *n.* gasolina *f.*
gasp /gæsp/ *n.* **1.** boqueada *f.* —*v.* **2.** boquear.
gas station gasolinera *f.*
gate /geit/ *n.* puerta; entrada; verja *f.*
gather /ˈgæðər/ *v.* recoger; inferir; reunir.
gaudy /ˈgɔdi/ *a.* brillante; llamativo.
gauge /geidʒ/ *n.* **1.** manómetro, indicador *m.* —*v.* **2.** medir; estimar.
gaunt /gɔnt/ *a.* flaco.
gauze /gɔz/ *n.* gasa *f.*
gay /gei/ *a.* **1.** alegre; homosexual. —*n.* **2.** homosexual.
gaze /geiz/ *n.* **1.** mirada *f.* —*v.* **2.** mirar con fijeza.
gear /gɪər/ *n.* engranaje *m.* **in g.,** en juego.
gearshift /ˈgɪərˌʃɪft/ *n.* palanca de cambio *f.*
gem /dʒɛm/ *n.* joya *f.*
gender /ˈdʒɛndər/ *n.* género *m.*
general /ˈdʒɛnərəl/ *a.* & *n.* general *m.*
generality /ˌdʒɛnəˈrælɪti/ *n.* generalidad *f.*
generalize /ˈdʒɛnərəˌlaiz/ *v.* generalizar.
generation /ˌdʒɛnəˈreiʃən/ *n.* generación *f.*
generator /ˈdʒɛnəˌreitər/ *n.* generador *m.*
generosity /ˌdʒɛnəˈrɒsɪti/ *n.* generosidad *f.*
generous /ˈdʒɛnərəs/ *a.* generoso.
genetic /dʒəˈnɛtɪk/ *a.* genético.
genial /ˈdʒinyəl/ *a.* genial.
genius /ˈdʒinyəs/ *n.* genio *m.*
genocide /ˈdʒɛnəˌsaid/ *n.* genocidio *m.*
gentle /ˈdʒɛntḷ/ *a.* suave; manso; benigno.
gentleman /ˈdʒɛntḷmən/ *n.* señor; caballero *m.*
gentleness /ˈdʒɛntḷnɪs/ *n.* suavidad *f.*
genuine /ˈdʒɛnyuɪn/ *a.* genuino.
genuineness /ˈdʒɛnyuɪnnɪs/ *n.* pureza *f.*
geographical /ˌdʒiəˈgræfɪkəl/ *a.* geográfico.
geography /dʒiˈɒgrəfi/ *n.* geografía *f.*
geometric /ˌdʒiəˈmɛtrɪk/ *a.* geométrico.
geranium /dʒəˈreiniəm/ *n.* geranio *m.*
germ /dʒɜrm/ *n.* germen; microbio *m.*
German /ˈdʒɜrmən/ *a.* & *n.* alemán -mana.
Germany /ˈdʒɜrməni/ *n.* Alemania *f.*
gesticulate /dʒɛˈstɪkyəˌleit/ *v.* gesticular.
gesture /ˈdʒɛstʃər/ *n.* **1.** gesto *m.* —*v.* **2.** gesticular, hacer gestos.
get /gɛt/ *v.* obtener; conseguir; (become) ponerse. **go and g.,** ir a buscar; **g. away,** irse; escaparse; **g. together,** reunirse; **g. on,** subirse; **g. off,** bajarse; **g. up,** levantarse; **g. there,** llegar.
ghastly /ˈgæstli/ *a.* pálido; espantoso.
ghost /goust/ *n.* espectro, fantasma *m.*
giant /ˈdʒaiənt/ *n.* gigante *m.*
gibberish /ˈdʒɪbərɪʃ/ *n.* galimatías, *m.*
gift /gɪft/ *n.* regalo, don; talento *m.*
gigabyte /ˈgɪgəˌbait, ˈdʒɪg-/ *n.* giga *m.*
gild /gɪld/ *v.* dorar.
gin /dʒɪn/ *n.* ginebra *f.*
ginger /ˈdʒɪndʒər/ *n.* jengibre *m.*
gingerbread /ˈdʒɪndʒərˌbrɛd/ *n.* pan de jengibre.
gingham /ˈgɪŋəm/ *n.* guinga *f.*
gird /gɜrd/ *v.* ceñir.
girdle /ˈgɜrdḷ/ *n.* faja *f.*
girl /gɜrl/ *n.* muchacha, niña, chica *f.*
give /gɪv/ *v.* dar; regalar. **g. back,** devolver. **g. up,** rendirse; renunciar.
giver /ˈgɪvər/ *n.* dador -ra; donador -ra.
glacier /ˈgleiʃər/ *n.* glaciar; ventisquero *m.*
glad /glæd/ *a.* alegre, contento. **be g.,** alegrarse.
gladly /ˈglædli/ *adj.* con mucho gusto.
gladness /ˈglædnɪs/ *n.* alegría *f.*; placer *m.*
glamor /ˈglæmər/ *n.* encanto *m.*; elegancia *f.*
glamorous /ˈglæmərəs/ *a.* encantador; elegante.
glamour /ˈglæmər/ *n.* encanto *m.*; elegancia *f.*
glance /glæns/ *n.* **1.** vistazo *m.*, ojeada *f.* —*v.* **2.** ojear.
gland /glænd/ *n.* glándula *f.*
glare /glɛər/ *n.* **1.** reflejo; brillo *m.* —*v.* **2.** deslumbrar; echar miradas indignadas.
glass /glæs/ *n.* vidrio; vaso *m.*; **(eyeglasses),** lentes, anteojos *m.pl.*
gleam /glim/ *n.* **1.** fulgor *m.* —*v.* **2.** fulgurar.
glee /gli/ *n.* alegría *f.*; júbilo *m.*
glide /glaid/ *v.* deslizarse.
glimpse /glɪmps/ *n.* **1.** vislumbre, vistazo *m.* —*v.* **2.** vislumbrar, ojear.
glisten /ˈglɪsən/ *n.* **1.** brillo *m.* —*v.* **2.** brillar.
glitter /ˈglɪtər/ *n.* **1.** resplandor *m.* —*v.* **2.** brillar.
globe /gloub/ *n.* globo; orbe *m.*
gloom /glum/ *n.* oscuridad; tristeza *f.*
gloomy /ˈglumi/ *a.* oscuro; sombrío, triste.
glorify /ˈglɔrəˌfai/ *v.* glorificar.
glorious /ˈglɔriəs/ *a.* glorioso.
glory /ˈglɔri/ *n.* gloria, fama *f.*
glossary /ˈglɒsəri/ *n.* glosario *m.*
glove /glʌv/ *n.* guante *m.*
glove compartment guantera *f.*
glow /glou/ *n.* **1.** fulgor *m.* —*v.* **2.** relucir; arder.
glucose /ˈglukous/ *f.* glucosa.
glue /glu/ *n.* **1.** cola *f.*, pegamento *m.* —*v.* **2.** encolar, pegar.
glum /glʌm/ *a.* de mal humor.
glutton /ˈglʌtn/ *n.* glotón -ona.
gnaw /nɔ/ *v.* roer.
GNP (*abbr.* **gross national product**), **PNB** (producto nacional bruto).
go /gou/ *v.* ir, irse. **g. away,** irse, marcharse. **g. back,** volver, regresar. **g. down,** bajar. **g. in,** entrar. **g. on,** seguir. **g. out,** salir. **g. up,** subir.
goal /goul/ *n.* meta *f.*; objeto *m.*
goalkeeper /ˈgoulˌkipər/ *n.* guardameta *mf.*
goat /gout/ *n.* cabra *f.*
goblet /ˈgɒblɪt/ *n.* copa *f.*
God /gɒd/ *n.* Dios *m.*
gold /gould/ *n.* oro *m.*
golden /ˈgouldən/ *a.* áureo.
gold-plated /ˈgould ˌpleitɪd/ *a.* chapado en oro.
golf /gɒlf/ *n.* golf *m.*
golf course campo de golf *m.*
golfer /ˈgɒlfər/ *n.* golfista *m.* & *f.*
good /gʊd/ *a.* **1.** bueno. —*n.* **2.** bienes *m.pl.*; *Com.* géneros *m.pl.*
good-bye /ˌgʊdˈbai/ *n.* **1.** adiós *m.* —*interj.* **2.** ¡adiós!, ¡hasta la vista!, ¡hasta luego! **say g. to,** despedirse de.
goodness /ˈgʊdnɪs/ *n.* bondad *f.*
goodwill /ˈgʊdˈwɪl/ *n.* buena voluntad. *f.*
goose /gus/ *n.* ganso *m.*
gooseberry /ˈgusˌbɛri/ *n.* uva crespa *f.*
gooseneck /ˈgusˌnɛk/ *n.* **1.** cuello de cisne *m.* —*a.* **2.** curvo.
goose step /ˈgusˌstɛp/ paso de ganso *m.*
gore /gɔr/ *n.* **1.** sangre *f.* —*v.* **2.** acornear.
gorge /gɔrdʒ/ *n.* **1.** gorja *f.* —*v.* **2.** engullir.
gorgeous /ˈgɔrdʒəs/ *a.* magnífico; precioso.
gorilla /gəˈrɪlə/ *n.* gorila *m.*
gory /ˈgɔri/ *a.* sangriento.
gosling /ˈgɒzlɪŋ/ *n.* gansarón *m.*
gospel /ˈgɒspəl/ *n.* evangelio *m.*
gossamer /ˈgɒsəmər/ *n.* **1.** telaraña *f.* —*a.* **2.** delgado.
gossip /ˈgɒsəp/ *n.* **1.** chisme *m.* —*v.* **2.** chismear.
Gothic /ˈgɒθɪk/ *a.* gótico.
gouge /gaudʒ/ *n.* **1.** gubia *f.* —*v.* **2.** escoplear.
gourd /gɔrd/ *n.* calabaza *f.*
gourmand /gʊrˈmɑnd/ *n.* glotón *m.*
gourmet /gʊrˈmei/ *a.* gastrónomo -ma.
govern /ˈgʌvərn/ *v.* gobernar.
governess /ˈgʌvərnɪs/ *n.* aya, institutriz *f.*
government /ˈgʌvərnmənt, -ərmənt/ *n.* gobierno *m.*
governmental /ˌgʌvərnˈmɛntḷ, ˌgʌvər-/ *a.* gubernamental.
governor /ˈgʌvərnər/ *n.* gobernador -ra.
governorship /ˈgʌvərnərˌʃɪp/ *n.* gobernatura *f.*
gown /gaun/ *n.* vestido *m.* **dressing g.,** bata *f.*
grab /græb/ *v.* agarrar, arrebatar.
grace /greis/ *n.* gracia; gentileza; merced *f.*
graceful /ˈgreisfəl/ *a.* agraciado.
graceless /ˈgreislɪs/ *a.* réprobo; torpe.
gracious /ˈgreiʃəs/ *a.* gentil, cortés.
grackle /ˈgrækəl/ *n.* grajo *m.*
grade /greid/ *n.* **1.** grado; nivel *m.*; pendiente; nota; calidad *f.* —*v.* **2.** graduar.
grade crossing *n.* paso a nivel *m.*
gradual /ˈgrædʒuəl/ *a.* gradual, paulatino.
gradually /ˈgrædʒuəli/ *adv.* gradualmente.
graduate /*n* ˈgrædʒuɪt; *v* -ˌeit/ *n.* **1.** graduado -da, diplomado -da. —*v.* **2.** graduar; diplomarse.
graft /græft/ *n.* **1.** injerto *m.*; soborno público. —*v.* **2.** injertar.
graham /ˈgreiəm/ *a.* centeno; acemita.
grail /greil/ *n.* grial *m.*
grain /grein/ *n.* grano; cereal *m.*
grain alcohol *n.* alcohol de madera *m.*
gram /græm/ *n.* gramo *m.*
grammar /ˈgræmər/ *n.* gramática *f.*
grammarian /grəˈmɛəriən/ *n.* gramático -ca.
grammar school *n.* escuela elemental *f.*
grammatical /grəˈmætɪkəl/ *a.* gramatical.
gramophone /ˈgræməˌfoun/ *n.* gramófono *m.*
granary /ˈgreinəri/ *n.* granero *m.*
grand /grænd/ *a.* grande, ilustre; estupendo.
grandchild /ˈgrænˌtʃaild/ *n.* nieto -ta.
granddaughter /ˈgrænˌdɔtər/ *n.* nieta *f.*
grandee /grænˈdi/ *n.* noble *m.*
grandeur /ˈgrændʒər/ *n.* grandeza *f.*
grandfather /ˈgrænˌfɑðər/ *n.* abuelo *m.*
grandiloquent /grænˈdɪləkwənt/ *a.* grandílocuo.
grandiose /ˈgrændiˌous/ *a.* grandioso.
grand jury jurado de acusación, jurado de juicio *m.*
grandly /ˈgrændli/ *adv.* grandiosamente.
grandmother /ˈgrænˌmʌðər/ *n.* abuela *f.*
grand opera ópera grande *f.*
grandparents /ˈgrændˌpɛərənts/ *n.* abuelos *m.pl.*
grandson /ˈgrænˌsʌn/ *n.* nieto *m.*
grandstand /ˈgrænˌstænd/ *n.* andanada *f.*, tribuna *f.*
grange /greindʒ/ *n.* granja *f.*
granger /ˈgreindʒər/ *n.* labriego *m.*
granite /ˈgrænɪt/ *n.* granito *m.*
granny /ˈgræni/ *n.* abuelita *f.*
grant /grænt/ *n.* **1.** concesión; subvención *f.* —*v.* **2.** otorgar; conceder; conferir. **take for granted,** tomar por cierto.
granular /ˈgrænyələr/ *a.* granular.
granulate /ˈgrænyəˌleit/ *v.* granular.
granulation /ˌgrænyəˈleiʃən/ *n.* granulación *f.*
granule /ˈgrænyul/ *n.* gránulo *m.*
grape /greip/ *n.* uva *f.*
grapefruit /ˈgreipˌfrut/ *n.* toronja *f.*
grape harvest vendimia *f.*
grapeshot /ˈgreipˌʃɒt/ *n.* metralla *f.*
grapevine /ˈgreipˌvain/ *n.* vid; parra *f.*
graph /græf/ *n.* gráfica *f.*
graphic /ˈgræfɪk/ *a.* gráfico.
graphite /ˈgræfait/ *n.* grafito *m.*
graphology /græˈfɒlədʒi/ *n.* grafología *f.*
grapple /ˈgræpəl/ *v.* agarrar.
grasp /græsp/ *n.* **1.** puño; poder; conocimiento *m.* —*v.* **2.** empuñar, agarrar; comprender.
grasping /ˈgræspɪŋ/ *a.* codicioso.
grass /græs/ *n.* hierba *f.*; (marijuana) marijuana *f.*
grasshopper /ˈgræsˌhɒpər/ *n.* saltamontes *m.*
grassy /ˈgræsi/ *a.* herboso.
grate /greit/ *n.* reja *f.*
grateful /ˈgreitfəl/ *a.* agradecido.
gratify /ˈgrætəˌfai/ *v.* satisfacer.
grating /ˈgreitɪŋ/ *n.* **1.** enrejado *m.* —*a.* **2.** discordante.
gratis /ˈgrætɪs/ *adv.* & *a.* gratis.
gratitude /ˈgrætɪˌtud/ *n.* agradecimiento *m.*
gratuitous /grəˈtuɪtəs/ *adj.* gratuito.
gratuity /grəˈtuɪti/ *n.* propina *f.*
grave /greiv/ *a.* **1.** grave. —*n.* **2.** sepultura; tumba *f.*
gravel /ˈgrævəl/ *n.* cascajo *m.*
gravely /ˈgreivli/ *adv.* gravemente.
gravestone /ˈgreivˌstoun/ *n.* lápida sepulcral *f.*
graveyard /ˈgreivˌyɑrd/ *n.* cementerio *m.*
gravitate /ˈgrævɪˌteit/ *v.* gravitar.
gravitation /ˌgrævɪˈteiʃən/ *n.* gravitación *f.*
gravity /ˈgrævɪti/ *n.* gravedad; seriedad *f.*
gravure /grəˈvyʊr/ *n.* fotograbado *m.*
gravy /ˈgreivi/ *n.* salsa *f.*
gray /grei/ *a.* gris; (hair) cano.
grayish /ˈgreiɪʃ/ *a.* pardusco.
gray matter substancia gris *f.*
graze /greiz/ *v.* rozar; (cattle) pastar.
grazing /ˈgreizɪŋ/ *a.* pastando.
grease /gris/ *n.* **1.** grasa *f.* —*v.* **2.** engrasar.
greasy /ˈgrisi/ *a.* grasiento.
great /greit/ *a.* grande, ilustre; estupendo.
Great Dane /dein/ mastín danés *m.*
great-grandfather /ˌgreit ˈgrænˌfɑðər/ *n.* bisabuelo.
great-grandmother /ˌgreit ˈgrænˌmʌðər/ *f.* bisabuela.
greatness /ˈgreitnɪs/ *n.* grandeza *f.*
Greece /gris/ *n.* Grecia *f.*
greed /grid/ **greediness** *n.* codicia, voracidad *f.*
greedy /ˈgridi/ *a.* voraz.
Greek /grik/ *a.* & *n.* griego -ga.
green /grin/ *a.* & *n.* verde *m.* **greens,** *n.* verduras *f.pl.*
greenery /ˈgrinəri/ *n.* verdor *m.*
greenhouse /ˈgrinˌhaus/ *n.* invernáculo *m.*
greenhouse effect *n.* efecto invernáculo *m.*
greet /grit/ *v.* saludar.
greeting /ˈgritɪŋ/ *n.* saludo *m.*
gregarious /grɪˈgɛəriəs/ *a.* gregario; sociable.
grenade /grɪˈneid/ *n.* granada; bomba *f.*
greyhound /ˈgreiˌhaund/ *n.* galgo *m.*
grid /grɪd/ *n.* parrilla *f.*
griddle /ˈgrɪdḷ/ *n.* tortera *f.*
griddlecake /ˈgrɪdḷˌkeik/ *n.* tortita de harina *f.*

gridiron /'grɪd,aiərn/ n. parrilla f.; campo de fútbol m.

grief /grif/ n. dolor m.; pena f.

grievance /'grivəns/ n. pesar; agravio m.

grieve /griv/ v. afligir.

grievous /'grivəs/ a. penoso.

grill /grɪl/ n. 1. parrilla f. —v. 2. asar a la parrilla.

grillroom /'grɪl,rum, -,rʊm/ n. parrilla f.

grim /grɪm/ a. ceñudo.

grimace /'grɪməs/ n. 1. mueca f. —v. 2. hacer muecas.

grime /graim/ n. mugre f.

grimy /'graimi/ a. sucio; mugroso.

grin /grɪn/ n. 1. sonrisa f. —v. 2. sonreír.

grind /graind/ v. moler; afilar.

grindstone /'graind,stoun/ n. amoladera f.

gringo /'grɪŋgou/ n. gringo; yanqui m.

grip /grɪp/ n. 1. maleta f. —v. 2. agarrar.

gripe /graip/ v. 1. agarrar. —n. 2. asimiento m., opresión f.

grippe /grɪp/ n. gripe f.

grisly /'grɪzli/ a. espantoso.

grist /grɪst/ n. molienda f.

gristle /'grɪsəl/ n. cartílago m.

grit /grɪt/ n. arena f.; entereza f.

grizzled /'grɪzəld/ a. tordillo.

groan /groun/ n. 1. gemido m. —v. 2. gemir.

grocer /'grousər/ n. abacero m.

grocery /'grousəri/ n. tienda de comestibles, abacería; (Carib.) bodega f.

grog /grɒg/ n. brebaje m.

groggy /'grɒgi/ a. medio borracho; vacilante.

groin /grɔin/ n. ingle f.

groom /grum/ n. 1. (of horses) establero; (at wedding) novio m.

groove /gruv/ n. 1. estría f. —v. 2. acanalar.

grope /group/ v. tentar; andar a tientas.

gross /grous/ a. 1. grueso; grosero. —n. 2. gruesa f.

grossly /'grousli/ adv. groseramente.

gross national product producto nacional bruto m.

grossness /'grousnɪs/ n. grosería f.

grotesque /grou'tɛsk/ a. grotesco.

grotto /'grɒtou/ n. gruta f.

grouch /grautʃ/ n. gruñón; descontento m.

ground /graund/ n. tierra f.; terreno; suelo; campo; fundamento m.

ground floor planta baja f.

groundhog /'graund,hɒg/ n. marmota f.

groundless /'graundlɪs/ a. infundado.

groundwork /'graund,wɜrk/ n. base f., fundamento m.

group /grup/ n. 1. grupo m. —v. 2. agrupar.

groupie /'grupi/ n. persona aficionada que acompaña a un grupo de música moderna.

grouse /graus/ v. quejarse.

grove /grouv/ n. arboleda f.

grovel /'grɒvəl/ v. rebajarse; envilecerse.

grow /grou/ v. crecer; cultivar.

growl /graul/ n. 1. gruñido m. —v. 2. gruñir.

grown /groun/ a. crecido; desarrollado.

grownup /'groun,ʌp/ n. adulto -ta.

growth /grouθ/ n. crecimiento m.; vegetación f.; Med. tumor m.

grub /grʌb/ n. gorgojo m., larva f.

grubby /'grʌbi/ a. gorgojoso, mugriento.

grudge /grʌdʒ/ n. rencor m. **bear a g.,** guardar rencor.

gruel /'gruəl/ n. 1. atole m. —v. 2. agotar.

gruesome /'grusəm/ a. horripilante.

gruff /grʌf/ a. ceñudo.

grumble /'grʌmbəl/ v. quejarse.

grumpy /'grʌmpi/ a. gruñón; quejoso.

grunt /grʌnt/ v. gruñir.

guarantee /,gærən'ti/ n. 1. garantía f. —v. 2. garantizar.

guarantor /'gærən,tɔr/ n. fiador -ra.

guaranty /'gærən,ti/ n. garantía f.

guard /gɑrd/ n. 1. guardia m. & f. —v. 2. vigilar.

guarded /'gɑrdɪd/ a. cauteloso.

guardhouse /'gɑrd,haus/ n. prisión militar f.

guardian /'gɑrdiən/ n. guardián -ana.

guardianship /'gɑrdiən,ʃɪp/ n. tutela f.

guardsman /'gɑrdzmən/ n. centinela m.

guava /'gwɑvə/ n. guayaba f.

gubernatorial /,gubərnə'tɔriəl/ a. gubernativo.

guerrilla /gə'rɪlə/ n. guerrilla f.; guerrillero, -ra.

guess /gɛs/ n. 1. conjetura f. —v. 2. adivinar; Colloq. creer.

guesswork /'gɛs,wɜrk/ n. conjetura f.

guest /gɛst/ n. huésped m. & f.

guest room alcoba de huéspedes f., alcoba de respeto f., cuarto para invitados m.

guffaw /gʌ'fɔ/ n. risotada f.

guidance /'gaidns/ n. dirección f.

guide /gaid/ n. 1. guía m. & f. —v. 2. guiar.

guidebook /'gaid,bʊk/ n. guía f.

guided tour /'gaidɪd/ visita explicada, visita programada, visita con guía f.

guideline /'gaid,lain/ n. pauta f.

guidepost /'gaid,poust/ n. poste indicador m.

guild /gɪld/ n. gremio m.

guile /gail/ n. engaño m.

guillotine /'gɪlə,tin/ n. 1. guillotina f. —v. 2. guillotinar.

guilt /gɪlt/ n. culpa f.

guiltily /'gɪltəli/ adv. culpablemente.

guiltless /'gɪltlɪs/ a. inocente.

guilty /'gɪlti/ a. culpable.

guinea fowl /'gɪni/ gallina de Guinea f.

guinea pig /'gɪni/ cobayo m., conejillo de Indias m.

guise /gaiz/ n. modo m.

guitar /gɪ'tɑr/ n. guitarra f.

guitarist /gɪ'tɑrɪst/ n. guitarrista m. & f.

gulch /gʌltʃ/ n. quebrada f.

gulf /gʌlf/ n. golfo m.

gull /gʌl/ n. gaviota f.

gullet /'gʌlɪt/ n. esófago m.; zanja f.

gullible /'gʌləbəl/ a. crédulo.

gully /'gʌli/ n. barranca f.

gulp /gʌlp/ n. 1. trago m. —v. 2. tragar.

gum /gʌm/ n. 1. goma f.; Anat. encía f. **chewing g.,** chicle m. —v. 2. engomar.

gumbo /'gʌmbou/ n. quimbombó m.

gummy /'gʌmi/ a. gomoso.

gun /gʌn/ n. fusil, revólver m.

gunboat /'gʌn,bout/ n. cañonero m.

gunman /'gʌnmən/ n. bandido m.

gunner /'gʌnər/ n. artillero m.

gun permit licencia de armas f.

gunpowder /'gʌn,paudər/ n. pólvora f.

gunshot /'gʌn,ʃɒt/ n. escopetazo m.

gunwale /'gʌnl/ n. borda f.

gurgle /'gɜrgəl/ n. 1. gorgoteo m. —v. 2. gorgotear.

guru /'guru, gʊ'ru/ n. gurú m.

gush /gʌʃ/ n. 1. chorro m. —v. 2. brotar, chorrear.

gusher /'gʌʃər/ n. pozo de petróleo m.

gust /gʌst/ n. soplo m.; ráfaga f.

gustatory /'gʌstə,tɔri/ a. gustativo.

gusto /'gʌstou/ n. gusto; placer m.

gusty /'gʌsti/ a. borrascoso.

gut /gʌt/ n. intestino m., tripa f.

gutter /'gʌtər/ n. canal; zanja f.

guttural /'gʌtərəl/ a. gutural.

guy /gai/ n. tipo m.

guzzle /'gʌzəl/ v. engullir; tragar.

gym /dʒɪm/ n. gimnasio m.

gymnasium /gɪm'nɑziəm/ n. gimnasio m.

gymnast /'dʒɪmnæst/ n. gimnasta m. & f.

gymnastic /dʒɪm'næstɪk/ a. gimnástico.

gymnastics /dʒɪm'næstɪks/ n. gimnasia f.

gynecologist /,gainɪ'kɒlədʒɪst/ n. ginecólogo, -ga m. & f.

gynecology /,gainɪ'kɒlədʒi/ n. ginecología f.

gypsum /'dʒɪpsəm/ n. yeso m.

Gypsy /'dʒɪpsi/ a. & n. gitano -na.

gyrate /'dʒaireit/ v. girar.

gyroscope /'dʒairə,skoup/ n. giroscopio m.

H

habeas corpus /'heibiəs 'kɔrpəs/ habeas corpus m.

haberdasher /'hæbər,dæʃər/ n. camisero m.

haberdashery /'hæbər,dæʃəri/ n. camisería f.

habiliment /hə'bɪləmənt/ n. vestuario m.

habit /'hæbɪt/ n. costumbre f., hábito m. **be in the h. of,** estar acostumbrado a; soler.

habitable /'hæbɪtəbəl/ a. habitable.

habitat /'hæbɪ,tæt/ n. habitación f., ambiente m.

habitation /,hæbɪ'teiʃən/ n. habitación f.

habitual /hə'bɪtʃuəl/ a. habitual.

habituate /hə'bɪtʃu,eit/ v. habituar.

habitué /hə'bɪtʃu,ei/ n. parroquiano m.

hack /hæk/ n. 1. coche de alquiler. —v. 2. tajar.

hacker /'hækər/ n. pirata m. & f.

hackneyed /'hæknid/ a. trillado.

hacksaw /'hæk,sɔ/ n. sierra para cortar metal f.

haddock /'hædək/ n. merluza f.

haft /hæft/ n. mango m.

hag /hæg, hɑg/ n. bruja f.

haggard /'hægərd/ a. trasnochado.

haggle /'hægəl/ v. regatear.

hail /heil/ n. 1. granizo; (greeting) saludo m. —v. 2. granizar; saludar.

Hail Mary /'mɛari/ Ave María m.

hailstone /'heil,stoun/ n. piedra de granizo f.

hailstorm /'heil,stɔrm/ n. granizada f.

hair /hɛr/ n. pelo; cabello m.

haircut /'hɛr,kʌt/ n. corte de pelo.

hairdo /'hɛr,du/ n. peinado m.

hairdresser /'hɛr,drɛsər/ n. peluquero m.

hair dryer /'draiər/ secador de pelo, secador m.

hairpin /'hɛr,pɪn/ n. horquilla f.; gancho m.

hair's-breadth /'hɛrz,brɛdθ/ n. ancho de un pelo m.

hairspray /'hɛrsprei/ n. aerosol para cabello.

hairy /'hɛri/ a. peludo.

halcyon /'hælsiən/ n. 1. alcedón f. —a. 2. tranquilo.

hale /heil/ a. sano.

half /hæf/ a. 1. medio. —n. 2. mitad f.

half-and-half /'hæf ən 'hæf/ a. mitad y mitad.

half-baked /'hæf 'beikt/ a. medio crudo.

half-breed /'hæf ,brid/ n. mestizo m.

half brother n. medio hermano m.

half-hearted /'hæf'hɑrtɪd/ a. sin entusiasmo.

half-mast /'hæf 'mæst/ a. & n. media asta m.

halfpenny /'heipəni/ n. medio penique m.

halfway /'hæf'wei/ adv. a medio camino.

half-wit /'hæf ,wɪt/ n. bobo m.

halibut /'hæləbət/ n. hipogloso m.

hall /hɔl/ n. corredor m.; (for assembling) sala f. **city h.,** ayuntamiento m.

hallmark /'hɔl,mɑrk/ n. marca del contraste f.

hallow /'hælou/ v. consagrar.

Halloween /,hælə'win/ n. víspera de Todos los Santos f.

hallucination /hə,lusə'neiʃən/ n. alucinación f.

hallway /'hɔl,wei/ n. pasadizo m.

halo /'heilou/ n. halo m.; corona f.

halt /hɔlt/ a. 1. cojo. —n. 2. parada f. —v. 3. parar. —interj. 4. ¡alto!

halter /'hɔltər/ n. cabestro m.

halve /hæv/ v. dividir en dos partes.

halyard /'hælyərd/ n. driza f.

ham /hæm/ n. jamón m.

hamburger /'hæm,bɜrgər/ n. albóndiga f.

hamlet /'hæmlɪt/ n. aldea f.

hammer /'hæmər/ n. 1. martillo m. —v. 2. martillar.

hammock /'hæmək/ n. hamaca f.

hamper /'hæmpər/ n. canasta f., cesto m.

hamstring /'hæm,strɪŋ/ n. 1. tendón de la corva m. —v. 2. desjarretar.

hand /hænd/ n. 1. mano f. **on the other h.,** en cambio. —v. 2. pasar. **h. over,** entregar.

handbag /'hænd,bæg/ n. cartera f.

handball /'hænd,bɔl/ n. pelota f.

handbook /'hænd,bʊk/ n. manual m.

handbrake /'hændbreik/ n. freno de mano m.

handcuff /'hænd,kʌf/ n. esposa v. esposar.

handful /'hændfʊl/ n. puñado m.

handicap /'hændi,kæp/ n. desventaja f.

handicraft /'hændi,kræft/ n. artífice m.; destreza manual.

handiwork /'hændi,wɜrk/ n. artefacto m.

handkerchief /'hæŋkərtʃɪf/ n. pañuelo m.

handle /'hændl/ n. 1. mango m. —v. 2. manejar.

hand luggage equipaje de mano m.

handmade /'hænd'meid/ a. hecho a mano.

handmaid /'hænd,meid/ n. criada de mano, sirvienta f.

hand organ organillo m.

handsome /'hænsəm/ a. guapo; hermoso.

hand-to-hand /'hænd tə 'hænd/ adv. de mano a mano.

handwriting /'hænd,raitɪŋ/ n. escritura f.

handy /'hændi/ a. diestro; útil; a la mano.

hang /hæŋ/ v. colgar; ahorcar.

hangar /'hæŋər/ n. hangar m.

hangdog /'hæŋ,dɒg/ a. & n. camastrón m.

hanger /'hæŋər/ n. colgador, gancho m.

hanger-on /'hæŋər 'ɒn/ n. dependiente; mogollón m.

hang glider /'glaidər/ aparato para vuelo libre, delta, ala delta.

hanging /'hæŋɪŋ/ n. 1. ahorcadura f. —a. 2. colgante.

hangman /'hæŋmən/ n. verdugo m.

hangnail /'hæŋ,neil/ n. padrastro m.

hang out v. enarbolar.

hangover /'hæŋ,ouvər/ n. resaca f.

hangup /'hæŋʌp/ n. tara (psicológica) f.

hank /hæŋk/ n. madeja f.

hanker /'hæŋkər/ v. ansiar; apetecer.

haphazard /'hæp'hæzərd/ a. casual.

happen /'hæpən/ v. acontecer, suceder, pasar.

happening /'hæpənɪŋ/ n. acontecimiento m.

happiness /'hæpɪnɪs/ n. felicidad; dicha f.

happy /'hæpi/ a. feliz; contento; dichoso.

happy-go-lucky /ˈhæpi gou ˈlʌki/ *a.* *&* *n.* descuidado *m.*
harakiri /ˈhɑrəˈkɪəri/ *n.* harakiri (suicidio japonés) *m.*
harangue /həˈræŋ/ *n.* **1.** arenga *f.* —*v.* **2.** arengar.
harass /həˈræs/ *v.* acosar; atormentar.
harbinger /ˈhɑrbɪndʒər/ *n.* presagio *m.*
harbor /ˈhɑrbər/ *n.* **1.** puerto; albergue *m.* —*v.* **2.** abrigar.
hard /hɑrd/ *a.* **1.** duro; difícil. —*adv.* **2.** mucho.
hard coal antracita *m.*
hard disk disco duro *m.*
harden /ˈhɑrdn̩/ *v.* endurecer.
hard-headed /ˈhɑrd ˈhɛdɪd/ *a.* terco.
hard-hearted /ˈhɑrdˈhɑrtɪd/ *a.* empedernido.
hardiness /ˈhɑrdinɪs/ *n.* vigor *m.*
hardly /ˈhɑrdli/ *adv.* apenas.
hardness /ˈhɑrdnɪs/ *n.* dureza; dificultad *f.*
hardship /ˈhɑrdʃɪp/ *n.* penalidad *f.*; trabajo *m.*
hardware /ˈhɑrdˌwɛər/ *n.* hardware *m.*; (computer) quincalla *f.*
hardwood /ˈhɑrdˌwʊd/ *n.* madera dura *f.*
hardy /ˈhɑrdi/ *a.* fuerte, robusto.
hare /hɛər/ *n.* liebre *f.*
harebrained /ˈhɛərˌbreind/ *a.* tolondro.
harelip /ˈhɛərˌlɪp/ *n.* **1.** labio leporino *m.* —*a.* **2.** labihendido.
harem /ˈhɛərəm/ *n.* harén *m.*
hark /hɑrk/ *v.* escuchar; atender.
Harlequin /ˈhɑrləkwɪn/ *n.* arlequín *m.*
harlot /ˈhɑrlət/ *n.* ramera *f.*
harm /hɑrm/ *n.* **1.** mal, daño; perjuicio *m.* —*v.* **2.** dañar.
harmful /ˈhɑrmfəl/ *a.* dañoso.
harmless /ˈhɑrmlɪs/ *a.* inocente.
harmonic /hɑrˈmɒnɪk/ *n.* armónico *m.*
harmonica /hɑrˈmɒnɪkə/ *n.* armónica *f.*
harmonious /hɑrˈmouniəs/ *a.* armonioso.
harmonize /ˈhɑrməˌnaiz/ *v.* armonizar.
harmony /ˈhɑrməni/ *n.* armonía *f.*
harness /ˈhɑrnɪs/ *n.* arnés *m.*
harp /hɑrp/ *n.* arpa *f.*
harpoon /hɑrˈpun/ *n.* arpón *m.*
harridan /ˈhærɪdn̩/ *n.* vieja regañona *f.*
harrow /ˈhærou/ *n.* **1.** rastro *m.*; grada *f.* —*v.* **2.** gradar.
harry /ˈhæri/ *v.* acosar.
harsh /hɑrʃ/ *a.* áspero.
harshness /ˈhɑrʃnɪs/ *n.* aspereza *f.*
harvest /ˈhɑrvɪst/ *n.* **1.** cosecha *f.* —*v.* **2.** cosechar.
hash /hæʃ/ *n.* picadillo *m.*
hashish /ˈhæʃiʃ/ *n.* haxis *m.*
hasn't /ˈhæzənt/ *v.* no tiene (neg. + tener).
hassle /ˈhæsəl/ *n.* lío *m.*, molestia *f.*; controversia *f.*
hassock /ˈhæsək/ *n.* cojín *m.*
haste /heist/ *n.* prisa *f.*
hasten /ˈheisən/ *v.* apresurarse, darse prisa.
hasty /ˈheisti/ *a.* apresurado.
hat /hæt/ *n.* sombrero *m.*
hat box /ˈhætˌbɒks/ sombrerera *f.*
hatch /hætʃ/ *n.* **1.** *Naut.* cuartel *m.* —*v.* **2.** incubar; *Fig.* tramar.
hatchery /ˈhætʃəri/ *n.* criadero *m.*
hatchet /ˈhætʃɪt/ *n.* hacha pequeña.
hate /heit/ *n.* **1.** odio *m.* —*v.* **2.** odiar, detestar.
hateful /ˈheitfəl/ *a.* detestable.
hatred /ˈheitrɪd/ *n.* odio *m.*
haughtiness /ˈhɔtinɪs/ *n.* arrogancia *f.*
haughty /ˈhɔti/ *a.* altivo.
haul /hɔl/ *n.* **1.** (fishery) redada *f.* —*v.* **2.** tirar, halar.
haunch /hɔntʃ/ *n.* anca *f.*
haunt /hɔnt/ *n.* **1.** lugar frecuentado. —*v.* **2.** frecuentar, andar por.
have /hæv; *unstressed* həv, əv/ *v.* tener; haber.
haven /ˈheivən/ *n.* puerto; asilo *m.*
haven't /ˈhævənt/ *v.* no tiene (neg. + tener).
havoc /ˈhævək/ *n.* ruina *f.*
hawk /hɔk/ *n.* halcón *m.*
hawker /ˈhɔkər/ *n.* buhonero *m.*
hawser /ˈhɔzər/ *n.* cable *m.*
hawthorn /ˈhɔˌθɔrn/ *n.* espino *m.*
hay /hei/ *n.* heno *m.*
hay fever *n.* fiebre del heno *f.*
hayfield /ˈheifild/ *n.* henar *m.*
hayloft /ˈheiˌlɔft/ *n.* henil *m.*
haystack /ˈheiˌstæk/ *n.* hacina de heno *f.*
hazard /ˈhæzərd/ *n.* **1.** azar *m.* —*v.* **2.** aventurar.
hazardous /ˈhæzərdəs/ *a.* peligroso.
haze /heiz/ *n.* niebla *f.*
hazel /ˈheizəl/ *n.* avellano *m.*
hazelnut /ˈheizəlˌnʌt/ avellana *f.*
hazy /ˈheizi/ *a.* brumoso.
he /hei/ *pron.* él *m.*
head /hɛd/ *n.* **1.** cabeza *f.*; jefe *m.* —*v.* **2.** dirigir; encabezar.
headache /ˈhɛdˌeik/ *n.* dolor de cabeza *m.*
headband /ˈhɛdˌbænd/ *n.* venda para cabeza *f.*
headfirst /ˈhɛdˈfɜrst/ *adv.* de cabeza.
headgear /ˈhɛdˌgɪər/ *n.* tocado *m.*
headlight /ˈhɛdˌlait/ *n.* linterna delantera *f.*, farol de tope *m.*
headline /ˈhɛdˌlain/ *n.* encabezado *m.*
headlong /ˈhɛdˌlɔŋ/ *a.* precipitoso.
head-on /ˈhɛd ˈɒn/ *adv.* de frente.
headphones /ˈhɛdˌfounz/ *n.pl.* auriculares *m.pl.*
headquarters /ˈhɛdˌkwɔrtərz/ *n.* jefatura *f.*; *Mil.* cuartel general.
headstone /ˈhɛdˌstoun/ *n.* lápida mortuoria *f.*
headstrong /ˈhɛdˌstrɔŋ/ *a.* terco.
headwaiter /ˈhɛdˈweitər/ jefe de comedor *m.* *&* *f.*
headwaters /ˈhɛdˌwɔtərz/ *n.* cabeceras *f.pl.*
headway /ˈhɛdˌwei/ *n.* avance *m.*, progreso *m.*
headwork /ˈhɛdˌwɜrk/ *n.* trabajo mental *m.*
heady /ˈhɛdi/ *a.* impetuoso.
heal /hil/ *v.* curar, sanar.
health /hɛlθ/ *n.* salud *f.*
healthful /ˈhɛlθfəl/ *a.* saludable.
healthy /ˈhɛlθi/ *a.* sano; salubre.
heap /hip/ *n.* montón *m.*
hear /hɪər/ *v.* oír. **h. from,** tener noticias de. **h. about, h. of,** oír hablar de.
hearing /ˈhɪərɪŋ/ *n.* oído *m.*
hearing aid audífono *m.*
hearsay /ˈhɪərˌsei/ *n.* rumor *m.*
hearse /hɜrs/ *n.* ataúd *m.*
heart /hɑrt/ *n.* corazón; ánimo *m.* **by h.,** de memoria. **have h. trouble** padecer del corazón.
heartache /ˈhɑrtˌeik/ *n.* angustia *f.*
heart attack ataque cardíaco, infarto, infarto de miocardio *m.*
heartbreak /ˈhɑrtˌbreik/ *n.* angustia *f.*; pesar *m.*
heartbroken /ˈhɑrtˌbroukən/ *a.* acongojado.
heartburn /ˈhɑrtˌbɜrn/ *n.* acedía *f.*, ardor de estómago *m.*
heartfelt /ˈhɑrtˌfɛlt/ *a.* sentido.
hearth /hɑrθ/ *n.* hogar *m.*, chimenea *f.*
heartless /ˈhɑrtlɪs/ *a.* empedernido.
heartsick /ˈhɑrtˌsɪk/ *a.* desconsolado.
heart-stricken /ˈhɑrt ˈstrɪkən/ *a.* afligido.
heart-to-heart /ˈhɑrt tə ˈhɑrt/ *adv.* franco; sincero.
hearty /ˈhɑrti/ *a.* cordial; vigoroso.
heat /hit/ *n.* **1.** calor; ardor *m.*; calefacción *f.* —*v.* **2.** calentar.
heated /ˈhitɪd/ *a.* acalorado.
heater /ˈhitər/ *n.* calentador *m.*
heath /hiθ/ *n.* matorral *m.*
heathen /ˈhiðən/ *a.* *&* *n.* pagano -na.
heather /ˈhɛðər/ *n.* brezo *m.*
heating /ˈhitɪŋ/ *n.* calefacción *f.*
heatstroke /ˈhitˌstrouk/ *n.* insolación *f.*
heat wave onda de calor *f.*
heave /hiv/ *v.* tirar.
heaven /ˈhɛvən/ *n.* cielo *m.*
heavenly /ˈhɛvənli/ *a.* divino.
heavy /ˈhɛvi/ *a.* pesado; oneroso.
Hebrew /ˈhibru/ *a.* *&* *n.* hebreo -ea.
hectic /ˈhɛktɪk/ *a.* turbulento.
hedge /hɛdʒ/ *n.* seto *m.*
hedgehog /ˈhɛdʒˌhɒg/ *n.* erizo *m.*
hedonism /ˈhidn̩ˌɪzəm/ *n.* hedonismo *m.*
heed /hid/ *n.* **1.** cuidado *m.* —*v.* **2.** atender.
heedless /ˈhidlɪs/ *a.* desatento; incauto.
heel /hil/ *n.* talón *m.*; (of shoe) tacón *m.*
heifer /ˈhɛfər/ *n.* novilla *f.*
height /hait/ *n.* altura *f.*
heighten /ˈhaitn̩/ *n.* elevar; exaltar.
heinous /ˈheinəs/ *a.* nefando.
heir /ɛər/ **heiress** *n.* heredero -ra.
helicopter /ˈhɛlɪˌkɒptər/ *n.* helicóptero *m.*
heliotrope /ˈhiliəˌtroup/ *n.* heliotropo *m.*
helium /ˈhiliəm/ *n.* helio *m.*
hell /hɛl/ *n.* infierno *m.*
Hellenism /ˈhɛləˌnɪzəm/ *n.* helenismo *m.*
hellish /ˈhɛlɪʃ/ *a.* infernal.
hello /hɛˈlou/ *interj.* ¡hola!; (on telephone) aló; bueno.
helm /hɛlm/ *n.* timón *m.*
helmet /ˈhɛlmɪt/ *n.* yelmo, casco *m.*
helmsman /ˈhɛlmzmən/ *n.* limonero *m.*
help /hɛlp/ *n.* **1.** ayuda *f.* **help!** ¡socorro! —*v.* **2.** ayudar. **h. oneself,** servirse. **can't help (but),** no poder menos de.
helper /ˈhɛlpər/ *n.* ayudante *m.*
helpful /ˈhɛlpfəl/ *a.* útil; servicial.
helpfulness /ˈhɛlpfəlnɪs/ *n.* utilidad *f.*
helpless /ˈhɛlplɪs/ *a.* imposibilitado.
hem /hɛm/ *n.* **1.** ribete *m.* —*v.* **2.** ribetear.
hemisphere /ˈhɛmɪˌsfɪər/ *n.* hemisferio *m.*
hemlock /ˈhɛmˌlɒk/ *n.* abeto *m.*
hemoglobin /ˈhiməˌgloubɪn/ *n.* hemoglobina *f.*
hemophilia /ˌhiməˈfɪliə/ *n.* hemofilia *f.*
hemorrhage /ˈhɛmərɪdʒ/ *n.* hemorragia *f.*
hemorrhoids /ˈhɛməˌrɔidz/ *n.* hemorroides *f.pl.*
hemp /hɛmp/ *n.* cáñamo *m.*
hemstitch /ˈhɛmˌstɪtʃ/ *n.* **1.** vainica *f.* —*v.* **2.** hacer una vainica.
hen /hɛn/ *n.* gallina *f.*
hence /hɛns/ *adv.* por lo tanto.
henceforth /ˌhɛnsˈfɔrθ/ *adv.* de aquí en adelante.
henchman /ˈhɛntʃmən/ *n.* paniaguado *m.*
henna /ˈhɛnə/ *n.* alheña *f.*
hepatitis /ˌhɛpəˈtaitɪs/ *n.* hepatitis *f.*
her /hɜr; *unstressed* hər, ər/ *a.* **1.** su. —*pron.* **2.** ella; la; le.
herald /ˈhɛrəld/ *n.* heraldo *m.*
heraldic /hɛˈrældɪk/ *a.* heráldico.
heraldry /ˈhɛrəldri/ *n.* heráldica *f.*
herb /ɜrb; *esp. Brit.* hɜrb/ *n.* yerba, hierba *f.*
herbaceous /hɜrˈbeiʃəs, ɜr-/ *a.* herbáceo.
herbarium /hɜrˈbɛəriəm, ɜr-/ *n.* herbario *m.*
herd /hɜrd/ *n.* **1.** hato, rebaño *m.* —*v.* **2.** reunir en hatos.
here /hɪər/ *adv.* aquí; acá.
hereafter /hɪərˈæftər/ *adv.* en lo futuro.
hereby /hɪərˈbai/ *adv.* por éstas, por la presente.
hereditary /həˈrɛdɪˌtɛri/ *a.* hereditario.
heredity /həˈrɛdɪti/ *n.* herencia *f.*
herein /hɪərˈɪn/ *adv.* aquí dentro; incluso.
heresy /ˈhɛrəsi/ *n.* herejía *f.*
heretic /ˈhɛrɪtɪk/ *a.* **1.** herético. —*n.* **2.** hereje *m.* *&* *f.*
heretical /həˈrɛtɪkəl/ *a.* herético.
heretofore /ˌhɪərtəˈfɔr/ *adv.* hasta ahora.
herewith /hɪərˈwɪθ/ *adv.* con esto, adjunto.
heritage /ˈhɛrɪtɪdʒ/ *n.* herencia *f.*
hermetic /hɜrˈmɛtɪk/ *a.* hermético.
hermit /ˈhɜrmɪt/ *n.* ermitaño *m.*
hernia /ˈhɜrniə/ *n.* hernia *f.*
hero /ˈhɪərou/ *n.* héroe *m.*
heroic /hɪˈrouɪk/ *a.* heroico.
heroically /hɪˈrouɪkəli/ *adv.* heroicamente.
heroin /ˈhɛrouɪn/ *n.* heroína *f.*
heroine /ˈhɛrouɪn/ *n.* heroína *f.*
heroism /ˈhɛrouˌɪzəm/ *n.* heroísmo *m.*
heron /ˈhɛrən/ *n.* garza *f.*
herring /ˈhɛrɪŋ/ *n.* arenque *m.*
hers /hɜrz/ *pron.* suyo, de ella.
herself /hərˈsɛlf/ *pron.* sí, sí misma, se. **she h.,** ella misma. **with h.,** consigo.
hertz /hɜrts/ *n.* hertzio *m.*
hesitancy /ˈhɛzɪtənsi/ *n.* hesitación *f.*
hesitant /ˈhɛzɪtənt/ *a.* indeciso.
hesitate /ˈhɛzɪˌteit/ *v.* vacilar.
hesitation /ˌhɛzɪˈteiʃən/ *n.* duda; vacilación *f.*
heterogeneous /ˌhɛtərəˈdʒiniəs/ *a.* heterogéneo.
heterosexual /ˌhɛtərəˈsɛkʃuəl/ *a.* heterosexual.
hexagon /ˈhɛksəˌgɒn/ *n.* hexágono *m.*
hibernate /ˈhaibərˌneit/ *v.* invernar.
hibernation /ˌhaibərˈneiʃən/ *n.* invernada *f.*
hibiscus /haiˈbɪskəs/ *n.* hibisco *m.*
hiccup /ˈhɪkʌp/ *n.* **1.** hipo *m.* —*v.* **2.** tener hipo.
hickory /ˈhɪkəri/ *n.* nogal americano *m.*
hidden /ˈhɪdn̩/ *a.* oculto; escondido.
hide /haid/ *n.* **1.** cuero *m.*; piel *f.* —*v.* **2.** esconder; ocultar.
hideous /ˈhɪdiəs/ *a.* horrible.
hide-out /ˈhaid ˌaut/ *n.* escondite *m.*
hiding place /ˈhaidɪŋ/ escondrijo *m.*
hierarchy /ˈhaiəˌrɑrki/ *n.* jerarquía *f.*
high /hai/ *a.* alto, elevado; (in price) caro.
highbrow /ˈhaiˌbrau/ *n.* erudito *m.*
highfalutin /ˌhaifəˈlutn̩/ *a.* pomposo, presumido.
high fidelity de alta fidelidad.
highlighter /ˈhaiˌlaitər/ *n.* marcador *m.*
highly /ˈhaili/ *adv.* altamente; sumamente.
high school escuela secundaria *f.*
highway /ˈhaiˌwei/ *n.* carretera *f.*; camino real *m.*
hijacker /ˈhaiˌdʒækər/ *n.* secuestrador, pirata de aviones *m.*
hike /haik/ *n.* caminata *f.*
hilarious /hɪˈlɛəriəs/ *a.* alegre, bullicioso.
hilarity /hɪˈlærɪti/ *n.* hilaridad *f.*
hill /hɪl/ *n.* colina *f.*; cerro *m.*; **down h.,** cuesta abajo. **up h.,** cuesta arriba.
hilly /ˈhɪli/ *a.* accidentado.
hilt /hɪlt/ *n.* puño *m.* **up to the h.,** a fondo.
him /hɪm/ *pron.* él; lo; le.
himself /hɪmˈsɛlf/ *pron.* sí, sí mismo; se. **he h.,** él mismo. **with h.,** consigo.
hinder /ˈhɪndər/ *v.* impedir.
hindmost /ˈhaindˌmoust/ *a.* último.
hindquarter /ˈhaindˌkwɔrtər/ *n.* cuarto trasero *m.*
hindrance /ˈhɪndrəns/ *n.* obstáculo *m.*
hinge /hɪndʒ/ *n.* **1.** gozne *m.* —*v.* **2.** engoznar. **h. on,** depender de.
hint /hɪnt/ *n.* **1.** insinuación *f.*; indicio *m.* —*v.* **2.** insinuar.

hip /hɪp/ n. cadera f.
hippopotamus /ˌhɪpə'pɒtəməs/ n. hipopótamo m.
hire /haɪʳ/ v. alquilar.
his /hɪz; unstressed ɪz/ a. **1.** su. —pron. **2.** suyo, de él.
Hispanic /hɪ'spænɪk/ a. hispano.
hiss /hɪs/ v. silbar, sisear.
historian /hɪ'stɔriən/ n. historiador m.
historic /hɪ'stɔrɪk/ **historical** a. histórico.
history /'hɪstəri/ n. historia f.
histrionic /ˌhɪstri'ɒnɪk/ a. histriónico.
hit /hɪt/ n. **1.** golpe m.; Colloq. éxito m.; (Internet) hit m. —v. **2.** golpear.
hitch /hɪtʃ/ v. amarrar; enganchar.
hitchhike /'hɪtʃ,haik/ v. hacer autostop.
hitchhiker /'hɪtʃ,haikər/ n. autostopista f.
hitchhiking /'hɪtʃ,haikɪŋ/ n. autostop m.
hither /'hɪðər/ adv. acá, hacia acá.
hitherto /'hɪðər,tu/ adv. hasta ahora.
hive /haiv/ n. colmena f.
hives /haivz/ n. urticaria f.
hoard /hɔrd/ n. **1.** acumulación f. —v. **2.** acaparar; atesorar.
hoarse /hɔrs/ a. ronco.
hoax /houks/ n. **1.** engaño m. —v. **2.** engañar.
hobby /'hɒbi/ n. afición f., pasatiempo m.
hobgoblin /hɒb,gɒblɪn/ n. trasgo m.
hobnob /'hɒb,nɒb/ v. tener intimidad.
hobo /'houbou/ n. vagabundo m.
hockey /'hɒki/ n. hockey m. **ice-h.**, hockey sobre hielo.
hod /hɒd/ n. esparavel m.
hodgepodge /'hɒdʒ,pɒdʒ/ n. baturrillo m.; mezcolanza f.
hoe /hou/ n. **1.** azada f. —v. **2.** cultivar con azada.
hog /hɔg/ n. cerdo, puerco m.
hoist /hɔist/ n. **1.** grúa f., elevador m. —v. **2.** elevar, enarbolar.
hold /hould/ n. **1.** presa f.; agarro m.; Naut. bodega f. **to get h. of,** conseguir, apoderarse de. —v. **2.** tener; detener; sujetar; celebrar.
holder /'houldər/ n. tenedor m. **cigarette h.,** boquilla f.
holdup /'hould,ʌp/ n. salteamiento m.
hole /houl/ n. agujero; hoyo; hueco m.
holiday /'hɒli,dei/ n. día de fiesta.
holiness /'houlinis/ n. santidad f.
Holland /'hɒlənd/ n. Holanda f.
hollow /'hɒlou/ a. **1.** hueco. —n. **2.** cavidad f. **3.** ahuecar; excavar.
holly /'hɒli/ n. acebo m.
hollyhock /'hɒli,hɒk/ n. malva real f.
holocaust /'hɒlə,kɔst/ n. holocausto m.
hologram /'hɒlə,græm/ n. holograma m.
holography /hə'lɒgrəfi/ n. holografía f.
holster /'houlstər/ n. pistolera f.
holy /'houli/ a. santo.
Holy See Santa Sede f.
Holy Spirit Espíritu Santo m.
Holy Week Semana Santa f.
homage /'hɒmɪdʒ/ n. homenaje m.
home /houm/ n. casa, morada f; hogar m. **at h.,** en casa. **to go h.,** ir a casa.
home appliance electrodoméstica m.
home computer ordenador doméstico m., computadora doméstica f.
homeland /'houm,lænd/ n. patria f.
homely /'houmli/ a. feo; casero.
home rule n. autonomía f.
homesick /'houm,sɪk/ a. nostálgico.
homespun /'houm,spʌn/ a. casero; tocho.
homeward /'houmwərd/ adv. hacia casa.
homework /'houm,wɜrk/ n. deberes m.pl.
homicide /'hɒmə,said/ n. homicida m. & f.

homily /'hɒməli/ n. homilía f.
homogeneous /ˌhoumə'dʒiniəs/ a. homogéneo.
homogenize /hə'mɒdʒə,naiz/ v. homogenizar.
homosexual /ˌhoumə'sɛkʃuəl/ n. & a. homosexual m.
Honduras /hɒn'dʊrəs/ n. Honduras f.
hone /houn/ n. **1.** piedra de afilar f. —v. **2.** afilar.
honest /'ɒnɪst/ a. honrado, honesto; sincero.
honestly /'ɒnɪstli/ adv. honradamente; de veras.
honesty /'ɒnəsti/ n. honradez, honestidad f.
honey /'hʌni/ n. miel f.
honeybee /'hʌni,bi/ n. abeja obrera f.
honeymoon /'hʌni,mun/ n. luna de miel.
honeysuckle /'hʌni,sʌkəl/ n. madreselva f.
honor /'ɒnər/ n. **1.** honra f.; honor m. —v. **2.** honrar.
honorable /'ɒnərəbəl/ a. honorable; ilustre.
honorary /'ɒnə,rɛri/ a. honorario.
hood /hʊd/ n. capota; capucha f.; Auto. cubierta del motor.
hoodlum /'hudləm/ n. pillo m., rufián m.
hoodwink /'hʊd,wɪŋk/ v. engañar.
hoof /hʊf/ n. pezuña f.
hook /hʊk/ n. **1.** gancho m. —v. **2.** enganchar.
hooligan /'huligən/ n. gamberro -rra.
hoop /hup/ n. cerco m.
hop /hɒp/ n. **1.** salto m. —v. **2.** saltar.
hope /houp/ n. **1.** esperanza f. —v. **2.** esperar.
hopeful /'houpfəl/ a. lleno de esperanzas.
hopeless /'houplɪs/ a. desesperado; sin remedio.
horde /hɔrd/ n. horda f.
horehound /'hɔr,haund/ n. marrubio m.
horizon /hə'raizən/ n. horizonte m.
horizontal /ˌhɔrə'zɒntl/ a. horizontal.
hormone /'hɔrmoun/ n. hormón m.
horn /hɔrn/ n. cuerno m.; (music) trompa f.; Auto. bocina f.
hornet /'hɔrnɪt/ n. avispón m.
horny /'hɔrni/ a. córneo; calloso.
horoscope /'hɔrə,skoup/ n. horóscopo m.
horrendous /hə'rɛndəs/ a. horrendo.
horrible /'hɔrəbəl/ a. horrible.
horrid /'hɔrɪd/ a. horrible.
horrify /'hɔrə,fai/ v. horrorizar.
horror /'hɔrər/ n. horror m.
horror film película de terror f.
hors d'oeuvre /ɔr 'dɜrv/ n. entremés m.
horse /hɔrs/ n. caballo m. **to ride a h.,** cabalgar.
horseback /'hɔrs,bæk/ n. **on h.,** a caballo. **to ride h.,** montar a caballo.
horseback riding equitación f.
horsefly /'hɔrs,flai/ n. tábano m.
horsehair /'hɔrs,hɛər/ n. pelo de caballo m.; tela de crin f.
horseman /'hɔrsmən/ n. jinete m.
horsemanship /'hɔrsmən,ʃɪp/ n. manejo m., equitación f.
horsepower /'hɔrs,pauər/ n. caballo de fuerza m.
horse race carrera de caballos f.
horseradish /'hɔrs,rædɪʃ/ n. rábano picante m.
horseshoe /'hɔrs,ʃu/ n. herradura f.
hortatory /'hɔrtə,tɔri/ a. exhortatorio.
horticulture /'hɔrtɪ,kʌltʃər/ n. horticultura f.
hose /houz/ n. medias f.pl; (garden) manguera f.
hosiery /'houʒəri/ n. calcetería f.
hospitable /'hɒspɪtəbəl/ a. hospitalario.
hospital /'hɒspɪtl/ n. hospital m.
hospitality /ˌhɒspɪ'tælɪti/ n. hospitalidad f.

hospitalization /ˌhɒspɪtlɪ'zeiʃən/ n. hospitalización f.
hospitalize /'hɒspɪtl,aiz/ v. hospitalizar.
host /houst/ n. anfitrión m., dueño de la casa; Relig. hostia f.
hostage /'hɒstɪdʒ/ n. rehén m.
hostel /'hɒstl/ n. hostería f.
hostelry /'hɒstlri/ n. fonda f., parador m.
hostess /'houstɪs/ n. anfitriona f., dueña de la casa.
hostile /'hɒstl/ a. hostil.
hostility /hɒ'stɪlɪti/ n. hostilidad f.
hot /hɒt/ a. caliente; (sauce) picante. **to be h.,** tener calor; (weather) hacer calor.
hotbed /'hɒt,bɛd/ n. estercolero m. Fig. foco m.
hot dog perrito caliente m.
hotel /hou'tɛl/ n. hotel m.
hotelier /ˌoutəl'yei, ˌhoutl'ɪər/ n. hotelero -ra.
hot-headed /'hɒt 'hɛdɪd/ a. turbulento, alborotadizo.
hothouse /'hɒt,haus/ n. invernáculo m.
hot-water bottle /'hɒt 'wɔtər/ bolsa de agua caliente f.
hound /haund/ n. **1.** sabueso m. —v. **2.** perseguir; seguir la pista.
hour /auʳ/ n. hora f.
hourglass /'auʳr,glæs/ n. reloj de arena m.
hourly /'auʳrli/ a. **1.** por horas. —adv. **2.** a cada hora.
house /n haus; v hauz/ n. **1.** casa f.; Theat. público m. —v. **2.** alojar, albergar.
housefly /'haus,flai/ n. mosca ordinaria f.
household /'haus,hould/ n. familia f.; casa f.
housekeeper /'haus,kipər/ n. ama de llaves.
housemaid /'haus,meid/ n. criada f., sirvienta f.
housewife /'haus,waif/ n. ama de casa.
housework /'haus,wɜrk/ n. tareas domésticas.
hovel /'hʌvəl/ n. choza f.
hover /'hʌvər/ v. revolotear.
hovercraft /'hʌvər,kræft/ n. aerodeslizador m.
how /hau/ adv. cómo. **h. much,** cuánto. **h. many,** cuántos. **h. far,** a qué distancia.
however /hau'ɛvər/ adv. como quiera; sin embargo.
howl /haul/ n. **1.** aullido m. —v. **2.** aullar.
HTML abbr. (HyperText Markup Language) Lenguaje de Marcado de Hipertexto m.
hub /hʌb/ n. centro m.; eje m. **h. of a wheel,** cubo de la rueda m.
hubbub /'hʌbʌb/ n. alboroto m., bulla f.
hue /hyu/ n. matiz; color m.
hug /hʌg/ n. **1.** abrazo m. —v. **2.** abrazar.
huge /hyudʒ/ a. enorme.
hulk /hʌlk/ n. casco de buque m.
hull /hʌl/ n. **1.** cáscara f.; (naval) casco m. —v. **2.** decascarar.
hum /hʌm/ n. **1.** zumbido m. —v. **2.** tararear; zumbar.
human /'hyumən/ a. & n. humano -na.
human being ser humano m.
humane /hyu'mein/ a. humano, humanitario.
humanism /'hyumə,nɪzəm/ n. humanidad f.; benevolencia f.
humanitarian /hyu,mænɪ'tɛəriən/ a. humanitario.
humanity /hyu'mænɪti/ n. humanidad f.
humanly /'hyumənli/ a. humanamente.
humble /'hʌmbəl/ a. humilde.

humbug /'hʌm,bʌg/ n. farsa f., embaucador m.
humdrum /'hʌm,drʌm/ a. monótono.
humid /'hyumɪd/ a. húmedo.
humidity /hyu'mɪdɪti/ n. humedad f.
humiliate /hyu'mɪli,eit/ v. humillar.
humiliation /hyu,mɪli'eiʃən/ n. mortificación f.; bochorno m.
humility /hyu'mɪlɪti/ n. humildad f.
humor /'hyumər/ n. **1.** humor; capricho m. —v. **2.** complacer.
humorist /'hyumərɪst/ n. humorista m.
humorous /'hyumərəs/ a. divertido.
hump /hʌmp/ n. joroba f.
humpback /'hʌmp,bæk/ n. jorobado m.
humus /'hyuməs/ n. humus m.
hunch /hʌntʃ/ n. giba f.; (idea) corazonada f.
hunchback /'hʌntʃ,bæk/ n. jorobado m.
hundred /'hʌndrɪd/ a. & pron. **1.** cien, ciento. **200,** doscientos. **300,** trescientos. **400,** cuatrocientos. **500,** quinientos. **600,** seiscientos. **700,** setecientos. **800,** ochocientos. **900,** novecientos. —n. **2.** centenar m.
hundredth /'hʌndrɪdθ/ n. & a. centésimo m.
Hungarian /hʌŋ'gɛəriən/ a. & n. húngaro -ra.
Hungary /'hʌŋgəri/ Hungría f.
hunger /'hʌŋgər/ n. hambre f.
hunger strike huelga de hambre f.
hungry /'hʌŋgri/ a. hambriento. **to be h.,** tener hambre.
hunt /hʌnt/ n. **1.** caza f. —v. **2.** cazar. **h. up,** buscar.
hunter /'hʌntər/ n. cazador m.
hunting /'hʌntɪŋ/ n. caza f. **to go h.,** ir de caza.
hurdle /'hɜrdl/ n. zarzo m., valla f.; dificultad f.
hurl /hɜrl/ v. arrojar.
hurricane /'hɜrɪ,kein/ n. huracán m.
hurry /'hɜri/ n. **1.** prisa f. **to be in a h.,** tener prisa. —v. **2.** apresurar; darse prisa.
hurt /hɜrt/ n. **1.** daño, perjuicio m. —v. **2.** dañar; lastimar; doler; ofender.
hurtful /'hɜrtfəl/ a. perjudicial, dañino.
hurtle /'hɜrtl/ v. lanzar.
husband /'hʌzbənd/ n. marido, esposo m.
husk /hʌsk/ n. **1.** cáscara f. —v. **2.** descascarar.
husky /'hʌski/ a. fornido.
hustle /'hʌsəl/ v. empujar.
hustle and bustle ajetreo m.
hut /hʌt/ n. choza f.
hyacinth /'haiəsɪnθ/ n. jacinto m.
hybrid /'haibrɪd/ a. híbrido.
hydrangea /hai'dreindʒə/ n. hortensia f.
hydraulic /hai'drɔlɪk/ a. hidráulico.
hydroelectric /ˌhaidrouɪ'lɛktrɪk/ a. hidroeléctrico.
hydrogen /'haidrədʒən/ n. hidrógeno m.
hydrophobia /ˌhaidrə'foubiə/ n. hidrofobia. f.
hydroplane /'haidrə,plein/ n. hidroavión m.
hydrotherapy /ˌhaidrə'θɛrəpi/ n. hidroterapia f.
hyena /hai'inə/ n. hiena f.
hygiene /'haidʒin/ n. higiene f.
hygienic /ˌhaidʒi'ɛnɪk/ a. higiénico.
hymn /hɪm/ n. himno m.
hymnal /'hɪmnl/ n. himnario m.
hype /haip/ n. Colloq. **1.** bomba publicitaria f. —v. **2.** promocionar a bombo y platillo.
hypercritical /ˌhaipər'krɪtɪkəl/ a. hipercrítico.
hyperlink /'haipər,lɪŋk/ n. (Internet) hiperenlace m.
hypermarket /'haipər,mɑrkɪt/ n. hipermercado m.
hypertension /ˌhaipər'tɛnʃən/ n. hipertensión f.

hypertext /'haɪpər,tɛkst/ *n.* (Internet) hipertexto *m.*

hyphen /'haɪfən/ *n.* guión *m.*

hyphenate /'haɪfə,neɪt/ *v.* separar con guión.

hypnosis /hɪp'noʊsɪs/ *n.* hipnosis *f.*

hypnotic /hɪp'nɒtɪk/ *a.* hipnótico.

hypnotism /'hɪpnə,tɪzəm/ *n.* hipnotismo *m.*

hypnotize /'hɪpnə,taɪz/ *v.* hipnotizar.

hypochondria /,haɪpə'kɒndriə/ *n.* hipocondría *f.*

hypochondriac /,haɪpə'kɒndri,æk/ *n.* & *a.* hipocondríaco *m.*

hypocrisy /hɪ'pɒkrəsi/ *n.* hipocresía *f.*

hypocrite /'hɪpəkrɪt/ *n.* hipócrita *m.* & *f.*

hypocritical /,hɪpə'krɪtɪkəl/ *a.* hipócrita.

hypodermic /,haɪpə'dɜrmɪk/ *a.* hipodérmico.

hypotenuse /haɪ'pɒtn,us/ *n.* hipotenusa *f.*

hypothesis /haɪ'pɒθəsɪs/ *n.* hipótesis *f.*

hypothetical /,haɪpə'θɛtɪkəl/ *a.* hipotético.

hysterectomy /,hɪstə'rɛktəmi/ *n.* histerectomía *f.*

hysteria /hɪ'stɛriə/ **hysterics** *n.* histeria *f.*

hysterical /hɪ'stɛrɪkəl/ *a.* histérico.

I

I /aɪ/ *pron.* yo.

iambic /aɪ'æmbɪk/ *a.* yámbico.

ice /aɪs/ *n.* hielo *m.*

iceberg /'aɪsbɜrg/ *n.* iceberg *m.*

icebox /'aɪs,bɒks/ *n.* refrigerador *m.*

ice cream helado, mantecado *m.;* **i.-c. cone,** barquillo de helado; **i.-c. parlor** heladería *f.*

ice cube cubito de hielo *m.*

ice skate patín de cuchilla *m.*

icon /'aɪkɒn/ *n.* icón *m.*

icy /'aɪsi/ *a.* helado; indiferente.

idea /aɪ'diə/ *n.* idea *f.*

ideal /aɪ'diəl/ *a.* ideal.

idealism /aɪ'diə,lɪzəm/ *n.* idealismo *m.*

idealist /aɪ'diəlɪst/ *n.* idealista *m.* & *f.*

idealistic /aɪ,diə'lɪstɪk/ *a.* idealista.

idealize /aɪ'diə,laɪz/ *v.* idealizar.

ideally /aɪ'diəli/ *adv.* idealmente.

identical /aɪ'dɛntɪkəl/ *a.* idéntico.

identifiable /aɪ,dɛntɪ'faɪəbəl/ *a.* identificable.

identification /aɪ,dɛntəfɪ'keɪʃən/ *n.* identificación *f.* **i. papers,** cédula de identidad *f.*

identify /aɪ'dɛntə,faɪ/ *v.* identificar.

identity /aɪ'dɛntɪti/ *n.* identidad *f.*

ideology /,aɪdi'ɒlədʒi/ *n.* ideología *f.*

idiocy /'ɪdiəsi/ *n.* idiotez *f.*

idiom /'ɪdiəm/ *n.* modismo *m.;* idioma *m.*

idiot /'ɪdiət/ *n.* idiota *m.* & *f.*

idiotic /,ɪdi'ɒtɪk/ *a.* idiota, tonto.

idle /'aɪdl/ *a.* desocupado; perezoso.

idleness /'aɪdlnɪs/ *n.* ociosidad, pereza *f.*

idol /'aɪdl/ *n.* ídolo *m.*

idolatry /aɪ'dɒlətri/ *n.* idolatría *f.*

idolize /'aɪdl,aɪz/ *v.* idolatrar.

idyl /'aɪdl/ *n.* idilio *m.*

idyllic /aɪ'dɪlɪk/ *a.* idílico.

if /ɪf/ *conj.* si. **even if,** aunque.

ignite /ɪg'naɪt/ *v.* encender.

ignition /ɪg'nɪʃən/ *n.* ignición *f.*

ignoble /ɪg'noʊbəl/ *a.* innoble, indigno.

ignominious /,ɪgnə'mɪniəs/ *a.* ignominioso.

ignoramus /,ɪgnə'reɪməs/ *n.* ignorante *m.*

ignorance /'ɪgnərəns/ *n.* ignorancia *f.*

ignorant /'ɪgnərənt/ *a.* ignorante. **to be i. of,** ignorar.

ignore /ɪg'nɔr/ *v.* desconocer, pasar por alto.

ill /ɪl/ *a.* enfermo, malo.

illegal /ɪ'ligəl/ *a.* ilegal.

illegible /ɪ'lɛdʒəbəl/ *a.* ilegible.

illegibly /ɪ'lɛdʒəbli/ *a.* ilegiblemente.

illegitimacy /,ɪlɪ'dʒɪtəməsi/ *n.* ilegitimidad *f.*

illegitimate /,ɪlɪ'dʒɪtəmɪt/ *a.* ilegítimo; desautorizado.

illicit /ɪ'lɪsɪt/ *a.* ilícito.

illiteracy /ɪ'lɪtərəsi/ *n.* analfabetismo *m.*

illiterate /ɪ'lɪtərɪt/ *a.* & *n.* analfabeto -ta.

illness /'ɪlnɪs/ *n.* enfermedad, maldad *f.*

illogical /ɪ'lɒdʒɪkəl/ *a.* ilógico.

illuminate /ɪ'lumə,neɪt/ *v.* iluminar.

illumination /ɪ,lumə'neɪʃən/ *n.* iluminación *f.*

illusion /ɪ'luʒən/ *n.* ilusión *f.;* ensueño *m.*

illusive /ɪ'lusɪv/ *a.* ilusivo.

illustrate /'ɪlə,streɪt/ *v.* ilustrar; ejemplificar.

illustration /,ɪlə'streɪʃən/ *n.* ilustración *f.;* ejemplo; grabado *m.*

illustrative /ɪ'lʌstrətɪv/ *a.* ilustrativo.

illustrious /ɪ'lʌstriəs/ *a.* ilustre.

ill will *n.* malevolencia *f.*

image /'ɪmɪdʒ/ *n.* imagen, estatua *f.*

imagery /'ɪmɪdʒri/ *n.* imaginación *f.*

imaginable /ɪ'mædʒənəbəl/ *a.* imaginable.

imaginary /ɪ'mædʒə,nɛri/ *a.* imaginario.

imagination /ɪ,mædʒə'neɪʃən/ *n.* imaginación *f.*

imaginative /ɪ'mædʒənətɪv/ *a.* imaginativo.

imagine /ɪ'mædʒɪn/ *v.* imaginarse, figurarse.

imam /ɪ'mɑm/ *n.* imán *m.*

imbecile /'ɪmbəsɪl/ *n.* & *a.* imbécil *m.*

imitate /'ɪmɪ,teɪt/ *v.* imitar.

imitation /,ɪmɪ'teɪʃən/ *n.* imitación *f.*

imitative /'ɪmɪ,teɪtɪv/ *a.* imitativo.

immaculate /ɪ'mækyəlɪt/ *a.* inmaculado.

immanent /'ɪmənənt/ *a.* inmanente.

immaterial /,ɪmə'tɪəriəl/ *a.* inmaterial; sin importancia.

immature /,ɪmə'tʃʊr/ *a.* inmaturo.

immediate /ɪ'midiɪt/ *a.* inmediato.

immediately /ɪ'midiɪtli/ *adv.* inmediatamente.

immense /ɪ'mɛns/ *a.* inmenso.

immerse /ɪ'mɜrs/ *v.* sumergir.

immigrant /'ɪmɪgrənt/ *n.* & *a.* inmigrante *m.* & *f.*

immigrate /'ɪmɪ,greɪt/ *v.* inmigrar.

imminent /'ɪmənənt/ *a.* inminente.

immobile /ɪ'moʊbəl/ *a.* inmóvil.

immoderate /ɪ'mɒdərɪt/ *a.* inmoderado.

immodest /ɪ'mɒdɪst/ *a.* inmodesto; atrevido.

immoral /ɪ'mɔrəl/ *a.* inmoral.

immorality /,ɪmə'rælɪti/ *n.* inmoralidad *f.*

immorally /ɪ'mɔrəli/ *adv.* licenciosamente.

immortal /ɪ'mɔrtl/ *a.* inmortal.

immortality /,ɪmɔr'tælɪti/ *n.* inmortalidad *f.*

immortalize /ɪ'mɔrtl,aɪz/ *v.* inmortalizar.

immune /ɪ'myun/ *a.* inmune.

immunity /ɪ'myunɪti/ *n.* inmunidad *f.*

immunize /'ɪmyə,naɪz/ *v.* inmunizar.

impact /'ɪmpækt/ *n.* impacto *m.*

impair /ɪm'pɛər/ *v.* empeorar, perjudicar.

impale /ɪm'peɪl/ *v.* empalar.

impart /ɪm'pɑrt/ *v.* impartir, comunicar.

impartial /ɪm'pɑrʃəl/ *a.* imparcial.

impatience /ɪm'peɪʃəns/ *n.* impaciencia *f.*

impatient /ɪm'peɪʃənt/ *a.* impaciente.

impede /ɪm'pid/ *v.* impedir, estorbar.

impediment /ɪm'pɛdəmənt/ *n.* impedimento *m.*

impel /ɪm'pɛl/ *v.* impeler.

impenetrable /ɪm'pɛnɪtrəbəl/ *a.* impenetrable.

impenitent /ɪm'pɛnɪtənt/ *n.* & *a.* impenitente *m.*

imperative /ɪm'pɛrətɪv/ *a.* imperativo.

imperceptible /,ɪmpər'sɛptəbəl/ *a.* imperceptible.

imperfect /ɪm'pɜrfɪkt/ *a.* imperfecto.

imperfection /,ɪmpər'fɛkʃən/ *n.* imperfección *f.*

imperial /ɪm'pɪəriəl/ *a.* imperial.

imperialism /ɪm'pɪəriə,lɪzəm/ *n.* imperialismo *m.*

imperious /ɪm'pɪəriəs/ *a.* imperioso.

impersonal /ɪm'pɜrsənl/ *a.* impersonal.

impersonate /ɪm'pɜrsə,neɪt/ *v.* personificar; imitar.

impersonation /ɪm,pɜrsə'neɪʃən/ *n.* personificación *f.;* imitación *f.*

impertinence /ɪm'pɜrtnəns/ *n.* impertinencia *f.*

impervious /ɪm'pɜrviəs/ *a.* impermeable.

impetuous /ɪm'pɛtʃuəs/ *a.* impetuoso.

impetus /'ɪmpɪtəs/ *n.* ímpetu *m.,* impulso *m.*

impinge /ɪm'pɪndʒ/ *v.* tropezar; infringir.

implacable /ɪm'plækəbəl/ *a.* implacable.

implant /ɪm'plænt/ *v.* implantar; inculcar.

implement /'ɪmpləmənt/ *n.* herramienta *f.*

implicate /'ɪmplɪ,keɪt/ *v.* implicar; embrollar.

implication /,ɪmplɪ'keɪʃən/ *n.* inferencia *f.;* complicidad *f.*

implicit /ɪm'plɪsɪt/ *a.* implícito.

implied /ɪm'plaɪd/ *a.* implícito.

implore /ɪm'plɔr/ *v.* implorar.

imply /ɪm'plaɪ/ *v.* significar; dar a entender.

impolite /,ɪmpə'laɪt/ *a.* descortés.

import /n. 'ɪmpɔrt; v. ɪm'pɔrt/ *n.* **1.** importación *f.* —*v.* **2.** importar.

importance /ɪm'pɔrtns/ *n.* importancia *f.*

important /ɪm'pɔrtnt/ *a.* importante.

importation /,ɪmpɔr'teɪʃən/ *n.* importación *f.*

importune /,ɪmpɔr'tun/ *v.* importunar.

impose /ɪm'poʊz/ *v.* imponer.

imposition /,ɪmpə'zɪʃən/ *n.* imposición *f.*

impossibility /ɪm,pɒsə'bɪlɪti/ *n.* imposibilidad *f.*

impossible /ɪm'pɒsəbəl/ *a.* imposible.

impotence /'ɪmpətəns/ *n.* impotencia *f.*

impotent /'ɪmpətənt/ *a.* impotente.

impregnable /ɪm'prɛgnəbəl/ *a.* impregnable.

impregnate /ɪm'prɛgneɪt/ *v.* impregnar; fecundizar.

impresario /,ɪmprə'sɑri,oʊ/ *n.* empresario *m.*

impress /ɪm'prɛs/ *v.* impresionar.

impression /ɪm'prɛʃən/ *n.* impresión *f.*

impressive /ɪm'prɛsɪv/ *a.* imponente.

imprison /ɪm'prɪzən/ *v.* encarcelar.

imprisonment /ɪm'prɪzənmənt/ *n.* prisión, encarcelación *f.*

improbable /ɪm'prɒbəbəl/ *a.* improbable.

impromptu /ɪm'prɒmptu/ *a.* extemporáneo.

improper /ɪm'prɒpər/ *a.* impropio.

improve /ɪm'pruv/ *v.* mejorar; progresar.

improvement /ɪm'pruvmənt/ *n.* mejoramiento; progreso *m.*

improvise /'ɪmprə,vaɪz/ *v.* improvisar.

impudent /'ɪmpyədənt/ *a.* descarado.

impugn /ɪm'pyun/ *v.* impugnar.

impulse /'ɪmpʌls/ *n.* impulso *m.*

impulsive /ɪm'pʌlsɪv/ *a.* impulsivo.

impunity /ɪm'pyunɪti/ *n.* impunidad *f.*

impure /ɪm'pyʊr/ *a.* impuro.

impurity /ɪm'pyʊrɪti/ *n.* impureza *f.;* deshonestidad *f.*

impute /ɪm'pyut/ *v.* imputar.

in /ɪn/ *prep.* **1.** en; dentro de. —*adv.* **2.** adentro.

inadvertent /,ɪnəd'vɜrtnt/ *a.* inadvertido.

inalienable /ɪn'eɪlyənəbəl/ *a.* inalienable.

inane /ɪ'neɪn/ *a.* mentecato.

inaugural /ɪn'ɔgyərəl/ *a.* inaugural.

inaugurate /ɪn'ɔgyə,reɪt/ *v.* inaugurar.

inauguration /ɪn,ɔgyə'reɪʃən/ *n.* inauguración *f.*

Inca /'ɪŋkə/ *n.* inca *m.*

incandescent /,ɪnkən'dɛsənt/ *a.* incandescente.

incantation /,ɪnkæn'teɪʃən/ *n.* encantación *f.,* conjuro *m.*

incapacitate /,ɪnkə'pæsɪ,teɪt/ *v.* incapacitar.

incarcerate /ɪn'kɑrsə,reɪt/ *v.* encarcelar.

incarnate /ɪn'kɑrnɪt/ *a.* encarnado; personificado.

incarnation /,ɪnkɑr'neɪʃən/ *n.* encarnación *f.*

incendiary /ɪn'sɛndi,ɛri/ *a.* incendiario.

incense /ɪn'sɛns/ *n.* **1.** incienso *m.* —*v.* **2.** indignar.

incentive /ɪn'sɛntɪv/ *n.* incentivo *m.*

inception /ɪn'sɛpʃən/ *n.* comienzo *m.*

incessant /ɪn'sɛsənt/ *a.* incesante.

incest /'ɪnsɛst/ *n.* incesto *m.*

inch /ɪntʃ/ *n.* pulgada *f.*

incidence /'ɪnsɪdəns/ *n.* incidencia *f.*

incident /'ɪnsɪdənt/ *n.* incidente *m.*

incidental /,ɪnsɪ'dɛntl/ *a.* incidental.

incidentally /,ɪnsɪ'dɛntli/ *adv.* incidentalmente; entre paréntesis.

incinerate /ɪn'sɪnə,reɪt/ *v.* incinerar.

incinerator /ɪn'sɪnə,reɪtər/ *n.* incinerador *m.*

incipient /ɪn'sɪpiənt/ *a.* incipiente.

incision /ɪn'sɪʒən/ *n.* incisión *f.;* cortadura *f.*

incisive /ɪn'saɪsɪv/ *a.* incisivo; mordaz.

incisor /ɪn'saɪzər/ *n.* incisivo *m.*

incite /ɪn'saɪt/ *v.* incitar, instigar.

inclination /,ɪnklə'neɪʃən/ *n.* inclinación *f.;* declive *m.*

incline /n. 'ɪnklaɪn; v. ɪn'klaɪn/ *n.* **1.** pendiente *f.* —*v.* **2.** inclinar.

inclose /ɪn'kloʊz/ *v.* incluir.

include /ɪn'klud/ *v.* incluir, englobar.

including /ɪn'kludɪŋ/ *prep.* incluso.

inclusive /ɪn'klusɪv/ *a.* inclusivo.

incognito /,ɪnkɒg'nitoʊ/ *n.* & *adv.* incógnito *m.*

income /'ɪnkʌm/ *n.* renta *f.;* ingresos *m.pl.*

income tax impuesto sobre la renta *m.*

incomparable /ɪn'kɒmpərəbəl/ *a.* incomparable.

inconvenience /,ɪnkən'vinyəns/ *n.* **1.** incomodidad *f.* —*v.* **2.** incomodar.

inconvenient /,ɪnkən'vinyənt/ *a.* incómodo.

incorporate /ɪn'kɔrpə,reɪt/ *v.* incorporar; dar cuerpo.

incorrigible /ɪn'kɔrɪdʒəbəl/ *a.* incorregible.

increase /ɪn'kris/ *v.* crecer; aumentar.

incredible /ɪn'krɛdəbəl/ *a.* increíble.

incredulity /,ɪnkrɪ'dulɪti/ *n.* incredulidad *f.*

incredulous /ɪn'krɛdʒələs/ *a.* incrédulo.

increment /'ɪnkrəmənt/ *n.* incremento *m.,* aumento *m.*

incriminate /ɪn'krɪmə,neɪt/ *v.* incriminar.

incrimination /ɪn,krɪmə'neɪʃən/ *n.* incriminación *f.*

incrust /ɪn'krʌst/ *v.* incrustar.

incubator /'ɪnkyə‚beitər/ n. incubadora f.

inculcate /ɪn'kʌlkeit/ v. inculcar.

incumbency /ɪn'kʌmbənsi/ n. incumbencia f.

incumbent /ɪn'kʌmbənt/ a. obligatorio; colocado sobre.

incur /ɪn'kɜr/ v. incurrir.

incurable /ɪn'kyurəbəl/ a. incurable.

indebted /ɪn'dɛtɪd/ a. obligado; adeudado.

indeed /ɪn'did/ adv. verdaderamente, de veras. **no i.**, de ninguna manera.

indefatigable /‚ɪndɪ'fætɪgəbəl/ a. incansable.

indefinite /ɪn'dɛfənɪt/ a. indefinido.

indefinitely /ɪn'dɛfənɪtli/ adv. indefinidamente.

indelible /ɪn'dɛləbəl/ a. indeleble.

indemnify /ɪn'dɛmnə‚fai/ v. indemnizar.

indemnity /ɪn'dɛmnɪti/ n. indemnificación f.

indent /ɪn'dɛnt/ n. **1.** diente f., mella f. —v. **2.** indentar, mellar.

indentation /‚ɪndɛn'teiʃən/ n. indentación f.

independence /‚ɪndɪ'pɛndəns/ n. independencia f.

independent /‚ɪndɪ'pɛndənt/ a. independiente.

in-depth /'ɪn 'dɛpθ/ adj. en profundidad.

index /'ɪndɛks/ n. índice m.; (of book) tabla f.

index card ficha f.

index finger dedo índice m.

India /'ɪndiə/ n. India f.

Indian /'ɪndiən/ a. & n. indio -dia.

indicate /'ɪndɪ‚keit/ v. indicar.

indication /‚ɪndɪ'keiʃən/ n. indicación f.

indicative /ɪn'dɪkətɪv/ a. & n. indicativo m.

indict /ɪn'dait/ v. encausar.

indictment /ɪn'daitmənt/ n. (law) sumaria; denuncia f.

indifference /ɪn'dɪfərəns/ n. indiferencia f.

indifferent /ɪn'dɪfərənt/ a. indiferente.

indigenous /ɪn'dɪdʒənəs/ a. indígena.

indigent /'ɪndɪdʒənt/ a. indigente, pobre.

indigestion /‚ɪndɪ'dʒɛstʃən/ n. indigestión f.

indignant /ɪn'dɪgnənt/ a. indignado.

indignation /‚ɪndɪg'neiʃən/ n. indignación f.

indignity /ɪn'dɪgnɪti/ n. indignidad f.

indirect /‚ɪndə'rɛkt/ a. indirecto.

indiscreet /‚ɪndɪ'skrit/ a. indiscreto.

indiscretion /‚ɪndɪ'skrɛʃən/ n. indiscreción f.

indiscriminate /‚ɪndɪ'skrɪmənɪt/ a. promiscuo.

indispensable /‚ɪndɪ'spɛnsəbəl/ a. indispensable.

indisposed /‚ɪndɪ'spouzd/ a. indispuesto.

individual /‚ɪndə'vɪdʒuəl/ a. & n. individuo m.

individuality /‚ɪndə‚vɪdʒu'ælɪti/ n. individualidad f.

individually /‚ɪndə'vɪdʒuəli/ adv. individualmente.

indivisible /‚ɪndə'vɪzəbəl/ a. indivisible.

indoctrinate /ɪn'dɒktrə‚neit/ v. doctrinar, enseñar.

indolent /'ɪndlənt/ a. indolente.

indoor /'ɪn‚dɔr/ a. **1.** interior. **indoors** —adv. **2.** en casa; bajo techo.

indorse /ɪn'dɔrs/ v. endosar.

induce /ɪn'dus/ v. inducir, persuadir.

induct /ɪn'dʌkt/ v. instalar, iniciar.

induction /ɪn'dʌkʃən/ n. introducción f.; instalación f.

inductive /ɪn'dʌktɪv/ a. inductivo; introductor.

indulge /ɪn'dʌldʒ/ v. favorecer. **i. in,** entregarse a.

indulgence /ɪn'dʌldʒəns/ n. indulgencia f.

indulgent /ɪn'dʌldʒənt/ a. indulgente.

industrial /ɪn'dʌstriəl/ a. industrial.

industrialist /ɪn'dʌstriəlɪst/ n. industrial m.

industrial park polígono industrial m.

industrious /ɪn'dʌstriəs/ a. industrioso, trabajador.

industry /'ɪndəstri/ n. industria f.

inedible /ɪn'ɛdəbəl/ a. incomible.

ineligible /ɪn'ɛlɪdʒəbəl/ a. inelegible.

inept /ɪn'ɛpt/ a. inepto.

inert /ɪn'ɜrt/ a. inerte.

inertia /ɪn'ɜrʃə/ n. inercia f.

inevitable /ɪn'ɛvɪtəbəl/ a. inevitable.

inexpensive /‚ɪnɪk'spɛnsɪv/ a. económico.

inexplicable /ɪn'ɛksplɪkəbəl/ a. inexplicable.

infallible /ɪn'fæləbəl/ a. infalible.

infamous /'ɪnfəməs/ a. infame.

infamy /'ɪnfəmi/ n. infamia f.

infancy /'ɪnfənsi/ n. infancia f.

infant /'ɪnfənt/ n. nene m.; criatura f.

infantile /'ɪnfən‚tail/ a. infantil.

infantry /'ɪnfəntri/ n. infantería f.

infatuated /ɪn'fætʃu‚eitɪd/ a. infatuado.

infatuation /ɪn‚fætʃu'eiʃən/ a. encaprichamiento m.

infect /ɪn'fɛkt/ v. infectar.

infection /ɪn'fɛkʃən/ n. infección f.

infectious /ɪn'fɛkʃəs/ a. infeccioso.

infer /ɪn'fɜr/ v. inferir.

inference /'ɪnfərəns/ n. inferencia f.

inferior /ɪn'fɪəriər/ a. inferior.

infernal /ɪn'fɜrnl/ a. infernal.

inferno /ɪn'fɜrnou/ n. infierno m.

infest /ɪn'fɛst/ v. infestar.

infidel /'ɪnfɪdl/ n. **1.** infiel m. & f.; pagano -na. —a. **2.** infiel.

infidelity /‚ɪnfɪ'dɛlɪti/ n. infidelidad f.

infiltrate /ɪn'fɪltreit/ v. infiltrar.

infinite /'ɪnfənɪt/ a. infinito.

infinitesimal /‚ɪnfɪnɪ'tɛsəməl/ a. infinitesimal.

infinitive /ɪn'fɪnɪtɪv/ n. & a. infinitivo m.

infinity /ɪn'fɪnɪti/ n. infinidad f.

infirm /ɪn'fɜrm/ a. enfermizo.

infirmary /ɪn'fɜrməri/ n. hospital m., enfermería f.

infirmity /ɪn'fɜrmɪti/ n. enfermedad f.

inflame /ɪn'fleim/ v. inflamar.

inflammable /ɪn'flæməbəl/ a. inflamable.

inflammation /‚ɪnflə'meiʃən/ n. inflamación f.

inflammatory /ɪn'flæmə‚tɔri/ a. inflamante; Med. inflamatorio.

inflate /ɪn'fleit/ v. inflar.

inflation /ɪn'fleiʃən/ n. inflación f.

inflection /ɪn'flɛkʃən/ n. inflexión f.; (of the voice) modulación de la voz f.

inflict /ɪn'flɪkt/ v. infligir.

infliction /ɪn'flɪkʃən/ n. imposición f.

influence /'ɪnfluəns/ n. **1.** influencia f. —v. **2.** influir en.

influential /‚ɪnflu'ɛnʃəl/ a. influyente.

influenza /‚ɪnflu'ɛnzə/ n. gripe f.

influx /'ɪn‚flʌks/ n. afluencia f.

inform /ɪn'fɔrm/ v. informar. **i. oneself,** enterarse.

informal /ɪn'fɔrməl/ a. informal.

information /‚ɪnfər'meiʃən/ n. informaciones f.pl.

information technology n. informática f.

infrastructure /'ɪnfrə‚strʌktʃər/ n. infraestructura f.

infringe /ɪn'frɪndʒ/ v. infringir.

infuriate /ɪn'fyuri‚eit/ v. enfurecer.

ingenious /ɪn'dʒinyəs/ a. ingenioso.

ingenuity /‚ɪndʒə'nuɪti/ n. ingeniosidad; destreza f.

ingredient /ɪn'gridiənt/ n. ingrediente m.

inhabit /ɪn'hæbɪt/ v. habitar.

inhabitant /ɪn'hæbɪtənt/ n. habitante m. & f.

inhale /ɪn'heil/ v. inhalar.

inherent /ɪn'hɪərənt/ a. inherente.

inherit /ɪn'hɛrɪt/ v. heredar.

inheritance /ɪn'hɛrɪtəns/ n. herencia f.

inhibit /ɪn'hɪbɪt/ v. inhibir.

inhibition /‚ɪnɪ'bɪʃən/ n. inhibición f.

inhuman /ɪn'hyumən/ a. inhumano.

inimical /ɪ'nɪmɪkəl/ a. hostil.

inimitable /ɪ'nɪmɪtəbəl/ a. inimitable.

iniquity /ɪ'nɪkwɪti/ n. iniquidad f.

initial /ɪ'nɪʃəl/ a. inicial f.

initiate /ɪ'nɪʃi‚eit/ v. iniciar.

initiation /ɪ‚nɪʃi'eiʃən/ n. iniciación f.

initiative /ɪ'nɪʃiətɪv/ n. iniciativa f.

inject /ɪn'dʒɛkt/ v. inyectar.

injection /ɪn'dʒɛkʃən/ n. inyección f.

injunction /ɪn'dʒʌŋkʃən/ n. mandato m.; (law) embargo m.

injure /'ɪndʒər/ v. herir; lastimar; ofender.

injurious /ɪn'dʒuriəs/ a. perjudicial.

injury /'ɪndʒəri/ n. herida; afrenta f.; perjuicio m.

injustice /ɪn'dʒʌstɪs/ n. injusticia f.

ink /ɪŋk/ n. tinta f.

inland /'ɪnlænd/ a. **1.** interior. —adv. **2.** tierra adentro.

inlet /'ɪnlɛt/ n. entrada f.; ensenada f.; estuario m.

inmate /'ɪn‚meit/ n. residente m. & f.; (of a prison) preso -sa.

inn /ɪn/ n. posada f.; mesón m.

inner /'ɪnər/ a. interior. **i. tube,** cámara de aire.

innocence /'ɪnəsəns/ n. inocencia f.

innocent /'ɪnəsənt/ a. inocente.

innocuous /ɪ'nɒkyuəs/ a. innocuo.

innovation /‚ɪnə'veiʃən/ n. innovación f.

innuendo /‚ɪnyu'ɛndou/ n. insinuación f.

innumerable /ɪ'numərəbəl/ a. innumerable.

inoculate /ɪ'nɒkyə‚leit/ v. inocular.

inoculation /ɪ‚nɒkyə'leiʃən/ n. inoculación f.

input /'ɪn‚put/ n. aducto m., ingreso m., entrada f.

inquest /'ɪnkwɛst/ n. indagación f.

inquire /ɪn'kwaiᵊr/ v. preguntar; inquirir.

inquiry /ɪn'kwaiᵊri/ n. pregunta; investigación f.

inquisition /‚ɪnkwə'zɪʃən/ n. escudriñamiento m.; (church) Inquisición f.

insane /ɪn'sein/ a. loco. **to go i.,** perder la razón; volverse loco.

insanity /ɪn'sænɪti/ n. locura f., demencia f.

inscribe /ɪn'skraib/ v. inscribir.

inscription /ɪn'skrɪpʃən/ n. inscripción; dedicatoria f.

insect /'ɪnsɛkt/ n. insecto m.

insecticide /ɪn'sɛktə‚said/ n. & a. insecticida m.

inseparable /ɪn'sɛpərəbəl/ a. inseparable.

insert /ɪn'sɜrt/ v. insertar, meter.

insertion /ɪn'sɜrʃən/ n. inserción f.

inside /‚ɪn'said/ a. & n. **1.** interior m. —adv. **2.** adentro, por dentro. **i. out,** al revés. —prep. **3.** dentro de.

insidious /ɪn'sɪdiəs/ a. insidioso.

insight /'ɪn‚sait/ n. perspicacia f.; comprensión f.

insignia /ɪn'sɪgniə/ n. insignias f.pl.

insignificance /‚ɪnsɪg'nɪfɪkəns/ n. insignificancia f.

insignificant /‚ɪnsɪg'nɪfɪkənt/ a. insignificante.

insinuate /ɪn'sɪnyu‚eit/ v. insinuar.

insinuation /ɪn‚sɪnyu'eiʃən/ n. insinuación f.

insipid /ɪn'sɪpɪd/ a. insípido.

insist /ɪn'sɪst/ v. insistir.

insistence /ɪn'sɪstəns/ n. insistencia f.

insistent /ɪn'sɪstənt/ a. insistente.

insolence /'ɪnsələns/ n. insolencia f.

insolent /'ɪnsələnt/ a. insolente.

insomnia /ɪn'sɒmniə/ n. insomnio m.

inspect /ɪn'spɛkt/ v. inspeccionar, examinar.

inspection /ɪn'spɛkʃən/ n. inspección f.

inspector /ɪn'spɛktər/ n. inspector -ora.

inspiration /‚ɪnspə'reiʃən/ n. inspiración f.

inspire /ɪn'spaiᵊr/ v. inspirar.

install /ɪn'stɔl/ v. instalar.

installation /‚ɪnstə'leiʃən/ n. instalación f.

installment /ɪn'stɔlmənt/ n. plazo m.

instance /'ɪnstəns/ n. ocasión f. **for i.,** por ejemplo.

instant /'ɪnstənt/ a. & n. instante m.

instantaneous /‚ɪnstən'teiniəs/ a. instantáneo.

instant coffee café soluble m.

instantly /'ɪnstəntli/ adv. al instante.

instead /ɪn'stɛd/ adv. en lugar de eso. **i. of,** en vez de, en lugar de.

instigate /'ɪnstɪ‚geit/ v. instigar.

instill /ɪn'stɪl/ v. instilar.

instinct /'ɪnstɪŋkt/ n. instinto m. **by i.,** por instinto.

instinctive /ɪn'stɪŋktɪv/ a. instintivo.

instinctively /ɪn'stɪŋktɪvli/ adv. por instinto.

institute /'ɪnstɪ‚tut/ n. **1.** instituto m. —v. **2.** instituir.

institution /‚ɪnstɪ'tuʃən/ n. institución f.

instruct /ɪn'strʌkt/ v. instruir.

instruction /ɪn'strʌkʃən/ n. instrucción f.

instructive /ɪn'strʌktɪv/ a. instructivo.

instructor /ɪn'strʌktər/ n. instructor -ora.

instrument /'ɪnstrəmənt/ n. instrumento m.

instrumental /‚ɪnstrə'mɛntl/ a. instrumental.

insufficient /‚ɪnsə'fɪʃənt/ a. insuficiente.

insular /'ɪnsələr/ a. insular; estrecho de miras.

insulate /'ɪnsə‚leit/ v. aislar.

insulation /‚ɪnsə'leiʃən/ n. aislamiento m.

insulator /'ɪnsə‚leitər/ n. aislador m.

insulin /'ɪnsəlɪn/ n. insulina f.

insult /n. 'ɪnsʌlt; v. ɪn'sʌlt/ n. **1.** insulto m. —v. **2.** insultar.

insuperable /ɪn'supərəbəl/ a. insuperable.

insurance /ɪn'ʃurəns/ n. seguro m.

insure /ɪn'ʃur, -'ʃɜr/ v. asegurar.

insurgent /ɪn'sɜrdʒənt/ a. & n. insurgente m. & f.

insurrection /‚ɪnsə'rɛkʃən/ n. insurrección f.

intact /ɪn'tækt/ a. intacto.

intangible /ɪn'tændʒəbəl/ a. intangible, impalpable.

integral /'ɪntɪgrəl/ a. íntegro.

integrate /'ɪntɪ‚greit/ v. integrar.

integrity /ɪn'tɛgrɪti/ n. integridad f.

intellect /'ɪntl‚ɛkt/ n. intelecto m.

intellectual /‚ɪntl'ɛktʃuəl/ a. & n. intelectual m. & f.

intelligence /ɪn'tɛlɪdʒəns/ n. inteligencia f.

intelligence quotient /'kwouʃənt/ coeficiente intelectual m.

intelligent /ɪn'tɛlɪdʒənt/ a. inteligente.

intelligible /ɪn'tɛlɪdʒəbəl/ a. inteligible.

intend /ɪn'tɛnd/ v. pensar; intentar; destinar.

intense /ɪn'tɛns/ a. intenso.

intensify /ɪn'tɛnsə‚fai/ v. intensificar.

intensity /ɪn'tɛnsɪti/ n. intensidad f.

intensive /ɪn'tɛnsɪv/ a. intensivo.

intensive-care unit /ɪn'tɛnsɪv'kɛər/ unidad de cuidados intensivos, unidad de vigilancia intensiva f.

intent /ɪn'tɛnt/ n. intento m.

intention /ɪn'tɛnʃən/ *n.* intención *f.*

intentional /ɪn'tɛnʃənl̩/ *a.* intencional.

intercede /ˌɪntər'sid/ *v.* interceder.

intercept /ˌɪntər'sɛpt/ *v.* interceptar; detener.

interchange /ˌɪntər'tʃendʒ/ *v.* intercambiar.

interchangeable /ˌɪntər'tʃeindʒəbəl/ *a.* intercambiable.

intercourse /'ɪntərˌkɔrs/ *n.* tráfico *m.;* comunicación *f.;* coito *m.*

interest /'ɪntərɪst/ *n.* **1.** interés *m.* —*v.* **2.** interesar.

interesting /'ɪntərəstɪŋ/ *a.* interesante.

interest rate *n.* tipo de interés *m.*

interface /'ɪntərˌfeis/ *n.* interfaz.

interfere /ˌɪntər'fɪər/ *v.* entrometerse, intervenir. **i. with,** estorbar.

interference /ˌɪntər'fɪərəns/ *n.* intervención *f.;* obstáculo *m.*

interior /ɪn'tɪəriər/ *a.* interior.

interject /ˌɪntər'dʒɛkt/ *v.* interponer; intervenir.

interjection /ˌɪntər'dʒɛkʃən/ *n.* interjección *f.;* interposición *f.*

interlude /'ɪntərˌlud/ *n.* intervalo *m.; Theat.* intermedio *m.;* (music) interludio *m.*

intermediary /ˌɪntər'midiˌɛri/ *n.* intermediario -ria.

intermediate /ˌɪntər'midiˌeit/ *a.* intermedio.

interment /ɪn'tɜrmənt/ *n.* entierro.

intermission /ˌɪntər'mɪʃən/ *n.* intermisión *f.; Theat.* entreacto *m.*

intermittent /ˌɪntər'mɪtn̩t/ *a.* intermitente.

intern /ɪn'tɜrn/ *n.* **1.** interno -na, internado -da. —*v.* **2.** internar.

internal /ɪn'tɜrnl̩/ *a.* interno.

international /ˌɪntər'næʃənl̩/ *a.* internacional.

internationalism /ˌɪntər'næʃənl̩ˌɪzəm/ *n.* internacionalismo *m.*

Internet, the /'ɪntərˌnɛt/ *n.* el Internet *m.*

interpose /ˌɪntər'pouz/ *v.* interponer.

interpret /ɪn'tɜrprɪt/ *v.* interpretar.

interpretation /ɪnˌtɜrprɪ'teiʃən/ *n.* interpretación *f.*

interpreter /ɪn'tɜrprɪtər/ *n.* intérprete *m.* & *f.*

interrogate /ɪn'tɛrəˌgeit/ *v.* interrogar.

interrogation /ɪnˌtɛrə'geiʃən/ *n.* interrogación; pregunta *f.*

interrogative /ˌɪntə'rɒgətɪv/ *a.* interrogativo.

interrupt /ˌɪntə'rʌpt/ *v.* interrumpir.

interruption /ˌɪntə'rʌpʃən/ *n.* interrupción *f.*

intersect /ˌɪntər'sɛkt/ *v.* cortar.

intersection /ˌɪntər'sɛkʃən/ *n.* intersección *f.;* (street) bocacalle *f.*

intersperse /ˌɪntər'spɜrs/ *v.* entremezclar.

interval /'ɪntərvəl/ *n.* intervalo *m.*

intervene /ˌɪntər'vin/ *v.* intervenir.

intervention /ˌɪntər'vɛnʃən/ *n.* intervención *f.*

interview /'ɪntərˌvyu/ *n.* **1.** entrevista *f.* —*v.* **2.** entrevistar.

interviewer /'ɪntərˌvyuər/ *n.* entrevistador -ora *m.* & *f.*

intestine /ɪn'tɛstɪn/ *n.* intestino *m.*

intimacy /'ɪntəməsi/ *n.* intimidad; familiaridad *f.*

intimate /'ɪntəmɪt/ *a.* **1.** íntimo, familiar. —*n.* **2.** amigo -ga íntimo -ma. —*v.* **3.** insinuar.

intimidate /ɪn'tɪmɪˌdeit/ *v.* intimidar.

intimidation /ɪnˌtɪmɪ'deiʃən/ *n.* intimidación *f.*

into /'ɪntu; *unstressed* -tʊ, -tə/ *prep.* en, dentro de.

intonation /ˌɪntou'neiʃən/ *n.* entonación *f.*

intone /ɪn'toun/ *v.* entonar.

intoxicate /ɪn'tɒksɪˌkeit/ *v.* embriagar.

intoxication /ɪnˌtɒksɪ'keiʃən/ *n.* embriaguez *f.*

intravenous /ˌɪntrə'vinəs/ *a.* intravenoso.

intrepid /ɪn'trɛpɪd/ *a.* intrépido.

intricacy /'ɪntrɪkəsi/ *n.* complejidad *f.;* enredo *m.*

intricate /'ɪntrɪkɪt/ *a.* intrincado; complejo.

intrigue /ɪn'trig; *n. also* 'ɪntrig/ *n.* **1.** intriga *f.* —*v.* **2.** intrigar.

intrinsic /ɪn'trɪnsɪk/ *a.* intrínseco.

introduce /ˌɪntrə'dus/ *v.* introducir; (a person) presentar.

introduction /ˌɪntrə'dʌkʃən/ *n.* presentación; introducción *f.*

introductory /ˌɪntrə'dʌktəri/ *a.* introductor; preliminar. **i. offer,** ofrecimiento de presentación *m.*

introvert /'ɪntrəˌvɜrt/ *n.* & *a.* introvertido -da.

intrude /ɪn'trud/ *v.* entremeterse.

intruder /ɪn'trudər/ *n.* intruso -sa.

intuition /ˌɪntu'ɪʃən/ *n.* intuición *f.*

intuitive /ɪn'tuɪtɪv/ *a.* intuitivo.

inundate /'ɪnənˌdeit/ *v.* inundar.

invade /ɪn'veid/ *v.* invadir.

invader /ɪn'veidər/ *n.* invasor -ra.

invalid /ɪn'vælɪd/ *a.* & *n.* inválido -da.

invariable /ɪn'vɛəriəbəl/ *a.* invariable.

invasion /ɪn'veiʒən/ *n.* invasión *f.*

invective /ɪn'vɛktɪv/ *n.* **1.** invectiva *f.* —*a.* **2.** ultrajante.

inveigle /ɪn'veigəl/ *v.* seducir.

invent /ɪn'vɛnt/ *v.* inventar.

invention /ɪn'vɛnʃən/ *n.* invención *f.*

inventive /ɪn'vɛntɪv/ *a.* inventivo.

inventor /ɪn'vɛntər/ *n.* inventor -ra.

inventory /'ɪnvənˌtɔri/ *n.* inventario *m.*

invertebrate /ɪn'vɜrtəbrɪt/ *n.* & *a.* invertebrado *m.*

invest /ɪn'vɛst/ *v.* investir; *Com.* invertir.

investigate /ɪn'vɛstɪˌgeit/ *v.* investigar.

investigation /ɪnˌvɛstɪ'geiʃən/ *n.* investigación *f.*

investment /ɪn'vɛstmənt/ *n.* inversión *f.*

investor /ɪn'vɛstər/ *n.* inversor, -ra.

inveterate /ɪn'vɛtərɪt/ *a.* inveterado.

invidious /ɪn'vɪdiəs/ *a.* abominable, odioso, injusto.

invigorate /ɪn'vɪgəˌreit/ *v.* vigorizar, fortificar.

invincible /ɪn'vɪnsəbəl/ *a.* invencible.

invisible /ɪn'vɪzəbəl/ *a.* invisible.

invitation /ˌɪnvɪ'teiʃən/ *n.* invitación *f.*

invite /ɪn'vait/ *v.* invitar, convidar.

invocation /ˌɪnvə'keiʃən/ *n.* invocación *f.*

invoice /'ɪnvɔis/ *n.* factura *f.*

invoke /ɪn'vouk/ *v.* invocar.

involuntary /ɪn'vɒlənˌtɛri/ *a.* involuntario.

involve /ɪn'vɒlv/ *v.* envolver; implicar.

involved /ɪn'vɒlvd/ *a.* complicado.

invulnerable /ɪn'vʌlnərəbəl/ *a.* invulnerable.

inward /'ɪnwərd/ *adv.* hacia adentro.

inwardly /'ɪnwərdli/ *adv.* interiormente.

iodine /'aiəˌdain/ *n.* iodo *m.*

IQ *abbr.* CI (coeficiente intelectual) *m.*

irate /ai'reit/ *a.* encolerizado.

Ireland /'aiərlənd/ *n.* Irlanda *f.*

iris /'airɪs/ *n. Anat.* iris *m.;* (botany) flor de lis *f.*

Irish /'airɪʃ/ *a.* irlandés.

irk /ɜrk/ *v.* fastidiar.

iron /'aiərn/ *n.* **1.** hierro *m.;* (appliance) plancha *f.* —*v.* **2.** planchar.

ironical /ai'rɒnɪkəl/ *a.* irónico.

ironing board /'aiərnɪŋ/ tabla de planchar *f.*

irony /'airəni/ *n.* ironía *f.*

irrational /ɪ'ræʃənl̩/ *a.* irracional; ilógico.

irregular /ɪ'rɛgyələr/ *a.* irregular.

irregularity /ɪˌrɛgyə'lærɪti/ *n.* irregularidad *f.*

irrelevant /ɪ'rɛləvənt/ *a.* ajeno.

irresistible /ˌɪrɪ'zɪstəbəl/ *a.* irresistible.

irresponsible /ˌɪrɪ'spɒnsəbəl/ *a.* irresponsable.

irreverent /ɪ'rɛvərənt/ *a.* irreverente.

irrevocable /ɪ'rɛvəkəbəl/ *a.* irrevocable.

irrigate /'ɪrɪˌgeit/ *v.* regar; *Med.* irrigar.

irrigation /ˌɪrɪ'geiʃən/ *n.* riego *m.*

irritability /ˌɪrɪtə'bɪlɪti/ *n.* irritabilidad *f.*

irritable /'ɪrɪtəbəl/ *a.* irritable.

irritant /'ɪrɪtn̩t/ *n.* & *a.* irritante *m.*

irritate /'ɪrɪˌteit/ *v.* irritar.

irritation /ˌɪrɪ'teiʃən/ *n.* irritación *f.*

island /'ailənd/ *n.* isla *f.*

isolate /'aisəˌleit/ *v.* aislar.

isolation /ˌaisə'leiʃən/ *n.* aislamiento *m.*

isosceles /ai'sɒsəˌliz/ *a.* isósceles.

issuance /'ɪʃuəns/ *n.* emisión *f.;* publicación *f.*

issue /'ɪʃu/ *n.* **1.** emisión; edición; progenie *f.;* número *m.;* punto en disputa. —*v.* **2.** emitir; publicar.

isthmus /'ɪsməs/ *n.* istmo *m.*

it /ɪt/ *pron.* ello; él, ella; lo, la.

Italian /ɪ'tælyən/ *a.* & *n.* italiano -na.

Italy /'ɪtl̩i/ *n.* Italia *f.*

itch /ɪtʃ/ *n.* **1.** picazón *f.* —*v.* **2.** picar.

item /'aitəm/ *n.* artículo; detalle *m.;* inserción *f.; Com.* renglón *m.*

itemize /'aitəˌmaiz/ *v.* detallar.

itinerant /ai'tɪnərənt/ *n.* **1.** viandante *m.* —*a.* **2.** ambulante.

itinerary /ai'tɪnəˌrɛri/ *n.* itinerario *m.*

its /ɪts/ *a.* su.

itself /ɪt'sɛlf/ *pron.* sí; se.

ivory /'aivəri/ *n.* marfil *m.*

ivy /'aivi/ *n.* hiedra *f.*

J

jab /dʒæb/ *n.* **1.** pinchazo *m.* —*v.* **2.** pinchar.

jack /dʒæk/ *n.* (for lifting) gato *m.;* (cards) sota *f.*

jackal /'dʒækəl/ *n.* chacal *m.*

jackass /'dʒækˌæs/ *n.* asno *m.*

jacket /'dʒækɪt/ *n.* chaqueta *f.;* saco *m.*

jack-of-all-trades /'dʒæk əv 'ɔl 'treidz/ *n.* estuche *m.*

jade /dʒeid/ *n.* (horse) rocín *m.;* (woman) picarona *f.;* (mineral) jade *m.*

jaded /'dʒeidɪd/ *a.* rendido.

jagged /dʒægɪd/ *a.* mellado.

jaguar /'dʒægwɑr/ *n.* jaguar *m.*

jail /dʒeil/ *n.* cárcel *f.*

jailer /'dʒeilər/ *n.* carcelero *m.*

jam /dʒæm/ *n.* **1.** conserva *f.;* aprieto, apretón *m.* —*v.* **2.** apiñar, apretar; trabar.

janitor /'dʒænɪtər/ *n.* portero *m.*

January /'dʒænyuˌɛri/ *n.* enero *m.*

Japan /dʒə'pæn/ *n.* Japón *m.*

Japanese /ˌdʒæpə'niz/ *a.* & *n.* japonés -esa.

jar /dʒɑr/ *n.* **1.** jarro *m.* —*v.* **2.** chocar; agitar.

jargon /'dʒɑrgən/ *n.* jerga *f.*

jasmine /'dʒæzmɪn/ *n.* jazmín *m.*

jaundice /'dʒɔndɪs/ *n.* ictericia *f.*

jaunt /dʒɔnt/ *n.* paseo *m.*

javelin /'dʒævlɪn/ *n.* jabalina *f.*

jaw /dʒɔ/ *n.* quijada *f.*

jay /dʒei/ *n.* grajo *m.*

jazz /dʒæz/ *n.* jazz *m.*

jealous /'dʒɛləs/ *a.* celoso. **to be j.,** tener celos.

jealousy /'dʒɛləsi/ *n.* celos *m.pl.*

jeans /dʒinz/ *n.* vaqueros, tejanos *m.pl.*

jeer /dʒɪər/ *n.* **1.** burla *f.,* mofa *f.* —*v.* **2.** burlar, mofar.

jelly /'dʒɛli/ *n.* jalea *f.*

jellyfish /'dʒɛliˌfɪʃ/ *n.* aguamar *m.*

jeopardize /'dʒɛpərˌdaiz/ *v.* arriesgar.

jeopardy /'dʒɛpərdi/ *n.* riesgo *m.*

jerk /dʒɜrk/ *n.* **1.** sacudida *f.* —*v.* **2.** sacudir.

jerky /'dʒɜrki/ *a.* espasmódico.

Jerusalem /dʒɪ'rusələm/ *n.* Jerusalén *m.*

jest /dʒɛst/ *n.* **1.** broma *f.* —*v.* **2.** bromear.

jester /'dʒɛstər/ *n.* bufón -ona; burlón -ona.

Jesuit /'dʒɛʒuɪt/ *a.* & *n.* jesuíta *m.*

Jesus Christ /'dʒizəs 'kraist/ *n.* Jesucristo *m.*

jet /dʒɛt/ *n.* chorro *m.;* (gas) mechero *m.*

jet lag *n.* defase horario *m.*, inadaptación horaria *f.*

jetsam /'dʒɛtsəm/ *n.* echazón *f.*

jettison /'dʒɛtəsən/ *v.* echar al mar.

jetty /'dʒɛti/ *n.* muelle *m.*

Jew /dʒu/ *n.* judío -día.

jewel /'dʒuəl/ *n.* joya *f.*

jeweler /'dʒuələr/ *n.* joyero -ra.

jewelry /'dʒuəlri/ *n.* joyas *f.pl.* **j. store,** joyería *f.*

Jewish /'dʒuɪʃ/ *a.* judío.

jib /dʒɪb/ *n. Naut.* foque *m.*

jiffy /'dʒɪfi/ *n.* instante *m.*

jig /dʒɪg/ *n.* jiga *f.* **j-saw,** sierra de vaivén *f.*

jilt /dʒɪlt/ *v.* dar calabazas.

jingle /'dʒɪŋgəl/ *n.* **1.** retintín *m.;* rima pueril *f.* —*v.* **2.** retiñir.

jinx /dʒɪŋks/ *n.* **1.** aojo *m.* —*v.* **2.** aojar.

jittery /'dʒɪtəri/ *a.* nervioso.

job /dʒɒb/ *n.* empleo *m.*

jobber /'dʒɒbər/ *n.* destajista *m.* & *f.,* corredor *m.*

jockey /'dʒɒki/ *n.* jockey *m.*

jocular /'dʒɒkyələr/ *a.* jocoso.

jog /dʒɒg/ *n.* empujoncito *m. v.* empujar; estimular. **j. along,** ir a un trote corto.

join /dʒɔin/ *v.* juntar; unir.

joiner /'dʒɔinər/ *n.* ebanista *m.*

joint /dʒɔint/ *n.* juntura *f.*

jointly /'dʒɔintli/ *adv.* conjuntamente.

joke /dʒouk/ *n.* **1.** broma, chanza *f.;* chiste *m.* —*v.* **2.** bromear.

joker /'dʒoukər/ *n.* bromista *m.* & *f.;* comodín *m.*

jolly /'dʒɒli/ *a.* alegre, jovial.

jolt /dʒoult/ *n.* **1.** sacudido *m.* —*v.* **2.** sacudir.

jonquil /'dʒɒŋkwɪl/ *n.* junquillo *m.*

jostle /'dʒɒsəl/ *v.* empujar.

journal /'dʒɜrnl̩/ *n.* diario *m.;* revista *f.*

journalism /'dʒɜrnl̩ˌɪzəm/ *n.* periodismo *m.*

journalist /'dʒɜrnl̩ɪst/ *n.* periodista *m.* & *f.*

journey /'dʒɜrni/ *n.* **1.** viaje *m.;* jornada *f.* —*v.* **2.** viajar.

journeyman /'dʒɜrnimən/ *n.* jornalero *m.*, oficial *m.*

jovial /'dʒouviəl/ *a.* jovial.

jowl /dʒaul/ *n.* carrillo *m.*

joy /dʒɔi/ *n.* alegría *f.*

joyful /'dʒɔifəl/ **joyous** *a.* alegre, gozoso.

jubilant /'dʒubələnt/ *a.* jubiloso.

jubilee /'dʒubəˌli/ *n.* jubileo *m.*

Judaism /'dʒudiˌɪzəm/ *n.* judaísmo *m.*

judge /dʒʌdʒ/ *n.* **1.** juez *m.* & *f.* —*v.* **2.** juzgar.

judgment /'dʒʌddʒmənt/ *n.* juicio *m.*

judicial /dʒu'dɪʃəl/ *a.* judicial.

judiciary /dʒu'dɪʃiˌɛri/ *a.* judiciario.

judicious /dʒu'dɪʃəs/ *a.* juicioso.

jug /dʒʌg/ *n.* jarro *m.*

juggle /'dʒʌgəl/ *v.* escamotear.

juice /dʒus/ *n.* jugo, zumo *m.*

juicy /'dʒusi/ *a.* jugoso.

July /dʒu'lai/ *n.* julio *m.*

jumble /'dʒʌmbəl/ *n.* **1.** revoltillo *m.* —*v.* **2.** arrebujar, revolver.

jump /dʒʌmp/ *n.* **1.** salto *m.* —*v.* **2.** saltar, brincar.

junction /ˈdʒʌŋkʃən/ *n.* confluencia *f.*; (railway) empalme *m.*
juncture /ˈdʒʌŋktʃər/ *n.* juntura *f.*; coyuntura *f.*
June /dʒun/ *n.* junio *m.*
jungle /ˈdʒʌŋgəl/ *n.* jungla, selva *f.*
junior /ˈdʒunyər/ *a.* menor; más joven. **Jr.,** hijo.
juniper /ˈdʒunəpər/ *n.* enebro *m.*
junk /dʒʌŋk/ *n.* basura *f.*
junket /ˈdʒʌŋkɪt/ *n.* **1.** leche cuajada *f.* —*v.* **2.** festejar.
junkie /ˈdʒʌŋki/ *n. Colloq.* yonqui *m. & f.*, toxicómano -na.
junk mail *n.* porpaganda indeseada *f.*, correo basura *m.*
jurisdiction /ˌdʒʊrɪsˈdɪkʃən/ *n.* jurisdicción *f.*
jurisprudence /ˌdʒʊrɪsˈprudns/ *n.* jurisprudencia *f.*
jurist /ˈdʒʊrɪst/ *n.* jurista *m. & f.*
juror /ˈdʒʊrər/ *n.* jurado -da.
jury /ˈdʒʊri/ *n.* jurado *m.*
just /dʒʌst/ *a.* **1.** justo; exacto. —*adv.* **2.** exactamente; (only) sólo. **j. now,** ahora mismo. **to have j.,** acabar de.
justice /ˈdʒʌstɪs/ *n.* justicia *f.*; (person) juez *m. & f.*
justifiable /ˈdʒʌstəˌfaiəbəl/ *a.* justificable.
justification /ˌdʒʌstəfɪˈkeiʃən/ *n.* justificación *f.*
justify /ˈdʒʌstəˌfai/ *v.* justificar.
jut /dʒʌt/ *v.* sobresalir.
jute /dʒut/ *n.* yute *m.*
juvenile /ˈdʒuvənl/ *a.* juvenil.
juvenile delinquency delincuencia de menores, delincuencia juvenil *f.*

K

kaleidoscope /kəˈlaidəˌskoup/ *n.* calidoscopio *m.*
kangaroo /ˌkæŋgəˈru/ *n.* canguro *m.*
karakul /ˈkærəkəl/ *n.* caracul *m.*
karat /ˈkærət/ *n.* quilate *m.*
karate /kəˈrɑti/ *n.* karate *m.*
keel /kil/ *n.* **1.** quilla *f.* —*v.* **2. to k. over,** volcarse.
keen /kin/ *a.* agudo; penetrante.
keep /kip/ *v.* mantener, retener; guardar; preservar. **k. on,** seguir, continuar.
keeper /ˈkipər/ *n.* guardián *m.*
keepsake /ˈkipˌseik/ *n.* recuerdo *m.*
keg /kɛg/ *n.* barrilito *m.*
kennel /ˈkɛnl/ *n.* perrera *f.*
kerchief /ˈkɜrtʃɪf/ *n.* pañuelo *m.*
kernel /ˈkɜrnl/ *n.* pepita *f.*; grano *m.*
kerosene /ˈkɛrəˌsin/ *n.* kerosén *m.*
ketchup /ˈkɛtʃəp/ *n.* salsa de tomate *f.*
kettle /ˈkɛtl/ *n.* caldera, olla *f.*
kettledrum /ˈkɛtlˌdrʌm/ *n.* tímpano *m.*
key /ki/ *n.* llave *f.*; (music) clave *f.*; (piano) tecla *f.*
keyboard /ˈkiˌbɔrd/ *n.* teclado *m.*
keyhole /ˈkiˌhoul/ *n.* bocallave *f.*
keypad /ˈkiˌpæd/ *n.* teclado *m.*
khaki /ˈkæki/ *a.* caqui.
kick /kɪk/ *n.* **1.** patada *f.* —*v.* **2.** patear; *Colloq.* quejarse.
kid /kɪd/ *n.* **1.** cabrito *m.*; *Colloq.* niño -ña, chico -ca. —*v.* **2.** *Colloq.* bromear.
kidnap /ˈkɪdnæp/ *v.* secuestrar.
kidnaper /ˈkɪdnæpər/ *n.* secuestrador -ora.
kidnaping /ˈkɪdnæpɪŋ/ *n.* rapto, secuestro *m.*
kidney /ˈkɪdni/ *n.* riñón *m.*
kidney bean *n.* frijol *m.*
kill /kɪl/ *v.* matar.
killer /ˈkɪlər/ *n.* matador -ora.
killjoy /ˈkɪlˌdʒɔi/ *n.* aguafiestas *m. & f.*
kiln /kɪl/ *n.* horno *m.*
kilogram /ˈkɪləˌgræm/ *n.* kilogramo *m.*
kilohertz /ˈkɪləˌhɜrts/ *n.* kilohercio *m.*
kilometer /kɪˈlɒmɪtər/ *n.* kilómetro *m.*
kilowatt /ˈkɪləˌwɒt/ *n.* kilovatio *m.*
kin /kɪn/ *n.* parentesco *m.*; parientes *m.pl.*
kind /kaind/ *a.* **1.** bondadoso, amable. —*n.* **2.** género *m.*; clase *f.* **k. of,** algo, un poco.
kindergarten /ˈkɪndərˌgɑrtn/ *n.* kindergarten *m.*
kindle /ˈkɪndl/ *v.* encender.
kindling /ˈkɪndlɪŋ/ *n.* encendimiento *m.* **k.-wood,** leña menuda *f.*
kindly /ˈkaindli/ *a.* bondadoso.
kindness /ˈkaindnɪs/ *n.* bondad *f.*
kindred /ˈkɪndrɪd/ *n.* parentesco *m.*
kinetic /kɪˈnɛtɪk/ *a.* cinético.
king /kɪŋ/ *n.* rey *m.*
kingdom /ˈkɪŋdəm/ *n.* reino *m.*
king prawn langostino *m.*
kink /kɪŋk/ *n.* retorcimiento *m.*
kinky /ˈkɪŋki/ *a. Colloq.* pervertidillo; (hair) rizado.
kiosk /ˈkiɒsk/ *n.* kiosco *m.*
kiss /kɪs/ *n.* **1.** beso *m.* —*v.* **2.** besar.
kitchen /ˈkɪtʃən/ *n.* cocina *f.*
kite /kait/ *n.* cometa *f.*
kitten /ˈkɪtn/ *n.* gatito -ta.
kleptomania /ˌklɛptəˈmeiniə/ *n.* cleptomanía *f.*
kleptomaniac /ˌklɛptəˈmeiniæk/ *n.* cleptómano -na.
klutz /klʌts/ *n. Colloq.* torpe, patoso -sa.
knack /næk/ *n.* don *m.*, destreza *f.*
knapsack /ˈnæpˌsæk/ *n.* alforja *f.*
knead /nid/ *v.* amasar.
knee /ni/ *n.* rodilla *f.*
kneecap /ˈniˌkæp/ *n.* rodillera, rótula *f.*
kneel /nil/ *v.* arrodillarse.
knickers /ˈnɪkərz/ *n.* calzón corto *m.*, pantalones *m.pl.*
knife /naif/ *n.* cuchillo *m.*
knight /nait/ *n.* caballero *m.*; (chess) caballo *m.*
knit /nɪt/ *v.* tejer.
knob /nɒb/ *n.* tirador *m.*
knock /nɒk/ *n.* **1.** golpe *m.*; llamada *f.* —*v.* **2.** golpear; tocar, llamar.
knot /nɒt/ *n.* **1.** nudo; lazo *m.* —*v.* **2.** anudar.
knotty /ˈnɒti/ *a.* nudoso.
know /nou/ *v.* saber; (a person) conocer.
knowledge /ˈnɒlɪdʒ/ *n.* conocimiento, saber *m.*
knuckle /ˈnʌkəl/ *n.* nudillo *m.* **k. bone,** jarrete *m.* **to k. under,** ceder a.
Koran /kəˈrɑn/ *n.* Corán *m.*
Korea /kəˈriə/ *n.* Corea *f.*
Korean /kəˈriən/ *a. & n.* coreano.

L

label /ˈleibəl/ *n.* **1.** rótulo *m.* —*v.* **2.** rotular; designar.
labor /ˈleibər/ *n.* **1.** trabajo *m.*; la clase obrera. —*v.* **2.** trabajar.
laboratory /ˈlæbrəˌtɔri/ *n.* laboratorio *m.*
laborer /ˈleibərər/ *n.* trabajador, obrero *m.*
laborious /ləˈbɔriəs/ *a.* laborioso, difícil.
labor union gremio obrero, sindicato *m.*
labyrinth /ˈlæbərɪnθ/ *n.* laberinto *m.*
lace /leis/ *n.* **1.** encaje *m.*; (of shoe) lazo *m.* —*v.* **2.** amarrar.
lacerate /ˈlæsəˌreit/ *v.* lacerar, lastimar.
laceration /ˌlæsəˈreiʃən/ *n.* laceración *f.*, desgarro *m.*
lack /læk/ *n.* **1.** falta *f.* **l. of respect,** desacato *m.* —*v.* **2.** faltar, carecer.
lackadaisical /ˌlækəˈdeizɪkəl/ *a.* indiferente; soñador.
laconic /ləˈkɒnɪk/ *a.* lacónico.
lacquer /ˈlækər/ *n.* **1.** laca *f.*, barniz *m.* —*v.* **2.** laquear, barnizar.
lactic /ˈlæktɪk/ *a.* láctico.
lactose /ˈlæktous/ *n.* lactosa *f.*
ladder /ˈlædər/ *n.* escalera *f.*
ladle /ˈleidl/ *n.* **1.** cucharón *m.* —*v.* **2.** servir con cucharón.
lady /ˈleidi/ *n.* señora, dama *f.*
ladybug /ˈleidiˌbʌg/ *n.* mariquita *f.*
lag /læg/ *n.* **1.** retraso *m.* —*v.* **2.** quedarse atrás.
lagoon /ləˈgun/ *n.* laguna *f.*
laid-back /ˈleid ˈbæk/ *a.* de buen talante, ecuánime, pacífico.
laity /ˈleiɪti/ *n.* laicado *m.*
lake /leik/ *n.* lago *m.*
lamb /læm/ *n.* cordero *m.*
lame /leim/ *a.* **1.** cojo; estropeado. —*v.* **2.** estropear, lisiar; incapacitar.
lament /ləˈmɛnt/ *n.* **1.** lamento *m.* —*v.* **2.** lamentar.
lamentable /ləˈmɛntəbəl/ *a.* lamentable.
lamentation /ˌlæmənˈteiʃən/ *n.* lamento *m.*; lamentación *f.*
laminate /ˈlæməˌneit/ *a.* laminado. *v.* laminar.
lamp /læmp/ *n.* lámpara *f.*
lampoon /læmˈpun/ *n.* **1.** pasquín *m.* —*v.* **2.** pasquinar.
lance /læns/ *n.* **1.** lanza *f.* —*v.* **2.** *Med.* abrir.
land /lænd/ *n.* **1.** país *m.*; tierra *f.* **native l.,** patria *f.* —*v.* **2.** desembarcar; (plane) aterrizar.
landholder /ˈlændˌhouldər/ *n.* hacendado -da.
landing /ˈlændɪŋ/ *n.* (of stairs) descanso, descansillo *m.*; (ship) desembarcadero *m.*; (airplane) aterrizaje *m.*
landlady /ˈlændˌleidi/ **landlord** *n.* propietario -ria.
landmark /ˈlændˌmɑrk/ *n.* mojón *m.*, señal *f.*; rasgo sobresaliente *m.*
landscape /ˈlændˌskeip/ *n.* paisaje *m.*
landslide /ˈlændˌslaid/ *n.* derrumbe *m.*
lane /lein/ *n.* senda *f.*
language /ˈlæŋgwɪdʒ/ *n.* lengua *f.*, idioma; lenguaje *m.*
languid /ˈlæŋgwɪd/ *a.* lánguido.
languish /ˈlæŋgwɪʃ/ *v.* languidecer.
languor /ˈlæŋgər/ *n.* languidez *f.*
lanky /ˈlæŋki/ *a.* larguirucho; desgarbado.
lanolin /ˈlænlɪn/ *n.* lanolina *f.*
lantern /ˈlæntərn/ *n.* linterna *f.*; farol *m.*
lap /læp/ *n.* **1.** regazo *m.*; falda *f.* —*v.* **2.** lamer.
lapel /ləˈpɛl/ *n.* solapa *f.*
lapse /læps/ *n.* **1.** lapso *m.* —*v.* **2.** pasar; decaer; caer en error.
laptop computer /ˈlæpˌtɒp/ ordenador portátil *m.*
larceny /ˈlɑrsəni/ *n.* ratería *f.*
lard /lɑrd/ *n.* manteca de cerdo *f.*
large /lɑrdʒ/ *a.* grande.
largely /ˈlɑrdʒli/ *adv.* ampliamente; mayormente; muy.
largo /ˈlɑrgou/ *n. & a. Mus.* largo *m.*
lariat /ˈlæriət/ *n.* lazo *m.*
lark /lɑrk/ *n.* (bird) alondra *f.*
larva /ˈlɑrvə/ *n.* larva *f.*
laryngitis /ˌlærənˈdʒaitɪs/ *n.* laringitis *f.*
larynx /ˈlærɪŋks/ *n.* laringe *f.*
lascivious /ləˈsɪviəs/ *a.* lascivo.
laser /ˈleizər/ *n.* láser *m.*
lash /læʃ/ *n.* **1.** azote, latigazo *m.* —*v.* **2.** azotar.
lass /læs/ *n.* doncella *f.*
lassitude /ˈlæsɪˌtud/ *n.* lasitud *f.*
lasso /ˈlæsou/ *n.* **1.** lazo *m.* —*v.* **2.** enlazar.
last /læst/ *a.* **1.** pasado; (final) último. **at l.,** por fin. **l. but one,** penúltimo. **l. but two,** antepenútimo. —*v.* **2.** durar.
lasting /ˈlæstɪŋ/ *a.* duradero.
latch /lætʃ/ *n.* aldaba *f.*
late /leit/ *a.* **1.** tardío; (deceased) difunto. **to be l.,** llegar tarde. —*adv.* **2.** tarde.
lately /ˈleitli/ *adv.* recientemente.
latent /ˈleitnt/ *a.* latente.
lateral /ˈlætərəl/ *a.* lateral.
lather /ˈlæðər/ *n.* **1.** espuma de jabón. —*v.* **2.** enjabonar.
Latin /ˈlætn/ *n.* latín *m.*
Latin America /əˈmɛrɪkə/ Hispanoamérica, América Latina *f.*
Latin American hispanoamericano -na.
latitude /ˈlætɪˌtud/ *n.* latitud *f.*
latrine /ləˈtrin/ *n.* letrina *f.*
latter /ˈlætər/ *a.* posterior. **the l.,** éste.
lattice /ˈlætɪs/ *n.* celosía *f.*
laud /lɔd/ *v.* loar.
laudable /ˈlɔdəbəl/ *a.* laudable.
laudanum /ˈlɔdnəm/ *n.* láudano *m.*
laudatory /ˈlɔdəˌtɔri/ *a.* laudatorio.
laugh /læf/ *n.* **1.** risa, risotada *f.* —*v.* **2.** reír. **l. at,** reírse de.
laughable /ˈlæfəbəl/ *a.* risible.
laughter /ˈlæftər/ *n.* risa *f.*
launch /lɔntʃ/ *n.* **1.** *Naut.* lancha *f.* —*v.* **2.** lanzar.
launder /ˈlɔndər/ *v.* lavar y planchar la ropa.
laundry /ˈlɔndri/ *n.* lavandería *f.*
laundryman /ˈlɔndriˌmæn/ *n.* lavandero -ra.
laureate /ˈlɔriɪt/ *n. & a.* laureado -da.
laurel /ˈlɔrəl/ *n.* laurel *m.*
lava /ˈlɑvə/ *n.* lava *f.*
lavatory /ˈlævəˌtɔri/ *n.* lavatorio *m.*
lavender /ˈlævəndər/ *n.* lavándula *f.*
lavish /ˈlævɪʃ/ *a.* **1.** pródigo. —*v.* **2.** prodigar.
law /lɔ/ *n.* ley *f.*; derecho *m.*
lawful /ˈlɔfəl/ *a.* legal.
lawless /ˈlɔlɪs/ *a.* sin ley.
lawn /lɔn/ *n.* césped; prado *m.*
lawn mower /ˈmouər/ *n.* cortacésped *m. & f.*
lawsuit /ˈlɔˌsut/ *n.* pleito *m.*
lawyer /ˈlɔyər/ *n.* abogado *m. & f.*
lax /læks/ *a.* flojo, laxo.
laxative /ˈlæksətɪv/ *n.* purgante *m.*
laxity /ˈlæksɪti/ *n.* laxidad *f.*; flojedad *f.*
lay /lei/ *a.* **1.** secular. —*v.* **2.** poner.
layer /ˈleiər/ *n.* capa *f.*
layman /ˈleimən/ *n.* lego, seglar *m.*
lazy /ˈleizi/ *a.* perezoso.
lead /lɛd, lid/ *n.* **1.** plomo *m.*; *Theat.* papel principal. **to take the l.,** tomar la delantera. —*v.* **2.** conducir; dirigir.
leaden /ˈlɛdn/ *a.* plomizo; pesado; abatido.
leader /ˈlidər/ *n.* líder *m. & f.*; jefe *m. & f.*; director -ora.
leadership /ˈlidərˌʃɪp/ *n.* dirección *f.*
leaf /lif/ *n.* hoja *f.*
leaflet /ˈliflɪt/ *n. Bot.* hojilla *f.*; folleto *m.*
league /lig/ *n.* liga; (measure) legua *f.*
leak /lik/ *n.* **1.** escape; goteo *m.* —*v.* **2.** gotear; *Naut.* hacer agua.
leakage /ˈlikɪdʒ/ *n.* goteo *m.*, escape *m.*, pérdida *f.*
leaky /ˈliki/ *a.* llovedizo, resquebrajado.
lean /lin/ *a.* **1.** flaco, magro. —*v.* **2.** apoyarse, arrimarse.
leap /lip/ *n.* **1.** salto *m.* —*v.* **2.** saltar.
leap year *n.* año bisiesto *m.*
learn /lɜrn/ *v.* aprender; saber.
learned /ˈlɜrnɪd/ *a.* erudito.
learning /ˈlɜrnɪŋ/ *n.* erudición *f.*, instrucción *f.*
lease /lis/ *n.* **1.** arriendo *m.* —*v.* **2.** arrendar.
leash /liʃ/ *n.* **1.** correa *f.* —*v.* **2.** atraillar.
least /list/ *a.* menor; mínimo. **the l.,** lo menos. **at l.,** por lo menos.
leather /ˈlɛðər/ *n.* cuero *m.*
leathery /ˈlɛðəri/ *a.* coriáceo.
leave /liv/ *n.* **1.** licencia *f.* **to take l.,** despedirse. —*v.* **2.** dejar; (depart) salir, irse. **l. out,** omitir.
leaven /ˈlɛvən/ *n.* **1.** levadura *f.* —*v.* **2.** fermentar, imbuir.
lecherous /ˈlɛtʃərəs/ *a.* lujurioso.
lecture /ˈlɛktʃər/ *n.* conferencia *f.*
lecturer /ˈlɛktʃərər/ *n.* conferencista *m. & f.*; catedrático -ca.
ledge /lɛdʒ/ *n.* borde *m.*; capa *f.*
ledger /ˈlɛdʒər/ *n.* libro mayor *m.*

lee /li/ *n.* sotavento *m.*
leech /litʃ/ *n.* sanguijuela *f.*
leek /lik/ *n.* puerro *m.*
leer /lɪər/ *v.* mirar de soslayo.
leeward /ˈliwərd/ *a.* sotavento.
left /lɛft/ *a.* izquierdo. **the l.,** la izquierda. **to be left,** quedarse.
left-handed /ˈlɛft ˈhændɪd/ *a.* zurdo.
leftist /ˈlɛftɪst/ *n.* izquierdista *m.* & *f.*
leftovers /ˈlɛftˌouvərz/ *n.* sobras *f.pl.*
leg /lɛg/ *n.* pierna *f.*
legacy /ˈlɛgəsi/ *n.* legado *m.*, herencia *f.*
legal /ˈligəl/ *a.* legal.
legalize /ˈligəˌlaiz/ *v.* legalizar.
legation /lɪˈgeiʃən/ *n.* legación, embajada *f.*
legend /ˈlɛdʒənd/ *n.* leyenda *f.*
legendary /ˈlɛdʒənˌdɛri/ *a.* legendario.
legible /ˈlɛdʒəbəl/ *a.* legible.
legion /ˈlidʒən/ *n.* legión *f.*
legislate /ˈlɛdʒɪsˌleit/ *v.* legislar.
legislation /ˌlɛdʒɪsˈleiʃən/ *n.* legislación *f.*
legislator /ˈlɛdʒɪsˌleitər/ *n.* legislador -ra.
legislature /ˈlɛdʒɪsˌleitʃər/ *n.* legislatura *f.*
legitimate /lɪˈdʒɪtəmɪt/ *a.* legítimo.
legume /ˈlɛgyum/ *n.* legumbre *f.*
leisure /ˈliʒər/ *n.* desocupación *f.*; horas libres.
leisurely /ˈliʒərli/ *a.* **1.** deliberado. —*adv.* **2.** despacio.
lemon /ˈlɛmən/ *n.* limón *m.*
lemonade /ˌlɛməˈneid/ *n.* limonada *f.*
lend /lɛnd/ *v.* prestar.
length /lɛŋkθ/ *n.* largo *m.*; duración *f.*
lengthen /ˈlɛŋkθən/ *v.* alargar.
lengthwise /ˈlɛŋkθˌwaiz/ *adv.* a lo largo.
lengthy /ˈlɛŋkθi/ *a.* largo.
lenient /ˈliniənt/ *a.* indulgente.
lens /lɛnz/ *n.* lente *m.* *or* *f.*
Lent /lɛnt/ *n.* cuaresma *f.*
Lenten /ˈlɛntn̩/ *a.* cuaresmal.
lentil /ˈlɛntɪl/ *n.* lenteja *f.*
leopard /ˈlɛpərd/ *n.* leopardo *m.*
leotard /ˈliəˌtɑrd/ *n.* mallas *f.pl.*
leper /ˈlɛpər/ *n.* leproso -sa.
leprosy /ˈlɛprəsi/ *n.* lepra *f.*
lesbian /ˈlɛzbiən/ *n.* lesbiana *f.*
lesion /ˈliʒən/ *n.* lesión *f.*
less /lɛs/ *a.* & *adv.* menos.
lessen /ˈlɛsən/ *v.* disminuir.
lesser /ˈlɛsər/ *a.* menor; más pequeño.
lesson /ˈlɛsən/ *n.* lección *f.*
lest /lɛst/ *conj.* para que no.
let /lɛt/ *v.* dejar; permitir; arrendar.
letdown /ˈlɛtˌdaun/ *n.* decepción *f.*
lethal /ˈliθəl/ *a.* letal.
lethargic /ləˈθɑrdʒɪk/ *a.* letárgico.
lethargy /ˈlɛθərdʒi/ *n.* letargo *m.*
letter /ˈlɛtər/ *n.* carta; (of alphabet) letra *f.*
letterhead /ˈlɛtərˌhɛd/ *n.* membrete *m.*
lettuce /ˈlɛtɪs/ *n.* lechuga *f.*
leukemia /luˈkimiə/ *n.* leucemia *f.*
levee /ˈlɛvi, lɛˈvi/ *n.* recepción *f.*
level /ˈlɛvəl/ *a.* **1.** llano, nivelado. —*n.* **2.** nivel *m.*; llanura *f.* —*v.* **3.** allanar; nivelar.
lever /ˈlɛvər/ *n.* palanca *f.*
levity /ˈlɛvɪti/ *n.* levedad *f.*
levy /ˈlɛvi/ *n.* **1.** leva *f.* —*v.* **2.** imponer.
lewd /lud/ *a.* lascivo.
lexicon /ˈlɛksɪˌkɒn/ *n.* léxico *m.*
liability /ˌlaiəˈbɪlɪti/ *n.* riesgo *m.*; obligación *f.*
liable /ˈlaiəbəl/ *a.* sujeto; responsable.
liaison /liˈeizən/ *n.* vinculación *f.*, enlace *m.*; concubinaje *m.*
liar /ˈlaiər/ *n.* embustero -ra.
libel /ˈlaibəl/ *n.* **1.** libelo *m.* —*v.* **2.** difamar.
libelous /ˈlaibələs/ *a.* difamatorio.
liberal /ˈlɪbərəl/ *a.* liberal; generoso.
liberalism /ˈlɪbərəˌlɪzəm/ *n.* liberalismo *m.*
liberality /ˌlɪbəˈrælɪti/ *n.* liberalidad *f.*
liberate /ˈlɪbəˌreit/ *v.* libertar.
liberty /ˈlɪbərti/ *n.* libertad *f.*
libidinous /lɪˈbɪdn̩əs/ *a.* libidinoso.
librarian /laiˈbrɛəriən/ *n.* bibliotecario -ria.
library /ˈlaiˌbrɛri/ *n.* biblioteca *f.*
libretto /lɪˈbrɛtou/ *n.* libreto *m.*
license /ˈlaisəns/ *n.* licencia *f.*; permiso *m.*
licentious /laiˈsɛnʃəs/ *a.* licencioso.
lick /lɪk/ *v.* lamer.
licorice /ˈlɪkərɪʃ, ˈlɪkrɪʃ, ˈlɪkərɪs/ *n.* regaliz *m.*
lid /lɪd/ *n.* tapa *f.*
lie /lai/ *n.* **1.** mentira *f.* —*v.* **2.** mentir. **l. down,** acostarse, echarse.
lieutenant /luˈtɛnənt/ *n.* teniente *m.*
life /laif/ *n.* vida *f.*
lifeboat /ˈlaifˌbout/ *n.* bote salvavidas *m.*
life buoy boya *f.*
lifeguard /ˈlaifˌgɑrd/ socorrista *m.* & *f.*
life insurance seguro de vida *m.*
life jacket chaleco salvavidas *m.*
lifeless /ˈlaiflɪs/ *a.* sin vida.
life preserver /prɪˈzɜrvər/ salvavidas *m.*
lifestyle /ˈlaifstail/ *n.* modo de vida *m.*
lift /lɪft/ *v.* levantar, alzar, elevar.
ligament /ˈlɪgəmənt/ *n.* ligamento *m.*
ligature /ˈlɪgətʃər/ *n.* ligadura *f.*
light /lait/ *a.* **1.** ligero; liviano; (in color) claro. —*n.* **2.** luz; candela *f.* —*v.* **3.** encender; iluminar.
light bulb bombilla *f.*
lighten /ˈlaitn̩/ *v.* aligerar; aclarar; iluminar.
lighter /ˈlaitər/ *n.* encendedor *m.*
lighthouse /ˈlaitˌhaus/ *n.* faro *m.*
lightness /ˈlaitnɪs/ *n.* ligereza; agilidad *f.*
lightning /ˈlaitnɪŋ/ *n.* relámpago *m.*
like /laik/ *a.* **1.** semejante. —*prep.* **2.** como. —*v.* **3. I like...** me gusta, me gustan... **I should like,** quisiera.
likeable /ˈlaikəbəl/ *a.* simpático, agradable.
likelihood /ˈlaikliˌhʊd/ *n.* probabilidad *f.*
likely /ˈlaikli/ *a.* probable; verosímil.
liken /ˈlaikən/ *v.* comparar; asemejar.
likeness /ˈlaiknɪs/ *n.* semejanza *f.*
likewise /ˈlaikˌwaiz/ *adv.* igualmente.
lilac /ˈlailək/ *n.* lila *f.*
lilt /lɪlt/ *n.* **1.** cadencia alegre *f.* —*v.* **2.** cantar alegremente.
lily /ˈlɪli/ *n.* lirio *m.*
lily of the valley muguete *m.*
limb /lɪm/ *n.* rama *f.*
limber /ˈlɪmbər/ *a.* flexible. **to l. up,** ponerse flexible.
limbo /ˈlɪmbou/ *n.* limbo *m.*
lime /laim/ *n.* cal *f.*; (fruit) limoncito *m.*, lima *f.*
limestone /ˈlaimˌstoun/ *n.* piedra caliza *f.*
limewater /ˈlaimˌwɔtər/ *n.* agua de cal *f.*
limit /ˈlɪmɪt/ *n.* **1.** límite *m.* —*v.* **2.** limitar.
limitation /ˌlɪmɪˈteiʃən/ *n.* limitación *f.*
limitless /ˈlɪmɪtlɪs/ *a.* ilimitado.
limousine /ˈlɪməˌzin/ *n.* limusina *f.*
limp /lɪmp/ *n.* **1.** cojera *f.* —*a.* **2.** flojo. —*v.* **3.** cojear.
limpid /ˈlɪmpɪd/ *a.* límpido.
line /lain/ *n.* **1.** línea; fila; raya *f.*; (of print) renglón *m.* —*v.* **2.** forrar; rayar.
lineage /ˈlɪniɪdʒ/ *n.* linaje *m.*
lineal /ˈlɪniəl/ *a.* lineal.
linear /ˈlɪniər/ *a.* linear, longitudinal.
linen /ˈlɪnən/ *n.* lienzo, lino *m.*; ropa blanca.
liner /ˈlainər/ *n.* vapor *m.*
linger /ˈlɪŋgər/ *v.* demorarse.
lingerie /ˌlɑnʒəˈrei/ *n.* ropa blanca *f.*
linguist /ˈlɪŋgwɪst/ *n.* lingüista *m.* & *f.*
linguistic /lɪŋˈgwɪstɪk/ *a.* lingüístico.
liniment /ˈlɪnəmənt/ *n.* linimento *m.*
lining /ˈlainɪŋ/ *n.* forro *m.*
link /lɪŋk/ *n.* **1.** eslabón; vínculo *m.* —*v.* **2.** vincular.
linoleum /lɪˈnouliəm/ *n.* linóleo *m.*
linseed /ˈlɪnˌsid/ *n.* linaza *f.*; simiente de lino *f.*
lint /lɪnt/ *n.* hilacha *f.*
lion /ˈlaiən/ *n.* león *m.*
lip /lɪp/ *n.* labio *m.*
liposuction /ˈlɪpəˌsʌkʃən, ˈlaipə-/ *n.* liposucción *f.*
lipstick /ˈlɪpˌstɪk/ *n.* lápiz de labios.
liqueur /lɪˈkɜr/ *n.* licor *m.*
liquid /ˈlɪkwɪd/ *a.* & *n.* líquido *m.*
liquidate /ˈlɪkwɪˌdeit/ *v.* liquidar.
liquidation /ˌlɪkwɪˈdeiʃən/ *n.* liquidación *f.*
liquor /ˈlɪkər/ *n.* licor *m.*
lisp /lɪsp/ *n.* **1.** ceceo *m.* —*v.* **2.** cecear.
list /lɪst/ *n.* **1.** lista *f.* —*v.* **2.** registrar.
listen (to) /ˈlɪsən/ *v.* escuchar.
listless /ˈlɪstlɪs/ *a.* indiferente.
litany /ˈlɪtn̩i/ *n.* letanía *f.*
liter /ˈlitər/ *n.* litro *m.*
literal /ˈlɪtərəl/ *a.* literal.
literary /ˈlɪtəˌrɛri/ *a.* literario.
literate /ˈlɪtərɪt/ *a.* alfabetizado.
literature /ˈlɪtərətʃər/ *n.* literatura *f.*
litigant /ˈlɪtɪgənt/ *n.* & *a.* litigante *m.* & *f.*
litigation /ˌlɪtɪˈgeiʃən/ *n.* litigio, pleito *m.*
litter /ˈlɪtər/ *n.* **1.** litera *f.*; cama de paja. —*v.* **2.** poner en desorden.
little /ˈlɪtl̩/ *a.* pequeño; (quantity) poco.
little finger meñique *m.*
liturgical /lɪˈtɜrdʒɪkəl/ *a.* litúrgico.
liturgy /ˈlɪtərdʒi/ *n.* liturgia *f.*
live /*a* laiv; *v* lɪv/ *a.* **1.** vivo. —*v.* **2.** vivir.
livelihood /ˈlaivliˌhʊd/ *n.* subsistencia *f.*
lively /ˈlaivli/ *a.* vivo; rápido; animado.
liver /ˈlɪvər/ *n.* hígado *m.*
livery /ˈlɪvəri/ *n.* librea *f.*
livestock /ˈlaivˌstɒk/ *n.* ganadería *f.*
livid /ˈlɪvɪd/ *a.* lívido.
living /ˈlɪvɪŋ/ *a.* **1.** vivo. —*n.* **2.** sustento *m.* **to earn (make) a living,** ganarse la vida.
living room salón *m.*
lizard /ˈlɪzərd/ *n.* lagarto *m.*, lagartija *f.*
llama /ˈlɑmə/ *n.* llama *f.*
load /loud/ *n.* **1.** carga *f.* —*v.* **2.** cargar.
loaf /louf/ *n.* **1.** pan *m.* —*v.* **2.** holgazanear.
loam /loum/ *n.* marga *f.*
loan /loun/ *n.* **1.** préstamo *m.* —*v.* **2.** prestar.
loathe /louð/ *v.* aborrecer, detestar.
loathsome /ˈlouðsəm/ *a.* repugnante.
lobby /ˈlɒbi/ *n.* vestíbulo *m.*
lobe /loub/ *n.* lóbulo *m.*
lobster /ˈlɒbstər/ *n.* langosta *f.*
local /ˈloukəl/ *a.* local.
local area network red local *f.*
locale /louˈkæl/ *n.* localidad *f.*
locality /louˈkælɪti/ *n.* localidad *f.*, lugar *m.*
localize /ˈloukəˌlaiz/ *v.* localizar.
locate /ˈloukeit/ *v.* situar; hallar.
location /louˈkeiʃən/ *n.* sitio *m.*; posición *f.*
lock /lɒk/ *n.* **1.** cerradura *f.*; *(pl.)* cabellos *m.pl.* —*v.* **2.** cerrar con llave.
locker /ˈlɒkər/ *n.* cajón *m.*; ropero *m.*
locket /ˈlɒkɪt/ *n.* guardapelo *m.*; medallón *m.*
lockjaw /ˈlɒkˌdʒɔ/ *n.* trismo *m.*
locksmith /ˈlɒkˌsmɪθ/ *n.* cerrajero -ra.
locomotive /ˌloukəˈmoutɪv/ *n.* locomotora *f.*
locust /ˈloukəst/ *n.* cigarra *f.*, saltamontes *m.*
locution /louˈkyuʃən/ *n.* locución *f.*
lode /loud/ *n.* filón *m.*, veta *f.*
lodge /lɒdʒ/ *n.* **1.** logia; (inn) posada *f.* —*v.* **2.** fijar; alojar, morar.
lodger /ˈlɒdʒər/ *n.* inquilino *m.*
lodging /ˈlɒdʒɪŋ/ *n.* alojamiento *m.*
loft /lɔft/ *n.* desván, sobrado *m.*
lofty /ˈlɔfti/ *a.* alto; altivo.
log /lɔg/ *n.* tronco de árbol; *Naut.* barquilla *f.*
loge /louʒ/ *n.* palco *m.*
logic /ˈlɒdʒɪk/ *n.* lógica *f.*
logical /ˈlɒdʒɪkəl/ *a.* lógico.
loin /lɔin/ *n.* lomo *m.*
loincloth /ˈlɔinˌklɔθ/ *n.* taparrabos *m.*
loiter /ˈlɔitər/ *v.* haraganear.
lone /loun/ *a.* solitario.
loneliness /ˈlounlinɪs/ *n.* soledad *f.*
lonely, /ˈlounli/ **lonesome** *a.* solo y triste.
lonesome /ˈlounsəm/ *a.* solitario, aislado.
long /lɔŋ/ *a.* **1.** largo. **a l. time,** mucho tiempo. —*adv.* **2.** mucho tiempo. **how l.,** cuánto tiempo. **no longer,** ya no. —*v.* **3. l. for,** anhelar.
long-distance call /ˈlɔŋ ˈdɪstəns/ conferencia interurbana *f.*
longevity /lɒnˈdʒɛvɪti/ *n.* longevidad *f.*
long-haired /ˈlɔŋ ˈhɛərd/ *a.* melenudo.
longing /ˈlɔŋɪŋ/ *n.* anhelo *m.*
longitude /ˈlɒndʒɪˌtud/ *n.* longitud *m.*
look /lʊk/ *n.* **1.** mirada *f.*; aspecto *m.* —*v.* **2.** parecer; mirar. **l. at,** mirar. **l. for,** buscar. **l. like,** parecerse a. **l. out!,** ¡cuidado! **l. up,** buscar; ir a ver, venir a ver.
looking glass /ˈlʊkɪŋ/ espejo *m.*
loom /lum/ *n.* **1.** telar *m.* —*v.* **2.** asomar.
loop /lup/ *n.* vuelta *f.*
loophole /ˈlupˌhoul/ *n.* aspillera *f.*; *Fig.* callejuela, evasiva *f.*, efugio *m.*
loose /lus/ *a.* suelto; flojo.
loose change suelto *m.*
loosen /ˈlusən/ *v.* soltar; aflojar.
loot /lut/ *n.* **1.** botín *m.*, saqueo *m.* —*v.* **2.** saquear.
lopsided /ˈlɒpˈsaidɪd/ *a.* desequilibrado.
loquacious /louˈkweiʃəs/ *a.* locuaz.
lord /lɔrd/ *n.* señor *m.*; (Brit. title) lord *m.*
lordship /ˈlɔrdʃɪp/ *n.* señorío *m.*
lose /luz/ *v.* perder. **l. consciousness,** perder el concimiento.
loss /lɔs/ *n.* pérdida *f.*
lost /lɔst/ *a.* perdido.
lot /lɒt/ *n.* suerte *f.* **building l.,** solar *m.* **a lot (of), lots of,** mucho.
lotion /ˈlouʃən/ *n.* loción *f.*
lottery /ˈlɒtəri/ *n.* lotería *f.*
loud /laud/ *a.* **1.** fuerte; ruidoso. —*adv.* **2.** alto.
loudspeaker /ˈlaudˌspikər/ *n.* altavoz *m.*
lounge /laundʒ/ *n.* sofá *m.*; salón de fumar *m.*
louse /laus/ *n.* piojo *m.*
love /lʌv/ *n.* **1.** amor *m.* **in l.,** enamorado. **to fall in l.,** enamorarse. **l. at first sight,** flechazo *m.* —*v.* **2.** querer; amar; adorar.
lovely /ˈlʌvli/ *a.* hermoso.
lover /ˈlʌvər/ *n.* amante *m.* & *f.*
low /lou/ *a.* bajo; vil.
low-cut /ˈlou ˈkʌt/ *a.* escotado.
lower /ˈlouər/ *v.* bajar; (in price) rebajar.
lower-case letter /ˈlouər ˈkeis/ minúscula *f.*
lowly /ˈlouli/ *a.* humilde.
low neckline /ˈnɛkˌlain/ escote *m.*
loyal /ˈlɔiəl/ *a.* leal, fiel.
loyalist /ˈlɔiəlɪst/ *n.* lealista *m.* & *f.*
loyalty /ˈlɔiəlti/ *n.* lealtad *f.*
lozenge /ˈlɒzɪndʒ/ *n.* pastilla *f.*
lubricant /ˈlubrɪkənt/ *n.* lubricante *m.*
lubricate /ˈlubrɪˌkeit/ *v.* engrasar, lubricar.
lucid /ˈlusɪd/ *a.* claro, lúcido.

luck /lʌk/ *n.* suerte; fortuna *f.*
lucky /'lʌki/ *a.* afortunado. **to be l.,** tener suerte.
lucrative /'lukrətɪv/ *a.* lucrativo.
ludicrous /'ludɪkrəs/ *a.* rídiculo.
luggage /'lʌgɪdʒ/ *n.* equipaje *m.*
lukewarm /'luk'wɔrm/ *a.* tibio.
lull /lʌl/ *n.* **1.** momento de calma. —*v.* **2.** calmar.
lullaby /'lʌlə,bai/ *n.* arrullo *m.*
lumbago /lʌm'beigou/ *n.* lumbago *m.*
lumber /'lʌmbər/ *n.* madera *f.*
luminous /'lumənəs/ *a.* luminoso.
lump /lʌmp/ *n.* protuberancia *f.;* (of sugar) terrón *m.*
lump sum suma global *f.*
lunacy /'lunəsi/ *n.* locura *f.*
lunar /'lunər/ *a.* lunar.
lunatic /'lunətɪk/ *a.* & *n.* loco -ca.
lunch, luncheon /lʌntʃ; 'lʌnteshən/ *n.* **1.** merienda *f.*, almuerzo *m.* —*v.* **2.** merendar, almorzar.
lunch box /'lʌntʃ,bɒks/ fiambrera *f.*
lung /lʌŋ/ *n.* pulmón *m.*
lunge /lʌndʒ/ *n.* **1.** estocada, arremetida *f.* —*v.* **2.** dar un estocada, arremeter.
lure /lʊr/ *v.* atraer.
lurid /'lʊrɪd/ *a.* sensacional; espeluznante.
lurk /lɜrk/ *v.* esconderse; espiar.
luscious /'lʌʃəs/ *a.* sabroso, delicioso.
lust /lʌst/ *n.* sensualidad; codicia *f.*
luster /'lʌstər/ *n.* lustre *m.*
lustful /'lʌstfəl/ *a.* sensual, lascivo.
lusty /'lʌsti/ *a.* vigoroso.
lute /lut/ *n.* laúd *m.*
Lutheran /'luθərən/ *n.* & *a.* luterano -na.
luxuriant /lʌg'ʒʊriənt/ *a.* exuberante, frondoso.
luxurious /lʌg'ʒʊriəs/ *a.* lujoso.
luxury /'lʌkʃəri/ *n.* lujo *m.*
lying /'laiɪŋ/ *a.* mentiroso.
lymph /lɪmf/ *n.* linfa *f.*
lynch /lɪntʃ/ *v.* linchar.
lyre /laiⁿr/ *n.* lira *f.*
lyric /'lɪrɪk/ *a.* lírico.
lyricism /'lɪrə,sɪzəm/ *n.* lirismo *m.*

M

macabre /mə'kɑbrə/ *a.* macabro.
macaroni /,mækə'rouni/ *n.* macarrones *m.*
machine /mə'ʃin/ *n.* máquina *f.*
machine gun ametralladora *f.*
machinery /mə'ʃinəri/ *n.* maquinaria *f.*
machinist /mə'ʃinɪst/ *n.* maquinista *m.* & *f.*, mecánico *m.*
macho /'mɑtʃou/ *a.* machista.
mackerel /'mækərəl/ *n.* escombro *m.*
macro /'mækrou/ *n.* (computer) macro *m.*
mad /mæd/ *a.* loco; furioso.
madam /'mædəm/ *n.* señora *f.*
mafia /'mɑfiə/ *n.* mafia *f.*
magazine /,mægə'zin/ *n.* revista *f.*
magic /'mædʒɪk/ *a.* **1.** mágico. —*n.* **2.** magia *f.*
magician /mə'dʒɪʃən/ *n.* mágico *m.*
magistrate /'mædʒə,streit/ *n.* magistrado, -da.
magnanimous /mæg'nænəməs/ *a.* magnánimo.
magnate /'mægneit/ *n.* magnate *m.*
magnesium /mæg'niziəm/ *n.* magnesio *m.*
magnet /'mægnɪt/ *n.* imán *m.*
magnetic /mæg'netɪk/ *a.* magnético.
magnificence /mæg'nɪfəsəns/ *n.* magnificencia *f.*
magnificent /mæg'nɪfəsənt/ *a.* magnífico.
magnify /'mægnə,fai/ *v.* magnificar.
magnifying glass /'mægnə,faiɪŋ/ lupa *f.*
magnitude /'mægnɪ,tud/ *n.* magnitud *f.*
magpie /'mæg,pai/ *n.* hurraca *f.*

mahogany /mə'hɒgəni/ *n.* caoba *f.*
maid /meid/ *n.* criada. *f.* **old m.,** solterona *f.*
maiden /'meidn/ *a.* soltera.
mail /meil/ *n.* **1.** correo *m.* **air m.,** correo aéreo. **by return m.,** a vuelta de correo. —*v.* **2.** echar al correo.
mailbox /'meil,bɒks/ *n.* buzón *m.*
mailman /'meil,mæn/ *n.* cartero *m.*
maim /meim/ *v.* mutilar.
main /mein/ *a.* principal.
mainframe /'mein,freim/ *n.* componente central de una computadora.
mainland /'mein,lænd/ *n.* continente *m.*
maintain /mein'tein/ *v.* mantener; sostener.
maintenance /'meintənəns/ *n.* mantenimiento; sustento *m.;* conservación *f.*
maître d' /,mei'tər di, ,meitrə, ,metrə/ *n.* jefe de sala *m.* & *f.*
maize /meiz/ *n.* maíz *m.*
majestic /mə'dʒestɪk/ *a.* majestuoso.
majesty /'mædʒəsti/ *n.* majestad *f.*
major /'meidʒər/ *a.* **1.** mayor. —*n.* **2.** *Mil.* comandante *m.;* (study) especialidad *f.*
majority /mə'dʒɔriti/ *n.* mayoría *f.*
make /meik/ *n.* **1.** marca *f.* —*v.* **2.** hacer; fabricar; (earn) ganar.
maker /'meikər/ *n.* fabricante *m.*
makeshift /'meik,ʃift/ *a.* provisional.
make-up /'meik,ʌp/ *n.* cosméticos *m.pl.*
malady /'mælədi/ *n.* mal *m.*, enfermedad *f.*
malaria /mə'lɛəriə/ *n.* paludismo *m.*
male /meil/ *a.* & *n.* macho *m.*
malevolent /mə'lɛvələnt/ *a.* malévolo.
malice /'mælɪs/ *n.* malicia *f.*
malicious /mə'lɪʃəs/ *a.* malicioso.
malign /mə'lain/ *v.* **1.** difamar. —*a.* **2.** maligno.
malignant /mə'lɪgnənt/ *a.* maligno.
malnutrition /,mælnu'trɪʃən/ *n.* desnutrición *f.*
malt /mɔlt/ *n.* malta *f.*
mammal /'mæməl/ *n.* mamífero *m.*
man /mæn/ *n.* hombre; varón *m. v.* tripular.
manage /'mænɪdʒ/ *v.* manejar; dirigir; administrar; arreglárselas. **m. to,** lograr.
management /'mænɪdʒmənt/ *n.* dirección, administración *f.*
manager /'mænɪdʒər/ *n.* director -ora.
mandate /'mændeit/ *n.* mandato *m.*
mandatory /'mændə,tɔri/ *a.* obligatorio.
mandolin /'mændlɪn/ *n.* mandolina *f.*
mane /mein/ *n.* crines *f.pl.*
maneuver /mə'nuvər/ *n.* **1.** maniobra *f.* —*v.* **2.** maniobrar.
manganese /'mæŋgə,nis, -,niz/ *n.* manganeso *m.*
manger /'meindʒər/ *n.* pesebre *m.*
mangle /'mæŋgəl/ *n.* **1.** rodillo, exprimidor *m.* —*v.* **2.** mutilar.
manhood /'mænhʊd/ *n.* virilidad *f.*
mania /'meiniə/ *n.* manía *f.*
maniac /'meini,æk/ *a.* & *n.* maniático -ca; maníaco -ca.
manicure /'mæni,kyʊr/ *v.* manicura *f.*
manifest /'mænə,fest/ *a.* **1.** manifiesto *m.* —*v.* **2.** manifestar.
manifesto /,mænə'festou/ *n.* manifiesto *m.*
manifold /'mænə,fould/ *a.* **1.** muchos. —*n.* **2.** *Auto.* tubo múltiple.
manipulate /mə'nɪpyə,leit/ *v.* manipular.
mankind /'mæn'kaind/ *n.* humanidad *f.*
manly /'mænli/ *a.* varonil.
manner /'mænər/ *n.* manera *f.*, modo *m.* **manners,** modales *m.pl.*
mannerism /'mænə,rɪzəm/ *n.* manerismo *m.*
mansion /'mænʃən/ *n.* mansión *f.*

mantel /'mæntl/ *n.* manto de chimenea.
mantle /'mæntl/ *n.* manto *m.*
manual /'mænyuəl/ *a.* & *n.* manual *m.*
manufacture /,mænyə'fæktʃər/ *v.* fabricar.
manufacturer /,mænyə'fæktʃərər/ *n.* fabricante *m.*
manufacturing /,mænyə'fæktʃərɪŋ/ *n.* fabricación *f.*
manure /mə'nʊr/ *n.* abono, estiércol *m.*
manuscript /'mænyə,skrɪpt/ *n.* manuscrito *m.*
many /'meni/ *a.* muchos. **how m.,** cuántos. **so m.,** tantos. **too m.,** demasiados. **as m. as,** tantos como.
map /mæp/ *n.* mapa *m.*
maple /'meipəl/ *n.* arce *m.*
mar /mɑr/ *v.* estropear; desfigurar.
marble /'mɑrbəl/ *n.* mármol *m.*
march /mɑrtʃ/ *n.* **1.** marcha *f.* —*v.* **2.** marchar.
March /mɑrtʃ/ *n.* marzo *m.*
mare /mɛər/ *n.* yegua *f.*
margarine /'mɑrdʒərɪn/ *n.* margarina *f.*
margin /'mɑrdʒɪn/ *n.* margen *m. or f.*
marijuana /,mærə'wɑnə/ *n.* marijuana *f.*
marine /mə'rin/ *a.* **1.** marino. —*n.* **2.** soldado de marina.
mariner /'mærənər/ *n.* marinero *m.*
marionette /,mæriə'net/ *n.* marioneta *f.*
marital /'mærɪtl/ *a.* marital.
maritime /'mærɪ,taim/ *a.* marítimo.
mark /mɑrk/ *n.* **1.** marca *f.* —*v.* **2.** marcar.
market /'mɑrkɪt/ *n.* mercado *m.* **meat m.,** carnicería *f.* **stock m.,** bolsa *f. v.* comercializar.
marmalade /'mɑrmə,leid/ *n.* mermelada *f.*
maroon /mə'run/ *a.* & *n.* color rojo oscuro. *v.* dejar abandonado.
marquis /'mɑrkwɪs/ *n.* marqués *m.*
marriage /'mærɪdʒ/ *n.* matrimonio *m.*
marriage certificate partida de matrimonio *f.*
married /'mærid/ *a.* casado. **to get m.,** casarse.
marrow /'mærou/ *n.* médula *f.;* substancia *f.*
marry /'mæri/ *v.* casarse con; casar.
marsh /mɑrʃ/ *n.* pantano *m.*
marshal /'mɑrʃəl/ *n.* mariscal *m.*
marshmallow /'mɑrʃ,melou/ *n.* malvarisco *m.;* bombón de altea *m.*
martial /'mɑrʃəl/ *a.* marcial. **m. law,** gobierno militar.
martyr /'mɑrtər/ *n.* mártir *m.* & *f.*
martyrdom /'mɑrtərdəm/ *n.* martirio *m.*
marvel /'mɑrvəl/ *n.* **1.** maravilla *f.* —*v.* **2.** maravillarse.
marvelous /'mɑrvələs/ *a.* maravilloso.
mascara /mæ'skærə/ *n.* rimel *m.*
mascot /'mæskɒt/ *n.* mascota *f.*
masculine /'mæskyəlɪn/ *a.* masculino.
mash /mæʃ/ *v.* majar. **mashed potatoes,** puré de papas *m.*
mask /mæsk/ *n.* máscara *f.*
mason /'meisən/ *n.* albañil *m.*
masquerade /,mæskə'reid/ *n.* mascarada *f.*
mass /mæs/ *n.* masa *f.; Relig.* misa *f.* **to say m.,** cantar misa. **m. production,** producción en serie.
massacre /'mæsəkər/ *n.* **1.** carnicería, matanza *f.* —*v.* **2.** matar atrozmente, destrozar.
massage /mə'sɑʒ/ *n.* **1.** masaje *m.;* soba. —*v.* **2.** sobar.
masseur /mə'sɜr/ *n.* masajista *m.* & *f.*
massive /'mæsɪv/ *a.* macizo, sólido.
mast /mæst/ *n.* palo, árbol *m.*
master /'mæstər/ *n.* **1.** amo; maestro *m.* —*v.* **2.** domar, dominar.

masterpiece /'mæstər,pis/ *n.* obra maestra *f.*
master's degree /'mæstərz/ maestría *f.*
mastery /'mæstəri/ *n.* maestría *f.*
mat /mæt/ *n.* **1.** estera; palleta *f.* —*v.* **2.** enredar.
match /mætʃ/ *n.* **1.** igual *m;* fósforo *m.;* (sport) partida, contienda *f.;* (marriage) noviazgo; casamiento. —*v.* **2.** ser igual a; igualar.
matchbox /'mætʃ,bɒks/ caja de cerillas, caja de fósforos *f.*
mate /meit/ *n.* **1.** consorte *m.* & *f.;* compañero -ra. —*v.* **2.** igualar; casar.
material /mə'tɪriəl/ *a.* & *n.* material *m.* **raw materials,** materias primas.
materialism /mə'tɪriə,lɪzəm/ *n.* materialismo *m.*
materialize /mə'tɪriə,laiz/ *v.* materializar.
maternal /mə'tɜrnl/ *a.* materno.
maternity /mə'tɜrniti/ *n.* maternidad *f.*
maternity hospital maternidad *f.*
mathematical /,mæθə'mætɪkəl/ *a.* matemático.
mathematics /,mæθə'mætɪks/ *n.* matemáticas *f.pl.*
matinee /,mætn'ei/ *n.* matiné *f.*
matrimony /'mætrə,mouni/ *n.* matrimonio *m.*
matron /'meitrən/ *n.* matrona; directora *f.*
matter /'mætər/ *n.* **1.** materia *f.;* asunto *m.* **what's the m.?,** ¿qué pasa? —*v.* **2.** importar.
mattress /'mætrɪs/ *n.* colchón *m.*
mature /mə'tʃʊr/ *a.* **1.** maduro. —*v.* **2.** madurar.
maturity /mə'tʃʊriti/ *n.* madurez *f.*
maudlin /'mɔdlɪn/ *a.* sentimental en exceso; sensiblero.
maul /mɔl/ *v.* aporrear.
maxim /'mæksɪm/ *n.* máxima *f.*
maximum /'mæksəməm/ *a.* & *n.* máximo.
may /mei/ *v.* poder.
May /mei/ *n.* mayo *f.*
maybe /'meibi/ *adv.* quizá, quizás, tal vez.
mayonnaise /,meiə'neiz/ *n.* mayonesa *f.*
mayor /'meiər/ *n.* alcalde *m.* alcaldesa *f.*
maze /meiz/ *n.* laberinto *m.*
me /mi/ *pron.* mí; me. **with me,** conmigo.
meadow /'medou/ *n.* prado *m.;* vega *f.*
meager /'migər/ *a.* magro; pobre.
meal /mil/ *n.* comida; (flour) harina *f.*
mean /min/ *a.* **1.** bajo; malo. —*n.* **2.** medio (see also **means**). —*v.* **3.** significar; querer decir.
meander /mi'ændər/ *v.* (river) serpentear; (person) deambular.
meaning /'minɪŋ/ *n.* sentido, significado *m.*
meaningless /'minɪŋlɪs/ *a.* sin sentido.
means /minz/ *n.pl.* medios, recursos *m.* **by all m.,** sin falta. **by no m.,** de ningún modo. **by m. of,** por medio de.
meanwhile /'min,wail/ *adv.* mientras tanto.
measles /'mizəlz/ *n.* sarampión *m.*
measure /'meʒər/ *n.* **1.** medida *f.;* (music) compás *m.* —*v.* **2.** medir.
measurement /'meʒərmənt/ *n.* medida, dimensión *f.*
meat /mit/ *n.* carne *f.*
mechanic /mə'kænɪk/ *n.* mecánico *m.* & *f.*
mechanical /mə'kænɪkəl/ *a.* mecánico.
mechanism /'mekə,nɪzəm/ *n.* mecanismo *m.*
mechanize /'mekə,naiz/ *v.* mecanizar.
medal /'medl/ *n.* medalla *f.*

meddle /'mɛdḷ/ v. meterse, entremeterse.

mediate /'midi,eit/ v. mediar.

medical /'mɛdɪkəl/ a. médico.

medicine /'mɛdəsɪn/ n. medicina f.

medicine chest botiquín m.

medieval /,midi'ivəl/ a. medieval.

mediocre /,midi'oukər/ a. mediocre.

mediocrity /,midi'ɒkrɪti/ n. mediocridad f.

meditate /'mɛdɪ,teit/ v. meditar.

meditation /,mɛdɪ'teiʃən/ n. meditación f.

Mediterranean /,mɛdɪtə'reiniən/ n. Mediterráneo m.

medium /'midiəm/ a. **1.** mediano, medio. —n. **2.** medio m.

medley /'mɛdli/ n. mezcla f., ensalada f.

meek /mik/ a. manso; humilde.

meekness /'miknɪs/ n. modestia; humildad f.

meet /mit/ a. **1.** apropiado. —n. **2.** concurso m. —v. **3.** encontrar; reunirse; conocer.

meeting /'mitɪŋ/ n. reunión f.; mitin m.

megahertz /'mɛgə,hɜrts/ n. megahercio m.

megaphone /'mɛgə,foun/ n. megáfono m.

melancholy /'mɛlən,kɒli/ a. **1.** melancólico. —n. **2.** melancolía f.

mellow /'mɛlou/ a. suave; blando; maduro.

melodious /mə'loudiəs/ a. melodioso.

melodrama /'mɛlə,dramə/ n. melodrama m.

melody /'mɛlədi/ n. melodía f.

melon /'mɛlən/ n. melón m.

melt /mɛlt/ v. derretir.

meltdown /'mɛlt,daun/ n. fundición resultante de un accidente en un reactor nuclear.

member /'mɛmbər/ n. socio -ia; miembro m. **m. of the crew,** tripulante m. & f.

membership /'mɛmbər,ʃɪp/ n. número de miembros.

membrane /'mɛmbrein/ n. membrana f.

memento /mə'mɛntou/ n. recuerdo m.

memoir /'mɛmwar/ n. memoria f.

memorable /'mɛmərəbəl/ a. memorable.

memorandum /,mɛmə'rændəm/ n. memorándum, volante m.

memorial /mə'mɔriəl/ a. **1.** conmemorativo. —n. **2.** memorial m.

memorize /'mɛmə,raiz/ v. aprender de memoria.

memory /'mɛməri/ n. memoria f.; recuerdo m.

menace /'mɛnɪs/ n. **1.** amenaza f. —v. **2.** amenazar.

mend /mɛnd/ v. reparar, remendar.

menial /'miniəl/ a. **1.** servil. —n. **2.** sirviente -ta.

meningitis /,mɛnɪn'dʒaitɪs/ n. meningitis. f.

menopause /'mɛnə,pɔz/ n. menopausia f.

menstruation /,mɛnstru'eiʃən/ n. menstruación f.

menswear /'mɛnz,wɛər/ n. ropa de caballeros f.

mental /'mɛntḷ/ a. mental.

mental disorder trastorno mental m.

mentality /mɛn'tælɪti/ n. mentalidad f.

menthol /'mɛnθɔl/ n. mentol m.

mention /'mɛnʃən/ n. **1.** mención f. —v. **2.** mencionar.

menu /'mɛnyu/ n. menú m., lista f.

mercantile /'mɜrkən,til/ a. mercantil.

mercenary /'mɜrsə,nɛri/ a. & n. mercenario -ria.

merchandise /'mɜrtʃən,daiz/ n. mercancía f.

merchant /'mɜrtʃənt/ a. **1.** mercante. —n. **2.** comerciante m.

merciful /'mɜrsɪfəl/ a. misericordioso, compasivo.

merciless /'mɜrsɪlɪs/ a. cruel, inhumano.

mercury /'mɜrkyəri/ n. mercurio m.

mercy /'mɜrsi/ n. misericordia; merced f.

mere /mɪər/ a. mero, puro.

merely /'mɪərli/ adv. solamente; simplemente.

merge /mɜrdʒ/ v. unir, combinar.

merger /'mɜrdʒər/ n. consolidación, fusión f.

meringue /mə'ræŋ/ n. merengue m.

merit /'mɛrɪt/ n. **1.** mérito m. —v. **2.** merecer.

meritorious /,mɛrɪ'tɔriəs/ a. meritorio.

mermaid /'mɜr,meid/ n. sirena f.

merriment /'mɛrɪmənt/ n. regocijo m.

merry /'mɛri/ a. alegre, festivo.

merry-go-round /'mɛri gou ,raund/ n. caballitos m. pl.; tiovivo m.

mesh /mɛʃ/ n. malla f.

mess /mɛs/ n. **1.** lío m.; confusión f.; Mil. salón comedor; rancho m. —v. **2. m. up,** ensuciar; enredar.

message /'mɛsɪdʒ/ n. mensaje, recado m.

messenger /'mɛsəndʒər/ n. mensajero -ra.

messy /'mɛsi/ a. confuso; desarreglado.

metabolism /mə'tæbə,lɪzəm/ n. metabolismo m.

metal /'mɛtḷ/ n. metal m.

metallic /mə'tælɪk/ a. metálico.

metaphysics /,mɛtə'fɪzɪks/ n. metafísica f.

meteor /'mitiər/ n. meteoro m.

meteorology /,mitiə'rɒlədʒi/ n. meteorología f.

meter /'mitər/ n. contador, medidor; (measure) metro m.

method /'mɛθəd/ n. método m.

meticulous /mə'tɪkyələs/ a. meticuloso.

metric /'mɛtrɪk/ a. métrico.

metropolis /mɪ'trɒpəlɪs/ n. metrópoli f.

metropolitan /,mɛtrə'pɒlɪtṇ/ a. metropolitano.

Mexican /'mɛksɪkən/ a. & n. mexicano -na.

Mexico /'mɛksɪ,kou/ n. México m.

mezzanine /'mɛzə,nin/ n. entresuelo m.

microbe /'maikroub/ n. microbio m.

microchip /'maikrou,tʃɪp/ n. microchip m.

microfiche /'maikrə,fiʃ/ n. microficha f.

microfilm /'maikrə,fɪlm/ n. microfilm m.

microform /'maikrə,fɔrm/ n. microforma f.

microphone /'maikrə,foun/ n. micrófono m.

microscope /'maikrə,skoup/ n. microscopio m.

microscopic /,maikrə'skɒpɪk/ a. microscópico.

mid /mɪd/ a. medio.

middle /'mɪdḷ/ a. & n. medio m. **in the m. of,** en medio de, a mediados de.

middle-aged /eidʒd/ a. de edad madura.

Middle East Medio Oriente m.

middle finger dedo corazón m.

midget /'mɪdʒɪt/ n. enano -na.

midnight /'mɪd,nait/ n. medianoche f.

midwife /'mɪd,waif/ n. comadrona, partera f.

might /mait/ n. poder m., fuerza f.

mighty /'maiti/ a. poderoso.

migraine /'maigrein/ n. migraña f.; jaqueca f.

migrate /'maigreit/ v. emigrar.

migration /mai'greiʃən/ n. emigración f.

migratory /'maigrə,tɔri/ a. migratorio.

mild /maild/ a. moderado, suave; templado.

mildew /'mɪl,du/ n. añublo m., moho m.

mile /mail/ n. milla f.

mileage /'mailɪdʒ/ n. kilometraje m.

militant /'mɪlɪtənt/ a. militante.

militarism /'mɪlɪtə,rɪzəm/ n. militarismo m.

military /'mɪlɪ,tɛri/ a. militar.

militia /mɪ'lɪʃə/ n. milicia f.

milk /mɪlk/ n. **1.** leche f. —v. **2.** ordeñar.

milk chocolate chocolate con leche m.

milkman /'mɪlk,mæn/ n. lechero -ra.

milk shake batido m.

milky /'mɪlki/ a. lácteo; lechoso.

mill /mɪl/ n. **1.** molino m.; fábrica f. —v. **2.** moler.

miller /'mɪlər/ n. molinero -ra.

millimeter /'mɪlə,mitər/ n. milímetro m.

milliner /'mɪlənər/ n. sombrerero -ra.

millinery /'mɪlə,nɛri/ n. sombrerería f.

million /'mɪlyən/ n. millón m.

millionaire /,mɪlyə'nɛər/ n. millonario -ria.

mimic /'mɪmɪk/ n. **1.** mimo -ma. —v. **2.** imitar.

mind /maind/ n. **1.** mente; opinión f. —v. **2.** obedecer. **never m.,** no se ocupe.

mindful /'maindfəl/ a. atento.

mine /main/ pron. **1.** mío. —n. **2.** mina f. —v. **3.** minar.

miner /'mainər/ n. minero m.

mineral /'mɪnərəl/ a. & n. mineral m.

mineral water agua mineral f.

mine sweeper /'main,swipər/ dragaminas f.

mingle /'mɪŋgəl/ v. mezclar.

miniature /'mɪniətʃər/ n. miniatura f.

miniaturize /'mɪniətʃə,raiz/ v. miniaturizar.

minibus /'mɪni,bʌs/ n. microbús m.

minicab /'mɪni,kæb/ n. microtaxi m.

minimize /'mɪnə,maiz/ v. menospreciar.

minimum /'mɪnəməm/ a. & n. mínimo m.

mining /'mainɪŋ/ n. minería f.

minister /'mɪnəstər/ n. **1.** ministro -tra; Relig. pastor m. —v. **2.** ministrar.

ministry /'mɪnəstri/ n. ministerio m.

mink /mɪŋk/ n. visón m.; (fur) piel de visón m.

minor /'mainər/ a. **1.** menor. —n. **2.** menor de edad.

minority /mɪ'nɔriti/ n. minoría f.

minstrel /'mɪnstrəl/ n. juglar m.

mint /mɪnt/ n. **1.** menta f.; casa de moneda. —v. **2.** acuñar.

minus /'mainəs/ prep. menos.

minute /mai'nut/ a. **1.** minucioso. —n. **2.** minuto, momento m.

miracle /'mɪrəkəl/ n. milagro m.

miraculous /mɪ'rækyələs/ a. milagroso.

mirage /mɪ'raʒ/ n. espejismo m.

mire /maiər/ n. lodo m.

mirror /'mɪrər/ n. espejo m.

mirth /mɜrθ/ n. alegría; risa f.

misbehave /,mɪsbɪ'heiv/ v. portarse mal.

miscellaneous /,mɪsə'leiniəs/ a. misceláneo.

mischief /'mɪstʃɪf/ n. travesura, diablura f.

mischievous /'mɪstʃəvəs/ a. travieso, dañino.

miser /'maizər/ n. avaro -ra.

miserable /'mɪzərəbəl/ a. miserable; infeliz.

miserly /'maizərli/ a. avariento, tacaño.

misfortune /mɪs'fɔrtʃən/ n. desgracia f., infortunio, revés m.

misgiving /mɪs'gɪvɪŋ/ n. recelo m., desconfianza f.

mishap /'mɪshæp/ n. desgracia f., contratiempo m.

mislay /mɪs'lei/ v. perder.

mislead /mɪs'lid/ v. extraviar, despistar; pervertir.

misplaced /mɪs'pleist/ a. extraviado.

mispronounce /,mɪsprə'nouns/ v. pronunciar mal.

miss /mɪs/ n. **1.** señorita f. —v. **2.** perder; echar de menos, extrañar. **be missing,** faltar.

missile /'mɪsəl/ n. proyectil m.

mission /'mɪʃən/ n. misión f.

missionary /'mɪʃə,nɛri/ n. misionero -ra.

mist /mɪst/ n. niebla, bruma f.

mistake /mɪ'steik/ n. equivocación f.; error m. **to make a m.,** equivocarse.

mistaken /mɪ'steikən/ a. equivocado.

mister /'mɪstər/ n. señor m.

mistletoe /'mɪsəl,tou/ n. muérdago m.

mistreat /mɪs'trit/ v. maltratar.

mistress /'mɪstrɪs/ n. ama; señora; concubina f.

mistrust /mɪs'trʌst/ v. desconfiar; sospechar.

misty /'mɪsti/ a. nebuloso, brumoso.

misunderstand /,mɪsʌndər'stænd/ v. entender mal.

misuse /mɪs'yuz/ v. maltratar; abusar.

mite /mait/ n. pizca f., blanca f.

mitten /'mɪtṇ/ n. mitón, confortante m.

mix /mɪks/ v. mezclar. **m. up,** confundir.

mixer /'mɪksər/ (for food), n. batidora f.

mixture /'mɪkstʃər/ n. mezcla, mixtura f.

mix-up /'mɪks,ʌp/ n. confusión f.

moan /moun/ n. **1.** quejido, gemido m. —v. **2.** gemir.

mob /mɒb/ n. muchedumbre f.; gentío m.

mobilization /,moubələ'zeiʃən/ n. movilización f.

mobilize /'moubə,laiz/ v. movilizar.

mock /mɒk/ v. burlar.

mockery /'mɒkəri/ n. burla f.

mod /mɒd/ a. a la última; en boga.

mode /moud/ n. modo m.

model /'mɒdḷ/ n. **1.** modelo m. —v. **2.** modelar.

modem /'moudəm/ n. módem m.

moderate /a 'mɒdərɪt; v -ə,reit/ a. **1.** moderado. —v. **2.** moderar.

moderation /,mɒdə'reiʃən/ n. moderación; sobriedad f.

modern /'mɒdərn/ a. moderno.

modernize /'mɒdər,naiz/ v. modernizar.

modest /'mɒdɪst/ a. modesto.

modesty /'mɒdəsti/ n. modestia f.

modify /'mɒdə,fai/ v. modificar.

modulate /'mɒdʒə,leit/ v. modular.

moist /mɔist/ a. húmedo.

moisten /'mɔisən/ v. humedecer.

moisture /'mɔistʃər/ n. humedad f.

moisturize /'mɔistʃə,raiz/ v. hidratar.

molar /'moulər/ n. molar m.

molasses /mə'læsɪz/ n. melaza f.

mold /mould/ n. **1.** molde; moho m. —v. **2.** moldar, formar; enmohecer.

moldy /'mouldi/ a. mohoso.

mole /'moulei/ n. lunar m.; (animal) topo m.

molecule /'mɒlɪ,kyul/ n. molécula f.

molest /mə'lɛst/ v. molestar.

mollify /'mɒlə,fai/ v. molificar.

moment /'moumənt/ n. momento m.

momentary /'moumən,tɛri/ a. momentáneo.

momentous /mou'mɛntəs/ a. importante.

monarch /'mɒnərk/ n. monarca m. & f.

monarchy /'mɒnərki/ n. monarquía f.

monastery /'mɒnə,stɛri/ n. monasterio m.

Monday /'mʌndei/ n. lunes m.

monetary /'mɒnɪ,tɛri/ a. monetario.

money /'mʌni/ n. dinero m. **m. order,** giro postal.

mongrel /'mʌŋgrəl/ n. **1.** mestizo m. —a. **2.** mestizo, cruzado.

monitor /'mɒnitər/ n. amonestador m.; (computer) consola f., pantalla f.

monk /mʌŋk/ n. monje m.

monkey /'mʌŋki/ n. mono -na.

monocle /'mɒnəkəl/ n. monóculo m.

monologue /'mɒnə,lɔg/ n. monólogo m.

monopolize /mə'nɒpə,laiz/ v. monopolizar.

monopoly /mə'nɒpəli/ n. monopolio m.

monosyllable /'mɒnə,siləbəl/ n. monosílabo m.

monotone /'mɒnə,toun/ n. monotonía f.

monotonous /mə'nɒtnəs/ a. monótono.

monotony /mə'nɒtni/ n. monotonía f.

monsoon /mɒn'sun/ n. monzón m.

monster /'mɒnstər/ n. monstruo m.

monstrosity /mɒn'strɒsiti/ n. monstruosidad f.

monstrous /'mɒnstrəs/ a. monstruoso.

month /mʌnθ/ n. mes m.

monthly /'mʌnθli/ a. mensual.

monument /'mɒnyəmənt/ n. monumento m.

monumental /,mɒnyə'mɛntḷ/ a. monumental.

mood /mud/ n. humor m.; Gram. modo m.

moody /'mudi/ a. caprichoso, taciturno.

moon /mun/ n. luna f.

moonlight /'mun,lait/ n. luz de la luna.

moonlighting /'mun,laitɪŋ/ n. pluriempleo m.

moor /mʊr/ n. **1.** párano m. —v. **2.** anclar.

Moor /mʊr/ n. moro -ra.

mop /mɒp/ n. **1.** fregasuelos m., fregona f., (S.A.) trapeador m. —v. **2.** fregar, (S.A.) trapear.

moped /'mou,pɛd/ n. (vehicle) velomotor m.

moral /'mɔrəl/ a. **1.** moral. —n. **2.** moraleja f. **morals, m.** moralidad f.

morale /mə'ræl/ n. espíritu m.

moralist /'mɔrəlɪst/ n. moralista m. & f.

morality /mə'ræliti/ n. moralidad, ética f.

morbid /'mɔrbid/ a. mórbido.

more /mɔr/ a. & adv. más. **m. and m.,** cada vez más.

moreover /mɔr'ouvər/ adv. además.

morgue /mɔrg/ n. necrocomio m.

morning /'mɔrnɪŋ/ n. mañana f. **good m.,** buenos días.

Morocco /mə'rɒkou/ n. Marruecos m.

morose /mə'rous/ a. malhumorado.

morphine /'mɔrfin/ n. morfina f.

morsel /'mɔrsəl/ n. bocado m.

mortal /'mɔrtḷ/ a. & n. mortal m. & f.

mortality /mɔr'tæliti/ n. mortalidad f.

mortar /'mɔrtər/ n. mortero m.

mortgage /'mɔrgɪdʒ/ n. **1.** hipoteca f. —v. **2.** hipotecar.

mortify /'mɔrtə,fai/ v. mortificar.

mosaic /mou'zeiik/ n. & a. mosaico m.

mosque /mɒsk/ n. mezquita f.

mosquito /mə'skitou/ n. mosquito m.

moss /mɔs/ n. musgo m.

most /moust/ a. **1.** más. —adv. **2.** más; sumamente. —pron. **3. m. of,** la mayor parte de.

mostly /'moustli/ adv. principalmente; en su mayor parte.

motel /mou'tɛl/ n. motel m.

moth /mɔθ/ n. polilla f.

mother /'mʌðər/ n. madre f.

mother-in-law /'mʌðər ɪn ,lɔ/ n. suegra f.

motif /mou'tif/ n. tema m.

motion /'mouʃən/ n. **1.** moción f.; movimiento m. —v. **2.** hacer señas.

motionless /'mouʃənlɪs/ a. inmóvil.

motion picture película f.

motivate /'moutə,veit/ v. motivar.

motive /'moutɪv/ n. motivo m.

motor /'moutər/ n. motor m.

motorboat /'moutər,bout/ n. lancha motora f., autobote, motorbote m., gasolinera f.

motorcycle /'moutər,saikəl/ n. motocicleta f.

motorcyclist /'moutər,saiklɪst/ n. motociclista m. & f.

motorist /'moutərɪst/ n. motorista m. & f.

motto /'mɒtou/ n. lema m.

mound /maund/ n. terrón; montón m.

mount /maunt/ n. **1.** monte m.; (horse) montura f. —v. **2.** montar; subir.

mountain /'mauntṇ/ n. montaña f.

mountaineer /,mauntṇ'ɪər/ n. montañés m.

mountainous /'mauntṇəs/ a. montañoso.

mourn /mɔrn/ v. lamentar, llorar; llevar luto.

mournful /'mɔrnfəl/ a. triste.

mourning /'mɔrnɪŋ/ n. luto; lamento m.

mouse /maus/ n. ratón, ratoncito m.

mouth /mauθ/ n. boca f.; (of river) desembocadura f.

mouthwash /'mauθ,wɔʃ/ n. enjuague bucal m.

movable /'muvəbəl/ a. movible, movedizo.

move /muv/ n. **1.** movimiento m.; mudanza f. —v. **2.** mover; mudarse; emocionar, conmover. **m. away,** quitar; alejarse; mudarse.

movement /'muvmənt/ n. movimiento m.

movie /'muvi/ n. película f. **m. theater, movies,** cine m.

moving /'muvɪŋ/ a. conmovedor; persuasivo.

mow /mou/ v. guadañar, segar.

Mr. /'mɪstər/ title. Señor (Sr.).

Mrs. /'mɪsəz/ title. Señora (Sra.).

much /mʌtʃ/ a. & adv. mucho. **how m.,** cuánto. **so m.,** tanto. **too m.,** demasiado. **as m. as,** tanto como.

mucilage /'myusəlɪdʒ/ n. mucílago m.

mucous /'myukəs/ a. mucoso.

mucous membrane n. membrana mucosa f.

mud /mʌd/ n. fango, lodo m.

muddy /'mʌdi/ a. **1.** lodoso; turbio. —v. **2.** ensuciar; enturbiar.

muff /mʌf/ n. manguito m.

muffin /'mʌfɪn/ n. panecillo m.

mug /mʌg/ n. cubilete m.

mugger /'mʌgər/ n. asaltante m. & f.

mulatto /mə'lætou/ n. mulato m.

mule /myul/ n. mula f.

mullah /'mʌlə/ n. mullah m.

multicultural /,mʌlti'kʌltʃərəl, ,mʌltai-/ a. multicultural.

multinational /,mʌlti'næʃənḷ, ,mʌltai-/ a. multinacional.

multiple /'mʌltəpəl/ a. múltiple.

multiplication /,mʌltəplɪ'keiʃən/ n. multiplicación f.

multiplicity /,mʌltə'plisiti/ n. multiplicidad f.

multiply /'mʌltəpli/ v. multiplicar.

multitasking /,mʌlti'tæskɪŋ, ,mʌltai-/ n. multitarea f.

multitude /'mʌlti,tud/ n. multitud f.

mummy /'mʌmi/ n. momia f.

mumps /mʌmps/ n. paperas f.pl.

municipal /myu'nɪsəpəl/ a. municipal.

munificent /myu'nɪfəsənt/ a. munífico.

munitions /myu'nɪʃənz/ n. municiones m.pl.

mural /'myʊrəl/ a. & n. mural m.

murder /'mɜrdər/ n. **1.** asesinato; homicidio m. —v. **2.** asesinar.

murderer /'mɜrdərər/ n. asesino -na.

murmur /'mɜrmər/ n. **1.** murmullo m. —v. **2.** murmurar.

muscle /'mʌsəl/ n. músculo m.

muscular /'mʌskyələr/ a. muscular.

muse /myuz/ n. **1.** musa f. —v. **2.** meditar.

museum /myu'ziəm/ n. museo m.

mushroom /'mʌʃrum/ n. seta f., hongo m.

music /'myuzɪk/ n. música f.

musical /'myuzɪkəl/ a. musical; melodioso.

musician /myu'zɪʃən/ n. músico -ca.

Muslim /'mʌzlɪm/ a. & n. musulmano.

muslin /'mʌzlɪn/ n. muselina f.; percal m.

mussel /'mʌsəl/ n. mejillón m.

must /mʌst/ v. deber; tener que.

mustache /'mʌstæʃ/ n. bigotes m.pl.

mustard /'mʌstərd/ n. mostaza f.

muster /'mʌstər/ n. **1.** Mil. revista f. —v. **2.** reunir, juntar.

mute /myut/ a. & n. mudo -da.

mutilate /'myutḷ,eit/ v. mutilar.

mutiny /'myutṇi/ n. **1.** motín m. —v. **2.** amotinarse.

mutt /mʌt/ n. Colloq. chucho m.

mutter /'mʌtər/ v. refunfuñar, gruñir.

mutton /'mʌtṇ/ n. carnero m.

mutual /'myutʃuəl/ a. mutuo.

muzzle /'mʌzəl/ n. **1.** hocico m.; bozal m. —v. **2.** embozar.

my /mai/ a. mi.

myriad /'mɪriəd/ n. miríada f.

myrtle /'mɜrtḷ/ n. mirto f.

myself /mai'sɛlf/ pron. mí, mí mismo; me. **I m.,** yo mismo.

mysterious /mɪ'stɪriəs/ a. misterioso.

mystery /'mɪstəri/ n. misterio m.

mystic /'mɪstɪk/ a. místico.

mystify /'mɪstə,fai/ v. confundir.

myth /mɪθ/ n. mito m.

mythical /'mɪθɪkəl/ a. mítico.

mythology /mɪ'θɒlədʒi/ n. mitología f.

N

nag /næg/ n. **1.** jaca f. —v. **2.** regañar; sermonear.

nail /neil/ n. **1.** clavo m.; (finger) uña f. **n. polish,** esmalte para las uñas. —v. **2.** clavar.

naïve /nɑ'iv/ a. ingenuo.

naked /'neikɪd/ a. desnudo.

name /neim/ n. **1.** nombre m.; reputación f. —v. **2.** nombrar, mencionar.

namely /'neimli/ adv. a saber; es decir.

namesake /'neim,seik/ n. tocayo m.

nanny /'næni/ n. niñera f.

nap /næp/ n. siesta f. **to take a n.,** echar una siesta.

naphtha /'næfθə, 'næp-/ n. nafta f.

napkin /'næpkɪn/ n. servilleta f.

narcissus /nɑr'sɪsəs/ n. narciso m.

narcotic /nɑr'kɒtɪk/ a. & n. narcótico m.

narrate /'næreit/ v. narrar.

narrative /'nærətɪv/ a. **1.** narrativo. —n. **2.** cuento, relato m.

narrow /'nærou/ a. estrecho, angosto. **n.-minded,** intolerante.

nasal /'neizəl/ a. nasal.

nasty /'næsti/ a. desagradable.

nation /'neiʃən/ n. nación f.

national /'næʃənḷ/ a. nacional.

nationalism /'næʃənḷ,ɪzəm/ n. nacionalismo m.

nationality /,næʃə'næliti/ n. nacionalidad f.

nationalization /,næʃənḷə'zeiʃən/ n. nacionalización f.

nationalize /'næʃənḷ,aiz, 'næʃnə,laiz/ v. nacionalizar.

native /'neitɪv/ a. **1.** nativo. —n. **2.** natural; indígena m. & f.

nativity /nə'tɪvɪti/ n. natividad f.

natural /'nætʃərəl/ a. natural.

naturalist /'nætʃərəlɪst/ n. naturalista m. & f.

naturalize /'nætʃərə,laiz/ v. naturalizar.

naturalness /,nætʃərəlnɪs/ n. naturalidad f.

nature /'neitʃər/ n. naturaleza f.; índole f.; humor m.

naughty /'nɔti/ a. travieso, desobediente.

nausea /'nɔziə, -ʒə/ n. náusea f.

nauseous /'nɔʃəs/ a. nauseoso.

nautical /'nɔtɪkəl/ a. náutico.

naval /'neivəl/ a. naval.

nave /neiv/ n. nave f.

navel /'neivəl/ n. ombligo m.

navigable /'nævɪgəbəl/ a. navegable.

navigate /'nævɪ,geit/ v. navegar.

navigation /,nævɪ'geiʃən/ n. navegación f.

navigator /'nævɪ,geitər/ n. navegante m. & f.

navy /'neivi/ n. marina f.

navy blue azul marino m.

near /nɪər/ a. **1.** cercano, próximo. —adv. **2.** cerca. —prep. **3.** cerca de.

nearby /'nɪər'bai/ a. **1.** cercano. —adv. **2.** cerca.

nearly /'nɪərli/ adv. casi.

nearsighted /'nɪər,saitɪd/ a. corto de vista.

neat /nit/ a. aseado; ordenado.

neatness /'nitnɪs/ n. aseo m.

nebulous /'nɛbyələs/ a. nebuloso.

necessary /'nɛsə,sɛri/ a. necesario.

necessity /nə'sɛsɪti/ n. necesidad f.

neck /nɛk/ n. cuello m.

necklace /'nɛklɪs/ n. collar m.

necktie /'nɛk,tai/ n. corbata f.

nectar /'nɛktər/ n. néctar m.

nectarine /,nɛktə'rin/ n. nectarina f.

need /nid/ n. **1.** necesidad; (poverty) pobreza f. —v. **2.** necesitar.

needle /'nidḷ/ n. aguja f.

needless /'nidlɪs/ a. innecesario, inútil.

needy /'nidi/ a. indigente, necesitado, pobre.

nefarious /nɪ'fɛəriəs/ a. nefario.

negative /'nɛgətɪv/ a. negativo. n. negativa f.

neglect /nɪ'glɛkt/ n. **1.** negligencia f.; descuido m. —v. **2.** descuidar.

negligee /,nɛglɪ'ʒei/ n. negligé m., bata de casa f.

negligent /'nɛglɪdʒənt/ a. negligente, descuidado.

negligible /'nɛglɪdʒəbəl/ a. insignificante.

negotiate /nɪ'gouʃi,eit/ v. negociar.

negotiation /nɪ,gouʃi'eiʃən/ n. negociación f.

Negro /'nigrou/ n. negro -ra.

neighbor /'neibər/ n. vecino -na.

neighborhood /'neibər,hʊd/ n. vecindad f.

neither /'niðər, 'nai-/ a. & pron. **1.** ninguno de los dos. —adv. **2.** tampoco. —conj. **3. neither... nor,** ni... ni.

neon /'niɒn/ n. neón m. **n. light,** tubo neón m.

nephew /'nɛfyu/ n. sobrino m.

nerve /nɜrv/ n. nervio m.; Colloq. audacia f.

nervous /'nɜrvəs/ a. nervioso.

nervous breakdown /'breik,daun/ crisis nerviosa f.

nest /nɛst/ n. nido m.

net /nɛt/ a. **1.** neto. —n. **2.** red f. **hair n.,** albanega, redecilla f. v. redar; Com. ganar.

netiquette /'nɛtɪkɪt/ n. etiqueta de la red f.

netting /'nɛtɪŋ/ n. red m.; obra de malla f.

network /'nɛt,wɜrk/ n. (radio) red radiodifusora f.

neuralgia /nʊ'rældʒə/ n. neuralgia f.

neurology /nʊ'rɒlədʒi/ n. neurología f.

neurotic /nʊ'rɒtɪk/ a. neurótico.

neutral /'nutrəl/ *a.* neutral.
neutrality /nu'trælɪti/ *n.* neutralidad *f.*
neutron /'nutrɒn/ *n.* neutrón *m.*
neutron bomb bomba de neutrones *f.*
never /'nɛvər/ *adv.* nunca, jamás; **n. mind,** no importa.
nevertheless /ˌnɛvərðə'lɛs/ *adv.* no obstante, sin embargo.
new /nu/ *a.* nuevo.
newbie /'nubi/ *n. Colloq.* novato -ta, inexperto -ta.
news /nuz/ *n.* noticias *f.pl.*
newsboy /'nuzˌbɔi/ *n.* vendedor -ra de periódicos.
news bulletin boletín informativo *m.*
news flash *n.* noticia de última hora *f.*
newsgroup /'nuzˌgrup/ *n.* grupo de discusion *m.*
newsletter /'nuzˌlɛtər/ *n.* hoja informativa *f.*
newspaper /'nuzˌpeipər/ *n.* periódico *m.*
New Testament Nuevo Testamento *m.*
new year *n.* año nuevo *m.*
next /nɛkst/ *a.* **1.** próximo; siguiente; contiguo. —*adv.* **2.** luego, después. **n. door,** al lado. **n. to,** al lado de.
next-to-the-last /'nɛkst tə ðə 'læst/ *a.* penúltimo.
nibble /'nɪbəl/ *v.* picar.
nice /nis/ *a.* simpático, agradable; amable; hermoso; exacto.
nick /nɪk/ *n.* muesca *f.*, picadura *f.* **in the n. of time,** a punto.
nickel /'nɪkəl/ *n.* níquel *m.*
nickname /'nɪkˌneim/ *n.* **1.** apodo, mote *m.* —*v.* **2.** apodar.
nicotine /'nɪkəˌtin/ *n.* nicotina *f.*
niece /nis/ *n.* sobrina *f.*
niggardly /'nɪgərdli/ *a.* mezquino.
night /nait/ *n.* noche *f.* **good n.,** buenas noches. **last n.,** anoche. **n. club,** cabaret *m.*
nightclub /'naitˌklʌb/ *n.* cabaret *m.*
nightclub owner cabaretero -ra *m.* & *f.*
nightgown /'naitˌgaun/ *n.* camisa de dormir.
nightingale /'naitn̩ˌgeil, 'naitɪŋ-/ *n.* ruiseñor *m.*
nightly /'naitli/ *adv.* todas las noches.
nightmare /'naitˌmɛər/ *n.* pesadilla *f.*
night school escuela nocturna *f.*
night watchman vigilante nocturno *m.*
nimble /'nɪmbəl/ *a.* ágil.
nine /nain/ *a.* & *pron.* nueve.
nineteen /'nain'tin/ *a.* & *pron.* diecinueve.
ninety /'nainti/ *a.* & *pron.* noventa.
ninth /nainθ/ *a.* noveno.
nipple /'nɪpəl/ *n.* teta *f.*; pezón *m.*
nitrogen /'naitrədʒən/ *n.* nitrógeno *m.*
no /nou/ *a.* **1.** ninguno. **no one,** nadie. —*adv.* **2.** no.
nobility /nou'bɪlɪti/ *n.* nobleza *f.*
noble /'noubəl/ *a.* & *n.* noble *m.*
nobleman /'noubəlmən/ *n.* noble *m.*
nobody /'nouˌbɒdi/ *pron.* nadie.
nocturnal /nɒk'tɜrnl̩/ *a.* nocturno.
nocturne /'nɒktɜrn/ *n.* nocturno *m.*
nod /nɒd/ *n.* **1.** seña con la cabeza. —*v.* **2.** inclinar la cabeza; (doze) dormitar.
no-frills /'nou 'frɪlz/ *a.* sin extras.
noise /nɔiz/ *n.* ruido *m.*
noiseless /'nɔizlɪs/ *a.* silencioso.
noisy /'nɔizi/ *a.* ruidoso.
nominal /'nɒmənl̩/ *a.* nominal.
nominate /'nɒməˌneit/ *v.* nombrar.
nomination /ˌnɒmə'neiʃən/ *n.* nombramiento *m.*, nominación *f.*
nominee /ˌnɒmə'ni/ *n.* candidato -ta.
nonaligned /ˌnɒnə'laind/ (in political sense), *a.* no alineado.
nonchalant /ˌnɒnʃə'lɑnt/ *a.* indiferente.
noncombatant /ˌnɒnkəm'bætnt/ *n.* no combatiente *m.*
noncommittal /ˌnɒnkə'mɪtl̩/ *a.* evasivo; reservado.
nondescript /ˌnɒndɪ'skrɪpt/ *a.* difícil de describir.
none /nʌn/ *pron.* ninguno.
nonentity /nɒn'ɛntɪti/ *n.* nulidad *f.*
nonpartisan /nɒn'pɑrtəzən/ *a.* sin afiliación.
non-proliferation /ˌnɒnprəˌlɪfə'reiʃən/ *n.* no proliferación *m.*
nonsense /'nɒnsɛns/ *n.* tontería *f.*
nonsmoker /nɒn'smoukər/ *n.* no fumador -dora.
noodle /'nudl̩/ *n.* fideo *m.*
noon /nun/ *n.* mediodía *m.*
noose /nus/ *n.* lazo corredizo *m.*; dogal *m.*
nor /nɔr; *unstressed* nər/ *conj.* ni.
normal /'nɔrməl/ *a.* normal.
north /nɔrθ/ *n.* norte *m.*
North America /ə'mɛrɪkə/ Norte América *f.*
North American *a.* & *n.* norteamericano -na.
northeast /ˌnɔrθ'ist; *Naut.* ˌnɔr-/ *n.* nordeste *m.*
northern /'nɔrðərn/ *a.* septentrional.
North Pole *n.* Polo Norte *m.*
northwest /ˌnɔrθ'wɛst; *Naut.* ˌnɔr-/ *n.* noroeste *m.*
Norway /'nɔrwei/ *n.* Noruega *f.*
Norwegian /nɔr'widʒən/ *a.* & *n.* noruego -ga.
nose /nouz/ *n.* nariz *f.*
nosebleed /'nouzˌblid/ *n.* hemorragia nasal *f.*
nostalgia /nɒ'stældʒə/ *n.* nostalgia *f.*
nostril /'nɒstrəl/ *n.* ventana de la nariz; (pl.) narices *f.pl.*
not /nɒt/ *adv.* no. **n. at all,** de ninguna manera. **n. even,** ni siquiera.
notable /'noutəbəl/ *a.* notable.
notary /'noutəri/ *n.* notario *m.*
notation /nou'teiʃən/ *a.* notación *f.*
notch /nɒtʃ/ *n.* muesca *f.*; corte *m.*
note /nout/ *n.* **1.** nota *f.*; apunte *m.* —*v.* **2.** notar.
notebook /'noutˌbʊk/ *n.* libreta *f.*, cuaderno *m.*
noted /'noutɪd/ *a.* célebre.
notepaper /'noutˌpeipər/ *n.* papel de notas *m.*
noteworthy /'noutˌwɜrði/ *a.* notable.
nothing /'nʌθɪŋ/ *pron.* nada.
notice /'noutɪs/ *n.* **1.** aviso *m.*; noticia *f.* —*v.* **2.** observar, fijarse en.
noticeable /'noutɪsəbəl/ *a.* notable.
notification /ˌnoutəfɪ'keiʃən/ *n.* notificación *f.*
notify /'noutəˌfai/ *v.* notificar.
notion /'nouʃən/ *n.* noción; idea *f.*; (pl.) novedades *f.pl.*
notoriety /ˌnoutə'raiɪti/ *n.* notoriedad *f.*
notorious /nou'tɔriəs/ *a.* notorio.
noun /naun/ *n.* nombre, sustantivo *m.*
nourish /'nɜrɪʃ/ *v.* nutrir, alimentar.
nourishment /'nɜrɪʃmənt/ *n.* nutrimento; alimento *m.*
novel /'nɒvəl/ *a.* **1.** nuevo, original. —*n.* **2.** novela *f.*
novelist /'nɒvəlɪst/ *n.* novelista *m.* & *f.*
novelty /'nɒvəlti/ *n.* novedad *f.*
November /nou'vɛmbər/ *n.* noviembre *m.*
novena /nou'vinə/ *n.* novena *f.*
novice /'nɒvɪs/ *n.* novicio -cia, novato -ta.
novocaine /'nouvəˌkein/ *n.* novocaína *f.*
now /nau/ *adv.* ahora. **n. and then,** de vez en cuando. **by n.,** ya. **from n. on,** de ahora en adelante. **just n.,** ahorita. **right n.,** ahora mismo.
nowadays /'nauəˌdeiz/ *adv.* hoy día, hoy en día, actualmente.
nowhere /'nouˌwɛər/ *adv.* en ninguna parte.
nozzle /'nɒzəl/ *n.* boquilla *f.*
nuance /'nuɑns/ *n.* matiz *m.*
nuclear /'nukliər/ *a.* nuclear.
nuclear energy energía nuclear *f.*
nuclear warhead /'wɔrˌhɛd/ cabeza nuclear *f.*
nuclear waste desechos nucleares *m.pl.*
nucleus /'nukliəs/ *n.* núcleo *m.*
nude /nud/ *a.* desnudo.
nuisance /'nusəns/ *n.* molestia *f.*
nuke /nuk/ *n.* bomba atómica *f.*
nullify /'nʌləˌfai/ *v.* anular.
number /'nʌmbər/ *n.* **1.** número *m.*; cifra *f.* **license n.,** matrícula *f.* —*v.* **2.** numerar, contar.
numeric /nu'mɛrɪk/ **numerical** *a.* numérico.
numeric keypad /nu'mɛrɪk/ teclado numérico *m.*
numerous /'numərəs/ *a.* numeroso.
nun /nʌn/ *n.* monja *f.*
nuptial /'nʌpʃəl/ *a.* nupcial.
nurse /nɜrs/ *n.* **1.** enfermera *f.*; (child's) ama, niñera *f.* —*v.* **2.** criar, alimentar, amamantar; cuidar.
nursery /'nɜrsəri/ *n.* cuarto destinado a los niños; *Agr.* plantel, criadero *m.*
nursery school jardín de infancia *m.*
nurture /'nɜrtʃər/ *v.* nutrir.
nut /nʌt/ *n.* nuez *f.*; *Mech.* tuerca *f.*
nutcracker /'nʌtˌkrækər/ *n.* cascanueces *m.*
nutrition /nu'trɪʃən/ *n.* nutrición *f.*
nutritious /nu'trɪʃəs/ *a.* nutritivo.
nylon /'nailɒn/ *n.* nilón *m.*
nymph /nɪmf/ *n.* ninfa *f.*

O

oak /ouk/ *n.* roble *m.*
oar /ɔr/ *n.* remo *m.*
OAS *abbr.* (Organization of American States) OEA (Organización de los Estados Americanos) *f.*
oasis /ou'eisɪs/ *n.* oasis *m.*
oat /out/ *n.* avena *f.*
oath /ouθ/ *n.* juramento *m.*
oatmeal /'outˌmil/ *n.* harina de avena *f.*
obedience /ou'bidiəns/ *n.* obediencia *f.*
obedient /ou'bidiənt/ *a.* obediente.
obese /ou'bis/ *a.* obeso, gordo.
obey /ou'bei/ *v.* obedecer.
obituary /ou'bɪtʃuˌeri/ *n.* obituario *m.*
object /*n* 'ɒbdʒɪkt; *v* əb'dʒɛkt/ *n.* **1.** objeto *m.*; *Gram.* complemento *m.* —*v.* **2.** oponerse; objetar.
objection /əb'dʒɛkʃən/ *n.* objeción *f.*
objectionable /əb'dʒɛkʃənəbəl/ *a.* censurable.
objective /əb'dʒɛktɪv/ *a.* & *n.* objetivo *m.*
obligation /ˌɒblɪ'geiʃən/ *n.* obligación *f.*
obligatory /ə'blɪgəˌtɔri/ *a.* obligatorio.
oblige /ə'blaidʒ/ *v.* obligar; complacer.
oblique /ə'blik/ *a.* oblicuo.
obliterate /ə'blɪtəˌreit/ *v.* borrar; destruir.
oblivion /ə'blɪviən/ *n.* olvido *m.*
oblong /'ɒbˌlɔŋ/ *a.* oblongo.
obnoxious /əb'nɒkʃəs/ *a.* ofensivo, odioso.
obscene /əb'sin/ *a.* obsceno, indecente.
obscure /əb'skyʊr/ *a.* **1.** obscuro. —*v.* **2.** obscurecer.
observance /əb'zɜrvəns/ *n.* observancia; ceremonia *f.*
observation /ˌɒbzɜr'veiʃən/ *n.* observación *f.*
observatory /əb'zɜrvəˌtɔri/ *n.* observatorio *m.*
observe /əb'zɜrv/ *v.* observar; celebrar.
observer /əb'zɜrvər/ *n.* observador -ra.
obsession /əb'sɛʃən/ *n.* obsesión *f.*
obsolete /ˌɒbsə'lit/ *a.* anticuado.
obstacle /'ɒbstəkəl/ *n.* obstáculo *m.*
obstetrician /ˌɒbstɪ'trɪʃən/ *n.* obstétrico -ca, tocólogo -ga *m.* & *f.*
obstinate /'ɒbstənɪt/ *a.* obstinado, terco.
obstruct /əb'strʌkt/ *v.* obstruir, impedir.
obstruction /əb'strʌkʃən/ *n.* obstrucción *f.*
obtain /əb'tein/ *v.* obtener, conseguir.
obtuse /əb'tus/ *a.* obtuso.
obviate /'ɒbviˌeit/ *v.* obviar.
obvious /'ɒbviəs/ *a.* evidente, obvio.
occasion /ə'keiʒən/ *n.* **1.** ocasión *f.* —*v.* **2.** ocasionar.
occasional /ə'keiʒənl̩/ *a.* ocasional.
occult /ə'kʌlt/ *a.* oculto.
occupant /'ɒkyəpənt/ *n.* ocupante *m.* & *f.*; inquilino -na.
occupation /ˌɒkyə'peiʃən/ *n.* ocupación *f.*; empleo *m.*
occupy /'ɒkyəˌpai/ *v.* ocupar; emplear.
occur /ə'kɜr/ *v.* ocurrir.
occurrence /ə'kɜrəns/ *n.* ocurrencia *f.*
ocean /'ouʃən/ *n.* océano *m.*
o'clock /ə'klɒk/ **it's one o.,** es la una. **it's two o.,** son las dos, etc. **at... o.,** a las...
octagon /'ɒktəˌgɒn/ *n.* octágono *m.*
octave /'ɒktɪv/ *n.* octava *f.*
October /ɒk'toubər/ *n.* octubre *m.*
octopus /'ɒktəpəs/ *n.* pulpo *m.*
oculist /'ɒkyəlɪst/ *n.* oculista *m.* & *f.*
odd /ɒd/ *a.* impar; suelto; raro.
odd number número impar *m.*
odious /'oudiəs/ *a.* odioso.
odor /'oudər/ *n.* olor *m.*; fragancia *f.*
of /əv/ *prep.* de.
off /ɔf/ *adv.* (see under verb: **stop off, take off,** etc.)
offend /ə'fɛnd/ *v.* ofender.
offender /ə'fɛndər/ *n.* ofensor -ra; delincuente *m.* & *f.*
offense /ə'fɛns/ *n.* ofensa *f.*; crimen *m.*
offensive /ə'fɛnsɪv/ *a.* **1.** ofensivo. —*n.* **2.** ofensiva *f.*
offer /'ɔfər/ *n.* **1.** oferta *f.* —*v.* **2.** ofrecer.
offering /'ɔfərɪŋ/ *n.* oferta *f.*
office /'ɔfɪs/ *n.* oficina *f.*; despacho *m.*; oficio, cargo *m.*
officer /'ɔfəsər/ *n.* oficial *m.* & *f.* **police o.,** agente de policía *m.* & *f.*
official /ə'fɪʃəl/ *a.* **1.** oficial. —*n.* **2.** oficial *m.* & *f.*, funcionario -ria.
officiate /ə'fɪʃiˌeit/ *v.* oficiar.
officious /ə'fɪʃəs/ *a.* oficioso.
offspring /'ɔfˌsprɪŋ/ *n.* hijos *m.pl.*; progenie *f.*
often /'ɔfən/ *adv.* muchas veces, a menudo. **how o.,** con qué frecuencia.
oil /ɔil/ *n.* **1.** aceite; óleo; petróleo *m.* —*v.* **2.** aceitar; engrasar.
oil refinery /rɪ'fainəri/ destilería de petróleo *f.*
oil tanker /'tæŋkər/ petrolero *m.*
oily /'ɔili/ *a.* aceitoso.
ointment /'ɔintmənt/ *n.* ungüento *m.*
okay /'ou'kei, ˌou'kei/ *adv.* bien; de acuerdo.
old /ould/ *a.* viejo; antiguo. **o. man, o. woman,** viejo -ja.
old-fashioned /'ould 'fæʃənd/ *a.* fuera de moda, anticuado.
Old Testament Antiguo Testamento *m.*
olive /'ɒlɪv/ *n.* aceituna, oliva *f.*
ombudsman /'ɒmbədzmən/ *n.* ombudsman *m.*
omelet /'ɒmlɪt/ *n.* tortilla de huevos.
omen /'oumən/ *n.* agüero *m.*
ominous /'ɒmənəs/ *a.* ominoso, siniestro.
omission /ou'mɪʃən/ *n.* omisión *f.*; olvido *m.*
omit /ou'mɪt/ *v.* omitir.
omnibus /'ɒmnəˌbʌs/ *n.* ómnibus *m.*
omnipotent /ɒm'nɪpətənt/ *a.* omnipotente.
on /ɒn/ *prep.* **1.** en, sobre, encima de. —*adv.* **2.** adelante.

once /wʌns/ *adv.* una vez. **at o.,** en seguida. **o. in a while,** de vez en cuando.

one /wʌn/ *a. & pron.* uno -na.

one-armed bandit /'wʌn ,armd/ tragaperras *f.*

oneself /wʌn'sɛlf/ *pron.* sí mismo -ma; se. **with o.,** consigo.

onion /'ʌnyən/ *n.* cebolla *f.*

on-line /'ɒn 'laɪn/ *a.* conectado.

only /'ounli/ *a.* **1.** único, solo. —*adv.* **2.** sólo, solamente.

onward /'ɒnwərd/ *adv.* adelante.

opal /'oupəl/ *n.* ópalo *m.*

opaque /ou'peik/ *a.* opaco.

open /'oupən/ *a.* **1.** abierto; franco. **o. air,** aire libre. —*v.* **2.** abrir.

opening /'oupənɪŋ/ *n.* abertura *f.*

opera /'ɒpərə/ *n.* ópera *f.* **o. glasses,** anteojos de ópera; gemelos *m.pl.*

operate /'ɒpə,reit/ *v.* operar.

operation /,ɒpə'reiʃən/ *n.* operación *f.* **to have an o.,** operarse, ser operado.

operative /'ɒpərətɪv/ *a.* eficaz, operativo.

operator /'ɒpə,reitər/ *n.* operario -ria. **elevator o.,** ascensorista *m. & f.* **telephone o.,** telefonista *m. & f.*

operetta /,ɒpə'rɛtə/ *n.* opereta *f.*

ophthalmic /ɒf'θælmɪk, ɒp-/ *a.* oftálmico.

opinion /ə'pɪnyən/ *n.* opinión *f.*

opponent /ə'pounənt/ *n.* antagonista *m. & f.*

opportunism /,ɒpər'tunɪzəm/ *n.* oportunismo *m.*

opportunity /,ɒpər'tunɪti/ *n.* ocasión, oportunidad *f.*

oppose /ə'pouz/ *v.* oponer.

opposite /'ɒpəzɪt/ *a.* **1.** opuesto, contrario. —*prep.* **2.** al frente de. —*n.* **3.** contrario *m.*

opposition /,ɒpə'zɪʃən/ *n.* oposición *f.*

oppress /ə'prɛs/ *v.* oprimir.

oppression /ə'prɛʃən/ *n.* opresión *f.*

oppressive /ə'prɛsɪv/ *a.* opresivo.

optic /'ɒptɪk/ *a.* óptico.

optical disc /'ɒptɪkəl 'dɪsk/ disco óptico *m.*

optical illusion /'ɒptɪkəl/ ilusión de óptica *f.*

optician /ɒp'tɪʃən/ *n.* óptico -ca.

optics /'ɒptɪks/ *n.* óptica *f.*

optimism /'ɒptə,mɪzəm/ *n.* optimismo.

optimistic /,ɒptə'mɪstɪk/ *a.* optimista.

option /'ɒpʃən/ *n.* opción, elección *f.*

optional /'ɒpʃənl/ *a.* discrecional, facultativo.

optometry /ɒp'tɒmɪtri/ *n.* optometría *f.*

opulent /'ɒpyələnt/ *a.* opulento.

or /ɔr/ *conj.* o, (before o-, ho-) u.

oracle /'ɔrəkəl/ *n.* oráculo *m.*

oral /'ɔrəl/ *a.* oral, vocal.

orange /'ɔrɪndʒ/ *n.* naranja *f.*

orange juice jugo de naranja, zumo de naranja *m.*

orange squeezer /'skwizər/ *n.* exprimidora de naranjas *f.*

oration /ɔ'reiʃən/ *n.* discurso *m.*; oración *f.*

orator /'ɔrətər/ *n.* orador -ra.

oratory /'ɔrə,tɔri/ *n.* oratoria *f.*; (church) oratorio *m.*

orbit /'ɔrbɪt/ *n.* órbita *f.*

orchard /'ɔrtʃərd/ *n.* huerto *m.*

orchestra /'ɔrkəstrə/ *n.* orquesta *f.* **o. seat,** butaca *f.*

orchid /'ɔrkɪd/ *n.* orquídea *f.*

ordain /ɔr'dein/ *v.* ordenar.

ordeal /ɔr'dil/ *n.* prueba *f.*

order /'ɔrdər/ *n.* orden, *m. or f.*; clase *f.*; *Com.* pedido *m.* **in o. that,** para que. *v.* ordenar; mandar; pedir.

order blank hoja de pedidos *f.*

orderly /'ɔrdərli/ *a.* ordenado.

ordinance /'ɔrdṇəns/ *n.* ordenanza *f.*

ordinary /'ɔrdṇ,ɛri/ *a.* ordinario.

ordination /,ɔrdṇ'eiʃən/ *n.* ordenación *f.*

ore /ɔr/ *n.* mineral *m.*

organ /'ɔrgən/ *n.* órgano *m.*

organdy /'ɔrgəndi/ *n.* organdí *m.*

organic /ɔr'gænɪk/ *a.* orgánico.

organism /'ɔrgə,nɪzəm/ *n.* organismo *m.*

organist /'ɔrgənɪst/ *n.* organista *m. & f.*

organization /,ɔrgənə'zeiʃən/ *n.* organización *f.*

organize /'ɔrgə,naiz/ *v.* organizar.

orgy /'ɔrdʒi/ *n.* orgía *f.*

orient /'ɔriənt/ *n.* **1.** oriente *m.* —*v.* **2.** orientar.

Orient /'ɔriənt/ *n.* Oriente *m.*

Oriental /,ɔri'ɛntḷ/ *a.* oriental.

orientation /,ɔriən'teiʃən/ *n.* orientación *f.*

origin /'ɔrɪdʒɪn/ *n.* origen *m.*

original /ə'rɪdʒənḷ/ *a. & n.* original *m.*

originality /ə,rɪdʒə'næliti/ *n.* originalidad *f.*

ornament /n 'ɔrnəmənt; v -,mɛnt/ *n.* **1.** ornamento *m.* —*v.* **2.** ornamentar.

ornamental /,ɔrnə'mɛntḷ/ *a.* ornamental, decorativo.

ornate /ɔr'neit/ *a.* ornado.

ornithology /,ɔrnə'θɒlədʒi/ *n.* ornitología *f.*

orphan /'ɔrfən/ *a. & n.* huérfano -na.

orphanage /'ɔrfənɪdʒ/ *n.* orfanato *m.*

orthodox /'ɔrθə,dɒks/ *a.* ortodoxo.

ostentation /,ɒstɛn'teiʃən/ *n.* ostentación *f.*

ostentatious /,ɒstɛn'teiʃəs/ *a.* ostentoso.

ostrich /'ɔstrɪtʃ/ *n.* avestruz *f.*

other /'ʌðər/ *a. & pron.* otro. **every o. day,** un día sí otro no.

otherwise /'ʌðər,waiz/ *adv.* de otra manera.

ought /ɔt/ *v.* deber.

ounce /auns/ *n.* onza *f.*

our /auər; *unstressed* ɑr/ **ours** *a. & pron.* nuestro.

ourselves /ɑr'sɛlvz/ *pron.* nosotros -as; mismos -as; nos.

oust /aust/ *v.* desalojar.

ouster /'austər/ *n.* desahucio *m.*

out /aut/ *adv.* **1.** fuera, afuera. **out of,** fuera de. —*prep.* **2.** por.

outbreak /'aut,breik/ *n.* erupción *f.*

outcast /'aut,kæst/ *n.* paria *m. & f.*

outcome /'aut,kʌm/ *n.* resultado *m.*

outdoors /,aut'dɔrz/ *adv.* fuera de casa; al aire libre.

outer /'autər/ *a.* exterior, externo.

outfit /'aut,fɪt/ *n.* **1.** equipo; traje *m.* —*v.* **2.** equipar.

outgrowth /'aut,grouθ/ *n.* resultado *m.*

outing /'autɪŋ/ *n.* paseo *m.*

outlaw /'aut,lɔ/ *n.* **1.** bandido *m.* —*v.* **2.** proscribir.

outlet /'autlɛt/ *n.* salida *f.*

outline /'aut,lain/ *n.* **1.** contorno; esbozo *m.*; silueta *f.* —*v.* **2.** esbozar.

outlive /,aut'lɪv/ *v.* sobrevivir.

out-of-court settlement /'autəv- ,kɔrt/ arreglo pacífico *m.*

out-of-date /'aut əv 'deit/ *a.* anticuado.

out of focus *a.* desenfocado.

outpost /'aut,poust/ *n.* puesto avanzado.

output /'aut,put/ *n.* capacidad *f.*; producción *f.*

outrage /'autreidʒ/ *n.* **1.** ultraje *m.*; atrocidad *f.* —*v.* **2.** ultrajar.

outrageous /aut'reidʒəs/ *a.* atroz.

outrun /,aut'rʌn/ *v.* exceder.

outside /a, prep, adv ,aut'said; n 'aut'said/ *n.* **1.** exterior *m.* —*adv.* **2.** afuera, por fuera. —*prep.* **3.** fuera de.

outskirt /'aut,skɔrt/ *n.* borde *m.*

outward /'autwərd/ *adv.* hacia afuera.

outwardly /'autwərdli/ *adv.* exteriormente.

oval /'ouvəl/ *a.* **1.** oval, ovalado. —*n.* **2.** óvalo *m.*

ovary /'ouvəri/ *n.* ovario *m.*

ovation /ou'veiʃən/ *n.* ovación *f.*

oven /'ʌvən/ *n.* horno *m.*

over /'ouvər/ *prep.* **1.** sobre, encima de; por. —*adv.* **2.** **o. here,** aquí. **o. there,** allí, por allí. **to be o.,** estar terminado.

overcoat /'ouvər,kout/ *n.* abrigo, sobretodo *m.*

overcome /,ouvər'kʌm/ *v.* superar, vencer.

overdose /'ouvər,dous/ *n.* sobredosis *f.*

overdue /,ouvər'du/ *a.* retrasado.

overflow /n 'ouvər,flou; v ,ouvər'flou/ *n.* **1.** inundación *f.* —*v.* **2.** inundar.

overhaul /,ouvər'hɔl/ *v.* repasar.

overhead /'ouvər,hɛd/ *adv.* arriba, en lo alto.

overkill /'ouvər,kɪl/ *n.* efecto mayor que el pretendido.

overlook /,ouvər'luk/ *v.* pasar por alto.

overnight /'ouvər'nait/ *adv.* **to stay or stop o.,** pasar la noche.

overpower /,ouvər'pauər/ *v.* vencer.

overrule /,ouvər'rul/ *v.* predominar.

overrun /,ouvər'rʌn/ *v.* invadir.

oversee /,ouvər'si/ *v.* superentender.

oversight /'ouvər,sait/ *n.* descuido *m.*

overt /ou'vɜrt/ *a.* abierto.

overtake /,ouvər'teik/ *v.* alcanzar.

overthrow /n 'ouvər,θrou; v ,ouvər'θrou/ *n.* **1.** trastorno *m.* —*v.* **2.** trastornar.

overture /'ouvərtʃər/ *n.* *Mus.* obertura *f.*

overturn /,ouvər'tɜrn/ *v.* trastornar.

overview /'ouvər,vyu/ *n.* visión de conjunto *f.*

overweight /'ouvər,weit/ *a.* demasiado pesado.

overwhelm /,ouvər'wɛlm/ *v.* abrumar.

overwork /,ouvər'wɜrk/ *v.* trabajar demasiado.

owe /ou/ *v.* deber. **owing to,** debido a.

owl /aul/ *n.* búho *m.*, lechuza *f.*

own /oun/ *a.* **1.** propio. —*v.* **2.** poseer.

owner /'ounər/ *n.* dueño -ña.

ox /ɒks/ *n.* buey *m.*

oxygen /'ɒksɪdʒən/ *n.* oxígeno *m.*

oxygen tent tienda de oxígeno *f.*

oyster /'ɔistər/ *n.* ostra *f.*

P

pace /peis/ *n.* **1.** paso *m.* —*v.* **2.** pasearse. **p. off,** medir a pasos.

pacific /pə'sɪfɪk/ *a.* pacífico.

Pacific Ocean Océano Pacífico *m.*

pacifier /'pæsə,faiər/ *n.* pacificador *m.*; (baby p.) chupete *m.*

pacifism /'pæsə,fɪzəm/ *n.* pacifismo *m.*

pacifist /'pæsəfɪst/ *n.* pacifista *m. & f.*

pacify /'pæsə,fai/ *v.* pacificar.

pack /pæk/ *n.* **1.** fardo; paquete *m.*; (animals) muta *f.* **p. of cards,** baraja *f.* —*v.* **2.** empaquetar; (baggage) empacar.

package /'pækɪdʒ/ *n.* paquete, bulto *m.*

package tour viaje todo incluido *m.*

pact /pækt/ *n.* pacto *m.*

pad /pæd/ *n.* **1.** colchoncillo *m.* **p. of paper,** bloc de papel. —*v.* **2.** rellenar.

paddle /'pædḷ/ *n.* **1.** canalete *m.* —*v.* **2.** remar.

padlock /'pæd,lɒk/ *n.* candado *m.*

pagan /'peigən/ *a. & n.* pagano -na.

page /peidʒ/ *n.* página *f.*; (boy) paje *m.*

pageant /'pædʒənt/ *n.* espectáculo *m.*; procesión *f.*

pail /peil/ *n.* cubo *m.*

pain /pein/ *n.* dolor *m.* **to take pains,** esmerarse.

painful /'peinfəl/ *a.* doloroso; penoso.

pain killer /'pein,kɪlər/ analgésico *m.*

paint /peint/ *n.* **1.** pintura *f.* —*v.* **2.** pintar.

painter /'peintər/ *n.* pintor -ra.

painting /'peintɪŋ/ *n.* pintura *f.*; cuadro *m.*

pair /pɛər/ *n.* **1.** par *m.*; pareja *f.* —*v.* **2.** parear. **p. off,** emparejarse.

pajamas /pə'dʒaməz, -'dʒæməz/ *n.* pijama *m.*

palace /'pælɪs/ *n.* palacio *m.*

palatable /'pælətəbəl/ *a.* sabroso, agradable.

palate /'pælɪt/ *n.* paladar *m.*

palatial /pə'leiʃəl/ *a.* palaciego, suntuoso.

pale /peil/ *a.* pálido. **to turn pale,** palidecer.

paleness /'peilnɪs/ *n.* palidez *f.*

palette /'pælɪt/ *n.* paleta *f.*

pallbearer /'pɔl,bɛərər/ *n.* portador del féretro, portaféretro *m.*

pallid /'pælɪd/ *a.* pálido.

palm /pam/ *n.* palma *f.* **p. tree,** palmera *f.*

palpitate /'pælpɪ,teit/ *v.* palpitar.

paltry /'pɔltri/ *a.* miserable.

pamper /'pæmpər/ *v.* mimar.

pamphlet /'pæmflɪt/ *n.* folleto *m.*

pan /pæn/ *n.* cacerola *f.*

panacea /,pænə'siə/ *n.* panacea *f.*

Pan-American /,pænə'mɛrɪkən/ *a.* panamericano.

pane /pein/ *n.* hoja de vidrio *f.*, cuadro *m.*

panel /'pænḷ/ *n.* tablero *m.*

pang /pæŋ/ *n.* dolor; remordimiento *m.*

panic /'pænɪk/ *n.* pánico *m.*

panorama /,pænə'ræmə, -'ramə/ *n.* panorama *m.*

pant /pænt/ *v.* jadear.

panther /'pænθər/ *n.* pantera *f.*

pantomime /'pæntə,maim/ *n.* pantomima *f.*; mímica *f.*

pantry /'pæntri/ *n.* despensa *f.*

pants /pænts/ *n.* pantalones, *m.pl.*

panty hose /'pænti,houz/ *n.* pantys; pantimedias *f.pl.* (medias hasta la cintura).

papal /'peipəl/ *a.* papal.

paper /'peipər/ *n.* papel; periódico; artículo *m.*

paperback /'peipər,bæk/ *n.* libro en rústica *m.*

paper clip sujetapapeles *m.*

paper cup vaso de papel *m.*

paper hanger /'peipər,hæŋər/ empapelador *m.*

paper money papel moneda *m.*

paperweight /'peipər,weit/ pisapapeles *m.*

papier-mâché /,peipərmə'ʃei, pɑ,pyei-/ *n.* cartón piedra *m.*

paprika /pæ'prikə, pə-, pɑ-, 'pæprikə/ *n.* pimentón *m.*

par /pɑr/ *n.* paridad *f.*; *Com.* par *f.*

parable /'pærəbəl/ *n.* parábola *f.*

parachute /'pærə,ʃut/ *n.* paracaídas *m.*

parade /pə'reid/ *n.* **1.** desfile *m.*, procesión *f.* —*v.* **2.** desfilar.

paradise /'pærə,dais/ *n.* paraíso *m.*

paradox /'pærə,dɒks/ *n.* paradoja *f.*

paraffin /'pærəfɪn/ *n.* parafina *f.*

paragraph /'pærə,græf/ *n.* párrafo *m.*

parakeet /'pærə,kit/ *n.* perico *m.*

parallel /'pærə,lɛl/ *a.* **1.** paralelo. —*v.* **2.** correr parejas con.

paralysis /pə'ræləsɪs/ *n.* parálisis *f.*

paralyze /'pærə,laiz/ *v.* paralizar.

paramedic /,pærə'mɛdɪk/ *n.* paramédico -ca.

parameter /pə'ræmɪtər/ *n.* parámetro *m.*

paramount /'pærə,maunt/ *a.* supremo.

paraphrase /'pærə,freiz/ *n.* **1.** paráfrasis *f.* —*v.* **2.** parafrasear.

paraplegic /'pærə'plidʒɪk/ *n.* parapléjico -ca.

parasite /'pærə,sait/ *n.* parásito *m.*

parboil /'par,bɔil/ v. sancochar.
parcel /'parsəl/ n. paquete m. **p. of land,** lote de terreno.
parchment /'partʃmənt/ n. pergamino m.
pardon /'pardn/ n. **1.** perdón m. —v. **2.** perdonar.
pare /pɛər/ v. pelar.
parentage /'pɛərəntɪdʒ, 'pær-/ n. origen m.; extracción f.
parenthesis /pə'rɛnθəsɪs/ n. paréntesis m.
parents /'pɛərənts/ n. padres m.pl.
parish /'pærɪʃ/ n. parroquia f.
Parisian /pə'rɪʒən, -'riʒən, -'rɪziən/ a. & n. parisiense m. & f.
parity /'pærɪti/ n. igualdad, paridad f.
park /park/ n. **1.** parque m. —v. **2.** estacionar.
parking lot /'parkɪŋ/ n. estacionamiento, aparcamiento m.
parking meter /'parkɪŋ/ parquímetro m.
parking space /'parkɪŋ/ estacionamiento, aparcamiento m.
parkway /'park,wei/ n. bulevar m.; autopista f.
parley /'parli/ n. conferencia f.; Mil. parlamento m.
parliament /'parləmənt/ n. parlamento m.
parliamentary /,parlə'mɛntəri, -tri; sometimes ,parlyə-/ a. parlamentario.
parlor /'parlər/ n. sala f., salón m.
parochial /pə'roukiəl/ a. parroquial.
parody /'pærədi/ n. **1.** parodia f. —v. **2.** parodiar.
parole /pə'roul/ n. **1.** palabra de honor f.; Mil. santo y seña. —v. **2.** poner en libertad bajo palabra.
paroxysm /'pærək,sɪzəm/ n. paroxismo m.
parrot /'pærət/ n. loro, papagayo m.
parsimony /'parsə,mouni/ n. parsimonia f.
parsley /'parsli/ n. perejil m.
parson /'parsən/ n. párroco m.
part /part/ n. **1.** parte f.; Theat. papel m. —v. **2.** separarse, partirse. **p. with,** desprenderse de.
partake /par'teik/ v. tomar parte.
partial /'parʃəl/ a. parcial.
participant /par'tɪsəpənt/ n. participante m. & f.
participate /par'tɪsə,peit/ v. participar.
participation /par,tɪsə'peiʃən/ n. participación f.
participle /'partə,sɪpəl, -səpəl/ n. participio m.
particle /'partɪkəl/ n. partícula f.
particular /pər'tɪkyələr/ a. & n. particular m.
parting /'partɪŋ/ n. despedida f.
partisan /'partəzən, -sən/ a. & n. partidario -ria.
partition /par'tɪʃən, pər-/ n. tabique m. v. dividir, partir.
partly /'partli/ adv. en parte.
partner /'partnər/ n. socio -cia; compañero -ra.
partridge /'partrɪdʒ/ n. perdiz f.
party /'parti/ n. tertulia, fiesta f.; grupo m.; (political) partido m.
pass /pæs/ n. **1.** pase; (mountain) paso m. —v. **2.** pasar. **p. away,** fallecer.
passable /'pæsəbəl/ a. transitable; regular.
passage /'pæsɪdʒ/ n. pasaje; (corridor) pasillo m.
passé /pæ'sei/ a. anticuado.
passenger /'pæsəndʒər/ n. pasajero -ra.
passenger ship buque de pasajeros m.
passerby /'pæsər'bai/ n. transeúnte m. & f.
passion /'pæʃən/ n. pasión f.
passionate /'pæʃənɪt/ a. apasionado.
passive /'pæsɪv/ a. pasivo.
passport /'pæsport/ n. pasaporte m.

password /'pæs,wɜrd/ n. código m., clave m., contraseña f.
past /pæst/ a. & n. **1.** pasado m. —prep. **2.** más allá de; después de.
paste /peist/ n. **1.** pasta f. —v. **2.** empastar; pegar.
pasteurize /'pæstʃə,raiz/ v. pasteurizar.
pastime /'pæs,taim/ n. pasatiempo m.; diversión f.
pastor /'pæstər/ n. pastor m.
pastrami /pə'strami/ n. pastrón m.
pastry /'peistri/ n. pastelería f.
pasture /'pæstʃər/ n. **1.** pasto m.; pradera f. —v. **2.** pastar.
pat /pæt/ n. **1.** golpecillo m. **to stand p.,** mantenerse firme. —v. **2.** dar golpecillos.
patch /pætʃ/ n. **1.** remiendo m. —v. **2.** remendar.
patent /'pætnt/ a. & n. **1.** patente m. —v. **2.** patentar.
patent leather /'pætnt, 'pætn/ charol m.
paternal /pə'tɜrnl/ a. paterno, paternal.
paternity /pə'tɜrniti/ n. paternidad f.
path /pæθ/ n. senda f.
pathetic /pə'θɛtɪk/ a. patético.
pathology /pə'θɒlədʒi/ n. patología f.
pathos /'peiθɒs/ n. rasgo conmovedor m.
patience /'peiʃəns/ n. paciencia f.
patient /'peiʃənt/ a. **1.** paciente. —n. **2.** enfermo -ma, paciente m. & f.
patio /'pæti,ou/ n. patio m.
patriarch /'peitri,ark/ n. patriarca m.
patriot /'peitriət/ n. patriota m. & f.
patriotic /,peitri'ɒtɪk/ a. patriótico.
patriotism /'peitriə,tɪzəm/ n. patriotismo m.
patrol /pə'troul/ n. **1.** patrulla f. —v. **2.** patrullar.
patrolman /pə'troulmən/ n. vigilante m.; patrullador m.
patron /'peitrən/ n. patrón m.
patronize /'peitrə,naiz/ v. condescender; patrocinar; ser cliente de.
pattern /'pætərn/ n. modelo m.
pauper /'pɔpər/ n. indigente m. & f.
pause /pɔz/ n. **1.** pausa f. —v. **2.** pausar.
pave /peiv/ v. pavimentar. **p. the way,** preparar el camino.
pavement /'peivmənt/ n. pavimento m.
pavilion /pə'vɪlyən/ n. pabellón m.
paw /pɔ/ n. **1.** pata f. —v. **2.** patear.
pawn /pɔn/ n. **1.** prenda f.; (chess) peón de ajedrez m. —v. **2.** empeñar.
pay /pei/ n. **1.** pago; sueldo, salario m.; —v. **2.** pagar. **p. back,** pagar; vengarse de. **p. cash,** pagar en metálico.
payee /pei'i/ n. destinatario -ria m. & f.
payment /'peimənt/ n. pago m.; recompensa f.
pay phone teléfono público m.
pea /pi/ n. guisante m.
peace /pis/ n. paz f.
peaceable /'pisəbəl/ a. pacífico.
peaceful /'pisfəl/ a. tranquilo.
peach /pitʃ/ n. durazno, melocotón m.
peacock /'pi,kɒk/ n. pavo real m.
peak /pik/ n. pico, cumbre; máximo m.
peal /pil/ n. repique; estruendo m. **p. of laughter,** risotada f.
peanut /'pi,nʌt/ n. maní, cacahuete m.
pear /pɛər/ n. pera f.
pearl /pɜrl/ n. perla f.
peasant /'pɛzənt/ n. campesino -na.
pebble /'pɛbəl/ n. guija f.
peck /pɛk/ n. **1.** picotazo m. —v. **2.** picotear.
peckish /'pɛkɪʃ/ a. tener un poco de hambre.
peculiar /pɪ'kyulyər/ a. peculiar.
pecuniary /pɪ'kyuni,ɛri/ a. pecuniario.
pedagogue /'pɛdə,gɒg/ n. pedagogo -ga.

pedagogy /'pɛdə,goudʒi, -,gɒdʒi/ n. pedagogía f.
pedal /'pɛdl/ n. pedal m.
pedant /'pɛdnt/ n. pedante m. & f.
peddler /'pɛdlər/ n. buhonero m.
pedestal /'pɛdəstl/ n. pedestal m.
pedestrian /pə'dɛstriən/ n. peatón -na.
pedestrian crossing paso de peatones m.
pediatrician /,pidiə'trɪʃən/ n. pediatra m. & f.
pediatrics /,pidi'ætrɪks/ n. puericultura f.
pedigree /'pɛdɪ,gri/ n. genealogía f.
peek /pik/ n. **1.** atisbo m. —v. **2.** atisbar.
peel /pil/ n. **1.** corteza f.; (fruit) pellejo m. —v. **2.** descortezar; pelar.
peep /pip/ n. **1.** ojeada f. —v. **2.** mirar, atisbar.
peer /pɪər/ n. **1.** par m. —v. **2.** mirar fijamente.
peg /pɛg/ n. clavija; estaquilla f.; gancho m.
pelt /pɛlt/ n. **1.** pellejo m. —v. **2.** apedrear; (rain) caer con fuerza.
pelvis /'pɛlvɪs/ n. pelvis f.
pen /pɛn/ n. pluma f.; corral m. **fountain p.,** pluma fuente.
penalty /'pɛnlti/ n. pena; multa f.; castigo m.
penance /'pɛnəns/ n. penitencia f. **to do p.,** penar.
penchant /'pɛntʃənt/ n. propensión f.
pencil /'pɛnsəl/ n. lápiz m.
pencil sharpener /'ʃarpənər/ sacapuntas m.
pending /'pɛndɪŋ/ a. pendiente. **to be p.,** pender.
penetrate /'pɛnɪ,treit/ v. penetrar.
penetration /,pɛnɪ'treiʃən/ n. penetración f.
penicillin /,pɛnə'sɪlɪn/ n. penicilina f.
peninsula /pə'nɪnsələ, -'nɪnsyələ/ n. península f.
penitent /'pɛnɪtənt/ n. & a. penitente m. & f.
penknife /'pɛn,naif/ n. cortaplumas f.
penniless /'pɛnɪlɪs/ a. indigente.
penny /'pɛni/ n. penique m.
pension /'pɛnʃən/ n. pensión f.
pensive /'pɛnsɪv/ a. pensativo.
penultimate /pɪ'nʌltəmɪt/ a. penúltimo.
penury /'pɛnyəri/ n. penuria f.
people /'pipəl/ n. **1.** gente f.; (of a nation) pueblo m. —v. **2.** poblar.
pepper /'pɛpər/ n. pimienta f.; (plant) pimiento m.
per /pɜr; unstressed pər/ prep. por.
perambulator /pər'æmbyə,leitər/ n. cochecillo de niño m.
perceive /pər'siv/ v. percibir.
percent /pər'sɛnt/ adv. por ciento.
percentage /pər'sɛntɪdʒ/ n. porcentaje m.
perceptible /pər'sɛptəbəl/ a. perceptible.
perception /pər'sɛpʃən/ n. percepción f.
perch /pɜrtʃ/ n. percha f.; (fish) perca f.
perdition /pər'dɪʃən/ n. perdición f.
peremptory /pə'rɛmptəri/ a. perentorio, terminante.
perennial /pə'rɛniəl/ a. perenne.
perfect /a. 'pɜrfɪkt; v. pər'fɛkt/ a. **1.** perfecto. —v. **2.** perfeccionar.
perfection /pər'fɛkʃən/ n. perfección f.
perfectionist /pər'fɛkʃənɪst/ a. & n. perfeccionista m. & f.
perforation /,pɜrfə'reiʃən/ n. perforación f.
perform /pər'fɔrm/ v. hacer; ejecutar; Theat. representar.
performance /pər'fɔrməns/ n. ejecución f.; Theat. representación f.
perfume /n. 'pɜrfyum; v. pər'fyum/ n. **1.** perfume m.; fragancia f. —v. **2.** perfumar.

perfunctory /pər'fʌŋktəri/ a. perfunctorio, superficial.
perhaps /pər'hæps/ adv. quizá, quizás, tal vez.
peril /'pɛrəl/ n. peligro m.
perilous /'pɛrələs/ a. peligroso.
perimeter /pə'rɪmɪtər/ n. perímetro m.
period /'pɪəriəd/ n. período m.; Punct. punto m.
periodic /,pɪəri'ɒdɪk/ a. periódico.
periodical /,pɪəri'ɒdɪkəl/ n. revista f.
periphery /pə'rɪfəri/ n. periferia f.
perish /'pɛrɪʃ/ v. perecer.
perishable /'pɛrɪʃəbəl/ a. perecedero.
perjury /'pɜrdʒəri/ n. perjurio m.
permanent /'pɜrmənənt/ a. permanente. **p. wave,** ondulado permanente.
permeate /'pɜrmi,eit/ v. penetrar.
permissible /pər'mɪsəbəl/ a. permisible.
permission /pər'mɪʃən/ n. permiso m.
permit /n. 'pɜrmɪt; v. pər'mɪt/ n. **1.** permiso m. —v. **2.** permitir.
pernicious /pər'nɪʃəs/ a. pernicioso.
perpendicular /,pɜrpən'dɪkyələr/ n. & a. perpendicular f.
perpetrate /'pɜrpɪ,treit/ v. perpetrar.
perpetual /pər'pɛtʃuəl/ a. perpetuo.
perplex /pər'plɛks/ v. confundir.
perplexity /pər'plɛksɪti/ n. perplejidad f.
persecute /'pɜrsɪ,kyut/ v. perseguir.
persecution /,pɜrsɪ'kyuʃən/ n. persecución f.
perseverance /,pɜrsə'vɪərəns/ n. perseverancia f.
persevere /,pɜrsə'vɪər/ v. perseverar.
persist /pər'sɪst/ v. persistir.
persistent /pər'sɪstənt/ a. persistente.
person /'pɜrsən/ n. persona f.
personage /'pɜrsənɪdʒ/ n. personaje m.
personal /'pɜrsənl/ a. personal.
personality /,pɜrsə'nælɪti/ n. personalidad f.
personnel /,pɜrsə'nɛl/ n. personal m.
perspective /pər'spɛktɪv/ n. perspectiva f.
perspiration /'pɜrspə'reiʃən/ n. sudor m.
perspire /pər'spaɪr/ v. sudar.
persuade /pər'sweid/ v. persuadir.
persuasive /pər'sweisɪv/ a. persuasivo.
pertain /pər'tein/ v. pertenecer.
pertinent /'pɜrtnənt/ a. pertinente.
perturb /pər'tɜrb/ v. perturbar.
peruse /pə'ruz/ v. leer con cuidado.
pervade /pər'veid/ v. penetrar; llenar.
perverse /pər'vɜrs/ a. perverso.
perversion /pər'vɜrʒən/ n. perversión f.
pessimism /'pɛsə,mɪzəm/ n. pesimismo m.
pester /'pɛstər/ v. molestar; fastidiar.
pesticide /'pɛstə,said/ n. pesticida m.
pestilence /'pɛstləns/ n. pestilencia f.
pet /pɛt/ n. **1.** favorito -ta; animal doméstico m. —v. **2.** mimar.
petal /'pɛtl/ n. pétalo m.
petition /pə'tɪʃən/ n. **1.** petición, súplica f. —v. **2.** pedir, suplicar.
petrify /'pɛtrə,fai/ v. petrificar.
petroleum /pə'trouliəm/ n. petróleo m.
petticoat /'pɛti,kout/ n. enagua f.
petty /'pɛti/ a. mezquino, insignificante.
petulant /'pɛtʃələnt/ a. quisquilloso.
pew /pyu/ n. banco de iglesia m.
pewter /'pyutər/ n. peltre m.
phantom /'fæntəm/ n. espectro, fantasma m.
pharmacist /'farməsɪst/ n. farmacéutico -ca, boticario -ria.
pharmacy /'farməsi/ n. farmacia, botica f.
phase /feiz/ n. fase f.
pheasant /'fɛzənt/ n. faisán m.

phenomenal /fɪˈnɒmənl̩/ *a.* fenomenal.

phenomenon /fɪˈnɒməˌnɒn/ *n.* fenómeno *f.*

philanthropy /fɪˈlænθrəpi/ *n.* filantropía *f.*

philately /fɪˈlætl̩i/ *n.* filatelia *f.*

philosopher /fɪˈlɒsəfər/ *n.* filósofo -fa.

philosophical /ˌfɪləˈsɒfɪkəl/ *a.* filosófico.

philosophy /fɪˈlɒsəfi/ *n.* filosofía *f.*

phlegm /flɛm/ *n.* flema *f.*

phlegmatic /flɛgˈmætɪk/ *a.* flemático.

phobia /ˈfoubiə/ *n.* fobia *f.*

phone /foun/ *n.* teléfono *m.*

phonetic /fəˈnɛtɪk/ *a.* fonético.

phonograph /ˈfounəˌgræf/ *n.* fonógrafo *m.*

phosphorus /ˈfɒsfərəs/ *n.* fósforo *m.*

photocopier /ˈfoutəˌkɒpiər/ *n.* fotocopiadora *f.*

photocopy /ˈfoutəˌkɒpi/ *n.* **1.** fotocopia *f.* —*v.* **2.** fotocopiar.

photoelectric /ˌfoutouɪˈlɛktrɪk/ *a.* fotoeléctrico.

photogenic /ˌfoutəˈdʒɛnɪk/ *a.* fotogénico.

photograph /ˈfoutəˌgræf/ *n.* **1.** fotografía *f.* —*v.* **2.** fotografiar; retratar.

photography /fəˈtɒgrəfi/ *n.* fotografía *f.*

phrase /freiz/ *n.* **1.** frase *f.* —*v.* **2.** expresar.

physical /ˈfɪzɪkəl/ *a.* físico.

physician /fɪˈzɪʃən/ *n.* médico *m.* & *f.*

physics /ˈfɪzɪks/ *n.* física *f.*

physiology /ˌfɪziˈɒlədʒi/ *n.* fisiología *f.*

physiotherapy /ˌfɪziouˈθɛrəpi/ *n.* fisioterapia *f.*

physique /fɪˈzik/ *n.* físico *m.*

pianist /piˈænɪst, ˈpiənɪst/ *n.* pianista *m.* & *f.*

piano /piˈænou/ *n.* piano *m.*

picayune /ˌpɪkəˈyun/ *a.* insignificante.

piccolo /ˈpɪkəˌlou/ *n.* flautín *m.*

pick /pɪk/ *n.* **1.** pico *m.* —*v.* **2.** escoger. **p. up,** recoger.

picket /ˈpɪkɪt/ *n.* piquete *m.*

pickle /ˈpɪkəl/ *n.* **1.** salmuera *f.*; encurtido *m.* —*v.* **2.** escabechar.

pickpocket /ˈpɪkˌpɒkɪt/ *n.* cortabolsas *m.* & *f.*

picnic /ˈpɪknɪk/ *n.* picnic *m.*

picture /ˈpɪktʃər/ *n.* **1.** cuadro; retrato *m.*; fotografía *f.*; (movie) película *f.* —*v.* **2.** imaginarse.

picturesque /ˌpɪktʃəˈrɛsk/ *a.* pintoresco.

pie /pai/ *n.* pastel *m.*

piece /pis/ *n.* pedazo *m.*; pieza *f.*

pieceworker /ˈpisˌwɜrkər/ *n.* destajero -ra, destajista *m.* & *f.*

pier /pɪər/ *n.* muelle *m.*

pierce /pɪərs/ *v.* perforar; pinchar; traspasar.

piety /ˈpaiɪti/ *n.* piedad *f.*

pig /pɪg/ *n.* puerco, cerdo, lechón *m.*

pigeon /ˈpɪdʒən/ *n.* paloma *f.*

pigeonhole /ˈpɪdʒənˌhoul/ *n.* casilla *f.*

pigment /ˈpɪgmənt/ *n.* pigmento *m.*

pile /pail/ *n.* **1.** pila *f.*; montón *m.*; *Med.* hemorroides *f.pl.* —*v.* **2.** amontonar.

pilfer /ˈpɪlfər/ *v.* ratear.

pilgrim /ˈpɪlgrɪm/ *n.* peregrino -na, romero -ra.

pilgrimage /ˈpɪlgrəmɪdʒ/ *n.* romería *f.*

pill /pɪl/ *n.* píldora *f.*

pillage /ˈpɪlɪdʒ/ *n.* **1.** pillaje *m.* —*v.* **2.** pillar.

pillar /ˈpɪlər/ *n.* columna *f.*

pillow /ˈpɪlou/ *n.* almohada *f.*

pillowcase /ˈpɪlouˌkeis/ *n.* funda de almohada *f.*

pilot /ˈpailət/ *n.* **1.** piloto *m.* & *f.* —*v.* **2.** pilotar.

pimple /ˈpɪmpəl/ *n.* grano *m.*

pin /pɪn/ *n.* **1.** alfiler; broche *m.*; *Mech.* clavija *f.* —*v.* **2.** prender. **p. up,** fijar.

pinafore /ˈpɪnəˌfɔr/ *n.* delantal (de niña) *m.*

pinch /pɪntʃ/ *n.* **1.** pellizco *m.* —*v.* **2.** pellizcar.

pine /pain/ *n.* **1.** pino *m.* —*v.* **2. p. away,** languidecer. **p. for,** anhelar.

pineapple /ˈpaiˌnæpəl/ *n.* piña *f.*, ananás *m.pl.*

pink /pɪŋk/ *a.* rosado.

pinky /ˈpɪŋki/ *n.* meñique *m.*

pinnacle /ˈpɪnəkəl/ *n.* pináculo *m.*; cumbre *f.*

pint /paint/ *n.* pinta *f.*

pioneer /ˌpaiəˈnɪər/ *n.* pionero -ra.

pious /ˈpaiəs/ *a.* piadoso.

pipe /paip/ *n.* pipa *f.*; tubo; (of organ) cañón *m.*

pipeline /ˈpaipˌlain/ *n.* oleoducto *m.*

piper /ˈpaipər/ *n.* flautista *m.* & *f.*

piquant /ˈpikənt/ *a.* picante.

pirate /ˈpairət/ *n.* pirata *m.*

pistol /ˈpɪstl̩/ *n.* pistola *f.*

piston /ˈpɪstən/ *n.* émbolo, pistón *m.*

pit /pɪt/ *n.* hoyo *m.*; (fruit) hueso *m.*

pitch /pɪtʃ/ *n.* **1.** brea *f.*; grado de inclinación; (music) tono *m.*; —*v.* **2.** lanzar; (ship) cabecear.

pitchblende /ˈpɪtʃˌblɛnd/ *n.* pechblenda *f.*

pitcher /ˈpɪtʃər/ *n.* cántaro *m.*; (baseball) lanzador -ra.

pitchfork /ˈpɪtʃˌfɔrk/ *n.* horca *f.*; tridente *m.*

pitfall /ˈpɪtˌfɔl/ *n.* trampa *f.*, hoya cubierta *f.*

pitiful /ˈpɪtɪfəl/ *a.* lastimoso.

pitiless /ˈpɪtɪlɪs/ *a.* cruel.

pituitary gland /pɪˈtuɪˌtɛri/ glándula pituitaria *f.*

pity /ˈpɪti/ *n.* **1.** compasión, piedad *f.* **to be a p.,** ser lástima. —*v.* **2.** compadecer.

pivot /ˈpɪvət/ *n.* **1.** espiga *f.*, pivote *m.*; punto de partida *m.* —*v.* **2.** girar sobre un pivote.

pizza /ˈpitsə/ *n.* pizza *f.*

placard /ˈplækɑrd/ *n.* **1.** cartel *m.* —*v.* **2.** fijar carteles.

placate /ˈpleikeit/ *v.* aplacar.

place /pleis/ *n.* **1.** lugar, sitio, puesto *m.* —*v.* **2.** colocar, poner.

placid /ˈplæsɪd/ *a.* plácido.

plagiarism /ˈpleidʒəˌrɪzəm/ *n.* plagio *m.*

plague /pleig/ *n.* **1.** plaga, peste *f.* —*v.* **2.** atormentar.

plain /plein/ *a.* **1.** sencillo; puro; evidente. —*n.* **2.** llano *m.*

plaintiff /ˈpleintɪf/ *n.* demandante *m.* & *f.*

plan /plæn/ *n.* **1.** plan, propósito *m.* —*v.* **2.** planear; pensar; planificar. **p. on,** contar con.

plane /plein/ *n.* **1.** plano; (tool) cepillo *m.* —*v.* **2.** allanar; acepillar.

planet /ˈplænɪt/ *n.* planeta *m.*

planetarium /ˌplænɪˈtɛəriəm/ *n.* planetario *m.*

plank /plæŋk/ *n.* tablón *m.*

planning /ˈplænɪŋ/ *n.* planificación *f.*

plant /plænt/ *n.* **1.** mata, planta *f.* —*v.* **2.** sembrar, plantar.

plantation /plænˈteiʃən/ *n.* plantación *f.* **coffee p.,** cafetal *m.*

planter /ˈplæntər/ *n.* plantador; hacendado *m.*

plasma /ˈplæzmə/ *n.* plasma *m.*

plaster /ˈplæstər/ *n.* **1.** yeso; emplasto *m.* —*v.* **2.** enyesar; emplastar.

plastic /ˈplæstɪk/ *a.* plástico.

plate /pleit/ *n.* **1.** plato *m.*; plancha de metal. —*v.* **2.** planchear.

plateau /plæˈtou/ *n.* meseta *f.*

platform /ˈplætfɔrm/ *n.* plataforma *f.*

platinum /ˈplætn̩əm/ *n.* platino *m.*

platitude /ˈplætɪˌtud/ *n.* perogrullada *f.*

platter /ˈplætər/ *n.* fuente *f.*, platel *m.*

plaudit /ˈplɔdɪt/ *n.* aplauso *m.*

plausible /ˈplɔzəbəl/ *a.* plausible.

play /plei/ *n.* **1.** juego *m.*; *Theat.* pieza *f.* —*v.* **2.** jugar; (music) tocar; *Theat.* representar. **p. a part,** hacer un papel.

player /ˈpleiər/ *n.* jugador -ra; (music) músico -ca.; *Theat.* actor *m.*, actriz *f.*

playful /ˈpleifəl/ *a.* juguetón.

playground /ˈpleiˌgraund/ *n.* campo de deportes; patio de recreo.

playmate /ˈpleiˌmeit/. *n.* compañero -ra de juego.

playwright /ˈpleiˌrait/ *n.* dramaturgo -ga.

plea /pli/ *n.* ruego *m.*; súplica *f.*; (legal) declaración *f.*

plead /plid/ *v.* suplicar; declararse. **p. a case,** defender un pleito.

pleasant /ˈplɛzənt/ *a.* agradable.

please /pliz/ *v.* **1.** gustar, agradar. **Pleased to meet you,** Mucho gusto en conocer a Vd. —*adv.* **2.** por favor. **Please...** Haga el favor de..., Tenga la bondad de..., Sírvase...

pleasure /ˈplɛʒər/ *n.* gusto, placer *m.*

pleat /plit/ *n.* **1.** pliegue *m.* —*v.* **2.** plegar.

plebiscite /ˈplɛbəˌsait/ *n.* plebiscito *m.*

pledge /plɛdʒ/ *n.* **1.** empeño *m.* —*v.* **2.** empeñar.

plentiful /ˈplɛntɪfəl/ *a.* abundante.

plenty /ˈplɛnti/ *n.* abundancia *f.* **p. of,** bastante. **p. more,** mucho más.

pleurisy /ˈplʊrəsi/ *n.* pleuritis *f.*

pliable, pliant /ˈplaiəbəl; ˈplaiənt/ *a.* flexible.

pliers /ˈplaiərz/ *n.pl.* alicates *m.pl.*

plight /plait/ *n.* apuro, aprieto *m.*

plot /plɒt/ *n.* **1.** conspiración; (of a story) trama; (of land) parcela *f.* —*v.* **2.** conspirar; tramar.

plow /plau/ *n.* **1.** arado *m.* —*v.* **2.** arar.

pluck /plʌk/ *n.* **1.** valor *m.* —*v.* **2.** arrancar; desplumar.

plug /plʌg/ *n.* **1.** tapón; *Elec.* enchufe *m.* **spark p.,** bujía *f.* —*v.* **2.** tapar.

plum /plʌm/ *n.* ciruela *f.*

plumage /ˈplumɪdʒ/ *n.* plumaje *m.*

plumber /ˈplʌmər/ *n.* fontanero -era, plomero -era.

plume /plum/ *n.* pluma *f.*

plump /plʌmp/ *a.* regordete.

plunder /ˈplʌndər/ *n.* **1.** botín *m.*; despojos *m.pl.* —*v.* **2.** saquear.

plunge /plʌndʒ/ *v.* zambullir; precipitar.

plural /ˈplʊrəl/ *a.* & *n.* plural *m.*

plus /plʌs/ *prep.* más.

plutocrat /ˈplutəˌkræt/ *n.* plutócrata *m.* & *f.*

pneumatic /nʊˈmætɪk/ *a.* neumático.

pneumonia /nʊˈmounyə/ *n.* pulmonía *f.*

poach /poutʃ/ *v.* (eggs) escalfar; invadir; cazar en vedado.

pocket /ˈpɒkɪt/ *n.* **1.** bolsillo *m.* —*v.* **2.** embolsar.

pocketbook /ˈpɒkɪtˌbʊk/ *n.* cartera *f.*

podiatry /pəˈdaiətri/ *n.* podiatría *f.*

poem /ˈpouəm/ *n.* poema *m.*

poet /ˈpouɪt/ *n.* poeta *m.* & *f.*

poetic /pouˈɛtɪk/ *a.* poético.

poetry /ˈpouɪtri/ *n.* poesía *f.*

poignant /ˈpɔinyənt/ *a.* conmovedor.

point /pɔint/ *n.* **1.** punta *f.*; punto *m.* —*v.* **2.** apuntar. **p. out,** señalar.

pointed /ˈpɔintɪd/ *a.* puntiagudo; directo.

pointless /ˈpɔintlɪs/ *a.* inútil.

poise /pɔiz/ *n.* **1.** equilibrio *m.*; serenidad *f.* —*v.* **2.** equilibrar; estar suspendido.

poison /ˈpɔizən/ *n.* **1.** veneno *m.* —*v.* **2.** envenenar.

poisonous /ˈpɔizənəs/ *a.* venenoso.

poke /pouk/ *n.* **1.** empuje *m.*, hurgonada *f.* —*v.* **2.** picar; haronear.

Poland /ˈpoulənd/ *n.* Polonia *f.*

polar /ˈpoulər/ *a.* polar.

pole /poul/ *n.* palo; *Geog.* polo *m.*

polemical /pəˈlɛmɪkəl/ *a.* polémico.

police /pəˈlis/ *n.* policía *f.*

policeman /pəˈlismən/ *n.* policía *m.*

policy /ˈpɒləsi/ *n.* política *f.* **insurance p.,** póliza de seguro.

Polish /ˈpɒlɪʃ/ *a.* & *n.* polaco -ca.

polish /ˈpɒlɪʃ/ *n.* **1.** lustre *m.* —*v.* **2.** pulir, lustrar.

polite /pəˈlait/ *a.* cortés.

politic /ˈpɒlɪtɪk/ **political** *a.* político.

politician /ˌpɒlɪˈtɪʃən/ *n.* político -ca.

politics /ˈpɒlɪtɪks/ *n.* política *f.*

poll /poul/ *n.* encuesta *f.*; (pl.) urnas *f.pl.*

pollen /ˈpɒlən/ *n.* polen *m.*

pollute /pəˈlut/ *v.* contaminar.

pollution /pəˈluʃən/ *n.* contaminación *f.*

polo /ˈpoulou/ *n.* polo *m.*

polyester /ˌpɒliˈɛstər/ *n.* poliéster *m.*

polygamy /pəˈlɪgəmi/ *n.* poligamia *f.*

polygon /ˈpɒliˌgɒn/ *n.* polígono *m.*

pomp /pɒmp/ *n.* pompa *f.*

pompous /ˈpɒmpəs/ *a.* pomposo.

poncho /ˈpɒntʃou/ *n.* poncho *m.*

pond /pɒnd/ *n.* charca *f.*

ponder /ˈpɒndər/ *v.* ponderar, meditar.

ponderous /ˈpɒndərəs/ *a.* ponderoso, pesado.

pontiff /ˈpɒntɪf/ *n.* pontífice *m.*

pontoon /pɒnˈtun/ *n.* pontón *m.*

pony /ˈpouni/ *n.* caballito *m.*

ponytail /ˈpouniˌteil/ *n.* cola de caballo *f.*

poodle /ˈpudl̩/ *n.* caniche *m.*

pool /pul/ *n.* charco *m.* **swimming p.,** piscina *f.*

poor /pʊr/ *a.* pobre; (not good) malo.

pop /pɒp/ *n.* chasquido *m.*

popcorn /ˈpɒpˌkɔrn/ *n.* rosetas de maíz, palomitas de maíz *f.pl.*

pope /poup/ *n.* papa *m.*

poppy /ˈpɒpi/ *n.* amapola *f.*

popsicle /ˈpɒpsɪkəl/ *n.* polo *m.*

popular /ˈpɒpyələr/ *a.* popular.

popularity /ˌpɒpyəˈlærɪti/ *n.* popularidad *f.*

population /ˌpɒpyəˈleiʃən/ *n.* población *f.*

porcelain /ˈpɔrsəlɪn/ *n.* porcelana *f.*

porch /pɔrtʃ/ *n.* pórtico *m.*; galería *f.*

pore /pɔr/ *n.* poro *m.*

pork /pɔrk/ *n.* carne de puerco.

pornography /pɔrˈnɒgrəfi/ *n.* pornografía *f.*

porous /ˈpɔrəs/ *a.* poroso, esponjoso.

port /pɔrt/ *n.* puerto; *Naut.* babor *m.* **p. wine,** oporto *m.*

portable /ˈpɔrtəbəl/ *a.* portátil.

portal /ˈpɔrtl̩/ *n.* portal *m.*

portend /pɔrˈtɛnd/ *v.* pronosticar.

portent /ˈpɔrtɛnt/ *n.* presagio *m.*, portento *m.*

porter /ˈpɔrtər/ *n.* portero *m.*

portfolio /pɔrtˈfouliˌou/ *n.* cartera *f.*

porthole /ˈpɔrtˌhoul/ *n.* porta *f.*

portion /ˈpɔrʃən/ *n.* porción *f.*

portly /ˈpɔrtli/ *a.* corpulento.

portrait /ˈpɔrtrɪt/ *n.* retrato *m.*

portray /pɔrˈtrei/ *v.* pintar.

Portugal /ˈpɔrtʃəgəl/ *n.* Portugal *m.*

Portuguese /ˌpɔrtʃəˈgiz/ *a.* & *n.* portugués -esa.

pose /pouz/ *n.* **1.** postura; actitud *f.* —*v.* **2.** posar. **p. as,** pretender ser.

position /pəˈzɪʃən/ *n.* posición *f.*

positive /ˈpɒzɪtɪv/ *a.* positivo.

possess /pəˈzɛs/ *v.* poseer.

possession /pəˈzɛʃən/ *n.* posesión *f.*

possessive /pəˈzɛsɪv/ *a.* posesivo.

possibility /ˌpɒsəˈbɪlɪti/ *n.* posibilidad *f.*

possible /ˈpɒsəbəl/ *a.* posible.

post /poust/ *n.* **1.** poste; puesto *m.* —*v.* **2.** fijar; situar; echar al correo.

postage /ˈpoustɪdʒ/ *n.* porte de correo. **p. stamp,** sello *m.*

postal /ˈpoustl̩/ *a.* postal.

post card tarjeta postal.

poster /ˈpoustər/ *n.* cartel, letrero *m.*

posterior /pɒˈstɪəriər/ *a.* posterior.

posterity /pɒˈstɛrɪti/ *n.* posteridad *f.*

postgraduate /poustˈgrædʒuɪt/ *a.* & *n.* postgraduado -da.

postmark /'poust,mɑrk/ n. matasellos m.

post office correos m.pl.

postpone /poust'poun/ v. posponer, aplazar.

postscript /'poust,skrɪpt/ n. posdata f.

posture /'pɒstʃər/ n. postura f.

pot /pɒt/ n. olla, marmita; (marijuana) marijuana, hierba f. **flower p.,** tiesto m.

potassium /pə'tæsiəm/ n. potasio m.

potato /pə'teitou/ n. patata, papa f. **sweet p.,** batata f.

potent /'poutṇt/ a. potente, poderoso.

potential /pə'tɛnʃəl/ a. & n. potencial f.

potion /'pouʃən/ n. poción, pócima f.

pottery /'pɒtəri/ n. alfarería f.

pouch /pautʃ/ n. saco m.; bolsa f.

poultry /'poultri/ n. aves de corral.

pound /paund/ n. **1.** libra f. —v. **2.** golpear.

pour /pɔr/ v. echar; verter; llover a cántaros.

poverty /'pɒvərti/ n. pobreza f.

powder /'paudər/ n. **1.** polvo m.; (gun) pólvora f. —v. **2.** empolvar; pulverizar.

power /'pauər/ n. poder m.; potencia f.

powerful /'pauərfəl/ a. poderoso, fuerte.

powerless /'pauərlıs/ a. impotente.

practical /'præktıkəl/ a. práctico.

practical joke inocentada f.

practically /'præktıkli/ adv. casi; prácticamente.

practice /'præktıs/ n. **1.** práctica; costumbre; clientela f. —v. **2.** practicar; ejercer.

practiced /'præktıst/ a. experto.

practitioner /præk'tıʃənər/ n. practicante m. & f.

pragmatic /præg'mætık/ a. pragmático.

prairie /'prɛəri/ n. llanura; S.A. pampa f.

praise /preiz/ n. **1.** alabanza f. —v. **2.** alabar.

prank /præŋk/ n. travesura f.

prawn /prɔn/ n. gamba f.

pray /prei/ v. rezar; (beg) rogar.

prayer /'preiər/ n. oración; súplica f., ruego m.

preach /pritʃ/ v. predicar; sermonear.

preacher /'pritʃər/ n. predicador m.

preamble /'pri,æmbəl/ n. preámbulo m.

precarious /prı'kɛəriəs/ a. precario.

precaution /prı'kɔʃən/ n. precaución f.

precede /prı'sid/ v. preceder, anteceder.

precedent /n. 'prɛsıdənt/ a. prı'sidnt/ n. & a. precedente m.

precept /'prisɛpt/ n. precepto m.

precinct /'prisıŋkt/ n. recinto m.

precious /'prɛʃəs/ a. precioso.

precipice /'prɛsəpıs/ n. precipicio m.

precipitate /prı'sıpı,teit/ v. precipitar.

precise /prı'sais/ a. preciso, exacto.

precision /prı'sıʒən/ n. precisión f.

preclude /prı'klud/ v. evitar.

precocious /prı'kouʃəs/ a. precoz.

precooked /'pri'kukt/ a. precocinado.

predatory /'prɛdə,tɔri/ a. de rapiña, rapaz.

predecessor /'prɛdə,sɛsər/ n. predecesor -ra, antecesor -ra.

predicament /prı'dıkəmənt/ n. dificultad f.; apuro m.

predict /prı'dıkt/ v. pronosticar, predecir.

predictable /prı'dıktəbəl/ a. previsible.

predilection /,prɛdḷ'ɛkʃən/ n. predilección f.

predispose /,pridı'spouz/ v. predisponer.

predominant /prı'dɒmənənt/ a. predominante.

prefabricate /pri'fæbrı,keit/ v. fabricar de antemano.

preface /'prɛfıs/ n. prefacio m.

prefer /prı'fɜr/ v. preferir.

preferable /'prɛfərəbəl/ a. preferible.

preference /'prɛfərəns/ n. preferencia f.

prefix /'prifıks/ n. **1.** prefijo m. —v. **2.** prefijar.

pregnant /'prɛgnənt/ a. preñada.

prehistoric /,prihı'stɔrık/ a. prehistórico.

prejudice /'prɛdʒədıs/ n. prejuicio m.

prejudiced /'prɛdʒədıst/ a. (S.A.) prejuiciado.

preliminary /prı'lımə,nɛri/ a. preliminar.

prelude /'prɛlyud/ n. preludio m.

premature /,primə'tʃur/ a. prematuro.

premeditate /pri'mɛdı,teit/ v. premeditar.

premier /prı'mıər/ n. primer ministro.

première /prı'mıər/ n. estreno m.

premise /'prɛmıs/ n. premisa f.

premium /'primiəm/ n. premio m.

premonition /,primə'nıʃən/ n. presentimiento m.

prenatal /pri'neitl/ a. prenatal.

preparation /,prɛpə'reiʃən/ n. preparativo m.; preparación f.

preparatory /prı'pærə,tɔri/ a. preparatorio. **p. to,** antes de.

prepare /prı'pɛər/ v. preparar.

preponderant /prı'pɒndərənt/ a. preponderante.

preposition /,prɛpə'zıʃən/ n. preposición f.

preposterous /prı'pɒstərəs/ a. prepóstero, absurdo.

prerequisite /prı'rɛkwəzıt/ n. requisito previo.

prerogative /prı'rɒgətıv/ n. prerrogativa f.

prescribe /prı'skraib/ v. prescribir; Med. recetar.

prescription /prı'skrıpʃən/ n. prescripción; Med. receta f.

presence /'prɛzəns/ n. presencia f.; porte m.

present /a, n 'prɛzənt/ v prı'zɛnt/ a. **1.** presente. **to be present at,** asistir a. —n. **2.** presente; (gift) regalo m. **at p.,** ahora, actualmente. **for the p.,** por ahora. —v. **3.** presentar.

presentable /prı'zɛntəbəl/ a. presentable.

presentation /,prɛzən'teiʃən/ n. presentación; introducción f.; Theat. representación f.

presently /'prɛzəntli/ adv. luego; dentro de poco.

preservative /prı'zɜrvətıv/ a. & n. preservativo m.

preserve /prı'zɜrv/ n. **1.** conserva f.; (hunting) vedado m. —v. **2.** preservar.

preside /prı'zaid/ v. presidir.

presidency /'prɛzıdənsi/ n. presidencia f.

president /'prɛzıdənt/ n. presidente -ta.

press /prɛs/ n. **1.** prensa f. —v. **2.** apretar; urgir; (clothes) planchar.

pressing /'prɛsıŋ/ a. urgente.

pressure /'prɛʃər/ n. presión f.

pressure cooker /'kukər/ cocina de presión f.

prestige /prɛ'stiʒ/ n. prestigio m.

presume /prı'zum/ v. presumir, suponer.

presumptuous /prı'zʌmptʃuəs/ a. presuntuoso.

presuppose /,prisə'pouz/ v. presuponer.

pretend /prı'tɛnd/ v. fingir. **p. to the throne,** aspirar al trono.

pretense /prı'tɛns, 'pritɛns/ n. pretensión f.; fingimiento m.

pretension /prı'tɛnʃən/ n. pretensión f.

pretentious /prı'tɛnʃəs/ a. presumido.

pretext /'pritɛkst/ n. pretexto m.

pretty /'prıti/ a. **1.** bonito, lindo. —adv. **2.** bastante.

prevail /prı'veil/ v. prevalecer.

prevailing /prı'veilıŋ/ **prevalent** a. predominante.

prevent /prı'vɛnt/ v. impedir; evitar.

prevention /prı'vɛnʃən/ n. prevención f.

preventive /prı'vɛntıv/ a. preventivo.

preview /'pri,vyu/ n. vista anticipada f.

previous /'priviəs/ a. anterior, previo.

prey /prei/ n. presa f.

price /prais/ n. precio m.

priceless /'praislıs/ a. sin precio.

prick /prık/ n. **1.** punzada f. —v. **2.** punzar.

pride /praid/ n. orgullo m.

priest /prist/ n. sacerdote, cura m.

prim /prım/ a. estirado, remilgado.

primary /'praimɛri/ a. primario, principal.

prime /praim/ a. **1.** primero. —n. **2.** flor f. —v. **3.** alistar.

prime minister primer ministro m. & f.

primitive /'prımıtıv/ a. primitivo.

prince /prıns/ n. príncipe m.

Prince Charming Príncipe Azul m.

princess /'prınsıs/ n. princesa f.

principal /'prınsəpəl/ a. **1.** principal. —n. **2.** principal m. & f.; director -ra.

principle /'prınsəpəl/ n. principio m.

print /prınt/ n. **1.** letra de molde f.; (art) grabado m. —v. **2.** imprimir, estampar.

printer /'prıntər/ n. impresora f.

printing /'prıntıŋ/ n. impresión; **p. office,** imprenta f.

printing press prensa f.

printout /'prınt,aut/ n. impreso producido por una computadora, impresión f.

priority /prai'ɔriti/ n. prioridad, precedencia f.

prism /'prızəm/ n. prisma m.

prison /'prızən/ n. prisión, cárcel f.

prisoner /'prızənər/ n. presidiario -ria, prisionero -ra, preso -sa.

pristine /'prıstin/ a. inmaculado.

privacy /'praivəsi/ n. soledad f.

private /'praivıt/ a. **1.** particular. —n. **2.** soldado raso. **in p.,** en particular.

privation /prai'veiʃən/ n. privación f.

privet /'prıvıt/ n. ligustro m.

privilege /'prıvəlıdʒ/ n. privilegio m.

privy /'prıvi/ n. letrina f.

prize /praiz/ n. **1.** premio m. —v. **2.** apreciar, estimar.

probability /,prɒbə'bılıti/ n. probabilidad f.

probable /'prɒbəbəl/ a. probable.

probate /'proubeit/ a. testamentario.

probation /prou'beiʃən/ n. prueba f.; probación f.; libertad condicional f.

probe /proub/ n. **1.** indagación f. —v. **2.** indagar; tentar.

probity /'proubıti/ n. probidad f.

problem /'prɒbləm/ n. problema m.

procedure /prə'sidʒər/ n. procedimiento m.

proceed /prə'sid/ v. proceder; proseguir.

process /'prɒsɛs/ n. proceso m.

procession /prə'sɛʃən/ n. procesión f.

proclaim /prou'kleim/ v. proclamar, anunciar.

proclamation /,prɒklə'meiʃən/ n. proclamación f.; decreto m.

procrastinate /prou'kræstə,neit/ v. dilatar.

procure /prou'kyur/ v. obtener, procurar.

prodigal /'prɒdıgəl/ n. & a. pródigo -ga.

prodigy /'prɒdıdʒi/ n. prodigio m.

produce /prə'dus/ v. producir.

product /'prɒdʌkt/ n. producto m.

production /prə'dʌkʃən/ n. producción f.

productive /prə'dʌktıv/ a. productivo.

profane /prə'fein/ a. **1.** profano. —v. **2.** profanar.

profanity /prə'fænıti/ n. profanidad f.

profess /prə'fɛs/ v. profesar; declarar.

profession /prə'fɛʃən/ n. profesión f.

professional /prə'fɛʃənl/ a. & n. profesional m. & f.

professor /prə'fɛsər/ n. profesor -ra; catedrático -ca.

proficient /prə'fıʃənt/ a. experto, proficiente.

profile /'proufail/ n. perfil m.

profit /'prɒfıt/ n. **1.** provecho m.; ventaja f.; Com. ganancia f. —v. **2.** aprovechar; beneficiar.

profitable /'prɒfıtəbəl/ a. provechoso, ventajoso, lucrativo.

profiteer /,prɒfı'tıər/ n. **1.** explotador -ra. —v. **2.** explotar.

profound /prə'faund/ a. profundo, hondo.

profuse /prə'fyus/ a. pródigo; profuso.

prognosis /prɒg'nousıs/ n. pronóstico m.

program /'prougræm/ n. programa m.

progress /n. 'prɒgrɛs; v. prə'grɛs/ n. **1.** progresos m.pl. **in p.,** en marcha. —v. **2.** progresar; marchar.

progressive /prə'grɛsıv/ a. progresivo; progresista.

prohibit /prou'hıbıt/ v. prohibir.

prohibition /,prouə'bıʃən/ n. prohibición f.

prohibitive /prou'hıbıtıv/ a. prohibitivo.

project / n. 'prɒdʒɛkt; v. prə'dʒɛkt/ n. **1.** proyecto m. —v. **2.** proyectar.

projectile /prə'dʒɛktıl/ n. proyectil m.

projection /prə'dʒɛkʃən/ n. proyección f.

projector /prə'dʒɛktər/ n. proyector m.

proliferation /prə,lıfə'reiʃən/ n. proliferación f.

prolific /prə'lıfık/ a. prolífico.

prologue /'proulɒg/ n. prólogo m.

prolong /prə'lɒŋ/ v. prolongar.

prominent /'prɒmənənt/ a. prominente; eminente.

promiscuous /prə'mıskyuəs/ a. promiscuo.

promise /'prɒmıs/ n. **1.** promesa f. —v. **2.** prometer.

promote /prə'mout/ v. fomentar; estimular; adelantar; promocionar.

promotion /prə'mouʃən/ n. promoción f.; adelanto m.

prompt /prɒmpt/ a. **1.** puntual. —v. **2.** impulsar; Theat. apuntar. —adv. **3.** pronto.

promulgate /'prɒməl,geit/ v. promulgar.

pronoun /'prou,naun/ n. pronombre m.

pronounce /prə'nauns/ v. pronunciar.

pronunciation /prə,nʌnsi'eiʃən/ n. pronunciación f.

proof /pruf/ n. prueba f.

proof of purchase certificado de compra m.

proofread /'pruf,rid/ v. corregir pruebas.

prop /prɒp/ n. **1.** apoyo m. —v. **2.** sostener.

propaganda /,prɒpə'gændə/ n. propaganda f.

propagate /'prɒpə,geit/ v. propagar.

propel /prə'pɛl/ v. propulsar.

propeller /prə'pɛlər/ n. hélice f.

propensity /prə'pɛnsıti/ n. tendencia f.

proper /'prɒpər/ a. propio; correcto.

property /'prɒpərti/ n. propiedad f.

prophecy /'prɒfəsi/ n. profecía f.

prophesy /'prɒfə,sai/ v. predecir, profetizar.

prophet /'prɒfıt/ n. profeta m.

prophetic /prə'fɛtık/ a. profético.

propitious /prə'pıʃəs/ a. propicio.

proponent /prə'pounənt/ *n.* & *a.* proponente *m.*

proportion /prə'pɔrʃən/ *n.* proporción *f.*

proportionate /prə'pɔrʃənɪt/ *a.* proporcionado.

proposal /prə'pouzəl/ *n.* propuesta; oferta *f.;* (marriage) declaración *f.*

propose /prə'pouz/ *v.* proponer; pensar; declararse.

proposition /ˌprɒpə'zɪʃən/ *n.* proposición *f.*

proprietor /prə'praiɪtər/ *n.* propietario -ria, dueño -ña.

propriety /prə'praiɪti/ *n.* corrección *f.*, decoro *m.*

prosaic /prou'zeiɪk/ *a.* prosaico.

proscribe /prou'skraib/ *v.* proscribir.

prose /prouz/ *n.* prosa *f.*

prosecute /'prɒsɪˌkyut/ *v.* acusar, procesar.

prospect /'prɒspɛkt/ *n.* perspectiva; esperanza *f.*

prospective /prə'spɛktɪv/ *a.* anticipado, presunto.

prosper /'prɒspər/ *v.* prosperar.

prosperity /prɒ'spɛrɪti/ *n.* prosperidad *f.*

prosperous /'prɒspərəs/ *a.* próspero.

prostate gland /'prɒsteit/ glándula prostática *f.*

prostitute /'prɒstɪˌtut/ *n.* **1.** prostituta *f.* —*v.* **2.** prostituir.

prostrate /'prɒstreit/ *a.* **1.** postrado. —*v.* **2.** postrar.

protect /prə'tɛkt/ *v.* proteger; amparar.

protection /prə'tɛkʃən/ *n.* protección *f.;* amparo *m.*

protective /prə'tɛktɪv/ *a.* protector.

protector /prə'tɛktər/ *n.* protector -ora.

protégé /'proutəˌʒei/ *n.* protegido -da.

protein /'proutin, -tiɪn/ *n.* proteína *f.*

protest /*n.* 'proutɛst; *v.* prə'tɛst, 'proutɛst/ *n.* **1.** protesta *f.* —*v.* **2.** protestar.

Protestant /'prɒtəstənt/ *a.* & *n.* protestante *m.* & *f.*

protocol /'proutəˌkɔl/ *n.* protocolo *m.*

proton /'proutɒn/ *n.* protón *m.*

protract /prou'trækt/ *v.* alargar, demorar.

protrude /prou'trud/ *v.* salir fuera.

protuberance /prou'tubərəns/ *n.* protuberancia *f.*

proud /praud/ *a.* orgulloso.

prove /pruv/ *v.* comprobar.

proverb /'prɒvərb/ *n.* proverbio, refrán *m.*

provide /prə'vaid/ *v.* proporcionar; proveer.

provided /prə'vaidɪd/ *conj.* con tal que.

providence /'prɒvɪdəns/ *n.* providencia *f.*

province /'prɒvɪns/ *n.* provincia *f.*

provincial /prə'vɪnʃəl/ *a.* **1.** provincial. —*n.* **2.** provinciano -na.

provision /prə'vɪʒən/ *n.* **1.** provisión *f.;* (pl.) comestibles *m.pl.* —*v.* **2.** abastecer.

provocation /ˌprɒvə'keiʃən/ *n.* provocación *f.*

provoke /prə'vouk/ *v.* provocar.

prowess /'prauɪs/ *n.* proeza *f.*

prowl /praul/ *v.* rondar.

prowler /'praulər/ *n.* merodeador -dora *m.* & *f.*

proximity /prɒk'sɪmɪti/ *n.* proximidad *f.*

proxy /'prɒksi/ *n.* delegado -da. **by p.,** mediante apoderado.

prudence /'prudns/ *n.* prudencia *f.*

prudent /'prudnt/ *a.* prudente, cauteloso.

prune /prun/ *n.* ciruela pasa *f.*

pry /prai/ *v.* atisbar; curiosear; *Mech.* alzaprimar.

psalm /sɑm/ *n.* salmo *m.*

pseudonym /'sudnɪm/ *n.* seudónimo *m.*

psychedelic /ˌsaikɪ'dɛlɪk/ *a.* psiquedélico.

psychiatrist /sɪ'kaiətrɪst, sai-/ *n.* psiquiatra *m.* & *f.*

psychiatry /sɪ'kaiətri, sai-/ *n.* psiquiatría *f.*

psychoanalysis /ˌsaikouə'næləsɪs/ *n.* psicoanálisis *m.*

psychoanalyst /ˌsaikou'ænlɪst/ *n.* psicoanalista *m.* & *f.*

psychological /ˌsaikə'lɒdʒɪkəl/ *a.* psicológico.

psychology /sai'kɒlədʒi/ *n.* psicología *f.*

psychosis /sai'kousɪs/ *n.* psicosis *f.*

ptomaine /'toumein/ *n.* tomaína *f.*

pub /pʌb/ *n.* bar *m.*

public /'pʌblɪk/ *a.* & *n.* público *m.*

publication /ˌpʌblɪ'keiʃən/ *n.* publicación; revista *f.*

publicity /pʌ'blɪsɪti/ *n.* publicidad *f.*

publicity agent publicista *m.* & *f.*

publish /'pʌblɪʃ/ *v.* publicar.

publisher /'pʌblɪʃər/ *n.* editor -ora.

pudding /'pʊdɪŋ/ *n.* pudín *m.*

puddle /'pʌdl/ *n.* charco, lodazal *m.*

Puerto Rican /'pwɛrtə 'rikən, 'pɔr-/ *a.* & *n.* puertorriqueño -ña.

Puerto Rico /'pwɛr'tə rikou, 'pɔrtə/ Puerto Rico *m.*

puff /pʌf/ *n.* **1.** soplo *m.;* (of smoke) bocanada *f.* **powder p.,** polvera *f.* —*v.* **2.** jadear; echar bocanadas. **p. up,** hinchar; *Fig.* engreír.

pugnacious /pʌg'neiʃəs/ *a.* pugnaz.

puh-lease! /pʌ 'liz/ ¡Favor!

pull /pʊl/ *n.* **1.** tirón *m.; Colloq.* influencia *f.* —*v.* **2.** tirar; halar.

pulley /'pʊli/ *n.* polea *f.*, motón *m.*

pulmonary /'pʌlməˌnɛri/ *a.* pulmonar.

pulp /pʌlp/ *n.* pulpa; (of fruit) carne *f.*

pulpit /'pʊlpɪt, 'pʌl-/ *n.* púlpito *m.*

pulsar /'pʌlsɑr/ *n.* pulsar *m.*

pulsate /'pʌlseit/ *v.* pulsar.

pulse /pʌls/ *n.* pulso *m.*

pump /pʌmp/ *n.* **1.** bomba *f.* —*v.* **2.** bombear. **p. up,** inflar.

pumpkin /'pʌmpkɪn/ *n.* calabaza *f.*

pun /pʌn/ *n.* juego de palabras.

punch /pʌntʃ/ *n.* **1.** puñetazo; *Mech.* punzón; (beverage) ponche *m.* —*v.* **2.** dar puñetazos; punzar.

punch bowl ponchera *f.*

punctual /'pʌŋktʃuəl/ *a.* puntual.

punctuate /'pʌŋktʃuˌeit/ *v.* puntuar.

puncture /'pʌŋktʃər/ *n.* **1.** pinchazo *m.*, perforación *f.* —*v.* **2.** pinchar, perforar.

pungent /'pʌndʒənt/ *a.* picante, pungente.

punish /'pʌnɪʃ/ *v.* castigar.

punishment /'pʌnɪʃmənt/ *n.* castigo *m.*

punitive /'pyunɪtɪv/ *a.* punitivo.

puny /'pyuni/ *a.* encanijado.

pupil /'pyupəl/ *n.* alumno -na; *Anat.* pupila *f.*

puppet /'pʌpɪt/ *n.* muñeco *m.*

puppy /'pʌpi/ *n.* perrito -ta.

purchase /'pɜrtʃəs/ *n.* **1.** compra *f.* —*v.* **2.** comprar.

purchasing power /'pɜrtʃəsɪŋ/ poder adquisitivo *m.*

pure /pyʊr/ *a.* puro.

purée /pyʊ'rei/ *n.* puré *m.*

purge /pɜrdʒ/ *v.* purgar.

purify /'pyʊrəˌfai/ *v.* purificar.

puritanical /ˌpyʊrɪ'tænɪkəl/ *a.* puritano.

purity /'pyʊrɪti/ *n.* pureza *f.*

purple /'pɜrpəl/ *a.* **1.** purpúreo. —*n.* **2.** púrpura *f.*

purport /*n.* 'pɜrpɔrt; *v.* pər'pɔrt/ *n.* **1.** significación *f.* —*v.* **2.** significar.

purpose /'pɜrpəs/ *n.* propósito *m.* **on p.,** de propósito.

purr /pɜr/ *v.* ronronear.

purse /pɜrs/ *n.* bolsa *f.*

pursue /pər'su/ *v.* perseguir.

pursuit /pər'sut/ *n.* caza; busca; ocupación *f.* **p. plane,** avión de caza *m.*

push /pʊʃ/ *n.* **1.** empuje; impulso *m.* —*v.* **2.** empujar.

put /pʊt/ *v.* poner, colocar. **p. away,** guardar. **p. in,** meter. **p. off,** dejar. **p. on,** ponerse. **p. out,** apagar. **p. up with,** aguantar.

putrid /'pyutrɪd/ *a.* podrido.

putt /pʌt/ *n.* (golf) golpe corto *m.*

puzzle /'pʌzəl/ *n.* **1.** enigma; rompecabezas *m.* —*v.* **2.** dejar perplejo. **p. out,** descifrar.

pyramid /'pɪrəmɪd/ *n.* pirámide *f.*

pyromania /ˌpairə'meiniə/ *n.* piromanía *f.*

Q

quack /kwæk/ *n.* **1.** (doctor) curandero -ra; (duck) graznido *m.* —*v.* **2.** graznar.

quadrangle /'kwɒdˌræŋgəl/ *n.* cuadrángulo *m.*

quadraphonic /ˌkwɒdrə'fɒnɪk/ *a.* cuatrifónico.

quadruped /'kwɒdrʊˌpɛd/ *a.* & *n.* cuadrúpedo *m.*

quail /kweil/ *n.* **1.** codorniz *f.* —*v.* **2.** descorazonarse.

quaint /kweint/ *a.* curioso.

quake /kweik/ *n.* **1.** temblor *m.* —*v.* **2.** temblar.

qualification /ˌkwɒləfɪ'keiʃən/ *n.* requisito *m.;* (pl.) preparaciones *f.pl.*

qualified /'kwɒləˌfaid/ *a.* calificado, competente; preparado.

qualify /'kwɒləˌfai/ *v.* calificar, modificar; llenar los requisitos.

quality /'kwɒlɪti/ *n.* calidad *f.*

quandary /'kwɒndəri, -dri/ *n.* incertidumbre *f.*

quantity /'kwɒntɪti/ *n.* cantidad *f.*

quarantine /'kwɔrənˌtin, 'kwɒr-, ˌkwɔrən'tin, ˌkwɒr-/ *n.* cuarentena *f.*

quarrel /'kwɔrəl, 'kwɒr-/ *n.* **1.** riña, disputa *f.* —*v.* **2.** reñir, disputar.

quarry /'kwɔri, 'kwɒri/ *n.* cantera; (hunting) presa *f.*

quarter /'kwɔrtər/ *n.* cuarto *m.;* (pl.) vivienda *f.*

quarterly /'kwɔrtərli/ *a.* **1.** trimestral. —*adv.* **2.** por cuartos.

quartet /kwɔr'tɛt/ *n.* cuarteto *m.*

quartz /kwɔrts/ *n.* cuarzo *m.*

quasar /'kweizɑr/ *n.* cuasar *m.*

quaver /'kweivər/ *v.* temblar.

queen /kwin/ *n.* reina *f.;* (chess) dama *f.*

queer /kwɪər/ *a.* extraño, raro.

quell /kwɛl/ *v.* reprimir.

quench /kwɛntʃ/ *v.* apagar.

query /'kwɪəri/ *n.* **1.** pregunta *f.* —*v.* **2.** preguntar.

quest /kwɛst/ *n.* busca *f.*

question /'kwɛstʃən/ *n.* **1.** pregunta; cuestión *f.* **q. mark,** signo de interrogación. —*v.* **2.** preguntar; interrogar; dudar.

questionable /'kwɛstʃənəbəl/ *a.* dudoso.

questionnaire /ˌkwɛstʃə'nɛər/ *n.* cuestionario *m.*

quiche /kiʃ/ *n.* quiche *f.*

quick /kwɪk/ *a.* rápido.

quicken /'kwɪkən/ *v.* acelerar.

quicksand /'kwɪkˌsænd/ *n.* arena movediza.

quiet /'kwaiɪt/ *a.* **1.** quieto, tranquilo; callado. **be q., keep q.,** callarse. —*n.* **2.** calma; quietud *f.* —*v.* **3.** tranquilizar. **q. down,** callarse; calmarse.

quilt /kwɪlt/ *n.* colcha *f.*

quinine /'kwainain/ *n.* quinina *f.*

quintet /kwɪn'tɛt/ *n.* *Mus.* quinteto *m.*

quip /kwɪp/ *n.* **1.** pulla *f.* —*v.* **2.** echar pullas.

quit /kwɪt/ *v.* dejar; renunciar a. **q. doing** (etc.) dejar de hacer (etc.).

quite /kwait/ *adv.* bastante; completamente. **not q.,** no precisamente; no completamente.

quiver /'kwɪvər/ *n.* **1.** aljaba *f.;* temblor *m.* —*v.* **2.** temblar.

quixotic /kwɪk'sɒtɪk/ *a.* quijotesco.

quorum /'kwɔrəm/ *n.* quórum *m.*

quota /'kwoutə/ *n.* cuota *f.*

quotation /kwou'teiʃən/ *n.* citación; *Com.* cotización *f.* **q. marks,** comillas *f.pl.*

quote /kwout/ *v.* citar; *Com.* cotizar.

R

rabbi /'ræbai/ *n.* rabí, rabino *m.*

rabbit /'ræbɪt/ *n.* conejo *m.*

rabble /'ræbəl/ *n.* canalla *f.*

rabid /'ræbɪd/ *a.* rabioso.

rabies /'reibiz/ *n.* hidrofobia *f.*

race /reis/ *n.* **1.** raza; carrera *f.* —*v.* **2.** echar una carrera; correr de prisa.

race track /'reisˌtræk/ hipódromo *m.*

rack /ræk/ *n.* **1.** (cooking) pesebre *m.;* (clothing) colgador *m.* —*v.* **2.** atormentar.

racket /'rækɪt/ *n.* (noise) ruido *m.;* (tennis) raqueta *f.;* (graft) fraude organizado.

radar /'reidɑr/ *n.* radar *m.*

radiance /'reidiəns/ *n.* brillo *m.*

radiant /'reidiənt/ *a.* radiante.

radiate /'reidiˌeit/ *v.* irradiar.

radiation /ˌreidi'eiʃən/ *n.* irradiación *f.*

radiator /'reidiˌeitər/ *n.* calorífero *m.;* *Auto.* radiador *m.*

radical /'rædɪkəl/ *a.* & *n.* radical *m.*

radio /'reidiˌou/ *n.* radio *m.* or *f.* **r. station,** estación radiodifusora *f.*

radioactive /ˌreidiou'æktɪv/ *a.* radioactivo.

radio cassette radiocasete *m.*

radish /'rædɪʃ/ *n.* rábano *m.*

radium /'reidiəm/ *n.* radio *m.*

radius /'reidiəs/ *n.* radio *m.*

raffle /'ræfəl/ *n.* **1.** rifa, lotería *f.* —*v.* **2.** rifar.

raft /ræft/ *n.* balsa *f.*

rafter /'ræftər/ *n.* viga *f.*

rag /ræg/ *n.* trapo *m.*

ragamuffin /'rægəˌmʌfɪn/ *n.* galopín *m.*

rage /reidʒ/ *n.* **1.** rabia *f.* —*v.* **2.** rabiar.

ragged /'rægɪd/ *a.* andrajoso; desigual.

raid /reid/ *n.* *Mil.* correría *f.*

rail /reil/ *n.* baranda *f.;* carril *m.* **by r.,** por ferrocarril.

railroad /'reilˌroud/ *n.* ferrocarril *m.*

rain /rein/ *n.* **1.** lluvia *f.* —*v.* **2.** llover.

rainbow /'reinˌbou/ *n.* arco iris *m.*

raincoat /'reinˌkout/ *n.* impermeable *m.;* gabardina *f.*

rainfall /'reinˌfɔl/ *n.* precipitación *f.*

rainy /'reini/ *a.* lluvioso.

raise /reiz/ *n.* **1.** aumento *m.* —*v.* **2.** levantar, alzar; criar.

raisin /'reizɪn/ *n.* pasa *f.*

rake /reik/ *n.* **1.** rastro *m.* —*v.* **2.** rastrillar.

rally /'ræli/ *n.* **1.** reunión *f.* —*v.* **2.** reunirse.

ram /ræm/ *n.* carnero *m.*

ramble /'ræmbəl/ *v.* vagar.

ramp /ræmp/ *n.* rampa *f.*

rampart /'ræmpɑrt/ *n.* terraplén *m.*

ranch /ræntʃ/ *n.* rancho *m.*

rancid /'rænsɪd/ *a.* rancio.

rancor /'ræŋkər/ *n.* rencor *m.*

random /'rændəm/ *a.* fortuito. **at r.,** a la ventura.

range /reindʒ/ *n.* **1.** extensión *f.;* alcance *m.;* estufa; sierra *f.;* terreno de pasto. —*v.* **2.** recorrer; extenderse.

rank /ræŋk/ *a.* **1.** espeso; rancio. —*n.* **2.** fila *f.;* grado *m.* —*v.* **3.** clasificar.

ransack /'rænsæk/ *v.* saquear.

ransom /'rænsəm/ *n.* **1.** rescate *m.* —*v.* **2.** rescatar.

rap /ræp/ *n.* **1.** golpecito *m.* —*v.* **2.** golpear.

rapid /'ræpɪd/ *a.* rápido.

rapist /ˈreipɪst/ *n.* violador -dora *m. & f.*
rapport /ræˈpɔr/ *n.* armonía *f.*
rapture /ˈræptʃər/ *n.* éxtasis *m.*
rare /rɛər/ *a.* raro; (of food) a medio cocer.
rascal /ˈræskəl/ *n.* pícaro, bribón *m.*
rash /ræʃ/ *a.* **1.** temerario. **—***n.* **2.** erupción *f.*
raspberry /ˈræzˌbɛri/ *n.* frambuesa *f.*
rat /ræt/ *n.* rata *f.*
rate /reit/ *n.* **1.** velocidad; tasa *f.;* precio *m.;* (of exchange; of interest) tipo *m.* **at any r.,** de todos modos. **—***v.* **2.** valuar.
rather /ˈræðər/ *adv.* bastante; más bien, mejor dicho.
ratify /ˈrætəˌfai/ *v.* ratificar.
ratio /ˈreiʃou/ *n.* razón; proporción *f.*
ration /ˈræʃən, ˈreiʃən/ *n.* **1.** ración *f.* **—***v.* **2.** racionar.
rational /ˈræʃənl/ *a.* racional.
rattle /ˈrætl/ *n.* **1.** ruido *m.;* matraca *f.* **r. snake,** culebra de cascabel, serpiente de cascabel *f.* **—***v.* **2.** matraquear; rechinar.
raucous /ˈrɔkəs/ *a.* ronco.
ravage /ˈrævɪdʒ/ *v.* pillar; destruir; asolar.
rave /reiv/ *v.* delirar; entusiasmarse.
ravel /ˈrævəl/ *v.* deshilar.
raven /ˈreivən/ *n.* cuervo *m.*
ravenous /ˈrævənəs/ *a.* voraz.
raw /rɔ/ *a.* crudo; verde.
ray /rei/ *n.* rayo *m.*
rayon /ˈreiɒn/ *n.* rayón *m.*
razor /ˈreizər/ *n.* navaja de afeitar. **r. blade,** hoja de afeitar.
reach /ritʃ/ *n.* **1.** alcance *m.* **—***v.* **2.** alcanzar.
react /riˈækt/ *v.* reaccionar.
reaction /riˈækʃən/ *n.* reacción *f.*
reactionary /riˈækʃəˌnɛri/ *a.* **1.** reaccionario. **—***n.* **2.** *Pol.* retrógrado *m.*
read /rid/ *v.* leer.
reader /ˈridər/ *n.* lector -ra; libro de lectura *m.*
readily /ˈrɛdḷi/ *adv.* fácilmente.
reading /ˈridɪŋ/ *n.* lectura *f.*
ready /ˈrɛdi/ *a.* listo, preparado; dispuesto.
ready-cooked /ˈrɛdi ˌkʊkt/ *a.* precocinado.
real /reiˈɑl/ *a.* verdadero; real.
real estate bienes inmuebles, *m.pl.*
real-estate agent /ˈriəl ɪˈsteit/ agente inmobiliario *m.*, agente inmobiliaria *f.*
realist /ˈriəlɪst/ *n.* realista *m. & f.*
realistic /ˌriəˈlɪstɪk/ *a.* realista.
reality /riˈælɪti/ *n.* realidad *f.*
realization /ˌriələˈzeiʃən/ *n.* comprensión; realización *f.*
realize /ˈriəˌlaiz/ *v.* darse cuenta de; realizar.
really /ˈriəli/ *adv.* de veras; en realidad.
realm /rɛlm/ *n.* reino; dominio *m.*
reap /rip/ *v.* segar, cosechar.
rear /rɪər/ *a.* **1.** posterior. **—***n.* **2.** parte posterior. **—***v.* **3.** criar; levantar.
reason /ˈrizən/ *n.* **1.** razón; causa *f.;* motivo *m.* **—***v.* **2.** razonar.
reasonable /ˈrizənəbəl/ *a.* razonable.
reassure /ˌriəˈʃʊr/ *v.* calmar, tranquilizar.
rebate /ˈribeit/ *n.* rebaja *f.*
rebel /*n.* ˈrɛbəl; *v.* rɪˈbɛl/ *n.* **1.** rebelde *m. & f.* **—***v.* **2.** rebelarse.
rebellion /rɪˈbɛlyən/ *n.* rebelión *f.*
rebellious /rɪˈbɛlyəs/ *a.* rebelde.
rebirth /riˈbɜrθ/ *n.* renacimiento *m.*
rebound /rɪˈbaund/ *v.* repercutir; resaltar.
rebuff /rɪˈbʌf/ *n.* **1.** repulsa *f.* **—***v.* **2.** rechazar.
rebuke /rɪˈbyuk/ *n.* **1.** reprensión *f.* **—***v.* **2.** reprender.
rebuttal /rɪˈbʌtl/ *n.* refutación *f.*
recalcitrant /rɪˈkælsɪtrənt/ *a.* recalcitrante.
recall /rɪˈkɔl/ *v.* recordar; acordarse de; hacer volver.
recapitulate /ˌrikəˈpɪtʃəˌleit/ *v.* recapitular.
recede /riˈsid/ *v.* retroceder.
receipt /rɪˈsit/ *n.* recibo *m.;* (com., pl.) ingresos *m.pl.*
receive /rɪˈsiv/ *v.* recibir.
receiver /rɪˈsivər/ *n.* receptor *m.*
recent /ˈrisənt/ *a.* reciente.
recently /ˈrisəntli/ *adv.* recién.
receptacle /rɪˈsɛptəkəl/ *n.* receptáculo *m.*
reception /rɪˈsɛpʃən/ *n.* acogida; recepción *f.*
receptionist /rɪˈsɛpʃənɪst/ *n.* recepcionista *m. & f.*
receptive /rɪˈsɛptɪv/ *a.* receptivo.
recess /rɪˈsɛs, ˈrisɛs/ *n.* nicho; retiro; recreo *m.*
recipe /ˈrɛsəpi/ *n.* receta *f.*
recipient /rɪˈsɪpiənt/ *n.* recibidor -ra, recipiente *m. & f.*
reciprocate /rɪˈsɪprəˌkeit/ *v.* corresponder; reciprocar.
recite /rɪˈsait/ *v.* recitar.
reckless /ˈrɛklɪs/ *a.* descuidado; imprudente.
reckon /ˈrɛkən/ *v.* contar; calcular.
reclaim /rɪˈkleim/ *v.* reformar; *Leg.* reclamar.
recline /rɪˈklain/ *v.* reclinar; recostar.
recognition /ˌrɛkəgˈnɪʃən/ *n.* reconocimiento *m.*
recognize /ˈrɛkəgˌnaiz/ *v.* reconocer.
recoil /*n.* ˈriˌkɔil; *v.* rɪˈkɔil/ *n.* **1.** culatada *f.* **—***v.* **2.** recular.
recollect /ˌrɛkəˈlɛkt/ *v.* recordar, acordarse de.
recommend /ˌrɛkəˈmɛnd/ *v.* recomendar.
recommendation /ˌrɛkəmɛnˈdeiʃən/ *n.* recomendación *f.*
recompense /ˈrɛkəmˌpɛns/ *n.* **1.** recompensa *f.* **—***v.* **2.** recompensar.
reconcile /ˈrɛkənˌsail/ *v.* reconciliar.
recondition /ˌrikənˈdɪʃən/ *v.* reacondicionar.
reconsider /ˌrikənˈsɪdər/ *v.* considerar de nuevo.
reconstruct /ˌrikənˈstrʌkt/ *v.* reconstruir.
record /*n.* ˈrɛkərd, *v.* rɪˈkɔrd/ *n.* **1.** registro; (sports) record *m.* **phonograph r.,** disco *m.* **—***v.* **2.** registrar.
record player tocadiscos *m.*
recount /rɪˈkaunt/ *v.* relatar; contar.
recover /rɪˈkʌvər/ *v.* recobrar; restablecerse.
recovery /rɪˈkʌvəri/ *n.* recobro *m.;* recuperación *f.*
recruit /rɪˈkrut/ *n.* **1.** recluta *m.* **—***v.* **2.** reclutar.
rectangle /ˈrɛkˌtæŋgəl/ *n.* rectángulo *m.*
rectify /ˈrɛktəˌfai/ *v.* rectificar.
recuperate /rɪˈkupəˌreit/ *v.* recuperar.
recur /rɪˈkɜr/ *v.* recurrir.
recycle /riˈsaikəl/ *v.* reciclar.
red /rɛd/ *a.* rojo, colorado.
redeem /rɪˈdim/ *v.* redimir, rescatar.
redemption /rɪˈdɛmpʃən/ *n.* redención *f.*
redhead /ˈrɛdˌhɛd/ *n.* pelirrojo -ja.
red mullet /ˈmʌlɪt/ salmonete *m.*
reduce /rɪˈdus/ *v.* reducir.
reduction /rɪˈdʌkʃən/ *n.* reducción *f.*
reed /rid/ *n.* caña *f.*, *S.A.* bejuco *m.*
reef /rif/ *n.* arrecife, escollo *m.*
reel /ril/ *n.* **1.** aspa *f.*, carrete *m.* **—***v.* **2.** aspar.
refer /rɪˈfɜr/ *v.* referir.
referee /ˌrɛfəˈri/ *n.* árbitro *m. & f.*
reference /ˈrɛfərəns/ *n.* referencia *f.*
refill /*n.* ˈriˌfɪl; *v.* riˈfɪl/ *n.* **1.** relleno *m.* **—***v.* **2.** rellenar.
refine /rɪˈfain/ *v.* refinar.
refinement /rɪˈfainmənt/ *n.* refinamiento *m.;* cultura *f.*
reflect /rɪˈflɛkt/ *v.* reflejar; reflexionar.
reflection /rɪˈflɛkʃən/ *n.* reflejo *m.;* reflexión *f.*
reflex /ˈriflɛks/ *a.* reflejo.
reform /rɪˈfɔrm/ *n.* **1.** reforma *f.* **—***v.* **2.** reformar.
reformation /ˌrɛfərˈmeiʃən/ *n.* reformación *f.*
refractory /rɪˈfræktəri/ *a.* refractario.
refrain /rɪˈfrein/ *n.* **1.** estribillo *m.* **—***v.* **2.** abstenerse.
refresh /rɪˈfrɛʃ/ *v.* refrescar.
refreshment /rɪˈfrɛʃmənt/ *n.* refresco *m.*
refrigerator /rɪˈfrɪdʒəˌreitər/ *n.* refrigerador *m.*
refuge /ˈrɛfyudʒ/ *n.* refugio *m.*
refugee /ˌrɛfyʊˈdʒi/ *n.* refugiado -da.
refund /*n* ˈrifʌnd; *v* riˈfʌnd/ *n.* **1.** reembolso *m.* **—***v.* **2.** reembolsar.
refusal /rɪˈfyuzəl/ *n.* negativa *f.*
refuse /*n* ˈrɛfyus; *v* rɪˈfyuz/ *n.* **1.** basura *f.* **—***v.* **2.** negarse, rehusar.
refute /rɪˈfyut/ *v.* refutar.
regain /riˈgein/ *v.* recobrar. **r. consciousness,** recobrar el conocimiento.
regal /ˈrigəl/ *a.* real.
regard /rɪˈgɑrd/ *n.* **1.** aprecio; respeto *m.* **with r. to,** con respecto a. **—***v.* **2.** considerar; estimar.
regarding /rɪˈgɑrdɪŋ/ *prep.* en cuanto a, acerca de.
regardless (of) /rɪˈgɑrdlɪs/ a pesar de.
regent /ˈridʒənt/ *n.* regente *m. & f.*
regime /rəˈʒim, rei-/ *n.* régimen *m.*
regiment /*n.* ˈrɛdʒəmənt; *v.* -ˌmɛnt/ *n.* **1.** regimiento *m.* **—***v.* **2.** regimentar.
region /ˈridʒən/ *n.* región *f.*
register /ˈrɛdʒəstər/ *n.* **1.** registro *m.* **cash r.,** caja registradora *f.* **—***v.* **2.** registrar; matricularse; (a letter) certificar.
registration /ˌrɛdʒəˈstreiʃən/ *n.* registro *m.;* matrícula *f.*
regret /rɪˈgrɛt/ *n.* **1.** pena *f.* **—***v.* **2.** sentir, lamentar.
regular /ˈrɛgyələr/ *a.* regular; ordinario.
regularity /ˌrɛgyəˈlærɪti/ *n.* regularidad *f.*
regulate /ˈrɛgyəˌleit/ *v.* regular.
regulation /ˌrɛgyəˈleiʃən/ *n.* regulación *f.*
regulator /ˈrɛgyəˌleitər/ *n.* regulador *m.*
rehabilitate /ˌrihəˈbɪlɪˌteit, ˌriə-/ *v.* rehabilitar.
rehearse /rɪˈhɜrs/ *v.* repasar; *Theat.* ensayar.
reheat /riˈhit/ *v.* recalentar.
reign /rein/ *n.* **1.** reino, reinado *m.* **—***v.* **2.** reinar.
reimburse /ˌriɪmˈbɜrs/ *v.* reembolsar.
rein /rein/ *n.* **1.** rienda *f.* **—***v.* **2.** refrenar.
reincarnation /ˌriɪnkɑrˈneiʃən/ *n.* reencarnación *f.*
reindeer /ˈreinˌdɪər/ *n.* reno *m.*
reinforce /ˌriɪnˈfɔrs, -ˈfours/ *v.* reforzar.
reinforcement /ˌriɪnˈfɔrsmənt, -ˈfours-/ *n.* refuerzo *m.;* armadura *f.*
reiterate /riˈɪtəˌreit/ *v.* reiterar.
reject /rɪˈdʒɛkt/ *v.* rechazar.
rejoice /rɪˈdʒɔis/ *v.* regocijarse.
rejoin /rɪˈdʒɔin/ *v.* reunirse con; replicar.
rejuvenate /rɪˈdʒuvəˌneit/ *v.* rejuvenecer.
relapse /*v.* rɪˈlæps; *n. also* ˈrilæps/ *v.* **1.** recaer. **—***n.* **2.** recaída *f.*
relate /rɪˈleit/ *v.* relatar, contar; relacionar. **r. to,** llevarse bien con.
relation /rɪˈleiʃən/ *n.* relación *f.;* pariente *m. & f.*
relative /ˈrɛlətɪv/ *a.* **1.** relativo. **—***n.* **2.** pariente *m. & f.*
relativity /ˌrɛləˈtɪvɪti/ *n.* relatividad *f.*
relax /rɪˈlæks/ *v.* descansar; relajar.
relay /ˈrilei; *v. also* rɪˈlei/ *n.* **1.** relevo *m.* **—***v.* **2.** retransmitir.
release /rɪˈlis/ *n.* **1.** liberación *f.* **—***v.* **2.** soltar.
relent /rɪˈlɛnt/ *v.* ceder.
relevant /ˈrɛləvənt/ *a.* pertinente.
reliability /rɪˌlaiəˈbɪlɪti/ *n.* veracidad *f.*
reliable /rɪˈlaiəbəl/ *a.* responsable; digno de confianza.
relic /ˈrɛlɪk/ *n.* reliquia *f.*
relief /rɪˈlif/ *n.* alivio; (sculpture) relieve *m.*
relieve /rɪˈliv/ *v.* aliviar.
religion /rɪˈlɪdʒən/ *n.* religión *f.*
religious /rɪˈlɪdʒəs/ *a.* religioso.
relinquish /rɪˈlɪŋkwɪʃ/ *v.* abandonar.
relish /ˈrɛlɪʃ/ *n.* **1.** sabor; condimento *m.* **—***v.* **2.** saborear.
reluctant /rɪˈlʌktənt/ *a.* renuente.
rely /rɪˈlai/ *v.* **r. on,** confiar en; contar con; depender de.
remain /rɪˈmein/ *n.* **1.** (pl.) restos *m.pl.* **—***v.* **2.** quedar, permanecer.
remainder /rɪˈmeindər/ *n.* resto *m.*
remark /rɪˈmɑrk/ *n.* **1.** observación *f.* **—***v.* **2.** observar.
remarkable /rɪˈmɑrkəbəl/ *a.* notable.
remedial /rɪˈmidiəl/ *a.* reparador.
remedy /ˈrɛmɪdi/ *n.* **1.** remedio *m.* **—***v.* **2.** remediar.
remember /rɪˈmɛmbər/ *v.* acordarse de, recordar.
remembrance /rɪˈmɛmbrəns/ *n.* recuerdo *m.*
remind /rɪˈmaind/ *v.* **r. of,** recordar.
reminisce /ˌrɛməˈnɪs/ *v.* pensar en o hablar de cosas pasadas.
remiss /rɪˈmɪs/ *a.* remiso; flojo.
remit /rɪˈmɪt/ *v.* remitir.
remorse /rɪˈmɔrs/ *n.* remordimiento *m.*
remote /rɪˈmout/ *a.* remoto.
remote control mando a distancia *m.*
removal /rɪˈmuvəl/ *n.* alejamiento *m.;* eliminación *f.*
remove /rɪˈmuv/ *v.* quitar; remover.
renaissance /ˌrɛnəˈsɑns/ *n.* renacimiento *m.*
rend /rɛnd/ *v.* hacer pedazos; separar.
render /ˈrɛndər/ *v.* dar; rendir; *Theat.* interpretar.
rendezvous /ˈrɑndəˌvu, -dei-/ *n.* cita *f.*
rendition /rɛnˈdɪʃən/ *n.* interpretación, rendición *f.*
renege /rɪˈnɪg, -ˈnɛg/ *v.* renunciar; faltar a su palabra, no cumplir una promesa.
renew /rɪˈnu, -ˈnyu/ *v.* renovar.
renewal /rɪˈnuəl, -ˈnyu-/ *n.* renovación; *Com.* prórroga *f.*
renounce /rɪˈnauns/ *v.* renunciar a.
renovate /ˈrɛnəˌveit/ *v.* renovar.
renown /rɪˈnaun/ *n.* renombre *m.*, fama *f.*
rent /rɛnt/ *n.* **1.** alquiler *m.* **—***v.* **2.** arrendar, alquilar.
repair /rɪˈpɛər/ *n.* **1.** reparo *m.* **—***v.* **2.** reparar.
repairman /rɪˈpɛərˌmæn/ *n.* técnico *m.*
repatriate /riˈpeitriˌeit/ *v.* repatriar.
repay /rɪˈpei/ *v.* pagar; devolver.
repeat /rɪˈpit/ *v.* repetir.
repel /rɪˈpɛl/ *v.* repeler, repulsar.
repent /ˈripənt, rɪˈpɛnt/ *v.* arrepentirse.
repentance /rɪˈpɛntns, -ˈpɛntəns/ *n.* arrepentimiento *m.*
repercussion /ˌripərˈkʌʃən, ˌrɛpər-/ *n.* repercusión *f.*
repertoire /ˈrɛpərˌtwɑr/ *n.* repertorio *m.*
repetition /ˌrɛpɪˈtɪʃən/ *n.* repetición *f.*
replace /rɪˈpleis/ *v.* reemplazar.
replenish /rɪˈplɛnɪʃ/ *v.* rellenar; surtir de nuevo.
reply /rɪˈplai/ *n.* **1.** respuesta *f.* **—***v.* **2.** replicar; contestar.
report /rɪˈpɔrt, -ˈpourt/ *n.* **1.** informe *m.* **—***v.* **2.** informar, contar; denunciar; presentarse.
reporter /rɪˈpɔrtər, -ˈpour-/ *n.* repórter *m. & f.*, reportero -ra.
repose /rɪˈpouz/ *n.* **1.** reposo *m.* **—***v.* **2.** reposar; reclinar.

reprehensible /ˌrɛprɪˈhɛnsəbəl/ *a.* reprensible.
represent /ˌrɛprɪˈzɛnt/ *v.* representar.
representation /ˌrɛprɪzɛnˈteiʃən, -zən-/ *n.* representación *f.*
representative /ˌrɛprɪˈzɛntətɪv/ *a.* **1.** representativo. —*n.* **2.** representante *m. & f.*
repress /rɪˈprɛs/ *v.* reprimir.
reprimand /ˈrɛprəˌmænd, -ˌmɑnd/ *n.* **1.** regaño *m.* —*v.* **2.** regañar.
reprisal /rɪˈpraizəl/ *n.* represalia *f.*
reproach /rɪˈproutʃ/ *n.* **1.** reproche *m.* —*v.* **2.** reprochar.
reproduce /ˌriprəˈdus, -ˈdyus/ *v.* reproducir.
reproduction /ˌriprəˈdʌkʃən/ *n.* reproducción *f.*
reproof /rɪˈpruf/ *n.* censura *f.*
reprove /rɪˈpruv/ *v.* censurar, regañar.
reptile /ˈrɛptɪl, -tail/ *n.* reptil *m.*
republic /rɪˈpʌblɪk/ *n.* república *f.*
republican /rɪˈpʌblɪkən/ *a. & n.* republicano -na.
repudiate /rɪˈpyudiˌeit/ *v.* repudiar.
repulsive /rɪˈpʌlsɪv/ *a.* repulsivo, repugnante.
reputation /ˌrɛpyəˈteiʃən/ *n.* reputación; fama *f.*
repute /rɪˈpyut/ *n.* **1.** reputación *f.* —*v.* **2.** reputar.
request /rɪˈkwɛst/ *n.* **1.** súplica *f.*, ruego *m.* —*v.* **2.** pedir; rogar, suplicar.
require /rɪˈkwaiᵊr/ *v.* requerir; exigir.
requirement /rɪˈkwaiᵊrmənt/ *n.* requisito *m.*
requisite /ˈrɛkwəzɪt/ *a.* **1.** necesario. —*n.* **2.** requisito *m.*
requisition /ˌrɛkwəˈzɪʃən/ *n.* requisición *f.*
rescind /rɪˈsɪnd/ *v.* rescindir, anular.
rescue /ˈrɛskyu/ *n.* **1.** rescate *m.* —*v.* **2.** rescatar.
research /rɪˈsɜrtʃ, ˈrisɜrtʃ/ *n.* investigación *f.*
researcher /rɪˈsɜrtʃər/ *n.* investigador -dora.
resemble /rɪˈzɛmbəl/ *v.* parecerse a, asemejarse a.
resent /rɪˈzɛnt/ *v.* resentirse de.
reservation /ˌrɛzərˈveiʃən/ *n.* reservación *f.*
reserve /rɪˈzɜrv/ *n.* **1.** reserva *f.* —*v.* **2.** reservar.
reservoir /ˈrɛzərˌvwɑr, -ˌvwɔr, -ˌvɔr, ˈrɛzə-/ *n* depósito; tanque *m.*
reside /rɪˈzaid/ *v.* residir, morar.
residence /ˈrɛzɪdəns/ *n.* residencia, morada *f.*
resident /ˈrɛzɪdənt/ *n.* residente *m. & f.*
residue /ˈrɛzɪˌdu/ *n.* residuo *m.*
resign /rɪˈzain/ *v.* dimitir; resignar.
resignation /ˌrɛzɪgˈneiʃən/ *n.* dimisión; resignación *f.*
resist /rɪˈzɪst/ *v.* resistir.
resistance /rɪˈzɪstəns/ *n.* resistencia *f.*
resolute /ˈrɛzəˌlut/ *a.* resuelto.
resolution /ˌrɛzəˈluʃən/ *n.* resolución *f.*
resolve /rɪˈzɒlv/ *v.* resolver.
resonant /ˈrɛzənənt/ *a.* resonante.
resort /rɪˈzɔrt/ *n.* **1.** recurso; expediente *m.* **summer r.,** lugar de veraneo. —*v.* **2.** acudir, recurrir.
resound /rɪˈzaund/ *v.* resonar.
resource /ˈrisɔrs/ *n.* recurso *m.*
respect /rɪˈspɛkt/ *n.* **1.** respeto *m.* **with r. to,** con respecto a. —*v.* **2.** respetar.
respectable /rɪˈspɛktəbəl/ *a.* respetable.
respectful /rɪˈspɛktfəl/ *a.* respetuoso.
respective /rɪˈspɛktɪv/ *a.* respectivo.
respiration /ˌrɛspəˈreiʃən/ *n.* respiración *f.*
respite /ˈrɛspɪt/ *n.* pausa, tregua *f.*
respond /rɪˈspɒnd/ *v.* responder.
response /rɪˈspɒns/ *n.* respuesta *f.*
responsibility /rɪˌspɒnsəˈbɪlɪti/ *n.* responsabilidad *f.*
responsible /rɪˈspɒnsəbəl/ *a.* responsable.
responsive /rɪˈspɒnsɪv/ *a.* sensible a.
rest /rɛst/ *n.* **1.** descanso; reposo *m.*; (music) pausa *f.* **the r.,** el resto, lo demás; los demás. —*v.* **2.** descansar; recostar.
restaurant /ˈrɛstərənt, -təˌrɑnt, -trɑnt/ *n.* restaurante *m.*
restful /ˈrɛstfəl/ *a.* tranquilo.
restitution /ˌrɛstɪˈtuʃən, -ˈtyu-/ *n.* restitución *f.*
restless /ˈrɛstlɪs/ *a.* inquieto.
restoration /ˌrɛstəˈreiʃən/ *n.* restauración *f.*
restore /rɪˈstɔr, -ˈstour/ *v.* restaurar.
restrain /rɪˈstrein/ *v.* refrenar.
restraint /rɪˈstreint/ *n.* limitación, restricción *f.*
restrict /rɪˈstrɪkt/ *v.* restringir, limitar.
rest room aseos *m.pl.*
result /rɪˈzʌlt/ *n.* **1.** resultado *m.* —*v.* **2.** resultar.
resume /rɪˈzum/ *v.* reasumir; empezar de nuevo.
résumé /ˈrɛzʊˌmei/ *n.* resumen *m.*
resurgent /rɪˈsɜrdʒənt/ *a.* resurgente.
resurrect /ˌrɛzəˈrɛkt/ *v.* resucitar.
resuscitate /rɪˈsʌsɪˌteit/ *v.* resucitar.
retail /ˈriteil/ *n.* **at r.,** al por menor.
retain /rɪˈtein/ *v.* retener.
retaliate /rɪˈtæliˌeit/ *v.* vengarse.
retard /rɪˈtɑrd/ *v.* retardar.
retention /rɪˈtɛnʃən/ *n.* retención *f.*
reticent /ˈrɛtəsənt/ *a.* reticente.
retire /rɪˈtaiᵊr/ *v.* retirar.
retirement /rɪˈtaiᵊrmənt/ *n.* jubilación *f.*
retort /rɪˈtɔrt/ *n.* **1.** réplica; *Chem.* retorta *f.* —*v.* **2.** replicar.
retreat /rɪˈtrit/ *n.* **1.** retiro *m.*; *Mil.* retirada, retreta *f.* —*v.* **2.** retirarse.
retribution /ˌrɛtrəˈbyuʃən/ *n.* retribución *f.*
retrieve /rɪˈtriv/ *v.* recobrar.
return /rɪˈtɜrn/ *n.* **1.** vuelta *f.*, regreso; retorno *m.* **by r. mail,** a vuelta de correo. —*v.* **2.** volver, regresar; devolver.
reunion /riˈyunyən/ *n.* reunión *f.*
rev /rɛv/ *n.* **1.** revolución *f.* —*v.* **2.** (motor) acelerar.
reveal /rɪˈvil/ *v.* revelar.
revelation /ˌrɛvəˈleiʃən/ *n.* revelación *f.*
revenge /rɪˈvɛndʒ/ *n.* venganza *f.* **to get r.,** vengarse.
revenue /ˈrɛvənˌyu, -əˌnu/ *n.* renta *f.*
revere /rɪˈvɪər/ *v.* reverenciar, venerar.
reverence /ˈrɛvərəns, ˈrɛvrəns/ *n.* **1.** reverencia *f.* —*v.* **2.** reverenciar.
reverend /ˈrɛvərənd, ˈrɛvrənd/ *a.* **1.** reverendo. —*n.* **2.** pastor *m.*
reverent /ˈrɛvərənt, ˈrɛvrənt/ *a.* reverente.
reverse /rɪˈvɜrs/ *a.* **1.** inverso. —*n.* **2.** revés, inverso *m.* —*v.* **3.** invertir; revocar.
revert /rɪˈvɜrt/ *v.* revertir.
review /rɪˈvyu/ *n.* **1.** repaso *m.*; revista *f.* —*v.* **2.** repasar; *Mil.* revistar.
revise /rɪˈvaiz/ *v.* revisar.
revision /rɪˈvɪʒən/ *n.* revisión *f.*
revival /rɪˈvaivəl/ *n.* reavivamiento *m.*
revive /rɪˈvaiv/ *v.* avivar; revivir, resucitar.
revoke /rɪˈvouk/ *v.* revocar.
revolt /rɪˈvoult/ *n.* **1.** rebelión *f.* —*v.* **2.** rebelarse.
revolting /rɪˈvoultɪŋ/ *a.* repugnante.
revolution /ˌrɛvəˈluʃən/ *n.* revolución *f.*
revolutionary /ˌrɛvəˈluʃəˌnɛri/ *a. & n.* revolucionario -ria.
revolve /rɪˈvɒlv/ *v.* girar; dar vueltas.
revolver /rɪˈvɒlvər/ *n.* revólver *m.*
revolving door /rɪˈvɒlvɪŋ/ puerta giratoria *f.*
reward /rɪˈwɔrd/ *n.* **1.** pago *m.*; recompensa *f.* —*v.* **2.** recompensar.
rhetoric /ˈrɛtərɪk/ *n.* retórica *f.*
rheumatism /ˈruməˌtɪzəm/ *n.* reumatismo *m.*
rhinoceros /raiˈnɒsərəs/ *n.* rinoceronte *m.*
rhubarb /ˈrubɑrb/ *n.* ruibarbo *m.*
rhyme /raim/ *n.* **1.** rima *f.* —*v.* **2.** rimar.
rhythm /ˈrɪðəm/ *n.* ritmo *m.*
rhythmical /ˈrɪðmɪkəl/ *a.* rítmico.
rib /rɪb/ *n.* costilla *f.*
ribbon /ˈrɪbən/ *n.* cinta *f.*
rib cage caja torácica *f.*
rice /rais/ *n.* arroz *m.*
rich /rɪtʃ/ *a.* rico.
rid /rɪd/ *v.* librar. **get r. of,** deshacerse de, quitarse.
riddle /ˈrɪdl/ *n.* enigma; rompecabezas *m.*
ride /raid/ *n.* **1.** paseo (a caballo, en coche, etc.) *m.* —*v.* **2.** cabalgar; ir en coche.
ridge /rɪdʒ/ *n.* cerro *m.*; arruga *f.*; (of a roof) caballete *m.*
ridicule /ˈrɪdɪˌkyul/ *n.* **1.** ridículo *m.* —*v.* **2.** ridiculizar.
ridiculous /rɪˈdɪkyələs/ *a.* ridículo.
riding /ˈraidɪŋ/ *n.* equitación *f.*
riding school picadero *m.*
rifle /ˈraifəl/ *n.* **1.** fusil *m.* —*v.* **2.** robar.
rig /rɪg/ *n.* **1.** aparejo *m.* —*v.* **2.** aparejar.
right /rait/ *a.* **1.** derecho; correcto. **to be r.,** tener razón. —*adv.* **2.** bien, correctamente. **r. here,** etc., aquí mismo, etc. **all r.,** está bien, muy bien. —*n.* **3.** derecho *m.*; justicia *f.* **to the r.,** a la derecha. —*v.* **4.** corregir; enderezar.
righteous /ˈraitʃəs/ *a.* justo.
rigid /ˈrɪdʒɪd/ *a.* rígido.
rigor /ˈrɪgər/ *n.* rigor *m.*
rigorous /ˈrɪgərəs/ *a.* riguroso.
rim /rɪm/ *n.* margen *m. or f.*; borde *m.*
ring /rɪŋ/ *n.* **1.** anillo *m.*; sortija *f.*; círculo; campaneo *m.* —*v.* **2.** cercar; sonar; tocar.
ring finger dedo anular *m.*
rinse /rɪns/ *v.* enjuagar, lavar.
riot /ˈraiət/ *n.* motín; alboroto *m.*
rip /rɪp/ *n.* **1.** rasgadura *f.* —*v.* **2.** rasgar; descoser.
ripe /raip/ *a.* maduro.
ripen /ˈraipən/ *v.* madurar.
ripoff /ˈrɪpˌɔf/ *n.* robo, atraco *m.*
ripple /ˈrɪpəl/ *n.* **1.** onda *f.* —*v.* **2.** ondear.
rise /raiz/ *n.* **1.** subida *f.* —*v.* **2.** ascender; levantarse; (moon) salir.
risk /rɪsk/ *n.* **1.** riesgo *m.* —*v.* **2.** arriesgar.
rite /rait/ *n.* rito *m.*
ritual /ˈrɪtʃuəl/ *a. & n.* ritual *m.*
rival /ˈraivəl/ *n.* rival *m. & f.*
rivalry /ˈraivəlri/ *n.* rivalidad *f.*
river /ˈraivər/ *n.* río *m.*
rivet /ˈrɪvɪt/ *n.* **1.** remache, roblón *m.* —*v.* **2.** remachar, roblar.
road /roud/ *n.* camino *m.*; carretera *f.*
roadside /ˈroudˌsaid/ *n.* borde de la carretera *m.*
roam /roum/ *v.* vagar.
roar /rɔr, rour/ *n.* **1.** rugido, bramido *m.* —*v.* **2.** rugir, bramar.
roast /roust/ *n.* **1.** asado *m.* —*v.* **2.** asar.
rob /rɒb/ *v.* robar.
robber /ˈrɒbər/ *n.* ladrón -na.
robbery /ˈrɒbəri/ *n.* robo *m.*
robe /roub/ *n.* manto *m.*
robin /ˈrɒbɪn/ *n.* petirrojo *m.*
robust /rouˈbʌst, ˈroubʌst/ *a.* robusto.
rock /rɒk/ *n.* **1.** roca, peña *f.*; (music) rock *m.*, música (de) rock *f.* —*v.* **2.** mecer; oscilar.
rocker /ˈrɒkər/ *n.* mecedora *f.*
rocket /ˈrɒkɪt/ *n.* cohete *m.*
rocking chair /ˈrɒkɪŋ/ mecedora *f.*
Rock of Gibraltar /dʒɪˈbrɔltər/ Peñón de Gibraltar *m.*
rocky /ˈrɒki/ *a.* pedregoso.
rod /rɒd/ *n.* varilla *f.*
rodent /ˈroudnt/ *n.* roedor *m.*
rogue /roug/ *n.* bribón, pícaro *m.*
roguish /ˈrougɪʃ/ *a.* pícaro.
role /roul/ *n.* papel *m.*
roll /roul/ **1.** rollo *m.*; lista *f.*; panecillo *m.* **to call the r.,** pasar lista. —*v.* **2.** rodar. **r. up,** enrollar. **r. up one's sleeves,** arremangarse.
roller /ˈroulər/ *n.* rodillo, cilindro *m.*
roller skate patín de ruedas *m.*
Roman /ˈroumən/ *a. & n.* romano -na.
romance /rouˈmæns, ˈroumæns/ *a.* **1.** románico. —*n.* **2.** romance *m.*; amorío *m.*
romantic /rouˈmæntɪk/ *a.* romántico.
romp /rɒmp/ *v.* retozar; jugar.
roof /ruf, rʊf/ *n.* **1.** techo *m.*; —*v.* **2.** techar.
room /rum, rʊm/ *n.* **1.** cuarto *m.*, habitación *f.*; lugar *m.* —*v.* **2.** alojarse.
roommate /ˈrumˌmeit, ˈrʊm-/ *n.* compañero -ra de cuarto.
rooster /ˈrustər/ *n.* gallo *m.*
root /rut/ *n.* raíz *f.* **to take r.,** arraigar.
rootless /ˈrutlɪs/ *a.* desarraigado.
rope /roup/ *n.* cuerda, soga *f.*
rose /rouz/ *n.* rosa *f.*
rosy /ˈrouzi/ *a.* róseo, rosado.
rot /rɒt/ *n.* **1.** putrefacción *f.* —*v.* **2.** pudrirse.
rotary /ˈroutəri/ *a.* giratorio; rotativo.
rotate /ˈrouteit/ *v.* girar; alternar.
rotation /rouˈteiʃən/ *n.* rotación *f.*
rotten /ˈrɒtn/ *a.* podrido.
rouge /ruʒ/ *n.* colorete *m.*
rough /rʌf/ *a.* áspero; rudo; grosero; aproximado.
round /raund/ *a.* **1.** redondo. **r. trip,** viaje de ida y vuelta. —*n.* **2.** ronda *f.*; (boxing) asalto *m.*
rouse /rauz/ *v.* despertar.
rout /raut, rut/ *n.* **1.** derrota *f.* —*v.* **2.** derrotar.
route /rut, raut/ *n.* ruta, vía *f.*
routine /ruˈtin/ *a.* **1.** rutinario. —*n.* **2.** rutina *f.*
rove /rouv/ *v.* vagar.
rover /ˈrouvər/ *n.* vagabundo -da.
row /rou/ *n.* **1.** fila *f.* —*v.* **2.** *Naut.* remar.
rowboat /ˈrouˌbout/ *n.* bote de remos.
rowdy /ˈraudi/ *a.* alborotado.
royal /ˈrɔiəl/ *a.* real.
royalty /ˈrɔiəlti/ *n.* realeza *f.*; (pl.) regalías *f.pl.*
rub /rʌb/ *v.* frotar. **r. against,** rozar. **r. out,** borrar.
rubber /ˈrʌbər/ *n.* goma *f.*; caucho *m.*; (pl.) chanclos *m.pl.*, zapatos de goma.
rubbish /ˈrʌbɪʃ/ *n.* basura *f.*; (nonsense) tonterías *f.pl.*
ruby /ˈrubi/ *n.* rubí *m.*
rudder /ˈrʌdər/ *n.* timón *m.*
ruddy /ˈrʌdi/ *a.* colorado.
rude /rud/ *a.* rudo; grosero; descortés.
rudiment /ˈrudəmənt/ *n.* rudimento *m.*
rudimentary /ˌrudəˈmɛntəri, -tri/ *a.* rudimentario.
rue /ru/ *v.* deplorar; lamentar.
ruffian /ˈrʌfiən, ˈrʌfyən/ *n.* rufián, bandolero *m.*
ruffle /ˈrʌfəl/ *n.* **1.** volante fruncido. —*v.* **2.** fruncir; irritar.
rug /rʌg/ *n.* alfombra *f.*
rugged /ˈrʌgɪd/ *a.* áspero; robusto.
ruin /ˈruɪn/ *n.* **1.** ruina *f.* —*v.* **2.** arruinar.
ruinous /ˈruənəs/ *a.* ruinoso.
rule /rul/ *n.* **1.** regla *f.* **as a r.,** por regla general. —*v.* **2.** gobernar; mandar; rayar.
ruler /ˈrulər/ *n.* gobernante *m. & f.*; soberano -na; regla *f.*
rum /rʌm/ *n.* ron *m.*
rumble /ˈrʌmbəl/ *v.* retumbar.
rumor /ˈrumər/ *n.* rumor *m.*
rumpus /ˈrʌmpəs/ *n.* lío, jaleo, escandalo *m.*
run /rʌn/ *v.* correr; hacer correr. **r. away,** escaparse. **r. into,** chocar con.

runner /'rʌnər/ n. corredor -ra; mensajero -ra.
runner-up /'rʌnər 'ʌp/ n. subcampeón -ona.
runproof /'rʌnpruf/ a. indesmallable.
rupture /'rʌptʃər/ n. **1.** rotura; hernia f. —v. **2.** reventar.
rural /'rʊrəl/ a. rural, campestre.
rush /rʌʃ/ n. **1.** prisa f.; Bot. junco m. —v. **2.** ir de prisa.
rush hour hora punta f.
Russia /'rʌʃə/ n. Rusia f.
Russian /'rʌʃən/ a. & n. ruso -sa.
rust /rʌst/ n. **1.** herrumbre f. —v. **2.** aherrumbrarse.
rustic /'rʌstɪk/ a. rústico.
rustle /'rʌsəl/ n. **1.** susurro m. —v. **2.** susurrar.
rusty /'rʌsti/ a. mohoso.
rut /rʌt/ n. surco m.
ruthless /'ruθlɪs/ a. cruel, inhumano.
rye /rai/ n. centeno m.
rye bread pan de centeno m.

S

saber /'seibər/ n. sable m.
sable /'seibəl/ n. cebellina f.
sabotage /'sæbə,taʒ/ n. sabotaje m.
sachet /sæ'ʃei/ n. perfumador m.
sack /sæk/ n. **1.** saco m. —v. **2.** Mil. saquear.
sacred /'seikrɪd/ a. sagrado, santo.
sacrifice /'sækrə,fais/ n. **1.** sacrificio m. —v. **2.** sacrificar.
sacrilege /'sækrəlɪdʒ/ n. sacrilegio m.
sad /sæd/ a. triste.
saddle /'sædl/ n. **1.** silla de montar. —v. **2.** ensillar.
sadness /'sædnɪs/ n. tristeza f.
safe /seif/ a. **1.** seguro; salvo. —n. **2.** caja de caudales.
safeguard /'seif,gard/ n. **1.** salvaguardia m. —v. **2.** proteger, poner a salvo.
safety / seifti/ n. seguridad, protección f.
safety belt cinturón de seguridad m.
safety pin imperdible m.
safety valve /vælv/ válvula de seguridad f.
sage /seidʒ/ a. **1.** sabio, sagaz. —n. **2.** sabio m.; Bot. salvia f.
sail /seil/ n. **1.** vela f.; paseo por mar. —v. **2.** navegar; embarcarse.
sailboat /'seil,bout/ n. barco de vela.
sailor /'seilər/ n. marinero m.
saint /seint/ n. santo -ta.
sake /seik/ n. **for the s. of,** por; por el bien de.
salad /'sæləd/ n. ensalada f. **s. bowl,** ensaladera f.
salad dressing aliño m.
salary /'sæləri/ n. sueldo, salario m.
sale /seil/ n. venta f.
salesman /'seilzmən/ n. vendedor m.; viajante de comercio.
sales tax /seilz/ impuesto sobre la venta.
saliva /sə'laivə/ n. saliva f.
salmon /'sæmən/ n. salmón m.
salt /sɔlt/ a. **1.** salado. —n. **2.** sal f. —v. **3.** salar.
salute /sə'lut/ n. **1.** saludo m. —v. **2.** saludar.
salvage /'sælvɪdʒ/ v. salvar; recobrar.
salvation /sæl'veiʃən/ n. salvación f.
salve /sælv/ n. emplasto, ungüento m.
same /seim/ a. & pron. mismo. **it's all the s.,** lo mismo da.
sample /'sæmpəl/ n. **1.** muestra f. —v. **2.** probar.
sanatorium /,sænə'tɔriəm/ n. sanatorio m.
sanctify /'sæŋktə,fai/ v. santificar.
sanction /'sæŋkʃən/ n. **1.** sanción f. —v. **2.** sancionar.
sanctity /'sæŋktɪti/ n. santidad f.
sanctuary /'sæŋktʃu,eri/ n. santuario, asilo m.
sand /sænd/ n. arena f.

sandal /'sændl/ n. sandalia f.
sandpaper /'sænd,peipər/ n. papel de lija m.
sandwich /'sændwɪtʃ, 'sæn-/ n. emparedado, sándwich m.
sandy /'sændi/ a. arenoso; (color) rufo.
sane /sein/ a. cuerdo; sano.
sanitary /'sænɪ,teri/ a. higiénico, sanitario. **s. napkin,** toalla sanitaria.
sanitation /,sænɪ'teiʃən/ n. saneamiento m.
sanity /'sænɪti/ n. cordura f.
Santa Claus /'sæntə klɔz/ Papá Noel m.
sap /sæp/ n. **1.** savia f.; Colloq. estúpido, bobo m. —v. **2.** agotar.
sapphire /'sæfaiər/ n. zafiro m.
sarcasm /'sarkæzəm/ n. sarcasmo m.
sardine /sar'din/ n. sardina f.
sash /sæʃ/ n. cinta f.
satellite /'sætl,ait/ n. satélite m.
satellite dish antena parabólica f.
satin /'sætn/ n. raso m.
satire /'sætaiər/ n. sátira f.
satisfaction /,sætɪs'fækʃən/ n. satisfacción; recompensa f.
satisfactory /,sætɪs'fæktəri/ a. satisfactorio.
satisfy /'sætɪs,fai/ v. satisfacer. **be satisfied that...,** estar convencido de que.
saturate /'sætʃə,reit/ v. saturar.
Saturday /'sætər,dei/ n. sábado m.
sauce /sɔs/ n. salsa; compota f.
saucer /'sɔsər/ n. platillo m.
saucy /'sɔsi/ a. descarado, insolente.
sauna /'sɔnə/ n. sauna f.
sausage /'sɔsɪdʒ/ n. salchicha f.
savage /'sævɪdʒ/ a. & n. salvaje m. & f.
save /seiv/ v. **1.** salvar; guardar; ahorrar, economizar. —prep. **2.** salvo, excepto.
savings /'seivɪŋz/ n. ahorros m.pl.
savings account cuenta de ahorros m.
savings bank caja de ahorros f.
savior /'seivyər/ n. salvador -ora.
savor /'seivər/ n. **1.** sabor m. —v. **2.** saborear.
savory /'seivəri/ a. sabroso.
saw /sɔ/ n. **1.** sierra f. —v. **2.** aserrar.
saxophone /'sæksə,foun/ n. saxofón, saxófono, m.
say /sei/ v. decir; recitar.
saying /'seiɪŋ/ n. dicho, refrán m.
scaffold /'skæfəld/ n. andamio; (gallows) patíbulo m.
scald /skɔld/ v. escaldar.
scale /skeil/ n. **1.** escala; (of fish) escama f.; (pl.) balanza f. —v. **2.** escalar; escamar.
scalp /skælp/ n. pericráneo m. v. escalpar.
scan /skæn/ v. hojear, repasar; (poetry) escandir; (computer) escanear, digitalizar.
scandal /'skændl/ n. escándalo m.
scanner /'skænər/ n. escáner m.
scant /skænt/ a. escaso.
scar /skar/ n. cicatriz f.
scarce /skeərs/ a. escaso; raro.
scarcely /'skeərsli/ adv. & conj. apenas.
scare /skeər/ n. **1.** susto m. —v. **2.** asustar. **s. away,** espantar.
scarf /skarf/ n. pañueleta, bufanda f.
scarlet /'skarlɪt/ n. escarlata f.
scarlet fever escarlatina f.
scatter /'skætər/ v. esparcir; dispersar.
scavenger /'skævɪndʒər/ n. basurero m.
scenario /sɪ'neəri,ou, -'nar-/ n. escenario m.
scene /sin/ n. vista f., paisaje m.; Theat. escena f. **behind the scenes,** entre bastidores.
scenery /'sinəri/ n. paisaje m.; Theat. decorado m.
scent /sɛnt/ n. **1.** olor, perfume;

(sense) olfato m. —v. **2.** perfumar; Fig. sospechar.
schedule /'skɛdʒul, -ʊl, -uəl/ n. **1.** programa, horario m. —v. **2.** fijar la hora para.
scheme /skim/ n. **1.** proyecto; esquema m. —v. **2.** intrigar.
scholar /'skɒlər/ n. erudito -ta; becado -da.
scholarship /'skɒlər,ʃip/ n. beca; erudición f.
school /skul/ n. **1.** escuela f.; colegio m.; (of fish) banco m. —v. **2.** enseñar.
sciatica /sai'ætɪkə/ n. ciática f.
science /'saiəns/ n. ciencia f.
science fiction ciencia ficción.
scientific /,saiən'tɪfɪk/ a. científico.
scientist /'saiəntɪst/ n. científico -ca.
scissors /'sɪzərz/ n. tijeras f.pl.
scoff /skɒf, skɒf/ v. mofarse, burlarse.
scold /skould/ v. regañar.
scoop /skup/ n. **1.** cucharón m.; cucharada f. —v. **2. s. out,** recoger, sacar.
scope /skoup/ n. alcance; campo m.
score /skɔr/ n. **1.** tantos m.pl.; (music) partitura f. —v. **2.** marcar, hacer tantos.
scorn /skɔrn/ n. **1.** desprecio m. —v. **2.** despreciar.
scornful /'skɔrnfəl/ a. desdeñoso.
Scotland /'skɒtlənd/ n. Escocia f.
Scottish /'skɒtɪʃ/ a. escocés.
scour /skauər/ v. fregar, estregar.
scourge /skɜrdʒ/ n. azote m.; plaga f.
scout /skaut/ n. **1.** explorador -ra. —v. **2.** explorar, reconocer.
scramble /'skræmbəl/ n. **1.** rebatiña f. —v. **2.** bregar. **scrambled eggs,** huevos revueltos.
scrap /skræp/ n. **1.** migaja f.; pedacito m.; Colloq. riña f. **s. metal,** hierro viejo m. **s. paper,** papel borrador. —v. **2.** desechar; Colloq. reñir.
scrapbook /'skræp,bʊk/ n. álbum de recortes m.
scrape /skreip/ n. **1.** lío, apuro m. —v. **2.** raspar; (feet) restregar.
scratch /skrætʃ/ n. **1.** rasguño m. —v. **2.** rasguñar; rayar.
scream /skrim/ n. **1.** grito, chillido m. —v. **2.** gritar, chillar.
screen /skrin/ n. **1.** biombo m.; (for window) tela metálica; (movie) pantalla f.
screw /skru/ n. **1.** tornillo m. —v. **2.** atornillar.
screwdriver /'skru,draivər/ n. destornillador m.
scribble /'skribəl/ v. hacer garabatos.
scroll /skroul/ n. rúbrica f.; rollo de papel.
scroll bar n. barra de enrollar f.
scrub /skrʌb/ v. fregar, estregar.
scruple /'skrupəl/ n. escrúpulo m.
scrupulous /'skrupyələs/ a. escrupuloso.
scuba diving /'skubə 'daivɪŋ/ submarinismo m.
sculptor /'skʌlptər/ n. escultor -ra.
sculpture /'skʌlptʃər/ n. **1.** escultura f. —v. **2.** esculpir.
scythe /saið/ n. guadaña f.
sea /si/ n. mar m. or f.
seabed /'si,bɛd/ n. lecho marino m.
sea breeze brisa marina f.
seafood /'si,fud/ n. mariscos m.pl.
seal /sil/ n. **1.** sello m.; (animal) foca f. —v. **2.** sellar.
seam /sim/ n. costura f.
seamy /'simi/ a. sórdido.
seaplane /'si,plein/ n. hidroavión m.
seaport /'si,pɔrt/ n. puerto de mar.
search /sɜrtʃ/ n. **1.** registro m. **in s. of,** en busca de. —v. **2.** registrar. **s. for,** buscar.
search engine motor de búsqueda m., buscador m., indexador de información m.
seasick /'si,sɪk/ a. mareado. **to get s.,** marearse.

season /'sizən/ n. **1.** estación; sazón; temporada f. —v. **2.** sazonar.
seasoning /'sizənɪŋ/ n. condimento m.
season ticket abono m.
seat /sit/ n. **1.** asiento m.; residencia, sede f.; Theat. localidad f. **s. belt,** cinturón de seguridad. —v. **2.** sentar. **be seated,** sentarse.
seaweed /'si,wid/ n. alga, alga marina f.
second /'sɪkɒnd/ a. & n. **1.** segundo m. —v. **2.** apoyar, segundar.
secondary /'sɛkən,deri/ a. secundario.
secret /'sikrɪt/ a. & n. secreto m.
secretary /'sɛkrɪ,teri/ n. secretario -ria; Govt. ministro -tra; (furniture) papelera f.
sect /sɛkt/ n. secta f.; partido m.
section /'sɛkʃən/ n. sección, parte f.
sectional /'sɛkʃənl/ a. regional, local.
secular /'sɛkyələr/ a. secular.
secure /sɪ'kyur/ a. **1.** seguro. —v. **2.** asegurar; obtener; Fin. garantizar.
security /sɪ'kyuriti/ n. seguridad; garantía f.
sedative /'sɛdətɪv/ a. & n. sedativo m.
seduce /sɪ'dus/ v. seducir.
see /si/ v. ver; comprender. **s. off,** despedirse de. **s. to,** encargarse de.
seed /sid/ n. **1.** semilla f. —v. **2.** sembrar.
seek /sik/ v. buscar. **s. to,** tratar de.
seem /sim/ v. parecer.
seep /sip/ v. colarse.
segment /'sɛgmənt/ n. segmento m.
segregate /'sɛgrɪ,geit/ v. segregar.
seize /siz/ v. agarrar; apoderarse de.
seldom /'sɛldəm/ adv. rara vez.
select /sɪ'lɛkt/ a. **1.** escogido, selecto. —v. **2.** elegir, seleccionar.
selection /sɪ'lɛkʃən/ n. selección f.
selective /sɪ'lɛktɪv/ a. selectivo.
selfish /'sɛlfɪʃ/ a. egoísta.
selfishness /'sɛlfɪnɪs/ n. egoísmo m.
sell /sɛl/ v. vender.
semester /sɪ'mɛstər/ n. semestre m.
semicircle /'sɛmɪ,sɜrkəl/ n. semicírculo m.
semolina /,sɛmə'linə/ n. sémola f.
senate /'sɛnɪt/ n. senado m.
senator /'sɛnətər/ n. senador -ra.
send /sɛnd/ v. mandar, enviar; (a wire) poner. **s. away,** despedir. **s. back,** devolver. **s. for,** mandar buscar. **s. off,** expedir. **s. word,** mandar recado.
senile /'sinail/ a. senil.
senior /'sinyər/ a. mayor; más viejo. Sr., padre.
senior citizen persona de edad avanzada.
sensation /sɛn'seiʃən/ n. sensación f.
sensational /sɛn'seiʃənl/ a. sensacional.
sense /sɛns/ n. **1.** sentido; juicio m. —v. **2.** percibir; sospechar.
sensible /'sɛnsəbəl/ a. sensato, razonable.
sensitive /'sɛnsɪtɪv/ a. sensible; sensitivo.
sensual /'sɛnʃuəl/ a. sensual.
sentence /'sɛntn̩s/ n. **1.** frase; Gram. oración; Leg. sentencia f. —v. **2.** condenar.
sentiment /'sɛntəmənt/ n. sentimiento m.
sentimental /,sɛntə'mɛntl̩/ a. sentimental.
separate /a. 'sɛpərɪt; v. -,reit/ a. **1.** separado; suelto. —v. **2.** separar, dividir.
separation /,sɛpə'reiʃən/ n. separación f.
September /sɛp'tɛmbər/ n. septiembre m.
sequence /'sikwəns/ n. serie f. **in s.,** seguidos.
serenade /,sɛrə'neid/ n. **1.** serenata f. —v. **2.** dar serenata a.
serene /sə'rin/ a. sereno; tranquilo.
sergeant /'sardʒənt/ n. sargento m.

serial /ˈsɪəriəl/ *a.* en serie, de serie.
series /ˈsɪəriz/ *n.* serie *f.*
serious /ˈsɪəriəs/ *a.* serio; grave.
sermon /ˈsɜrmən/ *n.* sermón *m.*
serpent /ˈsɜrpənt/ *n.* serpiente *f.*
servant /ˈsɜrvənt/ *n.* criado -da; servidor -ra.
serve /sɜrv/ *v.* servir.
server /ˈsɜrvər/ *n.* servidor *m.*
service /ˈsɜrvɪs/ *n.* **1.** servicio *m.* **at the s. of,** a las órdenes de. **be of s.,** servir; ser útil. —*v.* **2.** *Auto.* reparar.
service station estación de servicio *f.*
session /ˈsɛʃən/ *n.* sesión *f.*
set /sɛt/ *a.* **1.** fijo. —*n.* **2.** colección *f.*; (of a game) juego; *Mech.* aparato; *Theat.* decorado *m.* —*v.* **3.** poner, colocar; fijar; (sun) ponerse. **s. forth,** exponer. **s. off, s. out,** salir. **s. up,** instalar; establecer.
settle /ˈsɛtl̩/ *v.* solucionar; arreglar; establecerse.
settlement /ˈsɛtl̩mənt/ *n.* caserío; arreglo; acuerdo *m.*
settler /ˈsɛtlər/ *n.* poblador -ra.
seven /ˈsɛvən/ *a.* & *pron.* siete.
seventeen /ˈsɛvənˈtin/ *a.* & *pron.* diecisiete.
seventh /ˈsɛvənθ/ *a.* séptimo.
seventy /ˈsɛvənti/ *a.* & *pron.* setenta.
sever /ˈsɛvər/ *v.* desunir; romper.
several /ˈsɛvərəl/ *a.* & *pron.* varios.
severance pay /ˈsɛvərəns/ indemnización de despido.
severe /səˈvɪər/ *a.* severo; grave.
severity /səˈvɛrɪti/ *n.* severidad *f.*
sew /sou/ *v.* coser.
sewer /ˈsuər/ *n.* cloaca *f.*
sewing /ˈsouɪŋ/ *n.* costura *f.*
sewing basket costurero *m.*
sewing machine máquina de coser *f.*
sex /sɛks/ *n.* sexo *m.*
sexism /ˈsɛksɪzəm/ *n.* sexismo *m.*
sexist /ˈsɛksɪst/ *a.* & *n.* sexista *m.* & *f.*
sexton /ˈsɛkstən/ *n.* sacristán *m.*
sexual /ˈsɛkʃuəl/ *a.* sexual.
shabby /ˈʃæbi/ *a.* haraposo, desaliñado.
shade /ʃeid/ *n.* **1.** sombra *f.*; tinte *m.*; (window) transparente *m.* —*v.* **2.** sombrear.
shadow /ˈʃædou/ *n.* sombra *f.*
shady /ˈʃeidi/ *a.* sombroso; sospechoso.
shaft /ʃæft/ *n.* (columna) fuste; *Mech.* asta *f.*
shake /ʃeik/ *v.* sacudir; agitar; temblar. **s. hands with,** dar la mano a.
shallow /ˈʃælou/ *a.* poco hondo; superficial.
shame /ʃeim/ *n.* **1.** vergüenza *f.* **be a s.,** ser una lástima. —*v.* **2.** avergonzar.
shameful /ˈʃeimfəl/ *a.* vergonzoso.
shampoo /ʃæmˈpu/ *n.* champú *m.*
shape /ʃeip/ *n.* **1.** forma *f.*; estado *m.* —*v.* **2.** formar.
share /ʃɛər/ *n.* **1.** parte; (stock) acción *f.* **2** —*v.* **2.** compartir.
shareholder /ˈʃɛərˌhouldər/ *n.* accionista *m.* & *f.*
shareware /ˈʃɛərˌwɛər/ *n.* programas compartidos *m.pl.*
shark /ʃɑrk/ *n.* tiburón *m.*
sharp /ʃɑrp/ *a.* agudo; (blade) afilado.
sharpen /ˈʃɑrpən/ *v.* aguzar; afilar.
shatter /ˈʃætər/ *v.* estrellar; hacer pedazos.
shave /ʃeiv/ *n.* **1.** afeitada *f.* —*v.* **2.** afeitarse.
shawl /ʃɔl/ *n.* rebozo, chal *m.*
she /ʃi/ *pron.* ella *f.*
sheaf /ʃif/ *n.* gavilla *f.*
shear /ʃɪər/ *v.* cizallar.
shears /ʃɪərz/ *n.* cizallas *f.pl.*
sheath /ʃiθ/ *n.* vaina *f.*
shed /ʃɛd/ *n.* **1.** cobertizo *m.* —*v.* **2.** arrojar, quitarse.
sheep /ʃip/ *n.* oveja *f.*
sheet /ʃit/ *n.* sábana; (of paper) hoja *f.*
shelf /ʃɛlf/ *n.* estante, *m.*, repisa *f.*
shell /ʃɛl/ *n.* **1.** cáscara; (sea) concha *f.*; *Mil.* proyectil *m.* —*v.* **2.** desgranar; bombardear.
shellac /ʃəˈlæk/ *n.* laca *f.*
shelter /ˈʃɛltər/ *n.* **1.** albergue; refugio *m.* —*v.* **2.** albergar; amparar.
shepherd /ˈʃɛpərd/ *n.* pastor *m.*
sherry /ˈʃɛri/ *n.* jerez *m.*
shield /ʃild/ *n.* **1.** escudo *m.* —*v.* **2.** amparar.
shift /ʃɪft/ *n.* **1.** cambio; (work) turno *m.* —*v.* **2.** cambiar, mudar. **s. for oneself,** arreglárselas.
shine /ʃain/ *n.* **1.** brillo, lustre *m.* —*v.* **2.** brillar; (shoes) lustrar.
shiny /ˈʃaini/ *a.* brillante, lustroso.
ship /ʃɪp/ *n.* **1.** barco *m.*, nave *f.* —*v.* **2.** embarcar; *Com.* enviar.
shipment /ˈʃɪpmənt/ *n.* envío; embarque *m.*
shirk /ʃɜrk/ *v.* faltar al deber.
shirt /ʃɜrt/ *n.* camisa *f.*
shiver /ˈʃɪvər/ *n.* **1.** temblor *m.* —*v.* **2.** temblar.
shock /ʃɒk/ *n.* **1.** choque *m.* —*v.* **2.** chocar.
shoe /ʃu/ *n.* zapato *m.*
shoelace /ˈʃuˌleis/ *n.* lazo *m.*; cordón de zapato.
shoemaker /ˈʃuˌmeikər/ *n.* zapatero *m.*
shoot /ʃut/ *v.* tirar; (gun) disparar. **s. away, s. off,** salir disparado.
shop /ʃɒp/ *n.* tienda *f.*
shopping /ˈʃɒpɪŋ/ *n.* **to go s.,** hacer compras, ir de compras.
shop window escaparate *m.*
shore /ʃɔr/ *n.* orilla; playa *f.*
short /ʃɔrt/ *a.* corto; breve; (in stature) pequeño, bajo. **a s. time,** poco tiempo. **in s.,** en suma.
shortage /ˈʃɔrtɪdʒ/ *n.* escasez; falta *f.*
shorten /ˈʃɔrtn̩/ *v.* acortar, abreviar.
shortly /ˈʃɔrtli/ *adv.* en breve, dentro de poco.
shorts /ʃɔrts/ *n.* calzoncillos *m.pl.*
shot /ʃɒt/ *n.* tiro, disparo *m.*
shoulder /ˈʃouldər/ *n.* **1.** hombro *m.* —*v.* **2.** asumir; cargar con.
shoulder blade *n.* omóplato *m.*, paletilla *f.*
shout /ʃaut/ *n.* **1.** grito *m.* —*v.* **2.** gritar.
shove /ʃʌv/ *n.* **1.** empujón *m.* —*v.* **2.** empujar.
shovel /ˈʃʌvəl/ *n.* **1.** pala *f.* —*v.* **2.** traspalar.
show /ʃou/ *n.* **1.** ostentación *f.*; *Theat.* función *f.*; espectáculo *m.* —*v.* **2.** enseñar, mostrar; verse. **s. up,** destacarse; *Colloq.* asomar.
shower /ˈʃauər/ *n.* chubasco *m.*; (bath) ducha *f.* *v.* ducharse.
shrapnel /ˈʃræpnl̩/ *n.* metralla *f.*
shrewd /ʃrud/ *a.* astuto.
shriek /ʃrik/ *n.* **1.** chillido *m.* —*v.* **2.** chillar.
shrill /ʃrɪl/ *a.* chillón, agudo.
shrimp /ʃrɪmp/ *n.* camarón *m.*
shrine /ʃrain/ *n.* santuario *m.*
shrink /ʃrɪŋk/ *v.* encogerse, contraerse, **s. from,** huir de.
shroud /ʃraud/ *n.* **1.** mortaja *f.* —*v.* **2.** *Fig.* ocultar.
shrub /ʃrʌb/ *n.* arbusto *m.*
shudder /ˈʃʌdər/ *n.* **1.** estremecimiento *m.* —*v.* **2.** estremecerse.
shun /ʃʌn/ *v.* evitar, huir de.
shut /ʃʌt/ *v.* cerrar. **s. in,** encerrar. **s. up,** *Colloq.* callarse.
shutter /ˈʃʌtər/ *n.* persiana *f.*
shy /ʃai/ *a.* tímido, vergonzoso.
sick /sɪk/ *a.* enfermo. **s. of,** aburrido de, cansado de.
sickness /ˈsɪknɪs/ *n.* enfermedad *f.*
side /said/ *n.* **1.** lado; partido *m.*; parte *f.*; *Anat.* costado *m.* —*v.* **2. s. with,** ponerse del lado de.
sidewalk /ˈsaidˌwɔk/ *n.* acera, vereda *f.*
siege /sidʒ/ *n.* asedio *m.*
sieve /sɪv/ *n.* cedazo *m.*
sift /sɪft/ *v.* cerner.
sigh /sai/ *n.* **1.** suspiro *m.* —*v.* **2.** suspirar.
sight /sait/ *n.* **1.** vista *f.*; punto de interés *m.* **lose s. of,** perder de vista. —*v.* **2.** divisar.
sign /sain/ *n.* **1.** letrero; señal, seña *f.* —*v.* **2.** firmar. **s. up,** inscribirse.
signal /ˈsɪgnl̩/ *n.* **1.** señal *f.* —*v.* **2.** hacer señales.
signature /ˈsɪgnətʃər/ *n.* firma *f.*
significance /sɪgˈnɪfɪkəns/ *n.* significación *f.*
significant /sɪgˈnɪfɪkənt/ *a.* significativo.
significant other pareja *m.* & *f.*
signify /ˈsɪgnəˌfai/ *v.* significar.
silence /ˈsailəns/ *n.* **1.** silencio *m.* —*v.* **2.** hacer callar.
silent /ˈsailənt/ *a.* silencioso; callado.
silk /sɪlk/ *n.* seda *f.*
silken /ˈsɪlkən/ **silky** *a.* sedoso.
sill /sɪl/ *n.* umbral de puerta *m.*, solera *f.*
silly /ˈsɪli/ *a.* necio, tonto.
silo /ˈsailou/ *n.* silo *m.*
silver /ˈsɪlvər/ *n.* plata *f.*
silver-plated /ˈsɪlvər ˈpleitɪd/ *a.* chapado en plata.
silverware /ˈsɪlvərˌwɛər/ *n.* vajilla de plata *f.*
similar /ˈsɪmələr/ *a.* semejante, parecido.
similarity /ˌsɪməˈlærɪti/ *n.* semejanza *f.*
simple /ˈsɪmpəl/ *a.* sencillo, simple.
simplicity /sɪmˈplɪsɪti/ *n.* sencillez *f.*
simplify /ˈsɪmpləˌfai/ *v.* simplificar.
simulate /ˈsɪmyəˌleit/ *v.* simular.
simultaneous /ˌsaiməlˈteiniəs/ *a.* simultáneo.
sin /sɪn/ *n.* **1.** pecado *m.* —*v.* **2.** pecar.
since /sɪns/ *adv.* **1.** desde entonces. —*prep.* **2.** desde. —*conj.* **3.** desde que; puesto que.
sincere /sɪnˈsɪər/ *a.* sincero.
sincerely /sɪnˈsɪərli/ *adv.* sinceramente.
sincerity /sɪnˈsɛrɪti/ *n.* sinceridad *f.*
sinew /ˈsɪnyu/ *n.* tendón *m.*
sinful /ˈsɪnfəl/ *a.* pecador.
sing /sɪŋ/ *v.* cantar.
singe /sɪndʒ/ *v.* chamuscar.
singer /ˈsɪŋər/ *n.* cantante *m.* & *f.*
single /ˈsɪŋgəl/ *a.* solo; (room) sencillo; (unmarried) soltero. **s. room,** habitación individual.
singular /ˈsɪŋgyələr/ *a.* & *n.* singular *m.*
sinister /ˈsɪnəstər/ *a.* siniestro.
sink /sɪŋk/ *n.* **1.** fregadero *m.* —*v.* **2.** hundir; *Fig.* abatir.
sinner /ˈsɪnər/ *n.* pecador -ra.
sinuous /ˈsɪnyuəs/ *a.* sinuoso.
sinus /ˈsainəs/ *n.* seno *m.*
sip /sɪp/ *n.* **1.** sorbo *m.* —*v.* **2.** sorber.
siphon /ˈsaifən/ *n.* sifón *m.*
sir /sɜr/ *title.* señor.
siren /ˈsairən/ *n.* sirena *f.*
sirloin /ˈsɜrlɔin/ *n.* solomillo *m.*
sisal /ˈsaisəl, ˈsɪsəl/ *n.* henequén *m.*
sister /ˈsɪstər/ *n.* hermana *f.*
sister-in-law /ˈsɪstərɪnˌlɔ/ *n.* cuñada *f.*
sit /sɪt/ *v.* sentarse; posar. **be sitting,** estar sentado. **s. down,** sentarse. **s. up,** incorporarse; quedar levantado.
site /sait/ *n.* sitio, local *m.*
sitting /ˈsɪtɪŋ/ *n.* sesión *f.* *a.* sentado.
situate /ˈsɪtʃuˌeit/ *v.* situar.
situation /ˌsɪtʃuˈeiʃən/ *n.* situación *f.*
sit-up /ˈsɪt ˌʌp/ *n.* abdominal *m.*
six /sɪks/ *a.* & *pron.* seis.
sixteen /ˈsɪksˈtin/ *a.* & *pron.* dieciseis.
sixth /sɪksθ/ *a.* sexto.
sixty /ˈsɪksti/ *a.* & *pron.* sesenta.
size /saiz/ *n.* tamaño; (of shoe, etc.) número *m.*; talla *f.*
sizing /ˈsaizɪŋ/ *n.* upreso *m.*; sisa, cola de retazo *f.*
skate /skeit/ *n.* **1.** patín *m.* —*v.* **2.** patinar.
skateboard /ˈskeitˌbɔrd/ *n.* monopatín *m.*
skein /skein/ *n.* madeja *f.*
skeleton /ˈskɛlɪtn̩/ *n.* esqueleto *m.*
skeptic /ˈskɛptɪk/ *n.* escéptico -ca.
skeptical /ˈskɛptɪkəl/ *a.* escéptico.
sketch /skɛtʃ/ *n.* **1.** esbozo *m.* —*v.* **2.** esbozar.
ski /ski/ *n.* **1.** esquí *m.* —*v.* **2.** esquiar.
skid /skɪd/ *v.* **1.** resbalar. —*n.* **2.** varadera *f.*
skill /skɪl/ *n.* destreza, habilidad *f.*
skillful /ˈskɪlfəl/ *a.* diestro, hábil.
skim /skɪm/ *v.* rasar; (milk) desnatar. **s. over, s. through,** hojear.
skin /skɪn/ *n.* **1.** piel; (of fruit) corteza *f.* —*v.* **2.** desollar.
skin doctor dermatólogo -ga *m.* & *f.*
skip /skɪp/ *n.* **1.** brinco *m.* —*v.* **2.** brincar. **s. over,** pasar por alto.
skirmish /ˈskɜrmɪʃ/ *n.* escaramuza *f.*
skirt /skɜrt/ *n.* falda *f.*
skull /skʌl/ *n.* cráneo *m.*
skunk /skʌŋk/ *n.* zorrillo *m.*
sky /skai/ *n.* cielo *m.*
skylight /ˈskaiˌlait/ *n.* tragaluz *m.*
skyscraper /ˈskaiˌskreipər/ *n.* rascacielos *m.*
slab /slæb/ *n.* tabla *f.*
slack /slæk/ *a.* flojo; descuidado.
slacken /ˈslækən/ *v.* relajar.
slacks /slæks/ *n.* pantalones flojos.
slam /slæm/ *n.* **1.** portazo *m.* —*v.* **2.** cerrar de golpe. **slamming on the brakes,** frenazo *m.*
slander /ˈslændər/ *n.* **1.** calumnia *f.* —*v.* **2.** calumniar.
slang /slæŋ/ *n.* jerga *f.*
slant /slænt/ *n.* **1.** sesgo *m.* —*v.* **2.** sesgar.
slap /slæp/ *n.* **1.** bofetada, palmada *f.* —*v.* **2.** dar una bofetada.
slash /slæʃ/ *n.* **1.** cuchillada *f.* —*v.* **2.** acuchillar.
slat /slæt/ *n.* **1.** tablilla *f.* —*v.* **2.** lanzar.
slate /sleit/ *n.* **1.** pizarra *f.*; lista de candidatos. —*n.* **2.** destinar.
slaughter /ˈslɔtər/ *n.* **1.** matanza *f.* —*v.* **2.** matar.
slave /sleiv/ *n.* esclavo -va.
slavery /ˈsleivəri/ *n.* esclavitud *f.*
Slavic /ˈslɑvɪk/ *a.* eslavo.
slay /slei/ *v.* matar, asesinar.
sled /slɛd/ *n.* trineo *m.*
sleek /slik/ *a.* liso y brillante.
sleep /slip/ *n.* **1.** sueño *m.* **to get much s.,** dormir mucho. —*v.* **2.** dormir.
sleeping car /ˈslipɪŋ/ coche cama.
sleeping pill /ˈslipɪŋ/ pastilla para dormir, somnífero *m.*
sleepy /ˈslipi/ *a.* soñoliento. **to be s.,** tener sueño.
sleet /slit/ *n.* **1.** cellisca *f.* —*v.* **2.** cellisquear.
sleeve /sliv/ *n.* manga *f.*
slender /ˈslɛndər/ *a.* delgado.
slice /slais/ *n.* **1.** rebanada; (of meat) tajada *f.* —*v.* **2.** rebanar; tajar.
slide /slaid/ *v.* resbalar, deslizarse.
slide rule regla de cálculo *f.*
slight /slait/ *n.* **1.** desaire *m.* —*a.* **2.** pequeño; leve. —*v.* **3.** desairar.
slim /slɪm/ *a.* delgado.
slime /slaim/ *n.* lama *f.*
sling /slɪŋ/ *n.* **1.** honda *f.*; *Med.* cabestrillo *m.* —*v.* **2.** tirar.
slink /slɪŋk/ *v.* escabullirse.
slip /slɪp/ *n.* **1.** imprudencia; (garment) combinación *f.*; (of paper) trozo *m.*; ficha *f.* —*v.* **2.** resbalar; deslizar. **s. up,** equivocarse.
slipper /ˈslɪpər/ *n.* chinela *f.*
slippery /ˈslɪpəri/ *a.* resbaloso.
slit /slɪt/ *n.* **1.** abertura *f.* —*v.* **2.** cortar.
slogan /ˈslougən/ *n.* lema *m.*
slope /sloup/ *n.* **1.** declive *m.* —*v.* **2.** inclinarse.
sloppy /ˈslɒpi/ *a.* desaliñado, chapucero.
slot /slɒt/ *n.* ranura *f.*

slot machine tragaperras f.
slouch /slautʃ/ n. **1.** patán m. —v. **2.** estar gacho.
slovenly /ˈslʌvənli/ a. desaliñado.
slow /slou/ a. **1.** lento; (watch) atrasado. —v. **2. s. down, s. up,** retardar; ir más despacio.
slowly /ˈslouli/ adv. despacio.
slowness /ˈslounɪs/ n. lentitud f.
sluggish /ˈslʌgɪʃ/ a. perezoso, inactivo.
slum /slʌm/ n. barrio bajo m.
slumber /ˈslʌmbər/ v. dormitar.
slur /slɜr/ n. **1.** estigma m. —v. **2.** menospreciar.
slush /slʌʃ/ n. fango m.
sly /slai/ a. taimado. **on the s.** a hurtadillas.
smack /smæk/ n. **1.** manotada f. —v. **2.** manotear.
small /smɔl/ a. pequeño.
small letter minúscula f.
smallpox /ˈsmɔlˌpɒks/ n. viruela f.
smart /smɑrt/ a. **1.** listo; elegante. —v. **2.** escocer.
smash /smæʃ/ v. aplastar; hacer pedazos.
smear /smɪər/ n. **1.** mancha; difamación f. —v. **2.** manchar; difamar.
smell /smɛl/ n. **1.** olor; (sense) olfato m. —v. **2.** oler.
smelt /smɛlt/ n. **1.** eperlano m. —v. **2.** fundir.
smile /smail/ n. **1.** sonrisa f. —v. **2.** sonreír.
smite /smait/ v. afligir; apenar.
smock /smɒk/ n. camisa de mujer f.
smoke /smouk/ n. **1.** humo m. —v. **2.** fumar; (food) ahumar.
smokestack /ˈsmoukˌstæk/ n. chimenea f.
smolder /ˈsmouldər/ v. arder sin llama.
smooth /smuð/ a. **1.** liso; suave; tranquilo. —v. **2.** alisar.
smother /ˈsmʌðər/ v. sofocar.
smug /smʌg/ a. presumido.
smuggle /ˈsmʌgəl/ v. pasar de contrabando.
snack /snæk/ n. bocadillo m.
snag /snæg/ n. nudo; obstáculo m.
snail /sneil/ n. caracol m.
snake /sneik/ n. culebra, serpiente f.
snap /snæp/ n. **1.** trueno m. —v. **2.** tronar; romper.
snapshot /ˈsnæpˌʃɒt/ n. instantánea f.
snare /snɛər/ n. trampa f.
snarl /snɑrl/ n. **1.** gruñido m. —v. **2.** gruñir; (hair) enredar.
snatch /snætʃ/ v. arrebatar.
sneak /snik/ v. ir, entrar, salir (etc.) a hurtadillas.
sneaker /ˈsnikər/ n. sujeto ruín m. zapatilla de tenis.
sneer /snɪər/ n. **1.** mofa f. —v. **2.** mofarse.
sneeze /sniz/ n. **1.** estornudo m. —v. **2.** estornudar.
snicker /ˈsnɪkər/ n. risita m.
snob /snɒb/ n. esnob m.
snore /snɔr/ n. **1.** ronquido m. —v. **2.** roncar.
snow /snou/ n. **1.** nieve f. —v. **2.** nevar.
snowball /ˈsnouˌbɔl/ n. bola de nieve f.
snowdrift /ˈsnouˌdrɪft/ n. ventisquero m.
snowplow /ˈsnouˌplau/ n. quitanieves m.
snowstorm /ˈsnouˌstɔrm/ n. nevasca f.
snub /snʌb/ v. desairar.
snug /snʌg/ a. abrigado y cómodo.
so /sou/ adv. **1.** así; (also) también. **so as to,** para. **so that,** para que. **so... as,** tan... como. **so... that,** tan... que. —conj. **2.** así es que.
soak /souk/ v. empapar.
soap /soup/ n. **1.** jabón m. —v. **2.** enjabonar.
soap powder jabón en polvo m.
soar /sɔr/ v. remontarse.
sob /sɒb/ n. **1.** sollozo m. —v. **2.** sollozar.
sober /ˈsoubər/ a. sobrio; pensativo.
sociable /ˈsouʃəbəl/ a. sociable.
social /ˈsouʃəl/ a. **1.** social. —n. **2.** tertulia f.
socialism /ˈsouʃəˌlɪzəm/ n. socialismo m.
socialist /ˈsouʃəlɪst/ a. & n. socialista m. & f.
society /səˈsaiɪti/ n. sociedad; compañía f.
sociological /ˌsousiəˈlɒdʒɪkəl/ a. sociológico.
sociologist /ˌsousiˌɒlədʒɪst/ n. sociólogo -ga m. & f.
sociology /ˌsousiˈɒlədʒi/ n. sociología f.
sock /sɒk/ n. **1.** calcetín; puñetazo m. —v. **2.** dar un puñetazo a.
socket /ˈsɒkɪt/ n. cuenca f.; Elec. enchufe m.
sod /sɒd/ n. césped m.
soda /ˈsoudə/ n. soda; Chem. sosa f.
sodium /ˈsoudiəm/ n. sodio m.
sofa /ˈsoufə/ n. sofá m.
soft /sɔft/ a. blando; fino; suave.
soft drink bebida no alcohólica.
soften /ˈsɔfən/ v. ablandar; suavizar.
software /ˈsɔftˌwɛər/ n. software m., programa m.
soil /sɔil/ n. **1.** suelo m. —v. **2.** ensuciar.
sojourn /ˈsoudʒɜrn/ n. morada f., estancia f.
solace /ˈsɒlɪs/ n. **1.** solaz m. —v. **2.** solazar.
solar /ˈsoulər/ a. solar.
solar system sistema solar m.
solder /ˈsɒdər/ v. **1.** soldar. —n. **2.** soldadura f.
soldier /ˈsouldʒər/ n. soldado m. & f.
sole /soul/ n. **1.** suela; (of foot) planta f.; (fish) lenguado m. —a. **2.** único.
solemn /ˈsɒləm/ a. solemne.
solemnity /səˈlɛmnɪti/ n. solemnidad f.
solicit /səˈlɪsɪt/ v. solicitar.
solicitous /səˈlɪsɪtəs/ a. solícito.
solid /ˈsɒlɪd/ a. & n. sólido m.
solidify /səˈlɪdəˌfai/ v. solidificar.
solidity /səˈlɪdɪti/ n. solidez f.
solitary /ˈsɒlɪˌtɛri/ a. solitario.
solitude /ˈsɒlɪˌtud/ n. soledad f.
solo /ˈsoulou/ n. solo m.
soloist /ˈsoulouɪst/ n. solista m. & f.
soluble /ˈsɒlyəbəl/ a. soluble.
solution /səˈluʃən/ n. solución f.
solve /sɒlv/ v. solucionar; resolver.
solvent /ˈsɒlvənt/ a. solvente.
somber /ˈsɒmbər/ a. sombrío.
some /sʌm; unstressed səm/ a. & pron. algo (de), un poco (de); alguno; (pl.) algunos, unos.
somebody, someone /ˈsʌmbɒdi; ˈsʌmˌwʌn/ pron. alguien.
somehow /ˈsʌmˌhau/ adv. de algún modo.
someone /ˈsʌmˌwʌn/ n. alguien o alguno.
somersault /ˈsʌmərˌsɔlt/ n. salto mortal m.
something /ˈsʌmˌθɪŋ/ pron. algo, alguna cosa.
sometime /ˈsʌmˌtaim/ adv. alguna vez.
sometimes /ˈsʌmˌtaimz/ adv. a veces, algunas veces.
somewhat /ˈsʌmˌwʌt/ adv. algo, un poco.
somewhere /ˈsʌmˌwɛər/ adv. en (or a) alguna parte.
son /sʌn/ n. hijo m.
song /sɔŋ/ n. canción f.
son-in-law /ˈsʌn ɪn ˌlɔ/ n. yerno m.
soon /sun/ adv. pronto. **as s. as possible,** cuanto antes. **sooner or later,** tarde o temprano. **no sooner... than,** apenas... cuando.
soot /sʊt/ n. hollín m.
soothe /suð/ v. calmar.
soothingly /ˈsuðɪŋli/ adv. tiernamente.
sophisticated /səˈfɪstɪˌkeitɪd/ a. sofisticado.
sophomore /ˈsɒfəˌmɔr/ n. estudiante de segundo año m.
soprano /səˈprænou/ n. soprano m. & f.
sorcery /ˈsɔrsəri/ n. encantamiento m.
sordid /ˈsɔrdɪd/ a. sórdido.
sore /sɔr/ n. **1.** llaga f. —a. **2.** lastimado; Colloq. enojado. **to be s.,** doler.
sorority /səˈrɔrɪti, -ˈrɒr-/ n. hermandad de mujeres f.
sorrow /ˈsɒrou/ n. pesar, dolor m., aflicción f.
sorrowful /ˈsɒrəfəl/ a. doloroso; afligido.
sorry /ˈsɒri/ a. **to be s.,** sentir, lamentar. **to be s. for,** compadecer.
sort /sɔrt/ n. **1.** tipo m.; clase, especie f. **s. of,** algo, un poco. —v. **2.** clasificar.
soul /soul/ n. alma f.
sound /saund/ a. **1.** sano; razonable; firme. —n. **2.** sonido m. —v. **3.** sonar; parecer.
soundproof /ˈsaundˌpruf/ a. insonorizado. v. insonorizar.
soundtrack /ˈsaundˌtræk/ n. banda sonora f.
soup /sup/ n. sopa f.
sour /sauᵊr/ a. agrio; ácido; rancio.
source /sɔrs/ n. fuente; causa f.
south /sauθ/ n. sur m.
South Africa /ˈæfrɪkə/ Sudáfrica f.
South African a. & n. sudafricano.
South America /əˈmɛrɪkə/ Sud América, América del Sur.
South American a. & n. sudamericano -na.
southeast /ˌsauθˈist; Naut. ˌsau-/ n. sudeste m.
southern /ˈsʌðərn/ a. meridional.
South Pole n. Polo Sur m.
southwest /ˌsauθˈwɛst; Naut. ˌsau-/ n. sudoeste m.
souvenir /ˌsuvəˈnɪər/ n. recuerdo m.
sovereign /ˈsɒvrɪn/ n. soberano -na.
sovereignty /ˈsɒvrɪnti/ n. soberanía f.
Soviet Russia Rusia Soviética f.
sow /sau/ n. **1.** puerca f. —v. **2.** sembrar.
space /speis/ n. **1.** espacio m. —v. **2.** espaciar.
space out v. escalonar.
spaceship /ˈspeisˌʃɪp/ n. nave espacial, astronave f.
space shuttle /ˈʃʌtl/ transbordador espacial m.
spacious /ˈspeiʃəs/ a. espacioso.
spade /speid/ n. **1.** laya; (cards) espada f. —v. **2.** layar.
spaghetti /spəˈgɛti/ n. espaguetis m.pl.
Spain /spein/ n. España f.
span /spæn/ n. **1.** tramo m. —v. **2.** extenderse sobre.
Spaniard /ˈspænyərd/ n. español -ola.
Spanish /ˈspænɪʃ/ a. & n. español -ola.
spank /spæŋk/ v. pegar.
spanking /ˈspæŋkɪŋ/ n. tunda, zumba f.
spar /spɑr/ v. altercar.
spare /spɛər/ a. **1.** de repuesto. —v. **2.** perdonar; ahorrar; prestar. **have... to s.,** tener... de sobra.
spare tire neumático de recambio m.
spark /spɑrk/ n. chispa f.
sparkle /ˈspɑrkəl/ n. **1.** destello m. —v. **2.** chispear. **sparkling wine,** vino espumoso.
spark plug /ˈspɑrkˌplʌg/ n. bujía f.
sparrow /ˈspærou/ n. gorrión m.
sparse /spɑrs/ a. esparcido.
spasm /ˈspæzəm/ n. espasmo m.
spasmodic /spæzˈmɒdɪk/ a. espasmódico.
spatter /ˈspætər/ v. salpicar; manchar.
speak /spik/ v. hablar.
speaker /ˈspikər/ n. conferencista m. & f.
spear /spɪər/ n. lanza f.
spearmint /ˈspɪərˌmɪnt/ n. menta romana f.
special /ˈspɛʃəl/ a. especial. **s. delivery,** entrega inmediata, entrega urgente.
specialist /ˈspɛʃəlɪst/ n. especialista m. & f.
specialty /ˈspɛʃəlti/ n. especialidad f.
species /ˈspiʃiz, -siz/ n. especie f.
specific /spɪˈsɪfɪk/ a. específico.
specify /ˈspɛsəˌfai/ v. especificar.
specimen /ˈspɛsəmən/ n. espécimen m.; muestra f.
spectacle /ˈspɛktəkəl/ n. espectáculo m.; (pl.) lentes, anteojos m.pl.
spectacular /spɛkˈtækyələr/ a. espectacular, aparatoso.
spectator /ˈspɛkteitər/ n. espectador -ra.
spectrum /ˈspɛktrəm/ n. espectro m.
speculate /ˈspɛkyəˌleit/ v. especular.
speculation /ˌspɛkyəˈleiʃən/ n. especulación f.
speech /spitʃ/ n. habla f.; lenguaje; discurso m. **part of s.,** parte de la oración.
speechless /ˈspitʃlɪs/ a. mudo.
speed /spid/ n. **1.** velocidad; rapidez f. —v. **2. s. up,** acelerar, apresurar.
speed limit velocidad máxima f.
speedometer /spiˈdɒmɪtər/ n. velocímetro m.
speedy /ˈspidi/ a. veloz, rápido.
spell /spɛl/ n. **1.** hechizo; rato; Med. ataque m. —v. **2.** escribir; relevar.
spelling /ˈspɛlɪŋ/ n. ortografía f.
spend /spɛnd/ v. gastar; (time) pasar.
spendthrift /ˈspɛndˌθrɪft/ a. & n. pródigo; manirroto m.
sphere /sfɪər/ n. esfera f.
spice /spais/ n. **1.** especia f. —v. **2.** especiar.
spider /ˈspaidər/ n. araña f.
spider web telaraña f.
spike /spaik/ n. alcayata f.; punta f., clavo m.
spill /spɪl/ v. derramar. n. caída f., vuelco m.
spillway /ˈspɪlˌwei/ n. vertedero m.
spin /spɪn/ v. hilar; girar.
spinach /ˈspɪnɪtʃ/ n. espinaca f.
spine /spain/ n. espina dorsal f.
spinet /ˈspɪnɪt/ n. espineta m.
spinster /ˈspɪnstər/ n. solterona f.
spiral /ˈspairəl/ a. & n. espiral f.
spire /spaiᵊr/ n. caracol m., espiral f.
spirit /ˈspɪrɪt/ n. espíritu; ánimo m.
spiritual /ˈspɪrɪtʃuəl/ a. espiritual.
spiritualism /ˈspɪrɪtʃuəˌlɪzəm/ n. espiritismo m.
spirituality /ˌspɪrɪtʃuˈælɪti/ n. espiritualidad f.
spit /spɪt/ v. escupir.
spite /spait/ n. despecho m. **in s. of,** a pesar de.
splash /splæʃ/ n. **1.** salpicadura f. —v. **2.** salpicar.
splendid /ˈsplɛndɪd/ a. espléndido.
splendor /ˈsplɛndər/ n. esplendor m.
splice /splais/ v. **1.** empalmar. —n. **2.** empalme m.
splint /splɪnt/ n. tablilla f.
splinter /ˈsplɪntər/ n. **1.** astilla f. —v. **2.** astillar.
split /splɪt/ n. **1.** división f. —v. **2.** dividir, romper en dos.
splurge /splɜrdʒ/ v. **1.** fachendear. —n. **2.** fachenda f.
spoil /spɔil/ n. **1.** (pl.) botín m. —v. **2.** echar a perder; (a child) mimar.
spoke /spouk/ n. rayo (de rueda) m.
spokesman /ˈspouksmən/ n. portavoz m. & f.
spokesperson /ˈspouksˌpɜrsən/ n. portavoz m. & f.
sponge /spʌndʒ/ n. esponja f.
sponsor /ˈspɒnsər/ n. **1.** patrocinador m. —v. **2.** patrocinar; costear.
spontaneity /ˌspɒntəˈniɪti, -ˈnei-/ n. espontaneidad f.

spontaneous /spɒn'teiniəs/ *a.* espontáneo.
spool /spul/ *n.* carrete *m.*
spoon /spun/ *n.* cuchara *f.*
spoonful /'spunfʊl/ *n.* cucharada *f.*
sporadic /spə'rædɪk/ *a.* esporádico.
sport /spɔrt/ *n.* deporte *m.*
sport jacket chaqueta deportiva *f.*
sports center /spɔrts/ pabellón de deportes, polideportivo *m.*
sportsman /'spɔrtsmən/ *a.* **1.** deportivo. —*n.* **2.** deportista *m.* & *f.*
spot /spɒt/ *n.* **1.** mancha *f.*; lugar, punto *m.* —*v.* **2.** distinguir.
spouse /spaus/ *n.* esposo -sa.
spout /spaut/ *n.* **1.** chorro; (of teapot) pico *m.* —*v.* **2.** correr a chorro.
sprain /sprein/ *n.* **1.** torcedura *f.*, esguince *m.* —*v.* **2.** torcerse.
sprawl /sprɔl/ *v.* tenderse.
spray /sprei/ *n.* **1.** rociada *f.* —*v.* **2.** rociar.
spread /sprɛd/ *n.* **1.** propagación; extensión; (for bed) colcha *f.* —*v.* **2.** propagar; extender.
spreadsheet /'sprɛd,ʃit/ *n.* hoja de cálculo *f.*
spree /spri/ *n.* parranda *f.*
sprig /sprɪg/ *n.* ramita *f.*
sprightly /'spraitli/ *a.* garboso.
spring /sprɪŋ/ *n.* resorte, muelle *m.*; (season) primavera *f.*; (of water) manantial *m.*
springboard /'sprɪŋ,bɔrd/ *n.* trampolín *m.*
spring onion cebolleta *f.*
sprinkle /'sprɪŋkəl/ *v.* rociar; (rain) lloviznar.
sprint /sprɪnt/ *n.* carrera *f.*
sprout /spraut/ *n.* retoño *m.*
spry /sprai/ *a.* ágil.
spun /spʌn/ *a.* hilado.
spur /spɜr/ *n.* **1.** espuela *f.* **on the s. of the moment,** sin pensarlo. —*v.* **2.** espolear.
spurious /'spyʊriəs/ *a.* espurio.
spurn /spɜrn/ *v.* rechazar, despreciar.
spurt /spɜrt/ *n.* **1.** chorro *m.*; esfuerzo supremo. —*v.* **2.** salir en chorro.
spy /spai/ **1.** espía *m.* & *f.* —*v.* **2.** espiar.
squabble /'skwɒblɪŋ/ *n.* **1.** riña *f.* —*v.* **2.** reñir.
squad /skwɒd/ *n.* escuadra *f.*
squadron /'skwɒdrən/ *n.* escuadrón *m.*
squalid /'skwɒlɪd/ *a.* escuálido.
squall /skwɔl/ *n.* borrasca *f.*
squalor /'skwɒlər/ *n.* escualidez *f.*
squander /'skwɒndər/ *v.* malgastar.
square /skwɛər/ *a.* **1.** cuadrado. —*n.* **2.** cuadrado *m.*; plaza *f.*
square dance *n.* contradanza *f.*
squat /skwɒt/ *v.* agacharse.
squeak /skwik/ *n.* **1.** chirrido *m.* —*v.* **2.** chirriar.
squeamish /'skwimɪʃ/ *a.* escrupuloso.
squeeze /skwiz/ *n.* **1.** apretón *m.* —*v.* **2.** apretar; (fruit) exprimir.
squirrel /'skwɜrəl// *n.* ardilla *f.*
squirt /skwɜrt/ *n.* **1.** chisguete *m.* —*v.* **2.** jeringar.
stab /stæb/ *n.* **1.** puñalada *f.* —*v.* **2.** apuñalar.
stability /stə'bɪlɪti/ *n.* estabilidad *f.*
stabilize /'steibə,laiz/ *v.* estabilizar.
stable /'steibəl/ *a.* **1.** estable, equilibrado. —*n.* **2.** caballeriza *f.*
stack /stæk/ *n.* **1.** pila *f.* —*v.* **2.** apilar.
stadium /'steidiəm/ *n.* estadio *m.*
staff /stæf/ *n.* personal *m.* **editorial s.,** cuerpo de redacción. **general s.,** estado mayor.
stag /stæg/ *n.* ciervo *m.*
stage /steidʒ/ *n.* **1.** etapa; *Theat.* escena *f.* —*v.* **2.** representar.
stagflation /stæg'fleiʃən/ *n.* estagflación.
stagger /'stægər/ *v.* (teeter) tambalear; (space out) escalonar.
stagnant /'stægnənt/ *a.* estancado.
stagnate /'stægneit/ *v.* estancarse.
stain /stein/ *n.* **1.** mancha *f.* —*v.* **2.** manchar.
stainless steel /'steinlɪs/ acero inoxidable *m.*
staircase /'stɛər,keis/ **stairs** *n.* escalera *f.*
stake /steik/ *n.* estaca; (bet) apuesta *f.* **at s.,** en juego; en peligro.
stale /steil/ *a.* rancio.
stalemate /'steil,meit/ *n.* estancación *f.*; tablas *f.pl.*
stalk /stɔk/ *n.* caña *f.*; (of flower) tallo *m.* *v.* acechar.
stall /stɔl/ *n.* **1.** tenderete; (for horse) pesebre *m.* —*v.* **2.** demorar; (motor) atascar.
stallion /'stælyən/ *n. S.A.* garañón *m.*
stalwart /'stɔlwərt/ *a.* fornido.
stamina /'stæmənə/ *n.* vigor *m.*
stammer /'stæmər/ *v.* tartamudear.
stamp /stæmp/ *n.* **1.** sello *m.*, estampilla *f.* —*v.* **2.** sellar.
stamp collecting /kə'lɛktɪŋ/ filatelia *f.*
stampede /stæm'pid/ *n.* estampida *f.*
stand /stænd/ *n.* **1.** puesto *m.*; posición; (speaker's) tribuna; (furniture) mesita *f.* —*v.* **2.** estar; estar de pie; aguantar. **s. up,** pararse, levantarse.
standard /'stændərd/ *a.* **1.** normal, corriente. —*n.* **2.** norma *f.* **s. of living,** nivel de vida.
standardize /'stændər,daiz/ *v.* uniformar.
standing /'stændɪŋ/ *a.* fijo; establecido.
standpoint /'stænd,pɔint/ *n.* punto de vista *m.*
staple /'steipəl/ *n.* materia prima *f.*; grapa *f.*
stapler /'steiplər/ *n.* grapadora *f.*
star /stɑr/ *n.* estrella *f.*
starboard /'stɑrbərd/ *n.* estribor *m.*
starch /stɑrtʃ/ *n.* **1.** almidón *m.*; (in diet) fécula *f.* —*v.* **2.** almidonar.
stare /stɛər/ *v.* mirar fijamente.
stark /stɑrk/ *a.* **1.** severo. —*adv.* **2.** completamente.
start /stɑrt/ *n.* **1.** susto; principio *m.* —*v.* **2.** comenzar, empezar; salir; poner en marcha; causar.
startle /'stɑrtl/ *v.* asustar.
starvation /stɑr'veiʃən/ *n.* hambre *f.*
starve /stɑrv/ *v.* morir de hambre.
state /steit/ *n.* **1.** estado *m.* —*v.* **2.** declarar, decir.
statement /'steitmənt/ *n.* declaración *f.*
stateroom /'steit,rum/ *n.* camarote *m.*
statesman /'steitsmən/ *n.* estadista *m.*
static /'stætɪk/ *a.* **1.** estático. —*n.* **2.** estática *f.*
station /'steiʃən/ *n.* estación *f.*
stationary /'steiʃə,nɛri/ *a.* estacionario, fijo.
stationery /'steiʃə,nɛri/ *n.* papel de escribir.
statistics /stə'tɪstɪks/ *n.* estadística *f.*
statue /'stætʃu/ *n.* estatua *f.*
stature /'stætʃər/ *n.* estatura *f.*
status /'steitəs, 'stætəs/ *n.* condición, estado *m.*
statute /'stætʃut/ *n.* ley *f.*
staunch /stɔntʃ/ *a.* fiel; constante.
stay /stei/ *n.* **1.** estancia; visita *f.* —*v.* **2.** quedar, permanecer; parar, alojarse. **s. away,** ausentarse. **s. up,** velar.
steadfast /'stɛd,fæst/ *a.* inmutable.
steady /'stɛdi/ *a.* **1.** firme; permanente; regular. —*v.* **2.** sostener.
steak /steik/ *n.* biftec, bistec *m.*
steal /stil/ *v.* robar. **s. away,** escabullirse.
stealth /stɛlθ/ *n.* cautela *f.*
steam /stim/ *n.* vapor *m.*
steamboat /'stim,bout/ **steamer, steamship** *n.* vapor *m.*
steel /stil/ *n.* **1.** acero *m.* —*v.* **2. s. oneself,** fortalecerse.
steep /stip/ *a.* escarpado, empinado.
steeple /'stipəl/ *n.* campanario *m.*
steer /stɪər/ *n.* **1.** buey *m.* —*v.* **2.** guiar, manejar.
stellar /'stɛlər/ *a.* astral.
stem /stɛm/ *n.* **1.** tallo *m.* —*v.* **2.** parar. **s. from,** emanar de.
stencil /'stɛnsəl/ *n.* **1.** estarcido. —*v.* **2.** estarcir.
stenographer /stə'nɒgrəfər/ *n.* estenógrafo -fa.
stenography /stə'nɒgrəfi/ *n.* taquigrafía *f.*
step /stɛp/ *n.* **1.** paso *m.*; medida *f.*; (stairs) escalón *m.* —*v.* **2.** pisar. **s. back,** retirarse.
stepladder /'stɛp,lædər/ *n.* escalera de mano *f.*
stereophonic /,stɛriə'fɒnɪk/ *a.* estereofónico.
stereotype /'stɛriə,taip/ *n.* **1.** estereotipo *m.* —*v.* **2.** estereotipar.
sterile /'stɛrɪl/ *a.* estéril.
sterilize /'stɛrə,laiz/ *v.* esterilizar.
sterling /'stɜrlɪŋ/ *a.* esteriina, genuino.
stern /stɜrn/ *n.* **1.** popa *f.* —*a.* **2.** duro, severo.
stethoscope /'stɛθə,skoup/ *n.* estetoscopio *m.*
stevedore /'stivɪ,dɔr/ *n.* estibador *m.*
stew /stu/ *n.* **1.** guisado *m.* —*v.* **2.** estofar.
steward /'stuərd/ *n.* camarero.
stewardess /'stuərdɪs/ *n.* azafata *f.*, aeromoza *f.*
stick /stɪk/ *n.* **1.** palo, bastón *m.* —*v.* **2.** pegar; (put) poner, meter.
sticky /'stɪki/ *a.* pegajoso.
stiff /stɪf/ *a.* tieso; duro.
stiffness /'stɪfnɪs/ *n.* tiesura *f.*
stifle /'staifəl/ *v.* sofocar; *Fig.* suprimir.
stigma /'stɪgmə/ *n.* estigma *m.*
still /stɪl/ *a.* **1.** quieto; silencioso. **to keep s.,** quedarse quieto. —*adv.* **2.** todavía, aún; no obstante. —*n.* **3.** alambique *m.*
stillborn /'stɪl,bɔrn/ *n.* & *a.* nacido -da muerto -ta.
still life *n.* naturaleza muerta *f.*
stillness /'stɪlnɪs/ *n.* silencio *m.*
stilted /'stɪltɪd/ *a.* afectado, artificial.
stimulant /'stɪmyələnt/ *a.* & *n.* estimulante *m.*
stimulate /'stɪmyə,leit/ *v.* estimular.
stimulus /'stɪmyələs/ *n.* estímulo *m.*
sting /stɪŋ/ *n.* **1.** picadura *f.* —*v.* **2.** picar.
stingy /'stɪndʒi/ *a.* tacaño.
stipulate /'stɪpyə,leit/ *v.* estipular.
stir /stɜr/ *n.* **1.** conmoción *f.* —*v.* **2.** mover. **s. up,** conmover; suscitar.
stitch /stɪtʃ/ *n.* **1.** puntada *f.* —*v.* **2.** coser.
stock /stɒk/ *n.* surtido *f.*; raza *f.*; (finance) acciones. *f.pl.* **in s.,** en existencia. **to take s. in,** tener fe en.
stock exchange bolsa *f.*
stockholder /'stɒk,houldər/ *n.* accionista *m.* & *f.*
stocking /'stɒkɪŋ/ *n.* media *f.*
stockyard /'stɒk,yɑrd/ *n.* corral de ganado *m.*
stodgy /'stɒdʒi/ *a.* pesado.
stoical /'stouɪkəl/ *a.* estoico.
stole /stoul/ *n.* estola *f.*
stolid /'stɒlɪd/ *a.* impasible.
stomach /'stʌmək/ *n.* estómago *m.*
stomachache /'stʌmək,eik/ *n.* dolor de estómago *m.*
stone /stoun/ *n.* piedra *f.*
stool /stul/ *n.* banquillo *m.*
stoop /stup/ *v.* encorvarse; *Fig.* rebajarse. espaldas encorvadas *f.pl.*
stop /stɒp/ *n.* **1.** parada *f.* **to put a s. to,** poner fin a. —*v.* **2.** parar; suspender; detener; impedir. **s. doing** (etc.), dejar de hacer (etc.).
stopgap /'stɒp,gæp/ *n.* recurso provisional *m.*
stopover /'stɒp,ouvər/ *n.* parada *f.*
stopwatch /'stɒp,wɒtʃ/ *n.* cronómetro *m.*
storage /'stɔrɪdʒ/ *n.* almacenaje *m.*
store /stɔr/ *n.* **1.** tienda; provisión *f.* **department s.,** almacén *m.* —*v.* **2.** guardar; almacenar.
store window escaparate *m.*
stork /stɔrk/ *n.* cigüeña *f.*
storm /stɔrm/ *n.* tempestad, tormenta *f.*
stormy /'stɔrmi/ *a.* tempestuoso.
story /'stɔri/ *n.* cuento; relato *m.*; historia *f.* **short s.,** cuento.
stout /staut/ *a.* corpulento.
stove /stouv/ *n.* hornilla; estufa *f.*
straight /streit/ *a.* **1.** recto; derecho. —*adv.* **2.** directamente.
straighten /'streitn/ *v.* enderezar. **s. out,** poner en orden.
straightforward /,streit'fɔrwərd/ *a.* recto, sincero.
strain /strein/ *n.* **1.** tensión *f.* —*v.* **2.** colar.
strainer /'streinər/ *n.* colador *m.*
strait /streit/ *n.* estrecho *m.*
strand /strænd/ *n.* **1.** hilo *m.* —*v.* **2. be stranded,** encallarse.
strange /streindʒ/ *a.* extraño; raro.
stranger /'streindʒər/ *n.* extranjero -ra; forastero -ra; desconocido -da.
strangle /'stræŋgəl/ *v.* estrangular.
strap /stræp/ *n.* correa *f.*
stratagem /'strætədʒəm/ *n.* estratagema *f.*
strategic /strə'tidʒɪk/ *a.* estratégico.
strategy /'strætɪdʒi/ *n.* estrategia *f.*
stratosphere /'strætə,sfɪər/ *n.* estratosfera *f.*
straw /strɔ/ *n.* paja *f.*
strawberry /'strɔ,bɛri/ *n.* fresa *f.*
stray /strei/ *a.* **1.** vagabundo. —*v.* **2.** extraviarse.
streak /strik/ *n.* **1.** racha; raya *f.*; lado *m.* —*v.* **2.** rayar.
stream /strim/ *n.* corriente *f.*; arroyo *m.*
street /strit/ *n.* calle *f.*
streetcar /'strit,kɑr/ *n.* tranvía *m.*
street lamp /'strit,læmp/ *n.* farol *m.*
strength /strɛŋkθ, strɛnθ/ *n.* fuerza *m.*
strengthen /'strɛŋkθən, 'strɛn-/ *v.* reforzar.
strenuous /'strɛnyuəs/ *a.* estrenuo.
streptococcus /,strɛptə'kɒkəs/ *n.* estreptococo *m.*
stress /strɛs/ *n.* **1.** tensión *f.*; énfasis *m.* —*v.* **2.** recalcar; acentuar.
stretch /strɛtʃ/ *n.* **1.** trecho *m.* **at one s.,** de un tirón. —*v.* **2.** tender; extender; estirarse.
stretcher /'strɛtʃər/ *n.* camilla *f.*
strew /stru/ *v.* esparcir.
stricken /'strɪkən/ *a.* agobiado.
strict /strɪkt/ *a.* estricto; severo.
stride /straid/ *n.* **1.** tranco *m.*; (fig., pl.) progresos. —*v.* **2.** andar a trancos.
strife /straif/ *n.* contienda *f.*
strike /straik/ *n.* **1.** huelga *f.* —*v.* **2.** pegar; chocar con; (clock) dar.
striker /'straikər/ *n.* huelguista *m.* & *f.*
string /strɪŋ/ *n.* cuerda *f.*; cordel *m.*
string bean *n.* habichuela *f.*
stringent /'strɪndʒənt/ *a.* estricto.
strip /strɪp/ *n.* **1.** tira *f.* —*v.* **2.** despojar; desnudarse.
stripe /straip/ *n.* raya *f.*; *Mil.* galón *m.*
strive /straiv/ *v.* esforzarse.
stroke /strouk/ *n.* golpe *m.*; (swimming) brazada *f.*; *Med.* ataque *m.* **s. of luck,** suerte *f.*
stroll /stroul/ *n.* **1.** paseo *m.* —*v.* **2.** pasearse.
stroller /'stroulər/ *n.* vagabundo *m.*; cochecito (de niño).
strong /strɔŋ/ *a.* fuerte.
stronghold /'strɔŋ,hould/ *n.* fortificación *f.*
structure /'strʌktʃər/ *n.* estructura *f.*
struggle /'strʌgəl/ *n.* **1.** lucha *f.* —*v.* **2.** luchar.
strut /strʌt/ *n.* **1.** pavonada *f.* —*v.* **2.** pavonear.
stub /stʌb/ *n.* **1.** cabo; (ticket) talón

m. —*v.* 2. **s. on one's toes,** tropezar con.

stubborn /'stʌbərn/ *a.* testarudo.

stucco /'stʌkou/ *n.* 1. estuco *m.* —*v.* 2. estucar.

student /'studnt/ *n.* alumno -na, estudiante -ta.

studio /'studi,ou/ *n.* estudio *m.*

studious /'studiəs/ *a.* aplicado; estudioso.

study /'stʌdi/ *n.* 1. estudio *m.* —*v.* 2. estudiar.

stuff /stʌf/ *n.* 1. cosas *f.pl.* —*v.* 2. llenar; rellenar.

stuffing /'stʌfɪŋ/ *n.* relleno *m.*

stumble /'stʌmbəl/ *v.* tropezar.

stump /stʌmp/ *n.* cabo; tocón; muñón *m.*

stun /stʌn/ *v.* aturdir.

stunt /stʌnt/ *n.* 1. maniobra sensacional *f.* —*v.* 2. impedir crecimiento.

stupendous /stu'pɛndəs/ *a.* estupendo.

stupid /'stupɪd/ *a.* estúpido.

stupidity /stu'pɪdɪti/ *n.* estupidez *f.*

stupor /'stupər/ *n.* estupor *m.*

sturdy /'stɜrdi/ *a.* robusto.

stutter /'stʌtər/ *v.* 1. tartamudear. —*n.* 2. tartamudeo *m.*

sty /stai/ *n.* pocilga *f.*; *Med.* orzuelo.

style /stail/ *n.* estilo *m.*; moda *f.*

stylish /'stailɪʃ/ *a.* elegante; a la moda.

suave /swɑv/ *a.* afable, suave.

subconscious /sʌb'kɒnʃəs/ *a.* subconsciente.

subdue /səb'du/ *v.* dominar.

subject /*n.* 'sʌbdʒɪkt; *v.* səb'dʒɛkt/ *n.* 1. tema *m.*; (of study) materia *f.*; *Pol.* súbdito -ta; *Gram.* sujeto *m.* —*v.* 2. someter.

subjugate /'sʌbdʒə,geit/ *v.* sojuzgar, subyugar.

subjunctive /səb'dʒʌŋktɪv/ *a.* & *n.* subjuntivo *m.*

sublimate /'sʌblə,meit/ *v.* sublimar.

sublime /sə'blaim/ *a.* sublime.

submarine /,sʌbmə'rin/ *a.* & *n.* submarino *m.*

submerge /səb'mɜrdʒ/ *v.* sumergir.

submission /səb'mɪʃən/ *n.* sumisión *f.*

submit /səb'mɪt/ *v.* someter.

subnormal /sʌb'nɔrməl/ *a.* subnormal.

subordinate /*a, n* sə'bɔrdnɪt; *v* -dn,eit/ *a.* & *n.* 1. subordinado -da. —*v.* 2. subordinar.

subscribe /səb'skraib/ *v.* aprobar; abonarse.

subscriber /səb'skraibər/ *n.* abonado -da *m.* & *f.*

subscription /səb'skrɪpʃən/ *n.* abono *m.*

subsequent /'sʌbsɪkwənt/ *a.* subsiguiente.

subservient /səb'sɜrviənt/ *a.* servicial.

subside /səb'said/ *v.* apaciguarse, menguar.

subsidy /'sʌbsɪdi/ *n.* subvención *f.*

subsoil /'sʌb,sɔil/ *n.* subsuelo *m.*

substance /'sʌbstəns/ *n.* substancia *f.*

substantial /səb'stænʃəl/ *a.* substancial; considerable.

substitute /'sʌbstɪ,tut/ *a.* 1. substitutivo. —*n.* 2. substituto -ta. —*v.* 3. substituir.

substitution /,sʌbstɪ'tuʃən/ *n.* substitución *f.*

subterfuge /'sʌbtər,fyudʒ/ *n.* subterfugio *m.*

subtitle /'sʌb,taitl/ *n.* subtítulo *m.*

subtle /'sʌtl/ *a.* sutil.

subtract /səb'trækt/ *v.* substraer.

suburb /'sʌbɜrb/ *n.* suburbio *m.*; (pl.) afueras *f.pl.*

subversive /səb'vɜrsɪv/ *a.* subversivo.

subway /'sʌb,wei/ *n.* metro *m.*

succeed /sək'sid/ *v.* lograr, tener éxito; (in office) suceder a.

success /sək'sɛs/ *n.* éxito *m.*

successful /sək'sɛsfəl/ *a.* próspero; afortunado.

succession /sək'sɛʃən/ *n.* sucesión *f.*

successive /sək'sɛsɪv/ *a.* sucesivo.

successor /sək'sɛsər/ *n.* sucesor -ra; heredero -ra.

succor /'sʌkər/ *n.* 1. socorro *m.* —*v.* 2. socorrer.

succumb /sə'kʌm/ *v.* sucumbir.

such /sʌtʃ/ *a.* tal.

suck /sʌk/ *v.* chupar.

suction /'sʌkʃən/ *n.* succión *f.*

sudden /'sʌdn/ *a.* repentino, súbito. **all of a s.,** de repente.

suds /sʌdz/ *n.* jabonaduras *f.pl.*

sue /su/ *v.* demandar.

suffer /'sʌfər/ *v.* sufrir; padecer.

suffice /sə'fais/ *v.* bastar.

sufficient /sə'fɪʃənt/ *a.* suficiente.

suffocate /'sʌfə,keit/ *v.* sofocar.

sugar /'ʃʊgər/ *n.* azúcar *m.*

sugar bowl azucarero *m.*

suggest /səg'dʒɛst/ *v.* sugerir.

suggestion /səg'dʒɛstʃən/ *n.* sugerencia *f.*

suicide /'suə,said/ *n.* suicidio *m.*; (person) suicida *m.* & *f.* **to commit s.,** suicidarse.

suit /sut/ *n.* 1. traje; (cards) palo; (law) pleito *m.* —*v.* 2. convenir a.

suitable /'sutəbəl/ *a.* apropiado; que conviene.

suitcase /'sut,keis/ *n.* maleta *f.*

suite /swit/ *n.* serie *f.*, séquito *m.*

suitor /'sutər/ *n.* pretendiente *m.*

sullen /'sʌlən/ *a.* hosco.

sum /sʌm/ *n.* 1. suma *f.* —*v.* 2. **s. up,** resumir.

summarize /'sʌmə,raiz/ *v.* resumir.

summary /'sʌməri/ *n.* resumen *m.*

summer /'sʌmər/ *n.* verano *m.*

summon /'sʌmən/ *v.* llamar; (law) citar.

summons /'sʌmənz/ *n.* citación *f.*

sumptuous /'sʌmptʃuəs/ *a.* suntuoso.

sun /sʌn/ *n.* 1. sol *m.* —*v.* 2. tomar el sol.

sunbathe /'sʌn,beið/ *v.* tomar el sol.

sunburn /'sʌn,bɜrn/ *n.* quemadura de sol.

sunburned /'sʌn,bɜrnd/ *a.* quemado por el sol.

Sunday /'sʌndei/ *n.* domingo *m.*

sunken /'sʌŋkən/ *a.* hundido.

sunny /'sʌni/ *a.* asoleado. **s. day,** día de sol. **to be s.,** (weather) hacer sol.

sunshine /'sʌn,ʃain/ *n.* luz del sol.

suntan /'sʌn,tæn/ *n.* bronceado *m.* **s. lotion,** loción bronceadora *f.*, bronceador *m.*

superb /sʊ'pɜrb/ *a.* soberbio.

superficial /,supər'fɪʃəl/ *a.* superficial.

superfluous /sʊ'pɜrfluəs/ *a.* superfluo.

superhuman /,supər'hyumən/ *a.* sobrehumano.

superintendent /,supərɪn'tɛndənt/ *n.* superintendente *m.* & *f.*; (of building) conserje *m.*; (of school) director -ra general.

superior /sə'pɪəriər/ *a.* & *n.* superior *m.*

superiority /sə,pɪəri'ɔrɪti/ *n.* superioridad *f.*

superlative /sə'pɜrlətɪv/ *a.* superlativo.

supernatural /,supər'nætʃərəl/ *a.* sobrenatural.

supersede /,supər'sid/ *v.* reemplazar.

superstar /'supər,stɑr/ *n.* superestrella *m.* & *f.*

superstition /,supər'stɪʃən/ *n.* superstición *f.*

superstitious /,supər'stɪʃəs/ *a.* supersticioso.

supervise /'supər,vaiz/ *v.* supervisar.

supper /'sʌpər/ *n.* cena *f.*

supplement /'sʌpləmənt/ *n.* 1. suplemento *m.* —*v.* 2. suplementar.

supply /sə'plai/ *n.* 1. provisión *f.*; *Com.* surtido *m.*; *Econ.* existencia *f.* —*v.* 2. suplir; proporcionar.

support /sə'pɔrt/ *n.* 1. sustento; apoyo *m.* —*v.* 2. mantener; apoyar.

suppose /sə'pouz/ *v.* suponer. **be supposed to,** deber.

suppository /sə'pɒzɪ,tɔri/ *n.* supositorio *m.*

suppress /sə'prɛs/ *v.* suprimir.

suppression /sə'prɛʃən/ *n.* supresión *f.*

supreme /sə'prim/ *a.* supremo.

sure /ʃʊr, ʃɜr/ *a.* seguro, cierto. **for s.,** con seguridad. **to make s.,** asegurarse.

surety /'ʃʊrɪti, 'ʃɜr-/ *n.* garantía *f.*

surf /sɜrf/ *n.* 1. oleaje *m.* —*v.* 2. (Internet) navegar; (sport) surfear.

surface /'sɜrfɪs/ *n.* superficie *f.*

surfboard /'sɜrf,bɔrd/ *n.* tabla de surf *f.*

surfer /'sɜrfər/ *n.* (Internet) usuario -ria, navegante *m.* & *f.*; (sport) surfero -ra.

surge /sɜrdʒ/ *v.* surgir.

surgeon /'sɜrdʒən/ *n.* cirujano -na.

surgery /'sɜrdʒəri/ *n.* cirugía *f.*

surmise /sər'maiz/ *v.* suponer.

surmount /sər'maunt/ *v.* vencer.

surname /'sɜr,neim/ *n.* apellido *m.*

surpass /sər'pæs/ *v.* superar.

surplus /'sɜrplʌs/ *a.* & *n.* sobrante *m.*

surprise /sər'praiz, sə-/ *n.* 1. sorpresa —*v.* 2. sorprender. **I am surprised...,** me extraña...

surrender /sə'rɛndər/ *n.* 1. rendición *f.* —*v.* 2. rendir.

surround /sə'raund/ *v.* rodear, circundar.

surveillance /sər'veiləns/ *n.* vigilancia *f.*

survey /*n.* 'sɜrvei; *v.* sər'vei/ *n.* 1. examen; estudio *m.* —*v.* 2. examinar; (land) medir.

survival /sər'vaivəl/ *n.* supervivencia *f.*

survive /sər'vaiv/ *v.* sobrevivir.

susceptible /sə'sɛptəbəl/ *a.* susceptible.

suspect /*v.* sə'spɛkt; *n.* 'sʌspɛkt/ *v.* 1. sospechar. —*n.* 2. sospechoso -sa.

suspend /sə'spɛnd/ *v.* suspender.

suspense /sə'spɛns/ *n.* incertidumbre *f.* **in s.,** en suspenso.

suspension /sə'spɛnʃən/ *n.* suspensión *f.*

suspension bridge *n.* puente colgante *m.*

suspicion /sə'spɪʃən/ *n.* sospecha *f.*

suspicious /sə'spɪʃəs/ *a.* sospechoso.

sustain /sə'stein/ *v.* sustentar; mantener.

swallow /'swɒlou/ *n.* 1. trago *m.*; (bird) golondrina *f.* —*v.* 2. tragar.

swamp /swɒmp/ *n.* 1. pantano *m.* —*v.* 2. *Fig.* abrumar.

swan /swɒn/ *n.* cisne *m.*

swap /swɒp/ *n.* 1. trueque *m.* —*v.* 2. cambalachear.

swarm /swɔrm/ *n.* enjambre *m.*

swarthy /'swɔrði/ *a.* moreno.

sway /swei/ *n.* 1. predominio *m.* —*v.* 2. bambolearse; *Fig.* influir en.

swear /swɛər/ *v.* jurar. **s. off,** renunciar a.

sweat /swɛt/ *n.* 1. sudor *m.* —*v.* 2. sudar.

sweater /'swɛtər/ *n.* suéter *m.*

sweatshirt /'swɛt,ʃɜrt/ *n.* sudadera *f.*

Swede /swid/ *n.* sueco -ca.

Sweden /'swidn/ *n.* Suecia *f.*

Swedish /'swidɪʃ/ *a.* sueco.

sweep /swip/ *v.* barrer.

sweet /swit/ *a.* 1. dulce; amable, simpático. —*n.* 2. (pl.) dulces *m.pl.*

sweetheart /'swit,hɑrt/ *n.* novio -via.

sweetness /'switnɪs/ *n.* dulzura *f.*

sweet-toothed /'swit ,tuθt/ *a.* goloso.

swell /swɛl/ *a.* 1. *Colloq.* estupendo, excelente. —*n.* 2. (of the sea) oleada *f.* —*v.* 3. hincharse; aumentar.

swelter /'swɛltər/ *v.* sofocarse de calor.

swift /swɪft/ *a.* rápido, veloz.

swim /swɪm/ *n.* 1. nadada *f.* —*v.* 2. nadar.

swimming /'swɪmɪŋ/ *n.* natación *f.*

swimming pool alberca, piscina *f.*

swindle /'swɪndl/ *n.* 1. estafa *f.* —*v.* 2. estafar.

swine /swain/ *n.* puercos *m.pl.*

swing /swɪŋ/ *n.* 1. columpio *m.* **in full s.,** en plena actividad. —*v.* 2. mecer; balancear.

swirl /swɜrl/ *n.* 1. remolino *m.* —*v.* 2. arremolinar.

Swiss /swɪs/ *a.* & *n.* suizo -za.

switch /swɪtʃ/ *n.* 1. varilla *f.*; *Elec.* llave *f.*, conmutador *m.*; (railway) cambiavía *m.* —*v.* 2. cambiar; trocar.

switchboard /'swɪtʃ,bɔrd/ *n.* cuadro conmutador *m.*, centralita *f.*

Switzerland /'swɪtsərlənd/ *n.* Suiza *f.*

sword /sɔrd/ *n.* espada *f.*

syllable /'sɪləbəl/ *n.* sílaba *f.*

symbol /'sɪmbəl/ *n.* símbolo *m.*

sympathetic /,sɪmpə'θɛtɪk/ *a.* compasivo. **to be s.,** tener simpatía.

sympathy /'sɪmpəθi/ *n.* lástima; condolencia *f.*

symphony /'sɪmfəni/ *n.* sinfonía *f.*

symptom /'sɪmptəm/ *n.* síntoma *m.*

synagogue /'sɪnə,gɒg/ *n.* sinagoga *f.*

synchronize /'sɪŋkrə,naiz/ *v.* sincronizar.

syndicate /'sɪndɪkɪt/ *n.* sindicato *m.*

syndrome /'sɪndroum, -drəm/ *n.* síndrome *m.*

synonym /'sɪnənɪm/ *n.* sinónimo *m.*

synthetic /sɪn'θɛtɪk/ *a.* sintético.

syringe /sə'rɪndʒ/ *n.* jeringa *f.*

syrup /'sɪrəp, 'sɜr-/ *n.* almíbar; *Med.* jarabe *m.*

system /'sɪstəm/ *n.* sistema *m.*

systematic /,sɪstə'mætɪk/ *a.* sistemático.

T

tabernacle /'tæbər,nækəl/ *n.* tabernáculo *m.*

table /'teibəl/ *n.* mesa; (list) tabla *f.*

tablecloth /'teibəl,klɔθ/ *n.* mantel *m.*

table of contents /'kɒntɛnts/ índice de materias *m.*

tablespoon /'teibəl,spun/ *n.* cuchara *f.*

tablespoonful /'teibəlspun,fʊl/ *n.* cucharada *f.*

tablet /'tæblɪt/ *n.* tableta; *Med.* pastilla *f.*

tack /tæk/ *n.* tachuela *f.*

tact /tækt/ *n.* tacto *m.*

tag /tæg/ *n.* etiqueta *f.*, rótulo *m.*

tail /teil/ *n.* cola *f.*, rabo *m.*

tailor /'teilər/ *n.* sastre *m.*

take /teik/ *v.* tomar; llevar. **t. a bath,** bañarse. **t. a shower,** ducharse. **t. away,** quitar. **t. off,** quitarse. **t. out,** sacar. **t. long,** tardar mucho.

tale /teil/ *n.* cuento *m.*

talent /'tælənt/ *n.* talento *m.*

talk /tɔk/ *n.* 1. plática, habla *f.*; discurso *m.* —*v.* 2. hablar.

talkative /'tɔkətɪv/ *a.* locuaz.

tall /tɔl/ *a.* alto.

tame /teim/ *a.* 1. manso, domesticado. —*v.* 2. domesticar.

tamper /'tæmpər/ *v.* **t. with,** entremeterse en.

tampon /'tæmpɒn/ *n.* tampón *m.*

tan /tæn/ *a.* 1. color de arena. —*v.* 2. curtir; tostar. *n.* bronceado.

tangerine /,tændʒə'rin/ *n.* clementina *f.*

tangible /'tændʒəbəl/ *a.* tangible.

tangle /'tæŋgəl/ *n.* 1. enredo *m.* —*v.* 2. enredar.

tank /tæŋk/ *n.* tanque *m.*

tap /tæp/ *n.* 1. golpe ligero. —*v.* 2. golpear ligeramente; decentar.

tape /teip/ *n.* cinta *f.*

tape recorder /rɪ'kɔrdər/ magnetófono *m.*, grabadora *f.*
tapestry /'tæpəstri/ *n.* tapiz *m.;* tapicería *f.*
tar /tɑr/ *n.* **1.** brea *f.* —*v.* **2.** embrear.
target /'tɑrgɪt/ *n.* blanco *m.*
tarnish /'tɑrnɪʃ/ *n.* **1.** deslustre *m.* —*v.* **2.** deslustrar.
tarpaulin /tɑr'pɔlɪn, 'tɑrpəlɪn/ *n.* lona *f.*
task /tæsk/ *n.* tarea *f.*
taste /teist/ *n.* **1.** gusto; sabor *m.* —*v.* **2.** gustar; probar. **t. of,** saber a.
tasty /'teisti/ *a.* sabroso.
tattoo /tæ'tu/ *v.* tatuar.
taut /tɔt/ *a.* tieso.
tavern /'tævərn/ *n.* taberna *f.*
tax /tæks/ *n.* **1.** impuesto *m.* —*v.* **2.** imponer impuestos.
tax collector *n.* recaudador -ra *m.* & *f.*
taxi /'tæksi/ *n.* taxi, taxímetro *m.* **t. driver,** taxista *m.* & *f.*
taxpayer /'tæks,peiər/ *n.* contribuyente *m.* & *f.*
tax reform reforma tributaria *f.*
tax return declaración de la renta *f.*
tea /ti/ *n.* té *m.*
teach /titʃ/ *v.* enseñar.
teacher /'titʃər/ *n.* maestro -tra, profesor -ra.
team /tim/ *n.* equipo *m.;* pareja *f.*
tear /tɪər/ *n.* **1.** rasgón *m.;* lágrima *f.* —*v.* **2.** rasgar, lacerar. **t. apart,** separar.
tease /tiz/ *v.* atormentar; embromar.
teaspoon /'ti,spun/ *n.* cucharita *f.*
technical /'tɛknɪkəl/ *a.* técnico.
technician /tɛk'nɪʃən/ *n.* técnico -ca *m.* & *f.*
technique /tɛk'nik/ *n.* técnica *f.*
technology /tɛk'nɒlədʒi/ *n.* tecnología *f.*
teddy bear /'tɛdi/ oso de felpa *m.*
tedious /'tidiəs/ *a.* tedioso.
telegram /'tɛlɪ,græm/ *n.* telegrama *m.*
telegraph /'tɛlɪ,græf/ *n.* **1.** telégrafo *m.* —*v.* **2.** telegrafiar.
telephone /'tɛlə,foun/ *n.* **1.** teléfono *m.* **t. book,** directorio telefónico. —*v.* **2.** telefonear; llamar por teléfono.
telescope /'tɛlə,skoup/ *n.* **1.** telescopio *m.* —*v.* **2.** enchufar.
television /'tɛlə,vɪʒən/ *n.* televisión *f.*
tell /tɛl/ *v.* decir; contar; distinguir.
temper /'tɛmpər/ *n.* **1.** temperamento, genio *m.* —*v.* **2.** templar.
temperament /'tɛmpərəmənt, -prəmənt/ *n.* temperamento.
temperamental /,tɛmpərə'mɛntl̩, -prə'mɛn-/ *a.* sensitivo, emocional.
temperance /'tɛmpərəns/ *n.* moderación; sobriedad *f.*
temperate /'tɛmpərɪt/ *a.* templado.
temperature /'tɛmpərətʃər/ *n.* temperatura *f.*
tempest /'tɛmpɪst/ *n.* tempestad *f.*
tempestuous /tɛm'pɛstʃuəs/ *a.* tempestuoso.
temple /'tɛmpəl/ *n.* templo *m.*
temporary /'tɛmpə,rɛri/ *a.* temporal, temporario.
tempt /tɛmpt/ *v.* tentar.
temptation /tɛmp'teiʃən/ *n.* tentación *f.*
ten /tɛn/ *a.* & *pron.* diez.
tenant /'tɛnənt/ *n.* inquilino -na.
tend /tɛnd/ *v.* tender. **t. to,** atender.
tendency /'tɛndənsi/ *n.* tendencia *f.*
tender /'tɛndər/ *a.* **1.** tierno. —*v.* **2.** ofrecer.
tenderness /'tɛndərnɪs/ *n.* ternura *f.*
tennis /'tɛnɪs/ *n.* tenis *m.*
tennis court cancha de tenis, pista de tenis *f.*
tenor /'tɛnər/ *n.* tenor *m.*
tense /tɛns/ *a.* **1.** tenso. —*n.* **2.** *Gram.* tiempo *m.*
tent /tɛnt/ *n.* tienda, carpa *f.*
tenth /tɛnθ/ *a.* décimo.
term /tɜrm/ *n.* **1.** término; plazo *m.* —*v.* **2.** llamar.
terminal /'tɜrmənl̩/ *n.* terminal *f.*
terrace /'tɛrəs/ *n.* terraza *f.*
terrible /'tɛrəbəl/ *a.* terrible, espantoso; pésimo.
territory /'tɛrɪ,tɔri/ *n.* territorio *m.*
terror /'tɛrər/ *n.* terror, espanto, pavor *m.*
test /tɛst/ *n.* **1.** prueba *f.;* examen *m.* —*v.* **2.** probar; examinar.
testament /'tɛstəmənt/ *n.* testamento *m.*
testify /'tɛstə,fai/ *v.* atestiguar, testificar.
testimony /'tɛstə,mouni/ *n.* testimonio *m.*
test tube tubo de ensayo *m.*
text /tɛkst/ *n.* texto; tema *m.*
textbook /'tɛkst,bʊk/ *n.* libro de texto.
textile /'tɛkstail/ *a.* **1.** textil. —*n.* **2.** tejido *m.*
texture /'tɛkstʃər/ *n.* textura *f.;* tejido *m.*
than /ðæn, ðɛn; *unstressed* ðən, ən/ *conj.* que; de.
thank /θæŋk/ *v.* agradecer, dar gracias; **thanks, th. you,** gracias.
thankful /'θæŋkfəl/ *a.* agradecido; grato.
that /ðæt; *unstressed* ðət/ *a.* **1.** ese, aquel. —*dem. pron.* **2.** ése, aquél; eso, aquello. —*rel. pron.* & *conj.* **3.** que.
the /*stressed* ði; *unstressed before a consonant* ðə, *unstressed before a vowel* ði/ *art.* el, la, los, las; lo.
theater /'θiətər/ *n.* teatro *m.*
theft /θɛft/ *n.* robo *m.*
their /ðɛər; *unstressed* ðər/ *a.* su.
theirs /ðɛərz/ *pron.* suyo, de ellos.
them /ðɛm; *unstressed* ðəm, əm/ *pron.* ellos, ellas; los, las; les.
theme /θim/ *n.* tema; *Mus.* motivo *m.*
themselves /ðəm'sɛlvz, ,ðɛm-/ *pron.* sí, sí mismos -as. **they th.,** ellos mismos, ellas mismas. **with th.,** consigo.
then /ðɛn/ *adv.* entonces, después; pues.
thence /ðɛns/ *adv.* de allí.
theology /θi'ɒlədʒi/ *n.* teología *f.*
theory /'θiəri/ *n.* teoría *f.*
there /ðɛər; *unstressed* ðər/ *adv.* allí, allá, ahí. **there is, there are,** hay.
therefore /'ðɛər,fɔr/ *adv.* por lo tanto, por consiguiente.
thermometer /θər'mɒmɪtər/ *n.* termómetro *m.*
thermostat /'θɜrmə,stæt/ *n.* termostato *m.*
they /ðei/ *pron.* ellos, ellas.
thick /θɪk/ *a.* espeso, grueso, denso; torpe.
thicken /'θɪkən/ *v.* espesar, condensar.
thief /θif/ *n.* ladrón -na.
thigh /θai/ *n.* muslo *m.*
thimble /'θɪmbəl/ *n.* dedal *m.*
thin /θɪn/ *a.* **1.** delgado; raro; claro; escaso. —*v.* **2.** enrarecer; adelgazar.
thing /θɪŋ/ *n.* cosa *f.*
thingamabob /'θɪŋəmə,bɒb/ *n. Colloq.* chisme *m.*
think /θɪŋk/ *v.* pensar; creer.
thinker /'θɪŋkər/ *n.* pensador -ra.
third /θɜrd/ *a.* tercero.
Third World Tercer Mundo *m.*
thirst /θɜrst/ *n.* sed *f.*
thirsty /'θɜrsti/ *a.* sediento. **to be th.,** tener sed.
thirteen /'θɜr'tin/ *a.* & *pron.* trece.
thirty /'θɜrti/ *a.* & *pron.* treinta.
this /ðɪs/ *a.* **1.** este. —*pron.* **2.** éste; esto.
thoracic cage /θɔ'ræsɪk/ *n.* caja torácica *f.*
thorn /θɔrn/ *n.* espina *f.*
thorough /'θɜrou/ *a.* completo; cuidadoso.
though /ðou/ *adv.* **1.** sin embargo. —*conj.* **2.** aunque. **as th.,** como si.
thought /θɔt/ *n.* pensamiento *m.*
thoughtful /'θɔtfəl/ *a.* pensativo; considerado.
thousand /'θauzənd/ *a.* & *pron.* mil.
thread /θrɛd/ *n.* hilo *m.;* (of screw) rosca *f.*
threat /θrɛt/ *n.* amenaza *f.*
threaten /'θrɛtn̩/ *v.* amenazar.
three /θri/ *a.* & *pron.* tres.
thrift /θrɪft/ *n.* economía, frugalidad *f.*
thrill /θrɪl/ *n.* **1.** emoción *f.* —*v.* **2.** emocionar.
thrive /θraiv/ *v.* prosperar.
throat /θrout/ *n.* garganta *f.*
throne /θroun/ *n.* trono *m.*
through /θru/ *prep.* **1.** por; a través de; por medio de. —*a.* **2.** continuo. **th. train,** tren directo. **to be th.,** haber terminado.
throughout /θru'aut/ *prep.* **1.** por todo, durante todo. —*adv.* **2.** en todas partes; completamente.
throw /θrou/ *n.* **1.** tiro *m.* —*v.* **2.** tirar, lanzar. **th. away,** arrojar. **th. out,** echar.
thrust /θrʌst/ *n.* **1.** lanzada *f.* —*v.* **2.** empujar.
thumb /θʌm/ *n.* dedo pulgar, pulgar *m.*
thumbtack /'θʌm,tæk/ *n.* chincheta *f.*
thunder /'θʌndər/ *n.* **1.** trueno *m.* —*v.* **2.** tronar.
Thursday /'θɜrzdei/ *n.* jueves *m.*
thus /ðʌs/ *adv.* así, de este modo.
thwart /θwɔrt/ *v.* frustrar.
ticket /'tɪkɪt/ *n.* billete, boleto *m.* **t. window,** taquilla *f.* **round trip t.,** billete de ida y vuelta.
tickle /'tɪkəl/ *n.* **1.** cosquilla *f.* —*v.* **2.** hacer cosquillas a.
ticklish /'tɪklɪʃ/ *a.* cosquilloso.
tide /taid/ *n.* marea *f.*
tidy /'taidi/ *a.* **1.** limpio, ordenado. —*v.* **2.** poner en orden.
tie /tai/ *n.* **1.** corbata *f.;* lazo; (game) empate *m.* —*v.* **2.** atar; anudar.
tier /'tɪər/ *n.* hilera *f.*
tiger /'taigər/ *n.* tigre *m.*
tight /tait/ *a.* apretado; tacaño.
tighten /'taitn̩/ *v.* estrechar, apretar.
tile /tail/ *n.* teja *f.;* azulejo *m.*
till /tɪl/ *prep.* **1.** hasta. —*conj.* **2.** hasta que. —*n.* **3.** cajón *m.* —*v.* **4.** cultivar, labrar.
tilt /tɪlt/ *n.* **1.** inclinación; justa *f.* —*v.* **2.** inclinar; justar.
timber /'tɪmbər/ *n.* madera *f.;* (beam) madero *m.*
time /taim/ *n.* tiempo *m.;* vez *f.;* (of day) hora *f.;* *v. cronometrar.*
timetable /'taim,teibəl/ *n.* horario, itinerario *m.*
time zone huso horario *m.*
timid /'tɪmɪd/ *a.* tímido.
timidity /tɪ'mɪdɪti/ *n.* timidez *f.*
tin /tɪn/ *n.* estaño *m.;* hojalata *f.* **t. can,** lata *f.*
tin foil papel de estaño *m.*
tint /tɪnt/ *n.* **1.** tinte *m.* —*v.* **2.** teñir.
tiny /'taini/ *a.* chiquito, pequeñito.
tip /tɪp/ *n.* **1.** punta; propina *f.* —*v.* **2.** inclinar; dar propina a.
tire /taiᵊr/ *n.* **1.** llanta, goma *f.,* neumático *m.* —*v.* **2.** cansar.
tired /taiᵊrd/ *a.* cansado.
tissue /'tɪʃu/ *n.* tejido *m.* **t. paper,** papel de seda.
title /'taitl̩/ *n.* **1.** título *m.* —*v.* **2.** titular.
to /tu; *unstressed* tʊ, tə/ *prep.* a; para.
toast /toust/ *n.* **1.** tostada *f.;* (drink) brindis *m.* —*v.* **2.** tostar; brindar.
toaster /'toustər/ *n.* tostador *m.*
tobacco /tə'bækou/ *n.* tabaco *m.* **t. shop,** tabaquería *f.*
toboggan /tə'bɒgən/ *n.* tobogán *m.*
today /tə'dei/ *adv.* hoy.
toe /tou/ *n.* dedo del pie.
together /tə'gɛðər/ *a.* **1.** juntos. —*adv.* **2.** juntamente.
toil /tɔil/ *n.* **1.** trabajo *m.* —*v.* **2.** afanarse.
toilet /'tɔilɪt/ *n.* tocado; excusado, retrete *m.* **t. paper,** papel higiénico.
token /'toukən/ *n.* señal *f.*
tolerance /'tɒlərəns/ *n.* tolerancia *f.*
tolerate /'tɒlə,reit/ *v.* tolerar.
toll-free number /'toul 'fri/ teléfono gratuito *m.*
tomato /tə'meitou/ *n.* tomate *m.*
tomb /tum/ *n.* tumba *f.*
tomorrow /tə'mɔrou/ *adv.* mañana. **day after t.,** pasado mañana.
ton /tʌn/ *n.* tonelada *f.*
tone /toun/ *n.* tono *m.*
tongue /tʌŋ/ *n.* lengua *f.*
tonic /'tɒnɪk/ *n.* tónico *m.*
tonight /tə'nait/ *adv.* esta noche.
tonsil /'tɒnsəl/ *n.* amígdala *f.*
too /tu/ *adv.* también. **t. much,** demasiado. **t. many,** demasiados.
tool /tul/ *n.* herramienta *f.*
tooth /tuθ/ *n.* diente *m.;* (back) muela *f.*
toothache /'tuθ,eik/ *n.* dolor de muela.
toothbrush /'tuθ,brʌʃ/ *n.* cepillo de dientes.
toothpaste /'tuθ,peist/ *n.* crema dentífrica, pasta dentífrica.
top /tɒp/ *n.* **1.** parte de arriba. —*v.* **2.** cubrir; sobrepasar.
topic /'tɒpɪk/ *n. S.A.* tópico *m.*
topical /'tɒpɪkəl/ *a.* tópico.
torch /tɔrtʃ/ *n.* antorcha *f.*
torment /*n.* 'tɔrmɛnt; *v.* tɔr'mɛnt/ *n.* **1.** tormento *m.* —*v.* **2.** atormentar.
torrent /'tɔrənt/ *n.* torrente *m.*
torture /'tɔrtʃər/ *n.* **1.** tortura *f.* —*v.* **2.** torturar.
toss /tɔs/ *v.* tirar; agitar.
total /'toutl̩/ *a.* **1.** total, entero. —*n.* **2.** total *m.*
touch /tʌtʃ/ *n.* **1.** tacto *m.* **in t.,** en comunicación. —*v.* **2.** tocar; conmover.
tough /tʌf/ *a.* tosco; tieso; fuerte.
tour /tʊr/ *n.* **1.** viaje *m.* —*v.* **2.** viajar.
tourist /'tʊrɪst/ *n.* turista *m.* & *f.* *a.* turístico.
tournament /'tʊrnəmənt/ *n.* torneo *m.*
tow /tou/ *n.* **1.** remolque *m.* —*v.* **2.** remolcar.
toward /tɔrd, tə'wɔrd/ *prep.* hacia.
towel /'tauəl/ *n.* toalla *f.*
tower /'tauər/ *n.* torre *f.*
town /taun/ *n.* pueblo *m.*
town meeting cabildo abierto *m.*
tow truck grúa *f.*
toy /tɔi/ *n.* **1.** juguete *m.* —*v.* **2.** jugar.
trace /treis/ *n.* **1.** vestigio; rastro *m.* —*v.* **2.** trazar; rastrear; investigar.
track /træk/ *n.* **1.** huella, pista *f.* **race t.,** hipódromo *m.* —*v.* **2.** rastrear.
tract /trækt/ *n.* trecho; tracto *m.*
tractor /'træktər/ *n.* tractor *m.*
trade /treid/ *n.* **1.** comercio, negocio; oficio; canje *m.* —*v.* **2.** comerciar, negociar; cambiar.
trader /'treidər/ *n.* comerciante *m.*
tradition /trə'dɪʃən/ *n.* tradición *f.*
traditional /trə'dɪʃənl̩/ *a.* tradicional.
traffic /'træfɪk/ *n.* **1.** tráfico *m.* —*v.* **2.** traficar.
traffic jam atasco, embotellamiento *m.*
traffic light semáforo *m.*
tragedy /'trædʒɪdi/ *n.* tragedia *f.*
tragic /'trædʒɪk/ *a.* trágico.
trail /treil/ *n.* **1.** sendero; rastro *m.* —*v.* **2.** rastrear; arrastrar.
train /trein/ *n.* **1.** tren *m.* —*v.* **2.** enseñar; disciplinar; (sport) entrenarse.
traitor /'treitər/ *n.* traidor -ora.
tramp /træmp/ *n.* **1.** caminata *f.;* vagabundo *m.* —*v.* **2.** patear.
tranquil /'træŋkwɪl/ *a.* tranquilo.
tranquilizer /'træŋkwə,laizər/ *n.* tranquilizante *m.*
tranquillity /træŋ'kwɪlɪti/ *n.* tranquilidad *f.*
transaction /træn'sækʃən/ *n.* transacción *f.*
transfer /*n.* 'trænsfər, *v.* træns'fɜr/ *n.* **1.** traslado *m.;* boleto de transbordo. —*v.* **2.** trasladar, transferir.
transform /træns'fɔrm/ *v.* transformar.

transfusion /træns'fyuʒən/ n. transfusión f.

transistor /træn'zɪstər/ n. transistor m.

transition /træn'zɪʃən/ n. transición f.

translate /træns'leit/ v. traducir.

translation /træns'leiʃən/ n. traducción f.

transmit /træns'mɪt/ v. transmitir.

transparent /træns'pɛərənt/ a. transparente.

transport /n. 'trænspɔrt, v. træns'pɔrt/ n. **1.** transporte m. —v. **2.** transportar.

transportation /ˌtrænspər'teiʃən/ n. transporte m.

transsexual /træns'sɛkʃuəl/ a. & n. transexual m. & f.

transvestite /træns'vɛstait/ n. travestí m. & f.

trap /træp/ n. **1.** trampa f. —v. **2.** atrapar.

trash /træʃ/ n. desecho m.; basura f.

trash can cubo de la basura m.

travel /'trævəl/ n. **1.** tráfico m.; (pl.) viajes m.pl. —v. **2.** viajar.

travel agency agencia de viajes f.

traveler /'trævələr/ n. viajero -ra.

traveler's check /'trævələrz/ cheque de viaje m.

tray /trei/ n. bandeja f.

tread /trɛd/ n. **1.** pisada f.; (of a tire) cubierta f. —v. **2.** pisar.

treason /'trizən/ n. traición f.

treasure /'trɛʒər/ n. tesoro m.

treasurer /'trɛʒərər/ n. tesorero -ra.

treasury /'trɛʒəri/ n. tesorería f.

treat /trit/ v. tratar; convidar.

treatment /'tritmənt/ n. trato, tratamiento m.

treaty /'triti/ n. tratado, pacto m.

tree /tri/ n. árbol m.

tremble /'trɛmbəl/ v. temblar.

tremendous /trɪ'mɛndəs/ a. tremendo.

trench /trɛntʃ/ n. foso m.; Mil. trinchera f.

trend /trɛnd/ n. **1.** tendencia f. —v. **2.** tender.

trespass /'trɛspəs, -pæs/ v. traspasar; violar.

triage /tri'ɑʒ/ n. clasificación de los heridos después del combate.

trial /'traiəl/ n. prueba f.; Leg. proceso, juicio m.

triangle /'trai,æŋgəl/ n. triángulo m.

tribulation /ˌtrɪbyə'leiʃən/ n. tribulación f.

tributary /'trɪbyə,tɛri/ a. & n. tributario m.

tribute /'trɪbyut/ n. tributo m.

trick /trɪk/ n. **1.** engaño m.; maña f.; (cards) baza f. —v. **2.** engañar.

trifle /'traifəl/ n. **1.** pequeñez f. —v. **2.** juguetear.

trigger /'trɪgər/ n. gatillo m.

trim /trɪm/ a. **1.** ajustado; acicalado. —n. **2.** adorno m. —v. **3.** adornar; ajustar; cortar un poco.

trinket /'trɪŋkɪt/ n. bagatela, chuchería f.

trip /trɪp/ n. **1.** viaje m. —v. **2.** tropezar.

triple /'trɪpəl/ a. **1.** triple —v. **2.** triplicar.

tripod /'traipɒd/ n. trípode m.

trite /trait/ a. banal.

triumph /'traiəmf/ n. **1.** triunfo m. —v. **2.** triunfar.

triumphant /trai'ʌmfənt/ a. triunfante.

trivial /'trɪviəl/ a. trivial.

trolley /'trɒli/ n. tranvía m.

trombone /trɒm'boun/ n. trombón m.

troop /trup/ n. tropa f.

trophy /'troufi/ n. trofeo m.

tropical /'trɒpɪkəl/ a. trópico.

tropics /'trɒpɪks/ n. trópico m.

trot /trɒt/ n. **1.** trote m. —v. **2.** trotar.

trouble /'trʌbəl/ n. **1.** apuro m.; congoja; aflicción f. —v. **2.** molestar; afligir.

troublesome /'trʌbəlsəm/ a. penoso, molesto.

trough /trɔf/ n. artesa f.

trousers /'trauzərz/ n. pantalones, calzones m.pl.

trout /traut/ n. trucha f.

truce /trus/ n. tregua f.

truck /trʌk/ n. camión m.

true /tru/ a. verdadero, cierto, verdad.

truffle /'trʌfəl/ n. trufa f.

trumpet /'trʌmpɪt/ n. trompeta, trompa f.

trunk /trʌŋk/ n. baúl m.; (of a tree) tronco m.

trust /trʌst/ n. **1.** confianza f. —v. **2.** confiar.

trustworthy /'trʌst,wɜrði/ a. digno de confianza.

truth /truθ/ n. verdad f.

truthful /'truθfəl/ a. veraz.

try /trai/ n. **1.** prueba f.; ensayo m. —v. **2.** tratar; probar; ensayar; Leg. juzgar. **t. on,** probarse.

T-shirt /'ti,ʃɜrt/ n. camiseta f.

tub /tʌb/ n. tina f.

tube /tub/ n. tubo m.

tuberculosis /tu,bɜrkyə'lousɪs/ n. tuberculosis f.

tuck /tʌk/ n. **1.** recogido m. —v. **2.** recoger.

Tuesday /'tuzdei/ n. martes m.

tug /tʌg/ n. **1.** tirada f.; (boat) remolcador m. —v. **2.** tirar de.

tuition /tu'ɪʃən/ n. matrícula, colegiatura f.

tumble /'tʌmbəl/ n. **1.** caída f. —v. **2.** caer, tumbar; voltear.

tumult /'tumʌlt/ n. tumulto, alboroto m.

tuna /'tʌni/ n. atún m.

tune /tun/ n. **1.** tono m.; melodía, canción f. —v. **2.** templar.

tunnel /'tʌnl/ n. túnel m.

turf /tɜrf/ n. césped m.

Turkey /'tɜrki/ n. Turquía f.

Turkish /'tɜrkɪʃ/ a. turco.

turmoil /'tɜrmɔil/ n. disturbio m.

turn /tɜrn/ n. **1.** vuelta f.; giro; turno m. —v. **2.** volver, tornear, girar; **t. into,** transformar. **t. around,** volverse. **t. on,** encender; abrir. **t. off, t. out,** apagar.

turnip /'tɜrnɪp/ n. nabo m.

turret /'tɜrɪt/ n. torrecilla f.

turtle /'tɜrtl/ n. tortuga f.

turtleneck sweater /'tɜrtl,nɛk/ jersey de cuello alto m.

tutor /'tutər/ n. **1.** tutor -ra. —v. **2.** enseñar.

tweezers /'twizərz/ n.pl. pinzas f.pl.

twelve /twɛlv/ a. & pron. doce.

twenty /'twɛnti/ a. & pron. veinte.

twice /twais/ adv. dos veces.

twig /twɪg/ n. varita; ramita f.; vástago m.

twilight /'twai,lait/ n. crepúsculo m.

twin /twɪn/ n. gemelo -la.

twine /twain/ n. **1.** guita f. —v. **2.** torcer.

twinkle /'twɪŋkəl/ v. centellear.

twist /twɪst/ v. torcer.

two /tu/ a. & pron. dos.

type /taip/ n. **1.** tipo m. —v. **2.** escribir a máquina.

typewriter /'taip,raitər/ n. máquina de escribir.

typhoid fever /'taifɔid/ fiebre tifoidea.

typical /'tɪpɪkəl/ a. típico.

typist /'taipɪst/ n. mecanógrafo -fa.

tyranny /'tɪrəni/ n. tiranía f.

tyrant /'tairənt/ n. tirano -na.

U

udder /'ʌdər/ n. ubre f.

UFO abbr. (unidentified flying object) OVNI m. (objeto volador no identificado).

ugly /'ʌgli/ a. feo.

Ukraine /yu'krein/ n. Ucrania f.

Ukrainian /yu'kreiniən/ a. & n. ucranio.

ulcer /'ʌlsər/ n. úlcera f.

ulterior /ʌl'tɪəriər/ a. ulterior.

ultimate /'ʌltəmɪt/ a. último.

ultrasonic /ˌʌltrə'sɒnik/ a. ultrasónico.

umbrella /ʌm'brɛlə/ n. paraguas m. **sun u.,** quitasol m.

umpire /'ʌmpaiᵊr/ n. árbitro m.

unable /ʌn'eibəl/ a. incapaz. **to be u.,** no poder.

unanimous /yu'nænəməs/ a. unánime.

uncertain /ʌn'sɜrtn/ a. incierto, inseguro.

uncle /'ʌŋkəl/ n. tío m.

unconscious /ʌn'kɒnʃəs/ a. inconsciente; desmayado.

uncover /ʌn'kʌvər/ v. descubrir.

undeniable /ˌʌndɪ'naiəbəl/ a. innegable.

under /'ʌndər/ adv. **1.** debajo, abajo. —prep. **2.** bajo, debajo de.

underestimate /ˌʌndər'ɛstə,meit/ v. menospreciar; subestimar.

undergo /ˌʌndər'gou/ v. sufrir.

underground /'ʌndər,graund/ a. subterráneo; clandestino.

underline /ˌʌndər,lain/ v. subrayar.

underneath /ˌʌndər'niθ/ adv. **1.** por debajo. —prep. **2.** debajo de.

undershirt /'ʌndər,ʃɜrt/ n. camiseta f.

understand /ˌʌndər'stænd/ v. entender, comprender.

undertake /ˌʌndər'teik/ v. emprender.

underwear /'ʌndər,wɛər/ n. ropa interior.

undo /ʌn'du/ v. deshacer; desatar.

undress /ʌn'drɛs/ v. desnudar, desvestir.

uneasy /ʌn'izi/ a. inquieto.

uneven /ʌn'ivən/ a. desigual.

unexpected /ˌʌnɪk'spɛktɪd/ a. inesperado.

unfair /ʌn'fɛər/ a. injusto.

unfit /ʌn'fɪt/ a. incapaz; inadecuado.

unfold /ʌn'fould/ v. desplegar; revelar.

unforgettable /ˌʌnfər'gɛtəbəl/ a. inolvidable.

unfortunate /ʌn'fɔrtʃənɪt/ a. desafortunado, desgraciado.

unfurnished /ʌn'fɜrnɪʃt/ a. desamueblado.

unhappy /ʌn'hæpi/ a. infeliz.

uniform /'yunə,fɔrm/ a. & n. uniforme m.

unify /'yunə,fai/ v. unificar.

union /'yunyən/ n. unión f. **labor u.,** sindicato de obreros.

unique /yu'nik/ a. único.

unisex /'yunə,sɛks/ a. unisex.

unit /'yunɪt/ n. unidad f.

unite /yu'nait/ v. unir.

United Nations /yu'naitɪd 'neiʃənz/ Naciones Unidas f.pl.

United States /yu'naitɪd 'steits/ Estados Unidos m.pl.

unity /'yunɪti/ n. unidad f.

universal /ˌyunə'vɜrsəl/ a. universal.

universe /'yunə,vɜrs/ n. universo m.

university /ˌyunə'vɜrsɪti/ n. universidad f.

unleaded /ʌn'lɛdɪd/ a. sin plomo.

unless /ʌn'lɛs/ conj. a menos que, si no es que.

unlike /ʌn'laik/ a. disímil.

unload /ʌn'loud/ v. descargar.

unlock /ʌn'lɒk/ v. abrir.

unplug /ʌn'plʌg/ v. desenchufar.

unpopular /ʌn'pɒpyələr/ a. impopular.

unreasonable /ʌn'rizənəbəl/ a. desrazonable.

unscrew /ʌn'skru/ v. desatornillar.

untie /ʌn'tai/ v. desatar; soltar.

until /ʌn'tɪl/ prep. **1.** hasta. —conj. **2.** hasta que.

unusual /ʌn'yuʒəl/ a. raro, inusitado.

up /ʌp/ adv. **1.** arriba. —prep. **2.** **u. the street,** etc. calle arriba, etc.

uphold /ʌp'hould/ v. apoyar; defender.

upholster /ʌp'houlstər, ə'poul-/ v. entapizar.

upload /'ʌp,loud/ n. **1.** ascenso de archivos m. —v. **2.** subir, cargar.

upon /ə'pɒn/ prep. sobre, encima de.

upper /'ʌpər/ a. superior.

upper-case letter /'ʌpər 'keis/ mayúscula f.

upright /'ʌp,rait/ a. derecho, recto.

upriver /'ʌp'rɪvər/ adv. río arriba.

uproar /'ʌp,rɔr/ n. alboroto, tumulto m.

upset /n. 'ʌp,sɛt; v. ʌp'sɛt/ n. **1.** trastorno m. —v. **2.** trastornar.

upsetting /ʌp'sɛtɪŋ/ a. inquietante.

upstream /'ʌp'strim/ adv. aguas arriba, contra la corriente, río arriba.

uptight /ʌp'tait/ a. (psicológicamente) tenso, tieso.

upward /'ʌpwərd/ adv. hacia arriba.

urge /ɜrdʒ/ n. **1.** deseo m. —v. **2.** instar.

urgency /'ɜrdʒənsi/ n. urgencia f.

urgent /'ɜrdʒənt/ a. urgente. **to be u.,** urgir.

us /ʌs/ pron. nosotros -as; nos.

use /n. yus; v. yuz/ n. **1.** uso m. —v. **2.** usar, emplear. **u. up,** gastar, agotar. **be used to,** estar acostumbrado a.

useful /'yusfəl/ a. útil.

useless /'yuslɪs/ a. inútil, inservible.

user-friendly /'yuzər 'frɛndli/ a. amigable.

username /'yuzər'neim/ n. nombre de usuario m.

usher /'ʌʃər/ n. **1.** acomodador -ora. —v. **2.** introducir.

usual /'yuʒuəl/ a. usual.

utensil /yu'tɛnsəl/ n. utensilio m.

utmost /'ʌt,moust/ a. sumo, extremo.

utter /'ʌtər/ a. **1.** completo. —v. **2.** proferir; dar.

utterance /'ʌtərəns/ n. expresión f.

V

vacancy /'veikənsi/ n. vacante f.

vacant /'veikənt/ a. desocupado, libre.

vacation /vei'keiʃən/ n. vacaciones f.pl.

vaccinate /'væksə,neit/ v. vacunar.

vacuum /'vækyum/ n. vacuo, vacío m. **v. cleaner,** aspiradora f.

vagrant /'veigrənt/ a. & n. vagabundo- da.

vague /veig/ a. vago.

vain /vein/ a. vano; vanidoso. **in v.,** en vano.

valiant /'vælyənt/ a. valiente.

valid /'vælɪd/ a. válido.

valley /'væli/ n. valle m.

valor /'vælər/ n. valor m., valentía f.

valuable /'vælyuəbəl/ a. valioso. **to be v.,** valer mucho.

value /'vælyu/ n. **1.** valor, importe m. —v. **2.** valorar; estimar.

van /væn/ n. furgoneta f.

vandal /'vændl/ n. vándalo m.

vandalism /'vændl,ɪzəm/ n. vandalismo m.

vanish /'vænɪʃ/ v. desaparecer.

vanity /'vænɪti/ n. vanidad f. **v. case,** polvera f.

vanquish /'væŋkwɪʃ/ v. vencer.

vapor /'veipər/ n. vapor m.

variation /ˌvɛəri'eiʃən/ n. variación f.

varicose vein /'væri,kous/ variz f.

variety /və'raiɪti/ n. variedad f.

various /'vɛəriəs/ a. varios; diversos.

varnish /'vɑrnɪʃ/ n. **1.** barniz m. —v. **2.** barnizar.

vary /'vɛəri/ v. variar; cambiar.

vase /veis, veiz, vɑz/ n. florero; jarrón m.

vasectomy /væ'sɛktəmi/ n. vasectomía f.

vassal /'væsəl/ n. vasallo m.

vast /væst/ a. vasto.

vat /væt/ n. tina f., tanque m.

VAT /væt/ n. IVA (impuesto sobre el valor añadido).

vault /vɔlt/ n. bóveda f.

vegetable /'vɛdʒtəbəl/ a. & n. vegetal m.; (pl.) legumbres, verduras f.pl.

vehement /'viəmənt/ a. vehemente.

vehicle /'viɪkəl or, sometimes, 'vihi-/ n. vehículo m.

veil /veil/ n. 1. velo m. —v. 2. velar.

vein /vein/ n. vena f.

velocity /və'lɒsiti/ n. velocidad f.

velvet /'vɛlvɪt/ n. terciopelo m.

Venetian /və'niʃən/ a. & n. veneciano.

vengeance /'vɛndʒəns/ n. venganza f.

Venice /'vɛnɪs/ n. Venecia f.

vent /vɛnt/ n. apertura f.

ventilate /'vɛntl̩,eit/ v. ventilar.

venture /'vɛntʃər/ n. ventura f.

verb /vɜrb/ n. verbo m.

verbose /vər'bous/ a. verboso.

verdict /'vɜrdɪkt/ n. veredicto, fallo m.

verge /vɜrdʒ/ n. borde m.

verify /'vɛrə,fai/ v. verificar.

versatile /'vɜrsətl̩/ a. versátil.

verse /vɜrs/ n. verso m.

version /'vɜrʒən/ n. versión f.

vertical /'vɜrtɪkəl/ a. vertical.

very /'vɛri/ a. 1. mismo. —adv. 2. muy.

vessel /'vɛsəl/ n. vasija f.; barco m.

vest /vɛst/ n. chaleco m.

veteran /'vɛtərən/ a. & n. veterano -na.

veto /'vitou/ n. veto m.

vex /vɛks/ v. molestar.

via /'vaiə, 'viə/ prep. por la vía de; por.

viaduct /'vaiə,dʌkt/ n. viaducto m.

vibrate /'vaibreit/ v. vibrar.

vibration /vai'breiʃən/ n. vibración f.

vice /vais/ n. vicio m.

vicinity /vɪ'sɪnɪti/ n. vecindad f.

vicious /'vɪʃəs/ a. vicioso.

victim /'vɪktəm/ n. víctima f.

victor /'vɪktər/ n. vencedor -ora.

victorious /vɪk'tɔriəs/ a. victorioso.

victory /'vɪktəri/ n. victoria f.

video camera /'vɪdi,ou/ videocámara f.

videoconference /'vɪdiou,kɒnfərəns/ videoconferencia f.

videodisc /'vɪdiou,dɪsk/ n. videodisco m.

video game /'vɪdi,ou/ videojuego m.

videotape /'vɪdiou,teip/ n. vídeo m., magnetoscopio m.

view /vyu/ n. 1. vista f. —v. 2. ver.

viewpoint /'vyu,pɔint/ n. punto de vista m.

vigil /'vɪdʒəl/ n. vigilia, vela f.

vigilant /'vɪdʒələnt/ a. vigilante.

vigor /'vɪgər/ n. vigor m.

vile /vail/ a. vil, bajo.

village /'vɪlɪdʒ/ n. aldea f.

villain /'vɪlən/ n. malvado -da.

vindicate /'vɪndɪ,keit/ v. vindicar.

vine /vain/ n. parra, vid f.

vinegar /'vɪnɪgər/ n. vinagre m.

vintage /'vɪntɪdʒ/ n. vendimia f.

violate /'vaiə,leit/ v. violar.

violation /,vaiə'leiʃən/ n. violación f.

violence /'vaiələns/ n. violencia f.

violent /'vaiələnt/ a. violento.

violin /,vaiə'lɪn/ n. violín m.

virgin /'vɜrdʒɪn/ n. virgen f.

virile /'vɪrəl/ a. viril.

virtual /'vɜrtʃuəl/ a. virtual.

virtual memory memoria virtual f.

virtual reality realidad virtual f.

virtue /'vɜrtʃu/ n. virtud f.

virtuous /'vɜrtʃuəs/ a. virtuoso.

virus /'vairəs/ n. virus m.

visa /'vizə/ n. visa f.

visible /'vɪzəbəl/ a. visible.

vision /'vɪʒən/ n. visión f.

visit /'vɪzɪt/ n. 1. visita f. —v. 2. visitar.

visitor /'vɪzɪtər/ n. visitante m. & f.

visual /'vɪʒuəl/ a. visual.

vital /'vaitl̩/ a. vital.

vitality /vai'tælɪti/ n. vitalidad, energía vital f.

vitamin /'vaitəmɪn/ n. vitamina f.

vivacious /vɪ'veiʃəs, vai-/ a. vivaz.

vivid /'vɪvɪd/ a. vivo; gráfico.

vocabulary /vou'kæbyə,lɛri/ n. vocabulario m.

vocal /'voukəl/ a. vocal.

vodka /'vɒdkə/ n. vodca m.

vogue /voug/ n. boga; moda f. **be in vogue** estilarse.

voice /vɔis/ n. 1. voz f. —v. 2. expresar.

voice mail correo de voz m.

voice recognition reconocimiento de voz m.

void /vɔid/ a. 1. vacío. —n. 2. vacío m. —v. 3. invalidar.

voltage /'voultɪdʒ/ n. voltaje m.

volume /'vɒlyum/ n. volumen; tomo m.

voluntary /'vɒlən,tɛri/ a. voluntario.

volunteer /,vɒlən'tɪər/ n. 1. voluntario -ria. —v. 2. ofrecerse.

vomit /'vɒmɪt/ v. vomitar.

vote /vout/ n. 1. voto m. —v. 2. votar.

voter /'voutər/ n. votante m. & f.

vouch /vautʃ/ v. **v. for,** garantizar.

vow /vau/ n. 1. voto m. —v. 2. jurar.

vowel /'vauəl/ n. vocal f.

voyage /'vɔiidʒ/ n. viaje m.

vulgar /'vʌlgər/ a. vulgar; común; soez.

vulnerable /'vʌlnərəbəl/ a. vulnerable.

W

wade /weid/ v. vadear.

wag /wæg/ v. menear.

wage /weidʒ/ n. 1. (pl.) sueldo, salario m. —v. 2. **w. war,** hacer guerra.

wagon /'wægən/ n. carreta f.

wail /weil/ n. 1. lamento, gemido m. —v. 2. lamentar, gemir.

waist /weist/ n. cintura f.

wait /weit/ n. 1. espera f. —v. 2. esperar. **w. for,** esperar. **w. on,** atender.

waiter /'weitər/ **waitress** n. camarero -ra.

waiting room /'weitɪŋ/ sala de espera.

wake /weik/ v. **w. up,** despertar.

walk /wɔk/ n. 1. paseo m.; vuelta; caminata f.; modo de andar. —v. 2. andar; caminar; ir a pie.

wall /wɔl/ n. pared; muralla f.

wallcovering /'wɔl,kʌvərɪŋ/ n. tapizado de pared m.

wallet /'wɒlɪt/ n. cartera f.

wallpaper /'wɔl,peipər/ n. 1. empapelado m. —v. 2. empapelar.

walnut /'wɔl,nʌt/ n. nuez f.

waltz /wɔlts/ n. vals m.

wander /'wɒndər/ v. vagar.

want /wɒnt/ n. 1. necesidad f. —v. 2. querer.

war /wɔr/ n. guerra f.

ward /wɔrd/ n. 1. Pol. barrio m.; (hospital) cuadra f. —v. 2. **w. off,** parar.

warehouse /'wɛər,haus/ n. almacén m.

wares /wɛərz/ n. mercancías f.pl.

warlike /'wɔr,laik/ a. belicoso.

warm /wɔrm/ a. 1. caliente; Fig. caluroso. **to be w.,** tener calor; (weather) hacer calor. —v. 2. calentar.

warmth /wɔrmθ/ n. calor m.

warn /wɔrn/ v. advertir.

warning /'wɔrnɪŋ/ n. aviso m.

warp /wɔrp/ v. alabear.

warrant /'wɔrənt, 'wɒr-/ v. justificar.

warrior /'wɔriər/ n. guerrero -ra.

warship /'wɔr,ʃɪp/ n. navío de guerra, buque de guerra m.

wash /wɒʃ/ v. lavar.

washing machine /'wɒʃɪŋ/ máquina de lavar, lavadora f.

wasp /wɒsp/ n. avispa f.

waste /weist/ n. 1. gasto m.; desechos m.pl. —v. 2. gastar; perder.

watch /wɒtʃ/ n. 1. reloj m.; Mil. guardia f. —v. 2. observar, mirar. **w. for,** esperar. **w. out for,** tener cuidado con. **w. over,** guardar; velar por.

watchful /'wɒtʃfəl/ a. desvelado.

watchmaker /'wɒtʃ,meikər/ n. relojero -ra.

watchman /'wɒtʃmən/ n. sereno m.

water /'wɔtər/ n. 1. agua f. **w. color,** acuarela f. —v. 2. aguar.

waterbed /'wɔtər,bɛd/ n. cama de agua f.

waterfall /'wɔtər,fɔl/ n. catarata f.

watering can /'wɔtərɪŋ/ regadera f.

waterproof /'wɔtər,pruf/ a. impermeable.

wave /weiv/ n. 1. onda; ola f. —v. 2. ondear; agitar; hacer señas.

waver /'weivər/ v. vacilar.

wax /wæks/ n. 1. cera f. —v. 2. encerar.

way /wei/ n. camino; modo m., manera f. **in a w.,** hasta cierto punto. **a long w.,** muy lejos. **by the w.,** a propósito. **this w.,** por aquí. **that w.,** por allí. **which w.,** por dónde.

we /wi/ pron. nosotros -as.

weak /wik/ a. débil.

weaken /'wikən/ v. debilitar.

weakness /'wiknɪs/ n. debilidad f.

wealth /wɛlθ/ n. riqueza f.

wealthy /'wɛlθi/ a. adinerado.

wean /win/ v. destetar.

weapon /'wɛpən/ n. arma f.

wear /wɛər/ n. 1. uso; desgaste m.; (clothes) ropa f. —v. 2. usar, llevar. **w. out,** gastar; cansar.

weary /'wiəri/ a. cansado, rendido.

weather /'wɛðər/ n. tiempo m.

weave /wiv/ v. tejer.

weaver /'wivər/ n. tejedor -ra.

web /wɛb/ n. tela f.

Web /wɛb/ n. (Internet) malla f., telaraña f., web m.

wedding /'wɛdɪŋ/ n. boda f.

wedge /wɛdʒ/ n. cuña f.

Wednesday /'wɛnzdei/ n. miércoles m.

weed /wid/ n. maleza f.

week /wik/ n. semana f.

weekday /'wik,dei/ n. día de trabajo.

weekend /'wik,ɛnd/ n. fin de semana.

weekly /'wikli/ a. semanal.

weep /wip/ v. llorar.

weigh /wei/ v. pesar.

weight /weit/ n. peso m.

weightless /'weitlɪs/ v. ingrávido.

weightlessness /'weitlɪsnɪs/ n. ingravidez f.

weird /wiərd/ a. misterioso, extraño.

welcome /'wɛlkəm/ a. 1. bienvenido. **you're w.,** de nada, no hay de qué. —n. 2. acogida, bienvenida f. —v. 3. acoger, recibir bien.

welfare /'wɛl,fɛər/ n. bienestar m.

well /wɛl/ a. 1. sano, bueno. —adv. 2. bien; pues. —n. 3. pozo m.

well-done /'wɛl 'dʌn/ a. (food) bien cocido.

well-known /'wɛl 'noun/ a. bien conocido.

well-mannered /'wɛl 'mænərd/ a. educado.

west /wɛst/ n. oeste, occidente m.

western /'wɛstərn/ a. occidental.

westward /'wɛstwərd/ adv. hacia el oeste.

wet /wɛt/ a. 1. mojado. **to get w.,** mojarse. —v. 2. mojar.

whale /weil/ n. ballena f.

what /wʌt; unstressed wət/ a. 1. qué; cuál. —interrog. pron. 2. qué. —rel. pron. 3. lo que.

whatever /wʌt'ɛvər/ a. 1. cualquier. —pron. 2. lo que; todo lo que.

wheat /wit/ n. trigo m.

wheel /wil/ n. rueda f. **steering w.,** volante m.

when /wɛn; unstressed wən/ adv. 1. cuándo. —conj. 2. cuando.

whenever /wɛn'ɛvər/ conj. siempre que, cuando quiera que.

where /wɛər/ adv. 1. dónde, adónde. —conj. 2. donde.

wherever /wɛər'ɛvər/ conj. dondequiera que, adondequiera que.

whether /'wɛðər/ conj. si.

which /wɪtʃ/ a. 1. qué. —interrog. pron. 2. cuál. —rel. pron. 3. que; el cual; lo cual.

whichever /wɪtʃ'ɛvər/ a. & pron. cualquiera que.

while /wail/ conj. 1. mientras; mientras que. —n. 2. rato m.

whip /wɪp/ n. 1. látigo m. —v. 2. azotar.

whipped cream /wɪpt/ nata batida f.

whirl /wɜrl/ v. girar.

whirlpool /'wɜrl,pul/ n. vórtice m.

whirlwind /'wɜrl,wɪnd/ n. torbellino m.

whisk broom /wɪsk/ escobilla f.

whisker /'wɪskər/ n. bigote m.

whiskey /'wɪski/ n. whisky m.

whisper /'wɪspər/ n. 1. cuchicheo m. —v. 2. cuchichear.

whistle /'wɪsəl/ n. 1. pito; silbido m. —v. 2. silbar.

white /wait/ a. 1. blanco. —n. 2. (of egg) clara f.

who /hu/ **whom** interrog. pron. 1. quién. —rel. pron. 2. que; quien.

whoever /hu'ɛvər/ **whomever** pron. quienquiera que.

whole /houl/ a. 1. entero. **the wh.,** todo el. —n. 2. totalidad f. **on the wh.,** por lo general.

wholesale /'houl,seil/ n. **at wh.,** al por mayor.

wholesaler /'houl,seilər/ n. mayorista m. & f.

wholesome /'houlsəm/ a. sano, saludable.

wholly /'houli/ adv. enteramente.

whose /huz/ interrog. adj. 1. de quién. —rel. adj. 2. cuyo.

why /wai/ adv. por qué; para qué.

wicked /'wɪkɪd/ a. malo, malvado.

wickedness /'wɪkɪdnɪs/ n. maldad f.

wide /waid/ a. 1. ancho; extenso. —adv. 2. **w. open,** abierto de par en par.

widen /'waidn̩/ v. ensanchar; extender.

widespread /'waid'sprɛd/ a. extenso.

widow /'wɪdou/ n. viuda f.

widower /'wɪdouər/ n. viudo m.

width /wɪdθ/ n. anchura f.

wield /wild/ v. manejar, empuñar.

wife /waif/ n. esposa, señora, mujer f.

wig /wɪg/ n. peluca f.

wild /waild/ a. salvaje; bárbaro.

wilderness /'wɪldərnɪs/ n. desierto m.

wildlife /'waild,laif/ n. fauna silvestre f.

will /wɪl/ n. 1. voluntad f.; testamento m. —v. 2. querer; determinar; Leg. legar.

willful /'wɪlfəl/ a. voluntarioso; premeditado.

willing /'wɪlɪŋ/ a. **to be w.,** estar dispuesto.

willingly /'wɪlɪŋli/ adv. de buena gana.

wilt /wɪlt/ v. marchitar.

win /wɪn/ v. ganar.

wind /wɪnd/ n. 1. viento m. —v. 2. torcer; dar cuerda a.

windmill /'wɪnd,mɪl/ n. molino de viento m.

window /'wɪndou/ n. ventana f.; (of car) ventanilla f.; (of shop or store) escaparate m.

windshield /'wɪnd,ʃild/ n. parabrisas m.

windy /'wɪndi/ *a.* ventoso. **to be w.,** (weather) hacer viento.

wine /wain/ *n.* vino *m.*

wing /wɪŋ/ *n.* ala *f.; Theat.* bastidor *m.*

wink /wɪŋk/ *n.* **1.** guiño *m.* —*v.* **2.** guiñar.

winner /'wɪnər/ *n.* ganador -ra.

winter /'wɪntər/ *n.* invierno *m.*

wipe /waip/ *v.* limpiar; (dry) secar. **w. out,** destruir.

wire /wai°r/ *n.* **1.** alambre; hilo; telegrama *m.* —*v.* **2.** telegrafiar.

wireless /'wai°rlɪs/ *n.* telégrafo sin hilos.

wisdom /'wɪzdəm/ *n.* juicio *m.;* sabiduría *f.*

wise /waiz/ *a.* sensato, juicioso; sabio.

wish /wɪʃ/ *n.* **1.** deseo; voto *m.* —*v.* **2.** desear; querer.

wit /wɪt/ *n.* ingenio *m.*, sal *f.*

witch /wɪtʃ/ *n.* bruja *f.*

with /wɪθ, wɪð/ *prep.* con.

withdraw /wɪð'drɔ, wɪθ-/ *v.* retirar.

wither /'wɪðər/ *v.* marchitar.

withhold /wɪθ'hould, wɪð-/ *v.* retener, suspender.

within /wɪð'ɪn, wɪθ-/ *adv.* **1.** dentro, por dentro. —*prep.* **2.** dentro de; en.

without /wɪð'aut, wɪθ-/ *adv.* **1.** fuera, por fuera. —*prep.* **2.** sin.

witness /'wɪtnɪs/ *n.* **1.** testigo; testimonio *m. & f.* —*v.* **2.** presenciar; atestar.

witty /'wɪti/ *a.* ingenioso, gracioso, ocurrente.

wizard /'wɪzərd/ *n.* hechicero *m.*

woe /wou/ *n.* dolor *m.;* pena *f.*

wolf /wʊlf/ *n.* lobo -ba.

woman /'wʊmən/ *n.* mujer *f.*

womb /wum/ *n.* entrañas *f.pl.*, matriz *f.*

wonder /'wʌndər/ *n.* **1.** maravilla; admiración *f.* **for a w.,** por milagro. **no w.,** no es extraño. —*v.* **2.** preguntarse; maravillarse.

wonderful /'wʌndərfəl/ *a.* maravilloso; estupendo.

woo /wu/ *v.* cortejar.

wood /wʊd/ *n.* madera; (for fire) leña *f.*

wooden /'wʊdn/ *a.* de madera.

wool /wʊl/ *n.* lana *f.*

word /wɜrd/ *n.* **1.** palabra *f.* **the words** (of a song), la letra. —*v.* **2.** expresar.

word processing /'prɒsɛsɪŋ/ procesamiento de textos *m.*

word processor /'prɒsɛsər/ procesador de textos *m.*

work /wɜrk/ *n.* **1.** trabajo *m.;* (of art) obra *f.* —*v.* **2.** trabajar; obrar; funcionar.

worker /'wɜrkər/ *n.* trabajador -ra; obrero -ra.

workman /'wɜrkmən/ *n.* obrero *m.*

work station estación de trabajo *f.*

work week /'wɜrk,wik/ semana laboral *f.*

world /wɜrld/ *n.* mundo *m.* **w. war,** guerra mundial.

worldly /'wɜrldli/ *a.* mundano.

worldwide /'wɜrld'waid/ *a.* mundial.

worm /wɜrm/ *n.* gusano *m.*

worn /wɜrn/ *a.* usado. **w. out,** gastado; cansado, rendido.

worrisome /'wʌrisəm/ *a.* inquietante.

worry /'wɜri/ *n.* **1.** preocupación *f.* —*v.* **2.** preocupar.

worrying /'wɜriɪŋ/ *a.* inquietante.

worse /wɜrs/ *a.* peor. **to get w.,** empeorar.

worship /'wɜrʃɪp/ *n.* **1.** adoración *f.* —*v.* **2.** adorar.

worst /wɜrst/ *a.* peor.

worth /wɜrθ/ *a.* **1. to be w.,** valer. —*n.* **2.** valor *m.*

worthless /'wɜrθlɪs/ *a.* sin valor.

worthy /'wɜrði/ *a.* digno.

wound /wund/ *n.* **1.** herida *f.* —*v.* **2.** herir.

wrap /ræp/ *n.* **1.** (pl.) abrigos *m.pl.* —*n.* **2.** envolver.

wrapping /'ræpɪŋ/ *n.* cubierta *f.*

wrath /ræθ/ *n.* ira, cólera *f.*

wreath /riθ/ *n.* guirnalda; corona *f.*

wreck /rɛk/ *n.* **1.** ruina *f.;* accidente *m.* —*v.* **2.** destrozar, arruinar.

wrench /rɛntʃ/ *n.* llave *f.* **monkey w.,** llave inglesa.

wrestle /'rɛsəl/ *v.* luchar.

wretched /'rɛtʃɪd/ *a.* miserable.

wring /rɪŋ/ *v.* retorcer.

wrinkle /'rɪŋkəl/ *n.* **1.** arruga *f.* —*v.* **2.** arrugar.

wrist /rɪst/ *n.* muñeca *f.* **w. watch,** reloj de pulsera.

write /rait/ *v.* escribir. **w. down,** apuntar.

writer /'raitər/ *n.* escritor -ra.

writhe /raið/ *v.* contorcerse.

writing paper /'raitɪŋ/ papel de escribir *m.*

wrong /rɔŋ/ *a.* **1.** equivocado; incorrecto. **to be w.,** equivocarse; no tener razón. —*adv.* **2.** mal, incorrectamente. —*n.* **3.** agravio *m.* **right and w.,** el bien y el mal. —*v.* **4.** agraviar, ofender.

WWW *abbr.* (World Wide Web) malla mundial *f.*

X Y Z

x-ray /'ɛks,rei/ *n.* **1.** rayo X *m.*, radiografía, *f.* —*v.* **2.** radiografiar.

xylophone /'zailə,foun/ *n.* xilófono *m.*

yacht /yɒt/ *n.* yate *m.*

yard /yɑrd/ *n.* patio, corral *m.;* (measure) yarda *f.*

yarn /yɑrn/ *n.* hilo.

yawn /yɔn/ *n.* **1.** bostezo *m.* —*v.* **2.** bostezar.

year /yɪər/ *n.* año *m.*

yearly /'yɪərli/ *a.* anual.

yearn /yɜrn/ *v.* anhelar.

yell /yɛl/ *n.* **1.** grito *m.* —*v.* **2.** gritar.

yellow /'yɛlou/ *a.* amarillo.

yes /yɛs/ *adv.* sí.

yesterday /'yɛstər,dei/ *adv.* ayer.

yet /yɛt/ *adv.* todavía, aún.

Yiddish /'yɪdɪʃ/ *n.* yídish *m.*

yield /yild/ *v.* producir; ceder.

yogurt /'yougərt/ *n.* yogur *m.*

yoke /youk/ *n.* yugo *m.*

yolk /youk/ *n.* yema *f.*

you /yu; *unstressed* yʊ, yə/ *pron.* usted, (pl.) ustedes; lo, la, los, las; le, les; (familiar) tú, (pl.) vosotros -as; ti; te, (pl.) os. **with y.,** contigo, con usted.

young /yʌŋ/ *a.* joven.

youngster /'yʌŋstər/ *n.* muchacho -cha *m. & f.*

your /yʊr, yɔr; *unstressed* yər/ *a.* su; (familiar) tu; (pl.) vuestro.

yours /yʊrz, yɔrz/ *pron.* suyo; (familiar) tuyo; (pl.) vuestro.

yourself -selves /yʊr'sɛlf, yɔr- yər-/ *pron.* sí; se; (familiar) ti; te. **with y.,** consigo; contigo. **you y.,** usted mismo, ustedes mismos; tú mismo, vosotros mismos.

youth /yuθ/ *n.* juventud *f.;* (person) joven *m. & f.*

youth club club juvenil *m.*

youthful /'yuθfəl/ *a.* juvenil.

yuppie /'yʌpi/ *n.* yuppie *m. & f.*

zap /zæp/ *v.* desintegrar, aniquilar.

zeal /zil/ *n.* celo, fervor *m.*

zealous /'zɛləs/ *a.* celoso, fervoroso.

zero /'zɪərou/ *n.* cero *m.*

zest /zɛst/ *n.* gusto *m.*

zip code /zɪp/ número de distrito postal.

zipper /'zɪpər/ *m.* cremallera *f.*

zone /zoun/ *n.* zona *f.*

zoo /zu/ *n.* jardín zoológico.

SPANISH IRREGULAR VERBS

Infinitive	Present	Future	Preterit	Past Part.
andar	ando	andaré	anduve	andado
caber	quepo	cabré	cupe	cabido
caer	caigo	caeré	caí	caído
conducir	conduzco	conduciré	conduje	conducido
dar	doy	daré	di	dado
decir	digo	diré	dije	dicho
estar	estoy	estaré	estuve	estado
haber	he	habré	hube	habido
hacer	hago	haré	hice	hecho
ir	voy	iré	fui	ido
jugar	juego	jugaré	jugué	jugado
morir	muero	moriré	morí	muerto
oir	oigo	oiré	oí	oído
poder	puedo	podré	pude	podido
poner	pongo	pondré	puse	puesto
querer	quiero	querré	quise	querido
saber	sé	sabré	supe	sabido
salir	salgo	saldré	salí	salido
ser	soy	seré	fui	sido
tener	tengo	tendré	tuve	tenido
traer	traigo	traeré	traje	traído
valer	valgo	valdré	valí	valido
venir	vengo	vendré	vine	venido
ver	veo	veré	vi	visto

LAS FORMAS DEL VERBO INGLÉS

1. Se forma la 3ª persona singular del tiempo presente exactamente al igual que el plural de los sustantivos, añadiendo **-es** o **-s** a la forma sencilla según las mismas reglas, así:

(1)	teach	pass	wish	fix	buzz		
	teaches	passes	wishes	fixes	buzzes		
(2)	place	change	judge	please	freeze		
	places	changes	judges	pleases	freezes		
(3a)	find	sell	clean	hear	love	buy	know
	finds	sells	cleans	hears	loves	buys	knows
(3b)	think	like	laugh	stop	hope	meet	want
	thinks	likes	laughs	stops	hopes	meets	wants
(4)	cry	try	dry	carry	deny		
	cries	tries	dries	carries	denies		

Cinco verbos muy comunes tienen 3ª persona singular irregular:

| (5) | go | do | say | have | be |
| | goes | does | says | has | is |

2. Se forman el tiempo pasado y el participio de modo igual, añadiendo a la forma sencilla la terminación **-ed** o **-d** según las reglas que siguen:

(1) Si la forma sencilla termina en **-d** o **-t**, se le pone **-ed** como sílaba aparte:

| end | fold | need | load | want | feast | wait | light |
| ended | folded | needed | loaded | wanted | feasted | waited | lighted |

(2) Si la forma sencilla termina en cualquier otra consonante, se añade también **-ed** pero sin hacer sílaba aparte:

(2a) bang   sail   seem   harm   earn   weigh
banged   sailed   seemed   harmed   earned   weighed

(2b) lunch   work   look   laugh   help   pass
lunched   worked   looked   laughed   helped   passed

(3) Si la forma sencilla termina en **-e,** se le pone sólo **-d:**

(3a) hate   taste   waste   guide   fade   trade
hated   tasted   wasted   guided   faded   traded

(3b) free   judge   rule   name   dine   scare
freed   judged   ruled   named   dined   scared

(3c) place   force   knife   like   hope   base
placed   forced   knifed   liked   hoped   based

(4) Una **-y** final que sigue a cualquier consonante se cambia en **-ie** al añadir la **-d** del pasado/participio:
cry   try   dry   carry   deny
cried   tried   dried   carried   denied

3. Varios verbos muy comunes forman el tiempo pasado y el participio de manera irregular. Pertenecen a tres grupos.

(1) Los que tienen una sola forma irregular para tiempo pasado y participio, como los siguientes:

bend	bleed	bring	build	buy	catch	creep	deal
bent	bled	brought	built	bought	caught	crept	dealt
dig	feed	feel	fight	find	flee	get	hang
dug	fed	felt	fought	found	fled	got	hung
have	hear	hold	keep	lead	leave	lend	lose
had	heard	held	kept	led	left	lent	lost
make	mean	meet	say	seek	sell	send	shine
made	meant	met	said	sought	sold	sent	shone
shoot	sit	sleep	spend	stand	strike	sweep	teach
shot	sat	slept	spent	stood	struck	swept	taught

(2) Los que tienen una forma irregular para el tiempo pasado y otra forma irregular para el participio, como los siguientes:

be	beat	become	begin	bite
was	beat	became	began	bit
been	beaten	become	begun	bitten
blow	break	choose	come	do
blew	broke	chose	came	did
blown	broken	chosen	come	done
draw	drink	drive	eat	fall
drew	drank	drove	ate	fell
drawn	drunk	driven	eaten	fallen
fly	forget	freeze	give	go
flew	forgot	froze	gave	went
flown	forgotten	frozen	given	gone
grow	hide	know	ride	ring
grew	hid	knew	rode	rang
grown	hidden	known	ridden	rung
rise	run	see	shake	shrink
rose	ran	saw	shook	shrank
risen	run	seen	shaken	shrunk
sing	sink	speak	steal	swear
sang	sank	spoke	stole	swore
sung	sunk	spoken	stolen	sworn

Las formas del verbo inglés

swim	tear	throw	wear	write
swam	tore	threw	wore	wrote
swum	torn	thrown	worn	written

(3) Los que no varían del todo, la forma sencilla funcionando también como pasado/participio; entre éstos son de mayor frecuencia:

bet	burst	cast	cost	cut
hit	hurt	let	put	quit
read	set	shed	shut	slit
spit	split	spread	thrust	wet

El plural del sustantivo inglés

A la forma singular se añade la terminición -es o -s de acuerdo con las reglas siguientes.

(1) Si el singular termina en -ch, -s, -sh, -x o -z, se le pone -es como sílaba aparte:

match	glass	dish	box	buzz
matches	glasses	dishes	boxes	buzzes

(2) Si el singular termina en -ce, -ge, -se, or -ze, se le pone una -s que con la vocal precedente forma sílaba aparte:

face	page	house	size
faces	pages	houses	sizes

(3) Una -y final que sigue a cualquier consonante se cambia en -ie a ponérsele la -s del plural:

sky	city	lady	ferry	penny
skies	cities	ladies	ferries	pennies

(4) Los siguientes sustantivos comunes tienen plural irregular:

man	woman	child	foot	mouse	goose
men	women	children	feet	mice	geese
wife	knife	life	half	leaf	deer
wives	knives	lives	halves	leaves	deer

Weights and Measures/Pesos y Medidas

1 centímetro	=	.3937 inches		1 kilolitro	=	264.18 gallons
1 metro	=	39.37 inches		1 inch	=	2.54 centímetros
1 kilómetro	=	.621 mile		1 foot	=	.305 metros
1 centigramo	=	.1543 grain		1 mile	=	1.61 kilómetros
1 gramo	=	15.432 grains		1 grain	=	.065 gramos
1 kilogramo	=	2.2046 pounds		1 pound	=	.455 kilogramos
1 tonelada	=	2.204 pounds		1 ton	=	.907 toneladas
1 centilitro	=	.338 ounces		1 ounce	=	2.96 centilitros
1 litro	=	1.0567 quart (liquid); .908 quart (dry)		1 quart	=	1.13 litros
				1 gallon	=	4.52 litros

Numbers/Números

Cardinal/Cardinales

one	1	uno, una
two	2	dos
three	3	tres
four	4	cuatro
five	5	cinco
six	6	seis
seven	7	siete
eight	8	ocho
nine	9	nueve
ten	10	diez
eleven	11	once
twelve	12	doce
thirteen	13	trece
fourteen	14	catorce
fifteen	15	quince
sixteen	16	dieciséis
seventeen	17	diecisiete
eighteen	18	dieciocho
nineteen	19	diecinueve
twenty	20	veinte
twenty-one	21	veinte y uno
twenty-two	22	veinte y dos (or veintiuno)
		(or veintidós)
thirty	30	treinta
thirty-one	31	treinta y uno
thirty-two	32	treinta y dos
forty	40	cuarenta
fifty	50	cincuenta
sixty	60	sesenta
seventy	70	setenta
eighty	80	ochenta
ninety	90	noventa
one hundred	100	cien
one hundred one	101	ciento uno
one hundred two	102	ciento dos
two hundred	200	doscientos, -as
three hundred	300	trescientos, -as
four hundred	400	cuatrocientos, -as
five hundred	500	quinientos, -as
six hundred	600	seiscientos, -as
seven hundred	700	setecientos, -as
eight hundred	800	ochocientos, -as
nine hundred	900	novecientos, -as
one thousand	1,000	mil
two thousand	2,000	dos mil
one hundred thousand	100,000	cien mil
one million	1,000,000	un millón
two million	2,000,000	dos millones

Ordinal/Ordinales

first	1st /	1°	primero
second	2nd /	2°	segundo
third	3rd /	3°	tercero
fourth	4th /	4°	cuarto
fifth	5th /	5°	quinto
sixth	6th /	6°	sexto
seventh	7th /	7°	séptimo
eighth	8th /	8°	octavo
ninth	9th /	9°	noveno
tenth	10th /	10°	décimo

Days of the Week/Días de la Semana

Sunday	domingo	Thursday	jueves
Monday	lunes	Friday	viernes
Tuesday	martes	Saturday	sábado
Wednesday	miércoles		

Months/Meses

January	enero	July	julio
February	febrero	August	agosto
March	marzo	September	septiembre
April	abril	October	octubre
May	mayo	November	noviembre
June	junio	December	diciembre

Signs/Señales

By appointment	Cita previa
Caution	Precaución
Closed	Cerrado
Closed for repairs	Cerrado por refaccíon
Danger	Peligro
Do not disturb	No molesten
Down (on elevator)	Para bajar
Driveway	Vado permante/Paso de carruajes
Dumping prohibited	Se prohibe arrojar la basura
Entrance	Entrada
Exit	Salida
For immediate occupancy	De ocupación inmediata
For sale	Se vende
Go (traffic)	Siga
Inquire within	Se dan informaciones
Keep to the left	Tome su izquierda
Keep to the right	Tome su derecha
Ladies'/Women's room	El cuarto de damas
Men	Señores, Hombres, Caballeros
Men's room	El servicio
Narrow road	Camino estrecho
No admittance	Entrada prohibida
No entry	Dirección prohibida
No thoroughfare	Prohibido el paso/Calle cerrada
No parking	Se prohibe estacionar
No smoking	Prohibido fumar
No tipping	No se admiten propinas
Not working	No funciona
One way	Dirección única
Open	Abierto
People working	Trabajadores
Post no bills	Se prohibe fijar carteles
Road closed	Paso cerrado
Road repairs	Camino en reparación
Same-day service	En el día
Slow	Despacio
Slow down	Moderar su velocidad
Stop	Alto
This way to...	Dirección a...
Town ahead	Poblado próximo
Up (on elevator)	Para subir
Wet paint	Recién pintado
Women	Señoras, Mujeres, Damas

Useful Phrases/Locuciones Útiles

Good day, Good morning. Buenos días.
Good afternoon. Buenas tardes.
Good night, Good evening. Buenas noches.
Hello. ¡Hola!
Welcome! ¡Bienvenido!
See you later. Hasta luego.
Goodbye. ¡Adiós!
How are you? ¿Cómo está usted?
I'm fine, thank you. Estoy bien, gracias.
I'm pleased to meet you. Mucho gusto en conocerle.
May I introduce . . . Quisiera presentar . . .
Thank you very much. Muchas gracias.
You're welcome. De nada *or* No hay de qué.
Please. Por favor.
Excuse me. Con permiso.
Good luck. ¡Buena suerte!
To your health. ¡Salud!

Please help me. Ayúdeme, por favor.
I don't know. No sé.
I don't understand. No entiendo.
Do you understand? ¿Entiende usted?
I don't speak Spanish. No hablo español.
Do you speak English? ¿Habla usted inglés?
How do you say . . . in Spanish? ¿Cómo se dice . . . en español?
What do you call this? ¿Cómo se llama esto?
Speak slowly, please. Hable despacio, por favor.
Please repeat. Repita, por favor.
I don't like it. No me gusta.
I am lost. Ando perdido; Me he extraviado.

What is your name? ¿Cómo se llama usted?
My name is . . . Me llamo . . .
I am an American. Soy norteamericano.
Where are you from? ¿De dónde es usted?
I'm from . . . Soy de . . .

How is the weather? ¿Qué tiempo hace?
It's cold (hot) today. Hace frío (calor) hoy.
What time is it? ¿Qué hora es?

How much is it? ¿Cuánto es?
It is too much. Es demasiado.
What do you wish? ¿Qué desea usted?
I want to buy . . . Quiero comprar . . .
May I see something better? ¿Podría ver algo mejor?
May I see something cheaper? ¿Podría ver algo menos caro?
It is not exactly what I want. No es exactamente lo que quiero.

I'm hungry. Tengo hambre.
I'm thirsty. Tengo sed.
Where is there a restaurant? ¿Dónde hay un restaurante?
I have a reservation. Tengo una reservación.

I would like . . . Quisiera . . .; Me gustaría . . .
Please give me . . . Por favor, déme usted . . .
Please bring me . . . Por favor, tráigame usted . . .
May I see the menu? ¿Podría ver el menú?
The bill, please. La cuenta, por favor.
Is service included in the bill? ¿El servicio está incluido en la cuenta?
Where is there a hotel? ¿Dónde hay un hotel?
Where is the post office? ¿Dónde está el correo?
Is there any mail for me? ¿Hay correo para mí?
Where can I mail this letter? ¿Dónde puedo echar esta carta al correo?

Take me to . . . Lléveme a . . .
I believe I am ill. Creo que estoy enfermo.
Please call a doctor. Por favor, llame al médico.
Please call the police. Por favor, llame a la policía.
I want to send a telegram. Quiero poner un telegrama.
As soon as possible. Cuanto antes.

Round trip. Ida y vuelta.
Please help me with my luggage. Por favor, ayúdeme con mi equipaje.
Where can I get a taxi? ¿Dónde hay taxi?
What is the fare to . . . ¿Cuánto es el pasaje hasta . . . ?
Please take me to this address. Por favor, lléveme a esta dirección.
Where can I change my money? ¿Dónde puedo cambiar mi dinero?
Where is the nearest bank? ¿Dónde está el banco más cercano?
Can you accept my check? ¿Puede aceptar usted mi cheque?
Do you accept traveler's checks? ¿Aceptan cheques de viaje?
What is the postage? ¿Cuánto es el franqueo?
Where is the nearest drugstore? ¿Dónde está la farmacia más cercana?
Where is the men's (women's) room? ¿Dónde está el servicio de caballeros (de señoras)?
Please let me off at . . . Por favor, déjeme bajar en . . .

Right away. ¡Pronto!
Help. ¡Socorro!
Who is it? ¿Quién es?
Just a minute! ¡Un momento no más!
Come in. ¡Pase usted!
Pardon me. Dispense usted.
Stop. ¡Pare!
Look out. ¡Cuidado!
Hurry. ¡De prisa! *or* ¡Dése prisa!
Go on. ¡Siga!
To (on, at) the right. A la derecha.
To (on, at) the left. A la izquierda.
Straight ahead. Adelante.

FOOD TERMS/ALIMENTOS

apple	manzana	lemonade	limonada
artichoke	alcachofa	lettuce	lechuga
asparagus	espárrago	liver	hígado
bacon	tocino	lobster	langosta
baked	al horno	meat	carne
banana	banana	melon	melón
bean	habichuela	milk	leche
beer	cerveza	mushroom	seta
beet	remolacha	noodle	fideo
biscuit	bizcocho	nut	nuez
boiled	hervido	omelet	tortilla de huevos
bread	pan	onion	cebolla
broccoli	brócoli	orange	naranja
broiled	a la parrilla	peach	melocotón
butter	manteca	pear	pera
cake	torta	pepper	pimienta
carrot	zanahoria	pie	pastel
cauliflower	coliflor	pork	carne de puerco
celery	apio	potato	patata
cheese	queso	rice	arroz
chicken	pollo	roast beef	rosbif
chocolate	chocolate	roasted	asado
coffee	café	salad	ensalada
cognac	coñac	salmon	salmón
cookie	galleta dulce	salt	sal
crab	cangrejo	sandwich	sandwich
cream	crema	sauce	salsa
cucumber	pepino	scrambled eggs	huevos revueltos
dessert	postre	shrimp	camarón
drink	bebida	soda	soda
duck	pato	sole	lenguado
egg	huevo	soup	sopa
fillet	filete	spinach	espinaca
fish	pescado	steak	biftec
fowl	ave	strawberry	fresa
fried	frito	stuffed	relleno
fruit	fruta	sugar	azúcar
goose	ganso	tea	té
grape	uva	tomato	tomate
grapefruit	toronja	trout	trucha
ham	jamón	tuna	atún
hamburger	hamburguesa	turkey	pavo
ice cream	helado	veal	ternera
jelly	jalea	vegetable	legumbre
juice	jugo	water	agua
lamb	cordero	wine	vino